Red Hat®
Fedora™ 4
UNLEASHED

Andrew Hudson
Paul Hudson
Bill Ball
Hoyt Duff

 800 East 96th Street, Indianapolis, Indiana 46240 USA

Red Hat Fedora 4 Unleashed

International Standard Book Number: 0-672-32792-9

Library of Congress Catalog Card Number: 2004195542

Printed in the United States of America

First Printing: June 2005

08   07   06   05   4   3   2   1

Trademarks

All terms mentioned in this book that are known to be trademarks or service marks have been appropriately capitalized. Sams Publishing cannot attest to the accuracy of this information. Use of a term in this book should not be regarded as affecting the validity of any trademark or service mark.

Red Hat is a registered trademark and Fedora is a trademark of Red Hat, Inc.

Warning and Disclaimer

Every effort has been made to make this book as complete and as accurate as possible, but no warranty or fitness is implied. The information provided is on an "as is" basis. The authors and the publisher shall have neither liability nor responsibility to any person or entity with respect to any loss or damages arising from the information contained in this book or from the use of the CDs or programs accompanying it.

Bulk Sales

Sams Publishing offers excellent discounts on this book when ordered in quantity for bulk purchases or special sales. For more information, please contact

U.S. Corporate and Government Sales
1-800-382-3419
corpsales@pearsontechgroup.com

For sales outside the United States, please contact

International Sales
international@pearsoned.com

Acquisitions Editors
Damon Jordan
Shelley Johnston

Development Editor
Damon Jordan

Managing Editor
Charlotte Clapp

Project Editor
Matt Purcell

Production Editor
Megan Wade

Indexer
Ken Johnson

Proofreader
Wendy Ostermeyer

Technical Editors
Jason Byars
Dee-Ann LeBlanc
Chris Newman
Dallas Releford
Dave Taylor
Christopher Young

Publishing Coordinator
Vanessa Evans

Multimedia Developer
Dan Scherf

Designer
Gary Adair

Contents at a Glance

Table of Contents

About the Authors

Andrew Hudson is a regular contributor to *Linux Format* magazine, the UK's largest Linux magazine. His particular area of expertise is Red Hat–based distributions, including Red Hat Enterprise Linux and the Fedora Project, having worked with the original Red Hat Linux since version 5. Seemingly obsessed with performance, he spends many an evening trying to squeeze more performance out of legacy hardware. Andrew lives in Wiltshire, England, with his wife Bernice who is currently expecting their first child. Andrew does not like Emacs. Andrew can be contacted at andy.hudson@gmail.com.

Paul Hudson is a recognized expert in open-source technologies. He is a professional developer and full-time journalist for Future Publishing. His articles have appeared in *Mac Format*, *PC Answers*, *PC Format*, *PC Plus*, and *Linux Format*. Paul is passionate about Free Software in all its forms and uses a mix of Linux and BSD to power his desktops and servers. Paul likes Emacs. Paul can be contacted through http://hudzilla.org.

Bill Ball is the best-selling author of nearly 20 books about Linux, including several editions of *Red Hat Linux Unleashed*, Que Publishing's *Using Linux*, and Sams Publishing's *SuSE Linux Unleashed*. He is a technical writer, editor, and magazine journalist and has been using computers for nearly 30 years. He first edited books for Que in 1986 and wrote one of the first best-selling Linux books, *Teach Yourself Linux in 24 Hours*, in 1997. He has authored articles and reviews in *Linux Journal*, developed technical online content for business websites, and developed and released open-source software for the Mac OS and Palm OS platforms. He has been a fan of Linux and XFree86 since 1994 and uses the software on Intel-based PCs, Apple PowerMacs, and MIPS platforms. Bill is an active member of the Northern Virginia Linux Users Group (NOVALUG); teaches Linux courses at Stratford University in Falls Church, Virginia; and lives in the Shirlington area of Arlington, Virginia. He can be contacted through http://www.tux.org/~bball.

Hoyt Duff feels that a good word to describe his life experience is "former"—former senior vice president and senior commercial loan officer for a bank, former community college instructor, former restaurateur, and former special education teacher. He currently meets the needs of his inner ADD child by spending the summer months tending to his family business, a sport fishing pier (the longest on the East Coast), and playing cocktail piano on weekends. Hoyt even finds time to write about Linux as a columnist and regular contributor of reviews and tutorial for *Linux Format* magazine. Active in the TideWater Unix Users Group (www.twuug.org), Hoyt enjoys the regular Linux installfests the most and will attempt to install Linux on anything that moves. Hoyt can be contacted at hoyt@maximumhoyt.com.

Dedication

To my wife—Paul

To my wife Bernice and our unborn baby—Andrew

Acknowledgments

Andrew Hudson

This book is the result of a long time working, revising, and editing material, and I would like to take this opportunity to thank a number of people who have helped me get through this. First of all, I'd like to thank Damon Jordan, our development editor. Despite working with a couple of Brits, Damon keeps his cool very well.

Shelley Johnston is the person my wife blames for holing me up in my office for more nights than she cares to remember—Shelley, thank you for allowing us to build upon the heritage of the Red Hat/Fedora *Unleashed* series. I'd like to also thank Megan Wade, our production editor who had to read all of this. I can imagine that she must definitely sleep well at night!

Dallas Releford was responsible for making sure everything was correct technically, and both Paul and I are privileged to have worked with someone of his caliber.

Of course, those who are nearest to you support you the most, and I'd like to put on record that Paul and I have not fought once over this book, which is amazing considering we are brothers. Paul, thank you for being a sounding board and a test bed for numerous things. We did it! Our parents are loved and cherished by us both for the support and love they give us. My dear wife Bernice, who has been pregnant all the way through this book, thank you for being a part of my life and encouraging me in what I do. I also want to thank our unborn child, due in June, for showing me that there is more to life than Linux.

Finally I want to thank Almighty God for the many blessings he has given to me—I only hope I use them for His glory.

Paul Hudson

Although there are only a few names on the cover of this book, it is the culmination of many years of writing, refining, testing, rewriting, exploration, and passion from many people. I feel lucky to be part of the team and want to thank the others for their enthusiasm and humor—it makes a huge difference to know that everyone who works on this book enjoys the topic!

I'm grateful to the entire team at Pearson for their help and feedback, but there are a few special thanks: Shelley Johnston lassoed Andrew and I into writing this book, and we have had a great time. Without Shelley, this book would not be what it is. Damon Jordan worked hard to make sure that readers like you get the most value from our content. I think you will agree he did a great job!

On the technical side, we were blessed to have Dallas Releford scouring our every word, adding suggestions, making improvements, and ruthlessly correcting mistakes. Dallas is a supremely experienced Linux guru who eats, sleeps, and breathes Fedora. I hope I get to work with him again.

Our production editor was Megan Wade, and she turned our stilted, broken English into flowing prose. At the most basic level, she checks and corrects spelling, grammar, and style, but she went above and beyond the call of duty with this particular comment I got back during the author review process: "The title of The The's album is actually two words—Mind Bomb (I double-checked my copy of the album to make sure)." What author could ask for more?

Outside of Pearson, I owe a debt of gratitude to Nick Veitch at *Linux Format* magazine. It is because of him that I get paid to play around with Linux all day, which is my ideal job. I guess he also taught me a thing or two about writing, but I consider that a fair trade for all the lessons I have given him in *Unreal Tournament*!

My family's contribution to this work has been immense. Andrew was brave in accepting the job of co-writing, but it turns out that we work in tandem very well—he has done a marvelous job, and we are both very proud of this end result. My wife, Ildiko, managed to put up with months of me doing no housework, although I think that the minute I am finished with this it is back to the grindstone for me (why do you think these acknowledgements are so long?). My parents have been immensely supportive throughout, and I love them dearly.

Finally, none of this work would have been possible without the grace of God. Andrew and I have been blessed to be able to write this book, and I pray it blesses you even more.

We Want to Hear from You!

As the reader of this book, you are our most important critic and commentator. We value your opinion and want to know what we're doing right, what we could do better, what areas you'd like to see us publish in, and any other words of wisdom you're willing to pass our way.

You can email or write me directly to let me know what you did or didn't like about this book—as well as what we can do to make our books stronger.

Please note that I cannot help you with technical problems related to the topic of this book, and that due to the high volume of mail I receive, I might not be able to reply to every message.

When you write, please be sure to include this book's title and authors as well as your name and phone or email address. I will carefully review your comments and share them with the authors and editors who worked on the book.

Email: opensource@samspublishing.com

Mail: Mark Taber
Associate Publisher
Sams Publishing
800 East 96th Street
Indianapolis, IN 46240 USA

Reader Services

For more information about this book or others from Sams Publishing, visit our website at www.samspublishing.com. Type the ISBN (excluding hyphens) or the title of the book in the Search box to find the book you're looking for.

Introduction

Welcome to *Red Hat Fedora 4 Unleashed*! This book covers the free Linux distribution named Fedora Core and includes a fully functional and complete operating system produced by the Fedora Project, sponsored by Red Hat.

Fedora Core continues the strong legacy left behind by Red Hat Linux and has benefited from contributions from the global open-source community as well as from the sponsorship of Red Hat. This makes it the most exciting Linux distribution currently available, and one that is very easy to get to grips with.

If you're new to Linux and to Sams Publishing's *Unleashed* books about Linux, congratulations—you've picked one of the best books on the market about Fedora Core. Get ready for an exciting, safe, and productive journey as you read this book and install the included software.

This book provides information to match the latest developments found in Fedora and, as always, includes a free copy of the latest distribution on DVD and CD-ROM. Linux, the kernel of a free operating system, is no longer the new kid on the block because it has been available for more than 10 years now. Linux forms the core of a stable, mature, and secure operating system. From embedded devices (such as PDAs) to laptops, desktops to servers, and mainframes to new 64-bit CPUs, Linux continues to be in the vanguard and a major force in the free software marketplace.

Make no mistake: While Linux has been deployed in many corporate- and enterprise-level environments, it is also steadily advancing toward use on millions of desktops. Thousands of open-source programmers around the world improve, test, and update the Linux kernel and Linux-related software packages. Their efforts have contributed much to the success of Linux for many types of users. Fedora Core incorporates many of these software packages, along with the latest stable version of the Linux kernel. This means you can put Fedora to work right away.

This book contains everything you need to plan, install, configure, maintain, administer, rebuild, and use Fedora. You can use this software at school, at home, or in the workplace. You can also make as many copies of Fedora as you want and freely distribute those copies to anyone interested in using Linux.

After an introduction to Red Hat and the Fedora Core project, you will see to how to set up and plan for an install. You will then get step-by-step directions on how to install Fedora in a variety of ways. Following directions on configuration, you will be introduced to basic system administration, followed by instructions on advanced administration techniques and concepts. Sections on programming, productivity, and multimedia round out the host of skills you'll acquire and learn when you use this book. Keep in mind, however, that this book assumes you have at least some experience with using a computer operating system.

What Is Linux?

Linux is the core, or *kernel*, of a free operating system first developed and released to the world by Linus Benedict Torvalds in 1991. Torvalds, then a graduate student at the University of Helsinki, Finland, is now a Fellow at the Open Source Development Lab (http://www.osdl.org). He is an engineer and had previously worked for the CPU design and fabrication company Transmeta, Inc. Fortunately for all Linux users, Torvalds chose to distribute Linux under a free software license named the GNU General Public License (GPL).

> **NOTE**
>
> The free online resource Wikipedia has a great biography of Linus Torvalds that examines his life and notable achievements. It even includes a transcript of his first announcement of Linux. It can be found at http://en.wikipedia.org/wiki/Linux_Torvalds.

The GNU GPL is the brainchild of Richard M. Stallman, the founder of the Free Software Foundation. Stallman, the famous author of the Emacs editing environment and GCC compiler system, crafted the GPL to ensure that covered software would always be free and available in source code form. The GPL is the guiding document for Linux and its ownership, distribution, and copyright. Torvalds holds the rights to the Linux trademark, but thanks to a combination of his generosity, the Internet, thousands of programmers around the world, GNU software, and the GNU GPL, Linux will remain forever free and unencumbered by licensing or royalty issues. See the later section "Licensing" to learn more about the GNU GPL and other software licenses.

Linux, pronounced "lih-nucks," is free software. Combining the Linux kernel with GNU software tools—drivers, utilities, user interfaces, and other software such as The X.Org Foundation's X Window System—creates a Linux distribution. There are many different Linux distributions from different vendors, but many are derived from or closely mimic Red Hat's distribution of Linux—Red Hat Linux.

> **NOTE**
>
> To see just how many distributions are based on Red Hat Linux, go to http://www.linux.org, click Distributions, and search for "Red Hat-based." At the time of writing, there were 35 distributions that owe their existence to Red Hat Linux.

What Is Fedora Core?

Fedora Core (or more simply, Fedora) is an operating system based on the Linux kernel, created, improved, and distributed by the Fedora Project at http://fedora.redhat.com. The Fedora Project, sponsored by Red Hat, is an open-source project supported by a worldwide community of software developers. Although Fedora is not supported by Red Hat, it incorporates improvements made to the Linux kernel and helps contribute to Red Hat's commercial Linux distributions and software. At the same time, Fedora also benefits from improvements made by Red Hat software engineers to Red Hat's products. Despite this symbiotic relationship, Fedora Core is a free operating system, built entirely from free software, and is guided by a process open to all free software developers.

Roots of Red Hat and Fedora

In 1994, Marc Ewing and Bob Young combined forces to create Red Hat (named after a Cornell University lacrosse team hat) to develop, release, and market an easily installed, easily managed, and easy-to-use Linux distribution. Five years later, Durham, North Carolina–based Red Hat would have one of the most successful initial public offerings (IPOs) on the stock market. In 2001, Red Hat introduced a line of products aimed at the corporate and enterprise markets and created versions of its Red Hat Linux distributions and associated software in a product line known as Red Hat Enterprise Linux. Additional software, services, and distributions were added to the product over the next several years, such as the Advanced Server (with support for seven CPU architectures), ES (for small- to mid-range enterprise use), and WorkStation (WS) releases.

Following the release of Red Hat Linux 9 in mid-2003, Red Hat announced that it was discontinuing the sale of consumer-based Linux distributions. Previously, the distributions had been available in boxed sets with manuals on store shelves or in CD-ROM image format for free download over the Internet. Red Hat then created the Fedora Project and formally opened its new home on October 22, 2003.

Today, the company has grown from a handful of employees to more than 600 in 22 locations around the world.

Red Hat was one of the first companies to adopt, promote, and use open source as a business model for supporting development, technical service, support, and sales of free software to the computer industry. Its business practices have spawned a shift in paradigm of proprietary attitudes prevalent in the monopolistic software industry, and the company is a role model and business leader in the open source movement. You learn more about Red Hat and Fedora Core in Chapter 1, "Introducing Fedora."

> **CAUTION**
>
> The Fedora Core CD-ROMs and DVD distribution included with this book are not supported by Red Hat. If you want technical support when using a Red Hat release, purchase a copy of Red Hat Enterprise Linux from Red Hat at http://www.redhat.com.
>
> You can also call to order. In the United States, call 1-866-273-3428, extension 4555.
>
> Elsewhere in the world, check http://www.redhat.com/about/corporate/wwoffices/ for a list of local offices.
>
> Red Hat is a trademark of Red Hat. Linux is a trademark owned by Linus Torvalds.
>
> Do NOT contact Red Hat for any type of support when using or attempting to install the software included with this book. Although every effort has been made to ensure that information in this book matches the included software, you should instead contact Sams Publishing for any problems related to the CD-ROMs contained in this book:
>
> userservices@samspublishing.com
>
> Only users who purchase the "official" Red Hat Enterprise Linux products from Red Hat are entitled to support from Red Hat.

If you purchase an official Red Hat Enterprise Linux distribution from Red Hat, you might find commercial software included on the distribution's CD-ROMs or DVD. These software packages are often included as an enticement to purchase more feature-laden or corporate versions, but you should carefully read any accompanying licensing agreements and be careful to not make unauthorized copies.

Licensing

Software licensing is an important issue for all computer users and can entail moral, legal, and financial considerations. Many consumers think that purchasing a copy of a commercial or proprietary operating system, productivity application, utility, or game conveys ownership, but this is not true. In the majority of cases, the End User License Agreement (EULA) included with a commercial software package states that you have only paid for the right to use the software according to specific terms. This generally means you may not examine, make copies, share, resell, or transfer ownership of the software package. More onerous software licenses enforce terms that preclude you from distributing or publishing comparative performance reviews of the software. Even more insidious licensing schemes (and supporting legislation, especially in the United States), contain provisions allowing onsite auditing of the software's use!

This is not the case with the software included with this book. Although you cannot resell copies of this book's CD-ROMs labeled as "Fedora Core Linux," you are entirely free to make copies, share them with friends, and install the software on as many computers as you want—we encourage you to purchase additional copies of this book to give them as gifts, however. Be sure to read the README file on the first CD-ROM included with this book for important information regarding the included software and disk contents. Look under the /usr/share/apps/LICENSES directory after you install Fedora to find a copy of the GNU GPL (along with copies of other software licenses). You will see that the GPL provides unrestricted freedom to use, duplicate, share, study, modify, improve, and even sell the software.

You can put your copy of Fedora to work right away in your home or at your place of business without having to worry about software licensing, per-seat workstation or client licenses, software auditing, royalty payments, or any other types of payments to third parties. However, you should be aware that although much of the software included with Fedora is licensed under the GPL, some packages on this book's CD-ROMs are licensed under other terms. There is a variety of related software licenses, and many software packages fall under a broad definition known as *open source*. Some of these include the Artistic License, the BSD License, the Mozilla Public License, and the Q Public License.

For additional information about the various GNU software licenses, browse to http://www.gnu.org. For a definition of open-source and licensing guidelines, along with links to the terms of nearly three dozen open-source licenses, browse to http://www.opensource.org/.

Why Use Linux?

Millions of savvy computer users have been putting Linux to work for more than 10 years. Over the last year, many individuals; small office/home office (SOHO) users; businesses; corporations; colleges; nonprofits; and local, state, and federal agencies in a number of countries have incorporated Linux with great success. And today, Linux is being incorporated into many IS/IT environments as part of improvements in efficiency, security, and cost savings. Using Linux is a good idea for a number of reasons. These reasons include

- **Linux provides an excellent return on investment (ROI)**—There is little or no cost on a per-seat basis. Unlike commercial operating systems, Linux has no royalty or licensing fees and a single Linux distribution on CD-ROM can form the basis of an enterprise-wide software distribution, replete with applications and productivity software. Custom corporate CD-ROMs can be easily crafted to provide specific installs on enterprise-wide hardware. This feature alone can save hundreds of thousands, if not millions, of dollars in information service/information technology costs—all without the threat of a software audit from the commercial software monopoly or the need for licensing accounting and controls of base operating system installations.

- **Linux can be put to work on the desktop**—Linux, in conjunction with its supporting graphical networking protocol and interface (the X Window System), has worked well as a consumer Unix-like desktop operating system since the mid-1990s. The fact that Unix is ready for the consumer desktop is now confirmed with the introduction, adoption, and rapid maturation of Apple Computer's BSD Unix-based Mac OS X—supported, according to Apple, by more than 3,000 OS X-specific programs that are known as *native applications*. This book's CD-ROMs contain more than 1,300 software packages, including Internet connection utilities, games, a choice of three office suites, thousands of fonts, and hundreds of graphics applications.

- **Linux can be put to work as a server platform**—Linux is fast, secure, stable, scalable, and robust. Latest versions of the Linux kernel easily support multiple-processor computers (optimized for eight CPUs), large amounts of system memory (up to 64GB RAM), individual file sizes in excess of hundreds of gigabytes, a choice of modern journaling file systems, hundreds of process monitoring and control utilities, and the (theoretical) capability to simultaneously support more than four billion users. IBM, Oracle, and other major database vendors all have versions of their enterprise software available for Linux.

- **Linux has a low entry and deployment cost barrier**—Maintenance costs can also be reduced because Linux works well on a variety of PCs, including legacy hardware, such as some Intel-based 486 and early Pentium CPUs. Although the best program performance will be realized with newer hardware because clients can be recompiled and optimized for Pentium-class CPUs, base installs can even be performed on lower-end computers or embedded devices with only 8MB of RAM. This feature provides for a much wider user base; extends the life of older working hardware; and can help save money for home, small business, and corporate users.

- **Linux appeals to a wide hardware and software industry audience**—Versions of Linux exist for nearly every CPU. Embedded systems developers now turn to Linux when crafting custom solutions using ARM, MIPS, and other low-power processors. Linux is the first full operating system available for Intel's Itanium CPU, as well as the AMD64 group of CPUs; ports have also been available for HP/Compaq's Alpha and Sun Microsystem's SPARC CPUs for some time. PowerPC users regularly use the PPC port of Linux on IBM and Apple hardware.

- **Linux provides a royalty-free development platform for cross-platform development**—Because of the open-source development model and availability of free, high-quality development tools, Linux provides a low-cost entry point to budding developers and tech industry startups.

- **Big-player support in the computer hardware industry from such titans as IBM now lends credibility to Linux as a viable platform**—IBM has enabled Linux on the company's entire line of computers, from low-end laptops through "Big Iron" mainframes. New corporate customers are lining up and using Linux as part of enterprise-level computing solutions. It has been used on some of the world's fastest computers, including IBM's Blue Gene.

Look forward to even more support as usage spreads worldwide throughout all levels of business in search of lower costs, better performance, and stable and secure implementations.

Who This Book Is For

This book is for anyone searching for guidance on using Fedora Core, which is for Intel-based PC platforms. Although the contents are aimed at intermediate to advanced users, even new users with a bit of computer savvy will benefit from the advice, tips, tricks, traps, and techniques presented in each chapter. Pointers to more detailed or related information are also provided at the end of each chapter.

Fedora's installer program, named Anaconda, makes the job of installing Linux as easy as possible. However, if you are new to Linux, you might need to learn some new computer skills, such as how to research your computer's hardware, how to partition a hard drive, and occasionally how to use a command line. This book will help you learn these skills and show you how to learn more about your computer, Linux, and the software included with Fedora. System administrators with experience using other operating systems will be able to use the information presented in this book to install, set up, and run common Linux software services, such as the Network File System (NFS), a File Transfer Protocol (FTP) server, and a web server (using Apache, amongst others).

What This Book Contains

Red Hat Fedora 4 Unleashed is organized into seven parts, covering installation and configuration, Fedora on the desktop, system administration, Fedora as a server, programming and housekeeping, and a reference section. A two-CD set of the Fedora Core CD-ROMs is included, as is a DVD, so you will have everything you need to get started. This book starts by covering the initial and essential tasks required to get Fedora installed and running on a target system.

If you're new to Linux, and more specifically, Fedora, first read the chapters in Part I, "Installation and Configuration." You'll get valuable information on

- An overview of Fedora and Linux and their roles in various computing environments

- Planning for an installation by examining hardware requirements and the need for organizing how the system is installed

- Detailed steps that take you by the hand through various types of installations

- Critical advice on key configuration steps to fully install and configure Linux to work with your system's subsystems or peripherals, such as pointers, keyboards, modems, USB devices, power management, and—for laptop users—PCMCIA devices

- Initial steps needed by new users transitioning from other computing environments

- Configuration and use of the X Window System, the graphical interface for Linux

Part II, "Fedora Desktop," is aimed at users who want to get productive with Fedora and covers the following:

- Becoming familiar with the X Window system and looking at GNOME and KDE

- Discovering the many productivity applications that come with Fedora

- Surfing the Internet and working with email and newsgroups

- Using Fedora to listen to music and watch video

- Setting up local printers for Fedora

- A look at the current state of gaming for Linux

Moving beyond the productivity and desktop areas of Fedora, Part III, "System Administration," covers

- Managing users and groups

- Automating tasks and using shell scripts

- Monitoring system resources and availability

- Backup strategies and software

- Network connectivity, including sharing folders and securing the network
- Internet connectivity via dial-up and broadband connections

Part IV, "Fedora As a Server," looks at the opportunities provided by every Fedora system by covering

- Building and deploying web servers
- Database creation, management, and manipulation
- File and print servers
- Using FTP for serving files across the Internet and local networks
- Building and deploying email servers using Postfix as well as managing mailing lists
- Creating remote access gateways and services
- Configuring DNS for your network
- Using LDAP for storing information on users and security
- Configuring a local news server

Part V, "Programming Linux," provides a great introduction into ways in which you can extend Fedora's capabilities even further using the development tools supplied with it. This part covers

- Programming in Perl, using variables and scripting
- An introduction to the Python language
- Writing PHP scripts and linking them to databases
- C and C++ programming tools available with Fedora, and how to use the GNU C Compiler (gcc)

Part VI, "Fedora Housekeeping," looks at some of the more advanced skills you need to keep your system running in perfect condition, including

- Securing your machine against attack from outsiders and viruses
- Performance tuning
- Command-line masterclass
- Advanced yum
- Kernel and module management and compilation
- Managing the file system

There is also an extensive reference in Part VII, "Appendix," which gives you scope to explore in even more depth some of the topics covered in this book.

Conventions Used in This Book

A lot of documentation is included with every Linux distribution, and Fedora Core is certainly no exception. Although the intent of *Red Hat Fedora 4 Unleashed* is to be as complete as possible, it is impossible to cover every option of every command included in the distribution. However, this book offers numerous tables of various options, commands, or keystrokes to help condense, organize, and present information about a variety of subjects.

This edition is also packed full of screenshots to illustrate nearly all Fedora-specific graphical utilities—especially those related to system administration or the configuration and administration of various system and network services.

To help you better understand code listing examples and sample command lines, several formatting techniques are used to show input and ownership. For example, if the command or code listing example shows typed input, the input is formatted in boldface like this:

$ ls

If typed input is required, as in response to a prompt, the example typed input also is in boldface, like so:

Delete files? [Y/n] y

All statements, variables, and text that should appear on your display use the same boldface formatting. Additionally, command lines that require root or superuser access are prefaced with a pound sign like this:

```
# printtool &
```

Command-line examples that can be run by any user are prefaced with a dollar sign ($), like so:

```
$ ls
```

The following elements provide you with useful tidbits of information that relate to the discussion of the text:

> **NOTE**
>
> Notes provide additional information you might want to make note of as you are working; augment a discussion with ancillary details; or point you to an article, a whitepaper, or another online reference for more information about a specific topic.

> **TIP**
>
> A tip can contain special insight or a timesaving technique, as well as information about items of particular interest to you that you might not find elsewhere.

CAUTION

A caution warns you about pitfalls or problems before you run a command, edit a configuration file, or choose a setting when administering your system.

Sidebars Can Be Goldmines

Just because it is in a sidebar doesn't mean that you won't find something new here. Be sure to watch for these elements that bring in outside content that is an aside to the discussion in the text. You will read about other technologies, Linux-based hardware, or special procedures to make your system more robust and efficient.

Other formatting techniques used to increase readability include the use of italics for placeholders in computer command syntax. Computer terms or concepts also are italicized upon first introduction in text.

Finally, you should know that all text, sample code, and screenshots in *Red Hat Fedora 4 Unleashed* were developed using Fedora and open-source tools.

Read on to start learning about and using the latest version of Fedora Core. Experienced users will want to consider the new information presented in this edition when planning or considering upgrades. New users, or users new to Fedora, will benefit from the details presented in this book.

PART I

Installation and Configuration

IN THIS PART

Introducing Fedora

Welcome to *Red Hat Fedora 4 Unleashed!* Fedora Core is a unique Linux distribution and is the first and primary product of The Fedora Project, an open-source, community-driven project sponsored by Red Hat. Fedora Core, or more simply, *Fedora*, is a base Linux distribution available free over the Internet at http://fedora.redhat.com. Alternatively, places like linuxcentral.com or even your local Linux user group can supply you with a copy if you don't have a good Internet connection.

Fedora represents an evolution in the business direction of its sponsor, Red Hat. For nearly 10 years, Red Hat provided copies of its commercial Linux distribution, Red Hat Linux, free over the Internet. All that changed in October 2003, when Red Hat discontinued the sale and free distribution of its consumer-oriented Red Hat Linux.

As the company has since its inception, Red Hat then released all its work on the freely licensed software in the former consumer distribution. The work, which was to be a new version of Red Hat Linux, was then merged with an existing Fedora Linux project and was reborn as Fedora Core. Red Hat now focuses its efforts on enterprise and corporate Linux-based products and services, but again, continues to make source code available for all its products that are under an open-source license.

Red Hat's Enterprise Linux is a series of software products aimed for corporate and enterprise migration, deployment, and use. Although all Linux distributions could be considered the same underneath because all use the Linux kernel, Red Hat takes special pains to create, test, sell, and support commercial Linux distributions optimized for deployment on multiple hardware and CPU architectures. These high-performance enhancements include hardware-tweaked Linux kernels, fail-over and load-balancing clustering, and integrated Java support—essential for mission-critical applications and production environments.

About Red Hat

Red Hat is one of the world's foremost open-source development houses and returns nearly all its development efforts back to the Linux development community.

The company has been involved in many open-source and GNU GPL projects, such as the Apache web server, the `glibc` software libraries, the GNU Network Object Model Environment (GNOME), various GNU software tools and packages, the Linux kernel and device drivers, the PostgreSQL database system, and the Red Hat Package Manager (RPM).

Red Hat also supports many other projects by providing FTP service and web hosting and is one of the few companies actively promoting and using the open source business development model. This means that, although many of its products are free, revenue streams are derived from spin-off and related technologies and services. These pursuits include embedded development (the open-source eCos operating system); training and certification programs such as the Red Hat Certified Engineer (RHCE) track; commercial software development; fee- and subscription-based support; consulting; and advanced software products, such as an advanced e-commerce platform, a secure web server, a credit card verification system (CCVS), and the Red Hat Database.

One possible reason for the success of Linux could be "Best hack wins." In other words, software that works well, fills a critical need, is readily available in source form, and is distributed under a free software license (such as the GNU GPL) will quickly spread and see extensive use. The growth in popularity and widespread adoption of Linux around the world is a testament to quality, licensing, and need for Linux.

Unix enjoyed a similar rapid-fire adoption after it was distributed in the early 1970s and fulfilled user needs on a number of fronts. However, its licensing was restrictive, caused much grief in some open-source communities (such as education), and continues to spawn problems to this day.

Here is the bottom line: You are holding nearly $1 billion worth of software in your hands. That is one estimate of what it would cost to develop as complete an operating system, graphical interface, and related software to equal the operating system included with this book.

It was not long ago that any new major project involving use of Linux by big business, government (on any level), or academia would have been big news. Today, Linux is increasingly used by IS/IT strategists for computing solutions. Linux and related open-source software rule the Internet. It is the host platform of choice for traditional server operations. Linux is poised to take over the desktop, occupying the number two spot behind a monolithic software entity.

NOTE

The list of Linux projects, efforts, and partnerships reads like a Who's Who of the software industry: Amazon, Ameritrade, Borland, Computer Associates, Dell, Hewlett-Packard/Compaq,

IBM, Oracle, and SAP are just some of the enterprise-level players using Linux. Linux is also a key ingredient and shares an ever-increasing portion of server hardware sales from all large vendors, such as IBM, Hewlett-Packard/Compaq, and Dell.

What Is Fedora Core?

Fedora is the natural successor to Red Hat Linux and incorporates many of the features and software tools included with previous Red Hat Linux distributions. Red Hat Linux spawned many imitators in the Linux world in the past decade, and many of these imitators have gone on to create credible products and distributions.

As you learn in this chapter, Fedora is one of the most up-to-date Linux distributions available on the Internet. Here, you see why Fedora can be a good choice for a variety of computing environments and how, when combined with advances provided by the latest Linux kernel, it can provide multitiered support for the academic, home, small business, and even corporate user.

Inside Fedora Core

A complete copy of the Fedora Core distribution requires eight CD-ROMs, but only the first four are necessary for a full install of the operating system. Half of the distribution consists of source code for all the included software. More than 1,450 separate software packages are in Fedora Core. This distribution comprises the Linux kernel, installation utilities, thousands of pages of documentation, several thousand fonts, a comprehensive graphical networking interface, and several thousand individual commands and clients.

Fedora provides a base, or core, framework operating system and desktop comprised entirely of free software. Fedora includes the Bluecurve desktop theme and has an improved consistency in the two major graphical desktops available for use: the GNU Network Object Model Environment (GNOME) and the K Desktop Environment (KDE).

You can expect an extensive amount of Linux software to be supported by Fedora, and it is eventually expected to have an extensive library of contributed software packages outside the Fedora Core release. This means your first four Fedora Core CD-ROMs or DVD are just the beginning of a large collection of Linux software!

> **NOTE**
>
> Read more about GNOME and KDE in Chapter 6, "The X Window System."

Fedora provides the latest version of the X Window System and its server, X11R6 6.8.2, which sports improved and integral font handling. The Linux desktop has never looked better, and you will notice the difference when you browse the Web, use one of the dozen or so word processors and text editors included with Fedora, or view text at the command line in a terminal window.

If you are a veteran Red Hat user, you will feel at home with Fedora because it includes Red Hat's comprehensive suite of graphical administrative programs. The tools, shown in Table 1.1, combine and expand on the capabilities of standard Linux system utilities and are intended for use by the root operator (known as the *superuser*) to administer a Fedora system. The software takes the place of (and in some cases upgrades and augments) many of the legacy command-line-based tools traditionally used on a Unix system. You will learn how to use these tools throughout this book.

TABLE 1.1   Red Hat Software Tools Included with Fedora Core Graphical Administration Tools

Name	Description
neat	Creates, edits, and manages network devices
system-config-authentication	Manages user information and authentication protocol
system-config-bind	Configures Domain Name Service
system-config-boot	Manages boot loading
system-config-date	Sets date and time zone
system-config-display	Configures X to work with your PC hardware
system-config-httpd	Apache web server administration
system-config-keyboard	Configures keyboard type
system-config-kickstart	Creates automated install script
system-config-language	Sets system language
system-config-mouse	Configures mouse type and features
system-config-netboot	Configures network booting
system-config-network	Manages system network devices and settings
system-config-nfs	Configures Network File System
system-config-packages	Manages system software
system-config-printer	Creates, edits, and manages printers
system-config-proc	Manages kernel settings and processes
system-config-rootpassword	Sets and changes root password
system-config-samba	Manages a Session Message Block (SMB) server
system-config-securitylevel	Configures firewall service
system-config-services	Starts, stops, restarts, or sets boot services
system-config-soundcard	Configures Fedora for sound
system-config-time	Sets system date and time zone
system-config-users	Manages system users
system-switch-mail	Toggles use of Sendmail or Postfix email services

Fedora includes Internet programs such as Mozilla's open-source web browser, Firefox, along with productivity applications such as Ximian's Evolution (a mail, contact, and calendaring client) and OpenOffice.org (a Microsoft-compatible open-source office suite). You'll find all these and many more applications on this book's CD-ROMs and DVD.

Other major features are the inclusion of the latest GNU gcc compiler system, supporting C/C++ language program development. You will also get the newest version of the Apache web server, and the Common Unix Printing System (CUPS), which supports more than a thousand different printers.

Fedora Core, as the next generation of Red Hat Linux, is slated for upgrades two or three times a year, according to the Fedora Project. In reality, however, work never ceases on the distribution because open-source developers, along with Red Hat engineers, cross-pollinate Red Hat's Enterprise Linux and Fedora with software package upgrades, security updates, and bug fixes. Fedora's free, online upgrade system will be available via the Internet.

Red Hat uses a 12- to 18-month release cycle for Enterprise Linux. This cycle is required to provide third-party application developers time to test, deploy, and market products. In the past, Red Hat has used a 6-month release schedule for the consumer version of Red Hat Linux, with a 3- to 4-month beta cycle for development and testing. Fedora Core will have a similar schedule; the Fedora Project has stated it intends to "produce time-based releases of Fedora Core about two to three times a year."

As a Fedora user, you will be able to obtain the latest software for your system at any time using a variety of commands and software management tools:

yum—The Yellowdog Updater Modified, an automated software package manager based on RPM technology that resolves RPM dependencies.

apt-get—The APT command-line software package tool from The Debian Project, it's used to upgrade, install, check, or remove software.

system-config-packages—Red Hat's graphical package manager, it's used to install or remove applications (refer to Table 1.1).

rpm—The Red Hat Package Manager, which uses a database of installed packages to manage software on your system.

up2date—Red Hat's Red Hat Network update manager.

Distribution Version and Kernel Numbering Schema

There is a specific numbering system for Linux kernels, kernel development, and Fedora's kernel versions. Note that these numbers bear no relation to the version number of your Fedora Linux distribution. Fedora distribution version numbers are assigned by the Fedora Project, whereas most of the Linux kernel version numbers are assigned by Linus Torvalds and his legion of kernel developers.

To see the date your Linux kernel was compiled, use the uname command with its -v command-line option. To see the version of your Linux kernel, use the -r option. The numbers, such as 2.6.7-1, represent the major version (2), minor version (6), and patch level (7). The final number, (1), is the developer patch level and is assigned by the Fedora Project.

Even minor numbers are considered "stable" and generally fit for use in production environments, while odd minor numbers (such as a Linux 2.7 source tree) represent versions of the Linux kernel under development and testing. You will only find stable versions of the Linux kernel included with this book. You can choose to download and install a beta (test) version of the kernel, but this is not recommended for a system destined for everyday use. Most often, beta kernels are installed to provide support and testing of new hardware or operating system features.

Features of the Fedora Install

Installing Fedora can be accomplished in a number of ways. Many new users choose to simply boot from the first CD-ROM or from the DVD. The Fedora installer, named Anaconda (because it is written in the Python programming language), provides a default graphical interface for the installation process. The installer can be used to perform various initial actions before proceeding to an install, such as

- **Testing the installation media**—Useful for testing the integrity of your copies of the Fedora CD-ROMs/DVD. If you download .iso images of the Fedora CDs or DVD, you can also use an MD5SUM client to compare the prepublished checksums for the media against your .iso files.

- **Testing your PC's memory**—Useful for ensuring that your PC is in good form with functioning memory. Linux will use every available byte of RAM, and you should ensure that you do not run into problems after the operating system is installed.

- **Updating the installer before the install**—In some cases, you might need to use the latest version of the installer to work around a bug or problematic hardware, and this option can be used to use a new version of the installer even though it is not on the CD-ROM or DVD.

- **Rescuing the system**—In instances where a boot loader configuration has failed, or for some reason the system will not boot, the installer can be used to boot to a rescue mode; the existing file system can then be mounted and data can be rescued or the system reconfigured to resolve the problem.

- **Specifying hardware workarounds**—Various options at the installer command line can be used to get around problematic or unsupported hardware posing an obstacle to your install.

- **Specifying an install method**—Fedora Core can be installed from a hard drive partition or over a network using FTP, NFS, HTTP, or virtual networking.

See Chapter 3, "Installing Fedora," for specific details about various installer options. After the initial install and several screens to set install options, you can choose a class of installation, such as

- **Custom**—This option is used to install your own selection of software packages, which can be useful to trim unwanted software from your new Fedora system.

- **Upgrade**—Use this option to upgrade an existing Red Hat/Fedora system with the new Fedora desktop and software packages.

- **Server**—Select this option to create a web, File Transfer Protocol (FTP), network file system (NFS), or other server.

- **Personal Desktop**—Choose this install use the new Fedora desktop and create an Internet or multimedia workstation.

- **Workstation**—Choose this class to install development software, such as the gcc compiler suite and other programming tools to create a development system.

Fedora's installation process also allows you to install Linux in a variety of ways, using a text-based or graphical interface. See Chapter 3 to learn how to install using CD-ROM/DVD, a hard drive, or a network. See Chapter 2, "Preparing to Install Fedora," for some important considerations to help you prepare to install Fedora.

Fedora File System Features

Fedora also uses the ext3 file system, developed by Dr. Stephen C. Tweedie and used by Red Hat's Enterprise Linux products. ext3 supports a form of low-level storage data handling known as *journaling*, previously available only under very expensive computer platforms. Journaling is accomplished using a variety of techniques, but the end result aims to ensure that data remains intact on the disk despite a system crash, a power outage, or other mishap.

However, because Fedora is designed to be flexible and accommodating of all new Linux technologies, you can use other file systems for your workstation or server. This includes IBM JFS, a journaled file system designed for servers and used on many enterprise-level platforms. If you want to take advantage of fast restarts and enjoy good performance and reliability, JFS can be used as an alternative to ext3. However, ext3 offers benefits such as quick switching between legacy ext2 file systems and widespread use in the Linux community.

> **NOTE**
>
> More information about IBM's JFS file system for Linux can be found at http://oss.software.ibm.com/jfs/.

> **NOTE**
>
> Read Dr. Stephen Tweedie's presentation, "EXT3, Journaling File System," at http://olstrans.sourceforge.net/release/OLS2000-ext3/OLS2000-ext3.html for more details. You can also read how ext3 is used with the 2.4-series Linux kernel by browsing to Andrew Morton's page at http://www.zip.com.au/~akpm/linux/ext3/index.html.

Other journaling file systems should be supported by Fedora (such as reiserfs) and have similar features.

Fedora also supports the creation of large RAID arrays, both via software using one or more storage devices and using hardware with specific device controllers. You can also use logical volume management (LVM), a sophisticated file system handling feature that allows parts of the file system (directory layout) to span one or more portions of separate physical storage media. This feature also allows resizing of the resulting partitions if system resource requirements change after initial configuration, and while the pertinent file systems are unmounted or mounted.

Other benefits of using Fedora are the inclusion of digital signature verification of RPM packages (for enhanced security), RPM package dependency resolution suggestion (to more easily fix dependency diagnosis), and the privoxy server (to help filter out unwanted web page pop-ups and so on).

Fedora for Business

Linux has matured over the last 10 years, and features considered essential for use in enterprise-level environments, such as CPU architecture support, file systems, and memory handling, have been added and improved. The addition of virtual memory (the capability to swap portions of RAM to disk) was one of the first necessary ingredients, along with a copyright-free implementation of the TCP/IP stack (mainly due to BSD Unix being tied up in legal entanglements at the time). Other features quickly followed, such as support for a variety of network protocols.

Fedora includes a Linux kernel that has the capability to use multiple processors. This allows you to use Fedora in more advanced computing environments with greater demands on CPU power. This kernel will support at least 16 CPUs, but in reality, small business servers typically only use dual-CPU workstations or servers. However, Fedora has the capability to run Linux on more powerful hardware.

Fedora will automatically support your multiple-CPU Intel-based motherboard, and you will be able to take advantage of the benefits of symmetric multiprocessors (SMPs) for software development and other operations.

The Linux kernels included with Fedora can use system RAM sizes up to 64GB, allow individual file sizes in excess of 2GB, and host the demands of—theoretically—billions of users.

Businesses that depend on large-scale, high-volume, and high-availability systems can now turn to Red Hat's Enterprise Linux products for stable, robust, scalable, and inexpensive solutions for various platform hosting. Storage requirements in the terabyte range, no lengthy file system checks, and no downtime are just a few of the minimum requirements in such environments.

However, Fedora can be used in many of these environments by customers with widely disparate computing needs. Some of the applications for Fedora include desktop support; small file, print, or mail servers; intranet web servers; and security firewalls deployed at strategic points inside and outside company LANs.

Commercial Red Hat customers will benefit from Red Hat's engineering and support teams because Red Hat works closely with many computer industry leaders, such as HP, Fujitsu Limited, and IBM. This enables Red Hat Enterprise Linux to work well on a wide range of computers such as laptops, mid-range Intel Xeon and Itanium platforms, and some of the most powerful enterprise-class servers in the world.

Red Hat also develops platform and development tools for other CPUs, such as the Xstormy16 CPU from Sanyo, NEC's VR5500 MIPS, Motorola's 128-bit AltiVec and Book E PowerPC e500, SuperH's SuperH SH-5, and Intel's Xscale-based chips.

Red Hat Enterprise Linux in Government

Red Hat Enterprise Linux has a presence in many government entities at various levels across the world. For example, the New Jersey State Police use a Red Hat–based Oracle system, whereas India's Centre for Development of Advanced Computing uses Red Hat Linux in its high-performance computing lab.

Use of Linux is expanding rapidly in the U.S. federal sector. Red Hat Enterprise Linux is on the General Services Administration Schedule, and the U.S. National Security Agency has offered a series of kernel patches to assist in building secure versions of Linux. This has quickened the development of SELinux within both Fedora and Red Hat Enterprise Linux. Other agencies and departments, such as the U.S. Air Force; U.S. Marine Corps; Federal Aviation Administration; NASA; and the Departments of Defense, Agriculture, and Energy also use Linux-enabled platform solutions from IBM and Hewlett-Packard/Compaq.

Small business owners can earn great rewards by stepping off the software licensing and upgrade treadmill and adopting a Linux-based solution. Using Fedora not only avoids the need for licensing accounting and the threat of software audits, but also provides viable alternatives to many types of commercial productivity software.

Using Fedora in a small business setting makes a lot of sense for other reasons as well, such as not having to invest in cutting-edge hardware to set up a productive shop. Fedora easily supports older, or *legacy*, hardware, and savings are compounded over time by avoiding unnecessary hardware upgrades.

Additional savings will be realized because software and upgrades are free. New versions of applications can be downloaded and installed at little or no cost, and office suite software is free.

Fedora is easy to install and network and plays well with others, meaning it works well in a mixed-computing situation with other operating systems.

A simple Fedora server can be put to work as an initial partial solution or made to mimic file, mail, or print servers of other operating systems. Clerical help will quickly adapt to using familiar Internet and productivity tools, while your business gets the additional benefits of stability, security, and a virus-free computing platform.

By carefully allocating monies spent on server hardware, a productive and efficient multi-user system can be built for much less than the cost of comparable commercial software. Combine these benefits with support for laptops, PDAs, and remote access, and you'll find that Fedora supports the creation and use of an inexpensive yet efficient work environment.

Fedora in Your Home

Fedora's Personal Desktop install copies a special set of preselected software packages onto your hard drive; these are suitable for small office/home office (SOHO) users. This option provides a wealth of productivity tools for document management, printing, communication, and personal productivity.

NOTE

Don't confuse Personal Desktop with Red Hat Enterprise Linux. Fedora is a free community project, so it can only include nonproprietary software. RHEL comes with specialist business applications that Red Hat licenses from other companies. Fedora and RHEL mirror each other in a number of ways but are not identical!

The Personal Desktop installation requires nearly 2GB of hard drive space but should easily fit onto smaller hard drives in older Pentium-class PCs. The install also contains administrative tools, additional authoring and publishing clients, a variety of editors, a GNOME-based X11 desktop, support for sound, graphics editing programs, and graphical and text-based Internet tools. You can customize the selection to include or sidestep installation of unwanted software. See Chapter 3 for details.

Connecting to the Internet is a snap, and Fedora supports modem dialup and other broadband connections, such as cable modems or digital subscriber line (DSL). See Chapter 18, "Internet Connectivity," for more information. When you do connect, you can do so in relative confidence because firewall protection from malicious intruders and other attackers can be thwarted by running the lokkit or system-config-securitylevel clients. See Chapter 17, "Network Connectivity," to learn how to set up a network.

If you have a digital camera, run the gphoto2 client to download, organize, and manage your digital images. You can then fine-tune your pictures by editing them using one of the finest digital image editors in the world: The GIMP. See Chapter 10, "Multimedia Applications," for details on editing graphics.

Fedora can be used for a variety of purposes, and every user has different needs. Some of them might be esoteric. For example, I use Fedora to program and manage thousands of frequencies on various radio scanners and amateur radio transceivers, run a high-frequency shortwave radio via a graphical interface on the desktop, host wireless (802.11a/b/g) printing for several workstations, manage digital recording of my favorite TV episodes, provide secure remote access via a firewall, and listen to my favorite music playlists via a server.

64-bit Fedora

Recent advances in computing saw the introduction of 64-bit x86-compatible CPUs from AMD in the spring of 2003. The only platform at launch to support the new technology was Linux, and even at the time of writing, it is still the only mainstream operating system actively using the power of the 64-bit x86 architecture. Intel's EM64T extensions for x86, which largely mirror the advances made by AMD, have further increased the availability of commodity x86-64 hardware.

As a direct response to the growing 64-bit user base, the Fedora project released an x86_64 version of Fedora Core 2, allowing the use of Fedora on AMD64 and Intel hardware. If you have a 64-bit CPU, you are strongly encouraged to get involved and have a go—just bear in mind that, because the architecture is still quite new, there might not be 64-bit versions of all the software you require.

Getting the Most from Fedora and Linux Documentation

Nearly all commercial Linux distributions include shrink-wrapped manuals and documentation covering installation and configuration. You will not find official documentation included on the CD-ROMs or DVD provided with this book. However, you can read or get copies of assorted manuals or topic discussions online at http://fedora.redhat.com/projects/docs/. There you will find the Fedora Project's links to various documentation projects.

You can also turn to Red Hat's official manuals and guides, particularly for Red Hat Linux 9, for interim information about Red Hat tools (such as those listed in Table 1.1) at http://www.redhat.com/docs/manuals/linux/RHL-9-Manual/. Note that the names that began with `redhat-config` in Red Hat Linux 9 now begin with `system-config` in Fedora Core.

Documentation for Fedora (and many Linux software packages) is distributed and available in a variety of formats.

Some guides are available in Portable Document Format (PDF) and can be read using Adobe's Acrobat Reader for Linux or the xpdf client. Guides are also available as bundled HTML files for reading with a web browser such as links, KDE's Konqueror, GNOME's Epiphany, or Firefox. Along with these guides, Red Hat provides various tips, frequently asked questions (FAQs), and HOWTO documents.

You will find traditional Linux software package documentation, such as manual pages, under the `/usr/share/man` directory, with documentation for each installed software package under `/usr/share/doc`.

Linux manual pages are compressed text files containing succinct information about how to use a program. Each manual page generally provides a short summary of a command's use, a synopsis of command-line options, an explanation of the command's purpose, potential caveats or bugs, the name of the author, and a list of related configuration files and programs.

For example, you can learn how to read manual pages by using the `man` command to display its own manual page like so:

```
$ man man
```

After you press Enter, you see a page of text appear on the screen or in your window on the desktop. You can then scroll through the information using your keyboard's cursor keys, read, and then press the Q key to quit reading. More information about using the command line can be found in Chapter 5, "First Steps with Fedora."

Many of the software packages also include separate documents known as HOWTOs that contain information regarding specific subjects or software.

If the HOWTO documents are simple text files in compressed form (with filenames ending in `.gz`), you can easily read the document by using the `zless` command, which is a text pager that allows you to scroll back and forth through documents (use the `less` command to read plain-text files). You can start the command by using `less`, followed by the complete directory specification and name of the file, or *pathname*, like this:

```
$ less /usr/share/doc/httpd-2.0.50/README
```

To read a compressed version of this file, use the `zless` command in the same way:

```
$ zless /usr/share/doc/attr-2.4.1/CHANGES.gz
```

After you press Enter, you can scroll through the document using your cursor keys. Press the Q key to quit.

If the HOWTO document is in HTML format, you can simply read the information using a web browser, such as Firefox. Or if you're reading from a console, you can use the links or lynx text-only web browsers, like this:

```
$ links /usr/share/doc/stunnel-4.0.5/stunnel.html
```

The links browser offers drop-down menus, accessed by clicking at the top of the screen. You can also press the Q key to quit.

If the documentation is in PostScript format (with filenames ending in `.ps`), you can use the gv client to read or view the document like this:

```
$ gv /usr/share/doc/iproute-2.4.7/ip-crefs.ps
```

Finally, if you want to read a document in Portable Document Format (with a filename ending in `.pdf`), use the xpdf client like this:

```
$ xpdf /usr/share/doc/xfig/xfig-howto.pdf
```

> **NOTE**
>
> This book was developed and written using a complete install of all the software included with Fedora. You can use the CD-ROMs and DVD included with this book for your install or download your own copy, available as ISO9660 images (with filenames ending in `.iso`), and burn it onto 700MB CDRs or a DVD.
>
> Along with the full distribution, you will get the complete source code to the Linux kernel and source for all software in the distribution—more than 21 million lines of C and nearly 5 million lines of C++ code. Browse to http://fedora.redhat.com/download/ to get started.

Fedora Developers and Documentation

If you are interested in helping with the Fedora Project, you can assist in the effort by testing beta releases, writing documentation, and contributing software for the core or contributed software repositories. You should have some experience in installing Linux distributions, a desire to help with translation of documentation into different languages, or be able to use various software project management system, such as CVS.

Going beyond future versions of Fedora, you can also get involved with the continuing support of legacy versions. The Fedora Legacy project aims to provide security and critical bug fixes for retired versions of Fedora. Fedora Core 1 was the first version to be moved to the Fedora Legacy project, and future versions will be moved across once their operational lifetime is up. Because Red Hat views Fedora as a sand pit in which to test new technologies for possible inclusion into Red Hat Enterprise Linux, it is frequently updated and versions supersede each other. A rough guide of each version is supported for about 11 months, at which time it is moved into the Fedora Legacy Project. The project can be found at http://fedoralegacy.org—bear in mind that it is a community-supported project and, as such, is reliant upon the contributions of people just like you.

Reporting problems with Fedora Core during development is also part of the process! Bug reports are welcome and can be submitted according to guidelines outlined in Tammy Fox's and Havoc Pennington's *Fedora Project Developer's Guide*, found at http://fedora.redhat.com/participate/developers-guide/.

Writing documentation for Fedora requires a bit of discipline and experience with open-source document publishing tools. You can read more about the process by browsing to http://fedora.redhat.com/participate/documentation-guide/.

Mailing lists are also available as an outlet or forum for discussions about Fedora. The lists are categorized. For example, general users of Fedora Core can discuss issues on the fedora-list mailing list. Beta testers communicate via the fedora-test-list, developers via the fedora-devel-list, and documentation contributors via the fedora-docs-list. Mailing lists can be subscribed to by sending mail to `name_of_the_list-request@redhat.com`.

Reference

Each chapter in this book includes a "Reference" section listing links to additional or related information covered in the text. You can use these links to learn more about Fedora, Linux, and related technologies. You can also use the "Reference" section material to build custom sets of bookmarks to use while browsing or researching for more information about Linux.

http://www-1.ibm.com/linux/—Information from IBM regarding its efforts and offerings of Linux hardware, software, and services.

http://www.dwheeler.com/sloc—David A. Wheeler's amazing white paper covering the current state of GNU/Linux, its size, worth, components, market penetration.

http://fedora.redhat.com—Home page for the Fedora Project, sponsored by Red Hat, and your starting point for learning more about Fedora.

http://www.redhat.com/solutions/info/casestudies/—A listing of government and corporate Red Hat customers.

http://fedora.redhat.com/docs/—Web page with links to current Fedora documentation and release notes.

http://www.tldp.org—The definitive starting point for the latest updates to generic Linux FAQs, guides, and HOWTO documents.

http://www.ciac.org/ciac/—The U.S. Dept. of Energy's Computer Incident Advisory website, with details of security problems and fixes pertaining not only to Red Hat Linux, but many other operating systems. This site is useful for federal software contractors, developers, and system administrators.

http://www.justlinux.com/—One site to which new Linux users can browse to learn more about Linux.

http://fedorafaq.org/basics/—Another site that provides an easy introduction to Linux and Fedora.

# CHAPTER 2

Preparing to Install Fedora

Proper preparation and planning before installation can pay big dividends later on. If you are deploying Linux using Fedora Core, you will need to decide how you want to put it to use.

Installing Linux for the first time can seem daunting to inexperienced users or system administrators, but this chapter shows you how easy the installation can be if you make some simple preinstallation plans and decisions. Disk partitioning can be one of the most unfamiliar parts of the installation process, but it's an essential step toward configuring a multiplatform system. As you learn in this chapter, disk partitioning also is a manageable process when you take the time to plan ahead.

In this chapter, you learn how to prepare for an effective, efficient Fedora Core installation. The chapter begins with a checklist of considerations that can help you to plan how you will use Linux after installation, so you can plan for making the right choices during the installation itself. This chapter also outlines some of the basic hardware requirements for using Linux (with some specifics for the Fedora Core release on this book's CD-ROMs and DVD), and it highlights some potential hardware problems you can plan for—and avoid. The chapter also walks you through a general overview of the installation process, and it offers in-depth planning advice for partitioning your hard disk to support different configurations.

As you are about to learn, Fedora is a flexible Linux distribution that can adapt to a variety of hardware configurations and can be installed in a number of ways.

Planning Your Fedora Deployment

Before planning the specific steps of an installation, you need to make decisions about the type of deployment you want to undertake. Computing needs dictate the type of hardware and software solutions required for a successful deployment, but before making the plunge, some hard questions need to have been asked and answered, such as, "How will you use Fedora?" You learn more about these issues in the sections that follow. These sections also include a table you can use as a pre-deployment planning checklist and some final advice for planning the installation.

Business Considerations

Choosing an operating system for use in your business is an important decision. Migration to or adoption of a new hardware or software platform can have immediate and long-term effects on your organization. There is no magic formula to use in the decision-making process when contemplating a move, and freelance consultants, small business owners, medium-sized business, corporations, and other large business organizations will have different computing resources, objectives, and needs. For many businesses, computers are a critical and sometimes central component of business operations.

> **NOTE**
>
> Browse to Red Hat's Migration Center at http://www.redhat.com/business/utol/success/ to read success stories, market analyses, and technical reports on using Red Hat's Enterprise Linux products for business.

Fortunately, Linux is flexible enough to provide a full or partial migration and supports all of the major computing services required in today's business operations. Some of the more traditional services include electronic mail, file servers, network services (including firewalls), printing, web hosting (Internet and intranet-based), and database servers. If you desire commercial support, Red Hat can provide one, more, or all of these services. Linux can also be put to work in stages to ease migration issues such as training or support.

Some of the ideas, issues, and concerns surrounding the Linux deployment are listed in Table 2.1, titled "Deploying Fedora." One consideration is the context of how Fedora will be put to work. In other words, how will the new operating system fit in with your existing hardware and software needs? Another consideration is the level of consensus in management and user willingness to change to or adopt a new software environment. However, this issue can be sidestepped by making the transition as invisible as possible to users, such as when Linux-based web, file, or printing services replace existing servers.

The transition cost is another issue to consider. Fedora offers flexibility and reliability, but transitioning to a new platform can have unforeseen costs. Linux detractors sometimes point to added Total Cost of Ownership (TCO) factors, such as support and training, and argue that these issues add significantly to the cost of a Linux migration. Although there might be some additional support costs, again, training might not be an issue, especially if Linux is invisibly deployed. Hidden charges might be offset by the low cost in licensing, deployment, scaling, maintenance, resource requirements, and support of legacy hardware.

You should know what you are going to do with Linux before you install it. In other words, what is the objective of your migration? If Fedora will be used as a replacement platform for network services, what services will be replaced? What types of applications will need support If Fedora is deployed as a new desktop for administrative users?

Some research might be required beforehand, and you might want to compare software performance of desired services against your existing infrastructure, using a time-lined prototype install or deployment. Such testing is not a special requirement unique to a Linux migration, but a normal part of a careful consideration process before investing time and effort—which will represent your major costs because Linux and its major software is free.

System Considerations

Fedora is a perfect solution for many computing needs. However, choosing an operating system platform mandates consideration of a number of issues. Some of these issues are listed in Table 2.1. For example, how you choose to use Fedora will affect your choice of computer hardware, might affect your network configuration, and could dictate software policy issues (such as access, security, and allowable protocols).

Linux-based operating systems can be used to provide many different services. For example, one server might be boot management for a thin-client network in which workstations boot to a desktop by drawing a kernel and remotely mounted file systems over a network. This mechanism is not supported out of the box, so some effort can be expended if such a system is required. Other services more easily implemented (literally in an hour or less) could be centralized server environments for file serving, web hosting for a company intranet, or bridging of networks and routing services.

Linux supports nearly every network protocol, which enables it to be used to good effect even in mixed operating system environments. The security features of the Linux kernel and companion security software also make Linux a good choice when security is a top priority. Although no operating system or software package is perfect, the benefit of open source of the kernel and other software for Linux allows peer review of pertinent code and rapid implementation of any necessary fixes. Even with the secure features of Linux, some effort will have to be made in designing and implementing gateways, firewalls, or secure network routers.

Fedora can serve as a development platform for applications, e-commerce sites, new operating systems, foreign hardware systems, or design of new network devices using Linux as an embedded operating system. Setting up workstations, required servers, source code control systems, and industrial security will require additional effort.

Hardware compatibility can be an issue to consider when setting up a Linux server or building a Linux-based network. Fortunately, enlightened computer equipment manufacturers are beginning to realize that Linux-based operating systems (like other open-source operating systems such as BSD) are increasingly popular, support open standards, and offer technologies that can help rapid introduction of products into the market (through third-party developer communities).

Fedora can help ease system administration issues during migration. The latest suite of Fedora's configuration utilities provide intuitive and easy to use graphical interfaces for system administration of many common services, such as networking, printing, and Windows-based file sharing. Fedora can also be used to support legacy application environment, such as DOS, if required.

User Considerations

Humans are creatures of habit. So it can be hard to transition a workforce, customer base, or other community to a new environment. The Fedora desktop, however, provides a friendly and familiar interface with menus and icons that new users can readily learn and put to work.

Part of the migration process can involve addressing user concerns, especially if Linux will take over the desktop. Fedora can be deployed in stages to make the migration process a bit easier, but the issue of user training will need to be addressed early on. This is especially true if users will be required to develop new skills or be aware of any caveats when using Linux (such as deleting all files in one's home directory). Although Fedora can be configured to provide a "turn-key" desktop in which only several graphical applications (such as a web browser, organizer, or word processor) can be used, some users will want and need to learn more about Linux.

You can turn to formal Linux training from commercial vendors. System administrators can get training directly from Red Hat (go to http://www.redhat.com/training). For other issues concerning Linux in larger computing environments, browse to Linas Vepstas's Linux Enterprise Computing pages at http://linas.org/linux/.

A Predeployment Planning Checklist

Table 2.1 provides a minimal checklist you can use to help plan a deployment.

TABLE 2.1   Deploying Fedora

Consideration	Description
Applicability	How is Fedora going to be used?
Boot Management	Will remote booting be required?
Connectivity	Will the system be an intranet? Bandwidth requirements? Wireless? Mobile?
Context	How does this install fit in with academic, business, or corporate needs?
Consensus	Are managers and potential users on board with the project?
Comparison	Is this install part of platform comparison or benchmarking?
Development Platform	Will development tools be used?
Embedded Device	Is it an embedded device project?
Hardware	Are there any special hardware or device interfacing requirements?
Finance	How much is in the budget? Will cost comparison be required?
Marketing	Will a product or service be offered as a result?

TABLE 2.1   Continued

Consideration	Description
Networking	What type of networking will be required?
Objective	Is there a specific objective of the install?
Power Management	Any special power or energy requirements?
Prototype Project	Is this a prototype or test install?
Public Relations	Does the public need to know?
Quality of Service	Is high availability or data integrity an issue?
Roadmap	What other steps might precede or follow the install?
Reporting	Are follow-up reports required?
Security	What level or type of security will be required?
Server	Is this a server installation?
Site Considerations	Does the location provide needed temperature and security, or does it even matter?
Software	Are any special device drivers needed for success?
Storage	Are there size or integrity needs? Has a backup plan been devised?
Timeline	Are there time constraints or deadlines to the install?
Training	Will special training be required for users or administrators?
Users	How many and what type of users are expected?
Workstation	Is this a workstation or personal desktop install? Is the workstation portable?

Do not forget to address follow-up issues on your migration roadmap. You should pay attention to how satisfied or how well new users, especially those new to Linux, are adapting if a new desktop is used. However, if Fedora is deployed in a mixed environment, many users might not even know (or need to know) that Linux is being used!

Planning the Installation

There are many factors in favor of using Fedora Core as a computing solution. The current distribution can fill many different roles on various tiers and hardware platforms because its preconfigured installation scripts are a tailored fit for development, workstation, e-commerce, server, and mobile platforms—only the required software will be installed.

Addressing concerns beforehand can help quell any worries or fears felt by new users. Some key factors for a successful installation include

- **Preparation**—Thoroughly discuss the migration or deployment, along with benefits, such as greater stability and availability of service.

- **Preconfiguration**—If possible, give users a voice in software choices or categories and poll for comments regarding concerns.

- **Correct installation**—Ensure that the installed systems are working properly, including access permissions, password systems, or other user-related issues and interaction with the deployment.

- **The right hardware to do the job**—Make sure that users have the hardware they need for their work, and that computers match the tasks required. For example, developers will have workstation requirements vastly different from administrative personnel.

Hardware Requirements

Fedora can be installed on and will run on a wide variety of Intel-based hardware. This does not include pre-Pentium legacy platforms, but many older PCs, workstations, rack-mounted systems, and multiprocessor servers are supported. Small, medium-sized, and even large-scale deployments of specially tuned Linux distributions are available through a number of companies such as IBM, which offers hardware, software, and service solutions (with more than 200 software solutions for clustering applications alone).

> **TIP**
>
> It is always a good idea to explore your hardware options extensively before jumping on board with a specific vendor. You can buy computer hardware with a Linux distribution preinstalled. At the time of this writing, Dell Computers offered Linux systems (such as desktop PCs and notebooks) through http://www.dell.com/redhat/. IBM also offers Linux on its product line, and more information can be found through http://www.ibm.com/linux/. To find HP and preinstalled Linux systems, browse to http://www.hp.com/linux/. You can also buy low-cost desktop PCs with Linux through Wal-Mart's online store at http://www.walmart.com (click to select the electronics department).

In the first section of this chapter, you learned to consider how Linux can be used in your environment and how you can prepare for its installation and deployment. These considerations also play a role in determining the types of hardware you need in your installation. But the type of deployment you choose also determines the hardware required for a successful deployment of Linux—and post-deployment satisfaction. The range of Linux hardware requirements and compatible hardware types is quite wide, especially when you consider that Linux can be used with mainframe computers as well as embedded devices.

Meeting the Minimum Fedora Core Hardware Requirements

The Fedora Project publishes general minimum hardware requirements for installing and using its base distribution in a file named RELEASE NOTES on the first CD-ROM, or available at http://fedora.redhat.com/docs/release-notes/. For the current release, your PC should at least have a 200MHz Pentium CPU, 620MB hard drive space, and 64MB RAM for using (and installing) Fedora without a graphical interface. For obvious reasons, a faster CPU, larger capacity hard drive, and more RAM are desired. Servers and development workstations require more storage and RAM.

Using Legacy Hardware

If you have an older PC based on an Intel 486 CPU with only 32MB RAM and a 500MB hard drive (which can be hard to find nowadays), you can install other Linux distributions such as Debian from The Debian Project at http://www.debian.org.

> **CAUTION**
>
> One caveat is that if you prepare a hard drive with Linux in a PC with one CPU, such as a Pentium, and then install the drive in a PC with a 486 CPU, you should either make sure that a 486-based Linux kernel is installed, or perform a post-install of an appropriate kernel after moving the hard drive.

Installing Fedora on legacy hardware will be easier if you choose to use more recent Pentium-class PCs, but even older Pentium PCs can be used and purchased at a fraction of their original cost. Such PCs can easily handle many mundane but useful tasks. Some of the tasks suitable for older hardware include

- Acting as a firewall, router, or gateway
- Audio jukebox and music file storage server
- Handling electronic mail
- Hosting a remote printer and providing remote printing services
- Network font server
- Providing FTP server access
- Remote logging capture
- Secondary network-attached backup server
- Serving as an Intranet (internal LAN) web server
- Unattended dial-up gateway, voice mailbox, or fax machine
- Use as a "thin client" workstation for basic desktop tasks

Older PCs can handle any task that does not require a CPU with a lot of horsepower. To get the most out of your hardware, do not install any more software than required (a good idea in any case, especially if you are building a server). To get a little performance boost, add as much RAM as economically and practically feasible. If you cannot do this then cut down on memory usage by turning off unwanted or unneeded services. You can also recompile a custom Linux kernel to save a bit more memory and increase performance (see Chapter 38, "Kernel and Module Management").

> **NOTE**
>
> Fedora does not include XFree86 3.3.6. This version might be important because older, legacy video cards are no longer supported in the newer X11R6 7.0 distribution. You can download version 3.3.6 from The XFree86 Project, Inc. through http://ftp.xfree86.org/pub/XFree86/3.3.6/ binaries/. Make sure to choose the appropriate version for your operating system!

Planning for Hard Drive Storage for Your Fedora Installation Class

Making room for Fedora requires you to decide on how to use existing hard drive space. You might decide to replace existing hard drives entirely, for example, or you might decide to use only one operating system on your computer, making partitioning unnecessary. A full install from this book's CD-ROMs or DVD will require at least 7GB hard drive space just for the software, so if you plan to install everything, a 10GB hard drive could be ideal for a workstation. Note that depending on how you plan to use Linux, a smaller capacity disk can be used, or a disk capacity many times the size of your system will be required.

> **NOTE**
>
> The following recommended installations and minimal storage requirements are based on a full install of the freely available version of Fedora Core distributed on the Internet. The copy of Fedora included with this book is the same, but you may find many additional software packages available from third-party Fedora contributors. Installing additional software will impact your storage requirements.

The Fedora installer offers a choice of installation types or classes, and each has its own hard drive storage requirements:

- **Workstation**—You'll need a minimum of 3GB hard drive storage, but much more if you choose to install everything. This installation is intended for developers and other users who want to use the entire spectrum of Linux software offered by the distribution.

- **Personal Desktop**—This is a new installation class for SOHO (small office/home office) users that installs a basic graphical desktop, along with requisite office and Internet productivity software; you'll need around 2.3GB of storage if you don't customize the default software selections.

- **Server**—You need at least 1.1GB of storage for the operating system and server software, but you also must take into consideration other storage requirements. For example, if you plan to run a website with a lot of graphics or serve other files, you might need to add storage to your system or accommodate remotely mounted storage locally.

- **Custom**—This installation supports a minimal install requiring a little over 600MB; however, you can also choose to install all the software in the distribution; in which case, you'll need 7GB or more of storage, along with several hundred megabytes of free space for temporary files.

The storage requirements for each of these classes can be revised somewhat, depending on the X desktop environment you choose (such as KDE or GNOME). Choosing the Custom install will let you choose specific software packages from the group package categories. Here are some software packages you might want to consider passing up in the installation process for a minimalist system:

- X Window System
- GNOME Desktop Environment
- KDE Desktop Environment
- Graphical Internet
- Office/Productivity
- Documentation
- Sound and Video
- Graphics
- All Development software or libraries

Checking Hardware Compatibility

Fedora software for Intel-based PCs is compiled for the minimum x86 platform supported by the Linux kernel.

> **NOTE**
>
> The compatibility information in this chapter relates to Fedora Core. Other distributions might have different storage and CPU requirements.

Specific issues regarding Linux hardware compatibility can be researched online at a number of sites. Red Hat, Inc. offers a hardware compatibility database at http://hardware.redhat.com/hcl/. You can select hardware class, manufacturer, the version of Red Hat Linux, platform, and status of support.

Other sites, such as the Linux-USB device overview at http://www.qbik.ch/usb/devices/, offer an interactive browsing of supported devices, and printer compatibility can be researched at LinuxPrinting.org at http://linuxprinting.org/. Some hardware categories to consider in your research include

- **Controller cards**—Such as SCSI, IDE, FireWire
- **CPUs**—Intel, AMD, and others
- **Input devices**—Keyboards
- **Modems**—External, PCMCIA, PCI, and controllerless workarounds
- **Network cards**—ISA, PCI, USB, and others

- **Pointing devices**—Mice, tablets, and possibly touchscreens

- **Printers**—Various printer models

- **RAM**—Issues regarding types of system memory

- **Sound cards**—Issues regarding support

- **Specific motherboard models**—Compatibility or other issues

- **Specific PCs, servers, and laptop models**—Compatibility reports

- **Storage devices**—Removables, fixed, and others

- **Video cards**—Console issues (X compatibility depends on version of X11R6 or vendor-based X distribution used)

If you have a particular laptop or PC model, you should also check with its manufacturer for Linux support issues. Some enlightened manufacturers now offer a Linux operating system preinstalled, or have an in-house Linux hardware certification program. Laptop users will definitely want to browse to Linux on Laptops at http://linux-laptop.net/.

If you cannot find compatibility answers in various on-line databases, continue your research by reading the Linux Hardware HOWTO at http://www.tldp.org/HOWTO/ Hardware-HOWTO/.

At that address, you will find loads of general information and links to additional sources of information. Keep in mind that when PC hardware is unsupported under Linux, it is generally because the manufacturer cannot or will not release technical specifications or because no one has taken the time and effort to develop a driver. If you hit a roadblock with a particular piece of hardware, check the hardware manufacturer's support web pages, or Google.com's Linux pages at http://www.google.com/linux. You can then type in a specific search request and hopefully find answers to how to make the hardware work with Linux. This is also a good way to research answers to questions about software issues.

Preparing for Potential Hardware Problems

Fedora Core will work "out-of-the-box" with nearly every Intel-based Pentium PC motherboard and laptop; drivers for thousands of different types of hardware peripherals are included. But you can sometimes run into problems if Linux does not recognize a hardware item, if Fedora does not correctly initialize the hardware, or if an initialized item is incorrectly configured. For these reasons, some hardware items are prone to creating problems during an install. In the sections that follow, you learn some important pointers for avoiding these problems or resolving those that do occur.

Controllerless Modems

As you read earlier, most Linux hardware-related installation problems stem from a lack of technical specifications from the manufacturer, thwarting efforts of open-source developers to create a driver. In the recent past, one hardware item that triggered both types of difficulties was the controllerless modem, also colloquially known as a WinModem. The good news is that modem chipset manufacturers have been more forthcoming with driver details. Some original equipment manufacturers, such as IBM, have made a concerted effort to provide Linux support. Support for the ACP Mwave modem, used in ThinkPad 600/Es and 770s, is included in the Linux kernel. Drivers have been developed for many of the controllerless modem chipsets that formally did not work with Linux.

If a driver is not available for your controllerless modem, you have a few options. You can download the driver's source code and build the driver yourself. Alternatively, you can download a binary-only software package and install the driver.

Some controllerless modems might also need to be initialized and configured using a separate utility program. The modem, if supported, should work normally after installing and configuring the driver.

You can research Linux support for controllerless modems by browsing to http://www.linmodems.org/.

Universal Serial Bus Devices

Fedora supports hundreds of different Universal Serial Bus devices. USB is a design specification and a protocol used to enable a host computer to talk to attached peripherals. Because of lack of manufacturer and device ID information or lack of technical specifications regarding certain chipsets, some devices might not work with Fedora. USB 1.1 devices are designed to support data transfer speeds between 1.5 and 12Mbps.

Common USB devices include cameras, keyboards, mice, modems, network interfaces, printers, scanners, storage devices, video (such as webcams), and hubs (to chain additional devices). Some problematic USB devices (at the time of this writing) include

- **Wireless**—Many 802.11b wireless USB network adapters, with the exception of those using Atmel chipsets.

- **Scanners**—Many Canon, Visioneer, and Hewlett-Packard USB scanners

- **Webcams**—Selected Logitech and Creative Labs webcams

Although some enlightened manufacturers are aware of opportunities in the Linux marketplace, most still do not support Linux. It pays to determine Linux support before you buy any USB device; again, research Linux USB support and its current state of development by browsing to http://www.qbik.ch/usb/devices/.

The newer USB 2.0 specification enables devices (such as hard and CD drives) to use speeds up to 480Mbps. Fedora supports USB 2.0 with the ehci-hcd kernel module. This driver, in development since early 2001, enables the use of many forms of newer USB 2.0 devices as long as you have a supported USB controller. Check out the current state of Linux USB 2.0 support by browsing to http://www.linux-usb.org/usb2.html.

Motherboard-based Hardware

Small form factor PCs, thin-clients, notebooks, and embedded devices are part of a growing trend in the PC industry. Manufacturers are cramming more functionality into fewer chips in order to simplify design and lower power requirements. Today, many computers come with built-in video graphics, audio chipsets, and network interfaces, along with a host of peripheral support.

Common modern (1996-onward) PC motherboard form factors are designed according to industry-assigned specifications (usually from Intel), and are ATX (12–9.6 inches); MicroATX (9.6–9.6 inches); and FlexATX (9–7.5 inches). One of the newest and even smaller motherboard forms is from VIA Technologies, Inc.—the mini-ITX (approximately 6.5–6.5 inches), which has an embedded CPU. CPUs commonly used in all these mother-boards will vary, and have different socketing requirements based on chipset pins: Socket 478 for K7-type CPUs (from AMD); Socket 370 for Pentium IIIs and Celerons from Intel, or C3s from VIA; and Socket 478 for Intel's Pentium 4s (early versions of which used a 423-pin socket). Older socket types are Socket A, Socket 7 (and Super 7), Slot 1, and Slot 2.

Fortunately, nearly all controllers, bridges, and other chipsets are supported by Linux. Although flaky or unsupported built-in hardware can (usually) be sidestepped by installing a comparable PCI card component, cutting-edge notebook users are at the most risk for compatibility problems because internal components are not user-replaceable. Potential pitfalls can be avoided through careful research (vote with your money for Linux-compatible hardware), or by choosing PC motherboards with a minimum of built-in features, and then using PCI (Peripheral Component Interconnect) or AGP (Accelerated Graphics Port) cards known to work.

CPU, Symmetric Multiprocessing, and Memory Problems

Fedora supports all Intel-based Pentium CPUs. Code is included in the Linux kernel to recognize the CPU type when booting, and to then implement any required fixes to over-come architecture bugs (such as the now-infamous divide-by-zero error). After you install Fedora Core, you can also rebuild the Linux kernel to specifically support and take advan-tage of the host PC's CPU. You might not realize extreme improvements in computational speed, but you'll be assured that Linux is crafted for your CPU's architecture, which can help stability and reliability. Details about rebuilding the Linux kernel are in Chapter 38. Some of the Intel-based CPUs with specific supporting code for Linux include those from Advanced Micro Devices, Transmeta, and VIA Technologies.

Fedora's Linux kernel also should automatically recognize and use the amount of installed RAM. The Linux kernel should also recognize and map out any memory holes in system memory (perhaps used for video graphics).

If you are installing Fedora on a working, stable PC, you should not have any problems related to the system's memory. If you are putting together a new system, you need to avoid combining or configuring the system in ways that will interfere with its ability to process data. Some issues to be aware of are

- Do not expect similar CPU performance across product lines from different manu-facturers, such as AMD or VIA. Some CPU models offer better floating point or integer math operations, which are important for a number of CPU-intensive tasks (such as graphics, audio, and video rendering or conversion). If you need better performance, try to find a faster CPU compatible with your motherboard, or switch to a CPU with better Floating Point Unit (FPU) performance.

- Overclocking can cause problems with overheating, memory access, and other hardware performance, and it is not a good idea for any Linux system. Overclocking is a popular geek pastime and a great way to get a bit of performance boost out of slower CPUs by altering voltage settings and/or clock timings via the BIOS. You can try to push your CPU to higher speeds, but this approach is not recommended if your aim is system stability. The Linux kernel will report the recognized CPU speed upon booting (which you can view using the dmesg command).

- Along the same lines, CPU and motherboard overheating will cause problems. Proper attachment of the CPU's heatsink using a quality thermal paste (never use thermal tape), along with one or more fans providing adequate airflow will lessen the chance of hardware damage and system failure.

- You can run into problems if you switch the type of CPU installed in your computer, and especially if your PC's BIOS does not automatically recognize or configure for newly installed mainboard hardware and components. In some instances, a system reinstall is warranted, but BIOS issues should be resolved first.

- Not all CPUs support Symmetric Multiprocessing, or SMP. Fedora readily supports use of two or more CPUs, and during installation will automatically install an appropriate Linux kernel. You can avoid problems by reading the Linux SMP HOWTO (available through http://www.tldp.org). Note that some CPUs, such as the current crop of VIA C3s, may not be used for SMP. Also, SMP motherboards require that all CPUs be identical. This means that you will need two identical CPUs to take advantage of SMP.

- Faulty or bad memory will cause Linux kernel panics or Signal 11 errors (segmentation faults) causing a system crash or a program to abort execution. Linux is quite sensitive to faulty hardware, but will run with great stability in a correctly configured system with good hardware. Problems can arise from incorrect BIOS settings, especially if video memory must occupy and use a portion of system RAM. Always install quality (and appropriate) memory in your PC to avoid problems.

Preparing and Using a Hardware Inventory

Buying a turn-key Linux solution is one way to avoid hardware problems, and many vendors are standing by, ready to prescribe solutions. However, managing deployments aimed at using existing hardware requires some information collection.

If you are a small business or individual user, you are well-advised to prepare detailed checklists of existing hardware before attempting a migration to Linux. Not only will you benefit from the collected information, but you might also be able to sidestep or anticipate problems before, during, or after installation. Problems are most likely to occur with newer hardware, cutting-edge hardware such as new motherboard chipsets and video cards, or extraneous hardware such as operating system–specific scanners, printers, or wireless devices.

Table 2.2 provides a comprehensive checklist you can use to take inventory of target hardware, such as the computer and any peripherals. Veteran Linux users can take the collected information to build custom systems by adding known hardware or substituting cheaper but equivalent hardware.

TABLE 2.2   System and Peripheral Inventory Checklist

Item	Errata
Audio Devices	Microphone:
	Line out:
	Line in:
BIOS	Type:
	Revision:
	ACPI:
	APM:
CD-ROM Drive	Brand:
	Type:
CD-RW Drive	Brand:
	Type:
	CDR Write Speed:
	CD Re-Write Speed:
	CD-ROM Read Speed:
DVD Drive	Brand:
	Type:
DVD+/-RW Drive	Brand:
	Type:
Digital Camera	Brand:
	Model:
	Interface:
CPU	Brand:
	Socket Type:
	Speed:
Firewire (IEEE 1394)	Chipset:
	Device(s):
IrDA Port	Device number:
	Port IRQ:
Keyboard	Brand:
	Type:
Laptop	Brand:
	Model:
	Hibernation partition:

TABLE 2.2   Continued

Item	Errata
Legacy Ports	Parallel type:
	Parallel IRQ:
	RS-232 number(s):
	RS-232 IRQ(s):
Mice	Brand:
	Type:
Modem	Brand:
	Type:
Motherboard	Brand:
	Type:
	Chipset:
Monitor(s)	Brand:
	Model:
	Horizontal freq:
	Vertical freq:
	Max. Resolution:
Network Card	Wireless:
	Brand:
	Type:
	Speed:
PCI Bus	Version:
	Model:
	Type:
PCMCIA	Controller:
	Cardbus:
	Brand:
	Type:
Printer(s)	Brand:
	Model:
System RAM	Amount:
	Type:
	Speed:
S-Video Port	X Support:
Scanner	Brand:
	Model:
	Interface type:
Sound Card	Chipset:
	Type:
	I/O Addr:
	IRQ:
	DMA:
	MPU Addr:

2

TABLE 2.2   Continued

Item	Errata
Storage Device(s)	Removable:
	Size:
	Brand:
	Model:
	Controller(s):
	Rotational Speed:
Storage Device Controller	Type:
Tablet	Brand:
	Model:
	Interface:
Universal Serial Bus	Controller:
	BIOS MPS Setting:
	BIOS Plug-n-Play Setting:
	Device(s):
Video Device(s)	Brand:
	Model:
	Xinerama:
	Chipset:
	VRAM:

Use the checklist in Table 2.2 as a general guideline for recording your computer's hardware and other capabilities. You can get quite a bit of information through hardware manuals or other documentation included with your PC, video, sound, or network interface card. Don't worry if you cannot fill out the entire checklist; Fedora will most likely recognize and automatically configure your PC's hardware during installation. Much of this information can be displayed by the dmesg command after booting. However, some of these details, such as your video card's graphics chipset and installed video RAM, can come in handy if you need to perform troubleshooting. You can also use the list as a post-installation check-off sheet to see how well Fedora works with your system.

Preparing for the Install Process

The basic steps in installing Fedora are to plan, install, and configure. You'll need to decide on how to boot to an install and how much room to devote to Linux. Then perform the install (a sample step-by-step installation is in Chapter 3, "Installing Fedora") and afterward, configure your system to host new users and specific software services. Much of the initial work will be done during the install process because the installer, Anaconda, will walk you through partitioning, configuring the desktop, and configuration of any recognized network adapter.

There are many different ways to install Fedora Core, and selecting an installation method might depend on the equipment on hand, existing bandwidth, or equipment limitations.

Here are some of the most commonly used installation methods:

- **CD-ROM/DVD**—Using a compatible CD-ROM or DVD drive attached to the computer (laptop users with an external CD-ROM drive will need PCMCIA support from a driver disk image included under the first CD-ROM's images directory).

- **DOS**—By using LOADLIN, you can boot to a Linux install by pointing LOADLIN to use a Fedora installation kernel and ramdisk. Run the DOS batch file, autoboot.bat, found under the dosutils directory on the first Fedora CD-ROM or DVD.

- **Network File System (NFS)**—You can install Fedora from a remotely mounted hard drive containing the Fedora Core software. To do this installation, you need to have an installed and supported network interface card, along with a boot floppy with network support. (You learn how to make boot floppies later in this section of the chapter.)

- **File Transfer Protocol (FTP)**—As with an NFS install, installation via FTP requires that the Fedora software be available on a public FTP server. You also need an installed and supported network interface card, along with a boot floppy with network support.

- **Hypertext Transport Protocol (HTTP)**—As with the FTP and NFS installs, installation via HTTP requires that the Fedora software be available on an accessible website. You also need an installed and supported network interface card, along with a boot floppy with network support.

- **Installation via the Internet**—If you have the bandwidth, it may also be possible to install Fedora via the Internet; however, this method might not be as reliable as using a Local Area Network (LAN) because of availability and current use of Fedora Project or other servers on mirror sites.

- **A hard drive partition**—By copying the .iso images to a hard drive partition, you can then boot to an install.

- **Preinstalled media**—It is also possible to install Linux on another hard drive and then transfer the hard drive to your computer. This is handy, especially if your site uses removable hard drives or other media.

> **NOTE**
>
> More esoteric installations may be possible. Some Linux distributions support booting to an install via an Iomega Zip drive, via the Parallel Port Internet Protocol (PLIP), and even a null-modem cable supporting the Serial Line Internet Protocol (SLIP) or Point-to-Point Protocol (PPP). Browse to http://www.tldp.org and read Gilles Lamiral's PLIP Install HOWTO to see how to install Red Hat 7.0 using your PC's parallel port. Once installed, you can then try to upgrade to Fedora.

After booting and choosing to use either a graphical or text-based install interface, the installation procedure is nearly the same for each type of install. Chapter 3 walks you through a typical CD/DVD–based installation.

Preparing to Install from a CD-ROM

Installing Fedora can be as simple as inserting the first CD/DVD into your computer's CD drive and rebooting the computer. But if you choose this method, you should first make sure that your system's BIOS is set to boot from CD-ROM.

Entering the BIOS to make this change is usually accomplished by depressing a particular key immediately after turning on the computer, such as Del or F2. After entering the BIOS, navigate to the BIOS Boot menu, perhaps such as that shown in Figure 2.1.

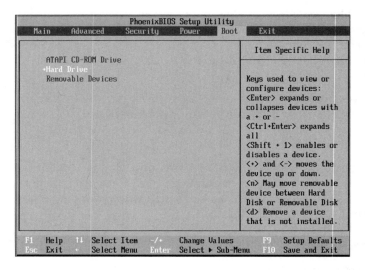

FIGURE 2.1 To boot to an install using your Fedora Core CD-ROM or DVD, set your BIOS to have your computer boot using its CD drive.

Partitioning Before and During Installation

Partitioning your hard drive for Linux can be done before or during installation.

If you plan to prepare your partitions before installing Linux, you'll need to use commercial partitioning software. Some of the popular commercial software you can use to create Linux partitions are Symantec's PartitionMagic or VCOM Products' Partition Commander. Alternatively, it may be possible to prepare partitions before installing Fedora by using the free FIPS.EXE command.

If you want to partition a hard drive using an existing Linux system, you can attach the hard drive to a spare IDE channel, and then use the Linux `fdisk` or GNU `parted` partitioning utilities. Both utilities offer a way to interactively partition and prepare storage media. Linux recognizes IDE hard drives using a device name such as `/dev/hda` (for the master device on IDE channel 0), `/dev/hdb` (for the slave device on IDE channel 0), `/dev/hdc` (for the master device on IDE channel 1), and `/dev/hdd` (for the slave device on IDE channel 1).

If a new hard drive is properly attached to your PC and you then boot Linux, you can see if the kernel recognizes the device by viewing the output of the dmesg command. You can then use fdisk with the device name to begin partitioning like so:

```
# fdisk /dev/hdb
```

Note that you will need root permission, and in this example, the new drive is attached as a slave on IDE channel 0. Do not change partitioning on your root device, or you'll hork your system! The fdisk command is interactive, and you can press m to get help when using the utility. You can use parted in much the same way if you specify the i, or interactive option on the command line like so:

```
# parted -i /dev/hdb
```

To get help when using parted interactively, press ? or type help followed a command keyword. The parted command has other helpful features, such as the ability to copy a file system directly from one partition to another.

Finally, you can prepare partitions ahead of installation by booting your system using a live Linux distribution (such as the LNX Bootable Business Card, available at http://www.lnx-bbc.org/) and then using a native Linux utility such as fdisk to partition your drive. For details on using the fdisk partitioning utility and alternative software tools to partition your hard drive, see the section "How to Access and Manipulate the Partition Table" in Chapter 37, "Managing the File System."

TIP

You can use the first Fedora CD or the DVD to perform other tasks aside from installing Linux. The CD-ROM/DVD features a rescue mode and can also be used to partition and prepare a hard drive for Linux. See Chapter 3.

NOTE

It is possible to create a dual-boot configuration, which allows the choice of booting Fedora and another operating system, such as Windows XP. To configure your system for dual-booting, you must first install Windows and then install Linux. Note that many Windows system-restore CD-ROMs will wipe out all data on your hard drive, including Linux. During installation of Fedora, you install the GRUB Linux bootloader in the primary drive's Master Boot Record, or MBR. When properly configured, GRUB allows your system to reboot to Windows or Linux. See Chapter 16, "Backing Up, Restoring, and Recovery," for information on using GRUB, or browse to http://www.gnu.org/software/grub/manual/ to read the GRUB manual.

CAUTION

Before you begin partitioning your drive, get your safety nets in order. First, back up all critical data! Any changes to your system's hard drive or operating system put your existing data at risk. To prevent the loss of time and resources that inevitably follow data loss, do full backups before you make any changes to your system. Create a bootdisk during the install (you will be asked before the install finishes), so you will be able to at least boot Linux if something goes wrong. See Chapter 16 for information on backups with Linux.

Choosing a Partitioning Scheme

Likedeployment and installation of Linux, partitioning your hard drive to accept Fedora requires some forethought, especially if the target computer is going to be used other than as a home PC on which to learn Linux.

If Linux is to be the only resident operating system, you can have the installer automatically create and use a partition scheme according to the type of installation you select during the install. If you plan to have a dual-boot system in which you can boot Linux or another operating system, you'll need to manually partition your hard drive before and possibly during the install.

The simplest and most basic partitioning scheme for a Linux system requires a Linux native root partition and a swap partition. On a single-drive system with 10GB storage and 128MB RAM, the scheme might look like this:

```
Hard Drive Partition    Mount Point    Size
/dev/hda1               /              9.74GB
/dev/hda2               swap           256MB
```

On a system running Windows, the scheme might look like this:

```
Hard Drive Partition    Mount Point    Size
/dev/hda1               /mnt/dos       2GB
/dev/hda2               /              7.74GB
/dev/hda3               swap           256MB
```

> **CAUTION**
>
> Notebook users should be careful when partitioning. Many notebooks use a special partition equal to the size of install RAM in order to perform suspend-to-disk or other hibernation operations. Always examine your computer's initial partitioning scheme if configuring a dual-boot system, and leave the special partition alone! One way around this problem is to use a software suspend approach as outlined at http://swsusp.sourceforge.net/.

Hosting Parts of the Linux File System on Separate Partitions

Your specific partitioning scheme will depend on how Fedora will be used. On a system being designed for expansion, greater capacity, or the capability to host additional software or users, you can use separate partitions to host various parts of the Linux file system. Some candidates for these separate partitions include

- /home—Users will store hundreds upon hundreds of megabytes of data under their directories. This is important data, perhaps even more so than the system itself. Using a separate partition (on a different volume) to store this user data helps make the data easier to find, and it segregates user and system data. You will have to decide ahead of time how much storage to allocate to users. For a single workstation, you should reserve several gigabytes of storage.

- /opt—As the home directory for additional software packages, this directory can have its own partition or remote file system. Fedora does not populate this directory, but it might be used by other software packages you install later on. One gigabyte of storage should be adequate, depending on applications to be installed.

- /tmp—This directory can be used as temporary storage by users, especially if disk quotas are enforced; as such, it could be placed on its own partition. This directory can be as small as 100MB.

- /usr—This directory holds nearly all the software on a Fedora system and can become quite large if additional software is added, especially on a workstation configuration. Using a separate partition can make sense. A full install will require at least 6GB for this directory or more if additional software is added.

- /var—Placing this directory (or perhaps some of its subdirectories) on a separate partition can be a good idea, especially because security logs, mail, and print spooling take place under this tree. You should reserve at least one gigabyte of storage for /var, especially if using Fedora as a print server (as spooled documents will reside under /var/spool) .

TIP

As a general rule, it is a good idea to segregate user and system data. Although a Linux system can be quickly restored, user data has a much greater value and can be much more difficult to replace. Segregating data can make the job of backing up and restoring much easier. If you ever have a problem accessing your partition, we recommend that you get the excellent Knoppix distribution that boots and runs entirely from CD. This will enable you to access your partitions and make any necessary repairs.

Using Fedora's kickstart Installation Method

Automating the installation process can save system administrators a lot of time and effort during an initial deployment, upgrade, or maintenance cycle by managing multiple computers at one time. Fedora offers a highly automated installation technique called kickstart, developed by Red Hat, which can be used for unattended installation of Linux.

Fedora's kickstart installation uses a single configuration file with a special, extensive syntax on a server, boot floppy, or other medium to install Fedora via CD/DVD, a hard drive partition, or a network connection. Using kickstart is easy and involves passing a kernel argument to the Fedora Linux boot kernel. The various arguments tell the boot kernel to look for a configuration file on floppy, a designated server, via a network, specific file, or CD/DVD.

You can use kickstart to install Fedora on one or more computers at the same time. First, set up a web or FTP server with Fedora's installation files. For directions, see the section "Installing Using a Network" in Chapter 3. Next, create a network boot floppy using the techniques described in this chapter's "Creating a Boot and Auxiliary Driver Disk" section. Follow the directions given here (choosing an FTP install) and then copy the custom kickstart file to the network boot floppy. You can then use this floppy (and copies) to boot one or more PCs to a network install using your FTP server.

TIP

Fedora does not automatically install ksconfig, the utility used to create and customize kickstart files. Be sure you install it using either yum or the Add/Remove Programs tool.

To begin the automated installation process, you create the configuration file that will be used by kickstart as an installation profile. You can configure the complex configuration file with Fedora's Kickstart Configurator. To start the configuration, click the Kickstart item from the System Tools menu on the desktop, or run the system-config-kickstart or ksconfig command, like so:

```
# /usr/sbin/ksconfig
```

After you press Enter, you see the Kickstart Configurator dialog box, as shown in Figure 2.2.

Click to select various options, and then enter the specifics desired for the target system. Start by selecting the default system language, type of keyboard, mouse, and so on. Of course, automated installations work best when installing to similar equipment. When finished, press Ctrl+S, or use the Save file item from the File menu. The configuration will be saved with the name ks.cfg. When you use the kickstart installation method, the kickstart file will be read by computers booting to the install. The kickstart language covers nearly every aspect of an install with the exception of sound card, printer, or modem setup.

For example, a portion of a kickstart file generated for an install might look like

```
#Generated by Kickstart Configurator

#System language
lang en_US

#Language modules to install
langsupport en_US
```

```
#System keyboard
keyboard us

#System mouse
mouse genericps/2

#System timezone
timezone --utc America/New_York

#Root password
rootpw --iscrypted $1$/n3yjyDV$AWoBZgRQq/lAxyRhX1JSM1
...
```

FIGURE 2.2   Fedora's kickstart configuration tool, ksconfig, can be used to quickly and easily create installation profiles for use in automated installations.

Note that not all the output of a sample ks.cfg is shown. However, you can see that this file will feed kickstart directions for an install, including an encrypted root password to be installed on the target system.

The next step is to copy your new ks.cfg to a boot disk created using one of the boot floppy images (found under the images directory on the first Fedora CD/DVD). You can do this with Linux by using the mount and cp commands. For example, take your boot disk, insert it into your PC, and then use the mount command (as root) like so:

```
# mount /mnt floppy
```

If Fedora has mounted your floppy automatically, you'll receive an error message such as /dev/fd0 already mounted. You can then simply copy the ks.cfg file to your floppy like so:

```
# cp ks.cfg /mnt/floppy
```

You can verify the contents of the floppy using the ls command like this:

```
# ls /mnt/floppy
boot.msg        general.msg      initrd.img       ks.cfg           ldlinux.sys
options.msg    param.msg        rescue.msg    snake.msg   splash.lss
syslinux.cfg    syslinux.png     vmlinuz
```

Then unmount the floppy using the umount command like so:

```
# umount /mnt/floppy
```

Remove the disk. It is now ready for use. When you use the disk to boot a PC, after booting, tell the install boot image that you'd like to perform a kickstart install like this:

```
linux ks=floppy
```

The installer will then use the specifications you outlined in the Kickstart Configurator and saved in ks.cfg to install Fedora.

Reference

The following is a list of references you can use to learn a bit more about partitioning, installation tools, and installing Fedora Core and Linux variants on a variety of hardware. You'll also find information about installation on hardware employed for embedded and mainframe solutions.

http://www.redhat.com/solutions/migration/—Red Hat's helpful Migration Center, with news, views, white papers, and other tips and research on migrating to a Linux solution.

http://www.yale.edu/pclt/BOOT/DEFAULT.HTM—A basic primer to partitioning that is operating system nonspecific.

http://www-1.ibm.com/linux/—Home page for Linux at IBM, with links to products, services, and downloads.

http://www-124.ibm.com/developerworks/opensource/linux390/—Home page for IBM S/390 Linux solutions.

http://www.dell.com/linux/—Dell Computer's Linux information pages.

http://hardware.redhat.com/hcl/—Entry point to Red Hat's hardware compatibility database.

http://www.linux1394.org/—Home page for the Linux Firewire Project, with information regarding the status of drivers and devices for this port.

http://www.linux-usb.org—Home page for the Linux USB Project, with lists of supported devices and links to drivers.

http://elks.sourceforge.net/—Home page for Linux for x286 and below CPUs, ELKS Linux.

http://www.lnx-bbc.org—Home page for the Bootable Business Card, a 50MB compressed Linux distribution that offers hundreds of networking clients, a live X session, web browsing, PDA backup, wireless networking, rescue sessions, and file recovery.

http://www.coyotelinux.com—Home page for several compact Linux distributions offering firewalling and VPN services; the floppy-based distribution works quite well on older PCs and does not require a hard drive.

http://www.freesco.org/—Home page for a floppy-based Linux router solution that works on 386 PCs, requires only 6MB RAM, and provides bridging, firewalling, IP masquerading, DNS, DHCP, web, telnet, print, time, and remote access functions.

http://www.bitwizard.nl/sig11/—A detailed overview of some root causes of Linux Signal 11 errors.

http://www.gnu.org/software/parted/parted.html#introduction—Home page for the GNU parted utility.

http://www.linux.org/vendors/systems.html—One place to check for a vendor near you selling Linux preinstalled on a PC, laptop, server, or hard drive.

Installing Fedora

In this chapter, you learn how to do a basic installation of Fedora. You will see how to boot and then install Fedora using the CD-ROMs included with this book. The chapter first shows how to prepare and research your install, choose a strategy on how Fedora will use your computer's hard drive, decide how to boot Fedora, and then how to complete the Fedora installation. You will get a step-by-step walkthrough of a sample installation, and then learn how to log in to Fedora and shutdown or reboot the system.

Before You Begin the Installation

Part of the process of installing Fedora (or any operating system for that matter) is to research how well the new operating system will fit into an existing hardware environment, or if new hardware will be required to host the operating system. The following sections provide some basic points to consider when installing Fedora and augment the checklists and ideas presented in Chapter 2, "Preparing to Install Fedora."

You start by researching and documenting your hardware. This information will prove helpful later on during the installation.

Research Your Hardware Specifications

You should first have a basic understanding of your system's hardware, such as the type of mouse, keyboard, or monitor, the amount of installed system memory, and the size of the hard drive. You need to know the storage capacity of your hard drive in order to choose a partitioning scheme, for example. Knowing the difference between a PS/2 and USB mouse will ensure proper pointer configuration—something that Fedora should do for you, but there is no harm being prepared. Such information will help make the installation as trouble-free as possible.

Use the checklist shown in Table 2.2 in Chapter 2 to inventory or at least record some basic features of your system. Some items you will need to know include the amount of installed memory, size of your hard drive, type of mouse, capabilities of the display monitor (such as maximum resolution), and number of installed network interfaces (if any).

Choose an Installation Type

You should also know what type of installation you plan to do beforehand (such as a workstation, server, firewall, gateway, router, development system, and so on). The type of install, or rather, the purpose of your intended install, will dictate the type and amount of software installed, and also influence hard drive storage requirements.

For convenience, the Fedora installer offers quick presets for a personal desktop, workstation, and server installation. Each type will install a set of preselected software libraries and applications. Use the custom installation option to select individual software packages and fine-tune your software selection. See Chapter 2 for details and hardware requirements for these installs.

> **NOTE**
>
> Although you can support nearly any operation (such as a development workstation or server) by installing all the software included with this book's CD-ROMs and DVD, this approach generally is not a good idea unless you are testing new hardware or learning how to use Linux at home. The reason for this is that installing extraneous software not relevant to support specific operations, especially in a business or production environment, can introduce security risks.

Choose Software Installation Options

Most new users with standalone Linux workstations will install all the software included with Fedora and depend on Red Hat's RPM technology (using up2date) or Fedora's support of yum to sort out and handle software dependencies (see Chapter 7, "Managing Software and System Resources," for more details about using these programs). Although Fedora is very stable and robust, crafting an efficient, stable, and working system can sometimes require consideration about the type of software to use given your existing hardware. For example, don't expect to run a fully loaded multimedia workstation if you plan to use Fedora Core on an early Pentium-based PC. However, that same PC can easily support email, print, or FTP server operations and even perform light duty as an intranet documentation web server.

Planning Partition Strategies

Part of planning a custom system involves implementing a partitioning strategy based on how you plan to use Fedora and, as previously mentioned, the capabilities of your existing hardware. For example, if you plan to host thousands of images or audio files, how much storage will you need? If you plan to back up this collection, will you use a tape drive, burn copies of directories onto optical media, transfer files across a network, or will you simply copy the files to another hard drive?

If you are planning an installation for a corporate or environment, you must also consider future expansion of the system. You will want to craft a flexible system that can evolve with your business and its system needs.

Knowing how software is allocated on your hard drive for Linux involves knowing how Fedora organizes its filesystem, or layout of directories on storage media. This knowledge will help you make the most out of hard drive space; and in some instances, such as planning to have user directories mounted via NFS or other means, can help head off data loss, increase security, and accommodate future needs. Create a great system, and you'll be the hero of information services.

To plan the best partitioning scheme, research and know the answers to these questions:

- How much disk space does your system require?
- Do you expect your disk space needs to grow significantly in the future?
- Will the system boot just Fedora, or do you need a dual-boot system?
- How much data will require backup, and what backup system will work best? (See Chapter 16, "Backing Up, Restoring, and Recovery," for more information on backing up your system.)

CD-ROM Installation Jumpstart

To install Fedora from the CDs or DVD included with this book, you must have at least a Pentium-class CPU, 800MB hard drive, and 64MB RAM. You will need at least 128MB to install using Fedora's graphical installer. A 10GB hard drive can easily host the entire distribution, leaving about 3GB free for other data. That said, hard disks are so cheap now that it costs almost the same to get an 80GB drive as it is to get a 20GB—even 250GB drives are affordable.

To begin the installation, set your PC's BIOS to boot from CD-ROM. Next, insert the first CD-ROM and boot your computer. Press Enter at the first screen and follow through the subsequent dialogs to install.

Remember or write down your system's root password. Also, even if you thoroughly test configuration of a graphical desktop during installation, you can choose to have Fedora boot to a text-based login (see the section "Step-by-Step Installation" later in this chapter). You can then start a graphical session after you finish the install, reboot, and log in. You can always set Fedora to boot to a graphical login later (see Chapter 6, "The X Window System," to see how).

If you have a floppy drive, create a boot disk during the install (see the "Step-by-Step Installation" section). Finally, finish the install, remove the CD-ROM from your computer, and reboot. Then log in and enjoy Fedora!

The Boot Loader

You will need to decide how to boot your system. For example, you can boot Fedora from a hard drive or floppy disk using the default boot loader, the Grand Unified Boot Loader (known as GRUB), use a commercial boot loader (as discussed in Chapter 2), or choose to not use a boot loader at all. Not using a boot loader can make booting Fedora difficult, but not impossible. For example, you can use another operating system such as DOS to jump-start to a Fedora session.

A boot loader is most often installed in the Master Boot Record (MBR) of an IDE hard drive, but can also be installed in the root Linux partition, or on a floppy disk. The boot loader can be used to pass essential kernel arguments to the Linux kernel for use during the boot process. Some arguments might include special disk geometry settings or specifying additional network interfaces. Fedora's boot loader, GRUB, supports special operations, such as booting from read-only memory (ROM) or flashed memory chips containing boot-loading code. Using a bootloader from floppy disk will work with many PCs, but you should be aware that not all PC hardware BIOS supports booting via Universal Serial Bus (USB) removable media or from a floppy disk. In fact, many PCs no longer include a floppy disk drive!

The GRUB loader works with all BSD Unix variants and many proprietary operating systems. This utility also supports menuing, command lines, installed RAM detection, and diskless and remote network booting. GRUB also offers password protection.

NOTE

Fedora's `mkbootdisk` command can be used to create floppy and CD-ROM boot media while using Linux. To do so, use the Linux kernel release number (returned by using the uname `-r` command) and a specified device. For example, to create a boot floppy, use the command like this:

```
# mkbootdisk --device /dev/fd0 `uname -r`
```

To create a CD-ROM boot image (which must then be burned onto a CD-R or CD-RW blank), use the command with its `-iso` option like this:

```
# mkbootdisk --iso --device boot_cd.img `uname -r`
```

Fedora can also be booted from a DOS session using the LOADLIN program, a DOS PATH to the Linux kernel, and the location of Linux kernel, such as

```
LOADLIN c:\KERNEL\VMLINUZ root=/dev/hda2 ro
```

In this example, the kernel named VMLINUZ is loaded, and the second primary partition of the first IDE hard drive is specified at the root (/) partition of a Linux system.

> **NOTE**
>
> If you find that LOADLIN fails to boot Linux and complains about a large kernel size, you can either try using make bzimage to build a smaller kernel or rebuild a kernel that relies less on built-in features and more on loadable modules. See Chapter 38, "Kernel and Module Management," for more information.

When choosing a commercial boot loader, weigh its capabilities and options. A good boot loader will support multiple operating systems, the ability to boot different Linux kernels (in order to change the characteristics of a system or easily accommodate new hardware), password protection, custom boot displays, and sane defaults, such as requiring verification before overwriting existing configurations and accommodating other recognized filesystems or previously installed boot code.

If you run into trouble after installing Fedora Core, make sure to read the documentation for your boot loader to acquire any diagnostic information. Most boot loaders will report on any problems, and the solution might be commonly fixed. Your best (and least expensive) bet is to use GRUB because it is the default boot loader for Fedora Core.

Choosing How to Install Fedora

Fedora can be installed in a variety of ways using different techniques and hardware.

Most users will install Fedora by booting to the installation directly from a CD or DVD. Other options include

- Booting to an installation using a floppy disk.

- Booting to an installation using Fedora's mini CD-ROM.

- Using a hard drive partition to hold the installation software.

- Booting from a DOS command line.

- Booting via a virtual network session. (See the file Release Notes included on the first Fedora CD-ROM for details.)

- Booting to an installation and installing software over a network using FTP or HTTP protocols.

- Booting to an installation and installing software from an NFS-mounted hard drive.

How you choose to install (and use) Fedora depends on your system's hardware, networking capabilities, corporate information service policy, or personal preference. The following sections describe the issues surrounding each of these types of installation.

Installing from CD or DVD

Most PCs' BIOS support booting directly from a CD or DVD drive, and offer the capability to set a specific order of devices (such as floppy, hard drive, CD-ROM, or USB) to search for bootable software. Turn on your PC, set your PC's BIOS if required (usually accessed by pressing an F or Del key after powering on); then insert Fedora's first disc, and boot to install Fedora.

To use this installation method, your computer must support booting from your optical drive, and the drive itself must be recognizable by the Linux kernel. You can verify this by checking your BIOS and then booting your PC.

Older PCs might prove problematic when you desire to boot to an install using optical media. The good news is that this should no longer be a problem with most post-1995 personal computers.

The file `boot.iso` is a 4.5MB CD-ROM image found under the `images` directory on the first Fedora CD-ROM. The image can be burned onto a CDR, mini CDR, or business-card sized CDR and supports booting to a network install. This is a convenient way to boot to a network install on a PC with a bootable CD-ROM drive, but no installed floppy drive, or when you don't want to use multiple floppies during an install requiring driver disks.

You burn the image onto optical media using the `cdrecord` command. For example, copy the file to your hard drive, insert a blank CDR into your CDRW drive, and then use a command line like so:

```
# cdrecord -v speed=4 dev=0,0,0 -data -eject boot.iso
```

This example will create a bootable CD-ROM, and then eject the new CD-ROM after writing the image. The speed (4 in this example) depends on the capabilities of your CD writing device. The device numbers are those returned by running `cdrecord` with its scanbus option, like so:

```
# cdrecord -scanbus
```

Installing Using a Network

Fedora can be installed using a local network (or even over the Internet if you have broadband access). You will need access to a web, FTP, or NFS server hosting the installation packages. To boot to a network install, use a network boot floppy, a bootable CD-ROM created using the `boot.iso` boot image, or the first Fedora Core CD-ROM included with this book. Boot your PC with the boot floppy or, if you use CD-ROM, type **linux askmethod** at the boot prompt. Follow the prompts, and you'll then be asked to choose the type of network installation.

> **TIP**
>
> Just press Enter at the boot prompt if you boot to a network install using a CD-R created with the `boot.iso` image. You will boot a graphical network install.

To install using FTP, select the network IP address assignment for your target PC, such as DHCP, or manually enter an IP address along with optional gateway IP address and nameserver addresses. You will then be asked for the FTP site name. You can enter the name or IP address of a remote FTP server hosting the Fedora release. The name of the remote directory will depend on where the Fedora install files are located on the remote server.

Installing Fedora using the File Transfer Protocol (FTP) will require access to an FTP server (see Chapter 22, "Remote File Serving with FTP," to see how to set up a server and use FTP). You'll need to know the hostname or IP address of the server, along with the path (directory) holding the Fedora Core software. One way to prepare a server to host installs is to

1. Create a directory named `Fedora` under the FTP server's `pub` directory. The directory will usually be `/var/ftp/pub` on a Linux server.

2. Create a directory named `base` and a directory named `RPMS` underneath the `Fedora` directory.

3. Copy or download all RPM packages included with Fedora Core into the `pub/Fedora/RPMS` directory.

4. Copy all original base files (`comps.rpm`, `comps.xml`, `hdlist`, `hdlist2`, `hdstg2.img`, `netstg2.img`, `stage2.img`, `TRANS.TBL`) from the first CD-ROM's base directory into the `pub/Fedora/base` directory.

Using this approach, enter **pub** when asked for the name of the remote directory holding the Fedora Core install software.

Installing Fedora using a remotely mounted Network File System (NFS) is similar to a hard drive installation, but requires access to an NFS server. You will need access permission, a permitted IP address or hostname for your computer, the hostname or IP address of the NFS server, and the path to the Fedora software. See Chapter 17, "Network Connectivity," for more information about NFS and network addressing.

To install Fedora using HTTP, you will need the hostname or IP address of the remote web server, along with the directory containing Fedora's software. See Chapter 19, "Apache Web Server Management," to see how to set up a web server.

> **NOTE**
>
> See Chapter 22 for details on how to configure the `vsftpd` FTP server. Chapter 19 provides information on how to set up and configure Apache for web service. See Chapter 17 for Samba settings. Note that you can have your server perform all three duties.

Step-by-Step Installation

This section provides a basic step-by-step installation of Fedora from CD-ROM. There are many different ways to proceed with an install, and the installer can provide a graphical or text-based interface in a variety of modes.

This example installation prepares a computer for general duties as a server, perhaps to host a File Transfer Protocol (FTP) site, a web server using Apache, or Session Message Block (SMB) services using Samba.

Before you begin, you should ensure that your computer is not connected to the Internet. Although you can use the installer to set up network protection during the install, it is best to check your system settings after any install and before opening up any public services (see the section "Firewall and Security Configuration" later in this chapter).

> **TIP**
>
> If you are installing to a system that has an older display monitor, it is a good idea to have your monitor's manual handy during the installation. If the install does not detect your monitor settings, you might need to specify the monitor's vertical and horizontal frequencies. This does not happen often, but if it does, you will be prepared.

> **NOTE**
>
> Fedora's graphical installation dialogs are convenient and easy to use. However, you can use a text-based installation, which works with any PC. Simply specify `linux text` at the install boot prompt. Use the graphical install outlined here as a starting point for learning more about installing Fedora.

Starting the Install

To get started, insert the first Fedora disc and reboot your computer. You'll first see a boot screen that offers a variety of options for booting (see Figure 3.1). Options may be passed to the Linux install kernel by typing special keywords at the boot prompt. Note that the install kernel is different from the kernel that will be installed on your system during installation!

The basic options most often used are

- <ENTER>—Starts the install using a graphical interface. The graphical interface supports a mouse and offers check boxes and text fields for choosing software, configuring options, and entering information.

- `linux text`—Starts the install using a graphical text interface.

To install using a text-based interface (used for our example), type `linux text` and press Enter; otherwise, just press Enter to start the install.

Several function keys can be used at this first boot screen to cycle through four help screens providing additional install information. Use these function keys at the boot prompt to jump to different screens describing alternative installation options and modes:

- Pressing F1 returns to the initial boot screen.

- Pressing F2 details some boot options.

- Pressing F3 gives general installation information (described next in this chapter).

- Pressing F4 describes how to pass kernel video arguments, useful for configuring video hardware to support a graphical install at a specific resolution (such as 800 × 600 pixels).

- Pressing F5 describes Fedora's rescue mode.

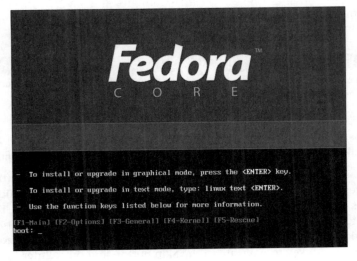

FIGURE 3.1   Select an installation option in this first Fedora Core boot screen.

Some of the options you can use at the boot prompt include

- `linux noprobe`—Disables probing of the system's hardware.

- `linux mediacheck`—Verifies the integrity of one or more install CD-ROMs.

- `linux rescue`—Boots to single-user mode with a root operator prompt, disabling X, multitasking, and networking; this option can be used if you need to reconfigure your boot loader or to rescue data from your system.

- `linux dd`—Uses a driver disk (a floppy image) and possibly one or more kernel arguments (such as `linux mem=512M expert`) to enable certain types of hardware, such as networking cards.

- `linux askmethod`—Prompts for the type of install to perform, such as over a network.

- `linux updates`—Starts an installation update.

- `memtest86`—Starts a cyclical, intensive series of memory tests of your PC's RAM.

- `linux nofb`—Starts a graphical installation, but does not use a framebuffer (helpful with problematic or unsupported video).

- `linux resolution=width x height`—Installs using a graphical display of width-by-height pixels (such as `resolution=800x600`), which can help match older or less capable display monitors and video cards.

The F4 screen lists options that can be used at the boot prompt to set a specific resolution for the installation. For example, this is done by typing `linux resolution=` at the boot prompt, along with an option such as `"800x600"`. Other options, such as optional arguments for kernel modules (in order to properly configure or initialize hardware) may be passed to the install kernel if you use the `noprobe` option.

> **TIP**
>
> The installer will start automatically in 60 seconds. Press the spacebar, reboot, or turn off your PC if you need to halt the install.

After you press Enter, the installer's kernel loads, and you're asked (in a text-based screen) if you would like to perform a media check of your CD-ROM, as shown in Figure 3.2.

This check can take quite some time (depending on the speed of your CD drive), but can ensure the integrity of the CD-ROM's contents, as an `md5sum` value is embedded on each CD-ROM. This check can help foil installation of malicious software from CD-ROMs with tampered contents. The check can also be helpful to make sure that the CD-ROM you are using will work on your PC and in your CD drive. To perform the check, choose OK; otherwise, use the Tab key to navigate to the Skip button and press Enter to choose it.

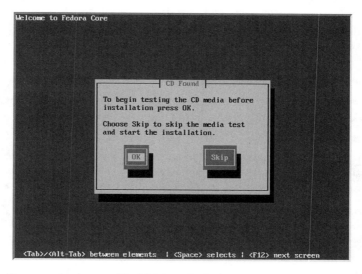

FIGURE 3.2   You can check your CD-ROM media before installing Fedora.

After checking your CD-ROM or skipping the check, the display will clear. The Fedora installer, Anaconda, will load, and you are presented with a graphical welcome screen as show in Figure 3.3. The installer should recognize your PC's graphics hardware and mouse. You can then click on the Release Notes button to get detailed information about Fedora Core, along with tips on hardware requirements and how to perform various installs.

If your pointing device (mouse) is not recognized, you can press Alt+R to "press" the Release Notes button. Similarly, you can click Alt+H to hide text shown on the left side of the screen, but you should take a minute to read frame's contents.

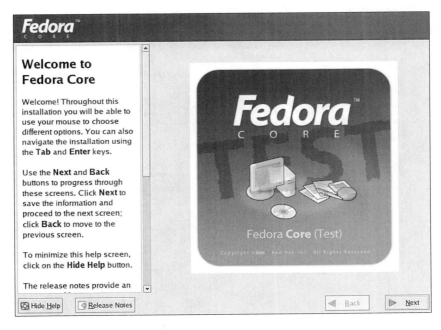

FIGURE 3.3   Read Help or Release Notes before installing Fedora.

Click Next (or press Alt+N) to continue, and the installer asks you to select one of 31 different languages for the installation, as shown in Figure 3.4.

You can navigate the installer's dialogs (during a text-based or graphical install) using the Tab key. You can scroll through lists using your cursor keys. Note that you can now "step backward" through the install by using a Back button. Select a language and click the Next button.

You'll then be asked to select a keyboard for the install, as shown in Figure 3.5.

Scroll to the appropriate keyboard option. You use this option to configure the install to support one of 53 different language keyboards. Click Next after making your selection.

FIGURE 3.4   Select a language to use when installing Fedora.

FIGURE 3.5   Select a default keyboard to use when installing and using Fedora.

If your PC's monitor was not detected, you might be asked to select your model from 132 different manufacturers. In rare instances, you might have to specify your monitor's exact horizontal and vertical frequencies. This can happen with older displays.

If an existing Linux install is detected, you'll be asked if you want to upgrade and reinstall; otherwise, you're then asked to select a type of installation, as shown in Figure 3.6.

FIGURE 3.6   Select a type of installation.

Select a type of installation suitable for your intended use—we'll use a Server install for our example. As we mentioned earlier, you can use the Custom install instead to select the specific packages to be installed. This can be helpful in order to prune unnecessary software from your system and might save some time later on. After you select the installation type, click Next to continue. You will then see a screen that offers a choice of partitioning schemes and tools.

> **NOTE**
>
> Fedora's installer also supports the ability to monitor background and install processes running during an installation. You can watch the progress of an install and hardware information reported by the Linux install kernel by navigating to a different console display or virtual console by simultaneously pressing the Ctrl, Alt, and appropriate Fn key (such as F1–F5).
>
> Use this approach to watch for kernel messages, monitor hardware detection, gain access to a single-user shell, and view the progress of the installer script.
>
> When using a graphical installer, press Ctrl+Alt+F4 (then Alt+F2 or Alt+F3) to navigate to the various screens. Press Alt+F7 to jump back to the installer. When performing a text-based installation, use Alt+F2 (then Alt+F3 or Alt+F4). Use Alt+F1 to jump back to a text-based install.

Partitioning Your Drive

You learned how to choose and plan a partitioning scheme in "Planning Partition Strategies," earlier in this chapter, based on the more specific partitioning information offered in Chapter 2. The Disk Partitioning Setup screen, shown in Figure 3.7, offers two options for disk partitioning. Here is what the options do:

- Using the Automatically Partition button conveniently partitions your hard drive according to the type of installation you selected and configures the partitions for use with Linux.

- Choosing the Manually Partition with Disk Druid button launches a graphical partition editor that enables the creation of custom partition schemes.

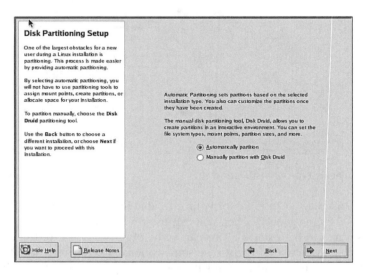

FIGURE 3.7   Select a partitioning scheme or tool.

For this example, select Manually Partition with Disk Druid button and click Next. If you are using a new hard drive that hasn't previously been partitioned, you will be asked if you would like to create new partitions on the drive. Click the Yes button to initialize the drive. If you are using a hard drive that has been previously partitioned or formatted and the partitions are recognized, Disk Druid will present the partitions in its partition dialog. Figure 3.8 shows the graphical interface presented for a 6GB hard drive that hasn't been partitioned.

To use Disk Druid, select any listed free space, and then click the New button (or press Alt+W) to create a new partition. Alternatively,

- To get help, see the help frame on the left.

- To create free space, scroll to an existing partition and use the Delete button to delete the partition.

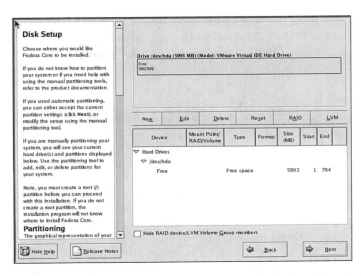

FIGURE 3.8   You can use Disk Druid to partition your drive before installing Fedora.

After you choose the New button, you see a screen as shown in Figure 3.9.

FIGURE 3.9   Set partition information about a selected or new partition on a hard drive.

You use the Add Partition dialog to assign a mount point (such as /boot or /), assign a filesystem (such as ext2, ext3, RAID, swap, or vfat) by using the drop-down menu set at ext3 by default, and assign the size of the partition. Remember that, at a minimum, your system should have a root (/) and swap partition. The ext3 filesystem is the best choice for your Linux partitions because it is the default and specifically supported by Fedora, but you can also use `ext2` (and convert to `ext3` later on—see Chapter 37, "Managing the File System"). The size of the partition can be fixed by entering a number (in megabytes), or if you select the Fill All Available Space field, will use all remaining free space (but not yet, as you need to create a partition for swap). Click OK to save the new partition information.

TIP

You can perform diagnostic checks on your storage media after installing Fedora by using various Linux software tools, as shown in Chapter 37.

Remember: Linux requires at least a root (/) and swap partition. The swap partition should be about twice as large as the amount of installed memory (or more) in order to get the most from your computer if you run a lot of programs or host many users. After you create an initial partition for the root filesystem, repeat the steps to create a new partition, but select swap as the filesystem type using the drop-down menu. Figure 3.10 shows a simple, completed partitioning scheme with a separate /home partition on a server using a 6GB hard drive.

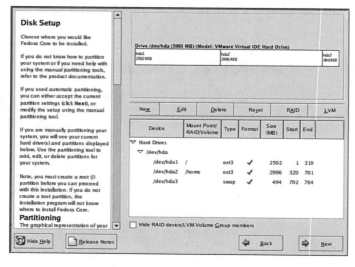

FIGURE 3.10   Review your partitioning scheme for your hard drive.

Take a moment to review your partitioning scheme. If you are not satisfied with the partitioning, you can make changes by selecting a partition and then using the Edit button to change the partition's information (such as mount point or type of filesystem). Use the Delete button to delete the partition entry and to free up partition space. You can then use the New button again to create partitions in the space that is now free. When satisfied, click Next to continue the install.

Choosing, Configuring, and Installing the Boot Loader

After you accept the partitioning scheme, a screen appears asking you to select a boot loader for booting Fedora (see Figure 3.11). This screen also enables you to choose not to use a boot loader (when booting from floppy, a commercial boot utility, a DOS partition, or over a network), and the ability to boot other operating systems if you have configured a dual-boot system. Review "Choosing a Boot Loader," shown previously in this chapter, for more information on making this choice.

> **TIP**
>
> Fedora will work well with other operating systems, but the reverse is not always true. If you need specialized help with configuring a dual-boot system, check various HOWTOs at http://www.tldp.org for hints and tips.

Select the GRUB boot loader. GRUB is typically installed in the MBR of the first IDE hard drive in a PC. However, the boot loader can also be installed in the first sector of the Linux boot partition, or even not installed on the hard drive. In this situation, you will need to create a boot floppy during the install; see "Create a Boot Disk," later in this chapter. Note that you can also backtrack through the install process to change any settings.

FIGURE 3.11   Select whether you want to use a boot loader and configure other boot options.

Note that you can assign a password for the boot loader. If you choose to use this option, you will need to enter a password at the GRUB boot screen (see the section "Login and Shutdown" at the end of this chapter for information on graphical logins). Carefully note the password! It does not have to be the same password used to log in, but if you password protect booting through your computer's BIOS and use a boot loader password here, you will subsequently need to enter three passwords (BIOS, boot loader, and login) in order to access Linux. Type in a password of at least eight characters twice (once on each line); then click OK or Cancel to exit the dialog.

If you click the Configure Advanced Boot Loader Options button, you're asked for arguments to pass to the Linux kernel before booting. Kernel arguments are used to enable or disable various features of Linux at boot time. If you install the source to the Linux kernel, you'll find documentation about the more than 200 different kernel arguments in the file kernel-parameters.txt under the /usr/src/linux/Documentation directory.

Click Next to set your boot loader configuration. You'll then proceed to network interface configuration, as shown in Figure 3.12.

Network Configuration

If you have an installed network adapter, you are asked for network configuration details, as shown in Figure 3.12. Fedora can be set to automatically configure networking upon booting. Note that you can also configure networking following installation using Fedora's system-config-network graphical network administration tool (see Chapter 13, "Managing Users," for details about using these tools).

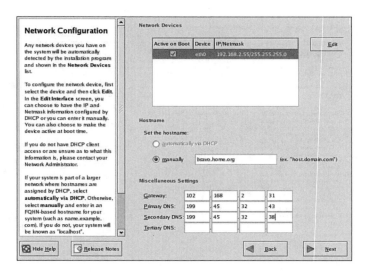

FIGURE 3.12   Select or enter networking configuration information.

> **NOTE**
>
> If the Linux kernel finds more than one network interface installed on your computer, you might be asked to configure a second Ethernet device. This might be the case, for example, if you are installing Fedora on a computer that will serve as a gateway or firewall. If you configure more than one Ethernet device, the device named eth0 will be the first active interface when you start Fedora.

You can choose to have your interface information automatically set using DHCP. Otherwise, especially if you are configuring a DHCP server, manually enter an IP address, hostname, or gateway address (such as for a router), along with DNS information if you click the Edit button listed by the interface (such as eth0 in the example).

After making your selection, click Next to continue. You'll be asked to select a firewall configuration.

Firewall and Security Configuration

Figure 3.13 shows the Fedora installer Firewall Configuration dialog, which offers an opportunity to set default security policies for the new server. Protecting your system using a firewall is especially important if your server is connected to a network (although it is best to first install Linux, set security policies, and then connect to a network). These settings in this installation screen determine how remote computers or users will be able to access your server. You can change these policies after finishing the install and logging in. Also on this screen is the option to either enable or disable SELinux, the more secure version of Fedora. If you have not come across SELinux before, you should consider setting it to either warn or disable because it will enable you to learn how SELinux could potentially impact your installation.

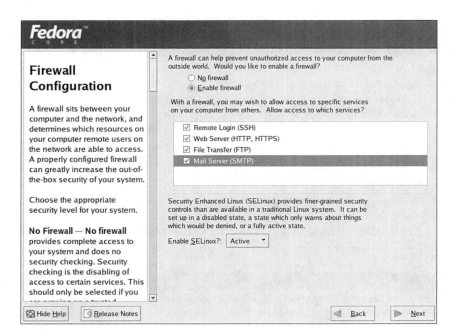

FIGURE 3.13   Select a desired security level and allowed services.

If you have a general idea of how you want to protect your computer, use the dialog shown in Figure 3.14 to turn on firewalling.

Choosing the No Firewall setting is not recommended; use this setting only if Fedora will be used as a non-networked workstation.

NOTE

Note that you can also manually configure security settings after installation using the text-based `lokkit` command, `system-config-securitylevel` client, or graphical `gnome-lokkit` client. See Chapter 33, "Securing Your Machines," for details on how to protect your system using these clients and various security level settings.

Click any allowable services, as shown in Figure 3.14. For some servers, HTTP, FTP, and Simple Mail Transport Protocol (SMTP) requests are acceptable and reasonable. Do not select or use the Telnet service, which is used to allow remote network logins. For security reasons, the Secure SHell (SSH) service is a much better choice (see Chapter 5, "First Steps with Fedora," on how to use the `ssh` client).

Click Next to install the firewall security settings. You will then be asked to select additional language support on your server. Again click Next when finished.

Setting the Time Zone

You are next shown a Time Zone Selection dialog (see Figure 3.14). There are two "clocks," or times, when using a PC: the hardware clock, maintained by hardware in the computer and a backup battery; and the system time, set upon booting and used by the Linux kernel. It is important to keep the two times accurate and in synchronization because automated system administration might need to take place at critical times. Many computer installations use computers with hardware clocks set to GMT, which stands for Greenwich Mean Time. The more modern designation is UTC or Coordinated Universal Time. The Linux system time is then set relative to this time and the default time zone, such as Eastern Standard Time, which is –5 hours of UTC.

Setting the computer's hardware clock to UTC (GMT) has the advantage of allowing the Linux system time to be easily set relative to the geographic position of the computer and resident time zone (such as a Linux laptop user who would like to create files or send electronic mail with correct time stamps, and who has traveled from New York to Tokyo). See Chapter 4, "Post-Installation Configuration," for details on setting the date and time for Linux.

TIP

Read the manual page for the `hwclock` command to learn how to keep a running Linux system synchronized with a PC's hardware clock. See Chapter 4 for more details on using the `hwclock` command and Linux time-related software.

Choose your time configuration, and then click Next.

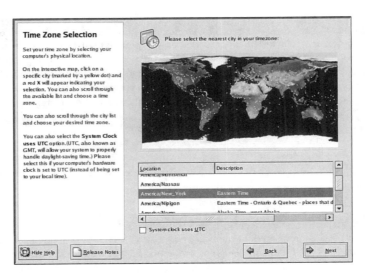

FIGURE 3.14 Select your time zone.

Creating a Root Password and User Accounts

You are next asked to enter a root operator password, as shown in Figure 3.15. Type in a password, press Tab or Enter, and then type it again to make sure that it is verified. The password, which is case sensitive, should be at least eight characters (or more) and consist of letters and numbers. Note that the password is not echoed back to the display. Your root password is important because you will need it to perform any system administration or user management with Fedora.

FIGURE 3.15 Type in, and do not forget, your root password.

> **CAUTION**
>
> Do not forget your system's BIOS, boot loader, or root passwords! Some equipment, such as notebook computers, might require factory replacement of motherboard components if the owner forgets the BIOS password. The BIOS settings on most desktop PCs can usually be reset via a jumper or removal and insertion of the motherboard battery. If you forget your boot loader password, use a boot disk (perhaps created during installation as shown later on in this chapter) or boot to a rescue mode using your first Fedora Core CD-ROM and reset the root password using the passwd command.

When finished, click Next to continue on to software package selection for your new server.

> **NOTE**
>
> You can only create a root account during a Fedora install. You will have to create user accounts later on after booting, using command-line programs (such as adduser) or the graphical system-config-users client. Create an account for yourself and any additional users. Usernames traditionally consist of the first letter of a person's first name and the last name. For example, Cathy Taulbee would have a username of *ctaulbee*. Do not forget to enter a password for any new user! If you create a user without a creating a password, the new user will not be able to log in.
>
> You should create at least one user for your server besides the root operator. This is for security purposes and to avoid logging in as root, either through the keyboard at the server or remotely over the network. The default shell and home directory settings should remain set at the defaults, which are the Bourne Again SHell (bash) and the /home directory.

> **NOTE**
>
> See Chapter 5 for how to become the root user or run root commands as a regular user. See Chapter 13, "Managing Users," for details on managing users.

Software Selection and Installation

The Package Group Selection dialog shown in Figure 3.16 displays the installer's suggested software for your class of installation (a server in our example).

If you choose to install a personal desktop, workstation, or other installation type, the software packages appropriate for that installation will be automatically selected for you. Each package (actually a Group) provides many different individual software packages (refer to "Choosing Software Installation Options," earlier in the chapter).

Scroll through the list of package groups, and then click a software package check box to select or deselect software to be installed. Note that the entire size (drive space requirements) of the installed software will be dynamically reflected by your choices.

Click the Next button when finished to start installing Linux and the Fedora Core software.

FIGURE 3.16   Select software package groups for installation.

The installer will then perform a quick dependency check and present a dialog informing you that a log of the install will be saved under the /root directory in the file named install.log. Press the Enter key to begin the installation of the software on your system. Be certain that you are ready when you confirm the process, as you cannot step back from this point on!

The installer will then format and prepare your new Linux partitions.

Next, the installer will prepare for the install by gathering a list of the RPM files and will start placing the software on the newly formatted partitions. This process can take anywhere from several minutes to two or more hours, depending on your PC and the amount of software you have chosen to be installed. The installer reports on the name of the current package being installed and the remaining time, as shown in Figure 3.17.

If you are installing over a network, go take a break because the install will proceed unattended through the software installation. If you are using this book's CD-ROMs, you might be prompted to remove the first CD-ROM and insert another. You might also be asked to repeat this operation using the third CD-ROM at some point.

Creating a Boot Disk

When the software installation finishes, the installer will perform some temporary file cleanup, install the boot loader, and then ask if you would like to create a boot disk for possible use later on, as shown in Figure 3.18.

You can create this boot disk now, or, as mentioned earlier, you can use Fedora's mkbootdisk command later on while using Fedora. Select Yes or No. Having a boot disk can be handy, especially if an error was made during the install and the boot loader fails to boot Linux.

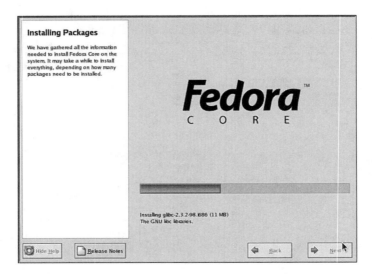

FIGURE 3.17   The Fedora installer formats your drive, and then installs selected software package groups.

If you choose to create a boot disk, you will need to have a blank disk on hand. Select Yes, insert a blank disk when prompted, create the boot disk, and continue the install.

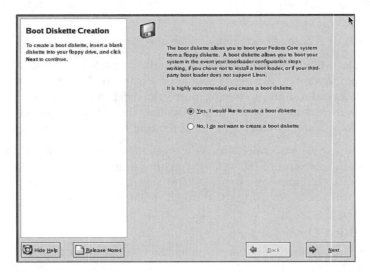

FIGURE 3.18   Create a boot disk for use with Fedora.

> **TIP**
>
> If you chose the X Window System, you can skip X configuration during the install and configure X after installation. This might be a better approach if the install fails to accurately probe your hardware or cannot configure X during the install, but you still desire to have X software installed. See Chapter 6 for details on configuring X to work with your PC's graphics card.

Finishing the Install

You are done! Press the Exit button, and the installer will eject any inserted CD-ROM and reboot. The GRUB boot loader will present a boot prompt as shown in Figure 3.19.

If you have set a GRUB password, press the p key, type your password, and press Enter. If you do nothing for 10 seconds or press Enter, either boot loader will boot Linux.

> **NOTE**
>
> After installation, you can edit the file /boot/grub/grub.conf and change the timeout= setting to change the boot time to a value other than 10 seconds.

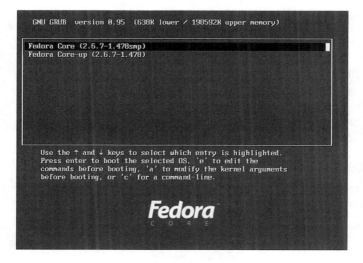

FIGURE 3.19   Boot Fedora with GRUB by pressing the Enter key or waiting 10 seconds.

Logging In and Shutting Down

After rebooting your PC, you will be able to log in to a Linux session. If you did not choose to use X11 software during the installation, you will log in at a text-based login prompt. If you configured X and enabled a graphical login, the screen will clear after your system boots, and you will be presented with a graphical login screen, as shown previously in Figure 3.19.

To log in at the text-based prompt, type your username and press Enter. You will then be prompted for your password. After you press Enter, you will be at the Linux command line. If you use a graphical login, you can use the shutdown or reboot menus in the screen's dialog to shut down or reboot your system. To immediately shut down your system from the command line of a text-based session, use the `su` command and its `-c` option to run the `halt` command, like this:

```
$ su - c halt
```

You can also use the `reboot` command to restart your computer like this:

```
$ su -c reboot
```

For new users, installing Fedora is just the beginning of a new and highly rewarding journey on the path to learning Linux. See Chapter 5 for additional information about using Linux commands. For Fedora system administrators, the task ahead is to fine-tune the installation and to customize the server or user environment.

Related Fedora and Linux Commands

You might use the following commands while installing Fedora:

dd—Convert and copy data

fdisk—The Linux disk partitioning utility

grub—The GNU boot loader for Linux and other operating systems

LOADLIN—A Linux boot loader for DOS

mkbootdisk—Red Hat's Linux boot disk creation utility

RAWRITE—A disk image utility for DOS

Reference

http://fedora.redhat.com—The place to start when looking for news, information, and documentation about installing, configuring, and using Fedora.

http://www.powerquest.com/partitionmagic/—Powerquest's PartitionMagic utility includes BootMagic, which can be used to support booting of Linux or, regrettably, other less-capable operating systems, such as Windows XP.

http://www.v-com.com/product/System_Commander_Home.html—V Communications, Inc.'s System Commander, a commercial 4.2MB download that can be used to support booting of any operating system capable of running on today's PCs. An intelligent partitioning utility, Partition Commander, is included.

http://www.nwc.com/columnists/1101colron.html—How to use Intel's Pre-execution Environment (PXE) protocol to remote boot workstations.

http://www.gnu.org/software/grub/—Home page for the GRUB boot loader.

http://elserv.ffm.fgan.de/~lermen/HOME.html—The somewhat outdated home of the LOADLIN Linux loader.

http://www.ibiblio.org/pub/Linux/docs/HOWTO/other-formats/html_single/ BootPrompt-HOWTO.html—The BootPrompt-HOWTO, a guide to using the boot prompt for passing kernel arguments.

http://www.tldp.org/HOWTO/Installation-HOWTO/index.html—The Linux Installation-HOWTO, a guide to installing Linux by Eric S. Raymond.

3

Post-Installation Configuration

As Chapter 3, "Installing Fedora," demonstrates, installing Fedora is an easy task in most situations. The installation process includes hardware probing, in which the installer surveys your system's hardware and then configures system settings accordingly. This process ensures that when the system boots, nearly all hardware is recognized and ready to operate.

If you are a system administrator (which you are even if you use Linux on a standalone workstation), you can expect to perform some post-installation configuration of your system. This chapter starts with some general advice on troubleshooting, and then offers some insight on how Fedora is set up to track your system's hardware. You will then see how to start and use the command line or the desktop to display and diagnose the Linux kernel's output regarding several common PC hardware components. You will also see several graphical configuration clients in action.

Troubleshooting Post-Installation Configuration Problems

As Linux continues to be developed, it has become increasingly fault-tolerant, meaning that if errors are encountered during the boot process, the errors will not cause a complete kernel or boot failure. Often, your computer might appear to be running fine, even though some device or process is not working correctly. The sources of such problems might include modules that did not load, services that did not start, or devices that are being used at sub-optimum levels (such as hard drive transfer speeds).

You will find clues to many problems in dmesg output, or in the /var/log/messages file, a simple text file containing constantly updated kernel and system information that you can view in any editor. Take a moment to review this file or dmesg output after installing or configuring new hardware; you will see that they show the progress of booting and starting services on your system.

The messages are generated by the kernel, other software run by /etc/rc.d/rc.sysinit, and Fedora's runlevel scripts. You might find what appear to be errors at first glance, but some errors are not really problems (for example, if a piece of hardware is configured but not present on your system).

When troubleshooting error messages, remember that "Google is your friend." Simply copy part or all of the error message and paste the information into a search field at http://www.google.com/linux/ and at http://marc.theaimsgroup.com/. You might find links to pages with information to help you solve your problem. It is quite likely that you are not the first person to encounter the problem. Reading the manual page for modprobe.conf and having perused /usr/src/linux-2.6/Documentation/devices.txt (and other files) will go a long way in helping you troubleshoot any problems.

Remember to only solve one problem at a time and always make a backup copy of any system file before you modify it. Do not use the common extension .bak because files with that extension can sometimes be overwritten. Here is a good method of copying the file:

```
# cp filename filename.original
```

And when restoring from that backup, do not rename the file, just copy it, like so:

```
# cp filename.original filename
```

(When these tips have saved you countless hours of frustration, thank us by purchasing copies of this book as gifts for your friends.)

Your Hardware and Kudzu

When you add or replace hardware, for example, you will need to configure the operating system to recognize and boot with the new components working properly. If you have enabled the kudzu service, Fedora will automatically detect new hardware upon rebooting; Kudzu then enables you to remove configuration information about missing hardware and configure the new device. If you do not use Kudzu, however, you might need to perform configuration manually without the support of automated hardware detection and configuration.

> **NOTE**
>
> The kudzu service maintains a database of your system's hardware information under the /etc/sysconfig directory in a file named hwconf. This service can be started, stopped, or restarted (like other operating system services) from the command line by using a script under

the `/etc/rc.d/init.d` directory (named `kudzu`). You can add options or enable various features of Kudzu, such as timeouts, by editing the `KUDZU_ARGS=` entry in the `kudzu` script (see the kudzu man page for the options). You can also use the command-line based `service` command or the graphical `system-config-services` client to control `kudzu`. See Chapter 14, "Automating Tasks," for more information on using these commands.

You can perform many post-installation tasks without rebooting or downtime. With proper planning, you also can create a server or workstation configuration that allows "hot-swapping" of system storage and other components, eliminating the need for downtime. In this chapter, you learn how to configure various USB and Firewire (IEEE-1394) devices in addition to keyboards, modems, and notebook PCMCIA services.

Information about your system's installed hardware is contained in a number of files under the Fedora directory system. Aside from one or two *symbolic links*, or shortcut-type files created under the `/dev` directory for the convenience of system utilities, nearly all these hardware settings are in text files under the `/etc` directory. The contents of these files are used by various software services to manage your system's hardware, save changes to your hardware, ensure that settings are saved between reboots, and to properly configure your system upon booting. A number of these files are used by the `/etc/rc.d/rc.sysinit` script when Linux starts. For example, some of these files include

`/etc/sysconfig/hwconf`—Lists the currently configured system hardware (used by kudzu)

`/etc/sysconfig/apmd`—Lists system power-management settings (used by the apmd deamon)

`/etc/sysconfig/clock`—Contains time zone, clock, and hardware clock settings (used by the hwclock command)

`/etc/sysconfig/harddisks`—System hard drive tuning parameters (using options available with the hdparm command)

`/etc/sysconfig/irda`—Provides configuration data concerning Infrared Data Association (IrDA) hardware

`/etc/sysconfig/keyboard`—Lists current keyboard mapping (and provides language settings)

`/etc/sysconfig/mouse`—Details the current system pointing device (such as whether or not a PS2 or USB mouse is used)

`/etc/modprobe.conf`—Defines device names, kernel hardware support modules to load, and any optional parameters (see Chapter 38, "Kernel and Module Management," for more information about Linux kernel modules)

`/etc/pcmcia`—A directory containing a Personal Computer Memory Card International Association (PCMCIA) hardware database and device settings (see the section "Managing PCMCIA" later in this chapter)

You will find additional information about the files in `/etc/sysconfig` in the file named `sysconfig.txt` under the `/usr/share/doc/initscripts` directory.

> **CAUTION**
>
> Do not edit kudzu's text-file database of installed hardware; these files are updated dynamically by Kudzu. If you have trouble with a device, however, you can check the information in these files when troubleshooting to see if the device is properly recognized and its definition matches the actual hardware.

Pointer and Keyboard Configuration

Fedora includes graphical tools that can quickly and easily change existing mouse and keyboard configuration settings. You also can use these tools to add support for a new keyboard or mouse on your system. These tools include

- mouseconfig—A dialog-based graphical mouse configuration tool for text-only consoles
- system-config-mouse—A graphical mouse configuration tool for the Red Hat desktop
- system-config-keyboard—A graphical keyboard configuration tool for the Fedora desktop or to configure a keyboard using a text console

The following sections explain how to use these tools to configure keyboards and pointing devices in Fedora.

Configuring Keyboards with Linux

> **NOTE**
>
> Linux supports many different types of keyboards. Up to the last few years, most keyboards used the PS/2 protocol (originally developed by IBM) and attached to a PC with a 6-pin mini-connector. Today, however, nearly all computers use Universal Serial Bus (USB) connectors for user input devices. Although many of today's PCs (and notebooks) continue to provide PS/2 ports, most manufacturers are now introducing "legacy free" computers without direct PS/2 support.

You can make a number of keyboard configuration choices in Fedora. You can choose a keyboard language that supplies the keyboard letters, diacritical marks, and layout appropriate for the language you will be typing in during your console or graphical sessions. Other configuration options include changing the keyboard's translation table to remap the order of keys on your keyboard, swapping specific keys (such as Caps Lock and Ctrl), or changing the delay period between the press of the key and the appearance of the character onscreen. (This configuration can help you synch the character entry to your typing speed.)

You can make keyboard configuration changes through text-based (console) keyboard commands or by using the graphical user interface.

If you do not use X, use Red Hat's `system-config-keyboard` command to change your keyboard type and language. This command can be used without an active X session (or if you are using X, from inside a terminal window) like this:

```
# system-config-keyboard
```

After you press Enter, you will see the Configure Keyboard dialog, as shown in Figure 4.1.

FIGURE 4.1   The `system-config-keyboard` command can be used to choose a keyboard map (language) for Fedora.

This dialog enables you to choose a new keyboard type.

Scroll through the list to highlight a desired keyboard type, and then use the Tab key to highlight the OK button and press Enter. The listings represent entries under the `/lib/kbd/keymaps/i386` directory, which are used to associate your keyboard's layout and keys with a language. The keyboard configuration is stored in the file `/etc/sysconfig/keyboard`, which might look like this:

```
KEYBOARDTYPE="pc"
KEYTABLE="us"
```

If you are using the Fedora desktop during an X session, you can use the graphical interface to select a keyboard language. To open the keyboard configuration dialog box, click the desktop panel System Settings Keyboard menu item, or use the `system-config-keyboard` client at the command line of a terminal window, like so:

```
$ system-config-keyboard
```

After you press Enter, you will be prompted for the root password. Enter the password and click OK. You will then see the Keyboard dialog box shown in Figure 4.2. This dialog box is similar to that displayed by `system-config-keyboard`.

FIGURE 4.2   The `system-config-keyboard` client is used during an X session to choose the language you will be keyboarding in during your desktop sessions.

Scroll through the list of languages, highlight a language, and then click OK to save your change.

Table 4.1 lists text-based and graphical commands you can use to manipulate or get information about your keyboard.

TABLE 4.1   Linux and X Keyboard-Related Commands

dumpkeys	Displays keyboard translation tables
kbd_mode	Modifies current keyboard mode
kbdrate	Changes keypress delay, repeats
loadkeys	Loads new keyboard table
showkey	Prints character, keycode, and other keystroke information
setleds	Displays, changes keyboard light-emitting diode (LED) settings
xkbcomp	Shows, sets keyboard character translations for X
xkbprint	Displays or saves X keyboard mappings
xset	Modifies keyboard settings for X
xmodmap	Changes key mappings for X

The X11 keyboard and other clients can be used to input a keyboard description into a running X server, show current keyboard character translations, change a keyboard map, and set other keyboard (and pointer) preferences. X11 settings are generally contained in a system's `xorg.conf` file (see Chapter 6, "The X Window System," for more information).

As a trivial example, the following short shell script (see Chapter 14 for more information on how to use shell scripts) can be used to blink the keyboard Caps Lock LED on and off each second (press Ctrl+C to stop the blinking) while using the console:

```
#!/bin/sh
while :
  do
    setleds -L +caps ; sleep 1 ; setleds -L -caps ; sleep 1;
done
```

Perhaps a more useful example is to switch the Caps Lock and Ctrl keys on your keyboard. Some users might find typing sessions a bit more comfortable if the locations are swapped. There are a number of ways to swap the keys. For your console-based sessions, use the loadkeys command to read in a file containing reverse key values for the keys:

```
keymaps 0-15
keycode 58 = Control
keycode 29 = Caps_Lock
```

You can then immediately swap the keys by using loadkeys to read in the file (perhaps named swapkeys) like so:

```
# loadkeys <swapkeys
```

The same swapping can be used for your Red Hat desktop by editing your /etc/X11/xorg.conf file's keyboard InputDevice section and adding

```
    Option      "XkbOptions"  "ctrl:swapcaps"
```

Yet another way to get the same results is to create a file named .Xmodmap in your home directory that contains

```
remove Lock = Caps_Lock
remove Control = Control_L
keysym Control_L = Caps_Lock
keysym Caps_Lock = Control_L
add Lock = Caps_Lock
add Control = Control_L
```

Or you can save the settings in a file (such as mykeyswap) and use the xmodmap client to directly read in the new keys like so:

```
$ xmodmap mykeyswap
```

Note that this will only work if you use the xterm or rxvt terminal clients. See Chapter 6 for more information about the Fedora desktop.

TIP

The system-config-keyboard command will present its graphical interface if launched from the command line during a graphical desktop session (that is, while using the X Window System).

However, you can force `system-config-keyboard` to use its text-based console interface by including the `--text` option on the command line like this:

```
# system-config-keyboard --text
```

This technique can also be used with the `system-config-mouse` client discussed next and the `sndconfig` command discussed later in this chapter. Using a console-based interface with one of these commands can be handy if you do not want the client to launch over a network after you have connected from a remote host.

Configuring Pointing Devices in Fedora

This section introduces pointer device configuration for Fedora Core. You will see how to use the `mouseconfig` command to configure a mouse from a text-based console, or the graphical `system-config-mouse` client for configuring a mouse for your desktop.

> **NOTE**
>
> Many pointing devices, such as the IBM Trackpoint (found in several versions of IBM non-notebook keyboards) work fine with Fedora. However, if you use a trackball, joystick, or other devices such as the Synaptics TouchPad, the Cirque GlidePoint, and wireless or infrared (IrDA) pointers, you might need to experiment with different configuration settings or use a driver provided (hopefully) by the manufacturer.
>
> Linux PC tablet users will have good reason to rejoice with the release of the Linux 2.6–series kernel. The new kernel will feature built-in touchscreen support and other improvements to make life easier when using Linux on a tablet PC. Compaq Tablet TC1000 users can browse to http://linux-tablet-pc.dhs.org/ for links to various drivers and supporting software. Some manufacturers provide direct links to Linux drivers or support reports. For example, Toshiba 3501 Tablet PC users can browse to http://linux.toshiba-dme.co.jp/linux/eng/pc/ptg3501_report.htm for additional information.
>
> Fedora does include some support for joystick use through the `jsattach`, `jscal`, and `jstest` commands (installed from the `joystick*.rpm` package). You can use these commands to support, calibrate, and test certain joystick makes and models.

The Fedora installer generally recognizes and correctly configures a computer's pointing device, but if you install a new pointing device, you will need to reconfigure the system for its use.

When using a PS/2 pointing device, a file named `/dev/mouse` will point to `/dev/psaux`; when using a USB pointing device, `/dev/mouse` will point to `/dev/input/mice`. A serial mouse will have `/dev/mouse` point to a specific serial port, perhaps `/dev/ttyS0`. The `/dev/mouse` file is a symbolic link, used for the convenience of many Linux applications. It is much more convenient for a program to look for `/dev/mouse` instead of `/dev/input/mice`, `/dev/psaux`, or `/dev/ttyS0`.

USB service (most likely initially configured by the installer) is started during the boot process by an entry in the system's module configuration file, /etc/modprobe.conf:

```
alias usb-controller usb-uhci
```

In this example, the PC platform uses a Universal Host Controller Interface (uhci), and the uhci.o kernel module will be loaded from the /lib/modules/2.6-X/kernel/ drivers/usb directory when Linux boots. Another USB controller commonly in use is the Open Host Controller Interface (ohci), requiring loading of the ohci.o module to enable USB service.

If your pointing device does not work, you can use the dmesg command to see if Linux has recognized the device during the boot process. This can provide some diagnostic information because Linux or the driver (perhaps a module) usually outputs diagnostic information:

```
...
usb-uhci.c: USB UHCI at I/O 0xd800, IRQ 15
usb-uhci.c: Detected 2 ports
usb.c: new USB bus registered, assigned bus number 2
hub.c: USB hub found
hub.c: 2 ports detected
usb-uhci.c: v1.275:USB Universal Host Controller Interface driver
hub.c: USB new device connect on bus1/1, assigned device number 2
usb.c: USB device 2 (vend/prod 0x1241/0x1122) is not claimed by any \
active driver.
usb.c: registered new driver hiddev
usb.c: registered new driver hid
input0: USB HID v1.00 Mouse [1241:1122] on usb1:2.0
hid-core.c: v1.8 Andreas Gal, Vojtech Pavlik <vojtech@suse.cz>
hid-core.c: USB HID support drivers
mice: PS/2 mouse device common for all mice
...
```

In this example (your output might look different), the kernel has recognized a generic USB mouse. USB support is initially enabled by the usbcore.o kernel module. In this example, the USB controller interface is initialized and configured by loading the usb-uhci.o kernel module, and then additional modules, such as input.o and hid.o, will be loaded to support a mouse (and/or keyboard) USB device.

You can see what modules have been loaded by using the output of the lsmod command. Note that you might see different memory size values, depending on your computer and module version:

```
# lsmod
...
mousedev        4288   1
hid            18720   0 (unused)
```

```
input           3744  0 [mousedev hid]
usb-uhci       21636  0 (unused)
usbcore        59072  1 [hid usb-uhci]
```

As you can see, USB device support, especially for pointing devices, involves proper loading of a chain of modules rather than a single driver.

> **TIP**
>
> Upon booting or connection, every USB device reports a pair of numbers representing a vendor and associated product (model). Problems can arise if the vendor and product ID are not recognized by a pertinent Linux kernel module. If a device is not properly recognized, it might not work with Linux. It is sometimes possible to rebuild a USB kernel module and include your device's vendor and product ID in order to get the device to work. For example, if you have installed the Linux kernel source, the file named scanner.h under the /usr/src/linux-2.6/ drivers/usb directory contains many popular USB scanner vendor and product IDs that are used by the kernel's scanner.o kernel module. See Chapter 38 for more information about rebuilding the Linux kernel and kernel modules. For a list of the latest USB devices supported with Linux, browse to http://www.qbik.ch/usb/devices/.

After Linux has recognized your hardware, you can use the mouseconfig command to configure a new pointer. Start the command like this:

```
# mouseconfig
```

> **TIP**
>
> If Linux recognizes a two-button pointer, the mouseconfig command automatically selects three-button emulation. (A simultaneous depress of both buttons will send a middle-button click.)
>
> Using a three-button mouse is essential for copy and paste operations—either at a text console or during X sessions. The left mouse button is most often used for clicking and selection, whereas the right mouse button is generally used for configuration or property display. The middle button is used for scrolling and pasting text or graphics.

After you press Enter, the Configure Mouse dialog appears, as shown in Figure 4.3.

Scroll through the list of pointers. Tab to select the OK button and press Enter when finished.

If you're using X, use the desktop panel System Settings Mouse menu item, or the system-config-mouse client at the command line of a terminal window, like so:

```
$ system-config-mouse
```

After you press Enter, you will be prompted for the root password. Type the password and then click the OK button; a graphical interface similar to mouseconfig's Configure Mouse dialog appears. Scroll through the listings, select an entry corresponding to your pointer, and then click the OK button.

FIGURE 4.3   The `mouseconfig` command can be used to configure a new pointing device.

Pointer configuration entries are stored in the file `/etc/sysconfig/mouse`, and can be examined like this:

```
# cat /etc/sysconfig/mouse
MOUSETYPE="ps/2"
XMOUSETYPE="PS/2"
FULLNAME="Generic Mouse (USB)"
XEMU3=yes
DEVICE=/dev/mouse
```

In this example, a two-button USB pointer emulates a PS/2 pointing device.

The corresponding entry contained in the `/etc/X11/xorg.conf`, used by X.org for the Fedora desktop looks like

```
Section "InputDevice"
    Identifier    "Mouse0"
    # Modified by mouseconfig
    Driver        "mouse"
    Option        "Device"          "/dev/mouse"
    Option        "Protocol"        "PS/2"
    Option        "Emulate3Buttons"    "yes"
    #Option        "ZAxisMapping"      "4 5"
EndSection
```

This entry enables the use of a USB pointing device during X sessions. See Chapter 6 to learn about X.

The ZAxisMapping entry (disabled in the preceding example) enables scrolling with a mouse that has a combination scroll-wheel and middle button. Many other types of input devices can be used with Linux and X.org. For information about using a mouse with X.org, read the file README.mouse under the /usr/X11R6/lib/X11/doc directory.

Mouse support for copy and paste operations during a Linux console session is provided by the General Purpose Mouse driver (gpm). gpm is a *daemon*, or software that runs in memory as a background process while you use Linux. If you make the appropriate configuration choices, the /etc/rc.d/init.d/gpm script starts the gpm daemon when Fedora boots. If you're not using X, you can configure Linux to start gpm when booting by using the ntsysv command from the console. Run the ntsysv command as root, like this:

```
# ntsysv
```

After you press Enter, you will see the Services dialog, as shown in Figure 4.4.

FIGURE 4.4   Use the ntsysv command to produce the Services dialog, in which you can select the gpm driver to start at boot time.

Scroll through the list of services using the Up or Down cursor keys to highlight the gpm service. Press the spacebar to toggle use of the service on (an asterisk will appear between the brackets) or off (no asterisk). Then tap the Tab key to highlight the OK button and press Enter to save your changes. The changes will take effect the next time you boot Red Hat.

> **NOTE**
>
> You can use the `chkconfig` command or the `system-config-services` client to configure Linux to run the gpm daemon when you're working in console mode (but not during X Window System sessions). Use the `chkconfig` command like this:
>
> ```
> # chkconfig --level 3 gpm on
> # chkconfig --level 5 gpm off
> ```
>
> See Chapter 14 to see how to configure when services run under Fedora.

Configuring Display Graphics

When you add or change the graphics devices used in your system after the initial installation, you must configure those devices. Adding or changing the display for your system can be as simple as swapping out the monitor or replacing a display adapter. For Intel-based PCs, this can mean switching from the use of the motherboard's built-in display adapter (if available)—by inserting a graphics card in the Accelerated Graphics Port (AGP) or Peripheral Component Interface (PCI) slot—or perhaps adding a second display adapter to support the use of multiple display monitors for X sessions.

Although a display monitor can be easily disconnected or reattached to a running system, insertion or removal of a graphics display adapter will require downtime—the bane of academic, enterprise, corporate, or small-business operations.

> **Linux and KVM**
>
> Keyboard, video, and mouse (KVM) hardware provides the capability to quickly switch display and control between banks of individual computers using a single monitor, keyboard, and pointer. This provides efficient organization, diagnostics and use of computers in larger installations, and allows a single operator to perform system administration tasks without physically moving to each computer.
>
> Using KVM can bring other cost savings. Eliminating the need for some monitors reduces the amount of storage required for the system and the amount of energy used to run and cool the system.
>
> Linux system administrators should be careful to research any hardware compatibility issues before implementing KVM. Many switches work regardless of the operating system and application used; however, take time to research what keyboard and pointer devices you will need to use (such as whether serial I/O, PS/2, or USB devices might be required). Some KVM switches come with some form of an embedded operating system (even Linux) that provides hardware emulation; these switches will have power requirements.
>
> Other issues to consider include cable construction, compatibility, and distance limitations, hardware or software switch configuration (such as providing push-button or key-combination switching), security, and scalability.
>
> If you use X and want to control the graphical desktops of remote hosts on your network, use the Xvnc server and `vncviewer` clients, discussed in "Remote X" in Chapter 25, "Remote Access with SSH and Telnet." You can also try the x2x and X2vnc clients. Although not included with

Red Hat, you can find these clients at http://ftp.digital.com/pub/Digital/SRC/x2x/ and http://www.hubbe.net/~hubbe/x2vnc.html.

Smaller Linux–based operations can avoid the use of KVM switching hardware by instead leveraging the graphical networking features of X11, multiple terminal sessions, and virtual desktops. Text-based virtual consoles can also be used on servers or workstations that do not use X11 to manage multiple computers or to receive logging messages from various services (such as email or web servers and the kernel). See Chapter 5, "First Steps with Fedora," to learn more about using virtual consoles. If you are limited to a single remote session window, use the screen command, a text-based window manager that enables a single terminal session to manage several shells. For additional information on using virtual consoles, see http://www.tldp.org/HOWTO/Keyboard-and-Console-HOWTO.html.

Your Fedora desktop is provided by the X Window System, a client and server software package that is configured to use your computer's video card, monitor, keyboard, and mouse. If you use the graphical desktop and kudzu (discussed earlier in this chapter) and change your graphics card, monitor, keyboard, or mouse, you might be asked to remove existing hardware configuration and reconfigure the new equipment the next time you boot.

The details about configuring X.org for Linux are covered in Chapter 6, but the basic utility used to configure a new xorg.conf file is system-config-display, Red Hat's graphical X configuration tool. You can also use Xorg -configure, which can generate an xorg.conf file by probing installed hardware.

> **NOTE**
>
> Connecting and using an external monitor with a notebook can be convenient, especially if the external monitor provides a larger desktop than the notebook's built-in display. However, configuring an external display for a notebook can sometimes be a problem when using X11. The notebook's graphics chipset must be supported by an X.org driver module, and the module must enable switching or concurrent use of an external monitor. Fortunately, many notebook chipsets are supported, and some notebook manufacturers provide support information for configuring external displays. For example, if your notebook has a Neomagic chipset, use the internDisp and externDisp options in the notebook's xorg.conf to enable use of an external display. Keep in mind that although Red Hat, Inc. encourages and supports X.org development efforts, The X.Org Foundation LLC controls X.org development and X graphics support. See Chapter 6 for more information about Linux and X11.

Fortunately, creating a working xorg.conf file (found in the directory /etc/X11) is usually easily accomplished when installing Fedora. If a new video card or monitor is put in use before installation, it will most likely work because X.org supports many families and types of graphics chipsets. Although newer graphics chipsets might cause some display compatibility problems, it is usually possible to configure a basic working display using existing software. The X.Org Foundation and contributing developers do a great job of providing software that works with nearly every product on the market.

If you are experiencing X11 configuration problems during installation, skip the configuration. Boot Fedora, and then look for a document under the /usr/X11R6/lib/X11/doc directory with information about your computer's graphics card. Various README files with specifics about a particular chipset are included with X.org. You can also check the X.Org Foundation website (see the "Reference" section at the end of this chapter) for any errata, changes, updates, or new releases.

> **TIP**
>
> Before running any X configuration tool, be sure to make a copy or back up any working xorg.conf configuration file.

Configuring Sound Devices

Most workstation users want to have a configured sound card working with Linux. Sound support is generally configured when Linux first boots (or during the install process if the sound card is recognized). Fedora Core uses the Advanced Linux Sound Architecture (ALSA) to enable sound support on your workstation.

To use sound, you should then use ALSA's alsamixer command to unmute your sound card's channels and save the settings using the alsactl command:

```
# alsactl store 0
```

The state of your sound card will be saved in the file /etc/asound.state. These settings, such as channel volumes, can be retrieved later by using the restore option instead of store.

> **NOTE**
>
> You will find complete documentation about the Linux kernel's sound support in various text files under the /usr/src/linux-2.6/Documentation/sound/alsa directory if you install the source code to Linux.

Configuration problems can arise, especially if your sound card's manufacturer will not or cannot release specifications to help open-source developers create working drivers. If your sound card is not recognized, or is recognized but will not work, and using ALSA fails, you can turn to commercial sound drivers from 4Front Technologies. These relatively inexpensive drivers support more than 350 sound systems and are installed, configured, and controlled using shell scripts. Browse to http://www.opensound.com for more information.

Fedora also includes a Red Hat-derived graphical sound card configuration client that can be used during an X session. Start the system-config-soundcard client by clicking your desktop panel's System Settings Soundcard Detection menu or item, or by using the command at a terminal window like so:

```
$ system-config-soundcard
```

After you press Enter, you will be prompted for the root password. Enter the password and click OK. The `system-config-soundcard` will try to automatically detect and configure your sound card. You will then see a dialog you can use to test your sound card settings, as shown in Figure 4.5. Click on the Play test sound button to listen to a sample sound.

FIGURE 4.5   The `system-config-soundcard` client is used during an X session to configure a sound card for Fedora.

Detecting and Configuring a Modem

More than 33 million users in the United States now connect to the Internet with cable or DSL service, but for many users a modem is the standard way to connect with an Internet service provider (ISP) using the Point-to-Point Protocol (PPP). Other common tasks for modems include sending and receiving faxes. If you add or change your modem after the initial installation, you will need to configure Fedora to use the new modem to perform all these tasks.

Fedora includes several tools you can use to configure and use an internal or external modem in your notebook or PC. Chapter 18, "Internet Connectivity," contains the details about configuring Fedora to connect to the Internet using a modem. This section covers how to configure and use modems using serial ports (using a standard formerly known as RS232, but now termed EIA232) or USB.

Configuring a Serial-Port Modem

Linux uses `/dev/ttySX`, `/dev/ttyUSBX`, or `/dev/usb/ttyUSBX` for serial ports, where *X* can range from 0 to 15. Many additional ports can be added to a system using multiport cards or chained USB devices. A PC's integral serial ports are generally recognized at boot time. To see a list of recognized ports for your system, pipe the `dmesg` command output through the `fgrep` command like so:

```
# dmesg | grep tty
ttyS00 at 0x03f8 (irq = 4) is a 16550A
ttyS01 at 0x02f8 (irq = 3) is a 16550A
```

In this example, the `grep` command reports that two serial ports have been recognized in the `dmesg` output. Note that the device matching `ttyS00` is `/dev/ttyS0`, despite the kernel output. The PC's external modem can be attached (most likely using a male DB9 adapter) to either port. Under Linux, nearly all modem-dependent software clients look for a symbolic link named `/dev/modem` that points to the desired device. This link is not created by default, but as root, you can create this device manually using the `ln` command like this:

```
# ln -s /dev/ttyS0 /dev/modem
```

In this example, `/dev/modem` will point to the first serial port.

You can also use the graphical X client `neat` to configure a modem after the initial installation. Internet connection software such as Fedora's `system-config-network` client (shown in Figure 4.6) will try to probe the system for an available modem. If a modem is not found, you can manually enter modem data.

KDE provides the `kppp` client (shown in Figure 4.7) that can also be used to look for and set up a modem when you set up a new Point-to-Point Protocol (PPP) connection. Click the Query Modem button in `kppp`'s dialog to search for an installed modem.

Fedora includes command-line–based diagnostic and serial port configuration tools for the system administrator. For example, to get more information about a specific port, you can use the `statserial` command, along with a designated device like this:

```
# statserial /dev/ttyS0
Device: /dev/ttyS0

Signal Pin Pin Direction Status Full
Name  (25) (9) (computer)        Name
-----  ---  ---  ---------  ------  -----
FG      1    -    -           -    Frame Ground
TxD     2    3    out         -    Transmit Data
RxD     3    2    in          -    Receive Data
RTS     4    7    out         1    Request To Send
CTS     5    8    in          0    Clear To Send
DSR     6    6    in          0    Data Set Ready
GND     7    5    -           -    Signal Ground
DCD     8    1    in          0    Data Carrier Detect
DTR     20   4    out         1    Data Terminal Ready
RI      22   9    in          0    Ring Indicator
```

The sample output is a display of the associated device's port signals. Another tool is the `setserial` command that can be used to display port statistics and reconfigure a serial port's system interrupt or speed. This can be handy when using some serial devices, such as a cellular phone that requires specific serial port characteristics. To get information about a specific port, use `setserial`, along with the device name like this:

```
# setserial -a /dev/ttyS0
/dev/ttyS0, Line 0, UART: 16550A, Port: 0x03f8, IRQ: 4
   Baud_base: 115200, close_delay: 50, divisor: 0
   closing_wait: 3000
   Flags: spd_normal skip_test
```

FIGURE 4.6   Red Hat's `system-config-network` client will probe for an available modem.

FIGURE 4.7   KDE's kppp client can be used to find and configure an available modem.

In this example, the characteristics of /dev/ttyS0 are displayed. The setserial command can also be used to configure or fine-tune a port's characteristics using 32 different command-line options and values.

One option for using a legacy serial device such as a modem on PC that does not have a serial port but supports USB is to use a USB-to-serial converter. These devices provide a serial port dongle and plug in to a USB hub or port. You can see the output and designated serial port by looking at the output of the dmesg command:

```
usb.c: registered new driver serial
usbserial.c: USB Serial support registered for Generic
usbserial.c: USB Serial Driver core v1.4
usbserial.c: USB Serial support registered for Keyspan PDA
usbserial.c: Keyspan PDA converter detected
usbserial.c: Keyspan PDA converter now attached to ttyUSB0 \
(or usb/tts/0 for devfs)
usbserial.c: USB Serial support registered for Keyspan PDA - (prerenumeration)
usbserial.c: USB Serial support registered for Xircom PGS - (prerenumeration)
usbserial.c: USB Serial support registered for Entregra PGS - (prerenumeration)
keyspan_pda.c: USB Keyspan PDA Converter driver v1.1
```

Configuring a Fax Modem

Linux should recognize and configure a designated serial port (such as /dev/ttyUSBX in the example) when the device is plugged in. Fedora also comes with a number of fax utilities that can be used to configure a system to send or receive phone faxes. One of the easier to configure fax utilities is the fax command. As root, you can configure the software by editing a few entries in the /usr/bin/fax shell script:

```
DEV=modem
FROM="1 555 555-1212"
NAME="Company Name"
```

The most important entry is DEV=, which will not need to be changed as long as /dev/modem points to an active fax-capable modem. You can also edit /usr/bin/fax to customize other entries, such as the fax viewing command. Use the test command-line option to check the settings like this:

```
# fax test
```

Sending a fax using the fax command is straightforward:

```
# fax send 5551212 document.txt
```

Configuring minicom for Modem Use

Use the minicom or xminicom script (used for launching minicom in a terminal window during an X session) for dial-up connections and terminal sessions to remote Linux systems. To configure this terminal program for use with an attached modem, start the client as root with its -s or setup option like this:

```
# minicom -s
```

After you press Enter, you will see a setup dialog. Select Serial-Port Configuration and press Enter. You will then see a Configuration Settings dialog as shown in Figure 4.8 that you can use to configure the program to work with an attached modem.

FIGURE 4.8   Use minicom's setup dialog to configure the program to work with an attached modem.

Configuring WinModems for Laptops

Other issues regarding modems focus on Linux notebook users with laptops using *controllerless* modems. These modems use proprietary software to emulate a hardware modem and are commonly referred to as *WinModems* due to the software being available only on Windows. Despite the release of binary-only drivers to enable use of some of these modems, these devices remain the bane of Linux notebook and some desktop users.

You might find some support for Lucent (but not Lucent AMR), Motorola SM56-type, the IBM Mwave, and Conexant HSF (not HCF) controllers. At the time of this writing, there was no support for any 3Com or U.S. Robotics controllerless modems. For links to drivers and more information, browse to the Linux Winmodem web page at http://www. linmodems.org.

Configuring Power-Management in Fedora

Advanced Power Management (APM) enables workstations and servers to automatically turn off when instructed to shut down. Most often used by Linux mobile users, APM can help extend battery sessions through the use of intelligent storage-cell circuitry, CPU "throttling" (similar to, but not the same as safety thermal throttling incorporated by Intel in Pentium III and IV CPUs), and control of displays and hard drives.

Most PCs support APM via the BIOS and hardware. APM support is configured, enabled, and then incorporated in the Linux kernel.

APM information is constantly updated in the file /proc/apm, which can look like this:

```
# cat /proc/apm
1.14 1.2 0x03 0x01 0x03 0x09 100% 10800 sec
```

This example provides information such as battery charge, along with time and percentage of time remaining. From left to right in the example is the driver version, BIOS version, status, AC status, battery status, battery state, remaining battery life, and number of seconds of life remaining. Some X11 clients, such as the asapm, xapmload, or GKrellM clients, parse this file and display icons or graphical power LEDs to present the information in an easier to digest form. These clients can be especially helpful for notebook users.

APM is supported by all kernels included with Fedora. However, problematic hardware or APM misconfiguration can cause kernel panics with some hardware, resulting in the inability to boot Linux. When this happens, you must reconfigure APM, and then build and install a new Linux kernel. (Refer to Chapter 38 for more information.)

Basic Linux kernel APM configuration options include

- CONFIG_APM—Whether or not to configure APM support
- CONFIG_APM_IGNORE_USER_SUSPEND—Ignores keyboard suspend instruction
- CONFIG_APM_DO_ENABLE—Enables APM at boot
- CONFIG_APM_CPU_IDLE—Idle CPU when not used
- CONFIG_APM_DISPLAY_BLANK—Enables monitor or LCD panel blanking
- CONFIG_APM_RTC_IS_GMT—Determines clock setting
- CONFIG_APM_ALLOW_INTS—Allows interrupts during APM use (such as serial-port activity)
- CONFIG_APM_REAL_MODE_POWER_OFF—Enables powering down

Fedora includes several APM-related commands—such as apm that prints APM information and apmsleep, used to suspend and then awake notebook hardware at a specific time. Linux notebook users can use the apm command like this:

```
$ apm -v
APM BIOS 1.2 (kernel driver 1.16)
AC on-line, battery status high: 95%
```

Other power management incorporated in the kernel includes control of Peripheral Control Interface (PCI) devices and Display Power Management Signaling (DPMS) for enabled monitors, which can help energy costs by placing devices in a low-power state after a preset time. Screen saving, as most astute Linux system administrators and users know, is no longer necessary to protect displays from image "burn-in." And password protection enabled by the screensaver only provides a modicum of physical security.

Hardware health monitoring is supported by the lm_sensors software package, which acquired some notoriety when early versions allegedly caused IBM ThinkPad notebooks to suffer permanent damage. However, system administrators managing desktop PCs can benefit from using applications, such as the sensors command that takes advantage of the hardware monitoring features of the lm_sensors libraries.

You can customize the output of the sensors command by editing (as root) the /etc/ sensors.conf file, but the default settings should work for your computer. To enable sensor reading, use the sensors-detect command to determine which kernel modules to load to enable sensor output:

```
# /usr/sbin/sensors-detect
This program will help you determine which I2C/SMBus modules you need to
load to use lm_sensors most effectively. You need to have i2c and
lm_sensors installed before running this program.
Also, you need to be `root', or at least have access to the /dev/i2c-*
files, for most things.
If you have patched your kernel and have some drivers built in, you can
safely answer NO if asked to load some modules. In this case, things may
seem a bit confusing, but they will still work.

It is generally safe and recommended to accept the default answers to all
questions, unless you know what you're doing.

We can start with probing for (PCI) I2C or SMBus adapters.
You do not need any special privileges for this.
Do you want to probe now? (YES/no):
```

Type YES and press Enter to begin the probe (*do not* if you have an IBM ThinkPad notebook; see http://www2.lm-sensors.nu/~lm78/cvs/browse.cgi/lm_sensors2/ README.thinkpad for more information). The command will then begin a series of probes of your PC's motherboard and report on found hardware. After you answer the prompts, the program will display one or more recommended command lines (and perhaps a new entry to /etc/modprobe.conf) to enable sensor reporting. For example,

```
modprobe i2c-isa
modprobe via686a
```

You can then use the `sensors` command's `-f` option to view various component temperatures in Fahrenheit, like this:

```
$ sensors -f
via686a-isa-6000
Adapter: ISA adapter
Algorithm: ISA algorithm
2.0V:    +1.36 V (min = +1.79 V, max = +2.18 V)
2.5V:    +2.49 V (min = +2.24 V, max = +2.74 V)
I/O:     +3.28 V (min = +2.95 V, max = +3.62 V)
+5V:     +5.02 V (min = +4.47 V, max = +5.49 V)
+12V:    +11.62 V (min = +10.79 V, max = +13.18 V)
Case Fan: 2700 RPM (min = 48214 RPM, div = 2)
CPU Fan: 3497 RPM (min = 67500 RPM, div = 2)
SYS Temp: +98.8°F (limit = +295°F, hysteresis = -95°F)
CPU Temp: +98.8°F (limit = +295°F, hysteresis = -95°F)
SBr Temp: +79.3°F (limit = -74°F, hysteresis = -95°F)
```

Monitoring your system's hardware can be critically important, especially if you overclock the Central Processing Unit (CPU) in order to gain performance.

Resetting the Date and Time

The Fedora installer will query you during installation for default time zone settings, and whether or not your computer's hardware clock is set to Greenwich Mean Time (GMT)—more properly known as *UTC*, or Coordinated Universal Time.

Linux provides a system date and time; your computer hardware provides a hardware clock-based time. In many cases, it is possible for the two times to drift apart. Linux system time is based on the number of seconds elapsed since Jan. 1, 1970. Your computer's hardware time depends on the type of clock chips installed on your PC's motherboard, and many motherboard chipsets are notoriously subject to drift.

Keeping accurate time is not only important on a single workstation, but also critically important in a network environment. Backups, scheduled downtimes, and other network-wide actions need to be accurately coordinated.

Fedora provides several date and time utilities you can use at the command line or during an X session, including these:

date—Used to display, set, or adjust the system date and time from the command line

hwclock—A root command to display, set, adjust, and synchronize hardware and system clocks

system-config-date—Red Hat's graphical date, time, and network time configuration tool

Using the date Command

Use the date command to display or set your Linux system time. This command requires you to use a specific sequence of numbers to represent the desired date and time. To see your Linux system's idea of the current date and time, use the date command like this:

```
# date
Wed Jan 10 14:17:01 EDT 2005
```

To adjust your system's time (say, to January 23, 2005 at 8 a.m.), use a command line with the month, day, hour, minute, and year, like so:

```
# date 092308002003
Tue Sep 23 08:00:00 EDT 2003
```

Using the hwclock Command

Use the hwclock command to display or set your Linux system time, display or set your PC's hardware clock, or to synchronize the system and hardware times. To see your hardware date and time, use hwclock with its --show option like so:

```
# hwclock --show
Wed 10 Sep 2003 02:17:53 PM EDT   -0.193809 seconds
```

Use hwclock with its --set and --date options to manually set the hardware clock like so:

```
# hwclock --set --date "09/23/03 08:00:00"
# hwclock --show
Tue 23 Sep 2003 08:00:08 AM EDT -0.151718 seconds
```

In these examples, the hardware clock has been set using hwclock, which is then used again to verify the new hardware date and time. You can also hwclock to set the Linux system date and time date using your hardware clock's values with the Linux system date and time.

For example, to set the system time from your PC's hardware clock, use the --hctosys option like so:

```
# hwclock --hctosys
```

To set your hardware clock using the system time, use the --systohc option like so:

```
# hwclock --systohc
```

Using the system-config-date Client

Fedora's graphical X tool named system-config-date can be used to set your system date and time. Start the client by clicking the desktop menu's System Settings Date & Time menu item, or from the command line of an X11 terminal window like this:

```
$ system-config-date &
```

After you press Enter, you will be asked to enter the root password. Type in the root password and click the OK button. You will then see a window, as shown in Figure 4.9.

FIGURE 4.9   Use Fedora's `system-config-date` client to set your system date and time.

Set the date and time by using the calendar and time fields. You can also have your workstation obtain updated date and time information via the network by entering a remote time server hostname in the Network Time Protocol field. This will require that the `ntpd` time daemon be properly configured and running.

> **NOTE**
>
> HTML documentation for using the `ntpd` daemon is in `/usr/share/doc/ntp*/ntpd.htm` (if `ntpd` is installed on your system).

Click on the Time Zone tab to change or verify your system's time zone. The current system time zone is designated by a file named `localtime` in the `/etc` directory, and is a copy of the pertinent time zone database file under the `/usr/share/zoneinfo` directory. For example,

```
$ ls -l /etc/localtime
-rw-r--r--   1 root     root         1267 Apr  1 16:39 /etc/localtime
```

```
$ ls -l /usr/share/zoneinfo/America/New_York
-rw-r--r--   5 root     root          1267 Mar 13 18:00
/usr/share/zoneinfo/_America/New_York
```

This file will change if you make a time zone change using `system-config-date`.

Managing PCMCIA

Mobile Linux users take advantage of notebook PCMCIA slots to add 70-pin, credit-card-sized devices to support Ethernet LAN connectivity, wireless operations, Firewire devices, Compact Flash hard drives, external storage devices, serial ports, and modems. Many different types of PCMCIA cards and Compact Flash form-factor cards in a PCMCIA caddy are supported by the Linux kernel and David Hinds' Card Services software.

Power is provided to PCMCIA devices and adapters directly through the card slot, although some external hardware might require an additional power source. PCMCIA support is enabled and configured at boot time according to the `/etc/sysconfig/pcmcia` file and `/etc/rc.d/init.d/pcmcia` startup script. The `/etc/sysconfig/pcmcia` file might look something like

```
PCMCIA=yes
PCIC=yenta_socket
PCIC_OPTS=
CORE_OPTS=
```

Previous incarnations of Linux distros from Red Hat and PCMCIA used specific controller information in this file. With the newer Linux kernels; however, support is provided by kernel modules or direct Linux kernel support.

Using PCMCIA

The PCMCIA Card Services software provides diagnostic information by one or more high or low beeps upon card insertion. One high and one low beep indicate that a card is recognized, but failed to be configured. A single beep indicates that the card was only recognized. Two high beeps indicate that a card was recognized and configured.

For example, if you use a compact flash storage device and insert it into your notebook while using Fedora, you should hear two high beeps. You can then check to see what device has been assigned to the card by using the `dmesg` command:

```
$ dmesg
...
hde: SunDisk SDCFB-8, ATA DISK drive
ide2 at 0x100-0x107,0x10e on irq 3
ide-floppy driver 0.99.newide
hde: 15680 sectors (8 MB) w/1KiB Cache, CHS=245/2/32
 hde: hde1
...
```

Not all the output is shown here (and yours may look different), but this example shows that the card has been recognized and configured as the /dev/hde device (with a single partition, /dev/hde1). You can then use the device as any other storage medium (see Chapter 37, "Managing the File System," for more information on using hard drives with Linux).

Other devices can be similarly recognized and configured. For example, if you have a combination Ethernet and modem PCMCIA card and insert it into your notebook, you should hear two sets of high beeps (to indicate successful recognition and configuration of the network interface and modem). The Linux kernel will report the interface and device information:

```
$ dmesg
...
eth0: NE2000 (DL10019 rev 05): io 0x300, irq 3, hw_addr 00:E0:98:06:84:C5
ttyS04 at port 0x0af8 (irq = 3) is a 16450
..
```

Here, the network interface has been recognized as eth0 (see Chapter 17, "Network Connectivity," to see how to connect to a network). The modem is configured to use /dev/ttyS04.

Again, troubleshooting problems with PCMCIA cards can be difficult, especially with the explosion in popularity and type of 802.11b/g wireless networking cards. Such troubleshooting is likely to require downloading, building, and installing new drivers.

Fortunately, however, nearly all serial, modem, and Compact Flash storage cards are easily recognized and configured. Many Ethernet cards are also supported. To check on the current support status for many cards, read the file SUPPORTED.CARDS. You will find a copy under the /usr/share/doc/kernel-pcmcia-cs-3.X.XX/ directory (where X.XX is the version of the package) if you install the pcmcia-cs RPM package.

> **NOTE**
>
> If you have trouble configuring and using a PCMCIA card, browse to the Linux PCMCIA home page at http://pcmcia-cs.sourceforge.net/. Click the SUPPORTED.CARDS link to see if your card is supported. Click the known problems link to see if other users with the same card are having problems, or if the card is not fully supported. If a new version of the PCMCIA kernel drivers are available and changes have been made to your card's drivers (or if a new driver has been developed), download and install the newer software. See Chapter 38 for information on installing the new PCMCIA modules, or follow the directions included with the PCMCIA software.

Controlling PCMCIA Service

Although PCMCIA cards can be inserted or removed while using Red Hat, be careful when using these cards. For example, do not remove a network card while connected to a remote computer. Don't pull a compact flash card or other storage media card (such as an

IBM microdrive) while the card's filesystem is mounted and in use—you could corrupt the media's filesystem and experience loss of data.

You can control a PCMCIA device from the command line, and insert and remove the card without physically removing and then inserting the card. Use the `cardctl` command to control PCMCIA service to one or more card slots on your notebook or desktop PC with a PCMCIA adapter. The `cardctl` command is used to get and print information about an inserted card, suspend or resume power to a card, reset a card, perform a software insertion or removal, or to configure a card according to a particular, predefined "scheme" (such as using a network in the office or at home). The format of the command is `cardctl command slot_number` (such as 0 or 1).

For example, if you have inserted a compact flash card, eject the card (after unmounting its filesystem) using the `cardctl` command and its `eject` option, along with the card's slot number like this:

```
# cardctl eject 0
```

This can save power when running a notebook. When the card is again needed, you can subsequently "insert" the card like so:

```
# cardctl insert 0
```

Configuring and Using CD, DVD, and CD-RW Drives

Linux provides support for using a variety of CD and DVD devices and media. This section shows how to determine what device has been assigned to your CD drive and how to get additional drive information if the drive supports recording on optical media.

AT Attachment Packet Interface, or ATAPI IDE-based CD drives, are recognized during installation and work through the `ide-cd` kernel module. A symbolic link named `/dev/cdrom` will be created and will point to your CD's device (perhaps `/dev/hdb` or `/dev/hdc`). You can use many different types of CD drives with Linux, and you can easily replace, add, or upgrade your system to use a new drive. Part of a successful configuration involves the proper installation of the hardware and being able to determine the drive's device when using Linux.

Checking Drive Assignment

Linux recognizes CD and DVD drives upon booting if they are attached to your computer's motherboard with proper cabling and if they are assigned as either a master or slave on an IDE channel. Look through your kernel boot message for the drive device assignment, such as

```
hdd: DVDROM 10X, ATAPI CD/DVD-ROM drive
```

If you have a DVD-capable drive, you generally should also have a symbolic link named `/dev/dvd` that points to your drive's device because many DVD clients, such as `xine` or vlc, will look for /dev/dvd by default. If you have a CD-RW drive, the Fedora installer will insert a kernel argument into your boot loader's configuration file that specifies use of the ide-scsi kernel. For example,

```
append="hdb=ide-scsi"
```

A similar entry in the grub boot loader's /etc/grub.conf file would look like this:

```
kernel boot/vmlinuz-6.5-1.358 ro root=/dev/hda2 hdb=ide-scsi
```

The first CD-RW drive will be assigned to the device /dev/scd0 (although it might still be initially recognized while booting as an IDE device), with subsequent drives assigned to /dev/scd1, and so on. In order to initialize your drive for use, the following modules should be loaded:

```
Module          Size Used by  Not tainted
sg              30244  0 (autoclean)
sr_mod          15192  0 (autoclean)
cdrom           27872  0 (autoclean) [sr_mod]
ide-scsi         8128  0
scsi_mod        96572  2 [sr_mod ide-scsi]
```

Look for kernel message output regarding the device such as this:

```
Attached scsi CD-ROM sr0 at scsi0, channel 0, id 0, lun 0
sr0: scsi3-mmc drive: 0x/32x writer cd/rw xa/form2 cdda tray
Uniform CD-ROM driver Revision: 3.12
```

Your ATAPI-based CD-RW drive will then work as a SCSI device under emulation, and the symbolic link /dev/cdrom should point to /dev/scd0. You can also use the cdrecord command (included with Red Hat's multimedia software packages) to acquire SCSI device information about your drive for later use during burning operation like this:

```
# cdrecord -scanbus
Cdrecord 1.10 (i686-pc-linux-gnu) Copyright (C) 1995-2001 Jörg Schilling
Linux sg driver version: 3.1.22
Using libscg version 'schily-0.5'
scsibus0:
    0,0,0    0) 'HL-DT-ST' 'RW/DVD GCC-4120B' '2.01' Removable CD-ROM
    0,1,0    1) *
    0,2,0    2) *
    0,3,0    3) *
    0,4,0    4) *
    0,5,0    5) *
    0,6,0    6) *
    0,7,0    7) *
```

The pertinent information—0,0,0 in the example (SCSI bus, device ID, and Logical Unit Number, or lun)—can then be used during a burn operation like this:

```
# cdrecord -v speed=8 dev=0,0,0 -data -eject file_name.img
```

In this example, a CD-ROM data image named file_name.img is created on a CD-R or CD-RW media at a speed of 8, and the new disk will be ejected after the write operation has completed. See "Burning CDs in Fedora Core Linux" in Chapter 10, "Multimedia Applications," for other ways to create CD-ROMs.

> **NOTE**
>
> Fedora also includes the dvdrecord, dvd+rw-format, and growisofs commands, which can be used with DVD-R and DVD-RW drives.

Initializing FireWire CD Drives

This section provides some basic information you can use if you attach a FireWire CD drive to your system. These drives use a high-speed serial interface, otherwise known as IEEE 1394, which supports data transfers more than 30 times faster than the first version of USB (at speeds up to 400Mbps), although USB 2.0 devices are a bit faster.

Linux has supported FireWire since the advent of the 2.4-series kernel, and now works with many different devices, such as video cameras, VCRs, hard drives, scanners, PCMCIA cards, and CD, DVD, or CD-RW drives. The Fedora Core installer should recognize most FireWire interface hardware; if so, you will be able to use the device with Linux. One Linux FireWire component, the video1394 kernel module, currently supports more than 120 different digital video cameras. General support exists for many different hard drives and DVD or CD-RW drives.

If you install an FireWire interface after Fedora has been installed, you can initialize support for your device, such as a CD-RW drive, by loading the ieee1394 and ohci1394 kernel modules like this:

```
# insmod ieee1394
# insmod ohci1394
```

Next, look for relevant device information from the Linux kernel using the dmesg command:

```
ohci1394: $Revision: 1.80 $ Ben Collins <bcollins@debian.org>
PCI: Found IRQ 10 for device 00:0b.0
PCI: Sharing IRQ 10 with 00:07.5
ohci1394_0: OHCI-1394 1.0 (PCI): IRQ=[10] MMIO=[ee000000-ee000800] \
 Max Packet=[2048]
ieee1394: Device added: node 2:1023, GUID 00d0010500007d8e
```

```
ieee1394: sbp2: Driver forced to serialize I/O (serialize_io = 1)
ieee1394: sbp2: Node 2:1023: Max speed [S400] - Max payload [2048]
scsi1 : IEEE-1394 SBP-2 protocol driver
 Vendor: TEAC    Model: CD-W28E      Rev: 1.1A
 Type:  CD-ROM                 ANSI SCSI revision: 02
```

In this example, the FireWire drivers have recognized a CD-RW drive (which will be
assigned to /dev/scd1 because another CD-RW is also present on the system). You might
also find that the sbp2 kernel module has loaded:

```
Module          Size Used by  Not tainted
sbp2           14400  0
ohci1394       15872  0 (unused)
ieee1394       25768  0 [sbp2 ohci1394]
```

> **NOTE**
>
> Fedora's installer should recognize any FireWire hardware in your PC during installation.
> Depending on your computer's hardware, you might find an entry in /etc/modprobe.conf such
> as alias ieee1394-controller ohci1394.

Again, use the cdrecord command and its –scanbus option to obtain information needed
to use the drive under SCSI emulation:

```
# cdrecord -scanbus
Cdrecord 1.10 (i686-pc-linux-gnu) Copyright (C) 1995-2001 Jörg Schilling
Linux sg driver version: 3.1.22
Using libscg version 'schily-0.5'
scsibus0:
    0,0,0   0) 'HL-DT-ST' 'RW/DVD GCC-4120B' '2.01' Removable CD-ROM
    0,1,0   1) *
    0,2,0   2) *
    0,3,0   3) *
    0,4,0   4) *
    0,5,0   5) *
    0,6,0   6) *
    0,7,0   7) *
scsibus1:
    1,0,0 100) 'TEAC  ' 'CD-W28E     ' '1.1A' Removable CD-ROM
    1,1,0 101) *
    1,2,0 102) *
    1,3,0 103) *
    1,4,0 104) *
    1,5,0 105) *
    1,6,0 106) *
    1,7,0 107) *
```

The pertinent information for the FireWire drive—1,0,0 in the example (a drive attached to SCSI bus 1, assigned device 0 and a lun of 0)—can then be used during a read operation like this:

```
# export CDDA_DEVICE=1,0,0
# cdda2wav -B
Type: ROM, Vendor 'TEAC  ' Model 'CD-W28E     ' Revision '1.1A' MMC+CDDA
724992 bytes buffer memory requested, 4 buffers, 75 sectors
#Cdda2wav version 1.10_linux_2.4.17-0.13smp_i686_i686 real time sched. \
soundcard support
AUDIOtrack pre-emphasis copy-permitted tracktype channels
  1- 8     no      no    audio  2
Table of Contents: total tracks:8, (total time 52:12.72)
 1.( 5:25.67), 2.( 9:06.65), 3.( 5:50.68), 4.( 5:35.57), 5.( 7:28.35)
 6.( 6:34.60), 7.( 6:07.15), 8.( 6:01.05),

Table of Contents: starting sectors
 1.(    0), 2.( 24442), 3.( 65457), 4.( 91775), 5.( 116957)
 6.( 150592), 7.( 180202), 8.( 207742), lead-out( 234822)
CDINDEX discid: SBRXDC1u_.D2S6U1MWq7ksIYOUE-
CDDB discid: 0x5e0c3a08
CD-Text: not detected
CD-Extra: not detected
samplefile size will be 552301388 bytes.
recording 3130.09600 seconds stereo with 16 bits @ 44100.0 Hz ->'audio'...
percent_done:
100% track 1 successfully recorded
100% track 2 successfully recorded
...
```

In this example, an environment variable named CDDA_DEVICE with the drive's SCSI information is created, and the cdda2wav command is used to extract the entire contents of an audio CD into .wav file format, with each track saved in a separate file. Other utilities might only need to know the name of the device, such as /dev/scd1, like this:

```
# cdparanoia -d /dev/scd1 -B
cdparanoia III release 9.8 (March 23, 2001)
(C) 2001 Monty <monty@xiph.org> and Xiphophorus

Report bugs to paranoia@xiph.org
http://www.xiph.org/paranoia/
```

```
    Couldn't disable kernel command translation layer
Ripping from sector     0 (track 1 [0:00.00])
    to sector 234821 (track 8 [6:01.04])

outputting to track01.cdda.wav
...
```

> **NOTE**
>
> Fedora also includes the cdrdao command, which can create "Disk-At-Once" (DAO) audio and data CD-ROMs. Other types of CD recording supported by Linux drivers and various CD drives include "Track-At-Once" and "Session-At-Once," which turn the drive's laser on and off during various stages of the recording process.

In this example, the CD-RW device name is used, and again, all tracks from an audio CD will be extracted and saved as .wav audio files. Other graphical clients, such as xine, grip, and xcdroast, are included with Fedora and can be used to create or copy audio and data CDs. See Chapter 10 for more details on burning CDs.

> **Related Fedora and Linux Commands**
>
> You will use these commands when performing post-installation configuration tasks:
>
> apm—Views or uses power management settings and commands
>
> cardctl—Controls PCMCIA slots and services
>
> cdda2wav—Extracts audio files from audio CDs
>
> cdparanoia—Extracts audio files from audio CDs
>
> cdrecord—Gets SCSI device information and burns CD-ROMs
>
> chkconfig—Controls services at each Linux runlevel
>
> dmesg—Views information reported by the Linux kernel
>
> insmod—Loads a kernel module into memory
>
> internet-druid—Red Hat's graphical X client (also run as system-config-network) used to detect and configure a modem when configuring a dialup Internet connection
>
> kppp—KDE's X PPP connection utility can detect and use a modem
>
> lsmod—Views loaded kernel modules
>
> mouseconfig—Configures a pointing device for Linux
>
> ntsysv—Controls services started when booting Linux
>
> system-config-date—Red Hat's graphical date and time client
>
> system-config-display—Red Hat's graphical X configuration client
>
> system-config-soundcard—Red Hat's graphical sound card configuration tool
>
> system-config-keyboard—Red Hat's graphical keyboard map configuration tool
>
> system-config-mouse—Red Hat's graphical pointer configuration tool

4

sensors—Gets the system's power, fan speed, and CPU temperatures

setserial—Configures a serial port from the command line

sndconfig—Configures a sound card for Fedora from the console

Reference

The *Linux Keyboard and Console HOWTO*—Andries Brouwer's tome on keyboard and console issues; includes many troubleshooting tips.

http://www.avocent.com/Cybex/PublicW2.nsf/gwMain?OpenFrameset—Product details for a KVM switch running Linux.

http://www.luv.asn.au/overheads/virtualconsoles.html—Using virtual consoles with Linux.

http://www.synaptics.com/products/touchpad.cfm—Information about TouchPad pointing devices.

http://www.compass.com/synaptics/—Site for a Linux TouchPad driver.

http://www.x.org/—The X.Org Foundation, home of X11R6 7.0.

http://www.alsa-project.org—Home page for the Advanced Linux Sound Architecture project, an alternative set of sound drivers for Linux.

http://www.opensound.com—Commercial sound drivers for Linux.

/usr/src/linux-2.6/Documentation/power/pci.txt—Patrick Mochel's document regarding PCI power-management routes for Linux kernel and PCI hardware support programmers.

http://www.tldp.org/pub/Linux/docs/HOWTO/Modem-HOWTO—One of the newest HOWTOs on using modems with Linux.

http://www.tldp.org/pub/Linux/docs/HOWTO/Serial-HOWTO—David S. Lawyer's Serial HOWTO, with additional information about Linux and serial port use.

http://www2.lm-sensors.nu/~lm78/cvs/lm_sensors2/doc/FAQ—Information regarding the lm-sensors software for Linux.

http://pcmcia-cs.sourceforge.net/—Source for the latest PCMCIA drivers for Linux.

http://www.camiresearch.com/Data_Com_Basics/RS232_standard.html—A description and tutorial on the EIA232 (formerly RS232) standard.

http://www.qbik.ch/usb/devices/—The place to check for compatibility of USB devices for Linux.

http://www.linmodems.org—This site provides links to several drivers for controllerless modem use under Linux.

http://www.linux1394.org/—Home page for the Linux IEEE 1394 project with new information, links to updated drivers, and lists of compatible chipsets and devices.

http://www.faqchest.com/—The FAQchest, a searchable archive of FAQ's HOWTO's and mailing lists; an alternative to http://marc.theaimsgroup.com/.

http://groups.google.com/—Search Usenet group through Google; another alternative to http://marc.theaimsgroup.com/.

http://www.linuxquestions.org/—The Linux Questions site, a useful set of community forums that can help you find answers to your more frustrating problems.

http://www.fokus.gmd.de/research/cc/glone/employees/joerg.schilling/private/_cdrecord.html—Home page for the cdrecord command and related utilities.

http://arstechnica.com/guide/building/bios/bios-1.html—An excellent discussion of BIOS options at ArsTechnica.

http://www.linuxnetmag.com/en/issue5/m5devs1.html—A brief article on how to make use of the information found in devices.txt.

4

First Steps with Fedora

Fedora Core Linux offers a wonderful graphical interface for the desktop (see Chapter 6, "The X Window System"), along with many capable graphical administration tools. However, there are times when you can't manage or use Linux effectively if you don't know how to use text-based programs at the command line. In some situations and with some software packages, the command line offers the only means of interacting with a running system or reconfiguring server software.

In this chapter, you learn the basics of how to use Linux and how to accomplish many routine tasks at the command line. These basic operations include how to read text files or other Linux documentation, list directories, or move, copy, and rename files. New Linux system administrators will get an introduction to using the command line to create new users, manage file permissions, and to properly reboot or shut down a Linux system.

Some of the basic command-line skills covered in this chapter include

- **Performing routine tasks**—Logging in and out, using the text console, changing passwords, listing and navigating directories.

- **Basic file management**—Creating, renaming, or deleting files and directories.

- **Basic user management**—Creating or deleting users from the command line.

- **Basic system management**—Shutting down or rebooting, reading manual pages or other documentation, and using text-based tools to edit system configuration files.

Read this chapter if you are migrating to Linux from another platform; the information here is valuable for individual users or system administrators who are new to Linux and learning to use the command line for the first time.

TIP

When you have learned how to use the command line with Linux, you will be comfortable using a Unix command line. This chapter, then, can help provide the foundation information you need to work with other Unix-like operating systems, such as FreeBSD.

NOTE

There are two types of users on a Linux system: normal users (see the section "Basic Linux User Skills") and the *root* operator, also known as the *superuser*. At big computing installations, one or more system administrators might have root access or superuser power on the system (perhaps for one-time only tasks). Normal users may rarely, if ever, interact with the root operator.

However, if you use Linux on your PC or notebook as a standalone workstation, you will be both a user and the root operator. Under Linux, root access is required to perform nearly all system and hardware configuration. This might be one of the primary reasons that some new users hold the view that using Linux requires a steep learning curve. Red Hat and other Linux developers have put a lot of effort into making system administration easier for new users by developing improved graphical administration utilities. Because of the way Linux is designed, however, you must become comfortable working with the command line and doing some root-level work, especially if using Linux on a standalone PC. The benefits of learning how to use the command line and work as the superuser far outweigh the disadvantages of allowing your operating system to make important system, file, and user decisions for you. You are in charge of your operating system, not the other way around!

Working with the Linux File System

Fedora uses a *file system*, or layout of hierarchical directories similar to that used by other Unix variants (such as Mac OS X). Nearly all Linux distributions use a similar directory structure, and Linux distribution vendors have generally agreed on the naming and location of critical Linux files and directories.

NOTE

The effort to build a consensus regarding the Linux directory structure began in 1993 with the Filesystem Hierarchy Standard (FHS), a draft proposal that addressed not only Linux issues, but also for other operating systems, such as BSD. Red Hat has stated that it is committed to stay compliant with the FHS, which specifies the location and names of files and directories. Fedora uses the current 2.3 standard. Key additions to this include the creation of a /media directory for removable storage devices (while keeping /mnt as a temporary mount point). udev has also been added to Fedora; although it's not a part of FHS 2.3, it enables /dev to become a dynamically managed folder allowing the hot-plugging of devices onto the system and the creation (on demand) of device nodes.

The universal layout of directories and file locations for Linux is extremely helpful for individual developers or companies creating distributions, packaging applications, and crafting system administration utilities. For example, knowing that the useradd command is always found under the /usr/sbin directory can simplify the creation of administrative shell scripts designed to be used by system administrators. This information can also help you if you use other Unix-like operating systems or other Linux distributions and need to troubleshoot software installation, or plan the addition of major software packages onto your Fedora system.

To gain the full benefits of this universal layout, you must know how Linux-based operating systems are organized, what the contents are of files and directories on your system, and where files and software should be installed. Understanding the Linux file system is part of learning how to administer and use Linux. As the root operator, you should know the name and proper location of all files (aside from user data) not only to ensure a smoothly running system, but also especially for security reasons.

Viewing the Linux File System

Look at the layout of Fedora Core Linux system by using the list directory contents command, ls, like this:

```
$ ls /
bin   dev   home    lib          media   mnt   proc   sbin      srv   tftpboot   usr
boot  etc   initrd  lost+found   misc    opt   root   selinux   sys   tmp        var
```

> **NOTE**
>
> This section provides an overview of the Fedora Core file system. You might find fewer or more directories than discussed here in your own system. When some software packages are installed, they create new directories. Updating software packages might also remove or change the name of some directories. See Chapter 7, "Managing Software and System Resources," for more information on installing, upgrading, or removing software from your Linux system.

To get a more detailed picture, use the tree command to show the root or base directory layout, along with associated subdirectories, like this (note that your system's /usr/src directory might be somewhat different, depending on the version of Fedora you have installed or if you have updated Fedora with a new kernel, and that not all subdirectories are listed):

```
$ tree -dx /
/
¦-- bin
¦-- boot
¦-- dev
¦-- etc
¦   ¦-- X11
¦   ¦-- cron.d
```

```
¦     ¦-- ppp
¦     ¦-- rc.d
¦     ¦-- ssh
¦     ¦-- sysconfig
¦-- home
¦     `-- bball
¦-- lib
¦     `-- modules
¦-- lost+found
¦-- media
¦     ¦-- cdrom
¦     ¦-- floppy
¦-- misc
¦-- mnt
¦     ¦-- cdrom
¦     `-- floppy
¦-- opt
¦-- proc
¦-- root
¦-- sbin
¦-- tftpboot
¦-- tmp
¦-- usr
¦     ¦-- X11R6
¦     ¦     ¦-- bin
¦     ¦     ¦-- include
¦     ¦     ¦-- lib
¦     ¦-- bin
¦     ¦-- doc
¦     ¦-- include
¦     ¦-- lib
¦     ¦-- local
¦     ¦-- sbin
¦     ¦-- share
¦     ¦-- src
¦     ¦     ¦-- redhat
¦     ¦     `-- sys
¦
`-- var
      ¦-- ftp
      ¦-- log
      `-- spool
```

This example (pruned from more than 30,000 directories) shows the higher-level directories and corresponds to the directories and descriptions in Table 5.1.

Table 5.1   Basic Linux Directories

Name	Description
/	The root directory
/bin	Essential commands
/boot	Boot loader files, Linux kernel
/dev	Device files
/etc	System configuration files
/home	User home directories
/initrd	Initial RAM disk boot support (used during boot time)
/lib	Shared libraries, kernel modules
/lost+found	Directory for recovered files (if found after a filesystem check)
/media	Mount point for removable media such as CD-ROMs and floppy disks
/mnt	Usual mount point for local, remote filesystems
/opt	Add-on software packages
/proc	Kernel information, process control
/root	Superuser (root home)
/sbin	System commands (mostly root only)
/selinux	Holds the data for SELinux, the security component of Fedora
/sys	Real-time information on devices used by the kernel
/tftpboot	Network boot support
/tmp	Temporary files
/usr	Secondary software file hierarchy
/var	Variable data (such as logs); spooled files

Some of the important directories in Table 5.1, such as those containing user and root commands or system configuration files, are discussed in the following sections. You will use and edit files under these directories when you use Fedora.

Use Essential Commands from the /bin and /sbin Directories

The /bin directory (about 5MB if you do a full install) contains essential commands used by the system when running and booting Linux. In general, only the root operator uses the commands in the /sbin directory. Many (though not all) of these commands are *statically* linked; such commands do not depend on software libraries residing under the /lib or /usr/lib directories. Nearly all the other applications on your system are *dynamically* linked—meaning that they require external software libraries (also known as *shared* libraries) in order to run.

> **TIP**
>
> Because the system contains dynamically linked applications, you might sometimes get "dependency errors" when installing or upgrading software packages; in those situations, a supporting library (or application) might not be present. See Chapter 7 for more information on working with dynamically linked applications and other methods of avoiding such problems.

Store the Booted Kernel and View Stored Devices in the /boot and /dev Directories

The /boot directory contains a compressed version of the Linux kernel (loaded at boot time), along with other files that describe the kernel or provide information for booting Linux. When you rebuild or install a new kernel, the kernel and related files are placed in this directory (see Chapter 38, "Kernel and Module Management," for more information on rebuilding or installing a kernel).

Linux device files are contained under the /dev directory. Note that under Linux, nearly everything on your system is a file. This means that (with the exception of network interfaces; see note that follows list) regular files; directories; hard drive partitions; serial, printer, or USB ports; and video and sound devices all are files!

The /dev directory contains more than 7,500 files representing devices that may or may not be in use on your system. Some of the most commonly used devices in this directory include

- IDE (Integrated Drive Electronics) hard drives, such as /dev/hda and /dev/hdb.

- CD-ROM drives; some of which are IDE, whereas others are CD-RW (CD read/write) drives emulated as SCSI (Small Computer Systems Interface) devices such as /dev/scd0.

- Serial ports, such as /dev/ttyS0 for COM1, /dev/ttyS1 for COM2, and so on.

- Pointing devices, including /dev/input/mice and others.

- Printers, such as /dev/lp0.

> **NOTE**
>
> Network interfaces (such as eth0 or ppp0) are not represented by Linux device files, but are created in memory when activated. See Chapter 17, "Network Connectivity," for more information.

Use and Edit Files in the /etc Directory

More than 65MB of system configuration files and directories reside under the /etc directory if you install all the software included with this book. Some major software packages, such as Apache, OpenSSH, and xinetd, have directories of configuration files under /etc. Other important system-related configuration files in /etc are

- fstab—The system filesystem table is a text file listing each hard drive, CD-ROM, floppy, or other storage device attached to your PC. The table indexes each device's partition information with a place in your Linux file system (directory layout) and lists other options for each device when used with Linux (see Chapter 37, "Managing the File System"). Nearly all entries in fstab can be manipulated by root using the mount command.

- `inittab`—The system initialization table defines the default runlevel, also known as *run-control* level or *system state*. Changes to this file can determine whether your system boots to a graphical or text login, as well as whether dial-up remote access is enabled. (You learn about default runlevels in the section "System Services and Runlevels" located in Chapter 14, "Automating Tasks." See the section "Starting X" located in Chapter 6 to learn more about changing inittab to boot to a graphical interface. Chapter 18, "Internet Connectivity," in the section "Configuring a Dial-In PPP Server" discusses editing `inittab` to enable dial-up remote access).

- `modprobe.conf`—This configuration file contains directions and options used when loading kernel modules to enable various types of hardware, such as sound, USB, networking, and so on (discussed in the section "Managing Modules" in Chapter 38). The contents of this file are used during boot time, and the file can be manually edited or automatically updated by Red Hat's `kudzu` hardware management server (if enabled, as you learn later in this section).

- `passwd`—The list of users for the system, along with user account information. The contents of this file can be changed by various programs, such as `useradd` or `chsh`.

- `printcap`—The system's printer capabilities database (discussed in the section "Overview of Fedora Linux Printing" in Chapter 11, "Printing with Fedora").

- `shells`—A list of approved shells (command-line interfaces).

One of the most important directories under /etc for Fedora is `sysconfig`. This directory contains network activation scripts and hardware- and software-related information:

```
$ tree -afx /etc/sysconfig
/etc/sysconfig
¦-- /etc/sysconfig/amd
¦-- /etc/sysconfig/apm-scripts
¦    `-- /etc/sysconfig/apm-scripts/apmscript
¦-- /etc/sysconfig/apmd
...
¦-- /etc/sysconfig/clock
¦-- /etc/sysconfig/console
...
¦-- /etc/sysconfig/dhcpd
¦-- /etc/sysconfig/dhcrelay
...
¦-- /etc/sysconfig/grub
¦-- /etc/sysconfig/harddisks
¦-- /etc/sysconfig/hidd
¦-- /etc/sysconfig/httpd
¦-- /etc/sysconfig/hwconf
...
¦-- /etc/sysconfig/init
...
```

```
¦-- /etc/sysconfig/keyboard
¦-- /etc/sysconfig/kudzu
¦-- /etc/sysconfig/lm_sensors
¦-- /etc/sysconfig/mouse
¦-- /etc/sysconfig/named
¦-- /etc/sysconfig/netdump
...
¦-- /etc/sysconfig/network
¦-- /etc/sysconfig/network-scripts
¦    ¦-- /etc/sysconfig/network-scripts/ifcfg-eth0
...
¦    ¦-- /etc/sysconfig/network-scripts/ifup-wireless
¦    ¦-- /etc/sysconfig/network-scripts/init.ipv6-global
¦    ¦-- /etc/sysconfig/network-scripts/network-functions
¦    `-- /etc/sysconfig/network-scripts/network-functions-ipv6
¦-- /etc/sysconfig/networking
¦    ¦-- /etc/sysconfig/networking/devices
¦    ¦-- /etc/sysconfig/networking/devices/ifcfg-eth0
...
¦    `-- /etc/sysconfig/networking/profiles
¦        `-- /etc/sysconfig/networking/profiles/default
¦-- /etc/sysconfig/ntpd
¦-- /etc/sysconfig/pand
¦-- /etc/sysconfig/pcmcia
...
¦-- /etc/sysconfig/redhat-config-users
¦-- /etc/sysconfig/redhat-logviewer
¦-- /etc/sysconfig/rhn
¦    ¦-- /etc/sysconfig/rhn/rhnsd
¦    ¦-- /etc/sysconfig/rhn/up2date
¦    `-- /etc/sysconfig/rhn/up2date-keyring.gpg
¦-- /etc/sysconfig/samba
¦-- /etc/sysconfig/sendmail
¦-- /etc/sysconfig/spamassassin
¦-- /etc/sysconfig/squid
¦-- /etc/sysconfig/syslog
...
¦-- /etc/sysconfig/ups
¦-- /etc/sysconfig/vncservers
¦-- /etc/sysconfig/xinetd
`-- /etc/sysconfig/yppasswdd
```

For brevity, not all directories and files are discussed here or listed in the example.
/etc/sysconfig contains many different hardware and software settings critical to the
operation of your Fedora system. Knowing the location and contents of these files can be
helpful if you need to troubleshoot new hardware configurations.

The settings in various files under /etc/sysconfig (such as keyboard, mouse, sound, and so on) are usually created automatically by a related Red Hat or Fedora graphical or console-based configuration utility.

These contents might dynamically change if you use the kudzu hardware configuration service. The kudzu service also prompts you at boot time to remove, configure, or ignore a related setting if kudzu detects new or different hardware (such as a new USB keyboard, network card, or monitor). kudzu creates a file called hwconf that contains a hardware profile of your PC's current state. Note that if kudzu is not enabled or running, you can use device-specific configuration utilities such as system-config-keyboard, or you can manually edit configuration files.

Information about the type of pointing device attached to the PC, for example, is contained in the file /etc/sysconfig/mouse:

```
MOUSETYPE="ps/2"
XMOUSETYPE="PS/2"
FULLNAME="Generic 3 Button Mouse (PS/2)"
XEMU3=no
```

If a different mouse, say a three-button USB device, is attached to the computer, you can edit this information to reflect the hardware change:

```
MOUSETYPE="ps/2"
XMOUSETYPE="IMPS/2"
FULLNAME="Generic 3 Button Mouse (USB)"
XEMU3=no
```

> **CAUTION**
>
> If you're new to Linux, the system-config-mouse client is the best tool to use to configure a new mouse. You should only manually edit system hardware configuration files used by graphical management clients as a last resort.

Protect the Contents of User Directories—/home

The most important data on a Linux system reside in user's directories, found under the /home directory. Segregating the system and user data can be helpful in preventing data loss and making the process of backing up easier. For example, having user data reside on a separate filesystem or mounted from a remote computer on the network might help shield users from data loss in the event of a system hardware failure.

Use the Contents of the /proc Directory to Interact with the Kernel

The content of the /proc directory is created from memory and only exists while Linux is running. This directory contains special "files" that either extract information from or send information to the kernel. Many Linux utilities extract information from dynamically created directories and files under this directory, also known as a *virtual filesystem*. For example, the free command obtains its information from a file named meminfo:

```
$ free
              total      used       free     shared    buffers     cached
Mem:         223260    157800      65460          0      55400      58872
-/+ buffers/cache:      43528     179732
Swap:        491392       400     490992
```

This information constantly changes as the system is used. You can get the same information by using the cat command to see the contents of the meminfo file:

```
$ cat /proc/meminfo
           total:      used:      free:  shared: buffers:   cached:
Mem:   228618240 161673216 66945024          0 56750080 60694528
Swap: 503185408    409600 502775808
MemTotal:       223260 kB
MemFree:         65376 kB
MemShared:           0 kB
Buffers:         55420 kB
Cached:          58872 kB
SwapCached:        400 kB
Active:         100328 kB
Inact_dirty:     25044 kB
Inact_clean:     19012 kB
Inact_target:    28876 kB
HighTotal:           0 kB
HighFree:            0 kB
LowTotal:       223260 kB
LowFree:         65376 kB
SwapTotal:      491392 kB
SwapFree:       490992 kB
Committed_AS:    51424 kB
```

The /proc directory can also be used to dynamically alter the behavior of a running Linux kernel by "echoing" numerical values to specific files under the /proc/sys directory. For example, to "turn on" kernel protection against one type of Denial Of Service (DOS) attack known as *SYN flooding*, use the echo command to send the number 1 (one) to the following /proc path:

```
# echo 1 >/proc/sys/net/ipv4/tcp_syncookies
```

> **NOTE**
>
> The Linux kernel has a number of built-in protections, but good system administration security policies and a secure firewall protecting your gateway, router, or Internet-connected system are

the best protection you can use. See the section "Securing Your Network" in Chapter 17 for an overview of firewalling and examples of how to implement Red Hat's network security tools included with Fedora.

Other ways to use the /proc directory include

- Getting CPU information, such as the family, type, and speed from /proc/cpuinfo.

- Viewing important networking information under /proc/net, such as active interfaces in tion under /proc/net/dev, routing information in /proc/net/route, and network statistics in /proc/net/netstat.

- Retrieving filesystem information.

- Reporting media mount point information via USB; for example, the Linux kernel will report what device to use to access files (such as /dev/sda) if a USB camera or hard drive is detected on the system. You can use the dmesg command to see this information or find information about these devices under the Device File System directory /proc/devfs (see the Linux Devfs FAQ in the file /usr/src/linux-2.6/Documentation/filesystems/devfs/README if the source code for the Linux kernel is installed). The file /usr/src/linux-2.6/Documentation/usb/proc_usb_info.txt contains general information about USB and the /proc directory, as well as what to expect in files under this directory. Note that devfs might be supported, but will generally be superseded in the upcoming 2.6 kernel by /proc/udev, as a way of managing hot-plug devices on your system.

- Getting the kernel version in /proc/version, performance information such as uptime in /proc/uptime, or other statistics such as CPU load, swap file usage, and processes in /proc/stat.

Work with Shared Data in the /usr Directory

The /usr directory (nearly 5GB in size if you do a full install) contains software applications, libraries, and other types of shared data for use by anyone on the system. Many Linux system administrators give /usr its own partition. A number of subdirectories under /usr contain the X Window System (/usr/X11R6), manual pages (/usr/share/man), software package shared files (/usr/share/name_of_package, such as /usr/share/emacs), additional application or software package documentation (/usr/share/doc), and an entire subdirectory tree of locally built and installed software, /usr/local.

Temporary File Storage in the /tmp Directory

As its name implies, the /tmp directory is used for temporary file storage; as you use Linux, various programs create files in this directory. The /tmp directory is cleaned of stale files each day by the tmpwatch command. (A stale file is any file not used after 10 days.) Fedora is configured by default to use tmpwatch to check /tmp each day by settings in your system's scheduling table, /etc/crontab.

Access Variable Data Files in the /var Directory

The /var directory contains subdirectories used by various system services for spooling and logging. Many of these variable data files, such as print spooler queues, are temporary, whereas others, such as system and kernel logs, are renamed and rotated in use. Incoming electronic mail is usually directed to files under /var/spool/mail.

Linux also uses /var for other important system services. These include the top-most File Transfer Protocol (FTP) directory under /var/ftp (see Chapter 22, "Remote File Serving with FTP"), and the Apache web server's initial home page directory for the system, /var/www/html. (See Chapter 19, "Apache Web Server Management," for more information on using Apache).

Logging In to and Working with Linux

You can access and use a Linux system in a number of ways. One way is at the console with a monitor, keyboard, and mouse attached to the PC. Another way might be via a serial console, either by dial-up via a modem or a PC running a terminal emulator and connected to the Linux PC via a null modem cable. You can also connect to your system through a wired or wireless network using the telnet or ssh commands. The information in this section shows you how to access and use the Linux system using physical and remote text-based logins.

> **NOTE**
>
> This chapter focuses on text-based logins and use of Linux. Graphical logins and using a graphical desktop are described in the section "Starting X" in Chapter 6.

Text-based Console Login

If you sit down at your PC and log in to a Linux system that has not been booted to a graphical login, you see a prompt similar to this one:

```
Fedora Core release 3 (Heidelberg)
Kernel 2.6.10-1.760_FC3 on an i686

login:
```

Your prompt might vary, depending on the version of Fedora Core you are using. In any event, at this prompt, type in your username and press Enter. When you are prompted for your password, type it in and press Enter.

> **NOTE**
>
> Note that your password is not echoed back to you, which is a good idea.

Working with Virtual Consoles

After logging in, you will be using an interactive command prompt known as a *shell* in the Linux text-based or *console* mode.

While you're sitting at your command prompt, you can also use one or more *virtual* consoles or terminals. Virtual consoles allow you to log in to Linux multiple times. (Each login is called a *session*.) This can be useful if you are not using a graphical desktop, but want to use several interactive programs, such as a text editor and web browser, at the same time. To do so, after you log in, run a program and then jump to another login prompt, log in, and start another session. Linux supports 63 virtual consoles, but only the first 6 are configured for use. (You can use 7 if you don't run X11.) Here's how to use virtual Linux consoles:

1. Log in. You'll be using the first virtual console, or vt1 by default.

2. Press F2. You should then see another login prompt. Log in again, and you are then using vt2, the second Linux console.

3. Press Alt+F1 to jump back to vt1.

4. Press Alt+F2 to jump back to vt2.

You can jump back and forth between sessions by using the Alt key plus the F key number of the desired session, such as F3, F4, F5, or F6.

One caveat when using virtual consoles is that there is a default limit on the available number (usually six) if an active X Window session is occupying vt7. To jump to a virtual console from an X session, press Ctrl+Alt+F2; you'll be at vt2. You can then jump back to your X session from the text-console by pressing Alt+F7 (to go to vt7, in use by X). You should also be careful to save any work in progress before you exit each session and to log out of each session when finished. If you do not, you could leave an open login and shell prompt available at the keyboard to anyone who walks by!

> **NOTE**
>
> In addition to virtual console keystrokes, the Linux console might also recognize the three-fingered salute (or Vulcan neck pinch), Ctrl+Alt+Del. This behavior (and the number of virtual terminals) can be controlled by the system administrator by editing the system's *initialization table,* /etc/inittab. See the Keyboard and Console HOWTO at http://www.tldp.org/ for more details.

Using Simple Keyboard and Mouse Techniques in a Linux Console Session

Working with Linux in a console-based session usually involves entering commands from the keyboard. However, you can also use simple mouse controls as well. Linux keyboard combinations and mouse support help provide virtual console navigation, start special system actions (such as rebooting or shutting down), provide shortcuts to save typing, and can aid in reading files or viewing program output.

For example, you can scroll the contents of your screen from the console by pressing Shift+PageUp or Shift+PageDown, and can copy and paste text using your mouse buttons. This section shows you how to access default or custom menus at the text console, which can be helpful to get system information or to launch new programs.

If you use a mouse with Linux (and you most likely do), you can use your pointing device for copy and paste operations. This support is provided by gpm, the general purpose mouse server. The gpm server must be enabled or started while booting Linux (see Chapter 14 for more details in the section "Controlling Services at Boot Using Administrative Tools"). To copy a section of text, click and drag text with the left mouse button (button 1) held down. To paste text, click an insertion point, and then press the middle mouse button (button 2).

Button assignment, like all mouse controls during text console use, is managed by command-line options given to gpm when it is started. For example, if you look at the gpm startup script named gpm under the /etc/rc.d/init.d/ directory, you'll see that it uses the file named mouse under the /etc/sysconfig directory to hold options:

```
# Additional options for gpm (e.g. acceleration), device
OPTIONS=""
DEVICE="/dev/mouse"
```

You can add options, detailed in the gpm manual page to change how your mouse works, enable or disable features, or assign special commands to a specific mouse button click. For example, to change your button order from 123 (left, middle, and right) to 321, edit the /etc/sysconfig/mouse file as root and change the OPTIONS entry like so:

```
OPTIONS="-B 321"
```

After saving your changes, restart gpm like so:

```
# /etc/rc.d/init.d/gpm restart
```

Your mouse buttons will now be reversed!

To aid users with a two-button mouse, Linux supports three-button *emulation*; emulation lets users simultaneously press the right and left mouse buttons to simulate a press of the middle button. You can enable this feature during installation or by using the mouseconfig command. See the section "Configuring Pointing Devices in Linux" in Chapter 4, "Post-Installation Configuration," to see how to use mouseconfig.

The gpm server also provides the ability to reboot or shut down the system with the mouse. Depending on the combination of mouse buttons you press, you have several reboot or shutdown options. Begin by holding down either the left or right mouse button and triple-clicking the opposite button; depending on which mouse button you press next, one of these actions occurs:

- Pressing the left button causes an immediate reboot using the `init` command.

- Pressing the middle button reboots the system using the `shutdown` command.

- Pressing the right button causes the system to shut down immediately with the `shutdown` command.

You can also create custom menus that will pop up at a text-based Linux console by editing the file `/etc/gpm-root.conf` (as root) and starting the `gpm-root` command. When you run `gpm-root` without making changes to its configuration file, by default a system status dialog (with the date, time, CPU load, free memory, and swap file usage) will appear if you hold down the Ctrl key and press the middle mouse button.

You can change your keyboard layouts by using the `loadkeys` command. To use a different font for the console, try the `setfont` command. Fedora Core Linux comes with nearly 150 different console fonts, which are found under the `/lib/kbd/consolefonts` directory. See the section "Configuring Keyboards with Linux" in Chapter 4 to see how to use these commands.

> **NOTE**
>
> A text-based, dial-up login, also known as a *shell* account, looks much the same as a text-based login at a PC running Linux. Details about setting up Linux to answer the phone and provide a login prompt via a modem are in Chapter 18. Using dial-up access has some limitations, such as the inability to use virtual consoles. From a shell account, however, you can start programs in the background (using the ampersand, &), run programs after logging out with the `nohup` command, or use the `screen` command to simulate virtual terminals (an approach that works much like using virtual consoles). For more information on different shells included with Linux, see Chapter 14.

Logging Out

Use the `exit` or `logout` commands to exit your session. Type the command and press Enter. You'll then be returned to the login prompt. If you use virtual consoles, remember to exit each console before leaving your PC. (Otherwise, someone could easily sit down and use your account.)

Logging In and Out from a Remote Computer

Although you can happily log in on your computer, an act known as a *local* log in, you can also log in to your computer via a network connection from a remote computer. Linux-based operating systems provide a number of remote access commands you can use to log in to other computers on your local area network (LAN), wide area network (WAN), or the Internet. Note that not only must you have an account on the remote computer, but also the remote computer must be configured to support remote logins—otherwise, you won't be able to log in.

See Chapter 17 to see how to set up network interfaces with Linux to support remote network logins and Chapter 14 to see how to start remote access services (such as sshd).

The best and most secure way (barring future exploits) to log in to a remote Linux computer is to use the ssh or Secure Shell client. Your login and session are encrypted while you work on the remote computer. The ssh client features many different command-line options, but can be simply used with the name of the remote computer, like this:

```
[andrew@laptop ~]$ ssh desktop
The authenticity of host 'desktop (192.168.2.3)' can't be established.
RSA key fingerprint is 91:7d:74:4b:1c:a1:96:06:ba:2f:d4:cf:78:44:ff:d7.
Are you sure you want to continue connecting (yes/no)? yes
```

The first time you connect with a remote computer using ssh, Linux displays the remote computer's encrypted identity key and asks you to verify the connection. After you type **yes** and press Enter, you're warned that the remote computer's identity (key) has been entered in a file named known_hosts under the .ssh directory in your home directory. You're also prompted to enter your password:

```
Warning: Permanently added 'desktop,192.168.2.3' (RSA) \
to the list of known hosts.
andrew@'desktop's password:
/usr/X11R6/bin/xauth:  creating new authority file /home/winky/.Xauthority
[andrew@desktop andrew]$
```

After entering your password, you can then work on the remote computer. Again, everything you enter on the keyboard in communication with the remote computer is encrypted. Use the exit or logout commands to exit your session and return to the shell on your computer.

The next remote access command, telnet, is shown as an example because it is included with most Linux distributions, but you shouldn't use it: telnet transmits your username and password in clear text across the network, posing a huge security risk for your system. Also, note that this service must be explicitly turned on and allowed on the remote computer (by editing the file named telnet under the /etc/xinetd.d directory and then restarting xinetd; see the section "Starting and Stopping Services Manually" in Chapter 14 for more information on starting or restarting a system service).

The telnet command can be used, along with the name of a remote host or Internet Protocol (IP) address, to log in to a remote computer. For example, to log in to the host named desktop from the host named laptop,

```
[andrew@laptop andrew]$ telnet desktop
```

After you press Enter, you'll see some information presented by the remote computer, and you will then be prompted for your username on the remote system:

```
Trying 192.168.2.70...
Connected to desktop.andbhudson.co.uk (192.168.2.73).
Escape character is '^]'.

Linux 2.6.10-1.741_FC3 (desktop.andbhudson.co.uk) (15:43 on Friday, 4 February
2005)

login: andrew
```

After you type your username (andrew in this example), press Enter, and you'll be prompted for your password on the remote system:

```
Password:
Last login: Fri Feb 4 15:42:26 from 192.168.2.2
[andrew@desktop andrew]$
```

After you type your password and press Enter (your password is not echoed back), you'll be informed of the last time you logged in, and you can then work on the remote computer. Use the exit or logout commands to exit your session and return to the shell on your computer.

Although it is possible to use telnet to log in to a remote computer over a wired and wireless network, such use is not recommended, especially via the Internet. When you type your username and then press Enter and type your password, your username and password are transmitted without encryption over the network. Transmitting usernames and passwords over a network without encryption is a bad idea for obvious reasons. However, if you have a physically secure internal network not connected to the Internet, have firewall policies in place, and don't use wireless networking, there is nothing wrong with using telnet. In fact, the encryption overhead of using ssh can reduce network transmission rates in some cases.

> **NOTE**
>
> It is possible to use telnet securely over an encrypted Virtual Private Network (VPN), but that is beyond the scope of this chapter and book. Besides, why bother when you can use SSH?

Changing Your User Information

Linux users are assigned a name, known as a *username*, by the root operator. One method of assigning usernames is to use one's first initial and last name in lowercase; for example, Bernice Hudson would have a username of *bhudson*. Each user must also have a password, which is used with the username either at a graphical or text-based login.

NOTE

Older versions of Linux operating systems limited the length of usernames to 8 characters. The current version of Fedora limits usernames to 32 characters. Good passwords should be a minimum of 8 characters long and contain upper- and lowercase letters, along with numbers. Random passwords for users can be generated using the mkpasswd command (which is included with the expect software package). For example, to generate a 10-character password automatically with three numbers and three digits, use mkpasswd -l 10 -d 3 -C 3. Good passwords are not birthdays, anniversaries, your pet's name, the name of your significant other, or the model of your first car!

You cannot change your username, but you can change your user information, such as address, phone, and so on. You make these changes using the chfn or *change finger information* command. This command will modify the contents of your entry in the system password file /etc/passwd, which is used by the finger command to display information about a system's user. For example, type **chfn** at the command line and press Enter:

```
$ chfn
Changing finger information for bhudson.
Password:
Name []: Bernice Hudson
Office []: Suite 56 N. Centennial Blvd.
Office Phone []: 919 555-1212
Home Phone []: 919 555-1213
Finger information changed.
```

You're led through a series of prompts to enter new or updated information. Note that the chfn command will not let you use any commas when entering information. You can verify this information in a couple ways, for example, by looking at the contents of /etc/passwd:

```
$ grep bhdudson /etc/passwd
bhudson:x:501:501:Bernice Hudson,Suite 56 N. Centennial Blvd.,\
919 555-1212,919 555-1213:/home/bhudson:/bin/bash
```

You also can verify the updated user information by using the finger command:

```
$ finger bhudson
Login: bhudson                      Name: Bernice Hudson
Directory: /home/bhudson             Shell: /bin/bash
Office: Suite 56 N. Centennial Blvd.  Office Phone: 919 555-1212
Home Phone: 919 555-1213
Never logged in.
No mail.
No Plan.
```

Reading Documentation

Although you learn the basics of using Fedora in this book, you need time and practice to master and troubleshoot more complex aspects of the Linux operating system and your distribution. As with any operating system, you can expect to encounter some problems or perplexing questions as you continue to work with Linux. The first place to turn for help with these issues is the documentation included with your system; if you cannot find the information you need there, check Fedora's website.

> **NOTE**
>
> Checking Fedora's website for security updates and bug fixes is a good idea. Browse to http://fedora.redhat.com/download/. Alternatively, you can always do a quick yum update to make sure your system has the most up-to-date software available.

Linux, like Unix, is a self-documenting system, with manual pages accessible through the man command. Linux offers many other helpful commands for accessing its documentation. You can use the apropos command—for example, with a keyword such as partition—to find commands related to partitioning, like this:

```
$ apropos partition
GNU Parted [parted]   (8) - a partition manipulation program
fdisk                 (8) - Partition table manipulator for Linux
jfs_mkfs              (8) - create a JFS formatted partition
jfs_mkfs [mkfs]       (8) - create a JFS formatted partition
lvmdiskscan          (8) - scan for all disks / multiple devices / partitions
➥ available
mpartition           (1) - partition an MSDOS hard disk
partprobe            (8) - inform the OS of partition table changes
pvcreate             (8) - initialize a disk or partition for use by LVM
sfdisk               (8) - Partition table manipulator for Linux
```

To find a command and its documentation, you can use the whereis command. For example, if you are looking for the fdisk command, you can do this:

```
$ whereis fdisk
fdisk: /sbin/fdisk /usr/share/man/man8/fdisk.8.gz
```

Using man Pages

To learn more about a command or program, use the man command, followed by the name of the command. Manual pages for Linux and X Window commands are within the /usr/share/man, /usr/local/share/man, and /usr/X11R6/man directories; so, for example, to read the rm command's man page, use the man command like this:

```
$ man rm
```

After you press Enter, the `less` command (a Linux command known as a pager) displays the manual page. The `less` command is a text browser you can use to scroll forward and backward (even sideways) through the document to learn more about the command. Type the letter **h** to get help, use the forward slash to enter a search string, or press **q** to quit.

NOTE

Although nearly all the hundreds of GNU commands included with Linux each have a manual page, detailed information about using a GNU command must be read using the `info` command. For example, to learn even more about `bash` (which has a rather extensive manual page), use the `info` command like this:

```
$ info bash
```

Press the **n** and **p** keys to navigate through the document, or scroll down to a menu item on the screen and press Enter to read about a specific feature. Press **q** to quit reading.

Finding and Reading Software Packages Documentation

Documentation for various software packages is included in the `/usr/share/doc` directory; that directory is stored in another directory that's labeled with the associated package's name. You can find other Linux documentation, known as HOWTOs and Frequently Asked Questions (FAQs), online by browsing to http://www.tldp.org. HOWTO documents contain specific information related to a particular subject, such as printing, setting up a network, programming a serial port, or using a CD-ROM drive with Linux. These documents can be read by using your web browser. Of course, one of the best online tools you can use is a good search engine, such as Google.

You can read document formats such as text with `less` or another pager or text reader. For example, to read a copy of the GNU General Public License (GPL), a file named GPL_V2 under the `/usr/share/apps/LICENSES` directory, use `less` like this:

```
$ less /usr/share/apps/LICENSES/GPL_V2
```

After you press Enter, you can scroll back and forth through the file. Press q to quit reading. If a document is in compressed form (ending in `.gz`), use the `zless` pager, which will decompress a document first:

```
$ zless /usr/share/man/es/man1/README.gz
```

Most users read document formats such as HTML using a web browser in a graphical desktop. Fedora includes at least two versatile text-based web browsers, however, accessed with the `lynx` and `links` commands. To browse an HTML file on your system without using X11, use either command, along with the path to the file. For example, to read an HTML version of the GNU GPL with `links`, use the command like this:

```
$ links /usr/share/doc/HTML/en/common/gpl-license.html
```

After you press Enter, use your Up and Down cursor keys to scroll back and forth through the file. Press *q*, Enter to quit reading. If you have configured a mouse, click the left button near the top of the screen, and links will display its menus.

Using the Shell

The shell is an interactive command prompt with many different features:

- Input and output redirection
- Background processing
- Job control
- History editing
- Built-in help
- Command-line completion
- Command-line editing

The shell interprets keyboard commands and is generally used to launch other commands or programs using the shell's interpreter language known as *shell scripts*.

> **NOTE**
>
> Shell scripts are discussed in Chapter 14.

The shell you use is assigned by the last field in your entry in the system's /etc/passwd file. This example, for a user named andrew, shows that the login shell is bash:

```
andrew:x:502:502::/home/andrew:/bin/bash
```

The default shell for most Linux distributions, including Fedora, is the GNU bash or Bourne Again SHell, but other shells, such as tcsh, ksh, and zsh are available for use. You can use a different shell by typing its name at the command line. Alternatively, the root operator might assign a user to another shell when creating that user account (see "Working as Root," later in this chapter).

> **CAUTION**
>
> If you're interested in trying a different shell with Linux, you can change your login shell using the chsh command, but make sure that the shell is actually installed on your system. For example, to change your default shell to tcsh, first use the which command to verify that it is installed:
>
> ```
> $ which tcsh
> /bin/tcsh
> ```

This example shows that the tcsh shell is installed under the /bin directory. The tcsh shell should also be listed in your system's list of approved shells, /etc/shells. Check to make sure that it is listed:

```
$ grep tcsh /etc/shells
/bin/tcsh
```

You can also use the chsh command's -l option to list valid system shells in order to verify that using tcsh is allowed. Because tcsh is installed and listed in /etc/shells, you can then change your shell using the chsh command:

```
$ chsh
Changing shell for andrew.
Password:
New shell [/bin/bash]: /bin/ksh
chsh: "/bin/ksh" does not exist.
```

Note that the chsh command will report an error if you enter the name of a shell not installed on your system.

```
$ chsh -s /bin/tcsh
Changing shell for andrew.
Password:
Shell changed.
```

If you now take a look at your /etc/passwd entry, you will see /bin/tcsh as your default shell. The next time you log in, you'll use tcsh.

Using Environment Variables

A number of in-memory variables are assigned and loaded by default when the user logs in. These variables are known as shell *environment variables*, which can be used by various commands to get information about your environment, such as the type of system you are running, your home directory, and the shell in use. Environment variables are used by Linux operating systems to help tailor the computing environment of your system, and include helpful specifications and setup, such as default locations of executable files and software libraries. If you begin writing shell scripts, you might use environment variables in your scripts. Until then, you only need to be aware of what environment variables are and do.

The following list includes a number of environment variables, along with descriptions of how the shell uses them:

- PWD—To provide the name of the current working directory, used by the pwd command (such as /home/andrew/foo)

- USER—To declare the user's name, such as andrew

- LANG—To set language defaults, such as English

- SHELL—To declare the name and location of the current shell, such as /bin/bash

- PATH—To set the default location of executable files, such as /bin, /usr/bin, and so on

- LD_LIBRARY_PATH—To declare the location of important software libraries (because most, but not all, Linux commands use shared resources)

- TERM—To set the type of terminal in use, such as vt100, which can be important when using screen-oriented programs, such as text editors

- MACHINE—To declare system type, system architecture, and so on

> **NOTE**
>
> Each shell can have its own feature set and language syntax, as well as a unique set of default environment variables. See Chapter 14 for more information about using the different shells included with Fedora.

At the command line, you can use the env or printenv commands to display these environment variables, like so:

```
$ env
PWD=/home/andrew
HOSTNAME=laptop.andbhudson.co.uk
USER=andrew
MACHTYPE=i386-redhat-linux-gnu
MAIL=/var/spool/mail/andrew
BASH_ENV=/home/andrew/.bashrc
LANG=en_GB
DISPLAY=0:0
LOGNAME=andrew
SHLVL=1
PATH=/usr/kerberos/bin:/usr/local/bin:/bin:/usr/bin: \
/usr/X11R6/bin:/home/bball/bin
SHELL=/bin/bash
HOSTTYPE=i386
OSTYPE=linux-gnu
HISTSIZE=1000
TERM=xterm
HOME=/home/andrew
```

This abbreviated list shows a few common variables. These variables are set by configuration or *resource* files contained in the /etc, /etc/skel, or user /home directory. You can find default settings for bash, for example, in /etc/profile, /etc/bashrc, the .bashrc, or .bash_profile files installed in your home directory. Read the man page for bash for details about using these configuration files.

One of the most important environment variables is $PATH, which defines the location of executable files. For example, if as a regular user, you try to use a command that is not located in your $PATH, such as the `ifconfig` command, you'll see something like this:

```
$ ifconfig
-bash: ifconfig: command not found
```

However, you might know that `ifconfig` is definitely installed on your system, and you can verify this using the `whereis` command like so:

```
$ whereis ifconfig
ifconfig: /sbin/ifconfig /usr/share/man/man8/ifconfig.8.gz
```

You can also run the command by typing its full *pathname*, or complete directory specification like this:

```
$ /sbin/ifconfig
```

As you can see in this example, the `ifconfig` command is indeed installed. What happened is that by default, the /sbin directory is not in your $PATH. One of the reasons for this is that commands under the /sbin directory are normally intended to only be run by root. You can add /sbin to your $PATH by editing the file .bash_profile in your home directory (if you use the bash shell by default, like most Linux users). Look for the following line:

```
PATH=$PATH:$HOME/bin
```

You can then edit this file, perhaps using the `vi` editor (discussed in this chapter), to add the /sbin directory like so:

```
PATH=$PATH:/sbin:$HOME/bin
```

Save the file. The next time you log in, the /sbin directory will be in your $PATH. One way to use this change right away is to read in the new settings in .bash_profile by using the bash shell's `source` command like so:

```
$ source .bash_profile
```

You'll now be able to run `ifconfig` without the need to explicitly type its full pathname.

Some Linux commands also use environment variables, for example, to acquire configuration information (such as a communications program looking for a variable such as BAUD_RATE, which might denote a default modem speed).

To experiment with the environment variables, you can modify the PS1 variable to manipulate the appearance of your shell prompt. If you are working with `bash`, you can use its built-in `export` command to change the shell prompt. For example, if your default shell prompt looks like

```
[andrew@laptop ~]$
```

You can change its appearance by using the PS1 variable like this:

```
$  PS1='$OSTYPE r00lz ->'
```

After you press Enter, you'll see

```
linux-gnu r00lz ->
```

> **NOTE**
>
> See the bash manual page for other variables you can use for prompt settings.

Navigating and Searching with the Shell

Use the `cd` command (built into the shell) to navigate through the Fedora file system. This command is generally used with a specific directory location, or *pathname* like this:

```
$ cd /usr/X11R6/lib/X11/doc
```

Under Fedora, the `cd` command can also be used with several shortcuts. For example, to quickly move up to the *parent* (higher-level) directory, use the `cd` command like this:

```
$ cd ..
```

To return to one's home directory from anywhere in the Linux file system, use the `cd` command like this:

```
$ cd
```

You can also use the `$HOME` shell environment variable to accomplish the same thing. Type this command and press Enter to return to your home directory:

```
$ cd $HOME
```

You can accomplish the same thing by using the tilde (~) like this:

```
$ cd ~
```

Linux also includes a number of GNU commands you can use to search the file system. These include

- `whereis` *command*—Returns the location of the command and its man page.
- `whatis` *command*—Returns a one-line synopsis from the command's man page.
- `locate` *file*—Returns locations of all matching file(s); an extremely fast method of searching your system, as `locate` searches a database containing an index of all files on your system; however, this database (about 4MB in size and named `slocate.db`

under the /var/lib/slocate directory) is built daily at 4:20 a.m. by default, and will not contain pathnames to files created during the workday or in the evening.

- apropos *subject*—Returns a list of commands related to subject.

Managing Files with the Shell

Managing files in your home directory involves using one or more easily remembered commands. If you have any familiarity with the now ancient DOS, you'll recognize some of these commands (though their names are different from those you remember). Basic file management operations include paging (reading), moving, renaming, copying, searching, and deleting files and directories. These commands include

- cat *filename*—Outputs contents of filename to display
- less *filename*—Allows scrolling while reading contents of filename
- mv *file1 file2*—Renames file1 to file2
- mv *file dir*—Moves file to specified directory
- cp *file1 file2*—Copies file1 and creates file2
- rm *file*—Deletes file
- rmdir *dir*—Deletes directory (if empty)
- grep *string file(s)*—Searches through files(s) and displays lines containing matching string

Note that each of these commands can be used with pattern-matching strings known as wildcards or *expressions*. For example, to delete all files in the current directory beginning with the letters abc, you can use an expression beginning with the first three letters of the desired filenames. An asterisk (*) is then appended to match all these files. Use a command line with the rm command like this:

```
$ rm abc*
```

Linux shells recognize many types of filenaming wildcards, but this is different from the capabilities of Linux commands supporting the use of more complex expressions. You learn more about using wildcards in Chapter 14.

> **NOTE**
>
> Learn more about using expressions by reading the ex or grep manual pages.

Compressing and Decompressing Files Through the Shell

Another file management operation is compression and decompression of files, or the creation, listing, and expansion of file and directory archives. Linux distros usually include several compression utilities that you can use to create, compress, expand, or list the contents of compressed files and archives. These commands include

- `bunzip2`—Expands a compressed file

- `bzip2`—Compresses or expands files and directories

- `gunzip`—Expands a compressed file

- `gzip`—Compresses or expands files and directories

- `shar` file—Creates a shell archive of files

- `tar`—Creates, expands, or lists the contents of compressed or uncompressed file or directory archives known as *tape archives* or "tarballs"

- `unshar`—Reassembles files from the shell archive

- `uudecode` file.uu—Decodes an uuencoded text file to its binary form

- `uuencode` file—Encodes a binary file to text file format for transmission via email

> **NOTE**
>
> The `rpm` command can also be used to manage archived data, but is generally used for software development and management. See Chapter 7 for more information on using RPM.

Most of these commands are easy to use. The `tar` command, however, has a somewhat complex (though capable) set of command-line options and syntax. Even so, you can quickly learn to use `tar` by remembering a few simple invocations on the command line. For example, to create a compressed archive of a directory, use `tar`'s `czf` options like this:

```
$ tar czf dirname.tgz dirname
```

The result will be a compressed archive (a file ending in `.tgz`) of the specified directory (and all files and directories under it). Add the letter `v` to the preceding options to view the list of files being added during compression and archiving. To list the contents of the compressed archive, substitute the `c` option with the letter `t`, like this:

```
$ tar tzf archive
```

Of course, if many files are in the archive, a better invocation (in order to easily read or scroll through the output) is

```
$ tar tzf archive ¦ less
```

To expand the contents of a compressed archive, use `tar`'s `xzf` options, like so:

```
$ tar xzf archive
```

`tar` decompresses the specified archive and extracts the contents in the current directory.

Using the Text Editors

Linux distributions include a number of applications known as *text editors* that you can use to create text files or edit system configuration files. Text editors are similar to word processing programs, but generally have fewer features, only work with text files, and might or might not support spell checking or formatting. The text editors range in features and ease of use, but are found on nearly every Linux distribution. The number of editors installed on your system depends on what software packages you've installed on the system.

Some of the console-based text editors are

- ed—A simple line editor without cursor support

- emacs—The comprehensive GNU emacs editing environment, which is much more than an editor; see the section "Working with emacs" later

- jed—A programmer's text editor with features such as colorized highlighting of text to help syntax checking and editing of programs

- joe—Joe's Own Editor, a text editor, which can be used to emulate other editors

- mcedit—A DOS-like text editor for Unix-like systems

- nano—A simple text editor similar to the pico text editor included with the pine email program

- sed—A stream editor usually used in shell scripts (discussed in Chapter 14)

- vim—An improved, compatible version of the vi text editor (which we'll call vi in the rest of this chapter because it has a symbolic link named vi and a symbolically linked manual page)

Note that not all text editors described here are *screen-oriented*; editors such as ed and sed work on a line-by-line basis, or a stream of text, and do not support movement of a cursor on the screen. Some of the text editors for the X Window System, which provide a graphical interface, such as menu bars, buttons, scrollbars and so on, are

- gedit—A GUI text editor for GNOME

- kate—A simple KDE text editor

- kedit—A simple KDE text editor

- nedit—A programming text editor

- kwrite—A simple KDE text editor

A good reason to learn how to use a text-based editor, such as vi, is that system maintenance and recovery operations generally never take place during X Window sessions (negating the use of a GUI editor). Many larger, more complex and capable editors will not work when Linux is booted to its single-user or maintenance mode. See Chapter 14 for more information about how Fedora boots. If anything does go wrong with your system, you probably won't be able to get into the X Window system, making knowledge and experience of using both the command line and text editors such as vi important. Make a point of opening some of the editors and playing around with them; you never know, you might just thank me someday!

Another reason to learn how to use a text-based editor under the Linux console mode is that you will be able to edit text files through dial-up or network shell sessions because many servers do not host graphical desktops.

Working with vi

The editor found on nearly every Unix and Linux system is, without a doubt, the vi editor, originally written by Bill Joy. This simple to use but incredibly capable editor features a somewhat cryptic command set, but you can put it to use with only a few commands. Although older, more experienced Unix and Linux users continue to use vi extensively during computing sessions, many newer users might prefer learning an easier to use text editor such as pico or GNU nano. Die-hard GNU fans and programmers definitely use emacs.

That said, learning how to use vi is a good idea. You might need to edit files on a Linux system with a minimal install, or a remote server without a more extensive offering of installed text editors. Chances are better than good that vi will be available.

You can start an editing session by using the vi command like this:

```
$ vi file.txt
```

The vi command works by using an insert, or editing mode, and a viewing (or command) mode.

When you first start editing, you'll be in the viewing mode. You can use your cursor or other navigation keys (as shown later) to scroll through the text. To start editing, tap the i key to insert text, or the a key to append text. When finished, use the Esc key to toggle out of the insert or append modes and into the viewing (or command) mode. To enter a command, type a colon (:), followed by the command, such as w to write the file, and press Enter.

Although vi supports many complex editing operations and numerous commands, you can accomplish work by using a few basic commands. These basic vi commands are

- **Cursor movement**—h, j, k, l (left, down, up, and right)
- **Delete character**—x
- **Delete line**—dd
- **Mode toggle**—ESC, Insert (or i)
- **Quit**—:q
- **Quit without saving**—:q!

- **Run a shell command**—:sh (use 'exit' to return)
- **Save file**—:w
- **Text search**—/

NOTE

Use the vimtutor command to quickly learn how to use vi's keyboard commands. The tutorial takes less than 30 minutes, and it teaches new users how to start or stop the editor, navigate files, insert and delete text and perform search, replace, and insert operations.

Working with emacs

Richard M. Stallman's GNU emacs editor, like vi, is included with Linux and nearly every other Linux distribution. Unlike other Unix and Linux text editors, emacs is much more than a simple text editor—it is an editing environment and can be used to compile and build programs, act as an electronic diary, appointment book and calendar, compose and send electronic mail, read Usenet news, and even play games. The reason for this capability is the emacs contains a built-in language interpreter that uses the Elisp (emacs LISP) programming language.

The GNU version of this editor requires more than 30MB of hard drive space. However, there are versions with less resource requirements, and at least one other text editor included with Linux, named joe, can be used as a emacs clone (albeit with fewer features).

You can start an emacs editing session like this:

```
$ emacs file.txt
```

TIP

If you start emacs when using X11, the editor will launch in its own floating window. To force emacs to display inside a terminal window instead of its own window (which can be useful if the window is a login at a remote computer), use the -nw command-line option like this: **emacs -nw file.txt**.

The emacs editor uses an extensive set of keystroke and named commands, but you can work with it using a basic command subset. Many of these basic commands require you to hold down the Ctrl key, or to first press a *meta* key (generally mapped to the Alt key). The basic commands are listed in Table 5.2.

TABLE 5.2   Emacs Editing Commands

Action	Command
Abort	Ctrl+g
Cursor left	Ctrl+b
Cursor down	Ctrl+n

TABLE 5.2   Continued

Action	Command
Cursor right	Ctrl+f
Cursor up	Ctrl+p
Delete character	Ctrl+d
Delete line	Ctrl+k
Go to start of line	Ctrl+a
Go to end of line	Ctrl+e
Help	Ctrl+h
Quit	Ctrl+x, Ctrl+c
Save As	Ctrl+x, Ctrl+w
Save file	Ctrl+x, Ctrl+s
Search backward	Ctrl+r
Search forward	Ctrl+s
Start tutorial	Ctrl+h, t
Undo	Ctrl+x, u

TIP

One of the best reasons to learn how to use emacs is that you can use nearly all the same keystrokes to edit commands on the bash shell command line. Another reason is that like vi, emacs is universally available on nearly every Unix and Linux system, including Apple's Mac OS X.

Working with Permissions

Under Linux (and Unix), everything in the file system, including directories and devices, is a file. And every file on your system has an accompanying set of permissions based on ownership. These permissions form the basis for security under Linux, and designate each file's read, write, and execute permission for you, members of your group, and all others on the system.

You can examine the default permissions for a file you create by using the umask command, or as a practical example, by using the touch command and then the ls command's long-format listing like this:

```
$ touch file
$ ls -l file
-rw-rw-r--   1 andrew    andrew          0 Jul 23 12:28 file
```

In this example, the touch command is used to quickly create a file. The ls command then reports on the file, displaying information (from left to right) in the first field of output (such as -rw-rw-r-- previously)

- **The first character of the field is the type of file created**—Common indicators of the type of file are a leading letter in the output. A blank (in the preceding example, which is represented by a dash) designates a plain file, d designates a directory, c designates a character device (such as /dev/ttyS0), and b is used for a block device (such as /dev/hda).

- **Permissions**—Read, write, and execute permissions for the owner, group, and all others on the system. (You learn more about these permissions later in this section.)

- **Number of links to the file**—The number one (1) designates that there is only one file, whereas any other number indicates that there might be one or more hard-linked files. Links are created with the ln command. A hard-linked file is an exact copy of the file, but it might be located elsewhere on the system. Symbolic links of directories can also be created, but only the root operator can create a hard link of a directory.

- **The owner**—The account that created or owns the file; you can change this designation by using the chown command.

- **The group**—The group of users who are allowed to access the file; you can change this designation by using the chgrp command.

- **File size and creation/modification date**—The last two elements indicate the size of the file in bytes and the date the file was created or last modified.

Assigning Permissions

Under Linux, permissions are grouped by owner, group, and others, with read, write, and execute permission assigned to each, like so:

```
Owner    Group    Others
rwx      rwx      rxw
```

Permissions can be indicated by mnemonic or octal characters. Mnemonic characters are

- r indicates permission for an owner, member of the owner's group, or others to open and read the file.

- w indicates permission for an owner, member of the owner's group, or others to open and write to the file.

- x indicates permission for an owner, member of the owner's group, or others to execute the file (or read a directory)

In the previous example for the file named file, the owner, andrew, has read and write permission, as does any member of the group named andrew. All other users may only read the file. Also note that default permissions for files created by the root operator will be different! This is because of umask settings assigned by the shell.

Many users prefer to represent permissions using numeric codes, based on octal (base-8) values. Here's what these values mean:

- 4 indicates read permission.

- 2 indicates write permission.

- 1 indicates execute permission.

In octal notation, the previous example file has a permission setting of 664 (read+write or 4+2, read+write or 4+2, read-only or 4). Although you can use either form of permissions notation, octal is easy to use quickly after you visualize and understand how permissions are numbered.

> **NOTE**
>
> In Linux, you can create groups to assign a number of users access to common directories and files, based on permissions. You might assign everyone in accounting to a group named accounting, for example, and allow that group access to accounts payable files while disallowing access by other departments. Defined groups are maintained by the root operator, but you can use the newgrp command to temporarily join other groups in order to access files (as long as the root operator has added you to the other groups). You can also allow or deny access to your files by other groups by modifying the group permissions of your files.

Directory Permissions

Directories are also files under Linux. For example, again use the ls command to show permissions like this:

```
$ mkdir foo
$ ls -ld foo
drwxrwxr-x   2 andrew    andrew        4096 Jan 23 12:37 foo
```

In this example, the mkdir command is used to create a directory. The ls command and its -ld option is used to show the permissions and other information about the directory (not its contents). Here you can see that the directory has permission values of 775 (read+write+execute or 4+2+1, read+write+execute or 4+2+1, and read+execute or 4+1).

This shows that the owner and group members can read and write to the directory and, because of execute permission, also list the directory's contents. All other users can only list the directory contents. Note that directories require execute permission in order for anyone to be able to view their contents.

You should also notice that the ls command's output shows a leading d in the permissions field. This letter specifies that this file is a directory; normal files will have a blank field in place. Other files, such as those specifying a block or character device, will have a different letter (see the section "Managing Files for Character Devices, Block Devices, and Special Devices" in Chapter 37 for more information about block devices).

For example, if you examine the device file for a Linux serial port, you will see

```
$ ls -l /dev/ttyS0
crw-rw----   1 root      uucp       4,  64 Jan 23 23:38 /dev/ttyS0
```

Here, /dev/ttyS0 is a character device (such as a serial communications port and designated by a c) owned by root and available to anyone in the uucp group. The device has permissions of 660 (read+write, read+write, no permission).

On the other hand, if you examine the device file for an IDE hard drive, you'll see

```
$ ls -l /dev/hda
brw-rw----   1 root      disk       3,   0 Jan 23 23:37 /dev/hda
```

In this example, b designates a block device (a device that transfers and caches data in blocks) with similar permissions. Other device entries you will run across on your Linux system include symbolic links, designated by s.

You can use the chmod command to alter a file's permissions. This command uses various forms of command syntax, including octal or a mnemonic form (such as u, g, o, or a and rwx, and so on) to specify a desired change. The chmod command can be used to add, remove, or modify file or directory permissions in order to protect, hide, or open up access to a file by other users (except for root, who can access any file or directory on a Linux system).

The mnemonic forms of chmod's options (when used with a plus character, +, to add, or a minus sign, -, to take away) designate the following:

> u—Adds or removes user (owner) read, write, or execute permission
>
> g—Adds or removes group read, write, or execute permission
>
> o—Adds or removes read, write, or execute permission for others not in a file's group
>
> a—Adds or removes read, write, or execute permission for all users
>
> r—Adds or removes read permission
>
> w—Adds or removes write permission
>
> x—Adds or removes execution permission

For example, if you create a file, such as a readme.txt, the file will have default permissions (set by the umask setting in /etc/bashrc) of

```
-rw-rw-r--   1 andrew    andrew         12 Jan  2 16:48 readme.txt
```

As you can see, you and members of your group can read and write the file. Anyone else can only read the file (and only if it is outside of your home directory, which will have read, write, and execute permission set only for you, the owner). You can remove all write permission for anyone by using chmod, the minus sign, and aw like so:

```
$ chmod -aw readme.txt
$ ls -l readme.txt
-r--r--r--   1 andrew    andrew        12 Jan  2 16:48 readme.txt
```

Now, no one will be able to write to the file (except you, if the file is in your home or
/tmp directory because of directory permissions). To restore read and write permission for
only you as the owner, use the plus sign and the u and rw options like so:

```
$ chmod u+rw readme.txt
$ ls -l readme.txt
-rw-------   1 andrew    andrew        12 Jan  2 16:48 readme.txt
```

You can also use the octal form of the chmod command, for example, to modify a file's
permissions so that only you, the owner, can read and write a file. Use the chmod
command and a file permission of 600, like this:

$ chmod 600 readme.txt

If you take away execution permission for a directory, files might be hidden inside and
may not be listed or accessed by anyone else (except the root operator, of course, who has
access to any file on your system). By using various combinations of permission settings,
you can quickly and easily set up a more secure environment, even as a normal user in
your home directory.

Understanding Set User ID and Set Group ID Permissions

Another type of permission is "set user ID", known as *suid*, and "set group ID" (*sgid*)
permissions. These settings, when used in a program, enable any user running that
program to have program owner or group owner permissions for that program. These
settings enable the program to be run effectively by anyone, without requiring that each
user's permissions be altered to include specific permissions for that program.

One commonly used program with suid permissions is the passwd command:

```
$ ls -l /usr/bin/passwd
-r-s--x--x   1 root      root       13536 Jan 12  2000 /usr/bin/passwd
```

This setting allows normal users to execute the command (as root) in order to make
changes to a root-only accessible file, /etc/passwd.

You also can assign similar permission using the chfn command. This command allows
users to update or change finger information in /etc/passwd. You accomplish this
permission modification by using a leading 4 (or the mnemonic s) in front of the three
octal values.

> **NOTE**
>
> Other files that might have suid or guid permissions include at, rcp, rlogin, rsh, chage, chsh,
> ssh, crontab, sudo, sendmail, ping, mount, and several Unix-to-Unix Copy (UUCP) utilities.
> Many programs (such as games) might also have this type of permission in order to access a
> sound device.

Files or programs that have suid or guid permissions can sometimes present security holes because they bypass normal permissions. This problem is especially compounded if the permission extends to an executable binary (a command) with an inherent security flaw because it could lead to any system user or intruder gaining root access. In past exploits, this typically happened when a user fed a vulnerable command with unexpected input (such as a long pathname or option); the command would bomb out, and the user would be presented a root prompt. Although Linux developers are constantly on the lookout for poor programming practices, new exploits are found all the time, and can crop up unexpectedly, especially in newer software packages that haven't had the benefit of peer developer review.

Savvy Linux system administrators will keep the number of suid or guid files present on a system to a minimum. The find command can be used to display all such files on your system:

```
# find / -type f -perm +6000 -exec ls -l {} \;
```

> **NOTE**
>
> The find command is quite helpful and can be used for many purposes, such as before or
> during backup operations. See the section "Using Backup Software" in Chapter 16, "Backing Up,
> Restoring, and Recovery."

Note that the programs do not necessarily have to be removed from your system. If your users really do not need to use the program, you can remove execute permission of the program for anyone. You will have to decide, as the root operator, whether your users are allowed to, for example, mount and unmount CD-ROMs or other media on your system. Although Linux-based operating systems can be set up to accommodate ease of use and convenience, allowing programs such as mount to be suid might not be the best security policy. Other candidates for suid permission change could include the chsh, at, or chage commands.

Working As root

The root, or superuser account, is a special account and user on Unix and Linux systems. Superuser permissions are required in part because of the restrictive file permissions assigned to important system configuration files. You will need root permission in order to edit these files or to access or modify certain devices (such as hard drives). When logged in as root, you have total control over your system, which can be dangerous.

When you work in root, you have the ability to destroy a running system with a simple invocation of the rm command like this:

```
# rm -fr /
```

This command line will not only delete files and directories, but also could wipe out file systems on other partitions and even remote computers. This alone is reason enough to take precautions when using root access.

The only time you should run Linux as the superuser is when booting to runlevel 1, or system maintenance mode, to configure the filesystem, for example, or to repair or maintain the system. Logging in and using Linux as the root operator isn't a good idea because it defeats the entire concept of file permissions.

Knowing how to run commands as root without logging in as root can help avoid serious missteps when configuring your system. Linux comes with a command named su that allows you to run one or more commands as root and then quickly return you to normal user status. For example, if you would like to edit your system's filesystem table (a simple text file that describes local or remote storage devices, their type, and location), you can use the su command like this:

```
$ su -c "nano -w /etc/fstab"
Password:
```

After you press Enter, you will be prompted for a password that gives you access to root. This extra step can also help you "think before you leap" into the command. Enter the root password, and you will then be editing /etc/fstab using the nano editor with line wrapping disabled.

> **CAUTION**
>
> Before editing any important system or software service configuration file, make a backup copy. Then make sure to launch your text editor with line wrapping disabled. If you edit a configuration file without disabling line wrapping, you could insert spurious carriage returns and line feeds into its contents, causing the configured service to fail when restarting. By convention, nearly all configuration files are formatted for 80-character text width, but this is not always the case. By default, the vi and emacs editors don't use line wrap.

You can use sudo to assign specific users permission to perform specific tasks (similar to BSD Unix and its "wheel" group of users) . The sudo command works by first examining the file named sudoers under the /etc directory; you modify this file with the visudo command. See the section "Granting Root Privileges on Occasion—The sudo Command" in Chapter 13, "Managing Users," for details on how to configure and use sudo.

Creating Users

When a Linux system administrator creates a user, an entry in /etc/passwd for the user is created. The system also creates a directory, labeled with the user's username, in the /home

directory. For example, if you create a user named *bernice*, the user's home directory is
/home/bernice.

> **NOTE**
>
> In this chapter, you learn how to manage users from the command line. See Chapter 13 for
> more information on user administration with Fedora using graphical administration utilities,
> such as the system-config-users client.

Use the useradd command, along with a user's name to quickly create a user:

```
# useradd andrew
```

After creating the user, you must also create the user's initial password with the passwd
command:

```
# passwd andrew
Changing password for user andrew.
New password:
Retype new password:
passwd: all authentication tokens updated successfully.
```

Enter the new password twice. If you do not create an initial password for a new user, the
user won't be able to log in.

You can view useradd's default new user settings by using the command and its -D option
like this:

```
# useradd -D
GROUP=100
HOME=/home
INACTIVE=-1
EXPIRE=
SHELL=/bin/bash
SKEL=/etc/skel
```

These options display the default group ID, home directory, account and password policy
(active forever with no password expiration), the default shell, and the directory containing defaults for the shell.

The useradd command has many different command-line options. The command can be
used to set policies and dates for the new user's password, assign a login shell, assign
group membership, and other aspects of a user's account.

Deleting Users

Use the userdel command to delete users from your system. This command will remove
a user's entry in the system's /etc/passwd file. You should also user the command's -r

option to remove all the user's files and directories (such as the user's mail spool file under /var/spool/mail):

```
# userdel -r winky
```

If you do not use the -r option, you will have to manually delete the user's directory under /home, along with the user's /var/spool/mail queue.

Shutting Down the System

Use the shutdown command to shut down your system. The shutdown command has a number of different command-line options (such as shutting down at a predetermined time), but the fastest way to cleanly shut down Linux is to use the -h or halt option, followed by the word now or the numeral zero (0), like this:

```
# shutdown -h now
```

or

```
# shutdown -h 0
```

To incorporate a timed shutdown and a pertinent message to all active users, use shutdown's time and message options, like so:

```
# shutdown -h 18:30 "System is going down for maintenance this evening"
```

This example will shut down your system and provide a warning to all active users 15 minutes before the shutdown (or reboot). Shutting down a running server can be considered drastic, especially if there are active users or exchanges of important data occurring (such as a backup in progress). One good approach is to warn users ahead of time. This can be done by editing the system Message of the Day (MOTD) motd file, which displays a message to users after login. To create your custom MOTD, use a text editor and change the contents of /etc/motd. You can also make downtimes part of a regular schedule, perhaps to coincide with security audits, software updates, or hardware maintenance.

You should shut down Fedora only for a few very specific reasons:

- You are not using the computer and want to conserve electrical power.
- You need to perform system maintenance that requires any or all system services to be stopped.
- You want to replace integral hardware.

TIP

Do not shut down your computer if you suspect that one or more intruders has infiltrated your system; instead, disconnect the machine from any or all networks and make a backup copy of your hard drives. You might want to also keep the machine running to examine the contents of memory and to examine system logs. See Chapter 17 and the section "Securing Your Network" on how to protect and monitor a network-connected system.

Rebooting the System

You should also use the `shutdown` command to reboot your system. The fastest way to cleanly reboot Linux is to use the `-r` option, and the word `now` or the numeral zero (0):

```
# shutdown -r now
```

or

```
# shutdown -r 0
```

Rebooting or shutting down can both have dire consequences if performed at the wrong time (such as during backups or critical file transfers, which arouse the ire of your system's users). However, Linux-based operating systems are designed to properly stop active system services in an orderly fashion. Other commands you can use to shut down and reboot Linux are the `halt` and `reboot` commands, but the `shutdown` command is more flexible.

Related Fedora and Linux Commands

The following programs and built-in shell commands are commonly used when working at the command line. These commands are organized by category to help you understand the command's purpose. If you need to find full information for using the command, you can find that information under the command's man page.

Managing users and groups—chage, chfn, chsh, edquota, gpasswd, groupadd, groupdel, groupmod, groups, mkpasswd, newgrp, newusers, passwd, umask, useradd, userdel, usermod

Managing files and filesystems—cat, cd, chattr, chmod, chown, compress, cp, dd, fdisk, find, gzip, ln, mkdir, mksfs, mount, mv, rm, rmdir, rpm, sort, swapon, swapoff, tar, touch, umount, uncompress, uniq, unzip, zip

Managing running programs—bg, fg, kill, killall, nice, ps, pstree, renice, top, watch

Getting information—apropos, cal, cat, cmp, date, diff, df, dir, dmesg, du, env, file, free, grep, head, info, last, less, locate, ls, lsattr, man, more, pinfo, ps, pwd, stat, strings, tac, tail, top, uname, uptime, vdir, vmstat, w, wc, whatis, whereis, which, who, whoami

Console text editors—ed, jed, joe, mcedit, nano, red, sed, vim

Console Internet and network commands—bing, elm, ftp, host, hostname, ifconfig, links, lynx, mail, mutt, ncftp, netconfig, netstat, pine, ping, pump, rdate, route, scp, sftp, ssh, tcpdump, traceroute, whois, wire-test

---

Reference

The migration to a new computer operating system doesn't have to be painful to management and users. Providing easy-to-understand directions, some background information, and pre-configuration of an installed system can help the transition.

This section lists some additional points of reference with background information on the standards and commands discussed in this chapter. Browse these links to learn more about some of the concepts discussed in this chapter and to expand your knowledge of your new Linux community.

http://www.winntmag.com/Articles/Index.cfm?ArticleID=7420—An article by a Windows NT user who, when experimenting with Linux, blithely confesses to rebooting the system after not knowing how to read a text file at the Linux console.

http://standards.ieee.org/regauth/posix/—IEEE's POSIX information page.

http://www.itworld.com/Comp/2362/lw-01-government/#sidebar—Discussion of Linux and POSIX compliance.

http://www.pathname.com/fhs/—Home page for the Linux FHS, Linux Filesystem Hierarchy Standard.

http://www.tldp.org—Browse the HOWTO section to find and read The Linux Keyboard and Console HOWTO—Andries Brouwer's somewhat dated but eminently useful guide to using the Linux keyboard and console.

http://www.gnu.org/software/emacs/emacs.html—Home page for the FSF's GNU emacs editing environment; you'll find additional documentation and links to the source code for the latest version here.

http://www.vim.org/—Home page for the vim (vi clone) editor included with Linux distros. Check here for updates, bug fixes, and news about this editor.

http://www.courtesan.com/sudo/—Home page for the sudo command. Check here for the latest updates, security features, and bug fixes.

PART II

Fedora Desktop

IN THIS PART

The X Window System

The X Window System, also known as X11R6, X11, and simply X, provides the graphical networking interface for your Fedora desktop. X started as a consortium-based project at the Massachusetts Institute of Technology in the early 1980s, and over the years it has gone through several major revisions. X is managed in open-source form by an organization named X.org.

X uses a client/server model. *Clients* are simply X programs written to take advantage of the network communication and graphics drawing protocols available in supporting software libraries. The X server communicates with clients and manages many different aspects of a local or remote desktop session. The X server used with Fedora is X11R6 8.2, an open-source version of the X Window System provided by The X.Org Foundation.

Today there are X.Org distributions for many platforms besides Intel-based PCs. The open-source version of X from The X.Org Foundation included with Fedora is a merger of the previous releases of X11R6 and XFree86, the version of X Windows shipped with earlier versions of Fedora and Red Hat Linux.

This chapter shows you how to work with the version of X11 included with Fedora. After a brief overview of X and X.org, you will learn how to configure X to work with Linux on your computer, useful if you install a new video card or attach a new LCD panel. You will learn how to start X and select and use X window managers—the X clients that draw and manage window displays, decorations, and onscreen icons. You will also get an introduction to Fedora's graphical desktop environment.

The Red Hat and Fedora Desktop

Red Hat initially caused quite a stir among veteran Linux users because of the decision to introduce consistency in the menus, dialogs, and client look and feel of GNOME and the K Desktop Environment (KDE), starting with Red Hat Linux 8.0. This action, part of the natural evolution of Red Hat's product line, provides a basic framework for the Red Hat desktop as a base Linux product in future commercial product lines. The new desktop is evolving, and enables Red Hat, Inc. to more easily integrate advanced products, such as enterprise-level web, database, application, or development server software.

Bluecurve, the new Red Hat desktop theme, was also used with Red Hat Linux 9 and now Fedora. While considered heresy by some die-hard users on both sides of the GNOME and KDE camps, the theme consistency actually helps novice Red Hat and Fedora users easily migrate from other operating systems by enabling them to learn a single set of controls and preferences while working in the new graphical interface.

The truth is that Fedora offers you the choice of whether to use the Red Hat desktop or another theme. You are entirely free to use a different desktop and to configure GNOME or KDE to look entirely different from the default graphical desktop. Fedora also includes alternative and legacy window managers, such as the Motif Window Manager mwm, and the twm window manager (which are discussed later in this chapter).

Basic X Concepts

The underlying engine of X11 is the X protocol, which provides a system of managing displays on local and remote desktops. The protocol uses a client/server model that allows an abstraction of the drawing of client windows and other decorations locally and over a network. An X server draws client windows, dialog boxes, and buttons that are specific to the local hardware and in response to client requests. The client, however, does not have to be specific to the local hardware. This means that system administrators can set up a network with a large server and clients and enable users to view and use those clients on workstations with totally different CPUs and graphics displays.

NOTE

As an example of X's support for remote client use, much of the original text of this chapter was written using the OpenOffice.org office suite, but the keyboard and display used for writing were part of a Sony VAIO laptop running Fedora; OpenOffice.org was launched from a Dell notebook running Fedora Core 3. Subsequent revisions were made on a workstation running Fedora Core 4, using the open-source OpenOffice.org office suite via a remote 802.11g connection from an IBM ThinkPad running Red Hat Enterprise Linux 4 WS.

X11's form of distributed processing means that Fedora, along with X11R6, can be used as a stable, cost-efficient desktop PC platform for using clients launched from a more powerful server, minicomputer, or mainframe. The X model provides a way to continue to use legacy PCs when more powerful systems are put in place, and it can help centralize the job of system management.

X is popular with Unix and Linux users, system administrators, and network engineers for a number of reasons. X is extremely portable and works with nearly every hardware-based graphics system on the market. This allows X to be deployed and used with high-end workstations and diminutive embedded devices. X also provides portable and multi-platform programming standards that truly allow write-once, cross-platform development.

Another attractive feature of X is its networking capabilities, which easily allow management of thousands of workstations, deployment of thin-client desktops, remote launching of applications, and standardization of installations—all working over a variety of media, such as Ethernet and wireless network connections. Although early releases of X supported only a handful of display architectures, subsequent versions have enabled the use of compressed fonts, *shaped* (that is, non-rectangular) windows, and a graphical login manager, known as a *display manager* (see the section "Using a Display Manager," later in this chapter). X also provides a mechanism for customizing how X clients appear: It allows you to edit text files that contain window or button appearance settings. These settings, known as *resources*, are available for nearly every X11 client.

Many small office/home office (SOHO) environments and computer hobbyists run Linux and X locally on non-networked PCs. But small business, academic, corporate, and enterprise-class environments can also reap the benefits of adopting and using X and Fedora for network computing. By using X, administrative staff, users, and in-house developers can enjoy custom or standardized desktops, and applications can be stored in and launched from a single location. This can make the job of system and software maintenance a lot easier.

Using X11R6

X11R6 8.2 is the X server that is used with Fedora. The base X.Org distribution consists of 30 RPM packages (almost 120MB), which contain the server, along with support and development libraries, fonts, various clients, and documentation. An additional 1,000 or more X clients, fonts, and documentation are also included with Fedora.

> **NOTE**
>
> A full installation of X and related X11R6 files can consume more—usually much more—than 170MB of hard drive space. This is because additional clients, configuration files, and graphics (such as icons) are under the /usr/bin and /usr/share directory trees. You can pare excessive disk requirements by judiciously choosing which X-related packages (such as games) to not install on workstations. However, with the increased capacity of most desktop PC hard drives today, the size requirements are rarely a problem, except in configuring thin-client desktops or embedded systems.

The /usr/X11R6 directory and its subdirectories contain the majority of XFree86's software. Some important subdirectories are

- /usr/X11R6/bin—This is the location of the X server and various X clients. (Note that not all X clients require active X sessions.)

- `/usr/X11R6/include`—This is the path to the files necessary for developing X clients and graphics such as icons.

- `/usr/X11R6/lib`—This directory contains required software libraries to support the X server and clients.

- `/usr/X11R6/lib/X11`—This directory contains fonts, default client resources, system resources, documentation, and other files that are used during X sessions and for various X clients. You will also find a symbolic link to this directory, named `X11`, under the `/usr/lib` directory.

- `/usr/X11R6/lib/modules`—This path to drivers and the X server modules used by the X server enables use of various graphics cards.

- `/usr/X11R6/man`—This directory contains directories of manual pages for X11 programming and clients.

The main components required for an active local X session will be installed on your system if you choose to use a graphical desktop. These components are the X server, miscellaneous fonts, a *terminal client* (that is, a program that provides access to a shell prompt), and a client known as a *window manager*. Window managers, which are discussed later in this chapter (see the section "Selecting and Using X Window Managers"), administer onscreen displays, including overlapping and tiling windows, command buttons, title bars, and other onscreen decorations and features.

Elements of the `xorg.conf` File

The single most important file required to launch X on a desktop is the `xorg.conf` configuration file. This text file can be created during installation or modified post-installation by using the `system-config-display` client (see "Configuring X," later in this chapter). `xorg.conf` is located under the `/etc/X11` directory and contains file locations, hardware descriptions, and specifications needed by the `xorg` server in order to work with the computer's graphics card and display monitor.

You will be better equipped to troubleshoot configuration problems and add or remove features of the X session if you understand the contents of the `xorg.conf` file. The components, or sections, of `xorg.conf` specify the X session or *server layout*, along with paths for files used by the server, server options, optional support modules to load, descriptions of the mouse and keyboard, graphics device, monitor, screen layout, and video modes to use. Of the 12 sections of an `xorg.conf` file, these are the essential components:

- `ServerLayout`—Defines the display, defines one or more screen layouts, and names input devices.

- `Files`—Defines the location of colors, fonts, or port number of the font server.

- `Module`—Tells the X server what graphics display support code modules to load.

- InputDevice—Defines the input devices, such as the keyboard and mouse; multiple devices can be used.

- Monitor—Defines the capabilities of any attached display; multiple monitors can be used.

- Device—Defines one or more graphics cards and specifies what optional (if any) features to enable or disable.

- Screen—Defines one or more resolutions, color depths, perhaps a default color depth, and other settings.

The following sections provide short descriptions of these elements; the xorg.conf manual page contains full documentation of all the options and other keywords you can use to customize your desktop settings.

The ServerLayout **Section**
As noted previously, the ServerLayout section of the xorg.conf file defines the display and screen layouts, and it names the input devices. A typical ServerLayout section from an automatically configured xorg.conf file might look like this:

```
Section "ServerLayout"
        Identifier       "single head configuration"
        Screen       0   "Screen0" 0 0
        InputDevice      "Mouse0" "CorePointer"
        InputDevice      "Keyboard0" "CoreKeyboard"
        InputDevice      "DevInputMice" "AlwaysCore"
EndSection
```

In this example, a single display is used (the numbers designate position of a screen), and two default input devices, Mouse0 and Keyboard0, are used for the session.

The Files **Section**
The Files section of the xorg.conf file might look like this:

```
Section "Files"
    RgbPath       "/usr/X11R6/lib/X11/rgb"
    FontPath      "unix/:7100"
EndSection
```

This section lists available session colors (by name, in the text file rgb.txt) and the port number to the X font server. The font server, xfs, is started at boot time and does not require an active X session. If a font server is not used, the FontPath entry could instead list each font directory under the /usr/X11R6/lib/X11/fonts directory, as in this example:

```
FontPath "/usr/X11R6/lib/X11/fonts/100dpi"
FontPath "/usr/X11R6/lib/X11/fonts/misc"
```

```
FontPath "/usr/X11R6/lib/X11/fonts/75dpi"
FontPath "/usr/X11R6/lib/X11/fonts/type1"
FontPath "/usr/X11R6/lib/X11/fonts/Speedo"
...
```

These directories contain the default compressed fonts that are available for use during the X session. The font server is configured by using the file named `config` under the `/etc/X11/fs` directory. This file contains a listing, or catalog, of fonts for use by the font server. By adding an `alternate-server` entry in this file and restarting the font server, you can specify remote font servers for use during X sessions. This can help centralize font support and reduce local storage requirements (even though only 25MB is required for the almost 5,000 fonts installed with Red Hat Linux and X).

The `Module` Section

The `Module` section of the `xorg.conf` file specifies loadable modules or drivers to load for the X session. This section might look like this:

```
Section "Module"
        Load    "dbe"
        Load    "extmod"
        Load    "fbdevhw"
        Load "glx"
        Load "record"
        Load    "freetype"
        Load    "type1"
        Load    "dri"


EndSection
```

These modules can range from special video card support to font rasterizers. The modules are located in subdirectories under the `/usr/X11R6/lib/modules` directory.

The `InputDevice` Section

The `InputDevice` section configures a specific device, such as a keyboard or mouse, as in this example:

```
Section "InputDevice"
        Identifier  "Keyboard0"
        Driver      "kbd"

        Option  "XkbModel"      "pc105"
        Option  "XkbLayout"     "us"
EndSection
Section "InputDevice"
        Identifier  "Mouse0"
        Driver      "mouse"
        Option      "Protocol" "IMPS/2"
```

```
        Option        "Device" "/dev/input/mice"
        Option        "ZAxisMapping" "4 5"
        Option        "Emulate3Buttons" "yes"
EndSection
```

You can configure multiple devices, and there might be multiple `InputDevice` sections. The preceding example specifies a basic keyboard and a two button PS/2 mouse (actually, a Dell touchpad pointer). An `InputDevice` section that specifies use of a USB device could be used at the same time (to enable mousing with PS/2 and USB pointers) and might look like this:

```
Section "InputDevice"
        Identifier    "Mouse0"
        Driver        "mouse"
        Option        "Device" "/dev/input/mice"
        Option        "Protocol" "IMPS/2"
        Option        "Emulate3Buttons" "off"
        Option        "ZAxisMapping" "4 5"
EndSection
```

> **NOTE**
>
> If you change your computer's pointing device, you should then run Fedora's `system-config-mouse` client, which automatically updates your system's `xorg.conf` file.

> **CAUTION**
>
> From Fedora Core 3 onward, the location for the mouse device changed from `/dev/mouse` to `/dev/input/mice`. Unfortunately, when `system-config-display` writes the `xorg.conf` file, it sometimes gets a little confused and still maps the mouse to `/dev/mouse` rather than `/dev/input/mice`. This is where a little knowledge of `vi` comes in!

The Monitor **Section**

The `Monitor` section configures the designated display device as declared in the `ServerLayout` section, as shown in this example:

```
Section "Monitor"
        Identifier    "Monitor0"
        VendorName    "Monitor Vendor"
        ModelName     "Monitor Model"
        DisplaySize   300     220
        HorizSync     31.5-48.5
        VertRefresh 50-70
        Option "dpms"
EndSection
```

Note that the X server automatically determines the best video timings according to the horizontal and vertical sync and refresh values in this section. If required, old-style mode-line entries (used by distributions and servers prior to XFree86 4.0) might still be used. If the monitor is automatically detected when you configure X (see the section "Configuring X," later in this chapter), its definition and capabilities are inserted in your `xorg.conf` file from the `MonitorsDB` database. This database contains more than 600 monitors and is located in the `/usr/share/hwdata` directory.

The `Device` Section

The `Device` section provides details about the video graphics chipset used by the computer, as in this example:

```
Section "Device"
        Identifier   "Videocard0"
        Driver       "radeon"
        VendorName   "Videocard vendor"
        BoardName    "ATI Radeon Mobility M6"

EndSection
```

This example identifies an installed video card as using an ATI Mobility M6 graphics chipset. The `Driver` entry tells the Xorg server to load the `radeon_drv.o` module from the `/usr/X11R6/lib/modules/drivers` directory. Different chipsets have different options. For example, here's the entry for a NeoMagic video chipset:

```
Section "Device"
        Identifier    "NeoMagic (laptop/notebook)"
        Driver        "neomagic"
        VendorName    "NeoMagic (laptop/notebook)"
        BoardName     "NeoMagic (laptop/notebook)"
    Option      "externDisp"
    Option      "internDisp"
EndSection
```

In this example, the `Device` section specifies the driver for the graphics card (neomagic_drv.o) and enables two chipset options (`externDisp` and `internDisp`) to allow display on the laptop's LCD screen and an attached monitor.

The `Xorg` server supports hundreds of different video chipsets. If you configure X11 but subsequently change the installed video card, you need to edit the existing `Device` section or generate a new `xorg.conf` file, using one of the X configuration tools discussed in this chapter, to reflect the new card's capabilities. You can find details about options for some chipsets in a companion manual page or in a README file under the `/usr/X11R6/lib/_X11/doc` directory. You should look at these sources for hints about optimizations and troubleshooting.

The Screen **Section**

The Screen section ties together the information from the previous sections (using the Screen0, Device, and Monitor Identifier entries). It can also specify one or more color depths and resolutions for the session. Here's an example:

```
Section "Screen"
        Identifier  "Screen0"
        Device      "Videocard0"
        Monitor     "Monitor0"
        DefaultDepth    24
        SubSection "Display"
                Viewport   0 0
                Depth      16
                Modes      "1024x768" "800x600" "640x480"
        EndSubSection
EndSection
```

In this example a color depth of thousands of colors and a resolution of 1024×768 is the default, with optional resolutions of 800×600 and 640×480. Multiple Display subsection entries with different color depths and resolutions (with settings such as Depth 24 for millions of colors) can be used if supported by the graphics card and monitor combination. You can also use a DefaultDepth entry (which is 24, or thousands of colors, in the example), along with a specific color depth to standardize display depths in installations.

You can also specify a desktop resolution larger than that supported by the hardware in your monitor or notebook display. This setting is known as a *virtual* resolution in the Display subsection. This allows, for example, an 800×600 display to pan (that is, slide around inside) a virtual window of 1024×768.

> **NOTE**
>
> If your monitor and graphics card support multiple resolutions and the settings are properly configured, you can use the key combination of Ctrl+Alt+Keypad+ or Ctrl+Alt+Keypad- to change resolutions on-the-fly during your X session.

Configuring X

Although the Fedora installer can be used to configure X during installation, problems can arise if the PC's video card is not recognized. If you are unable to configure X during installation (see Chapter 3, "Installing Fedora"), do not specify booting to a graphical configuration and skip the X configuration portion of the installation. Note that some installs, such as for servers, don't require that X be configured for use in order to support active X sessions but might require installation of X and related software to support remote users and clients.

You can use the following configuration tools, among others, to create a working xorg.conf file:

- system-config-display—This is Fedora's graphical configuration tool, which launches an X session to create an xorg.conf file.

- Xorg—The X server itself can create a skeletal working configuration.

The following sections discuss how to use each of these software tools to create a working xorg.conf file.

Configuring X with the system-config-display Client

You can use the system-config-display client to create or update an xorg.conf file. You can start by clicking the Display menu item from the desktop panel's System Settings menu if you are already running X, but you can also begin, as root, by starting the client from the command line during a console session, like this:

```
# system-config-display
```

The screen clears, and system-config-display attempts to start an X session. If you start this client during an X session, its main window appears, as shown in Figure 6.1.

FIGURE 6.1   The system-config-display client provides a graphical configuration interface for creating or updating a system's xorg.conf file. Here you see the Display Settings main screen, offering resolution and color-depth settings.

The Display Settings main screen is a dialog showing the current monitor and video card settings (if configured). You can change the resolution (horizontal and vertical pixels) and color depth (number of supported colors) by clicking one or the other of the drop-down menus. Click the OK or Cancel button to save or cancel any change.

If you click the Hardware tab, other configuration options become available as shown in Figure 6.2.

FIGURE 6.2 `system-config-display`'s Hardware settings are used to configure a monitor and video card (and multihead video card) for X11R6.

Click the Configure button in the Monitor Type area of the Hardware tab dialog to change your Monitor settings, as shown in Figure 6.3. You can use this dialog to configure a different monitor or to change current monitor settings.

First, scroll through the list of monitor brands (from the `MonitorDB` database), and then click the small triangle to the left of the name of the manufacturer or type. You will then see a list of model names. Click to select one, and when you are finished, click the OK button to use the new settings or click the Cancel button to abort changes.

To configure a video card, you can click the Video Card area's Configure button in the Hardware tab dialog. The Video Card dialog appears, as shown in Figure 6.4.

You can scroll through the list of video cards. You can click one to select it and when you are finished, click the OK button to finalize your selection.

FIGURE 6.3   You can scroll to select a new monitor to use for your X sessions.

FIGURE 6.4   Use the Hardware tab's Video Card Configure button to choose a new video card for your X sessions.

If your video card supports the use of two or more monitors, you can use the Dual head tab toconfigure multiple monitor support. Xorg supports multiple displays using a feature named Xinerama. This feature enables multiple monitors to appear as a single display, and each display can be located in any quadrant of a screen's layout.

In order to use Xinerama for your desktop sessions, you must start the Xorg server with its +xinerama option. Your xorg.conf file must also have proper settings, and each display must be capable of supporting identical color depth (usually 16bpp or thousands of colors). Details about using Xinerama with Xorg can be found in the Xorg man page and in the Xinerama HOWTO at http://www.tldp.org/HOWTO/Xinerama-HOWTO/.

When you have finished your changes to your X server settings, click the OK button. You will then see a dialog advising that you will need to log out and then log back (or exit your X session and restart X) in order to use the new settings.

The new settings will be stored in a new xorg.conf file under the /etc/X11 directory. If you find that the new settings do not work, you can simply copy the backup xorg.conf file named xorg.conf.backup to xorg-conf in the same directory to revert to your original settings.

Using Xorg to Configure X

You can create the xorg.conf file manually by typing one from scratch using a text editor, but you can also create one automatically by using the Xorg server or configuration utilities (as discussed in the previous sections). As the root operator, you can use the following on the server to create a test configuration file:

```
# X -configure
```

After you press Enter, a file named xorg.conf .new is created in root's home directory, the /root directory. You can then use this file for a test session, like this:

```
# X -config /root/xorg.conf.new
```

Starting X

You can start X sessions in a variety of ways. The Fedora installer will set up the system initialization table /etc/inittab to have Linux boot directly to an X session using a *display manager* (that is, an X client that provides a graphical login). After you log in, you will use a local session (running on your computer) or, if the system is properly configured, an X session running on a remote computer on the network. Logging in via a display manager requires you to enter a username and password. You can also start X sessions from the command line. The following sections describe these two methods.

Using a Display Manager

An X display manager presents a graphical login that requires a username and password to be entered before access is granted to the X desktop. It also allows you to choose a different desktop for your X session. Whether or not an X display manager is presented after you boot Linux is controlled by a *runlevel*—a system state entry in /etc/inittab. The following runlevels are defined in the file:

```
# 0 - halt (Do NOT set initdefault to this)
# 1 - Single user mode
# 2 - Multiuser, without NFS (The same as 3, if you do not have networking)
# 3 - Full multiuser mode
# 4 - unused
# 5 - X11
# 6 - reboot (Do NOT set initdefault to this)
```

Runlevel 5 isused for multiuser mode with a graphical X login via a display manager; booting to runlevel 3 provides a console, or text-based, login. The initdefault setting in the /etc/inittab file determines the default runlevel:

```
id:5:initdefault:
```

In this example, Linux boots and then ends up running X.

The default display manager might also be specified in /etc/inittab, like this:

```
x:5:respawn:/usr/bin/xdm -nodaemon
```

However, Fedora uses a shell script named prefdm, found under the /etc/X11 directory, to set the display manager:

```
x:5:respawn:/etc/X11/prefdm -nodaemon
```

According to this script, the display manager is based on the file named desktop under the /etc/sysconfig directory. The words GNOME, KDE, and XDM following a DESKTOP= entry determine what display manager is used for login. The following sections describe how to configure the three most commonly used display managers: gdm, kdm, and xdm).

Configuring gdm

The gdm display manager is part of the GNOME library and client distribution included with Fedora and provides a graphical login when a system boots directly to X. Its login (which is actually displayed by the gdmlogin client) hosts pop-up menus of window managers, languages, and system options for shutting down (halting) or rebooting the workstation. Although you can edit (as root) gdm.conf under the /etc/X11/gdm directory to configure gdm, a much better way to configure GNOME's display manager is to use the gdmsetup client.

You can use the gdmsetup client, shown in Figure 6.5, to configure many aspects and features of the login display. You launch this client from the GNOME desktop panel's System Settings Login Screen menu item, or from the command line, like this:

```
# gdmsetup &
```

After you press Enter, you see the GDM Setup window, as shown in Figure 6.5.

You can specify settings for security, remote network logins, the X server, and session and session chooser setup by clicking on the tabs in the GDM Setup dialog.

FIGURE 6.5   You use gdmsetup to configure the gdmlogin screen when using gdm as a display manager.

Configuring kdm

The kdm client, which is part of the KDE X desktop suite, offers a graphical login similar to gdm. You configure kdm by running the KDE Control Center client kcontrol, as the root operator, by clicking the Control Center menu item from the KDE kicker or desktop panel menu. You can also start KDE Control Center by using the kcontrol client at the command line like so:

```
$ kcontrol &
```

In the Index tab of the left pane of the KDE Control Center window, you click the System Administration menu item to open its contents, and then you click the Login Manager menu item. The right pane of the Control Center window displays the tabs and configuration options for the kdm Login Manager, as shown in Figure 6.6.

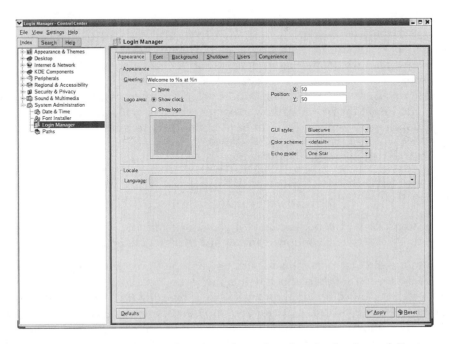

FIGURE 6.6   You configure kdm by choosing tabs and settings in the Control Center dialog box.

In order to make any changes to the KDE display manager while logged in as a regular user, you must first click the Administrator Mode button, and then enter the root operator password. You can click on a tab in the Control Center dialog to set configuration options. Options in these tabs allow you to control the login display, prompts, user icons, session management, and configuration of system options (for shutting down or rebooting). After you have made your configuration choices in each tab, click the Apply button to apply the changes immediately; otherwise, the changes are applied when the X server restarts.

Using the xdm Display Manager

The xdm display manager is part of the Xorg distribution and offers a bare-bones login for using X. Although it is possible to configure xdm by editing various files under the /etc/X11/xdm directory, GNOME and KDE offer a greater variety of options in display manager settings. The default xdm login screen's display is handled by the xsetroot client, which is included with Xorg, and Owen Taylor's xsri client, as specified in the file Xsetup_0 in the xdm directory under /etc/X11. The xsri client may be used to set the background color of the login display's desktop and to place an image in the initial display.

Starting X from the Console by Using startx

If you have Fedora set to boot to runlevel 3, a text-based console login, you can start an X session from the command line. You use the startx command (which is actually a shell script) to do so. You launch the X server and an X session by using startx, like this:

```
$ startx
```

startx first looks in your home directory for a file named .xinitrc. This file can contain settings that will launch an alternative desktop and X clients for your X session. The default system .xinitrc is found in the /etc/X11/xinit directory, but a local file can be used instead to customize an X session and launch default clients. For example, you can download and install the mlvwm window manager, which is available from http://www2u.biglobe.ne.jp/~y-miyata/mlvwm.html in the /usr/local/bin directory. You can then use the mlvwm desktop for your X session along the xterm terminal client by creating an .xinitrc file that contains the following:

```
xterm &
exec /usr/X11R6/bin/mlvwm
```

Using a custom .xinitrc is not necessary if you're using Fedora's desktop, which runs X and either a GNOME-aware window manager or KDE as a desktop environment.

You can also use the startx command with one or more command-line options. These options are passed to the X server before it launches an X session. For example, you can use startx to specify a color depth for an X session by using the -depth option, followed by a number such as 8, 16, 24, or 32 for 256, thousands, or millions of colors (as defined in the X configuration file and if supported). Using different color depths can be useful during development, for testing how X clients look on different displays, or to conserve use of video memory, such as when trying to get the highest resolution (increased color depth can sometimes affect the maximum resolution of older video cards).

For example, to start a session with thousands of colors, you use the startx command like this:

```
$ startx -- -depth 16
```

Another option that can be passed is a specific dots-per-inch (dpi) resolution that is to be used for the X session. For example, to use 100 dpi, you use the -dpi option followed by 100, like this:

```
$ startx -- -dpi 100
```

You can also use startx to launch multiple X sessions. This feature is due to Linux support for *virtual consoles*, or multiple text-based displays. To start the first X session, you use the startx command followed by a *display number*, or an X server instance (the first is 0, using screen 0) and a number that represents a virtual console. The default console used for X is number 7, so you can start the session like this:

```
$ startx -- :0 vt7
```

After X starts and the window manager appears, you press Ctrl+Alt+F2 and then log in again at the prompt. Next, you start another X session like this, specifying a different display number and virtual console:

```
$ startx -- :1 vt8
```

Another X session starts. To jump to the first X session, you press Ctrl+Alt+F7. You use Ctrl+Alt+F8 to return to the second session. If you exit the current session and go to another text-based login or shell, you use Alt+F7 or Alt+F8 to jump to the desired session.

Using startx is a flexible way to launch X sessions, but multiple sessions can be confusing, especially to new users, and are a horrific resource drain on a system that does not have enough CPU horsepower and memory. A better approach is to use multiple workspaces, also known as *virtual desktops*, as discussed in the following section.

Selecting and Using Window Managers

A window manager is launched immediately after the X server starts. The window manager handles the drawing and display of graphical session windows and their onscreen controls and features. Without a window manager, X client windows cannot be moved about the screen, resized, minimized or maximized, and so on.

Many different window managers are available for Linux, providing a number of choices for how the desktop appears and functions. This wealth of desktop choices appeals to many people who use Linux and X.

A window manager provides an X display and customized desktop by handling window decoration, movement, placement, and resizing operations. A window manager can also handle icons, and it can support icon-docking and other window operations such as tiling and overlays. Another important window manager task is *focus policy*—how and when a window becomes active. A window can become active when the pointer is over it, for example, or it might require a mouse click for activation.

A window manger might also provide menuing on the root desktop or after a button is clicked in a client's window title bar. Some window managers support the use of special keyboard keys to move the pointer and emulate mouse button clicks. Another feature is the capability to provide multiple workspaces, or a *virtual desktop*, which is not the same as the virtual screen; whereas a virtual screen is a desktop that is larger than the display, a virtual desktop offers two, four, or eight additional complete workspaces.

Some window managers support advanced features, such as drag and drop of icons that represent files or system devices. This allows the user to easily copy, print, delete, link, or move files—even over a network or the Internet.

Many different window managers are available for Linux. You do not have to use Fedora's default selection of window managers. This is part of the freedom of using Linux and a testament to the flexibility of the X architecture. You can download, install, and run nearly any other window manager for X without problems. One of the best places to find links and information to other window managers is Matt Chapman's Window Managers for X page, at http://xwinman.org/. Many of these window managers can be downloaded and installed by using RPM, apt, or yum, or built and installed from source. For those of you who do not realize, Fedora Core 4 ships with the Gnome 2.10 window manager as standard.

The following sections describe how to select a default desktop, switch to a different desktop, and configure different window managers for X.

Using Fedora's `switchdesk`

You can use Fedora's `switchdesk` client to change the default window manager or desktop environment such as GNOME or KDE. A *desktop environment* includes a window manager and a suite of related clients, such as productivity or utility applications. Most desktop environments also include the ability to save a session *state* (such as running applications, the applications' window size and positions, and so on), using a feature known as *session management*.

You can also use the `switchdesk` utility when running X or at a text-based console, along with a keyword (such as GNOME or KDE), to set the default X desktop before launching X. For example, to specify that you want to use the KDE desktop environment as the default, you use `switchdesk` like this:

```
$ switchdesk KDE
Red Hat Linux switchdesk 4.0
Copyright (C) 1999-2004 Red Hat, Inc
Redistributable under the terms of the GNU General Public License
Desktop now set up to run KDE.
For system defaults, remove /home/andrew/.Xclients
```

This example shows that the default X session will now use KDE. Settings are saving in the file named `.Xclients` in the home directory. You can launch `switchdesk` during an X session by clicking the Desktop Switching Tool menu item from the System Settings More System Setting menu or from the command line of an X11 terminal like this:

```
$ switchdesk &
```

After you press Enter, you get a graphical dialog offering a choice of window managers for X sessions (depending on the window managers that are installed on the system), as shown in Figure 6.7.

FIGURE 6.7   You use switchdesk to set the default window manager for X sessions.

Choosing a window manager is a matter of preference, necessity, or policy. You might prefer to use one of the older window managers—such as the Tab Window Manager (twm) or the Motif Window Manager (mwm)—on legacy PCs because they have fewer system resource requirements (that is, they require less hard drive space, CPU horsepower, and system memory). Newer desktop environments require 64MB or even more memory for good performance. The following sections describe some of the most popular window managers and their uses.

The Tab Window Manager (twm)

The Tab Window Manager (twm), which is included with Xorg and also sometimes known as Tom's Window Manager, is a legacy client that provides modest but essential features in a small (less than 1MB) memory footprint. It supports window decorations, menus, icons, and other features, but it does not support virtual desktops, session management, and other features, such as drag and drop.

The twm window manager is used as a fallback, or *failsafe*, window manager for Fedora as it requires much less video and system memory. It is included with the Xorg software distribution and will be used as your window manager after you log in or start X in the event the system or your default window manager settings are lost or unusable. The twm resource file, system.twmrc, is located under the /etc/X11/twm directory. You can configure this file to provide a default desktop with a custom application menu if you save your settings to a file named .twmrc in your home directory. The format of this configuration file is documented in the twm man page.

A sample twm desktop is shown in Figure 6.8, displaying the xosview, xclock, xcalc, and xterm clients. The default desktop color can be changed using the xsetroot client. You access the desktop menu in twm by left-clicking in a blank area of the main window, known as the root display.

FIGURE 6.8   twm is included with Xorg and offers basic window and icon management.

The Motif Window Manager (mwm)

mwm, the Motif Window Manager, is included with Fedora to provide a legacy X desktop. It is a clone window manager that closely mimics the original mwm window manager that was part of the OSF/Motif distribution from The Open Software Foundation. The mwm window manager is part of a Motif 1.2–compatible set of programming libraries and development files named LessTif.

mwm can even use the same configuration files as the OSF/Motif version. mwm's default resource file is located in /etc/X11/ system.mwmrc. You can edit this file to provide custom settings when it is located in your home directory and is named .mwmrc.

A sample mwm desktop is shown in Figure 6.9. Note that the Motif Window Manager offers more sophisticated window decorations (controls such as borders and title bar items) than the twm window manager.

FIGURE 6.9   The Motif Window Manager provides a simple desktop for Fedora.

The GNOME and KDE Desktop Environments

A desktop environment for X provides one or more window managers and a suite of clients that conform to a standard graphical interface based on a common set of software libraries. When they are used to develop associated clients, these libraries provide graphical consistency for the client windows, menus, buttons, and other onscreen components, along with some common keyboard controls and client dialogs. The following sections briefly discuss the two desktop environments that are included with Fedora Core: GNOME and KDE.

GNOME: The GNU Network Object Model Environment

The GNOME project, which was started in 1997, is the brainchild of programmer whiz Miguel de Icaza. GNOME provides a complete set of software libraries and clients. GNOME depends on a window manager that is GNOME aware. This means that in order to provide a graphical desktop with GNOME elements, the window manager needs to be written to recognize and use GNOME. Some compliant window managers that are GNOME-aware include Havoc Pennington's `metacity` (the default GNOME window manager), Enlightenment, Window Maker, IceWM, and `sawfish`.

Fedora uses GNOME's user-friendly suite of clients to provide a consistent and user-friendly desktop. GNOME is a staple feature of Red Hat's commercial Linux distributions and Fedora because Red Hat actively supports its development. GNOME clients are found under the /usr/bin directory, and GNOME configuration files are stored under the /etc/gnome and /usr/share/gnome directories, with user settings stored in the home directory under .gnome.

Ximian GNOME for Red Hat

In 1999, Miguel de Icaza and Nat Friedman, the original GNOME developers, created a company and a product now known as Ximian. Ximian is a polished GNOME environment that offers not only an updated suite of GNOME clients, but also groupware software that provides integrated mail, calendar, addressing, and instant messaging services.

In August 2003, Ximian was acquired by Novell, Inc. The Ximian GNOME distribution, now named Ximian Desktop 2, is not included with Red Hat's Linux distros or Fedora, but you may be able to install it via CD-ROM or, if you have broadband access, in about an hour or less over the Internet. Versions are available for many different Linux distributions (even those on non-Intel platforms).

To get started, you can go to Novell's Ximian Desktop website at http://www.novell.com/products/desktop/download.html. You first use wget to quickly download a graphical installer, which is then used to select a download site, selected files, and the base Ximian distribution. The download and installation are done as an automatic process, and Ximian replaces your default GNOME software with its own GNOME distribution. After installation, you can quickly install updates and bug fixes by using an update icon on the Ximian desktop.

A representative GNOME desktop, running the gconftool-2 client used for setting themes, is shown in Figure 6.10.

FIGURE 6.10   Fedora's GNOME desktop uses the metacity window manager and offers a selection of GNOME (and KDE) themes.

You can configure your desktop in various ways and by using different menu items under the Preferences menu. For a comprehensive icon view of preference items, click the Control Center menu item from the desktop panel's Preferences menu. A graphical shell named Nautilus then launches. Nautilus was originally developed by Eazel (which ceased operations shortly before summer 2001). The Nautilus shell is used for the Fedora desktop as a file browser and desktop utility.

The Nautilus main window, shown in Figure 6.11, shows Preference icons. You can then click any icon (such as Background or Screensaver) and its dialog to change your desktop's appearance, focus behavior, window behavior, placement, sound, and workspace settings.

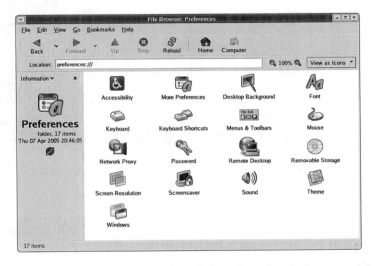

FIGURE 6.11   You can customize your Fedora desktop by using Preference settings that are available in the Nautilus graphical shell.

KDE: The K Desktop Environment

KDE, which is included with Fedora, has been available for Linux, Xorg, and XFree86 since 1996. KDE is a graphical desktop environment that offers a huge suite of clients, including a free office suite named KOffice. KDE clients are located under the /usr/bin directory, and nearly all clients have a name that begins with k.

The directory .kde in your home directory contains custom settings and session information. You can use KDE's Control Center, as shown in Figure 6.12, to customize desktop settings. You can launch this client by clicking the Control Center menu item from KDE's desktop menu (hosted by the panel along the bottom of your desktop, known as the *kicker*) or from the command line, like so:

```
$ kcontrol &
```

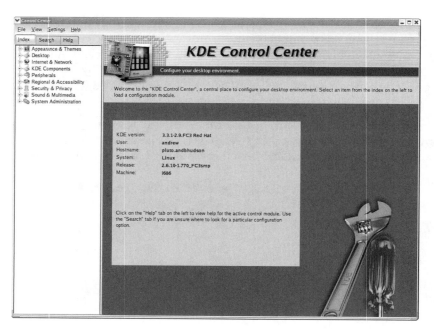

FIGURE 6.12   You can use the KDE Control Center to manage nearly every aspect of KDE desktop sessions.

Related Fedora and Linux Commands

You can use these commands to create and configure the X Window System in Fedora:

Xorg—The X server that is provided with the X Window System distribution from The X.Org Foundation

mouseconfig—RFedora's text-based GUI pointing-device–configuration program

kcontrol—The KDE Control Center client

system-config-display—Fedora's graphical X11R6 configuration tool

system-config-mouse—Fedora's graphical mouse configuration tool

gdmsetup—The GNOME display manager configuration client

startx—A shell script that is used to start one or more X sessions from the shell command line

xsri—A display manager root desktop decoration client

Reference

http://www.x.org—Curators of the X Window System.

http://www.x.org/Downloads_mirror.html—Want to download the source to the latest revision of X? Start at this list of mirror sites.

http://www.xfree86.org—Home of The XFree86 Project, Inc., which has provided a graphical interface for Linux for nearly 10 years.

http://www.kde.org—The place to get started when learning about KDE and the latest developments.

http://www.gnome.org—The launch point for more information about GNOME, links to new clients, and GNOME development projects.

http://people.redhat.com/~hp/metacity/—Havoc Pennington's `metacity` download page, where you can get the latest full-source version of this window manager.

http://sawmill.sourceforge.net—The home page for the `sawmill` window manager.

http://www.windowmaker.org—The source for the latest version of Window Maker.

http://www.icewm.org—IceWM's home page.

http://www.lesstif.org—The home page of the LessTif project, which aims to provide GNU GPL versions of OSF/Motif-compatible software libraries.

http://scwm.sourceforge.net—The home page of a lightweight, yet virtual desktop-enabled, window manager.

http://www.fvwm.org—The home page for FVWM2, where you can download the latest version.

http://www.novell.com/products/desktop/—The place to get started with Ximian GNOME.

CHAPTER **7**

Managing Software and System Resources

This chapter introduces concepts, procedures, and software you can use to manage installed system resources on a Fedora Core system. Managing the system resources—including software, storage, and memory—of your computer is important for a number of reasons. Good resource management promotes and supports efficient, productive sessions, a stable system, and satisfied users. Managing these resources involves installing, removing, upgrading, or rebuilding software packages—each a vital task that can contribute to your system's security.

As a Fedora Core system administrator, you should also know how to maximize your system's resources by managing memory and storage for the most efficient system use. Properly managing your system resources ensures that you will not run out of room for new software, and you can expand the system to fit changing needs and new projects. In other words, system resource management is essential to providing the best possible computing experience for your users.

Fedora Core provides a variety of tools for system resource management. The following sections introduce the RPM Package Manager (RPM), along with command-line and graphical software-management tools. You will also learn about monitoring and managing memory and disk storage on your system.

Using RPM for Software Management

RPM was derived (in part) from early Linux package management software—named RPP, PMS, and PM—that were written in Perl. RPM was first used with Red Hat Linux 2.0 in late 1995, and then rewritten in C for the Red Hat Linux 3.0.3 (Picasso) release in 1996. Since then, the rpm command has been the prime feature of Red Hat's unique software management system, which is based on the concept of pristine sources, or the capability to use a single, initial archive of a program's source code to build packages for different systems and to track versions. With the release of Red Hat 8.0 (Psyche) in 2002, Red Hat offered a slightly updated graphical management interface for its venerable RPM application.

In addition to improving the package management of early software management scripts, RPM version 4.1 introduced software features designed to ease the task of building software for different platforms from a single set of source-code files. Changes can be tracked and kept outside a developer's initial source code and multiple packages can be built from scratch and installed at the same time—simultaneously, RPM also verifies installation dependencies. Additional features, such as a checksum and GNU Privacy Guard (GPG) signatures, enable binary software packages to be safely distributed without the fear of virus infection or the inclusion of Trojan code.

The rpm command uses the RPM system to install, remove (erase), upgrade, verify, and build software archives known as .rpm files. These archives, or packages, contain package identification (a signature), checksums (mathematically derived validation values), and an archive of the software, either in source or binary form. A .rpm package also contains quite a bit of additional information, such as a name, version, and basic description, and can include pre- and post-installation scripts used for software installation, erasure, or upgrading.

The RPM database installed on your computer keeps track of which versions of which packages are installed. RPM uses your system's /var/lib/rpm directory to store files (actually databases) containing information about the software installed on your system. You can use the ls command to view these files (you might see file sizes different from those shown here, depending on the amount of software you have installed):

```
$ ls -l /var/lib/rpm
total 53820
-rw-r--r--  1 rpm     rpm       5423104 Oct 14 19:53 Basenames
-rw-r--r--  1 rpm     rpm         12288 Oct 14 12:32 Conflictname
-rw-r--r--  1 root    root        16384 Oct 14 17:31 __db.001
-rw-r--r--  1 root    root      1318912 Oct 14 17:31 __db.002
-rw-r--r--  1 root    root       458752 Oct 14 17:31 __db.003
-rw-r--r--  1 rpm     rpm       1179648 Oct 14 19:53 Dirnames
-rw-r--r--  1 rpm     rpm       5521408 Oct 14 19:53 Filemd5s
-rw-r--r--  1 rpm     rpm         24576 Oct 14 19:53 Group
-rw-r--r--  1 rpm     rpm         20480 Oct 14 19:53 Installtid
-rw-r--r--  1 rpm     rpm         45056 Oct 14 19:53 Name
-rw-r--r--  1 rpm     rpm      41070592 Oct 14 19:53 Packages
-rw-r--r--  1 rpm     rpm        348160 Oct 14 19:53 Providename
-rw-r--r--  1 rpm     rpm         98304 Oct 14 19:53 Provideversion
```

```
-rw-r--r--    1 rpm       rpm        12288 Oct 14 19:53 Pubkeys
-rw-r--r--    1 rpm       rpm       237568 Oct 14 19:53 Requirename
-rw-r--r--    1 rpm       rpm       176128 Oct 14 19:53 Requireversion
-rw-r--r--    1 rpm       rpm        94208 Oct 14 19:53 Sha1header
-rw-r--r--    1 rpm       rpm        49152 Oct 14 19:53 Sigmd57
-rw-r--r--    1 rpm       rpm        12288 Oct 14 19:53 Triggername
```

The primary database of installed software is contained in the file named Packages. As you can see from the preceding example, this database can grow to 33MB (and perhaps larger) if you perform a full installation of Fedora Core (more than 4GB of software). After you install Fedora Core Linux, rpm and related commands will use this directory during software management operations.

Command-Line and Graphical RPM Clients

As a Fedora Core Linux system administrator, you will use the rpm command or the Fedora Core graphical clients to perform one of five basic tasks. These operations, which must be conducted by the root operator, include the following:

- Installing new software

- Erasing or removing outdated or unneeded packages

- Upgrading an installed software package

- Querying to get information about a software package

- Verifying the installation or integrity of a package installation

The rpm command has more than 60 command-line options, but its administrative functions can be grouped according to the previous five types of action. Graphical RPM clients provide easy-to-use interfaces to these operations. As a system administrator, you will have a choice between using a graphical interface and using rpm's various command-line options. The general format of an rpm command is

```
# rpm option packagename
```

The basic options look like this:

- -i—Installs the selected package or packages.

- -e—Erases (removes) the selected package or packages.

- -U—Removes the currently installed package, and then installs software with the contents of the selected package or packages, leaving the existing configuration files.

- -q—Queries the system or selected package or packages.

- -V—Verifies installed or selected package or packages.

Two Handy Options

By appending vh to any option, you get

v   Some status feedback.

h   Hash marks as the work proceeds.

Many additional options can also be added to or used in conjunction with these options. These are summarized in the following table:

Option	Used To
rpm-i	Install a package
	Useful options to -i:
	--excludedocs: Does not install documentation to save space.
	--replacepkgs: Replaces the package with a new copy of itself.
	--force: The "big hammer"—Ignores all warnings and installs anyway.
	--noscripts: Does not execute any pre- or post-install scripts.
	--nodeps: Ignores any dependencies.
	--root *path*: Sets an alternative root to *path*.
rpm -e	Erases (deletes) a package.
	Useful option to -e:
	--nodeps: Ignores any dependencies.
rpm -U	Upgrades a package, removing the older one but keeping modified files, such as configurations.
	Useful options to -U:
	--oldpackage: Permits downgrading to an older version.
	Other options are the same as with rpm -i.
rpm -q	Queries about package information
	Useful options to -q:
	-p *file*: Displays all information about the package *file*.
	-f *file*: What package owns the file *file*?
	--whatprovides *x*: Determines what packages provide *x*.
	--whatrequires *x*: Determines what packages require *x*.
	-i: Summarizes the package information.
	-l: Lists the files in package.
	--scripts: Displays the contents of any install, uninstall, or verifies scripts.
	--provides: Displays the capabilities package provides.
	--requires: Displays the capabilities package requires.
rpm -V	Verifies packages against the RPM database
	Useful options to -V:
	-a: Verifies all installed packages.

Option	Used To
rpm -K	Uses GPG to verify a downloaded package.
	Useful options to -K:
	--nosignature: If you lack public GPG encryption keys, do not have GPG installed, or are legally prohibited from using GPG, this still verifies the package using size and MD5 checksums.

Details on obtaining the Fedora Core public GPG encryption key and using it are at http://www.rpm.org/max-rpm/s1-rpm-checksig-using-rpm-k.html.

RPM Is for Programmers, Too!

Remember that RPM was created not only to provide an easy to use administrative tool, but also as a developer's tool for use in multi-platform source-code package management. Programmers using rpm for development and distribution will use its rpmbuild command, along with a myriad of additional command-line flags. RPM can be used to build binaries, execute programs, test installations, verify and sign packages, build source packages, track versions, and target builds for specific architectures. Details can be found at the RPM home page (listed in the "Reference" section at the end of this chapter).

Using rpm on the Command Line

Because the new graphical RPM client can only install and uninstall RPM packages (for now—more functionality is promised), you will still end up administering RPM packages from the command line. You can perform all the five basic rpm operations using the rpm command from the command line. This section gives you an introduction to performing those operations. It also provides examples of how to install, verify, query, remove, and upgrade a software package.

The most common rpm operation is software installation. Using rpm is an easy way to keep track of installed software, and it can be used to quickly remove undesired packages. Use the -i option, along with the full or partial name (using regular expressions) of a software package, to install software with rpm. For example, to install the unace archiving package, use the rpm command like this:

```
# rpm -ivh http://mirrors.zoreil.com/plf.zarb.org/mandrake/10.0/
i586/unace-2.2-2plf.i586.rpm
Retrieving http://mirrors.zoreil.com/plf.zarb.org/mandrake/10.0/
i586/unace-2.2-2plf.i586.rpm
warning: /var/tmp/rpm-xfer.48amVs: V3 DSA signature: NOKEY, key ID 8df56d05
Preparing...                ########################################### [100%]
   1:unace
########################################### [100%]
```

This example uses the v and h options, which provide a more verbose output and display of hash marks to show the progress of the installation. The example also demonstrates the capability of rpm to use HTTP or FTP servers to fetch files for installation. It also shows that rpm can use GPG keys to validate a file. (The key was not installed in our example.)

You can also use rpm to query its database after installing packages to verify an installation. Use the -V option, along with the name of a software package, to verify installation of your system. For example, to verify the unace archiving package, use the rpm command like this:

```
# rpm -V unace
```

> **NOTE**
>
> If everything is correct with your software installation, your system will display no response to rpm -V after you run the command; only problems are displayed.

As you can see from the following program output, you can get additional information about a package by adding additional verification options (such as two more v's) to the -V option. To get more information about an installed package, use one or more forms of the rpm query options. For example, to display concise information about an installed package, use the -q option, along with the i option and the installed package name, like this (note that your version will be different from that shown here):

```
# rpm -qi unace
Name        : unace                  Relocations: (not relocateable)
Version     : 2.2                           Vendor: Penguin Liberation Front
Release     : 2plf                      Build Date: Sat 01
➥Mar 2003 12:13:48 PM EST
Install date: Tue 02 Sep 2003 03:46:28 PM EDT      Build Host:
➥baader.subversion.alt
Group       : Archiving/Compression      Source RPM: unace-2.2-2plf.src.rpm
Size        : 401368                        License: freeware
Packager    : Guillaume Rousse <guillomovitch@zarb.org>
URL         : http://www.winace.com
Summary     : Decompressor for .ace format archives
Description :
Unace is a utility to extract, view, and test the contents of an ACE archive.
```

This form of the rpm query provides quite a bit of information about the software package. (You can also query packages before installation by providing a pathname for them.)

If this package is not up-to-date, you can easily and quickly upgrade the package by downloading a newer version and then using rpm's -U or upgrade option like this:

```
# rpm -Uvh unace-2.2-2plf.i586.rpm
Preparing...            ######################################### [100%]
   1:unace               ######################################### [100%]
```

Note that it wasn't necessary to remove the currently installed software package—the U option removes the old version of the software (saving the old configuration files), and then automatically installs the new software.

You can also upgrade your system software by using the rpm command's -F or "freshen" option, which will fetch a designated package from a remote FTP or HTTP server. For example, to upgrade the fetchmail-conf package, use rpm like this:

```
# rpm -Fv ftp://ftp.tux.org/linux/redhat/updates/9/en/os/i386/\
initscripts-7.14-1.i386.rpm
Retrieving ftp://ftp.tux.org/linux/redhat/updates/9/en/os/i386/\
initscripts-7.14-1.i386.rpm
Preparing packages for installation...
initscripts-7.14-1
```

Use the -e option, along with the name of a software package, to remove or erase software from your system with rpm. For example, to remove the unace archiving package, use the rpm command like this:

```
# rpm -e unace
```

Note that if the operation succeeds, no messages will be displayed on your system. You can quickly search for the names of installed packages by piping the output of rpm -qa through the grep and sort commands (see Chapter 5, "First Steps with Fedora," for additional information on grep and sort); here's how to do that search:

```
# rpm -qa ¦ grep mail ¦ sort
fetchmail-6.2.0-7

mailcap-2.1.14-1.1
mailx-8.1.1-31.1
mozilla-mail-1.4.1-8
procmail-3.22-11
sendmail-8.12.10-1.1
sendmail-cf-8.12.10-1.1
```

This example returns a sorted list of all packages with names containing the word mail.

> **NOTE**
>
> Another essential feature of the rpm command is its --rebuilddb option. If your system's RPM database becomes corrupted, this is your first (and perhaps only) option for restoring software management services. We hope that you never have to use this option; help ensure that by always backing up your data!

Package Organization with RPM

Software packages on your Fedora Core Linux system are organized into various groups, as you see later in this chapter. Using a group organization helps Fedora Core keep software organized by category and provides for hierarchical listings of software when using graphical RPM clients. You never have to manipulate these groups, but understanding the concept of package organization can help you gain familiarity with the way Fedora Core Linux works.

Extracting a Single File from an RPM File

Occasionally, it is useful to extract a single file from an RPM package. You can do so using the command-line version of mc, the Midnight Commander. In Figure 7.1, the Midnight Commander is displaying the contents of the Yum .rpm file. The Midnight Commander is a UNIX clone of the famous DOS Norton Commander, a file management utility. Using mc, just highlight the RPM file and press Enter; the contents of the RPM file will be displayed. In the listing, you can browse the file structure of the RPM file and use mc to copy files from it.

FIGURE 7.1 A classic two-panel directory view and drop-down menus betray Midnight Commander's DOS inspiration, but it's a full-featured Linux file manager.

You might want to know what a .rpm script will do before you install the application. You can use the F3 key in mc to view the script files. If you want to look at the scripts without using mc, use this command:

```
# rpm -q --scripts filename > scripts.txt
```

This command pipes the scripts into a file, where you can examine it with a text editor. You could also pipe it to the less pagination command to view the scripts on your display:

```
# rpm -q --scripts filename | less
```

Graphical Package Management

The Fedora graphical package management tool identified in the menu as Add/Remove Software is actually an application named system-config-packages. This application replaces kpackage, gnorpm, and xrpm—all of which are no longer provided. Add/Remove Software allows you to select packages arranged in categories and install or remove them. With the addition of Yum to Fedora Core, you may now add your own packages to the Fedora Core graphical tools' database, improving its usefulness over earlier versions.

Launch the Fedora GUI package manager by clicking the Start button on your desktop, and then choose System Settings, Add/Remove Applications. The package management tool launches with the Add and Remove Software screen, shown in Figure 7.2.

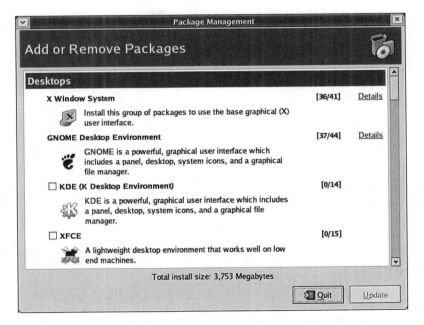

FIGURE 7.2   The initial screen of the package management tool will look familiar if you installed Fedora Core; it's the package selection screen used by the installation program.

The packages listed in the screen are organized into the Desktops, Applications, Servers, Development, and Systems groups. To choose individual package groups for installation or removal click details next to the subgroup. The numbers to the right of the package group name indicate the number of packages installed on your system and the total number of packages available in the group. In Figure 7.2, you can see that 37 of 44 possible GNOME packages have been installed.

Under the details for each subgroup, simply select the packages you want to remove. Note that you can only access the Extra Packages; to remove the base packages, you need to uncheck the box next to the name of the subgroup.

FIGURE 7.3   The Standard Packages listing (collapsed in this view) details the base packages installed when the main category is selected. Extra Packages are those that you have the option of installing.

Using Red Hat Network and Alternatives for Software Management

For the Red Hat 8 and 9 releases, the only command-line application for the management of system software provided by Red Hat was RPM; the only GUI tool for management was the Red Hat Packages graphical client (`system-config-packages`) now identified as Add/Remove Software. For the average person, RPM is hopelessly complicated; it includes extra complexity to allow it to be used as a general `.rpm` file-building and development tool, features not normally used by many people. The graphical software management client has been improved for Fedora Core to enable the use of local and remote Yum (that stands for YellowDog Updater modified, first used in the YellowDog [PPC] Linux distribution) repositories.

Not previously covered in this book is the Red Hat Network (https://rhn.redhat.com—see Figure 7.4). RHN has not been covered because it is not free to the users of this book (or to users of the freely-available FTP download version) and it is limited to managing only the software that is provided by Red Hat. Other alternatives are now available.

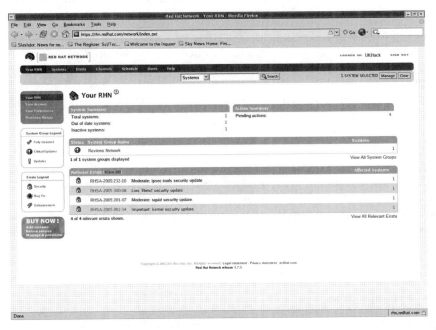

FIGURE 7.4   The Red Hat Network provides automated update subscription services. It only works with software provided by Red Hat and is designed for commercial users.

The RHN service is a client-server mechanism through which a user subscribes to a channel on the server (a repository of software for a specific release of Fedora Core). The local client (identified by a round icon at the right of the desktop panel) can manually or automatically connect to the Red Hat Network server, obtain a list of updates, errata, and security fixes and install them; one subscription is required for each client.

Although there are several alternatives for `rpm/system-config-packages`, two of the most useful are apt and Yum. These package management applications go a long way toward solving dependency problems and easing the use of RPM to manage software. Both can install software from either local or remote repositories. Interestingly, the Yum application is now provided in Fedora, and `system-config-packages` has been modified to be used as a graphical front end for it.

The benefit to installing and using either of these two applications is that they allow you easy access to and installation of programs that Red Hat nor Fedora Core cannot or will not provide (such as multimedia and non-GPL licensed applications). Since the apt and Yum mirrors for Fedora all have current Fedora updates, it is not necessary for you to use up2date or RHN to keep your computer software current. The following sections discuss the apt and Yum applications in more detail.

apt

Originally developed for Debian Linux and modified to use with `rpm` packages by Connectiva Linux, apt and its GUI interface Synaptic are easy to install and use. There are two primary providers of apt packages and repositories; either provider is a good choice. However, because of version conflicts between packages, the two projects' files should not be used together. FreshRPMs at http://www.freshrpms.net/ is one provider; the Fedora Project at http://fedora.mplug.org/ is the other. The Fedora Project has now been integrated into the briefly lived Red Hat Linux Project and renamed Fedora Core. We will use FreshRPMs as an example because they provide packages not available from Fedora.

Here is how you install and configure apt:

- Read the introduction to apt in the /apt/ section of the http://freshrpms.net site.

- Install the FreshRPMS GPG key (you need to have lynx installed, or simply download and gpg --import the downloaded text file):

  ```
  # lynx -source http://freshrpms.net/packages/RPM-GPG-KEY.txt ¦ gpg --import
  ```

- Install the correct version of apt from FreshRpms.

  ```
  # rpm -ivh http://ftp.freshrpms.net/pub/freshrpms/fedora/linux/2/apt/
  apt-0.5.15cnc6-1.1.fc4.fr.i386.rpm
  ```

- Review the man page of apt. The most important commands are apt-get update and apt-get install *packagename*:

  ```
  # man apt
  ```

- The list of apt repositories is preconfigured in /etc/apt/sources/list, but the index of packages that is available needs to be updated with

  ```
  # apt-get update
  ```

- Once the update of the packages list is completed, we suggest that you install Synaptic, the GUI package manager shown in Figure 7.5.

```
# apt-get install synaptic
```

- Launch synaptic from the command line, browse the available packages, and install what you like.

```
# synaptic &
```

The Synaptic graphical interface is nicely laid out (see Figure 7.5). It allows you to view a list of all available packages and any dependencies required for them. It also provides a graphical interface to add new repositories.

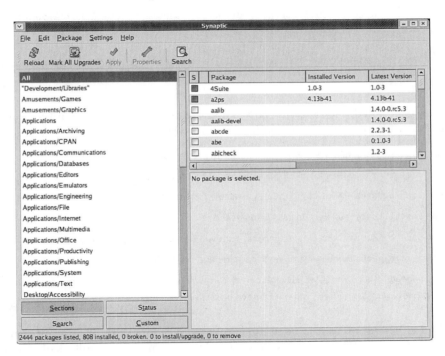

FIGURE 7.5   Synaptic is a graphical interface to the apt package management application making it incredibly easy to use.

Yum

Some developers believe that although apt is a good tool, using it for .rpm packages is a hack. apt also is believed to be bloated with unnecessary code used for the Debian .deb packages. A new tool, Yum, was developed using the Python language because the Fedora Core installer, Anaconda, was written in Python and much of the code could be shared. This decision is what has made Yum the choice for integration into the Fedora Core distribution. It works much the same as apt, but lacked a GUI tool. The Fedora developers have integrated support for Yum into the graphical Red Hat/Fedora package management tool. You can obtain Yum from the Fedora site as well as from FreshRPMs.net; the home page of Yum is at http://linux.duke.edu/projects/yum/.

Here's how you install and configure Yum:

- Read the HOWTO and Users FAQ at the Fedora site: http://fedora.mplug.org/.

- Install the Fedora GPG key:

  ```
  # lynx -source http://fedora.mplug.org/FEDORA-GPG-KEY ¦ gpg --import
  ```

- Install the correct version of Yum:

  ```
  # rpm -ivh http://ftp.freshrpms.net/pub/freshrpms/fedora/linux/2/yum/
  yum-2.0.7-3.1.fc.fr.noarch.rpm
  ```

- Review the man page for Yum to familiarize yourself with all available options:

  ```
  # man yum
  ```

Once Yum is installed, the following commands are useful (remember that the Fedora graphical client is available if you configure it to use Yum repositories):

yum list—A list of all packages available from the repository.

yum list installed—A list of all packages installed on your computer.

yum list updates—A list of all updates available for your computer.

yum install *packagename*—Installs *packagename*.

yum update—Run without a *packagename*, Yum will update all installed packages.

yum remove *packagename*—Removes a package and dependencies.

yum upgrade—Run without a package name, Yum will upgrade all packages and remove any obsoleted packages; yum update will not remove obsoleted packages.

You'll find either apt or Yum to be useful additions to Fedora Core. We suggest that you use the one from FreshRPMs.net if you want to install some of the multimedia applications described in Chapter 10, "Multimedia Applications." To learn more about yum, check out Chapter 36, "Advanced Yum."

Compiling Software from Source

Not all the software you might want to use is available in rpm packages or in the exact form that you desire. Many complicated programs have options that can only be selected at compile time and many smaller, special-purpose applications only exist as source code. Fedora Core provides all the tools necessary for you to compile source code into binary applications. First, we'll cover building from source rpm files, and then manipulating source rpm files and finally, building from source tarballs.

> **NOTE**
>
> For other software package formats, you can use the File Roller application (found in the Accessories menu) to easily display, browse, read, and extract contents of compressed files, including legacy archives such as tarballs or compressed tar archives (recognized by their .gz or .tgz extensions). Other compressed files, such as those created with the compress command (ending in .Z) or bzip2 files (ending in .bz2), are also supported by File Roller. The File Roller client will also convert compressed archives between gzip and bzip2 formats.

Building RPMS from src.rpm Files

A rule of thumb is that you never build rpms as the root user even though the directories are already set up at /usr/src/redhat as follows:

```
# tree /usr/src/redhat
/usr/src/redhat
|-- BUILD
|-- RPMS
|    |-- athlon
|    |-- i386
|    |-- i486
|    |-- i586
|    |-- i686
|    `-- noarch
|-- SOURCES
|-- SPECS
`-- SRPMS
```

Using the mkdir command, re-create this directory tree structure in your home directory; you can name the new directory redhat (or anything you like). You might even want to create a new user just to build rpms and source code. (You can compile without being root; you just can't install the software systemwide as a regular user.)

The configuration information for building rpms is kept in three places:

/usr/lib/rpm/*/macros—The systemwide defaults.

/etc/rpm/macros.*—Where systemwide changes are kept.

~/.rpmmacros—Where user-specific changes are kept.

Because we need to tell rpm that we will not be using the systemwide default build location for our user, we can

```
$ echo "%_topdir $HOME/redhat" > $HOME/.rpmmacros
```

> **TIP**
>
> Here, we use > instead of >> to blank the file in case there is already content in it. The >> construct appends information to a file.

To select a temporary directory

```
$ echo "%_tmppath $HOME/tmp" >> $HOME/.rpmmacros
```

To set any compiler optimization flags (here, we are using an Athlon processor as an example), we will use

```
$ echo "-o3 -march=athlon" >> $HOME/.rpmmacros
```

To rebuild a `src.rpm` file as a regular user, you would use

```
$ rpmbuild --recompile packagename.src.rpm
```

After a successful build, you will find the binary file(s) in `~/redhat/RPMS/athlon`.

You can install them as `root` with

```
# rpm -Uvh --replacepkgs --replacefiles packagename.rpm
```

If the build fails, the error message will point you to a solution (usually a dependency has not been satisfied). You will find that a lot of the packages named with `-devel` will be needed before you compile from source code. Install the package for the missing dependency and retry the compile.

Working with Source RPM Files

You might want to modify a source package for your own uses such as adding documentation, changing default settings, or patching the source code itself. Fedora Core provides the source code to its distribution in the form of source RPM files. You can access the source code on disks 4 and 5 of the downloadable CD images or obtain them from the Fedora Core FTP site.

> **TIP**
>
> An important part of the RPM file is called the `.spec` file, a specification file. It tells RPM how to behave with the particular source files during compilation, installation, and erasure.

As an example, we'll use information that was found at http://elektron.its.tudelft.nl/ ~rbos36/mdkfreetype2.html (the page has now been removed by the author) to modify the freetype2 library provided with Fedora Core in order to enable the bytecode interpreter. The code for the interpreter has been disabled by default because of redistribution licensing concerns that don't affect individual use. Enabling the interpreter will result in improved rendering of the TrueType fonts. We used the file from Red Hat 7.3 as our example, but the source file from FC4 should work as well.

Begin work by first installing the source RPM package with rpm -i. (Note that here we are building as root to follow the example from the web page; you should typically build packages as a regular user.) In our example, obtain the freetype-2.1.9-2.src.rpm and install it with rpm -i. The source code files are placed in /usr/src/redhat/SOURCES.

Copy the source file (it's a compressed tar file) to /tmp, and then cd (change directories) there to unpack and modify it:

```
# cp freetype-2.1.9.tar.bz2 /tmp
# cd /tmp
```

Because it's a .bz2 (BZip2 compressed) tar file, un-tar it with

```
# tar xjvf freetype-2.1.9.tar.bz2
```

and cd to the new directory:

```
# cd freetype-2.1.9
```

Using the text editor of your choice, edit the file include/freetype/config/ftoption.h and find the line

```
#undef TT_CONFIG_OPTION_BYTECODE_INTERPRETER
```

Change it to

```
#define TT_CONFIG_OPTION_BYTECODE_INTERPRETER
```

Save it and exit the text editor.

Next, re-create the compressed archive:

```
# cd /tmp
# tar cfj freetype-2.1.9.tar.bz2 ./freetype-2.1.9/
```

Put it back in your source directory:

```
# mv freetype-2.1.9.tar.bz2 /usr/src/SOURCES
```

Now edit the .spec file in /usr/src/redhat/SPECS to change the line beginning with Release to increment the number found there. (We are changing the version number by doing this, so it will not conflict with the version of the application we will be replacing.) Make any changes to the %description line to describe your changes if you desire, and save the file.

Build the binary RPM with

```
# rpmbuild -bb freetype.spec
```

During the build process, RPM will detect a patch and ask you about the patch; press y for "yes" to continue.

The new RPMs (actually four of them) are found in /usr/src/redhat/RPMS/i386. We only need the one named freetype-2.1.9; you can install it with rpm -Uvh. (This is why we changed the version number; if we had not, RPM would not upgrade to the "same" version. Had we not changed the version number, we could have forced the installation with the --replacepackages --replacefiles option.)

The font server needs to be restarted to use the new library, so we use the service command as shown in Chapter 14, "Automating Tasks."

```
# service xfs restart
```

Enjoy your new look—provided by better rendering of the fonts.

Compile from Source Tarballs

Compiling applications from source is not that difficult. Most source code is available as compressed source *tarballs*—that is, tar files that have been compressed using gzip or bzip. The compressed files will typically uncompress into a directory containing several files. It's always a good idea to compile source code as a regular user to limit any damage that broken or malicious code might inflict, so create a directory named source in your home directory.

From wherever you downloaded the source tarball, uncompress it into the ~/source directory using the -C option to tar:

```
$ tar zxvf packagename.tgz -C ~/source

$ tar zxvf packagename.tar.gz -C ~/source

$ tar jxvf packagename.bz -C ~/source

$ tar jxvf packagename.tar.bz2 -C ~/source
```

If you're not certain what file compression method was used, employ the file command to figure it out:

```
$ file packagename
```

Now, change directories to ~/source/*packagename* and look for a file named README, INSTALL, or a similar name. Print the file out if necessary because it will contain specific instructions on how to compile and install the software. Typically, the procedure to compile source code is

```
$ ./configure
```

which runs a script to check if all dependencies are met and the build environment is correct. Then,

```
$ make
```

to compile the software. And finally, as root:

```
# make install
```

If the compile fails, check the error messages for the reason and run

```
$ make clean
```

before you start again. You can also run

```
$ make uninstall
```

to remove the software if you do not like it.

An alternative to running `make install` is a program named CheckInstall, which will produce an `rpm` file for your installation. This method allows the RPM database to be aware of and keep track of all the files you are installing. See the following sidebar on CheckInstall for more information.

A Handy Software Installation Tool—CheckInstall

When you compile applications from source and install them, they won't show up in the RPM database and therefore can't be managed by RPM.

You can provide RPM management for these applications by using a program named CheckInstall. At its simplest, `checkinstall` is a drop-in substitute for the `make install` step in building from source code.

For example, when compiling from source code, you would traditionally use

```
# ./configure
# make
# make install
```

Using CheckInstall, the steps would look like this:

```
# ./configure
# make
# checkinstall
```

CheckInstall will create a binary `.rpm` package and install the application from it. This makes the new application part of the RPM database. The new `.rpm` file is left for you in `/usr/src/redhat/RPMS/i386`. The new application can later be uninstalled with `rpm -e`.

Some applications arrive in the form of a shell script wrapper. Using the shell script as the argument to CheckInstall will provide a `.rpm` file of the installed files and add them to your RPM database. Not all applications will install with CheckInstall. Read its accompanying documentation carefully.

CheckInstall can be downloaded from http://asic-linux.com.mx/~izto/checkinstall/index.php.

Reference

http://www.rpm.org—Home page for the Fedora Core Package Manager. This site provides essential links to the latest version of RPM software for Linux and X desktop environments, such as GNOME.

http://www.rpm.org/max-rpm/—Link to the start of an update to Ed Bailey's classic tome and RPM reference book, *Maximum RPM*.

http://linux.tnc.edu.tw/techdoc/maximum-rpm/rpmbook/node15.html—History of the Red Hat Package Manager.

http://www.smoogespace.com/documents/behind_the_names.html—A history of Red Hat Linux releases, and a good place to learn about the connection between the names of the releases.

http://www.gnupg.org/—Home page for GNU Privacy Guard, an unencumbered free replacement for Pretty Good Privacy.

http://www.debian.org/doc/manuals/project-history/ch-detailed.en.html—History of the Debian Linux package system.

http://www.nrh-up2date.org/index.html—A replacement for Red Hat's Up2Date application.

# CHAPTER 8

On the Internet: Surfing the Web, Writing Email, and Reading the News

The Internet has revolutionized our modern civilization within a very short time. Not long ago it was unheard of to be communicating through the Internet; nowadays you are deemed backwards if you do not have an email account or an instant messenger. This chapter introduces you to some of the more popular software that you can use to access the Internet, send and receive email, read network news, collaborate with others using an online collaboration tool, and talk in real time using instant messenging and even videoconferencing. You will find out how to set up each piece of software to access the resources you need.

Choosing a Web Browser

The Internet has forever changed how we access and share information. The ways in which we view the Internet have also changed and are continually improving to give better and richer experiences. In this section, we look at some of the popular open-source web browsers available for Fedora.

A Brief Introduction to the Internet

The Internet itself was first brought to life by the U.S. Department of Defense in 1969. It was called ARPANet after the Department of Defense's Advanced Research Projects Agency. Designed to build a network that would withstand major catastrophe (this was the peak of the Cold War), it soon grew to encompass more and more networks to build the Internet. Then, in 1991 Tim Berners-Lee of CERN developed the idea of the World Wide Web, including Hypertext Transfer Protocol (HTTP) and Hypertext Markup Language (HTML). This gave us what we now know to be the Internet.

Mozilla Firefox

One of the most popular web browsers, and in fact the default web browser in Fedora, is Mozilla Firefox (see Figure 8.1). Built on a solid code base that is derived from the Mozilla Suite, Firefox offers a new lease on life to surfing the Internet. Over 25 million people have downloaded Firefox since its release in late 2004, and it has grabbed significant market share from Internet Explorer.

In Fedora you will find Firefox under the Applications, Internet menu at the top of your screen. An even simpler way to start Firefox, though, is to click the small world icon next to the Actions menu. Either way, you will open Firefox.

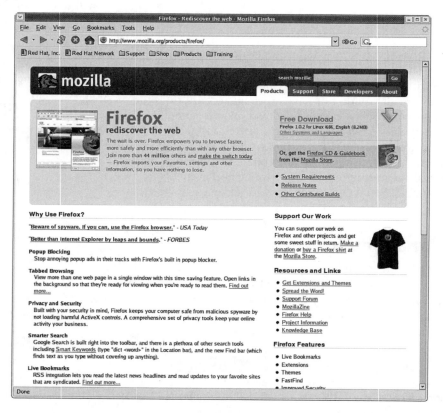

FIGURE 8.1   Mozilla Firefox—rediscover the Web. Firefox allows you to add on numerous upgrades, further enhancing your experience.

Beyond the basic program are a wealth of plug-ins and extensions that can increase the capabilities of Firefox beyond simple web browsing. Plug-ins such as Shockwave Flash and

Java are available, whereas extensions provide useful and sometimes humorous additions to the browsing experience. For example, ForecastFox is an extension that gives you your local weather conditions, and Bandwidth Tester is a tool that calculates your current bandwidth.

The Mozilla Suite

The Mozilla Suite is a tightly integrated web browsing and messaging application suite that was spun off from Netscape (see Figure 8.2). Since Netscape became dormant a few years ago, the Mozilla Foundation was set up by AOL and other companies to continue the now open-source development of the once-popular browser. The fruits of this labor can be seen in the Mozilla Suite. By default, Mozilla is not installed in Fedora; instead you have to specify it in the installation or install it later using Yum or apt.

Bear in mind that if you install Mozilla, you also get the other parts of the suite: the mail and newsgroup reader, the address book, and the IRC client. If you do not require all of this, you might be better off with Firefox.

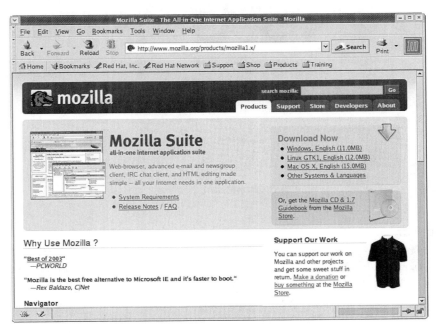

FIGURE 8.2   The Mozilla suite, the forefather of Firefox and a descendant of Netscape.

Epiphany

Epiphany is the browser supplied with the vanilla Gnome desktop (see Figure 8.3). Very basic and built on the same Gecko rendering engine as Firefox and Mozilla before it, Epiphany has advanced in a number of areas to the current version.

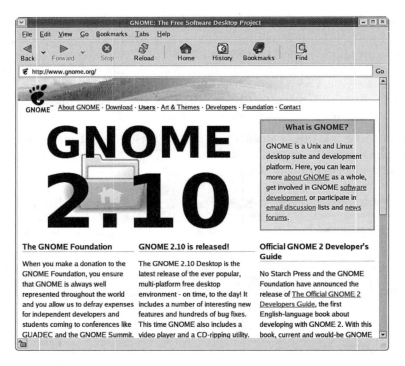

FIGURE 8.3   Epiphany, the standard Gnome web browser.

Konqueror

KDE users have the option to use Konqueror, which is the default browser for KDE (see Figure 8.4). As well as handling file system navigation, Konqueror can also be used to surf the Web. It, too, is based on the Gecko rendering engine as found in Firefox, Mozilla, and Epiphany.

FIGURE 8.4 Konqueror, the standard KDE web and file system browser.

Choosing an Email Client

Back in the days of Unix, there were various text-based email clients such as `elm` and `pine` (Pine Is Not Elm). Although they looked basic, they allowed the average user to interact with his email, both composing and reading correspondence. With the advent of mainstream computing and the realization that people needed friendly GUI interfaces to be productive, came a plethora of email clients, with some of them being cross-platform and compatible between Linux, Windows, and Mac OS X, not to mention Unix.

A Brief Introduction to Email Terms

The email world is filled with acronyms and technical terms. The first of these covered here describes the components of the email system. Some applications combine features from among these three groups.

The Mail User Agent (MUA), mail client, or mail reader allows the user to read and compose her email. This is the application most users are familiar with; it presents a text or graphical interface to the user. Examples would be Evolution, Balsa, mutt, Mozilla Mail, or KMail. All are provided by Fedora Core.

The mail transfer agent (MTA) works behind the scenes to send and receive email between computers. Examples would be Sendmail, Postfix, Fetchmail, Exim, or Qmail. All but the last two are provided by Fedora Core. The Mail Delivery Agent (MDA) is similar to an MTA, but does not handle deliveries between systems and does not provide an interface to the user like an MUA. Examples would be Procmail or Spamassassin; both provide filtering services to the MTA, and the latter is provided by Fedora Core.

The protocols used for email are a hotbed of acronyms; these are covered next.

RFC—The Request For Comments is as close to an Internet rulebook as one can get. See the "Reference" section at the end of this chapter for links to specific RFCs. By changing the number in the link, you can look at any particular RFC. If you have Fetchmail installed, author Eric S. Raymond has included a list of RFCs (with descriptions) that are relevant to email in the file `/usr/share/doc/fetchmail/NOTES`.

POP—Defined by RFC-1939, the Post Office Protocol is a mail server for delivering mail to clients. (It isn't used for sending mail to servers; that's SMTP, later.) POP3 is very useful when you have one mail client on one computer, such as a typical home user. POP3 is designed for local access to mail; it downloads all mail from a central server to the local client, and then deletes the files on the server. Most ISPs offer POP3 mail access.

IMAP—It is the Internet Mail Access Protocol, which allows a user to access his email stored on a remote server rather than a local disk. This means that email can be accessed from anywhere if the user is employing a mail client with IMAP support. IMAP is a good solution to providing mail for a LAN. The version supplied with Fedora Core is the University of Washington IMAP server, found at http://www.washington.edu/imap/.

SMTP—Defined by RFC-821, it is the Simple Mail Transport Protocol used for sending mail from one network to another. It is a sever-to-server protocol, so some other method must be used to deliver messages to a client application to be read by a user. Extensions to the protocol add authentication and error messages to the basic protocol.

MIME—Defined by RFC-1341, 1521, 1522, 1523, 1820, and many others, Multipurpose Internet Mail Extensions address the formatting of email messages to include non-ASCII text, encoded binary images, and multimedia content.

Certainly, this is not an exhaustive list, nor is it intended to be. You might find the Jargoogle search page useful to decipher other unfamiliar terms you encounter. It is found at http://www.tuxedo.org/~esr/jargon/jargoogle.html.

NOTE

The amazing deluge of spam and Internet scams using forged headers has spurred interest in a "better mousetrap." One such project is AMTP at http://amtp.bw.org/, an enhancement for SMTP. This specification calls for mail servers needing a signed security certificate and using TLS (Transport Layer Security, RFC2246). An AMTP mail server will not relay mail from an "untrusted source"—in other words, a mail server lacking the proper authentication. Although not eradicating SPAM, AMTP does provide a mechanism to identify the source.

Evolution

Evolution, a Ximian/Novell product, is the standard email client that comes with Fedora (see Figure 8.5). If you have used Microsoft Outlook, the interface Evolution has will come as no great shock. It really is a drop-in replacement for Outlook and encompasses many of Outlook's features and benefits, including email, calendaring, contact management, and task management. Here we examine how to get Evolution configured for email access.

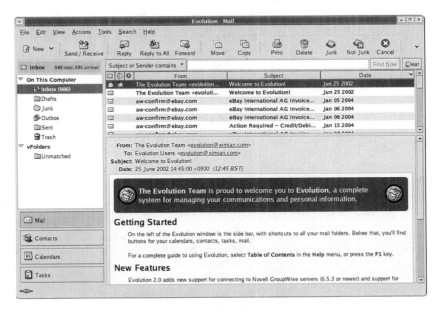

FIGURE 8.5   Ximian Evolution, the default and extremely powerful email client for Fedora.

You need to have the following information to hand to successfully configure Evolution:

- Your email address
- Your incoming email server name and type (that is, pop.email.com, POP, and IMAP)
- Your username and password for the incoming server
- Your outgoing email server name (that is, smtp.email.com)

After you have all the information, you can start Evolution. The first screen you are presented with is the Account Setup Assistance (see Figure 8.6).

The next screen permits you to configure Evolution to use your MTA. You can choose POP, IMAP, the local spools found in /var/mail in either mbox or maildir format, a local MTA, or None if you simply want to use the other features of Evolution. As shown in Figure 8.7, you can also set your password.

You must also choose between SMTP or Sendmail for sending your mail; enter your email address, and choose a time zone (very important for your calendar). Finally, you will see the opening Evolution window in Figure 8.8.

FIGURE 8.6 You can launch and configure Evolution with just a few simple commands. The Identity screen, the first of several screens, asks you to enter your information. Click Forward to proceed.

FIGURE 8.7 The Receiving Mail screen requires information from your ISP or system administrator.

Each icon in the left pane of mainEvolution window opens a different window when selected. Each view has options that can be configured to suit your needs; just click each window's Tools menu item, for example, to open the Tools screen, shown in Figure 8.9.

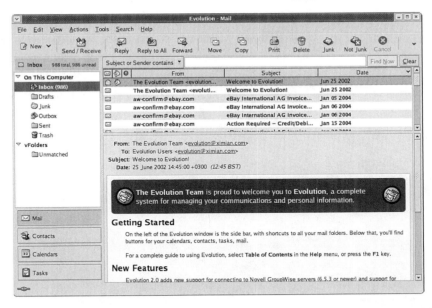

FIGURE 8.8   The standard Evolution display. On the left you can see buttons to choose Mail, Contacts, Calendars, and Tasks windows.

FIGURE 8.9   The calendar application Tools screen is where the information can be shared with others. Here, the times and dates can be configured.

Mozilla Thunderbird

Mozilla Thunderbird is the sister program to Firefox. Whereas Firefox is designed to browse the Web, Thunderbird's specialty is communication. It can handle email, network news (see later in this chapter), and RSS feeds.

Thunderbird is not installed by default with Fedora, so you will have to use either yum or apt to install it.

Balsa

Balsa is an email client designed to work with GNOME. Configuring Balsa is similar to configuring Evolution, although most of the configuration is done from the Preferences menu item, and the basic functionality is similar. Figure 8.10 shows a screenshot of the Balsa interface.

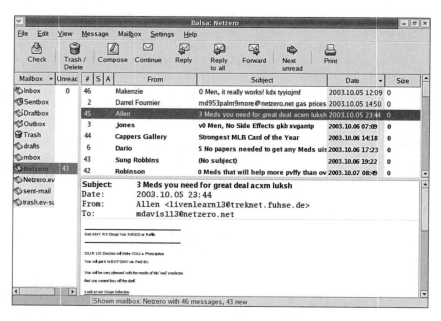

FIGURE 8.10   The Balsa email client. It should not take long for users of Outlook Express or Mozilla Mail to get comfortable with the interface.

KMail

If you are using the KDE Desktop Environment rather than the Fedora Core default GNOME desktop, you will also have KMail installed. As with Balsa, it won't take users of Outlook Express or Mozilla Mail very long to get used to the KMail interface. Some useful features found in KMail are the choice of mbox or maildir formats, improved filter creation, the ability to sort mail into threads, and the ability to apply filters at the MTA. Figure 8.11 shows the KMail email program. KMail offers IMAP access; extensive filtering;

`mbox` and `maildir` formats; and the ability to easily integrate MTAs such as Procmail, Spamassassin, or custom processing scripts.

FIGURE 8.11   The KMail email client, part of the KDE Desktop Environment.

Mozilla Mail

Mozilla is more than a browser: It is an Internet Relay Chat client and a mail and newsgroup reader. The Mail and News setup wizard and preferences can be found under the Edit menu item. When you select Mail & Newsgroup Account Setup and then click New Account, the wizard dialog appears, as shown in Figure 8.12.

Configuration via the wizard is easy: Mozilla prompts you for the necessary information. The Mail interface (shown in Figure 8.13) is familiar to many users. If you use Mozilla for web browsing, using it for email is a natural extension. Mozilla Mail is also a good choice for those who do not need all the features offered in the Evolution mail client.

The `mail` Application

A Unix utility named `mail` is included with all Unix and Linux distributions. Because it has a very Spartan interface, it is not commonly used interactively. However, `mail` is still an extremely useful program to use in shell scripting because it can take all the information it needs to send mail from the command line. No user interaction is required. `mail` is also useful for sending quick notes because it starts up quickly and doesn't require going through menus to send a message.

FIGURE 8.12   This is where your email and newsgroup configurations are set. Mozilla provides many choices to accommodate your individual needs.

FIGURE 8.13   The interface to Mozilla Mail is familiar to many; is similar to MS Outlook Express, KMail, and Balsa; and is easy to use.

Using mail

To begin sending a message in mail, simply type **mail** at the shell prompt, followed by the email address that you want to send mail to:

```
$ mail paul@hudzilla.org
```

mail will then prompt you for the subject of the message. Enter the subject and press Enter. The cursor will then move down to the next blank line. You can now start entering the body of your message. When you have finished, press Ctrl+D on a blank line to exit the mail program and send the message. (You might be prompted for Cc:. If you do not want to send carbon copies to anyone, simply press Enter here.) The message will be handed off to the MTA, and your shell prompt will return. To abandon a message you are currently writing, press Ctrl+C.

If you want to retrieve your email using the mail program, simply type **mail** at the shell prompt. The system will respond with something similar to the following:

```
Mail   Type ? for help.
"/var/mail/andrew": 1 message 1 unread
>U  1 paul@hudzilla.org   Sun Mar 20 07:15  18/551    "Birthday"
>N  2 spam@ebay.com       Sun Mar 20 08:25  18/542
"A large and obnoxious spam message"
>N  3 paul@hudzilla.org   Sun Mar 20 09:21  17/524    "Fedora 4 Update"
>N  4 nick@veitch.org     Sun Mar 20 09:24  17/528    "Issues"
&
```

The & prompt is mail's way of prompting you for input.

The first column in the list of messages is a flag that indicates the status of the message. For example, U means that the message is unread. N means that the message is new. The rest of the columns are self-explanatory.

To read one of these messages, simply type the message number and press Enter.

For example,

```
& 4
Message 4

From nick@veitch.org  Sun Mar 20 09:24:35 2003
Date: Tue, 23 Sep 2003 09:24:34 -0500
From: andrew@andbhudson.co.uk
To: nick@veitch.org
Subject: Issues
```

```
Hey Nick,

The new issue looks great! Where did you get the idea for the cover from?

Seeya

&
```

If you want to respond to this message, you can type **respond** and press Enter. You can also simply type **r** and press Enter. By default, the command will be applied to the currently active message, which is indicated in the message list by a > (and will be the last message that you read). If you want to have the command applied to a different message, you can simply specify the message number after the command. For example, typing **r 2** will respond to message number 2.

A complete list of commands is available within mail by typing **?** at the prompt. Note that you can abbreviate all commands to the shortest abbreviation that is not ambiguous.

Shell Scripting with `mail`

As mentioned previously, `mail`'s most useful application is its use in shell scripting. The complete instruction to create and send a message can be done from the command line. For example, suppose that we have a shell script that generates a report and stores it as a text file. Now we want to email that text file to a user at the end of the script. With `mail`, we could use a command such as the following:

```
$ mail andrew@andbhudson.co.uk -s "Report from shell script" < report.txt
```

The `-s` specifies a subject line on the command line, and then we use simple shell redirection to use the file `report.txt` as the body for the message (see Chapter 14, "Automating Tasks"). It is simple, clean, and requires no user interaction to send the message.

For other options available on the `mail` command line, see the `man` page for `mail`.

> **NOTE**
>
> The venerable pine email client is no longer provided by Fedora, not because it is not a good application; it just uses a license that is incompatible with distribution by Fedora and Red Hat.

Mutt

Mutt is a relatively new command-line mail client that is rapidly becoming popular with users. The client is called mutt because it is known as "the mongrel of email clients" in that it attempts to combine the best features of several other clients such as elm and pine. Mutt is an extremely feature-rich email client, although it is not as easy to use as pine. It is however, more secure than pine. Figure 8.14 shows the mutt interface.

To check the version and see the compile time options, use `mutt -v` like this:

```
$ mutt -v
Mutt 1.4.2.1i (2004-02-12)
Copyright (C) 1996-2002 Michael R. Elkins and others.
Mutt comes with ABSOLUTELY NO WARRANTY; for details type `mutt -vv'.
Mutt is free software, and you are welcome to redistribute it
under certain conditions; type `mutt -vv' for details.
System: Linux 2.6.11.1177_FC4 (i686) [using ncurses 5.4]
Compile options:
-DOMAIN
-DEBUG
-HOMESPOOL  -USE_SETGID  -USE_DOTLOCK  -DL_STANDALONE
+USE_FCNTL  -USE_FLOCK
+USE_POP  +USE_IMAP  +USE_GSS  +USE_SSL  +USE_SASL
+HAVE_REGCOMP  -USE_GNU_REGEX
+HAVE_COLOR  +HAVE_START_COLOR  +HAVE_TYPEAHEAD  +HAVE_BKGDSET
+HAVE_CURS_SET  +HAVE_META  +HAVE_RESIZETERM
+HAVE_PGP  -BUFFY_SIZE -EXACT_ADDRESS  -SUN_ATTACHMENT
+ENABLE_NLS  -LOCALES_HACK  +HAVE_WC_FUNCS  +HAVE_LANGINFO_CODESET
¬+HAVE_LANGINFO_YESEXPR
+HAVE_ICONV  -ICONV_NONTRANS  +HAVE_GETSID  +HAVE_GETADDRINFO
ISPELL="/usr/bin/ispell"
SENDMAIL="/usr/sbin/sendmail"
MAILPATH="/var/mail"
PKGDATADIR="/usr/share/mutt"
SYSCONFDIR="/etc"
EXECSHELL="/bin/sh"
-MIXMASTER
To contact the developers, please mail to <mutt-dev@mutt.org>.
To report a bug, please use the flea(1) utility.
```

If you want to change the options (such as any paths) you will need to recompile mutt from the source code.

The latest versions of mutt, as well as news and information about it, are available at http://www.mutt.org. Mutt is proud to be a bug-free program, but its authors believe it might have a few "fleas"—thankfully, these are few.

The systemwide configuration file is kept at /etc/Muttrc, and each user can have his own ~/.muttrc files. Mutt configuration is often an evolving process, as each user attempts to configure this feature-rich mail client.

Before you can use mutt, you need to configure a .muttrc file for each user's home directory. A sample file is found in /usr/share/doc/mutt-*/sample.muttrc, just copy it (or the systemwide file) to .muttrc in the appropriate home directory. There, edit it to reflect how you have your mail system configured and set your preferences; you will find mutt highly customizable, awkward to configure, and simple to use.

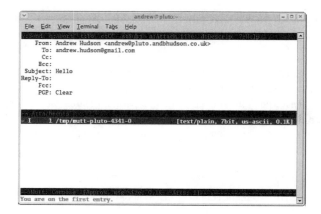

FIGURE 8.14   Mutt combines the best features of elm and pine (aside from ugly default screen colors). Fedora defaults the editor to vi, but you can choose any other editor.

Sending and receiving messages using mutt is very easy; the colorful display provides a subset of common commands, and F1 brings up the online help documents.

Other Mail Clients

The mail clients included by Fedora Core are only a few of those available. Sylpheed-claws (not included) is very popular because it offers spell check while typing and is well-suited for use in large network environments in which network overhead and RAM usage are important considerations. You can find other mail clients and applications suitable for use with Fedora Core Linux by searching http://freshmeat.net/.

An Overview of Network News

The concept of newsgroups revolutionized the way information was exchanged between people across a network. The Usenet network news system created a method for people to electronically communicate with large groups of people with similar interests.

The following sections describe the Usenet network newsgroup format and how newsgroup information is transmitted between hosts. As you will see, many of the concepts of Usenet news are embodied in other forms of collaborative communication.

Newsgroups

Usenet newsgroups act as a form of public bulletin board system. Any user can subscribe to individual newsgroups and send (or *post*) messages (called *articles*) to the newsgroup so that all the other subscribers of the newsgroup can read them. Some newsgroups include an administrator, who must approve each message before it is posted. These are called *moderated* newsgroups. Other newsgroups are *open*, allowing any subscribed member to post a message. When an article is posted to the newsgroup, it is transferred to all the other hosts in the news network.

Usenet newsgroups are divided into a hierarchy to make it easier to find individual newsgroups. The hierarchy levels are based on topics, such as computers, science, re-creation, and social issues. Each newsgroup is named as a subset of the higher-level topic. For example, the newsgroup comp relates to all computer topics. The newsgroup comp.laptops relates to laptop computer issues. Often the hierarchy goes several layers deep. For example, the newsgroup comp.databases.oracle.server relates to Oracle server database issues.

> **NOTE**
>
> The format of newsgroup articles follows the strict guidelines defined in the Internet standards document Request for Comments (RFC) 1036. Each article must contain two distinct parts: header lines and a message body.
>
> The header lines identify information about when and from whom the article was posted. The body of the message should contain only standard ASCII text characters. No binary characters or files should be posted within news articles. To get around this restriction, binary files are converted to text data by using either the standard Unix uuencode program or the newer Multipurpose Internet Mail Extensions (MIME) protocol. The resulting text file is then posted to the newsgroup. Newsgroup readers can then decode the posted text file back into its original binary form.

A collection of articles posted in response to a common topic is called a *thread*. A thread can contain many articles as users post messages in response to other posted messages. Some newsreader programs allow the user to track articles based on the threads they belong to. This helps simplify the organization of articles in the newsgroup.

> **TIP**
>
> The free news server news.gmane.org makes the Red Hat and Fedora mail lists available via newsgroups. The beta list is available as gmane.linux.redhat.rhl.beta. It is a handy way to read threaded discussions and easier than using the Fedora Core mail list archives.

The protocol used to transfer newsgroup articles from one host to another is Network News Transfer Protocol (NNTP), defined in RFC 977. (You can search RFCs at ftp:// metalab.unc.edu/pub/docs/rfc/;look at the file rfc-index.txt.) NNTP was designed as a simple client/server protocol that enables two hosts to exchange newsgroup articles in an efficient manner.

Selecting a Newsreader

Whether your Fedora server is or is not set up as a news server, you can use a newsreader program to read newsgroup articles. The newsreader programs just require a connection to a news server. It does not matter whether the news server is on the same machine or is a remote news server on the other side of the world.

Several programs are available for Unix systems to connect to news servers to read and post articles in newsgroups. The following sections describe the newsreaders that are available with the Fedora Core Linux distribution.

The `slrn` News Client

The `slrn` program is a text-based newsreader program included with the Fedora Core distribution. It uses the `ncurses` package to paint text-based windows on the terminal screen. `slrn` can be used to both read and post articles to newsgroups on a configured news server. If you want to use the same newsreader on different platforms, `slrn` runs on Linux, Mac, OS2, BeOS, Windows, and VMX. It now provides true offline reading capabilities.

The `slrn` program is included in the `slrn` RPM package; you install it by using the `yum` or `rpm` command. After you have installed `slrn`, you need to create a local configuration file. Begin by setting an environmental variable:

```
$ export NNTSERVER=news.andbhudson.co.uk
```

Of course, you will use your own news servers' domain name.

Then create you local configuration file with

```
$ slrn -f .jnewsrc -- create
```

and launch `slrn`. The configuration file, located at `/etc/slrn.rc`, is a well-commented file that is easy to modify and customize.

When `slrn` starts, it displays a list of the groups that are available on the news server. You select the group you want to read articles from, and then select the individual articles. Figure 8.15 shows a `slrn` screen example.

The Pan News Client

Pan is a graphical newsreader client that works with GNOME and is the default newsreader for Fedora. If you have the GNOME libraries installed (and they usually are installed by default), you can also use Pan with the K Desktop Environment (KDE). Pan has the capability to download and display all the newsgroups and display posted news articles. You can launch it by using the GNOME or KDE desktop panel or from the command line of an X terminal window with the command pan &. Pan supports combining multipart messages and the yenc encoding/decoding protocol. Figure 8.16 shows a sample Pan display. Unlike the `slrn` program, Pan does not require a systemwide default or user-defined NNTPSERVER environment variable to define the news server address, but you do need to configure Pan.

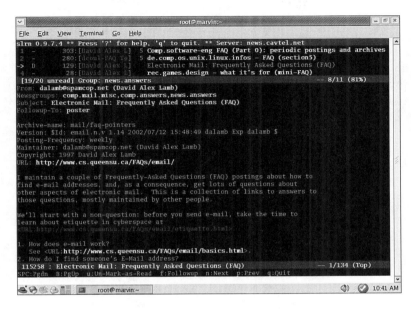

FIGURE 8.15   A `slrn` article display example showing a posted message about a FAQ for Internet mail.

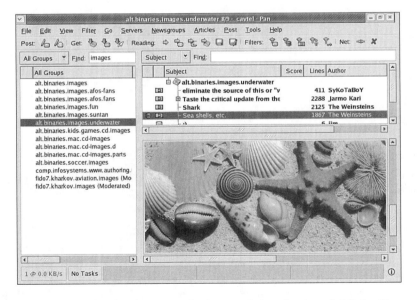

FIGURE 8.16   The Pan graphical newsreader is one of the nicest available for Linux, shown here displaying an image attached to a news article.

The first time you run Pan, a configuration wizard appears and prompts you for your name, the SMTP server name, the NNTP server name, and the name you want to use to identify the connection (in the example shown in Figure 8.17, we use Cavtel). After the wizard is finished, you will be prompted to download a list of the newsgroups the server provides; this may take a while. If you need to change the news server or add an additional server, you can access the Preferences item under the Edit menu to bring up the list of servers. Then, you highlight the appropriate one and click Edit to change it or just click the New button to add a new news server.

FIGURE 8.17   The Pan news server configuration window.

The KNode News Client

The KNode program is part of the kdenetwork RPM package—the KDE network package included in Fedora Core. KNode is usually installed by default if you select the KDE windows manager option in the Fedora Core installation.

The KNode program is an excellent graphical program (similar to MS Outlook Express) that allows you to connect to news servers (either a local or remote server) and select newsgroups where you can read and post articles. Before you can begin, though, you must configure the address of your news server in KNode. You do this from the Settings menu item on the main KNode window; select the Configure KNode item, and the KNode configuration window appears. Under the Accounts item, select the News item. A list of configured news servers appears in the window. To add a new news server, click the New button. Figure 8.18 shows the KNode New Account window, where you can enter the new news server information.

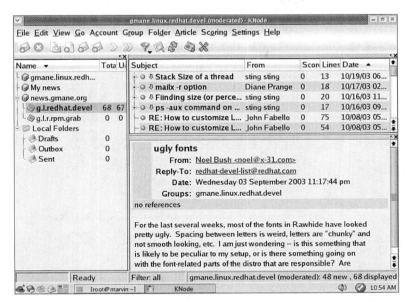

FIGURE 8.18   The KNode newsreader; setup is quick and easy. It's a great newsreader for text-only newsgroups.

The Mozilla News Client

The Mozilla web browser supports graphical Usenet news reading as well as web browsing. Having numerous news reading clients installed on a Fedora Core system offers users a wealth of choice and opportunities for developing favorites. In some cases, however, it can complicate the administrator's task of tracking and fixing client security liabilities. Using Mozilla can help simplify this task by offering an all-in-one client that provides web browsing, email, file transfer, and news reading capabilities. For these reasons, you might choose to use Mozilla as a browser, email client, and news client. Mozilla is the default browser for Fedora Core.

To begin news reading with Mozilla, you launch Mozilla and select Window, Mail and Newsgroups; the window shown in Figure 8.19 appears. The menu Edit, Mail & Newsgroups Account Settings is where you configure Mozilla for your news and mail server settings. Many people prefer to use Mozilla for all their web browsing, mail, news, and IRC.

To add accounts, under Edit, Mail & Newsgroups Account Settings, click the Add Account button and select either a mail or news account to add. The Account Settings dialog is shown in Figure 8.20.

When you finish entering this information, click OK, and you arrive at the newsreader window. Click the news server name in the left pane and then select Subscribe to Newsgroups in the right pane to begin downloading a list of newsgroups from your news server. At any time, you can update the list of newsgroups by clicking the Refresh button in that window.

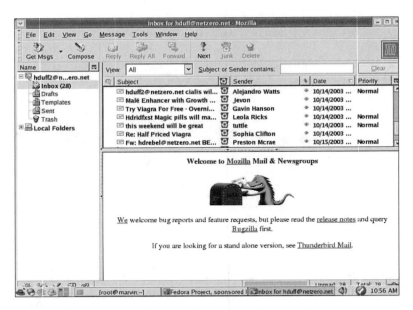

FIGURE 8.19   Mozilla is a handy, all-around integrated Internet client.

FIGURE 8.20   Here is where your configuration information is accessed. Note that we had to deliberately deselect the Compose Messages in HTML Format option, fixing a poorly chosen default.

The Thunderbird News Client

Along with Firefox, the Thunderbird mail and news client is a direct descendant of the Mozilla suite. Designed to be lightweight and with a clean interface, Thunderbird does many of the things that the Mozilla News client can do but is a separate application from Firefox.

To add a new account to Thunderbird, click Tools, Account Settings and select Add Account. Select the news account and follow the prompts giving Thunderbird all the information it needs.

When you have finished providing Thunderbird with all the relevant information, click OK, and you arrive at Thunderbird's default view. Along the left pane you will see the new news server account. Click it and then select Manage Newsgroup Subscriptions.

Collaborating with TWiki

Although Usenet is a useful interactive and collaboration tool, in some cases a web-based tool is better suited to your needs. TWiki (http://TWiki.org/) is a web-based interactive collaboration tool that can also be used as a bulletin board, knowledge base, bug tracker, and software archive.

> **TIP**
>
> You can examine the TWiki Success Stories on the company's home page for any encouragement you need to explore TWiki. You can also explore this Linux-related public TWiki site (http://TWiki.org/cgi-bin/view/Wikilearn/WebHome/).

TWiki is not available from Fedora, and you must download it from the TWiki website after completing a brief registration. You then receive email instructions explaining how to download a .zip file from the site. (You use unzip to extract the files.) The program is licensed under the GPL.

You might want to first read the installation instructions located at http://TWiki.org/cgi-bin/view/TWiki/TWikiDocumentation. The documentation has been improved over the past year and now includes directions for installing TWiki as the non-root user. Many details are provided on file ownership and file permissions. There is also an automatic installer—the O'Wiki Installer—referenced at http://TWiki.org/cgi-bin/view/Codev/TWikiUnixInstaller. This might be a good approach to use if you are skilled at Apache configuration, but the install script does not set the appropriate file ownership and permissions for Fedora as mentioned later.

Here is a short list of advice for moving smoothly through the installation process on a Fedora system (this list assumes that you are performing an installation as the root user and are reading the TWiki installation instructions from the TWiki website):

- You need to create the directory /home/httpd/twiki; unzip TWiki into this directory.
- The installation instructions mention the file /etc/httpd/httpd.conf. For Fedora, this file is found at /etc/httpd/conf/httpd.conf. You simply copy and paste the entries shown in the example supplied by the downloaded instructions.
- The path to Perl for Fedora is /usr/bin/perl.

- Fedora Core runs CGI scripts as the user apache, not the user nobody, as assumed in the default TWiki installation. You can browse to http://localhost/twiki/bin/testenv and read the warnings that are displayed onscreen. This is a special script run on your local machine to help you diagnose any problems with your installation. The messages should be specific to your installation, and any warning should be accompanied by a suggestion about how to fix the problem.

The TWiki installation directions suggest setting permissions and changing ownership. For Fedora, the permissions are set correctly, but the ownerships are wrong. To change the ownerships, implement the following steps (after each step, you should reload the http://localhost/twiki/bin/testenv page to check your progress):

1. Change the group ownership of everything to apache, but change the group owner-ship of /httpd/twiki/templates back to root:

```
# chgrp -r apache /home/httpd
# chgrp -r root /home/httpd/twiki/templates
```

2. Remember to edit /home/httpd/twiki/lib/TWiki.cfg to reflect your own domain name instead of http://your.domain.com.

3. Change the ownership of the RCS repository files to the user apache:

```
# cd /home/httpd/twiki/data
# perl -pi -e 's/nobody:/apache:/' */*,v
```

After you complete the installation, you should have a "virgin" TWiki installation that you can view at http://localhost/twiki/bin/view. As with any application, you need to further configure this file so that it suits your needs. The TWiki documentation explains the many configuration options and processes available to you. This documentation is included in the TWiki installation you just completed.

Internet Relay Chat

As documented in RC 2812 and RFC 2813, the IRC protocol is used for text conferencing. Like mail and news, IRC uses a client/server model. Although it is rare for an individual to establish an IRC server, it can be done. Most people use public IRC servers and access them with IRC clients.

Fedora Core provides a number of graphical IRC clients, including X-Chat, licq-kde, and Mozilla-chat, but there is no default chat client for Fedora Core. Fedora Core Linux also provides the console clients epic and licq for those who eschew X. If you don't already have a favorite, you should try them all.

> **CAUTION**
>
> You should never use an IRC client while you are the root user. It is better to create a special user just for IRC because of potential security problems. To use X-Chat in this manner, you open a terminal window, use su to change to your IRC user, and start the xchat client.

X-Chat is a popular IRC client, and it is the client that is used in this chapter's example. The HTML documents for X-Chat are available in /usr/share/docs/xchat. It is a good idea to read them before you begin because they include an introduction to and cover some of the basics of IRC. To launch the X-Chat client, select the IRC Client item from the Internet menu found under the Extras menu, or you can launch it from the command line, like this:

```
$ xchat &
```

The X-Chat application allows you to assign yourself up to three nicknames. You can also specify your real name and your username. Because many people choose not to use their real names in IRC chat, you are free to enter any names you desire in any of the spaces provided. You can select multiple nicknames; you might be banned from an IRC channel under one name, and you could then rejoin using another. If this seems slightly juvenile to you, you are beginning to get an idea of the type of behavior on many IRC channels.

When you open the main X-Chat screen, a list of IRC servers appears, as shown in Figure 8.21. After you choose a server by double-clicking it, you can view a list of channels available on that server by choosing Window, List Window. The X-Chat Channel List window appears. In that window, you can choose to join channels featuring topics that interest you. To join a channel, you double-click it.

FIGURE 8.21   The main X-Chat screen presents a list of available public servers from which to select.

The Wild Side of IRC

Do not be surprised at the number of lewd topics and the use of crude language on public IRC servers. For a humorous look at the topic of IRC cursing, see http://www.irc.org/fun_docs/ nocuss.html. This site also offers some tips for maintaining IRC etiquette, which is essential if you do not want to be the object of any of that profanity! Here are some of the most important IRC etiquette rules:

- Do not use colored text, all-capitalized text, blinking text, or "bells" (beeps caused by sending ^G to a terminal).
- Show respect for others.
- Ignore people who act inappropriately.

After you have selected a channel, you can join in the conversation, which appears as onscreen text. The messages scroll down the screen as new messages appear.

TIP

You can establish your own IRC server even though Fedora does not provide one. Setting up a server is not a task for anyone who is not well versed in Linux or IRC.

A popular server is IRCd, which you can obtain from ftp://ftp.irc.org/irc/server/. Before you download IRCd, you should look at the README file to determine what files you need to download and read the information at http://www.irchelp.org/irchelp/ircd/.

Internet Messaging with GAIM

IM has been popularized by America Online (AOL) as a way for AOL users to chat directly with each other rather than speak in chat rooms. As long as the IM clients for everyone involved in the conversation are running, they alert you to any incoming messages. The clients also announce to the server that you are active and listening for messages, so your friends can be made aware via *buddy lists* that you are available to chat with them.

You can use IM in place of IRC for interoffice collaboration. Fedora provides the GAIM IM client, for your use. To use them, you need to be communicating with a group of "buddies" who are active IM users as well.

GAIM is a GNOME (GTK-based) IM client that supports a wide range of protocols such as TOC, AIN/ICQ, Yahoo!, IRC, Jabber, Napster, Zephyr, and Gadu-Gadu. GAIM is a feature-rich message client, and it has support for plug-ins that extend the functionality of the application.

NOTE

GAIM supports Jabber, an open XML-based IM protocol that can be used to set up a corporate IM server. Jabber is not supplied with Fedora, but you can obtain additional information about it from the Jabber home page, at http://www.jabber.com/. You can obtain the Jabber server, Jabberd, from http://jabberd.jabberstudio.org/. If you want to use GAIM locally for collaboration, Jabber would be an excellent choice for a private local server.

Videoconferencing with GnomeMeeting

GnomeMeeting is an Internet videoconferencing application that provides two-way voice and pictures over the Internet by using the H.323 protocol for IP telephony (also known as Voice over IP [VoIP]). It is an application similar to Microsoft NetMeeting and is provided with Fedora Core as the default videoconferencing client.

Before you can take full advantage of the phone and videoconferencing capabilities of GnomeMeeting, you must configure a full-duplex–capable sound card and video device (see Chapter 10, "Multimedia Applications") as well as a camera.

GnomeMeeting is found in the Internet menu as Videoconferencing; you click on the icon to launch it. When you start the GnomeMeeting application for the first time, a configuration wizard (called a "druid") runs and you are greeted by the first of four configuration screens. You simply enter your name, email address, and location and select your connection type. The settings for your audio and video devices are automatically detected; you can view them by selecting the Preferences item from the Edit menu.

Figure 8.22 shows GnomeMeeting in action, looking at a list of users listed with the server who are currently online.

FIGURE 8.22   GnomeMeeting is surprisingly simple to use. A video source is not necessary; a static picture can be used as well.

When you have GnomeMeeting running, you must register (from within GnomeMeeting) with the server at http://ils.seconix.com/ to enable conferencing; GnomeMeeting does this automatically for you if you have told it to do so during the initial configuration. GnomeMeeting is capable of communicating with Microsoft NetMeeting; you should ask

NetMeeting users to register at http://ils.seconix.com/ so that you can see them because NetMeeting can see only other NetMeeting users.

You can find an informative FAQ at the GnomeMeeting home page at http://www.gnomemeeting.org/ that you should read in full before using GnomeMeeting. Also, an excellent article about VoIP is at http://freshmeat.net/articles/view/430/.

> **NOTE**
>
> If you frequently use VoIP applications such as GnomeMeeting, you will tire of repetitively typing in long IP addresses to make connections. To avoid this hassle, you can use a "gatekeeper"— similar in purpose to a DNS server—to translate names into IP addresses. OpenH323 Gatekeeper is one such popular gatekeeper application. It is not provided with Fedora, but you can obtain it from http://www.gnugk.org/.

> **Relevant Fedora Commands**
>
> You will use the following commands to manage electronic mail in Fedora Core Linux:
>
> `balsa`—A GNOME mail user agent for X.
>
> `biff`—A console-based mail notification utility.
>
> `evolution`—A comprehensive and capable Ximian GNOME mail PIM for X.
>
> `thunderbird`—A lightweight but powerful email application from Mozilla.
>
> `kmail`—A graphical mail user client for KDE and X
>
> `korn`—A `biff` applet for KDE and X.
>
> `mail`—A console-based mail user agent.
>
> `mutt`—A console-based mail user agent.

Reference

http://www.ximian.com—The home of Ximian Evolution, the standard email client for Fedora.

http://www.mozilla.org—The home page for Mozilla Firefox, Thunderbird, and the Mozilla Suite.

http://www.spreadfirefox.com/—The Firefox advocacy home page is useful for converting those Internet Explorer types.

# CHAPTER 9

Productivity Applications

Today's modern businesses are beginning to learn what experienced Linux users have known for years: There are great cost benefits when using Linux and free productivity software. Stepping off the software licensing and upgrade treadmill immediately contributes to the bottom line. This chapter provides some details about popular office productivity software included with and available for Fedora. Despite the nay-saying of a few tech industry pundits, Fedora can be used to support desktop operations in business settings. You can create efficient personal computing environments by carefully choosing and installing select productivity software packages. A wealth of usable, reliable, and free software is available for Fedora.

Productivity clients include free office suites and tools that can be used for creating documents and for scheduling, organizing, and calculating.

In this chapter, we examine the default office productivity applications that Fedora provides. You will see how easy it could be to migrate your employees to Linux desktops because similar applications are available that can make use of existing Microsoft-formatted data files. You will learn about alternative applications provided by Fedora, as well as some applications that you can install yourself. This chapter describes how to install, configure, and launch the applications; information on using the applications is provided only to make you aware of special issues associated with the use of a given application.

Office Suites for Fedora

Most office suites include productivity applications, such as word processors, spreadsheet programs, calculators, database programs, and drawing tools. A number of office suites have been created for use with Linux. Many of them are free, but a number of commercial products are available as well. Many of these office suites contain applications that mimic the functionality of popular Windows-based productivity applications, and many are designed to be compatible with the file formats of those applications.

Fedora has not developed its own office suite, but it has provided a default set of office applications that are designed to have wide appeal and provide useful functionality. The main components, OpenOffice.org, and the GNOME Office suite are included on this book's CD-ROMs and DVD. In the following sections, you will learn about the applications included in these productivity packages and get some tips for installing and configuring them. You will also learn about the KDE office suite (KOffice) that is included, as well as other office suites that are available for free download or by purchase for use with Linux.

Working with OpenOffice.org

If your primary need is to achieve compatibility with proprietary Microsoft file formats, the OpenOffice.org suite of applications is a front-runner for meeting that need. Microsoft file formats are the most commonly used in business settings, so compatibility with those formats is a primary concern of most businesses that are choosing office suites. OpenOffice.org contains applications that are largely compatible with Microsoft file formats, but they do not offer 100% compatibility. That level of compatibility is impossible for GNU Public License (GPL) applications because the file formats are proprietary and import/export filters must be reverse-engineered. There might be some esoteric formatting that does not import or export well—you can only judge that with a personal test on your own files—but all the basics work well.

Many home Fedora users prefer OpenOffice.org because its user interface is similar to (but not identical) that of the Microsoft applications they have used in the past. This interface familiarity is an important point if you are attempting to move from Microsoft Office in your home or office.

OpenOffice.org recognizes and opens nearly 120 file formats and types of documents, ranging from popular commercial office suites to various graphics file formats and is capable of exporting nearly 70 types of documents.

What Is in OpenOffice.org?

OpenOffice.org contains a number of productivity applications for use in creating text documents, preparing spreadsheets, organizing presentations, managing projects, and more. The following components of the OpenOffice.org package are included with Fedora:

- **Writer**—This word processing program enables you to compose, format, and organize text documents. If you are accustomed to using Microsoft Word, the functionality of OpenOffice.org Writer will be familiar to you. The presentation of these functions in the application menus is slightly different from Microsoft Word's, however, so you may have to hunt for familiar functions. Spell checking, a thesaurus, macros, styles, and a help facility are built in to Writer and work in a manner consistent with other word processors and applications.

- **Calc**—This spreadsheet program enables you to manipulate numbers in a spreadsheet format. Support for all but the most esoteric Microsoft Excel functions means that trading spreadsheets with Excel users should be successful. Calc offers some limited compatibility with Excel macros, but those macros will generally have to be rewritten. Calc also supports data exchange formats such as the Data Interchange Format and dBASE format.

- **Impress**—This presentation program is similar to Microsoft PowerPoint and enables you to create slide show presentations that include graphs, diagrams, and other graphics. Impress also works well with PowerPoint files. When it is opened, Impress starts with a wizard that steps you through the creation of a new presentation, lets you use an existing template (although none are provided) , or allows you to open an existing presentation.

- **Math**—This math formula editor enables you to write mathematical formulas with a number of math fonts and symbols for inclusion in a word processing document. Such symbols are highly specialized and not easily included in the basic functionality of a word processor. It is of interest primarily to math and science writers, but Math can be useful to anyone who needs to include a complex formula in their text.

- **Base**—This database was introduced with the OpenOffice.org 2.0 suite, released in early 2005. It provides a fully functional database application. When you open Base, you are asked to set up the database for use. The easy-to-use setup assistants take you through most of the hard work.

- **Draw**—This graphics application allows you to create images for inclusion in the documents produced with OpenOffice.org. It saves files only in OpenOffice.org format, but it can import most common image formats. It is not meant as a replacement for more general graphics applications, but it has enough features to meet most needs.

- **Dia**—This technical drawing editor from the GNOME Office suite enables you to create measured drawings, such as those used by architects and engineers. Its functionality is similar to that of Microsoft Visio.

- **Planner**—You can use this project management application for project planning, scheduling, and tracking; this application is similar to, but not compatible with, Microsoft Project. It is found in the Office menu as the Project Planner item.

A Brief History of OpenOffice.Org

The OpenOffice.org office suite has its roots in an application known as StarOffice. Originally developed by a German company, StarOffice was purchased by Sun Microsystems in the United States. One of the biggest complaints about the old StarOffice was that all the component applications were integrated under a StarOffice "desktop" that looked very much like a Microsoft Windows desktop, including a Start button and menus. This meant that in order to edit a simple document, unneeded applications had to be loaded, making the office suite slow to load, slow to run, and quite demanding on system resources.

After the purchase of StarOffice, Sun Microsystems released a large part of the StarOffice code under the GPL, and development began on what has become OpenOffice.org, which is freely available under the GPL. Sun continued development on StarOffice and released a commercial version as StarOffice 6.0. The significant differences between the free and commercial versions of the software are that StarOffice provides more fonts and more import/export file filters than OpenOffice.org (these filters cannot be provided in the GPL version because of licensing restrictions) and StarOffice provides its own relational database, Software AG's Adabas D database.

Installing and Configuring OpenOffice.org

Fedora provides an RPM package for OpenOffice.org. If you do not install the RPM package during your initial Fedora installation, you can install it later, using the Add/remove Applications tool or by using yum `install openoffice.org` from the command line.

TIP

OpenOffice.org is constantly improving its productivity applications. You can check the OpenOffice.org website (http://www.openoffice.org/) for the latest version. The website provides a link to download the source or a pre-compiled version of the most current working installation files. A more current version might offer file format support that you need. Should you need a Windows compatible version, you will also find it at the website.

The initial Fedora installation of OpenOffice.org is done on a systemwide basis, but no individual users are configured. To install local files and use OpenOffice.org, a user can simply click any OpenOffice.org icon on her desktop, and her files are installed by the installation wizard. This initial installation takes a little time, and OpenOffice.org unfortunately does not display a dialog about what is going on in the background. During the delay, some users might assume that the application has not started, but that is not the case.

Shown in Figure 9.1 are icons on the left of the top desktop panel that represent the different components of OpenOffice.org as well as other applications. From left to right, beginning with the Applications and Actions menus, the icons represent the Firefox web browser, Evolution email, OpenOffice.org Writer, OpenOffice.org Impress, and OpenOffice.org Calc. The icons displayed on your desktop might vary from those shown here. If you click the Applications icon, the main menu opens, and all the OpenOffice.org applications can be accessed from the Office menu.

FIGURE 9.1   The OpenOffice.org suite provided by Fedora Core is simple to configure and use. After you configure the address book, the application is ready to go to work.

As with many Linux applications, in OpenOffice.org you can be overwhelmed with configuration options. The dialog to configure those many options is well organized in the OpenOffice.org suite. From the Tools menu (which you open by selecting Tools from the menu bar in any OpenOffice.org application), you select Options to launch the Options dialog, as shown in Figure 9.2. All the settings for the entire suite of applications can be configured from this dialog, and each application provides access to this same dialog. For example, the default work path is set to your home directory, but you can change that default work path. To do so, select Tools, Options to open the dialog. Then click the Paths list item and click and edit the My Documents setting, as shown in Figure 9.2.

FIGURE 9.2   You can edit the OpenOffice.org path settings to change default locations of files and directories. This configuration dialog sets options for all the OpenOffice.org applications.

TIP

Two websites provide additional information on the functionality of OpenOffice.org:

http://lingucomponent.openoffice.org/download_dictionary.html—This site provides instructions and files for installing spelling and hyphenation dictionaries, which are not included with OpenOffice.org.

http://sourceforge.net/projects/ooextras/—This site provides templates, macros, and clip art, which are not provided with OpenOffice.org.

OpenOffice.org is a work in progress, but the current release is on a par with the Sun version of StarOffice 8.0. You can browse to the OpenOffice.org website to get documentation and answers to frequently asked questions and to offer feedback.

Working with GNOME Office

Rather than developing an integrated suite of applications from scratch, the GNOME project has brought together an offering of GTK-based applications from different developers to meet general office needs (see the following sidebar). Because Sun plans to integrate StarOffice/OpenOffice.org with GNOME, continued support and development for some of the GNOME Office components might be in doubt.

The GTK Widget Set

In order to make it easier to program GUI applications, small pieces of code are prewritten to describe some graphical functions of the graphical interface; these functions include drop-down lists, radio buttons, Save As dialogs, window buttons, and the like. Such functions are referred to as widgets, and the collection of widgets is referred to as a tool kit or a widget set. Rather than write the code for all these functions from scratch, programmers need only reference the widgets. This makes writing GUI applications easier. Whereas Windows and Mac programmers only have one set of widgets to work with, Unix and Linux programmers have many sets; unfortunately, these sets are incompatible with one another. The KDE desktop uses the QT widget set, Netscape uses the Motif widget set, and GNOME applications use the GTK widget set.

GTK is an acronym for Gimp Tool Kit. The GIMP (The GNU Image Manipulation Program) is a graphics application very similar to Adobe Photoshop. By using the GTK-based jargon, we save ourselves several hundred words of typing and help move along our discussion of GNOME Office. You might also see similar references to QT and Motif, as well as other widget sets, in these chapters.

Here are some of the primary components of the GNOME Office suite that are available in Fedora:

- **AbiWord**—This word processing program enables you to compose, format, and organize text documents and has some compatibility with the Microsoft Word file format. It uses plug-ins (programs that add functionality such as language translation) to enhance its functionality.

- **Gnumeric**—This spreadsheet program enables you to manipulate numbers in a spreadsheet format. Support for all but the most esoteric Microsoft Excel functions means that users should have little trouble trading spreadsheets with Excel users.

- **The GIMP**—This graphics application allows you to create images for general use. It can import and export all common graphic file formats. The GIMP is analogous to Adobe's Photoshop application and is described in Chapter 10, "Multimedia Applications."

- **Evolution**—Evolution is a mail client with an interface similar to Microsoft Outlook, providing email, scheduling, and calendaring. It is described in Chapter 8, "On The Internet: Surfing the Web, Writing Email, and Reading the News."

- **Balsa**—This lightweight mail client is in the mold of Microsoft Outlook Express. It is described in Chapter 8.

The loose association of applications known as GNOME Office includes several additional applications that duplicate the functionality of applications already provided by Fedora Core. Those extra GNOME applications are not included in a default installation of Fedora to eliminate redundancy. They are all available from the GNOME Office website, at http://www.gnome.org/projects/ooo/ and some are on the installation CDs.

Fedora provides the AbiWord editor as part of its Extras, shown in Figure 9.3. AbiWord can import XML, Microsoft Word, RTF, UTF8, plain text, WordPerfect, KWord, and a few other formats. AbiWord is notable for its use of plug-ins, or integrated helper applications, that extend its capabilities. These plug-ins add language translation, HTML editing, a thesaurus, a Linux command shell, and an online dictionary, among other functions and features. If you just need a lightweight but powerful word processing application, you should examine AbiWord.

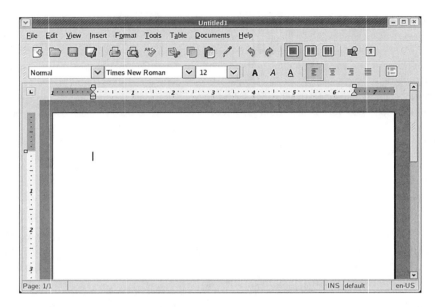

FIGURE 9.3   AbiWord is a word processing program for Fedora, GNOME, and X11. It handles some formats that OpenOffice.org cannot, but does not yet do well with MS Word formats.

The AbiWord application icon is found in the More Office Applications menu, under the Office menu (along with Gnumeric and the KOffice applications we will discuss later in this section) as the Word Processor item. Simply click on the icon to launch the application, or you can launch it from the command line, like this:

```
$ abiword &
```

If you are familiar with Microsoft Works, the AbiWord interface will be familiar to you because its designers used it as their model.

You can use the Gnumeric spreadsheet application to perform financial calculations and to graph data, as shown in Figure 9.4. It can import comma or tab-separated files, text, or files in the Gnumeric XML format, saving files only as XML or text. To launch Gnumeric from the menu, choose Office, More Office Applications, and then Gnumeric Spreadsheet. You can also launch the spreadsheet editor from the command line, like this:

```
$ gnumeric &
```

After you press Enter, the main Gnumeric window appears. You enter data in the spreadsheet by clicking a cell and then typing in the text box. To create a graph, you click and drag over the spreadsheet cells to highlight the desired data, and then you click the

Graph Wizard icon in Gnumeric's toolbar. Gnumeric's graphing component launches, and you are guided through a series of dialogs to create a graph. When you are finished, you can click and drag a blank area of your spreadsheet, and the graph appears.

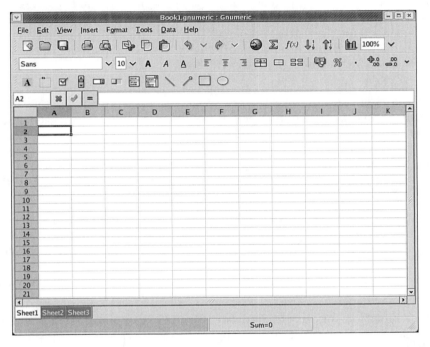

FIGURE 9.4   GNOME's Gnumeric is a capable financial data editor—here being used to track a 401K retirement account. OpenOffice.org also provides a spreadsheet application as does KOffice.

The Project Planner application is useful for tracking the progress of projects, much like its Windows counterpart Microsoft Project. When the main window is displayed, you can start a new project or import an existing project. The application provides three views: Resources, Gantt Chart, and Tasks.

NOTE

Some productivity applications fall into the category of "groupware"; these include shared calendars, files, notes, email, and the like. These applications are covered in detail in Chapter 8.

Working with KOffice

TheK Desktop Environment, known as KDE, is not the default desktop environment for Fedora. KDE comes with its own set of libraries, widgets, and a system of inter-application communication (drag-and-drop) that is incompatible with the default Gnome desktop environment. This does not mean that the KDE applications are not usable if you choose a GNOME desktop (or vice versa). Although KDE duplicates a lot of the functionality of the Gnome offerings, the KDE applications often present a unique approach to solving familiar problems and might be just what you are looking for.

The KDE office suite KOffice was developed to provide tight integration with the KDE desktop. Integration enables objects in one application to be inserted in other applications via drag-and-drop, and all the applications can communicate with each other, so a change in an object is instantly communicated to other applications. The application integration provided by KDE is a significant enhancement to productivity. (Some GNOME desktop applications share a similar communication facility with each other.) If you use the KDE desktop instead of the default GNOME desktop, you can enjoy the benefits of this integration, along with the Konqueror web and file browser.

The word processor for KOffice is KWord. KWord is a frames-based word processor, meaning that document pages can be formatted in framesets that hold text, graphics, and objects in enclosed areas. Framesets can be used to format text on a page that includes columnar text and images that the text needs to flow around, making KWord an excellent choice for creating documents other than standard business letters, such as newsletters and brochures.

KWord and other components of KOffice are still under development and lack all the polished features of OpenOffice.org and AbiWord, as well as the necessary Microsoft file format support. If Microsoft compatibility is unimportant to you and you and your associates use the KDE desktop environment rather than GNOME, KOffice is worth considering. The next version of KOffice will include the Kolab groupware applications referred to in Chapter 8; GNOME lacks similar groupware functionality at present.

You can access the KOffice components from the More Office Applications submenu under the Office menu. You can also access them from the KOffice shell, which can be launched from the command line, like this:

```
$ koshell &
```

After you press Enter, you see the main window of KOffice shell, as shown in Figure 9.5. On the left are icons representing all the KOffice applications available to you. Clicking on one starts a dialog to open an existing file or begin work in a new file.

You can click on icons on the left side of the main window to launch the KWord word processing client, the KSpread spreadsheet program, and other components. You can also launch individual clients from the command line without using the KOffice workspace. For example, to use KWord, enter the following:

```
$ kword &
```

FIGURE 9.5   KDE's KOffice provides a workspace office suite environment. Here is the Open File dialog.

KWord then asks you to select a document for your session. The KWord client, shown in Figure 9.6, offers sophisticated editing capabilities, including desktop publishing.

The KOffice KSpread client is a functional spreadsheet program that offers graphing capabilities. Like KWord, KSpread can also be launched from the command line. After you use a command like this, you are asked to choose a type of document (new or previous document):

```
$ kspread &
```

KSpread is still in development and (at the time of this writing) had difficulty importing the Gnumeric spreadsheet used in an earlier example in Gnumeric format. When developed, a strength of KSpread will be its ability to share data with other KOffice applications.

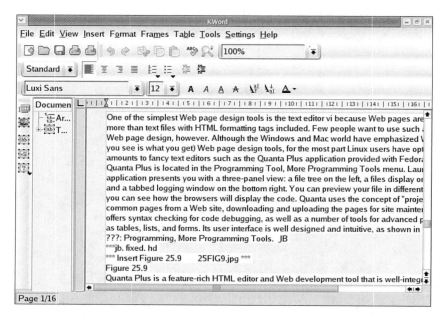

FIGURE 9.6 The KOffice KWord word processing component is a sophisticated frames-based WYSIWYG editor that is suitable for light desktop publishing, supporting several formats, including WordPerfect.

KDE includes other productivity clients in its collection of KOffice and related applications. These clients include an address book, time tracker, calculator, notepad, and scheduler. One popular client is KOrganizer, which provides daily, weekly, work week, and monthly views of tasks, to-do lists, and scheduled appointments with background alarms. A journal, or diary, function is also supported within it, and you can synchronize information with your Palm Pilot by using KPilot (discussed later in the section "GUI PDA Client Software"). You can launch this client from the KDE desktop panel's menu or from the command line, like this:

```
$ korganizer &
```

A typical KOrganizer window is shown in Figure 9.7.

Commercial Office Suites for Linux

Several commercial office suites are available for Fedora in addition to StarOffice, already mentioned. None of these commercial suites are provided with Fedora. Of note is Hancom Office. Using the same QT widget set found in the KDE desktop, Hancom Office scores well on Microsoft file format compatibility. The suite includes a word processor, a spreadsheet presentation tool, and a graphics application. Corel produced a version of its WordPerfect Office 2000 for Linux before it discontinued the release of any new Linux products. It still offers a support page, but the software is no longer available, nor is the excellent—but whiskered—WordPerfect8 for Linux.

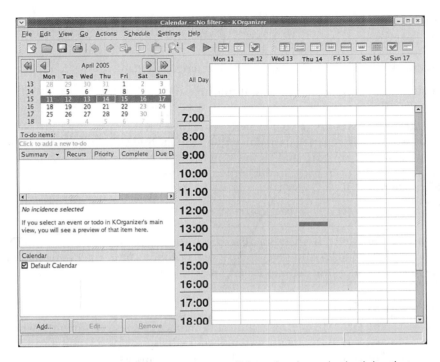

FIGURE 9.7   KDE's KOrganizer client supports editing of tasks and schedules that you can sync with your PDA. Shown here is the address book as well.

PDA Connectivity

Fedora provides programs and clients for use with Palm-type personal digital assistants (PDAs). You can use these programs to transfer information to and from a PDA, send and retrieve email, manage and sync your calendaring programs, and more.

Command-Line PDA Software for Fedora

The most popular PDA-related software suite is the collection of utilities included with the `pilot-link` package. . You can use this application from the command line to perform a variety of tasks with your Palm, Handspring, Handera, TRGPro, or Sony PDA, including the following:

- Extracting and uploading addresses
- Installing date book information
- Transferring text memos to and from the PDA
- Managing PDA to-do lists
- Managing user settings

- Sending and retrieving email documents

- Installing new PDA programs

- Backing up, syncing, and restoring the contents of a PDA

- Acquiring expense database account information.

You use `pilot-xfer` without. a GUI to perform many of these tasks; the suite of commands includes 31 separate programs. After configuring the software, determining the proper serial (or USB) port, and connecting the PDA to a desktop or notebook PC that is running Fedora, you can back up the contents of the PDA with the `pilot-xfer` command, like this:

```
$ pilot-xfer –p /dev/ttyS1 -b backupdirectory
```

This command automatically creates a directory according to the name following the `-b` option and then downloads and saves the contents of the PDA in the designated directory. The full set of pilot-link commands is explored in the `man` page for `pilot-link`.

GUI PDA Client Software

Fedora provides the GNOME `gpilot` graphical. interface to these commands, which is not included as an item in the menu system. Fedora does provide a Gnome panel applet that can be configured by starting it from the command line as

```
$ gpilotd-control-applet &
```

which leads you through a setup wizard that does little more than allow you to configure the port and sync the PDA.

We recommend either of the two following GUI applications, which provide more features.

Another graphical PDA client, shown in Figure 9.8, is the comprehensive J-Pilot application. It will manage, retrieve, install, back up, and sync any information for your Palm-related PDA. You can click on the Date Book, To-Do List, Address Book, and Memo Pad buttons to perform related tasks. You use the Sync and Backup buttons to update or preserve a copy of a PDA's data. Open this client by choosing J-Pilot from the Accessories, More Accessories menu.

NOTE

Fedora provides several mail clients for your use—with Evolution (a Microsoft Outlook work-alike) being provided as the default. All the mail clients were covered in detail in Chapter 8. Graphics applications, including The GIMP, are discussed in Chapter 10.

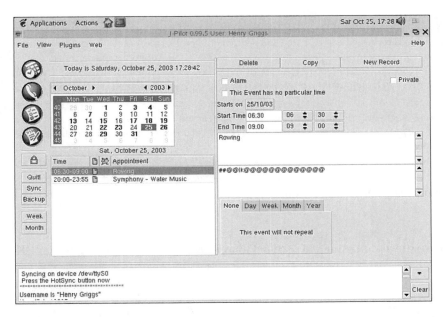

FIGURE 9.8   The J-Pilot PDA client supports PalmOS devices, shown here syncing with one.

Scanner Applications for Fedora

The use of a scanner provides a wealth of options to enhance productivity. You can manipulate scanned images in graphics applications such as The GIMP, Draw, and Kontour and then print, fax, or embed them in a word processing document. You can scan paper documents for archival purposes, or you can process them with optical character recognition (OCR) software to translate images into words that can be edited in a text editor or word processor. Fedora Core provides the Xsane and Kooka applications to assist you with scanning.

Scanner support is provided by Scanner Access Now Easy (SANE). If your scanner is supported, it is listed on the SANE support page at http://www.sane-project.org/.

> **NOTE**
>
> The development version of SANE supports scanners that are not supported in the regular version. If your scanner is supported only in the development version, you need to download and compile the CVS version of SANE. That is a complex operation suitable for advanced Linux users only, and it is beyond the scope of this chapter. For information on that process, see the CVS-RCS HOWTO Document for Linu (Source Code Control System) at http://www.tldp.org/HOWTO/_CVS-RCS-HOWTO.html.

The VueScan Scanner Application

If your scanner does not support SANE, you might consider the excellent VueScan scanner application. VueScan, available from http://www.hamrick.com/, supports more scanners than SANE. It is designed for photography professionals but is easy to use. A full list of VueScan's supported scanners can be found at http://www.hamrick.com/vuescan/vuescan.htm#supported.

You can download VueScan for evaluation. The program is unrestricted but places a watermark on any scan until you purchase a serial number (current cost: U.S. $60; U.S. $80 for upgrades past 12 months). The site offers some of the best documentation and support concerning scanner usage we have seen.

VueScan provides features in addition to scanning commands that allow you to crop, rotate, and color correct images. A detailed tutorial on using VueScan can be found at http://homepage.mac.com/onelucent/VS/vsm.html.

The Xsane application, as shown in Figure 9.9, is a graphical front end to SANE. It allows you to acquire and manipulate scanned images. It can be run as a plug-in from The GIMP. (The GIMP is discussed in more detail in Chapter 10.)

FIGURE 9.9   Upon starting, Xsane presents several related screens on your desktop: a control interface, a histogram, a preview screen, and an options dialog.

Kooka is a KDE application that provides similar functionality to Xsane, but it provides OCR capabilities as well as an image gallery function. Because Kooka is a KDE application, it can provide scanning services to other KDE applications (such as KOffice and KView) if they are written to use it. Kooka uses gocr (http://jocr.sourceforge.net/) as an application for character recognition, but support for Clara OCR (http://www.claraocr.org/) is planned for the future.

The configuration of scanner devices is covered in detail in Chapter 10.

Web Design Tools

One of the simplest web page design tools is the text editor vi because web pages are really nothing more than text files with HTML formatting tags included. Few people want to use such a simple tool for web page design, however. Although the Windows and Mac world have emphasized WYSIWYG (what you see is what you get) web page design tools, for the most part Linux users have opted for what amounts to fancy text editors such as the Quanta Plus application provided with Fedora Core.

Quanta Plus is located in the Programming Tool, More Programming Tools menu. Launching the application presents you with a three-panel view: a file tree on the left, a files display on the upper right, and a tabbed logging window on the bottom right. You can preview your file in different browsers so that you can see how the browsers will display the code. Quanta uses the concept of "projects" to manage common pages from a website, downloading and uploading the pages for site maintenance. Quanta offers syntax checking for code debugging, as well as a number of tools for advanced page elements such as tables, lists, and forms. Its user interface is well designed and intuitive, as shown in Figure 9.10.

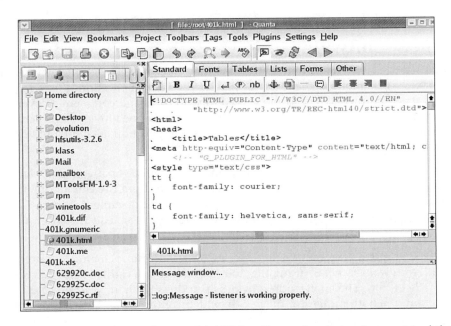

FIGURE 9.10   Quanta Plus is a feature-rich HTML editor and web development tool that is well-integrated into KDE.

The following are some of the many web development tools that are not provided with Fedora Core:

- **Bluefish**—Found at http://bluefish.openoffice.nl/, Bluefish is a GTK-based HTML editor similar in function to Quanta Plus. It supports anti-aliased fonts and UTF8 encoding, so it is compatible with Fedora Core Linux.

- **IBM WebSphere Studio Homepage Builder**—A commercial application, available at http://www-3.ibm.com/software/awdtools/hpbuilder/, is a WYSIWYG editor from Big Blue.

- **Coffee Cup**—A free commercial editor available at http://www.coffeecup.com/linux/, Coffee Cup provides a number of preconfigured templates and Java code examples.

OpenOffice.org (included with Fedora Core Linux) can also be used as an effective HTML editor. From the File:Autopilot menu in OpenOffice.org Writer, you select the Web Page Wizard to create HTML pages.

> **NOTE**
>
> Fedora includes a wealth of other tools you can use to create web pages or intranet content. See Chapter 19, "Apache Web Server Management," for information on how to set up, start, and run Apache, the web server for Fedora.

Fax Client Software

Fedora provides several clients that handle different aspects of composing, viewing, and sending faxes. Two graphical clients are available: The KFax application is used to view faxes, and the KdeprintFax application is used to send faxes and comment a cover sheet for them. The XSane application can also be used to fax scanned images. The actual sending and receiving of faxes is handled by the Efax application, a command line application (see Figure 9.11).

You can use any text editor to create the document you will be faxing. If you want something fancy, you can select the OpenOffice.org Fax Wizard from the File:Autopilot menu and it will step you through the creation of an elaborate fax document. You can also choose to simply select a plain-text document with KdeprintFax, edit the cover page, and send it.

You access KdeprintFax through the Accessories, More Accessories menu. To use it, you add the file you want to fax by using the Add File dialog. You can view the file by clicking the View File button. The application provides an address book for your use. Note the "Efax" field in the bottom right of the screen, which confirms that Efax will be used to actually send the fax.; KdeprintFax simply collects the information and uses Efax to actually do the sending.

FIGURE 9.11   KdeprintFax allows you to send faxes from your Linux desktop. It is a GUI front end to Efax, a command-line application.

NOTE

Using multiple fax applications might seems unnecessarily complicated to fax users who are used to sending and receiving their faxes on their own machine through a modem connected to that machine. The Linux (and Unix) approach is more complicated because it is network focused. A single computer can be set up to send and receive faxes for the entire network of hundreds of computers. None of the individual computers has a need for Efax or a fax modem; they just need a fax reader/viewer and a convenient way to send them a fax document to the central fax server.

The /usr/bin/fax script provides a simple command-line interface to Efax that allows you to send, receive, view, or print faxes without a GUI. You can view the commands available for faxing by entering **fax help** at the command line. You can use the **fax make** command to turn a text file into a fax file. Fedora Core also provides the efix command-line application to convert files formats from fax, text, bitmap, and grayscale formats, if necessary. All these applications can be called from scripts to automate the process of converting fax messages, so the end user never has to bother with it.

TIP

You can find more information on the workings of fax and Efax in the man pages and at the Efax home page at http://www.cce.com/efax/documentation/.

Efax is really designed for a single user; there are other fax applications mentioned here that can handle entire offices. If you have more that one fax user, Efax is likely to be too simple for your needs.

HylaFax is a fax management application that can utilize fax modems distributed around a network and service a large number of users because of its client/server architecture. A FAQ is maintained at the HylaFax website at http://www.hylafax.org/HylaFAQ/ index.html. RPM packages for Red Hat are available from the HylaFax FTP site at ftp:// ftp.hylafax.org/binary/linux/redhat/RPMS/i386/, as are a HOWTO, setup information, and a FAQ.

The traditional Linux way to handle faxes has been with `mgetty+sendfax`. The `mgetty+sendfax` application involves `mgetty`, a modem-aware `getty`. (`getty` is an application that interacts with a terminal, known as a "tty," from its Teletype heritage.). Unfortunately, the configuration of `mgetty+sendfax` is complex and beyond the scope of this chapter. You can find complete documentation for the installed version of `mgetty+sendfax` from the CD-ROMs that accompany this book, under the `/usr/share/ doc/mgetty-1.1.31` directory. The files also include a directory of instructions on how to set up voice mail by using the `vgetty` command (`vgetty` is included in the `mgetty+sendfax` package), which is discussed in more detail in Chapter 18, "Internet Connectivity." The documentation for `mgetty` can be found at http://alpha.greenie.net/ mgetty/, which includes a HOWTO and a FAQ and the `vgetty` documentation is at http://alpha.greenie.net/vgetty/.

Other Office and Productivity Tools Included with Fedora

Fedora is distributed with a number of other useful productivity tools. Under the Accessories menu choice, you can find a calculator, a web-based dictionary to access the MIT dictionary server (see Figure 9.12), and a lightweight text editor. You can also open the Graphics menu to access a PDF document viewer. (OpenOffice.org can create PDF documents for you.)

FIGURE 9.12   The web-enabled Dictionary, found under the Accessories menu, can also be conveniently called from a KDE panel applet.

Under the More Accessories menu, there are a multitude of useful small applications, including these:

- **KhexEdit**—An application that's an editor for hexadecimal code files

- **Kjots**—A note taking application

- **KTimer**—An application to time the execution time of other applications

The "More" menus also include items for other programming environments, graphics viewers, and dozens of other applications, including games. You should take some time to search through the "More" menus and experiment with some of the productivity (and non–productivity) tools you find there.

A Look at an Open-Source Office

Mark Davis, the director of Information Systems at Lake Taylor Transitional Care Hospital (LTH) in Norfolk, Virginia (http://www.laketaylor.org), has recently transitioned the facility from the use of SCO Unix to Linux and has enhanced office productivity.

Because LTH uses a thin-client topology and all applications are served from a central location to X terminals located throughout the facility, special attention to network bandwidth issues was necessary. Although it was recognized that commercial applications would be used when no viable open-source alternative was available, applications that emphasized nonproprietary, open standards were given the highest consideration. Using open-source applications allowed Davis to edit the source code and customize the applications for use at LTH, permitting the easy integration of applications into the overall system.

A common modification was to remove functionality that represented potential security compromises (such as access to command prompts or unneeded functions) and to reduce network bandwidth (such as removing animated icons and splash screens).

With the new Linux system in place, the LTH staff enjoys a work environment that presents all the productivity applications necessary in a modern business. The total cost of ownership (TCO) is significantly reduced, and the system is as stable as or more stable than when LTH used the commercial SCO Unix.

Among others, the open-source applications used at LTH are: Mozilla, Dillo, HylaFax, OpenOffice, Seyon, Sylpheed-claws, IceWM, The GIMP, Apache, Postfix, Gnumeric, Ghostscript, J-Pilot, Quanta, WebCal, Dia, gdict, and VNC. LTH uses a number of commercial applications, including Recital, Netscape, WordPerfect, FoxBASE, Merge, Applixware, Gerimenu, Context Codelink, Monette Ultracare, Kronos Time Keeper Central, and AIS Xess. Because one vendor (that could not be replaced) would not provide a Unix version of its application, a single computer running Microsoft Windows (modified to limit security problems) is now used along with VNC to run the application. (See Chapter 25, "Remote Access with SSH and Telnet," to learn more about VNC.)

Productivity Applications Written for Microsoft Windows

Microsoft Windows is fundamentally different from Linux yet you can install and run some Microsoft Windows applications in Linux by using an application named Wine. Wine enables you to use Microsoft Windows and DOS programs on Unix-based systems. Wine includes a program loader that you can use to execute a Windows binary, along with a .dll library that implements Windows command calls, translating them to the equivalent Unix and X11 command calls. Because of frequent updates to the Wine code base, Wine is not included with Fedora Core. Download a current version of Wine from http://www.winehq.org/.

To see if your favorite application is supported by Wine, you can look at the Wine application database at http://appdb.winehq.org/appbrowse.php.

As well, there are other solutions to enable use of Microsoft productivity applications, primarily Codeweaver's CrossoverOffice. If you are after a painless way of running not only Microsoft Office, but also Apple iTunes and other software, you should really pay Codeweaver's a visit. Crossover Office is one of the simplest programs you can use to get Windows-based programs to work. Check out www.codeweavers.com to download a trial version of the latest software. It requires registration, but don't worry—the guys at Codeweaver's are great and will not misuse your details. The big plus is that you get a whole month to play around with the trial before you decide whether to buy it. Of course, you might get to the end of the 30 days and realize that Linux does what you want it to do and you don't want to go back to Windows. Do not be afraid; take the plunge!

Relevant Fedora Commands

The following commands give you access to productivity applications, tools, and processes in Fedora:

fax—A script that acts as a front end to the Efax application

gimp—A graphical image editor for X

koshell—KDE's KOffice office suite shell

kspread—KDE's KSpread spreadsheet

oowriter—The word processor in OpenOffice.org

gnumeric—A spreadsheet editor for GNOME

planner—A project management client for GNOME

abiword—A graphical word processor for GNOME

pilot-xfer—A comprehensive command-line tool for PalmOS PDA users

---

Reference

http://www.openoffice.org—The home page for the OpenOffice.org office suite.

http://www.pclinuxonline.com/modules.php?name=News&file=article&sid=3199—A set of links to tips, tricks, and enhancements for OpenOffice.org. One link at the site is to a PDF file that explains how to use OpenOffice.org as a database front end for MySQL.

http://www.gnome.org/projects/ooo/—The GNOME Office site.

http://www.koffice.org—The home page for the KOffice suite.

http://en.hancom.com/—The home page for the Hancom Office suite.

http://www.sun.com/software/star/staroffice/6.0/—The StarOffice 6.0 site.

ftp://ftp.corel.com/pub/linux/Office2000/updates/installscript—A download site for an improved installer script that enables a less error-prone installation of Corel's WordPerfect Office 2000 suite under Red Hat Fedora Core Linux and other distributions.

http://bulldog.tzo.org/webcal/webcal.html—The home page of the excellent WebCal web-based calendar and scheduling program.

http://quanta.sourceforge.net—The Quanta Plus web development tool for KDE.

http://www.kronos.com/products/TKC.htm—A Linux-based timekeeping system that supports open standards and is more affordable that the competition.

http://www.hgriggs.com/palm.html—Tutorial and exposition on getting a Palm Pilot device working with Linux as well as several useful applications.

http://www.codeweavers.com—Website of the hugely popular CrossOverOffice from Codeweaver's that allows you to run Windows programs under Linux.

6

CHAPTER 10

Multimedia Applications

Movies, music, animation, live videoconferencing, and other multimedia functions have become essential capabilities for many home and business computing environments. Without question, multimedia has driven the growth of the Internet and the advances in computer hardware as much as the traditional services of mail, news, and other Internet-related services.

Fedora includes several different programs you can use to perform feats of magic that include graphics, video, and audio formats used on other, less capable operating systems.

This chapter provides an overview of some of the basic multimedia tools included with Fedora. You will see how to create your own CDs, watch TV, rip audio CDs into the open-source OGG audio format for playback, scan and manipulate graphics images, and perform other productive and enjoyable tasks.

> **NOTE**
>
> Continuing a move begun with the release of Red Hat 9, the Fedora Project maintains a philosophy that has been controversial with many longtime users. Because of concerns of potential liability arising from copyright and patent issues in the United States, Red Hat and the Fedora Project have voluntarily removed any functionality that could violate the intellectual property rights of others or subject Red Hat to any penalties. That does not mean individual users would be violating those same rights, so we have provided resources to the reader as to how some of that functionality can be restored; the choice is yours.

By installing and using apt or yum as described in Chapter 7, "Managing Software and System Resources," you can easily restore full multimedia functionality to Fedora.

Because Fedora uses UTF-8 language encoding, some non-Fedora applications will have display problems if they are not UTF-8 compliant. You can fix this by placing the following line in /etc/bashrc:

```
export LANG=en_US SUPPORTED="en_US"
LC_MESSAGES=C LC_ALL=C
```

Burning CDs and DVDs in Fedora Core Linux

Burning (or creating) your own CDs is a fundamental skill for Linux multimedia enthusiasts. The CD and DVD (digital versatile disc) have become the standard media for multimedia content because of the increasingly larger size of typical media files. (Individual songs, even in compressed audio format, usually require several megabytes of storage space.) You can use CDs to

- Record and store multimedia data, such as backup files, graphics images, and music, on a CD.

- Rip audio tracks from a music CD (ripping refers to extracting music tracks from a music CD) and compile your own music CD for your personal use.

Linux audio clients and programs support the creation and use of many different types of audio formats. Later sections of this chapter discuss sound formats, sound cards, music players, and much more. Because CD burning is used for many other purposes in Fedora, we cover the essentials of that process first in this chapter. To record multimedia data on a CD, you must have installed a drive with CD writing capabilities on your system. Chapter 4, "Post-Installation Configuration," explains the rudiments of getting a CD writer configured and working properly. The hardware should have been set up properly during the initial Fedora installation or configured properly when detected by Kudzu. To make certain that your CD writer is working, use cdrecord -scanbus to get the information for using the CD drive under SCSI (small computer system interface) emulation:

```
# cdrecord -scanbus
Cdrecord-Clone 2.01a32-dvd (i686-pc-linux-gnu) Copyright (C) 1995-2001 Jörg
Schilling
Linux sg driver version: 3.5.27
Using libscg version 'schily-0.8'
scsibus0:
        0,0,0     0) 'HL-DT-ST' 'RW/DVD GCC-4120B' '2.01' Removable CD-ROM
        0,1,0     1) *
        0,2,0     2) *
        0,3,0     3) *
        0,4,0     4) *
```

```
0,5,0    5) *
0,6,0    6) *
0,7,0    7) *
```

Here, we see that the CD writer (in this example, a CD writer/DVD reader) is present and is known by the system as device 0,0,0. The numbers represent the scsibus/target/lun (logical unit number) of the device. You will need to know this device number when you burn the CD, so write it down or remember it.

TIP

An IDE drive used to create CDs and DVDs needs to be emulated as a SCSI drive. Fedora does this automatically when you first install it, but in case you need to do it manually, here are the few items you need to configure (assuming that the CD drive is at /dev/hdd):

- Add the following line to the /etc/modules.conf file:

  probeall ide-scsi

- Edit the /boot/grub/menu.lst file to add the following to the kernel commands:

  hdd=ide-scsi

- Reboot your computer.

These items will load the appropriate modules and provide SCSI emulation. You would no longer refer to the CD drive as /dev/hdd, but as /dev/scd0. Check the symbolic for /dev/cdrom to make certain that it points to /dev/scd0.

However, because Fedora now uses the 2.6 kernel, SCSI emulation is not necessary, although it is useful information should something not work correctly.

Creating CDs from the Command Line

In Linux, creating a CD is a two-step process. You first create the iso9660-formatted image, and you then burn or write the image onto the CD. The iso9660, as you will learn in Chapter 37, "Managing the File System," is the default file system for CD-ROMs.

Use the mkisofs command to create the ISO image. The mkisofs command has many options (see the man page for a full listing), but use the following for quick burns:

```
$ mkisofs -r -v -J -l -o /tmp/our_special_cd.iso /source_directory
```

The options used in this example are as follows:

-r—Sets the permission of the files to more useful values. UID and GID (individual and group user ID requirements) are set to zero, all files are globally readable and searchable, and all files are set as executable (for Windows systems) .

-v—Displays verbose messages (rather than terse messages) so that you can see what is occurring during the process; these messages can help you resolve problems if they occur.

-J—Uses the Joliet extensions to ISO9660 so that our Windows-using buddies can more easily read the CD. The Joliet (for Windows), Rock Ridge (for Unix), and HSF (for Mac) extensions to the iso9660 standard are used to accommodate long filenames rather than the eight-character DOS filenames that the iso9660 standard supports.

-l—Allows 31 character filenames; DOS will not like it, but everyone else does.

-o—Defines the directory where the image will be written (that is, the output) and its name. The /tmp directory is convenient for this purpose, but the image could go anywhere you have write permissions.

/source_directory—Indicates the path to the source directory; that is, the directory containing the files we want to include. There are ways to append additional paths and exclude directories (and files) under the specified path—it is all explained in the man page if you need that level of complexity. Our simple solution is to construct a new directory tree and populate it with the files we want to copy, and then make the image using that directory as the source.

Many more options are available, including options to make the CD bootable.

After you have created the ISO image, you can write it to the CD with the cdrecord command:

```
$ cdrecord -eject -v speed=12 dev=0,0,0 /tmp/our_special_cd.iso
```

The options used in this example are as follows:

-eject—Ejects the CD when the write operation is finished.

-v—Displays verbose messages.

speed=—Sets the speed; the rate depends on the individual drive's capabilities. If the drive or the recordable medium is poor, you can use lower speeds to get a good burn.

dev=—Specifies the device number of the CD writer (the number I told you to write down earlier).

NOTE

You can also use the blank= option with the cdrecord command to erase CD-RW disks. The cdrecord command has fewer options than does mkisofs, but it offers the -multi option, which enables you to make multi-session CDs. A multi-session CD enables you to write a data track, quit, and then add more data to the CD later. A single session CD can be written to only once; any leftover CD capacity is wasted. Read about other options in the cdrecord man page.

Current capacity for CD media is 700MB of data or 80 minutes of music. (There are 800MB/90-minute CDs, but they are rare.) Some CDs can be overburned; that is, recorded to a capacity in excess of the standard. The cdrecord command is capable of overburning if your CD-RW drive supports it. You can learn more about overburning CDs at http://www.cdmediaworld.com/hardware/cdrom/cd_oversize.shtml/.

Creating DVDs from the Command Line

There are several competing formats for DVD (Digital Versatile Disk), and with prices rapidly falling, it is more likely that DVD-writing drives will become commonplace. The formats are as follows:

DVD+R

DVD-R

DVD+RW

DVD-RW

Differences in the + and – formats have mostly to do with how the data is modulated onto the DVD itself with the + format having an edge in buffer underrun recovery. How this is achieved impacts the playability of the newly created DVD on any DVD player. The DVD+ format also has some advantages in recording on scratched or dirty media. Most drives support the DVD+ format. As with any relatively new technology, your mileage may vary.

We will focus on the DVD+RW drives because most drives sold support that standard. The software supplied with Fedora Core has support for writing to DVD-R/W (re-writable) media as well. It will be useful for you to review the DVD+RW/+R/-R[W] for Linux HOWTO at http://fy.chalmers.se/~appro/linux/DVD+RW/ before attempting to use the dvd+rw-tools that you will need to install to enable DVD creation (also known as "mastering") as well as the cdrtools package. You can ignore the discussion in the HOWTO about kernel patches, compiling the tools.

> **TIP**
>
> The 4.7GB size of DVD media is measured as 1000 megabytes per gigabyte, instead of the more commonly used 1024 megabytes per gigabyte, so don't be surprised when the actual formatted capacity, about 4.4GB, is less than you anticipated. The dvd+rw-tools will not allow you to exceed the capacity of the disk.

You need to have the dvd+rw-tools package installed (as well as the cdrtools package). The dvd+rw-tools package contains the growisofs application (that acts as a front end to mkisofs) as well as the DVD formatting utility.

You can use DVD media to record data in two ways. The first way is much the same as that used to record CDs in a "session," and the second way is to record the data as a true file system using packet writing.

Session Writing

To record data in a session, you use a two-phase process:

- Format the disk with dvd+rw-format /dev/scd0 (only necessary the first time you use a disk).

- Write your data to the disk with growisofs -Z /dev/scd0 -R -J /your_files.

The `growisofs` command simply streams the data to the disk. For subsequent sessions, use the -M argument instead of -Z. The -Z argument is used only for the initial session recording; if you use the -Z argument on an already used disk, it simply erases the existing files.

CAUTION

Some DVDs come preformatted; formatting them again when you use them for the first time can make the DVD useless. Always be sure to carefully read the packaging your DVD comes in to ensure that you are not about to create another coaster!

TIP

Writing a first session of at least 1GB helps maintain compatibility of your recorded data with other optical drives. This is because the DVD players calibrate themselves by attempting to read from specific locations on the disk; you need data there for the drive to read it and calibrate itself.

Also, because of limitations to the ISO9660 file system in Linux, do not start new sessions of a multi-session DVD that would create a directory past the 4GB boundary. If you do so, it will cause the offsets used to point to the files to "wrap around" and point to the wrong files.

Packet Writing

Packet writing treats the DVD disk like a hard drive in which you create a file system (like ext3) and "format" the disk, and then write to it randomly like a conventional hard drive. This method, although commonly available on MS Windows-based computers, is still experimental for Linux and is not yet covered in detail here.

TIP

DVD+RW media are capable of only about 1,000 writes, so it is very useful to mount them with the `noatime` option to eliminate any writing to update their inodes or simply mount them read-only when it's not necessary to write to them.

It is possible to pipe data to the `growisofs` command:

```
# your_application | growisofs -Z /dev/scd0=/dev/fd/0
```

It's also possible to burn from an existing image (or file, named pipe, or device):

```
# growisofs -Z /dev/scd0=image
```

The `dvd+rw-tools` documentation, found at /usr/share/doc/dvd+rw-tools-*/ index.html, is required reading before your first use of the program. We also suggest that you experiment with DVD-RW (re-writable) media first, as DVD-R (record once) media is not yet as inexpensive as CD-R media.

Currently, there are no GUI clients for DVD creation, so all your DVD work will be done at the command line. We suggest that you practice with a re-writable DVD because of the expense of DVD disks.

Creating CDs with Fedora's Graphical Clients

Although adequate for quick burns and use in shell scripting, the command-line technique for burning CDs is an awkward choice for many people until they become proficient at it and learn all the arcane commands. Fortunately, Fedora provides several graphical clients.

With Fedora, enhanced functionality has been included in the default file browser Nautilus. Under the Places menu item is a CD Creator selection. To use it, insert a blank CD into your CD-RW drive. You will need to have two Nautilus windows open: one showing the files you want to save to the CD, and a second one that is opened to the burn:/// location. Click on the Write CD button as shown in Figure 10.1 to bring up the Write dialog; click on the Write files to CD button to actually create the CD. It is that simple, or it should be. There are some reports of difficulty with Nautilus being able to burn CDs.

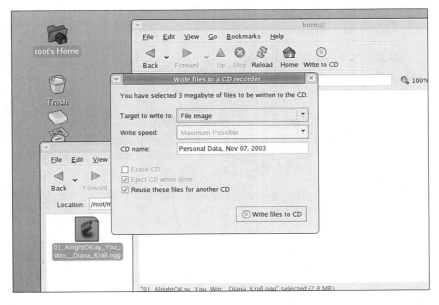

FIGURE 10.1   Creating a CD using the Nautilus browser is made easy with the drag-and-drop features it provides.

The following sections describe X-CD-Roast, as well as a number of other graphical clients for burning audio and data CDs.

> **TIP**
>
> An excellent Internet site for CD-related information is http://www.cdmediaworld.com/.
>
> Also, the Gracenote CDDB Music Recognition Service licenses a database service to software developers so that they can include additional functionality in their application by accessing the database and having their application display information about the music CD, including the artist and song title, the CD's track list, and so on. The database server at cddb.cddb.org will, when contacted by the appropriate software, identify the appropriate CD and send the information to be displayed locally. Many CD player applications provide this functionality. The service is interactive: If you have a CD that is not in the CDDB database, the website tells you how you can add the information to the database.

Each GUI application for burning CDs has different strengths and weaknesses. You should experiment with all the different graphical tools as well as try your hand at command-line burning and you will have a significantly richer multimedia experience with Fedora.

X-CD-Roast

X-CD-Roast, shown in Figure 10.2, is the default standalone CD creator provided with Fedora Core Linux. It can be found in the System Tools menu as the CD Writer menu item, or it can be launched from the command line, like this:

```
$ xcdroast &
```

When you first start it, X-CD-Roast is deceptively plain, giving little indication of the true power of this application. The very first time it is run, it begins with a dialog warning you to enter the Setup dialog, which will be the only button presented to you in the next screen other than Exit. The application autodetects your CD drive, but you must tell it which drive (if you have more than one) is the CD-RW drive and select the users who are allowed to use the application. The dialogs for setting this information are straightforward and easy to follow. Make certain that you choose a default directory for temporary image storage that offers enough room to store several images.

The main X-CD-Roast menu offers you the choice to duplicate or create CDs. The latter operation is shown in Figure 10.3.

Other Graphical CD Clients

Fedora provides the GNOME Grip client to advance ripping to a fine art. Working as both a player and a ripper, it uses cdparanoia and cdda2wav to rip music tracks and access Internet databases for retrieving track information from disc database servers. To launch Grip, click on its icon in the Sound & Video menu found in the More Sound & Video Applications menu. Use the options in the Grip dialog box tabs to choose, configure, and rip tracks. Also provided is the similar Sound Juicer application.

FIGURE 10.2 X-CD-Roast is the default CD creation client for Fedora, and it must be configured from the Setup dialog.

FIGURE 10.3 The X-CD-Roast Create CD window allows access to the full range of options, including creating music CDs.

Sound and Music

Linux has a reputation of lacking good support for sound and multimedia applications in general. Certainly, there is less sound card support than that found in Microsoft Windows. (However, Microsoft no longer supports the Microsoft Sound Card, but Linux users still enjoy support for it, no doubt just to annoy the folks in Redmond.) However, Unix has always had good multimedia support as David Taylor, Unix author and guru, points out:

> "The original graphics work for computers was done by Evans & Sutherland on Unix systems. The innovations at MIT's Media Lab were done on Unix workstations. In 1985, we at HP Labs were creating sophisticated multimedia immersive work environments on Unix workstations, so maybe Unix is more multimedia than suggested. Limitations in Linux support doesn't mean Unix had the same limitations. I think it was more a matter of logistics, with hundreds of sound cards and thousands of different possible PC configurations."

That last sentence sums it up quite well. Unix had a limited range of hardware to support; Linux has hundreds of sound cards. Sound card device driver support has been long lacking from manufacturers, and there is still no single standard for the sound subsystem in Linux.

In this section, you learn about sound cards, sound file formats, and the sound applications provided with Fedora Core Linux.

Sound Cards

Fedora supports a wide variety of sound hardware and software. Two models of sound card drivers compete for prominence in today's market:

- ALSA, the Advanced Linux Sound Architecture, which is entirely open source.

- OSS, the Open Sound System, which offers free and commercial drivers.

Fedora uses ALSA because ALSA is the sound architecture for the 2.6 series kernels.

ALSA supports a long list of sound cards. You can review the list at http://www. alsa-project.org/alsa-doc/. If your sound card is not supported, it might be supported in the commercial version of OSS. You can download a trial version of commercial software and test your sound card at http://www.opensound.com/download.cgi.

TIP

You can check the directory /usr/src/linux-2.6/ for documentation for each sound module. Be aware, however, that the documentation is likely to be out-of-date. Although even this out-of-date documentation can be useful, you should research any new sound card you might purchase to ascertain its level of support in Linux. Use http:/www.google.com/linux to search Linux websites and Linux newsgroups for mention of any sound card you are using.

Fedora detects most sound cards during the original installation. If you add or replace a sound card after the initial install, the Kudzu "new hardware configuration" utility will automatically detect and configure it at the next reboot. To configure the sound card at any other time, use the `system-config-soundcard` graphical tool. The graphical tool can be found under the System Settings menu as the Soundcard Detection menu item. For additional details about configuring your sound card, refer to Chapter 4.

Recording Sound

Fedora provides a number of tools that enable you to control volume, mix, and other sound recording functions. The Kmix sound mixer acts as a virtual mixing board, taking sound inputs from different sources, enabling you to adjust their individual volumes, mute them, and listen to them through your sound card.

If you need to control sound from command line, use the `alsamixer` command, which can be used to adjust balance or volume in text mode using the left and right cursor keys to select a channel and the up and down keys to adjust the volume.

```
$ alsamixer
```

The Sound Recorder, shown in Figure 10.4, along with the Volume Control application, is provided to enable you to play and record .wav files. You can use the SoX utility (covered later in this chapter) to convert the recorded sound if necessary.

FIGURE 10.4 Simplicity in design and layout make the Sound Recorder and Volume Control applications easy to use.

Sound Formats

A number of formats exist for storing sound recordings. Some of these formats are associated with specific technologies, and others are used strictly for proprietary reasons. Fedora supports several of the most popular sound formats, including

- **raw (.raw)**—More properly known as headerless format, audio files using this format contain an amorphous variety of specific settings and encodings. All other sound files contain a short section of code at the beginning—a header—that identifies the format type.

- **MP3 (.mp3)**—A popular, but commercially licensed, format for the digital encoding used by many Linux and Windows applications. MP3 is not supported by any software included with Fedora (which advises you to use the open source Ogg-Vorbis format instead).

- **WAV (.wav)**—The popular uncompressed Windows audio-visual sound format. It is often used as an intermediate file format when encoding audio.

- **Ogg-Vorbis (.ogg)**—Fedora preferred audio encoding format. You will enjoy better compression, audio playback, and freedom from lawsuits by using this open-source encoding format for your audio files.

> **NOTE**
>
> Because of patent and licensing issues, Fedora has removed support for the MPEG, MPEG2, and MPEG3 (MP3) file formats in Fedora Core Linux. Although we cannot offer any legal advice, it appears that individuals using MP3 software are okay; it's just that Fedora cannot distribute the code because it sells its distribution. It seems—at this point—perfectly all right for you to obtain an MP3-capable version of Xmms (for example), which is a Winamp clone that plays MPEG1/2/3 files. (You learn more about Xmms in the "Music Players" section later in this chapter.) You can get Xmms directly from http://www.xmms.org/ because that group has permission to distribute the MP3 code.
>
> Another alternative is to use the Ogg-Vorbis format; it is completely free of restrictions. A ripper for CD music is available from http://www.thekompany.com/projects/tkcoggripper/ and an MP3-to-Ogg converter is available from http://faceprint.com/code/. Or, you could download and install the non-crippled versions of multimedia applications from FreshRPMs at http://www.freshrpms.net/.

Fedora includes software (such as the sox command used to convert between sound formats) so that you can more easily listen to audio files provided in a wide variety of formats, such as AU (from NeXT and Sun), AIFF (from Apple and SGI), IFF (originally from Commodore's Amiga, RA (from Real Audio), and VOC (from Creative Labs).

TIP

To learn more about the technical details of audio formats, read Chris Bagwell's Audio Format FAQ at http://www.cnpbagwell.com/audio.html.

Fedora also offers utilities for converting sound files from one format to another. Conversion utilities come in handy when you want to use a sound in a format not accepted by your current application of choice. A repository of conversion utilities resides at http://ibiblio.org/pub/linux/apps/sound/convert/!INDEX.html and includes MP3 and music CD–oriented utilities not found in Fedora. You will have to know how to compile and install from source, however. If you see something useful, have a look at http://www.rpmfind.net/ to locate a binary RPM if you don't feel up to the task.

Fedora does provide sox, a self-described sound translator that will convert music between the AIFF, AU, VAR, DAT, OGG, and WAV formats, among others. It also can be used to change many other parameters of the sound files.

Timidity is a MIDI to WAV converter and player. If you are interested in MIDI and musical instruments, Timidity is a handy application; it handles karaoke files as well, displaying the words to accompany your efforts at singing.

Music Players

Fedora provides music players. One of the most popular is Xmms, a Winamp clone, which in the full version can play not only music, but MPEG1/2/3 video as well. Xmms supports a number of plug-ins that can add dancing, lighted oscilloscope-like displays, redirect its output to other devices, support unusual file formats, sync animations to the music, and otherwise increase its geek appeal exponentially. You can find Xmms as the Media Player item in the Sound & Video menu.

The default music player is Rhythmbox, which is designed to play music files from playlists and Internet radio stations much like Xmms. It is found in the Sound & Video menu as the Music Player menu item.

Kmid, found in the More Sound & Video Applications submenu, is a karaoke and MIDI mapper; it supports external synthesizers. MIDI mappers enable you to map MIDI channels to the synthesizer instruments you want them to control. If you enjoy karaoke, Kmid will also enable you to change the tempo of songs without changing the pitch, and permits the organization of your songs into collections with a selectable play order.

Gnome-CD is the CD Player menu item found in the Sound & Video menu. As the default CD player application, it provides a basic GUI interface for playing CDs in your CD-ROM drive.

Other music and sound-related applications can be found in the Sound & Video menu, and, of course, you are free to install your own selection of applications as well. You might have a problem adding them to the menu, however, so we provide the following tip to enable menu editing in Fedora.

10

> **TIP**
>
> Menu editing is available in the GNOME/metacity desktop provided as the default Fedora Core desktop, but it is inexplicably disabled. To enable it, workingas root perform the following steps:
>
> ```
> # cd /etc/gnome-vfs-2.0/modules
> # mv default-modules.conf default-modules.conf.without-menu-editing
> # cp default-modules.conf.with-menu-editing  default-modules.conf
> ```
>
> Upon restarting GNOME, you can edit the menu by right-clicking on the menu item or by using the URL applications:/// in Nautilus.

Streaming Audio

Streaming audio is for playing games, listening to Internet radio, and other online audio content. Streaming audio is designed to produce an uninterrupted sound output, but it requires the system to perform a content "juggling act." Essentially, the system's audio buffer is continually filled with audio information, which is fed to the buffer through the system's Internet connection. Because of server and connection capabilities, the rate of input might vary. Because audio is used at a constant rate, the trick to managing streaming audio is to always keep the buffer full, although you might not be able to fill it at a constant rate.

Streaming audio is handled in Fedora Core Linux in the .m3u format. The MPEG formats are also used for streaming audio. Although Xmms supports streaming audio, another popular application is the Real Player, available from http://www.real.com/linux/. An excellent resource for music and sound in Linux is http://linux-sound.org/. The Network Audio section of that website contains an extensive list of streaming audio applications.

The Icecast application, not provided with Fedora Core Linux, is a popular streaming audio server. You can use Icecast to serve your MP3 music collection over your home LAN. You can learn more about Icecast at http://www.icecast.org/. A nice tutorial on Icecast is available at http://www.linuxnetmag.com/en/issue4/m4icecast1.html.

> **TIP**
>
> You can also read Chapter 17, "Network Connectivity," to see how to use the Network File System (NFS) to mount a remote directory of music files over your network.

Viewing TV and Video

You can use Fedora tools and applications to view movies and other video presentations on your PC. This section presents some TV and motion picture video software tools included with the Fedora Core Linux distribution you received with this book.

In addition to the information you read here, you should review Chapter 3, "Installing Fedora," and Chapter 6, "The X Window System," to learn more about installing and configuring your video graphics card.

TV and Video Hardware

To watch TV and video content on your PC, you must install a supported TV card or have a video/TV combo card installed. A complete list of TV and video cards supported by Fedora Core Linux is at http://www.exploits.org/v4l/. See the Gatos Project at http://gatos.sourceforge.net for information on ATI video combo cards.

Freely available Linux support for TV display from video cards that have a TV-out jack is poor. That support must come from the X11 driver, not from a video device that Video4Linux supports with a device driver. Some of the combo TV-tuner/video display cards have support, including the Matrox Marvel, the Matrox Rainbow Runner G-Series, and the RivaTV cards. Many other combo cards lack support, although an independent developer might have hacked something together to support his own card. Your best course of action is to perform a thorough Internet search using Google.

Many of the TV-only PCI cards are supported. In Linux, however, they are supported by the video chipset they use, and not by the name some manufacturer has slapped on a generic board (the same board is typically sold by different manufacturers under different names). The most common chipset is the Brooktree Bt*** series of chips; they are supported by the bttv device driver.

If you have a supported card in your computer, it should be detected during installation. If you add it later, the Kudzu hardware detection utility should detect it and configure it. You can always configure it by hand.

To determine what chipset your card has, use the lspci command to list the PCI device information, find the TV card listing, and look for the chipset that the card uses. For example, the lspci output for our computer shows

```
# lspci
00:00.0 Host bridge: Advanced Micro Devices [AMD] AMD-760 [IGD4-1P]
➥System Controller (rev 13)
00:01.0 PCI bridge: Advanced Micro Devices [AMD] AMD-760 [IGD4-1P]
➥ AGP Bridge
00:07.0 ISA bridge: VIA Technologies, Inc. VT82C686 [Apollo Super South]
➥ (rev 40)
00:07.1 IDE interface: VIA Technologies, Inc. VT82C586B PIPC Bus Master IDE
➥ (rev 06)
00:07.2 USB Controller: VIA Technologies, Inc. USB (rev 1a)
00:07.3 USB Controller: VIA Technologies, Inc. USB (rev 1a)
00:07.4 SMBus: VIA Technologies, Inc. VT82C686 [Apollo Super ACPI]
➥ (rev 40)
00:09.0 Multimedia audio controller: Ensoniq 5880 AudioPCI (rev 02)
00:0b.0 Multimedia video controller: Brooktree Corporation Bt878 Video Capture
➥ (rev 02)
```

```
00:0b.1 Multimedia controller: Brooktree Corporation Bt878 Audio Capture
➥ (rev 02)
00:0d.0 Ethernet controller: Realtek Semiconductor Co., Ltd. RTL-8029(AS)
00:0f.0 FireWire (IEEE 1394): Texas Instruments TSB12LV23 IEEE-1394
➥ Controller
00:11.0 Network controller: Standard Microsystems Corp [SMC]
➥ SMC2602W EZConnect
01:05.0 VGA compatible controller: nVidia Corporation NV15 [GeForce2 Ti]
➥ (rev a4)
```

Here, the lines listing the multimedia video controller and multimedia controller say that our TV board uses a Brooktree Bt878 Video Capture chip and a Brooktree Bt878 Audio Capture chip. This card uses the Bt878 chipset. Your results will be different, depending on what card and chipset your computer has. This card happened to be an ATI All-in-Wonder VE (also known as ATI TV-Wonder). (The VE means Value Edition; hence, there is no TV-out connector and no radio chip on the card; what a value!) The name of the chipset tells us that the card uses the bttv driver.

The documentation for the bt878 kernel sound module used for recording sound is found in /usr/src/linux-2.6/Documentation/sound/ossbtaudio. The documentation for the video driver is found under /usr/src/linux-2.6/Documentation/video4linux/bttv.

In the documentation directory, we find a file named CARDLIST, and in that file is the following entry, among others:

```
card=64 - ATI TV-Wonder VE
```

There are 105 cards listed as well as 41 radio cards, including:

```
card=0 -  *** UNKNOWN/GENERIC ***
```

which is what we would have used had we not known the manufacturer's name for our card.

The file named Modules.conf, located in the same directory, gives us the following example of information to place in our /etc/modules.conf file:

```
# i2c
alias char-major-89    i2c-dev
options i2c-core       i2c_debug=1
options i2c-algo-bit   bit_test=1

# bttv
alias char-major-81    videodev
alias char-major-81-0  bttv
options bttv           card=2 radio=1
options tuner          debug=1
```

All we need do is enter this information into `/etc/modules.conf` and change the value for `card=2` to `card=64` to match our hardware. We can delete the reference to the radio card (`radio=2`) because we do not have one and leave the other values alone. Then we must execute

```
# depmod -a
```

to rebuild the modules dependency list so that all our modules are loaded automatically. When finished, all we need do is execute

```
# modprobe bttv
```

and our TV card should be fully functional. All the correct modules will be automatically loaded every time we reboot. Fedora is clever enough to detect and configure a supported TV card that is present during installation.

> **TIP**
>
> Other useful documentation can be found in `/usr/src/linux-2.6/Documentation/`
> `_video4linux`. After you have identified a driver for a device, it will not hurt to look at the source code for it because so little formal documentation exists for many drivers; much of it is in the source code comments.

The development of support for TV cards in Linux has coalesced under the Video4Linux project. The Video4Linux software provides support for video capture, radio, and Teletext devices in Fedora Core.

Video Formats

Fedora recognizes a variety of video formats. The formats created by the MPEG group, Apple, and Microsoft dominate, however. At the heart of video formats are the *codecs*—the encoders and decoders of the video and audio information. These codecs are typically proprietary, but free codecs do exist. Here is a list of the most common video formats and their associated file extensions:

- `.mpeg`—The MPEG video format; also known as `.mpg`
- `.qt`—The QuickTime video format from Apple
- `.mov`—Another QuickTime video format
- `.avi`—The Windows audio visual format

> **TIP**
>
> An RPM that provides a DivX codec for Linux can be found at http://www.freshrpms.net/. DivX is a patented MPEG-4 video codec that is the most widely used codec of its type. It allows for compression of MPEG-2 video by a factor of 8. See http://www.divx.com/ for more information.

> The GetCodecs application is a Python script with a GUI interface that will download, install, and configure your Fedora system with multimedia codecs not provided by Fedora, such as MP3, DivX and DVD codecs. The script can be obtained from http://sourceforge.net/projects/ getcodecs/.

If you need to convert video from one format to another, you use encoder applications called *grabbers*. These applications take raw video data from a video device such as a camera or TV card, and convert it to one of the standard MPEG formats or to a still image format, such as JPEG or GIF. Fedora does not supply any encoder applications (other than ppmtompeg which encodes MPEG-1 video), but you can find them at http://www.freshrpms.net/ or another online source (see the "Reference" section at the end of this chapter).

Viewing Video in Linux

Because of the patent and licensing issues mentioned earlier, the ability to play video files has been removed from Fedora. This functionality can be restored if you install the full version of the applications described in this section from FreshRPMs at http://www.freshrpms.net/. There, you will find multimedia applications such as Ogle, Xine, AlsaPlayer, Gstreamer, Grip, Mplayer, VCDImager, VideoLAN-client, Xmms, and Zapping.

You can use Linux software to watch TV, save individual images (take snapshots) from a televised broadcast, save a series of snapshots to build animation sequences, or capture video, audio, or both. The following sections describe some of the ways in which you can put Linux multimedia software to work for you.

The noatun viewer is provided with Fedora to use as an embedded viewer in the Konqueror browser. noatun is set up as the default association for the video file formats it plays. Open a video file in Konqueror or Nautilus, and the video will be shown in the viewer if it is supported. The viewer provides basic Start, Stop, and Fast-Forward VCR-type functions.

You can watch MPEG and DVD video with Xine. Xine is a versatile and popular media player that is not included with Fedora. Xine is used to watch AVI, QuickTime, OGG, and MP3 files (the latter disabled in Fedora Core).

Macromedia Flash

The Macromedia Flash plug-in for the Mozilla browser is a commercial multimedia application that isn't provided with Fedora, but many people find it useful. Macromedia Flash enables you to view Flash content at websites that support it. The Mozilla plug-in can be obtained from http://macromedia.mplug.org/. Both .rpm and .tar.gz files are provided.

Download the file for Linux and, if using the .tar.gz file, uncompress it with

```
# tar zxvf install_flash_player_6_linux.tar.gz
```

This produces a directory named `flashplayer_installer`. Install the plug-in with

```
# ./install_flash_player_6_linux/flashplayer-installer
```

and follow the screen prompts to install it and make it available to the Mozilla browser.

Having trouble with the Macromedia Flash plugin for Mozilla? Just manually copy the files `flashplayer.xpt` and `libflashplayer.so` to `/usr/lib/mozilla/plugins`. An `.rpm` file for Flash that should install without problems is available from http://macromedia.mplug.org/.

Another interesting video viewer application is MPlayer (not provided by Fedora), a movie player for Linux. MPlayer can use Win32 codecs and it supports a wider range of video formats than Xine, including DivX and some RealMedia files. MPlayer also uses some special display drivers that support Matrox, 3Dfx, and Radeon cards and can make use of some hardware MPEG decoder boards for better MPEG decoding. Look for Fedora packages at http://www.MPlayerHQ.hu/homepage/; a Win32 codec package is also available, as well as other codec packages and a GUI interface.

Viewing Television with Linux

You can configure a number of video input sources to feed television images to your computer. You can use any supported TV device as described previously to connect cable TV, an Xbox, Sega Dreamcast, PS/2, or even an external television antenna to your computer and view the images on your video display.

Fedora provides the `tvtime` TV viewing application to enable you to watch *South Park* without leaving your computer.

> **NOTE**
>
> The kdetv application (formerly known as QtVision) is steadily growing in terms of both popularity and features and is worth a look. It can be downloaded from http://www.kdetv.org/.

Start `tvtime` from the command line:

```
$ tvtime &
```

Right-clicking on it will toggle the display of the Options menu. Adjust the settings to suit your hardware.

```
$ scantv
```

The `tvtime` configuration file details are contained in the man page for `tvtime`.

An alternative TV-viewing application available at FreshRPMs.Net is Zapping, a GNOME viewer that supports Vide4Linux, Vide4Linux2, and Xvideo and is extensible in functionality through plug-ins. The home page is http://zapping.sourceforge.net/.

10

Personal Video Recorders

The best reason to attach a television antenna to your computer, however, is to use the video card and the computer as a personal video recorder.

The commercial personal video recorder, TiVo, uses Linux running on a PowerPC processor to record television programming with a variety of customizations. TiVo has a clever interface and wonderful features, including a record/playback buffer, programmed recording and pause, slow motion, and reverse effects. Fedora does not provide any of the many applications that attempt to mimic the TiVo functionality on a desktop PC running Linux. However, several such applications, including DVR, The Linux TV Project, and OpenPVR, are listed at http://www.exploits.org/v4l/. These projects are in development and do not provide .rpm files, so you will need to know how to download from CVS and compile your own binaries. For something a little easier, check out MythTV at http://www.mythtv.org/; a Fedora .rpm file should be available from FreshRPMs.Net.

Linux, TiVo, and PVRs

Some TiVo users say that using this Linux-based device has changed their lives. Indeed, the convenience of using a personal video recorder (PVR) can make life a lot easier for inveterate channel surfers. Although PVR applications are not included with Fedora Core Linux, open-source developers are working on newer and better versions of easy-to-install and easy-to-use PVR software for Linux. For more information about TiVo, which requires a monthly charge and a phone line (or broadband connection with a newer TiVo2), browse to http://www.tivo.com/. Unrepentant Linux hardware hackers aiming to disembowel or upgrade a TiVo can browse to http://www.9thtee.com/tivoupgrades.htm or read the TiVo Hack FAQ at http://www.tivofaq.com/hack/faq.html. A PVR makes viewing television a lot more fun!

A number of Linux sites are devoted to PVR software development. Browse to the DVR project page at http://dvr.sourceforge.net/.

DVD and Video Players

You can now easily play DVDs using Fedora as long as you install the appropriate software. (Fedora doesn't provide any.) Browse to http://www.videolan.org/, and then download, build, and install the vlc client.

You will need a CPU of at least 450MHz and a working sound card to use a DVD player. The default Fedora kernel supports the DVD CD-ROM file system. As mentioned earlier, Xine and MPlayer do a great job of playing DVD files.

NOTE

The VideoLAN HOWTO found at http://videolan.org/ discusses the construction of a network for streaming video. Although you might not want to do that, a great deal of useful information about the software and hardware involved in the enterprise can be generalized for use elsewhere, so it is worth a look. The site also contains a link to a HOWTO about cross-compiling on Linux to produce a Windows binary.

Using Still Cameras with Fedora Core Linux

Most still cameras used in connection with Fedora fall into one of two categories: webcams (small, low-resolution cameras connected to the computer's interface) or hand-held digital cameras that record image data on disks or memory cards for downloading and viewing on a PC. Fedora supports both types. Other types of cameras, such as surveillance cameras that connect directly to a network via wire or wireless connections, need no special support (other than a network connection and viewing software) to be used with a Linux computer.

Fedora supports hundreds of different digital cameras, from early parallel-port (CPiA chipset-based) cameras to today's newer USB-based cameras. You can even use Intel's QX3 USB microscope with Fedora. If you prefer a standalone network-based webcam, explore the capabilities of Linux-based cameras from Axis (at http://www.axis.com/products/video/camera/productguide.htm). The following sections describe some of the more commonly used still camera hardware and software supported by Fedora.

Webcams

Webcams are typically small, low-resolution cameras connected to your computer via a parallel port or USB port. The camera can act in two modes: streaming (for a series of images of a moving object) and grabbing (for a single still image) . The most common uses for webcams include videoconferencing and web voyeurism. The latter is not as lurid as it might sound, although some webcam sites are notorious for their pornographic content. Webcams can be used to send almost-live images to an online correspondent; many people include screen grabs of themselves at their computer workstations just because they can.

> ### Coffee Pot Cam
>
> One of the more interesting uses of a webcam was the legendary "Internet coffee pot" cam (started in 1991, but turned off on August 22, 2001—a day that will live in infamy). A webcam was trained on a coffee maker, and the sysadmin could see whether fresh coffee was available without leaving his cubicle. Some webcams take grabs of intersections in various cities. You will likely find some similar worthwhile use for your webcam.

You can use any of the video applications that can access a video4linux device to view webcam or still camera images in Fedora. You also can use GnomeMeeting (discussed in Chapter 8, "On the Internet: Surfing the Web, Writing Email, and Reading the News") as a viewer for your webcam.

Not all webcams are supported in Linux and the drivers are based on the chipset used, rather than the model or manufacturer. Some of the files in /usr/src/linux-2.6/ Documentation/usb contain information about USB webcams and drivers supported by Fedora Core Linux, including:

10

- `ibmcam.txt`

- `ov511.txt`

- `phillips.txt`

- `se401.txt`

- `stv0608.txt`

Documentation on parallel port cameras, including the CQ cam (`Cqcam.txt`) and CPiA camera (`README.cpia`), is found in `/usr/src/linux-2.6/Documentation/video4linux/` if you have installed the kernel documentation on your computer.

> **TIP**
>
> Unfortunately, most of the documentation provided for webcams is abysmal, and it is difficult to associate the webcam you just purchased with a related driver. If you are interested in a particular USB webcam, but are not sure whether it is supported by Linux, browse to http://www.qbik.ch/usb/devices/showdevcat.php?id=9.

Handheld Digital Cameras

Handheld cameras have been a hit with consumers since they were introduced, especially digital cameras. You can capture your photographs to a disk or memory card, view and print photos on your computer screen, and store and edit the images on a CD. Unfortunately, the instant gratification afforded by digital cameras is often overcome with frustration when users try to link those devices to a Linux workstation. Most software provided by digital camera manufacturers is designed for use with Microsoft's operating systems.

Fedora does provide some useful camera applications, but you must use them with a supported device. Most USB cameras, when connected to a computer as SCSI storage devices, are detected during the initial Fedora Core Linux or after reboot. To see whether your camera is detected when connected, look at the output of

`# cat /proc/bus/usb/devices`

or

`# lsusb`

Your camera will likely be detected as `/dev/sda1`, the first SCSI data device.

Fedora also includes the GNOME `gtkam` digital camera support client, listed as Digital Camera Tool in the Graphics menu selection. When you first launch `gtkam` by clicking on the menu icon, you are asked to select the type of camera and connection port it uses. The Select Camera drop-down menu demonstrates that an extensive list of digital cameras is supported.

After saving your configuration, you can download selected images from your camera or download an index of thumbnail views. You can retrieve images in batches from your camera by clicking on individual thumbnail images. The images will then be displayed in individual windows, which you can access in full view by choosing them from gtkam's main window with your mouse.

The GIMP graphics program, included with Fedora Core Linux, also can import images from cameras. You can use The GIMP's extensive options to edit images by adjusting the contrast, brightness, and color. You also can use The GIMP to edit out content and alter images with special effects.

Using Scanners in Fedora Core Linux

You can also use many types of image scanners with The GIMP. In the recent past, the most capable scanners required a SCSI port. Today, however, many scanners work through a USB port. You must have scanner-support enabled for Linux (usually through a loaded kernel module, scanner.o) before using a scanner with The GIMP.

Although some scanners can work via the command line, you will enjoy more productive scanning sessions using a graphical interface because image manipulation tasks, such as previewing and cropping, can save time before actually scanning an image. Most scanners in use with Linux use the Scanner Access Now Easy (SANE) package that supports and enables graphical scanning sessions.

SANE consists of two software components. A low-level driver enables the hardware support and is specific to each scanner. Next, a graphical scanner interface X client known as xsane is used as a plug-in, or ancillary program (or script) that adds features to The GIMP.

> **NOTE**
>
> Although xsane is commonly used as a GIMP plug-in, it can also be used as a standalone program. Another useful program is Joerg Schulenburg's gocr client, used for optical character recognition (OCR). Although not a standalone application, it is included in the Kooka scanning application. This program works best with 300 dots per inch (dpi) scans in several different graphics formats. OCR is a resource-intensive task and can require hundreds of megabytes of disk storage!

A list of currently supported scanners can be found at http://www.sane-project.org/sane-supported-devices.html. Unfortunately, if your scanner doesn't appear on the list, you should not expect it to work with the SANE software. There is also a list on that same page for drivers not yet included, but you must be able to compile the application from source to use them.

Supported USB scanners are automatically detected and the appropriate driver is loaded automatically. The USB devices "tell" the USB system several pieces of information when they are connected—the most important of which is the vendor ID and the device ID. This identification is used to look up the device in a table and load the appropriate driver.

10

Many scanners are supported in Linux. If yours is not, it still might be possible to use it. The Kooka and Xsane scanner applications are included with Fedora Core Linux, and are covered in detail in Chapter 9, "Productivity Applications." They can be found in the Graphics menu as the Scanning and Scan & OCR Program menu items.

USB Scanner Success Is Elusive

Because a failure is sometimes more educational than a success, for previous editions of this book, we attempted to configure a USB scanner that wasn't supported: the Canon N650U. With the release of the version of SANE included with Fedora, the scanner is now supported, and it is automatically detected!

However, here are the manual steps we used for detecting and configuring this scanner in Linux when it did not work properly:

First, connect the scanner. For this USB scanner, look at the output of:

```
# cat /proc/bus/usb/devices/
```

(We have truncated the output here to show only the scanner. You can also use the `lsusb` command.)

```
T:  Bus=01 Lev=01 Prnt=01 Port=00 Cnt=01 Dev#=  2 Spd=12  MxCh=
D:  Ver= 1.00 Cls=00(>ifc ) Sub=00 Prot=00 MxPS= 8 #Cfgs=  1
P:  Vendor=04a9 ProdID=2206 Rev= 1.00
S:  Manufacturer=Canon
S:  Product=CanoScan
C:* #Ifs= 1 Cfg#= 1 Atr=80 MxPwr=500mA
I:  If#= 0 Alt= 0 #EPs= 3 Cls=ff(vend.) Sub=00 Prot=ff Driver=(none)
E:  Ad=81(I) Atr=03(Int.) MxPS=   1 Ivl=16ms
E:  Ad=82(I) Atr=02(Bulk) MxPS=  64 Ivl=0ms
E:  Ad=03(O) Atr=02(Bulk) MxPS=  64 Ivl=0ms
```

`Driver=(none)` at the end of the seventh line tells us that the device was not found in the lookup table. Because we now have the "magic" vendor ID and device ID, we can attempt to load the driver manually with

```
# /sbin/modprobe scanner vendor=0x04a9 product=0x2206
```

Now the output of the `catlsusb` command from before tells us that the scanner device driver is associated with our scanner:

```
I:  If#= 0 Alt= 0 #EPs= 3 Cls=ff(vend.) Sub=00 Prot=ff Driver=usbscanner
```

and the Kooka and Xsane applications now recognize the scanner.

Graphics Manipulation

If you have ever wished you could change a photograph slightly—red eyes returned to their normal color, dark areas lightened, funny Uncle Bert removed—and longed for a way to accomplish that task, you have been granted your wish. Now, you can accomplish all of these tasks with the tools provided with Fedora (and a digital image from a digital camera or from a scanner).

This section of the chapter discusses The GIMP, a powerful graphics manipulation tool. (You learned about the other graphics tools that Fedora provides in Chapter 9.) In this section of the chapter, you also learn about graphic file formats supported by Fedora, as well as some tools you can use to convert them if the application you want to use requires a different format.

The GNU Image Manipulation Program

One of the best graphics clients is The GIMP. The GIMP is a free, GPLed image editor with sophisticated capabilities that can import and export more than 30 different graphics formats, including files created with Adobe Photoshop. It is often compared with Photoshop, and The GIMP represents one of the GNU Projects' first significant successes. You will see many images in Linux that have been prepared with The GIMP.

The GIMP can be started by clicking a desktop panel menu item or by using the command line, like this:

```
$ gimp &
```

You will see an installation dialog box when The GIMP is started for the first time, and then a series of dialog boxes that display information regarding the creation and contents of a local GIMP directory. This directory can contain personal settings, preferences, external application resource files, temporary files, and symbolic links to external software tools used by the editor.

What Does Photoshop Have That Isn't in The GIMP?

Although The GIMP is powerful, it does lack two features Adobe Photoshop offers that are important to some graphics professionals.

The first of these is the ability to generate color separations for commercial press printers (CMYK for the cyan, magenta, yellow, key, or black colors). The GIMP uses RGB (red, green, and blue) which is great for video display, not so great for printing presses. The second feature GIMP lacks is the use of Pantone colors (a patented color specification) to ensure accurate color matching.

If these features are unimportant to you, The GIMP is an excellent tool. If you must use Adobe Photoshop, the current version of Codeweaver's Crossover Office will run Photoshop in Linux.

These deficiencies might not last long. A CMYK plugin is in the works, and the Pantone issues will likely be addressed in the near future as well.

After the initial configuration has finished, The GIMP's main windows and toolboxes appear. The GIMP's main window contains tools used for selection, drawing, movement, view enlargement or reduction, airbrushing, painting, smudging, copying, filling, and color selection. Depending on the version installed on your system, the toolbox can host more than 25 different tools.

10

The toolbox's File, Xtns, and Help menus are used for file operations (including the ability to send the current image by electronic mail), image acquisition or manipulation, and documentation, respectively. If you right-click an open image window, you'll see the wealth of The GIMP's menus, as shown in Figure 10.5.

FIGURE 10.5   Right-click on an image window to access The GIMP's cascading menus.

Working with Graphics Formats

Image file formats are developed to serve a specific technical purpose (lossless compression, for example, where the file size is reduced without sacrificing image quality) or to meet a need for a proprietary format for competitive reasons. Many file formats are covered by one or more patents. For example, the GIF format has fallen into disfavor with the open-source crowd because the patent holder has only recently decided to begin enforcing his patent rights.

If you want to view or manipulate an image, you need to identify the file format in order to choose the right tool for working with the image. The file's extension is your first indicator of the file's format. The graphics image formats supported by the applications included with Red Hat include

- .bmp—Bitmapped graphics, commonly used in Microsoft Windows

- .cgm—Computer graphics metafile

- .g3—CCITT Group 3 FAX image

- .gif—CompuServe Graphics Interchange Format

- .ico—Microsoft Windows icon image

- .jpg—Joint Photographic Experts Group

- .mng—Multiple-image Network Graphic image

- .pbm—Portable Bitmap File Format

- .pcx—IBM Paintbrush

- .pgm—Portable Graymap File Format

- .png—Portable Network Graphics

- .pnm—Portable Anymap

- .ppm—Portable Pixmap File Format

- .rgb—Raw red, green, and blue samples

- .rs—Sun raster image

- .svg—Scalable Vector Graphics

- .tif—Tagged Image File Format

- .xbm—X bitmap image

- .xpm—X Pixmap image, commonly used for Linux icons images

An extensive list of image file extensions can be found in the man page for ImageMagick, an excellent application included with Fedora, which you learn more about in upcoming sections of this chapter.

> **TIP**
>
> Fedora includes dozens of graphics conversion programs, and there are few, if any, graphics file formats that cannot be manipulated when using Linux. These commands can be used in Perl scripts, shell scripts, or command-line pipes to support many types of complex format conversion and image manipulation tasks. See the manual pages for the ppm, pbm, pnm, and pgm families of commands. Also see the man page for the convert command, which is part of a suite of extremely capable programs included with the ImageMagick suite.

Often, a file you want to manipulate in some way is in a format that cannot be used by either your graphics application or the final application. The solution is to convert the image file—sometimes through several formats. The convert utility from ImageMagick is useful as are the netpbm family of utilities. If it is not already installed, ImageMagick can be installed with the Add Remove Software GUI found in the System Settings menu; the netpbm tools are always installed by default.

The convert utility converts between image formats recognized by ImageMagick. Color depth and size also can be manipulated during the conversion process. You can use ImageMagick to append images, surround them with borders, labels, rotate and shade

10

them, and perform other manipulations well-suited to scripting. Commands associated with ImageMagick include `display`, `animate`, `identify`, and `import`. The application supports more than 130 different image formats—(all listed in the `man` page for ImageMagick).

Fun with ImageMagick's `identify`

You can use ImageMagick's `identify` command to identify details about image files. The welcoming splash image used for the GRUB bootloader is located in `/boot/grub` and is a gzipped `.xpm` image. If you run `identify` on the image, you'll discover that it's a 640x480 xpm image with 16-bit color depth. That's all you need to know to construct a replacement image of your own. Using The GIMP or another graphics tool, crop or resize your chosen image to 640x480 and change the color depth to 16 bits. Save the image as `splash.xpm` and then `gzip` the resulting file. Replace the original Red Hat file, and you now have a custom boot image. The use of `identify` helped you duplicate the parameters of the original image to comply with the requirements of GRUB.

The `identify` command is useful to identify unknown image files and to determine whether they're corrupt.

The `netpbm` tools are installed by default because they compose the underpinnings of graphics format manipulation. The `man` page for each image format lists related conversion utilities; the number of those utilities gives you some indication of the way that format is used and shows how one is built on another:

- The `man` page for `ppm`, the portable pixmap file format, lists 47 conversion utilities related to ppm. This makes sense because ppm, or portable pixmap, is considered the lowest common denominator for color image files. Because of this, it is often used as an intermediate format.

- The `man` page for `pgm`, the portable graymap file format, lists 22 conversion utilities. This makes sense because pgm is the lowest common denominator for grayscale image files.

- The `man` page for `pnm`, the portable anymap file format, lists 31 conversion utilities related to it. However, there is no format associated with PNM because it operates in concert with ppm, pgm, and pbm.

- An examination of the `man` page for `pbm`, the portable bitmap file format, reveals no conversion utilities. It's a monochrome format and serves as the foundation of the other related formats.

Capturing Screen Images

You can use graphics manipulation tools to capture images that are displayed on your computer screen. Although this technique was used for the production of this book, it has broader uses; there is truth to the cliché that a picture is worth a thousand words. Sometimes, it is easier to show an example than it is to describe it.

A captured screen image (also called a screen grab or a screenshot) can be used to illustrate an error in the display of an application (a font problem, for example) or an error dialog that is too complex to copy down by hand. You might just want to share an image of your beautifully crafted custom desktop configuration with your friends or illustrate your written documents. In this section, you learn how to capture screen images for these and other purposes.

When using the GNOME desktop, you can take advantage of the built-in screenshot mechanism (gnome-panel-screenshot). Access this tool by pressing the Print Screen key. (Alt+Print Screen takes a screenshot of only the window that has "focus" on a desktop.) Captured images are saved in .png format.

You also can capture screen images from a remote computer using tools supported by Red Hat Linux. The import command (one of ImageMagick's commands) was used to take the screenshots for this book, for example, using a local computer and a remote computer on a LAN.

First, we ran $ **xhost +** on the remote computer to allow another computer access to the X server on the remote machine; the command to take the screenshot is run on our local machine like this:

```
$ import -window root -display 192.168.2.4:0 12fig07.jpg
```

This utility made a difficult task easy because the publisher required the screenshots be done from an 800 × 600 screen (too small to comfortably work in) to accommodate their printing and production equipment.

We could also have used the classic Unix tool xwd to take screenshots. The command would have looked similar to that of import:

```
$ xwd -root -display 192.168.2.4:0 -out 12fig07.jpg
```

Although the screenshots could have been taken with The GIMP and saved in the appropriate format, we would have had to be running The GIMP on that computer and navigating the menus every time we captured an image—the remote option of import was very convenient.

We did not use Ksnapshot (not included in the menus, but available from the command line) because it does not support the .pcx format the publisher used to use and it must be run locally, but it can take screenshots easily and is our preferred tool for use on a single machine.

Enabling Java

Some multimedia content relies on Sun's Java and Java web browser plug-ins.

Getting the Java plug-in to work correctly with the Mozilla browser can be a challenge. Download the latest version (versions prior to 1.4.1 will not work) from http://java.sun.com/. (You can find a modified .rpm version of the files at http://dag.wieers.com/packages/j2re/.) As root, make the downloaded file executable with chmod +x and unpack it with ./j2re-1_4_2_05linux-i586-rpm.bin; install the resulting rpm file with

```
# rpm ivh j2re-1_4_2_05 -linux-i586.rpm
```

To make the Java plug-in work with Mozilla, you need to link it correctly:

```
# ln -s /usr/java/j2re1.4.2_05/plugin/i386/ns610-gcc32/libjavaplugin_oji.so
 /usr/lib/mozilla/plugins/
```

You might also need to link the Java binary into /usr/bin:

```
# ln -s /usr/java/j2re1.4.2_05/bin/java /usr/bin/java
```

Java can be difficult to install properly because of PATH problems. Here's a way to do it correctly:

Edit your /etc/profile file to add the following lines. This will inform the system where the Java executable is found.

```
JAVA_HOME=/usr/java/j2re1.4.2_05
PATH=/usr/java/j2re1.4.2_05/bin:$PATH
```

You can also find numerous multimedia goodies at http://freshrpms.net/ and at http://www.cs.trinity.edu/ftp/pub/FC2-Software-Additions//. The multimedia applications that used to be part of Fedora before its merger with Red Hat are now housed at http://rpm.livna.org. To add this repository to YUM, add to /etc/yum.conf the lines

```
[livna-stable]
name=Livna.org Fedora Compatible Packages (stable)
baseurl=
  http://rpm.livna.org/fedora/$releasever/$basearch/yum/stable
gpgcheck=1
```

and for APT, add this line to /etc/apt/sources:

```
rpm http://rpm.livna.org/ fedora/1/i386 stable
```

and for Up2date,

```
yum livna-stable
http://rpm.livna.org/fedora/1/i386/yum/stable
```

Add the GPG key as detailed on the Livna home page. See Chapter 7 for details on using these package management tools.

Relevant Fedora Core Linux Commands

You will use these commands when working with multimedia applications for Fedora Core Linux:

CD/DVD Disks

cdda2wav—Copies WAV files from CDs; used by other applications

cdlabelgen—Creates labels for CD jewel cases; used in scripts

cdp—A text-mode CD player

cdparanoia—A CD ripper

cdrecord—A command-line tool to record CDs

dvd+rw-tools—A command-line tool to create DVDs

grip—A CD music ripper

mkisofs—Creates ISO files

xcdroast—A CD recorder

Sound and Music

alsamixer—A console audio mixer

kmid—A MIDI player

mikmod—A MOD music player

rhythmbox—The default music player; it can play from playlists or Internet radio stations

sox—A sound conversion tool

sound-juicer—A CD ripping tool

system-config-soundcard—Default sound card configuration utility

vorbis-tools—The OGG Vorbis codecs

xmms—An MP3 player

Video

kaboodle—A KDE media player

noatun—KDE media player

tvtime—A television viewer

xine—A video player

xmms—An MPEG1/2/3 player

Cameras

gtkam—A front end for gPhoto2

kamera—The KDE digital camera utility

dvgrab—A video camera capture utility using a Firewire connection

Scanners

kooka—The KDE scanner application

xsane—A scanner application

10

Graphics

`eog`—Eye of Gnome image viewer

`ImageMagick`—An image manipulation application

`gimp`—The GNU Image Manipulation Program

`gqview`—GNOME image viewer

`kcoloredit`—KDE palette editor

`kiconedit`—KDE icon editor

`kpaint`—A graphics application

`kuickshow`—KDE image-viewing application

`kview`—KDE embedded image viewer.

`ntpbm-progs`—Tools for manipulating `netpbm`-formatted graphics

`xfig`—A vector graphic application

Reference

http://www.cdcopyworld.com/—A resource for technical information about CD media and CD writers.

http://hardware.redhat.com/hcl/—A database of supported hardware.

http://www.opensound.com/download.cgi—The commercial OSS sound driver trial version download.

http:/www.xmms.org/—Home to the Xmms audio player.

http://www.thekompany.com/projects/tkcoggripper/—A free (but not GPL) OGG CD ripper.

http://faceprint.com/code/—An MP3 to OGG converter named mp32ogg.

http://www.ibiblio.org/pub/linux/apps/sound/convert/!INDEX.html—Home to several sound conversion utilities.

http://linux-sound.org/—An excellent resource for Linux music and sound.

http://www.cnpbagwell.com/audio.html—The Audio Format FAQ.

http://www.icecast.org/—A streaming audio server.

http://www.linuxnetmag.com/en/issue4/m4icecast1.html—An Icecast tutorial.

http://linuxselfhelp.com/HOWTO/MP3-HOWTO-7.html—The MP3 HOWTO contains brief descriptions of many audio applications and, although it focuses on the MP3 format, the information is easily generalized to other music formats.

http://www.exploits.org/v4l/—Video for Linux resources.

http://fame.sourceforge.net/—Video encoding tools.

http://teletext.mb21.co.uk/faq.shtml—The Teletext FAQ.

http://xine.sourceforge.net/—Home of the Xine DVD/video player.

http://www.MPlayerHQ.hu/homepage/—Home to the MPlayer video player.

http://www.videolan.org/—A VideoLAN project with good documentation.

http://fy.chalmers.se/~appro/linux/DVD+RW/—The DVD+RW/+R/-R[W] for Linux, a HOWTO for creating DVDs under Linux.

10

Printing with Fedora

Fedora supports more than 600 printers from more than 40 manufacturers, and it is possible to mix and match printing hardware with newer computers. In this chapter, you learn about printing services offered in Fedora. Here, you also learn about the many different programs, files, and directories that are integral to supporting printing under Fedora. The chapter also shows you simple techniques for configuring new printers. You learn a variety of methods for making printers available for use quickly and easily, and you learn some important workarounds for connecting printer and system hardware with differing port configurations.

Fedora uses the Common Unix Printing System (CUPS). Other printing systems, such as LPRng, can be used as the printing system, but you might not be able to use some of the graphical print management utilities included with Fedora. For information on avoiding printer headaches refer to "Avoiding Printer-Support Problems" in Chapter 21, "File and Print."

> **The Internet Printing Protocol**
>
> CUPS supports the Internet Printing Protocol, known as *IPP*, and offers a number of unique features, such as network printer directory (printer browsing) services, support for encryption, and support for PostScript Printer Description (.ppd) files.
>
> According to the Internet Engineering Task Force (IETF), IPP grew out of a 1996 proposal by Novell to create a printing protocol for use over the Internet. Since then, the system has been developed and has matured into a stable print system for use on a variety of Linux and Unix-like operating platforms.

Overview of Fedora Printing

Fedora's print filter system is the main engine that enables the printing of many types of documents. The heart of that engine is the GNU GPL version of Aladdin's Ghostscript interpreter, the gs client. The system administrator's printer configuration tool is the system-config-printer client.

> **NOTE**
>
> Fedora's print system can be used to print to local (attached) or remote (network) printers. If you use a local printer, it is represented by a printer device, such as /dev/lp0 or /dev/usb/lp0 (if you have a USB printer). Local and remote printers use print *queues* defined in your system's printer capabilities database, /etc/printcap. A document being printed is known as a print *job*, and you can view and control your list, or queue, of current print jobs in the spool directory, which is /var/spool/cups. Note that you may only control your print jobs; only the root operator can control print jobs of any user on the system.

To add a printer to your system, you use the system-config-printer client to create, configure, and save the printer's definition. The client saves the definition as an entry in your system's printer capabilities database, /etc/printcap. Each definition contains a text field with the name of the printer, its host, and name of the print queue. Printed documents will be spooled to the /var/spool/cups directory. A sample printcap definition might look like

```
# This file was automatically generated by cupsd(8) from the
# /etc/cups/printers.conf file.  All changes to this file
# will be lost.
lp¦lp:rm=stinky:rp=lp:¨
```

CUPS maintains its own database of defined printers under the /etc/cups directory in a file named printers.conf. For example, an associated printer defined in /etc/printcap previously might have the following entry in /etc/cups/printers.conf:

```
<DefaultPrinter lp>
Info Created by redhat-config-printer 0.6.x
DeviceURI parallel:/dev/lp0
Location HP 648 local printer
State Idle
Accepting Yes
JobSheets none none
QuotaPeriod 0
PageLimit 0
KLimit 0
</Printer>
```

This example shows the definition for the printer named lp, along with its associated device, description, state, and other information. The various possible fields and entries in this file are documented in the printer.conf man page.

CUPS uses a print server (daemon) named cupsd, also called a *scheduler* in the CUPS documentation. The server can be controlled, like other Fedora services, by the service command or system-config-services client. How the server works on a system is determined by settings in its configuration file, cupsd.conf, found under the /etc/cups directory. CUPS executables are found under the /usr/lib/cups directory.

The cupsd.conf man page documents more than 80 different settings for the server, which you can configure to match your system, network, or printing environment. Default CUPS-related files and directories are stored under the /usr/share/cups directory. Logging can be set to seven different levels, with information about access and errors stored in log files under the /var/log/cups directory.

Resource requirements can be tailored through other settings, such as MaxCopies to set the maximum number of copies of a print job by a user, MaxJobs to set a limit on the number of active print jobs, and MaxJobsPerUser to set a limit on the number of active jobs per user. The RIPCache setting (8MB by default) controls the amount of memory used for graphics cache during printing.

For example, if you want to limit printing to 20 copies of a document or page at a time and only 10 simultaneous print jobs per user, use settings such as

```
MaxCopies 20
MaxJobsPerUser 10
```

> **TIP**
>
> Don't forget to restart the CUPS server after making any changes to its configuration file. Changes are only activated when the service is restarted (when the daemon rereads its configuration file). See the section "GUI-Based Printer Configuration Quickstart" later on.

Because CUPS does not use the traditional Berkeley-style print spooling system, lpd, you can change the name of the printer capabilities database from the default /etc/printcap. Encryption can be used for printing, with secure access behavior determined by settings in /etc/cups/client.conf. Network access settings include port, connection, IP address, domains, and limits to the number and size of client requests.

Configuring and Managing Print Services

Your task as a system administrator (or root operator of your workstation) is to properly define local or remote printers and to ensure that printing services are enabled and running properly. Fortunately, Fedora includes Red Hat's graphical print service configuration tools that make this job easy. You should use these tools to configure printing, as you learn in this section of the chapter. But first, take a moment to read through a quick overview of the configuration process.

> **CAUTION**
>
> Do not manually edit your /etc/printcap. Any changes will be lost when printing service is restarted or if your system is rebooted. If you need to create customized printer entries, save the entries in /etc/printcap.local and then restart print service.

You can configure printing services using either the command line system-config-printer-tui program or the system-config-printer-gui graphical interface. Most of the detailed information in this chapter refers to the use of the GUI. The overview sections that follow, however, give you solid foundation in both configuration approaches. You learn the details of these processes in later sections of the chapter.

GUI-based Printer Configuration Quickstart

Configuring a printer for Fedora is easy but must be done using root permission. Make sure that the cupsd daemon is installed and running. If you elect to use printing support when you install Fedora, the daemon and related software will be installed. If you're not sure if cupsd is running, you can use the service command with the name of the service and the status keyword like so:

 # service cups status

You will either see

cupsd is stopped

or if cupsd is running, an acknowledgement, along with its process ID, such as:

cupsd (pid 2923) is running...

If cupsd is installed but not running, start the daemon like so:

 # /etc/rc.d/init.d/cups start

You can also start the daemon using the service command like so:

 # service cups start

If you are using the desktop, select the Printing menu item from the System Settings menu. You will be asked to enter the root password. If not, you are using X as root, which is a bad idea. Log out, and then log back in as a regular user! After entering the root password, the printer configuration dialog appears.

You then simply follow the prompts to define your printer and add local or remote printing services. You should print a test page before saving your changes. Use the printer configuration client or the File menu's Print menu item from a GNOME or KDE client.

> **NOTE**
>
> The `system-config-printer` utility is an update to the now-legacy `printtool` client included with previous Red Hat Linux distributions. Although you might also find related tools (or symbolic links), such as `printtool`, `printconf-tui`, and `/usr/sbin/printconf-gui` installed on your system, you should use the `system-config-printer` client to manage printers under Fedora.

Console-based Printer Configuration Quickstart

Local or remote print services can also be configured locally or on a server without the X Window System. To do so, you use Fedora's text-based `system-config-printer-tui` printer configuration utility. You need to run this command as root:

```
# system-config-printer-tui
```

The screen clears after you press Enter, and you will see the command's main dialog. (You see this screen in the section titled "Console-based Print Commands," later in this chapter.)

> **NOTE**
>
> If you launch `system-config-printer` as root when not using X at a console, the `system-config-printer-tui` interface will be used.

You use the Tab key and spacebar to navigate the dialogs and expand lists of devices. You can create a new printer entry by highlighting the New button and pressing Enter. Use the Up or Down cursor keys to select and highlight an existing entry; then highlight the Edit button and press Enter to edit a previously defined printer.

You can then print documents from the command line using the `lpr` command, view any active jobs using the `lpq` command, and control the print queue by using the `lrpm` command.

Managing Printing Services

After defining a printer, you can use the command line to view and control your print jobs, or if root, all print jobs and printers on your system.

Table 11.1 contains a partial list of CUPS and related printing commands and drivers included with Fedora.

TABLE 11.1   Print-related Commands and Drivers

Name	Description
a2ps	Formats text files for PostScript printing
accept	Controls CUPS print job destinations
cancel	Cancels a CUPS print job

TABLE 11.1   Continued

Name	Description
disable	Controls CUPS printers
dvi	Converts TeX DVI files to specific PCL format
enable	Controls CUPS printers
encscript	Converts text files to PostScript
escputil	Epson Stylus inkjet printer utility
grolbp	groff driver for Canon LBP-4 and LBP-8 laser printers
gs	The Ghostscript interpreter
gsbj	Ghostscript BubbleJet printer drivers
gsdj	Ghostscript DeskJet printer drivers
lpadmin	CUPS command-line based printer utility
lp	Starts a CUPS print job
lpc	A Berkeley-subset CUPS printer control client
lpf	General printer filter
lprm	A Berkeley-compatible CUPS job queue utility
lpstat	Displays CUPS print jobs and printer status
mpage	PostScript text formatting utility
pbm	Portable bitmap conversion utilities
pr	Text formatting command
psmandup	Duplex printing utility for non-duplex printers
reject	Controls CUPS print job destinations
setup	Launches printer configuration tool
smbclient	SMB print spooler
smbprint	SMB print shell script
smbspool	SMB printer spooler
thinkjettopbm	Portable bitmap to ThinkJet printer conversion utility

Most Linux systems use PostScript as the default document format for printing. Fedora uses the gs command along with CUPS to manage local and remote print jobs and the type of data transferred during a print job. The gs command is used to translate the document stream into a format accepted by the destination printer (which most likely uses HPCL).

You can use the Ghostscript interpreter gs to display its built-in printer devices by using the gs interpreter with its --help command-line option like this:

```
# gs --help
```

NOTE

Fedora includes graphical clients you can use to view many different types of documents. For example, to display PostScript documents (including compressed PostScript documents) or PostScript images, use the gv client. To display Portable Document Format (PDF) documents, you can use gv or the xpdf client.

The gs command outputs many lines of help text on command-line usage and then lists built-in printer and graphics devices. Another way to get this information is to start gs and then use the devicenames == command like this:

```
# gs
GNU Ghostscript 7.05 (2002-04-22)
Copyright (C) 2002 artofcode LLC, Benicia, CA.  All rights reserved.
This software comes with NO WARRANTY: see the file PUBLIC for details.
Loading NimbusRomNo9L-Regu font from /usr/share/fonts/default/Type1/
¬n021003l.pfb... \
2410668 1053956 1642520 347466 0 done.
Loading NimbusSanL-Regu font from /usr/share/fonts/default/Type1/n019003l.pfb...
 2785628 1379834 1662616 358654 0 done.
Using NimbusSansL-Regu font for NimbusSanL-Regu.
[/miff24 /psmono /alc8500 /lp2563 /pkmraw /stp /iwlq /pbm /md1xMono /epson /bjc600
¬/lbp310 \
/coslw2p /cdjcolor /bj10v /cdj1600 /djet500 /x11rg16x /atx23 /x11gray4 /st800
¬/jpeggray /necp6 \
/psgray /alc2000 /lp8000 /pksm /lxm3200 /jetp3852 /pbmraw /DJ630 /epsonc /bjc800
¬/lbp320 \
/coslwxl /cdjmono /bj10vh /cdj500 /laserjet /x11rg32x /atx24 /x11mono /stcolor
¬/pdfwrite /oce9050 \
/psrgb /cups /lq850 /pksmraw /lx5000 /la50 /pgm /DJ6xx /escp /faxg3 /lips2p /cp50
¬/cdj550 \
/mag16 /cdj670 /ljetplus /ljet4pjl /atx38 /bmpmono /sunhmono /pswrite /oki182 /bit
¬/cljet5 /lxm5700m \
/tiffcrle /lex7000 /la70 /pgmraw /DJ6xxP /fs600 /faxg32d /bjc880j /declj250 /pj
¬/mag256 /cdj850 /ljet2p\
 /lj4dithp /bmpa16 /bmpgray /t4693d2 /epswrite /okiibm /bitrgb /cljet5c /m8510
¬/tiffg3 /lex5700 /la75
...
```

Not all the devices are listed in this example.

Aladdin or GNU?

At least two versions of Ghostscript are available for Linux. One version is named "AFPL Ghostscript," which went by the former name "Aladdin Ghostscript." This version is licensed under the Aladdin Free Public License, which disallows commercial distribution. The other version is called "GNU Ghostscript," which is distributed under the GNU General Public License. For details about the different versions or for answers to questions regarding licensing, see the Ghostscript home page at http://www.cs.wisc.edu/~ghost/.

Creating and Configuring Local Printers

Creating a local printer for your Fedora system can be accomplished in six easy steps. You must have root permission to use the `system-config-printer` client. The cupsd daemon should also be running before you begin (start the daemon manually as shown earlier in this chapter, or use the `ntsysv`, `chkconfig`, or `system-config-services` commands to ensure that `lpd` is started at boot time).

To launch `system-config-printer`, select the Printing menu item from the GNOME or KDE desktop panel's System Settings menu or use the command line of an X terminal window like this:

```
# system-config-printer &
```

Creating the Print Queue

The Fedora `system-config-printer` tool walks you through a process to create a new print queue, which effectively defines a new printer on your system. To begin configuration of a local (attached) printer, click the New toolbar button in `system-config-printer`'s main window. An Add a New Print Queue configuration dialog appears, as shown in Figure 11.1.

FIGURE 11.1   Click the New toolbar button to start the configuration of a new printer for your system; when the wizard's dialog appears, click the Forward button to begin.

Click the Forward button; the Queue Name dialog appears. Type a desired name for the new printer (such as `lp`), enter a short description, and then click the Forward button. The Queue type dialog appears, as shown in Figure 11.2. Click the queue type drop-down menu to select the type of printer you're adding. You can configure a local or networked printer supported by the Common Unix Printing System (CUPS), the `lpd` daemon on a remote server, a Session Message Block (SMB) server, Netware Core Protocol (Novell), or a JetDirect interface. To configure a printer attached to your computer, select the locally connected Queue type, click to select the printer device (which might be `/dev/lp0` or `/dev/usb/lp0`), and then click Forward. You can also use the Custom device button to enter a different port, such as `/dev/ttyS0`, for a serial printer.

FIGURE 11.2   Click the drop-down menu to select a locally connected printer queue type.

The Printer model dialog shown in Figure 11.3 presents a drop-down menu you can use to choose the manufacturer of your printer, or you can simply choose a generic type of connected printer.

FIGURE 11.3   Click the drop-down menu to select your printer's manufacturer or printer type.

Note that you can configure a printer for Fedora even if it is not attached to your computer. After you select your printer's manufacturer, a list of printers from that manufacturer (such as HP, as shown in Figure 11.4) will appear. Select your printer from the list, and then click the Forward button.

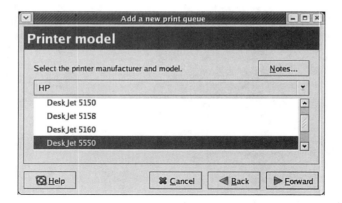

FIGURE 11.4   Select your printer from the list and click the Forward button to finish the configuration of a locally connected printer.

Do not worry if you do not see your printer listed in the selection; it is possible to select a related, though different, printer model and still be able to print to your printer. For example, many HP printers can be used by selecting the Deskjet 500 for monochrome or 500C model for color printing.

> **NOTE**
>
> You can also browse to http://www.linuxprinting.org/ to find out what drivers to use with your printer or to see a cross-referenced listing of printers supported by each driver. You might also find new and improved drivers for the latest printers on the market.

You can experiment to see which printer selection works best for your printer if its model is not listed. You might not be able to use all the features of your printer, but you will be able to set up printing service. Click Forward when you have made your choice.

The Finish and Create New Print Queue dialog shows you the printer type, printer device, and selected printer, so you can confirm that the information is correct (see Figure 11.5). If you need to change the options, click Back to return to previous dialogs. To create the new print queue, click Finish.

When the print queue has been created, you will be asked if you would like to print a test page. Click Yes to save your new printer setup and to print a test page. If you click No, a test page will not be printed, and you will need to delete the new printer entry or save or cancel your changes before you quit system-config-printer.

You can see the new printer defined in the system-config-printer main window as shown in Figure 11.6.

FIGURE 11.5   Double-check your settings before you commit to creating a new printer entry in /etc/printcap; when the settings are right, click Finish to create the new print queue.

FIGURE 11.6   New printer entries created in /etc/printcap will be displayed in system-config-printer's main window.

> **TIP**
>
> You can also configure multiple print queues for the same printer. Use this technique to test printing using different print drivers with the same printer. Create a new queue, give it a specific name, (such as testpcl3), and select a different printer. Finish the configuration and print a test page to compare the results against other entries to find the best output. You can also use this technique to define a monochrome or color printer entry for the same printer or to use different drivers for different types of media (such as regular or photo paper).

Editing Printer Settings

You also use the system-config-printer tool to edit the newly defined printers. To edit the printer settings, highlight the printer's listing in the Printer configuration dialog, and then click on the toolbar's Edit button. The Edit a Print Queue dialog appears, as shown in Figure 11.7.

The first tab in this dialog enables you to assign a new name for the printer.

FIGURE 11.7   Edit a printer's settings by using tabs in `system-config-printer`'s Edit a Print Queue window.

In this example, the printer has the name `lp`. Other tabs in this dialog enable you to change the queue type or queue options (such as whether to print a banner page or set the image area of a page), to select or update the driver, or to choose available driver options for the printer (shown in Figure 11.8).

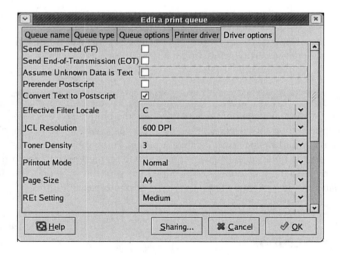

FIGURE 11.8   A printer's driver settings can be changed in the Driver Options tab of `system-config-printer`'s Edit a Print Queue window.

Click the Help button to read detailed information about the different options, which are used to force a page eject, support character rendering, and set a different resolution or a default page orientation. Printer/driver notes are available if you are selecting a different driver in the Printer Driver tab.

When you have finished editing your printer definition (or *queue*), click the OK button. Use the Apply command in the Action menu to save the definition and automatically restart the cupsd daemon. This step is extremely important; you need to update the printer settings and restart the cupsd daemon to force it to reread your new settings. Click Quit from the Action menu when finished.

Related Fedora and Linux Commands

The following commands help you manage printing services:

accept—Controls print job access to the CUPS server via the command line

cancel—Cancels a print job from the command line

cancel—Command-line control of print queues

disable—Controls printing from the command line

enable—Command-line control CUPS printers

lp—Command-line control of printers and print service

lpc—Displays status of printers and print service at the console

lpq—Views print queues (pending print jobs) at the console

lprm—Removes print jobs from the print queue via the command line

lpstat—Displays printer and server status

system-config-printer—Red Hat's graphical printer configuration tool

system-config-printer-tui—Red Hat text-dialog printer configuration tool

---

Reference

http://www.linuxprinting.org/—Browse here for specific drivers and information about USB and other types of printers.

http://www.hp.com/wwsolutions/linux/products/printing_imaging/index.html—Short, but definitive information from HP regarding printing product support under Linux.

http://www.linuxdoc.org/HOWTO/Printing-HOWTO/—Grant Taylor's Printing HOWTO, with information on using various print services under Linux.

http://www.cups.org/—A comprehensive repository of CUPS software, including versions for Red Hat Linux.

http://www.pwg.org/ipp/—Home page for the Internet Printing Protocol standards.

http://www.linuxprinting.org/cups-doc.html—Information about the Common Unix Printing System (CUPS).

http://www.cs.wisc.edu/~ghost/—Home page for the Ghostscript interpreter.

CHAPTER 12

Games

For any operating system to become truly mass market, it has to have a number of games that are compatible with it. Let's face it, no one wants to use computers just for word processing or databases—they want to be able to use them as a source of relaxation and even fun! In this chapter we will examine the state of Linux gaming and tell you how to get some of the current blockbusters up and running in a Linux environment. We will even show you how to run Windows-based games under Linux.

Linux Gaming

Fedora has a number of games that come as part of the distribution, and they are divided into three distinct camps: KDE games, GNOME games, and X games. Our favorites are *Tux-Racer* and *Maelstrom* (see Figure 12.1), but there are a few for you to choose from. The best part, of course, is trying each one and seeing what you think. Many other free games are available across the Web, so go to Google and see what you come up with.

However, games for Linux do not stop there—a few versions of popular Windows-based games are being ported across to the Linux platform, including *Doom 3* and *Unreal Tournament 2004*. These two popular games have native Linux support and in some cases can run at similar, if not better, speeds than their Windows counterparts. Even the U.S. Army produces a simulation called *America's Army* that is available for Linux.

Finally, an implementation of the Wine code, called WineX, is optimized especially for games. This uses application interfaces to make Windows games believe they are running on a Windows platform and not a Linux platform. Bear in mind that Wine stands for *wine is not an emulator*, so do not start thinking of it as such—the community can get touchy about it!

FIGURE 12.1   Zapping asteroids in the highly unpredictable *Maelstrom*.

Because of their popularity, we will examine the process of installing proprietary drivers for an NVIDIA graphics display card and show you how to install *Unreal Tournament 2004* from Epic Games and *Doom 3* from id Software.

Installing Proprietary Video Drivers

Fedora does not provide the official NVIDIA display drivers because they are closed source. The latest drivers can be downloaded from http://www.nvidia.com/object/ linux.html. The Linux 2.6 kernel series did not actually support the NVIDIA graphics drivers when it was released, but advancements made by NVIDIA do get around this problem, with the current kernel (at time of writing, it's 2.6.11) working with little or no problems. If you do encounter problems with the NVIDIA drivers, check out http:// www.nvnews.net/vbulletin/forumdisplay.php?f=14 for more help. The NVIDIA staff do contribute to that forum, so you should be able to find expert help when you need it.

As for ATI, the other principal graphics card maker, the story is not quite the same. Although ATI is committed to producing Linux drivers, it's not as quick to update them as NVIDIA is. At the time of writing, ATI had just released versions of its driver for Linux. Go to http://www.ati.com/support/infobase/linuxhowto-ati.html to get detailed instructions on installing them for use.

Installing *Doom 3*

The follow-up to the infamous *Doom* and *Doom II* was released in the second half of 2004 (see Figure 12.2), and it provides a way to run it under Linux. You still need to purchase the Windows version because you need some of the files that are on the CDs. The rest of the files are available from id Software at http://zerowing.idsoftware.com/linux/doom. You can find other information about graphics cards on there too.

You can download the file doom3-linux-1.1.1282.x86.run from their FTP server or by using BitTorrent. Once finished, open a terminal and change to the directory in which you saved the file. Type the following command:

```
# sh doom3-linux-1.1.1282.x86.run
```

This begins the installation of the demo. As with other commercial games, you must agree to an EULA before you can install. Follow the installation procedure and, when it finishes, you need to get the Windows CDs ready.

The files you need to copy across are the following:

- pak000.pk4

- pak001.pk4

- pak002.pk4

- pak003.pk4

- pak004.pk4

They must be saved in the /usr/local/games/doom3/base/ directory. After you have copied these, you can start the game by typing **doom3** or starting the dedicated server for multiplayer games by typing **doom3-dedicated**.

FIGURE 12.2 Descending into the pits of hell. *Doom 3* is one of the most graphic computer games available.

Installing *Unreal Tournament 2004*

Unreal Tournament 2004 (or UT2004, as it is affectionately known) from Epic natively supports Linux in both its 32-bit and 64-bit incarnations (see Figure 12.3). Be aware that if you run the 64-bit version, you need to ensure that your graphics drivers are supported under 64-bit mode.

Installation is easy, and there are two ways to do it. You can insert the DVD and mount it, or you can open the DVD in GNOME and double-click the linux-installer.sh icon. When you are asked if you want to run it or display its contents, click Run in Terminal to launch the graphical installer. As with *Doom 3*, you must read and accept the terms of the EULA before being allowed to install *UT2004*. You are given the option of where you want to install the software; the default is in your home directory. After it's installed, click Begin Install and *UT2004* does the rest.

The alternative way of accessing the graphical installer is via the command line. Change directory to /media/cdrom/ and type

```
$ sh linux-install.sh
```

This brings up the graphical installer. Continue through this and, when finished, you should find *Unreal Tournament 2004* in /home/username/ut2004.

If you want to uninstall *UT2004*, you can use the uninstall script in the ut2004 directory. Type

```
$ sh uninstall.sh
```

After confirmation, *Unreal Tournament* removes itself from your system.

Installing *Wolfenstein—Enemy Territory*

Whereas the earlier *Return to Castle Wolfenstein* was both single- and multiplayer, the freely available *Wolfenstein—Enemy Territory* is multiplayer only. Available in Win32 and Linux native versions, it can be downloaded through http://www.SplashDamage.com/. After you download the 260MB file named et-linux-2.55.x86.run, install the game by typing

```
# sh et-linux-2.55.x86.run
```

Then accept the defaults. A symlink exists in /usr/local/bin to the script that loads the game. When using the KDE desktop, we had difficulty with sound due to a conflict with the KDE sound daemon artsd. The fix was prepending a line to the et script that read killall artsd.

Wolfenstein—Enemy Territory, as shown in Figure 12.4, does not require an NVIDIA graphics card to play the game, unlike *UT2003*. We found the game playable on a 16MB Voodoo 3-3000 AGP video card.

FIGURE 12.3 *Unreal Tournament* builds on the classic death-match scenario with more enemies and more combatants!

FIGURE 12.4 Teamwork is the key to victory in this lush but hostile graphical environment.

Playing Windows Games with Cedega

As mentioned earlier, the key to mass-market appeal of an operating system is in the applications available for it. A group of developers saw that the vast majority of the computing world was using Windows-based productivity and gaming software and decided to develop a way to run this software on Linux, thereby giving Linux users access to this large application base. The developers came up with a program called Wine, which has been updated regularly and forms the basis of the gaming variant called Cedega. This is a commercial product available from developers Transgaming (www.transgaming.com) so you can't retrieve it using yum.

However, it is a very popular and up-to-date product with support for recent releases such as *Half-Life 2*, *Sid Meier's Pirates!*, and *World of Warcraft*.

So, if you cannot wait for Linux to become more popular with the games developers, use Cedega as a stop-gap until they can be persuaded to support Linux directly.

> **TIP**
>
> The keys to successful gaming in Linux are to always read the documentation thoroughly, always investigate the Internet resources thoroughly, and always understand your system. Installing games is a great way to learn about your system because the reward of success is so much fun.

Reference

- http://www.transgaming.com/—The Official Transgaming website provides details of games that are directly supported under Cedega.

- http://www.linuxgames.com/—A good source of up-to-date information about the state of Linux gaming.

- http://zerowing.idsoftware.com/linux/doom/—Includes a complete how-to and troubleshooting guide for running *Doom 3* under Linux.

- http://www.unrealtournament.com/—The official site of *Unreal Tournament*.

- http://www.nvnews.net/vbulletin/forumdisplay.php?f=14—The Official NVIDIA Linux driver support forum.

- http://www.nvidia.com/object/linux.html—Home page for the NVIDIA Linux drivers.

- http://www.ati.com/support/drivers/linux/radeon-linux.html/—Home page for the ATI Linux drivers.

PART III

System Administration

IN THIS PART

Managing Users

In this chapter, you learn how to perform the tasks necessary to manage users of your Fedora system. Controlling users is a critical part of your job as a system administrator, and you need to be aware that allowing someone access to a computer is more than just permitting him to sit at a terminal and type. You need to know how to establish new user accounts and place them in groups, how to create new home directories for those users, and how to populate the directories with an initial set of files. Managing users also requires that you know how to establish user passwords and how to grant users file and directory permissions, so they can have access to files they need and are prohibited from accessing files they have no business using.

In this chapter, you learn how to accomplish all these tasks and others for managing user accounts. You will learn about the different types of users and the responsibilities of the superuser so you will have a better idea of what roles you will play as a system administrator. In addition, you will learn how to delegate superuser power to others when it's appropriate.

User Accounts

Three kinds of users are at work in the typical Fedora system environment: the superuser, the regular user, and the system user. All three have important roles and must work cooperatively to accomplish their tasks.

All users have accounts. Fedora Core uses the /etc/passwd file to hold user account information. Each user, regardless of type, will have a one-line entry of account information stored in the /etc/passwd text file. Each account entry contains a username (used for logging in), a password field containing an x (as passwords are actually contained in /etc/shadow), a User ID (UID), and a Group ID (GID). The fifth field contains optional human ID information, such as real name, office location, phone number, and so on. The last two fields are the location of the user's home directory and the user's default login shell. See the section "The Password File" later in this chapter for more information.

Fedora uses the traditional form of Unix file ownership and permissions. Each file (which includes directories and devices) can be assigned read, write, and/or execution permission to an owner, a member of a group, or anyone on the system. This information can be viewed with the ls command, using -l for files or -ld for directories. Fedora's file security is derived by combining ownerships and permissions. It is the superuser's responsibility to make sure that all users have proper filename, UIDs, and GIDs and that sensitive system files are protected from improperly permissive write permission assignment.

Although many system administrators might exist on a large system, only one root user has (and grants) all privileges on the system. The root user is defined as having a User ID of zero and a Group ID of zero. (We will discuss those IDs later in the chapter, but you can see how that ID is unique to root.)

The root user can use any program, manipulate any file, go anywhere in the file system, and do anything within the Fedora Core Linux system. For reasons of security, that kind of raw power should only be given to a single trusted individual.

It is often practical for that power to be delegated by the root user to other users. This delegation is referred to as an elevation of privileges, and these individuals are known as superusers because they enjoy the same powers that root enjoys. This approach is normally only used on large systems in which one person cannot effectively act as the system administrator.

> **NOTE**
>
> On your Fedora system, when you log in as root, you are root or the superuser. In this chapter, the terms root, superuser, system administrator, and sysadmin are used interchangeably, although they need not all refer to a single person.

The regular user is a person who logs onto and uses the computer to accomplish some non-administrative task. Regular users do not participate in the management or administration of the computer on a global scale, but they may be permitted to manage their own personal settings and configurations—if the root user does not take that privilege away.

The superuser grants privileges to regular users by means of file and directory permissions. (Those are covered in Chapter 5, "First Steps with Fedora.") For example, if the superuser does not want you to change your settings in ~/.profile (the ~ is a shell shortcut representing your home directory; see Chapter 14, "Automating Tasks"), root can alter the permissions so that you may read from, but not write to, that file.

> **CAUTION**
>
> Because of the potential for making a catastrophic error as the superuser (using the command `rm -rf /*` is the classic example, but do not ever try it!), always use your system as a regular user and become root only temporarily to do sysadmin duties. While you are on a multiuser system, you should consider this advice an absolute rule; if root were to delete the wrong file or kill the wrong process, the results could be disastrous for the business. On your home system, you can do as you please and running as root makes many things easier, but less safe. In any setting, however, the risks of running as root are significant.

The system user is not a person, but a process running on the computer. The system user requires ownership of files and processes so that it can do its job in a secure manner. (Fedora calls these users logical users.) For example, the system user named apache owns the web server (assuming that you are using Apache) and all the associated files. No one else (except root) may have access to those files in a way that Apache does not permit. Unlike regular users, system users do not have a home directory or password and cannot log in like a regular user.

You will find a list of all the users on a system in the /etc/passwd file. Fedora refers to these users as the standard users because they will be found on every Fedora computer as the default set of system (or logical) users provided during the initial installation. This "standard" set differs between Linux distributions.

User IDs and Group IDs

A computer is a number oriented machine. It identifies users and groups by numbers known as the User ID (UID) and Group ID (GID) . The alphabetic names displayed on your screen are there exclusively for the convenience of the biological entities that so often annoy the computer.

As was already mentioned, the root user is UID 0. Numbers from 1 through 499 and 65,534 are the system, or logical, users. Regular users have UIDs beginning with 500; Fedora assigns them sequentially beginning with this number.

With only a few exceptions, the GID is the same as the UID. Those exceptions are system users who need to act with root permissions: sync, shutdown, halt, and operator.

Fedora creates a private GID for every UID of 500 and greater. The system administrator can add other users to a GID or create a totally new group and add users to it. Unlike Windows NT and some Unix variants, a group cannot be a member of another group in Linux.

File Permissions

As you learned in Chapter 5, permissions are of three types: read, write, and execute (r, w, x). For any file or directory, permissions can be established in three categories: user, group, and global. In this section, we focus on group permissions, buthere's a highlight of the commands used to change the group, user, or access permissions of a file or directory:

318 CHAPTER 13 Managing Users

- `chgrp`—Changes the group ownership of a file or directory.

- `chown`—Changes the owner of a file or directory.

- `chmod`—Changes the access permissions of a file or directory.

These commands, which modify file ownerships and permissions, can be used to model organizational structure and permissions in the real world onto your Fedora system (see the next section, "Managing Groups"). For example, a human resources department can share health-benefit memos to all company employees by making the files readable (but not writable) by anyone in an accessible directory. On the other hand, programmers in the company's research and development section, while being able to access each other's source code files, would not have read or write access to HR pay-scale or personnel files (and certainly would not want HR or Marketing poking around R&D).

These commands are used to manage group and file ownerships and permissions from the command line. Use the `chgrp` command to allow (or restrict) groups of users access to specific directories and files. The `chown` command can be used to set ownerships, but may only be used by root. Use the `chmod` command to set read and write permissions for files you own. Refer to Chapter 5 of this book or the man page of each command for details on these commands.

User Stereotypes

As is the case in many professions, exaggerated characterizations (stereotypes or caricatures) have emerged for users and system administrators. Many stereotypes contain elements of truth mixed with generous amounts of hyperbole and humor and serve to assist us in understanding the characteristics of and differences in the stereotyped subjects. The stereotypes of the "luser" and the "BOFH" (users and administrators, respectively) also serve as cautionary tales describing what behavior is acceptable and unacceptable in the computing community.

Understanding these stereotypes allows you to better define the appropriate and inappropriate roles of system administrators, users, and others. The canonical reference to these terms is found in the alt.sysadmin.recovery FAQ found at http://www.ctrl-c.liu.se/~ingvar/asr/overview.html.

Managing Groups

Groups establish relationships among users in which they share a common set of permissions. An individual cannot read or write to a file owned by another user. But if users are in the same group, they may both read and write to files owned by the group (depending on the group permissions) while retaining the privacy and security of their own files.

Group permissions can be used to facilitate group work on a project involving common files and to control access to devices such as the modem and floppy drive. This approach also represents a secure method of limiting access to system resources to only those users who need them. As an example, the sysadmin could put the users andrew, paul, damon, bernice, mark, and shelley in a new group named unleashed. Those users could each create files intended for their group work and chgrp those files to unleashed.

Now, everyone in the unleashed group—but no one else except root—can work with those files. The sysadmin would probably create a directory owned by that group so they could have an easily accessed place to store those files. The sysadmin could also add other users like bernice and ildiko to the group and remove existing users when their part of the work is done. The sysadmin could make the user shelley the group administrator so that shelley could decide how group membership should be changed.

Different Unix operating systems implement the group concept in various ways. Fedora uses a scheme called UPG, the User Private Group, in which all users are assigned to a group with their own name by default. (The user's username and group name are identical.) All the groups are listed in /etc/group file.

Here is a partial list of a sample /etc/group file:

```
# cat /etc/group
root:x:0:root
bin:x:1:root,bin,daemon
daemon:x:2:root,bin,daemon
sys:x:3:root,bin,adm
adm:x:4:root,adm,daemon
tty:x:5:
disk:x:6:root
lp:x:7:daemon,lp
mem:x:8:
kmem:x:9:
wheel:x:10:root
mail:x:12:mail,postfix
news:x:13:news
uucp:x:14:uucp
man:x:15:
games:x:20:
gopher:x:30:
dip:x:40:
ftp:x:50:
lock:x:54:
nobody:x:99:
users:x:100:
dbus:x:81:
floppy:x:19:
vcsa:x:69:
nscd:x:28:
rpm:x:37:
```

```
haldaemon:x:68:
utmp:x:22:
netdump:x:34:
slocate:x:21:
sshd:x:74:
rpc:x:32:
rpcuser:x:29:
nfsnobody:x:65534:
mailnull:x:47:
smmsp:x:51:
pcap:x:77:
apache:x:48:
xfs:x:43:
ntp:x:38:
gdm:x:42:
named:x:25:
dovecot:x:97:
postdrop:x:90:
postfix:x:89:
andrew:x:500:
```

In this example, there are a number of groups, mostly for services (mail, ssh, and so on) and devices (floppy, disk, and so on). As previously mentioned, the system services groups enable those services to have ownership and control of their files. For example, adding postfix to the mail group, as shown previously, enables the postfix application to access mail's files in the manner that mail would decide for group access to its file. Adding a regular user to a device's group permits the regular user to use the device with permissions granted by the group owner. Adding user andrew to the group floppy, for example, would allow andrew to use the floppy drive device. You will learn how to add and remove users from groups in the next section.

Group Management Tools

Fedora provides several command-line tools for managing groups as well as graphical tools. Many experienced sysadmins prefer the command-line tools because they are quick and easy to use and they can be included in scripts if the sysadmin desires to script a repetitive task.

Here are the most commonly used group management command-line tools:

> groupadd—This command creates and adds a new group.
>
> groupdel—This command removes an existing group.
>
> groupmod—This command creates a group name or GIDs, but doesn't add or delete members from a group.

gpasswd—This command creates a group password. Every group can have a group password and an administrator. Use the -A argument to assign a user as group administrator.

useradd -G—The -G argument adds a user to a group during the initial user creation. (More arguments are used to create a user.)

usermod -G—This command allows you to add a user to a group as long as the user is not logged in at the time.

grpck—A command for checking the /etc/group file for typos.

As an example, there is a CD-RW device (/dev/scd0) on our computer that the sysadmin wants a regular user named shelley to have access to. To grant shelley that access, we would use these steps:

1. Add a new group with the groupadd command:

   ```
   # groupadd cdrw
   ```

2. Change the group ownership of the device to the new group with the chgrp command:

   ```
   # chgrp cdrw /dev/scd0
   ```

3. Add the approved user to the group with the usermod command:

   ```
   # usermod -G cdrw  shelley
   ```

4. Make user shelley the group administrator with the gpasswd command so that she can add new users to the group:

   ```
   # gpasswd -A shelley
   ```

Now, the user shelley has permission to use the CD-RW drive, as would anyone else added to the group by the superuser or shelley because she is now also the group administrator and can add users to the group.

The sysadmin can also use the graphical interface that Fedora provides, as shown in Figure 13.1. It is accessed as the Users and Groups item from the System Settings menu item.

You will note that the full set of group commands and options are not available from the graphical interface, limiting the usefulness of the GUI to a subset of the most frequently used commands. You learn more about using the Fedora User Manager GUI in the next section of this chapter.

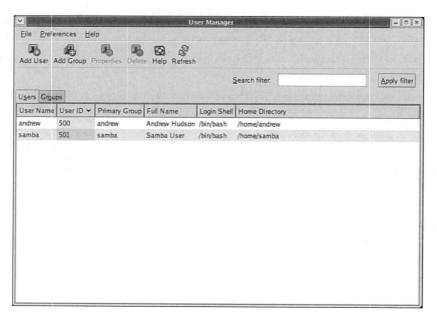

FIGURE 13.1   Just check the box to add a user to a group.

Managing Users

We have mentioned users previously, but in this section we will examine how the sysadmin can manage the users. Users must be created, assigned a UID, provided a home directory, provided an initial set of files for their home directory, and assigned to groups so that they may use the system resources securely and efficiently. The system administrator might elect to restrict a user's access not only to files, but to the amount of disk space they use as well. (You learn more about that in the "Managing Disk Quotas" section in Chapter 7, "Managing Software and System Resources.")

User Management Tools

Fedora provides several command-line tools for managing users as well as graphical tools. Many experienced sysadmins prefer the command-line tools because they are quick and easy to use and they can be included in scripts if the sysadmin desires to script a repetitive task.

Here are the most commonly used commands used to manage users:

useradd—This command is used to add a new user account to the system. Its options permit the sysadmin to specify the user's home directory and initial group or to create the user with the default home directory and group assignments.

useradd -G—This command sets the system defaults for creating the user's home directory, account expiration date, default group, and command shell. See the specific options in man useradd. Used without any arguments, it displays the defaults for the system. The default set of files for a user are found in /etc/skel.

13

> **NOTE**
>
> The set of files initially used to populate a new user's home directory are kept in /etc/skel. This is very convenient for the system administrator because any special files, links, or directories that need to be universally applied can be placed in /etc/skel and will be duplicated automatically with appropriate permissions for each new user.
>
> ```
> # ls -al /etc/skel
> total 76
>
> drwxr-xr-x   3 root root  4096 Feb 21 19:25 .
> drwxr-xr-x  83 root root 12288 Feb 26 19:06 ..
> -rw-r--r--   1 root root   302 Nov  5 16:54 .bash_logout
> -rw-r--r--   1 root root   191 Nov  5 16:54 .bash_profile
> -rw-r--r--   1 root root   124 Nov  5 16:54 .bashrc
> -rw-r--r--   1 root root   438 Feb  4 15:41 .emacs
> -rw-r--r--   1 root root   120 Oct 19 21:28 .gtkrc
> drwxr-xr-x   3 root root  4096 Aug 12  2002 .kde
> -rw-r--r--   1 root root   658 Jul  5  2004 .zshrc
> ```
>
> Each line provides the file permissions, the number of files housed under that file or directory name, the file owner, the file group, the file size, the creation date, and the filename.
>
> As you can see, root owns every file here, but the adduser command (a symbolic link to the actual command named useradd) copies everything in /etc/skel to the new home directory and resets file ownership and permissions to the new user.
>
> Certain user files may exist that the system administrator doesn't want the user to change; the permissions for those files in /home/username can be reset so that the user can read them but can't write to them.

userdel—This command will completely remove a user's account (thereby eliminating that user's home directory and all files it contains).

passwd—This command updates the "authentication tokens" used by the password management system.

> **TIP**
>
> To lock a user out of his account, use the command
>
> ```
> # passwd -l username
> ```
>
> This prepends a ! to the user's encrypted password; the command to reverse the process uses the -u option. This is a more elegant and preferred solution to the problem than the traditional Unix way of manually editing the file.

usermod—This command changes several user attributes. The most commonly used arguments are -s to change the shell and -u to change the UID. No changes can be made while the user is logged in or running a process.

chsh—This command changes the user's default shell. For Fedora Core Linux, the default shell is /bin/bash, known as the Bash, or Bourne Again Shell.

Adding New Users

The command-line approach to adding this user is actually quite simple and can be accomplished on a single line. In the example shown here, the sysadmin will use the useradd command to add the new user bernice. The command adduser (a variant found on some Unix systems) is a symbolic link to useradd, so both commands work the same. In this example, we use the -p option to set the password the user requested; we use the -s to set his special shell, and the -u option to specify his UID. (If we created a user with the default settings, we would not need to use these options.) All we want to do can be accomplished on one line:

```
# useradd bernice -p sTitcher -s /bin/zsh -u 507
```

The sysadmin can also use the graphical interface that Fedora provides, as shown in Figure 13.2. It is accessed as the Users and Groups item from the System Settings menu item. Here, the sysadmin is adding a new user to the system where user bernice uses the bash command shell.

These are the steps we used to add the same account as shown in the preceding command, but using the graphical User Manager interface:

1. Launch the Fedora User Manager graphical interface by clicking on the Users and Groups menu item found in the System Settings menu.

2. Click on the Add User button to bring up the Add User dialog window.

3. Fill in the form with the appropriate information as described in the first paragraph in this section.

4. Click on the drop-down Login Shell menu to select the bash shell.

5. Check the Specify User ID box to permit access to the UID dialog.

6. Using the arrows found in the UID dialog, increment the UID to 5413.

7. Click OK to save the settings.

Note that the user is being manually assigned the UID of 549 because that is her UID on another system machine that will be connected to this machine. Because the system only knows her as 549 and not as bernice, the two machines would not recognize bernice as the same user if two different UIDs were assigned.

FIGURE 13.2 Adding a new user is simple. The GUI provides a more complete set of commands for user management than for group management.

> **NOTE**
>
> A Linux username can be any alphanumeric combination that does not begin with a special character reserved for shell script use (see Chapter 14 for disallowed characters, mostly punctuation characters). In Chapter 5, we told you that usernames are typically the user's first name plus the first initial of her last name. That is a common practice on larger systems with many users because it makes life simpler for the sysadmin, but is not a rule nor a requirement.

Monitoring User Activity on the System

Monitoring user activity is part of the sysadmin's duties and an essential task in tracking how system resources are being used. The w command will tell the sysadmin who is logged in, where he is logged in, and what he is doing. No one is able to hide from the superuser. The w command can be followed by a specific user's name to show only that user.

The ac command provides information about the total connect time of a user measured in hours. It accesses the /var/log/wtmp file for the source of its information.

> **TIP**
>
> Interestingly, a phenomenon known as "timewarp" can occur in which an entry in the wtmp files jumps back into the past and ac will show unusual amounts of time accounted for users. Although this can be attributed to some innocuous factors having to do with the system clock, it is worthy of investigation by the sysadmin since it can also be the result of a security breach.

The ac command is most useful in shell scripts to generate reports on operating system usage for management review.

The last command searches through the /var/log/wtmp file and will list all the users logged in and out since that file was first created. The user reboot exists so that you might know who has logged in since the last reboot. A companion to last is the command lastb, which shows all failed, or bad, logins. It is useful for determining if a legitimate user is having trouble or if a hacker is attempting access.

> **NOTE**
>
> The accounting system on your computer keeps track of usage user statistics and is kept in the current /var/log/wtmp file. That file is managed by the init and login processes. If you want to explore the depths of the accounting system, use the GNU info system: info accounting.

Managing Passwords

Passwords are an integral part of Linux security, and they are the most visible part to the user. In this section, you will learn how to establish a minimal password policy for your system, where the passwords are stored, and how to manage passwords for your users.

System Password Policy

An effective password policy is a fundamental part of a good system administration plan. The policy should cover:

- Allowed and forbidden passwords

- The frequency of mandated password changes

- The retrieval or replacement of lost or forgotten passwords

- Password handling by users

The Password File

The password file is /etc/passwd, and it is the database file for all users on the system. The format of each line is as follows:

```
username:password:uid:gid:gecos:homedir:shell
```

The fields are self-explanatory except for the GECOS field. This field is for miscellaneous information about the user, such as the users' full name, his office location, office and home phone numbers, and possibly a brief text message. For security and privacy reasons, this field is little used nowadays, but the system administrator should be aware of its existence since the GECOS field is used by traditional Unix programs such as finger and mail. For that reason, it is commonly referred to as the *finger information field*. The data in this field will be comma delimited; the GECOS field can be changed with the cgfn (change finger) command.

Note that a colon separates all fields in the /etc/passwd file. If no information is available for a field, that field is empty, but all the colons remain.

If an asterisk appears in the password field, that user will not be permitted to log on. Why does this feature exist? So a user can be easily disabled and (possibly) reinstated later without having to be created all over again. The system administrator manually edits this field, which is the traditional Unix way of accomplishing this task. Fedora provides improved functionality with the passwd -l command mentioned earlier.

Several services run as pseudo-users, usually with root permissions. These are the system, or logical, users mentioned previously. You would not want these accounts available for general login for security reasons, so they are assigned /sbin/nologin as their shell, which prohibits any logins from those "users."

A list of /etc/passwd reveals

```
# cat /etc/passwd
root:x:0:0:root:/root:/bin/bash
bin:x:1:1:bin:/bin:/sbin/nologin
daemon:x:2:2:daemon:/sbin:/sbin/nologin
adm:x:3:4:adm:/var/adm:/sbin/nologin
lp:x:4:7:lp:/var/spool/lpd:/sbin/nologin
sync:x:5:0:sync:/sbin:/bin/sync
shutdown:x:6:0:shutdown:/sbin:/sbin/shutdown
halt:x:7:0:halt:/sbin:/sbin/halt
mail:x:8:12:mail:/var/spool/mail:/sbin/nologin
news:x:9:13:news:/etc/news:
uucp:x:10:14:uucp:/var/spool/uucp:/sbin/nologin
operator:x:11:0:operator:/root:/sbin/nologin
games:x:12:100:games:/usr/games:/sbin/nologin
gopher:x:13:30:gopher:/var/gopher:/sbin/nologin
ftp:x:14:50:FTP User:/var/ftp:/sbin/nologin
nobody:x:99:99:Nobody:/:/sbin/nologin
dbus:x:81:81:System message bus:/:/sbin/nologin
vcsa:x:69:69:virtual console memory owner:/dev:/sbin/nologin
nscd:x:28:28:NSCD Daemon:/:/sbin/nologin
rpm:x:37:37::/var/lib/rpm:/sbin/nologin
haldaemon:x:68:68:HAL daemon:/:/sbin/nologin
netdump:x:34:34:Network Crash Dump user:/var/crash:/bin/bash
sshd:x:74:74:Privilege-separated SSH:/var/empty/sshd:/sbin/nologin
rpc:x:32:32:Portmapper RPC user:/:/sbin/nologin
rpcuser:x:29:29:RPC Service User:/var/lib/nfs:/sbin/nologin
nfsnobody:x:65534:65534:Anonymous NFS User:/var/lib/nfs:/sbin/nologin
mailnull:x:47:47::/var/spool/mqueue:/sbin/nologin
smmsp:x:51:51::/var/spool/mqueue:/sbin/nologin
pcap:x:77:77::/var/arpwatch:/sbin/nologin
apache:x:48:48:Apache:/var/www:/sbin/nologin
```

13

```
xfs:x:43:43:X Font Server:/etc/X11/fs:/sbin/nologin
ntp:x:38:38::/etc/ntp:/sbin/nologin
gdm:x:42:42::/var/gdm:/sbin/nologin
named:x:25:25:Named:/var/named:/sbin/nologin
dovecot:x:97:97:dovecot:/usr/libexec/dovecot:/sbin/nologin
postfix:x:89:89::/var/spool/postfix:/sbin/nologin
andrew:x:500:500:Andrew Hudson:/home/andrew:/bin/bash
```

Note that all the password fields do not show a password, but contain an x because they
are *shadow passwords*, a useful security enhancement to Linux, discussed in the following
section.

Shadow Passwords

It is considered a security risk to keep any password in /etc/passwd because anyone with
read access can run a cracking program on the file and obtain the passwords with little
trouble. To avoid this risk, *shadow passwords* are used so that only an x appears in the
password field of /etc/passwd; the real passwords are kept in /etc/shadow, a file that can
only be read by the sysadmin (and PAM, the Pluggable Authentication Modules authentication manager; see the "PAM Explained" sidebar for an explanation of PAM).

Special versions of the traditional password and login programs must be used to enable
shadow passwords. Shadow passwords are automatically enabled during the installation
phase of the operating system on Fedora systems.

Let's examine a listing of the shadow companion to /etc/passwd, the /etc/shadow file:

```
# cat /etc/shadow
root:$1$QmG67w3D$B7/xVSB3sehbK8.DL4y.w0:12782:0:99999:7:::
bin:*:12782:0:99999:7:::
daemon:*:12782:0:99999:7:::
adm:*:12782:0:99999:7:::
lp:*:12782:0:99999:7:::
sync:*:12782:0:99999:7:::
shutdown:*:12782:0:99999:7:::
halt:*:12782:0:99999:7:::
mail:*:12782:0:99999:7:::
news:*:12782:0:99999:7:::
uucp:*:12782:0:99999:7:::
operator:*:12782:0:99999:7:::
games:*:12782:0:99999:7:::
gopher:*:12782:0:99999:7:::
ftp:*:12782:0:99999:7:::
nobody:*:12782:0:99999:7:::
dbus:!!:12782:0:99999:7:::
vcsa:!!:12782:0:99999:7:::
nscd:!!:12782:0:99999:7:::
```

```
rpm:!!:12782:0:99999:7:::
haldaemon:!!:12782:0:99999:7:::
netdump:!!:12782:0:99999:7:::
sshd:!!:12782:0:99999:7:::
rpc:!!:12782:0:99999:7:::
rpcuser:!!:12782:0:99999:7:::
nfsnobody:!!:12782:0:99999:7:::
mailnull:!!:12782:0:99999:7:::
smmsp:!!:12782:0:99999:7:::
pcap:!!:12782:0:99999:7:::
apache:!!:12782:0:99999:7:::
xfs:!!:12782:0:99999:7:::
ntp:!!:12782:0:99999:7:::
gdm:!!:12782:0:99999:7:::
named:!!:12782:0:99999:7:::
dovecot:!!:12782:0:99999:7:::
postfix:!!:12782:0:99999:7:::
andrew:$1$TIkBJRsW$444QX2igYBlUj.l3I9cyA.:12782:0:99999:7:::
```

The fields are separated by colons and are, in order:

The user's login name.

The encrypted password for the user.

The number of days since Jan 1, 1970 that the password was last changed. This date is know in Unix circles as the "epoch." Just so you know, the billionth second since the epoch occurred was in September 2001; that was the Unix version of Y2K; not much happened because of it.

The number of days before the password can be changed (prevents changing a password and then changing it back to the old password right away—a dangerous security practice).

The number of days after which the password must be changed. This can be set to force the change of a newly issued password known to the system administrator.

The number of days before the password expiration that the user is warned it will expire.

The number of days after the password expires that the account is disabled (for security).

The number of days since Jan 1, 1970 that account has been disabled.

The final field is a "reserved" field and is not currently allocated for any use.

Note that password expiration dates and warnings are disabled by default in Fedora. These features are not used on home systems and usually not used for small offices. It is the sysadmin's responsibility to establish and enforce password expiration policies.

The permissions on the /etc/shadow file should be set so that it is not writable or readable by regular users: The permissions should be 600.

PAM Explained

Pluggable Authentication Modules (PAM) is a system of libraries that handle the tasks of authentication on your computer. It uses four management groups: account management, authentication management, password management, and session management. This allows the system administrator to choose how individual applications will authenticate users. Fedora has preinstalled and preconfigured all the necessary PAM files for you.

The configuration files in Fedora Core are found in /etc/pam.d. These files are named for the service they control, and the format is as follows:

```
type control module-path module-arguments
```

The type field is the management group that the rule corresponds to. The control field tells PAM what to do if authentication fails. The final two items deal with the PAM module used and any arguments it needs. Programs that use PAM typically come packaged with appropriate entries for the /etc/pam.d directory. To achieve greater security, the system administrator can modify the default entries. Misconfiguration can have unpredictable results, so back up the configuration files before you modify them. The defaults provided by Fedora Core are adequate for home and small office users.

As an example of a PAM configuration file with the formatted entries as described previously is shown next. Here are the contents of /etc/pam.d/system-config-users:

```
#%PAM-1.0
auth       sufficient    /lib/security/pam_rootok.so
auth       required      /lib/security/pam_stack.so service=system-auth
session    required      /lib/security/pam_permit.so
session    optional      /lib/security/pam_xauth.so
account    required      /lib/security/pam_permit.so
```

Amusingly, even the PAM documents state that you do not really need (or want) to know a lot about PAM to use it effectively.

You will likely only need the PAM system administrators guide. Look under the /usr/share/doc/pam* directory for additional documents in PostScript, text, and HTML formats.

If you configure you system to use LDAP or kerberos authentication during install and are unable to log on to the machine using the local root account, be aware that there is a known bug in the /etc/pam.d/system-auth file. As a temporary fix, change the line that reads

```
account required /lib/security/$ISA/pam_unix.so
```

to

```
account sufficient /lib/security/$ISA/pam_unix.so
```

The underlying problem appears to be a flaw in the way that PAM handles intervals for requests for authorization. This issue has existed since Red Hat 7.3 and does not appear to be fixed in Fedora Core.

Managing Password Security for Users

Selecting appropriate user passwords is always an exercise in trade-offs. A password such as *password* (don't laugh, it has been used too often before in the real world) is just too easy to guess by an intruder as are simple words or number combinations (a street address, for example). A security auditor for one of my former employers would take the cover sheet from the employees' personnel file (which contained the usual personal information of name, address, birth date, and so on) and would then attempt to log on to a terminal with passwords constructed from that information—and often succeeded in logging on.

On the other hand, a password such as `2a56u'"F($84u&#^Hiu44Ik%$([#EJD` is sure to present great difficulty to an intruder (or an auditor). However, that password is so difficult to remember that it would be likely that the password owner would write that password down and tape it next to her keyboard. I worked for a business in which the safe combination was written on the ceiling tile over the safe; the manager could not remember it and was told he should not keep it on a piece of paper in his wallet. This is but one of many examples of poor security in the field.

The sysadmin has control, with settings in the `/etc/shadow` file, over how often the password must be changed. The settings can be changed using a text editor, the change command, or a configuration tool such as Fedora's User Manager, as shown in Figure 13.1. Click on the Password Info tab under that particular user's Properties to set individual password policies.

Changing Passwords in a Batch

On a large system, there might be times when a large number of users and their passwords need some attention. The superuser can change passwords in a batch by using the `chpasswd` command, which accepts input as a name/password pair per line in the following form:

```
# chpasswd username:password
```

Passwords can be changed *en masse* by redirecting a list of name and password pairs to the command. An appropriate shell script can be constructed with the information gleaned from Chapter 14.

However, Fedora also provides the `newusers` command to add users in a batch from a text file. This command also allows a user to be added to a group, and a new directory can be added for the user as well.

Granting System Administrator Privileges to Regular Users

On occasion, it is necessary for regular users to run a command as if they were the root user. They usually do not need these powers, but they might on occasion—for example, to temporarily access certain devices or run a command for testing purposes.

There are two ways to run commands with root privileges: The first is useful if you are the superuser and the user; the second if you are not the regular user (as on a large, multiuser network).

Temporarily Changing User Identity with the su Command

What if you are also root, but are logged on as a regular user because you are performing non-administrative tasks and you need to do something that only the superuser can do? The su command is available for this purpose.

> **NOTE**
>
> A popular misconception is that the su command is short for *super user*; it just means *substitute user*. An important but often overlooked distinction is that between su and su -. In the former instance, you become that user but keep your own environmental variables (like paths). In the latter, you inherit the environment of that user. This is most noticeable when you use su to become the super user, root. Without appending the -, you do not inherit the path variable that includes /bin or /sbin, so you must always enter the full path to those commands when you just su to root.

Because almost all Linux file system security revolves around file permissions, it can be useful to occasionally become a different user with permission to access files belonging to other users or groups or to access special files (such as the communications port /dev/ttyS0 when using a modem or the sound device /dev/audio when playing a game). You can use the su command to temporarily switch to another user identity, and then switch back.

> **TIP**
>
> It is never a good idea to use an Internet Relay Chat (IRC) client as the root user, and you might not want to run it using your regular user account. Simply create a special new user just for IRC and su to that user in a terminal widow to launch your IRC client.

The su command spawns a new shell, changing both the UID and GID of the existing user and automatically changes the environmental variables associated with that user, known as inheriting the environment. See Chapter 5 for more information on environmental variables.

The syntax for the su command is

```
$ su option  username  arguments
```

The man page for su gives more details, but some highlights of the su command are

```
-c, --command COMMAND
    pass a single COMMAND to the shell with -c
```

```
-m, --preserve-environment
   do not reset environment variables

-l   a full login simulation for the substituted user,
the same as specifying the dash alone
```

You can invoke the su command in different ways that yield diverse results. By using su alone, you can become root, but you keep your regular user environment. This can be verified by using the printenv command before and after the change. Note that the working directory (you can execute pwd as a command line to print the current working directory) has not changed. By executing the following, you become root and inherit root's environment:

```
$ su -
```

By executing the following, you become that user and inherit the superuser's environment—a pretty handy tool. (Remember: Inheriting the environment comes from using the dash in the command; omit that, and you keep your "old" environment.) To become another user, specify a different user's name on the command line:

```
$ su - other_user
```

When leaving an identity to return to your usual user identity, use the exit command. For example, while logged on as a regular user,

```
$ su - root
```

the system prompts for a password:

```
Password:
```

When the password is entered correctly, the root user's prompt appears:

```
#
```

To return to the regular user's identity, just type

```
# exit
```

This takes you to the regular user's prompt:

```
$
```

If you need to allow other users access to certain commands with root privileges, it is necessary to give them the root password so that they can use su—that definitely is not a very secure solution. The next section describes a more flexible and secure method of allowing normal users to perform selected root tasks.

Granting Root Privileges on Occasion—The sudo Command

Often it is necessary to delegate some of the authority that root wields on a system. For a large system, this makes sense because no single individual will always be available to perform superuser functions. The problem is that Unix permissions come with an "all or nothing" authority. Enter sudo, an application that permits the assignment of one, several, or all of the root-only system commands.

Once configured, using sudo is simple. An authorized user merely precedes the superuser-authority–needed command with the sudo command, like so

```
$ sudo command
```

After getting the user's password, sudo checks the /etc/sudoers file to see if that user is authorized to execute that particular command; if so, sudo generates a "ticket" for a specific length of time that authorizes the use of that command. The user is then prompted for his own password (to preserve accountability and provide some measure of security) and then the command is run as if root had issued it. During the life of the ticket, the command can be used again without a password prompt. If an unauthorized user attempts to execute a sudo command, a record of the unauthorized attempt is kept in the system log and a mail message is sent to the superuser.

Three man pages are associated with sudo: sudo, sudoers, and visudo. The first covers the command itself, the second the format of the /etc/sudoers file, and the third the use of the special editor for /etc/sudoers. You should use the special editing command because it will check the file for parse errors and lock the file to prevent others from editing it at the same time. The visudo command uses the vi editor, so you might need a quick review of the vi editing commands found in Chapter 5 in the section "Working with vi." You begin the editing by executing the visudo command with

```
# visudo
```

The default /etc/sudoers file looks like this:

```
# sudoers file.
#
#
# This file MUST be edited with the 'visudo' command as root.
#
# See the sudoers man page for the details on how to write a sudoers file.
#

# Host alias specification

# User alias specification

# Cmnd alias specification
```

```
# Defaults specification

# User privilege specification
root    ALL=(ALL) ALL

# Uncomment to allow people in group wheel to run all commands
# %wheel        ALL=(ALL)       ALL

# Same thing without a password
# %wheel        ALL=(ALL)       NOPASSWD: ALL

# Samples
# %users  ALL=/sbin/mount /cdrom,/sbin/umount /cdrom
# %users  localhost=/sbin/shutdown -h now
```

The basic format of a sudoers line in the file is

```
user host_computer=command
```

The user can be an individual user or a group (prepended by a % to identify the name as a group). The host_computer is normally ALL for all hosts on the network and localhost for the local machine, but the host computer can be referenced as a subnet or any specific host. The command in the sudoers line can be ALL, a list of specific commands, or a restriction on specific commands (formed by prepending a ! to the command). A number of options are available for use with the sudoers line, and aliases can be used to simplify the assignment of privileges. Again, the sudoers man page will give the details, but here are a few examples:

If we uncomment the line:

```
# %wheel        ALL=(ALL)       NOPASSWD: ALL
```

any user we add to the wheel group can execute any command without a password.

Suppose that we want to give user shelley permission across the network to be able to add users with the graphical interface. We would add the line

```
shelley ALL=/system-config-users
```

or perhaps grant permission only on her local computer:

```
shelley 192.168.1.87=/usr/bin/system-config-users
```

If we want to give the editor group systemwide permission with no password required to delete files:

```
%editors ALL=NOPASSWD: /bin/rm
```

If we want to give every user permission with no password required to mount the CD drive on the localhost:

```
ALL localhost=NOPASSWD:/sbin/mount /dev/scd0 /mnt/cdrom /sbin/umount /mnt/cdrom
```

It is also possible to use wildcards in the construction of the sudoers file. Aliases can be used as well to make it easier to define users and groups. Although the man page for sudoers contains some examples, http://www.komar.org/pres/sudo/toc.html provides illustrative notes and comments of sudo use at a large aerospace company. The sudo home page at http://www.sudo.ws/ is also a useful resource for additional explanations and examples.

The following command presents users with a list of the commands they are entitled to use

```
$ sudo -l
```

Control Via Restricted Shells

Using restricted shells is actually the opposite of granting additional privileges to users. There might be situations in which you want to restrict a user to a very specific subset of privileges permitted to other users. If you have a desire to severely restrict what a user can do (for reasons of security, distribution of a turnkey system, or custom system installation), you can provide him with a restricted shell. To run a restricted bash shell, you would use the -r option. It is easy to try yourself, just enter the following at your prompt:

```
$ bash -r
```

Then try to do something that you could do before as a regular user, such as listing the files in your home directory:

```
$ ls -a
```

You then see

```
bash: ls: No such file or directory
```

The cd command, redirection, using / in command names, and several other commands and options are also disabled in the restricted shell. (The man page for bash details specific restrictions; the appropriate information is at the very end of the very long man page.) Do not rely on a restricted shell as your only means of controlling user activity; although using restricted shells applies some tight restrictions, a very determined user might find a way to confound the restrictions. Always use appropriate permission and password controls as well.

The User Login Process

It is useful to know what happens during the process when a user attempts to log in—if for nothing else than troubleshooting for that one user in the accounting department who cannot get logged on to run the payroll program and get the payroll checks printed on time. Understanding this process also involves understanding the purpose of the default user installation files that are found in /etc/skel. This section helps illuminate the login process for you.

The login process is used for entering, or "signing on" to a system and is summarized in steps as follows:

1. Login prompts for a username.

2. If the /etc/nologin file exists and the user is not root, a warning message is issued and the login process is halted. The /etc/nologin file is typically used when the system will be shut down shortly and new logins should be restricted.

3. The /etc/usertty file is examined to see if any restrictions are specified for the user. As a security measure, root logons can be restricted to specific terminals and regular users can have the same restrictions placed on them as necessary.

4. The system prompts for a password; it is checked against the encrypted password kept in /etc/shadow. Unsuccessful attempts are logged via the syslog facility and can be reviewed with the lastd command.

5. The UID and the GID of the tty (terminal) being used are set.

6. The TERM environment, if it has been set, is preserved.

7. The HOME, PATH, SHELL, TERM, MAIL, and LOGNAME environment variables are set. (If the -p option is used, all preexisting environmental variables are preserved.)

8. The PATH defaults to /usr/local/bin:/bin:/usr/bin: for normal users and to /sbin:/bin:/usr/sbin:/usr/bin for root.

9. Normal greeting messages and mail checking are disabled if the file .hushlogin exists in the users' home directory; otherwise, those messages are displayed at the end of the logon process.

10. The user's command shell is started at this point, presenting the user with a command prompt. If no shell is specified for the user in /etc/passwd, /bin/sh is used by default. (Some Unix operating systems will just log you back out.) If no home directory is specified in /etc/passwd, / is used.

When you log in as a regular user, the files that control your environment are found in your /home/username directory. These configuration files are normally hidden from view because their filename is preceded by a period (as in .bashrc—these are known as "dot files").

The name of the file indicates which program it is associated with. The files .bash_logout, .bash_profile, and .bashrc all determine how the bash shell is used by the user. (These files can, of course, be preset by the system administrator with the user given only read access, so the files cannot be changed. Other shells have their own associated files.)

338 CHAPTER 13 Managing Users

The .screenrc file determines the console screen environment, and the .Xdefaults file determines much the same thing for X11. For Fedora Core, the .dmrc file sources the file /etc/X11/dm/Sessions/Default.desktop, which sets the default desktop for the entire system. The .Xclients-default file is created by running the switchdesk command (the Desktop Switching Tool is the name of the GUI interface) to change the default desktop for that user. You would use this command if you occasionally launched X11 from the command line and desired to change your default desktop. Fedora Core sets the default as GNOME.

Other files might be present depending on the system and the system administrator. The point is that the environment of each user can be set globally through the use of files in /etc/skel and individually by allowing user modification of the files in their /home directory (or not, depending on the system administration policies).

The system logs all user logins, as well as all uses of su and sudo commands for the sysadmin's review. (The init, syslogd, and klogd applications create the logs.) Modern security monitoring programs (or simple scripts you create) can scan these files (such as /var/log/messages) for anomalies and signal possible security violations.

Disk Quotas

On large systems with many users, you need to control the amount of disk space a user has access to. Disk quotas are designed for this purpose. Quotas, managed per each partition, can be set for both individual users as well as groups; quotas for the group need not be as large as the aggregate quotas for the individuals in the groups.

When files are created, both a user and a group own them; ownership of the files is always part of the metadata about the files. This makes quotas based on both users and groups easy to manage.

> **NOTE**
>
> Disk quota management is never done on a home system and rarely, if ever, done on a small office system.

To manage disk quotas, you must have the quota package installed on your system; it is usually installed by default. Quota management with Fedora is not enabled by default and has traditionally been enabled and configured manually by system administrators. Sysadmins use the family of quota commands, such as quotacheck to initialize the quota database files, edquota to set and edit user quotas, setquota to configure disk quotas, and quotaon or quotaoff to control the service. (Other utilities include warnquota for automatically sending mail to users over their disks pace usage limit.)

Implementing Quotas

To reiterate, quotas might not be enabled by default, even if the quota software package is installed on your system. When quotas are installed and enabled, you can see which partitions have either user quotas, group quotas, or both by looking at the fourth field in the /etc/fstab file. For example, one line in /etc/fstab shows that quotas are enabled for the /home partition:

```
/dev/hda5      /home      ext3          defaults,usrquota,grpquota 1 1
```

The root of the partition with quotas enabled will have the files quota.user or quota.group in them (or both files if both types of quotas are enabled), and the files will contain the actual quotas. The permissions of these files should be 600 so that users cannot read or write to them. (Otherwise, users would change them to allow ample space for their music files and Internet art collections.) In order to initialize disk quotas, the partitions must be remounted. This is easily accomplished with the following:

```
# mount -o ro,remount partition_to_be_remounted mount_point
```

The underlying console tools (complete with man pages) are

- quotaon, quotaoff—Toggles quotas on a partition.

- repquota—A summary status report on users and groups.

- quotacheck—Updates the status of quotas (compares new and old tables of disk usage); it is run after fsck.

- edquota—A very basic quota management command.

Manually Configuring Quotas

Manual configuration of quotas involves changing entries in your system's file system table, /etc/fstab, to add the usrquota mount option to the desired portion of your file system. As an example in a simple file system, quota management can be enabled like this:

```
LABEL=/              /                    ext3      defaults,usrquota     1 1
```

Group-level quotas can also be enabled by using the grpquota option. As the root operator, you must then create a file (using our example of creating user quotas) named quota.user in the designated portion of the file system, like so:

```
# touch /quota.user
```

You should then turn on the use of quotas using the quotaon command:

```
# quotaon -av
```

You can then edit user quotas with the edquota command to set hard and soft limits on file system use. The default system editor (vi unless you change your EDITOR environment variable) will be launched when editing a user's quota.

Any user can find out what their own quotas are with

```
$ quota -v
```

NOTE

There are no graphical tools supported by Fedora Core that can be used to configure disk quotas. A Quota mini HOWTO is maintained at http://www.tldp.org/HOWTO/mini/Quota.html.

Related Fedora Commands

You will use these commands to manage user accounts in Fedora:

ac—A user account-statistics command

chage—Sets or modifies user password expiration policies

chfn—Creates or modifies user finger information in /etc/passwd

chgrp—Modifies group memberships

chmod—Changes file permissions

chown—Changes file ownerships

chpasswd—Batch command to modify user passwords

chsh—Modifies a user's shell

groups—Displays existing group memberships

logname—Displays a user's login name

newusers—Batches user management command

passwd—Creates or modifies user passwords

su—Executes shell or command as another user

sudo—Manages selected user execution permissions

system-config-users—Fedora's graphical user management tool

useradd—Creates, modifies, or manages users

userinfo—Fedora's graphical chfn command

usermod—Edits a user's login profile

userpasswd—Fedora's graphical user password command

Reference

http://www.ibiblio.org/pub/Linux/docs/HOWTO/other-formats/html_single/_User-Authentication-HOWTO.html—The User-Authentication HOWTO describes how user and group information is stored and used for authentication.

http://www.ibiblio.org/pub/Linux/docs/HOWTO/other-formats/html_single/Shadow-Password-HOWTO.html—The Shadow-Password HOWTO delves into the murky depths of shadow passwords and even discusses why you might not want to use them.

http://www.ibiblio.org/pub/Linux/docs/HOWTO/other-formats/html_single/
_Security-HOWTO.html—A "must read" HOWTO, the Security HOWTO is a good
overview of security issues. Especially applicable to this chapter are sections on creating
accounts, file permissions, and password security.

http://www.secinf.net/unix_security/Linux_Administrators_Security_Guide/—A general
guide, the Linux System Administrator's Security Guide has interesting sections on limiting and monitoring users.

http://www.ibiblio.org/pub/Linux/docs/HOWTO/other-formats/html_single/
Config-HOWTO.html—How can you customize some user-specific settings? The
Config HOWTO Software Configuration gives some advice.

http://www.ibiblio.org/pub/Linux/docs/HOWTO/other-formats/html_single/Path.html—
How can one know the true path? The Path HOWTO sheds light on this issue. You need
to understand paths if you want to guide the users to their data and applications.

http://www.courtesan.com/sudo/—The SUperuser DO command is a powerful and elegant
way to delegate authority to regular users for specific commands.

http://www.kernel.org/pub/linux/libs/pam/index.html—The Pluggable Authentication
Modules are complex and highly useful applications that provide additional security and
logging for passwords. PAM is installed by default in Fedora Core. It isn't necessary to
understand the intricacies of PAM in order to use it effectively.

http://localhost/localdomain/—Your Fedora Core system contains man and info pages on
just about everything covered here. Use man -k to search on a keyword.

13

CHAPTER **14**

Automating Tasks

In this chapter you learn about the five ways to automate tasks on your system: making them services that run as your system starts, making them services you start and stop by hand, scheduling them to run at specific times, connecting multiple commands together on the shell, and writing custom scripts that group everything together under one command.

After you turn on the power switch, the boot process begins with the computer executing code stored in a chip called the BIOS; this process occurs no matter what operating system you have installed. The Linux boot process begins when the code known as the boot loader starts loading the Linux kernel and ends only when the login prompt appears.

As a system administrator, you will use the skills you learn in this chapter to control your system's services and manage runlevels on your computer. Understanding the management of the system services and states is essential to understanding how Linux works (especially in a multiuser environment) and will help untangle the mysteries of a few of your Fedora Core Linux system's configuration files. Furthermore, a good knowledge of the cron daemon that handles task scheduling is essential for administrators at all skill levels.

This chapter is also an introduction to the basics of creating *shell scripts*, or executable text files written to conform to shell syntax. Shell scripts run like any other command under Linux and can contain complex logic or a simple series of Linux command-line instructions. You can also run other shell scripts from within a shell program. The features and functions for several Linux shells are discussed in this chapter after a short introduction to working from the shell command line. You learn how to write and execute a simple shell program using bash, one of the most popular Linux shells.

Running Services at Bootup

Although most people consider a computer to be either on or off, in Fedora there are a number of states in between. Known as *runlevels*, they control what system services are started upon bootup. These services are simply applications running in the background that provide some needed function to your system, such as getting information from your mouse and sending it to the display; or a service could monitor the partitions to see whether they have enough free space left on them. Services are typically loaded and run (also referred to as being started) during the boot process, in the same way as Microsoft Windows services are.

You can manage nearly every aspect of your computer and how it behaves after booting via configuring and ordering boot scripts, as well as by using various system administration utilities included with Fedora Core Linux. In this chapter, you learn how to work with these boot scripts and system administration utilities. This chapter also offers advice for troubleshooting and fixing problems that might arise with software configuration or the introduction or removal of various types of hardware from your system.

Beginning the Boot Loading Process

Although the actual boot loading mechanism for Linux varies on different hardware platforms (such as the SPARC, Alpha, or PowerPC systems), Intel-based PCs running Fedora Core Linux most often use the same mechanism throughout product lines. This process is accomplished through a Basic Input Output System, or BIOS. The BIOS is an application stored in a chip on the motherboard that initializes the hardware on the motherboard (and often the hardware that's attached to the motherboard). The BIOS gets the system ready to load and run the software that we recognize as the operating system.

As a last step, the BIOS code looks for a special program known as the boot loader or boot code. The instructions in this little bit of code tell the BIOS where the Linux kernel is located, how it should be loaded into memory, and how it should be started.

If all goes well, the BIOS looks for a bootable volume such as a floppy disk, CD-ROM, hard drive, RAM disk, or other media. The bootable volume contains a special hexadecimal value written to the volume by the boot loader application (likely either GRUB or LILO, although LILO is not provided with Fedora Core) when the boot loader code was first installed in the system's drives. The BIOS searches volumes in the order established by the BIOS settings (for example, the floppy first, followed by a CD-ROM, and then a hard drive) and then boots from the first bootable volume it finds. Modern BIOS's allow considerable flexibility in choosing the device used for booting the system.

> **NOTE**
>
> If the BIOS does detect a hardware problem, the boot process will fail and the BIOS will generate a few beeps from the system speaker. These "beep codes" indicate the nature of the

problem the BIOS has encountered. The codes vary among manufacturers, and the diagnosis of problems occurring during this phase of the boot process is beyond the scope of this book and does not involve Linux. If you encounter a problem, you should consult the motherboard manual or contact the manufacturer of the motherboard.

Next, the BIOS looks on the bootable volume for boot code in the partition boot sector also known as the Master Boot Record (MBR) of the first hard disk. The MBR contains the boot loader code and the partition table—think of it as an index for a book, plus a few comments on how to start reading the book. (We cover the MBR in more detail in Chapter 37, "Managing the File System.") If the BIOS finds a boot loader, it loads the boot loader code into memory. At that point, the BIOS's job is completed, and it passes control of the system to the boot loader.

The boot loader locates the Linux kernel on the disk and loads it into memory. After that task is completed, the boot loader passes control of the system to the Linux kernel. You can see how one process builds on another in an approach that enables many different operating systems to work with the same hardware.

Fedora Core Linux can use a variety of boot loaders, including GRUB (the default for Fedora Core), LILO (a long-time standard but not available with Fedora Core), BootMagic (a commercial program), and others.

> **NOTE**
>
> Linux is very flexible and can be booted from multiple images on a CD-ROM, over a network using PXE (pronounced "pixie") or NetBoot, or on a headless server with the console display sent over a serial or network connection. Work is even underway to create a special Linux BIOS at http://www.linuxbios.org/ that will expedite the boot process because Linux does not need many of the services offered by the typical BIOS.
>
> This kind of flexibility enables Linux to be used in a variety of ways, such as remote servers or diskless workstations, which are not generally seen in personal home use.

Loading the Linux Kernel

In a general sense, the kernel manages the system resources. As the user, you do not often interact with the kernel, but instead just the applications that you are using. Unix refers to each application as a process, and the kernel assigns each process a number called a *process ID (PID)*. First, the Linux kernel loads and runs a process named init, which is also known as the "father of all processes" because it starts every subsequent process. The init process looks for a list of instructions in a file named /etc/rc.d/rc.sysinit. That script issues a number of commands that are only run once—each time the system is turned on.

> **NOTE**
>
> Details about the sequence of events that occur when the Linux kernel is loaded can be found in the file /usr/src/linux-2.6/init/main.c if you have installed the Linux kernel documentation.

This next step of the boot process begins with a message that the Linux kernel is loading, and a series of messages will be printed to the screen, giving you the status of each command in rc.sysinit script language. A failure should display an error message. The -quiet option may be passed to the kernel at boot time to suppress many of these messages.

Although it is not intended that you modify the rc.sysinit script, knowledge of the contents of the file might aid you in diagnosing a problem if the boot process fails during this step. Look at /etc/rc.d/rc.sysinit, and you will discover that it's just a text file filled with shell script language.

After the rc.sysinit script has been run, the basic system is configured and the kernel is in control of the system. If the boot process were halted at this point, the system would just sit idle and the screen would be blank. In order to make the system useful for users, we need to start the system services. Those services are some of the applications that allow us to interact with the system.

System Services and Runlevels

After finishing with rc.sysinit script during the bootloading process, the init command uses the Linux system initialization table found in /etc/inittab to boot Fedora Core Linux to a specific system state. The state of the system is commonly referred to as its runlevel.

Several different ways of starting and stopping system services exist, and Fedora Core uses a method derived from System V Unix. The System V (pronounced "System Five") method uses runlevels and different combinations of services to define different states of operation. Runlevels determine which of the many available system services are started, as well as in which order they start. A special runlevel is used to stop the system, and a special runlevel is used for system maintenance. As you will see, there are other runlevels for special purposes.

> **NOTE**
>
> The System V method makes extensive use of symbolic links, which are ways to reference a file in another location and make it appear as if it were in two or more places at once. The benefit is that you only need to edit one file to change them all. In addition, any reorganization to be done means that only links need to be changed, not the files themselves.

You will use runlevels to manage the system services running on your computer. All these special files and scripts are set up during your installation of Fedora Core Linux, and they receive their initial values based on your choices during the installation—as described in Chapter 3, "Installing Fedora," and Chapter 4, "Post-Installation Configuration." You can change and control them manually, as you learn later in this chapter using tools of varying sophistication.

Runlevel Definitions

The Fedora Core Linux runlevels are defined for the Fedora Core system in /etc/inittab.

> **NOTE**
>
> Not all Linux distributions use the same runlevel configurations or runlevel definitions! For example, although Fedora Core Linux uses runlevel 3 for a full, console-based multiuser mode, pre-7.1 versions of SUSE Linux defined this system state as runlevel 2. Red Hat, Fedora Core and SUSE now use the same runlevels to conform to the Linux Standards Base, or LSB. As a system administrator, you should be aware of this issue, especially if you have devised any administrative scripts or tools that deal with system states.

Each runlevel tells the init command what services to start or stop. Although runlevels might all have custom definitions, Fedora Core Linux has adopted some standards for runlevels:

- **Runlevel 0**—Known as "halt," this runlevel is used to shut down the system.

- **Runlevel 1**—This is a special runlevel, defined as "single," which boots Fedora Core Linux to a root access shell prompt where only the root user may log in. It has networking, X, and multiuser access turned off. This is the maintenance or rescue mode. It allows the system administrator to perform work on the system, make backups, or repair configuration or other files.

- **Runlevel 2**—This runlevel dictates that Fedora Core Linux be booted to a console, or text-based mode, with multiuser access.

- **Runlevel 3**—This runlevel is identical to runlevel 2, except that it also starts any networking services.

- **Runlevel 4**—This runlevel is undefined, and it can readily be configured to boot Fedora Core Linux to a custom system state.

- **Runlevel 5**—This runlevel boots Fedora Core Linux to a networking, multiuser state with an active X session. This is the most common runlevel for home users who want a graphical interface.

- **Runlevel 6**—This runlevel is used to reboot the system.

Runlevel 1 (also know as single-user mode or maintenance mode) is most commonly used to repair file systems and change the root password on a system when the password has been forgotten. Trespassers with physical access to the machine can also use runlevel 1 to access your system.

> **CAUTION**
>
> Never forget that uncontrolled physical access is virtually a guarantee of access to your data by an intruder.

Booting into the Default Runlevel

Entries in /etc/inittab use a field-based notation that determines the runlevel—when to execute the process, whether or not the process is executed when booting, whether or not to wait for the process to complete, and when to execute the process during booting. The default choices are adequate and only need be changed in unique circumstances that the average user is not likely to encounter.

The value of the default entry, or the initdefault line in /etc/inittab, determines the particular system state in which Fedora Core Linux will be when the login prompt is finally presented. For example,

```
id:5:initdefault:
```

In this example, Fedora Core Linux boots to runlevel 5, a network-enabled, multiuser mode with an active X session and a graphical login. The value 5 is forwarded to the script named rc under the /etc/rc.d directory. This script is used when booting or changing runlevels; it also acts as an interpreter when you boot Fedora Core Linux in "Interactive" mode by pressing **i** during the boot.

After /etc/rc.d/rc.sysinit has finished, init uses the corresponding /etc/inittab entry that matches the designated default runlevel. Using the previous example, the line in /etc/inittab would then be

```
l5:5:wait:/etc/rc.d/rc 5
```

Under the /etc/rc.d directory are a series of directories that correspond to each runlevel:

```
# ls /etc/rc.d
init.d  rc0.d  rc2.d  rc4.d  rc6.d       rc.sysinit
rc      rc1.d  rc3.d  rc5.d  rc.local
```

Assuming that the value is 5, the rc script then executes all the scripts under the /etc/rc.d/rc.5 directory and then launches the graphical login.

If Fedora Core Linux is booted to runlevel 5, for example, scripts beginning with the letter K followed by scripts beginning with the letter S under the /etc/rc.d/rc5.d directory are then executed:

```
# ls /etc/rc.d/rc5.d/
K01yum         K20bootparamd      K28amd         K45named       K61ldap
K74ypxfrd         S05kudzu        S24pcmcia      S85gpm  K05innd
K20iscsi          K30sendmail   K46radvd         K65identd     K84bgpd
S08ip6tables   S25netfs       S90crond K05saslauthd    K20netdump-server
K34dhcrelay    K50netdump    K65kadmin    K84ospf6d          S08ipchains
S26apmd        S90FreeWnn    K10psacct      K20nfs             K34yppasswdd
K50snmpd       K65kprop     K84ospfd         S08iptables    S28autofs
S90xfs  K10radiusd     K20rstatd         K35atalk       K50snmptrapd
K65krb524   K84ripd         S10network    S40smartd      S92lisa
```

```
K12canna      K20rusersd       K35dhcpd       K50tux       K65krb5kdc
K84ripngd     S12syslog        S44acpid       S95anacron  K12mailman
K20rwalld     K35smb           K50vsftpd      K70aep1000  K85zebra
S13irqbalance S55cups          S95atd  K12mysqld     K20rwhod
K35vncserver  K54dovecot   K70bcm5820  K90isicom        S13portmap
S55sshd        S97messagebus K15httpd     K20spamassassin   K35winbind
K54pxe        K74ntpd    K91isdn       S14nfslock     S56rawdevices
S97rhnsd K15postgresql  K24irda      K40mars-nwe   K55routed
K74ups        K95firstboot     S17keytable   S56xinetd      S99local
K16rarpd      K25squid         K45arpwatch   K61hpoj       K74ypserv
S00microcode_ctl  S20random       S84privoxy     S99mdmonitor
```

These scripts are actually symbolic links to system service scripts under the
/etc/rc.d/init.d directory (yours might look different, depending on whether you are
working with a workstation or server installation and the services or software packages
installed on your system):

```
# ls /etc/rc.d/init.d/
acpid      bgpd         firstboot  ip6tables   keytable     mars-nwe       nfs
postgresql  ripd         smartd      vncserver  zebra  aep1000    bluetooth
FreeWnn    ipchains     killall     mdmonitor      nfslock  privoxy
ripngd      smb           vsftpd  amd        bootparamd  functions  iptables
kprop        messagebus   nscd       psacct      routed       snmpd        winbind
anacron    canna         gkrellmd   irda        krb524       microcode_ctl  ntpd
pxe          rstatd       snmptrapd  xfs  apmd        cpqarrayd    gpm
irqbalance  krb5kdc      mysqld      ospf6d  radiusd       rusersd
spamassassin xinetd  arpwatch  crond       halt        iscsi        kudzu
named        ospfd        radvd       rwalld       squid        ypbind
atalk        cups         hpoj       isdn        ldap        netdump       pand
random      rwhod        sshd        yppasswd  atd        dhcpd
httpd        isicom       lisa        netdump-server  pcmcia     rarpd
saslauthd  syslog       ypserv  autofs  dhcrelay  identd       kadmin
lm_sensors  netfs            portmap  rawdevices  sendmail    tux
ypxfrd  bcm5820  dovecot       innd        kdcrotate    mailman
network          postfix  rhnsd       single      ups                     yum
```

The rc5.d links are prefaced with a letter and number, such as K15 or S10. The (K) or (S)
in these prefixes indicate whether or not a particular service should be killed (K) or started
(S) and pass a value of stop or start to the appropriate /etc/rc.d/init.d script. The
number in the prefix executes the specific /etc/rc.d/init.d script in a particular order.
The symlinks have numbers to delineate the order in which they are started. Nothing is
sacred about a specific number, but some services need to be running before others are
started. You wouldn't want your Fedora Core Linux system to attempt, for example, to
mount a remote Network File System (NFS) volume without first starting networking and
NFS services.

After all the system services are started for our runlevel, `init` starts the graphical login (because we are in runlevel 5). The graphical login's definition appears toward the end of /etc/inittab and looks like this:

```
# Run xdm in runlevel 5

x:5:respawn:/etc/X11/prefdm -nodaemon
```

This example shows that the shell script named `prefdm` executes the proper X11 display manager when Fedora Core Linux is booted to runlevel 5.

Booting to a Non-Default Runlevel with GRUB

After you select a default runlevel, that runlevel will be selected every time you restart the system from a power-off state. There might come a time when you do not want to boot into that runlevel. You might want to enter the maintenance mode or start the system without an active X server and graphical login in order to modify or repair the X server or desktop manager. You'll need to follow several specific steps to boot to a non-default runlevel if you use the default boot loader for Fedora Core, GRUB.

> **NOTE**
>
> If you have enabled a GRUB password, you must first press **p**, type your password, and then press Enter before using this boot method.

The GRUB boot loader passes arguments, or commands, to the kernel at boot time. These arguments are used, among other things, to tell GRUB where the kernel is located and also to pass specific parameters to the kernel, such as how much memory is available or how special hardware should be configured.

To override the default runlevel, you can add an additional kernel argument to GRUB as follows:

At the graphical boot screen, press **e** (for edit), scroll down to select the kernel, and press **e** again.

Press the spacebar, type **single** or **1** (Fedora Core allows **S** and s as well), and press Enter.

Finally, press **b** to boot, and you'll boot into runlevel 1 instead of the default runlevel listed in /etc/inittab.

Fedora Core Linux includes several command-line and graphical system administration utilities you can use to start, stop, reorder, or restart various services in different runlevels. These commands (discussed later in this chapter) work by renaming, removing, or creating symbolic links from /etc/rc.d/init.d to /etc/rc.d/rc.* as appropriate. Many administrators use these commands to change the symbolic links to the scripts under each /etc/rc.d/rc* directory rather than do it by hand.

The locations of symbolic links can also be confusing. Red Hat (and now Fedora Core) has traditionally kept them in one place, and the Linux Standards Base (LSB) requires that they now be located elsewhere. Because other scripts reference these files and it would be difficult to change them all, Fedora Core places symbolic links in the places specified by the LSB.

As you might surmise, symbolic links are very powerful tools in the system administrator's toolbox.

Understanding `init` Scripts and the Final Stage of Initialization

Each `/etc/rc.d/init.d` script, or `init` script, contains logic that determines what to do when receiving a start or stop value. The logic might be a simple switch statement for execution, as in this example:

```
case "$1" in
  start)
        start
        ;;
  stop)
        stop
        ;;
  restart)
        restart
        ;;
  reload)
        reload
        ;;
  status)
        rhstatus
        ;;
  condrestart)
        [ -f /var/lock/subsys/smb ] && restart ¦¦ :
        ;;
  *)
        echo $"Usage: $0 {start¦stop¦restart¦status¦condrestart}"
        exit 1
esac
```

Although the scripts can be used to customize the way that the system runs from power-on, absent the replacement of the kernel, this script approach also means that the system does not have to be halted in total to start, stop, upgrade, or install new services.

Note that not all scripts will use this approach, and that other messages might be passed to the service script, such as restart, reload, or status. Also, not all scripts will respond to the same set of messages (with the exception of start and stop, which they all have to accept by convention) because each service might require special commands.

14

> **TIP**
>
> You can write your own `init` scripts using the existing scripts as examples. Example scripts can also be found in `/usr/share/doc/initscripts/sysvinitfiles`, along with a brief tutorial written by Red Hat and a brief explanation of all the options available to use in `init` scripts.

After all the system scripts have been run, your system is configured and all the necessary system services have been started. If you are using a runlevel other then 5, the final act of the `init` process is to launch the user shell—`bash`, `tcsh`, `zsh`, or any of the many command shells available. The shell launches and you see a login prompt on the screen.

Controlling Services at Boot with Administrative Tools

As the master control file for system startup, `/etc/inittab` and its corresponding system of symbolic links control system services. You can manage `/etc/inittab` and its symbolic links using these graphical and non-graphical administrative tools:

- `chkconfig`—A small script that helps you configure system services

- `ntsysv`—A graphical interface for the `chkconfig` configuration script

- `system-config-services`—A full graphical services configuration client. This application is found in the System Services/Sever settings menu as the Services menu item.

The following sections explain how to use all these administrative tools to configure and manage services in Fedora Core Linux.

Using the `chkconfig` Text-Based Command-Line Tool

Traditionally, the command-line tool `chkconfig` has been used to effect administration of the services and their associations in the different runlevels. `chkconfig` was a major improvement over the process of configuring the symbolic links by hand. It is an effective, text-based command-line tool that you can use to display, diagnose, or change the starting or stopping of system services (as available under `/etc/rc.d/init.d`) in each runlevel.

For example, to list all services that will be turned on in runlevel 5, you can pipe the output of `chkconfig` through the `grep` command like this:

```
# /sbin/chkconfig --list ¦ grep '5:on' ¦ sort
anacron       0:off   1:off   2:on    3:on    4:on    5:on    6:off
apmd          0:off   1:off   2:on    3:on    4:on    5:on    6:off
atd           0:off   1:off   2:off   3:on    4:on    5:on    6:off
autofs        0:off   1:off   2:off   3:on    4:on    5:on    6:off
canna         0:off   1:off   2:on    3:off   4:on    5:on    6:off
crond         0:off   1:off   2:on    3:on    4:on    5:on    6:off
```

Not all the output is shown here, but as you can see, chkconfig can display the value of off or on for each service and each runlevel. The sample output only shows those services that will be started in runlevel 5. The chkconfig command can be used to reassign start or stop values for each runlevel and each service. As an example, to alter the scripts to start power management (controlled by the apmd script under /etc/rc.d/init.d) when using Fedora Core Linux during runlevel 5, use chkconfig like this:

```
# chkconfig --level 5 apmd on
```

You can then verify this action by again grepping chkconfig's output like this:

```
# chkconfig --list ¦ grep apmd
apmd              0:off   1:off   2:on    3:on    4:on    5:on    6:off
```

The chkconfig command does not start or stop a service; instead, it alters the scripts that start or stop a service, or it can report on the status of a service. Affecting only the current runlevel by default, other runlevels can be modified by using the –levels option. You would use the ntsysv or service commands or run the daemons directly in order to actually start or stop services (as described later in this chapter). All these tools have useful man pages to refresh your memory of all the available options.

ntsysv is a graphical interface you can use to access chkconfig and use a graphical interface. ntsysv is an ncurses-based interface, meaning that it offers crude, block graphics and elements you can tab through and select by pressing the spacebar (see Figure 14.1).

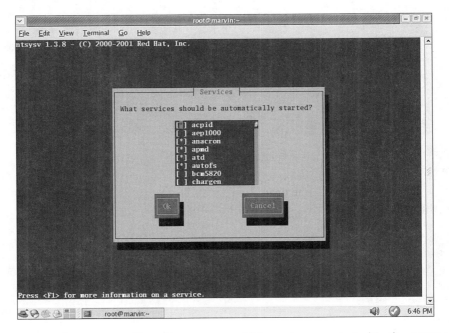

FIGURE 14.1   The ntsysv utility only manages which services are started in the current runlevel. Use the --level option to modify other runlevels.

When you have the ntsysv application open, you can scroll through the list of services and toggle a service on or off by pressing the spacebar on the keyboard. When finished, use the Tab key to highlight the OK or Cancel button. Your changes will be saved and used the next time Fedora Core Linux is booted.

> **NOTE**
>
> ntsysv is simple to use and it's an excellent tool for a system without X, but it only works for the runlevel you are currently in. Use the --level option to modify other runlevels.

The Fedora Core tool setup is an ncurses-based menu for all the available ncurses-based command-line configuration tools (see Figure 14.2). It can be used to access ntsysv and all the other command-line configuration tools.

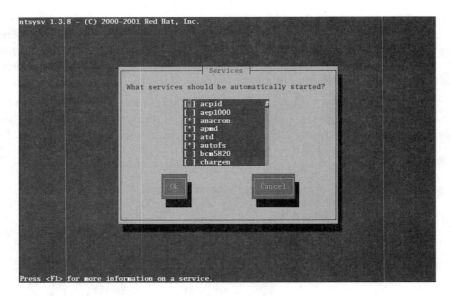

FIGURE 14.2   Use the setup command's System Services item to access the ntsysv command.

Using the GUI-Based Service Configuration Tool

Fedora Core's developers have added GUIs to many text-only, command-line–based system administration tools as Linux has matured. These tools provide an easier-to-use interface and don't require memorization or lookup of command-line options. Fedora Core provides its own Service Configuration tool for the control and administration of services (see Figure 14.3). You can access the GUI menu selection from the System Settings/Server Settings menu, and then select Services. The command-line name of this tool is system-config-services.

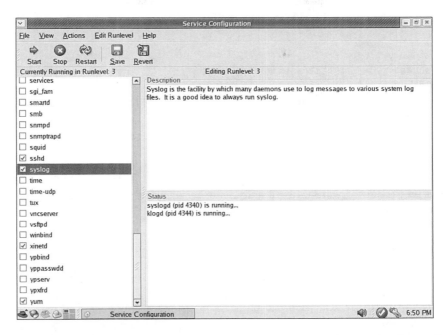

FIGURE 14.3 The new Service Configuration tool allows you to select runlevels to edit, displays all the available services, and provides an explanation of what the service does.

Running Services Through xinetd

The xinetd daemonis a replacement for inetd, and is a daemon that listens for requests for services on certain ports and starts those services as required. It is called a super server because it controls other servers; its purpose is to conserve resources by not running services when not needed. The xinetd daemon is more secure than the older inetd, offers better logging facilities than inetd, and can redirect service requests to another machine. It does not require the root user to start any services.

The configuration file for xinetd is found at /etc/xinetd.conf, configuration files for individual services are located in /etc/xinet.d/; the particulars of its format are covered in the man page for xinetd.conf, which also provides an example file listing. Fedora Core provides the appropriate server RPM packages already configured to use xinetd if possible. If you are installing servers manually from source code, the included documentation will describe the appropriate xinetd configuration. Services run under xinetd cannot be started and stopped in the same manner as the services run from scripts in /etc/rc.d/init.d; you must restart the xinetd service itself and let it control those services.

Here is a sample listing of the rsync file /etc/xinet.d/rsync:

```
# default: off
# description: The rsync server is a good addition to an ftp server, as it \
#       allows crc checksumming etc.
```

```
service rsync
{
        disable = yes
        socket_type      = stream
        wait             = no
        user             = root
        server           = /usr/bin/rsync
        server_args      = --daemon
        log_on_failure   += USERID
}
```

The items are straightforward and will vary from service to service. Although you can edit this by hand, it can be configured via the command-line or graphical service configuration clients.

Changing Runlevels

After making changes to system services and runlevels, you can use the telinit command to change runlevels on-the-fly on a running Fedora Core Linux system. Changing runlevels this way allows system administrators to alter selected parts of a running system in order to make changes to the services or to put changes into effect that have already been made (such as reassignment of network addresses for a networking interface).

For example, a system administrator can quickly change the system to maintenance or single-user mode by using the telinit command with its **S** option like this:

```
# telinit S
```

The telinit command uses the init command to change runlevels and shut down currently running services. The command then starts services for the specified runlevel, where in this example, the single-user runlevel is the same as runlevel 2. The init command can only be run from a console, not from an xterm running in an X session.

After booting to single-user mode, you can then return to multiuser mode without X, like this:

```
# telinit 3
```

If you have made changes to the system initialization table itself, /etc/inittab, use the telinit command's **q** command-line option to force init to re-examine the table.

> **TIP**
>
> Linux is full of shortcuts: If you exit the single-user shell by typing **exit** at the prompt, you'll go back to the default runlevel without worrying about using telinit.

Troubleshooting Runlevel Problems

Reordering or changing system services during a particular runlevel is rarely necessary when using Fedora Core Linux unless some disaster occurs. But system administrators should have a basic understanding of how Linux boots and how services are controlled in order to perform troubleshooting or to diagnose problems. By using additional utilities such as the `dmesg ¦ less` command to read kernel output after booting or by examining system logging with `cat /var/log/messages ¦ less`, it is possible to gain a bit more detail about what is going on when faced with troublesome drivers or service failure.

To better understand how to troubleshoot service problems in Fedora Core Linux, look at the diagnosis and resolution of a typical service-related issue.

In this example, X won't start: You don't see a desktop displayed, nor does the computer seem to respond to keyboard input. The X server might either be hung in a loop, repeatedly failing, or might exit to a shell prompt with or without an error message.

The X server only attempts to restart itself in runlevel 5, so to determine whether the X server is hung in a loop, try switching to runlevel 3.

> **TIP**
>
> If you are working on a multiuser system and might inadvertently interrupt the work of other users, ask them to save their current work; then change to a safer runlevel, such as single user mode.

Change to runlevel 3 by switching to another virtual console with Ctrl+Alt+F2, logging in as root, and running the command `telinit 3`. This switch to runlevel 3 will stop the X server from attempting to restart itself.

Now you can easily examine the error and attempt to fix it.

First, try to start the X server "naked" (without also launching the window manager). If you are successful, you will get a gray screen with a large X in the middle. If so, kill X with the Ctrl+Alt+Backspace key combination, and look at your window manager configuration. (This configuration varies according to which window manager you have chosen.)

Let's assume that X won't run "naked." If we look at the log file for Xorg (it's clearly identified in the `/var/log` directory), we'll pay attention to any line that begins with `(EE)`, the special error code. We can also examine the error log file, `.xsessions-error`, in our home directory if such a file exists.

If we find an error line, the cause of the error might or might not be apparent to us. The nice thing about the Linux community is that it is very unlikely that you are the first person to experience that error. Enter the error message (or better, a unique part of it) into http://www.google.com/linux and discover what others have had to say about the problem. You might need to adjust your search to yield usable results, but that level of detail is beyond the scope of this chapter. Make adjustments and retest as before until you achieve success.

Fix the X configuration and start X with **startx**. Repeat as necessary.

CAUTION

Before making any changes to any configuration file, always make a backup copy of the original, unmodified file. Our practice is to append the extension .original to the copy because that is a unique and unambiguous identifier.

If you need to restore the original configuration file, do not rename it, but copy it back to its original name.

Starting and Stopping Services Manually

If you change a configuration file for a system service, it is usually necessary to stop and restart the service to make it read the new configuration. If you are reconfiguring the X server, it is often convenient to change from runlevel 5 to runlevel 3 to make testing easier and then switch back to runlevel 5 to re-enable the graphical login. If a service is improperly configured, it is easier to stop and restart it until you have it configured correctly than it is to reboot the entire machine.

There are several ways to manually start or stop services or to change runlevels while using Fedora Core Linux. The traditional way to manage a service (as root) is to call the service's /etc/rc.d/init.d name on the command line with an appropriate keyword, such as start, status, or stop. For example, to start the automated nightly update of the YUM RPM package database, call the /etc/rc.d/init.d/yum script like this:

```
# /etc/rc.d/init.d/yum start
Enabling nightly yum update:                              [  OK  ]
```

The script will execute the proper program(s) and report the status of it. Stopping services is equally easy, and in fact, you can also check the status of some services by using the status keyword like this:

```
# /etc/rc.d/init.d/yum status
Nightly yum update is enabled.
```

In this example, the yum script reports that the daemon is running. This information might be useful for other system management tasks.

A much easier way to manually start or stop a service is to use a script named service. Using service, you do not have to know the full pathname to the system service; you only need know the name of the system service you want to manipulate. Using this approach, the previous Yum example looks like this:

```
# service yum start
Nightly yum update is enabled:                            [  OK  ]
```

Of course, the GUI tools mentioned before also have the functionality to start and stop specific services in your current runlevel. The tool you choose is a matter of personal preference; a good system administrator will be aware of them all.

Relevant Fedora Core Linux Commands

Here are some of the commands you learned so far:

chkconfig—Fedora Core's text-only command-line runlevel configuration utility.

ntsysv—Fedora Core's text-based system services configuration tool for the command line.

setup—Actually a BASH script, it is a menu to all the individual ncurses-based configuration tools, including ntsysv.

system-config-services—Fedora Core's GUI runlevel configuration tool, named Configure Services.

telinit—Changes the current runlevel.

14

Scheduling Tasks

There are three ways to schedule commands in Fedora Core Linux, all of which work in different ways. The first is the at command, which specifies a command to run at a specific time and date relative to today. The second is the batch command, which is actually a script that redirects you to the at command with some extra options set so your command runs when the system is quiet. The last option is the cron daemon, which is the Linux way of executing tasks at a given time.

Using at and batch to Schedule Tasks for Later

If there is a time-intensive task you want to run, but you do not want to do it while you are still logged in, you can tell Fedora to run it later with the at command. To use at, you need to tell it the time at which you want to run and then press Enter. You will then see a new prompt that start with at>, and everything you type there until you press Ctrl+D will be the commands you want at to run.

When the designated time arrives, at will perform each action individually and in order, which means later commands can rely on the results of earlier commands. In this next example, run at just after 5 p.m., at is used to download and extract the latest Linux kernel at a time when the network should be quiet:

```
[paul@caitlin ~]$ at now + 7 hours
at> wget http://www.kernel.org/pub/linux/kernel/v2.6/linux-2.6.10.tar.bz2
at> tar xvfjp linux-2.6.10.tar.bz2
at> <EOT>
job 2 at 2005-01-09 17:01
```

Specifying now + 7 hours as the time does what you would expect: at was run at 5 p.m., so the command will run just after midnight that night. When your job has finished, at will send you a mail with a full log of your job's output; type mail at the console to bring up your mailbox and then press the relevant number to read at's mail.

If you have a more complex job, you can use the -f parameter to have at read its commands from a file, like this:

```
echo wget http://www.kernel.org/pub/linux/kernel/v2.6/linux-2.6.10.tar.bz2\;
tar xvfjp linux-2.6.10.tar.bz2 > myjob.job
at -f myjob.job tomorrow
```

As you can see, at is flexible about the time format it takes; you can specify it in three ways:

- Using the now parameter, you can specify how many minutes, hours, days, or weeks relative to the current time—for example, now + 4 weeks would run the command one month from today.

- You can also specify several special times, including tomorrow, midnight, noon, or teatime (4 p.m.). If you do not specify a time with tomorrow, your job is set for precisely 24 hours from the current time.

- You can specify an exact date and time using HH:MM MM/DD/YY format—for example, 16:40 22/12/05 for 4:40 p.m. on the 22nd of December 2005.

When your job is submitted, at will report the job number, date, and time that the job will be executed; the queue identifier; plus the job owner (you). It will also capture all your environment variables and store them along with the job so that, when your job runs, it can restore the variables, preserving your execution environment.

The job number and job queue identifier are both important. When you schedule a job using at, it is placed into queue "a" by default, which means it runs at your specified time and taking up a normal amount of resources.

There is an alternative command, batch, which is really just a shell script that calls at with a few extra options. These options (-q b -m now, if you were interested) set at to run on queue b (-q b), mailing the user on completion (-m), and running immediately (now). The queue part is what is important: Jobs scheduled on queue b will only be executed when system load falls below 0.8—that is, when the system is not running at full load. Furthermore, it will run with a lower niceness, meaning a queue jobs usually have a niceness of 2, whereas b queue jobs have a niceness of 4.

Because batch always specifies now as its time, you need not specify your own time; it will simply run as soon as the system is quiet. Having a default niceness of 4 means that batched commands will get less system resources than a queue jobs (at's default) and less system resources than most other programs. You can optionally specify other queues using at. Queue c runs at niceness 6, queue d runs at niceness 8, and so on. However, it is important to note that the system load is only checked before the command is run. If the load is lower than 0.8, your batch job will be run. If the system load subsequently rises beyond 0.8, your batch job will continue to run, albeit in the background, thanks to its niceness value.

When you submit a job for execution, you will also be returned a job number. If you forget this or just want to see a list of other jobs you have scheduled to be run later, use the atq command with no parameters. If you run this as a normal user, it will print only your jobs; running it as a superuser will print everyone's jobs. The output is in the same format as when you submit a job, so you get the ID number, execution time, queue ID, and owner of each job.

If you want to delete a job, use the atrm command followed by the ID number of the job you want to delete. This next example shows atq and atrm being used to list jobs and delete one:

```
[paul@caitlin ~]$ atq
14      2005-01-20 23:33 a paul
16      2005-02-03 22:34 a paul
17      2005-01-25 22:34 a paul
15      2005-01-22 04:34 a paul
18      2005-01-22 01:35 b paul
[paul@caitlin ~]$ atrm 16
[paul@caitlin ~]$ atq
14      2005-01-20 23:33 a paul
17      2005-01-25 22:34 a paul
15      2005-01-22 04:34 a paul
18      2005-01-22 01:35 b paul
```

In that example, job 16 is deleted using atrm, and so it does not show up in the second call to atq.

The default configuration for at and batch is to allow everyone to use it, which is not always the desired behavior. Access is controlled through two files: /etc/at.allow, and /etc/at.deny. By default, at.deny exists but is empty, which allows everyone to use at and batch. You can enter usernames into at.deny, one per line, to stop those users scheduling jobs.

Alternatively, you can use the at.allow file; this does not exist by default. If you have a blank at.allow file, no one except root is allowed to schedule jobs. As with at.deny, you can add usernames to at.allow one per line, and those users will be able to schedule jobs. You should use either at.deny or at.allow: When someone tries to run at or batch, Fedora checks for her username in at.allow. If it is in there, or if at.allow does not exist, Fedora checks for her username in at.deny. If her username is in at.deny or at.deny does not exist, she is not allowed to schedule jobs.

Using cron to Run Jobs Repeatedly

The at and batch commands work well if you just want to execute a single task at a later date, but they are less useful if you want to run a task frequently. Instead, there is the crond daemon for running tasks repeatedly based upon system—and user—requests. Cron has a similar permissions system to at: Users listed in the cron.deny file are not allowed to use Cron, and users listed in the cron.allow file are. An empty cron.deny file—the default—means everyone can set jobs. An empty cron.allow file means that no one (except root) can set jobs.

There are two types of jobs: system jobs and user jobs. Only root can edit *system* jobs, whereas any user whose name appears in cron.allow or does not appear in cron.deny can run *user* jobs. System jobs are controlled through the /etc/crontab file, which by default looks like this:

```
SHELL=/bin/bash
PATH=/sbin:/bin:/usr/sbin:/usr/bin
MAILTO=root
HOME=/

# run-parts
01 * * * * root run-parts /etc/cron.hourly
02 4 * * * root run-parts /etc/cron.daily
22 4 * * 0 root run-parts /etc/cron.weekly
42 4 1 * * root run-parts /etc/cron.monthly
```

The first four lines are optional: SHELL specifies which shell should be used to execute the job (defaults to the shell of the user who owns the crontab file, usually /bin/bash), PATH specifies the search path for executables that will be used, and you should avoid using environment variables here. MAILTO defines who mail should be sent to. If this is not set, it uses the owner of the crontab, but if you do not want to receive mail when your job runs, just set it to "". Finally, HOME specifies the home directory of the user; again, this defaults to the user's home directory if left unspecified.

The next line, # run-parts, starts with a pound sign (#) and so is treated as a comment and ignored. The next four lines are the important parts: They are the jobs themselves.

Each job is specified in seven fields that define the time to run, owner, and command. The first five commands specify the execution time in quite a quirky order: minute (0–59), hour (0–23), day of the month (1–31), month of the year (1–12), and day of the week (0–7). For day of the week, both 0 and 7 are Sunday, which means that 1 is Monday, 3 is Wednesday, and so on. If you want to specify "all values" (that is, every minute, every hour, every day, and so on), use an asterisk, *.

The next field specifies the username of the owner of the job. When a job is executed, it uses the username specified here. The last field is the command to execute.

So, the first job runs at minute 1, every hour of every day of every month and executes the command run-parts /etc/cron.hourly. The run-parts command is a simple script that runs all programs inside a given directory—in this case, /etc/cron.hourly. So, in this case, the job will execute at 00:01 (1 minute past midnight), 01:01, 02:01, 03:01, and so on, and will use all the programs listed in the cron.hourly directory.

The next job runs at minute 2 and hour 4 of every day of every month, running run-parts /etc/cron.daily. Because of the hour limitation, this script will run only once per day, at 4:02 a.m. Note that it uses minute 2 rather than minute 1 so that daily jobs do not clash with hourly jobs. You should be able to guess what the next two jobs do, simply by looking at the commands they run!

Inside each of those four directories (cron.hourly, cron.daily, cron.weekly, and cron.monthly) are a collection of shell scripts that will be run by run-parts. For example, in cron.daily you will have scripts like rpm; which saves a list of your packages in /var/log/rpmpkgs every day, logrotate, which handles backing up of log files; and makewhatis, which updates the whatis database. You can add other system tasks to these directories if you want to, but you should be careful to ensure your scripts are correct.

> **CAUTION**
>
> The cron daemon reads all the system crontab files and all user crontab files once a minute (on the minute, i.e. at 6:00:00, 6:01:00, and so on) to check for changes. However, any new jobs it finds will not be executed until at least 1 minute has passed.
>
> For example, if it is 6:01:49 (that is, 49 seconds past 1 minute past 6 a.m.) and you set a cron job to run at 6:02, it will not execute. At 6:02, the cron daemon will reread its configuration files and see the new job, but it will not be able to execute it. If you set the job to run at 6:02 a.m. every day, it will be executed the following morning and every subsequent morning.
>
> This same situation exists when deleting jobs. If it is 6:01:49 and you have a job scheduled to run at 6:02, deleting it will make no difference: cron will run it before it rereads the crontab files for changes. However, after it has reread the crontab file and noticed the job is no longer there, it will not be executed in subsequent days.

There are alternative ways of specifying dates. For example, you can use sets of dates and times by using hyphens of commas, such as hours 9–15 would execute at 9, 10, 11, 12, 13, 14, and 15 (from 9 a.m. to 3 p.m.), whereas 9,11,13,15 would miss out at the even hours. Note that it is important you do not put spaces into these sets because the cron daemon will interpret them as the next field. You can define a step value with a slash (/) to show time division: */4 for hours means "every four hours all day", and 0-12/3 means "every three hours from midnight to noon." You can also specify day and month names rather than numbers, using three-character abbreviations: Sun, Mon, Tue, Fri, Sat for days, or Jan, Feb, Mar, Oct, Nov, Dec for months.

As well as system jobs, there are also user jobs for those users who have the correct permissions. User jobs are stored in the /var/spool/cron directory, with each user having his own file in his named after his username—for instance, /var/spool/cron/paul or /var/spool/cron/root. The contents of these files contain the jobs the user wants to run and take roughly the same format as the /etc/crontab file, with the exception that the owner of the job should not be specified because it will always be the same as the filename.

To edit your own `crontab` file, type **`crontab -e`**. This brings up a text editor (`vim` by default, but you can set the `EDITOR` environment variable to change that) where you can enter your entries. The format of this file is a little different from the format for the main `crontab` because this time there is no need to specify the owner of the job—it is always you.

So, this time each line is made up of six fields: minute (0–59), hour (0–23), day of the month (1–31), month of the year (1–12), day of the week (0–7), and then the command to run. If you are using `vim` and are new to it, press `i` to enter insert mode to edit your text; then press Esc to exit insert mode. To save and quit, type a colon followed by `wq` and press Enter.

When programming, we tend to use a `sandbox` subdirectory in our home directory where we keep all sorts of temporary files that we were just playing around with. We can use a personal job to empty that directory ever morning at 6 a.m. so that we get a fresh start each morning. Here is how that would like in our `crontab` file:

```
0 6 * * * rm -rf /home/paul/sandbox/*
```

If you are not allowed to schedule jobs, you will be stopped from editing your `crontab` file.

Once your jobs are placed, you can use the command `crontab -l` to list your jobs. This just prints the contents of your `crontab` file, so its output will be the same as the line you just entered.

If you want to remove just one job, the easiest thing to do is type `crontab -e` to edit your `crontab` file in `vim`; then, after having moved the cursor to the job you want to delete, type `dd` (two *d*s) to delete that line. If you want to delete all your jobs, you can use `crontab -r` to delete your `crontab` file.

Basic Shell Control

Fedora Core Linux includes a rich assortment of capable, flexible, and powerful shells. Each shell is different but has numerous built-in commands and configurable command-line prompts and might include features such as command-line history, the ability to recall and use a previous command line, and command-line editing. As an example, the `bash` shell is so powerful that it is possible to write a minimal web server entirely in `bash`'s language using 114 lines of script (see the link at the end of this chapter).

Although there are many shells to choose from, most people stick with the default, `bash`. This is because `bash` does everything most people need to do, and more. Only change your shell if you really need to.

Table 14.1 lists each shell, along with its description and location, in your Fedora file system.

TABLE 14.1   Shells with Fedora Core

Name	Description	Location
ash	A small shell (sh-like)	/bin/ash
ash.static	A version of ash not dependent on software libraries	/bin/ash.static
bash	The Bourne Again SHell	/bin/bash
bsh	A symbolic link to ash	/bin/bsh
csh	The C shell, a symbolic link to tcsh	/bin/csh
ksh	The Korn shell	/bin/ksh, /usr/bin/ksh
pdksh	A symbolic link to ksh	/usr/bin/pdksh
rsh	The restricted shell (for network operation)	/usr/bin/rsh
sash	A standalone shell	/sbin/sash
sh	A symbolic link to bash	/bin/sh
tcsh	A csh-compatible shell	/bin/tcsh
zsh	A compatible csh, ksh, and sh shell	/bin/zsh

Learning More About Your Shell

All the shells listed in Table 14.1 have accompanying man pages, along with other documentation under the /usr/share/doc directory. Some of the documentation can be quite lengthy, but it is generally much better to have too much documentation than too little! The bash shell includes more than 100 pages in its manual, and the zsh shell documentation is so extensive that it includes the zshall meta man page (use man zshall to read this overview)!

The Shell Command Line

Having a basic understanding of the capabilities of the shell command line can help you write better shell scripts. You can use the shell command line to perform a number of different tasks, including

- Searching files or directories with programs using pattern-matching, or *expressions*; these commands include the GNU gawk (linked as awk) and the grep family of commands, including egrep and fgrep.

- Getting data from and sending data to a file or command, known as *input* and *output redirection*.

- Feeding or filtering a program's output to another command (called using *pipes*).

A shell can also have built-in *job-control* commands to launch the command line as a background process, suspend a running program, selectively retrieve or kill running or suspended programs, and perform other types of process control.

Multiple commands can be run on a single command line using a semicolon to separate commands:

```
$ w ; free ; df
  6:02pm  up 4 days, 24 min,  1 user,  load average: 0.00, 0.00, 0.00
USER     TTY        FROM              LOGIN@   IDLE   JCPU   PCPU  WHAT
bball    pts/0      shuttle.home.org 1:14pm   0.00s  0.57s  0.01s  w
total        used        free      shared    buffers     cached
Mem:        190684      184420        6264          76      17620        142820
-/+ buffers/cache:       23980      166704
Swap:     1277156        2516     1274640
Filesystem          1k-blocks      Used Available Use% Mounted on
/dev/hda1            11788296   4478228   6711248  41% /
none                    95340         0     95340   0% /dev/shm
```

This example displays the output of the w, free, and df commands. Long shell command lines can be extended inside shell scripts or at the command line by using the backslash character (\). For example,

```
$ echo ""this is a long \
> command line and"" ; echo ""shows that multiple commands \
> may be strung out.""
this is a long command line and
shows that multiple commands may be strung out.
```

The first three lines of this example are a single command line. In that single line are two instances of the echo command. Note that when you use the backslash as a line-continuation character, it must be the last character on the command line (or in your shell script, as you will see later on in this chapter).

Using the basic features of the shell command line is easy, but mastering use of all features can be difficult. Entire books have been devoted to using shells, writing shell scripts, and using pattern-matching expressions. The following sections provide an overview of some features of the shell command line relating to writing scripts.

Grokking grep

If you plan to develop shell scripts to expand the capabilities of pattern-matching commands such as grep, you will benefit from learning more about using expressions. One of the definitive guides to using the pattern-matching capabilities of Unix and Linux commands is *Mastering Regular Expressions* by Jeffrey E. F. Freidl (O'Reilly), ISBN: 0-596-00289-0.

Shell Pattern-Matching Support

The shell command line allows you to use strings of specially constructed character patterns for wildcard matches. This is a different simpler capability than that supported by GNU utilities such as grep, which can use more complex patterns, known as *expressions*, to search through files or directories or to filter data input to or out of commands.

The shell's pattern strings can be simple or complex, but even using a small subset of the available characters in simple wildcards can yield constructive results at the command line. Some common characters used for shell pattern matching are

- *—Matches any character. For example, to find all files in the current directory ending in .txt, you could use

  $ ls *.txt

- ?—Matches a single character. For example, to find all files in the current directory ending in the extension .d?c (where ? could be 0–9, a–z, or A–Z):

  $ ls *.d?c

- [xxx] or [x-x]—Matches a range of characters. For example, to list all files in a directory with names containing numbers:

  $ ls *[0-9]*

- \x—Matches or escapes a character such as ? or a tab character. For example, to create a file with a name containing question mark:

  $ touch foo\?

Note that the shell might not interpret some characters or regular expressions in the same manner as a Linux command, and mixing wildcards and regular expressions in shell scripts can lead to problems unless you're careful. For example, finding patterns in text is best left to regular expressions used with commands such as grep; simple wildcards should be used for filtering or matching filenames on the command line. And although both Linux command expressions and shell scripts can recognize the backslash as an escape character in patterns, the dollar sign ($) will have two wildly different meanings (single-character pattern matching in expressions and variable assignment in scripts).

> **CAUTION**
>
> Make sure you read your command carefully when using wildcards; an all-too-common error is to type something like rm -rf * .txt with a space between the * and the .txt. By the time you wonder why the command is taking so long, Bash will already have deleted most of your files. The problem is that it will treat the * and the .txt separately. * will match everything, so Bash will delete all your files.

Redirecting Input and Output

You can create, overwrite, and append data to files at the command line, using a process called *input* and *output redirection*. The shell recognizes several special characters for this process, such as >, <, or >>.

In this example, the output of the ls command is redirected to create a file named textfiles.listing:

```
$ ls *.txt >textfiles.listing
```

Use output redirection with care because it is possible to overwrite existing files. For example, specifying a different directory but using the same output filename will over-write the existing textfiles.listing:

```
$ ls /usr/share/doc/mutt-1.4/*.txt >textfiles.listing
```

Fortunately, most shells are smart enough to recognize when you might do something foolish. Here, the bash shell warns that the command is attempting to redirect output to a directory:

```
$ mkdir foo
$ ls >foo
bash: foo: Is a directory
```

Output can be appended to a file without overwriting existing content by using the append operator, >>. In> append operator> this example, the directory listing will be appended to the end of textfiles.listing instead of overwriting its contents:

```
$ ls /usr/share/doc/mutt-1.4/*.txt >>textfiles.listing
```

You can use *input redirection* to feed data into a command by using the < like this:

```
$ cat < textfiles.listing
```

You can use the shell *here* operator, <<, to specify the end of input on the shell command line:

```
$ cat >simple_script <<DONE
> echo ""this is a simple script""
> DONE
$ cat simple_script
echo ""this is a simple script""
```

In this example, the shell will feed the cat command you are typing (input) until the pattern DONE is recognized. The output file simple_script is then saved and its contents verified. This same technique can be used in scripts to create content based on the output of various commands and define an end-of-input or delimiter.

Piping Data

Many Linux commands can be used in concert in a single, connected command line to transform data from one form to another. Stringing Linux commands together in this fashion is known as using or creating *pipes*. Pipes are created on the command line with the bar operator ($\mid$). For example, a pipe can be used to perform a complex task from a single command line like this:

```
$ find /d2 -name '*.txt' -print | xargs cat | \
tr ' ' '\n' | sort | uniq >output.txt
```

This example takes the output of the find command to feed the cat command (via xargs) the name all text files under the /d2 command. The content of all matching files is then fed through the tr command to change each space in the data stream into a carriage return. The stream of words is then sorted, and identical adjacent lines are removed using the uniq command. The output, a raw list of words, is then saved in the file named output.txt.

Background Processing

The shell allows you to start a command and then launch it into the background as a process by using an ampersand (&) at the end of a command line. This technique is often used at the command line of an X terminal window to start a client and return to the command line. For example, to launch another terminal window using the xterm client use

```
$ xterm &
[3] 1437
```

The numbers echoed back show a number (3 in this example), which is a *job* number, or reference number for a shell process, and a *Process ID* number, or PID (1437 in this example). The xterm window session can be killed by using the shell's built-in kill command, along with the job number like this:

```
$ kill %3
```

Or the process can be killed by using the kill command, along with the PID, like so:

```
$ kill 1437
```

Background processing can be used in shell scripts to start commands that take a long time, such as backups:

```
# tar -czf /backup/home.tgz /home &
```

Writing and Executing a Shell Script

Why should you write and use shell scripts? Shell scripts can save you time and typing, especially if you routinely use the same command lines multiple times every day. Although you could also use the history function (press the Up or Down keys while using bash or use the history command), a shell script can add flexibility with command-line argument substitution and built-in help.

Although a shell script won't execute faster than a program written in a computer language such as C, a shell program can be smaller in size than a compiled program. The shell program does not require any additional library support other than the shell or, if used, existing commands installed on your system. The process of creating and testing shell scripts is also generally simpler and faster than the development process for equivalent C language commands.

> **NOTE**
>
> Hundreds of commands included with Fedora are actually shell scripts, and many other good shell script examples are available over the Internet—a quick search will yield numerous links to online tutorials and scripting guides from fellow Linux users and developers. For example, the startx command, used to start an X Window session from the text console, is a shell script used every day by many Linux (and Unix) users. Sending faxes can be accomplished by using the fax command, which is a shell script you can customize to include your name, phone number, and other information. To learn more about shell scripting with bash, see the Advanced Bash-Scripting Guide, listed in the "Reference" section at the end of this chapter. You'll also find *Sams Teach Yourself Shell Programming in 24 Hours* a helpful guide to learning more about using the shell to build your own commands.

When you are learning to write and execute your first shell scripts, start with scripts for simple, but useful tasks. Begin with short examples, and then expand the scripts as you build on your experience and knowledge. Make liberal use of comments (lines preceded with a pound # sign) to document each section of your script. Include an author statement and overview of the script as additional help, along with a creation date or version number. Write shell scripts using a text editor such as vi because it does not automatically wrap lines of text. Line wrapping can break script syntax and cause problems. If you use the nano editor, include its -w flag to disable line wrap.

In this section, you learn how to write a simple shell script to set up a number of *aliases* (command synonyms) whenever you log on. Instead of typing all the aliases every time you log on, you can put them in a file by using a text editor, such as vi, and then execute the file. Normally these changes are saved in systemwide shell configuration files under the /etc directory to make the changes active for all users or in your .bashrc, .cshrc (if you use tcsh), or .bash_profile files in your home directory.

Here is what is contained in myenv, a sample shell script created for this purpose (for bash):

```
#!/bin/sh
alias ll='ls -l'
alias ldir='ls -aF'
alias copy='cp'
```

This simple script creates command *aliases*, or convenient shorthand forms of commands, for the ls and cp commands. The ll alias provides a long directory listing: The ldir alias is the ls command, but prints indicators (for directories or executable files) in listings. The copy alias is the same as the cp command. You can experiment and add your own options or create aliases of other commands with options you frequently use.

You can execute myenv in a variety of ways under Linux. As shown in this example, you can make myenv executable by using the chmod command and then execute it as you would any other native Linux command:

```
$ chmod +x myenv
```

This line turns on the executable permission of myenv, which can be checked with the ls command and its -l option like this:

```
$ ls -l myenv
-rwxrwxr-x    1 winky    winky            11 Aug 26 17:38 myenv
```

Running the New Shell Program

You can run your new shell program in several ways. Each method will produce the same results, which is a testament to the flexibility of using the shell with Linux. One way to run your shell program is to execute the file myenv from the command line as if it were a Linux command:

```
$ ./myenv
```

A second way to execute myenv under a particular shell, such as pdksh, is as follows:

```
$ pdksh myenv
```

This invokes a new pdksh shell and passes the filename myenv as a parameter to execute the file. A third way will require you to create a directory named bin in your home directory, and to then copy the new shell program into this directory. You can then run the program without the need to specify a specific location or to use a shell. You do this like so:

```
$ mkdir bin
$ mv myenv bin
$ myenv
```

This works because Fedora is set up by default to include the executable path $HOME/bin in your shell's environment. You can view this environment variable, named PATH, by piping the output of the env command through fgrep like so:

```
$ env ¦ fgrep PATH
/usr/kerberos/bin:/usr/local/bin:/bin:/usr/bin: \
/usr/X11R6/bin:/sbin:/home/paul/bin
```

As you can see, the user (paul in this example) can use the new bin directory to hold executable files. Another way to bring up an environment variable is to use the echo command along with the variable name (in this case, $PATH):

```
$ echo $PATH
/usr/kerberos/bin:/usr/local/bin:/usr/bin:/bin:/usr/X11R6/bin:/home/bball/bin
```

The Public Domain Korn Shell

The pdksh shell was originally created by Eric Gisin, and, like the original Korn shell by David Korn, is in the public domain. In Fedora, pdksh is named ksh. Two symbolic links, /usr/bin/pdksh and /usr/bin/ksh, point to the pdksh shell, named /bin/ksh. For more information about pdksh, see the /usr/share/doc/pdksh directory or read the ksh man page. You can download the latest copy of pdksh (in source-code form) by browsing to ftp://ftp.cs.mun.ca/pub/pdksh/.

On March 1, 2000, AT&T released the official version of the korn shell, named KornShell 93, as open source. If you are interested in trying the original korn shell by David Korn, download a copy from the KornShell web page at http://www.kornshell.com/.

CAUTION

Never put . in your $PATH in order to execute files or a command in the current directory—this presents a serious security risk, especially for the root operator, and even more so if . is first in your $PATH search order. Trojan scripts placed by crackers in directories such as /tmp can be used for malicious purposes, and will be executed immediately if the current working directory is part of your $PATH.

Storing Shell Scripts for Systemwide Access

After you execute the command myenv, you should be able to use ldir from the command line to get a list of files under the current directory and ll to get a list of files with attributes displayed. However, the best way to use the new commands in myenv is to put them into your shell's login or profile file. For Fedora, and nearly all Linux users, the default shell is bash, so you can make these commands available for everyone on your system by putting them in the /etc/bashrc file. Systemwide aliases for tcsh are contained in files with the extension .csh under the /etc/profile.d directory. The pdksh shell can use these command aliases as well.

NOTE

To use a shell other than bash after logging in, use the chsh command from the command line or the system-config-users client during an X session. You'll be asked for your password (or the root password if using system-config-users), as well as the location and name of the new shell (refer to Table 14.1). The new shell will become your default shell, but only if its name is in the list of acceptable system shells in /etc/shells. See Chapter 5, "First Steps with Fedora," for details on changing your shell.

Interpreting Shell Scripts Through Specific Shells

The majority of shell scripts use a she*bang line* (#!) at the beginning to control the type of shell used to run the script; this bang line calls for an sh-incantation of bash:

```
#!/bin/sh
```

A shebang line (it is short for "sharp" and "bang", two names for # and !) tells the Linux kernel that a specific command (a shell, or in the case of other scripts, perhaps awk or Perl) is to be used to interpret the contents of the file. Using a shebang line is common practice for all shell scripting. For example, if you write a shell script using bash, but want the script to execute as if run by the Bourne shell, sh, the first line of your script will contain #!/bin/sh, which is a link to the bash shell. Running bash as sh will cause bash to act as a Bourne shell. This is the reason for the symbolic link sh, which points to bash.

The Shebang Line

The shebang line is a magic number, as defined in /usr/share/magic—a text database of magic numbers for the Linux file command. Magic numbers are used by many different Linux commands to quickly identify a type of file, and the database format is documented in the section five manual page named magic (read by using man 5 magic). For example, magic numbers can be used by the Linux file command to display the identity of a script (no matter what filename is used) as a shell script using a specific shell or other interpreter such as awk or Perl.

You might also find different or new environment variables available to your scripts by using different shells. For example, if you launch csh from the bash command line, you will find several new variables or variables with slightly different definitions, such as

```
$ env
...
VENDOR=intel
MACHTYPE=i386
HOSTTYPE=i386-linux
HOST=thinkpad.home.org
```

On the other hand, bash might provide these variables or variables of the same name with a slightly different definition, such as

```
$ env
...
HOSTTYPE=i386
HOSTNAME=thinkpad.home.org
```

Although the behavior of a shebang line is not defined by POSIX, variations of its use can be helpful when you are writing shell scripts. For example, as described in the wish man page, you can use a shell to help execute programs called within a shell script without needing to hard code pathnames of programs. The wish command is a windowing Tool Control Language (tcl) interpreter that can be used to write graphical clients. Avoiding the use of specific pathnames to programs increases shell script portability because not every Unix or Linux system has programs in the same location.

14

For example, if you want to use the `wish` command, your first inclination might be to write

```
#!/usr/local/bin/wish
```

Although this will work on many other operating systems, the script will fail under Linux because `wish` is located under the `/usr/bin` directory. However, if you write the command line this way,

```
#!/bin/sh
exec wish "$@"
```

you can use the `wish` command (as a binary or a shell script itself) `wish` command; your first inclination might be to write in Linux.

Using Variables in Shell Scripts

When writing shell scripts for Linux, you work with three types of variables:

- **Environment variables**—Part of the system environment, you can use them in your shell program. New variables can be defined, and some of them, such as PATH, can also be modified within a shell program.

- **Built-in variables**—These are variables such as options used on the command (interpreted by the shell as a *positional argument*) are provided by Linux. Unlike environment variables, you cannot modify them.

- **User variables**—Defined by you when you write a shell script. You can use and modify them at will within the shell program.

A major difference between shell programming and other programming languages is that in shell programming, variables are not *typed*—that is, you do not have to specify whether a variable is a number or a string, and so on.

Assigning a Value to a Variable

Say that you want to use a variable called `lcount` to count the number of iterations in a loop within a shell program. You can declare and initialize this variable as follows:

Command	Environment
lcount=0	pdksh and bash
set lcount=0	tcsh

> **NOTE**
>
> Under pdksh and bash, you must ensure that the equal sign (=) does not have spaces before and after it.

To store a string in a variable, you can use the following:

Command	Environment
myname=Sanjiv	pdksh and bash
set myname=Sanjiv	tcsh

Use the preceding variable form if the string doesn't have embedded spaces. If a string has embedded spaces, you can do the assignment as follows:

Command	Environment
myname="Sanjiv Guha"	pdksh and bash
set myname="Sanjiv Guha"	tcsh

Accessing Variable Values

You can access the value of a variable by prefixing the variable name with a $ (dollar sign). That is, if the variable name is var, you can access the variable by using $var.

If you want to assign the value of var to the variable lcount, you can do so as follows:

Command	Environment
lcount=$var	pdksh and bash
set lcount=$var	tcsh

Positional Parameters

It is possible to pass options from the command line or from another shell script to your shell program.

These options are supplied to the shell program by Linux as *positional parameters*, which have special names provided by the system. The first parameter is stored in a variable called 1 (number 1) and can be accessed by using $1 within the program. The second parameter is stored in a variable called 2 and can be accessed by using $2 within the program, and so on. One or more of the higher numbered positional parameters can be omitted while you're invoking a shell program.

Understanding how to use these positional parameters and how to access and use variables retrieved from the command line is necessary when developing more advanced shell programs.

A Simple Example of a Positional Parameter

For example, if a shell program mypgm expects two parameters—such as a first name and a last name—you can invoke the shell program with only one parameter, the first name. However, you cannot invoke it with only the second parameter, the last name.

Here is a shell program called mypgm1, which takes only one parameter (a name) and displays it on the screen:

```
#!/bin/sh
#Name display program
if [ $# -eq 0 ]
then
    echo "Name not provided"
else
    echo "Your name is "$1
fi
```

If you execute mypgm1, as follows,

```
$ bash  mypgm1
```

you get the following output:

```
Name not provided
```

However, if you execute mypgm1, as follows,

```
$ bash  mypgm1 Sanjiv
```

you get the following output:

```
Your name is Sanjiv
```

The shell program mypgm1 also illustrates another aspect of shell programming: the built-in variables provided to the shell by the Linux kernel. In mypgm1, the built-in variable $# provides the number of positional parameters passed to the shell program. You learn more about working with built-in variables in the next major section of this chapter.

Using Positional Parameters to Access and Retrieve Variables from the Command Line

Using positional parameters in scripts can be helpful if you need to use command lines with piped commands requiring complex arguments. Shell programs containing positional parameters can be even more convenient if the commands are infrequently used. For example, if you use your Fedora system with an attached voice modem as an answering machine, you can write a script to issue a command that retrieves and plays the voice messages. The following lines convert a saved sound file (in .rmd or voice-phone format) and pipe the result to your system's audio device:

```
#!/bin/sh
# play voice message in /var/spool/voice/incoming
rmdtopvf /var/spool/voice/incoming/$1 ¦ pvfspeed -s 8000 ¦ \
pvftobasic >/dev/audio
```

A voice message can then easily be played back using this script (perhaps named pmm):

$ **pmm** name_of_message

Shell scripts that contain positional parameters are often used for automating routine and mundane jobs, such as system log report generation, file system checks, user resource accounting, printer use accounting, and other system, network, or security administration tasks.

Using a Simple Script to Automate Tasks

You could use a simple script, for example, to examine your system log for certain keywords. If the script is run via your system's scheduling table, /etc/crontab, it can help automate security monitoring. By combining the output capabilities of existing Linux commands with the language facilities of the shell, you can quickly build a useful script to perform a task normally requiring a number of command lines. For example, you can create a short script, named greplog, like this:

```
#!/bin/sh
#    name:  greplog
#     use:  mail grep of designated log using keyword
# version:  v.01 08aug02
#
#  author: bb
#
# usage: greplog [keyword] [logpathname]
#
#  bugs: does not check for correct number of arguments

# build report name using keyword search and date
log_report=/tmp/$1.logreport.`date '+%m%d%y'`

# build report header with system type, hostname, date and time
echo "=========================================================" \
     >$log_report
echo "          S Y S T E M   M O N I T O R   L O G" >>$log_report
echo uname -a >>$log_report
echo "Log report for" `hostname -f` "on" `date '+%c'`      >>$log_report
echo "=========================================================" \
     >>$log_report ; echo "" >>$log_report

# record log search start
echo "Search for->" $1 "starting" `date '+%r'` >>$log_report
echo "" >>$log_report
```

```
# get and save grep results of keyword ($1) from logfile ($2)
grep -i $1 $2 >>$log_report

# build report footer with time
echo "" >>$log_report
echo "End of" $log_report at `date '+%r'` >>$log_report

# mail report to root
mail -s "Log Analysis for $1" root <$log_report

# clean up and remove report
rm $log_report
exit 0
```

In this example, the script creates the variable $log_report, which will be the filename of the temporary report. The keyword ($1) and first argument on the command line is used as part of the filename, along with the current date (with perhaps a better approach to use $$ instead of the date, which will append the script's PID as a file extension). Next, the report header containing some formatted text, the output of the uname command, and the hostname and date is added to the report. The start of the search is then recorded, and any matches of the keyword in the log are added to the report. A footer containing the name of the report and the time is then added. The report is mailed to root with the search term as the subject of the message, and the temporary file is deleted.

> **NOTE**
>
> By default, Fedora uses the logwatch log monitoring command (actually a Perl script) in your system's /etc/cron.daily directory to generate various reports each day at 0402 (4:02 a.m.). Configure logwatch by editing the file /etc/log.d/logwatch.conf. Other system monitoring tools are included, such as tripwire. System logging can be controlled by editing /etc/syslog.conf.

You can test the script by running it manually and feeding it a keyword and a pathname to the system log, /var/log/messages, like this:

```
# greplog FAILED /var/log/messages
```

Note that your system should be running the syslogd daemon. If any login failures have occurred on your system, the root operator might get an email message that looks like this:

```
Date: Thu, 23 Oct 2003 16:23:24 -0400
From: root <root@stinkpad.home.org>
To: root@stinkpad.home.org
Subject: FAILED
```

```
================================================================
          S Y S T E M   M O N I T O R   L O G
Linux stinky 2.4.22-1.2088.nptl #1 Thu Oct 9 20:21:24 EDT 2003 i686 i686 i386
+GNU/Linux
Log report for stinkpad.home.org on Thu 23 Oct 2003 04:23:24 PM EDT
================================================================

Search for-> FAILED starting 04:23:24 PM

Oct 23 16:23:04 stinkpad login[1769]: FAILED LOGIN 3 FROM (null) FOR bball,
+Authentication failure

End of /tmp/FAILED.logreport.102303 at 04:23:24 PM
```

To further automate the process, you can include command lines using the script in another script to generate a series of searches and reports.

Built-in Variables

Built-in variables are special variables provided to shell by Linux that can be used to make decisions within a shell program. You cannot modify the values of these variables within the shell program.

Some of these variables are

$#—Number of positional parameters passed to the shell program

$?—Completion code of the last command or shell program executed within the shell program (returned value)

$0—The name of the shell program

$*—A single string of all arguments passed at the time of invocation of the shell program

To show these built-in variables in use, here is a sample program called mypgm2:

```
#!/bin/sh
#my test program
echo "Number of parameters is $#"
echo "Program name is $0"
echo "Parameters as a single string is $*"
```

If you execute mypgm2 from the command line in pdksh and bash as follows,

```
$ bash mypgm2 Sanjiv Guha
```

you get the following result:

```
Number of parameters is 2
Program name is mypgm2
Parameters as a single string is Sanjiv Guha
```

Special Characters

Some characters have special meaning to Linux shells; these characters represent commands, denote specific use for surrounding text, or provide search parameters. Special characters provide a sort of shorthand by incorporating these rather complex meanings into a simple character. Some special characters are shown in Table 14.2.

TABLE 14.2 Special Shell Characters

Character	Explanation
$	Indicates the beginning of a shell variable name
¦	Pipes standard output to next command
#	Starts a comment
&	Executes a process in the background
?	Matches one character
*	Matches one or more characters
>	Output redirection operator
<	Input redirection operator
`	Command substitution (the backquote or backtick—the key above the Tab key on most keyboards)
>>	Output redirection operator (to append to a file)
<<	Wait until following end-of-input string (HERE operator)
[ ]	Range of characters
[a-z]	All characters a through z
[a,z] or [az]	Characters a or z
Space	Delimiter between two words

Special characters are very useful to you when you're creating shell scripts, but if you inadvertently use a special character as part of variable names or strings, your program will behave incorrectly. As you learn in later parts of this section, you can use one of the special characters in a string if you precede it with an *escape character* (/, or backslash) to indicate that it isn't being used as a special character and shouldn't be treated as such by the program.

A few special characters deserve special note. They are the double quotes ("), the single quotes ('), the backslash (\), and the backtick (`)—all discussed in the following sections.

Use Double Quotes to Resolve Variables in Strings with Embedded Spaces

If a string contains embedded spaces, you can enclose the string in double quotes (") so that the shell interprets the whole string as one entity instead of more than one.

For example, if you assigned the value of abc def (abc followed by one space, followed by def) to a variable called x in a shell program as follows, you would get an error because the shell would try to execute def as a separate command:

Command	Environment
x=abc def	pdksh and bash
set x=abc def	tcsh

The shell will execute the string as a single command if you surround the string in double quotes as follows:

Command	Environment
x="abc def"	pdksh and bash
set x="abc def"	tcsh

The double quotes resolve all variables within the string. Here is an example for pdksh and bash:

```
var="test string"
newvar="Value of var is $var"
echo $newvar
```

Here is the same example for tcsh:

```
set var="test string"
set newvar="Value of var is $var"
echo $newvar
```

If you execute a shell program containing the preceding three lines, you get the following result:

```
Value of var is test string
```

Using Single Quotes to Maintain Unexpanded Variables

You can surround a string with single quotes (') to stop the shell from expanding variables and interpreting special characters. When used for the latter purpose, the single quote is an *escape character*, similar to the backslash, which you learn about in the next section. Here, you learn how to use the single quote to avoid expanding a variable in a shell script. An unexpanded variable maintains its original form in the output.

In the following examples, the double quotes in the preceding examples have been changed to single quotes:

pdksh and bash:

```
var='test string'
newvar='Value of var is $var'
echo $newvar
```

tcsh:

```
set var = 'test string'
set newvar = 'Value of var is $var'
echo $newvar
```

If you execute a shell program containing these three lines, you get the following result:

```
Value of var is $var
```

As you can see, the variable var maintains its original format in the results, rather than having been expanded.

Using the Backslash As an Escape Character

As you learned earlier, the backslash (\) serves as an escape character that stops the shell from interpreting the succeeding character as a special character. Say that you want to assign a value of $test to a variable called var. If you use the following command, the shell reads the special character $ and interprets $test as the value of the variable test. No value has been assigned to test; a null value is stored in var as follows:

Command	Environment
var=$test	pdksh and bash
set var=$test	tcsh

Unfortunately, this assignment may work for bash and pdksh, but it returns an error of "undefined variable" if you use it with tcsh. Use the following commands to correctly store $test in var:

Command	Environment
var=\$test	pdksh and bash
set var = \$test	tcsh

The backslash before the dollar sign (\$) signals the shell to interpret the $ as any other ordinary character and not to associate any special meaning to it. You could also use single quotes (') around the $test variable to get the same result.

Using the Backtick to Replace a String with Output

You can use the backtick (`) character to signal the shell to replace a string with its output when executed. This special character can be used in shell programs when you want the result of the execution of a command to be stored in a variable. For example, if you want to count the number of lines in a file called test.txt in the current directory and store the result in a variable called var, you can use the following command:

Command	Environment
var=`wc -l test.txt`	pdksh and bash
set var = `wc -l test.txt`	tcsh

Comparison of Expressions in pdksh and bash

Comparing values or evaluating the differences between similar bits of data—such as file information, character strings, or numbers—is a task known as *comparison of expressions*. Comparison of expressions is an integral part of using logic in shell programs to accomplish tasks. The way the logical comparison of two operators (numeric or string) is done varies slightly in different shells. In pdksh and bash, a command called test can be used to achieve comparisons of expressions. In tcsh, you can write an expression to accomplish the same thing.

The following section covers comparison operations using the pdksh or bash shells. Later in the chapter, you learn how to compare expressions in the tcsh shell.

The pdksh and bash shell syntax provide a command named test to compare strings, numbers, and files. The syntax of the test command is as follows:

```
test expression
```

or

```
[ expression ]
```

Both forms of the test commands are processed the same way by pdksh and bash. The test commands support the following types of comparisons:

- String comparison
- Numeric comparison
- File operators
- Logical operators

14

String Comparison

The following operators can be used to compare two string expressions:

=—To compare whether two strings are equal

!=—To compare whether two strings are not equal

-n—To evaluate whether the string length is greater than zero

-z—To evaluate whether the string length is equal to zero

Next are some examples using these operators when comparing two strings, string1 and string2, in a shell program called compare1:

```
#!/bin/sh
string1="abc"
string2="abd"
if [ $string1 = $string2 ]; then
   echo "string1 equal to string2"
else
   echo "string1 not equal to string2"
fi

if [ $string2 != string1 ]; then
   echo "string2 not equal to string1"
else
   echo "string2 equal to string2"
fi

if [ $string1 ]; then
   echo "string1 is not empty"
else
   echo "string1 is empty"
fi

if [ -n $string2 ]; then
   echo "string2 has a length greater than zero"
else
   echo "string2 has length equal to zero"
fi

if [ -z $string1 ]; then
   echo "string1 has a length equal to zero"
else
  echo "string1 has a length greater than zero"
fi
```

If you execute compare1, you get the following result:

```
string1 not equal to string2
string2 not equal to string1
string1 is not empty
string2 has a length greater than zero
string1 has a length greater than zero
```

If two strings are not equal in size, the system pads out the shorter string with trailing spaces for comparison. That is, if the value of string1 is abc and that of string2 is ab, string2 will be padded with a trailing space for comparison purposes—it will have a value of ab.

Number Comparison

The following operators can be used to compare two numbers:

> -eq—To compare whether two numbers are equal

> -ge—To compare whether one number is greater than or equal to the other number

> -le—To compare whether one number is less than or equal to the other number

> -ne—To compare whether two numbers are not equal

> -gt—To compare whether one number is greater than the other number

> -lt—To compare whether one number is less than the other number

The following shell program compares three numbers, number1, number2, and number3:

```
#!/bin/sh
number1=5
number2=10
number3=5

if [ $number1 -eq $number3 ]; then
    echo "number1 is equal to number3"
else
    echo "number1 is not equal to number3"
fi

if [ $number1 -ne $number2 ]; then
    echo "number1 is not equal to number2"
else
    echo "number1 is equal to number2"
fi

if [ $number1 -gt $number2 ]; then
    echo "number1 is greater than number2"
```

14

```
else
   echo "number1 is not greater than number2"
fi


if [ $number1 -ge $number3 ]; then
   echo "number1 is greater than or equal to number3"
else
   echo "number1 is not greater than or equal to number3"
fi


if [ $number1 -lt $number2 ]; then
   echo "number1 is less than number2"
else
   echo "number1 is not less than number2"
fi


if [ $number1 -le $number3 ]; then
   echo "number1 is less than or equal to number3"
else
   echo "number1 is not less than or equal to number3"
fi
```

When you execute the shell program, you get the following results:

```
number1 is equal to number3
number1 is not equal to number2
number1 is not greater than number2
number1 is greater than or equal to number3
number1 is less than number2
number1 is less than or equal to number3
```

File Operators

The following operators can be used as file comparison operators:

- -d—To ascertain whether a file is a directory

- -f—To ascertain whether a file is a regular file

- -r—To ascertain whether read permission is set for a file

- -s—To ascertain whether a file exists and has a length greater than zero

- -w—To ascertain whether write permission is set for a file

- -x—To ascertain whether execute permission is set for a file

Assume that a shell program called compare3 is in a directory with a file called file1 and a subdirectory dir1 under the current directory. Assume that file1 has a permission of r-x (read and execute permission) and dir1 has a permission of rwx (read, write, and execute permission). The code for the shell program would look like this:

```
#!/bin/sh
if [ -d $dir1 ]; then
    echo "dir1 is a directory"
else
    echo "dir1 is not a directory"
fi

if [ -f $dir1 ]; then
    echo "dir1 is a regular file"
else
    echo "dir1 is not a regular file"
fi

if [ -r $file1 ]; then
    echo "file1 has read permission"
else
    echo "file1 does not have read permission"
fi

if [ -w $file1 ]; then
    echo "file1 has write permission"
else
    echo "file1 does not have write permission"
fi

if [ -x $dir1 ]; then
    echo "dir1 has execute permission"
else
    echo "dir1 does not have execute permission"
fi
```

If you execute the shell program, you get the following results:

```
dir1 is a directory
file1 is a regular file
file1 has read permission
file1 does not have write permission
dir1 has execute permission
```

Logical Operators
Logical operators are used to compare expressions using Boolean logic, which compares values using characters representing NOT, AND, and OR.

!—To negate a logical expression

-a—To logically AND two logical expressions

-o—To logically OR two logical expressions

This example named `logic` uses the file and directory mentioned in the previous compare3 example:

```
#!/bin/sh
if [ -x file1 -a -x dir1 ]; then
    echo file1 and dir1 are executable
else
    echo at least one of file1 or dir1 are not executable
fi

if [ -w file1 -o -w dir1 ]; then
    echo file1 or dir1 are writable
else
    echo neither file1 or dir1 are executable
fi

if [ ! -w file1 ]; then
    echo file1 is not writable
else
    echo file1 is writable
fi
```

If you execute `logic`, it will yield the following result:

```
file1 and dir1 are executable
file1 or dir1 are writable
file1 is not writable
```

Comparing Expressions with `tcsh`

As stated earlier, the method for comparing expressions in `tcsh` is different from the method used under `pdksh` and `bash`. The comparison of expression demonstrated in this section uses the syntax necessary for the `tcsh` shell environment.

String Comparison

The following operators can be used to compare two string expressions:

==—To compare whether two strings are equal

!=—To compare whether two strings are not equal

The following examples compare two strings, string1 and string2, in the shell program compare1:

```tcsh
#!/bin/tcsh
set string1 = "abc"
set string2 = "abd"

if  (string1 == string2)  then
   echo "string1 equal to string2"
else
   echo "string1 not equal to string2"
endif

if  (string2 != string1)  then
   echo "string2 not equal to string1"
else
   echo "string2 equal to string1"
endif
```

If you execute compare1, you get the following results:

```
string1 not equal to string2
string2 not equal to string1
```

Number Comparison

These operators can be used to compare two numbers:

>=—To= number comparison operators> compare whether one number is greater than or equal to the other number

<=—To compare whether one number is less than or equal to the other number

>—To (less than) number comparison operators>) number comparison operators> compare whether one number is greater than the other number

<—To compare whether one number is less than the other number

The next examples compare two numbers, number1 and number2, in a shell program called compare2:

```tcsh
#!/bin/tcsh
set number1=5
set number2=10
set number3=5

if  ($number1 > $number2)  then
   echo "number1 is greater than number2"
```

```
else
   echo "number1 is not greater than number2"
endif

if  ($number1 >= $number3) then
   echo "number1 is greater than or equal to number3"
else
   echo "number1 is not greater than or equal to number3"
endif

if  ($number1 < $number2)  then
   echo "number1 is less than number2"
else
   echo "number1 is not less than number2"
endif

if  ($number1 <= $number3) then
   echo "number1 is less than or equal to number3"
else
   echo "number1 is not less than or equal to number3"
endif
```

When executing the shell program compare2, you get the following results:

```
number1 is not greater than number2
number1 is greater than or equal to number3
number1 is less than number2
number1 is less than or equal to number3
```

File Operators
These operators can be used as file comparison operators:

- -d—To ascertain whether a file is a directory
- -e—To ascertain whether a file exists
- -f—To ascertain whether a file is a regular file
- -o—To ascertain whether a user is the owner of a file
- -r—To ascertain whether read permission is set for a file
- -w—To ascertain whether write permission is set for a file
- -x—To ascertain whether execute permission is set for a file
- -z—To ascertain whether the file size is zero

The following examples are based on a shell program called compare3, which is in a directory with a file called file1 and a subdirectory dir1 under the current directory. Assume that file1 has a permission of r-x (read and execute permission) and dir1 has a permission of rwx (read, write, and execute permission).

The following is the code for the compare3 shell program:

```tcsh
#!/bin/tcsh
if  (-d dir1) then
    echo "dir1 is a directory"
else
    echo "dir1 is not a directory"
endif

if (-f dir1)  then
    echo "file1 is a regular file"
else
    echo "file1 is not a regular file"
endif

if (-r file1) then
    echo "file1 has read permission"
else
    echo "file1 does not have read permission"
endif

if (-w file1) then
    echo "file1 has write permission"
else
    echo "file1 does not have write permission"
endif

if (-x dir1) then
    echo "dir1 has execute permission"
else
    echo "dir1 does not have execute permission"
endif

if (-z file1) then
    echo "file1 has zero length"
else
    echo "file1 has greater than zero length"
endif
```

If you execute the file compare3, you get the following results:

```
dir1 is a directory
file1 is a regular file
file1 has read permission
```

14

```
file1 does not have write permission
dir1 has execute permission
file1 has greater than zero length
```

Logical Operators

Logical operators are used with conditional statements. These operators are used to negate a logical expression or to perform logical ANDs and ORs:

> !—To negate a logical expression

> &&—To logically AND two logical expressions

> ¦¦—To logically OR two logical expressions

This example named `logic` uses the file and directory mentioned in the previous compare3 example:

```
#!/bin/tcsh
if ( -x file1 && -x dir1 ) then
   echo file1 and dir1 are executable
else
   echo at least one of file1 or dir1 are not executable
endif

if ( -w file1 ¦¦ -w dir1 ) then
   echo file1 or dir1 are writable
else
   echo neither file1 or dir1 are executable
endif

if ( ! -w file1 ) then
   echo file1 is not writable
else
   echo file1 is writable
endif
```

If you execute `logic`, it will yield the following result:

```
file1 and dir1 are executable
file1 or dir1 are writable
file1 is not writable
```

The for Statement

The for statement is used to execute a set of commands once each time a specified condition is true. The for statement has a number of formats. The first format used by pdksh and bash is as follows:

```
for curvar in list
do
    statements
done
```

This form should be used if you want to execute statements once for each value in list. For each iteration, the current value of the list is assigned to vcurvar. list can be a variable containing a number of items or a list of values separated by spaces. The second format is as follows:

```
for curvar
do
    statements
done
```

In this form, the statements are executed once for each of the positional parameters passed to the shell program. For each iteration, the current value of the positional parameter is assigned to the variable curvar.

This form can also be written as follows:

```
for curvar in $@
do
    statements
done
```

Remember that $@ gives you a list of positional parameters passed to the shell program, quoted in a manner consistent with the way the user originally invoked the command.

Under tcsh, the for statement is called foreach. The format is as follows:

```
foreach curvar (list)
    statements
end
```

In this form, statements are executed once for each value in list, and, for each iteration, the current value of list is assigned to curvar.

Suppose that you want to create a backup version of each file in a directory to a subdirectory called backup. You can do the following in pdksh and bash:

```
#!/bin/sh
for filename in *
do
    cp $filename backup/$filename
    if [ $? -ne 0 ]; then
        echo "copy for $filename failed"
    fi
done
```

In the preceding example, a backup copy of each file is created. If the copy fails, a message is generated.

The same example in `tcsh` is as follows:

```
#!/bin/tcsh
foreach filename (`/bin/ls`)
   cp $filename backup/$filename
   if ($? != 0) then
      echo "copy for $filename failed"
   endif
end
```

The `while` Statement

The `while` statement can be used to execute a series of commands while a specified condition is true. The loop terminates as soon as the specified condition evaluates to false. It is possible that the loop will not execute at all if the specified condition initially evaluates to false. You should be careful with the `while` command because the loop will never terminate if the specified condition never evaluates to false.

Endless Loops Have Their Place in Shell Programs

Endless loops can sometimes be useful. For example, you can easily construct a simple command that constantly monitors the 802.11b link quality of a network interface by using a few lines of script:

```
#!/bin/sh
while :
 do
   /sbin/iwconfig eth0 ¦  grep Link ¦ tr '\n' '\r'
 done
```

The script outputs the search, and then the `tr` command formats the output. The result is a simple animation of a constantly updated single line of information:

```
Link Quality:92/92  Signal level:-11 dBm  Noise level:-102 dBm
```

This technique can also be used to create a graphical monitoring client for X that outputs traffic information and activity about a network interface:

```
#!/bin/sh
xterm -geometry 75x2 -e \
bash -c \
"while :; do \
    /sbin/ifconfig eth0 ¦ \
    grep 'TX bytes' ¦
     tr '\n' '\r' ; \
done"
```

The simple example uses a `bash` command-line script (enabled by `-c`) to execute a command line repeatedly. The command line pipes the output of the `ifconfig` command through `grep`, which searches `ifconfig`'s output and then pipes a line containing the string `"TX bytes"` to the `tr` command. The `tr` command then removes the carriage return at the end of the line to display the information inside an `/xterm` X11 terminal window, automatically sized by the `-geometry` option:

```
RX bytes:4117594780 (3926.8 Mb)  TX bytes:452230967 (431.2 Mb)
```

Endless loops can be so useful that Linux includes a command that will repeatedly execute a given command line. For example, you can get a quick report about a system's hardware health by using the `sensors` command. But instead of using a shell script to loop the output endlessly, you can use the `watch` command to repeat the information and provide simple animation:

```
$ watch "sensors -f ¦ cut -c 1-20"
```

In `pdksh` and `bash`, the following format is used for the `while` flow control construct:

```
while expression
do
    statements
done
```

In `tcsh`, the following format is used:

```
while (expression)
    Statements
end
```

If you want to add the first five even numbers, you can use the following shell program in `pdksh` and `bash`:

```
#!/bin/bash
loopcount=0
result=0
while [ $loopcount -lt 5 ]
do
    loopcount=`expr $loopcount + 1`
    increment=`expr $loopcount \* 2`
    result=`expr $result + $increment`
done

echo "result is $result"
```

In `tcsh`, this program can be written as follows:

```
#!/bin/tcsh
set loopcount = 0
set result = 0
```

```
while ($loopcount < 5)
   set loopcount = `expr $loopcount + 1`
   set increment = `expr $loopcount \* 2`
   set result = `expr $result + $increment`

end

echo "result is $result"
```

The until Statement

The until statement can be used to execute a series of commands until a specified condition is true.

The loop terminates as soon as the specified condition evaluates to True.

In pdksh and bash, the following format is used:

```
until expression
do
    statements
done
```

As you can see, the format of the until statement is similar to that of the while statement, but the logic is different: In a while loop, you execute until an expression is False, but in an until loop, you loop until the expression is True.

If you want to add the first five even numbers, you can use the following shell program in pdksh and bash:

```
#!/bin/bash
loopcount=0
result=0
until [ $loopcount -ge 5 ]
do
   loopcount=`expr $loopcount + 1`
   increment=`expr $loopcount \* 2`
   result=`expr $result + $increment`
done

echo "result is $result"
```

The example here is identical to the example for the while statement, except that the condition being tested is just the opposite of the condition specified in the while statement.

The tcsh shell does not support the until statement.

The repeat Statement (tcsh)

The repeat statement is used to execute only one command a fixed number of times.

If you want to print a hyphen (-) 80 times with one hyphen per line on the screen, you can use the following command:

```
repeat  80 echo '-'
```

The select Statement (pdksh)

The select statement is used to generate a menu list if you are writing a shell program that expects input from the user online. The format of the select statement is as follows:

```
select  item in itemlist
do
     Statements
done
```

itemlist is optional. If it isn't provided, the system iterates through the item entries one at a time. If itemlist is provided, however, the system iterates for each entry in itemlist and the current value of itemlist is assigned to item for each iteration, which then can be used as part of the statements being executed.

If you want to write a menu that gives the user a choice of picking a Continue or a Finish, you can write the following shell program:

```
#!/bin/ksh
select  item in Continue Finish
do
   if [ $item = "Finish" ]; then
      break
   fi
done
```

When the select command is executed, the system displays a menu with numeric choices to the user—in this case, 1 for Continue and 2 for Finish. If the user chooses 1, the variable item contains a value of Continue; if the user chooses 2, the variable item contains a value of Finish. When the user chooses 2, the if statement is executed and the loop terminates.

The shift Statement

The shift statement is used to process the positional parameters, one at a time, from left to right. As you'll remember, the positional parameters are identified as $1, $2, $3, and so on. The effect of the shift command is that each positional parameter is moved one position to the left and the current $1 parameter is lost.

The shift statement is useful when you are writing shell programs in which a user can pass various options. Depending on the specified option, the parameters that follow can mean different things or might not be there at all.

The format of the shift command is as follows:

```
shift   number
```

The parameter number is the number of places to be shifted and is optional. If not specified, the default is 1; that is, the parameters are shifted one position to the left. If specified, the parameters are shifted number positions to the left.

The if Statement

The if statement evaluates a logical expression to make a decision. An if condition has the following format in pdksh and bash:

```
if [ expression ]; then
    Statements
elif [ expression ]; then
    Statements
else
    Statements
fi
```

The if conditions can be nested. That is, an if condition can contain another if condition within it. It isn't necessary for an if condition to have an elif or else part. The else part is executed if none of the expressions that are specified in the if statement and are optional in subsequent elif statements are true. The word fi is used to indicate the end of the if statements, which is very useful if you have nested if conditions. In such a case, you should be able to match fi to if to ensure that all if statements are properly coded.

In the following example for bash or pdksh, a variable var can have either of two values: Yes or No. Any other value is invalid. This can be coded as follows:

```
if [ $var = "Yes" ]; then
   echo "Value is Yes"
elif [ $var = "No" ]; then
   echo "Value is No"
else
   echo "Invalid value"
fi
```

In tcsh, the if statement has two forms. The first form, similar to the one for pdksh and bash, is as follows:

```
if (expression) then
    Statements
```

```
else if (expression) then
    Statements
else
    Statements
endif
```

The if conditions can be nested—that is, an if condition can contain another if condition within it. It isn't necessary for an if condition to have an else part. The else part is executed if none of the expressions specified in any of the if statements are true. The optional if part of the statement (else if (expression) then) is executed if the condition following it is true and the previous if statement is not true. The word endif is used to indicate the end of the if statements, which is very useful if you have nested if conditions. In such a case, you should be able to match endif to if to ensure that all if statements are properly coded.

Using the example of the variable var having only two values, Yes and No, here is how it would be coded with tcsh:

```
if ($var == "Yes") then
    echo "Value is Yes"
else if ($var == "No" ) then
    echo "Value is No"
else
    echo "Invalid value"
endif
```

The second form of the if condition for tcsh is as follows:

```
if (expression) command
```

In this format, only a single command can be executed if the expression evaluates to true.

The case Statement

The case statement is used to execute statements depending on a discrete value or a range of values matching the specified variable. In most cases, you can use a case statement instead of an if statement if you have a large number of conditions.

The format of a case statement for pdksh and bash is as follows:

```
case str in
    str1 ¦ str2)
        Statements;;
    str3¦str4)
        Statements;;
    *)
        Statements;;
esac
```

14

You can specify a number of discrete values—such as str1, str2, and so on—for each condition, or you can specify a value with a wildcard. The last condition should be * (asterisk) and is executed if none of the other conditions are met. For each of the specified conditions, all the associated statements until the double semicolon (;;) are executed.

You can write a script that will echo the name of the month if you provide the month number as a parameter. If you provide a number that isn't between 1 and 12, you will get an error message. The script is as follows:

```
#!/bin/sh

case $1 in
    01 | 1) echo "Month is January";;
    02 | 2) echo "Month is February";;
    03 | 3) echo "Month is March";;
    04 | 4) echo "Month is April";;
    05 | 5) echo "Month is May";;
    06 | 6) echo "Month is June";;
    07 | 7) echo "Month is July";;
    08 | 8) echo "Month is August";;
    09 | 9) echo "Month is September";;
    10) echo "Month is October";;
    11) echo "Month is November";;
    12) echo "Month is December";;
    *) echo "Invalid parameter";;
esac
```

You need to end the statements under each condition with a double semicolon (;;). If you do not, the statements under the next condition will also be executed.

The format for a case statement for tcsh is as follows:

```
switch (str)
    case str1|str2:
        Statements
        breaksw
    case str3|str4:
        Statements
        breaksw
    default:
        Statements
        breaksw
endsw
```

You can specify a number of discrete values—such as str1, str2, and so on—for each condition, or you can specify a value with a wildcard. The last condition should be default and is executed if none of the other conditions are met. For each of the specified conditions, all the associated statements until breaksw are executed.

The example that echoes the month when a number is given, shown earlier for pdksh and bash, can be written in tcsh as follows:

```
#!/bin/tcsh
```

```
set month = 5
switch  ( $month )
   case 1: echo "Month is January" ;  breaksw
   case 2: echo "Month is February" ;  breaksw
   case 3: echo "Month is March" ;  breaksw
   case 4: echo "Month is April" ;  breaksw
   case 5: echo "Month is May" ;  breaksw
   case 6: echo "Month is June" ;  breaksw
   case 7: echo "Month is July" ;  breaksw
   case 8: echo "Month is August"  ;  breaksw
   case 9: echo "Month is September" ;  breaksw
   case 10: echo "Month is October" ;  breaksw
   case 11: echo "Month is November" ;  breaksw
   case 12: echo "Month is December" ;  breaksw
   default: echo "Oops! Month is Octember!" ;  breaksw
endsw
```

You need to end the statements under each condition with breaksw. If you do not, the statements under the next condition will also be executed.

The break **and** exit **Statements**

You should be aware of two other statements: the break statement and the exit statement.

The break statement can be used to terminate an iteration loop, such as a for, until, or repeat command.

exit statements can be used to exit a shell program. You can optionally use a number after exit. If the current shell program has been called by another shell program, the calling program can check for the code (the $? or $status variable, depending on shell) and make a decision accordingly.

Using Functions in Shell Scripts

As with other programming languages, shell programs also support *functions*. A function is a piece of a shell program that performs a particular process; you can reuse the same function multiple times within the shell program. Functions help eliminate the need for duplicating code as you write shell programs.

The following is the format of a function in pdksh and bash:

```
func(){
    Statements
}
```

You can call a function as follows:

```
func param1 param2 param3
```

The parameters *param1*, *param2*, and so on are optional. You can also pass the parameters as a single string—for example, $@. A function can parse the parameters as if they were positional parameters passed to a shell program from the command line as command-line arguments, but instead use values passed inside the script. For example, the following script uses a function named Displaymonth() that displays the name of the month or an error message if you pass a month number out of the range 1 to 12. This example works with pdksh and bash:

```
#!/bin/sh
Displaymonth() {
    case $1 in
        01 ¦ 1) echo "Month is January";;
        02 ¦ 2) echo "Month is February";;
        03 ¦ 3) echo "Month is March";;
        04 ¦ 4) echo "Month is April";;
        05 ¦ 5) echo "Month is May";;
        06 ¦ 6) echo "Month is June";;
        07 ¦ 7) echo "Month is July";;
        08 ¦ 8) echo "Month is August";;
        09 ¦ 9) echo "Month is September";;
        10) echo "Month is October";;
        11) echo "Month is November";;
        12) echo "Month is December";;
        *) echo "Invalid parameter";;
    esac
}
Displaymonth 8
```

The preceding program displays the following output:

```
Month is August
```

Related Fedora and Linux Commands

You can use these commands and tools when using the shell or writing shell scripts:

chsh—Command used to change one's login shell

kibitz—Allows two-person interaction with a single shell

mc—A visual shell named the GNU Midnight Commander

nano—An easy-to-use text editor for the console

system-config-users—A graphical user-management utility that can be used to change one or more user login shells

shar—Command used to create shell archives

vi—The vi (actually vim) text editor

Reference

http://www.linuxgazette.com/issue70/ghosh.html—A Linux Gazette article on "Bootstrapping Linux," which includes much detail on the BIOS and MBR aspects of the boot process.

http://www.lostcircuits.com/advice/bios2/1.shtml—the LostCircuits BIOS guide; much detail on the meaning of all those BIOS settings.

http://www.rojakpot.com/default.aspx?location=1—The BIOS Optimization Guide; details on tweaking those BIOS settings to your heart's content.

http://www-106.ibm.com/developerworks/linux/library/l-slack.html—A link through IBM's website to an article on booting Slackware Linux, along with a sidebar about the history of System V versus BSD init scripts.

/usr/src/linux/init/main.c—The best place to learn about how Linux boots. Fascinating reading, really. Get it from the source!

http://sunsite.dk/linux-newbie/—Home page for the Linux Newbie Administrator Guide—A gentle introduction to Linux System Administration.

The GRUB Manual—The still yet-to-be-completed manual can be found at http://www.gnu.org/software/grub/manual/. On your Fedora Core system, info grub provides a plethora of information and a sample grub.conf file (/boot/grub/menu.lst is a symbolic link to /boot/grub/grub.conf; use either name) can be found in /usr/doc/grub.

"LILO User's Guide"—Werner Almesberger's definitive technical tome on the LInux LOader, or LILO, and how it works on Intel-based PCs. Look under the /usr/share/doc/lilo*/doc directory for the file User_Guide.ps, which can be viewed using the gv client. LILO has been dropped from Fedora Core; GRUB is now the default boot loader supported in the distribution.

"Managing Initscripts with Red Hat's chkconfig"—by Jimmy Ball, *Linux Journal*, April 2001; pp. 128–132.

"Grub, Glorious Grub"—Hoyt Duff, *Linux Format*, August 2001; pp. 58–61. A tutorial on the GRUB boot leader.

http://www.redhat.com/docs/manuals/linux/RHL-9-Manual/custom-guide/ s1-services-serviceconf.html—Red Hat's guide to use the system-config-service client (then called redhat-config-service).

http://www.linuxbase.org/spec/refspecs/LSB_1.0.0/gLSB/sysinit.html—The Linux Standard Base description of system initialization; this is the standard.

http://www.gnu.org/software/bash/bash.html—The bash home page at the GNU Software Project.

http://www.tldp.org/LDP/abs/html/—Mendel Cooper's "Advanced Bash-Scripting Guide."

http://www.linuxnewbie.org/nhf/intel/shells/basic.html—Learn basic shell commands at this site.

http://www.cs.princeton.edu/~jlk/lj/—"The New Korn Shell—ksh93," an article by David G. Korn, Charles J. Northrup, and Jeffery Korn regarding the korn shell.

http://web.cs.mun.ca/~michael/pdksh/—The pdksh home page.

http://lug.umbc.edu/~mabzug1/bash-httpd.html—The Bash-httpd FAQ, with links to the latest version of the bash web server, bash-httpd-0.02.

http://www.tcsh.org/—Find out more about tcsh here.

http://www.zsh.org/—Examine zsh in more detail here.

# CHAPTER 15

System Resources

System Monitoring Tools

Monitoring your server or workstation is an important task, especially in a commercial or corporate environment. Whether you are working on critical application programming or conducting e-commerce on the Internet, you will want to track your system's health signs while it's running. Good Fedora Core Linux system administrators are also quite vigilant about watching running processes on their systems, including resources such as CPU and disk, memory, network, and printer usage. Even though the task is not strictly part of standard security operations, such as examining system logs and network traffic, monitoring resource usage can help you spot misuse and avoid developing problems, such as unwanted intruder connections to your network.

This chapter introduces just a few of the basic tools and approaches used to monitor a running Linux system. Some of the tools focus on in-memory processes, whereas others, such as filesystem reporting and network monitoring, have more comprehensive uses. You will also see how to control some system processes using various command-line and graphical tools included with Fedora Core.

Console-based Monitoring

Traditional Unix systems have always included the ps or process display command. This command lists the running processes on the system and identifies who owns them and how much of the system resources are being used.

Because of the architecture of the Linux kernel and its memory management, Linux also provides much process reporting and control via the command line. This feature can be accessed manually through the /proc filesystem, a pseudo-filesystem used as a direct interface to the kernel. (You see how it's used in the upcoming discussion of the ps command.) The /proc filesystem is frequently used by application programmers who construct an interface for the raw information it provides. This filesystem is too complex to adequately deal with in the context of this chapter, but you can benefit from reading the proc man page to examine the list and description of the scores of kernel values available. You then can write shell scripts (refer to Chapter 14, "Automating Tasks") to use those values as needed.

Processes can be controlled at the command line as well. Whenever a program or command is launched on your Fedora Core Linux system, the process started by the kernel is assigned an identification number, called a PID or Process ID. This number is (generally) displayed by the shell if the program is launched in the background, like this:

```
$ xosview &
[1] 11670
```

In this example, the xosview client has been launched in the background, and the (bash) shell reported a shell job number ([1] in this case). A job number or job control is a shell-specific feature that allows a different form of process control (such as sending or suspending programs to the background and retrieving background jobs to the foreground; see your shell's manual pages for more information if you are not using bash).

The second number displayed (11670, in this example) represents the Process ID. You can get a quick list of your processes by using the ps command like this:

```
$ ps
  PID TTY          TIME CMD
  736 tty1     00:00:00 bash
  743 tty1     00:00:00 startx
  744 tty1     00:00:00 tee
  752 tty1     00:00:00 xinit
  756 tty1     00:00:09 kwm
  ...
11670 pts/4    00:00:00 xosview
11671 pts/4    00:00:00 ps
```

Note that not all output from the display is shown here. But as you can see, the output includes the process ID, abbreviated as PID, along with other information, such as the name of the running program. Like any Unix command, many options are available; the proc man page has a full list. A most useful option is aux, which provides a friendly list of all the processes. You should also know that ps works not by polling memory, but through the interrogation of the Linux /proc or process filesystem. (ps is one of the interfaces mentioned at the beginning of this section.)

The /proc directory contains quite a few files—some of which include constantly updated hardware information (such as battery power levels, and so on). Linux administrators will often pipe the output of ps through a member of the grep family of commands in order to display information about a specific program, perhaps like this:

```
$ ps aux ¦ grep xosview
USER        PID %CPU %MEM   VSZ  RSS TTY     STAT START   TIME COMMAND
andrew          11670  0.3   1.1        2940 1412 pts/4
➥S    14:04          0:00    xosview
```

This example returns the owner (the user who launched the program) and the PID, along with other information, such as the percentage of CPU and memory usage, size of the command (code, data, and stack), time (or date) the command was launched, and name of the command. Processes can also be queried by PID like this:

```
$ ps 11670
  PID TTY     STAT   TIME COMMAND
11670 pts/4   S      0:00 xosview
```

You can use the PID to stop a running process by using the shell's built-in kill command. This command will ask the kernel to stop a running process and reclaim system memory. For example, to stop the xosview client in the example, use the kill command like this:

```
$ kill 11670
```

After you press Enter (or perhaps press Enter again), the shell might report

```
 [1]+  Terminated            xosview
```

Note that users can only kill their own processes, but root can kill them all. Controlling any other running process requires root permission, which should be used judiciously (especially when forcing a kill by using the -9 option); by inadvertently killing the wrong process through a typo in the command, you could bring down an active system.

Using the kill Command to Control Processes

The kill command is a basic Unix system command. We can communicate with a running process by entering a command into its interface, such as when we type into a text editor. But some processes (usually system processes rather than application processes) run without such an interface, and we need a way to communicate with them as well, so we use a system of signals. The kill system accomplishes just that by sending a signal to a process, and we can use it to communicate with any process. The general format of the kill command is

```
# kill option PID
```

A number of signal options can be sent as words or numbers, but most are of interest only to programmers. One of the most common ones you will use is

```
# kill PID
```

This tells the process with PID to stop; you supply the actual PID.

```
# kill -9 PID
```

This is the signal for `kill` (9 is the number of the SIGKILL signal); use this combination when the plain `kill` shown previously doesn't work.

```
# kill -SIGHUP PID
```

This is the signal to "hangup"—stop—and then clean up all associated processes as well. (Its number is -1.)

As you become proficient at process control and job control, you will learn the utility of a number of `kill` options. A full list of signal options can be found in the man `signal` page.

Using Priority Scheduling and Control

Every process cannot make use of the systems resources (CPU, memory, disk access, and so on) as it pleases. After all, the kernel's primary function is to manage the system resources equitably. It does this by assigning a priority to each process so that some processes get better access to system resources and some processes might have to wait longer until their turn arrives. Priority scheduling can be an important tool in managing a system supporting critical applications or in a situation in which CPU and RAM usage must be reserved or allocated for a specific task. Two legacy applications included with Red Linux include the `nice` and re-`nice` commands. (`nice` is part of the GNU sh-utils package, whereas re-`nice` is inherited from BSD Unix.)

The `nice` command is used with its -n option, along with an argument in the range of -20 to 19, in order from highest to lowest priority (the lower the number, the higher the priority). For example, to run the `xosview` client with a low priority, use the `nice` command like this:

```
$ nice -n 12 xosview &
```

The `nice` command is typically used for disk or CPU-intensive tasks that might be obtrusive or cause system slowdown. The re-`nice` command can be used to reset the priority of running processes or control the priority and scheduling of all processes owned by a user. Regular users can only numerically increase process priorities (for example, make tasks less important) using this command, but the root operator can use the full `nice` range of scheduling (–20–19).

System administrators can also use the `time` command (here, `time` is used to measure the duration of elapsed time; the command that deals with civil and sidereal time is the `date` command) to get an idea about how long and how much of a system's resources will be required for a task (such as a shell script). This command is used with the name of another command (or script) as an argument like this:

```
# time -p find / -name core -print
/dev/core
/proc/sys/net/core

real 1.20
user 0.14
sys 0.71
```

Output of the command displays the time from start to finish, along with user and system time required. Other factors you can query include memory, CPU usage, and filesystem Input/Output (I/O) statistics. See the `time` command's manual page for more details.

Nearly all graphical process monitoring tools include some form of process control or management. Many of the early tools ported to Linux were clones of legacy Unix utilities. One familiar monitoring (and control) program is `top`. Based on the `ps` command, the `top` command provides a text-based display, constantly updated console-based output showing the most CPU-intensive processes currently running. It can be started like this:

```
# top
```

After you press Enter, you will see a display as shown in Figure 15.1. The `top` command has a few interactive commands: pressing `h` displays the help screen; pressing `k` prompts you to enter the `pid` of a process to kill; pressing `n` prompts you to enter the `pid` of a process to change its nice value. The `top` man page describes other commands and includes a detailed description of what all the columns of information `top` can display actually represent; have a look at top's well-written `man` page.

FIGURE 15.1   The `top` command can be used to monitor and control processes. Here, we are being prompted to re-nice a process.

15

The top command displays quite a bit of information about your system. Processes can be sorted by PID, age, CPU or memory usage, time, or user. This command also provides process management, and system administrators can use its k or r keypress commands to kill or reschedule running tasks.

The top command uses a fair amount of memory, so you might want to be judicious in its use and not leave it running all the time.

After you have finished, simply press q to quit top.

Displaying Free and Used Memory with free

Although top includes some memory information, the free utility will display the amount of free and used memory in the system in kilobytes (the -m switch displays in megabytes). On one system, the output looks like this:

```
# free
                    total     used      free      shared    buffers    cached
Mem               255452    251132      4320         0       19688      77548
-/+ buffers/cache: 153896    101556
Swap:             136512     31528    104984
```

This output describes a machine with 256MB of RAM memory and a swap partition of 137MB. Note that some swap is being used although the machine is not heavily loaded. Linux is very good at memory management and "grabs" all the memory it can in anticipation of future work.

> **TIP**
>
> A useful trick is to employ the watch command; it will repeatedly rerun a command every 2 seconds by default. If you use
>
> ```
> #  watch free
> ```
>
> you'll see the output of the free command updated every 2 seconds.

Another useful system monitoring tool is vmstat (virtual memory statistics). This command reports on processes, memory, I/O, and CPU typically providing an average since the last reboot, or you can make it report usage for a current period of time by telling it the time interval in seconds and the number of iterations you desire, like

```
# vmstat 5 10
```

which will run vmstat every 5 seconds for 10 iterations.

Use the uptime command to see how long it has been since the last reboot and to get an idea of what the load average has been; higher numbers mean higher loads.

Disk Quotas

Disk quotas are a way to restrict the usage of disk space either by user or by groups. Although rarely—if ever—used on a local or standalone workstation, quotas are definitely a way of life at the enterprise level of computing. Usage limits on disk space not only conserve resources, but also provide a measure of operational safety by limiting the amount of disk space any user can consume.

Disk quotas are more fully covered in Chapter 13, "Managing Users."

Graphical Process and System Management Tools

The GNOME and KDE desktop environments offer a rich set of network and system monitoring tools. Graphical interface elements, such as menus and buttons, and graphical output, including metering and real-time load charts, make these tools easy to use. These clients, which require an active X session and in some cases (but not all) root permission, are included with Fedora Core.

If you view the graphical tools locally while they are being run on a server, you must have X properly installed and configured on your local machine. Although some tools can be used to remotely monitor systems or locally mounted remote filesystems, you'll need to properly configure pertinent X11 environment variables, such as $DISPLAY, to use the software or use the ssh client's -X option when connecting to the remote host.

Fedora Core includes the xosview client, which provides load, CPU, memory and swap usage, disk I/O usage and activity, page swapping information, network activity, I/O activity, I/O rates, serial port status, and if APM is enabled, the battery level (such as for a laptop).

For example, to see most of these options, start the client like this:

```
# xosview -geometry 406x488 -font 8x16 +load +cpu +mem +swap \
 +page +disk +int +net &
```

After you press Enter, you will see a display as shown in Figure 15.2.

The display can be customized for a variety of hardware and information, and the xosview client (like most well-behaved X clients) obeys geometry settings such as size, placement, or font. If you have similar monitoring requirements, but want to try a similar but different client from xosview, try xcpustate, which has features that enable it to monitor network CPU statistics foreign to Linux. Neither of these applications is installed with the base set of packages; you need to install them manually if you want to use them.

Some of the graphical system and process monitoring tools included with Fedora Core Linux include the following:

- vncviewer—AT&T's open-source remote session manager (part of the Xvnc package), which can be used to view and run a remote desktop session locally. This software (discussed in more detail in Chapter 25, "Remote System Access with SSH and Telnet") requires an active, but background X session on the remote computer.

- nmapfe—A GTK+ graphical front end to the nmap command. This client provides system administrators with the ability to scan networks to monitor the availability of hosts and services.

- ethereal—This graphical network protocol analyzer can be used to save or display packet data in real time and has intelligent filtering to recognize data signatures or patterns from a variety of hardware and data captures from third-party, data-capture programs, including compressed files. Some protocols include AppleTalk, Andrew File System (AFS), AOL's Instant Messenger, various Cisco protocols, and many more.

- gnome-system-monitor—Replacing gtop, this tool is a simple process monitor offering two views: a list view and a moving graph. It is accessed via the System Tool menu selection as the System Monitor item (see Figure 15.3).

FIGURE 15.2   The xosview client displays basic system stats in a small window. You can choose from several options to determine what it will monitor for you.

The System Monitor menu item (shown in Figure 15.3) is found in the System Tools menu. It can be launched from the command line with

```
# gnome-system-monitor
```

From the Process Listing view (chosen via the tab in the upper left portion of the window), select a process and click on More Info at the bottom left of the screen to display details on that process at the bottom of the display. You can select from three views to filter the display, available in the drop-down View list: All Processes, My Processes (those you alone own), or Active Processes (All Processes that are active).

FIGURE 15.3   The Process Listing view of the System Monitor.

Choose Hidden Processes under the Edit command accessible from the top of the display to show any hidden processes (those that the kernel does not enable the normal monitoring tools to see). Select any process and kill it with End Process.

The processes can be re-niced by selecting Edit, Change Priority. The View selection from the menu bar also provides a memory map. In the Resource Monitor tab, you can view a moving graph representing CPU and memory usage (see Figure 15.4).

KDE Process and System Monitoring Tools

KDE provides several process and system monitoring clients. The KDE graphical clients are integrated into the desktop taskbar by right-clicking on the taskbar and following the menus.

These KDE monitoring clients include the following:

- kdf—A graphical interface to your system's filesystem table that displays free disk space and enables you to mount and unmount filesystems using a pointing device.

- ksysguard—Another panel applet that provides CPU load and memory use information in animated graphs.

15

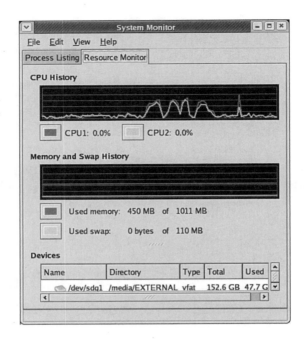

FIGURE 15.4   The Graph view of the System Monitor. It shows CPU usage, Memory/Swap usage, and disk usage. To get this view, select the Resource Monitor tab.

Reference

http://and.sourceforge.net/—Home page of the and auto nice daemon, which can be used to prioritize and reschedule processes automatically.

http://sourceforge.net/projects/schedutils/—Home page for various projects offering scheduling utilities for real-time scheduling.

http://freetype.sourceforge.net/patents.html—A discussion of the FreeType bytecode interpreter patents.

http://www.ethereal.com—Home page for the Ethereal client.

http://www.realvnc.com/—The home page for the Virtual Network Computing remote desktop software, available for a variety of platforms, including Fedora Core Linux. This software has become so popular that it is now included with nearly every Linux distribution.

# CHAPTER 16

Backing Up, Restoring, and Recovery

This chapter examines the practice of safeguarding data through backups, restoring that same data if necessary, and recovering data in case of a catastrophic hardware or software failure. After reading this chapter, you will have a full understanding of the reasons for sound backup practices. You can use the information in this chapter to make intelligent choices about which strategies are best for you. The chapter also shows you how to perform some types of data recovery and system restoration on your own and when to seek professional assistance.

Choosing a Backup Strategy

Backups are always trade-offs. Any backup will consume time, money, and effort on an ongoing basis; backups must be monitored, validated, indexed, stored, and new media continuously purchased. Sound expensive? The cost of not having backups is the loss of your critical data. Re-creating the data from scratch will cost time and money, and if the cost of doing it all again is greater than the cost associated with backing up, you should be performing backups. At the where-the-rubber-meets-the-road level, backups are nothing more than insurance against financial loss for you or your business.

Your first step in formulating and learning to use an effective backup strategy is to choose the strategy that is right for you. First, you must understand some of the most common (and not so common) causes of data loss so that you are better able to understand the threats your system faces. Then, you need to assess your own system, how it is used and by whom, your available hardware and software resources, and your budget constraints. The following sections look at each of these issues in detail, as well as offering some sample backup systems and discussing their use.

Why Data Loss Occurs

Files disappear for any number of reasons: They can be lost because the hardware fails and causes data loss; your attention might wander and you accidentally delete or over-write a file. Some data loss occurs as a result of natural disasters and other circumstances beyond your control. A tornado, flood, or earthquake could strike, the water pipes could burst, or the building could catch on fire. Your data, as well as the hardware, would likely be destroyed in such a disaster. A disgruntled employee might destroy files or hardware in an attempt at retribution. And any equipment might fail, and it all will fail at some time—most likely when it is extremely important for it not to fail.

A Case in Point

A recent Harris poll of Fortune 500 executives found that roughly two-thirds of them had prob-lems with their backups and disaster-recovery plans. How about you?

Data can also be lost because of malfunctions that corrupt the data as it attempts to write to the disk. Other applications, utilities, and drivers might be poorly written, buggy (the phrase most often heard is "still beta quality"), or might suffer some corruption and fail to correctly write that all-important data you have just created. If that happened, the contents of your data file would be indecipherable garbage of no use to anyone.

All of these accidents and disasters offer important reasons for having a good backup strategy; however, the most frequent cause of data loss is human error. Who among us has not overwritten a new file with an older version or unintentionally deleted a needed file? This applies not only to data files, but also to configuration files and binaries. While perusing the mail lists or the Usenet newsgroup postings, stories about deleting entire directories such as /home, /usr, or /lib seem all too common. Incorrectly changing a configuration file and not saving the original in case it has to be restored (which it does more often than not because the person reconfigured it incorrectly) is another common error.

TIP

To make a backup of a configuration file you are about to edit, use the cp command:

```
$ cp filename filename.original
```

And to restore it:

```
$ cp filename.original filename
```

Never edit or move the *.original file, or the original copy will be lost. If it is, you can extract the configuration files from an .rpm file to at least provide the out-of-the-box configuration; Chapter 7, "Managing Software and System Resources," explains how to do that.

Proper backups can help you recover from these problems with a minimum of hassle, but you have to put in the effort to keep backups current, verify their intactness, and practice restoring the data in different disaster scenarios.

Assessing Your Backup Needs and Resources

By now you have realized that some kind of plan is needed to safeguard your data, and, like most people, you are overwhelmed by the prospect. Entire books, as well as countless articles and whitepapers, have been written on the subject of backing up and restoring data. What makes the topic so complex is that each solution is truly individual.

Yet, the proper approach to making the decision is very straightforward. You start the process by asking

- What data must be safeguarded?

- How often does the data change?

The answers to these two questions determine how important the data is, determine the volume of the data, and determine the frequency of the backups. This in turn will determine the backup medium. Only then can the software be selected that will accommodate all these considerations. (You learn about choosing backup software, hardware, and media later in this chapter.)

Available resources are another important consideration when selecting a backup strategy. Backups require time, money, and personnel. Begin your planning activities by determining what limitations you face for all of these resources. Then, construct your plan to fit those limitations, or be prepared to justify the need for more resources with a careful assessment of both backup needs and costs.

> **TIP**
>
> If you are not willing or capable of assessing your backup needs and choosing a backup solution, there exists a legion of consultants, hardware vendors, and software vendors who would love to assist you. The best way to choose one in your area is to query other Unix and Linux system administrators (located through user groups, discussion groups, or mail lists) who are willing to share their experiences and make recommendations. If you cannot get a referral, ask the consultant for references and check them out.

Many people also fail to consider the element of time when formulating their plan. Some backup devices are faster than others, and some recovery methods are faster than others. You need to consider that when making choices.

It is a good idea to examine incidents of data loss in the past and decide if your chosen scheme will adequately address that loss. Finally, examine what effect a total disaster might have. In each case, ask yourself: What data am I protecting? How will it be safe? How will it be restored, and how long will that take? The answers to all these questions should help you form your plan.

To formulate your backup plan, you need to determine the frequency of backups. The necessary frequency of backups should be determined by how quickly the important data on your system changes. On a home system, most files never change, a few change daily, and some change weekly. No elaborate strategy needs to be created to deal with that. A good strategy for home use is to back up (to any kind of removable media) critical data frequently and back up configuration and other files weekly.

At the enterprise level on a larger system with multiple users, a different approach is called for. Some critical data is changing constantly, and it could be expensive to re-create; this typically involves elaborate and expensive solutions. Most of us exist somewhere in between these extremes. Assess your system and its use to determine where you fall in this spectrum.

Backup schemes and hardware can be elaborate or simple, but they all require a workable plan and faithful follow-through. Even the best backup plan is useless if the process is not carried out, data is not verified, and data restoration is not practiced on a regular basis. Whatever backup scheme you choose, be sure to incorporate in it these three principles:

- **Have a plan**—Design a plan that is right for your needs and have equipment appropriate to the task. This involves assessing all the factors that affect the data you are backing up. We will get into more detail later in the chapter.

- **Follow the plan**—Faithfully complete each part of your backup strategy, and then verify the data stored in the backups. Backups with corrupt data are of no use to anyone. Even backup operations can go wrong.

- **Practice your skills**—Practice restoring data from your backup systems, so when the time comes, you are ready (and able) to benefit from the strength of your backup plan. (For restoring data, see the section "Using Backup Software.") Keep in mind that it is entirely possible that the flaws in your backup plan will only become apparent when you try restoring!

NOTE

If you are a system administrator serving other users (as opposed to being both the system administrator and the sole user), your insistence on following system policies and adhering to backup procedures might make you the object of cruel jokes or cause you to be shunned at the office holiday party. However, when you recover a file for those same people, you will become their best friend (for the moment, at least).

Sound Practices

You have to create your own best-backup plan, but here are some building blocks that go into the foundation of any sound backup program:

- Maintain more than one copy of critical data.
- Label the backups.
- Store the backups in a climate-controlled and secure area.

- Use secure, offsite storage of critical data. Many companies choose bank vaults for their offsite storage, and this is highly recommended.

- Establish a backup policy that makes sense and can be followed religiously. Try to back up your data when the system is consistent (that is, no data is being written), which is usually overnight.

- Keep track of who has access to your backup media, and keep the total number of people as low as possible. If you can, allow only trusted personnel near your backups.

- Routinely verify backups and practice restoring data from them.

- Routinely inspect backup media for defects and regularly replace them (after destroying the data on them if it is sensitive).

Evaluating Backup Strategies

Now that you are convinced you need backups, you need a strategy. It is difficult to be specific about an ideal strategy because each user or administrator's strategy will be highly individualized, but here are a few general examples:

- **Home user**—At home, the user has the Fedora Core installation CDs that take an hour or so to reinstall, so the time issue is not a major concern. The home user will want to back up any configuration files that have altered, keep an archive of any files that have been downloaded, and keep an archive of any data files created while using any applications. Unless the home user has a special project (such as writing this book) in which constant backups are useful, a weekly backup is adequate. The home user will likely use a floppy disk, CD-RW drive, or other removable media for backups.

- **Small office**—Many small offices tend to use the same strategy as the home user, but are more likely to back up critical data daily and use manually changed tape drives. If they have a tape drive with adequate storage, they will likely have a full system backup as well because restoring from the tape is quicker than reinstalling from the CDs. They also might be using CD-RW or DVD writers for backups. Although they will use scripts to automate backups, most of it is probably done by hand.

- **Small enterprise**—Here is where backups begin to require higher-end equipment such as autoloading tape drives with fully automated backups. Commercial backup software usually makes an introduction at this level, but a skillful system administrator on a budget can use one of the basic applications discussed in this chapter. Backups are highly structured and supervised by a dedicated system administrator.

- **Large enterprise**—These are the most likely settings for the use of expensive, proprietary, highly automated backup solutions. At this level, data means money, lost data means lost money, and delays in restoring data means money lost as well. These system administrators know that backups are necessary insurance and plan accordingly.

16

Does all this mean that enterprise-level backups are better than those done by a home user? Not at all. The "little guy" with Fedora Core Linux can do just as well as the enterprise operation at the expense of investing more time in the process. By examining the higher-end strategies, we can apply useful concepts across the board.

NOTE

If you are a new sysadmin, you might be inheriting an existing backup strategy. Take some time to examine it and see if it meets the current needs of the organization. Think about what backup protection your organization really needs, and determine if the current strategy meets that need. If it does not, change the strategy. Consider whether the current policy is being practiced by the users, and, if not, why it is not.

Backup Levels

Unix uses the concept of backup levels as a shorthand way of referring to how much data is backed up in relation to a previous backup. It works this way:

A level 0 backup is a full backup. The next backup level would be 1.

Backups at the other numbered levels will back up everything that has changed since the last backup at that level or a numerically higher level (the dump command, for example, offers 10 different backup levels). For example, a level 3 followed by a level 4 will generate an incremental backup from the full backup, whereas a level 4 followed by a level 3 will generate a differential backup between the two.

The following sections examine a few of the many strategies in use today. Many strategies are based on these sample schemes; one of them can serve as a foundation for the strategy you construct for your own system.

Simple Strategy

If you need to back up just a few configuration files and some small data files, copy them to a USB stick, engage the write-protect tab, and keep it someplace safe. If you need just a bit more backup storage capacity, you can copy the important files to a Zip disk (100, 250, and 750MB in size), CD-RW disk (up to 700MB in size), or DVD-R disk (up to 4.4GB for data).

In addition to configuration and data files, you should archive each user's home directory, as well as the entire /etc directory. Between the two, that backup would contain most of the important files for a small system. Then, you can easily restore this data from the backup media device you have chosen, after a complete reinstall of Fedora Core Linux, if necessary.

Experts believe that if you have more data than can fit on a floppy disk, you really need a formal backup strategy. Some of those are discussed in the following sections. We use a tape media backup as an example.

Full Backup on a Periodic Basis

This backup strategy involves a backup of the complete file system on a weekly, bi-weekly, or other periodic basis. The frequency of the backup depends on the amount of data being backed up, the frequency of changes to the data, and the cost of losing those changes.

This backup strategy is not complicated to perform, and it can be accomplished with the swappable disk drives discussed later in the chapter. If you are connected to a network, it is possible to mirror the data on another machine (preferably offsite); the rsync tool is particularly well suited to this task. Recognize that this does not address the need for archives of the recent state of files; it only presents a snapshot of the system at the time the update is done.

Full Backups with Incremental Backups

This scheme involves performing a full backup of the entire system once a week, along with a daily incremental backup of only those files that have changed in the previous day, and it begins to resemble what a sysadmin of a medium to large system would traditionally use.

This backup scheme can be advanced in two ways. In one way, each incremental backup can be made with reference to the original full backup. In other words, a level 0 backup is followed by a series of level 1 backups. The benefit of this backup scheme is that a restoration requires only two tapes (the full backup and the most recent incremental backup). But because it references the full backup, each incremental backup might be large (and grow ever larger) on a heavily used system.

Alternatively, each incremental backup could reference the previous incremental backup. This would be a level 0 backup followed by a level 1, followed by a level 2, and so on. Incremental backups are quicker (less data each time), but require every tape to restore a full system. Again, it is a classic trade-off decision.

You might need to retrieve the version of a file from six days ago or a file that was deleted last week. Such requests from users are not uncommon or unreasonable, and you need to be prepared to meet their needs.

Modern commercial backup applications such as Amanda or BRU assist in organizing the process of managing complex backup schedules and tracking backup media. Doing it yourself using the classic dump or employing shell scripts to run the tar, pax, or cpio applications requires that the system administrator handle all the organization herself. For this reason, complex backup situations are typically handled with commercial software and specialized hardware that are packaged, sold, and supported by vendors.

Mirroring Data or RAID Arrays

Given adequate (and often expensive) hardware resources, you can always mirror the data somewhere else, essentially maintaining a real-time copy of your data on hand. This is often a cheap, workable solution if no large amounts of data are involved. The use of RAID arrays (in some of their incarnations—see Chapter 37, "Managing the File System," for more information on RAID) provides for a recovery if a disk fails.

Note that RAID arrays and mirroring systems will just as happily write corrupt data as valid data. Moreover, if a file is deleted, a RAID array will not save it. RAID arrays are best suited for protecting the current state of a running system, not for backup needs.

Making the Choice

Only you can decide what is best for your situation. After reading about the backup options in this book, put together some sample backup plans; run through a few likely scenarios and assess the effectiveness of your choice.

In addition to all the other information you have learned about backup strategies, here are a couple of good rules of thumb to remember when making your choice:

- If the backup strategy and policy is too complicated (and this holds true for most security issues), it will eventually be disregarded and fall into disuse.

- The best scheme is often a combination of strategies; use what works.

Choosing Backup Hardware and Media

Any device that can store data can be used to back it up, but that is like saying that anything with wheels can take you on a cross-country trip. Trying to fit a gigabyte worth of data on a big stack of 1.4MB floppy disks is an exercise in frustration, and using a $5,000 automated tape device to save a single copy of an email is a waste of resources.

Many people use what hardware they already have for their backup operations. Many consumer-grade workstations have a floppy drive and possibly a CD-RW drive, but they typically do not have the abundant free disk space necessary for performing and storing multiple full backups.

In this section, you learn about some of the most common backup hardware available and how to evaluate its appropriateness for your backup needs. With large storage devices becoming increasingly affordable (160GB IDE drives can be had for around $100) and prices falling on DVD recorders, decisions about backup hardware for the small business and home users has become more interesting.

Removable Storage Media

At one time, every computer came with a floppy drive, but those drives are becoming less common and are no longer being provided as standard equipment with many new computers. Some sysadmins remove them because they can be used as a means of penetrating system security. (Remember that physical access to a machine means that it is insecure; a floppy drive provides a way to bypass the system administrator to load and run malicious programs.) Many modern laptops do not provide floppy drives except as an option.

Floppy drives are cheap and disposable solutions for making simple, quick backups of a few files by the user, but the media are easily damaged, lost, and accidentally overwritten.

They also unexpectedly fail at times. Floppies now represent the low-rent district for data storage.

Zip Drives

You can use removable or portable drives as part of your backup strategy. Of all the removable hard drive manufacturers, Iomega seems to have acquired some staying power with its Zip (100, 250, and 750MB) drive. Although these drives have good support in Fedora Core Linux, in the past they have been plagued with mechanical problems that have rendered data irretrievable. Their reliability has improved, but shy away from any older drives. These drives have been ubiquitous and are common in the publishing industry. They are now less frequently encountered and are being supplanted by CD writers.

USB and Solid-State Drives

USB hard drives and solid-state "pen" drives are the new kids on the block with prices dropping over the last year or two; a 64MB "pen" drive costs slightly less than $30 and capacities up to 1GB are available for around $90. USB drives have a large capacity for their size. If your machine supports them (or if you have purchased a card reader), you can also use Compact Flash devices, which come in sizes up to 8GB in the Flash memory versions and 4GB for Hitachi Microdrives. Both USB hard drives and solid-state drives are highly portable. Support for these drives under Fedora Core Linux is very good, accommodating these drives by emulating them as SCSI drives—the system usually sees them as /dev/scd1. Watch for improved support and ever falling prices in the future. The newer USB 2.0 hard drives are significantly faster than the older USB 1.0 hard drives. A 100GB USB hard drive will cost about $150. The biggest benefits of USB drives are data transfer speed and portability.

FireWire Drives

FireWire (IEEE-1394) hard drives are similar to USB drives; they just use a different interface to your computer. Many digital cameras and portable MP3 players use FireWire. Kernel support is available if you have this hardware; a 100GB FireWire drive will cost about $180, roughly twice IDE drive prices. Found mostly on the Mac, controller and drive hardware exists for the PC platform as well.

CD-RW and DVD+RW/-RW Drives

Compared to floppy drives and some removable drives, CD-RW drives and their cousins, DVD+RW/-RW drives, can store large amounts of data and are useful for a home or small business. Once very expensive, CD writers and media are at commodity prices today, although automated CD changing machines, necessary for automatically backing up large amounts of data, are still quite costly. A benefit of CD and DVD storage over tape devices is that the archived uncompressed file system can be mounted and its files accessed randomly just like a hard drive (you do this when you create a data CD, refer to Chapter 10, "Multimedia Applications"), making the recovery of individual files easier.

Each CD-RW disk can hold 650MB–700MB of data (the media comes in both capacities at roughly the same cost); larger chunks of data can be split to fit on multiple disks. Some backup programs support this method of storage. Once burned and verified, the shelf life for the media is at least a decade or longer. Prices increase with writing speed, but a serviceable CD-RW drive can be purchased for less than $100.

DVD+RW/-RW is similar to CD-RW, but it is more expensive and can store up to 4.4GB of uncompressed data per disk. These drives are selling for less than $100. Writing to DVD drives requires special software, and, unfortunately, Linux development is somewhat behind the curve for DVD writing. Fedora Core does provide the latest software to write to DVD+RW drives. (DVD-RW support is still experimental.)

Network Storage

For network backup storage, remote arrays of hard drives provide one solution to data storage. With the declining cost of mass storage devices and the increasing need for larger storage space, network storage (NAS, or Network Attached Storage) is available and supported in Linux. These are cabinets full of hard drives and their associated controlling circuitry, as well as special software to manage all of it. These NAS systems are connected to the network and act as a huge (and expensive) mass storage device.

More modest and simple network storage can be done on a remote desktop-style machine that has adequate storage space (up to eight 250GB IDE drives is a lot of storage space, easily accomplished with off-the-shelf parts), but then that machine (and the local system administrator) has to deal with all the problems of backing up, preserving, and restoring its own data, doesn't it? Several hardware vendors offer such products in varying sizes.

Tape Drive Backup

Tape drives have been used in the computer industry from the beginning. Tape drive storage has been so prevalent in the industry that the `tar` command (the most commonly used command for archiving) is derived from the words Tape ARchive. Modern tape drives use tape cartridges that can hold 70GB of data (or more in compressed format). Capacities and durability of tapes vary from type to type and range from a few gigabytes to hundreds of gigabytes with commensurate increases in cost for the equipment and media. Autoloading tape-drive systems can accommodate archives that exceed the capacity of the file systems.

> **TIP**
>
> Older tape equipment is often available in the used equipment market and might be useful for smaller operations that have outgrown more limited backup device options.

Tape equipment is well supported in Linux and, when properly maintained, is extremely reliable. The tapes themselves are inexpensive, given their storage capacity and the ability to reuse them. Be aware, however, that tapes do deteriorate over time and, being mechanical, tape drives can and will fail.

> **CAUTION**
>
> Neglecting to clean, align, and maintain tape drives puts your data at risk. The tapes themselves are also susceptible to mechanical wear and degradation. Hardware maintenance is part of a good backup policy. Do not ever forget that it is a question of when—not if—hardware will fail.

Using Backup Software

Because there are thousands of unique situations requiring as many unique backup solutions, it comes as no surprise that Linux offers many backup tools. Fedora Core provides the classic command-line backup software tar, dump, and cpio. The following sections discuss each of those tools and examine how dd and cp commands can be used to copy files. (Those copies can be considered backups if you store them safely.) Fedora Core provides a graphical interface for tar named Kdat that exploits the KDE desktop's drag-and-drop functionality. Fedora Core Linux also provides a graphical archiving tool, File Roller, that can create and extract files from archives. Finally, Fedora Core provides support for the Amanda backup application—a sophisticated backup application that works well over network connections and can be configured to automatically back up all the computers on your network. Amanda works with drives as well as tapes. The book *Unix Backup and Recovery* by W. Curtis Preston includes a whole chapter on setting up and using Amanda, and this chapter is available online at http://www.backupcentral.com/amanda.html.

> **NOTE**
>
> The software in a backup system must support the hardware, and this relationship can determine which hardware or software choices you make. Many sysadmins choose a particular backup software not because they prefer it to other options, but because it supports the hardware they own.
>
> The price seems right for free backup tools, but consider the software's ease of use and automation when assessing costs. If you must spend several hours implementing, debugging, documenting, and otherwise dealing with overly elaborate automation scripts, the real costs go up.

tar: **The Most Basic Backup Tool**

The tar tool, the bewhiskered old man of archiving utilities, is installed by default. It is an excellent tool for saving entire directories full of files. For example, here is the command used to back up the /etc directory:

```
# tar cvf etc.tar /etc
```

Here, the options use tar to create an archive, be verbose in the message output, and use the filename etc.tar as the archive name for the contents of the directory /etc.

Alternatively, if the output of tar is sent to the standard output and redirected to a file, the command appears as follows:

```
# tar cv /etc > etc.tar
```

and the result is the same.

All files in the /etc directory will be saved to a file named etc.tar. With an impressive array of options (see the man page), tar is quite flexible and powerful in combination with shell scripts. With the -z option, it can even create and restore gzip compressed archives while the -j option works with bzipped files.

> **TIP**
>
> Do you have backup tapes made with MTF that you would like to extract a file from? The Microsoft Tape Format is used to back up Windows NT files and can be read with a Linux utility named mtf.
>
> This Linux program works with SCSI tape drives. Software compression and archives that span tapes are not yet supported. Download the source code from http://www.layton-graphics.com/mtf/.

Creating Full and Incremental Backups with tar

If you want to create a full backup,

```
# tar cjvf fullbackup.tar.bz2 /
```

will create a bzip2 compressed tarball (the j option) of the entire system.

To perform an incremental backup, you must locate all the files that have been changed since the last backup. For simplicity, assume that you do incremental backups on a daily basis. To locate the files, use the find command:

```
# find / -newer name_of_last_backup_file ! -a -type f -print
```

When run alone, find will generate a list of files systemwide and print it to the screen. The ! -a -type eliminates everything but regular files from the list; otherwise, the entire directory would be sent to tar even if the contents was not all changed.

Pipe the output of our find command to tar as follows:

```
# find / -newer name_of_last_backup_file ! -type d -print |\
  tar czT - backup_file_name_or_device_name
```

Here, the T - option gets the filenames from a buffer (where the - is the shorthand name for the buffer).

> **NOTE**
>
> The `tar` command can back up to a raw device (one with no file system) as well as a formatted partition. For example,
>
> ```
> # tar cvzf /dev/hdd  /boot  /etc /home
> ```
>
> backs up those directories to device /dev/hdd (not /dev/hda1, but to the unformatted device itself).
>
> The `tar` command can also back up over multiple floppy disks:
>
> ```
> # tar czvMf /dev/fd0 /home
> ```
>
> will back up the contents of /home and spread the file out over multiple floppies, prompting you with this message:
>
> ```
> Prepare volume #2 for `/dev/fd0' and hit return:
> ```

Restoring Files from an Archive with `tar`

The `xp` option in `tar` will restore the files from a backup and preserve the file attributes as well, and `tar` will create any subdirectories it needs. Be careful when using this option because the backups might have been created with either relative or absolute paths. You should use the `tvf` option with `tar` to list the files in the archive before extracting them so that you will know where they will be placed.

For example, to restore a tar archive compressed with `bzip2`,

```
# tar xjvf fedoratest.tar.bz2
```

To list the contents of a tar archive compressed with `bzip2`,

```
# tar tjvf fedoratest.tar.bz2
drwxrwxr-x paul/paul       0 2003-09-04 18:15:05 fedoratest/
-rw-rw-r-- paul/paul     163 2003-09-03 22:30:49
                         ¬fedoratest/fedora_screenshots.txt
-rw-rw-r-- paul/paul     840 2003-09-01 19:27:59
                         ¬fedoratest/fedora_guideline.txt
-rw-rw-r-- paul/paul    1485 2003-09-01 18:14:23 fedoratest/style-sheet.txt
-rw-rw-r-- paul/paul     931 2003-09-01 19:02:00 fedoratest/fedora_TOC.txt
```

Note that because the pathnames do not start with a backslash, they are relative pathnames and will install in your current working directory. If they were absolute pathnames, they would install exactly where the paths state.

Backing Up Files with `cpio`

The `cpio` tool (installed by default) is great for saving individual files scattered throughout a file system as opposed to all the files that are located in a single directory. You can generate a list of files and pipe them to `cpio`; those files then become part of the archive.

Interestingly, RPM files (Red Hat Package Manager) are modified cpio files. The rpm2cpio command can be used to unpack (rather than install) RPM files if needed; refer to Chapter 7 for more information on RPM files.

Create a cpio Archive

To see how cpio works, you can create a list of files from the /etc directory and then use that list to create the cpio archive:

```
# find /etc -print > filelist
# cat filelist ¦ cpio -o > backup.cpio
```

To do it all on one line (Unix people like to do that), try this:

```
# find /etc -print ¦ cpio -o > backup.cpio
```

Note that you can concatenate several file lists together and use grep to search for and remove files you do not want in the archive. (Using cat and grep are covered in Chapter 5, "First Steps with Fedora.") You can use these basic commands to build scripts (refer to Chapter 14, "Automating Tasks") that can perform complex and elaborate backups tailored to your particular needs; such is the power of the GNU tools provided with Linux. The man page for cpio lists an impressive array of options for backing up and restoring files.

> **NOTE**
>
> You can name your backups anything you want, but it is a good idea to follow the filename conventions of using the .tar, .tgz, and .cpio extensions, for example. Also, include the current date and time in the filename—easily done when using shell scripts and cron to perform backups. (Refer to Chapter 14 for examples of shell scripting.)

Restoring Files from an Archive with cpio

The -im option in cpio will restore the files from a backup and preserve the file attributes as well. Whereas tar will create any subdirectories it needs, the -d option needs to be explicitly added to cpio for the same result. Be careful because the backups might have been created with relative or absolute paths. You should use -otv with cpio to list the files in the archive before extracting them so that you will know where they will be placed.

To restore a cpio archive,

```
# cpio -imd fedoratest.cpio
```

To list the contents of a cpio file,

```
# cpio -otv fedoratest.cpio
drwxrwxr-x paul/paul         0 2003-09-04 18:15:05 fedoratest/
-rw-rw-r-- paul/paul       163 2003-09-03 22:30:49
                              ¬fedoratest/fedora_screenshots.txt
```

```
-rw-rw-r-- paul/paul         840 2003-09-01 19:27:59
                             ¬fedoratest/fedora_guideline.txt
-rw-rw-r-- paul/paul        1485 2003-09-01 18:14:23 fedoratest/style-sheet.txt
-rw-rw-r-- paul/paul         931 2003-09-01 19:02:00 fedoratest/fedora_TOC.txt
```

Note that because the pathnames do not start with a backslash, they are relative pathnames and will install in your current working directory. If they were absolute pathnames, they would install exactly where the paths state.

> **NOTE**
>
> Two of the oldest and most primitive Unix applications are the dump and restore commands. dump examines files on an ext2 and ext3 file system and determines which files need to be backed up. The backups can span multiple media and levels (dump levels determine the amount of data to be backed up). The dump archives are restored using the restore program. You can use restore across a network and use it to restore full and incremental backups. These bare-metal Unix applications are feature-rich but awkward to use, even for some Unix old-timers; for that reason, we do not cover their use in this chapter. Most users prefer the simpler GUI network backup utilities, such as those you learn about in "Alternative Backup Software," later in this chapter, or prefer to use tar.

The GNOME File Roller

The GNOME desktop file archiving graphical application File Roller (file-roller) will view, extract, and create archive files using tar, gzip, bzip, compress, zip, rar, lha, and several other compression formats. Note that File Roller is only a front-end to the command-line utilities that actually provide these compression formats; if they are not installed, File Roller cannot use that format.

> **CAUTION**
>
> File Roller will not complain if you select a compression format that is not supported by installed software until after you attempt to create the archive. Install any needed compression utilities first.

File Roller is well-integrated with the GNOME desktop environment to provide convenient drag-and-drop functionality with the Nautilus file manager. To create a new archive, select Archive, New to open the New Archive dialog box and navigate to the directory where you want the archive to be kept. Type your archive's name in the Selection: /root text box at the bottom of the New Archive dialog box. Use the Archive type drop-down menu to select a compression method. Now, drag the files that you want to be included from Nautilus into the empty space of the File Roller window, and the animated icons will show that files are being included in the new archive. When you are done, a list of files will be shown in the previously blank File Roller window (see Figure 16.1). To save the archive, simply select Archive, Close. Opening an archive is as easy as using the Archive, Open dialog to select the appropriate archive file.

FIGURE 16.1   Drag and drop files to build an archive with the GNOME File Roller.

The KDE Archiving Tools (KDE ark and kdat)

Fedora Core provides you with the KDE ark and kdat GUI tools for backups; they are installed only if you select the KDE desktop during installation. Archiving has traditionally been a function of the system administrator and not seen as a task for the individual user, so no elaborate GUI was believed necessary. Backing up has also been seen as a script driven, automated task in which a GUI is not as useful.

The KDE ark Archiving Tool

You launch ark by launching it from the command line. It is integrated with the KDE desktop (like File Roller is with GNOME), so it might be a better choice if you use KDE. This application provides a graphical interface to viewing, creating, adding to, and extracting from archived files as shown in Figure 16.2. Several configuration options are available with ark to ensure its compatibility with MS Windows. You can drag and drop from the KDE desktop or Konqueror file browser to add or extract files, or you can use the ark menus.

As long as the associated command-line programs are installed, ark can work with tar, gzip, bzip2, zip, and lha files (the latter four being compression methods used to save space by compaction of the archived files).

Existing archives are opened after launching the application itself. You can add files and directories to the archive or delete them from the archive, as shown in Figure 16.3. After opening the archive, you can extract all of its contents or individual files. You can also perform searches using patterns (all *.jpg files, for example) to select files.

FIGURE 16.2   Here, the contents of a `.zip` file containing the screenshots used for Chapter 7 are displayed.

FIGURE 16.3   The opening view of ark presented as a simple GUI browser. Here, several files are being selected to add to the new archive.

Choosing New from the File menu creates new archives. You then type the name of the archive, providing the appropriate extension (`.tar`, `.gz`, and so on), and then proceed to add files and directories as you desire.

Using the `dd` Command for Archiving

Although the dd command is not normally thought of as an archiving tool, it can be used to mirror a partition or entire disk, regardless of the information either contains. dd is useful for archiving copies of floppy disks while retaining the capability to restore the data to a floppy intact. For example,

```
# dd if=/dev/fd0 of=floppyimage1.img
```

Swapping the `if=` and `of=` values reverses the process. Although best known for copying images, `dd` can also be used to convert data, and it is especially useful when restoring older archives or moving data between big endian and little endian systems. Although such esoteric details are beyond the scope of this chapter, remember `dd` if you need to convert data from obsolete formats.

> **CAUTION**
>
> Do not confuse the `if=` and `of=` assignments; if you do, `dd` will be more than happy to overwrite your valid data with garbage. Use the Carpenter's Rule: "Measure twice—cut once."

Using the Amanda Backup Application

Provided with Fedora Core, Amanda is a powerful, network backup application created by the University of Maryland at College Park. Amanda is a robust backup and restore application best suited to unattended backups with an autoloading tape drive of adequate capacity. It benefits from good user support and documentation.

Amanda's features include compression and encryption. It is intended for use with high-capacity tape drives, floptical, CD-R, and CD-RW devices.

Amanda uses GNU `tar` and `dump`; it is intended for unattended, automated tape backups, and is not well-suited for interactive or ad hoc backups. The support for tape devices in Amanda is robust, and file restoration is relatively simple. Although Amanda does not support older Macintosh clients, it will use Samba to back up Microsoft Windows clients, as well as any Unix client that can use GNU tools (which includes Mac OS X). Because Amanda runs on top of standard GNU tools, file restoration can be made using those tools on a recovery disk even if the Amanda server is not available. File compression can be done on either the client or server, thus lightening the computational load on less powerful machines that need backing up.

> **CAUTION**
>
> Amanda does not support `dump` images larger than a single tape and requires a new tape for each run. If you forget to change a tape, Amanda continues to attempt backups until you insert a new tape, but those backups will not capture the data as you intended them to. Do not use too small a tape or forget to change a tape, or you will not be happy with the results.

There is no GUI interface for Amanda. Configuration is done in the time-honored Unix tradition of editing text configuration files located in `/etc/amanda`. The default installation in Fedora Core includes a sample `cron` file because it is expected that you will be using `cron` to run Amanda regularly. The client utilities are installed with the package `am-utils`; the Amanda server must be obtained from the Amanda website. As far as backup schemes are concerned, Amanda calculates an optimal scheme on-the-fly and schedules it accordingly. It can be forced to adhere to a traditional scheme, but other tools are possibly better suited for that job.

The `man` page for Amanda (the client is `amdump`) is well written and useful, explaining both the configuration of Amanda as well as detailing the several programs that actually make up Amanda. The configuration files found in `/etc/amanda` are well commented; they provide a number of examples to assist you in configuration.

The program's home page is http://www.amanda.org. There, you will find information on subscribing to the mail list, as well as links to Amanda-related projects and a FAQ.

Alternative Backup Software

The free download version of Fedora Core does not provide any other sophisticated backup applications, but the version targeted to businesses usually does. Commercial and other freeware backup products do exist; BRU and Veritas are good examples of effective commercial backup products. Here are some useful free software backup tools that are not installed with Fedora Core Linux:

- `flexbackup`—This backup tool is a large file of Perl scripts that makes `dump` and `restore` easier to use. `flexbackup`'s command syntax can be accessed by using the command with the `-help` argument. It also can use `afio`, `cpio`, and `tar` to create and restore archives locally or over a network using `rsh` or `ssh` if security is a concern. Its home page is http://www.flexbackup.org/.

- `afio`—This tool creates `cpio`-formatted archives, but handles input data corruption better than `cpio` (which does not handle data input corruption very well at all). It supports multi-volume archives during interactive operation and can make compressed archives. If you feel the need to use `cpio`, you might want to check out `afio` at http://freshmeat.net/projects/afio/.

- `cdbackup`—Designed for the home or small office user, `cdbackup` will work with any backup and will restore software that can read from `stdin`, write to `stdout`, and can handle linear devices such as tape drives. It makes it easier to use CD-Rs as the storage medium. Similar applications are available elsewhere as well; the home page for this application is at http://www.muempf.de/index.html.

Many other alternative backup tools exist, but covering all of them is beyond the scope of this book. Two good places to look for free backup software are Freshmeat (http://www.freshmeat.net) and Google (http://www.google.com/linux).

Copying Files

Often, when you have only a few files that you need to protect from loss or corruption, it might make better sense to simply copy the individual files to another storage medium rather than to create an archive of them. You can use the tar, cp, rsync, or even the cpio commands to do this, as well as a handy file management tool known as mc. Using tar is the traditional choice because older versions of cp did not handle symbolic links and permissions well at times, causing those attributes (characteristics of the file) to be lost; tar handled those file attributes in a better manner. cp has been improved to fix those problems, but tar is still more widely used. rsync has recently been added to Fedora Core and is an excellent choice for mirroring sets of files, especially when done over a network.

Many choices exist for using file copying as a backup technique, and your choice will depend on your priorities. If you are interested in the simplest method, choose cp -a. The tar alternative is the next best option. cpio is better suited to creating archives than it is to simply copying files. mc might offer the best combination of ease, power, and flexibility, but it cannot be counted on to be found on every system; you should find tar and cp everywhere. The following sections describe how to use each of these methods so that you can better determine which is best for your situation.

To illustrate how to use file copying as a backup technique, the examples here show how to copy (not archive) a directory tree. This tree includes symbolic links and files that have special file permissions we need to keep intact.

Copying Files Using tar

One choice for copying files into another location would be to use the tar command where you would create a tar file that would be piped to tar to be uncompressed in the new location. To accomplish this, first change to the source directory. Then, the entire command resembles

```
# tar cvf - files ¦ (cd target_directory ; tar xpf -)
```

where *files* are the filenames you want to include; use * to include the entire current directory.

Here is how the command shown works: You have already changed to the source directory and executed tar with the cvf - arguments that tell tar to

> c—Create an archive.
>
> v—Verbose; lists the files processed so we can see that it is working.
>
> f—The filename of the archive will be what follows. (In this case, it is -.)
>
> - —A buffer; a place to hold our data temporarily.

The following tar commands can be useful for creating file copies for backup purposes:

> l—Stay in the local file system (so you do not include remote volumes).
>
> atime-preserve—Do not change access times on files, even though you are accessing them now, to preserve the old access information for archival purposes.

The contents of the tar file (held for us temporarily in the buffer, which is named -) are then piped to the second expression, which will extract the files to the target directory. In shell programming (refer to Chapter 14), enclosing an expression in parentheses causes it to operate in a subshell and be executed first.

First we change to the target directory, and then

> x—Extract files from a tar archive.
>
> p—Preserve permissions.
>
> f—The filename will be -, the temporary buffer that holds the tar'ed files.

Compressing, Encrypting, and Sending tar Streams

The file copy techniques using the tar command in the previous section can also be used to quickly and securely copy a directory structure across a LAN or the Internet (using the ssh command). One way to make use of these techniques is to use the following command line to first compress the contents of a designated directory, and then decompress the compressed and encrypted archive stream into a designated directory on a remote host:

```
$ tar cvzf - data_folder | ssh remote_host `( cd ~/mybackup_dir; tar xvzf - )'
```

The tar command is used to create, list, and compress the files in the directory named data_folder. The output is piped through the ssh (secure shell) command and sent to the remote computer named *remote_host*. On the remote computer, the stream is then extracted and saved in the directory named */mybackup_dir*. You will be prompted for a password in order to send the stream.

Copying Files Using cp

To copy files, we could use the cp command. The general format of the command when used for simple copying is

```
$ cp -a source_directory target_directory
```

The -a argument is the same as giving -dpR, which would be

> -d—Dereferences symbolic links (never follows symbolic links) and copies the files that they point to instead of copying the links.
>
> -p—Preserves all file attributes if possible. (File ownership might interfere.)
>
> -R—Copies directories recursively.

The cp command can also be used to quickly replicate directories and retain permissions by using the -avR command-line options. Using these options preserves file and directory permissions, gives verbose output, and recursively copies and re-creates subdirectories. A log of the backup can also created during the backup by redirecting the standard output like this:

```
# cp -avR directory_to_backup destination_vol_or_dir 1>/root/backup_log.txt
```

or

```
# cp -avR fedora /test2 1>/root/backup_log.txt
```

This example makes an exact copy of the directory named /fedora on the volume named /test2, and saves a backup report named backup_log.txt under /root.

Copying Files Using cpio

You can use cpio instead of tar to make backup file copies, but remember that cpio really works with lists of files. So you must first create the list and feed it to cpio.

```
# find source_directory -print ¦ cpio -pudv target_directory
```

Here, use the find command on the current directory with the -print option to generate a list of files in that directory. Then pipe that file list to cpio. When cpio gets the file list, it

- p—Runs in copy-pass mode. (We are not creating an archive file here.)

- u—Replaces all files without asking (unconditional).

- d—Creates directories if needed.

- v—Lists all files copied (verbose).

Copying Files Using mc

The Midnight Commander is a command-line file manager that is useful for copying, moving, and archiving files and directories. The Midnight Commander has a look and feel similar to the Norton Commander of DOS fame. By executing mc at a shell prompt, a dual-pane view of the files is displayed. It contains drop-down menu choices and function keys to manipulate files. It also uses its own virtual file system, enabling it to mount FTP directories and display the contents of tar files, gzipped tar files (.tar.gz or .tgz), bzip files, DEB files, and RPM files, as well as extract individual files from them. As if that was not enough, mc contains a File Undelete virtual file system for ext2/3 partitions. By using cd to "change directories" to an FTP server's URL, you can transfer files using the FTP protocol. The default font chosen for Fedora Core makes the display of mc ugly when used in a tty console (as opposed to an xterm), but does not affect its performance.

Figure 16.4 shows a shot of the default dual-panel display. Pressing the F9 key drops down the menu, and pressing F1 displays the Help file. A "feature" in the default GNOME terminal intercepts the F10 key used to exit mc, so use F9 instead to access the menu item to quit, or simply click on the menu bar at the bottom with your mouse. The configuration files are well documented, and it would appear easy to extend the functionality of mc for your system if you understand shell scripting and regular expressions. It is an excellent choice for file management on servers not running X.

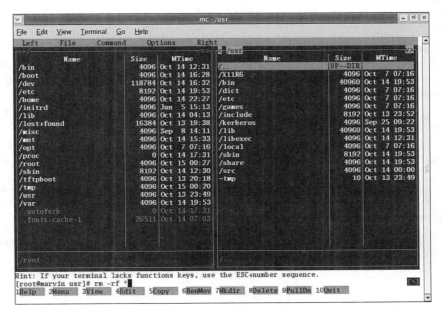

FIGURE 16.4   The Midnight Commander is a highly versatile file tool. If it does not display properly on your screen, launch it with the -a argument to force ASCII mode.

Copying Files Using scp

The traditional way to copy files from one computer to another is to use uucp, the Unix-to-Unix copy program, or to use one of the rtools, rcp. The rtools are insecure over a public network and are subject to several exploits. It is best not to use them at all because they have been supplanted by more secure tools based on the secure shell, ssh.

> **NOTE**
>
> The file transfer protocol known as FTP can be used to copy files from one computer to another, but this requires that an FTP server be running, and the server is subject to security problems of its own.
>
> See Chapter 22, " Remote File Serving with FTP," for more details on FTP.

The scp command uses ssh for file copying. Useful arguments for this command include

-p—Preserves modification times, access times, and modes from the original file.

-r—Recursively copies entire directories.

-v—Verbose mode for debugging problems.

-C—Enables file compression.

The syntax of an scp copy command is

```
scp [arguments] [source] [target]
```

For example, if we want to copy the file /home/paul/fedora.txt to ~/docs on our account on a remote host

```
$ scp -p /home/paul/fedora.txt paul@192.168.168.4:/home/paul/docs
```

After it prompts us for a password, we see

```
fedora.txt    100% ************************    0    00:00
```

This indicates that the transfer was completed. If we had subdirectories to transfer, we would have used the -r (recursive) argument.

Actually, it can be much easier than the example because scp assumes that all paths are relative to the home directory of the user unless the full path is given.

Taking this into consideration, our example becomes

```
$ scp -p fedora.txt paul@192.168.168.5:docs
```

And it can be made even easier. Creating a file named ~/.ssh/config with the following contents:

```
Host = titan
HostName = 192.168.168.5
User = paul
ForwardAgent = yes
ForwardX11 = yes
Compression = yes
```

allows us to simply use

```
$ scp -p fedora.txt titan:docs
```

NOTE

If you are comfortable with FTP, you might want to consider a cousin of scp: sftp. It provides the common FTP command set. If no sftp server is running on the remote host, simply use scp to copy the sftpserv binary to your remote home directory. (Often, ~/bin is in your path.) The FTP client gftp supports sftp and gives you a GUI client as well.

You can find more information on both scp and sftp in Chapter 25, "Remote Access with SSH and Telnet."

Copying Files Using rsync

rsync is a file transfer tool now included with Fedora Core. According to the rsync man page, it is a "faster, flexible replacement for rcp, the traditional remote copy application." We have already mentioned that rcp is not a secure method of transferring files.

A significant benefit of using rsync is that it speeds up file transfers by transferring only the differences between the two sites across a network link. rsync can copy links, devices, owners, groups, and permissions, and it can be told to exclude certain files. rsync can use ssh (via the command line or setting the RSYNC_RSH variable) and does not require root privileges. rsync has support for anonymous or authenticated rsync servers for use in mirroring.

The man page is extremely well-written and provides four excellent examples of how rsync can be used to transfer files matching a pattern, can recursively transfer files, and can be used locally (without a server).

The rsync command has some 62 options (not including short and long variants of the same option). A few particularly useful options are

-z—Uses gzip compression.

-P—Keeps partial files and reports on the progress of the transfer.

--bwlimit=KBPS—Sets a maximum bandwidth rsync might use.

--exclude-from=FILE—All excluded files listed in a separate file; pattern matching is enabled.

-x—Does not cross file system boundaries.

-n—Dry run for testing.

-l—Copies symlinks, not the files themselves.

-L—Copies the file, not the symlink.

-r—Copies recursively.

-v—Verbose output.

The rsync utility can be run as a daemon to establish an rsync server, listening on TCP port 873 by default. The configuration of the server is handled by the contents of the /etc/rsyncd.conf file; the man page for rsyncd.conf provides the details. The daemon can be launched standalone or via xinetd to suit your·needs.

The rsync website provides an examples page showing examples of

- Backing up to a central server with a seven-day increment

- Backing up to a spare disk

- Mirroring a CVS tree

- Automated backup at home over a modem

16

A time and bandwidth saving trick is to use `rsync` to only re-download that part of an ISO file that is incorrect, rather than downloading the entire 650MB–700MB of the file. First, you must locate an `rsync` server that is offering the `.iso` images you seek. Look at the Fedora Core mirrors at http://www.redhat.com/download/mirror.html and select one that offers "`D`", the identifier for `.iso` images.

An `rsync` server will provide *modules*, or directory trees as symbolic names. To determine if a server provides an `rsync` module, use the query:

```
rsync some.site.com::
```

If an `rsync` server is running on that site, you will see a list of available `rsync` modules. If we try

```
$ rsync ftp-linux.cc.gatech.edu::

GEORGIA TECH SOFTWARE LIBRARY

Unauthorized use is prohibited.  Your access is being logged.

If you run a publicly accessible mirror, and are interested in
mirroring from us, please contact lxmirror@cc.gatech.edu.

- - - - - - - - - - - - - - - - - - - - - - - - - - - - - - - - - - - - - - - - - - - - - - - - - - - - - - - - - - - - - - -


altlinux        mirror of ftp.altlinux.ru
arklinux        mirror of arklinux.org
asplinux        mirror of ftp.asp-linux.com
debian          mirror of ftp.debian.org
debian-cd       mirror of ftp.debian.org
mandrake        mirror of ftp.mandrake.com
redhat          mirror of ftp.redhat.com
<SNIP>
```

To use this `rsync` service, we would explore the *redhat* module to discover the file path to the .iso images using `rsync -r` and the module name to explore it recursively.

To use `rsync` to repair our defective .iso images, we point `rsync` at the "good" image and at our "bad" image like so:

```
# rsync -a -vvv --progress ftp-linux.cc.gatech.edu::\
redhat/linux/9/en/iso/i386/shrike-i386-disc1.iso\
 ~/downloads/shrike-i386-disc1.iso
```

`rsync` compares the two files and will download only the needed replacement parts for our local file much faster than downloading the entire image again.

Undeleting Files

Up to this point, we have discussed backing up data and restoring that data. In some situations, however, you need to restore data that has not been backed up because you just accidentally deleted it. File recovery (and system recovery, which you learn about in a later section) requires a high level of expertise to successfully complete. There are data recovery businesses that are good at data and system recovery, and they prosper because the task is so difficult. The information presented here, along with practice on your part, can assist you in attempting to do-it-yourself or enable you to recognize when a professional service is warranted.

Using the `ext2fs` Undeletion Process

On multiuser systems, when files are deleted, their inodes are made available immediately for use by the system. In that case, recovering that data intact is very unlikely, although not impossible. The first rule in undeleting a file is to stop all disk writes as soon as possible. If the system is heavily used, the old inode will likely be overwritten quite soon. The sooner you stop disk writes after deleting a file, the better chance you have of restoring at least some of the file.

After you have unmounted the file system containing the deleted files, you must attempt to methodically find the deleted parts of the file and reassemble them. Essentially, this involves examining the raw data on the disk using pattern matching to identify candidates for recovery, and then decoding the candidates' inode information to relink the files if possible. It is a time-consuming process and should be reason enough to encourage you to back up the files in the first place. On a single-user system, the chances of recovery are better because fewer writes to the disk have occurred after the file deletion.

File recovery is not something to be attempted without preparation and practice; both will improve your chances of recovering more of the data. The Ext2fs Undeletion mini-HOWTO (see "Reference") has been written to detail the process. Again, file recovery *requires some practice* before you would be ready to use it in the real world.

> **TIP**
>
> If you want to experiment with learning to restore files, use the information in the Examples section of Chapter 37 to create a loopback file system to experiment with. Using that, you can safely delete and undelete files without taking a chance on damaging your system by inadvertently changing critical files or deleting directories.

Reformatting with the `-S` Option When Experiencing Unrecoverable File System Errors

In attempting to recover data from a damaged disk with file system errors that cannot be fixed with `fsck`, you can run the `mke2fs` command with the `-S` option like this (for example, if you are having trouble with the ext2/3 partition on `/dev/hda2`):

```
# mke2fs -S /dev/hda2
```

The -S argument writes new superblock information, but does not write new inodes; this might make the missing data salvageable, or it might not depending on the damage. You must run e2fsck on the unmounted partition after using the mke2fs command in this manner.

Because a directory is a file as well, the same techniques for file recovery can be used to recover entire directories. The Ext2fs Undeletion of Directory Structures mini-HOWTO (see "Reference") is written as a companion to the Ext2fs Undeletion mini-HOWTO—both of which should be on everyone's required reading list if you want to successfully undelete any files. The manual technique described in the HOWTOs is too long and complex to be covered in this book.

Undeleting Files Using mc

The Midnight Commander can make use of a virtual file system and includes a special undelete file system that can be used on ext2/3 partitions. The mc utility is just an inter- face to the ext2fs library, and the virtual file system handles for you the nitty-gritty details of the file system that the previous paragraph alluded to. As with any simplified solution to complex issues, mc must make some assumptions for you that might result in less data being recovered than if you use the manual method. For that reason, using mc for recovering deleted files is not a standard method.

To use the recovery file system, you must cd in one of the panels to the special filename formed by combining the prefix /#undel: with the partition name where your deleted file resides. For example, to attempt to recover a deleted file on /dev/hda2, do this:

```
# cd /#undel:hda2
```

Be patient because it will take quite a while for the deleted files to be displayed. You will see a list of inodes that you can examine with the text editor (using the F4 key); then use the F12 key to perform a Save As operation, renaming the file to something appropriate for your use. Repeat this process until you have renamed and saved all the files. Press the Shift+F10 key to exit when done. Note that you might be able to recover only pieces of files and might not be able to recover any at all.

> **NOTE**
>
> If you need to know what is on a drive or disk that cannot be easily mounted (it could be a non-Linux format, or could contain un-formatted, raw data), use
>
> ```
> # dd if=/dev/hda1 count=1 bs=512 ¦ file -
> ```
>
> which produces output similar to the following:
>
> ```
> 1+0 records in
> 1+0 records out
> standard input:              x86 boot sector, \
> system MSWIN4.1, FAT (16 bit)
> ```

To discover what an unknown floppy disk is, use this:

```
# dd if=/dev/fd0 count=1 bs=512 ¦ file -
```

which produces output similar to the following:

```
1+0 records in
1+0 records out
standard input:              x86 boot sector, system )\
_3oEIHC, FAT (12 bit)
```

System Rescue

There will come a time when you need to engage in system rescue efforts. This need arises when the system will not even start Linux so that you can recover any files. This problem is most frequently associated with the boot loader program or partition table, but it could be that critical system files have been inadvertently deleted or corrupted. If you have been making backups properly, these kinds of system failures are easily, though not quickly, recoverable through a full restore. Still, valuable current data might not have been backed up since the last scheduled backup, and the backup archives are found to be corrupt, incomplete, or missing. A full restore also takes time you might not have. If the problem causing the system failure is simply a damaged boot loader, a damaged partition table, a missing library, or misconfiguration, a quick fix can get the system up and running and the data can then be easily retrieved.

In this section, we will first examine a way to back up and restore the boot loader itself or, having failed to do that, restore it by hand. Then we will look at a few alternatives to booting the damaged system so that we can inspect it, fix it, or retrieve data from it.

The Fedora Core Rescue Disc

Fedora Core provides a rescue disc hidden in the first installation CD. To use it, insert the first installation CD and reboot the computer, booting from the CD just as you did when you installed Fedora originally. At the intro screen, press the F1 key to see all the available choices, but simply enter linux rescue at the LILO boot prompt to enter rescue mode like

```
boot: linux rescue
```

You will learn more about the rescue mode later in this section, but feel free to explore it at any time. A graphical interface is not available, so you will need to bone up on your command-line skills. If necessary, you can perform all the operations discussed in this section from rescue mode.

Backing Up and Restoring the Master Boot Record

The Master Boot Record (MBR) is the first 512 bytes of a hard disk. It contains the boot loader code in the first 446 bytes and the partition table in the next 64 bytes; the last two bytes identify that sector as the MBR. The MBR can become corrupted, so it makes sense to back it up.

This example uses the dd command as root to back up the entire MBR. If the boot loader code changes from the time you make this image and restore the old code, the system will not boot when you restore it all; it is easy enough to keep a boot floppy handy and then re-run LILO if that is what you are using.

To copy the entire MBR to a file, use this:

```
# dd if=/dev/hda of=/tmp/hdambr bs=512 count=1
```

To restore the entire MBR, use this:

```
# dd if=/tmp/hdambr of=/dev/hda bs=512 count=1
```

To restore only the partition table, skipping the boot loader code, use this:

```
# dd if=/tmp/hdambr of=/dev/hda bs=1 skip=446 count=66
```

Of course, it would be prudent to move the copy of the MBR to a floppy or other appropriate storage device. (The file is only 512 bytes in size.) You will need to be able to run dd on the system in order to restore it (which means that you will be using the Fedora Core rescue disk as described later, or any equivalent to it).

Manually Restoring the Partition Table

A different way of approaching the problem is to have a printed copy of the partition table that can then be used to restore the partition table by hand using the Fedora Core rescue disk and the fdisk program.

We can create a listing of the printout of the partition table with fdisk using the -l option (for list), as follows:

```
# fdisk /dev/hda -l > /tmp/hdaconfig.txt
```

or send the listing of the partition table to the printer:

```
# fdisk /dev/hda -l ¦ kprinter
```

We could also copy the file /tmp/hdaconfig.txt to the same backup floppy as the MBR for safekeeping.

Now that we have a hard copy of the partition table (as well as having saved the file itself somewhere), it is possible to restore the MBR by hand at some future date.

Use the Fedora Core Rescue Disk for this process. After booting into rescue mode, you will have the opportunity to use a menu to mount your system read/write, not to mount your system, or to mount any found Linux partitions as read-only. If you plan to make any changes, you will need to have any desired partitions mounted with write permission.

Once logged on (you are `root` by default), start `fdisk` on the first drive:

```
# fdisk /dev/had
```

Use the p command to display the partition information and compare it to the hard copy you have. If the entries are identical, you have a problem somewhere else; it is not the partition table.

If there is a problem, use the d command to delete all the listed partitions.

Now use the n command to create new partitions that will match the partition table from your hard copy. Make certain that the partition types (`ext2`, `FAT`, `swap` and so on) are the same. If you have a `FAT` partition at `/dev/hda1`, make certain that you set the bootable flag for it; otherwise, Windows or DOS will not boot.

If you find that you have made an error somewhere along the way, just use the q command to quit `fdisk` without saving any changes and start over. Without specifically telling `fdisk` to write to the partition table, no changes are actually made to it.

When the partition table information shown on your screen matches your printed version, write the changes to the disk with the w command; you will be automatically exited from `fdisk`. Restart `fdisk` to verify your handiwork, and then remove the rescue disk and reboot.

It helps to practice manually restoring the partition table on an old drive before you have to do it in an emergency situation.

Booting the System from the Rescue CD

For advanced Linux users, you can use the rescue CD to boot the system (rather than boot the rescue operating system on the CD-ROM) if the boot loader code on your computer is damaged or incorrect. To use the Rescue CD to boot your system from `/dev/hda1`, for example, first boot the CD and press the F1 key. At the LILO prompt, enter something similar to this example. Note that you are simply telling the boot loader what your root partition is.

```
boot: linux rescue root=/dev/hda1
```

Booting the System from a Generic Boot Floppy

If you failed to make a boot floppy or cannot locate the one you did make, any Linux boot floppy (a slightly older version or one borrowed from a friend) can be pressed into service as long as it has a reasonably similar kernel version. (The major and minor numbers match—for example, 2.6.5 would likely work with any 2.6 system, but not with a 2.4 system.) You would boot your system by manually specifying the root and boot partitions as described previously. Although you are almost guaranteed to get some error messages, you might at least be able to get a base system running enough to replace files and recover the system.

> **TIP**
>
> In both preceding cases, it is assumed that you do not need any special file system or device drivers to access the root partition. If you do, add the `initrd=` argument to the LILO line pointing to the appropriate `initrd` file on your system. If you do not know the exact name of the `initrd` file, you are out of luck with LILO, so learn to use a GRUB boot floppy as well.

Using a GRUB Boot Floppy

The GRand Unified Boot loader (GRUB) can attempt to boot a system from a floppy without a viable custom-made boot floppy. The image for the floppy can be downloaded from ftp://alpha.gnu.org/gnu/grub/grub-0.95-i386-pc.ext2fs and copied to a floppy using dd. (`rawrite.exe` would be used on a Microsoft system.) Or, if you have a boot floppy from an existing system using GRUB, that one will work as well.

GRUB has its own command shell, file system drivers, and search function (much like command completion in the bash shell). It is possible to boot using the GRUB floppy, examine the drive partitions, and search for the kernel and `initrd` image as well, using them to boot the system. Worthy of a chapter all its own, the GRUB documentation is extensive: In addition to `info grub` (the `info` system is similar to the `man` system for documentation), the GRUB documents contain a tutorial worth reading. The flexibility and power of GRUB are what influenced Red Hat to make it the default boot loader for Fedora Core Linux. The GRUB boot loader is shown in Figure 16.5.

FIGURE 16.5   The GRUB boot loader gives you incredible flexibility in booting even unfamiliar systems.

Using the Recovery Facility from the Installation Disc

As in the previous example, use the `linux rescue` command at the LILO boot prompt (`:`) to launch the CD in rescue mode. Rescue mode runs a version of Fedora Core from the CD-ROM that is independent from your system. It permits you to mount your root partition for maintenance. This alternative is useful when your root partition is no longer bootable because something has gone wrong. Fedora Core is constantly improving the features of the Recovery Facility.

Upon beginning the rescue mode, you get your choice of language and keyboard layouts. You are given an opportunity to configure networking in rescue mode and are presented with a nice ncurses-based form to fill in the information. The application will attempt to find your existing partitions and will offer you a choice of mounting them read-write, read-only (always a wise choice the first time), or skip any mounting and drop to a command prompt. With multiple partitions, you must then indicate which is the root partition. That partition is then mounted at /mnt/sysimage. When you are finally presented with a command prompt, it is then possible to make your system the root file system with

```
# chroot /mnt/sysimage
```

To get back to the rescue file system, type **exit** at the prompt. To reboot, type **exit** at the rescue system's prompt.

The rescue function does offer support for software RAID arrays (RAID 0, 1, and 5), as well as IDE or SCSI partitions formatted as ext2/3. After asking for input if it is unsure how to proceed, you eventually arrive at a command shell as root; there is no login or password. Depending on your configuration, you might or might not see prompts for additional information. If you get lost or confused, you can always reboot. (It helps to practice the use of the rescue mode.)

In rescue mode, a number of command-line tools are available for you, but no GUI tools are provided. For networking, you have the ifconfig, route, rcp, rlogin, rsh, and ftp commands. For archiving (and restoring archives), cpio, uncpio, gzip, gunzip, dd, zcat, and md5sum commands are there. As for editors, vi is emulated by BusyBox and pico, jmacs, and joe are provided by the joe editor. There are other useful system commands. A closer look at these commands reveals that they are all links to a program called BusyBox (home page at http://www.busybox.net/).

BusyBox provides a reasonably complete POSIX environment for any small or embedded system. The utilities in BusyBox generally have fewer options than their full-featured GNU cousins; however, the included options "provide the expected functionality and behave very much like their GNU counterparts." This means that you should test the rescue mode first to see if it can restore your data and see which options are available to you because the BusyBox version will behave slightly differently from the full GNU version. (Some options are missing; some options do not work quite the same—you need to know if this will affect you *before* you are in an emergency situation.)

There are a few useful tricks to know when using rescue mode. If your system is functional, you can use the chroot command to change the root file system from the CD to your system in this manner:

```
# chroot /mnt/sysimage
```

You will find yourself at a new command prompt with all your old files in—hopefully—the right place. Your familiar tools—if intact—should be available to you. To exit the chrooted environment, use the exit command to return to the rescue system prompt. If you use the exit command again, the system will reboot.

The rescue environment provides a nice set of networking commands and network-enabled tools such as scp, sftp, and some of the rtools. It also provides rpm, which can fetch packages over a network connection. Installing them is tricky because you want them installed in the file system mounted at /mnt/sysimage, not at /. To accomplish that, use the --root argument to set an alternate path to root:

```
# rpm -ivh --root /mnt/sysimage ftp://location/package.rpm
```

Alternatives to the Fedora Core Rescue CD

The Fedora Core rescue CD might be inadequate for your system restoration needs; it might lack specific Ethernet device support, file system support, or the kind of full utility functionality that you require for a successful recovery operation. An alternative exists in the SuperRescue CD created by H. Peter Anvin.

Essentially, the SuperRescue CD is a reasonably full and robust Red Hat distribution (based on Red Hat 7.2 and the 2.4.20-rc1 kernel) that runs completely from a bootable CD. The best thing about the SuperRescue CD is that it comes with build scripts, so it is incredibly easy to add new software (that special driver or application) and create a new CD. The home page is at http://freshmeat.net/projects/superrescue/, but you can grab a copy directly at http://www.kernel.org/pub/dist/superrescue/v2/.

Relevant Fedora Core Commands

The following commands are useful in performing backup, recovery, and restore operations in Fedora Core Linux:

amdump—Amanda is a network-based backup system, consisting of 18 separate commands, for use with Linux.

ark—A KDE desktop GUI archiving utility.

cp—The copy command.

scp—The secure shell copy command.

cpio—A data archive utility.

dd—A data copy and conversion utility.

gzip—The GNU compression utility.

tar—The GNU tape archive utility.

Reference

http://www.tldp.org/LDP/solrhe/Securing-Optimizing-Linux-RH-Edition-v1.3/ whywhen.html—A thorough discussion with examples of using dump and restore for backups.

http://en.tldp.org/LDP/solrhe/Securing-Optimizing-Linux-RH-Edition-v1.3/ chap29sec306.html—Making automatic backups with tar using cron.

http://kmself.home.netcom.com/Linux/FAQs/backups.html—The Linux Backups mini FAQ contains some useful, although brief, comments on backup media, compression, encryption, and security.

http://www.tldp.org/—The Linux Documentation Project offers several useful HOWTO documents that discuss backups and disk recovery.

http://www.ibiblio.org/pub/Linux/docs/HOWTO/other-formats/html_single/ Ext2fs-Undeletion.html—If you need to undelete a file from an ext2/3 file system, the Linux Ext2fs Undeletion mini HOWTO is the document for you. You will be more successful if you practice.

http://www.ibiblio.org/pub/Linux/docs/HOWTO/other-formats/html_single/ Ext2fs-Undeletion-Dir-Struct.html—The Ext2fs Undeletion of Directory Structures is a companion HOWTO to the Linux Ext2fs Undeletion mini HOWTO, helping you cope with an errant rm -rf *.

http://www.ibiblio.org/pub/Linux/docs/HOWTO/other-formats/html_single/ Bootdisk-HOWTO.html#AEN1483—Here is a list of LILO Boot error codes to help you debug a cranky system that will not boot.

http://www.ibiblio.org/pub/Linux/docs/HOWTO/other-formats/html_single/ Ftape-HOWTO.html—This is a HOWTO for the floppy tape device driver.

http://www.linux-usb.org/USB-guide/x498.html—The USB Guide for mass storage devices. If you have a USB device and need to know if it is supported, check here.

http://www.backupcentral.com/amanda.html—This is the Amanda chapter of *Unix Backup and Recovery* (written by John R. Jackson and published by O'Reilly and Associates). The chapter is available online and covers every aspect of using Amanda. The site features a handy search tool for the chapter.

http://twiki.org/cgi-bin/view/Wikilearn/RsyncingALargeFileBeginner—Rsyncing a large file to "repair" a local ISO image that does not pass the md5sum check.

http://www.lycoris.org/sections.php?op=viewarticle&artid=8—Lycoris ISO rsync mini HOWTO. A step-by-step tutorial on using rsync to sync files.

http://www.mikerubel.org/computers/rsync_snapshots/—Automated snapshot-style backups using rsync.

http://www.mondorescue.org/—Mondo Rescue is a bare-metal backup/rescue tool independent of Fedora Core, using CD, DVD, tape, or NFS; it can produce bootable CDs to restore the system.

http://www.ccp14.ac.uk/ccp14admin/linux-server/mondorescue/dvd_mondo.html—A HOWTO for using MondoRescue to back up on a DVD.

http://www.linuxorbit.com/modules.php?op=modload&name=Sections&file=index&req= viewarticle&artid=222&page=1—A HOWTO using split and mkisofs to manually back up large archives to CD.

Network Connectivity

One of Linux's strongest features is its networking capabilities. Linux can emulate or share files with almost every operating system. Linux can talk to Mac OS X, Netware, BSD, all flavors of Unix, and even Windows (with the help of Samba). Linux servers can be easily and quickly deployed in heterogeneous networks and will run for weeks or even months without failures. It is that kind of flexibility and performance that can account for Linux's increased wired and wireless presence in the workplace and in homes.

This chapter introduces some basic concepts about networking with Linux and shows you how to configure, manage, and use *network interface cards (NICs)* and various network services with Fedora. You will see how to use command-line programs to control networking on your system, as well as how to launch and use several of Fedora's graphical network management clients. You will need to perform many of these tasks using root permission, but you'll see how easily network management can be performed when using Linux. You will also see how to protect your system on any network using Red Hat's graphical firewall configuration utility.

Networking with TCP/IP

The basic building block for any network based on Unix hosts is the Transport Control Protocol/Internet Protocol (TCP/IP) suite of three protocols. The suite consists of the Internet Protocol (IP), Transport Control Protocol (TCP), and Universal Datagram Protocol (UDP). IP is the base protocol. The TCP/IP suite is *packet*-based, which means that data is broken into little chunks on the transmit end for transmission to the receiving end. Breaking data up into manageable packets allows for faster and more accurate transfers. In TCP/IP, all data travels via IP packets, which is why addresses are referred to as IP addresses. It is the lowest level of the suite.

TCP is a connection-based protocol. Before data is transmitted between two machines, a connection is established between them. When a connection is made, a stream of data is sent to the IP to be broken into the packets that are then transmitted. At the receiving end, the packets are put back in order and sent to the proper application port.

On the other hand, UDP is a connectionless protocol. Applications using this protocol just choose their destination and start sending. UDP is normally used for small amounts of data or on fast and reliable networks. If you are interested in the internals of TCP/IP, see the "Reference" section at the end of this chapter for places to look for more information.

Fedora and Networking

Chances are that your network card was configured during the installation of Fedora. You can however, use the `ifconfig` command at the shell prompt or Fedora's graphical network configuration tools, such as `system-config-network`, to edit your system's network device information or to add or remove network devices on your system. Hundreds of networking commands and utilities are included with Fedora—far too many to cover in this chapter and more than enough for coverage in two or three volumes.

Nearly all Ethernet cards can be used with Linux, along with many PCMCIA wired and wireless network cards. The great news is that many USB wireless network devices also work just fine with Linux, and more will be supported with upcoming versions of the Linux kernel. Check the Linux USB Project at http://www.linux-usb.org for the latest developments or to verify support for your device.

After reading this chapter, you might want to learn more about other graphical network clients for use with Linux. The GNOME `ethereal` client, for example, can be used to monitor all traffic on your LAN or specific types of traffic. Another client, NmapFE, can be used to scan a specific host for open ports and other running services.

TCP/IP Addressing

To understand networking with Linux, you need to know the basics of TCP/IP addressing. Internet IP addresses (also known as public IP addresses) are different from those used internally on a Local Area Network, or LAN. Internet IP addresses are assigned (for the United States and some other hosts) by the American Registry for Internet Numbers, available at http://www.arin.net/. Entities that need an Internet address apply to this agency to be assigned an address. The agency assigns Internet service providers (ISPs) one or more blocks of IP addresses, which the ISPs can then assign to their subscribers.

You will quickly recognize the current form of TCP/IP addressing, known as IPv4 (IP version 4). In this method, a TCP/IP address is expressed of a series of four decimal numbers—a 32-bit value expressed in a format known as dotted decimal format, such as 192.168.120.135. Each set of numbers is known as an *octet* (eight ones and zeros, such as 10000000 to represent 128) and ranges from zero to 255.

The first octet usually determines what *class* the network belongs to. There are three classes of networks. The classes are

> Class A—Consists of networks with the first octet ranging from 1 to 126. There are only 126 Class A networks—each composed of up to 16,777,214 hosts. (If you are doing the math, there are potentially 16,777,216 addresses, but no host portion of an address can be all zeros or 255s.) The "10." network is reserved for local network use, and the "127." network is reserved for the *loopback* address of 127.0.0.1. Loopback addressing is used by TCP/IP to enable Linux network-related client and server programs to communicate on the same host. This address will not appear and is not accessible on your LAN.

> **NOTE**
>
> Notice that zero is not included in Class A. The zero address is used for network-to-network broadcasts. Also, note that there are two other classes of networks, Classes D and E. Class D networks are reserved for multicast addresses and not for use by network hosts. Class E addresses are deemed experimental, and thus are not open for public addressing.

> Class B—Consists of networks defined by the first two octets with the first ranging from 128 to 191. The "128." network is also reserved for local network use. There are 16,382 Class B networks—each with 65,534 possible hosts.

> Class C—Consists of a network defined by the first three octets with the first ranging from 192 to 223. The "192." network is another that is reserved for local network use. There are a possible 2,097,150 Class C networks of up to 254 hosts each.

No host portion of an IP address can be all zeros or 255s. These addresses are reserved for broadcast addresses. IP addresses with all zeros in the host portion are reserved for network-to-network broadcast addresses. IP addresses with all 255s in the host portion are reserved for local network broadcasts. Broadcast messages are not typically seen by users.

These classes are the standard, but a *netmask* also determines what class your network is in. The netmask determines what part of an IP address represents the network and what part represents the host. Common netmasks for the different classes are

> **Class A**—255.0.0.0
>
> **Class B**—255.255.0.0
>
> **Class C**—255.255.255.0

Because of the allocation of IP addresses for Internet hosts, it is now impossible to get a Class A network. It is also nearly impossible to get a Class B network (all the addresses have been given out, but some companies are said to be willing to sell theirs), and Class C network availability is dropping rapidly with the current growth of Internet use worldwide. See the following sidebar.

Limits of Current IP Addressing

The current IPv4 address scheme is based on 32-bit numbering and limits the number of available IP addresses to about 4.1 billion. Many companies and organizations (particularly in the United States) were assigned very large blocks of IP addresses in the early stages of the growth of the Internet, which has left a shortage of "open" addresses. Even with careful allocation of Internet-connected host IP addresses and the use of *network address translation (NAT)* to provide communication to and from machines behind an Internet-connected computer, the Internet might run out of available addresses.

To solve this problem, a newer scheme named IPv6 (IP version 6) is being implemented. It uses a much larger addressing solution based on 128-bit addresses, with enough room to include much more information about a specific host or device, such as Global Positioning Server (GPS) or serial numbering. Although the specific details about the entire contents of the an IPv6 address have yet to be finalized, all Internet-related organizations appear to agree that something must be done to provide more addresses. According to Vint Cerf, one of the primary developers of the TCP/IP protocol, "There will be nearly 2.5 billion devices on the Internet by 2006, and by 2010 half the world's population will have access to the Internet."

You can get a good overview of the differences between IPv4 and IPv6, policies regarding IP address assignments, and the registration process of obtaining IP addresses by browsing to http://www.arin.net/library/index.html. Read the Linux IPv6 HOWTO by browsing to http://tldp.org/HOWTO/Linux+IPv6-HOWTO/.

Fedora supports the use of IPv6 and includes a number of networking tools conforming to IPv6 addressing. Support for IPv6 can be configured by using settings and options in the file named `network` under the `/etc/sysconfig` directory, along with changes to related network configuration files, such as `/etc/hosts`. Many IPv6-based tools, such as `ipcalc6`, `ping6`, and `traceroute6`, are available for Fedora. See various files under the `/usr/share/doc/initscripts` directory for more information specific to setting up IPv6 addressing with Linux and Fedora.

Migration to IPv6 is slow in coming, however, because the majority of computer operating systems, software, hardware, firmware, and users are still in the IPv4 mindset. Supporting IPv6 will require rewrites to many networking utilities, portions of operating systems currently in use, and firmware in routing and firewall hardware.

Using IP Masquerading in Fedora

Three blocks of IP addresses are reserved for use on internal networks and hosts not directly connected to the Internet. The address ranges are from `10.0.0.0` to `10.255.255.255`, or 1 Class A network; from `172.16.0.0` to `172.31.255.255`, or 16 Class B networks; and from `192.168.0.0` to `192.168.255.255`, or 256 Class C networks. Use these IP addresses when building a LAN for your business or home. Which class you choose can depend on the number of hosts on your network.

Internet access for your internal network can be provided by a PC running Fedora or other broadband or dial-up router. The host or device is connected to the Internet and is used as an Internet gateway to forward information to and from your LAN. The host should also be used as a *firewall* to protect your network from malicious data and users while functioning as an Internet gateway. A PC used in this fashion will typically have at least two network interfaces. One is connected to the Internet with the other connected to the computers on the LAN (via a hub or switch). Some broadband devices also incorporate four or more switching network interfaces. Data is then passed between the LAN and the Internet using *NAT*, better known in Linux circles as *IP Masquerading*. See Chapter 33, "Securing Your Machines," for more information.

> **NOTE**
>
> Do not rely on a single point of protection for your LAN, especially if you use wireless networking, provide dial-in services, or allow mobile (laptop or PDA) users internal or external access to your network. Companies, institutions, and individuals relying on a "moat mentality" have often discovered to their dismay that such an approach to security is easily breached. Make sure that your network operation is accompanied by a security policy that stresses multiple levels of secure access, with protection built into every server and workstation—something easily accomplished when using Linux.

Ports

Most servers on your network have more than one task. For example, web servers have to serve both standard and secure pages. You might also be running an FTP server on the same host. For this reason, applications are provided *ports* to use to make "direct" connections for specific software services. These ports help TCP/IP distinguish services so that data can get to the correct application. If you check the file /etc/services, you will see the common ports and their usage. For example, for FTP, HTTP, and Post Office Protocol (email retrieval server), you will see

```
ftp        21/tcp
http       80/tcp      www www-http  # WorldWideWeb HTTP
pop3       110/tcp     pop-3         # POP version 3
```

The ports defined in /etc/services in this example are 21 for FTP, 80 for HTTP, and 110 for POP3. Other common port assignments are 25 for *Simple Mail Transport Protocol (SMTP)* and 22 for *secure shell (SSH)* remote login. Note that these ports are not set in stone, and you can set up your server to respond to different ports. For example, although port 22 is listed in /etc/services as a common default for SSH, the sshd server can be configured to listen on a different port by editing its configuration file /etc/ssh/sshd_config. The default setting (commented out with a pound sign) looks like this:

```
#Port 22
```

Edit the entry to use a different port, making sure to select an unused port number, such as

```
Port 2224
```

Save your changes, and then restart the sshd server. (Refer to Chapter 14, "Automating Tasks," to see how to restart a service.) Remote users must now access the host through port 2224, which can be done using ssh's -p (port) option like so:

```
$ ssh -p 2224 remote_host_name_or_IP
```

Network Organization

Properly organizing your network addressing process grows more difficult as the size of your network grows. Setting up network addressing for a Class C network with fewer than 254 devices is simple. Setting up addressing for a large, worldwide company with a Class A network and many different users can be extremely complex. If your company has fewer than 254 *hosts* (meaning any device that requires an IP address, including computers, printers, routers, switches, and other devices) and all your workgroups can share information, a single Class C network will be sufficient.

Subnetting

Within Class A and B networks, there can be separate networks called *subnets*. Subnets are considered part of the host portion of an address for network class definitions. For example, in the 128. Class B network, you can have one computer with an address of 128.10.10.10 and another with an address of 128.10.200.20; these computers are on the same network (128.10.), but they have different subnets (128.10.10. and 128.10.200.). Because of this, communication between the two computers requires either a router or a switch. Subnets can be helpful for separating workgroups within your company.

Often subnets can be used to separate workgroups that have no real need to interact with or to shield from other groups information passing among members of a specific workgroup. For example, if your company is large enough to have its own HR department and payroll section, you could put those departments' hosts on their own subnet and use your router configuration to limit the hosts that can connect to this subnet. This configuration prevents networked workers who are not members of the designated departments from being able to view some of the confidential information the HR and payroll personnel work with.

Subnet use also enables your network to grow beyond 254 hosts and share IP addresses. With proper routing configuration, users might not even know they are on a different subnet from their co-workers. Another common use for subnetting is with networks that cover a wide geographic area. It is not practical for a company with offices in Chicago and London to have both offices on the same subnet, so using a separate subnet for each office is the best solution.

Subnet Masks

Subnet masks are used by TCP/IP to show which part of an IP address is the network portion and which part is the host. Subnet masks are usually referred to as *netmasks*. For a pure Class A network, the netmask would be 255.0.0.0; for a Class B network, the netmask would be 255.255.0.0; and for a Class C network, the netmask would be 255.255.255.0. Netmasks can also be used to deviate from the standard classes.

By using customized netmasks, you can subnet your network to fit your needs. For example, your network has a single Class C address. You have a need to subnet your network. Although this isn't possible with a normal Class C subnet mask, you can change the mask to break your network into subnets. By changing the last octet to a number greater than zero, you can break the network into as many subnets as you need.

For more information on how to create customized subnet masks, see Day 6, "The Art of Subnet Masking," in *Sams Teach Yourself TCP/IP Network Administration in 21 Days*. This chapter goes into great detail on how to create custom netmasks and explains how to create an addressing cheat sheet for hosts on each subnet. You can also browse to the Linux Network Administrator's Guide and read about how to create subnets at http://www.tldp.org/LDP/nag2/index.html.

Broadcast, Unicast, and Multicast Addressing

Information can get to systems through three types of addresses: unicast, multicast, and broadcast. Each type of address is used according to the purpose of the information being sent, as explained here:

- **Unicast**—Sends information to one specific host. Unicast addresses are used for telnet, FTP, SSH, or any other information that needs to be shared in a one-to-one exchange of information. Although it is possible that any host on the subnet/ network can see the information being passed, only one host is the intended recipient and will take action on the information being received.

- **Multicasting**—Broadcasts information to groups of computers sharing an application, such as a video conferencing client or online gaming application. All the machines participating in the conference or game require the same information at precisely the same time to be effective.

- **Broadcasting**—Transmits information to all the hosts on a network or subnet. *Dynamic Host Configuration Protocol (DHCP)* uses broadcast messages when the DHCP client looks for a DHCP server to get its network settings, and *Reverse Address Resolution Protocol (RARP)* uses broadcast messages for hardware address to IP address resolution. Broadcast messages use .255 in all the host octets of the network IP address. (10.2.255.255 will broadcast to every host in your Class B network.)

17

Hardware Devices for Networking

As stated at the beginning of this chapter, networking is one of the strong points of the Linux operating system. This section covers the classes of devices used for basic networking. Note that this section talks about hardware devices, and not Linux networking devices, which are discussed in the section, "Using Network Configuration Tools."

Network Interface Cards

A computer must have a *network interface card (NIC)* to connect to a network. Currently, there are several topologies (ways of connecting computers) for network connections. These topologies range from the old and mostly outdated 10BASE-2 to the much newer and popular wireless Wi-Fi or 802.11 networking.

A Dual-host No-NIC Network

The truly frugal can also "network" two Linux workstations using a null-modem or LPT cable and PPP, as shown in the PPP HOWTO at http://tldp.org/HOWTO/PPP-HOWTO/direct.html. Just connect two PCs running Linux together with a null-modem cable, and use the pppd daemon on each end. If one Linux host is connected to a network or has a dialup connection, that PC will become a gateway for the other host. You will need to use pppd's defaultroute option on the serial-only host when connecting.

Each NIC has a unique address (the hardware address, known as Media Access Control, or MAC), which identifies that NIC. This address is six pairs of hexadecimal bits separated by colons (:). A MAC address looks similar to this: 00:60:08:8F:5A:D9. The hardware address is used by DHCP (see "DHCP" later in this chapter) to identify a specific host. It is also used by the *Address Resolution Protocol (ARP)* and *Reverse Address Resolution Protocol (RARP)* to map hosts to IP addresses.

This section covers some of the different types of NIC used to connect to your network.

Token Ring

Token ring networking was developed by IBM. As the name implies, the network is set up in a ring. A single "token" is passed from host to host, indicating the receiving host's "permission" to transmit data.

Token ring has a maximum transfer rate of 16Mbps (16 million bits per second). Unlike 10BASE-2 and 10BASE-5, token ring uses what is called *unshielded twisted pair (UTP)* cable. This cable looks a lot like the cable that connects your phone to the wall. Almost all token ring NICs are recognized by Linux.

10BASE-T

10BASE-T was the standard for a long time. A large number of networks still use it. 10BASE-T also uses UTP cable. Instead of being configured in a ring, 10BASE-T mostly uses a star architecture. In this architecture, the hosts all connect to a central location (usually a hub, which you learn about later in the section titled "Hubs"). All the data is sent to all hosts, but only the destination host takes action on individual packets. 10BASE-T has a transfer rate of 10Mbps.

10BASE-T has a maximum segment length of 100 meters. There are many manufacturers of 10BASE-T NICs, and most are recognized by Fedora.

100BASE-T

100BASE-T was popular around the turn of the millennium, keeping the same ease of administration as 10BASE-T while increasing the speed by a factor of 10. For most networks, the step from 10BASE-T to 100BASE-T is as simple as replacing NICs and hubs. Most 100BASE-T NICs and hubs can also handle 10BASE-T and can automatically detect which is in use. This allows for a gradual network upgrade and usually does not require rewiring your whole network. Nearly every known 100BASE-T NIC and most generic NICs are compatible with Linux, thanks to Donald Becker of http://www.scyld.com. 100BASE-T requires category 5 unshielded twisted pair cabling.

1000BASE-T

1000BASE-T—usually referred to as *Gigabit Ethernet*—is the accepted standard in enterprise networking, with most NICs being detected and configured correctly by Fedora. Like 100BASE-T NICs, gigabit NICs automatically downgrade if they are plugged in to a slower network. Also like 100BASE-T, gigabit NICs require category 5 unshielded twisted pair cabling; however, many institutions are now deploying category 6 cables because they have much longer range and so are often worth the extra cost.

Fiber Optic and Gigabit ethernet

Fiber optic is more commonly used in newer and high-end installations because the cost of upgrading can be prohibitive for older sites.

Fiber optics were originally used on *fiber distributed data interface (FDDI)* networks, similar to token ring in structure except that there are two rings—one is primary, whereas the other is secondary. The primary ring is used exclusively, and the secondary sits idle until there is a break in the primary ring. At this point, the secondary ring takes over, keeping the network alive. FDDI has a speed of 100Mbps and has a maximum ring length of 62 miles. FDDI uses several tokens at the same time that, along with the faster speed of fiber optics, account for the drastic increase in network speed.

As stated, switching to a fiber optic network can be very costly. To make the upgrade, the whole network has to be rewired (as much as U.S. $150 per network connection), and all NICs must be replaced at the same time. Most FDDI NICs are recognized by Linux.

Fiber-related gigabit is termed 1000BASE-X, whereas 1000BASE-T Gigabit Ethernet uses twisted-pair (see the section, "Unshielded Twisted Pair").

Wireless Network Interfaces

Wireless has really taken off in the past year or two. Wireless networking, as the name states, works without network cables. Upgrading is as easy as replacing network cards and equipment, such as routers and switches. Wireless networking equipment can also work along with the traditional wired networking using existing equipment.

It might not be practical to upgrade a desktop or large server to wireless just yet if the wiring is already in place. Wireless networking is still generally slower than a traditional wired network. However, this situation is changing with wider adoption of newer protocols, such as 802.11g (supporting the common 802.11b and faster but less popular 802.11a), along with the introduction of more compliant and inexpensive wireless NICs. Some 802.11g NICs work at up to 108Mbps, which appears faster than 100BASE-T wired networking on the surface. However, in practice it is a great deal slower: Unless your networking environment has paper thin walls, you can usually halve the reported speed of Wi-Fi network devices. 108Mbps works about half the speed of 100BASE-T.

As of this writing, the price for wireless networking equipment is low enough that many home users are using wireless networking to eliminate the need to run cable throughout their houses. With each new version of Linux, more and more wireless NICs are compatible. That said, it is usually better to get brand name wireless NICs, because you have a

17

better chance of compatibility.) Check the http://www.hpl.hp.com/personal/
Jean_Tourrilhes/Linux/ web page for more specific hardware compatibility information.
More on wireless networking is discussed later in this chapter.

Network Cable

Currently, three types of network cable exist—coaxial, unshielded twisted pair (UTP), and
fiber. Coaxial cable (rarely used today) looks a lot like the coaxial cable used to connect
your television to the cable jack or antenna. UTP looks a lot like the cable that runs from
your phone to the wall jack (the jacks are a bit wider). Fiber cable looks sort of like the
RCA cables used on your stereo or like the cable used on your electrical appliances in your
house (two separate segments connected together). The following sections discuss UTP
and fiber network cable in more detail.

Unshielded Twisted Pair

Unshielded twisted pair (UTP) uses color-coded pairs of thin copper wire to transmit data.
Six categories of UTP exist—each serving a different purpose:

- **Category 1 (Cat1)**—Used for voice transmissions such as your phone. Only one pair
  is used per line—one wire to transmit and one to receive. An RJ-11 plug is used to
  connect the cable to your phone and the wall.

- **Category 2 (Cat2)**—Used in early token ring networks. Has a transmission rate of
  4Mbps (million bits per second) and has the slowest data transfer rate. An RJ-11
  plug is also used for cable connections.

- **Category 3 (Cat3)**—Used for 10BASE-T networks. It has a transmission rate of
  10Mbps. Three pairs of cables are used to send and receive signals. RJ-11 or RJ-45
  plugs can be used for Cat3 cables, usually deferring to the smaller RJ-11. RJ-45 plugs
  are similar in design to RJ-11, but are larger to handle up to four pairs of wire and
  are used more commonly on Cat5 cables.

- **Category 4 (Cat4)**—Used in modern token ring networks. It has a transmission rate
  of 16Mbps and is less and less common as companies are switching to better alternatives. RJ-45 plugs are used for cable connections.

- **Category 5 (Cat5)**—The fastest of the UTP categories with a transmission rate of up
  to 1000Mbps. It is used in both 100BASE-T and 1000BASE-T networks and uses four
  pairs of wire. Cat5 cable came out just as 10BASE-T networks were becoming
  popular and isn't much more expensive than Cat3 cable. As a result, most 10BASE-T
  networks use Cat5 UTP instead of Cat3. Cat5 cable uses RJ-45 plugs.

- **Category 6 (Cat6)**—Also rated at 1000Mbps, this cable is available in two forms:
  stranded for short runs (25-meter) and solid for up to 100-meter runs, but which
  should not be flexed.

Fiber Optic Cable

Fiber optic cable (fiber) is usually orange or red in color. The transmission rate is 100Mbps and has a maximum length of 62 miles. Fiber uses a two-pronged plug to connect to devices. A couple of advantages to fiber are that because it uses light instead of electricity to transmit its signal, it is free from the possibility of electromagnetic interference and is also more difficult to tap into and eavesdrop.

Hubs

Hubs are used to connect several hosts together on a star architecture network. Hubs can have any number of connections; the common sizes are 4, 8, 16, 24, and 48 connections (ports)—each port has a light that comes on when a network connection is made (link light). The use of hubs enables you to expand your network easily; you can just add new hubs when you need to add new connections. Each hub can connect to the other hubs on the network, typically, through a port on the hub called an *uplink* port. This enables two hubs, connected by their uplink ports, to act as one hub. Having a central location where all the hosts on your network can connect allows for easier troubleshooting of problems. If one host goes down, none of the other hosts are affected (depending on the purpose of the downed host). Because hubs are not directly involved with the Linux operating system, compatibility is not an issue.

> **TIP**
>
> Troubleshooting network connections can be a challenge, especially on large networks. If a user complains that he has lost his network connection, the hub is a good place to start. If the link light for the user's port is lit, chances are the problem is with the user's network configuration. If the link light is not on, either the host's NIC is bad, the cable is not inserted properly, or the cable has gone bad for some reason.

17

Routers and Bridges

Routers and bridges are used to connect different networks to your network and to connect different subnets within your network. Routers and bridges both serve the same purpose of connecting networks and subnets, but they do so with different techniques. The information in the following sections will help you choose the connection method that best suits your needs.

Bridges

Bridges are used within a network to connect different subnets. A bridge will blindly relay all information from one subnet to another without any filtering and is often referred to as a *dumb gateway*. This can be helpful if one subnet in your network is becoming over-burdened and you need to lighten the load. A bridge is not very good for connecting to the Internet, however, because it lacks filtering. You really do not want all traffic traveling the Internet to be able to get through to your network.

Routers

Routers can pass data from one network to another, and they allow for filtering of data. Routers are best suited to connect your network to an outside network, such as the Internet. If you have a web server for an internal intranet that you do not want people to access from the Internet, for example, you can use a router's filter to block port 80 from your network. These filters can be used to block specific hosts from accessing the Internet as well. For these reasons, routers are also called *smart gateways*.

Routers range in complexity and price from a Cisco brand router that can cost thousands of dollars to other brands that can be less than two hundred dollars.

Initializing New Network Hardware

All the initial network configuration and hardware initialization for Fedora is normally done during installation. At times, however, you will need to reconfigure networking on your system, such as when a host needs to be moved to a different subnet or a different network, or if you replace any of your computer's networking hardware.

Linux creates network interfaces in memory when the kernel recognizes that a NIC or other network device is attached to the system. These interfaces are unlike other Linux interfaces, such as serial communications ports, and will not have a corresponding device file in the /dev directory. Unless support for a particular NIC is built in to your kernel, Linux must be told to load a specific kernel module to support your NIC. More than 100 such modules are located in the /lib/modules/2.6.XX-XX/kernel/drivers/net directory (where XX-XX is your version of the kernel).

You can initialize a NIC in several ways when using Linux. When you first install Fedora, automatic hardware probing detects and configures your system to use any installed NICs. If you remove the original NIC and replace it with a different make and model, your system will not automatically detect and initialize the device unless you configure Fedora to use automatic hardware detection when booting. If you have enabled the kudzu hardware daemon, (refer to Chapters 14, "Automating Tasks," and 7, "Managing Software and System Resources"), it will detect the absence of the old NIC and the presence of the new NIC at boot time and prompt you for permission to change your system's NIC configuration information.

If you do not use automatic hardware detection and configuration, you can initialize network hardware by

- Manually editing the /etc/modprobe.conf file to prompt the system to recognize and support the new hardware upon reboot

- Write a script or insert commands into the /etc/rc.d/rc.local file to initialize the new hardware upon booting, taking care to avoid software service dependencies; in other words, not attempting remote connections or file system mounting until hardware is initialized and configured

- Manually load or unload the new device's kernel module with the `modprobe` command

The following sections explain the first and last of the preceding methods.

Editing the `/etc/modprobe.conf` File

You can manually edit the `/etc/modprobe.conf` file to add a module dependency entry (also known as a *directive*) to support a new NIC or other network device. This entry includes the device's name and its corresponding kernel module. After you add this entry, the Linux kernel recognizes your new networking hardware upon reboot. Fedora runs a module dependency check upon booting.

For example, if your system uses a RealTek NIC, you could use an entry like this:

```
alias eth0 8139too
```

The example entry tells the Linux kernel to load the `8139too.o` kernel module to support the `eth0` network device. On the other hand, if you have an Intel Ethernet Pro NIC installed, you would use an entry like this:

```
alias eth0 eepro100
```

Other parameters can be passed to a kernel module using one or more option entries, if need be, to properly configure your NIC. See the `modprobe.conf` manual page for more information on using entries. For more specifics regarding NIC kernel modules, examine the module's source code because no manual pages exist (a good opportunity for anyone willing to write the documentation).

> **TIP**
>
> Linux kernel and network tools can be used to diagnose problems or troubleshoot problematic NICs. However, if you browse to Don Becker's Linux Ethercard Status, Diagnostic and Setup Utilities page at http://www.scyld.com/ethercard_diag.html, you will find more than two dozen hardware-specific utilities for a variety of PCI and legacy ISA Ethernet network cards. These tools can be extremely helpful if you run into trouble during NIC recognition or configuration.

Using `modprobe` to Manually Load Kernel Modules

You do not have to use an `/etc/modprobe.conf` entry to initialize kernel support for your new network device. As root, you can manually load or unload the device's kernel module using the `modprobe` command, along with the module's name. For example, use the following command line to enable the example RealTek NIC:

```
# modprobe 8139too
```

After you press Enter, you will see this device reported from the kernel's ring buffer messages, which can be displayed by the `dmesg` command. Here's a portion of that command's output:

```
$ dmesg
...
eth0: RealTek RTL8139 Fast Ethernet at 0xce8ee000, 00:30:1b:0b:07:0d, IRQ 11
eth0: Identified 8139 chip type 'RTL-8139C'
eth0: Setting half-duplex based on auto-negotiated partner ability 0000.
...
```

Note that at this point, an IP address or other settings have not been assigned to the device. Linux can use multiple Ethernet interfaces, and the first Ethernet device will be numbered eth0, the second eth1, and so on. Each different Ethernet device recognized by the kernel might have additional or different information reported, depending on its kernel module. For example,

```
$ dmesg
...
eepro100.c:v1.09j-t 9/29/99 Donald Becker http://cesdis.gsfc.nasa.gov/linux/drive
rs/eepro100.html
eepro100.c: $Revision: 1.36 $ 2000/11/17 Modified by Andrey V. Savochkin <saw@saw
.sw.com.sg> and others
PCI: Found IRQ 10 for device 00:0d.0
eth0: Intel Corporation 82557 [Ethernet Pro 100], 00:90:27:91:92:B5, IRQ 10.
 Board assembly 721383-007, Physical connectors present: RJ45
 Primary interface chip i82555 PHY #1.
 General self-test: passed.
 Serial sub-system self-test: passed.
 Internal registers self-test: passed.
 ROM checksum self-test: passed (0x04f4518b).
...
```

In this example, an Intel Ethernet Pro 100 NIC has been recognized. To disable support for a NIC, the kernel module can be unloaded, but usually only after the device is no longer in use. Read the next section to learn how to configure a NIC once it has been recognized by the Linux kernel and how to control its behavior.

Using Network Configuration Tools

If you add or replace networking hardware after your initial installation, you must configure the new hardware. You can do so using either the command line or the graphical configuration tools. To configure a network client host using the command line, you can use a combination of commands or edit specific files under the /etc/sysconfig directory. To configure the hardware through a graphical interface, you can use Red Hat's graphical tool for X11 called system-config-network or the console-based netconfig command. This section introduces command-line and graphical software tools you can use to configure a network interface and network settings on your Red Hat system. You'll see how to control your NIC and manage how your system interacts with your network.

Using the command-line configuration tools can seem difficult if you are new to Linux. For anyone new to networking, the `system-config-network` graphical tool is the way to go. Both manual and graphical methods require root access to work. If you do not have root access, get it before trying any of these actions. You should not edit any scripts or settings files used by graphical network administration tools on your system. Your changes will be lost the next time the tool, such as `system-config-network`, is run! Either use a manual approach and write your own network setup script, or stick to using graphical configuration utilities.

> **NOTE**
>
> The network configuration process described in this section is for client hosts. You cannot perform server network configuration, such as Domain Name System (DNS) and DHCP during installation. (See Chapter 26, "DNS," for more information on configuring DNS; see the "DHCP" section later in this chapter for more information on that item.)

Command-Line Network Interface Configuration

You can configure a network interface from the command line using the basic Linux networking utilities. You configure your network client hosts with the command line by using commands to change your current settings or by editing a number of system files. Two commands, `ifconfig` and `route`, are used for network configuration. The `netstat` command displays information about the network connections.

`/sbin/ifconfig`
`ifconfig` is used to configure your network interface. You can use it to

- Activate or deactivate your NIC or change your NIC's mode.

- Change your machine's IP address, netmask, or broadcast address.

- Create an IP alias to allow more than one IP address on your NIC.

- Set a destination address for a point-to-point connection.

You can change as many or as few of these options as you'd like with a single command. The basic structure for the command is as follows:

`/sbin/ifconfig [network device] options`

Table 17.1 shows a subset of `ifconfig` options and examples of their uses.

TABLE 17.1   `ifconfig` Options

Use	Option	Example
Create alias	-[network device] 10.10.10.10	ifconfig eth0:0_:[number]
Change IP address		ifconfig eth0 10.10.10.12
Change the netmask	netmask [netmask]	fconfig eth0 netmask 255.255.255.0

TABLE 17.1   Continued

Use	Option	Example
Change the broadcast	broadcast [address]	ifconfig eth0 broadcast 10.10.10.255
Take interface down	down	ifconfig eth0 down
Bring interface up	up (add IP address)	ifconfig eth0 up (ifconfig eth0 10.10.10.10)
Set NIC promiscuous	[-]promisc [ifconfig eth0 -promisc]	ifconfig eth0 promisc mode on [off]
Set multicasting mode	[-]allmulti	ifconfig eth0_on [off] allmulti [ifconfig eth0 -allmulti]
Enable [disable] [address]	[-]pointopoint eth0_pointopoint	ifconfig_point-to-point address 10.10.10.20 [ifconfig eth0 pointopoint_10.10.10.20]

The ifconfig man page shows other options that enable your machine to interface with a number of network types such as AppleTalk, Novell, IPv6, and others. Again, read the man page for details on these network types.

> **NOTE**
>
> Promiscuous mode causes the NIC to receive all packets on the network. It is often used to sniff a network. Multicasting mode enables the NIC to receive all multicast traffic on the network.

If no argument is given, ifconfig displays the status of active interfaces. For example, the output of ifconfig, without arguments and one active and configured NIC, looks similar to this:

/sbin/ifconfig

```
eth0    Link encap:Ethernet HWaddr 00:30:1B:0B:07:0D
        inet addr:192.168.2.70 Bcast:192.168.2.255 Mask:255.255.255.0
        UP BROADCAST RUNNING MULTICAST MTU:1500 Metric:1
        RX packets:127948 errors:0 dropped:0 overruns:0 frame:0
        TX packets:172675 errors:0 dropped:0 overruns:0 carrier:0
        collisions:7874 txqueuelen:100
        RX bytes:19098389 (18.2 Mb) TX bytes:73768657 (70.3 Mb)
        Interrupt:11 Base address:0x2000

lo      Link encap:Local Loopback
        inet addr:127.0.0.1 Mask:255.0.0.0
        UP LOOPBACK RUNNING MTU:16436 Metric:1
        RX packets:215214 errors:0 dropped:0 overruns:0 frame:0
```

```
TX packets:215214 errors:0 dropped:0 overruns:0 carrier:0
collisions:0 txqueuelen:0
RX bytes:68739080 (65.5 Mb) TX bytes:68739080 (65.5 Mb)
```

The output is easily understood. The inet entry displays the IP address for the interface. UP signifies that the interface is ready for use, BROADCAST denotes that the interface is connected to a network that supports broadcast messaging (ethernet), RUNNING means that the interface is operating, and LOOPBACK shows which device (lo) is the loopback address. The *maximum transmission unit (MTU)* on eth0 is 1500 bytes. This determines the size of the largest packet that can be transmitted over this interface (and is sometimes "tuned" to other values for performance enhancement). Metric is a number from 0 to 3 that relates to how much information from the interface is placed in the routing table. The lower the number, the smaller the amount of information.

The ifconfig command can be used to display information about or control a specific interface using commands as listed in Table 17.1. For example, to deactivate the first Ethernet device on a host, use the ifconfig command, the interface name, and the command down like so:

ifconfig eth0 down

You can also configure and activate the device by specifying a hostname or IP address and network information. For example to configure and activate ("bring up") the eth0 interface with a specific IP address, use the ifconfig command like this:

ifconfig eth0 192.168.2.35 netmask 255.255.255.0 up

If you have a host defined in your system's /etc/hosts file (see the section "Network Configuration Files" later in this chapter), you can configure and activate the interface according to the defined hostname like this:

ifconfig eth0 trusty.home.org up

Read the next section to see how to configure your system to work with your LAN.

/sbin/route
The second command used to configure your network is the route command. route is used to build the routing tables (in memory) implemented for routing packets as well as displaying the routing information. It is used after ifconfig has initialized the interface. route is normally used to set up static routes to other networks via the gateway or to other hosts. The command configuration is like this:

/sbin/route [options] [commands] [parameters]

To display the routing table, use the route command with no options. The display will look similar to this:

17

```
# /sbin/route
Kernel IP routing table
Destination     Gateway         Genmask         Flags Metric Ref Use Iface
149.112.50.64   *               255.255.255.192 U     0      0   0   eth0
208.59.243.0    *               255.255.255.0   U     0      0   0   eth0
127.0.0.0       *               255.0.0.0       U     0      0   0   lo
default         149.112.50.65   0.0.0.0         UG    0      0   0   eth0
```

In the first column, Destination is the IP address (or, if the host is in /etc/hosts or /etc/networks, the hostname) of the receiving host. The default entry is the default gateway for this machine. The Gateway column lists the gateway that the packets must go through to reach their destination. An asterisk (*) means that packets go directly to the host. Genmask is the netmask. The Flags column can have several possible entries. In our example, U verifies that the route is enabled and G specifies that Destination requires the use of a gateway. The Metric column displays the distance to the Destination. Some daemons use this to figure the easiest route to the Destination. The Ref column is used by some Unix flavors to convey the references to the route. It isn't used by Linux. The Use column indicates the number of times this entry has been looked up. Finally, the Iface column is the name of the interface for the corresponding entry.

Using the -n option to the route command will give the same information substituting IP addresses for names and asterisks (*) and looks like this:

```
# /sbin/route -n
Kernel IP routing table
Destination     Gateway         Genmask         Flags Metric Ref Use Iface
149.112.50.64   0.0.0.0         255.255.255.192 U     0      0   0   eth0
208.59.243.0    0.0.0.0         255.255.255.0   U     0      0   0   eth0
127.0.0.0       0.0.0.0         255.0.0.0       U     0      0   0   lo
0.0.0.0         149.112.50.65   0.0.0.0         UG    0      0   0   eth0
```

The route command can add to the table using the add option. With the add option, you can specify a host (-host) or a network (-net) as the destination. If no option is used, the route command assumes that you are configuring the host issuing the command. The most common uses for the route command is to add the default gateway for a host, for a host that has lost its routing table, or if the gateway address has changed. For example, to add a gateway with a specific IP address, you could use the following:

```
# /sbin/route add default gw 149.112.50.65
```

Note that you could use a hostname instead of an IP address if desired. Another common use is to add the network to the routing table right after using the ifconfig command to configure the interface. Assuming that the 208.59.243.0 entry from the previous examples was missing, replace it use the following command:

```
# /sbin/route add -net 208.59.243.0 netmask 255.255.255.0 dev eth0
```

You also can use /sbin/route to configure a specific host for a direct (point-to-point) connection. For example, say that you have a home network of two computers. One of the computers has a modem through which it connects to your business network. You typically work at the other computer. You can use the route command to establish a connection through specific hosts using the following command:

```
# /sbin/route add -host 198.135.62.25 gw 149.112.50.65
```

The preceding example makes the computer with the modem the gateway for the computer you are using. This type of command line is useful if you have a gateway or firewall connected to the Internet. There are many additional uses for the route command, such as manipulating the default packet size. See the man page for those uses.

/bin/netstat

The netstat command is used to display the status of your network. It has several parameters that can display as much or as little information as you prefer. The services are listed by *sockets* (application-to-application connections between two computers). You can use netstat to display the information in Table 17.2.

TABLE 17.2   netstat Options

Option	Output
-g	Displays the multicast groups configured
-i	Displays the interfaces configured by ifconfig
-s	Lists a summary of activity for each protocol
-v	Gives verbose output, listing both active and inactive sockets
-c	Updates output every second (good for testing and troubleshooting)
-e	Gives verbose output for active connections only
-C	Displays information from the route cache and is good for looking at past connections

Several other options are available for this command, but they are used less often. As with the /sbin/route command, the man page can give you details about all options and parameters.

Network Configuration Files

As previously stated, seven network configuration files can be modified to make changes to basic network interaction of your system. The files are

/etc/hosts—A listing of addresses, hostnames, and aliases

/etc/services—Network service and port connections

/etc/nsswitch.conf—Linux network information service configuration

/etc/resolv.conf—Domain name service domain (search) settings

/etc/host.conf—Network information search order (by default, /etc/hosts and then DNS)

`/etc/sysconfig/network`—The hostname, IP address, boot activation control, and gateway settings (along with optional IPv6 settings)

`/etc/sysconfig/network-scripts/ifcfg-eth0`—Network settings for the `eth0` network device; see the file `sysconfig.txt` under the `/usr/share/doc/initscripts/` directory for details about optional settings

After the first six of these files are modified, the changes are active. As with most configuration files, comments can be added with a hash mark (#) preceding the comment. The last file (`/etc/sysconfig/network`) requires the networking daemons to be restarted before the file is used. All seven of these files have a man page written about them for more information.

Adding Hosts to `/etc/hosts`

The `/etc/hosts` file is a map of IP to hostnames. If you aren't using DNS or another naming service, and you are connected to a large network, this file can get quite large and can be a real headache to manage. A small `/etc/hosts` file can look something like this:

```
127.0.0.1       localhost.localdomain  localhost
128.112.50.69  myhost.mydomain.com    myhost
128.112.50.169 yourhost.mydomain.com  yourhost
```

The first entry is for the loopback entry. The second is for the name of the machine. The third is another machine on the network. If no naming service is in use on the network, the only host that myhost will recognize by name is yourhost. (IP addresses on the network can still be used.)

If your network is using a naming service, the last line is not needed and can be deleted. However, if myhost connects to yourhost frequently, it might be good to leave the entry so that myhost doesn't need to consult the naming service each time. This can save time and reduce the strain on the network or the name service server. Edit this file if you need to change your hostname or IP address or if you aren't using a naming service and a host has been added to your network.

Service Settings in `/etc/services`

The `/etc/services` file maps port numbers to services. The first few lines look similar to this (the `/etc/services` file can be quite long, more than 500 lines):

```
# Each line describes one service, and is of the form:
#
# service-name port/protocol [aliases ...]   [# comment]

tcpmux      1/tcp               # TCP port service multiplexer
tcpmux      1/udp               # TCP port service multiplexer
rje         5/tcp               # Remote Job Entry
rje         5/udp               # Remote Job Entry
echo        7/tcp
```

```
echo        7/udp
discard     9/tcp      sink null
discard     9/udp      sink null
systat      11/tcp     users
```

Typically, there are two entries for each service because most services can use either TCP or UDP for their transmissions. Usually once /etc/services is initially configured, you will not need to change it.

Using /etc/nsswitch.conf After Changing Naming Services

This file was initially developed by Sun Microsystems to specify the order that services are accessed on the system. A number of services are listed in the /etc/nsswitch.conf file, but the most commonly modified entry is the hosts entry. A portion of the file can look like this:

```
passwd:     files
shadow:     files
group:      files

#hosts:     db files nisplus nis dns
hosts:      files dns
```

This tells services that they should consult standard Unix/Linux files for passwd, shadow, and group (/etc/passwd, /etc/shadow, /etc/group, respectively) lookups. For host lookups, the system will check /etc/hosts and if there is no entry, it will check DNS. The commented hosts entry lists the possible values for hosts. Only edit this file if your naming service has changed.

Setting a Name Server with /etc/resolv.conf

/etc/resolv.conf is used by DNS, the domain name service. (DNS is covered in detail in Chapter 26.) The following is an example of resolv.conf:

```
nameserver 192.172.3.8
nameserver 192.172.3.9
search mydomain.com
```

This sets the nameservers and the order of domains for DNS to use. The contents of this file will be set automatically if you use Dynamic Host Configuration Protocol, or DHCP (see the section on "DHCP" later in this chapter).

Setting DNS Search Order with /etc/host.conf

The /etc/host.conf file lists the order in which your machine will search for hostname resolution. The following is the default /etc/host.conf file:

```
order hosts, bind
```

17

In this example, the host will check the /etc/hosts file first and then perform a DNS lookup. A couple more options control how the name service is used. The only reason to modify this file is if you use NIS for your name service or you want one of the optional services. The nospoof option can be a good option for system security. It will compare a standard DNS lookup to a reverse lookup (host-to-IP then IP-to-host) and fail if the two don't match. The drawback is that often when proxy services are used, the lookup will fail, so you will want to use this with caution.

Examining Host Network Settings in /etc/sysconfig/network

Changes to /etc/sysconfig/network will not take effect until you restart the networking daemons or reboot the system. If you use Fedora's graphical configuration network tools (described in the next section), you should not edit this file. The file might look like this:

```
NETWORKING=yes
HOSTNAME=myhost
GATEWAY=192.112.50.99
```

A GATEWAYDEV setting is also available to associate a specific network device (such as eth0 or eth1 and so on). An additional optional entry to /etc/sysconfig/network is for NIS domain machines and would look like this:

```
NISDOMAIN=rebel
```

The network file previously supported a FORWARD_IPV4 value, which determined whether the host forwarded IP packets (usually "yes" for routers). This setting is now saved in /etc/sysctl.conf as a net.ipv4.ip_forward setting, which can be modified if the forwarding changes are required. See the sysctl.conf man page for more information.

Using Graphical Configuration Tools

As mentioned earlier, if you are new to networking or still becoming proficient with the command line, the graphical configuration tool is your best method for configuring new hardware in Fedora. Like most graphical tools, system-config-network allows you to fill in the blanks; press the proper buttons, and the tool will modify the required files and issue the proper commands. Remember, you must be root to run system-config-network.

There are two ways to start system-config-network: from the command line of an X11 terminal window with the command system-config-network, using the panel's Run Application menu item, or by clicking the System Setting's Network menu item from a GNOME or KDE desktop panel menu. (In either case, you'll be prompted to enter the root password.)

Once started, system-config-network might ask if you would like to create a new device. If you've installed Fedora on a computer with an existing network card, however, the screen shown in Figure 17.1 appears after you start system-config-network.

FIGURE 17.1   Use the initial `system-config-network` networking screen to begin configuring your network client host.

Click the DNS tab to configure your system's DNS settings, hostname, or DNS search path. Click the Hosts tab, and then either click the New or Edit button (after selecting a host) to create or edit an entry in your system's `/etc/hosts` file, for example, to add the IP addresses, hostnames, and aliases of hosts on your network see Figure 17.2 for an example of editing a host entry.

Click on the Devices tab, and then either click New or select an existing setting and click Edit to automatically or manually set up an Ethernet device. Figure 17.3 shows the Add New Device Type dialog box with all necessary information in place for a *static*, or fixed IP address assignment. Choose how your card will get its configuration, manually from Dynamic Host Control Protocol (see the next section) or from Bootp. Just fill in the blanks as needed.

> **NOTE**
>
> Bootp is the initial protocol that DHCP was built on, and it has mostly been replaced by DHCP.

When you have finished configuring your NIC or editing an IP address or assignment scheme for a NIC, save your changes using the File menu's Save menu item. Note that you can also use the Profile menu (as shown previously in Figure 17.1) to create different network configurations and IP address assignments for your installed NICs. This is handy if you want to create, for example, a different network setup for home or work on a laptop running Fedora.

FIGURE 17.2   Highlight an existing entry, and then click the Edit button to change /etc/hosts entries in the Hosts tab of the Network Configuration screen.

FIGURE 17.3   Configure an Ethernet device in the Configure Network Setting screen of the Add New Device Type dialog.

Dynamic Host Configuration Protocol

As the name implies, *Dynamic Host Configuration Protocol (DHCP)* configures hosts for connection to your network. DHCP allows a network administrator to configure all TCP/IP parameters for each host as he connects to the network after activation of a NIC. These parameters include automatically assigning an IP address to a NIC, setting name server entries in /etc/resolv.conf, and configuring default routing and gateway information for a host. This section first describes how to use DHCP to obtain IP address assignment for your NIC, and then how to quickly set up and start a DHCP server using Fedora.

> **NOTE**
>
> You can learn more about DHCP by reading RFC2131 "Dynamic Host Configuration Protocol." Browse to http://www.ietf.org/rfc/rfc2131.txt.

How DHCP Works

DHCP provides persistent storage of network parameters by holding identifying information for each network client that might connect to the network. The three most common pairs of identifying information are

- **Network subnet/host address**—Used by hosts to connect to the network at will

- **Subnet/hostname**—Enables the specified host to connect to the subnet

- **Subnet/hardware address**—Enables a specific client to connect to the network after getting the hostname from DHCP

DHCP also allocates to clients temporary or permanent network (IP) addresses. Once a temporary assignment, known as a *lease*, has elapsed, the client can request to have the lease extended, or, if the address is no longer needed, the client can relinquish the address. For hosts that will be permanently connected to a network with adequate addresses available, DHCP allocates infinite leases.

DHCP offers your network some advantages. First, it shifts responsibility for assigning IP addresses from the network administrator (who can accidentally assign duplicate IP addresses) to the DHCP server. Second, DHCP makes better use of limited IP addresses. If a user is away from the office for whatever reason, the user's host can release its IP address for use by other hosts.

Like most things in life, DHCP is not perfect. Servers cannot be configured through DHCP alone because DNS does not know what addresses that DHCP assigns to a host. This means that DNS lookups are not possible on machines configured through DHCP alone; therefore, services cannot be provided. However, DHCP can make assignments based on DNS entries when using subnet/hostname or subnet/hardware address identifiers.

> **NOTE**
>
> The problem of using DHCP to configure servers using registered hostnames is being addressed by Dynamic DNS which, when fully developed, will enable DHCP to register IP addresses with DNS. This will allow you, for example, to register a domain name (such as imalinuxuser.com) and be able to easily access that domain's web server without needing to use static IP addressing of a specific host. The largest hurdle to overcome is the security implication of enabling each host connecting to the system to update DNS. A few companies, such as http://www.dyndns.org, are already offering Dynamic DNS services and have clients for Linux.

Activating DHCP at Installation and Boot Time

During installation, you can instruct the Fedora installer to save DHCP settings for your NIC. After installation, you can also use the system-config-network client to edit the TCP/IP configuration information required to properly initialize and configure your NIC to connect your system to the local network and Internet. When you select a *dynamic*, or DHCP-assigned IP addressing scheme for your NIC, the broadcast address is set at 255.255.255.255 because dhclient, the DHCP client used for IP configuration, is initially unaware of where the DHCP server is located, so the request must travel every network until a server replies.

DHCP-specific information is simply saved as a BOOTPROTO=dhcp entry for your NIC under the /etc/sysconfig/network directory (in settings and scripts for a specific device, such as eth0).

Other settings specific to obtaining DHCP settings are saved in the file named dhclient.conf under the /etc directory and are documented in the dhclient.conf man page. More than 100 options are also documented in the dhcp-options man page.

However, using DHCP is not that complicated. If you want to use DHCP and know that there is a server on your network, you can quickly configure your NIC by using the dhclient like so:

```
# dhclient
Internet Software Consortium DHCP Client V3.0pl2
Copyright 1995-2001 Internet Software Consortium.
All rights reserved.
For info, please visit http://www.isc.org/products/DHCP

Listening on LPF/lo/
Sending on   LPF/lo/
Listening on LPF/eth0/00:a0:24:aa:f5:17
Sending on   LPF/eth0/00:a0:24:aa:f5:17
Sending on   Socket/fallback
DHCPREQUEST on eth0 to 255.255.255.255 port 67
DHCPACK from 192.168.2.254
save_previous /etc/yp.conf
save_previous /etc/resolv.conf
bound to 192.168.2.253 -- renewal in 9906 seconds.
```

In this example, the first Ethernet device, eth0, has been assigned an IP address of 192.168.2.253 from a DHCP server at 192.168.2.54. The renewal will take place in about two hours and 45 minutes.

> **NOTE**
>
> The file named dhcpd under the /etc/sysconfig directory can contain any optional command-line arguments, such as NIC lease times (the amount of time an interface has an assigned address). See the dhcpd manual page for options.

DHCP Software Installation and Configuration

Installation of the DHCP client and server might be easiest during the initial install of Fedora, but you can also use RPMs later on, or download and build the source code yourself. The RPMs are available on your Fedora CD-ROMs or from a mirror FTP site (refer to Chapter 7 for more information). This section describes configuring the dhclient and setting up and running the dhpcd daemon.

DHCP dhclient

As previously mentioned, DHCP use for an installed NIC is easily accomplished when installing Fedora on your host (read more about installation in Chapter 3, "Installing Fedora"), and during the network step of installation, you can choose to have DHCP initiated at boot time. If you choose to do this (and choose to install the DHCP client package), the DHCP client, dhclient, will send a broadcast message that the DHCP server will reply to with networking information for your host. That is it; you're done.

If you choose to install from source, you will have to (as root) download and install the server packages that include dhclient. Unpack the source file, run ./configure from the root of the source directory, run make, and then run make install. This should put the DHCP client binaries where they will start at the correct time in the boot process.

You can however, fine-tune how dhclient works, and where and how it obtains or looks for DHCP information. You probably will not need to take this additional effort; but if you do, you can create and edit a file named dhclient.conf, and save it in the /etc directory with your settings. A few of the dhclient.conf options include

- timeout *time* ;—How long to wait before giving up trying (60 seconds is the default)

- retry *time* ;—How long to wait before retrying (5 minutes is the default)

- select-timeout *time* ;—How long to wait before selecting a DHCP offer (0 seconds is the default)

- reboot *time* ;—How long to wait before trying to get a previously set IP (10 seconds is the default)

- renew *date* ;—When to renew an IP lease, where *date* is in the form of <weekday> <year>/<month>/<day> <hour>:<minute>:<second>, such as 4 2004/1/1 22:01:01 for Thursday, January 4, 2004 at 10:01 p.m.

See the dhclient.conf man page for more information on additional settings.

DHCP Server

Again, the easiest way to install the DHCP server on your computer is to include the RPMs at install time or to use RPMs if you've installed your machine without installing the DHCP server RPMs. If you are so inclined, you can go to the Internet Software Consortium (ISC) website and download and build the source code yourself (http://www.isc.org).

If you decide to install from a source downloaded from the ISC website, the installation is very straightforward. Just unpack your `tar` file, run `./configure` from the root of the source directory, run `make`, and finally, if there are no errors, run `make install`. This will put all the files used by the DHCP daemon in the correct places. If you have the disk space, it's best to leave the source files in place until you are sure that DHCP is running correctly; otherwise, you can delete the source tree.

> **NOTE**
>
> For whichever installation method you choose, be sure that a file called `/etc/dhcpd.leases` is created. The file can be empty, but it does need to exist in order for `dhcpd` to start properly.

Using DHCP to Configure Network Hosts

Configuring your network with DHCP can look difficult, but is actually easy if your needs are simple. The server configuration can take a bit more work if your network is more complex and depending on how much you want DHCP to do.

DHCP Server Configuration

Configuring the server takes some thought and a little bit of work. Luckily, the work only involves editing a single configuration file, `/etc/dhcpd.conf`. To start the server at boot time, use the `service`, `ntsysv`, or `system-config-services` commands.

The `/etc/dhcpd.conf` file contains all the information needed to run `dhcpd`. Fedora includes a sample `dhcpd.conf` in `/usr/share/doc/dhcp*/dhcpd.conf.sample`. The DHCP server source files also contain a sample `dhcpd.conf` file.

The `/etc/dhcpd.conf` file can be looked at as a three-part file. The first part contains configurations for DHCP itself. The configurations include

- **Setting the domain name**—`option domain-name "example.org"`.

- **Setting DNS servers**—`option domain-name-servers ns1.example.org, ns2.example.org` (IP addresses can be substituted.)

- **Setting the default and maximum lease times**—`default-lease-time 3600` and `max-lease-time 14400`.

Other settings in the first part include whether the server is the primary (authoritative) server and what type of logging DHCP should use. These settings are considered default and can be overridden by the subnet and host portion of the configuration in more complex situations.

> **NOTE**
>
> The `dhcpd.conf` file requires semicolons (;) after each command statement. If your configuration file has errors or runs improperly, check for this.

The next part of the dhcpd.conf deals with the different subnets that your DHCP server serves; this section is quite straightforward. Each subnet is defined separately and can look like this:

```
subnet 10.5.5.0 netmask 255.255.255.224 {
 range 10.5.5.26 10.5.5.30;
 option domain-name-servers ns1.internal.example.org;
 option domain-name "internal.example.org";
 option routers 10.5.5.1;
 option broadcast-address 10.5.5.31;
 default-lease-time 600;
 max-lease-time 7200;
}
```

This defines the IP addressing for the 10.5.5.0 subnet. It defines the IP address ranging from 10.5.5.26 through 10.5.5.30 to be dynamically assigned to hosts that reside on that subnet. This example shows that any TCP/IP option can be set from the subnet portion of the configuration file. It shows which DNS server the subnet will connect to, which can be good for DNS server load balancing, or which can be used to limit the hosts that can be reached through DNS. It defines the domain name, so you can have more than one domain on your network. It can also change the default and maximum lease time.

If you want your server to ignore a specific subnet, the following entry can be used to accomplish this:

```
subnet 10.152.187.0 netmask 255.255.255.0 {
}
```

This defines no options for the 10.152.187.0 subnet; therefore, the DHCP server ignores it.

The last part of your dhcp.conf is for defining hosts. This can be good if you want a computer on your network to have a specific IP address or other information specific to that host. The key to completing the host section is to know the hardware address of the host. As you learned in "Hardware Devices for Networking," earlier in this chapter, the hardware address is used to differentiate the host for configuration. Your hardware address can be obtained by using the ifconfig command as described previously. The hardware address is on the eth0 line labeled "Hwaddr":

```
host fantasia {
  hardware ethernet 08:00:07:26:c0:a5;
  fixed-address fantasia.fugue.com;
}
```

This example takes the host with the hardware address 08:00:07:26:c0:a5 and does a DNS lookup to assign the IP address for fantasia.fugue.com to the host.

17

DHCP can also define and configure booting for diskless clients like this:

```
host passacaglia {
  hardware ethernet 0:0:c0:5d:bd:95;
  filename "vmunix.passacaglia";
  server-name "toccata.fugue.com";
}
```

The diskless host `passacaglia` will get its boot information from server `toccata.fugue.com` and use `vmunix.passacaglia` kernel. All other TCP/IP configuration can also be included.

CAUTION

Remember, only one DHCP server should exist on a local network to avoid problems. Your DHCP might not work correctly on a LAN with hosts running outdated legacy operating systems. Often Windows NT servers will have the Windows DHCP server installed by default. Because there is no configuration file for NT to sort through, that DHCP server will configure your host before the Linux server if both machines are on the same LAN. Check your NT servers for this situation and disable DHCP on the NT server; afterward, your other DHCP-enabled hosts should configure correctly. Also, check to make sure there are no conflicts if you use a cable or DSL modem, wireless access point (WAP), or other intelligent router on your LAN that can provide DHCP.

Other Uses for DHCP

A whole host of options can be used in `dhcpd.conf`: Entire books are dedicated to DHCP. The most comprehensive book is *The DHCP Handbook*, available at http://www.dhcp-handbook.com/. You can define NIS domains, configure NETBIOS, set subnet masks, and define time servers, or many other types of servers—to name a few of the DHCP options you can use. The preceding example will get your DHCP server and client up and running.

The DHCP server distribution contains an example of the `dhcpd.conf` file that you can use as a template for your network. The file shows a basic configuration that can get you started with explanations for the options used.

Wireless Networking

As stated earlier, Linux has had support for wireless networking since the first standards were developed in the early 1990s. With computers getting smaller and smaller, the uses for wireless networking increased; meanwhile, the transmission speeds are increasing all the time. There are several different ways to create a wireless network. The following sections introduce you to several Linux commands you can use to initialize, configure, and manage wireless networking on your Fedora system.

Support for Wireless Networking in Fedora

The Linux kernel that ships with Fedora provides extensive support for wireless networking. Related wireless tools for configuring, managing, or displaying information about a wireless connection include

- iwconfig—Used to set the network name, encryption, transmission rate, and other features of a wireless network interface

- iwlist—Displays information about a wireless interface, such as rate, power level, or frequency used

- iwpriv—Uses i to set optional features, such as roaming, of a wireless network interface

- iwspy—Shows wireless statistics of a number of nodes

Support will vary for wireless devices—most likely in the form of a PCMCIA adapter—although some USB wireless devices now work with Linux. In general, Linux wireless device software (usually in the form of a kernel module) will support the creation of an Ethernet device that can be managed by traditional interface tools such as ifconfig—with wireless features of the device managed by the various wireless software tools.

For example, when a wireless networking device is first recognized and initialized for use, the driver will most likely report a new device:

```
wvlan_cs: WaveLAN/IEEE PCMCIA driver v1.0.6
wvlan_cs: (c) Andreas Neuhaus <andy@fasta.fh-dortmund.de>
wvlan_cs: index 0x01: Vcc 3.3, irq 3, io 0x0100-0x013f
wvlan_cs: Registered netdevice eth0
wvlan_cs: MAC address on eth0 is 00 05 5d f3 1d da
```

This output (from the dmesg command) shows that the eth0 device has been reported. If DHCP is in use, the device should automatically join the nearest wireless subnet and will be automatically assigned an IP address. If not, the next step is to use a wireless tool such as iwconfig to set various parameters of the wireless device. The iwconfig command, along with the device name (eth0 in this example), will show the status:

```
# iwconfig eth0
eth0    IEEE 802.11-DS ESSID:"GreyUFO" Nickname:"Prism I"
        Mode:Managed Frequency:2.412GHz Access Point: 00:02:2D:2E:FA:3C
        Bit Rate:2Mb/s  Tx-Power=15 dBm  Sensitivity:1/3
        RTS thr:off  Fragment thr:off
        Encryption key:off
        Power Management:off
        Link Quality:92/92 Signal level:-11 dBm Noise level:-102 dBm
        Rx invalid nwid:0 Rx invalid crypt:0 Rx invalid frag:0
        Tx excessive retries:0 Invalid misc:4  Missed beacon:0
```

17

This example shows a 2Mbps connection to a network named GreyUFO. To change a parameter, such as the transmission rate, use a command-line option with the iwconfig command like so:

```
# iwconfig eth0 rate 11M
```

Other options supported by the iwconfig command include essid, used to set the NIC to connect to a specific network by named; mode, used to enable the NIC to automatically retrieve settings from an access point or connect to another wireless host; or freq, to set a frequency to use for communication. Additional options include channel, frag, enc (for encryption), power, and txpower. Details and examples of these options are in the iwconfig manual page.

You can then use the ifconfig command or perhaps a graphical Red Hat tool to set the device networking parameters, and the interface will work as on a hardwired LAN. One handy output of the iwconfig command is the link quality output, which can be used in shell scripts or other graphical utilities for signal monitoring purposes (refer to Chapter 14 for an example).

Cellular Networking

The ads are starting to crop up on TV: This cellular service will allow you to check your email anywhere your cellular phone can reach; that cellular company will provide news and other information via the Internet to your phone. Personal digital assistants have cellular add-ons or even built-in options.

For example, if your laptop has a cellular modem, you can use it to dial in to your network. This is not truly wireless networking if the network dialed in to is wired, but it illustrates how far-reaching wireless networks can go. As long as your cellular service follows you, you can dial in to any network you have access to (be it home or office) from any location in the world to check your email and use it to send electronic files to your associates. And many newer cell phones can be used as a modem by attaching a cable from the phone to a serial or USB port on a laptop. As with most devices, the majority of brand-name PCMCIA cards will work with Linux. A lot of generic equipment (such as serial I/O cards) should work, but you are taking a chance if the card is not supported (see the section "Managing PCMCIA" in Chapter 4, "Post-Installation Configuration").

Advantages of Wireless Networking

Advantages to wireless networking are the mobility and the potential range. If you have a large enough antenna network, your network can stretch many miles. This would be an expensive network, but one that would easily break out of the brick and mortar confines of the office.

Wireless networking would also be a great advantage to college campuses to eliminate the need to tear through walls to install cabling because more and more students expect to have a network connection in their dorm rooms. Wireless networking cards are becoming more reasonable in price and can easily be issued to each student as he requires them.

Home networkers can also benefit from wireless networking. For those who cannot do wired network modifications to their homes, wireless networking removes the unsightly wires running along baseboards and ceilings that are required to connect computers in different rooms. With a wireless home network, you are not even confined to inside the house. Depending on the transmit power of your router, you can sit out in your backyard and watch clouds drifting by as you type away. Wireless routers are coming down in price with each passing day.

Choosing the right types of wireless devices is an important decision. The next sections discuss some of the basic differences between current protocols used for wireless networking.

Choosing from Among Available Wireless Protocols

The Institute of Electrical and Electronics Engineers (IEEE) started to look seriously at wireless networking in 1990. This is when the 802.11 Standard was first introduced by the Wireless Local Area Networks Standards Working Group. The group based the standard roughly around the architecture used in cellular phone networks. The wireless network is controlled by a base station, which can be just a transmitter attached to the network or, more commonly these days, a router.

Larger networks can use more than one base station. Networks with more than one base station are usually referred to as distribution systems. Use of a distribution system can be used to increase coverage area and support roaming of wireless hosts. You can also employ external omnidirectional antennas to increase coverage area, or if required, use point-to-point, or directional antennas to connect distant computers or networks. Right now, the least expensive wireless Linux networks are built using devices (such as access points or NICs) supporting 802.11b, although prices are rapidly dropping for faster 802.11g devices.

An early standard, 802.11a, offers greater transmission rates than 802.11b, and a number of 802.11a wireless NICs are available (some products provide up to 72Mbps, but will not work with 802.11b devices). Wireless networking devices based on 802.11g, which has the speed improvement of 802.11a and is compatible with 802.11b, are becoming more widely available. Other wireless protocols include Bluetooth, which provides up to 720Kbps data transfers. Bluetooth is intended for short-range device communications (such as for a printer) and only supports a typical range of 10 meters. Bluetooth is unlike IrDA, which requires line-of-sight (devices that are aimed at each other). Bluetooth use will conflict with 802.11 networks because it also uses the 2.4GHz band. You can find out more by browsing to http://www.bluetooth.com.

The 802.11 standard specifies that wireless devices use a frequency range of 2400–2483.5MHz. This is the standard used in North America and Europe. In Japan however, wireless networks are limited to a frequency range of 2471MHz–2479MHz because of Japanese regulations. Within these ranges, each network is given up to 79 non-overlapping frequency channels to use. This reduces the chance of two closely located wireless networks using the same channel at the same time. It also allows for channel hopping, which can be used for security.

17

Related Fedora and Linux Commands

You will use these commands when managing network connectivity in your Fedora system:

dhclient—Automatically acquire, and then set IP info for a NIC

ethereal—GNOME graphical network scanner

gnome-lokkit—Fedora's basic graphical firewalling tool for X

ifconfig—Displays and manages Linux networking devices

iwconfig—Displays and sets wireless network device parameters

lokkit—Fedora's basic graphical firewalling tool

netconfig—Fedora's console-based graphical network interface configuration tool

route—Displays and manages Linux kernel routing table

setup—Fedora's console-based graphical management tool

ssh—The OpenSSH remote-login client and preferred replacement for telnet

system-config-nfs—Fedora's graphical Network File System configuration tool

system-config-network—Fedora's graphical network and service management client for X

system-config-securitylevel—Fedora's graphical firewall configuration utility

---

Using Patches/Upgrades to Keep Your Network Secure

One of the keys to security not mentioned previously is to keep up-to-date with at least the latest stable versions of your software. Each time a new version of a software package comes out, it corrects any known security holes found in the previous release. Also be sure to keep your operating systems patched to the latest patch level. Your network security is only as strong as the weakest host.

Refer to Chapter 7 for details on how to use RPM to update Fedora with newer software packages. See Chapter 38, "Kernel and Module Management," to see how to update your Linux kernel (even if you use RPM).

With effort, your system can be secure enough to keep most intruders out. Just keep your software up-to-date and keep yourself informed of potential security threats to your software, and you should be fine.

Reference

The following websites and books are great resources for more information on the topics covered in this chapter. Networking is complex. The more you take the time to learn, the easier setting up and maintaining your network will be.

General

http://fedora.redhat.com/docs—Links to additional documentation for Fedora.

http://www.ietf.org/rfc.html—Go here to search for, or get a list of, Request for Comments (RFC).

DHCP

http://www.oth.net/dyndns.html—For a list of Dynamic DNS service providers, go to this site.

http://www.isc.org/products/DHCP/dhcpv3-README.html—The DHCP README is available at this site.

Wireless

http://www.ieee.org—The Institute of Electrical and Electronics Engineers (IEEE) website.

http://www.mozillaquest.com/Network_02/Wireless_Network_Technology_03_Story-01.html—Wireless networking with Red Hat 7.2.

http://crl.cs.uiuc.edu/doc/wireless_redhat.html—Wireless networking using Red Hat Linux at the Computing Research Laboratory (CRL), the information technology support group for the Department of Computer Science at the University of Illinois at Urbana-Champaign.

http://www.sorgonet.com/network/wirelessnoap/—Building a wireless network without using an access point, using Red Hat 8.0.

Books

Sams Teach Yourself TCP/IP Network Administration in 21 Days, Sams Publishing, ISBN: 0-672-31250-6

TCP/IP Network Administration, O'Reilly Publishing, ISBN: 1-56592-322-7

Practical Networking, Que Publishing, ISBN: 0-7897-2252-6

Samba Unleashed, Sams Publishing, ISBN: 0-672-31862-8

The DHCP Handbook, Sams Publishing, ISBN: 0-672-32327-3

17

CHAPTER **18**

Internet Connectivity

Fedora Core supports Internet connections and the use of Internet resources in many different ways. You will find a wealth of Internet-related software included with this book's version of Fedora Core, and you can download hundreds of additional free utilities from a variety of sources. To use them, you will need to have a working Internet connection.

In this chapter, you will learn how to set up an Internet connection in Fedora Core Linux using a modem and Point-to-Point Protocol (PPP) as well as other connection methods, including Digital Subscriber Line (DSL) and cable modem services. Just a few years ago, getting a dial-up connection working was difficult—hence, an entire chapter of this book was devoted to it. Nowadays, as long as you have a hardware modem, dial-up configuration is simple. The Red Hat engineers and the Linux community have made great progress in making connectivity easier.

Although many experienced Linux users continue to use manual scripts to establish their Internet connectivity, new users and experienced system administrators alike will find Fedora Core's graphical network configuration interface, the Internet Connection Wizard, much easier to use. You learn how to use the Internet Connection Wizard in this chapter, as well as how to configure Fedora Core Linux to provide dial-in PPP support. The chapter also describes how to use Roaring Penguin's DSL utilities for managing connectivity through a cable modem connection.

Linux and America Online

The America Online service (AOL) is often cited as a reason that many more people don't use Linux. Why? Because AOL uses a proprietary protocol to connect and a proprietary user interface to access AOL content; no Linux interface is available (although one has been rumored for a while). Simply put, if you wanted to use Linux, you were forced to choose some Internet connection other than AOL.

Not surprisingly, an enterprising group of people are working on a Linux dialer that will access a legitimate AOL account. It does not provide the unique AOL user interface or access AOL email and suggests that you use AOL's web-based email interface, but the Linux dialer does provide connectivity to the Internet via an AOL account.

The Penggy (formerly Pengaol) page at http://www.peng.apinc.org/eng/ provides links to binary RPM packages as well as source tarballs and HOWTOs. This software is not sanctioned by AOL, but it might allow an AOL user to experiment with Linux.

However, the situation is different if you connect via DSL. AOL now supports the use of routers, allowing you to connect Linux boxes and access the Internet through the router. Granted, you will not be able to access any of AOL's unique content, but are you really going to miss it?

Common Configuration Information

Although Fedora Core enables great flexibility in configuring Internet connections, that flexibility comes at the price of an increase in complexity. To configure Internet connectivity in Fedora Core Linux, you must know more about the details of the connection process than you can learn from the information typically provided by your Internet service provider (ISP). In this section of the chapter, you learn what to ask about and how to use the information.

Some ISPs are unaware of Linux or unwilling to support its use with their service. Fortunately, that attitude is rapidly changing, and the majority of ISPs offer services using standard protocols that are compatible with Linux, even if they (or their technical support people) aren't aware that their own ISPs are Linux friendly. You just need to press a little for the information you require.

If you are using a dial-up modem account (referred to in Linux as PPP for the Point-to-Point Protocol it uses), your ISP will provide your computer with a static or dynamic IP (Internet Protocol) address. A dynamic IP address changes each time you dial in, whereas a static IP address remains the same. The ISP also might automatically provide your computer with the names of the Domain Name Service servers (DNS). You will need to know the telephone number that your computer will dial in to for making the connection; your ISP supplies that number, too. You'll also need a working modem and need to know the device name of the modem (usually /dev/modem).

> **NOTE**
>
> Most IP addresses are dynamically assigned by ISPs; they have a pool of addresses, and you get whatever address is available. From the ISP's viewpoint, a small number of addresses can serve a large number of people because not everyone will be online at the same time. For most Internet services, a dynamic IP works well because it's the ISP's job to route that information to you, and they sit in the middle—between you and the service you want to use. But a dynamic IP address changes, and if someone needs to find you at the same address (if you run a website or a file transfer site, for example), an IP that changes every time you log on will not work well. For that,

you need a static IP. Because your ISP cannot reuse that IP with its other customers, it will likely charge you more for a static IP than a dynamic IP. The average consumer doesn't need the benefit of a static IP, so he is happy paying less for a dynamically assigned IP. Also, the DNS information can be provided automatically by the ISP by the Dynamic Host Configuration Protocol, or DHCP. This is discussed in depth in Chapter 17, "Network Connectivity."

If you are using DSL access or a cable modem, you might have a dynamic IP provided through DHCP, or you might be assigned a static IP. You might automatically be provided with the names of the DNS servers if you use DHCP, or you will need to set up DNS manually (in which case, you will need to know the IP addresses of the DNS servers).

In all cases, you will need to know your username, your password, and for the configuration of other services, the names of the mail servers and the news server. This information can be obtained from your ISP if you specifically ask for it.

> **NOTE**
>
> The information in this book will help you understand and avoid many connection issues, but you might experience connection problems. Keep the telephone number of the technical help service for your ISP on hand in case you are not able to establish a connection. But be aware that few ISPs offer Linux support, and you might need to seek help from a Linux-savvy friend or a Linux user's group if your special circumstances cannot be handled from the knowledge you gain from this book.

Laying the Foundation: The localhost Interface

Prior to connecting to the Internet or network, you must create a dummy or localhost interface. This interface, known as lo (the loopback interface), is used by the TCP/IP protocol to assign an IP address to your machine and is required for establishing a PPP interface. The lo interface is also used by many network-aware applications and is easy to set up.

Checking for the Availability of the Loopback Interface

Fedora Core normally takes care of setting up this interface during the installation. You can use the ifconfig command as root to see if it is already available. The command and its response will look similar to this if lo is available:

```
# /sbin/ifconfig
lo        Link encap:Local Loopback
          inet addr:127.0.0.1  Mask:255.0.0.0
          UP LOOPBACK RUNNING  MTU:16436  Metric:1
          RX packets:12 errors:0 dropped:0 overruns:0 frame:0
          TX packets:12 errors:0 dropped:0 overruns:0 carrier:0
          collisions:0 txqueuelen:0
          RX bytes:760 (760.0 b)  TX bytes:760 (760.0 b)
```

The sample output shows that the loopback interface is active and running, that it has been assigned the typical loopback IP address 127.0.0.1, that the broadcast mask of 255.0.0.0 is used, and that the interface hasn't had much traffic (RX = receive and TX = transmit). If you don't see something similar to the example, you'll need to configure the localhost interface by hand after reading the remainder of this section. Otherwise, you can skip to the next section.

Configuring the Loopback Interface Manually

The localhost interface's IP address is defined in a text file that can be used by Fedora Core Linux to store network IP address information. This file is called /etc/hosts and should exist on a system even if it's empty. The file provides IP addresses and associated hostnames to the Linux kernel and other network-related utilities. Prior to configuring network interfaces, you might find that the /etc/hosts file only contains a single line:

```
127.0.0.1        localhost.localdomain            localhost
```

This line defines the special localhost interface and assigns it an IP address of 127.0.0.1. You might hear or read about terms such as localhost, loopback, and dummy interface; all these terms refer to the use of the IP address 127.0.0.1. The term *loopback interface* indicates that to Linux networking drivers, it looks as though the machine is talking to a network that consists of only one machine; the kernel sends network traffic to and from itself on the same computer. *Dummy* interface indicates that the interface doesn't really exist as far as the outside world is concerned; it exists only for the local machine. You can read more about networking in Chapter 17.

Each networked Fedora Core Linux machine on a LAN will use this same IP address for its localhost. If for some reason a Fedora Core Linux computer does not have this interface, edit the /etc/hosts file to add the localhost entry, and then use the ifconfig and route commands as root to create the interface like this:

```
# /sbin/ifconfig lo 127.0.0.1
# /sbin/route add 127.0.0.1 lo
```

These commands will create the localhost interface in memory (all interfaces, such as eth0 or ppp0, are created in memory when using Linux), and then add the IP address 127.0.0.1 to an internal (in-memory) table so that the Linux kernel's networking code can keep track of routes to different addresses.

Use the ifconfig command as shown previously to test the interface.

You should now be able to use the ping to check that the interface is responding properly like this (using either localhost or its IP address):

```
# /bin/ping -c 3 localhost
PING localhost.localdomain (127.0.0.1) from 127.0.0.1 : 56(84) bytes of data.
64 bytes from localhost.localdomain (127.0.0.1): icmp_seq=0 ttl=255 time=212 \
usec
```

```
64 bytes from localhost.localdomain (127.0.0.1): icmp_seq=1 ttl=255 time=80 usec
64 bytes from localhost.localdomain (127.0.0.1): icmp_seq=2 ttl=255 time=50 usec

--- localhost.localdomain ping statistics ---
3 packets transmitted, 3 packets received, 0% packet loss
round-trip min/avg/max/mdev = 0.050/0.114/0.212/0.070 ms
```

The -c option is used to set the number of pings, and the command, if successful (as it was previously), will return information regarding the round-trip speed of sending a test packet to the specified host.

Configuring Dial-up Internet Access

Most ISPs provide dial-up connections supporting PPP because it is a fast and efficient protocol for using TCP/IP over serial lines. PPP is designed for two-way networking; TCP/IP provides the transport protocol for data. One hurdle faced by new Fedora Core Linux users is how to set up PPP and connect to the Internet. It is not necessary to understand the details of the PPP protocol in order to use it, and setting up a PPP connection is easy. You can configure the PPP connections manually using the command line or graphically during an X session using Fedora's Internet Configuration Wizard. Each approach produces the same results.

PPP uses several components on your system. The first is a daemon called pppd, which controls the use of PPP. The second is a driver called the high-level data link control (HDLC), which controls the flow of information between two machines. A third component of PPP is a routine called chat that dials the other end of the connection for you when you want it to. Although PPP has many "tunable" parameters, the default settings work well for most people.

> **NOTE**
>
> You can check to see whether PPP is installed on your system by running the pppd command as root from a command line with the --help argument, like this:
>
> # pppd --help
>
> That will list the current version number and describe a few available options if PPP is installed.
>
> If PPP isn't installed on your system, use the rpm command to install the PPP package from the Fedora Core CD-ROM or use the Packages menu item from the System Settings menu. Chapter 7, "Managing Software and System Resources," covers the details of using rpm and the graphical package manager.

18

Configuring a Dial-up Connection Manually

The first step in manually configuring PPP is to log in as root in order to copy and edit the necessary files. After you are logged in, you'll use the chat command, the pppd daemon, and several files to configure PPP:

`/etc/ppp/ppp-on`—Used to start a PPP connection. This file contains the ISP's phone number, your username and password, as well as various options such as IP address options, the modem device, and its settings (such as baud rate) for the connection.

`/etc/ppp/ppp-off`—Used to terminate a PPP connection.

`/etc/ppp/ppp-on-dialer`—Used to perform dialing and connection with the `chat` command; this script contains error-handling and negotiation responses between the remote system and the `chat` command script.

CAUTION

Many software modems will not work with Linux because the manufacturers won't release programming information about them or provide Linux drivers. An external serial port modem or ISA bus modem will almost always work; USB and PCI modems are still problematic. It is suggested that you do a thorough Google search using your modem's name and model number to see how others have solved problems with that particular modem. Links to software modem compatibility sites appear at the end of this chapter.

Begin by copying the scripts from the `/usr/share/doc/ppp*/scripts` directory to the `/etc/ppp` directory, like so:

```
# cp -ar /usr/share/doc/ppp*/scripts/ppp-o* /etc/ppp
```

Using your favorite text editor, edit the `ppp-on` file (making sure to disable the line wrapping function in your editor—that varies from editor to editor—and line wrapping inserts carriage returns that cause these scripts to stop working) and change the first four entries to reflect your ISP's phone number and your username and password, like this:

```
TELEPHONE=555-1212      # The telephone number for the connection
ACCOUNT=beau          # The account name for logon
PASSWORD=pulley       # The password for this account
LOCAL_IP=0.0.0.0      # Local IP address if known. Dynamic = 0.0.0.0
```

Change the values for TELEPHONE, ACCOUNT, and PASSWORD, substituting your ISP's phone number and your username and password. Change the LOCAL_IP entry to an IP address only if your ISP provides one for use. (Dynamic IPs are typical of dial-up accounts.) Otherwise, leave the entry blank. Next, scroll through the script until you find the dialing setup, which can look like this:

```
exec /usr/sbin/pppd debug lock modem crtscts /dev/ttyS0 38400 \
      asyncmap 20A0000 escape FF kdebug 0 $LOCAL_IP:$REMOTE_IP \
      noipdefault netmask $NETMASK defaultroute connect $DIALER_SCRIPT
```

These lines (actually a single script line) contain modem options for the chat script used in the `ppp-on-dialer` script and will start the `pppd` daemon on your computer after establishing a connection. Using a text editor, change the modem device (`/dev/ttyS0` in this example) to `/dev/modem`.

> **CAUTION**
>
> You can use /dev/modem only if Fedora Core's kudzu utility has recognized and configured the computer's modem. (If /dev/modem does not exist, use the ln command to create the file as a symbolic link pointing to the correct serial port.) To create the symlink (from /dev/ttyS2, for example):
>
> ```
> # ln -s /dev/ttyS2 /dev/modem
> ```
>
> If your modem was not automatically detected and the /dev/modem link configured, it is possible that you have a software modem, also known as a Winmodem or HSF modem (see earlier note).

Set the baud rate (38400 in the default case) to the desired connection speed—most likely 115200 or 57600. When finished, save the file.

Next, use the chmod command to make these scripts executable, like this:

```
# chmod +x /etc/ppp/ppp-o*
```

To debug or check the progress of your modem connection, dialing, and connection to your ISP, monitor the syslog messages by using the tail command with its -f "loop forever" option, like this:

```
# /sbin/tail -f /var/log/messages
```

To connect to your ISP, run the ppp- script:

```
# /etc/ppp/ppp-on
```

Use the ppp-off script to stop the PPP connection like so:

```
# /etc/ppp/ppp-off
```

You can also move the ppp-on and ppp-off scripts to a recognized $PATH, such as /usr/local/bin. Enabling use of these scripts by normal users will entail changing permissions of the serial port and other files (which can be a security problem because unauthorized users can access it).

> **TIP**
>
> If your modem is installed and working, you can access it using a terminal program such as minicom, which usually is not installed by default. After you install it from the .rpm file or from source code, start it the very first time with the -s argument to configure it:
>
> ```
> $ minicom -s
> ```
>
> Set the serial port to that of your modem, and then save the configuration. You can then use minicom to communicate with your modem using the AT command set and see its responses.

18

If you don't want to go to that trouble, you can use the echo command to send commands to the modem, but the modem won't be capable of responding to you. For example, the AT&W command can be sent as follows:

```
# echo "AT&W" > /dev/modem
```

Using the Fedora Core Internet Configuration Wizard

The Fedora Core Internet Configuration Wizard can be used to set up the many kinds of network connection types that exist. Fedora Core provides wizards for the following connections:

CIPE (VPN) connection (Virtual Private Network using Crypto IP Encapsulation)

Ethernet connection

ISDN connection

Modem connection

Token Ring connection

Wireless connection

xDSL connection

The example provided here uses the Wizard to configure a modem connection, the most commonly encountered home network connection. The other types are configured in essentially the same manner.

From the System Tools menu, select the Internet Configuration Wizard to configure a new Internet connection. Highlight your selection and click Forward. The Select Modem screen, shown in Figure 18.1, is then displayed.

Select "Modem connection" in the Device Type list, and then click the Forward button. You will then be asked to select a provider, designate a name for the service, enter your ISP's phone number, and enter your username and password on the remote system, as shown in Figure 18.2. A dialing prefix (to disable call waiting, for example) can be added in the Prefix field. Additional special settings are also included for PPP users in various countries with different ISPs, as shown by the country flags on the left.

Enter the telephone number of your ISP's remote computer's modem. Enter a country code if needed, along with an area code and telephone number. Note that some areas require a 10-digit number for local telephone service. When finished, click the Forward button. You'll then be able to confirm the settings. Click the Finish button to create the interface. When you are done, you will see a new ppp0 entry in the Network Configuration window, as shown in Figure 18.3.

To edit the new connection identified as ppp0, select the interface, and then click the Edit button. A configuration dialog will appear as shown in Figure 18.4. Each tab presents an easy-to-use interface for setting dial-up options.

FIGURE 18.1   The Internet Connection Wizard can be used to quickly and easily configure many different kinds of Internet connections.

FIGURE 18.2   Enter a name for your ISP's service, along with the telephone number, username, and password for the service.

This window can be reached later from the System Settings menu as the Network menu item. Fedora Core also provides a simple control interface via the System Tools menu as the Network Device Control menu item, as shown in Figure 18.5.

FIGURE 18.3   Your new PPP dial-up connection appears in the Network Configuration dialog, which also shows the status of the connection.

FIGURE 18.4   Here, you can edit the dial-up configuration if necessary to set IP addresses and other custom values; the defaults work for most people.

FIGURE 18.5   The Network Device Control allows you to start and stop a network interface.

Launch a PPP connection by selecting the ppp0 interface and then clicking the Activate button.

You can also use the ifup command manually (only as root) to bring up the connection like this:

```
# /sbin/ifup ppp0
```

To close the connection manually, use ifdown:

```
# /sbin/ifdown ppp0
```

If you named the dial-up connection something other than ppp0, use that name instead. Because we named ours *Cavtel*, we can bring it up manually with

```
# /sbin/ifup Cavtel
```

18

Configuring Digital Subscriber Line Access

Fedora Core also supports the use of a digital subscriber line (DSL) service. Although it refers to the different types of DSL available as xDSL, that name includes ADSL, IDSL, SDSL, and other flavors of DSL service; they can all be configured using the Internet Connection Wizard. DSL service generally provides 128Kbps to 1.0Mbps transfer speeds and transmits data over copper telephone lines from a central office to individual subscriber sites (such as your home). Many DSL services provide asymmetric speeds with download speed greater than upload speeds.

> **NOTE**
>
> DSL service is an "always on" type of Internet service, although you can turn off the connection under Fedora Core using the Network Device Control. An always on connection exposes your computer to malicious abuse from crackers who trawl the Internet attempting to gain access to

other computer systems. In addition to the capability to turn off such connections, Fedora Core provides a firewall to keep crackers out; you configured a simple firewall during the original installation. The firewall can also be configured from the Security Level Configuration tool found in the System Settings menu selection as Security Level.

A DSL connection requires that you have an Ethernet network interface card (sometimes a USB interface that is not easily supported in Linux) in your computer or notebook. Many users also configure a gateway, firewall, or other computer with at least two network interface cards in order to share a connection with a LAN. Chapter 17 discusses the hardware and protocol issues in detail. Advanced configuration of a firewall or router, other than what was addressed during your initial installation of Fedora Core, is beyond the scope of this book.

Understanding Point-to-Point Protocol over Ethernet

Establishing a DSL connection with an ISP providing a static IP address is easy. Unfortunately, many DSL providers use a type of PPP protocol named Point-to-Point Protocol over Ethernet (PPPoE) that provides dynamic IP address assignment and authentication by encapsulating PPP information inside Ethernet frames. Roaring Penguin's rp-pppoe clients are included with Fedora Core Linux, and these clients make the difficult-to-configure PPPoE connection much easier to deal with. You can download and install newer versions (see the Roaring Penguin link in the "Reference" section at the end of this chapter).

Configuring a PPPoE Connection Manually

The basic steps involved in manually setting up a DSL connection using Fedora Core Linux involve connecting the proper hardware, and then running a simple configuration script if you use rp-pppoe from Roaring Penguin.

First, connect your DSL modem to your telephone line, and then plug in your Ethernet cable from the modem to your computer's network interface card. If you plan to share your DSL connection with the rest of your LAN, you'll need at least two network cards—designated eth0 (for your LAN) and eth1 (for the DSL connection).

The following example assumes that you have more than one computer and will share your DSL connection on a LAN.

First, log in as root, and ensure that your first eth0 device is enabled and up (perhaps using the ifconfig command). Next, bring up the other interface, but assign a null IP address like this:

```
# /sbin/ifconfig eth1 0.0.0.0 up
```

Now use the adsl-setup command to set up your system. Type the command like this:

```
# /sbin/adsl-setup
```

You will be presented with a text script and be asked to enter your username and the Ethernet interface used for the connection (such as eth1). You'll then be asked to use "on demand" service or have the connection stay up all the time (until brought down by the root operator). You can also set a timeout in seconds, if desired. You'll then be asked to enter the IP addresses of your ISP's DNS servers if you haven't configured the system's /etc/resolv.conf file.

After that, you will be prompted to enter your password two times, and will then have to choose the type of firewall and IP masquerading to use. (You learned about IP masquerading in the section "Using IP Masquerading in Fedora Core Linux," in Chapter 17.) The actual configuration is done automatically. Using a firewall is essential nowadays, so you should choose this option unless you intend to craft your own set of firewall rules—a discussion of which is beyond the scope of this book. After you have chosen your firewall and IP masquerading setup, you will be asked to confirm, save, and implement your settings. You are also given a choice to allow users to manage the connection, a handy option for home users.

Changes will be made to your system's /etc/sysconfig/network-scripts/ifcfg-ppp0, /etc/resolv.conf, /etc/ppp/pap-secrets, and /etc/ppp/chap-secrets files.

After configuration has finished, use the adsl-start command to start a connection and DSL session, like this:

```
# /sbin/adsl-start
```

The DSL connection should be nearly instantaneous, but if problems occur, check to make sure that your DSL modem is communicating with the phone company's central office by examining the status LEDs on the modem. Because this varies from modem to modem, consult your modem user's manual.

Check to make certain that all cables are properly attached, that your interfaces are properly configured, and that you have entered the correct information to the setup script.

If IP masquerading is enabled, other computers on your LAN on the same subnet address (such as 192.168.1.*XXX*) can use the Internet, but must have the same /etc/resolv.conf nameserver entries and a routing entry with the DSL-connected computer as a gateway. For example, if the host computer with the DSL connection has an IP address of 192.168.1.1, and other computers on your LAN use addresses in the 192.168.1.*XXX* range, use the route command on each computer like this:

```
# /sbin/route add default gw 192.168.1.1
```

Note that you can also use a hostname instead if each computer has an /etc/hosts file with hostname and IP address entries for your LAN. To stop your connection, use the adsl-stop command like this:

```
# /sbin/adsl-stop
```

18

Troubleshooting Connection Problems

The Internet Configuration Wizard does not offer any Help dialogs, but the Linux Documentation Project at http://www.tldp.org/ offers many in-depth resources for configuring and troubleshooting these connections. The Internet search engine Google is also an invaluable tool for dealing with specific questions about these connections. For many other useful references, see the "Reference" section at the end of this chapter.

Here are a few troubleshooting tips culled from many years of experience:

- If your modem connects and then hangs up, you are probably using the wrong password or dialing the wrong number. If the password and phone number are correct, it is likely an authentication protocol problem.

- If you get connected but cannot reach websites, it is likely a domain name resolver problem, meaning that DNS is not working. If it worked yesterday and you haven't "adjusted" the associated files, it is probably a problem at the ISP's end. Call and ask.

- Always make certain that everything is plugged in. Check again—and again.

- If the modem works in Windows, but not in Linux no matter what you do, it is probably a software modem no matter what it said on the box.

- If everything just stops working (and you do not see smoke), it is probably a glitch at the ISP or the telephone company. Take a break and give them some time to fix it.

- Never configure a network connection when you have had too little sleep or too much caffeine; you will just have to redo it tomorrow.

Configuring a Dial-in PPP Server

If you want to access your high-speed Internet connection when you are away from home, a simple dial-up PPP service can be quickly configured on your Fedora Core Linux system by configuring Linux to answer a call from a remote modem and start PPP. This is handy if you have high-speed access at home and need to use it while you are on the road. For example, our DSL connection is made through the telephone lines to our home. While at our winter vacation home, that DSL connection is not available. With a dial-in server, we use the modem in our laptop to dial home and the dial-up server connects us to the Internet (as well as our home LAN); it is like a private ISP. Not everyone will want to configure a dial-in PPP server to do this, but it does illustrate the kind of power that Linux offers a user.

You will need a second phone line (for convenience, it is not really necessary), a serial port, and an attached modem. The modem must be set to answer incoming calls using the AT commands specific to the modem you are using (consult its manual), and with the configuration saved using the AT&W modem command. A line-monitoring application such as agetty, getty, or mgetty is then used to watch the serial port by editing an entry in the system's initialization table, /etc/inittab. You then create a special user account and script to configure Fedora Core Linux to automatically start the pppd daemon and PPP service after a user logs in.

Many modems can use a modem string such as ATE1Q0V1&C1&S0S0=1&W to auto answer calls, but this varies by modem manufacturer. Some terminal monitors, such as uugetty, have configuration files that automatically set up the modem for a particular serial port and use an entry in /etc/inittab that looks like this:

```
3:2345:respawn:/sbin/uugetty ttyS1 38400 vt100
```

This entry assumes that a modem is attached to /dev/ttyS1.

Other commands, such as agetty, can directly configure a modem port and might use an /etc/inittab entry like this:

```
3:2345:respawn:/usr/local/bin/agetty -w -I 'ATE0Q1&D2&C1S0=1\015' \
115200 ttyS1 vt100
```

If you would prefer to use the mgetty command, which is included with Fedora Core, use an entry like this:

```
3:2345:respawn:/sbin/mgetty -a -n 1 -D ttyS1
```

You will also need to edit the file /etc/mgetty+sendfax/mgetty.config to set connection speeds and whether data, fax, or data-only or fax-only connections are to be allowed.

Linux Voice Modem Support

If you are the fortunate owner of a vgetty-supported voice modem, such as the Elsa MicroLink 56K Internet modem, you can download, install, and use the vgetty command to monitor the modem and have your system provide voice, data, and fax services. Edit the file /etc/mgetty+sendfax/voice.conf, create your answering voice messages in /var/spool/voice/messages, and then use a vgetty /etc/inittab entry such as

```
S0:345:respawn:/sbin/vgetty ttyS2
```

To host voice messages, you will need to use the wavtopvf and pvfspeed commands to convert your voice sound files into a format used by the modem, like this:

```
# wavtopvf mymessage.wav mymessage.pvf
# pvfspeed -s 7200 mymessage.pvf ¦ pvftormd Elsa 4 > mymessage.rmd
```

To play your outgoing message (which should be stored in /var/spool/voice/messages with the name standard.rmd), use the following command line (needed to convert sound formats so we can play it):

```
# rmdtopvf mymessage.rmd ¦ pvfspeed -s 8000 ¦ pvftobasic >/dev/audio
```

18

This technique can be used to listen to any messages left by callers (which end up in the `/var/spool/voice/incoming` directory).

Browse to http://alpha.greenie.net/vgetty/ to download `vgetty` and its documentation. Also, look at the Linux Answering machine HOWTO at http://linuxindia.virtualave.net/lamhowto.html.

The next step is to create a user named ppp and then to assign a password to it. Although it is possible to allow remote users to log in and start pppd from the command line (assuming that you have set pppd to SUID root), the pppd daemon can be started automatically by creating a short shell script and then assigning the shell script to the user for the default shell in the user's `/etc/passwd` entry, like this:

```
ppp:x:500:500::/home/ppp:/usr/local/bin/dopppdoppp
```

(made executable with chmod +x) would contain the following:

```
exec /usr/sbin/pppd -detach
```

Using this approach, pppd will start automatically after the ppp dial-in user connects and logs in (perhaps using the `ppp-on` scripts or other clients on the remote computer). The file options under the `/etc/ppp` directory should include general dial-in options for PPP service on your system, and specific options files (such as `options.ttyS1` for this example) should be created for each enabled dial-in port. For example, `/etc/ppp/options` could contain

```
asyncmap 0
netmask 255.255.255.0
proxyarp
lock
crtscts
modem
```

There are many approaches to providing your own PPP service. IP addresses can be assigned dynamically, or a static IP address can be doled out for a user. For example, `/etc/ppp/options.ttyS1` could contain

```
IPofPPPserver:assignedIPofdialinuser
```

In this example, the first IP address is for the host computer, whereas the second IP address will be assigned to the remote user. For details about configuring PPP for Linux, read the pppd manual page or documentation under the `/usr/share/doc/pppd*` directory. If you're a Linux developer, browse the source code files ppp_async.c, ppp_deflate.c, ppp_generic.c, and ppp_synctty.c under the `/usr/src/linux-2.6/drivers/net` directory.

Saving Even More Bandwidth

If you elect to use a dial-in server, one of the problems you face when using it is that you are using a connection with narrower bandwidth. Wouldn't it be nice if you could strip out all the advertising images and compress the HTML pages before sending them over the modem? Here's how it can be done:

One approach is to use the Fedora Core–supplied `privoxy` proxy server or squid proxy server to filter ads and the Ziproxy (http://ziproxy.sourceforge.net/) server to convert the images to smaller, low-quality images and compress the HTML pages before sending them on to the dial-in user. A Red Hat 9 version is available at http://www.ai.mit.edu/people/wang/ziproxy-1.2.rh9.tgz, as well as a statically compiled version (requires no additional files) at http://aleron.dl. sourceforge.net/sourceforge/ziproxy/ziproxy-1.2b-static.i586.tar.bz2. Ziproxy requires a library not provided by Red Hat or Fedora Core, libconfuse (available at http://www.nongnu.org/ confuse/, where you'll find a src.rpm file to compile on your system; refer to Chapter 8, "On the Internet: Surfing the Web, Writing Email, and Reading the News," for information on compiling source RPM files).

Another approach is to use RabbIT (http://www.khelekore.org/rabbit/), a Java web proxy server that handles both tasks. The site mentions that 2.9MB of original data was compressed to 1.3MB and transmitted in 17 minutes instead of 75 minutes, a considerable saving. The site offers a Getting Started link on the main page describing downloading, installing, configuring, and using the application.

Both applications require ImageMagick to be installed to use the `convert` function to process images into low-resolution version to save bandwidth.

Relevant Fedora Core and Linux Commands

`internet-druid`—Fedora Core's command-line name for its graphical Internet Connection Wizard.

`mgetty`—An advanced serial port monitoring tool that supports data and fax modem operations with Linux.

`neat`—Fedora Core's command-line name for the Network Configuration tool.

`system-control-network`—Red Hat's command-line name for its graphical Network Device Control tool.

`system-config-network-druid`—Red Hat's command-line name for its Internet Connection Wizard.

`system-config-network`—Red Hat's command-line name for its graphical Network Configuration tool. It offers a graphical interface and a command-line interface (when used as `system-config-network-tui`.

Reference

http://www.tldp.org/HOWTO/Modem-HOWTO.html—The Linux Modem HOWTO provides a wealth of information. For example, Chapter 8 deals with locating your modem; Chapters 12 and 13 deal with dial-in use; Chapter 17 offers troubleshooting advice.

http://www.roaringpenguin.com/pppoe/—Home page for the fabulous rp-pppoe software package that enables DSL users to connect to the Internet using Linux. This is a "must-have" software package for Fedora Core and DSL users. You might want to grab a source RPM and rebuild it; their download page gives directions on how to do that.

http://axion.physics.ubc.ca/ppp-linux.html—W.G. Unruh's extensive web page describing how to use PPP and Linux to connect to an ISP, figuring out their connection protocol, and testing the connection.

http://www.tldp.org/HOWTO/PPP-HOWTO/—A great place to start reading about PPP and Linux; includes directions on configuring various clients, linking LANs, and setting up a PPP server.

http://www.tldp.org/HOWTO/DSL-HOWTO—Information about using DSL and Linux, with details about DSL hardware, setting up a network, using USB modems, DSL use and security, and other helpful tips. Highly recommended reading for any Fedora Core Linux user contemplating use of DSL service.

http://www.knowplace.org/ppp.html—The 5-minute Linux PPP HOWTO. A wonderful no-frills guide to setting up PPP manually.

http://www.tldp.org/FAQ/Linux-FAQ/index.html—Linux Frequently Asked Questions with Answers. Section 11, "How Do Configure Dial-up PPP?" is very useful. Section 17 has answers to common general problems.

http://www.tldp.org/HOWTO/Serial-HOWTO.html—The Serial HOWTO covers all aspects of the serial ports used by modems.

http://www.tldp.org/HOWTO/PCMCIA-HOWTO.html—The Linux PCMCIA HOWTO covers PCMCIA modems used in laptop computers.

http://www.tldp.org/HOWTO/PPP-HOWTO/index.html—The Linux PPP HOWTO is the canonical reference for PPP.

http://www.tldp.org/FAQ/PPP-FAQ.html—The FAQ supplements the HOWTO and delves into troubleshooting modems in detail.

http://walbran.org/sean/linux/linmodem-howto.html—The Linmodem HOWTO helps you with your software modem with tips on identification, modules compiling, and a good FAQ.

http://www.pcquest.com/content/linux/handson/102082101.asp—Winmodems and Linux: An overview of software modems with a list of manufacturers and links to their drivers.

http://www.linmodems.org/—The "official" software modem site for Linux.

http://linmodems.technion.ac.il/pctel-linux/—The unofficial PCTEL modem site for Linux.

http://pctelcompdb.sourceforge.net/—An unofficial database for PCTEL modems.

http://linmodems.technion.ac.il/—A linmodem support page.

http://www-124.ibm.com/acpmodem/—The ACP modem driver for Linux.

http://www.swcp.com/~jgentry/pers.html—The Linux Dialin Server Setup Guide, a step-by-step guide to configuring a dial-in server.

https://www.redhat.com/docs/manuals/linux/RHL-9-Manual/security-guide/ s1-vpn-cipe.html—The Red Hat Guide to using Crypto IP Encapsulation (CIPE) over a Virtual Private Network (VPN) to establish a secure Ethernet connection between any two hosts.

18

PART IV

Fedora As a Server

IN THIS PART

Apache Web Server Management

This chapter covers the configuration and management of the Apache web server. The chapter includes an overview of some of the major components of the server and discussions of text-based and graphical server configuration. You will see how to start, stop, and restart Apache using the command line and the Red Hat utilities included with Fedora. The chapter begins with some introductory information about this popular server and then shows you how to install, configure, and start using Apache.

About the Apache Web Server

Apache is the most widely used web server on the Internet today, according to a Netcraft survey of active websites in January 2005, which is shown in Table 19.1.

TABLE 19.1   Netcraft Survey Results (January 2005)

Web Server	Number	Percentage
Apache	39,821,368	68.43%
Microsoft*	12,137,446	20.86%
SunONE	1,830,008	3.14%
Zeus	690,193	1.19%
*All web server products		

Note that these statistics do not reflect Apache's use on internal networks, known as *intranets*.

The name *Apache* appeared during the early development of the software because it was "a patchy" server, made up of patches for the freely available source code of the NCSA HTTPd web server. For a while after the NCSA HTTPd project was discontinued, a number of people wrote a variety of patches for the code, to either fix bugs or add features they wanted. A lot of this code was floating around and people were freely sharing it, but it was completely unmanaged.

After a while, Bob Behlendorf and Cliff Skolnick set up a centralized repository of these patches, and the Apache project was born. The project is still composed of a small core group of programmers, but anyone is welcome to submit patches to the group for possible inclusion in the code.

There's been a surge of interest in the Apache project over the past several years, partially buoyed by a new interest in open source on the part of enterprise-level information services. It's also due in part to crippling security flaws found in Microsoft's Internet Information Services (IIS); the existence of malicious web task exploits; and operating system and networking vulnerabilities to the now-infamous Code Red, Blaster, and Nimda worms. IBM made an early commitment to support and use Apache as the basis for its web offerings and has dedicated substantial resources to the project because it makes more sense to use an established, proven web server.

In mid-1999, The Apache Software Foundation was incorporated as a nonprofit company. A board of directors, who are elected on an annual basis by the ASF members, oversees the company. This company provides a foundation for several open-source software development projects, including the Apache Web Server project.

The best places to find out about Apache are the Apache Group's website, http://www.apache.org/, and the Apache Week website, http://www.apacheweek.com/, where you can subscribe to receive Apache Week by email to keep up on the latest developments in the project, keep abreast of security advisories, and research bug fixes.

> **TIP**
>
> You'll find an overview of Apache in its frequently asked questions (FAQs) at http://httpd.apache.org/docs-2.0/faq/. In addition to extensive online documentation, you'll also find the complete documentation for Apache in the HTML directory of your Apache server. You can access this documentation by looking at http://localhost/manual/index.html on your new Fedora

---

system with one of the web browsers included on your system. You'll need to have Apache
running on your system!

Fedora ships with Apache 2.0, and the server (named httpd) is included on this book's
CD-ROMs and DVD. You can obtain the latest version of Apache as an RPM installation
file from a Fedora FTP server; upgrade using up2date, yum, or apt-get; or get the source
code from the Apache website and, in true Linux tradition, build it for yourself.

To determine the version of Apache included with your system, use the web server's -V
command-line option like this:

```
$ /usr/sbin/httpd -V ¦ cat
Server version: Apache/2.0.50
Server built:    Jun 29 2004 11:11:55
Server's Module Magic Number: 20020903:8
Architecture:    32-bit
Server compiled with....
```

The output displays the version number, build date and time, platform, and various
options used during the build. You can use the -v option to see terser version information.

> **TIP**
>
> In the previous command, we pipe to the cat command because your machine might have
> SELinux configured to stop Apache writing to the terminal.

Installing the Apache Server

You can install Apache from RPMs or build it yourself from source code. The Apache
source builds on just about any Unix-like operating system and on Win32. If you elect to
install the Web Server group of files when first installing Fedora, Apache and related software and documentation in 17 packages are installed automatically.

If you're about to install a new version of Apache, you should shut down the old server.
Even if it's unlikely that the old server will interfere with the installation procedure, shut-
ting it down ensures that there will be no problems. If you don't know how to stop
Apache, see the "Starting and Stopping Apache" section later in this chapter.

Installing from the RPM

You can find the Apache RPM on the Fedora Core installation media, on the Fedora FTP
server, or at one of its many mirror sites. Check the fedora.redhat.com site as often as
possible to download updates as they become available. Updated RPM files usually
contain important bug and security fixes. When an updated version is released, install it
as quickly as possible to keep your system secure.

NOTE

Check the Apache site for security reports. Browse to http://httpd.apache.org/
security_report.html for links to security vulnerabilities for Apache 1.3 and 2.0. Subscribe to a
support list or browse through up-to-date archives of all Apache mailing lists at http://
httpd.apache.org/mail/ (for various articles) or http://httpd.apache.org/lists.html (for comprehensive and organized archives).

If you want the most recent, experimental version of Apache for testing, check Red Hat's
Rawhide distribution, which is also available on the Fedora FTP server (http://
download.fedora.redhat.com/pub/fedora/linux/core/development/). This distribution is experimental and always contains the latest versions of all RPMs. However, note that the Apache
package might depend on new functionality available in other RPMs. Therefore, you might need
to install many new RPMs to be able to use packages from Rawhide. If you still want to use an
Apache version from the Rawhide distribution for testing, a better option might be to download
the source code RPM (SRPM) and compile it yourself. That way, you avoid dependencies on
other new packages. (Refer to the "Working with Source RPM Files" section in Chapter 7,
"Managing Software and System Resources," for information about building and installing packages from SRPM files.)

CAUTION

You should be wary of installing experimental packages, and never install them on production
servers (that is, servers used in "real life"). Very carefully test the packages beforehand on a host
that isn't connected to a network!

After you have obtained an Apache RPM, you can install it with the command-line rpm
tool by typing the following:

```
rpm -Uvh latest_apache.rpm
```

where *latest_apache.rpm* is the name of the latest Apache RPM. For more information
on installing packages with RPM, refer to Chapter 7.

The Apache RPM installs files in the following directories:

- /etc/httpd/conf—This directory contains the Apache configuration file,
  httpd.conf. See the section "Configuring Apache for Peak Performance," later in
  this chapter, for more information.

- /etc/rc.d/—The tree under this directory contains the system startup scripts. The
  Apache RPM installs a startup script named httpd for the web server under the
  /etc/rc.d/init.d directory. This script, which you can use to start and stop
  the server from the command line, also automatically starts and stops the server
  when the computer is halted, started, or rebooted.

- /var/www—The RPM installs the default server icons, Common Gateway Interface
  (CGI) programs, and HTML files in this location. If you want to keep web content
  elsewhere, you can do so by making the appropriate changes in the server configuration files.

- /var/www/ manual/—If you've installed the apache-manual RPM, you'll find a copy of the Apache documentation in HTML format here. You can access it with a web browser by going to http://localhost/manual/.

- /usr/share/man—Fedora's Apache RPM also contains manual pages, which are placed underneath this directory. For example, the httpd man page is in section 8 of the man directory.

- /usr/sbin—The executable programs are placed in this directory. This includes the server executable itself, as well as various utilities.

- /usr/bin—Some of the utilities from the Apache package are placed here—for example, the htpasswd program, which is used for generating authentication password files.

- /var/log/httpd—The server log files are placed in this directory. By default, there are two important log files (among several others): access_log and error_log. However, you can define any number of custom logs containing a variety of information. See the section "Logging," later in this chapter, for more detail.

- /usr/src/redhat/SOURCES/—This directory might contain a tar archive containing the source code for Apache and, in some cases, patches for the source. You must have installed the Apache SRPM for these files to be created.

When Apache is being run, it also creates the file httpd.pid, containing the process ID of Apache's parent process in the /var/run/ directory.

> **NOTE**
>
> If you are upgrading to a newer version of Apache, RPM doesn't write over your current configuration files. RPM moves your current files and appends the extension .rpmnew to them. For example, srm.conf becomes srm.conf.rpmnew.

Building the Source Yourself

There are several ways to obtain the source code for Apache. The Fedora Project provides SRPMs containing the source of Apache, which includes patches to make it work better with the Fedora Core distribution. The most up-to-date, stable binary version for Fedora can be installed via RPM packages using the up2date command or by installing a source RPM from Fedora's source repository (browse to http://fedora.redhat.com and then click the Download link). When you install one of these SRPMs, a tar archive containing the Apache source is created in /usr/src/redhat/SOURCES/.

You can also download the source directly from http://www.apache.org/. The latest version at the time of this writing (2.0.50) is a 6MB compressed tape archive, and the latest pre-2.0 version of Apache is 1.3.31. Although many sites continue to use the older version (for script and other compatibility reasons), many new sites are migrating to or starting out using the latest stable version.

19

After you have the `tar` file, you must unroll it in a temporary directory, such as `/tmp`. Unrolling this `tar` file creates a directory called `apache_version_number`, where `version_number` is the version you've downloaded (for example, `apache_1.3.21`).

There are two ways to compile the source—the old, familiar way (at least, to those of us who have been using Apache for many years) by editing Makefile templates, and the new, easy way using a `configure` script. You'll first see how to build Apache from source the easy way. The `configure` script offers a way to have the source software automatically configured according to your system. However, manually editing the configuration files before building and installing Apache provides more control over where the software is installed and which capabilities or features are built in to Apache.

> **TIP**
>
> As with many software packages distributed in source code form for Linux and other Unix-like operating systems, extracting the source code results in a directory that contains a `README` and an `INSTALL` file. Be sure to peruse the `INSTALL` file before attempting to build and install the software.

Using `./configure` to Build Apache

To build Apache the easy way, run the `./configure` script in the directory just created. You can provide it with a `--prefix` argument to install it in a directory other than the default, which is `/usr/local/apache/`. Use this command:

```
# ./configure --prefix=/preferred/directory/
```

This generates the Makefile that's used to compile the server code.

Next, type **make** to compile the server code. After the compilation is complete, type **make install** as root to install the server. You can now configure the server via the configuration files. See the "Runtime Server Configuration Settings" section for more information.

> **TIP**
>
> A safer way to install a new version of Apache from source is to use the `ln` command to create symbolic links of the existing file locations (listed in the "Installing from the RPM" section earlier in this chapter) to the new locations of the files. This method is safer because the default install locations are different from those used when the RPM installs the files. Failure to use this installation method could result in your web server process not being started automatically at system startup.
>
> Another safe way to install a new version of Apache is to first back up any important configuration directories and files (such as `/etc/httpd`) and then use the `rpm` command to remove the server. You can then install and test your new version and, if needed, easily restore your original server and settings.
>
> It is strongly recommended that you use Fedora's RPM version of Apache until you really know what happens at system startup. No "uninstall" option is available when installing Apache from source!

Apache File Locations After a Build and Install

Files are placed in various subdirectories of /usr/local/apache (or whatever directory you specified with the --prefix parameter) if you build the server from source. Before version 1.3.4, files were placed in /usr/local/etc/httpd.

The following is a list of the directories used by Apache, as well as brief comments on their usage:

- /usr/local/apache/conf—This contains several subdirectories and the Apache configuration file, httpd.conf. See the section "Editing httpd.conf" later in this chapter to learn more about configuration files.

- /usr/local/apache—The cgi-bin, icons, and htdocs subdirectories contain the CGI programs, standard icons, and default HTML documents, respectively.

- /usr/local/apache/bin—The executable programs are placed in this directory.

- /usr/local/apache/logs—The server log files are placed in this directory. By default, there are two log files—access_log and error_log—but you can define any number of custom logs containing a variety of information (see the "Logging" section later in this chapter). The default location for Apache's logs as installed by Fedora is /var/log/httpd.

A Quick Guide to Getting Started with Apache

Setting up, testing a web page, and starting Apache using Fedora can be accomplished in just a few steps. First, make sure that Apache is installed on your system. Either select it during installation or install the server and related RPM files (refer to Chapter 7 if you need to install the server software).

Next, set up a home page for your system by editing (as root) the file named index.html under the /var/http/www/html directory on your system. Make a backup copy of the original page or www directory before you begin so you can restore your web server to its default state if necessary.

Start Apache (again, as root) by using the service command with the keywords httpd and start, like this:

```
# service httpd start
```

You can also use the httpd script under the /etc/rc.d/init.d/ directory, like this:

```
# /etc/rc.d/init.d/httpd start
```

You can then check your home page by running a favorite browser and using localhost, your system's hostname, or its Internet Protocol (IP) address in the URL. For example, with the links text browser, use a command line like this:

```
# links http://localhost/
```

For security reasons, you shouldn't start and run Apache as root if your host is connected to the Internet or a company intranet. Fortunately, Apache is set to run as the user and group apache no matter how it's started (by the User and Group settings in /etc/httpd/httpd.conf). Despite this safe default, Apache should be started and managed by the user named apache, defined in /etc/passwd as

```
apache:x:48:48:Apache:/var/www:/sbin/nologin
```

After you are satisfied with your website, use the setup (select Services) or ntsysv (select httpd) command to ensure that Apache is started properly.

Starting and Stopping Apache

At this point, you have installed your Apache server with its default configuration. Fedora provides a default home page named index.html as a test under the /var/www/html/usage directory. The proper way to run Apache is to set system initialization to have the server run after booting, network configuration, and any firewall configuration. See Chapter 14, "Automating Tasks," for more information about how Fedora boots.

It is time to start it up for the first time. The following sections show how to either start and stop Apache or configure Fedora to start or not start Apache when booting.

Starting the Apache Server Manually

You can start Apache from the command line of a text-based console or X terminal window, and you must have root permission to do so. The server daemon, httpd, recognizes several command-line options you can use to set some defaults, such as specifying where httpd reads its configuration directives. The Apache httpd executable also understands other options that enable you to selectively use parts of its configuration file, specify a different location of the actual server and supporting files, use a different configuration file (perhaps for testing), and save startup errors to a specific log. The -v option causes Apache to print its development version and quit. The -V option shows all the settings that were in effect when the server was compiled.

The -h option prints the following usage information for the server (assuming that you're running the command as root):

```
# httpd -h
Usage: httpd [-D name] [-d directory] [-f file]
             [-C "directive"] [-c "directive"]
             [-k start|restart|graceful|stop]
             [-v] [-V] [-h] [-l] [-L] [-t]
Options:
  -D name            : define a name for use in <IfDefine name> directives
  -d directory       : specify an alternate initial ServerRoot
  -f file            : specify an alternate ServerConfigFile
  -C "directive"     : process directive before reading config files
  -c "directive"     : process directive after reading config files
  -e level           : show startup errors of level (see LogLevel)
  -E file            : log startup errors to file
```

```
  -v                  : show version number
  -V                  : show compile settings
  -h                  : list available command line options (this page)
  -l                  : list compiled in modules
  -L                  : list available configuration directives
  -t -D DUMP_VHOSTS : show parsed settings (currently only vhost settings)
-t                    : run syntax check for config files
```

Other options include listing Apache's *static modules*, or special, built-in independent parts of the server, along with options that can be used with the modules. These options are called *configuration directives* and are commands that control how a static module works. Note that Apache also includes nearly 50 *dynamic modules*, or software portions of the server that can be optionally loaded and used while the server is running.

The -t option is used to check your configuration files. It's a good idea to run this check before restarting your server, especially if you've made changes to your configuration files. Such tests are important because a configuration file error can result in your server shutting down when you try to restart it.

> **NOTE**
>
> When you build and install Apache from source and don't use Fedora's Apache RPM files, start the server manually from the command line as root (such as when testing). You do this for two reasons:
>
> - The standalone server uses the default HTTP port (port 80), and only the superuser can bind to Internet ports that are lower than 1024.
> - Only processes owned by root can change their UID and GID as specified by Apache's User and Group directives. If you start the server under another UID, it runs with the permissions of the user starting the process.
>
> Note that although some of the following examples show how to start the server as root, you should do so only for testing after building and installing Apache. Fedora is set up to run web service as the apache user if you install Apache using Fedora RPM files.

Using /etc/rc.d/init.d/httpd

Fedora uses the scripts in the /etc/rc.d/init.d directory to control the startup and shutdown of various services, including the Apache web server. The main script installed for the Apache web server is /etc/rc.d/init.d/httpd, although the actual work is done by the apachectl shell script included with Apache.

> **NOTE**
>
> /etc/rc.d/init.d/httpd is a shell script and isn't the same as the Apache server located in /usr/sbin. That is, /usr/sbin/httpd is the program executable file (the server); /etc/rc.d/init.d/httpd is a shell script that uses another shell script, apachectl, to control the server. See Chapter 14 for a description of some service scripts under /etc/rc.d/init.d and how the scripts are used to manage services such as httpd.

You can use the /etc/rc.d/init.d/httpd script and the following options to control the web server:

- start—The system uses this option to start the web server during bootup. You, as root, can also use this script to start the server.

- stop—The system uses this option to stop the server gracefully. You should use this script, rather than the kill command, to stop the server.

- reload—You can use this option to send the HUP signal to the httpd server to have it reread the configuration files after modification.

- restart—This option is a convenient way to stop and then immediately start the web server. If the httpd server isn't running, it is started.

- condrestart—The same as the restart parameter, except that it restarts the httpd server only if it's actually running.

- status—This option indicates whether the server is running; if it is, it provides the various PIDs for each instance of the server.

For example, to check on the status of your server, use the command

```
# /etc/rc.d/init.d/httpd status
```

This prints the following for me:

```
httpd (pid 15997 1791 1790 1789 1788 1787 1786 1785 1784 1781) is running...
```

This indicates that the web server is running; in fact, 10 instances of the server are currently running in this configuration.

In addition to the previous options, the httpd script also offers these features:

- help—Prints a list of valid options to the httpd script (which are passed onto the server as if called from the command line).

- configtest—A simple test of the server's configuration, which reports Status OK if the setup is correct. You can also use httpd's -t option to perform the same test, like this:

```
# httpd -t
```

- fullstatus—Displays a verbose status report.

- graceful—The same as the restart parameter, except that the configtest option is used first and open connections are not aborted.

> **TIP**
>
> Use the `reload` option if you're making many changes to the various server configuration files. This saves time when you're stopping and starting the server by having the system simply reread the configuration files.

Controlling Apache with Red Hat's `service` **Command**

Instead of directly calling the `/etc/rc.d/init.d/httpd` script, you can use Red Hat's `service` command to start, stop, and restart Apache. The `service` command is used with the name of a service (listed under `/etc/rc.d/init.d`) and an optional keyword:

```
# service <name_of_script> <option>
```

For example, you can use `service` with `httpd` and any option discussed in the previous section, like so:

```
# service httpd restart
```

This restarts Apache if it's running or starts the server if it isn't running.

Controlling Apache with Red Hat's `chkconfig` **Command**

The `chkconfig` command provides a command-line–based interface to Fedora's service scripts. The command can be used to list and control which software services will be started, restarted, and stopped for a specific system state (such as when booting up, restarting, or shutting down) and runlevel (such as single-user mode, networking with multitasking, or graphical login with X).

For example, to view your system's current settings, take a look at Fedora's default runlevel as defined in the system initialization table `/etc/inittab` using the `grep` command:

```
# grep id: /etc/inittab
id:3:initdefault:
```

This example shows that this Fedora system will boot to a text-based login without running X11. You can then use the `chkconfig` command to look at the behavior of Apache for that runlevel:

```
# chkconfig --list ¦ grep httpd
httpd           0:off   1:off   2:off   3:off   4:off   5:off   6:off
```

Here you can see that Apache is turned off for runlevels 3 and 5 (the only two practical runlevels in a default Fedora system, although you could create a custom runlevel 4 for Apache). Use `--level`, `httpd`, and the control keyword on to set Apache to automatically start when booting to runlevel 3:

```
# chkconfig --level 3 httpd on
```

19

You can then again use chkconfig to verify this setting:

```
# chkconfig --list | grep httpd
httpd           0:off   1:off   2:off   3:on    4:off   5:off   6:off
```

To have Apache also start when your system is booted to a graphical login using X, again use level, httpd, and the control keyword on, but this time, specify runlevel 5 like so:

```
# chkconfig --level 5 httpd on
```

Again, to verify your system settings, use

```
# chkconfig --list | grep httpd
httpd           0:off   1:off   2:off   3:on    4:off   5:on    6:off
```

Use the off keyword to stop Apache from starting at a particular runlevel.

Controlling Apache with Red Hat's system-config-services Client

You can also use a graphical version of the chkconfig command named system-config-services during an X session to set when Apache is started or stopped and at which runlevel. To start system-config-services, select the Services on the Server Settings menu from your desktop panel's System Settings menu, or type the command in a terminal window like so:

```
$ system-config-services &
```

After you press Enter, you're prompted for the root password (because you shouldn't be running X as root).

> **NOTE**
>
> You can also use the ntsysv command to set Apache to start at boot time or start system-config-services using the serviceconf command.

This client is a graphical runlevel editor. To have Apache start when using runlevel 3, first use the Edit Runlevel menu to select runlevel 3 and then scroll through the list of services to find httpd. If you click the httpd check box, as shown in Figure 19.1, and then click the toolbar's Save button, Apache is started at that runlevel the next time the system starts or reboots.

You can also use the Service Configuration client to instantly control a service. Use the Edit Runlevel menu to select the current runlevel in use; highlight httpd; and then click the Start, Stop, or Restart toolbar button.

FIGURE 19.1 Use the `system-config-services` client to set when Apache is started or stopped on your Fedora system.

Runtime Server Configuration Settings

At this point, the Apache server will run, but perhaps you want to change a behavior, such as the default location of your website's files. This section talks about the basics of configuring the server to work the way you want it to work.

Runtime configurations are stored in just one file—`httpd.conf`, which is found under the `/etc/httpd/conf` directory. This configuration file can be used to control the default behavior of Apache, such as the web server's base configuration directory (`/etc/httpd`), the name of the server's process identification (PID) file (`/etc/httpd/run/httpd.pid`), or its response timeout (300 seconds). Apache reads the data from the configuration file when started (or restarted). You can also cause Apache to reload configuration information with the command `/etc/rc.d/init.d/httpd reload`, which is necessary after making changes to its configuration file. (You learned how to accomplish this in the earlier section, "Starting and Stopping Apache.")

Runtime Configuration Directives

You perform runtime configuration of your server with configuration directives, which are commands that set options for the `httpd` daemon. The directives are used to tell the server about various options you want to enable, such as the location of files important to the server configuration and operation. Apache supports nearly 300 configuration directives using the following syntax:

```
directive option option...
```

Each directive is specified on a single line. See the following sections for some sample directives and how to use them. Some directives only set a value such as a filename, whereas others enable you to specify various options. Some special directives, called sections, look like HTML tags. Section directives are surrounded by angle brackets, such as

`<directive>`. Sections usually enclose a group of directives that apply only to the directory specified in the section:

```
<Directory somedir/in/your/tree>
  directive option option
  directive option option
</Directory>
```

All sections are closed with a matching section tag that looks like this: `</directive>`. Note that section tags, like any other directives, are specified one per line.

TIP

After installing and starting Apache, you'll find an index of directives at http://localhost/manual/mod/directives.html.

Editing `httpd.conf`

Most of the default settings in the config file are okay to keep, particularly if you've installed the server in a default location and aren't doing anything unusual on your server. In general, if you don't understand what a particular directive is for, you should leave it set to the default value.

The following sections describe some of the configuration file settings you *might* want to change concerning operation of your server.

ServerRoot

The `ServerRoot` directive sets the absolute path to your server directory. This directive tells the server where to find all the resources and configuration files. Many of these resources are specified in the configuration files relative to the `ServerRoot` directory.

Your `ServerRoot` directive should be set to `/etc/httpd` if you installed the RPM or `/usr/local/apache` (or whatever directory you chose when you compiled Apache) if you installed from the source.

Listen

The `Listen` directive indicates on which port you want your server to run. By default, this is set to 80, which is the standard HTTP port number. You might want to run your server on another port—for example, when running a test server that you don't want people to find by accident. Don't confuse this with real security! See the "File System Authentication and Access Control" section for more information about how to secure parts of your web server.

User **and** Group

The `User` and `Group` directives should be set to the UID and group ID (GID) the server will use to process requests.

In Fedora, set these configurations to a user with few or no privileges. In this case, they're set to user apache and group apache—a user defined specifically to run Apache. If you want to use a different UID or GID, be aware that the server will run with the permissions of the user and group set here. That means in the event of a security breach, whether on the server or (more likely) in your own CGI programs, those programs will run with the assigned UID. If the server runs as root or some other privileged user, someone can exploit the security holes and do nasty things to your site. Always think in terms of the specified user running a command such as rm -rf / because that would wipe all files from your system. That should convince you that leaving apache as a user with no privileges is probably a good thing.

Instead of specifying the User and Group directives using names, you can specify them using the UID and GID numbers. If you use numbers, be sure that the numbers you specify correspond to the user and group you want and that they're preceded by the pound (#) symbol.

Here's how these directives look if specified by name:

```
User apache
Group apache
```

Here's the same specification by UID and GID:

```
User #48
Group #48
```

> **TIP**
>
> If you find a user on your system (other than root) with a UID and GID of 0, your system has been compromised by a malicious user.

ServerAdmin
The ServerAdmin directive should be set to the address of the webmaster managing the server. This address should be a valid email address or alias, such as webmaster@gnulix.org, because this address is returned to a visitor when a problem occurs on the server.

ServerName
The ServerName directive sets the hostname the server will return. Set it to a fully qualified domain name (FQDN). For example, set it to www.your.domain rather than simply www. This is particularly important if this machine will be accessible from the Internet rather than just on your local network.

You don't need to set this unless you want a name other than the machine's canonical name returned. If this value isn't set, the server will figure out the name by itself and set it to its canonical name. However, you might want the server to return a friendlier address, such as www.your.domain. Whatever you do, ServerName should be a real domain name service (DNS) name for your network. If you're administering your own DNS, remember to add an alias for your host. If someone else manages the DNS for you, ask that person to set this name for you.

DocumentRoot

Set this directive to the absolute path of your document tree, which is the top directory from which Apache will serve files. By default, it's set to /var/www/html/usage. If you built the source code yourself, DocumentRoot is set to /usr/local/apache/htdocs (if you didn't choose another directory when you compiled Apache). Prior to version 1.3.4, this directive appears in srm.conf.

UserDir

The UserDir directive disables or enables and defines the directory (relative to a local user's home directory) where that user can put public HTML documents. It's relative because each user has her own HTML directory. This setting is disabled by default but can be enabled to store user web content under any directory.

The default setting for this directive, if enabled, is public_html. Each user can create a directory called public_html under her home directory, and HTML documents placed in that directory are available as http://servername/~username, where *username* is the user-name of the particular user. Prior to version Apache version 1.3.4, this directive appears in srm.conf.

DirectoryIndex

The DirectoryIndex directive indicates which file should be served as the index for a directory, such as which file should be served if the URL http://servername/_SomeDirectory/ is requested.

It's often useful to put a list of files here so that if index.html (the default value) isn't found, another file can be served instead. The most useful application of this is to have a CGI program run as the default action in a directory. If you have users who make their web pages on Windows, you might want to add index.htm as well. In that case, the directive would look like DirectoryIndex index.html index.cgi index.htm. Prior to version 1.3.4, this directive appears in srm.conf.

Apache Multiprocessing Modules

Apache version 2.0 and greater now uses a new internal architecture supporting multiprocessing modules (MPMs). These modules are used by the server for a variety of tasks, such as network and process management, and are compiled into Apache. MPMs enable Apache to work much better on a wider variety of computer platforms, and they can help improve server stability, compatibility, and scalability.

Apache can use only one MPM at any time. These modules are different from the base set included with Apache (see the "Apache Modules" section later in this chapter) but are used to implement settings, limits, or other server actions. Each module in turn supports numerous additional settings, called *directives*, which further refine server operation.

The internal MPM modules relevant for Linux include

- `mpm_common`—A set of 20 directives common to all MPM modules

- `prefork`—A nonthreaded, preforking web server that works similar to earlier (1.3) versions of Apache

- `worker`—Provides a hybrid multiprocess multithreaded server

MPM enables Apache to be used on equipment with fewer resources yet still handle massive numbers of hits and provide stable service. The `worker` module provides directives to control how many simultaneous connections your server can handle.

> **NOTE**
>
> Other MPMs are available for Apache related to other platforms, such as `mpm_netware` for NetWare hosts and `mpm_winnt` for NT platforms. An MPM named `perchild`, which provides user ID assignment to selected daemon processes, is under development. For more information, browse to the Apache Software Foundation's home page at http://www.apache.org.

Using `.htaccess` Configuration Files

Apache also supports special configuration files, known as `.htaccess` files. Almost any directive that appears in `httpd.conf` can appear in a `.htaccess` file. This file, specified in the `AccessFileName` directive in `httpd.conf` (or `srm.conf` prior to version 1.3.4) sets configurations on a per-directory (usually in a user directory) basis. As the system administrator, you can specify both the name of this file and which of the server configurations can be overridden by the contents of this file. This is especially useful for sites in which there are multiple content providers and you want to control what these people can do with their space.

To limit which server configurations the `.htaccess` files can override, use the `AllowOverride` directive. `AllowOverride` can be set globally or per directory. For example, in your `httpd.conf` file, you could use the following:

```
# Each directory to which Apache has access can be configured with respect
# to which services and features are allowed and/or disabled in that
# directory (and its subdirectories).
#
# First, we configure the "default" to be a very restrictive set of
# permissions.
#
<Directory />
    Options FollowSymLinks
    AllowOverride None
</Directory>
```

Options **Directives**

To configure which configuration options are available to Apache by default, you must use the Options directive. Options can be None; All; or any combination of Indexes, Includes, FollowSymLinks, ExecCGI, and MultiViews. MultiViews isn't included in All and must be specified explicitly. These options are explained in Table 19.2.

TABLE 19.2   Switches Used by the Options Directive

Switch	Description
None	None of the available options are enabled for this directory.
All	All the available options, except for MultiViews, are enabled for this directory.
Indexes	In the absence of an index.html file or another DirectoryIndex file, a listing of the files in the directory is generated as an HTML page for display to the user.
Includes	Server-side includes (SSIs) are permitted in this directory. This can also be written as IncludesNoExec if you want to allow includes but don't want to allow the exec option in them. For security reasons, this is usually a good idea in directories over which you don't have complete control, such as UserDir directories.
FollowSymLinks	Allows access to directories that are symbolically linked to a document directory. You should never set this globally for the whole server and only rarely for individual directories. This option is a potential security risk because it allows web users to escape from the document directory and could potentially allow them access to portions of your file system where you really don't want people poking around.
ExecCGI	CGI programs are permitted in this directory, even if it isn't a directory defined in the ScriptAlias directive.
MultiViews	This is part of the mod_negotiation module. When a client requests a document that can't be found, the server tries to figure out which document best suits the client's requirements. See http://localhost/manuals/mod/_mod_negotiation.html for your local copy of the Apache documentation.

> **NOTE**
>
> These directives also affect all subdirectories of the specified directory.

AllowOverrides **Directives**

The AllowOverrides directives specify which configuration options .htaccess files can override. You can set this directive individually for each directory. For example, you can have different standards about what can be overridden in the main document root and in UserDir directories.

This capability is particularly useful for user directories, where the user doesn't have access to the main server configuration files.

AllowOverrides can be set to All or any combination of Options, FileInfo, AuthConfig, and Limit. These options are explained in Table 19.3.

TABLE 19.3   Switches Used by the `AllowOverrides` Directive

Switch	Description
`Options`	The `.htaccess` file can add options not listed in the `Options` directive for this directory.
`FileInfo`	The `.htaccess` file can include directives for modifying document type information.
`AuthConfig`	The `.htaccess` file might contain authorization directives.
`Limit`	The `.htaccess` file might contain `allow`, `deny`, and `order` directives.

File System Authentication and Access Control

You're likely to include material on your website that isn't supposed to be available to the public. You must be able to lock out this material from public access and provide designated users with the means to unlock the material. Apache provides two methods for accomplishing this type of access: authentication and authorization. You can use different criteria to control access to sections of your website, including checking the client's IP address or hostname, or requiring a username and password. This section briefly covers some of these methods.

> **CAUTION**
>
> Allowing individual users to put web content on your server poses several important security risks. If you're operating a web server on the Internet rather than on a private network, you should read the WWW Security FAQ at http://www.w3.org/Security/Faq/www-security-faq.html.

Restricting Access with `allow` and `deny`

One of the simplest ways to limit access to website material is to restrict access to a specific group of users, based on IP addresses or hostnames. Apache uses the `allow` and `deny` directives to accomplish this.

Both directives take an address expression as a parameter. The following list provides the possible values and use of the address expression:

- `all` can be used to affect all hosts.

- A hostname or domain name, which can either be a partially or a fully qualified domain name; for example, `test.gnulix.org` or `gnulix.org`.

- An IP address, which can be either full or partial; for example, `212.85.67` or `212.85.67.66`.

- A network/netmask pair, such as `212.85.67.0/255.255.255.0`.

- A network address specified in classless inter-domain routing (CIDR) format; for example, `212.85.67.0/24`. This is the CIDR notation for the same network and netmask that were used in the previous example.

If you have the choice, it's preferable to base your access control on IP addresses rather than hostnames. Doing so results in faster performance because no name lookup is necessary—the IP address of the client is included with each request.

You also can use `allow` and `deny` to provide or deny access to website material based on the presence or absence of a specific environment variable. For example, the following statement denies access to a request with a context that contains an environment variable named NOACCESS:

```
deny from env=NOACCESS
```

The default behavior of Apache is to apply all the `deny` directives first and then check the `allow` directives. If you want to change this order, you can use the `order` statement. Apache might interpret this statement in three different ways:

- `Order deny,allow`—The deny directives are evaluated before the `allow` directives. If a host isn't specifically denied access, it is allowed to access the resource. This is the default ordering if nothing else is specified.

- `Order allow,deny`—All `allow` directives are evaluated before deny directives. If a host isn't specifically allowed access, it is denied access to the resource.

- `Order mutual-failure`—Only hosts that are specified in an `allow` directive and at the same time do not appear in a deny directive are allowed access. If a host doesn't appear in either directive, it is not granted access.

Consider this example. Suppose you want to allow only persons from within your own domain to access the `server-status` resource on your web. If your domain were named gnulix.org, you could add these lines to your configuration file:

```
<Location /server-status>
    SetHandler server-status
    Order deny,allow
    Deny from all
    Allow from gnulix.org
</Location>
```

Authentication

Authentication is the process of ensuring that visitors really are who they claim to be. You can configure Apache to allow access to specific areas of web content only to clients who can authenticate their identity. There are several methods of authentication in Apache; Basic Authentication is the most common (and the method discussed in this chapter).

Under Basic Authentication, Apache requires a user to supply a username and a password to access the protected resources. Apache then verifies that the user is allowed to access the resource in question. If the username is acceptable, Apache verifies the password. If the password also checks out, the user is authorized and Apache serves the request.

HTTP is a stateless protocol; each request sent to the server and each response is handled individually, and not in an intelligent fashion. Therefore, the authentication information must be included with each request. That means each request to a password-protected area is larger and therefore somewhat slower. To avoid unnecessary system use and delays, protect only those areas of your website that absolutely need protection.

To use Basic Authentication, you need a file that lists which users are allowed to access the resources. This file is composed of a plain text list containing name and password pairs. It looks very much like the /etc/passwd user file of your Linux system.

CAUTION

Don't use /etc/passwd as a user list for authentication. When you're using Basic Authentication, passwords and usernames are sent as base64-encoded text from the client to the server—which is just as readable as plain text. The username and password are included in each request that is sent to the server. So, anyone who might be snooping on Net traffic would be able to get this information!

To create a user file for Apache, use the htpasswd command. This is included with the Apache package. If you installed using the RPMs, it's in /usr/bin. Running htpasswd without any options produces the following output:

```
Usage:
        htpasswd [-cmdps] passwordfile username
        htpasswd -b[cmdps] passwordfile username password

        htpasswd -n[mdps] username
        htpasswd -nb[mdps] username password
 -c  Create a new file.
 -n  Don't update file; display results on stdout.
 -m  Force MD5 encryption of the password.
 -d  Force CRYPT encryption of the password (default).
 -p  Do not encrypt the password (plaintext).
 -s  Force SHA encryption of the password.
 -b  Use the password from the command line rather than prompting for it.
 -D  Delete the specified user.
On Windows, TPF and NetWare systems the '-m' flag is used by default.
On all other systems, the '-p' flag will probably not work.
```

As you can see, it isn't a very difficult command to use. For example, to create a new user file named gnulixusers with a user named wsb, you need do something like this:

```
# htpasswd -c gnulixusers wsb
```

You would then be prompted for a password for the user. To add more users, you would repeat the same procedure, only omitting the -c flag.

19

You can also create user group files. The format of these files is similar to that of /etc/groups. On each line, enter the group name, followed by a colon, and then list all users, with each user separated by spaces. For example, an entry in a user group file might look like this:

```
gnulixusers: wsb pgj jp ajje nadia rkr hak
```

Now that you know how to create a user file, it's time to look at how Apache might use this to protect web resources.

To point Apache to the user file, use the AuthUserFile directive. AuthUserFile takes the file path to the user file as its parameter. If the file path isn't absolute—that is, beginning with a /—it's assumed that the path is relative to the ServerRoot. Using the AuthGroupFile directive, you can specify a group file in the same manner.

Next, use the AuthType directive to set the type of authentication to be used for this resource. Here, the type is set to Basic.

Now you need to decide to which realm the resource will belong. Realms are used to group different resources that will share the same users for authorization. A realm can consist of just about any string. The realm is shown in the Authentication dialog box on the user's web browser. Therefore, you should set the realm string to something informative. The realm is defined with the AuthName directive.

Finally, state which type of user is authorized to use the resource. You do this with the require directive. The three ways to use this directive are as follows:

- If you specify valid-user as an option, any user in the user file is allowed to access the resource (that is, provided she also enters the correct password).

- You can specify a list of users who are allowed access with the users option.

- You can specify a list of groups with the group option. Entries in the group list, as well as the user list, are separated by a space.

Returning to the server-status example you saw earlier, instead of letting users access the server-status resource based on hostname, you can require the users to be authenticated to access the resource. You can do so with the following entry in the configuration file:

```
<Location /server-status>
    SetHandler server-status
    AuthType Basic
    AuthName "Server status"
    AuthUserFile "gnulixusers"
    Require valid-user
</Location>
```

Final Words on Access Control

If you have host-based as well as user-based access protection on a resource, the default behavior of Apache is to require the requester to satisfy both controls. But assume that you want to mix host-based and user-based protection and allow access to a resource if either method succeeds. You can do so using the `satisfy` directive. You can set the `satisfy` directive to `All` (this is the default) or `Any`. When set to `All`, all access control methods must be satisfied before the resource is served. If `satisfy` is set to `Any`, the resource is served if any access condition is met.

Here's another access control example, again using the previous `server-status` example. This time, you combine access methods so all users from the `Gnulix` domain are allowed access and those from outside the domain must identify themselves before gaining access. You can do so with the following:

```
<Location /server-status>
    SetHandler server-status
    Order deny,allow
    Deny from all
    Allow from gnulix.org
    AuthType Basic
    AuthName "Server status"
    AuthUserFile "gnulixusers"
    Require valid-user
    Satisfy Any
</Location>
```

There are more ways to protect material on your web server, but the methods discussed here should get you started and will probably be more than adequate for most circumstances. Look to Apache's online documentation for more examples of how to secure areas of your site.

Apache Modules

The Apache core does relatively little; Apache gains its functionality from modules. Each module solves a well-defined problem by adding necessary features. By adding or removing modules to supply the functionality you want Apache to have, you can tailor Apache server to suit your exact needs.

Nearly 50 core modules are included with the basic Apache server. Many more are available from other developers. The Apache Module Registry is a repository for add-on modules for Apache, and it can be found at http://modules.apache.org/. The modules are listed in the `modules` directory under `/etc/httpd/`, but this directory is a link to the `/usr/lib/httpd/modules` directory where the modules reside (your list might look different):

mod_access.so	mod_cern_meta.so	mod_log_config.so	mod_setenvif.so
mod_actions.so	mod_cgi.so	mod_mime_magic.so	mod_speling.so
mod_alias.so	mod_dav_fs.so	mod_mime.so	mod_ssl.so

mod_asis.so	mod_dav.so	mod_negotiation.so	mod_status.so
mod_auth_anon.so	mod_dir.so	mod_perl.so	mod_suexec.so
mod_auth_dbm.so	mod_env.so	mod_proxy_connect.so	mod_unique_id.so
mod_auth_digest.so	mod_expires.so	mod_proxy_ftp.so	mod_userdir.so
mod_auth_mysql.so	mod_headers.so	mod_proxy_http.so	mod_usertrack.so
mod_auth_pgsql.so	mod_imap.so	mod_proxy.so	mod_vhost_alias.so
mod_auth.so	mod_include.so	mod_python.so	mod_autoindex.so
mod_info.so	mod_rewrite.so		

Each module adds new directives that can be used in your configuration files. As you might guess, there are far too many extra commands, switches, and options to describe them all in this chapter. The following sections briefly describe a subset of those modules available with Fedora's Apache installation.

mod_access

mod_access controls access to areas on your web server based on IP addresses, hostnames, or environment variables. For example, you might want to allow anyone from within your own domain to access certain areas of your web. Refer to the "File System Authentication and Access Control" section for more information.

mod_alias

mod_alias manipulates the URLs of incoming HTTP requests, such as redirecting a client request to another URL. It also can map a part of the file system into your web hierarchy. For example,

```
Alias /images/ /home/wsb/graphics/
```

fetches contents from the /home/wsb/graphics directory for any URL that starts with /images/. This is done without the client knowing anything about it. If you use a redirection, the client is instructed to go to another URL to find the requested content. More advanced URL manipulation can be accomplished with mod_rewrite.

mod_asis

mod_asis is used to specify, in fine detail, all the information to be included in a response. This completely bypasses any headers Apache might have otherwise added to the response. All files with an .asis extension are sent straight to the client without any changes.

As a short example of the use of mod_asis, assume you've moved content from one location to another on your site. Now you must inform people who try to access this resource that it has moved, as well as automatically redirect them to the new location. To provide this information and redirection, you can add the following code to a file with a .asis extension:

```
Status: 301 No more old stuff!
Location: http://gnulix.org/newstuff/
Content-type: text/html

<HTML>
 <HEAD>
  <TITLE>We've moved...</TITLE>
 </HEAD>
 <BODY>
   <P>We've moved the old stuff and now you'll find it at:</P>
   <A HREF="http://gnulix.org/newstuff/">New stuff</A>!.
 </BODY>
</HTML>
```

mod_auth

mod_auth uses a simple user authentication scheme, referred to as Basic Authentication, which is based on storing usernames and encrypted passwords in a text file. This file looks very much like Unix's /etc/passwd file and is created with the htpasswd command. Refer to the "File System Authentication and Access Control" section earlier in this chapter for more information about this subject.

mod_auth_anon

The mod_auth_anon module provides anonymous authentication similar to that of anonymous FTP. The module enables you to define user IDs of those who are to be handled as guest users. When such a user tries to log on, he is prompted to enter his email address as his password. You can have Apache check the password to ensure that it's a (more or less) proper email address. Basically, it ensures that the password contains an @ character and at least one . character.

mod_auth_dbm

mod_auth_dbm uses Berkeley DB files instead of text for user authentication files.

mod_auth_digest

An extension of the basic mod_auth module, instead of sending the user information in plain text, mod_auth_digest is sent via the MD5 Digest Authentication process. This authentication scheme is defined in RFC 2617. Compared to using Basic Authentication, this is a much more secure way of sending user data over the Internet. Unfortunately, not all web browsers support this authentication scheme.

To create password files for use with mod_auth_dbm, you must use the htdigest utility. It has more or less the same functionality as the htpasswd utility. See the man page of htdigest for further information.

19

mod_autoindex

The mod_autoindex module dynamically creates a file list for directory indexing. The list is rendered in a user-friendly manner similar to those lists provided by FTP's built-in ls command.

mod_cgi

mod_cgi allows execution of CGI programs on your server. CGI programs are executable files residing in the /var/www/cgi-bin directory and are used to dynamically generate data (usually HTML) for the remote browser when requested.

mod_dir and mod_env

The mod_dir module is used to determine which files are returned automatically when a user tries to access a directory. The default is index.html. If you have users who create web pages on Windows systems, you should also include index.htm, like this:

```
DirectoryIndex index.html index.htm
```

mod_env controls how environment variables are passed to CGI and SSI scripts.

mod_expires

mod_expires is used to add an expiration date to content on your site by adding an Expires header to the HTTP response. Web browsers or cache servers won't cache expired content.

mod_headers

mod_headers is used to manipulate the HTTP headers of your server's responses. You can replace, add, merge, or delete headers as you see fit. The module supplies a Header directive for this. Ordering of the Header directive is important. A set followed by an unset for the same HTTP header removes the header altogether. You can place Header directives almost anywhere within your configuration files. These directives are processed in the following order:

1. Core server

2. Virtual host

3. <Directory> and .htaccess files

4. <Location>

5. <Files>

mod_imap

The mod_imap module provides for server-side handling of imagemap files. Clickable regions are defined in a .map file. Six directives are available for use in the .map file. The directives are used to describe the layout of the clickable regions as well as the URLs to which they lead.

mod_include

mod_include enables the use of server-side includes on your server. See the "Dynamic Content" section later in the chapter for more information about how to use SSI.

mod_info and mod_log_config

mod_info provides comprehensive information about your server's configuration. For example, it displays all the installed modules, as well as all the directives used in its configuration files.

mod_log_config defines how your log files should look. See the "Logging" section for further information about this subject.

mod_mime and mod_mime_magic

The mod_mime module tries to determine the MIME type of files from their extensions.

The mod_mime_magic module tries to determine the MIME type of files by examining portions of their content.

mod_negotiation

Using the mod_negotiation module, you can select one of several document versions that best suits the client's capabilities. There are several options to select which criteria to use in the negotiation process. You can, for example, choose among different languages, graphics file formats, and compression methods.

mod_proxy

mod_proxy implements proxy and caching capabilities for an Apache server. It can proxy and cache FTP, CONNECT, HTTP/0.9, and HTTP/1.0 requests. This isn't an ideal solution for sites that have a large number of users and therefore have high proxy and cache requirements. However, it's more than adequate for a small number of users.

mod_rewrite

mod_rewrite is the Swiss army knife of URL manipulation. It enables you to perform any imaginable manipulation of URLs using powerful regular expressions. It provides rewrites, redirection, proxying, and so on. There's very little that you can't accomplish using this module.

> **TIP**
>
> See http://localhost/manual/misc/rewriteguide.html for a cookbook that gives you an in-depth explanation of what the .mod_rewrite module is capable of.

mod_setenvif

mod_setenvif allows manipulation of environment variables. Using small snippets of text-matching code known as *regular expressions*, you can conditionally change the content of environment variables. The order in which SetEnvIf directives appear in the configuration files is important. Each SetEnvIf directive can reset an earlier SetEnvIf directive when used on the same environment variable. Be sure to keep that in mind when using the directives from this module.

mod_speling

mod_speling is used to enable correction of minor typos in URLs. If no file matches the requested URL, this module builds a list of the files in the requested directory and extracts those files that are the closest matches. It tries to correct only one spelling mistake.

mod_status

You can use mod_status to create a web page containing a plethora of information about a running Apache server. The page contains information about the internal status as well as statistics about the running Apache processes. This can be a great aid when you're trying to configure your server for maximum performance. It's also a good indicator of when something's amiss with your Apache server.

mod_ssl

mod_ssl provides Secure Sockets Layer (version 2 and 3) and transport layer security (version 1) support for Apache. At least 30 directives exist that deal with options for encryption and client authorization and that can be used with this module.

mod_unique_id

mod_unique_id generates a unique request identifier for every incoming request. This ID is put into the UNIQUE_ID environment variable.

mod_userdir

The mod_userdir module enables mapping of a subdirectory in each user's home directory into your web tree. The module provides several ways to accomplish this.

mod_usertrack

mod_usertrack is used to generate a cookie for each user session. This can be used to track the user's click stream within your web tree. You must enable a custom log that logs this cookie into a log file.

mod_vhost_alias

mod_vhost_alias supports dynamically configured mass virtual hosting, which is useful for Internet service providers (ISPs) with many virtual hosts. However, for the average user, Apache's ordinary virtual hosting support should be more than sufficient.

There are two ways to host virtual hosts on an Apache server. You can have one IP address with multiple CNAMEs, or you can have multiple IP addresses with one name per address. Apache has different sets of directives to handle each of these options. (You learn more about virtual hosting in Apache in the next section of this chapter.)

Again, the available options and features for Apache modules are too numerous to describe completely in this chapter. You can find complete information about the Apache modules in the online documentation for the server included with Fedora or at the Apache Group's website.

Virtual Hosting

One of the more popular services to provide with a web server is to host a virtual domain. Also known as a *virtual host*, a virtual domain is a complete website with its own domain name, as if it were a standalone machine, but it's hosted on the same machine as other websites. Apache implements this capability in a simple way with directives in the httpd.conf configuration file.

Apache now can dynamically host virtual servers by using the mod_vhost_alias module you read about in the preceding section of the chapter. The module is primarily intended for ISPs and similar large sites that host a large number of virtual sites. This module is for more advanced users and, as such, it is outside the scope of this introductory chapter. Instead, this section concentrates on the traditional ways of hosting virtual servers.

Address-Based Virtual Hosts

After you've configured your Linux machine with multiple IP addresses, setting up Apache to serve them as different websites is simple. You need only put a VirtualHost directive in your httpd.conf file for each of the addresses you want to make an independent website:

```
<VirtualHost 212.85.67.67>
ServerName gnulix.org
DocumentRoot /home/virtual/gnulix/public_html
TransferLog /home/virtual/gnulix/logs/access_log
ErrorLog /home/virtual/gnulix/logs/error_log
</VirtualHost>
```

Use the IP address, rather than the hostname, in the VirtualHost tag.

You can specify any configuration directives within the <VirtualHost> tags. For example, you might want to set AllowOverrides directives differently for virtual hosts than you do for your main server. Any directives that aren't specified default to the settings for the main server.

Name-Based Virtual Hosts

Name-based virtual hosts enable you to run more than one host on the same IP address. You must add the names to your DNS as CNAMEs of the machine in question. When an

HTTP client (web browser) requests a document from your server, it sends with the request a variable indicating the server name from which it's requesting the document. Based on this variable, the server determines from which of the virtual hosts it should serve content.

> **NOTE**
>
> Some older browsers are unable to see name-based virtual hosts because this is a feature of HTTP 1.1 and the older browsers are strictly HTTP 1.0–compliant. However, many other older browsers are partially HTTP 1.1–compliant, and this is one of the parts of HTTP 1.1 that most browsers have supported for a while.

Name-based virtual hosts require just one step more than IP address-based virtual hosts. You must first indicate which IP address has the multiple DNS names on it. This is done with the `NameVirtualHost` directive:

```
NameVirtualHost 212.85.67.67
```

You must then have a section for each name on that address, setting the configuration for that name. As with IP-based virtual hosts, you need to set only those configurations that must be different for the host. You must set the `ServerName` directive because it's the only thing that distinguishes one host from another:

```
<VirtualHost 212.85.67.67>
ServerName bugserver.gnulix.org
ServerAlias bugserver
DocumentRoot /home/bugserver/htdocs
ScriptAlias /home/bugserver/cgi-bin
TransferLog /home/bugserver/logs/access_log
</VirtualHost>

<VirtualHost 212.85.67.67>
ServerName pts.gnulix.org
ServerAlias pts
DocumentRoot /home/pts/htdocs
ScriptAlias /home/pts/cgi-bin
TransferLog /home/pts/logs/access_log
ErrorLog /home/pts/logs/error_log
</VirtualHost>
```

> **TIP**
>
> If you're hosting websites on an intranet or internal network, users will likely use the shortened name of the machine rather than the FQDN. For example, users might type http://bugserver/index.html in their browser location field rather than http://bugserver.gnulix.org/index.html. In that case, Apache would not recognize that those two addresses should go to the same virtual host. You could get around this by setting up `VirtualHost` directives for both bugserver and

bugserver.gnulix.org, but the easy way around it is to use the `ServerAlias` directive, which lists all valid aliases for the machine:

```
ServerAlias bugserver
```

For more information about `VirtualHost`, refer to the help system on http://localhost/_manual.

Logging

Apache provides for logging just about any web access information you might be interested in. Logging can help with

- System resource management, by tracking usage
- Intrusion detection, by documenting bad HTTP requests
- Diagnostics, by recording errors in processing requests

Two standard log files are generated when you run your Apache server: `access_log` and `error_log`. They are found under the `/var/log/httpd` directory. (Others include the SSL logs `ssl_access_log`, `ssl_error_log`, and `ssl_request_log`.) All logs except for the `error_log` (by default, this is just the `access_log`) are generated in a format specified by the `CustomLog` and `LogFormat` directives. These directives appear in your `httpd.conf` file.

A new log format can be defined with the `LogFormat` directive:

```
LogFormat "%h %l %u %t \"%r\" %>s %b" common
```

The `common` log format is a good starting place for creating your own custom log formats. Note that most of the available log analysis tools assume you're using the `common` log format or the `combined` log format—both of which are defined in the default configuration files.

The following variables are available for `LogFormat` statements:

%a	Remote IP address.
%A	Local IP address.
%b	Bytes sent, excluding HTTP headers. This is shown in Apache's Combined Log Format (CLF). For a request without any data content, a - is shown instead of 0.
%B	Bytes sent, excluding HTTP headers.
%{VARIABLE}e	The contents of the environment variable VARIABLE.
%f	The filename of the output log.
%h	Remote host.
%H	Request protocol.

19

%{HEADER}i	The contents of HEADER; header line(s) in the request sent to the server.
%l	Remote log name (from identd, if supplied).
%m	Request method.
%{NOTE}n	The contents of note NOTE from another module.
%{HEADER}o	The contents of HEADER; header line(s) in the reply.
%p	The canonical port of the server serving the request.
%P	The process ID of the child that serviced the request.
%q	The contents of the query string, prepended with a ? character. If there's no query string, this evaluates to an empty string.
%r	The first line of request.
%s	Status. For requests that were internally redirected, this is the status of the original request—%>s for the last.
%t	The time, in common log time format.
%{format}t	The time, in the form given by format, which should be in strftime(3) format. See the section "Basic SSI Directives" later in this chapter for a complete list of available formatting options.
%T	The seconds taken to serve the request.
%u	Remote user from auth; this might be bogus if the return status (%s) is 401.
%U	The URL path requested.
%V	The server name according to the UseCanonicalName directive.
%v	The canonical ServerName of the server serving the request.

You can put a conditional in front of each variable to determine whether the variable is displayed. If the variable isn't displayed, - is displayed instead. These conditionals are in the form of a list of numerical return values. For example, %!401u displays the value of REMOTE_USER unless the return code is 401.

You can then specify the location and format of a log file using the CustomLog directive:

```
CustomLog logs/access_log common
```

If it isn't specified as an absolute path, the location of the log file is assumed to be relative to the ServerRoot.

Dynamic Content

The most common way to provide dynamic content on websites is with CGI programs. CGI is a specification of communication between server processes (such as programs that generate dynamic documents) and the server itself. SSIs allow output from CGI programs, or other programs, to be inserted into existing HTML pages.

Another way to add dynamic content to your website is to use PHP (PHP Hypertext Preprocessor [the name is recursive]). PHP is an HTML-embedded scripting language designed specifically for web usage. The PHP module for Apache is one of the most popular third-party modules available.

CGI

By default, you can put any CGI program on your server in the directory defined by the ScriptAlias directive.

CGI programs can be written in any language. The most popular languages for CGI programming are Perl and C. Chapter 29, "Using Perl," provides more information about using the Perl scripting language.

These programs must be executable by the default Apache user, which means you must change the mode of the files to 555 so the Apache user can execute them. By default, Apache runs in Fedora as a user named apache:

```
chmod 555 program.cgi
```

To execute CGI programs outside the ScriptAlias directory., you must enable the ExecCGI option for that directory. This is done either in your httpd.conf file or in an .htaccess file in the directory.

To test whether you have CGI configured correctly, try the CGI program in Listing 19.1. This program is written in Perl and displays the values of the HTTP environment variables.

LISTING 19.1 environment.pl

```
#!/usr/bin/perl -w

print <<EOF;
"Content-type: text/html"

<HTML>
 <HEAD>
  <TITLE>Simple CGI program</TITLE>
 </HEAD>
 <BODY>
EOF
for (keys %ENV)    {
    print "  $_ = $ENV{$_}<BR>\n";
}
print <<EOF;
 </BODY>
</HTML>
EOF
```

If you're going to write CGI programs in Perl, take some time to study the CGI modules that come bundled with Perl. An extensive Perl module library, which contains many modules designed to be used when writing CGIs, is accessible at http://www.cpan.org.

If you are using many CGIs written in Perl, examine the mod_perl module. It embeds a Perl interpreter within the Apache server. Using this module results in faster execution times for your CGIs because you don't need to start a new Perl interpreter for each request. You'll find information about using mod_perl under the /usr/share/ doc/_mod_perl-1.99_12/docs/ directory if you install it from this book's CD-ROMs.

> **NOTE**
>
> Always check for security updates and bug fixes if you use CGIs developed by other users or outside developers. Poorly updated and improperly implemented or written CGIs can pose significant security threats in your system.

SSI

Server-side includes are directives written directly into an HTML page, which the server parses when the page is served to the web client. SSIs can be used to include other files, the output from programs, or environment variables.

You can enable SSI with the XBitHack directive. XBitHack can be set to a value of on or off and can be set in either your configuration file or .htaccess files. If the XBitHack directive is on, it indicates that all files with the user execute bit set should be parsed for SSI directives. This has two main advantages. One is that you don't need to rename a file and change all links to that file simply because you want to add a little dynamic content to it. The other reason is more cosmetic: Users looking at your web content can't tell by looking at the filename that you're generating a page dynamically, so your wizardry is just a tiny bit more impressive.

Another positive side effect of using XBitHack is that it enables you to control how clients should cache your page. Pages containing SSI statements do not usually contain a Last-modified HTTP header. Therefore, they won't be cached by proxies or web browsers. If you enable XBitHack, the group-execute bit for files control whether a Last-modified header should be generated. It is set to the same value as the last modified time of the file. Be sure to use this only on files that really are supposed to be cached.

Another way to enable SSI is to indicate that files with a certain filename extension (typically .shtml) are to be parsed by the server when they're served. This is accomplished with the following lines in your httpd.conf file:

```
# To use server-parsed HTML files
#
#AddType text/html .shtml
#AddHandler server-parsed .shtml
```

If you uncomment the AddType and AddHandler lines, you tell the server to parse all .shtml files for SSI directives.

In addition to these directives, the following directive must be specified for directories in which you want to permit SSI:

```
Options Includes
```

This can be set in the server configuration file or in a .htaccess file.

Basic SSI Directives

SSI directives look rather like HTML comment tags. The syntax is as follows:

```
<!--#element attribute=value attribute=value ... -->
```

The element can be one of several directives, including

- config
- echo
- exec
- fsize
- flastmod
- include
- printenv
- set

The following sections describe each of these directives and their uses.

config

The config directive enables you to set various configuration options to determine how the document parsing is handled. Because the page is parsed from top to bottom, config directives should appear at the top of the HTML document. Three configurations can be set with this command:

- errmsg—Sets the error message that's returned to the client if something goes wrong while parsing the document. The default message is [an error occurred while processing this directive], but you can set the message to any text with this directive. For example,

  ```
  <!--#config errmsg="[It's broken, dude]" -->
  ```

- `sizefmt`—Sets the format used to display file sizes. You can set the value to `bytes` to display the exact file size in bytes or set it to `abbrev` to display the size in KB or MB. For example,

  `<!--#config sizefmt="bytes" -->`

- `timefmtU`—Sets the format used to display times. The format of the value is the same as that of the `strftime` function used by C (and Perl) to display dates, as shown in the following list:

  - `%%`—PERCENT

  - `%a`—Day of the week abbreviation

  - `%A`—Day of the week

  - `%b`—Month abbreviation

  - `%B`—Month

  - `%c`—ctime format: `Sat Nov 19 21:05:57 1994`

  - `%d`—Numeric day of the month

  - `%e`—DD

  - `%D`—MM/DD/YY

  - `%h`—Month abbreviation

  - `%H`—Hour, 24-hour clock, leading zeroes

  - `%I`—Hour, 12-hour clock, leading zeroes

  - `%j`—Day of the year

  - `%k`—Hour

  - `%l`—Hour, 12-hour clock

  - `%m`—Month number, starting with 1

  - `%M`—Minute, leading zeroes

  - `%n`—NEWLINE

  - `%o`—Ordinal day of month—1st, 2nd, 25th, and so on

  - `%p`—AM or PM

  - `%r`—Time format: `09:05:57 PM`

  - `%R`—Time format: `21:05`

  - `%S`—Seconds, leading zeroes

  - `%t`—Tab

- %T—Time format: `21:05:57`

- %U—Week number; Sunday as first day of week

- %w—Day of the week, numerically; Sunday = 0

- %W—Week number; Monday as first day of week

- %x—Date format: `11/19/94`

- %X—Time format: `21:05:57`

- %y—Year (two digits)

- %Y—Year (four digits)

- %Z—Time zone in ASCII, such as PST

echo

The `echo` directive displays any one of the include variables in the following list. Times are displayed in the time format specified by `timefmt`. Use the `var` attribute to indicate the variable to be displayed:

- `DATE_GMT`—The current date in Greenwich mean time.

- `DATE_LOCAL`—The current date in the local time zone.

- `DOCUMENT_NAME`—The filename (excluding directories) of the document requested by the user.

- `DOCUMENT_URI`—The (%-decoded) URL path of the document requested by the user. Note that in the case of nested include files, this isn't the URL for the current document.

- `LAST_MODIFIED`—The last modification date of the document requested by the user.

exec

The `exec` directive executes a shell command or a CGI program, depending on the parameters you provide. Valid attributes are `cgi` and `cmd`:

- `cgi`—The URL of a CGI program to be executed. The URL must be a local CGI, not one located on another machine. The CGI program is passed the `QUERY_STRING` and `PATH_INFO` that were originally passed to the requested document, so the URL specified cannot contain this information. You should use `include virtual` instead of this directive.

- `cmd`—A shell command to be executed. The results are displayed on the HTML page.

fsize

The `fsize` directive displays the size of a file specified by either the `file` or `virtual` attribute. Size is displayed as specified with the `sizefmt` directive:

19

- `file`—The path (file system path) to a file, either relative to the root if the value starts with / or relative to the current directory if it doesn't

- `virtual`—The relative URL path to a file

`flastmod`
Displays the last modified date of a file. The desired file is specified as with the `fsize` directive.

`include`
The `include` directive includes the contents of a file. The file is specified with the `file` and `virtual` attributes, as with `fsize` and `flastmod`.

If the file specified is a CGI program and `IncludesNOEXEC` isn't set, the program is executed and the results are displayed. This is to be used in preference to the `exec` directive. You can pass a `QUERY_STRING` with this directive—something you can't do with the `exec` directive.

`printenv`
It displays all existing variables and has no attributes. For example,

`<!--#printenv -->`

`set`
This sets the value of a variable, and its attributes are `var` and `value`. For example,

`<!--#set var="animal" value="cow" -->`

> **NOTE**
>
> All defined CGI environment variables are also allowed as `include` variables.

> **NOTE**
>
> In your configuration files (or in `.htaccess`), you can specify `Options IncludesNOEXEC` to disallow the `exec` directive because this is the least secure of the SSI directives. Be especially cautious when web users are able to create content (such as a guest book or discussion board) and these options are enabled!

The variables whose attributes have been set by `var` and `value` can also be used elsewhere with some of the following directives.

Flow Control

Using the variables set with the set directive and the various environment and include variables, a limited flow control syntax can be used to generate a certain amount of dynamic content on server-parsed pages.

The syntax of the if/else functions is as follows:

```
<!--#if expr="test_condition" -->
<!--#elif expr="test_condition" -->
<!--#else -->
<!--#endif -->
```

expr can be a string, which is considered true if nonempty, or a variety of comparisons between two strings. Available comparison operators are =, !=, <, <=, >, and >=. If the second string has the format /string/, the strings are compared with regular expressions. Multiple comparisons can be strung together with && (AND) and ¦¦ (OR). Any text appearing between the if/elif/else directives are displayed on the resulting page. An example of such a flow structure follows:

```
<!--#set var="agent" value="$HTTP_USER_AGENT" -->
<!--#if expr="$agent = /Mozilla/" -->
Mozilla!
<!--#else -->
Something else!
<!--#endif -->
```

This code displays Mozilla! if you're using a browser that passes Mozilla as part of its USER_AGENT string, and it displays Something else! otherwise.

Graphic Interface Configuration of Apache

Some of Apache's basic behavior can be configured using Red Hat's system-config-httpd, a GUI tool for the X Window System. This can provide an easy way to configure settings, such as Apache's user and group name, the location of PID and process lock files, or performance settings (such as the maximum number of connections), without manually editing configuration files.

> **CAUTION**
>
> If you use system-config-httpd, you shouldn't try to manually edit the httpd.conf file. Manual changes are overwritten by the GUI client if you again use system-config-httpd!

Launch this client by using your X desktop panel's Server Settings' HTTP Server menu item or from the command line of an X terminal window, like this:

```
$ system-config-httpd &
```

19

After you press Enter, you're asked to type the root password. You then see the main client window shown in Figure 19.2.

FIGURE 19.2   The system-config-httpd main dialog box provides access to basic configuration of the Apache web server.

In the Main tab, you can set the server name, indicate where to send email addressed to the webmaster, and set the port that Apache will use. If you want, you can also configure specific virtual hosts to listen on different ports.

Configuring Virtual Host Properties

In the Virtual Hosts tab, you can configure the properties of each virtual host. The Name list box contains a list of all virtual hosts operating in Apache. Edit a virtual host by opening the Virtual Hosts Properties dialog box, shown in Figure 19.3. You do this by highlighting the name of a virtual host in the Name list box of the Virtual Hosts tab and clicking the Edit button at the right of the tab. Use the General Options item in the Virtual Hosts Properties dialog box to configure basic virtual host settings.

Click the Site Configuration listing in the General Options list of this dialog box to set defaults, such as which files are loaded by default when no files are specified (the default is index.*) in the URL.

The SSL listing in the General Options pane gives you access to settings used to enable or disable SSL, specify certificate settings, and define the SSL log filename and location. Select the Logging listing to access options for configuring where the error messages are logged, as well as where the transfer log file is kept and how much information is put in it.

Use the Environment Variables options to configure settings for the env_mod module, used to pass environment directives to CGI programs.

The Directories section configures the directory options (such as whether CGI programs are allowed to run) as well as the order entries mentioned in the httpd.conf section.

FIGURE 19.3 `system-config-httpd`'s Virtual Host Properties dialog box gives you access to numerous options for configuring the properties of an Apache virtual host.

Configuring the Server

The Server tab, shown in Figure 19.4, enables you to configure things such as where the lock file and the PID file are kept.

In both cases, you should use the defaults. You can also configure the directory where any potential core dumps will be placed.

Finally, you can set which user and group Apache is to run as. As mentioned in a previous note, for security reasons, you should run Apache as the user named apache and as a member of the group apache.

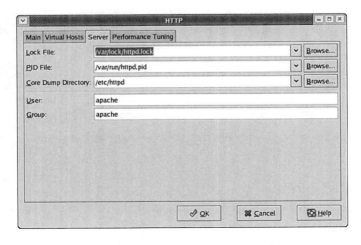

FIGURE 19.4 `system-config-httpd`'s Server configuration tab.

Configuring Apache for Peak Performance

Use the options in the Performance Tuning tab to configure Apache to provide peak performance in your system. Options in this tab set the maximum number of connections, connection timeouts, and number of requests per connection. When setting this number, keep in mind that, for each connection to your server, another instance of the HTTPD program might be run, depending on how Apache is built. Each instance takes resources such as CPU time and memory. You can also configure details about each connection such as how long, in seconds, before a connection times out and how many requests each connection can make to the server.

Other Web Servers for Use with Fedora

Of course, other web servers can be used with Fedora. Apache is by far the most popular, but this does not rule out the others.

To determine the best web server for your use, consider the needs of the website you manage. Does it need heavy security (for e-commerce), multimedia (music, video, and pictures), or the capability to download files easily? How much are you willing to spend for the software? Do you need software that is easy to maintain and troubleshoot or that includes tech support? The answers to these questions might steer you to something other than Apache.

The following sections list some of the more popular alternatives to using Apache as your web server.

thttpd

It is not entirely clear what the *t* in thttpd stands for. Meanings alternate between *tiny*, *turbo*, and *throttling*, depending on whom you ask. Whatever meaning you opt for, it is clear that thttpd is *not* big and slow.

Throttling, in the context of thttpd, is a process in which incoming URL calls are kept under control for a certain page or collection of pages on the website. If traffic to these pages hits a defined limit, the requesters for the page are sent a `try again` code until the traffic returns to a more manageable level.

thttpd is, on the surface, a simple little HTTP server that can handle a fair amount of traffic with minimal strain. Although not as robust as Apache, it does feature a throttling control—something that is not readily available for Apache.

thttpd is available as freeware from the thttpd website (http://www.acme.com/software/thttpd).

Sun ONE Web Server

Despite the Netcraft numbers shown previously in Table 19.1, there is evidence that the Sun Java System Web Server (formerly known as the iPlanet Web Server, and subsequently Sun ONE Web Server) might be even more popular than Apache in strictly corporate arenas. Netcraft has rated Sun Java System Web Server number one in market share among Fortune 100 websites.

The server got its start as the Netscape Enterprise Server—one of the first powerful web servers ever to hit the market. Sun ONE Web Server comes in many flavors, and all of them are big. In addition to the enterprise-level web server that can be run on Red Hat, the software features application, messaging, calendar, and directory servers—just to name a few.

Sun ONE Web Server is great for handling big web needs, and it comes with an appropriately big price tag: $1,495 (U.S.) per CPU. It's definitely not something to run the school website—unless your school happens to be a major state university with several regional campuses. For more information on Sun Java System Web Server, you can visit its website (http://wwws.sun.com/software/products/web_srvr/home_web_srvr.html).

Stronghold

If you're looking for something a little more secure than Apache but still don't want to lose the Apache functionality, you can purchase Stronghold from Red Hat Software.

Although not a web server as such, Stronghold is a server add-on that provides 128-bit cryptography and security certificates to the Apache web server (which is included in your purchase of Stronghold).

Stronghold supports SSL and TLS security standards, as well as many of the certificate standards on the market today.

The price for this kind of security is not particularly cheap. The software, which can be previewed at http://www.redhat.com/software/stronghold/, was advertised in 2004 at $995 (U.S.) per year.

Zope

Zope is another open-source web server. Although it is still relatively young and might not have as much flexibility as Apache, it is making strong inroads in the web server market.

What makes Zope different from Apache is the fact that it is managed through a completely web-based graphic interface. This has broad appeal for those who are not enthused about a command-line–only interface.

Zope is a product of the Zope Corporation (formerly Digital Creations), the same firm that made the Python programming language. And, like all things open source, it is free. Information on Zope can be found at both http://www.zope.com (for the commercial version) and http://www.zope.org (for the open-source version).

Zeus Web Server

Fedora sites can also use the Zeus Web Server from Zeus Technology. This server offers a scalable SSL implementation, security settings across multiple websites, and an online administration server. The current price is $1,700 for a host platform with up to two

CPUs, but load balancing via the Zeus Load Balancer costs $12,000 for each pair of load-balancing computers.

You can get more information about the Zeus Web Server at http://www.zeus.com/products/zws/.

TWiki

TWiki is a web-based collaboration tool. In use, it provides pages that resemble a regular website, but logged-in users can add content or make other modifications using a web browser. Content is generated while maintaining a log of all changes. TWiki is a collection of Perl scripts that can extend and complement Apache's capabilities. TWiki is available at no cost under the GPL from http://www.TWiki.org. You learn more about this tool in "Collaborating with TWiki," in Chapter 8, "On the Internet: Surfing the Web, Writing Email, and Reading the News."

Related Fedora and Linux Commands

You will use these commands when managing your Apache web Server in Fedora:

- `apachectl`—Server control shell script included with Apache
- `system-config-httpd`—Red Hat's graphical web server configuration tool
- `httpd`—The Apache web server
- `konqueror`—KDE's graphical web browser
- `elinks`—A text-based, graphical menu web browser
- `firefox`—The premier open-source web browser

Reference

There's a plethora of Apache documentation online. For more information about Apache and the subjects discussed in this chapter, look at some of the following resources:

- http://news.netcraft.com/archives/web_server_survey.html—A statistical graph of web server usage by 53,341,867 servers (as of August 2004). The research points out that Apache is by far the most widely used server for Internet sites.

- http://www.apache.org/—Extensive documentation and information about Apache are available at The Apache Project website.

- http://www.apacheweek.com/—You can obtain breaking news about Apache and great technical articles at the Apache Week site.

- http://apachetoday.com/—Another good Apache site. Original content as well as links to Apache-related stories on other sites can be found at Apache Today's site.

- http://www.hwg.org/—HTML, CGI, and related subjects are available at The HTML Writers Guild site.

- http://modules.apache.org/—Available add-on modules for Apache can be found at The Apache Module Registry website.

There are several good books about Apache. For example, *Apache Server Unleashed* (Sams Publishing), ISBN 0-672-31808-3.

For more information on Zope, see *The Zope Book* (New Riders Publishing), ISBN: 0-7357-11372.

# CHAPTER 20

Administering Database Services

This chapter is an introduction to MySQL and PostgreSQL, two database systems that are included with Fedora. You'll learn what these systems do, how the two programs compare, and how to consider their advantages and disadvantages. This information can help you choose which one to use for your organization's database needs. Finally, you will learn how to install, initialize, and configure these popular client/server database programs and how to administer those databases to maintain tight security and full integrity of the data.

The database administrator (DBA) for an organization has several responsibilities, which vary according to the size and operations of the organization, supporting staff, and so on. Depending on the particular organization's structure, if you are the organization's DBA, your responsibilities might include the following:

- **Installing and maintaining database servers**—You might need to install and maintain the database server software. Maintenance can involve such tasks as installing patches that fix bugs and security issues as well as upgrading the software at the appropriate times. As DBA, you might need to have root access to your system and perhaps know how to manage software (see Chapter 7, "Managing Software and System Resources"). You also need to be aware of kernel, file system, and other security issues.

- **Installing and maintaining database clients**—The database client is the program users use to access the database (you'll learn more on that later in this chapter, in the section "Database Clients"), either locally or remotely over a network. Your responsibilities might include installing and maintaining these client programs on users' systems. This chapter discusses how to install and work with the clients from both the Linux command line and through its graphical interface database tools.

- **Managing accounts and users**—Account and user management include adding and deleting users from the database, assigning and administering passwords, and so on. In this chapter, you will learn how to grant and revoke user privileges and passwords for MySQL and PostgreSQL while using Fedora.

- **Ensuring database security**—To ensure database security, you need to be concerned with things such as access control, which ensures that only authorized people can access the database, and permissions, which ensure that people who can access the database cannot do things they should not do. In this chapter, you will learn how to manage Secure Shell (SSH), web, and local GUI client access to the database. Planning and overseeing the regular backup of an organization's database and restoring data from those backups is another critical component of securing the database.

- **Ensuring data integrity**—Of all the information stored on a server's hard disk storage, chances are the information in the database is the most critical. Ensuring data integrity involves planning for multiple-user access and ensuring that changes are not lost or duplicated when more than one user is making changes to the database at the same time.

A Brief Review of Database Basics

Database services under Linux that use the software discussed in this chapter are based on a *client/server* model. Database clients are often used to input data and to query or display query results from the server. You can use the command line or a graphical client to access a running server. Databases generally come in two forms: flat file and relational. A *flat file* database can be as simple as a text file with a space, tab, or some other character delimiting different parts of the information. One example of a simple flat file database is the Fedora /etc/passwd file. Another example could be a simple address book that might look something like this:

```
Doe~John~505 Some Street~Anytown~NY~12345~555-555-1212
```

You can use standard Unix tools such as grep, awk, and perl to search for and extract information from this primitive database. Although this might work well for a small database such as an address book that only one person uses, flat file databases of this type have several limitations:

- **They do not scale well**—Flat file databases cannot perform random access on data. They can only perform sequential access. This means they have to scan each line in the file, one by one, to look for specific information. As the size of the database grows, access times increase and performance decreases.

- **Flat file databases are unsuitable for multiuser environments**—Depending on how the database is set up, it either enables only one user to access it at a time or allows two users to make changes simultaneously, and the changes could end up overwriting each other and cause data loss.

These limitations obviously make the flat file database unsuitable for any kind of serious work in even a small business—much less in an enterprise environment. Relational databases, or relational database management systems (RDBMSs) to give them their full name, are good at finding the relationships between individual pieces of data. An RDBMS stores data in tables with fields much like those in spreadsheets, making the data searchable and sortable. RDBMSs are the focus of this chapter.

Oracle, DB2, Microsoft SQL Server, and the freely available PostgreSQL and MySQL are all examples of RDBMSs. The following sections discuss how relational databases work and provide a closer look at some of the basic processes involved in administering and using databases. You will also learn about SQL, the standard language used to store, retrieve, and manipulate database data.

How Relational Databases Work

To effectively set up and administer an RDBMS, you need to know a little bit about how relational databases store information and how users can access and work with that data. This section doesn't offer a detailed lesson in relational database theory and management, but it does provide a good overview of the essential concepts and processes.

An RDBMS stores data in tables, which you can visualize as spreadsheets. Each column in the table is a field; for example, a column might contain a name or an address. Each row in the table is an individual record. The table itself has a name you use to refer to that table when you want to get data out of it or put data into it. Figure 20.1 shows an example of a simple relational database that stores name and address information.

last_name	first_name	address	city	state	zip	phone
Doe	John	501 Somestreet	Anytown	NY	55011	555-555-1212
Doe	Jane	501 Somestreet	Anytown	NY	55011	555-555-1212
Palmer	John	205 Anystreet	Sometown	NY	55055	123-456-7890
Johnson	Robert	100 Easystreet	Easytown	CT	12345	111-222-3333

FIGURE 20.1   In this visualization of how an RDBMS stores data, the database stores four records (rows) that include name and address information, divided into seven fields (columns) of data.

In the example shown in Figure 20.1, the database contains only a single table. Most RDBMS setups are much more complex than this, with a single database containing multiple tables. Figure 20.2 shows an example of a database named `sample_database` that contains two tables.

20

phonebook

last_name	first_name	phone
Doe	John	555-555-1212
Doe	Jane	555-555-1212
Palmer	John	555-123-4567
Johnson	Richard	555-111-4321

cd_collection

id	title	artist	year	rating
1	Mindbomb	The The	1989	4
2	For All You've Done	Hillsong	2004	
3	Trouser Jazz	Mr Scruff	2002	5
4	Natural Elements	Acoustic Alchemy	1988	3
5	Combat Rock	The Clash	1982	4
6	Life for Rent	Dido	2003	5
7	Adiemus 4	Karl Jenkins	2000	4
8	The Two Towers	Howard Shore	2002	5

FIGURE 20.2   A single database can contain two tables—in this case, phonebook and cd_collection.

In the sample_database example, the phonebook table contains four records (rows) and each record hold three fields (columns) of data. The cd_collection table holds eight records, divided into five fields of data.

If you are thinking that there is no logical relationship between the phonebook table and the cd_collection table in the sample_database example, you are correct. In a relational database, users can store multiple tables of data in a single database—even if the data in one table is unrelated to the data in others.

For example, suppose you run a small company that sells widgets and you have a computerized database of customers. In addition to storing each customer's name, address, and phone number, you want to be able to look up outstanding order and invoice information for any of your customers. You could use three related tables in an RDBMS to store and organize customer data for just those purposes. Figure 20.3 shows an example of such a database.

In the example in Figure 20.3, we have added a customer ID field to each customer record. This field holds a customer ID number that is the unique piece of information that can be used to link all other information for each customer to track orders and invoices. Each customer is given an ID unique to him; two customers might have the same data in their name fields, but their ID field values will never be the same. The Customer ID field data in the Orders and Overdue tables replaces the Last Name, First Name, and Shipping Address field information from the Customers table. Now, when you want to run a search for any customer's order and invoice data, you can search based on one key rather than multiple keys. You get more accurate results in faster, easier-to-conduct data searches.

customers

cid	last_name	first_name	shipping_address
1	Doe	John	505 Somestreet
2	Doe	Jane	505 Somestreet
3	Palmer	John	200 Anystreet
4	Johnson	Richard	1000 Another Street

orders

cid	order_num	stock_num	priority	shipped	date
1	1002	100,252,342	3	Y	8/31/01
1	1221	200,352	1	N	10/2/01
3	1223	200,121	2	Y	10/2/01
2	1225	221,152	1	N	10/3/01

overdue

cid	order_num	days_overdue	action
1	1002	32	sent letter

FIGURE 20.3   You can use three related tables to track customers, orders, and outstanding invoices.

Now that you have an idea of how data is stored in an RDBMS and how the RDBMS structure enables you to work with that data, you are ready to learn how to input and output data from the database. This is where SQL comes in.

Understanding SQL Basics

SQL (pronounced either "S-Q-L," or "se-quel") is a database query language understood by virtually all RDBMSs available today. You use SQL statements to get data into and retrieve data from a database. As with statements in any language, SQL statements have a defined structure that determines their meanings and functions.

In most settings, SQL is programmed into front-end or middleware applications that end users do not directly manipulate. Thus, most end users are unaware of SQL and its role and have little reason to be concerned about the structure of SQL statements.

However, as a DBA, you should understand the basics of SQL, even if you will not be doing any of the actual programming yourself. Fortunately, SQL is similar to standard English, so learning the basics is simple.

20

> **TIP**
>
> The following sections are not intended to be a tutorial on SQL. They are simply intended to introduce you to the basics of the language. If you need a full tutorial on SQL programming, check out one of the several available books on this topic, including *MySQL, Sams Teach Yourself MySQL in 21 Days*, and *PostgreSQL* (all from Sams Publishing).

Creating Tables

As mentioned previously, an RDBMS stores data in tables that look similar to spread-sheets. Of course, before you can store any data in a database, you need to create the necessary tables and columns to store the data. You do this by using the CREATE statement.

For example, the cd_collection table from Figure 20.2 has five columns, or fields: id, title, artist, year, and rating.

SQL provides several column types for data that define what kind of data will be stored in the column. Some of the available types are INT, FLOAT, CHAR, and VARCHAR. Both CHAR and VARCHAR hold text strings, with the difference being that CHAR holds a fixed-length string, whereas VARCHAR holds a variable-length string.

There are also special column types, such as DATE, that only take data in a date format, and ENUMs (enumerations), which can be used to specify that only certain values are allowed. If, for example, you wanted to record the genre of your CDs, you could use an ENUM column that accepts only the values POP, ROCK, EASY_LISTENING, and so on. You will learn more about ENUM later in this chapter.

Looking at the cd_collection table, you can see that three of the columns hold numeri-cal data and the other two hold string data. In addition, the character strings are of vari-able length. Based on this information, you can discern that the best type to use for the text columns is type VARCHAR, and the best type to use for the others is INT. You should notice something else about the cd_collection table: One of the CDs is missing a rating, perhaps because we have not listened to it yet. This value, therefore, is optional; it starts empty and can be filled in later.

You are now ready to create a table. As mentioned before, you do this by using the CREATE statement, which uses the following syntax:

```
CREATE TABLE table_name (column_name column_type(parameters) options, ...);
```

You should know the following about the CREATE statement:

- **SQL commands are not case sensitive**—For example, CREATE TABLE, create table, and Create Table are all valid. You should get in the habit of using all uppercase for commands because later, when you start writing front ends to your databases in C, Perl, and so on, using all uppercase will make it easier to pick out the SQL code. (Keywords in C, Perl, and so on are almost always lowercase.)

- **Whitespace is generally ignored**—This means you should use it to make your SQL commands clearer.

The following example shows how to create the table for the cd_collection database:

```
CREATE TABLE cd_collection
(
id INT NOT NULL,
```

```
title VARCHAR(50) NOT NULL,
artist VARCHAR(50) NOT NULL,
year VARCHAR(50) NOT NULL,
rating VARCHAR(50) NULL
);
```

Notice that the statement terminates with a semicolon. This is how SQL knows you are finished with all the entries in the statement. In some cases, the semicolon can be omitted, and we will point out these cases when they arise.

TIP

SQL has a large number of reserved keywords that cannot be used in table names or field names. For example, if you keep track of CDs you want to take with you on vacation, you would not be able to use the field name `select` because that is a reserved keyword. Instead, you should either choose a different name (`selected`?) or just prefix the field name with an `f`, such as `fselect`.

Inserting Data into Tables

After you create the tables, you can put data into them. You can insert data manually with the `INSERT` statement, which uses the following syntax:

```
INSERT INTO table_name VALUES('value1', 'value2', 'value3', ...);
```

This statement inserts *value1*, *value2*, and so on into the table *table_name*. The values that are inserted constitute one row, or *record*, in the database. Unless specified otherwise, values are inserted in the order in which the columns are listed in the database table. If, for some reason, you want to insert values in a different order (or if you want to insert only a few values and they are not in sequential order), you can specify which columns you want the data to go in by using the following syntax:

```
INSERT INTO table_name (column1,column4) VALUES('value1', 'value2');
```

You can also fill multiple rows with a single `INSERT` statement, using syntax such as the following:

```
INSERT INTO table_name VALUES('value1', 'value2'),('value3', 'value4');
```

In this statement, *value1* and *value2* are inserted into the first row and *value3* and *value4* are inserted into the second row.

The following example shows how you would insert the `Nevermind` entry into the `cd_collection` table:

```
INSERT INTO cd_collection VALUES(9, 'Nevermind', ''Nirvana', '1991,
''NULL);
```

20

MySQL requires the NULL value for the last column (rating) if you do not want to include a rating. PostgreSQL, on the other hand, lets you get away with just omitting the last column. Of course, if you had columns in the middle that were null, you would need to explicitly state NULL in the INSERT statement.

Normally, INSERT statements are coded into a front-end program so users adding data to the database do not have to worry about the SQL statements involved.

Retrieving Data from a Database

Of course, the main reason for storing data in a database is so you can later look up, sort, and generate reports on that data. Basic data retrieval is done with the SELECT statement, which has the following syntax:

```
SELECT column1, column2, column3 FROM table_name WHERE search_criteria;
```

The first two parts of the statement—the SELECT and FROM parts—are required. The WHERE portion of the statement is optional. If it is omitted, all rows in the table *table_name* are returned.

The *column1*, *column2*, *column3* indicates the name of the columns you want to see. If you want to see all columns, you can also use the wildcard * to show all the columns that match the search criteria. For example, the following statement displays all columns from the cd_collection table:

```
SELECT * FROM cd_collection;
```

If you wanted to see only the titles of all the CDs in the table, you would use a statement such as the following:

```
SELECT title FROM cd_collection;
```

To select the title and year of a CD, you would use the following:

```
SELECT title, year FROM cd_collection;
```

If you wanted something a little fancier, you can use SQL to print the CD title followed by the year in parentheses, as is the convention. Both MySQL and PostgreSQL provide string concatenation functions to handle problems such as this. However, the syntax is different in the two systems.

In MySQL, you can use the CONCAT() function to combine the title and year columns into one output column, along with parentheses. The following statement is an example:

```
SELECT CONCAT(title," (",year, ")") AS TitleYear FROM cd_collection;
```

That statement lists both the title and year under one column that has the label TitleYear. Note that there are two strings in the CONCAT() function along with the fields—these add whitespace and the parentheses.

In PostgreSQL, the string concatenation function is simply a double pipe (¦¦). The following command is the PostgreSQL equivalent of the preceding MySQL command:

```
SELECT (genus¦¦'' ('¦¦species¦¦')') AS TitleYear FROM cd_collection;
```

Note that the parentheses are optional, but they make the statement easier to read. Once again, the strings in the middle and at the end (note the space between the quotes) are used to insert spacing and parentheses between the title and year.

Of course, more often than not, you do not want a list of every single row in the database. Rather, you only want to find rows that match certain characteristics. For this, you add the WHERE statement to the SELECT statement. For example, suppose you want to find all the CDs in the cd_collection table that have a rating of 5. You would use a statement like the following:

```
SELECT * FROM cd_collection WHERE rating = 5;
```

Using the table from Figure 20.2, you can see that this query would return the rows for *Trouser Jazz*, *Life for Rent*, and *The Two Towers*. This is a simple query, and SQL is capable of handling queries much more complex than this. Complex queries can be written using logical AND and logical OR statements. For example, suppose you want to refine the query so it lists only those CDs that were not released in 2003. You would use a query like the following:

```
SELECT * FROM cd_collection WHERE rating = 5 AND year != 2003;
```

In SQL, != means "is not equal to." So once again looking at the table from Figure 20.2, you can see that this query returns the rows for *Trouser Jazz* and *The Two Towers* but doesn't return the row for *Life for Rent* because it was released in 2003.

So, what if you want to list all the CDs that have a rating of 3 or 4 except those released in the year 2000? This time, you combine logical AND and logical OR statements:

```
SELECT * FROM cd_collection WHERE rating = 3 OR rating = 4 AND year != 2000;
```

This query would return entries for *Mind Bomb*, *Natural Elements*, and *Combat Rock*. However, it wouldn't return entries for *Adiemus 4* because it was released in 2000.

TIP

One of the most common errors among new database programmers is confusing logical AND and logical OR. For example, in everyday speech, you might say "Find me all CDs released in 2003 and 2004." At first glance, you might think that if you fed this statement to the database in SQL format, it would return the rows for *For All You've Done* and *Life for Rent*. In fact, it would return no rows at all. This is because the database interprets the statement as "Find all rows in which the CD was released in 2003 and was released in 2004." It is, of course, impossible for the same CD to be released twice, so this statement would never return any rows, no matter how many CDs were stored in the table. The correct way to form this statement is with an OR statement instead of an AND statement.

SQL is capable of far more than is demonstrated here. But as mentioned before, this section is not intended to teach you all there is to know about SQL programming; rather, it teaches you the basics so you can be a more effective DBA.

Choosing a Database: MySQL Versus PostgreSQL

If you are just starting out and learning about using a database with Linux, the first logical step is to research which database will best serve your needs. Many database software packages are available for Linux; some are free, and others cost hundreds of thousands of dollars. Expensive commercial databases, such as Oracle, are beyond the scope of this book. Instead, this chapter focuses on two freely available databases: MySQL and PostgreSQL.

Both of these high-quality databases are included on this book's CD-ROMs and DVD. But just because MySQL and PostgreSQL are free does not mean they lack power. Both of these databases (PostgreSQL in particular) can handle very complex projects. They are used in commercial organizations (like Yahoo!), government agencies (such as NASA), research institutions, and educational institutions.

Both of these databases are quite capable, and either one could probably serve your needs. However, each database has a unique set of features and capabilities that might serve your needs better or make developing database applications easier for you. The following sections look at some of the key features of any database and discuss how those features are implemented in MySQL and PostgreSQL. You should use the information in these sections to compare the two databases so you can choose the one that's right for your project.

Speed

Until recently, the speed choice was simple: If the speed of performing queries was paramount to your application, you used MySQL. MySQL has a reputation for being an extremely fast database. Until recently, PostgreSQL was quite slow by comparison.

Newer versions of PostgreSQL have improved in terms of speed (when it comes to disk access, sorting, and so on). In certain situations, such as periods of heavy simultaneous access, PostgreSQL can be significantly faster than MySQL, as you will see in the next section. However, MySQL is still extremely fast when compared to many other databases.

Data Locking

To prevent data corruption, a database needs to put a lock on data while it is being accessed. As long as the lock is on, no other process can access the data until the first process has released the lock. This means that any other processes trying to access the data have to wait until the current process completes. The next process in line then locks the data until it is finished, and the remaining processes have to wait their turn, and so on.

Of course, operations on a database generally complete quickly, so in environments with a small number of users simultaneously accessing the database, the locks are usually of such short duration that they do not cause any significant delays. However, in environments in which many people are accessing the database simultaneously, locking can create performance problems as people wait their turn to access the database.

MySQL uses a data-locking method that is fundamentally different from the data-locking method used by PostgreSQL.

Older versions of MySQL lock data at the table level, which can be considered a bottleneck for updates during periods of heavy access. This means that when someone writes a row of data in the table, the entire table is locked so no one else can enter data. If your table has 500,000 rows (or records) in it, all 500,000 rows are locked any time 1 row is accessed. Once again, in environments with a relatively small number of simultaneous users, this doesn't cause serious performance problems because most operations complete so quickly that the lock time is extremely short. However, in environments in which many people are accessing the data simultaneously, MySQL's table-level locking can be a significant performance bottleneck.

PostgreSQL, on the other hand, locks data at the row level. In PostgreSQL, only the row currently being accessed is locked. The rest of the table can be accessed by other users. This row-level locking significantly reduces the performance impact of locking in environments that have a large number of simultaneous users. Therefore, as a general rule, PostgreSQL is better suited for high-load environments than MySQL.

The MySQL release bundled with Fedora Core gives you the choice of using tables with table-level or row-level locking. In MySQL terminology, MyISAM tables use table-level locking and InnoDB tables use row-level locking.

> **NOTE**
>
> MySQL's data locking methods are discussed in more depth at http://www.mysql.com/doc/en/Internal_locking.html.
>
> You can find more information on PostgreSQL's locking at http://www.postgresql.org/idocs/index.php?locking-tables.html.

ACID Compliance in Transaction Processing to Protect Data Integrity

Another way MySQL and PostgreSQL differ is in the amount of protection they provide for keeping data from becoming corrupted. The acronym ACID is commonly used to describe several aspects of data protection:

- **Atomicity**—A term derived from the word *atom*, which, as you might know, means "indivisible." In the database world, this means that several database operations are treated as an atomic unit, often called a *transaction*. In a transaction, either all unit operations are carried out or none of them are. In other words, if any operation in the atomic unit fails, the entire atomic unit is canceled.

  If you have a power failure or server crash after an original record has been deleted, for example, but before the updated one has been added, you don't lose the record

20

because atomic transactions ensure that the original record isn't deleted if the update portion of the atomic unit fails.

- **Consistency**—Ensures that no transaction can cause the database to be left in an inconsistent state. Inconsistent states can be caused by database client crashes, network failures, and similar situations. Consistency ensures that, in such a situation, any transaction or partially completed transaction that would cause the database to be left in an inconsistent state is *rolled back*, or undone. This prevents, for example, the deletion of one critical field of a database record when all other fields for that record remain (referred to as *orphaned* data). Incomplete transactions are rolled back to maintain consistency.

- **Isolation**—Ensures that multiple transactions operating on the same data are completely isolated from each other. This prevents data corruption if two users try to write to the same record at the same time. The way isolation is handled can generally be configured by the database programmer. One way that isolation can be handled is through locking, as discussed previously.

- **Durability**—Ensures that, after a transaction has been committed to the database, it cannot be lost in the event of a system crash, network failure, or other problem. This is usually accomplished through transaction logs. Durability means, for example, that if the server crashes, the database can examine the logs when it comes back up and it can commit any transactions that were not yet complete into the database.

PostgreSQL is ACID-compliant, but again MySQL gives you the choice of using ACID-compliant tables or not. MyISAM tables are not ACID-compliant, whereas InnoDB tables are. Note that ACID compliancy is no easy task: All the extra precautions incur a performance overhead.

SQL Subqueries

Subqueries allow you to combine several operations into one atomic unit, and they enable those operations to access each other's data. By using SQL subqueries, you can perform some extremely complex operations on a database. In addition, using SQL subqueries eliminates the potential problem of data changing between two operations as a result of another user performing some operation on the same set of data. Both PostgreSQL and MySQL have support for subqueries in this release of Fedora, but this was not true in earlier releases. MySQL has only recently implemented the technology.

Importing Text Files into Tables

In MySQL and PostgreSQL, the SQL statements used to create a database table can be entered directly into the command-line clients. However, doing so introduces a lot of opportunity for error; if you make a mistake, you have to type the entire table again from the beginning. Fortunately, both MySQL and PostgreSQL can read a list of SQL statements from a plain-text file. You could also enter SQL statements into a text editor and save the file with the filename extension .sql. (The .sql extension is helpful because it makes it easy to see that this file contains SQL statements when doing a directory listing.)

Statements saved in a text file can be imported into the database with the following commands in MySQL and PostgreSQL, respectively, where mammal.sql is the name of the saved text file:

```
$ mysql database_name < mammal.sql
$ psql database_name < mammal.sql
```

Of course, for this to work, mysql or psql must be invoked by a user who has permission to create tables in the database represented by database_name. For more information, see the sections "Granting and Revoking Privileges in MySQL" and "Creating a Database in MySQL," later in this chapter.

Procedural Languages and Triggers

A *procedural language* is an external programming language that can be used to write functions and procedures. This allows you to do things that aren't supported by simple SQL. A *trigger* allows you to define an event that will invoke the external function or procedure you have written. For example, a trigger can be used to cause an exception if an INSERT statement containing an unexpected or out-of-range value for a column is given.

For example, in the CD tracking database, you could use a trigger to cause an exception if a user entered data that did not make sense. PostgreSQL has a procedural language called PL/pgSQL. Although MySQL has support for a limited number of built-in procedures and triggers, it does not have any procedural language. This means you cannot create custom procedures or triggers in MySQL, although the same effects can often be achieved through creative client-side programming.

Getting Started with Databases and Fedora

A number of steps are required before database services can be used with Fedora. The first step is to ensure that the database server has been properly started (usually at boot time). The root operator needs to make sure that Fedora starts the server during any anticipated system runlevel (see Chapter 14, "Automating Tasks," for more information). A root database user must then be created, and the database server needs to be initialized. A root database user password is then created, along with one or more databases. The root database user can then grant authorized users various levels of access to each database.

Configuring MySQL

A free and stable version of MySQL is included with Fedora. MySQL is also available from the website http://www.mysql.com. The software is available in source code, binary, and RPM format for Linux. You can elect to have MySQL installed when you install Fedora or later use the redhat-config-packages client to add the software to your system. See Chapter 7 for the details on adding (or removing) software.

After you have MySQL installed, you need to initialize the *grant tables,* or permissions to access any or all databases and tables and column data within a database. You can do this by issuing `mysql_install_db` as root. This command initializes the grant tables and creates a MySQL root user.

> **CAUTION**
>
> The MySQL data directory needs to be owned by the user as which MySQL will run (changing ownership using the `chown` command). In addition, only this user should have any permissions on this directory. (In other words, the permissions should be set to 700 by using `chmod`.) Setting up the data directory any other way creates a security hole.

Running `mysql_install_db` should generate output similar to the following:

```
# mysql_install_db
Preparing db table
Preparing host table
Preparing user table
Preparing func table
Preparing tables_priv table
Preparing columns_priv table
Installing all prepared tables
020916 17:39:05 /usr/libexec/mysqld: Shutdown Complete
...
```

The command prepares MySQL for use on the system and reports helpful information. The next step is to set the password for the MySQL root user, which is discussed in the following section.

> **CAUTION**
>
> By default, the MySQL root user is created with no password. This is one of the first things you must change because the MySQL root user has access to all aspects of the database. The following section explains how to change the password of the user.

Setting a Password for the MySQL Root User

To set a password for the root MySQL user, you need to connect to the MySQL server as the root MySQL user; you can use the command `mysql -u root` to do so. This command connects you to the server with the MySQL client. When you have the MySQL command prompt, issue a command like the following to set a password for the root user:

```
mysql> SET PASSWORD FOR root = PASSWORD("secretword");
```

secretword should be replaced by whatever you want to be the password for the root user. You can use this same command with other usernames to set or change passwords for other database users.

After you enter a password, you can exit the MySQL client by typing `exit` at the command prompt.

Creating a Database in MySQL

In MySQL you create a database by using the `CREATE DATABASE` statement. To create a database, you connect to the server by typing **`mysql -u root -p`** and pressing Enter. After you do so, you are connected to the database as the MySQL root user and prompted for a password. After you enter the password, you are placed at the MySQL command prompt. Then you use the `CREATE DATABASE` command. For example, the following commands create a database called `animals`:

```
# mysql -u root -p
Enter password:
Welcome to the MySQL monitor. Commands end with ; or \g.
Your MySQL connection id is 1 to server version: 3.23.58

Type 'help;' or '\h' for help. Type '\c' to clear the buffer.

mysql> CREATE DATABASE animals;
Query OK, 1 row affected (0.00 sec)
mysql>
```

Another way to create a database is to use the `mysqladmin` command, as the root user, with the `create` keyword and the name of a new database. For example, to create a new database named `reptiles`, you use a command line like this:

```
# mysqladmin -u root -p create reptiles
```

Granting and Revoking Privileges in MySQL

You probably want to grant yourself some privileges, and eventually you will probably want to grant privileges to other users. Privileges, also known as *rights*, are granted and revoked on four levels:

- **Global-level**—These rights allow access to any database on a server.

- **Database-level**—These rights allow access to all tables in a database.

- **Table-level**—These rights allow access to all columns within a table in a database.

- **Column-level**—These rights allow access to a single column within a database's table.

20

> **NOTE**
>
> Listing all the available privileges is beyond the scope of this chapter. See the MySQL documentation for more information.

To add a user account, you connect to the database by typing `mysql -u root -p` and pressing Enter. You are then connected as the root user and prompted for a password. (You did set a password for the root user, as instructed in the last section, right?) After you enter the root password, you are placed at the MySQL command prompt.

To grant privileges to a user, you use the `GRANT` statement, which has the following syntax:

```
grant what_to_grant ON where_to_grant TO user_name IDENTIFIED BY 'password';
```

The first option, *what_to_grant*, is the privileges you are granting to the user. These privileges are specified with keywords. For example, the `ALL` keyword is used to grant global-, database-, table-, and column-level rights for a specified user.

The second option, *where_to_grant*, specifies the resources on which the privileges should be granted. The third option, *user_name*, is the username to which you want to grant the privileges. Finally, the fourth option, *password*, is a password that should be assigned to this user. If this is an existing user who already has a password and you are modifying permissions, you can omit the `IDENTIFIED BY` portion of the statement.

For example, to grant all privileges on a database named `sampledata` to a user named `foobar`, you could use the following command:

```
GRANT ALL ON animals.* TO foobar IDENTIFIED BY 'secretword';
```

The user `foobar` can now connect to the database `sampledata` by using the password `secretword`, and `foobar` has all privileges on the database, including the ability to create and destroy tables. For example, the user `foobar` can now log in to the server (by using the current hostname—`shuttle2`, in this example), and access the database like so:

```
$ mysql -h shuttle2 -u foobar -p animals
Enter password:
Welcome to the MySQL monitor. Commands end with ; or \g.
Your MySQL connection id is 43 to server version: 3.23.58

Type 'help;' or '\h' for help. Type '\c' to clear the buffer.

mysql>
```

> **NOTE**
>
> See the section "The MySQL Command-Line Client" for additional command-line options.

Later, if you need to revoke privileges from `foobar`, you can use the `REVOKE` statement. For example, the following statement revokes all privileges from the user `foobar`:

```
REVOKE ALL ON animals FROM foobar;
```

Advanced database administration, privileges, and security are very complex topics that are beyond the scope of this book. See the section "Reference" at the end of this chapter for links to online documentation. You can also check out Luke Welling's and Laura Thompson's book *PHP and MySQL Development* from Sams Publishing.

Configuring PostgreSQL

If you do not want to use the version of PostgreSQL bundled with Fedora, the latest PostgreSQL binary files and source are available at http://www.postgresql.org. The PostgreSQL RPMs are distributed as several files. At a minimum, you probably want the `postgresql`, `postgresql-server`, and `postgresql-libs` RPMs. You should see the `README.rpm-dist` file in the FTP directory ftp://ftp.postgresql.org/pub/ to determine whether you need any other packages.

If you are installing from the Fedora RPM files, a necessary `postgres` user account (that is, an account with the name of the user running the server on your system) is created for you automatically:

```
$ fgrep postgres /etc/passwd
postgres:x:26:26:PostgreSQL Server:/var/lib/pgsql:/bin/bash
```

Otherwise, you need to create a user called `postgres` during the installation. This user shouldn't have login privileges because only root should be able to use su to become this user and no one will ever log in directly as the user. (See Chapter 13, "Managing Users," for more information on how to add users to a Fedora system.) After you have added the user, you can install each of the PostgreSQL RPMs you downloaded using the standard `rpm -i` command for a default installation.

Initializing the Data Directory in PostgreSQL

After the RPMs have been installed, you need to initialize the data directory. To do so, you must first create the data directory and you must be the root user. The following example assumes that the data directory is `/usr/local/pgsql/data`.

Create the `/usr/local/pgsql/data` directory (using `mkdir`) and change the ownerships of the directory (using `chown` and `chgrp`) so it is owned by the user `postgres`. Then use su and, as the user `postgres`, issue the following commands:

```
# mkdir /usr/local/pgsql
# chown postgres /usr/local/pgsql
# chgrp postgres /usr/local/pgsql
# su - postgres
-bash-2.05b$ initdb -D /usr/local/pgsql/data
The files belonging to this database system will be owned by user "postgres".
This user must also own the server process.

The database cluster will be initialized with locale en_US.UTF-8.
This locale setting will prevent the use of indexes for pattern matching
```

20

operations. If that is a concern, rerun initdb with the collation order
set to "C". For more information see the Administrator's Guide.

```
creating directory /usr/local/pgsql/data... ok
creating directory /usr/local/pgsql/data/base... ok
creating directory /usr/local/pgsql/data/global... ok
creating directory /usr/local/pgsql/data/pg_xlog... ok
creating directory /usr/local/pgsql/data/pg_clog... ok
creating template1 database in /usr/local/pgsql/data/base/1... ok
creating configuration files... ok
initializing pg_shadow... ok
enabling unlimited row size for system tables... ok
initializing pg_depend... ok
creating system views... ok
loading pg_description... ok
creating conversions... ok
setting privileges on built-in objects... ok
vacuuming database template1... ok
copying template1 to template0... ok


Success. You can now start the database server using:

 /usr/bin/postmaster -D /usr/local/pgsql/data
or
 /usr/bin/pg_ctl -D /usr/local/pgsql/data -l logfile start
```

This initializes the database and sets the permissions on the data directory to their correct
values.

CAUTION

The initdb program sets the permissions on the data directory to 700. You should not change
these permissions to anything else to avoid creating a security hole.

You can start the postmaster program with the following command (make sure you are
still the user postgres):

```
$ postmaster -D /usr/local/pgsql/data &
```

If you have decided to use a directory other than /usr/local/pgsql/data as the data
directory, you should replace the directory in the postmaster command line with whatever directory you are using.

> **TIP**
>
> By default, Fedora makes the PostgreSQL data directory /var/lib/pgsql/data. This isn't a very good place to store the data, however, because most people do not have the necessary space in the /var partition for any kind of serious data storage. Note that if you do change the data directory to something else (such as /usr/local/pgsql/data, as in the examples in this section), you need to edit the PostgreSQL startup file (named postgres) located in /etc/rc.d/init.d to reflect the change.

Creating a Database in PostgreSQL

Creating a database in PostgreSQL is straightforward, but it must be performed by a user who has permissions to create databases in PostgreSQL—for example, initially the user named postgres. You can then simply issue the following command from the shell prompt (not the PSQL client prompt, but a normal shell prompt):

```
# su - postgres
-bash-2.05b$ createdb database
```

where *database* is the name of the database you want to create.

The createdb program is actually a wrapper that makes it easier to create databases without having to log in and use psql. However, you can also create databases from within psql with the CREATE DATABASE statement. Here's an example:

```
CREATE DATABASE database;
```

You need to create at least one database before you can start the pgsql client program. You should create this database while you're logged in as the user postgres. To log in as this user, you need to use su to become root and then use su to become the user postgres. To connect to the new database, you start the psql client program with the name of the new database as a command-line argument, like so:

```
$ psql sampledata
```

If you don't specify the name of a database when you invoke psql, the command attempts to connect to a database that has the same name as the user as which you invoke psql (that is, the default database).

Creating Database Users in PostgreSQL

To create a database user, you use su to become the user postgres from the Linux root account. You can then use the PostgreSQL createuser command to quickly create a user who is allowed to access databases or create new database users, like this:

```
$ createuser phudson
Shall the new user be allowed to create databases? (y/n) y
Shall the new user be allowed to create more new users? (y/n) y
CREATE USER
```

In this example, the new user named phudson is created and allowed to create new databases and database users (you should carefully consider who is allowed to create new databases or additional users).

You can also use the PostgreSQL command-line client to create a new user by typing psql along with name of the database and then use the CREATE USER command to create a new user. Here is an example:

```
CREATE USER foobar ;
```

> **CAUTION**
>
> PostgreSQL allows you to omit the WITH PASSWORD portion of the statement. However, doing so causes the user to be created with no password. This is a security hole, so you should always use the WITH PASSWORD option when creating users.

> **NOTE**
>
> When you are finished working in the psql command-line client, you can type \q to get out of it and return to the shell prompt.

Deleting Database Users in PostgreSQL

To delete a database user, you use the dropuser command, along with the user's name, and the user's access is removed from the default database, like this:

```
$ dropuser msmith
DROP USER
```

You can also log in to your database by using psql and then use the DROP USER commands. Here's an example:

```
$ psql demodb
Welcome to psql, the PostgreSQL interactive terminal.

Type: \copyright for distribution terms
 \h for help with SQL commands
 \? for help on internal slash commands
 \g or terminate with semicolon to execute query
 \q to quit

demodb=# DROP USER msmith ;
DROP USER
demodb=# \q
$
```

Granting and Revoking Privileges in PostgreSQL

As in MySQL, granting and revoking privileges in PostgreSQL is done with the GRANT and REVOKE statements. The syntax is the same as in MySQL except that PostgreSQL doesn't use the IDENTIFIED BY portion of the statement because with PostgreSQL, passwords are assigned when you create the user with the CREATE USER statement, as discussed previously. Here is the syntax of the GRANT statement:

```
GRANT what_to_grant ON where_to_grant TO user_name;
```

The following command, for example, grants all privileges to the user foobar on the database sampledata:

```
GRANT ALL ON sampledata TO foobar;
```

To revoke privileges, you use the REVOKE statement. Here is an example:

```
REVOKE ALL ON sampledata FROM foobar;
```

This command removes all privileges from the user foobar on the database sampledata.

Advanced administration and user configuration are complex topics. This section cannot begin to cover all the aspects of PostgreSQL administration or of privileges and users. For more information on administering PostgreSQL, see the PostgreSQL documentation or consult a book on PostgreSQL, such as *PostgreSQL* (Sams Publishing).

Database Clients

Both MySQL and PostgreSQL use a client/server system for accessing databases. In the simplest terms, the database server handles the requests that come into the database and the database client handles getting the requests to the server as well as getting the output from the server to the user.

Users never interact directly with the database server even if it happens to be located on the same machine they are using. All requests to the database server are handled by a database client, which might or might not be running on the same machine as the database server.

Both MySQL and PostgreSQL have command-line clients. A command-line client is a very primitive way of interfacing with a database and generally isn't used by end users. As a DBA, however, you use the command-line client to test new queries interactively without having to write front-end programs for that purpose. In later sections of this chapter, you will learn a bit about the MySQL graphical client and the web-based database administration interfaces available for both MySQL and PostgreSQL.

The following sections examine two common methods of accessing a remote database, a method of local access to a database server, and the concept of web access to a database.

> **NOTE**
>
> You should consider access and permission issues when setting up a database. Should users be able to create and destroy databases? Or should they only be able to use existing databases? Will users be able to add records to the database and modify existing records? Or should users be limited to read-only access to the database? And what about the rest of the world? Will the general public need to have any kind of access to your database through the Internet? As DBA, you must determine the answers to these questions.

SSH Access to a Database

Two types of remote database access scenarios are briefly discussed in this section. In the first scenario, the user directly logs in to the database server through SSH (to take advantage of the security benefits of encrypted sessions) and then starts a program on the server to access the database. In this case, shown in Figure 20.4, the database client is running on the database server itself.

FIGURE 20.4   The user logs in to the database server located on host `simba` from the workstation (host `cheetah`). The database client is running on `simba`.

In the other scenario, shown in Figure 20.5, the user logs in to a remote host through SSH and starts a program on it to access the database, but the database is actually running on a different system. Three systems are now involved—the user's workstation, the remote host running the database client, and the remote host running the database server.

The important thing to note in Figure 20.5 is the middleman system `leopard`. Although the client is no longer running on the database server itself, it isn't running on the user's local workstation, either.

FIGURE 20.5   The user logs in to the remote host `leopard` from the workstation (host `cheetah`) and starts a database client on `leopard`. The client on `leopard` then connects to the database server running on host `simba`. The database client is running on `leopard`.

Local GUI Client Access to a Database

A user can log in to the database server by using a graphical client (which could be running on Windows, Macintosh, or a Unix workstation). The graphical client then connects to the database server. In this case, the client is running on the user's workstation. Figure 20.6 shows an example.

FIGURE 20.6   The user starts a GUI database program on his workstation (hostname `cheetah`). This program, which is the database client, then connects to the database server running on the host `lion`.

Web Access to a Database

In this section, we look at two basic examples of web access to the database server. In the first example, a user accesses the database through a form located on the World Wide Web. At first glance, it might appear that the client is running on the user's workstation. Of course, in reality it is not; the client is actually running on the web server. The web browser on the user's workstation simply provides a way for the user to enter the data that he wants to send to the database and a way for the results sent from the database to be displayed to the user. The software that actually handles sending the request to the database is running on the web server in the form of a CGI script; a Java servlet; or embedded scripting such as the PHP or Sun Microsystems, Inc.'s JavaServer Pages (JSP).

Often, the terms *client* and *front end* are used interchangeably when speaking of database structures. However, Figure 20.7 shows an example of a form of access in which the client and the front end aren't the same thing at all. In this example, the front end is the form displayed in the user's web browser. In such cases, the client is referred to as *middleware*.

FIGURE 20.7   The user accesses the database through the World Wide Web. The front end is the user's web browser, the client is running on `leopard`, and the server is running on `simba`.

In another possible web access scenario, it could be said that the client is a two-piece application in which part of it is running on the user's workstation and the other part is running on the web server. For example, the database programmer can use JavaScript in the web form to ensure that the user has entered a valid query. In this case, the user's query is partially processed on her own workstation and partially on the web server. Error checking is done on the user's own workstation, which helps reduce the load on the server and also helps reduce network traffic because the query is checked for errors before being sent across the network to the server.

The MySQL Command-Line Client

The MySQL command-line client is `mysql`, and it has the following syntax:

```
mysql [options] [database]
```

Some of the available options for `mysql` are discussed in Table 20.1. *database* is optional, and if given, it should be the name of the database to which you want to connect.

TABLE 20.1   Command-Line Options to Use When Invoking `mysql`

Option	Action
`-h` *hostname*	Connects to the remote host *hostname* (if the database server isn't located on the local system).
`-u` *username*	Connects to the database as the user *username*.
`-p`	Prompts for a password. This option is required if the user you are connecting as needs a password to access the database. Note that this is a lowercase p.
`-P` *n*	Specifies *n* as the number of the port that the client should connect to. Note that this is an uppercase P.
`-?`	Displays a help message.

More options are available than are listed in Table 20.1, but these are the most common options. See the man page for `mysql` for more information on the available options.

> **CAUTION**
>
> Although `mysql` allows you to specify the password on the command line after the `-p` option, and thus allows you to avoid having to type the password at the prompt, you should never invoke the client this way. Doing so causes your password to display in the process list, and the process list can be accessed by any user on the system. This is a major security hole, so you should never give your password on the `mysql` command line.

You can access the MySQL server without specifying a database to use. After you log in, you use the `help` command to get a list of available commands, like this:

```
mysql> help

MySQL commands:
Note that all text commands must be first on line and end with ';'
help    (\h) Display this help.
?       (\?) Synonym for `help'.
clear   (\c) Clear command.
connect (\r) Reconnect to the server. Optional arguments are db and host.
edit    (\e) Edit command with $EDITOR.
ego     (\G) Send command to mysql server, display result vertically.
exit    (\q) Exit mysql. Same as quit.
go      (\g) Send command to mysql server.
nopager (\n) Disable pager, print to stdout.
notee   (\t) Don't write into outfile.
pager   (\P) Set PAGER [to_pager]. Print the query results via PAGER.
print   (\p) Print current command.
quit    (\q) Quit mysql.
rehash  (\#) Rebuild completion hash.
source  (\.) Execute a SQL script file. Takes a file name as an argument.
```

20

```
status (\s) Get status information from the server.
tee (\T) Set outfile [to_outfile]. Append everything into given outfile.
use (\u) Use another database. Takes database name as argument.
```

You can then access a database by using the use command and the name of a database that has been created (such as animals) and that you are authorized to connect to, like this:

```
mysql> use animals
Database changed
mysql>
```

The PostgreSQL Command-Line Client

You invoke the PostgreSQL command-line client with the command psql. Like mysql, psql can be invoked with the name of the database to which you would like to connect. Also like mysql, psql can take several options. These options are listed in Table 20.2.

TABLE 20.2   Command-Line Options to Use When Invoking psql

Option	Action
-h *hostname*	Connects to the remote host *hostname* (if the database server isn't located on the local system).
-p *n*	Specifies *n* as the number of the port that the client should connect to. Note that this is a lowercase p.
-U *username*	Connects to the database as the user *username*.
-W	Prompts for a password after connecting to the database. In PostgreSQL 7 and later, password prompting is automatic if the server requests a password after a connection has been established.
-?	Displays a help message.

Several more options are available in addition to those listed in Table 20.2. See the psql's man page for details on all the available options.

Graphical Clients

If you'd rather interact with a database by using a graphical database client than with the command-line clients discussed in the previous section, you're in luck: A few options are available.

MySQL has an official graphical client, called MySQLGUI. MySQLGUI is available in both source and binary formats from the MySQL website at http://www.mysql.com.

Web-based administration interfaces are also available for MySQL and PostgreSQL. phpMyAdmin and phpPgAdmin are two such products. Both of these products are based on the PHP-embedded scripting language and therefore require you to have PHP installed. Of course, you also need to have a web server installed.

Related Fedora and Database Commands

The following commands are useful for creating and manipulating databases in Fedora:

createdb—Creates a new PostgreSQL database

createuser—Creates a new PostgreSQL user account

dropdb—Deletes a PostgreSQL database

dropuser—Deletes a PostgreSQL user account

mysql—Interactively queries the mysqld server

mysqladmin—Administers the mysqld server

mysqldump—Dumps or backs up MySQL data or tables

pgaccess—Accesses a PostgreSQL database server

pg_ctl—Controls a PostgreSQL server or queries its status

psql—Accesses PostgreSQL via an interactive terminal

Reference

The following are references for the databases mentioned in this chapter:

- http://www.mysql.com—This is the official website of the MySQL database server. Here you can find the latest versions as well as up-to-date information and online documentation for MySQL. You can also purchase support contracts here. You might want to look into this if you will be using MySQL in a corporate setting. (Many corporations balk at the idea of using software for which the company has no support contract in place.)

- http://www.postgresql.org—This is the official website of the PostgreSQL database server. You are asked to select a mirror when you arrive at this site. After you select a mirror, you are taken to the main site. From there, you can find information on the latest versions of PostgreSQL and read the online documentation.

- http://www.postgresql.org/idocs/index.php?tutorial-start.html—This interactive HTML documentation tree is a great place to get started with learning how to use PostgreSQL.

- http://www.pgsql.com—This is a commercial company that provides fee-based support contracts for the PostgreSQL database.

# CHAPTER 21

File and Print

There are many reasons to share files and printers across a network. Perhaps you have a set of documents that need to be accessible to more than one person at a time, or you need to be able to print to a laser printer or a color printer. Fortunately, Fedora comes with a host of tools that allow you to share files with one another and access remote printers.

For the most part, graphical tools are available to help you configure your machine, but sometimes you might need to delve into the command line and some of the configuration files to tweak it just how you want it. This chapter takes you through setting up file sharing using both NFS and Samba and explains how to add users for Samba sharing as well as working with access levels, configuring Samba using SWAT (a handy web-based configuration tool), setting up and accessing remote printers on a print queue, and configuring Network Attached Printers that use interfaces such as JetDirect.

So, whether you are sharing ogg files across the network or setting up a corporate file server to hold office documents, you will find the answers here.

Using the Network File System

The Network File System (NFS) was developed by Sun Microsystems as a way for computers to share files as if they were local to the remote machine. NFS is commonly used to share home directories between hosts within a network. This reduces the need to have a home directory on every computer and ensures that no matter which computer you log in to, your home directory will be consistent.

Another popular use for NFS is to share binary files between similar computers. If you have a new version of a package that you want all machines to have, you only have to do the upgrade on the NFS server, and all hosts running the same version of Fedora will have the same upgraded package.

Installing and Starting or Stopping NFS

NFS is installed by default on Fedora and consists of several programs that work together to provide the NFS server service. One is rpc.portmapper, which maps NFS requests to the correct daemon. Two others are rpc.nfsd, which is the NFS daemon, and rpc.mountd, which controls the mounts and unmounts of file systems.

To have NFS automatically started when Fedora boots, use command-line or graphical administrative utilities, such as chkconfig, ntsysv, or system-config-services. Make sure you have the portmap service started because it is used as part of the service. One way to manually start or stop NFS is by directly calling its service control script nfs like this:

```
# /etc/rc.d/init.d/nfs start
Starting NFS services:              [ OK ]
Starting NFS quotas:                [ OK ]
Starting NFS daemon:                [ OK ]
Starting NFS mountd:                [ OK ]
```

In this example, NFS has been started. Use the stop keyword instead to stop the service. This approach to controlling NFS is handy, especially after configuration changes have been made. You can also use the service command or the graphical system-config-services client in the same way. See the next section on how to configure NFS support on your Fedora system.

NFS Server Configuration

The NFS server can be configured by editing the /etc/exports file. This file is similar to the /etc/fstab file in that it is used to set the permissions for the file systems being exported. The entries look like this:

```
/file/system yourhost(options) *.yourdomain.com(options) 192.15.69.0/24(options)
```

This shows three common clients to which to share /file/system. The first, yourhost, shares /file/system to just one host. The second, .yourdomain.com, uses the asterisk (*) as a wildcard to enable all hosts in yourdomain.com to access /file/system. The third share enables all hosts of the Class C network, 192.15.69.0, to access /file/share. For security, it is best not to use shares like the last two across the Internet because all data will be readable by any network the data passes by.

Some common options are shown in Table 21.1.

TABLE 21.1 /etc/fstab Options

Option	Purpose
rw	Gives read and write access
ro	Gives read-only access
async	Writes data when the server feels the need, not the client
sync	Writes data as it is received

The following is an example of an /etc/exports file:

```
# /etc/exports file for myhost.mydomain.com
/usr/local        yourhost(ro,show)
/home/jkennedy    *.yourdomain.com(rw,hide,sync)
```

This file *exports* (makes available) /usr/local to yourhost. The mount is read-only (which is good for a directory of binary files that don't get written to). It also allows users on yourhost to see the contents of file systems that might be mounted on /usr/local. The second export mounts /home/jkennedy to any host in yourdomain.com. It doesn't allow subsidiary file systems to be viewed, but you can read and write to the file system.

After you have finished with the /etc/exports file, the following command

/usr/sbin/exportfs -r

exports all the file systems in the /etc/exports file to a list named xtab under the /var/lib/nfs directory, which is used as a guide for mounting when a remote computer asks for a directory to be exported. The -r option to the command reads the entire /etc/exports file and mounts all the entries. The exportfs command can also be used to export specific files temporarily. Here's an example using exportfs to export a file system:

```
/usr/sbin/exportfs -o async yourhost:/usr/tmp
```

This command exports /usr/tmp to yourhost with the async option.

Be sure to restart the NFS server after making any changes to /etc/exports. If you prefer, you can use Red Hat's system-config-nfs graphical client to set up NFS while using the X Window System. Start the client by clicking the System Settings menu and then selecting the NFS Server menu item from the Server Settings menu. You can also start the client from the command line of an X terminal window, like so:

$ **system-config-nfs &**

After you press Enter, you are prompted for the root password. Type in the password and click OK, and you see the main window. Click the Add button, and you see the Add NFS Share dialog box, as shown in Figure 21.1.

FIGURE 21.1   Red Hat's `system-config-nfs` client can be used to quickly set up local directories for export using NFS.

In the Directory text box, type in a name of a directory to be exported; in the Host(s) text box, type in a hostname or the IP address of a remote host that is to be allowed access to the directory. By default, a directory is exported as read-only, but you can choose read and write access by clicking either option in the Basic Permissions area of the dialog box. When finished, click the OK button, click the Apply button, and then use the File menu to quit.

NFS Client Configuration

To configure your host as an NFS client (to acquire remote files or directories), edit the /etc/fstab file as you would to mount any local file system. However, instead of using a device name to be mounted (such as /dev/hda1), enter the remote hostname and the desired file system to be imported. For example, one entry might look like this:

```
# Device           Mount Point   Type   Options        Freq Pass
yourhost:/usr/local  /usr/local    nfs    nfsvers=3,ro  0    0
```

> **NOTE**
>
> If you use autofs on your system, you need to use proper autofs entries for your remote NFS mounts. See the section 5 man page for autofs.

The options column uses the same options as standard fstab file entries with some additional entries, such as nfsvers=3, which specifies the third version of NFS. You can also use the `mount` command, as root, to quickly attach a remote directory to a local file system by using a remote host's name and exported directory. For example,

```
# mount -t nfs 192.168.2.67:/music /music
```

After you press Enter, the entire remote directory appears on your file system. You can verify the imported file system using the `df` command like so:

```
# df
Filesystem              1k-blocks       Used Available Use% Mounted on
/dev/hda2               18714368    9642600   8121124  55% /
/dev/hda1                  46636      13247     30981  30% /boot
none                      120016          0    120016   0% /dev/shm
192.168.2.67:/music     36875376   20895920  14106280  60% /music
```

Make sure that the desired mount point exists before using the `mount` command. When finished using the directory (perhaps for copying backups), the `umount` command can be used to remove the remote file system. Note that if you specify the root directory (/) as a mount point, you will not be able to unmount the NFS directory until you reboot (because Linux will complain that the file system is in use).

Putting Samba to Work

Samba uses the Session Message Block (SMB) protocol to enable the Windows operating system (or any operating system) to access Linux files. Using Samba, you can make your Fedora machine look just like a Windows computer to other Windows computers on your network. You do not need to install Windows on your PC.

Samba is a very complex program—so much so that the book *Samba Unleashed* (Sams Publishing, 2000, ISBN 0-672-31862-8) is more than 1,200 pages long. The Samba man page (when converted to text) for just the configuration file is 330KB and 7,013 lines long. Although Samba is complex, setting it up and using it does not have to be difficult. There are many options, which accounts for some of Samba's complexity. Depending on what you want, Samba's use can be as easy or as difficult as you would like it to be.

Fortunately, Fedora includes the Samba Web Administration Tool (SWAT), which can be used to configure Samba by using the Mozilla web browser. SWAT provides an easy way to start and stop the Samba server; set up printing services; define remote access permissions; and create Samba usernames, passwords, and shared directories. This section delves into the basics of configuring Samba, and you should first read how to manually configure Samba to get an understanding of how the software works. At the end of this section, you will see how to enable, start, and use SWAT to set up simple file sharing.

Like most of the software that comes with Fedora, Samba is licensed under the GPL and is free. It comes as both an RPM and as source code. In both cases, installation is straightforward and the software can be installed when you install Fedora or use RPM software packages. The Samba RPMs should be on one of your Fedora install disks, or the latest version can be downloaded from the Internet, preferably from the Fedora Project (at fedora.redhat.com) or an authorized mirror site. See Chapter 7, "Managing Software and System Resources," for more information on using RPM packages.

Installing from source code can be more time-consuming. If you do not want to install using Fedora's default locations, however, installing from the source code is a more configurable method. Just download the source from http://www.samba.org and unpack the files. Change into the source directory and, as root, run the command ./configure along with any changes from the defaults. Then run make, make test (if you want), followed by make install to install Samba in the specified locations.

If you install Samba using your Fedora CD-ROMs, you can find a large amount of documentation in the directory tree starting at /usr/share/doc/samba*/doc/ in several formats, including PDF, HTML, and text, among others. Altogether, almost 3MB of documentation is included with the source code.

After Samba is installed, you can either create the file /etc/smb.conf or use the smb.conf file supplied with Samba, which is located by default under the /etc/samba directory with Fedora. Nearly a dozen sample configuration files can be found under the /usr/share/doc/samba*/examples directory.

> **NOTE**
>
> Depending on your needs, smb.conf can be a simple file of less than 20 lines or a huge file spanning many pages of text. If your needs are complex, I suggest picking up a copy of *Samba Unleashed*.

Manually Configuring Samba with /etc/samba/smb.conf

The /etc/samba/smb.conf file is broken into sections. Each section is a description of the resource shared (share) and should be titled appropriately. The three special sections are

- [global]—Establishes the global configuration settings (defined in detail in the smb.conf manual page and Samba documentation, found under the /usr/share/doc/samba/docs directory)

- [homes]—Shares users' home directories and specifies directory paths and permissions

- [printers]—Handles printing by defining shared printers and printer access

Each section in your /etc/samba/smb.conf configuration file should be named for the resource being shared. For example, if the resource /usr/local/programs is being shared, you could call the section [programs]. When Windows sees the share, it is called by whatever you name the section (programs in this example). The easiest and fastest way to set up this share is with the following example from smb.conf:

```
[programs]
path = /usr/local/programs
writeable = true
```

This bit shares the /usr/local/programs directory with any valid user who asks for it and makes that directory writable. It is the most basic share because it sets no limits on the directory.

Here are some parameters you can set in the sections:

- Requiring a user to enter a password before accessing a shared directory

- Limiting the hosts allowed to access the shared directory

- Altering permissions users are allowed to have on the directory

- Limiting the time of day during which the directory is accessible

The possibilities are almost endless. Any parameters set in the individual sections override the parameters set in the [global] section. The following section adds a few restrictions to the [programs] section:

```
[programs]
path = /usr/local/programs
writeable = true
valid users = jkennedy
browseable = yes
create mode = 0700
```

The valid users entry limits userid to just jkennedy. All other users can browse the directory because of the browseable = yes entry, but only jkennedy can write to the directory. Any files created by jkennedy in the directory give jkennedy full permissions, but no one else will have access to the file. This is exactly the same as setting permissions with the chmod command. Again, there are numerous options, so you can be as creative as you want to when developing sections.

Setting Global Samba Behavior with the [global] Section

The [global] section set parameters establishes configuration settings for all of Samba. If a given parameter isn't specifically set in another section, Samba uses the default setting in the [global] section. The [global] section also sets the general security configuration for Samba. The [global] section is the only section that doesn't require the name in brackets.

Samba assumes that anything before the first bracketed section not labeled [global] is part of the global configuration. (Using bracketed headings in /etc/samba/smb.conf makes your configuration file more readable.) The following sections discuss common Samba settings to share directories and printers. You will then see how to test your Samba configuration.

Sharing Home Directories Using the [homes] Section

The [homes] section shares out Fedora home directories for the users. The home directory is shared automatically when a user's Windows computer connects to the Linux server holding the home directory. The one problem with using the default configuration is that the user sees all the configuration files (such as .profile and others with a leading period in the filename) that he normally wouldn't see when logging on through Linux. One quick way to avoid this is to include a path option in the [homes] section. To use this solution, each user who requires a Samba share of his home directory needs a separate "home directory" to act as his Windows home directory.

For example, this pseudo home directory could be a directory named share in each user's home directory on your Fedora system. You can specify the path option when using SWAT by using the %u option when specifying a path for the default homes shares (see the section "Configuring Samba Using SWAT" later in this chapter). The complete path setting would be

```
/home/%u/share
```

This setting specifies that the directory named share under each user's directory will be the shared Samba directory. The corresponding manual smb.conf setting to provide a separate "home directory" looks like this:

```
[homes]
        comment = Home Directories
        path = /home/%u/share
        valid users = %S
        read only = No
        create mask = 0664
        directory mask = 0775
        browseable = No
```

If you have a default [homes] section, the share shows up in the user's Network Neighborhood as the user's name. When the user connects, Samba scans the existing sections in smb.conf for a specific instance of the user's home directory. If there isn't one, Samba looks up the username in /etc/passwd. If the correct username and password have been given, the home directory listed in /etc/passwd is shared out at the user's home directory. Typically the [homes] section looks like this (the browseable = no entry prevents other users from being able to browse your home directory and is a good security practice):

```
[homes]
browseable = no
writable = yes
```

This example shares out the home directory and makes it writable to the user. Here's how you specify a separate Windows home directory for each user:

```
[homes]
browseable = no
writable = yes
path = /path/to/windows/directories
```

Sharing Printers by Editing the `[printers]` Section

The `[printers]` section works much like the `[homes]` section but defines shared printers for use on your network. If the section exists, users have access to any printer listed in your Fedora `/etc/printcap` file.

Like the `[homes]` section, when a print request is received, all the sections are scanned for the printer. If no share is found (with careful naming, there should not be unless you create a section for a specific printer), the `/etc/printcap` file is scanned for the printer name that is then used to send the print request.

For printing to work properly, printing services must be set up correctly on your Fedora computer. A typical `[printers]` section looks like the following:

```
[printers]
comment = Red Hat Printers
browseable = no
printable = yes
path = /var/spool/samba
```

The `/var/spool/samba` is a spool path set just for Samba printing.

Testing Samba with the `testparm` Command

After you have created your `/etc/smb.conf` file, you can check it for correctness. This is done with the `testparm` command. This command parses through your `/etc/smb.conf` file and checks for any syntax errors. If none are found, your configuration file will probably work correctly. It does not, however, guarantee that the services specified in the file will work. It is merely making sure that the file is correctly written.

As with all configuration files, if you are modifying an existing, working file, it is always prudent to copy the working file to a different location and modify that file. Then, you can check the file with the `testparm` utility. The command syntax is as follows:

```
# testparm /path/to/smb.conf.back-up
Load smb config files from smb.conf.back-up
Processing section "[homes]"
Processing section "[printers]"
Loaded services file OK.
```

This output shows that the Samba configuration file is correct, and, as long as all the services are running correctly on your Fedora machine, Samba should be working correctly. Now copy your old `smb.conf` file to a new location, put the new one in its place, and restart Samba with the command /etc/init.d/smb restart. Your new or modified Samba configuration should now be in place.

Starting the smbd **Daemon**

Now that your smb.conf file is correctly configured, you can start your Samba server daemon. This can be done with the /usr/sbin/smbd command, which (with no options) starts the Samba server with all the defaults. The most common option you will change in this command is the location of the smb.conf file; you change this option if you don't want to use the default location /etc/smb/smb.conf. The -s option allows you to change the smb.conf file Samba uses; this option is also useful for testing whether a new smb.conf file actually works. Another useful option is the -l option, which specifies the log file Samba uses to store information.

To start, stop, or restart Samba from the command line, use the service command; the system-config-services client; or the /etc/rc.d/init.d/smb script with a proper keyword, such as start, like so:

```
# /etc/rc.d/init.d/smb start
```

Using the smbstatus **Command**

The smbstatus command reports on the current status of your Samba connections. The syntax is

```
/usr/bin/smbstatus [options]
```

Some of the available options are shown in Table 21.2.

TABLE 21.2   smbstatus Options

Option	Result
-b	Brief output.
-d	Verbose output.
-s /path/to/config	Used if the configuration file used at startup is not the standard one.
-u *username*	Shows the status of a specific user's connection.
-p	Lists current smb processes. This can be useful in scripts.

Connecting with the smbclient **Command**

The smbclient command allows users on other Linux hosts to access your smb shares. You can't mount the share on your host, but you can use it in a way that's similar to an FTP client. Several options can be used with the smbclient command. The most frequently used is -I followed by the IP address of the computer to which you are connecting. The smbclient command does not require root access to run:

```
smbclient -I 10.10.10.20 -Uusername%password
```

This gives you the following prompt:

```
smb: <current directory on share>
```

From here, the commands are almost identical to the standard Unix/Linux FTP commands. Note that you can omit a password on the `smbclient` command line. You are then prompted to enter the Samba share password.

Mounting Samba Shares

There are two ways to mount Samba shares to your Linux host. Mounting a share is the same as mounting an available media partition or remote NFS directory except that the Samba share is accessed using SMB. (See Chapter 37, "Managing the File System," to see how to mount partitions.) The first method uses the standard Linux mount command:

```
mount -t smbfs //10.10.10.20/homes /mount/point -o username=jkennedy,dmask=777,\
 fmask=777
```

> **NOTE**
>
> The hostname can be substituted for an IP address if your name service is running or the host is in your /etc/hosts file.

This command mounts `jkennedy`'s home directory on your host and gives all users full permissions to the mount. The permissions are equal to the permissions on the `chmod` command.

The second method produces the same results using the `smbmount` command as follows:

```
# smbmount //10.10.10.20/homes /mount/point -o username=jkennedy,dmask-777,\
 fmask=777
```

To unmount the share, use the standard

```
# umount /mount/point
```

These `mount` commands can also be used to mount true Windows client shares to your Fedora host. Using Samba, you can configure your server to provide any service Windows can serve, and no one but you will ever know.

Configuring Samba Using SWAT

The Samba team of developers has made administering Samba a snap with the Samba Web Administration Tool (SWAT). SWAT is a web-based configuration and maintenance interface that gets as close to a point-and-click Samba environment as possible. This section provides a simple example of how to use SWAT to set up SMB access to a user's home directory and how to share a directory.

You need to perform a few steps before you can start using SWAT. First, make sure you have the Samba and the samba-swat RPM packages installed. You then enable SWAT access to your system by editing the /etc/xinetd.d/swat file by changing the following line:

```
disable = yes
```

Change the word yes to the word no, like so:

```
disable = no
```

Save the file, and then restart the xinetd daemon, using either the system-config-services client or the xinetd shell script under /etc/rc.d/init.d like so:

 # /etc/rc.d/init.d/xinetd restart

Next, start an X session, launch the Mozilla web browser, and browse to the http://localhost:901 uniform resource locator (URL). You are presented a login prompt. Enter the root username and password, and then click the OK button. The screen clears, and you see the main SWAT page, as shown in Figure 21.2.

TIP

You can also configure Samba using Red Hat's system-config-samba client. Launch the client from the command line of an X terminal window or select the System Settings, Samba Server menu item (as shown later in Figure 21.9).

---

sample_database

phonebook

last_name	first_name	phone
Doe	John	555-555-1212
Doe	Jane	555-555-1212
Palmer	John	555-123-4567
Johnson	Richard	555-111-4321

cd_collection

id	title	artist	year	rating
1	Mind Bomb	The The	1989	4
2	For All You've Done	Hillsong	2004	
3	Trouser Jazz	Mr Scruff	2002	5
4	Natural Elements	Acoustic Alchemy	1988	3
5	Combat Rock	The Clash	1982	4
6	Life for Rent	Dido	2003	5
7	Adiemus 4	Karl Jenkins	2000	4
8	The Two Towers	Howard Shore	2002	5

FIGURE 21.2   SWAT can be used to easily configure and administer Samba on your system.

First, click the GLOBALS icon in SWAT's main page. You see a page similar to the one shown in Figure 21.3. Many options are in the window, but you can quickly set up access for hosts from your LAN by simply entering one or more IP addresses or a subnet address (such as 192.168.2.—note the trailing period, which allows access for all hosts; in this example, on the 192.168.2 subnet) in the Hosts Allow field under the Security Options section. If you need help on how to format the entry, click the Help link to the left of the field. A new web page appears with the pertinent information.

When finished, click the Commit Changes button to save the global access settings. The next step is to create a Samba user and set the user's password. Click the PASSWORD icon on the main SWAT page (refer to Figure 21.2). The Server Password Management page opens, as shown in Figure 21.4. Type a new username in the User Name field; then type a password in the New Password and Re-type New Password fields.

> **NOTE**
>
> You need to supply a username of an existing system user, but the password used for Samba access does not need to match the existing user's password.

When finished, click the Add New User button. SWAT then creates the username and password and displays Added user *username* (where *username* is the name you entered). The new Samba user should now be able to gain access to the home directory from any allowed host if the Samba (smb) server is running.

FIGURE 21.3   Configure Samba to allow access from specific hosts or subnets on your LAN.

FIGURE 21.4   Enter a Samba username and password in the SWAT Password page.

For example, if you have set up Samba on a host named `shuttle2` that has a user named `sprice`, the user can access the home directory on `shuttle2` from any remote host (if allowed by the GLOBALS settings), perhaps by using the `smbclient` command like so:

```
$ smbclient //shuttle2/sprice -U sprice
added interface ip=192.168.2.68 bcast=192.168.2.255 nmask=255.255.255.0
Password:
Domain=[MYGROUP] OS=[Unix] Server=[Samba 2.2.5]
smb: \> pwd
Current directory is \\shuttle2\sprice\
smb: \> quit
```

Click the Status icon (as shown in Figure 21.2 or 21.4) to view Samba's status or to start, stop, or restart the server. You can use various buttons on the resulting web page to control the server and view periodic or continuous status updates.

You can also use SWAT to share a Linux directory. First, click the Shares icon in the toolbar at the top of the main Samba page (refer to Figure 21.2). Type a share name in the Create Shares field, and then click the Create Shares button. The SWAT page displays the detailed configuration information in a dialog box as shown in Figure 21.5, providing access to detailed configuration for the new Samba share.

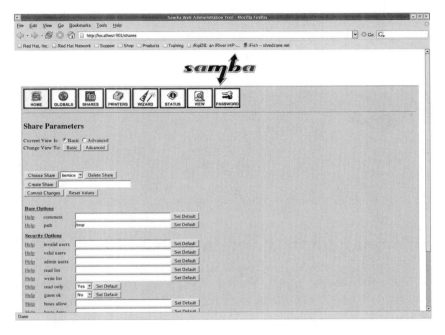

FIGURE 21.5   Use the SWAT Shares page to set up sharing of a portion of your Linux file system.

Type the directory name (such as /music) you want to share in the Path field under the Base options. Select No or Yes in the Read Only field under Security options to allow or deny read and write access. Select Yes in the Guest OK option to allow access from other users and specify a hostname, IP address, or subnet in the Hosts Allow field to allow access. Click the Commit Changes button when finished. Remote users can then access the shared volume. This is how a Linux server running Samba can easily mimic shared volumes in a mixed computing environment!

Alternatively, use the system-config-samba client (from the command line or the Server Settings Samba Server menu item on the System Settings menu). Figure 21.6 shows the properties of a shared directory named /music. Use the Add button to create new shares and the Properties button to edit the share's access options. Use the Preferences menu to edit your Samba server's general settings or to create and manage Samba users.

FIGURE 21.6 Configure a Samba share by editing the share defaults.

Network and Remote Printing with Fedora

In Chapter 11, "Printing with Fedora," we discussed how to set up and configure local printers as well as the associated print services. This section covers configuring printers for sharing and access across a network.

Offices all over the world benefit from using print servers and shared printers. In my office I have two printers connected to the network via an old PC with Linux so my wife can print from downstairs using a wireless link and I can print from my three computers in my office. It's a simple thing to do and can bring real productivity benefits, even in small settings.

Creating Network Printers

Setting up remote printing service involves configuring a print server and then creating a remote printer entry on one or more computers on your network. This section introduces a quick method of enabling printing from one Linux workstation to another Linux computer on a LAN. You also learn about SMB printing using Samba and its utilities. Finally, this section discusses how to configure network-attached printers and use them to print single or multiple documents.

Enabling Network Printing on a LAN

To set up printing from one Linux workstation to another across a LAN, you need root permission and access to both computers, but the process is simple and easy to perform.

First, log in or ssh to the computer to which the printer is attached. This computer will be the printer server. Use the hostname or ifconfig commands to obtain the hostname or IP address and write down or note the name of the printer queue. If the system uses LPRng instead of CUPS, you need to edit the file named /etc/lpd.perms. Scroll to the end of the file and look for the remote permission entry:

```
# allow local job submissions only
REJECT SERVICE=X NOT SERVER
```

Remote printing is not enabled by default, so you must comment out the service reject line with a pound sign (#):

```
# allow local job submissions only
#REJECT SERVICE=X NOT SERVER
```

Save the file, and then restart the lpd daemon.

This enables incoming print requests with the proper queue name (name of the local printer) from any remote host to be routed to the printer. After you have finished, log out and go to a remote computer on your LAN without an attached printer.

TIP

LPRng, like CUPS, can be configured to restrict Print services to single hosts, one or more specific local or remote users, all or part of a domain, or a LAN segment (by specifying an IP address range). An entry in /etc/lpd.perms, for example, to allow print requests only from hosts on 192.168.2.0, would look like this:

```
ACCEPT SERVICE=X REMOTEIP=192.168.2.0/255.255.255.0
```

The lpd.perms man page (included as part of the LPRng documentation) contains an index of keywords you can use to craft custom permissions. Don't forget to restart the lpd daemon after making any changes to /etc/lpd.perms (or /etc/lpd.conf).

If the computer with an attached printer is using Fedora and you want to set up the system for print serving, again use the system-config-printer client. You can create a new print queue, but the easiest approach is to edit settings for an existing queue and enable sharing of the printer.

To enable sharing, start the system-config-printer, and then click the name of the printer to be shared over your network. Click Sharing from the Action menu to open the dialog box shown in Figure 21.7.

FIGURE 21.7   Sharing allows you to offer a locally attached printer as a remote printer on your network.

Click the check box in the dialog box to allow sharing of the printer. By default, all remote hosts will be allowed access, but you can edit the settings to add, remove, or specify host access to your printer. Click the Edit button to specify access over a network interface (such as eth0, eth1, and so on), a range of IP addresses, or a specific host.

TIP

If you will share your CUPS-managed printer with other Linux hosts on a LAN using the Berkeley-type print spooling daemon, lpd, check the Enable LPD Protocol item under the Sharing dialog box's General tab. Next, check that the file cups-lpd under the /etc/xinetd.d directory contains the setting disable = no and then restart xinetd. This enables CUPS to run the cups-lpd server and accept remote print jobs sent by lpd from remote hosts. Do not forget to save your changes and restart CUPS!

When finished, click the OK button and then select Quit from the Action menu to exit.

To create a printer queue to access a remote Unix print server, use system-config-printer to create a printer but select the Networked Unix (LPD) type. Click Forward and enter a printer name and description; you are then asked to enter the hostname (or IP address) of the remote computer with a printer, along with the printer's queue name, as shown in Figure 21.8.

FIGURE 21.8   Enter the hostname or IP address of the remote computer with a printer, along with the remote printer's queue name.

NOTE

Browse to http://www.faqs.org/rfcs/rfc1179.html to read more about using the Strict RFC1179 Compliance option when configuring Fedora to be able to print to a remote Unix printer. This 13-year-old Request For Comments (RFC) document describes printing protocols for the BSD line print spooling system. The option is used to allow your documents to print to remote servers using the older print system or software conforming to the standard.

Click the Forward button after entering this information; then continue to configure the new entry as if the remote printer were attached locally (use the same print driver setting as the remote printer). When finished, don't forget to save the changes!

You can also test the new remote printer by clicking the Tests menu item and using one of the test page items, such as the ASCII or PostScript test pages. The ASCII test page prints a short amount of text to test the spacing and page width; the PostScript test page prints a page of text with some information about your printer, a set of radial lines one degree apart, and a color wheel (if you use a color printer).

Session Message Block Printing

Printing to an SMB printer requires Samba, along with its utilities such as the smbclient and associated smbprint printing filter. You can use the Samba software included with Fedora to print to a shared printer on a Windows network or set up a printer attached to your system as an SMB printer. This section describes how to create a local printer entry to print to a remote shared printer using SMB.

Setting up an SMB or shared printer is usually accomplished under Windows operating systems through configuration settings using the Control Panel's Network device. After enabling print sharing, reboot the computer. In the My Computer, Printers folder, right-click the name or icon of the printer you want to share and select Sharing from the pop-up menu. Set the Shared As item; then enter a descriptive shared name, such as **HP4100**, and a password.

You must enter a shared name and password to configure the printer when running Linux. You also need to know the printer's workgroup name, IP address, and printer name and have the username and password on hand. To find this information, select Start, Settings, Printers; then right-click the shared printer's listing in the Printers window and select Properties from the pop-up window.

On your Fedora system, use system-config-printer to create a new local printer queue and assign it a name; then select the Networked Windows (SMB) type in the Add a New Print Queue dialog box. Click the drop-down list by the name of any active Samba server on your LAN (CELLO in example shown in Figure 21.9). SMB printers offered by the server appear in the drop-down list and can be selected for use, or you can click the Specify button and create your own entry. When you click Forward, you are asked to enter a username and password for the remote share if passwords are required.

Click Forward, and then create a printer queue with characteristics that match the remote printer. (For example, if the remote printer is an HP 400 Deskjet, select the driver listed for that device in your configuration.)

Network-Attached Printer Configuration and Printing

Fedora supports other methods of remote printing, such as using a Novell Netware–based print queue or using a printer attached directly to your network with an HP JetDirect adapter. Some manufacturers even offer Linux-specific drivers and help. For example,

HP/Compaq provides graphical printer configuration tools and software drivers for other Linux distributions at http://h20000.www2.hp.com/bizsupport/TechSupport/Home.jsp.

FIGURE 21.9   Create a shared remote printer using required information for Windows.

You can set up network-attached printing quickly and easily using a variety of devices. For example, NETGEAR's PS101 print server adapter works well with Linux. This tiny device (a self-hosted print server) is an adapter that directly attaches to a printer's Centronics port, eliminates the use of a parallel-port cable, and enables the use of the printer over a network. The PS101 offers a single 10Mbps Ethernet jack and, after initial configuration and assignment of a static IP address, can be used to print to any attached printer supported by Fedora.

A JetDirect- or Unix-based configuration using `system-config-printer` can be used to allow you to print to the device from Fedora or other remote Linux hosts. To see any open ports or services on the device, use the `nmap` command with the print server adapter's IP address like this:

```
$ nmap 192.168.2.52
Starting nmap V. 2.54BETA22 ( www.insecure.org/nmap/ )
Interesting ports on  (192.168.2.52):
(The 1536 ports scanned but not shown below are in state: closed)
Port      State      Service
21/tcp    open       ftp
23/tcp    open       telnet
80/tcp    open       http
139/tcp   open       netbios-ssn
515/tcp   open       printer
9100/tcp  open       jetdirect
Nmap run completed -- 1 IP address (1 host up) scanned in 10 seconds
```

To configure printing, select `system-config-printer`'s JetDirect option; then specify the device's IP address (192.168.2.52 in the example) and port 9100 (as shown previously— you're clued that this is the right port by the Service entry, which states `jetdirect` in the example). Alternatively, you can configure the device and attached printer as a Unix-based print server, but you need to use PS1 as the name of the remote printer queue. Note that the device hosts a built-in web server (HTTP on port 80); you can administer the device by browsing to its IP address (such as http://192.168.2.52 in the example). Other services, such as FTP and Telnet, are supported but undocumented:

```
$ telnet 192.168.2.52
Trying 192.168.2.52...
Connected to 192.168.2.52 (192.168.2.52).
Escape character is '^]'.

Welcome to Print Server

PS>monitor
(P1)STATE: Idle
TYPE: Parallel
PRINTER STATUS: On-Line

PS>exit
Connection closed by foreign host.
```

> **TIP**
>
> Curiously, NETGEAR does not promote the PS101 as Linux-supported hardware even though it works. Other types of network-attached print devices include Bluetooth-enabled printers and 802.11b wireless Ethernet print servers such as Trendware's TEW-PS3, HP/Compaq's parallel port-based WP 110, and the JetDirect 380x with USB. As always, research how well a product, such as a printer or print server, works with Linux before purchasing!

Console Print Control

Older versions of Red Hat Linux used the 4.3BSD line-printer spooling system and its suite of text-based printing utilities. Newer versions of these utilities, with the same names, are included with your Fedora CD-ROMs, but are part of the CUPS package. The commands support the launching of print jobs in the background (as a background process), the printing of multiple documents, the capability to specify local and networked printers, control of the printers, and management of the queued documents waiting in the printer's spool queue.

Console-based Printer Configuration

The system-config-printer-tui tool offers all the convenience and features of Red Hat's graphical printer configuration client without the need for a currently running X session. As you learned earlier, you run this command as root:

```
# system-config-printer-tui
```

After you press Enter, the command's main dialog box appears, as shown in Figure 21.10. You use the Tab and spacebar keys to navigate among and choose controls in this dialog box.

FIGURE 21.10   Use Red Hat's `system-config-printer-tui` printer configuration utility to create or edit printers during console-based Linux sessions.

Using Basic Print Commands

After configuring your printer, you can print from the desktop using any printer-capable graphical clients. If you don't use the desktop but prefer to use or access your Fedora system using a text-based interface, you can enter a number of print commands from the command line, as well. The main CUPS commands used to print and control printing from the command line are as follows:

- `lp`—The line printer spooling command; used to print documents using a specific printer

- `lpq`—The line printer queue display command; used to view the existing list of documents waiting to be printed

- `lpstat`—Displays server and printer status information

- `lprm`—The line printer queue management command; used to remove print jobs from a printer's queue

- `lpc`—The line printer control program; used by the root operator to manage print spooling, the `lpd` daemon, and printer activity

These commands offer a subset of the features provided by CUPS but can be used to start and control printers and print queues from the command line.

You print files (documents or images) using the lp command, along with a designated printer and filename. For example, to print the file mydoc.txt using the printer named lp, use the lp command, its -d command-line option, and the printer's name, like this:

```
# lp -dlp mydoc.txt
```

Managing Print Jobs

You can also print multiple documents from the command line. For example, to simultaneously print a number of files to the lp printer, use lpr like so:

```
# lp -dlp *.txt
```

This approach uses the wildcard capabilities of the shell to feed the lpr command all files in the current directory with a name ending in .txt for printing. Use the lpq command to view the printer's queue like so:

```
# lpq
lp is ready and printing
Rank    Owner   Job     File(s)                    Total Size
active  root    7       classes.conf               3072 bytes
```

The lpq command reports on the job, owner, job number, file being printed, and size of job. The job number (7 in this example) is used by CUPS to keep track of documents printing or waiting to be printed. Each job has a unique job number. To stop the print job in this example, use the lprm command, followed by the job number, like this:

```
# lprm 7
```

The lprm command removes the spooled files from the printer's queue and kills the job. Print job owners, such as regular users, can only remove spooled jobs that they own. As the root operator, you can kill any job.

Only the root operator can use the lpc command to administer printers and queues because the command is primarily used for printer and queue control. You, as a regular user, cannot use it to rearrange the order of your print jobs, but you can get a display of the status of any system printer. Start lpc on the command line like this:

```
# /usr/sbin/lpc
```

The lpc command has built-in help, but it consists of only five commands: exit, help, quit, status, and ?. The status command shows the status of a specified printer or all printers:

```
# lpc
lpc> ?
Commands may be abbreviated.  Commands are:
```

```
exit    help    quit    status  ?
lpc> status
lp:
        printer is on device 'parallel' speed -1
        queuing is enabled
        printing is enabled
        no entries
        daemon present
netlp:
        printer is on device 'parallel' speed -1
        queuing is enabled
        printing is enabled
        no entries
        daemon present
lpc> quit
```

The preceding sample session shows a status report for two printers: lp and netlp. Another helpful command is lpstat, which you use like this with its -t option:

```
# lpstat -t
scheduler is running
system default destination: lp
device for lp: parallel:/dev/lp0
device for netlp: parallel:/dev/lp0
lp accepting requests since Jan 01 00:00
netlp accepting requests since Jan 01 00:00
printer lp is idle.  enabled since Jan 01 00:00
printer netlp is idle.  enabled since Jan 01 00:00!)
```

This command lists all status information about printer queues on the local system.

Using the Common Unix Printing System GUI

You can use CUPS to create printer queues, get print server information, and manage queues by launching a browser (such as Mozilla) and browsing to http://localhost:631. CUPS provides a web-based administration interface, as shown in Figure 12.11.

If you click the Do Administration Tasks item in the browser page, you are asked to enter the root password, as shown in Figure 21.12.

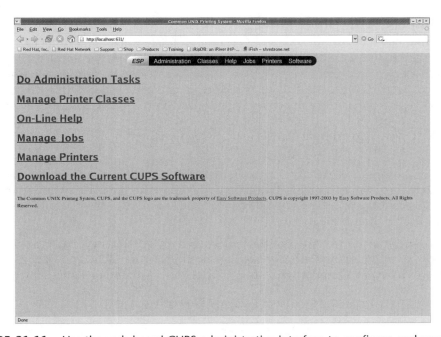

FIGURE 21.11 Use the web-based CUPS administrative interface to configure and manage printing.

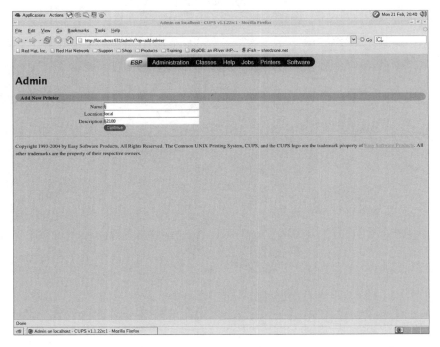

FIGURE 21.12 Enter the root password to perform printer administration with CUPS.

Creating a CUPS Printer Entry

This section provides a short example of creating a Linux printer entry using CUPS's web-based interface. Use the CUPS interface to create a printer and device queue type (such as local, remote, serial port, or Internet); then you enter a device uniform resource identifier (URI), such as `lpd://192.168.2.35/lp`, which represents the IP address of a remote Unix print server, and the name of the remote print queue on the server. You also need to specify the model or make of printer and its driver. A Printers page link allows you to print a test page, stop printing service, manage the local print queue, modify the printer entry, or add another printer.

In the Admin page, click the Add Printer button and then enter a printer name in the Name: field (such as `lp`), a physical location of the printer in the Location: field, and a short note about the printer (such as its type) in the Description: field. Figure 21.13 shows a sample entry for an HP648C.

Click the Continue button. You can then select the type of printer access (local, remote, serial port, or Internet) in the Device page, as shown in Figure 21.14. For example, to configure printing to a local printer, select Parallel Port #1 or, for a remote printer, select the LPD/LPR Host or Printer entry.

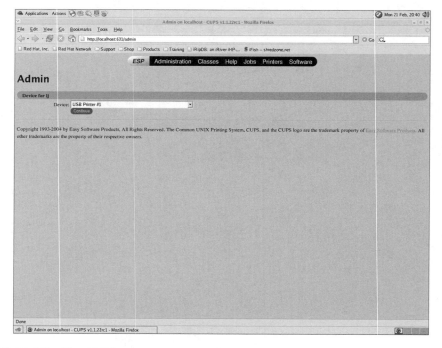

FIGURE 21.13   Use CUPS to create a new printer queue.

Again click Continue and select a printer make as requested in the dialog box shown in Figure 21.15.

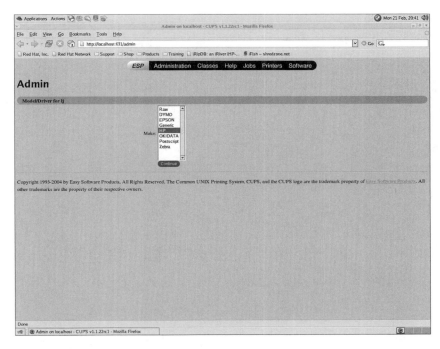

FIGURE 21.14   Select a printer device in the CUPS administrative page.

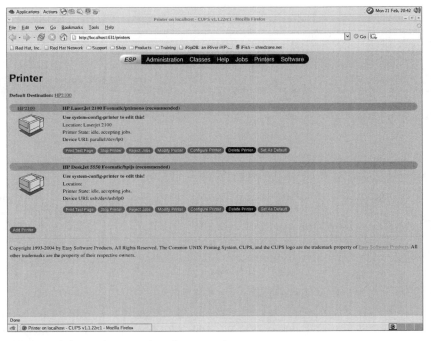

FIGURE 21.15   Select printer make when creating a new queue.

After you click Continue, you then select the driver. After creating the printer, you can then use the Printer page, as shown in Figure 21.16, to print a test page, stop printing service, manage the local print queue, modify the printer entry, or add another printer.

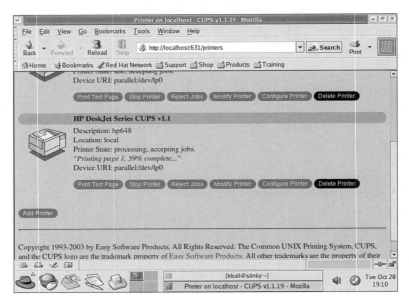

FIGURE 21.16   Manage printers easily using the CUPS Printer page.

CUPS offers many additional features and once installed, configured, and running, provides transparent traditional Unix printing support for Fedora.

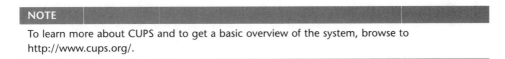

> **NOTE**
>
> To learn more about CUPS and to get a basic overview of the system, browse to http://www.cups.org/.

Avoiding Printer Support Problems

Troubleshooting printer problems can be frustrating, especially if you find that your new printer is not working properly with Linux. First, keep in mind that nearly all printers on the market today work with Linux. However, some vendors have higher batting averages in the game of supporting Linux. If you care to see a scorecard, browse to http://www.linuxprinting.org/vendors.html.

All-in-One (Print/Fax/Scan) Devices

Problematic printers, or printing devices that might or might not work with Fedora, include multifunction (or *all-in-one*) printers that combine scanning, faxing, and printing services. You should research any planned purchase, and avoid any vendor unwilling to support Linux with drivers or development information.

One shining star in the field of Linux support for multifunction printers is HP support of the HP OfficeJet Linux driver project at http://hpoj.sourceforge.net/. Printing and scanning are supported on many models, with fax support in development.

Using USB and Legacy Printers

Other problems can arise because of a lack of a printer's USB vendor and device ID information—a problem shared by some USB scanners under Linux. For information regarding USB printer support, you can check with the Linux printing folks (at the URL in the start of this section) or with the Linux USB project at http://www.linux-usb.org.

Although many newer printers require universal serial bus (USB), excellent support still exists for legacy parallel-port (IEEE-1284) printers with Linux, enabling sites to continue to use older hardware. You can take advantage of Linux workarounds to set up printing even if the host computer does not have a traditional parallel printer port or if you want to use a newer USB printer on an older computer.

For example, to host a parallel port–based printer on a USB-only computer, attach the printer to the computer using an inexpensive USB-to-parallel converter. USB-to-parallel converters typically provide a Centronics connector; one end of that connector is plugged in to the older printer, whereas the other end is plugged in to a USB connector. The USB connector is then plugged in to your hub, desktop, or notebook USB port. On the other hand, you can use an add-on PCI card to add USB support for printing (and other devices) if the legacy computer does not have a built-in USB. Most PCI USB interface cards add at least two ports, and devices can be chained via a hub.

Related Fedora and Linux Commands

The following commands help you manage printing services:

`accept`—Controls print job access to the CUPS server via the command line

`cancel`—Cancels a print job from the command line

`disable`—Controls printing from the command line

`enable`—Controls CUPS printers

`lp`—Sends a specified file to the printer and allows control of the prince service

`lpc`—Displays the status of printers and print service at the console

`lpq`—Views print queues (pending print jobs) at the console

`lprm`—Removes print jobs from the print queue via the command line

`lpstat`—Displays printer and server status

`system-config-printer`—Displays Fedora's graphical printer configuration tool

`system-config-printer-tui`—Displays Fedora's text-dialog printer configuration tool

---

Reference

- http://www.linuxprinting.org/—Browse here for specific drivers and information about USB and other types of printers.

- http://www.hp.com/wwsolutions/linux/products/printing_imaging/index.html— Short but definitive information from HP regarding printing product support under Linux.

- http://www.linuxdoc.org/HOWTO/Printing-HOWTO/—Grant Taylor's Printing HOWTO, with information on using various print services under Linux.

- http://www.cups.org/—A comprehensive repository of CUPS software, including versions for Red Hat Linux.

- http://www.pwg.org/ipp/—Home page for the Internet Printing Protocol standards.

- http://www.linuxprinting.org/cups-doc.html—Information about CUPS.

- http://www.cs.wisc.edu/~ghost/—Home page for the Ghostscript interpreter.

- http://www.samba.org/—Base entry point for getting more information about Samba and using the SMB protocol with Linux, Unix, Mac OS, and other operating systems.

In addition, an excellent book on Samba to help you learn more is *Samba Unleashed* (Sams Publishing, ISBN: 0-672-31862-8).

# CHAPTER 22

Remote File Serving with FTP

F*ile Transfer Protocol (FTP)* was once considered the primary method used to transfer files over a network from computer to computer. FTP is still heavily used today, although many graphical FTP clients now supplement the original text-based interface command. As computers have evolved, so has FTP, and Fedora Core includes many ways with which to use a graphical interface to transfer files over FTP.

This chapter contains an overview of the available FTP software included with Fedora, along with some details concerning initial set up, configuration, and use of FTP-specific clients. Fedora also includes an FTP server software package named vsftpd, the Very Secure FTP Daemon, and a number of associated programs you can use to serve and transfer files with the FTP protocol.

The following sections provide an overview of how to use FTP clients, then how to install and configure the vsftpd FTP server.

Using FTP Clients

The basic FTP protocol allows users to connect to a server, read directories and filenames, and download and upload data. If the correct access rights are set, users can also create new folders and set access permissions on them.

However, using FTP poses a security risk: Usernames and passwords are transmitted unencrypted across a LAN or the Internet. To stop users from taking the risk of giving their authentication details to anyone listening on the wire, many sites only enable anonymous FTP login and file retrieval. Many Linux users have turned to more secure alternatives, such as sshd and sftp or scp, included with the OpenSSH suite. The following sections discuss the different types of newer and traditional interfaces to FTP and their usage. Because they are part of the larger OpenSSH collection, the sftp and scp commands are covered in Chapter 25, "Remote Access with SSH and Telnet."

The FTP Client Interface

Fedora provides FTP clients that support a graphical or a text-based FTP interface. No matter which type you choose, you can improve your understanding and use of FTP if you learn how to use the FTP client at the command line.

Using the text-based interface helps you understand what each action in a graphical FTP session does. This understanding can be handy when, for example, the graphic client does not automatically detect the file type being transferred. In this situation, a binary file is transferred as an ASCII file and is therefore useless. Conversely, an ASCII file transferred as a binary prints the ^M control character at the end of each line. This error typically occurs when transferring files from older Microsoft Windows operating systems to Linux, as the Windows FTP client defaulted to ASCII, not binary transfers.

The following sections describe how to use the text-based FTP client interface. After this explanation, you learn how to use the many graphical FTP clients available for Fedora.

Using the Text-Based FTP Client Interface

Some of the following common commands may be used in a typical FTP session:

- ascii—Sets an ASCII file transfer type for the FTP session. You use this command before file transfers when sending or receiving text files.

- bin—Sets a binary file-type transfer for the FTP session. Use it before file transfers to send or receive binary files such as graphics images or compressed archives.

- bye—Use this command to close the FTP connection and quit the ftp command.

- close—Closes a connection to a remote server during an FTP session. Use this command instead of quit or bye to return to the ftp command prompt.

- get—Initiates a transfer of a single file from the FTP server to the user's local machine. Use this command to retrieve a single file (such as get cartoon.jpg).

- hash—Sets use of a hash mark (#) during file transfer. Use this command to get a visual indication of the progress of a transfer.

- mget—Initiates a transfer of multiple files from the FTP server to the user's local machine. Use this command to download (receive) multiple files with a single command (such as mget *.jpg).

- mput—Initiates a transfer of multiple files from the user's local machine to the FTP server. Use this command to upload (send) multiple files with a single command (such as mput *.jpg)

- open—Opens a connection to a remote server using an IP address or hostname. Use this command when working at the `ftp` command prompt (such as `open ftp.redhat.com`).

- prompt—Is an interactive command that asks the user for input on whether to get a specific file when the `mput` or `mget` command is issued. If the user initiates an `mget *`, with prompting on, the FTP client will prompt the user to transfer each file that the * wildcard matches. This can be particularly useful when several files in a directory need to be transferred, with one or two files that are unwanted. By default, prompting is turned on.

- put—Initiates the transfer of a single file from the user's local machine to the FTP server. Use this command to upload (send) a single file (such as `put inventory.doc`).

- send—The same command as `put`.

- quit—The same command as `bye`.

> **TIP**
>
> Although this section of the chapter discusses the use of the standard `ftp` client, other text-based FTP clients are available for Linux. Nc-FTP, which is included on the Fedora Core CD-ROM or available from www.ncftp.com, gives users extra functionality, such as the ability to get multiple directories at one time (without performing recursive `mget`s) and reconstructing the directory structure on their local machines. The website for this product has a list of all features this client offers to the user—in addition to the standard set of actions descriptor in the example.

These are just some of the commands available during an FTP session. By typing **help**, the user can see a full list of valid commands. Typing `help command-name` displays a brief description of what that command does. Listing 22.1 shows the `help` output.

LISTING 22.1   The Commands Listed by `help` in an FTP Session

```
Commands may be abbreviated.  Commands are:
```

!	cr	mdir	proxy	send
$	delete	mget	sendport	site
account	debug	mkdir	put	size
append	dir	mls	pwd	status
ascii	disconnect	mode	quit	struct
bell	form	modtime	quote	system
binary	get	mput	recv	sunique
bye	glob	newer	reget	tenex
case	hash	nmap	rstatus	trace
ccc	help	nlist	rhelp	type
cd	idle	ntrans	rename	user
cdup	image	open	reset	umask

LISTING 22.1   Continued

chmod	lcd	passive	restart	verbose
clear	ls	private	rmdir	?
close	macdef	prompt	runique	
cprotect	mdelete	protect	safe	

A Typical FTP Session Using the `ftp` Command

Connecting to a remote FTP server can require a username and password, but many servers also provide anonymous access. A properly configured remote FTP server responds quickly to FTP requests, and will display shared directories and files. This section shows a sample FTP session with a typical server found at many Internet sites (in this case, running the wu-ftpd server).

You connect to a remote FTP server by using the `ftp` command along with either the IP address or hostname of the remote computer, like so:

```
$ ftp pheniox
Connected to pheniox.
220 pheniox FTP server (Version wu-2.6.1-18) ready.
Name (pheniox:tdc): anonymous
331 Guest login ok, send your complete e-mail address as password.
Password:
230 Guest login ok, access restrictions apply.
Remote system type is Unix.
Using binary mode to transfer files.
ftp>
```

In this example, `ftp` is used to connect and then login using anonymous access. This is done by entering the word anonymous at the Name prompt. After pressing Enter, a password prompt is displayed. When using anonymous access, it is considered "good form" to enter your email address as a courtesy. There is no validation of the address entered, but many FTP servers are configured to only accept a valid email address form (that is, user@somewhere.com) if any text is typed at the prompt.

TIP

Many FTP servers will accept a simple press of the Enter key at the password prompt if accessed anonymously.

Now that a connection has been established and authenticated to the server, you can then set up your FTP session to work the way you want it to. As mentioned in the previous section, the `ftp` command has many different built-in commands, which you can view by typing a question mark at the `ftp>` prompt. These commands can affect the session display, set the type of file transfer, or obtain information about the remote server.

```
ftp> hash
Hash mark printing on (1024 bytes/hash mark).
ftp> prompt
Interactive mode off.
ftp> bin
200 Type set to I.
```

In this example, you have told ftp to print a hash (#) character for every 1024 bytes that are transferred, turn off prompting, and set the transfer type to binary (which should be on by default). The hash character display provides a visual indicator of the progress of your downloads and uploads. Turning off prompting will allow you to send and retrieve multiple files without the need to confirm each transfer. Setting the transfer type to binary will ensure that binary files are transferred in the proper format instead of text, which means that executable files and pictures will transfer correctly.

Next, you ask the server to show a listing of what directories and files are available on the server:

```
ftp> ls
200 PORT command successful.
150 Opening ASCII mode data connection for directory listing.
total 32
d--x--x--x   2 root     root         4096 Aug 31 07:15 bin
d--x--x--x   2 root     root         4096 Aug 31 07:15 etc
d--x--x--x   2 root     root         4096 Aug 31 04:44 lib
d--x-x---x   2 root     50           4096 Sep  3 07:34 pub
226 Transfer complete.
```

If directory permissions in the FTP repository are set correctly, the pub directory should be the only directory that shows any files under it. To verify this, change directories to etc and list the contents:

```
ftp> cd etc
250 CWD command successful.
ftp> ls
200 PORT command successful.
150 Opening ASCII mode data connection for directory listing.
total 0
226 Transfer complete.
```

By setting the permissions to execute only on the directories bin, lib, and etc, a system administrator can restrict users from seeing any files in that directory. Good security dictates that remote users be denied information about a system, as any information could aid in hacking attempts.

Now that you see the server is relatively secure, change directories to pub and list the contents of that directory:

```
ftp> cd pub
250-Please read the file README
250-  it was last modified on Sun Sep  2 19:25:47 2001 - 1 day ago
250 CWD command successful.
ftp> ls
200 PORT command successful.
150 Opening ASCII mode data connection for directory listing.
total 552
-rw-r--r--   1 root      50               100 Sep  2 19:25 README
-rw-r--r--   1 root      50                 8 Sep  3 07:33 configuration
-rw-r--r--   1 root      50                 8 Sep  3 07:33 temp.txt
-rw-r--r--   1 root      50             15798 Sep  3 10:29 tftp-0.17-14.i386.rpm
-rw-r--r--   1 root      50             26011 Sep  3 10:30 tftp-
server-0.17-14.i386.rpm
-rw-r--r--   1 root      50            219332 Sep  3 10:29 wu-ftpd-
2.6.1-22.i386.rpm226 Transfer complete.
```

To transfer all the RPM files to your local machine, issue the mget *.rpm command:

```
ftp> mget *.rpm
local: tftp-0.17-14.i386.rpm remote: tftp-0.17-14.i386.rpm
200 PORT command successful.
150 Opening BINARY mode data connection for tftp-0.17-14.i386.rpm
(15798 bytes).##############
226 Transfer complete.
15798 bytes received in 0.974 secs (16 Kbytes/sec)
local: tftp-server-0.17-14.i386.rpm remote: tftp-server-0.17-
14.i386.rpm
200 PORT command successful.
150 Opening BINARY mode data connection for tftp-server-0.17-
14.i386.rpm (26011 bytes).
#######################
226 Transfer complete.
26011 bytes received in 2.5 secs (10 Kbytes/sec)
local: wu-ftpd-2.6.1-22.i386.rpm remote: wu-ftpd-2.6.1-
22.i386.rpm
200 PORT command successful.
150 Opening BINARY mode data connection for wu-ftpd-2.6.1-
22.i386.rpm (219332 bytes).
################################################################
################################################################
################################################################
##################
226 Transfer complete.
219332 bytes received in 50.3 secs (4.3 Kbytes/sec)
```

As described before, the mget command transferred all files with the .rpm extension to our local machine. Furthermore, it did not prompt us to confirm each file because we turned off prompting. The ftp client printed a # for each 1024 bytes transferred to our machine. This is helpful when transferring over a slow connection because you get a visual reminder that your connection is still active.

22

> **TIP**
>
> After every action, the FTP server will return a status code and brief message showing the result of the command you issued. You can find a listing of all status codes and their corresponding messages in Request For Comment 959; you can access a copy of this listing at http://www.ietf.org/rfc/rfc959.txt.

Now you are finished with this session; you can issue the command quit or bye to end the session. Additionally, the FTP server will inform you of how many bytes your session transfers, how many files, and the total transferred data (in bytes) between your local machine and the server:

```
ftp> bye
221-You have transferred 503818 bytes in 5 files.
221-Total traffic for this session was 506422 bytes in 7 transfers.
221 Thank you for using the FTP service on pheniox.
```

This is a simple example, but average FTP sessions are similarly trivial. Several other commands are available during an FTP session, but they are rarely used. FTP has the capability to take scripted input and define macros that allow for a much more complicated session.

> **TIP**
>
> The FTP info pages are much like the man (manual) pages shipped with almost every command in Linux. More detailed information may be found in the command's source code package.

Using the lftp Command for File Transfers

The lftp command can be used for file transfers using FTP, HTTP, and various secure protocols such as HTTPS and HFTP if a remote proxy is enabled. Two great features of this command are the ability to restart a stalled download in the middle of a file transfer, as well as to start and run multiple downloads in a single session (with job control).

For example, here is a simple session showing an HTTP retrieval from a remote computer running the Apache web server:

```
$ lftp http://192.168.2.37
cd ok, cwd=/
lftp 192.168.2.37:/> ls
-rw-r--r--    --  manual/mod/core.html
-rw-r--r--    --  manual/index.html
```

```
-rw-r--r--  --  icons/apache_pb.gif
-rw-r--r--  --  poweredby.png
lftp 192.168.2.37:/> get poweredby.png
1154 bytes transferred
lftp 192.168.2.37:/> bye
```

The lftp command can also be used as a "traditional" FTP client, but with some interesting features:

```
$ lftp 192.168.2.67 -u phudson
Password:
lftp phudson@192.168.2.67:~> cd /d2/isos/redhat/limbo
cd ok, cwd=/d2/isos/redhat/limbo
lftp phudson@192.168.2.67:/d2/isos/redhat/limbo> mget disc1 &
[0] mget *disc1* &
lftp phudson@192.168.2.67:/d2/isos/redhat/limbo> jobs
[0] mget *disc1*
        `limbo-i386-disc1.iso' at 56436448 (8%) 1.08M/s eta:9m [Receiving data]
lftp phudson@192.168.2.67:/d2/isos/redhat/limbo> bye
[1843] Moving to background to complete transfers...
$ ps aux ¦ fgrep lftp
phudson     1843  7.6  1.0  5456 2404 ?         S    19:09   0:02 lftp 192.168.2.67
```

A username (and password) can be passed on the command line using the -u option. You can use this feature to reduce the amount of interactive typing required when retrieving remote files, as an aid when using lftp in shell scripts, and when retrieving files with lftp as a background process.

By using an ampersand (&), the retrieval is conducted in the background, as shown in the preceding example. The jobs command is then used to show current transfers. If one logs out of the session (using the bye command), the file transfer continues as a background process if it has not completed. (This is verified by using the ps command.)

The lftp client has many additional features that can make the job of transferring files easier than using other FTP clients.

> **NOTE**
>
> Another handy text-based file transfer utility included with Fedora is curl, which supports HTTP for file retrieval.

Using the wget Command for File Transfers

The wget command is used for file transfers using FTP, HTTP, and various secure protocols such as HTTPS and HFTP if a remote proxy is enabled. However, wget only supports non-interactive transfers, unlike other FTP clients. This is actually a feature, as wget can be used to download files as a background process and to recursively replicate remote file directories. The command also supports download completion of partially downloaded files, which can save a lot of time during periods of intermittent connectivity or broken connections.

For example, here is a simple invocation showing FTP retrieval from a remote computer using wget and an FTP URL:

```
$ wget ftp://phudson:mypasswd@stinky/mp3/*
--13:13:28--  ftp://phudson:*password*@stinky/mp3/*
           => `.listing'
Resolving stinky... done.
Connecting to stinky[192.168.2.33]:21... connected.
Logging in as phudson ... Logged in!
==> SYST ... done.    ==> PWD ... done.
==> TYPE I ... done.   ==> CWD /home/paul/mp3 ... done.
==> PORT ... done.    ==> LIST ... done.

   [ <=>                              ] 648         632.81K/s

13:13:28 (632.81 KB/s) - `.listing' saved [648]

Removed `.listing'.
--13:13:28--  ftp://phudson:*password*@stinky/mp3/C31821-01A.mp3
           => `C31821-01A.mp3'
==> CWD not required.
==> PORT ... done.    ==> RETR C31821-01A.mp3 ... done.
Length: 5,172,089

60% [=====================>            ] 3,123,680   264.80K/s   ETA 00:07
```

In this example, the user retrieves all files in a directory named mp3 (under /home/paul) on the remote host named stinky. The wget command will first retrieve a directory listing, then proceed to download the specified files (all marked with '*' in this example). Note that you can specify a username and password (mypasswd in the example) on the command. This generally is not a good idea. A better, but still not really secure, approach is to save the password in a file named .wgetrc in your home directory. See the wget man page for more information, or check the only documentation at http://www.gnu.org/software/wget/manual/wget-1.8.1/html_mono/wget.html.

> **TIP**
>
> Another popular use for wget is downloading complete copies of websites for offline reading, although it is not very friendly toward website owners who have to pay for all the bandwidth!
>
> To download an entire site, you need to specify the --mirror, --convert-links, and -p parameters, followed by the URL of the site to download. The first parameter tells wget to download all the pages and pictures from the site, following links as it can. The second tells it to rewrite the HTML so that it works when browsed locally. The last parameter, -p, tells wget to download all

the files referenced in the HTML, such as sounds, CSS files, and other related documents. You might also want to specify the –w parameter, which allows you to specify a number of seconds between individual wget requests; this stops your download from overloading the web server.

So, the complete command to download a website (for example, www.example.com) would be
wget --mirror --convert-links –p –w 2 http://www.example.com/.

Using Graphical FTP Clients

Many graphical FTP clients are available for Linux. Fedora includes the graphical gFTP client and network-aware browsers included with GNOME and KDE. These browsers feature built-in drag-and-drop capability, thus ensuring FTP functionality. Other graphical interface clients that can be used for FTP include the Mozilla web browser, KDE's Konqueror, GNOME's Epiphany, and the Nautilus file manager.

Using the gFTP Interface

The GNOME gFTP client provides all the typical features of FTP, including the ability to save profiles of common connections. Figure 22.1 shows a typical gFTP session in action. On the left panel is the local host, and on the right panel is the remote server. A connection is initiated by typing the address of the host into the host field, a specific port if not the standard FTP port (21), a valid username for the server, and a password. After the information has been entered, clicking the icon that looks like a monitor will start the connection to the server. The bottom panel displays session information, such as changing directories, as seen in Figure 22.1.

FIGURE 22.1   A typical gFTP session.

gFTP sets the file type as binary by default, which can be changed by clicking on ASCII in the FTP drop-down menu. To upload a file to the server, the user clicks on a filename in the left panel and clicks on the right arrow icon. The file is then transferred to the server, and the right panel will be updated to reflect this new file being added to the server. Similarly, to download a file from the server, the user selects the correct file type from the drop-down menu, selects the file to be downloaded, and clicks the left arrow icon. The left panel will then be updated to show the result of the transfer, with logging information shown in the bottom panel.

After all files are uploaded or downloaded, you must close the session. Do this by clicking the red button on the top right of the application window to issue the quit command. gFTP displays the session summary information in the log panel at the bottom of the application. You can also close the session simply by exiting gFTP.

Although using a graphical interface, you still need to understand the basic functionality of FTP to use gFTP. Not knowing the file type that needs to be set can result in wasted time downloading a binary file in ASCII format, thus rendering the file unusable. gFTP defaults to a binary file type, but detects the file type during the transfer. gFTP is a robust application, providing all the necessary actions typical of an FTP session, in a pretty, easy-to-use format.

FTP Sessions with Konqueror and Nautilus

Both KDE and GNOME file browsers have integrated FTP functionality built in. Use an ftp:// URL followed by a server name or IP address to start an anonymous FTP session. The drag-and-drop feature of KDE and the GNOME window manager allow users to select remote files and drag them to the desktop.

KDE's Konqueror web browser is capable of handling a number of networking and file transfer protocols, including FTP. You can configure various settings for this browser, such as the appearance of the browser's toolbar, but one of Konqueror's best features is its flexibility for file transfers.

Start the browser by clicking its icon on the KDE's kicker desktop panel or by typing the following at the command line:

```
$ konqueror &
```

After launching the client, you can use the ftp:// URL form to access remote servers, as shown in Figure 22.2.

If your window manager does not support drag and drop, you can use Konqueror's Copy Files feature to retrieve a file. First, type in an FTP URL (such as ftp://ftp.tux.org). Next, navigate to a desired directory and click to select a desired file. You then click the Edit menu's Copy Files menu item (or press F7). A Save dialog will appear, and you can select your home directory to save the file. After you press Enter, a file download progress dialog will be displayed while the file is being retrieved.

You can also use the Nautilus browser to retrieve files from a remote server.

FIGURE 22.2   KDE's Konqueror web browser can access remote FTP servers.

Figure 22.3 shows an anonymous login to a remote FTP server using Nautilus. Browse to a remote FTP server using an FTP URL, then simply click to select a file, select Copy from the Edit menu (or press Ctrl+C), click to go to your home directory (using the icon in the Nautilus toolbar), and then click Paste (or press Ctrl+V) to retrieve and save the file.

FIGURE 22.3   The Nautilus file browser can be used for FTP sessions.

These types of intuitive features can shield users from needing to know the details of how FTP works or memorizing various commands.

FTP Servers

FTP uses a client/server model. As a client, FTP accesses a server, and as a server, FTP provides access to files or storage. Just about every computer platform available has software written to enable a computer to act as an FTP server, but Fedora provides the average user the ability to do this without paying hefty licensing fees and without regard for client usage limitations.

There are two types of FTP servers and access: anonymous and standard. A *standard* FTP server requires an account name and password from anyone trying to access the server. *Anonymous* servers allow anyone to connect to the server to retrieve files. Anonymous servers provide the most flexibility, but they can also present a security risk. Fortunately, as you will read in this chapter, Fedora is set up to use proper file and directory permissions and commonsense default configuration, such as disallowing root to perform an FTP login.

> **NOTE**
>
> Many Linux users now use OpenSSH and its suite of clients, such as the sftp command, for a more secure solution when transferring files. The OpenSSH suite provides the sshd daemon and enables encrypted remote logins (see Chapter 25 for more information).

Choosing an Authenticated or Anonymous Server

When you are preparing to set up your FTP server, you must first make the decision to install either the authenticated or anonymous service. *Authenticated* service requires the entry of a valid username and password for access. As previously mentioned, *anonymous* service allows the use of the username anonymous and an email address as a password for access.

Authenticated FTP servers are used to provide some measure of secure data transfer for remote users, but will require maintenance of user accounts as username and passwords are used. Anonymous FTP servers are used when user authentication is not needed or necessary, and can be helpful in providing an easily accessible platform for customer support or public distribution of documents, software, or other data.

If you use an anonymous FTP server in your home or business Linux system, it is vital that you properly install and configure it to retain a relatively secure environment. Generally, sites that host anonymous FTP servers place them outside of the firewall on a dedicated machine. The dedicated machine contains only the FTP server and should not contain data that cannot be restored quickly. This dedicated-machine setup prevents malicious users who compromise the server from obtaining critical or sensitive data. For an additional, but by no means a more secure setup, the FTP portion of the file system can be mounted read-only from a separate hard drive partition or volume, or mounted from read-only media, such as CD-ROM, DVD, or other optical storage.

Fedora Core Linux includes an FTP server package with its distribution, but other FTP packages also work with Fedora Linux. The following sections discuss FTP servers in both categories.

Fedora FTP Server Packages

The Very Secure vsftpd server, like wu-ftpd also discussed in this chapter, is licensed under the GNU GPL. The server can be used for personal or business purposes. Other FTP servers are available for Fedora, but only vsftpd comes bundled with this book's CD-ROMs. The wu-ftpd and vsftpd servers will be covered in the remainder of this chapter.

Other FTP Servers

One alternative server is NcFTPd, available from http://www.ncftp.com. This server operates independently of xinetd (typically used to enable and start the wu-ftp server) and provides its own optimized daemon. Additionally, NcFTPd has the capability to cache directory listings of the FTP server in memory, thereby increasing the speed at which users can obtain a list of available files and directories. Although NcFTPd has many advantages over wu-ftpd, NcFTPd is not GPL licensed software, and its licensing fees vary according to the maximum number of simultaneous server connections ($199 for 51 or more concurrent users and $129 for up to 50 concurrent users, but free to education institutions with a compliant domain name). Because of this licensing NcFTPd is not packaged with Fedora—you will not find it on this book's CD-ROMs.

> **NOTE**
>
> Do not confuse the ncftp client with ncftpd. The ncftp-3.1.7-4 package included with Fedora is the client software, a replacement for ftp-0.17-22, and includes the ncftpget and ncftpput commands for transferring files via the command line or by using a remote file uniform resource locator (URL) address. ncftpd is the FTP server, which can be downloaded from www.ncftpd.com.

Another FTP server package for Linux is ProFTPD, licensed under the GNU GPL. This server works well with most Linux distributions and has been used by a number of Linux sites, including ftp.kernel.org and ftp.sourceforge.net. ProFTPD is actively maintained and updated for bug fixes and security enhancements. Its developers recommend that you use the latest release (1.2.10 at the time of this writing) to avoid exposure to exploits and vulnerabilities. Browse to http://www.proftpd.org to download a copy.

Yet another FTP server package is Bsdftpd-ssl, which is based on the BSD ftpd (and distributed under the BSD license). Bsdftpd-ssl offers simultaneous standard and secure access using security extensions; secure access requires a special client. For more details, browse to http://bsdftpd-ssl.sc.ru/.

Finally, another alternative is to use Apache (and the HTTP protocol) for serving files. Using a web server to provide data downloads can reduce the need to monitor and maintain a separate software service (or directories) on your server. This approach to serving files also reduces system resource requirements and gives remote users a bit more flexibility when downloading (such as enabling them to download multiple files at once). See Chapter 19, "Apache Web Server Management," for more information about using Apache.

Installing FTP Software

As part of the Workstation installation, the client software for FTP is already installed. You can verify that FTP-related software is installed on your system by using the RPM (Red Hat Package Manager), grep, and sort commands in this query:

```
$ rpm -qa ¦ grep ftp ¦ sort
```

The example results might differ, depending on what software packages are installed. In your Fedora file system, you will find the file /usr/bin/pftp symbolically linked to /usr/bin/ftp as well as the vsftpd server under the /usr/sbin directory. The base anonymous FTP directory structure is located under the /var/ftp directory. Other installed packages include additional text-based and graphical FTP clients.

If vsftpd is not installed, you can find it under the Add/Remove Applications dialog, under FTP Server.

> **NOTE**
>
> If you host an FTP server connected to the Internet, make it a habit to always check the Fedora site, http://fedora.redhat.com for up-to-date system errata, and security and bug fixes for your server software.

> **TIP**
>
> The Computer Emergency Response Team (http://www.cert.org) provides security advisories about current attacks and vulnerabilities on multiple platforms. Checking this site regularly for updates is a must for any site administrator. As a Fedora administrator (or user), you should also subscribe to Red Hat's announcement lists (see Appendix A, "Fedora and Linux Internet Resources").

Because the anonftp and wu-ftpd RPM packages are not included with Fedora, you must download and install them if you wish to use the wu-ftpd server. Retrieve the most recent packages for Linux from http://www.wu-ftpd.org/ to build from the latest source code, or obtain RPM packages from a reputable mirror.

Refer to Chapter 7, "Managing Software and System Resources," for information on how to use RPM packages, and Chapter 32, "C/C++ Programming Tools for Fedora," on how to build software packages from source code archives.

The FTP User

After installing Fedora, an FTP user will be created. This user is not a normal user per se, but a name for anonymous FTP users. The FTP user entry in /etc/passwd looks like

```
ftp:x:14:50:FTP User:/var/ftp:/sbin/nologin
```

> **NOTE**
>
> The FTP user, as discussed here, applies to anonymous FTP configurations and server setup.
>
> Also, note that other Linux distributions might use a different default directory, such as /usr/local/ftp, for FTP files and anonymous users.

This entry follows the standard /etc/passwd entry: username, password, User ID, Group ID, comment field, home directory, and shell.

To learn more about /etc/password, see the section "The Password File" in Chapter 13, "Managing Users."

Each of the items in this entry is separated by colons. In the preceding example, you can see that the Fedora system hosting the server uses shadowed password because an x is present in the traditional password field. The shadow password system is important because it adds an additional level of security to Fedora; the shadow password system is normally installed during the Fedora installation.

The FTP server software uses this user account to assign permissions to users connecting to the server. By using a default shell of /sbin/nologin for anonymous FTP users versus /bin/bash or some other standard, interactive shell, an anonymous FTP user, will be unable to log in as a regular user. /sbin/nologin is not a shell, but a program usually assigned to an account that has been locked. As root inspection of the /etc/shadow file shows (see Listing 22.2), it is not possible to log in to this account, denoted by the * as the password.

LISTING 22.2   Shadow Password File ftp User Entry

```
# cat /etc/shadow
bin:*:11899:0:99999:7:::
daemon:*:11899:0:99999:7:::
adm:*:11899:0:99999:7:::
lp:*:11899:0:99999:7:::
...
ftp:*:12276:0:99999:7:::
...
```

The shadow file (only a portion of which is shown in Listing 22.2) contains additional information not found in the standard /etc/passwd file, such as account expiration, password expiration, whether the account is locked, and the encrypted password. The * in the password field indicates that the account is not a standard login account; thus, it does not have a password.

Although shadow passwords are in use on the system, passwords are not transmitted in a secure manner when using FTP. Because FTP was written before the necessity of encryption and security, it does not provide the mechanics necessary to send encrypted passwords. Account information is sent in plain text on FTP servers; anyone with enough technical knowledge and a network sniffer can find the password for the account you connect to on the server. Many sites use an anonymous-only FTP server specifically to prevent normal account passwords from being transmitted over the Internet.

Figure 22.4 shows a portion of an ethereal capture of an FTP session for the user named *cathy* and her password ("ilikecatz"). The ethereal client is a graphical browser used to display network traffic in real time, and it can be used to watch packet data, such as an FTP login on a LAN.

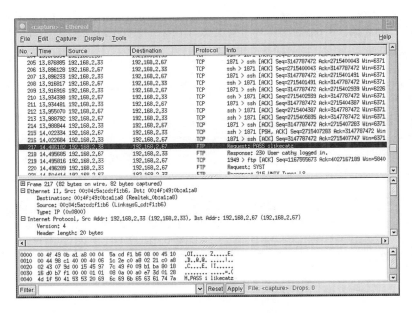

FIGURE 22.4   The ethereal client can filter and sniff FTP sessions to capture usernames and passwords.

Quick and Dirty FTP Service

Conscientious Linux administrators will take the time to carefully install, set up, and configure a production FTP server before offering public service or opening up for business on the Internet. However, you can set up a server very quickly on a secure LAN by following a few simple steps:

1. Ensure that the FTP server RPM package is installed, networking is enabled, and firewall rules on the server allow FTP access. See Chapter 17, "Network Connectivity," to see how to use Red Hat's system-config-securitylevel client for firewalling.

2. If anonymous access to server files is desired, populate the /var/ftp/pub directory. Do this by mounting or copying your content, such as directories and files under this directory.

3. Edit, and then save the appropriate configuration file (such as vsftpd.conf for vsftpd) to enable access.

4. If you are using wu-ftpd, you must then start or restart xinetd like so: /etc/rc.d/init.d/xinetd restart. If you are using vsftpd, you must then start or restart the server like so: service vsftpd start.

xinetd **Configuration for** wu-ftpd

xinetd (pronounced "zy-net-d") is the extended Internet services daemon, and handles incoming connections for network services. xinetd is the preferred replacement for a similar tool (used with other Linux distributions and older Red Hat releases) called inetd. However, in addition to several other improvements over inetd, xinetd allows you to apply individual access policies to different network connection requests, such as FTP.

This daemon controls a number of services on your system according to settings in configuration files under the /etc/xinetd.d directory. This section shows you how to edit the appropriate files to enable the use of the wu-ftpd FTP server.

Configuring xinetd **for the** wu-ftp **Server**

When installing wu-ftp using RPM, the RPM package may contain an xinetd configuration file, /etc/xinetd.d/wu-ftpd, as seen in Listing 22.3. You need to edit the file because its default settings disable incoming FTP requests.

> **NOTE**
>
> Do not be confused by the first line of the wu-ftpd file's text. Even though it reads default: on, FTP service is off unless you specifically configure its use. The line is a comment because it begins with a pound sign (#) and is ignored by xinetd. Whether FTP service is on is determined by the text line disable = yes.

LISTING 22.3   xinetd Configuration File for wu-ftpd

```
# default: on
# description: The wu-ftpd FTP server serves FTP connections. It uses \
#        normal, unencrypted usernames and passwords for authentication.
service ftp
{
disable = yes
        socket_type             = stream
        wait                    = no
        user                    = root
        server                  = /usr/sbin/in.ftpd
```

LISTING 22.3   Continued

```
        server_args             = -l -a
        log_on_success          += DURATION
        nice                    = 10


}
```

Using an editor, change the disable = yes line to disable = no. Save the file and exit the editor. You then must restart xinetd because configuration files are only parsed at startup. To restart xinetd as root, issue the command **/etc/rc.d/init.d/xinetd restart**. This makes a call to the same shell script that is called at any runlevel to start or stop the xinetd daemon (and thus start up or shut down the system). xinetd should report its status as

```
# /etc/rc.d/init.d/xinetd restart
Stopping xinetd:                                    [  OK  ]
Starting xinetd:                                    [  OK  ]
```

Once restarted, the FTP server is accessible to all incoming requests.

Starting the Very Secure FTP Server (vsftpd) Package

Previous versions of Red Hat's Linux distributions required you to edit a file named vsftp under the /etc/xinetd.d directory in order to enable and start the Very Secure FTP server, vsftpd. However, with Fedora you can now simply use the system-config-services client or service command to start vsftpd. For example, start the server using the service command like this:

```
# service vsftpd start
Starting vsftpd for vsftpd:                         [  OK  ]
```

Use the system-config-services client or service command to start, stop, or restart the vsftpd server. Do not run two FTP servers on your system at the same time!

> **TIP**
>
> You can also use the shell script named vsftpd under the /etc/rc.d/init.d directory to start, stop, restart, and query the vsftpd server. You must have root permission to use the vsftpd script to control the server, but any user can query the server (to see if it is running and to see its Process ID number) using the status keyword like this:
>
> ```
> $ /etc/rc.d/init.d/vsftpd status
> ```

Configuring the Very Secure FTP Server

The vsftpd server, although not as popular as Wu-FTPd, is used by Red Hat, Inc. for its FTP server operations. (The vsftpd server home page is located at http://vsftpd. beasts.org/.) The server offers features such as simplicity, security, and speed. It has been used by a number of sites, such as ftp.debian.org, ftp.gnu.org, rpmfind.net, and ftp.gimp.org. Note that despite its name, the Very Secure FTP server does not enable use of encrypted usernames or passwords.

Its main configuration file is vsftpd.conf, which resides under the /etc/vsftpd directory. The server has a number of features and default policies, but these can be overridden by changing the installed configuration file.

By default, anonymous logins are enabled, but users are not allowed to upload files, create new directories, or delete or rename files. The configuration file installed by Fedora allows local users (that is, users with a login and shell account) to log in and then access their home directory. This configuration presents potential security risks because usernames and passwords are passed without encryption over a network. The best policy is to deny your users access to the server from their user accounts. The standard vsftpd configuration disables this feature.

Controlling Anonymous Access

Toggling anonymous access features for your FTP server is done by editing the vsftpd.conf file and changing related entries to YES or NO in the file. Settings to control how the server works for anonymous logins include

> anonymous_enable—Enabled by default; use a setting of NO, and then restart the server to turn off anonymous access.
>
> anon_mkdir_write_enable—Allows or disallows creating of new directories.
>
> anon_other_write_enable—Allows or disallows deleting or renaming of files and directories.
>
> anon_upload_enable—Controls whether anonymous users can upload files (also depends on the global write_enable setting); this is a potential security and liability hazard and should rarely be used; if enabled, consistently monitor any designated upload directory.
>
> anon_world_readable_only—Only allows anonymous users to download files with world-readable (444) permission.

After making any changes to your server configuration file, make sure to restart the server; this forces vsftpd to reread its settings.

Other vsftpd Server Configuration Files

You can edit vsftpd.conf to enable, disable, and configure many features and settings of the vsftpd server, such as user access, filtering of bogus passwords, and access logging. Some features might require the creation and configuration of other files, such as

/etc/vsftpd.user_list—Used by the userlist_enable and/or the userlist_deny options; the file contains a list of usernames to be denied access to the server.

/etc/vsftpd.chroot_list—Used by the chroot_list_enable and/or chroot_local_user options, this file contains a list of users who are either allowed or denied access to a home directory. An alternate file can be specified using the chroot_list_file option.

/etc/vsftpd.banned_emails—A list of anonymous password entries used to deny access if the deny_email_enable setting is enabled. An alternate file can be specified using the banned_email option.

/var/log/vsftpd.log—Data transfer information is captured to this file if logging is enabled using the xferlog_enable setting.

Default vsftpd **Behaviors**

The contents of a file named .message (if it exists in the current directory) are displayed when a user enters the directory. This feature is enabled in the installed configuration file, but disabled by the daemon. FTP users are also not allowed to perform recursive directory listings, which can help reduce bandwidth use.

The PASV data connection method is enabled to let external users know the IP address of the FTP server. This is a common problem when using FTP from behind a firewall/gateway using IP masquerading or when incoming data connections are disabled. For example, here is a connection to an FTP server (running ProFTPD), an attempt to view a directory listing, and the resulting need to use ftp's internal passive command:

```
$ ftp ftp.tux.org
Connected to gwyn.tux.org.
220 ProFTPD 1.2.5rc1 Server (ProFTPD on ftp.tux.org) [gwyn.tux.org]
500 AUTH not understood.
KERBEROS_V4 rejected as an authentication type
Name (ftp.tux.org:gbush): gbush
331 Password required for gbush.
Password:
230 User gbush logged in.
Remote system type is Unix.
Using binary mode to transfer files.
ftp> cd public_html
250 CWD command successful.
ftp> ls
500 Illegal PORT command.
ftp: bind: Address already in use
ftp>
ftp> pass
Passive mode on.
ftp> ls
227 Entering Passive Mode (204,86,112,12,187,89).
```

```
150 Opening ASCII mode data connection for file list
-rw-r--r--  1 gbush    gbush        8470 Jan 10  2000 LinuxUnleashed.gif
-rw-r--r--  1 gbush    gbush        4407 Oct  4  2001 RHU72ed.gif
-rw-r--r--  1 gbush    gbush        6732 May 18  2000 SuSEUnleashed.jpg
-rw-r--r--  1 gbush    gbush        6175 Jan 10  2000 TYSUSE.gif
-rw-r--r--  1 gbush    gbush        3135 Jan 10  2000 TZones.gif
...
```

> **NOTE**
>
> Browse to http://slacksite.com/other/ftp.html for a detailed discussion regarding active and passive FTP modes and the effect of firewall blocking of service ports on FTP server and client connections.

Other default settings are that specific user login controls are not set, but you can configure the controls to deny access to one or more users.

The data transfer rate for anonymous client access is unlimited, but a maximum rate (in bytes per second) can be set using the anon_max_rate setting in vsftpd.conf. This can be useful for throttling bandwidth use during periods of heavy access. Another default is that remote clients will be logged out after five minutes of idle activity or a stalled data transfer. You can set idle and transfer timeouts (stalled connections) separately.

Other settings that might be important for managing your system's resources (networking bandwidth or memory) when offering FTP access include

dirlist_enable—Toggles directory listings on or off.

dirmessage_enable—Toggles display of a message when user enters a directory; a related setting is ls_recurse_enable, which can be used to disallow recursive directory listings.

download_enable—Toggles downloading on or off.

max_clients—Sets a limit on the maximum number of connections.

max_per_ip—Sets a limit on the number of connections from the same IP address.

> **TIP**
>
> A number of techniques, such as adjusting TCP socket buffers based on bandwidth characteristics, have been researched in an effort to speed up FTP file transfers. Many factors can slow FTP server performance. Disk I/O, system resources such as RAM, and network speeds are just some of these factors. Directories containing large numbers of files can cause bottlenecks. Even the underlying file system can slow file transfers. Tuning your system's disk I/O, interrupt priorities, network interfaces, and use of TCP are only a few approaches for improving transfer speeds. For additional ideas and a list of links to other system tuning information, browse to http://linuxperf.nl.linux.org/.

Configuring the Wu-FTPd Server

Wu-FTP uses a number of configuration files to control how it operates, including the following:

- `ftpaccess`—Contains the majority of server configuration settings
- `ftpconversions`—Contains definitions of file conversions during transfers
- `ftphosts`—Settings to control user access from specific hosts

These files may be created in the `/etc` directory during RPM installation, or may be created by a system administrator. The following sections describe each of these files and how to use the commands they contain to configure the Wu-FTP server is accessible to all incoming requests.

> **CAUTION**
>
> When configuring an anonymous FTP server, it is extremely important to ensure that all security precautions are taken to prevent malicious users from gaining privileged level access to the server. Although this chapter shows you how to configure your FTP server for secure use, all machines connected to the Internet are potential targets for malicious attacks. Vulnerable systems can be a source of potential liability, especially if anyone accesses and uses them to store illegal copies of proprietary software—even temporarily. There is little value in configuring a secure FTP server if the rest of the system is still vulnerable to attack. Use Red Hat's `lokkit` or `system-config-securitylevel` client to implement a firewall on your system.

> **TIP**
>
> Whenever editing the FTP server files, make a backup file first. Also, it is always a good idea to comment out (using a pound sign at the beginning of a line) what is changed instead of deleting or overwriting entries. Follow these comments with a brief description why the change was made. This leaves a nice audit trail of what was done, by whom, when, and why. If you have any problems with the configuration, these comments and details will help you troubleshoot and return to valid entries if necessary. You can use the `rpm` command or other Linux tools (such as `mc`) to extract a fresh copy of a configuration file from the software's RPM archive. Be aware, however, that the extracted version will replace the current version and overwrite your configuration changes.

> **NOTE**
>
> Back up the FTP server configuration files to another machine, should any of the working copies become corrupt. There might be a need to replicate server configurations across multiple hosts or revert back to an original copy of the defaults at some point in time. By making regular backups before changing a file, you guarantee that the changes can be undone and a working server restored with minimal down time.

Using Commands in the `ftpaccess` File to Configure `wu-ftpd`

The `ftpaccess` file contains most of the server configuration details. Each line contains a definition or parameter that is passed to the server to specify how the server is to operate. The directives can be broken down into the following categories, including

- **Access Control**—Settings that determine who can access the FTP server and how it is accessed

- **Information**—Settings that determine what information is provided by the server or displayed to a user

- **Logging**—Settings that determine if logging is enabled and what information is logged

- **Permission Control**—Settings that control the behavior of users when accessing the server; in other words, what actions users are allowed to perform, such as create a directory, upload a file, delete a file or directory, and so on

> **TIP**
>
> Many more options can be specified for the `wu-ftpd` FTP server in its `ftpaccess` file. The most common commands have been covered here. A full list of configuration options can be found in the `ftpaccess` man page after you install the server.

You can edit the `ftpaccess` file at the command line to make configuration changes in any of these categories. The following sections describe some configuration changes and how to edit these files to accomplish them.

Configure Access Control

Controlling which users can access the FTP server and how they can access it is a critical part of system security. Use the following entries in the `ftpaccess` file to specify to which group the user accessing the server is assigned.

Limit Access for Anonymous Users

This command imposes increased security on the anonymous user:

```
autogroup <groupname> <class> [<class>]
```

If the anonymous user is a member of a group, he will only be allowed access to files and directories owned by him or his group. The group must be a valid group from `/etc/groups` or `/var/ftp/etc/groups`.

Define User Classes

This command defines a class of users by the address to which the user is connected.

```
class <class> <typelist> <addrglob> [<addrglob>]
```

There might be multiple members for a class of users, and multiple classes might apply to individual members. When multiple classes apply to one user, the first class that applies will be used.

The typelist field is a comma-separated list of the keywords anonymous, guest, and real. anonymous applies to the anonymous user, and guest applies to the guest access account, as specified in the guestgroup directive. real defines those users who have a valid entry in the /etc/passwd file.

The addrglob field is a regular expression that specifies addresses to which the class is to be applied. The (*) entry specifies all hosts.

Block a Host's Access to the Server

Sometimes it is necessary to block access to the server to entire hosts. This can be useful in order to protect the system from individual hosts or entire blocks of IP addresses, or to force the use of other servers. Use this command to do so:

```
deny <addrglob> <message_file>
```

deny will always deny access to hosts that match a given address.

addr_glob is a regular expression field that contains a list of addresses, either numeric or a DNS name. This field can also be a file reference, which contains a listing of addresses. If the address is a file reference, it must be an absolute file reference; that is, starting with a /. To ensure that IP addresses can be mapped to a valid domain name, use the !nameserver parameter.

A sample deny line resembles the following:

```
deny *.exodous.net /home/ftp/.message_exodous_deny
```

This entry will deny access to the FTP server from all users who are coming from the exodous.net domain, and will display the message contained in the file .message_exoduous_deny in the /home/ftp directory.

---

ftpusers File Purpose Now Implemented in ftpaccess

Certain accounts are created during the installation of Linux that are for the system to segment and separate tasks with specific permissions. The ftpusers file (located in /etc/ftpusers) is where accounts for system purposes are listed. It is possible that the version of wu-ftp you will use with Fedora has depreciated the usage of this file, and instead implements the specific functionality of this file in the ftpaccess file with the commands of deny-uid/deny-gid.

Restrict Permissions Based on Group IDs

The guestgroup line assigns a given group name or group names to behave exactly like the anonymous user. Here is the command:

```
guestgroup <groupname> [<groupname>]
```

This command confines the user to a specific directory structure in the same way anonymous users are confined to /var/ftp. This command also limits these users to access files for which their assigned group has permissions.

The groupname parameter can be the name of a group or that group's corresponding GID (Group ID). If you use a GID as the groupname parameter, put a percentage symbol (%) in front of it. You can use this command to assign permissions to a range of group IDs, as in this example:

```
guestgroup %500-550
```

This entry would restrict all users with the group IDs 500–550 to be treated as a guest group, rather than individual users. In order for guestgroup to work, you must set up the user's home directories with the correct permissions, exactly like the anonymous FTP user.

Limit Permissions Based on Individual ID
The guestuser line works exactly like the guestgroup command you just read about, except it specifies a User ID (UID) instead of a group ID. Here's the command:

```
guestuser <username> [<username>]
```

This command limits the guest user to files for which the user has privileges. Generally, a user has more privileges than a group, so this type of assignment can be less restrictive than the guestgroup line.

Restrict the Number of Users in a Class
limit restricts the number of users in a class during given times. Here is the command, which contains fields for specifying a class, a number of users, a time range, and the name of a text file that contains an appropriate message:

```
limit <class> <n> <times> <message_file>
```

If the specified number of users from the listed class is exceeded during the given time period, the user sees the contents of the file given in the message_file parameter.

The times parameter is somewhat terse. The format for this is a comma-delimited string in the form of days, hours. Valid day strings are Su, Mo, Tu, We, Th, Fr, Sa, and Any. The hours are formatted in a 24-hour format. An example is as follows:

```
limit anonymous 10 MoTuWeThFr,Sa0000-2300 /home/ftp/.message_limit_anon_class
```

This line will limit the anonymous class to 10 concurrent connections on Monday through Friday, and on Saturday from midnight to 11:00 p.m. If the number of concurrent connections is exceeded or at 11:00 p.m. on Saturday, the users will see the contents of the file /home/ftp/.message_limit_anon_class.

Syntax for finer control over limiting user connections can be found in the ftpaccess man page.

Limit the Number of Invalid Password Entries

This line allows control over how many times a user can enter an invalid password before the FTP server terminates the session:

```
loginfails <number>
```

The default for `loginfails` is set to 5. This command prevents users without valid passwords from experimenting until they "get it right."

Configure User Information

Providing users with information about the server and its use is a good practice for any administrator of a public FTP server. Adequate user information can help prevent user problems and eliminate tech support calls. You also can use this information to inform users of restrictions governing the use of your FTP server. User information gives you an excellent way to document how your FTP server should be used.

You can use the commands detailed in the following sections to display messages to users as they log in to the server or as they perform specific actions. The following commands enable messages to be displayed to users when logging in to the server or when an action is performed.

Display a Prelogin Banner

This command is a reference to a file that is displayed before the user receives a login prompt from the FTP server:

```
banner <path>
```

Generally, this file contains information to identify the server. The path is an absolute pathname, relative to the system root (/), not the base of the anonymous FTP user's home. The entry might look like this:

```
banner /etc/rh8ftp.banner
```

This example uses the file named rh8ftp.banner under the /etc directory. The file can contain one or more lines of text, such as

```
Welcome to Widget, Inc.'s Red Hat Linux FTP server.
This server is only for use of authorized users.
Third-party developers should use a mirror site.
```

When an FTP user attempts to log in, the banner will be displayed like so:

```
$ ftp shuttle2
Connected to shuttle2.home.org.
220-Welcome to Widget, Inc.'s Red Hat Linux FTP server.
220-This server is only for use of authorized users.
220-Third-party developers should use a mirror site.
220-
```

```
220-
220 shuttle2 FTP server (Version wu-2.6.2-8) ready.
504 AUTH GSSAPI not supported.
504 AUTH KERBEROS_V4 not supported.
KERBEROS_V4 rejected as an authentication type
Name (shuttle2:phudson):
```

> **NOTE**
>
> Note that the banner does not replace the greeting text, which, by default, displays the host-name and server information, such as
>
> ```
> 220 shuttle2 FTP server (Version wu-2.6.2-8) ready.
> ```
>
> To hide version information, use the `greeting` command in `ftpaccess` with a keyword, such as terse, like so:
>
> ```
> greeting terse
> ```
>
> FTP users will then see a short messages like this as part of the login text:
>
> ```
> 220 FTP server ready.
> ```
>
> Also, not all FTP clients can handle multiline responses from the FTP server. The `banner<path>` command is how the banner line passes the file contents to the client. If a client cannot interrupt multiline responses, the FTP server will be useless to them. You should also edit the default banner to remove identity and version information.

Display a File

This line specifies a text file to be displayed to the user during login and when the user issues the cd command:

```
message <path> {<when> {<class> ...}}
```

The optional when clause can be LOGIN or CWD=(dir), where dir is the name of a directory that is current. The optional class parameter enables messages to be shown only to a given class or classes of users.

Using messages is a good way to give information about where things are on your site as well as information that is system dependent, such as alternative sites, general policies regarding available data, server availability times, and so on.

You can use *magic cookies* to breathe life into your displayed messages. Magic cookies are symbolic constants that are replaced by system information. Table 22.1 lists valid magic cookies for the message command and their representation.

TABLE 22.1   Magic Cookies and Their Descriptions

Cookie	Description
%T	Local time (form Thu Nov 15 17:12:42 1990)
%F	Free space in partition of CWD (kbytes)
	[Not supported on all systems]
%C	Current working directory
%E	The maintainer's email address as defined in ftpaccess
%R	Remote hostname
%L	Local hostname
%u	Username as determined via RFC931 authentication
%U	Username given at login time
%M	Maximum allowed number of users in this class
%N	Current number of users in this class
%B	Absolute limit on disk blocks allocated
%b	Preferred limit on disk blocks
%Q	Current block count
%I	Maximum number of allocated inodes (+1)
%i	Preferred inode limit
%q	Current number of allocated inodes
%H	Time limit for excessive disk use
%h	Time limit for excessive files
Ratios	
%xu	Uploaded bytes
%xd	Downloaded bytes
%xR	Upload/Download ratio (1:n)
%xc	Credit bytes
%xT	Time limit (minutes)
%xE	Elapsed time since login (minutes)
%xL	Time left
%xU	Upload limit
%xD	Download limit

To understand how this command works, imagine that you want to display a welcome message to everyone who logs in to the FTP server. An entry of

```
message /home/ftp/welcome.msg    login
message /welcome.msg             login
```

shows the contents of the welcome.msg file to all real users who log in to the server. The second entry shows the same message to the anonymous user.

The welcome.msg file is not created with the installation of the RPM, but you can create it using a text editor. Type the following:

```
Welcome to the anonymous ftp service on %L!

There are %N out of %M users logged in.

Current system time is %T

Please send email to %E if there are
any problems with this service.

Your current working directory is %C
```

Save this file as `/var/ftp/welcome.msg`. Verify that it works by connecting to the FTP server:

```
220 FTP server ready.
504 AUTH GSSAPI not supported.
504 AUTH KERBEROS_V4 not supported.
KERBEROS_V4 rejected as an authentication type
Name (shuttle:phudson): anonymous
331 Guest login ok, send your complete e-mail address as password.
Password:
230-Welcome to the anonymous ftp service on shuttle.home.org!
230-
230-There are 1 out of unlimited users logged in.
230-
230-Current system time is Mon Nov  3 10:57:06 2003
230-
230-Please send email to root@localhost if there are
230-any problems with this service.
230-Your current working directory is /
```

Display Administrator's Email Address

This line sets the email address for the FTP administrator:

```
email <name>
```

This string is printed whenever the %E magic cookie is specified. This magic cookie is used in the messages line or in the shutdown file. You should display this string to users in the login banner message so that they know how to contact you (the administrator) in case of problems with the FTP server.

CAUTION

Do not use your live email address in the display banner; you want others to be able to access user emails as necessary. Instead, use an alias address that routes the messages to the appropriate IT department or other address.

Notify User of Last Modification Date

The readme line tells the server if a notification should be displayed to the user when a specific file was last modified. Here's the command:

```
readme <path> {<when {<class>}}
```

The path parameter is any valid path for the user. The optional when parameter is exactly as seen in the message line. class can be one or more classes as defined in the class file. The path is absolute for real users. For the anonymous user, the path is relative to the anonymous home directory, which is /var/ftp by default.

Configure System Logging

Part of any system administration involves reviewing log files for what the server is doing, who accessed it, what files were transferred, and other pieces of important information. You can use a number of commands within /etc/ftpacess to control your FTP server logging actions.

Redirect Logging Records

This line allows the administrator to redirect where logging information from the FTP server will be recorded:

```
log <syslog>{+<xferlog>}
```

By default, the information for commands is stored in /var/log/messages, although the man pages packaged in some RPMs state that this information will be written to /var/log/xferlog. Check your server's settings for information regarding the location of your file transfer logs.

Log All User-Issued Commands

This line enables logging for all commands issued by the user:

```
log commands [<typelist>]
```

typelist is a comma-separated list of anonymous, guest, and real. If no typelist is given, commands are logged for all users. Some wu-ftpd RPMs set the logging of all file transfers to /var/log/xferlog (see the next section). However, you can add the log command to ftpaccess with the commands keyword to capture user actions. Logging will then be turned on and user actions captured in /var/log/messages. Here is an example of a sample log file:

```
Oct  6 12:21:42 shuttle2 ftpd[5229]: USER anonymous
Oct  6 12:21:51 shuttle2 ftpd[5229]: PASS phudson@widget.com
Oct  6 12:21:51 shuttle2 ftpd[5229]: ANONYMOUS FTP LOGIN FROM 192.168.2.31
➥[192.168.2.31], phudson@widget.com
Oct  6 12:21:51 shuttle2 ftpd[5229]: SYST
Oct  6 12:21:54 shuttle2 ftpd[5229]: CWD pub
```

```
Oct  6 12:21:57 shuttle2 ftpd[5229]: PASV
Oct  6 12:21:57 shuttle2 ftpd[5229]: LIST
Oct  6 12:21:59 shuttle2 ftpd[5229]: QUIT
Oct  6 12:21:59 shuttle2 ftpd[5229]: FTP session closed
```

The example log shows the username and password entries for an anonymous login. The CWD entry shows that a `cd` command is used to navigate to the `pub` directory. Note that the commands shown do not necessarily reflect the syntax the user typed in, but instead list corresponding system calls the FTP server received. For example, the `LIST` entry is actually the `ls` command.

Log Security Violations and File Transfers

Two other logging commands are useful in the `/etc/ftpaccess` configuration file. This line enables the logging of security violations:

```
log security [<typelist>]
```

Violations are logged for anonymous, guest, and real users, as specified in the `typelist`— the same as other `log` commands. If you do not specify a `typelist`, security violations for all users will be logged.

This line writes a log of all files transferred to and from the server:

```
log transfers [<typelist> [<directions>]]
```

`typelist` is the same as seen in log commands and log security lines. `directions` is a comma-separated list of the keywords `inbound` for uploaded files and `outbound` for downloaded files. If no directions are given, both uploaded and downloaded files will be logged. Inbound and outbound logging is turned on by default.

Configure Permission Control

Controlling user activity is an important component of securing your system's server. The `ftpaccess` file includes a number of commands that enable you to determine what users can and cannot execute during an FTP session. You can use these permission controls to allow users to change file permissions, delete or overwrite files, rename files, and to create new files with default permissions. You learn how to use all these `ftpaccess` file command lines in the following sections.

> **NOTE**
>
> By default, all the `ftpaccess` file command lines prohibit anonymous users from executing actions and enable authorized users to do so.

Allow Users to Change File Permissions

The chmod line determines if a user has the ability to change a file's permissions. Here is the command line:

```
chmod <yes¦no> <typelist>
```

This command acts the same as the standard chmod command.

The yes¦no parameter designates whether the command can be executed. typelist is a comma-delimited string of the keywords anonymous, guest, and real. If you do not specify a typelist string, the command will be applied to all users. An exhaustive description of its purpose and parameters can be found in the man page.

Assign Users File-Delete Permission

The delete line determines whether the user can delete files with the rm command. Here's the command line:

```
delete<yes¦no> <typelist>
```

The yes¦no parameter is used to turn this permission on or off, and typelist is the same as the chmod command.

Assign Users File-Overwrite Permission

This command line of the ftpaccess file allows or denies users the ability to overwrite an existing file. Here's the command line:

```
overwrite <yes¦no> <typelist>
```

The FTP client determines whether users can overwrite files on their own local machines; this line specifically controls overwrite permissions for uploads to the server. The yes¦no parameter toggles the permission on or off, and typelist is the same as seen in the chmod line.

Allow Users to Rename Files

You can enable or prevent a user from renaming files using this command line:

```
rename <yes¦no> <typelist>
```

The yes¦no parameter toggles the permission on or off, and typelist is the same comma-delimited string as seen in chmod.

Allow Users to Compress Files

This line determines whether the user will be able to use the compress command on files:

```
compress <yes¦no> [<classglob>]
```

The yes¦no parameter toggles the permission on or off, and classglob is a regular express string that specifies one or more defined classes of users. The conversions that result from the use of this command are specified in the ftpconversions file, which contains directions on what compression or extraction command is to be used on a file with a specific extension, such as .Z for the compress command, .gz for the gunzip command, and so on. See the section "Configure FTP Server File-Conversion Actions" later in this chapter.

Assign or Deny Permission to Use tar

This line determines whether the user will be able to use the tar (tape archive) command on files:

```
tar <yes¦no> [<classglob> ...]
```

The yes¦no parameter toggles the permission on or off, and classglob is a regular express string that specifies one or more defined classes of users. Again, the conversions that result from the use of this command are specified in the ftpconversions file.

Determine What Permissions Can Apply to User-Created Upload Files

This line is a bit different from the other commands in the permission control section. The umask command determines with what permissions a user can create new files; here it is.

```
umask <yes¦no> <typelist>
```

The yes¦no parameter toggles based on whether a user is allowed to create a file with his default permissions when uploading a file. Like the overwrite command you read about earlier in this section, this command line is specific to uploaded files because the client machine determines how new files are created from a download.

Configure Commands Directed Toward the cdpath

This alias command allows the administrator to provide another name for a directory other than its standard name:

```
alias <string> <dir>
```

The alias line only applies to the cd command. This line is particularly useful if a popular directory is buried deep within the anonymous FTP user's directory tree. A sample entry is the following:

```
alias linux-386 /pub/redhat/7.3/en/i386/
```

This line would allow the user to type cd linux-386 and be automatically taken to the /pub/redhat/7.3/en/i386 directory.

The cdpath <dir> line specifies in what order the cd command will look for a given string the user enters. The search path is done in the order in which the cdpath lines are entered in the ftpacess file.

For example, if the following cdpath entries are in the ftpaccess file,

```
cdpath /pub/redhat/
cdpath /pub/linux/
```

And the user types `cd i386`, the server will search for an entry in any defined aliases first in the `/pub/redhat` directory and then in the `/pub/linux` directory. If a large number of aliases are defined, it is recommended that symbolic links to the directories be created instead of aliases. This will reduce the amount of work on the FTP server and decrease wait time for the user.

Structure of the `shutdown` File

The `shutdown` command tells the server where to look for the `shutdown` message generated by the `ftpshut` command or by the user. The `shutdown` command is used with a pathname to a shutdown file, such as

```
shudown /etc/rh8ftpshutdown
```

If this file exists, the server will check the file to see when the server should shut down. The syntax of this file is as follows:

```
<year> <month> <day> <hour> <minute> <deny_offset> <disc_offset> <text>
```

`year` can be any year after 1970 (called the epoch), `month` is from 0–11, `hour` is 0–23, `minute` is 0–59, `deny_offset` is a number in minutes before shutdown in which the server will disable new connections, `disc_offset` is the number of minutes before connected users will be disconnected, and `text` is a message that will be displayed to the users at login. In addition to valid magic cookies defined in the messages section, those listed in Table 22.2 are also available.

TABLE 22.2   Magic Cookies for the Shutdown File

Cookie	Description
%s	The time the system will be shut down
%r	The time new connections will be denied
%d	The time current connections will be dropped

Configuring FTP Server File-Conversion Actions

The FTP server can convert files during transfer to compress and uncompress files automatically. Suppose that the user is transferring a file to his Microsoft Windows machine that was TARed and GZIPed on a Linux machine. If the user does not have an archive utility installed to uncompress these files, he cannot access or use the files.

As the FTP server administrator, you can configure the FTP server to automatically unarchive these files before download, should the site support users who might not have unarchive capabilities. Additionally, you can configure an upload area for the users, and then configure the FTP server to automatically compress any files transferred to the server.

CAUTION

Allowing users to upload files to the FTP server is highly dangerous unless restricted to authorized local users. Anonymous upload areas have often been the breeding ground for viruses, unlicensed software, and cracking software used by system crackers for malicious usage. Should an anonymous upload area be allowed, be sure to check it regularly.

The structure of the format of the `ftpconversions` file is

`1:2:3:4:5:6:7:8`

where 1 is the strip prefix, 2 is the strip postfix, 3 is the add-on prefix, 4 is the add-on postfix, 5 is the external command, 6 is the types, 7 is the options, and 8 is the description.

Strip Prefix

The *strip prefix* is one or more characters at the beginning of a filename that should be automatically removed by the server when the file is requested. By specifying a given prefix to strip in a conversions rule, such as devel, the user can request the file `devel_procman.tar.gz` by the command get `procman.tar.gz`, and the FTP server will perform any other rules that apply to that file and retrieve it from the server. Although this feature is documented, as of version 2.6.2, it has yet to be implemented.

Strip Postfix

The *strip postfix* works much the same as strip prefix, except one or more characters are taken from the end of the filename. Typically, this feature is used to strip the `.gz` extension from files that have been TARed and GZIPed when the server is performing automatic decompression before sending the file to the client.

Add-On Prefix

The *add-on prefix* conversion instructs the server to insert one or more characters to a filename before it is transferred to the server or client. For example, a user requests the file `procman.tar.gz`. The server has a conversion rule to add a prefix of gnome to all `.tar.gz` files; thus the server would append this string to the file before sending it to the client. The user would receive a file called `gnome_procman.tar.gz`. Keywords such as uppercase and lowercase can be used in this function to change the case of the filename for those operating systems in which case makes a difference. Similar to the strip prefix conversion, this feature is not yet implemented in version 2.6.2.

Add-On Postfix

An *add-on postfix* instructs the server to append one or more characters to the end of a filename during the transfer or reception of a file. A server can contain TARed packages of applications that are uncompressed. If an add-on postfix conversion was configured on the server, the server could compress the file, append a `.gz` extension after the file was compressed, and then send that file to the client. The server could also do the same action for uncompressed files sent to the server. This would have the effect of conserving disk space on the server.

External Command

The *external command* entries in the ftpconversions file contain the bulk of the FTP server conversion rules. The external command entry tells the server what should be done with a file after it is transferred to the server. The specified conversion utility can be any command on the server, although generally it is a compression utility. As the file is sent, the server passes the file through the external command. If the file is being uploaded to the server, the command needs to send the result to standard in, whereas a download will send the command to standard out. For example, here is an entry specifying the tar command:

```
:    : :.tar:/bin/tar -c -f - %s:T_REG¦T_DIR:O_TAR:TAR
```

The following sections describe the fields in a conversion entry.

Types

You must use the types field of the ftpconversions file to tell the server what types of files the conversion rules apply to. Separate the file type entries with the (¦) character, and give each type a value of T_REG, T_ASCII, and T_DIR.

T_REG signifies a regular file, T_ASCII an ASCII file, and T_DIR a directory. A typical entry is T_REG ¦ T_ASCII, which signifies a regular ASCII file.

Options

The options field informs the server what action is being done to the file. Similar to the types file, options are separated by the (¦) character. Here are the valid ranges you can assign to items in the options field:

- O_COMPRESS to compress the file

- O_UNCOMPRESS to uncompress the file

- O_TAR to tar the file

An example of this field would be O_COMPRESS ¦ O_TAR, where files are both compressed and TARed.

Description

The description field allows an administrator to quickly understand what the rule is doing. This field does not have any syntax restriction, although it is usually a one word entry—such as TAR, TAR+COMPRESS, or UNCOMPRESS—which is enough to get the concept across.

An Example of Conversions in Action

Crafting complex conversion entries is a task perhaps best left to the Linux/Unix expert, but the sample `ftpconversions` file included with `wu-ftpd` provides more than enough examples for the average Red Hat administrator. Building your own simple conversion entry is not really too difficult, so let's examine and decode an example:

```
:.Z:   :   :/bin/compress -d -c %s:T_REG¦T_ASCII:O_UNCOMPRESS:UNCOMPRESS
```

In this example, the strip prefix (field 1) is `null` because it is not yet implemented, so this rule does not apply to prefixes. The second field of this rule contains the `.Z` postfix; thus it deals with files that have been compressed with the compress utility. The rule does not address the add-on prefix or postfix, so fields 3 and 4 are `null`. Field 5, the external command field, tells the server to run the `compress` utility to decompress all files that have the `.Z` extension, as the `-d` parameter signifies. The `-c` options tells compress to write the output of the `compress` utility to the standard out, which is the server in this case. The `%s` is the name of the file that the rule was applied against. Field 6 specifies that this file is a regular file in ASCII format. Field 7, the options field, tells the server that this command uncompresses the file. Finally, the last field is a comment that gives the administrator a quick decode of what the conversion rule is doing, that is, uncompressing the file.

> **Examples**
>
> Several conversion rules may be specified in `wu-ftpd`'s default `ftpconversions` file. Additional examples, such as for Sun's Solaris operating system, might also be available in additional `wu-ftpd` documentation.

Using Commands in the `ftphosts` File to Allow or Deny FTP Server Connection

The purpose of the `ftphosts` file is to allow or deny specific users or addresses from connecting to the FTP server. The format of the file is the word `allow` or `deny` optionally followed by a username, followed by an IP or a DNS address.

```
allow username address
deny username address
```

Listing 22.4 shows a sample configuration of this file.

LISTING 22.4   `ftphosts` Configuration File for Allowing or Denying Users

```
# Example host access file
#
# Everything after a '#' is treated as comment,
# empty lines are ignored
allow tdc 128.0.0.1
```

LISTING 22.4   Continued

```
allow tdc 192.168.101.*
allow tdc insanepenguin.net
allow tdc *.exodous.net
deny anonymous 201.*
deny anonymous *.pilot.net
```

The * is a wildcard that will match any combination of that address. For example, `allow tdc *.exodous.net` will allow the user `tdc` to log in to the FTP server from any address that contains the domain name exodous.net. Similarly, the anonymous user will not be allowed to access the FTP if he is coming from a 201 public class C IP address.

Changes made to your system's FTP server configuration files only become active after you restart `xinetd` because configuration files are only parsed at startup. To restart `xinetd` as root, issue the command `/etc/rc.d/init.d/xinetd restart`. This makes a call to the same shell script that is called at system startup and shutdown for any runlevel to start or stop the `xinet` daemon. `xinetd` should report its status as

```
# /etc/rc.d/init.d/xinetd restart
Stopping xinetd:                                      [  OK  ]
Starting xinetd:                                      [  OK  ]
```

Once restarted, the FTP server is accessible to all incoming requests.

Server Administration

`wu-ftp` provides a few commands to aid in the administration of the server. These commands are

- `ftpwho`—Displays information about current FTP server users
- `ftpcount`—Displays information about current server users by class
- `ftpshut`—Provides automated server shutdown and user notification
- `ftprestart`—Provides automated server restart and shutdown message removal

Each of these commands must be executed with superuser privileges because they reference the `ftpaccess` configuration file to obtain information about the FTP server.

Display Information About Connected Users

command provides information about users who are currently connected to the FTP server. Here's the command line:

```
/usr/bin/ftpwho
```

Table 22.3 shows the format of the output `ftpwho` displays.

TABLE 22.3   `ftpwho` Fields

Name	Description
Process ID	The process ID of the FTP server process.
TTY	The terminal ID of the process. This will always be a ? because the FTP daemon is not an interactive login.
Status	Status of the FTP process. The values are S: sleeping Z: zombie, indicating a crash R: running N: normal process
Time	The elapsed processor time the process has used in minutes and seconds.
Details	Tells what host the process is connecting from, the user who connected, and the current command that is executing.

Listing 22.5 shows a typical output of this command. It lists the process ID for the `ftp` daemon handling requests, the class that the particular user belongs to, the total time connected, what username the user is connected as, and the status of his session.

In addition to the information given about each connected user, `ftpwho` will also display the total number of users connected out of any maximum that might have been set in the `ftpaccess` file. This information can be used to monitor the use of your FTP server.

You can pass one parameter to `ftpwho`. (You can find the parameter by using the `ftpwho--help` command.) The single parameter you can pass to `ftpwho` is `-v`. This parameter prints out version and licensing information for `wu-ftp`, as shown here:

```
# ftpwho
Service class all:
10447 ?         SN      0:00 ftpd: localhost: anonymous/winky@disney.com: IDLE
1 users (no maximum)
```

The output of `ftpwho`, using the `-V` option, which shows version information, is shown in Listing 22.5.

LISTING 22.5   `ftpwho -V` Command Output

```
Copyright © 1999,2000,2001 WU-FTPD Development Group.
All rights reserved.

Portions Copyright © 1980, 1985, 1988, 1989, 1990, 1991, 1993, 1994
  The Regents of the University of California.
Portions Copyright © 1993, 1994 Washington University in Saint Louis.
Portions Copyright © 1996, 1998 Berkeley Software Design, Inc.
Portions Copyright © 1989 Massachusetts Institute of Technology.
Portions Copyright © 1998 Sendmail, Inc.
Portions Copyright © 1983, 1995, 1996, 1997 Eric P.  Allman.
Portions Copyright © 1997 by Stan Barber.
```

LISTING 22.5 Continued

Portions Copyright © 1997 by Kent Landfield.
Portions Copyright © 1991, 1992, 1993, 1994, 1995, 1996, 1997
Free Software Foundation, Inc.

Use and distribution of this software and its source code are governed
by the terms and conditions of the WU-FTPD Software License ("LICENSE").

If you did not receive a copy of the license, it may be obtained online
at http://www.wu-ftpd.org/license.html.
Version wu-2.6.2-8

Count the Number of Connections

/usr/bin/ftpcount counts the number of connected users to the FTP server and the maximum number of users allowed. This same information is found at the end of the output for the ftpwho command. This command only takes one parameter, -V, which displays the same output as the previous ftpwho example.

```
# ftpcount
Service class all                    -    4 users (no maximum)
```

Use /usr/sbin/ftpshut to Schedule FTP Server Downtime

As with any public server administration, it is always good practice to let users of the FTP server know about upcoming outages, when the server will be updated, and other relevant site information. The ftpshut command allows the administrator to let the FTP server do much of this automatically.

The ftpshut command allows the administrator to take the FTP server down at a specific time based on some parameters passed to it. The format of the command is as follows and is documented in the ftpshut man page:

```
ftpshut  [ -V ] [ -l min] [ -d min] time [ warning-message ... ]
```

The -V parameter displays the version information of the command. The time parameter is the time when the ftpshut command will stop the FTP servers. This parameter will take either a + number for the number of minutes from the current time, or a specific hour and minute in 24-hour clock format with the syntax of *HH:MM*.

The -l parameter allows the FTP server administrator to specify how long, in minutes, before shutdown the server will disable new connections. The default for this is 10 minutes. If the time given to shut down the servers is less than 10 minutes, new connections will be disabled immediately.

The -d parameter is similar to the -l parameter, but controls when the FTP server will terminate the current connections. By default this will occur five minutes before the server shuts down. If the shutdown time is less than five minutes, the server will termi-nate the connections immediately.

When you execute this command, the FTP server creates a file containing the shutdown information in the location specified in the `ftpaccess` file under the shutdown section. The default configuration for this file is `/etc/shutmsg`. If you execute the `ftpshut` command with warning messages, the messages are displayed when the user logs in to the server.

```
Name (pheniox:tdc): anonymous
331 Guest login ok, send your complete e-mail address as password.
Password:
230-system doing down at Mon Sep  3 06:23:00 2001
230-0 users of unlimited on pheniox.
230 Guest login ok, access restrictions apply.
Remote system type is Unix.
Using binary mode to transfer files.
```

Here is a sample `ftpshut` command:

```
ftpshut -l 5 -d 5 +10 "system going down at %s %N users of %M on %R"
```

This command tells the FTP server to disconnect new connections in 5 minutes, drop all current connections in 5 minutes, shut down the server in 10 minutes, and display a warning message to the users at login. The message can be a mixture of text and magic cookies, defined in Table 22.4. It is important to keep in mind that the message can only be 75 characters in length. Additionally, it is not important to know how many characters the magic cookies will take because the system knows this information and will truncate the message at 75 characters.

TABLE 22.4   Magic Cookies for the `ftpshut` Command

Cookie	Description
%s	Time the system will be shut down
%r	Time new connections will be denied
%d	Time the current connections will be dropped
%C	Current working directory
%E	Server administrators email address as specified in the `ftpaccess` file
%F	Available free space in the current working directories partition in kilobytes
%L	Local host time
%M	Maximum number of allowed connections in this user class
%N	Current number of connections for this user class
%R	Remote hostname
%T	Local time, in the form of Fri Aug 31 21:04:00 2001
%U	Username given at login

When `ftpshut` is issued to the system, it creates a file that stores the necessary information. The `ftprestart` command removes this file for all servers, either canceling the impending shutdown or removing the shutdown file and restarting the FTP server. The `ftprestart` only has one optional argument, `-V`, to show version information.

Using `/var/log/xferlog` to View a Log of Server Transactions

The `xferlog` file gives a log of what transactions have occurred with the FTP server. Depending on the settings in the `/etc/ftpaccess` file, the contents of this file can contain the files sent or received by who with a date stamp. Table 22.5 lists the fields of this file. The same information can also be found in the corresponding man page included in the `wu-ftp` RPM.

TABLE 22.5   `/var/log/xferlog` Fields

Field	Description
current-time	Current local time in the form of *DDD MMM dd hh:mm:ss YYYY,* where *DDD* is the day of the week, *MMM* is the month, *dd* is the day of the month, *hh* is the hour, *mm* is the minutes, *ss* is the seconds, and *YYYY* is the year.
transfer-time	Total time in seconds for the transfer.
remote-host	Remote hostname.
file-size	Size of the transferred file in bytes.
filename	Name of the file.
transfer-type	A single character indicating the transfer type. The types are
	a for ascii transfers.
	b for binary transfers.
special-action-flag	One or more character flags indicating any special action taken by the server. The values are
	C for compressed files.
	U for uncompressed files.
	T for TARed files.
	- for no special action taken.
direction	Indicates whether the file was sent from or received by the server.
access-mode	The way in which the user logged in to the server. The values are
	a anonymous guest user.
	g guest user, corresponding to the guestgroup command in the /etc/ftpaccess file.
	r real user on the local machine.
username	If logged in as a real user, the username.
	If the access mode was guest, the password is given.
service-name	The name of the service used, usually FTP.
authentication-method	Type of authentication used. The values are
	0: none.
	1: RFC931 Authentication (a properly formed email address).

22

TABLE 22.5   Continued

Field	Description
authenticated-user-id	This is the user ID returned to the server based on the authentication method used to access the server. An * is used when an authenticated user ID cannot be found.
completion-status	A single character field indicating the status of the transfer. The values are c: completed transfer. i: incomplete transfer.

An example of this file is seen in Listing 22.6.

LISTING 22.6   Sample /var/log/xferlog File with Inbound and Outbound Logging

```
Mon Sep  3 07:13:05 2001 1 localhost.localdomain 100
 /var/ftp/pub/README b  o a testing@test.com ftp 0 * c
Mon Sep  3 02:35:35 2001 1 helios 8 /var/ftp/pub/configuration a
_ o a testing@test.com ftp 0 * c
Mon Sep  3 02:35:35 2001 1 helios 8 /var/ftp/pub/temp.txt a  o a
testing@test.com ftp 0 * c
Mon Sep  3 02:35:35 2001 1 helios 8 /var/ftp/pub/tftp-server-
0.17-14.i386.rpm a  o a testing@test.com ftp 0 * c
Mon Sep  3 02:35:35 2001 1 helios 8 /var/ftp/pub/wu-ftpd-2.6.1-
22.i386.rpm a  o a testing@test.com ftp 0 * c
```

Related Fedora and Linux Commands

You'll use these commands to install, configure, and manage FTP services in Fedora Core:

epiphany—A graphical GNOME browser supporting FTP

ftp—A text-based interactive FTP command

ftpcopy—Copy directories and files from a FTP server

ftpcp—Retrieve data from remote FTP server, but do not overwrite existing local files

gftp—A graphical FTP client for GNOME

konqueror—KDE's graphical web browser

lftp—An advanced text-based FTP program

nautilus—Red Hat's graphical file explorer and browser

ncftp—A sophisticated, text-based FTP program

sftp—Secure file transfer program

smbclient—Samba FTP client to access SMB/CIFS resources on servers

system-config-services—Red Hat's system service GUI admin utility

vsftpd—The Very Secure FTP daemon

webcam—A webcam-oriented FTP client included with xawtv

Reference

http://www.wu-ftpd.org/—WU-FTP Official website

http://fedora.redhat.com/—Red Hat's Official Fedora Core website

http://www.cert.org/—Computer Emergency Response Team

http://www.openssh.com/—The OpenSSH home page and source for the latest version of OpenSSH and its component clients, such as sftp

http://www.cert.org/tech_tips/anonymous_ftp_config.html—CERT Anonymous FTP Configuration Guidelines

http://vsftpd.beasts.org/—Home page for the `vsftd` FTP server

ftp://vsftpd.beasts.org/users/cevans/—Download site for the latest releases of the `vsftpd` server

22

Handling Electronic Mail

Communication by electronic mail—commonly referred to as *email*—is easily the most popular activity on the Internet and intranets. Email is fast, free (apparently), and easy to use. Hidden behind that seeming ease, however, is a complex infrastructure that can be accessed and controlled with the power of Fedora Core Linux.

In this chapter, you learn how to configure Fedora Core to act as an email server. You also take a close look at the various email clients that Fedora Core makes available for your use, and you learn some techniques for working with them. Although you might not ever need to administer a mail server, understanding how they work can make you a better mail user.

How Email Is Sent and Received

Email is sent as plain text across networks using SMTP. SMTP is used for sending mail from one network to another. Extensions to the protocol add authentication and error messages to the basic protocol. The mail transfer agent (MTA) works behind the scenes to send and receive email between computers. Some MTAs are Sendmail, Postfix, Fetchmail, Exim, or Qmail.

SMTP helps each computer along the way figure out how to get all the mail delivered to its destination. It is a remarkable system when you think about how complex a task it is asked to accomplish.

Here is a simplified example of how email is successfully processed and sent to its destination:

1. user1@lion.org composes and sends an email message to user2@cheetah.org.

2. The MTA at `lion.org` receives `user1`'s email message and queues it for delivery behind any other messages that are also waiting to go out.

3. The MTA at `lion.org` contacts the MTA at `cheetah.org` on port 25. After `cheetah.org` acknowledges the connection, the MTA at `lion.org` sends the mail message. After `cheetah.org` accepts and acknowledges receipt of the message, the connection is closed.

4. The MTA at `cheetah.org` places the mail message into `user2`'s incoming mailbox; `user2` is notified that she has new mail the next time she logs on.

Of course, several things can go wrong during this process. Here are a few examples:

What if `user2` doesn't exist at `cheetah.org`? In this case, the MTA at `cheetah.org` will reject the email and notify the MTA at `lion.org` of what the problem is. The MTA at `lion.org` will then generate an email message and send it to `user1@lion.org`, informing her that no `user2` exists at `cheetah.org` (or perhaps just silently discard the message and give the sender no indication of the problem, depending on how the email server is configured).

What happens if `cheetah.org` doesn't respond to `lion.org`'s connection attempts? (Perhaps the server is down for maintenance.) The MTA at `lion.org` notifies the sender that the initial delivery attempt has failed. Further attempts will be made at intervals decided by the server administrator until the deadline is reached, and the sender will be notified that the mail is undeliverable.

The Mail Transport Agent

Working behind the scenes to move mail between computers on different networks, several different MTAs are available for Fedora Core—each with its own strengths and weaknesses. Some are extremely powerful, but very difficult to configure and somewhat slow; others are very fast and easy to configure, but do not contain as many features. The following sections provide more details about some of the more common MTAs available for use with Fedora.

Sendmail

The vast majority of email traffic on the Internet is handled by an MTA called Sendmail, the default MTA shipped with Fedora (and a number of other Unix distributions). Sendmail has the advantage of being installed and well-supported in your Fedora system. The commercial version (not included with Fedora) sports a GUI configuration utility, as well.

Sendmail is one of the oldest and most powerful MTAs in existence, but it has a few disadvantages. It is somewhat slow; in a high load environment, other MTAs, including Postfix and Qmail, typically can handle a much greater volume of messages per second. Sendmail is also notoriously convoluted; configuration files are extremely cryptic. (The best-selling book on Sendmail is more than 1,000 pages in length.)

Fortunately, the default configuration of Sendmail as provided by Fedora Core works fine for most basic installations, and only minor changes are needed to configure it for a basic email server installation. However, because of the complexity of advanced Sendmail configuration, many administrators choose to replace it with one of the alternative MTAs. (You learn the basics of configuring and using Sendmail in "Basic Sendmail Configuration and Operation," later in this chapter).

Postfix

Postfix (originally released in 1998 as the IBM Secure Mailer) is a popular Sendmail alternative; it is fast, secure, and easy to administer. Postfix is a drop-in replacement for Sendmail (meaning that other applications that expect to use Sendmail will not notice that Postfix has replaced it and will continue to work correctly), and migrating a Sendmail installation to Postfix is relatively simple. To make all this magic work, Postfix uses a Sendmail wrapper (an interface for making other programs think that it is Sendmail) so that MUAs and such can communicate with it just as if they were communicating with Sendmail.

> **CAUTION**
>
> Fedora provides Postfix version 2, which uses a slightly different configuration than the earlier version. If you are upgrading Postfix from an earlier Red Hat version, check your configuration files.
>
> Fedora also now compiles Postfix and Sendmail against version 2 of the Cyrus SASL library (an authentication library). The Release Notes contain detailed information on file location and option changes that will affect you if you use these libraries.

For enhanced security, many Postfix processes used to use the `chroot` facility (which restricts access to only specific parts of the file system) for improved security, and there are no `setuid` components in Postfix. With the current release of Fedora, a `chroot` configuration *is no longer used* and is, in fact, discouraged by the Postfix author. You can manually reconfigure Postfix to a `chroot` configuration, but that is no longer supported by Fedora.

If you are starting from scratch, Postfix is considered a better choice than Sendmail.

Qmail and Exim

Qmail is a direct competitor to Postfix but is not provided with Fedora. Postfix is designed to be easier to use than Sendmail, as well as faster and more secure. However, Qmail isn't a drop-in replacement for Sendmail, so migrating an existing Sendmail installation to Qmail is not quite as simple as migrating from Sendmail to Postfix. Qmail is relatively easy to administer, and it integrates with a number of software add-ons, including web mail systems and POP3 servers. Qmail is available from http://www.qmail.org/.

Exim is yet another MTA, and it is available at http://www.exim.org/. Exim is considered faster and more secure that Sendmail or Postfix, but is much different to configure that either of those. Exim and Qmail use the `maildir` format rather than `mbox`, so both are considered "NFS safe" (see the following sidebar).

MDIR Versus Mailbox

Qmail also introduced `maildir`, which is an alternative to the standard Unix method of storing incoming mail. `maildir` is a more versatile system of handling incoming email, but it requires your email clients to be reconfigured, and it is not compatible with the traditional Unix way of storing incoming mail. You will need to use mail programs that recognize the `maildir` format. (The modern programs do.)

The traditional `mbox` format keeps all mail assigned to a folder concatenated as a single file and maintains an index of individual emails. With `maildir`, each mail folder has three subfolders: `/cur`, `/new`, and `/tmp`. Each email is kept in a separate, unique file. If you are running a mail server for a large number of people, you should select a file system that can efficiently handle a large number of small files.

`mbox` does offer one major disadvantage. While you are accessing the monolithic `mbox` file that contains all your email, suppose that some type of corruption occurs, either to the file itself or to the index. Recovery from this problem can be difficult. The `mbox` files are especially prone to problems if the files are being accessed over a network and can result in file corruption; one should avoid accessing `mbox` mail mounted over NFS, the network file system because file corruption can occur.

Depending on how you access your mail, `maildir` does permit the simultaneous access of `maildir` files by multiple applications; `mbox` does not.

The choice of an MUA also affects your choice of mail directory format. For example, the `pine` program does not cache any directory information and must reread the mail directory any time it accesses it. If you are using `pine`, `maildir` would be a poor choice. More advanced MUAs perform caching, so `maildir` might be a good choice, although the MUA cache can get out of synchronization. It seems that there is no perfect choice.

Fedora provides you with mail alternatives that have both strong and weak points. Be aware of the differences among the alternatives and frequently reevaluate your selection to make certain that it is the best one for your circumstances.

Choosing an MTA

Other MTAs are available for use with Fedora Core, but those discussed in the preceding sections are the most popular. Which one should you choose? That depends on what you need to do. Sendmail's main strengths are that it is considered the standard and it can do things that many other MTAs cannot. However, if ease of use or speed is a concern to you, you might want to consider replacing Sendmail with Postfix, Exim, or Qmail. Because Sendmail is the default MTA included with Fedora Core, it is covered in more detail in the following section.

The Mail Delivery Agent

SMTP is a server-to-server protocol that was designed to deliver mail to systems that are always connected to the Internet. Dial-up systems only connect at the user's command; they connect for specific operations, and are frequently disconnected. To accommodate this difference, many mail systems also include a mail delivery agent, or MDA. The MDA transfers mail to systems without permanent Internet connections. The MDA is similar to an MTA (see the following note), but does not handle deliveries between systems and does not provide an interface to the user.

> **NOTE**
>
> Procmail or Spamassassin are examples of MTAs; both provide filtering services to the MTA while they store messages locally and then make them available to the MUA or email client for reading by the user.

The MDA uses the POP3 or IMAP protocols for this process. In a manner similar to a post office box at the post office, POP3 and IMAP implement a "store and forward" process that alleviates the need to maintain a local mail server if all you want to do is read your mail. For example, dial-up Internet users can intermittently connect to their ISP's mail server to retrieve mail using Fetchmail—the MDA provided by Fedora (see the section "Using Fetchmail to Retrieve Mail," later in this chapter).

The Mail User Agent

The mail user agent, or MUA, is another necessary part of the email system. The MUA is a mail client, or mail reader, that allows the user to read and compose email and provides the user interface. (It is the email application itself that most users are familiar with as "email.") Some popular Unix command-line MUAs are elm, pine, and mutt. Fedora also provides modern GUI MUAs: Evolution, Thunderbird, Mozilla Mail, Balsa, Sylpheed, and KMail. For comparison, common non-Unix MUAs are Microsoft Outlook, Outlook Express, Pegasus, Eudora, or Netscape Messenger.

The Microsoft Windows and Macintosh MUAs often include some MTA functionality; Unix does not. For example, Microsoft Outlook can connect to your Internet provider's mail server to send messages. On the other hand, Unix MUAs generally rely on an external MTA such as Sendmail. This might seem like a needlessly complicated way to do things, and it is if used to connect a single user to her ISP. For any other situation, however, using an external MTA allows you much greater flexibility because you can use any number of external programs to handle and process your email functions and customize the service. Having the process handled by different applications gives you very great control over how you provide email service to users on your network, as well as to individual and SOHO users.

For example, you could

- Use Evolution to read and compose mail.

- Use Sendmail to send your mail.

- Use xbiff to notify you when you have new mail.

- Use Fetchmail to retrieve your mail from a remote mail server.

- Use Procmail to automatically sort your incoming mail based on sender, subject, or many other variables.

- Use Spamassassin to eliminate the unwanted messages before you read them.

Basic Sendmail Configuration and Operation

Because Sendmail is the Fedora default client (and the mostly widely used client), the following sections provide a brief explanation and examples for configuring and operating your email system. As mentioned earlier, however, Sendmail is an extremely complex program with a very convoluted configuration. As such, this chapter only covers some of the basics. For more information on Sendmail, as well as other MTAs, see the "Reference" section at the end of this chapter.

Sendmail configuration is handled by files in the /etc/mail directory with much of the configuration being handled by the file sendmail.cf. The actual syntax of the configuration file, sendmail.cf, is cryptic (see the following example). In an attempt to make it easier to configure Sendmail, the sendmail.mc file was created. The following example belies that goal, however. The sendmail.mc file must be processed with the m4 macro processor to create the sendmail.cf file; the needs of that processor account for the unusual syntax of the file. You will learn how to use it later, and we will look at a Perl script that automates and simplifies the entire process. First, let us examine some basic configuration you might want to do with Sendmail.

> **NOTE**
>
> sendmail.cf has some strange syntax because of the requirements of the m4 macro processor. You do not need to understand the details of m4 here, but note the quoting system. The starting quote is a backtick (`` ` ``), and the ending quote is simply a single quote ('). Also, the dnl sequence means to "delete to new line" and causes anything from the sequence up to and including the newline character to be deleted in the output.
>
> Here's a look at an excerpt from the sendmail.cf file:
>
> ```
> CP.
> # "Smart" relay host (may be null)
> DS
> # operators that cannot be in local usernames (i.e., network indicators)
> CO @ % !
> # a class with just dot (for identifying canonical names)
> C..
> # a class with just a left bracket (for identifying domain literals)
> C[[
> # access_db acceptance class
> C{Accept}OK RELAY
> C{ResOk}OKR
> # Hosts for which relaying is permitted ($=R)
> FR-o /etc/mail/relay-domains
> ```

And here's a quote from the `sendmail.mc` file for comparison:

```
dnl define(`SMART_HOST',`smtp.your.provider')
define(`confDEF_USER_ID',``8:12'')dnl
undefine(`UUCP_RELAY')dnl
undefine(`BITNET_RELAY')dnl
dnl define(`confAUTO_REBUILD')dnl
define(`confTO_CONNECT', `1m')dnl
define(`confTRY_NULL_MX_LIST',true)dnl
```

You can see why the file is described as "cryptic."

Rather than involve you in a detailed description of hand editing a file known to be among the most difficult to edit with success, we will examine a Perl script developed by Donncha O'Caoimh. The script automates the configuration of Sendmail by prompting you for information and then doing all the heavy work by modifying the Sendmail configuration file itself. The script sets up a network mail server on a home computer running Fedora. To use the script, you will need to know your email address, the login names and passwords of all mail users, your mail server addresses and the network's IP address. When you are done, Sendmail and Fetchmail will be configured. Running the script not only prompts you for all the necessary information, but it even provides some explanation and help along the way.

You should have Sendmail and Fetchmail installed on your system before you begin. The script is available for download at http://cork.linux.ie/projects/install-sendmail/. Simply uncompress the archive:

```
$ tar -zxvf install-sendmail-5.5.tar.gz
```

Now use the `cd` command to change to the newly created directory.

You can read a great description of this script and its use in the previously mentioned site's README, FAQ, and INSTALL files. You should read these files before you proceed with the installation; they are well-written and will answer all the questions you have. If you are interested in the power of programming with Perl, see Chapter 29, "Using Perl."

Of course, you can always configure Sendmail by hand, especially if you need any advanced options. The following five sections address some commonly used advanced options.

Configuring Masquerading

Sometimes you might want to have Sendmail masquerade as a host other than the actual hostname of your system. Such a situation could occur if you have a dial-up connection to the Internet and your ISP handles all your mail for you. In this case, you will want Sendmail to masquerade as the domain name of your ISP. For example,

```
MASQUERADE_AS(`samplenet.org')dnl
```

Using Smart Hosts

If you do not have a full-time connection to the Internet, you will probably want to have Sendmail send your messages to your ISP's mail server and let it handle delivery for you. Without a full-time Internet connection, you could find it difficult to deliver messages to some locations (such as some underdeveloped areas of the world where email services are unreliable and sporadic). In those situations, you can configure Sendmail to function as a smart host by passing email on to another sender rather than attempting to deliver the email directly. You can use a line such as the following in the `sendmail.mc` file to enable a smart host:

```
define(`SMART_HOST', `smtp.samplenet.org')
```

This line causes Sendmail to pass any mail it receives to the server `smtp.samplenet.org` rather than attempt to deliver it directly. Smart hosting will not work for you if your ISP, like many others, blocks any mail relaying. Some ISPs block relaying because it is frequently used to disseminate spam.

Setting Message Delivery Intervals

As mentioned earlier, Sendmail typically attempts to deliver messages as soon as it receives them, and again at regular intervals after that. If you have only periodic connections to the Internet, as with a dial-up connection, you likely would prefer that Sendmail hold all messages in the queue and attempt to deliver them at specific time intervals or at your prompt. You can configure Sendmail to do so by adding the following line to `sendmail.mc`:

```
define(`confDELIVERY_MODE', `d')dnl
```

This line will cause Sendmail to only attempt mail delivery at regularly scheduled queue processing intervals (by default, somewhere between 20 and 30 minutes).

However, this delay time might not be sufficient if you are offline for longer periods of time. In those situations, you can invoke Sendmail with no queue processing time. For example, by default, Sendmail might start with the following command:

```
# sendmail -bd -q30m
```

This tells Sendmail that it should process the mail queue (and attempt message delivery) every 30 minutes. You can change 30 to any other number to change the delivery interval. If you want Sendmail to wait for a specific prompt before processing the queue, you can invoke Sendmail with no queue time, like this:

```
# sendmail -bd -q
```

This command tells Sendmail to process the queue once when it is started, and again only when you manually direct it to do so. To manually tell Sendmail to process the queue, you can use a command like the following:

```
# sendmail -q
```

> **TIP**
>
> If you use networking over a modem, there is a configuration file for pppd called `ppp.linkup`, which is located in `/etc/ppp`. Any commands in this file will automatically be run each time the PPP daemon is started. You can add the line `sendmail -q` to this file to have your mail queue automatically processed each time you dial up your Internet connection.

Building the `sendmail.cf` File

Books are available to explore the depths of Sendmail configuration, but the Sendmail Installation and Operation Guide is the canonical reference. Configuration guidance can also be found through a Google search; many people use Sendmail in many different configurations. Fortunately, Fedora has provided a default Sendmail configuration that will work "out-of-the-box" for a home user as long as your networking is correctly configured and you do not require an ISP-like Sendmail configuration.

After you have made all your changes to `sendmail.mc`, you need to rebuild the `sendmail.cf` file. First, back up your old file:

```
# cp /etc/mail/sendmail.cf /etc/mail/sendmail.cf.old
```

You must run `sendmail.mc` through the m4 macro processor in order to generate a usable configuration file. A command, such as the following, is used to do this:

```
# m4 /etc/mail/sendmail.mc > /etc/mail/sendmail.cf
```

This command loads the `cf.m4` macro file from `/usr/share/sendmail-cf/m4/cf.m4` and then uses it to process the `sendmail.mc` file. The output, normally sent to STDOUT, is then redirected to the file `sendmail.cf`, and your new configuration file is ready. You will need to restart Sendmail before the changes will take effect.

> **TIP**
>
> Fedora also provides an alternative to using awk to rebuild the Sendmail configuration. As root, execute
>
> ```
> # make -C /etc/mail
> ```

Mail Relaying

By default, Sendmail will not relay mail that did not originate from the local domain. This means that if a Sendmail installation running at `lion.org` receives mail intended for `cheetah.org`, and that mail did not originate from `lion.org`, the mail will be rejected and will not be relayed. If you want to allow selected domains to relay through you, add an entry for the domain to the file `/etc/mail/relay-domains`. If the file does not exist, simply create it in your favorite text editor and add a line containing the name of the domain that you want to allow to relay through you. Sendmail will need to be restarted for this change to take effect.

> **CAUTION**
>
> You need a very good reason to relay mail; otherwise, do not do it. Allowing all domains to relay through you will make you a magnet for spammers who will use your mail server to send spam. This can lead to your site being blacklisted by many other sites, which then will not accept any mail from you or your site's users—even if the mail is legitimate!

Forwarding Email with Aliases

Aliases allow you to have an infinite number of valid recipient addresses on your system, without having to worry about creating accounts or other support files for each address. For example, most systems have "postmaster" defined as a valid recipient, yet do not have an actual login account named "postmaster." Aliases are configured in the file /etc/aliases. Here is an example of an alias entry:

```
postmaster: root
```

This entry will forward any mail received for "postmaster" to the root user. By default, almost all the aliases listed in the /etc/aliases file forward to root.

> **CAUTION**
>
> Reading email as root is a security hazard; a malicious email message can exploit an email client and cause it to execute arbitrary code as the user running the client. To avoid this danger, you can forward all of root's mail to another account and read it from there. You can choose one of two ways for doing this.
>
> You can add an entry to the /etc/mail/aliases file that sends root's mail to a different account. For example, root: foobar would forward all mail intended for root to the account foobar.
>
> The other way is to create a file named .forward in root's home directory that contains the address that the mail should forward to.

Anytime you make a change to the /etc/mail/aliases file, you will need to rebuild the aliases database before that change will take effect. This is done with

```
# newaliases
```

Rejecting Email from Specified Sites

You read earlier in this chapter that you must be careful with mail relaying to avoid becoming a spam magnet. But what do you do if you are having problems with a certain site sending you spam? You can use the /etc/mail/access file to automatically reject mail from certain sites.

You can use several rules in the access file. Table 23.1 gives a list of these rules.

TABLE 23.1 The Various Possible Options for Access Rules

Option	Action
OK	Accepts mail from this site, overriding any rules that would reject mail from this site.
RELAY	Allows this domain to relay through the server.
REJECT	Rejects mail from this site and sends a canned error message.
DISCARD	Simply discards any message received from the site.
ERROR: "n message"	Where n is an RFC821-compliant error code number and message can be any message that you would like to send back to the originating server.

The following is an example of three rules used to control access to a Sendmail account. The first rejects messages from spam.com. The second rejects messages from lamer.com and displays an error message to that site. The third allows mail from the specific host user5.lamer.com, even though there is a rule that rejects mail from the site lamer.com. (For a more personal example of why you would bother to do this, I find that I get a lot of spam from the Hotmail domain, so I would just as soon reject it all. However, my wife uses a Hotmail account for her mail. If I did not allow her mail through, that would be a problem for me.)

```
spam.com            REJECT
lamer.com           ERROR:"550 Mail from spammers is not accepted at this site."
user5.lamer.com     OK
```

Open the /etc/access file, enter the rules of your choice, and then restart Sendmail so that your changes to the access file take effect. That can be done with

```
# /sbin/service sendmail restart
```

or any of the other ways we discussed in Chapter 14, "Automating Tasks."

Introducing Postfix

Sendmail has been the de facto MTA of choice for the Internet for a long time. At one point, it was the power behind 90% of the email traffic across the world, although it has now become largely superceded by worthier programs.

One of the more popular programs that has become available is Postfix, which was developed and is exclusively maintained by Wietse Venema. Designed to be a drop-in replacement for Sendmail, Postfix allows the system administrator to literally replace Sendmail without any detriment to the system.

Postfix was designed from the ground up to retain compatibility with Sendmail but to work in a more efficient fashion. Sendmail is notoriously system intensive when handling either large volumes of mail or large numbers of clients. One command pretty much handles everything, making Sendmail something of a monolith. On the other hand, Postfix works with several individual modules all working together, only using modules when needed.

Making the Switch

Postfix is easy to install and configure. The first thing to do is to make a backup of all your Sendmail information that you want to keep just in case. After you have done this, you need to use Yum to remove `Sendmail` and install Postfix.

After Postfix has been successfully installed, you can begin configuring it. The scripts for Postfix are all located in `/etc/postfix` and include

- `install.cf`—The script generated when Postfix is installed. This file lists the locations Postfix uses and can be a big help when working with the `main.cf` file.

- `main.cf`—The principle configuration script for Postfix. Within the remarks at the start of the script, you are advised to change only a couple of options at any time. This is sage advice, given that there are more than 300 possibilities!

- `master.cf`—The throttle control for Postfix. This script allows you to change settings for Postfix that directly affect the speed at which it works. Unless you have a reason to tinker with this file, leave it alone. Trust me, you will know when you need to make changes.

- `postfix-script`—The script used by Postfix as a wrapper. You cannot execute it directly; instead it is called by Postfix itself.

You can keep your original Sendmail aliases file for use with Postfix because it will not make much difference to it.

You will also require the services of `system-switch-mail`, which can also be installed by using yum.

After `system-switch-mail` has been successfully installed, switch to a root terminal and type the following:

```
# system-switch-mail
```

You are then greeted with a simple text screen asking which MTA you want to use. Select Postfix and simply press Enter. After a few seconds, a new window appears informing you that your MTA has been successfully switched. All you then need to do is ensure that Postfix is enabled in runlevel 5 by checking the service (`system-config-services`).

Further configuration of Postfix focuses on the `main.cf` file, which is extensively documented throughout the file using comments.

The beauty of Postfix is that it can be used in any situation from a single home user to a large corporation that has thousands of clients, even up to the ISP level. It can even be linked to MySQL for authentication purposes and virtual hosting.

Using Fetchmail to Retrieve Mail

SMTP is designed to work with systems that have a full-time connection to the Internet. What if you are on a dial-up account? What if you have another system store your email for you and then you log in to pick it up once in awhile? (Most users who are not setting up servers will be in this situation.) In this case, you cannot easily receive email using SMTP, and you need to use a protocol, such as POP3 or IMAP, instead.

> **NOTE**
>
> Remember when we said that some mail clients can include some MTA functionality? MS Outlook and Outlook Express can be configured to use SMTP and, if you use a dial-up connection, will offer to start the connection and then use SMTP to send your mail, so a type of MTA functionality is included in those mail clients.

Unfortunately, many MUAs do not know anything about POP3 or IMAP. To eliminate that problem, you can use a program called Fetchmail to contact mail servers using POP3 or IMAP, download mail off the servers, and then inject those messages into the local MTA just as if they had come from a standard SMTP server. The following sections explain how to install, configure, and use the Fetchmail program.

Installing Fetchmail

Similar to other `.rpm` files, Fetchmail can be installed with the `rpm -i` command. This command will install all files to their default locations. If, for whatever reason, you need to perform a custom installation, see Chapter 7, "Managing Software and System Resources," for more information on changing the default options for `rpm`.

You can get the latest version of Fetchmail at http://tuxedo.org/~esr/fetchmail. It is available in both source and RPM binary formats. The version of Fedora on the CDs and DVD accompanying this book provides a reasonably current version of Fetchmail and installs useful Fetchmail documentation in the `/usr/share/doc/fetchmail` directory. That directory includes an `FAQ`, `features` list, and `Install` documentation.

Configuring Fetchmail

After you have installed Fetchmail, you must create the file `.fetchmailrc` in your home directory, which provides the configuration for the Fetchmail program.

There are two ways to create the `.fetchmailrc` file. The first is by simply creating and editing the file by hand with any text editor. The second is by using the graphical `fetchmailconf` program. The configuration file is straightforward and quite easy to create; the following sections explain the manual method for creating and editing the file. The information presented in the following sections does not discuss all the options available in the `.fetchmailrc` file, but covers the most common ones needed to get a basic Fetchmail installation up and running. You'll need to use a text editor to create the file to include entries like the ones shown as examples—modified for your personal information, of course. For advanced configuration, see the `man` page for Fetchmail. The `man` page is well written and documents all the configuration options in detail.

23

> **CAUTION**
>
> The `.fetchmailrc` file is divided into three different sections: global options, mail server options, and user options. It is very important that these sections appear in the order listed. Do not add options to the wrong section. Putting options in the wrong place is one of the most common problems that new users make with Fetchmail configuration files.

Configuring Global Options

The first section of `.fetchmailrc` contains the global options. These options affect all the mail servers and user accounts that you list later in the configuration file. Some of these global options can be overridden with local configuration options, as you learn later in this section. Here is an example of the options that might appear in the global section of the `.fetchmailrc` file:

```
set daemon 600
set postmaster foobar
set logfile ./.fetchmail.log
```

The first line in this example tells Fetchmail that it should start in daemon mode and check the mail servers for new mail every 600 seconds, or 10 minutes. Daemon mode means that after Fetchmail starts, it will move itself into the background and continue running. Without this line, Fetchmail would check for mail once when it started and would then terminate and never check again.

The second option tells Fetchmail to use the local account `foobar` as a last resort address. In other words, any email that it receives and cannot deliver to a specified account should be sent to `foobar`.

The third line tells Fetchmail to log its activity to the file `./.fetchmail.log`. Alternatively, you can use the line `set syslog`—in which case, Fetchmail will log through the `syslog` facility.

Configuring Mail Server Options

The second section of the `.fetchmailrc` file contains information on each of the mail servers that should be checked for new mail. Here is an example of what the mail section might look like:

```
poll mail.samplenet.org
proto pop3
no dns
```

The first line tells Fetchmail that it should check the mail server `mail.samplenet.org` at each poll interval that was set in the global options section (which was 600 seconds in our example). Alternatively, the first line can begin with `skip`. If a mail server line begins with `skip`, it will not be polled as the poll interval, but will only be polled when it is specifically specified on the Fetchmail command line.

The second line specifies the protocol that should be used when contacting the mail server. In this case, we are using the POP3 protocol. Other legal options are IMAP, APOP, and KPOP. You can also use AUTO here—in which case, Fetchmail will attempt to automatically determine the correct protocol to use with the mail server.

The third line tells Fetchmail that it should not attempt to do a DNS lookup. You will probably want to include this option if you are running over a dial-up connection.

Configuring User Accounts

The third and final section of .fetchmailrc contains information about the user account on the server specified in the previous section. Here is an example:

```
user foobar
pass secretword
fetchall
flush
```

The first line, of course, simply specifies the username that is used to log in to the email server, and the second line specifies the password for that user. Many security conscious people cringe at the thought of putting clear-text passwords in a configuration file, and they should if it is group or world-readable. The only protection for this information is to make certain that the file is readable only by the owner; that is, with file permissions of 600.

The third line tells Fetchmail that it should fetch all messages from the server, even if they have already been read.

The fourth line tells Fetchmail that it should delete the messages from the mail server after it has completed downloading them. This is the default, so we would not really have to specify this option. If you wanted to leave the messages on the server after downloading them, use the option no flush.

The configuration options you just inserted configured the entire .fetchmailrc file to look like this:

```
set daemon 600
set postmaster foobar
set logfile ./.fetchmail.log

poll mail.samplenet.org
proto pop3
no dns

user foobar
pass secretword
fetchall
flush
```

What this file tells Fetchmail to do is

- Check the POP3 server `mail.samplenet.org` for new mail every 600 seconds.
- Log in using the username `foobar` and the password `secretword`.
- Download all messages off the server.
- Delete the messages from the server after it has finished downloading them.
- Send any mail it receives that cannot be delivered to a local user to the account `foobar`.

TIP

You could use the graphical `fetchmailconf` client to configure, test, and use your Fetchmail settings. If you choose to install it, start the client from the command line of an X terminal window like this:

```
# fetchmailconf &
```

As mentioned before, many more options can be included in the `.fetchmailrc` file than are listed here. However, these options will get you up and running with a basic configuration.

For additional flexibility, you can define multiple `.fetchmailrc` files in order to retrieve mail from different remote mail servers while using the same Linux user account. For example, you can define settings for your most often used account and save them in the default `.fetchmailrc` file. Mail can then quickly be retrieved like so:

```
$ fetchmail -a
1 message for bball at mail.myserver.com (1108 octets).
reading message 1 of 1 (1108 octets) . flushed
```

By using Fetchmail's `-f` option, you can specify an alternative resource file and then easily retrieve mail from another server like this:

```
$ fetchmail -f .myothermailrc
2 messages for bball at othermail.otherserver.org (5407 octets).
reading message 1 of 2 (3440 octets) ... flushed
reading message 2 of 2 (1967 octets) . flushed
You have new mail in /var/spool/mail/bball
```

By using the `-d` option, along with a time interval (in seconds), you can use Fetchmail in its daemon, or background mode. The command will launch as a background process and retrieve mail from a designated remote server at a specified interval. For more advanced options, see the Fetchmail man page, which is very well-written and documents all options in detail.

> **CAUTION**
>
> Because the `.fetchmailrc` file contains your mail server password, it should be readable only by you. This means that it should be owned by you and should have permissions no greater than 600. Fetchmail will complain and refuse to start if the `.fetchmailrc` file has permissions greater than this.

Choosing a Mail Delivery Agent

Because of the modular nature of mail handling, it is possible to use multiple applications to process mail and accomplish more than simply deliver it. Getting mail from the storage area and displaying it to the user is the purpose of the mail delivery agent (MDA). MDA functionality can be found in some of the mail clients (MUAs), which can cause some confusion to those still unfamiliar with the concept of Unix mail. As an example, the Procmail MDA provide filtering based on rulesets; KMail and Evolution, both MUAs, provide filtering, but the MUAs pine, mutt, and Balsa do not. Some MDAs perform simple sorting, and other MDAs are designed to eliminate unwanted emails, such as spam and viruses.

You would choose an MDA based on what you want to do with your mail. We'll look at five MDAs that offer functions you might find useful in your particular situation. If you have simple needs (just organizing mail by rules), one of the MUAs that offers filtering might be better for your needs. Fedora provides the Evolution MUA as the default selection (and it contains some MDA functionality as previously noted), so try that first and see if it meets your needs. If not, investigate one of the following MDAs provided by Fedora.

Unless otherwise noted, all the MDA software is provided with the Fedora discs. Chapter 7 details the general installation of any software.

Procmail

As a tool for advanced users, the Procmail application acts as a filter for email as it is retrieved from a mail server. It uses rulesets (known as recipes) as it reads each email message. No default configuration is provided; you must manually create a `~/.procmail` file for each user, or each user can create her own.

There is no systemwide default configuration file. The creation of the rulesets is not trivial and requires an understanding of the use of regular expressions that is beyond the scope of this chapter. Fedora Core does provide three examples of the files in `/usr/share/doc/procmail/examples`, as well as a fully commented example in the `/usr/share/doc/procmail` directory, which also contains a README and FAQ. Details for the rulesets can be found in the man page for Procmail as well as the man pages for `procmailrc`, `procmailsc`, and `procmailex`, which contain examples of Procmail recipes.

Spamassassin

If you have used email for any length of time, you have likely been subjected to spam—unwanted email that is sent to thousands of people at the same time. Fedora provides an MDA named Spamassassin to assist you in reducing and eliminating unwanted emails. Easily integrated with Procmail and Sendmail, it can be configured for both systemwide and individual use. It employs a combination of rulesets and blacklists (Internet domains known to mail spam).

Enabling Spamassassin is simple. You must first have installed and configured Procmail. The README file found in /usr/share/doc/spamassassin provides details on configuring the .procmail file to process mail through Spamassassin. It will tag probable spam with a unique header; you can then have Procmail filter the mail in any manner you choose. One interesting use of Spamassasin is to use it to tag email received at special email accounts established solely for the purpose of attracting spam. This information is then shared with the Spamassassin site where these "spam trap" generated hits help the authors fine-tune the rulesets.

Squirrelmail

Perhaps you do not want to read your mail in an MUA. If you use your web browser often, it might make sense to read and send your mail via a web interface, such as the one used by Hotmail or Yahoo! mail. Fedora provides Squirrelmail for just that purpose. Squirrelmail is written in the PHP 4 language and supports IMAP and SMTP with all pages rendering in HTML 4.0 without using Java. It supports MIME attachments, as well as an address book and folders for segregating email.

You must configure your web server to work with PHP 4. Detailed installation instructions can be found in /usr/share/doc/squirrelmail/INSTALL. Once configured, point your web browser to http://www.yourdomain.com/squirellmail/ to read and send email.

Virus Scanners

Although the currently held belief is that Linux is immune to email viruses targeted at Microsoft Outlook users, it certainly makes no sense for Unix mail servers to permit infected email to be sent through them. Although Fedora does not provide a virus scanner, one of the more popular of many such scanners is MailScanner, available from http://www.sng.ecs.soton.ac.uk/mailscanner/; a Fedora RPM package is available as well as the source code. It supports Sendmail and Exim, but not Postfix or Qmail. Searching on the terms "virus" and "email" at Freshmeat.net will turn up a surprising list of GPLed virus scanners that might serve your needs.

Special Mail Delivery Agents

If you already use Hotmail or another web-based email account, the currently available MUAs will not be useful to you; formal POP3 access to a Hotmail account is not available free of charge. However, Microsoft Outlook Express can access Hotmail at no charge using a special protocol called HTTPMail. How that is done is covered in RFC-2518 as "WebDAV extensions to HTTP/1.1." No specific solution is provided by Fedora, but the basic tools it provides are adequate when supplemented by some clever Perl programming.

Hotwayd is available from http://sourceforge.net/projects/hotwayd/ and implements this functionality, allowing you to use your favorite mail client to read mail from Hotmail.

A newer Hotmail access tool is Gotmail from http://sourceforge.net/projects/gotmail. It is a Perl script that is easy to configure. There are brief tutorials on configuring it for use with KMail and Evolution at http://www.madpenguin.org/cms/?m=show&id=437.

A similar tool exists for Yahoo! mail. FetchYahoo is available from http://fetchyahoo.twizzler.org/.

Once implemented, you can use a regular MUA, or mail client, to access your web-based mail. None of them, however, enable you to send mail through Hotmail or Yahoo! mail.

Mail Daemons

Fedora provides an `imap` package that will install IMAP and POP daemons (servers) for your system. These servers facilitate receiving mail from a remote site. Once installed, the documentation will be found in `/usr/share/doc/imap` and the README is brief; Fedora has already done the configuration for you: You only need to start the services (see Chapter 14).

Biff and its KDE cousin KOrn are small daemons that monitor your mail folder and notify you when a message has been placed there. It is common to include `biff y` in the `.login` or `.profile` files to automatically start it upon user login if you want to use Biff. KOrn can be started by adding the applet to the KDE taskbar.

> **NOTE**
>
> Autoresponders automatically generate replies to received messages; they are commonly used to notify others that the recipient is out of the office. Mercifully, Fedora does not include one, but you can find and install an autoresponder at `Freshmeat.net`. If you are subscribed to a mailing list, be aware that automatic responses from your account can be very annoying to others on the list. Please unsubscribe from mail lists before you leave the office with your autoresponder activated.

Alternatives to Microsoft Exchange Server

One of the last areas in which a Microsoft product has yet to be usurped by Open Source software is a replacement for MS Exchange Server. Many businesses use MS Outlook and MS Exchange Server to access email, as well as to provide calendaring, notes, file sharing, and other collaborative functions. General industry complaints about Exchange Server center around scalability, administration (backup and restore in particular), and licensing fees.

A "drop-in" alternative needs to have compatibility with MS Outlook because it's intended to replace Exchange Server in an environment in which there are Microsoft desktops in existence using Outlook. A "work-alike" alternative provides similar features to Exchange Server, but does not offer compatibility with the MS Outlook client itself; the latter is typical of many of the open- source alternatives.

There are several "drop-in" alternatives, none of which are fully open source because some type of proprietary connector is needed to provide the services to MS Outlook clients (or provide Exchange services to the Linux Evolution client). For Outlook compatibility, the key seems to be the realization of a full, open implementation of MAPI, Microsoft's Messaging Application Program Interface. That goal is going to be difficult to achieve because MAPI is a poorly documented Microsoft protocol. For Linux-only solutions, the missing ingredient for many alternatives is a usable group calendaring/ scheduling system similar in function to that provided by Exchange Server/Outlook.

Of course, independent applications for these functions abound in the open-ource world, but one characteristic of "groupware" is its central administration; another is that all components can share information.

The following sections examine several of the available servers, beginning with MS Exchange Server itself and moving toward those applications that have increasing incompatibility with it. None of these servers are provided with Fedora.

Microsoft Exchange Server/Outlook Client

Exchange Server and Outlook seem to be the industry benchmark because of their widespread deployment. They offer a proprietary server providing email, contacts, scheduling, public folders, task lists, journaling, and notes using MS Outlook as the client and MAPI as the API. If you consider what MS Exchange offers as the "full" set of features, no other replacement offers 100% of the features exactly as provided by MS Exchange Server—even those considered "drop-in" replacements. The home page for the Microsoft Exchange server is http://www.microsoft.com/exchange/.

CommuniGate Pro

CommuniGate Pro is a proprietary, drop-in alternative to MS Exchange Server, providing, email, webmail, LDAP directories, a web server, file server, contacts, calendaring (third-party), and a list server. The CommuniGate Pro MAPI Connector provides access to the server from MS Outlook and other MAPI-enabled clients. The home page for this server is http://www.stalker.com/.

Samsung Contact (Formerly Known As HP OpenMail)

This is a proprietary, drop-in alternative to MS Exchange Server (and is also used by many Fortune 500 companies). The Samsung Contact server provides what is almost a full replacement for MS Exchange Server and will (once ITEF finishes the open "calendar spec") work with all the more common Linux email clients and web browsers. The home page is http://www.samsungcontact.com/en/.

Bynari

Bynari provides a proprietary group of servers to act as a drop-in replacement for MS Exchange Server for email, calendaring, public folders, scheduling, address book, webmail, and contacts. Although it runs on Linux, it offers no Linux clients and the Connector provides services to MS Outlook only. The home page is http://www.bynari.net/.

SuSE OpenExchange

The SuSE Linux OpenExchange message server is based on Cyrus-imap and Postfix. Most of the server's groupware features are provided by a proprietary web-based groupware server (ComFire). SuSE OpenExchange also uses Apache, OpenLDAP, Samba, and SuSE Linux Enterprise Server 8 to provide public directories, notes, webmail, scheduler, tasks, project management, document management, forums, and bookmarks. Some compatibility with MS Outlook is provided. The home page is http://www.suse.com/en/business/products/openexchange/.

Kroupware

The Kroupware project was begun to provide groupware functions such as email, group calendaring, notes and tasks, but Kroupware was not designed to be a total replacement for MS Exchange Server and Outlook. The result is composed of the Kolab Server and the KDE Kolab Client. The Kolab Server is based on the existing Open Source components of OpenLDAP, Cyrus-imapd, Postfix, and Apache. The KDE Kolab Client uses special versions of KMail, KOrganizer, KAddressBook, and KPilot that can communicate with the Kolab Server. It is necessary to use the Bynari Insight Connector to enable Outlook to communicate with the Kolab Server. The home page is http://www.kroupware.org/.

OpenGroupware (Formerly SKYRiX 4.1)

OpenGroupware (not affiliated with OpenOffice.org) focuses on groupware and collaboration (and does not provide its own mail server). It can replace Comfire in SuSE OpenExchange to save on the licensing cost or be used with a Cyrus-imap mail server and PostgreSQL and FrontBase (no MySQL) for the database. For connectivity to Outlook, OpenGroupware uses the ZideLook MAPI Storage Provider (proprietary, it maps MAPI to WebDAV) and the Open Source WebDAV middleware server ZideStore. ZideStore translates WebDAV requests to calls to OpenGroupware as well as clients such as Evolution and Mozilla. The home page is http://www.opengroupware.org/en/.

phpgroupware

phpgroupware is an open-source application written in PHP (and used with MySQL or postgresql plus a web server and an IMAP mail server). phpgroupware provides a web-based calendar, task list, address book, email, news headlines, and a file manager. Version 1.0 is expected to be released in 2004. The home page is http://www.phpgroupware.org/.

PHProjekt

PHProjekt is open-source software written in PHP (used with MySql, postgresql, Oracle, Informix, or MS-sql). PHProjekt provides calendaring, contact manager, time card system, project management, online chat, threaded discussion forum, trouble ticket system, email, public files, notes bookmarks, voting system, task lists, reminders, site-search, and integration with the PostNuke news site application. It provides no Exchange/Outlook compatibility whatsoever. The home page is http://www.PHProjekt.com/.

IMP/Horde

IMP/Horde is a PHP-based application framework. When combined with an HTTP server (Apache, Microsoft IIS, Netscape) and MySql database, IMP/Horde offers modules that provide webmail, contact manager, calendar, CVS viewer, file manager, time tracking, email filter rules manager, notes, tasks, chat, newsgroups, forms, bug tracking, FAQ repository, and presentations. The home page is http://www.horde.org/.

Conclusion

There are no open-source–only alternatives that can provide full Exchange-like services to MS Outlook clients. If you do not have Outlook clients to worry about, OpenGroupware, IMP/Horde and phprojekt look promising. None of them are provided with Fedora.

Relevant Fedora and Linux Commands

You will use the following commands to manage electronic mail in Fedora:

`balsa`—A GNOME mail user agent for X.

`biff`—A console-based mail notification utility.

`evolution`—A comprehensive and capable Ximian GNOME mail PIM for X.

`fetchmail`—A console-based and daemon-mode mail retrieval command for Linux.

`fetchmailconf`—A graphical `fetchmail` configuration client for X.

`kmail`—A graphical mail user client for KDE and X

`korn`—A `biff` applet for KDE and X.

`mail`—A console-based mail user agent.

`mutt`—A console-based mail user agent.

`sendmail`—A comprehensive mail transport agent for Unix and Linux.

`xbiff`—A mail notification X client.

Reference

The following references are recommended reading for email configuration. Of course, not all references will apply to you. Select the ones that apply to the email server that you are using.

Web Resources

http://www.sendmail.org/—This is the Sendmail home page. Here you will find configuration information and FAQs regarding the Sendmail MTA.

http://www.postfix.org/—This is the Postfix home page. If you are using the Postfix MTA, documentation and sample configurations can be found at this site.

http://www.qmail.org/—This is the home page for the Qmail MTA. It contains documentation and links to other resources on Qmail.

http://www.linuxgazette.com/issue35/jao.html—IMAP on Linux: A Practical Guide. The Internet Mail Access Protocol allows a user to access his email stored on a remote server rather than a local disk.

http://www.redhat.com/support/resources/faqa/RH-postfix-FAQ/book1.html—A slightly out-of-date but still very useful HOWTO about setting up Postfix in a Red Hat environment.

http://www.imap.org/about/whatisIMAP.html—A page describing what IMAP is.

http://www.rfc-editor.org/—A repository of RFCs—Request for Comments—that define the technical "rules" of modern computer usage.

http://www.procmail.org/—The Procmail home page.

http://www.moongroup.com/docs/procmail/—The Procmail FAQ, which includes suggestions for troubleshooting problems. The page also references a page of links that, in turn, reference other link collections as well as tidbits from the Procmail mail list.

http://www.ibiblio.org/pub/Linux/docs/HOWTO/other-formats/html_single/ Qmail-VMailMgr-Courier-imap-HOWTO.html—If you want some help configuring a mail system based on the lesser-used applications, this HOWTO will help.

Books

Sendmail from O'Reilly Publishing. This is the de facto standard guide for everything Sendmail. It is loaded with more than 1,000 pages, which gives you an idea of how complicated Sendmail really is.

Postfix from Sams Publishing. An excellent book from Sams Publishing that covers the Postfix MTA.

Running Qmail from Sams Publishing. This is similar to the Postfix book from Sams Publishing except that it covers the Qmail MTA.

24

Setting Up a Proxy Server

There are two things in this world that you can never have enough of: time and bandwidth. Fedora comes with a proxy server—Squid—that enables you to cache web traffic on your server so that websites load faster and users consume less bandwidth.

What Is a Proxy Server?

A *proxy server* lies between client machines—the desktops in your company—and the Internet. As clients request websites, they do not connect directly to the Web and send the HTTP request. Instead, they connect to the local proxy server. The proxy then forwards their request on to the Web, retrieves the result, and hands it back to the client. At its simplest, a proxy server really is just an extra layer between client and server, so why bother?

The three main reasons for deploying a proxy server are

- **Content control**—You want to stop people whiling away their work hours reading the news or downloading MP3s.

- **Speed**—You want to cache common sites to make the most of your bandwidth.

- **Security**—You want to monitor what people are doing.

Squid is capable of all of these, and more.

Installing Squid

Squid installation is handled through the Add/Remove Applications dialog under the System Settings menu. The Squid package is confusingly located under the Web Server group; this has the downside of installing Apache alongside Squid whether you like it or not. That said, you can (and should) deselect other autoinstall packages that you do not need from the Web Server category.

After Squid is installed, switch to the console and use su to get to the root account. You should run the command chkconfig --level 345 squid on to run Squid at runlevels 3, 4, and 5, like this:

```
[root@susannah ~]# chkconfig --list squid
squid    0:off 1:off 2:off 3:off 4:off 5:off 6:off
[root@susannah ~]# chkconfig --level 345 squid on
[root@susannah ~]# chkconfig --list squid
squid    0:off 1:off 2:off 3:on 4:on 5:on 6:off
```

That runs Squid the next time the system switches to runlevel 3, 4, or 5, but it will not run it just yet.

Configuring Clients

Before you configure your new Squid server, you should set up the local web browser to use it for its web access. This allows you to test your rules as you are working with the configuration file.

To configure Firefox, select Preferences from the Edit menu. From the dialog that appears, click the Connection Settings button (near the bottom on the General tab) and select the option Manual Proxy Configuration. Check the box beneath it, Use the Same Proxy for All Protocols; then enter **127.0.0.1** as the IP address and **3128** as the port number. See Figure 24.1 for how this should look. If you are configuring a remote client, specify the IP address of the Squid server instead of 127.0.0.1.

For Konqueror, go to the Settings menu and select Configure Konqueror. From the left tabs, scroll down to Proxy, select Manually Specify the Proxy Settings, and then click Setup. Enter **127.0.0.1** as the proxy IP address and **3128** as the port. As with Firefox, if you are configuring a remote client, specify the IP address of the Squid server instead of 127.0.0.1.

Internet Explorer's proxy settings are in Tools/Internet Options. From the Connections tab, click the LAN Settings button and enable the Use a Proxy Server for Your LAN option. Enter the address as the IP of your Squid machine, and then specify **3128** as the port.

FIGURE 24.1   Setting up Firefox to use 127.0.0.1 routes all its web requests through Squid.

Access Control Lists

The main Squid configuration file is /etc/squid/squid.conf, and the default Fedora configuration file is full of comments to help guide you. The default configuration file allows full access to the local machine but denies the rest of your network. This is a secure place to start; we recommend you try all the rules on yourself (localhost) before rolling them out to other machines.

Before you start, open two terminal windows as root. In the first, change to the directory /var/log/squid and run this command:

```
tail -f access.log cache.log
```

That reads the last few lines from both files and (thanks to the -f flag) follows them so that any changes appear in there. This allows you to watch what Squid is doing as people access it. We will refer to this window as the "log window," so keep it open. In the other window (as root, remember), bring up the file /etc/squid/squid.conf in your favorite editor. This window will be referred to as the "config editor," and you should keep it open also.

To get started, search for the string acl all—this brings you to the access control section, which is where most of the work needs to be done. There is a lot you can configure else-where, but unless you have unusual requirements, you can leave the defaults in place.

> **NOTE**
>
> The default port for Squid is 3128, but you can change that by editing the http_port line. Alternatively, you can have Squid listen on multiple ports by having multiple http_port lines: 80, 8000, and 8080 are all popular ports for proxy servers.

The acl lines make up your access control lists. The first 16 or so define the minimum recommended configuration that set up ports to listen to, and so on. You can safely ignore these. If you scroll down further (past another short block of comments), you come to the http_access lines, which are combined with the acl lines to dictate who can do what. You can (and should) mix and match acl and http_access lines to keep your configuration file easy to read.

Just below the first block of http_access lines is a comment like # INSERT YOUR OWN RULE(S) HERE TO ALLOW ACCESS FROM YOUR CLIENTS. This is just what we are going to do. First, though, scroll just a few lines further and you should see these two lines:

```
http_access allow localhost
http_access deny all
```

They are self-explanatory: The first says, "allow HTTP access to the local computer, but deny everyone else." This is the default rule, as mentioned earlier. Leave that in place for now, and run service squid start to start the server with the default settings. If you have not yet configured the local web browser to use your Squid server, do so now so you can test the default rules.

In your web browser (Firefox is assumed from here on, but it makes little difference), go to the URL http://fedora.redhat.com. You should see it appear as normal in the browser, but in the log window you should see a lot of messages scroll by as Squid downloads the site for you and stores it in its cache. This is all allowed because the default configuration allows access to the localhost.

Go back to the config editor window and add this before the last two http_access lines:

```
http_access deny localhost
```

So, the last three lines should look like this:

```
http_access deny localhost
http_access allow localhost
http_access deny all
```

Save the file and quit your editor. Then, run this command:

```
kill -SIGHUP `cat /var/run/squid.pid`
```

That looks for the PID of the Squid daemon and then sends the SIGHUP signal to it, which forces it to reread its configuration file while running. You should see a string of messages in the log window as Squid rereads its configuration files. If you now go back to Firefox and enter a new URL, you should see the Squid error page informing you that you do not have access to the requested site.

The reason you are now blocked from the proxy is because Squid reads its ACL lines in sequence, from top to bottom. If it finds a line that conclusively allows or denies a request, it stops reading and takes the appropriate action. So, in the previous lines localhost is being denied in the first line and then allowed in the second. When Squid sees localhost asking for a site, it reads the deny line first and immediately sends the error page—it does not even get to the allow line. Having a deny all line at the bottom is highly recommended so that only those you explicitly allow are able to use the proxy.

Go back to editing the configuration file and remove the deny localhost and allow localhost lines. This leaves only deny all, which blocks everyone (including the localhost) from accessing the proxy. Now we are going to add some conditional allow statements: We want to allow localhost only if it fits certain criteria.

Defining access criteria is done with the acl lines, so above the deny all line, add this:

```
acl newssites dstdomain news.bbc.co.uk slashdot.org
http_access allow newssites
```

The first line defines an access category called newssites, which contains a list of domains (dstdomain). The domains are news.bbc.co.uk and slashdot.org, so the full line reads, "create a new access category called newssites, that should filter on domain, and contain the two domains listed." It does *not* say whether access should be granted or denied to that category; that comes in the next line. The line http_access allow newssites means, "allow access to the category newssites with no further restrictions." It is not limited to localhost, which means that applies to every computer connecting to the proxy server.

Save the configuration file and rerun the kill -SIGHUP line from before to restart Squid; then go back to Firefox and try loading http://fedora.redhat.com. You should see the same error as before because that was not in our newssites category. Now try http://news.bbc.co.uk, and it should work. However, if you try http://www.slashdot.org, it will *not* work, and you might also have noticed that the images did not appear on the BBC News website either. The problem here is that specifying slashdot.org as the website is very specific: It means that http://slashdot.org will work, whereas http://www.slashdot.org will not. The BBC News site store its images on the site http://newsimg.bbc.co.uk, which is why they do not appear.

Go back to the configuration file, and edit the newssites ACL to this:

```
acl newssites dstdomain .bbc.co.uk .slashdot.org
```

Putting the period in front of the domains (and in the BBC's case, taking the news off also) means that Squid will allow any subdomain of the site to work, which is usually what you will want. If you want even more vagueness, you can just specify .com to match *.com addresses.

Moving on, you can also use time conditions for sites. For example, if you want to allow access to the news sites in the evenings, you can set up a time category using this line:

```
acl freetime time MTWHFAS 18:00-23:59
```

This time, the category is called freetime and the condition is time, which means we need to specify what time the category should contain. The seven characters following that are the days of the week: Monday, Tuesday, Wednesday, tHursday, Friday, sAturday, and sUnday. Thursday and Saturday use capital *H* and *A* so they do not clash with Tuesday and Sunday.

With that category defined, you can change the `http_access` line to include it, like this:

```
http_access allow newssites freetime
```

For Squid to allow access now, it must match both conditions—the request must be for either `*.bbc.co.uk` or `slashdot.org`, and during the time specified. If either condition does not match, the line is not matched and Squid continues looking for other matching rules beneath it. The times you specify here are inclusive on both sides, which means users in the `freetime` category will be able to surf from 18:00:00 until 23:59:59.

You can add as many rules as you like, although you should be careful to try to order them so they make sense. Keep in mind that all conditions in a line must be matched for the line to be matched. Here is a more complex example:

- You want a category `newssites` that contains serious websites people need for their work.

- You want a category `playsites` that contains websites people do not need for their work.

- You want a category `worktime` that stretches from 09:00 to 18:00.

- You want a category `freetime` that stretches from 18:00 to 20:00, when the office closes.

- You want people to be able to access the news sites, but not the play sites, during working hours.

- You want people to be able to access both the news sites and the play sites during the free time hours.

To do that, you need the following rules:

```
acl newssites dstdomain .bbc.co.uk .slashdot.org
acl playsites dstdomain .tomshardware.com fedora.redhat.com
acl worktime time MTWHF 9:00-18:00
acl freetime time MTWHF 18:00-20:00
http_access allow newssites worktime
http_access allow newssites freetime
http_access allow playsites freetime
```

> **NOTE**
>
> The letter D is equivalent to MTWHF in meaning "all the days of the working week."

Notice that there are two `http_access` lines for the `newssites` category: one for `worktime` and one for `freetime`. This is because all the conditions must be matched for a line to be matched. The alternative would be to write this:

```
http_access allow newssites worktime freetime
```

However, if you do that and someone visits news.bbc.co.uk at 2:30 p.m. (14:30) on a Tuesday, Squid will work like this:

- Is the site in the `newssites` category? Yes, continue.

- Is the time within the `worktime` category? Yes, continue.

- Is the time within the `freetime` category? No; do not match rule, and continue searching for rules.

It is because of this that two lines are needed for the `worktime` category.

One particularly powerful way to filter requests is with the `url_regex` ACL line. This allows you to specify a regular expression that is checked against each request: If the expression matches the request, the condition matches.

For example, if you want to stop people downloading Windows executable files, you would use this line:

```
acl nojpgs url_regex -i exe$
```

The dollar sign means "end of URL," which means it would match http:// www.somesite.com/virus.exe but not http://www.executable.com/innocent.html. The `-i` part means "case-insensitive," so the rule will match `.exe`, `.Exe`, `.EXE`, and so on. You can use the caret sign (^) for "start of URL."

For example, you could stop some pornography sites using this ACL:

```
acl noporn url_regex -i sex
```

Do not forget to run the `kill -SIGHUP` command each time you make changes to Squid; otherwise, it will not reread your changes. You can have Squid check your configuration files for errors by running `squid -k parse` as root. If you see no errors, it means your configuration is fine.

> **NOTE**
>
> It is critical that you run the command `kill -SIGHUP` and provide it the process ID of your Squid daemon each time you change the configuration; without this, Squid will not reread its configuration files.

24

Specifying Client IP Addresses

The configuration options so far have been basic, and there are many more you can use to enhance the proxying system you want.

After you are past deciding which rules work for you locally, it is time to spread them out to other machines. This is done by specifying IP ranges that should be allowed or disallowed access, and you enter these into Squid using more ACL lines.

If you want to, you can specify all the IP addresses on your network, one per line. However, for networks of more than about 20 people or using DHCP, that is more work than necessary. A better solution is to use classless interdomain routing (CIDR) notation, which allows you to specify addresses like this:

```
192.0.0.0/8
192.168.0.0/16
192.168.0.0/24
```

Each line has an IP address, followed by a slash and then a number. That last number defines the range of addresses you want covered and refers to the number of bits in an IP address. An IP address is a 32-bit number, but we are used to seeing it in dotted-quad notation: A.B.C.D. Each of those quads can be between 0 and 255 (although in practice some of these are reserved for special purposes), and each is stored as an 8-bit number.

The first line in the previous code covers IP addresses starting from 192.0.0.0; the /8 part means that the first 8 bits (the first quad, 192) is fixed and the rest is flexible. So, Squid treats that as addresses 192.0.0.0, 192.0.0.1, through to 192.0.0.255, then 192.0.1.0, 192.0.1.1, all the way through to 192.255.255.255.

The second line uses /16, which means Squid will allow IP addresses from 192.168.0.0 to 192.168.255.255. The last line has /24, which allows from 192.168.0.0 to 192.168.0.255.

These addresses are placed into Squid using the src ACL line, like this:

```
acl internal_network src 10.0.0.0/24
```

That line creates a category of addresses from 10.0.0.0 to 10.0.0.255. You can combine multiple address groups together, like this:

```
acl internal_network src 10.0.0.0/24 10.0.3.0/24 10.0.5.0/24 192.168.0.1
```

That example allows 10.0.0.0–10.0.0.255, then 10.0.3.0–10.0.3.255, and finally the single address 192.168.0.1.

Keep in mind that, if you are using the local machine and you have the web browser configured to use the proxy at 127.0.0.1, the client IP address will be 127.0.0.1, too. So, make sure you have rules in place for localhost.

As with other ACL lines, you need to enable them with appropriate http_access allow and http_access deny lines.

Sample Configurations

To help you fully understand how Squid access control works, and also to help give you a
head start developing your own rules, the following are some ACL lines you can try. Each
line is preceded with one or more comment lines (starting with a #) explaining what it
does:

```
# include the domains news.bbc.co.uk and slashdot.org
# and not newsimg.bbc.co.uk or www.slashdot.org.
acl newssites dstdomain news.bbc.co.uk slashdot.org

# include any subdomains or bbc.co.uk or slashdot.org
acl newssites dstdomain .bbc.co.uk .slashdot.org

# only include sites located in Canada
acl canadasites dstdomain .ca

# only include working hours
acl workhours time MTWHF 9:00-18:00

# only include lunchtimes
acl lunchtimes time MTWHF 13:00-14:00

# only include weekends
acl weekends time AS 00:00-23:59

# include URLs ending in ".zip". Note: the \ is important,
# because "." has a special meaning otherwise
acl zipfiles url_regex -i \.zip$

# include URLs starting with https
acl httpsurls url_regex -i ^https

# include all URLs that match "hotmail"
url_regex hotmail url_regex -i hotmail

# include three specific IP addresses
acl directors src 10.0.0.14 10.0.0.28 10.0.0.31

# include all IPs from 192.168.0.0 to 192.168.0.255
acl internal src 192.168.0.0/24

# include all IPs from 192.168.0.0 to 192.168.0.255
# and all IPs from 10.0.0.0 to 10.255.255.255
acl internal src 192.168.0.0/24 10.0.0.0/8
```

24

When you have your ACL lines in place, you can put together appropriate `http_access` lines. For example, you might want to use a multilayered access system so that certain users (for example, company directors) have full access, whereas others are filtered. For example:

```
http_access allow directors
http_access deny hotmail
http_access deny zipfiles
http_access allow internal lunchtimes
http_access deny all
```

Because Squid matches those in order, directors will have full, unfiltered access to the Web. If the client IP address is not in the directors list, the two `deny` lines are processed so that the user cannot download `.zip` files or read online mail at Hotmail. After blocking those two types of requests, the `allow` on line four allows internal users to access the Web, as long as they do so only at lunch time. The last line (which is highly recommended) blocks all other users from the proxy.

Reference

http://www.squid-cache.org/—The home page of the Squid Web Proxy Cache.

http://squid-docs.sourceforge.net/latest/book-full.html—The home page of *Squid: A User's Guide*, a free online book about Squid.

http://www.faqs.org/docs/securing/netproxy-squid.html—A brief online guide to configuring a local Squid server.

http://squid.visolve.com/squid/index.htm/—The home page of a company that can provide commercial support and deployment of Squid.

http://squid.visolve.com/squid/reverseproxy.htm—ViSolve's guide to setting up Squid to reverse proxy to cache a local web server for external visitors.

As well as these URLs, there are two excellent books on the topic of web caching. The first is *Squid: The Definitive Guide* (O'Reilly) by Duane Wessels, ISBN: 0-596-00162-2. The second is *Web Caching* (O'Reilly) also by Duane Wessels, ISBN: 1-56592-536-X.

Of the two, the former is more practical and covers the Squid server in depth. The latter is more theoretical, discussing how caching is implemented. Wessels is one of the leading developers on Squid, so both books are of impeccable technical accuracy.

# CHAPTER 25

Remote Access with SSH and Telnet

The ability to control your system remotely is one of the high points of Fedora Core Linux—you can connect from any Linux box to another Linux box in a variety of ways. If you just want to check something quickly or if you have limited bandwidth, you have the option of using only the command line, but you can also connect directly to the X server and get full graphical control.

Understanding the selection of tools available is largely a history lesson. For example, Telnet was an earlier way of connecting to another computer through the command line, but that has since been superseded by SSH. That is not to say that you should ignore Telnet; you need to know how to use it so you have it as a fallback. However, SSH is preferred because it is more secure. We cover both in this chapter.

Setting Up a Telnet Server

Having been superseded by SSH, you will find the Telnet server installation packages under Legacy Network Server in the Add or Remove Packages dialog box. You need to select it from the Details selection because it is not one of the default selections for the package group. Once installed, select System Settings, Server Settings, Services and enable Telnet for runlevel 5. Note your IP address while you are here (switch to root and run `ifconfig`).

With that done, you can now fire up your other Linux box and type **telnet <your IP>**. You are prompted to enter your username and password. The whole conversation should look like this:

```
[paul@susannah ~]$ telnet 10.0.0.1
Trying 10.0.0.1…
Connected to 10.0.0.1 (10.0.0.1)
Escape character is '^]'.

Welcome to Caitlin
Running Fedora Core

* All access is logged *

login: paul
Password:
Last login: Sat Jul 9 12:05:41 from 10.0.0.5
[paul@caitlin ~]$
```

> **TIP**
>
> Note that the server responds with `Welcome to Caitlin, running Fedora Core`, which is a customized message. Your machine will probably respond with `Fedora Core 4` and your kernel version. This is insecure: giving away version numbers is never a smart move. In fact, even saying `Fedora` is questionable. Edit the `issue` and `issue.net` files in your `/etc` directory to change these messages.

Running the w command now shows you as connecting from the external IP address.

Telnet Versus SSH

Although Telnet is worth keeping around as a fail-safe, last resort option, SSH is superior in virtually every way. Telnet is fast but also insecure. It sends all your text, including your password, in plain text that can be read by anyone with the right tools. SSH, on the other hand, encrypts all your communication and so is more resource intensive but secure—even a government security agency sniffing your packets for some reason would still have a hard time cracking the encryption.

Andy Green, posting to the `fedora-list` mailing list, summed up the Telnet situation perfectly when he said, "As Telnet is universally acknowledged to encourage evil, the service telnetd is not enabled by default." It is worthwhile taking the hint: Use Telnet as a last resort only.

Setting Up an SSH Server

The OpenSSH server is set up to be automatically installed and run in Fedora, which means it should already be working on your system. However, if you have disabled it, you can reenable it by selecting System Settings, Server Settings, Services and selecting the sshd box. As you might have gathered, sshd is the name for the SSH server daemon.

Two different versions of SSH exist, called SSH1 and SSH2. The latter is newer, is more secure, comes with more features, and is the default in Fedora Core Linux. However, support for SSH1 clients is also left enabled by default so older clients can connect. Because it is less secure, you should disable SSH1 if you have no one who specifically relies on it.

To do this, edit the `/etc/ssh/sshd_config` file and look for this line:

```
#Protocol 2,1
```

Edit this line so that it becomes

```
Protocol 2
```

This removes the comment sign (#) and tells sshd that you want it to only allow SSH2 connections. Save the file and exit your editor. The next step is to tell sshd to reread its configuration file, by executing this command:

```
kill -HUP `cat /var/run/sshd.pid`
```

If this returns `cat: /var/run/sshd.pid: No such file or directory`, it means you didn't have sshd running. Next time you start it, it reads the configuration file and uses SSH2 only.

You can test this change by trying to connect to your SSH server in SSH1 mode. From the same machine, type this:

```
ssh -1 localhost
```

The `-1` switch forces SSH1 mode. If you successfully forced the SSH2 protocol, you should get the message `Protocol major versions differ: 1 vs. 2`.

The SSH Tools

To the surprise of many, OpenSSH actually comprises a suite of tools. We have already seen ssh, the secure shell command that connects to other machines, and sshd, the SSH server daemon that accepts incoming SSH connections. However, there is also `sftp`, a replacement for `ftp`, and `scp`, a replacement for `rcp`.

You should already be familiar with the `ftp` command because it is the lowest-common-denominator system for handling FTP file transfers. Like Telnet, though, `ftp` is insecure: It sends your data in plain text across the network and anyone can sniff your packets to pick out a username and password. The SSH replacement, `sftp`, puts FTP traffic over an SSH link, thus securing it.

The `rcp` command might be new to you, largely because it is not used much anymore. Back in its day, `rcp` was the primary way of copying a single file to another server. As with `ftp`, `scp` replaces `rcp` by simply channeling the data over a secure SSH connection. The difference between `sftp` and `scp` is that the former allows you to copy many files, whereas the latter just sends one.

Using scp to Copy Individual Files Between Machines

The most basic use of the scp command is to copy a file from your current machine to a remote machine. You can do that with the following command:

```
scp test.txt 10.0.0.1:
```

The first parameter is the name of the file you want to send, and the second is the server to which you want to send it. Note that there is a colon at the end of the IP address. This is where you can specify an exact location for the file to be copied. If you have nothing after the colon, as in the previous example, scp copies the file to your home directory. As with SSH, scp prompts you for your password before copying takes place.

You can rewrite the previous command so you copy test.txt from the local machine and save it as newtest.txt on the server:

```
scp test.txt 10.0.0.1:newtest.txt
```

Alternatively, if there is a directory where you want the file to be saved, you can specify it like this:

```
scp test.txt 10.0.0.1:subdir/stuff/newtest.txt
```

The three commands so far have all assumed that your username on your local machine is the same as your username on the remote machine. If this is not the case, you need to specify your username before the remote address, like this:

```
scp test.txt japh@10.0.0.1:newtest.txt
```

You can use scp to copy remote files locally, simply by specifying the remote file as the source and the current directory (.) as the destination:

```
scp 10.0.0.1:remote.txt .
```

The scp command is nominally also capable of copying files from one remote machine to another remote machine, but this functionality has yet to be properly implemented in Fedora Core Linux. If a patch is released—and we hope one is eventually—the correct command to use would be this:

```
scp 10.0.0.1:test.txt 10.0.0.2:remotetest.txt
```

That copies test.txt from 10.0.0.1 to remotetest.txt on 10.0.0.2. If this works, you are asked for passwords for both servers.

Using sftp to Copy Many Files Between Machines

sftp is a mix between ftp and scp. Connecting to the server uses the same syntax as scp—you can just specify an IP address to connect using your current username, or you can specify a username using *username@ipaddress*. You can optionally add a colon and a directory, as with scp. After you are connected, the commands are the same as ftp: cd, put, mput, get, quit, and so on.

In one of the scp examples, we copied a remote file locally. You can do the same thing with sftp with the following conversation:

```
[paul@susannah ~]$ sftp 10.0.0.1
Connecting to 10.0.0.1...
paul@10.0.0.1's password:
sftp> get remote.txt
Fetching /home/paul/remote.txt to remote.txt
/home/paul/remote.txt        100%  23    0.0KB/s    00:00
sftp> quit
paul@susannah ~]$
```

Although FTP remains prominent because of the number of systems that do not have support for SSH (Windows, specifically), SFTP is gaining in popularity. Apart from the fact that it secures all communications between client and server, SFTP is popular because the initial connection between the client and server is made over port 22 through the sshd daemon. Someone using SFTP connects to the standard sshd daemon, verifies himself, and then is handed over to the SFTP server. The advantage to this is that it reduces the attack vectors because the SFTP server cannot be contacted directly and so cannot be attacked as long as the sshd daemon is secure.

Using ssh-keygen to Enable Key-based Logins

There is a weak link in the SSH system, and, inevitably, it lies with users. No matter what lengths system administrators go to in training users to be careful with their passwords, monitors around the world have Post-it notes attached to them with "passw0rd". Sure, it has a mix of letters and numbers, but it can be cracked in less than a second by any brute-force method. *Brute-forcing* is the method of trying every password possibility, starting with likely words (such as *password* and variants, or *god*) and then just trying random letters (for example, *a*, *aa*, *ab*, *ac*, and so on).

Even very strong passwords are no more than about 16 characters; such passwords take a long time to brute-force but can still be cracked. The solution is to use key-based logins, which generate a unique, 1024-bit private and public key pair for your machine. These keys take even the fastest computers a lifetime to crack, and you can back them up with a password to stop others from using them.

Creating an SSH key is done through the ssh-keygen command, like this:

```
ssh-keygen -t dsa
```

Press Enter when it prompts you where to save your key, and enter a passphrase when it asks you to. This passphrase is just a password used to protect the key—you can leave it blank if you want to, but doing so would allow other people to use your account to connect to remote machines if they manage to log in as you.

After the key is generated (it might take up to 30 seconds depending on the speed of your machine), change the directory to .ssh (cd ~/.ssh), which is a hidden directory where your key is stored and also where it keeps a list of safe SSH hosts. There you will see the files id_dsa and id_dsa.pub. The first is your private key and should never be given out. The second is your public key, which is safe for distribution. You need to copy the public key to each server you want to connect to via key-based SSH.

Using scp, you can copy the public key over to your server, like this:

```
scp id_dsa.pub 10.0.0.1:
```

This places id_dsa.pub in your home directory on 10.0.0.1. The next step is to SSH into 10.0.0.1 normally and set up that key as an authorized key. So, you can SSH in as yourself and then type

```
touch .ssh/authorized_keys
cat id_dsa.pub >> .ssh/authorized_keys
chmod 400 .ssh/authorized_keys
```

The touch command creates the authorized_keys file (if it does not exist already); then you use cat to append the contents of id_dsa.pub to the list of already authorized keys. Finally, chmod is used to make authorized_keys read only.

With that done, you can type exit to disconnect from the remote machine and return to your local machine. Then you can try running ssh again. If you are prompted for your passphrase, you have successfully configured key-based authentication.

That is the current machine secured, but what about every other machine? It is still possible to log in from another machine using only a password, which means your remote machine is still vulnerable.

The solution to this is to switch to root and edit the /etc/ssh/sshd_config file. Look for the PasswordAuthentication line and make sure it reads no (and that it is not commented out with a #). Save the file, and run kill -HUP `cat /var/run/sshd.pid` to have sshd reread its configuration files. With that done, sshd accepts only connections from clients with authorized keys, which stops crackers from brute-forcing their way in.

TIP

For extra security, consider setting PermitRootLogin to no in /etc/ssh/sshd_config. When this is set, it becomes impossible to SSH into your machine using the root account—you must connect with a normal user account and then use su or sudo to switch to root. This is advantageous because most brute-force attempts take place on the root account because it is the only account that is guaranteed to exist on a server.

Also, even if a cracker knows your user account, she has to guess both your user password and your root password to take control of your system.

Remote X

Everything we have looked at so far has been about command-line remoting, with no mention so far of how to bring up a graphical user interface. There are two ways of doing this in Linux: the X Display Manager Control Protocol (XDMCP) and Virtual Network Computing (VNC). The former is specific to X Windows and is very tightly integrated with the rest of the graphical system but is also very insecure. VNC is more modern and very widespread but insecure in some implementations. Both are being used with Fedora, so we will cover both here.

XDMCP

Unless you have Fedora configured to log in a specific user automatically, you will be familiar with the user login screen that appears at bootup. What you are seeing is the Gnome Display Manager (GDM), which runs your X sessions, checks passwords, and so forth. What you are doing is logging in to the local machine because that is the default configuration.

However, GDM is also equipped to allow other network users to connect to your machine through the XDMCP protocol. There are various reasons for using XDMCP, of which the most popular is that many modern machines are large and noisy. They have big hard drives, CPUs with huge fans, and powerful graphics cards, and so do not fit into a peaceful living room. On the flip side, a thin client (a machine with very little CPU power and no hard disk of its own) is silent but not powerful enough to run Gnome or OpenOffice.org.

The solution is to have your powerful machine locked away in a cupboard somewhere with a Wi-Fi connection attached and your quiet thin client sitting in the lounge also on the Wi-Fi link. The thin client connects to the powerful machine and runs all its programs from there, with all the graphics being relayed over the network.

With Fedora, this is incredibly easy to do. On the server side (the powerful machine), you need to check one box, and on the client side (the less-powerful machine), you need to check another box. We will start with the server side first. Select System Settings, Login Screen; then select the XDMCP tab and click Enable XDMCP. On the client side, select System Settings, Login Screen; then select the Security tab and click the Allow Running XDMCP Chooser from the Login Screen. You should also make sure the Show Actions Menu box is checked.

Now, from the client side, log out from your desktop so you return to the Fedora login screen. When it prompts you for your username, press F10. A menu appears with an option labeled XDMCP Chooser. Select that and a new dialog box appears with a list of local XDMCP servers that are willing to accept your connection—you should see your server in there. Select it and click Connect; you will see a login screen from that server, inviting you to log in. You will, of course, need a valid account on the server to be able to log in; however, that is the only thing you need.

As you can see, because XDMCP is so core to the X Windows system, it is easy to set up. However, as you will find as you use it, XDMCP is very slow—even on a Gigabit Ethernet network, it will chew up a substantial percentage of bandwidth. It is also insecure. Anyone can monitor what you are doing with very little work. Because of these two flaws, XDMCP should never be used outside a trusted network.

VNC

The next step up from XDMCP is VNC, which was developed at AT&T's Cambridge Research Laboratory in England. VNC is widespread in the Linux world and, to a lesser extent, in the Windows world. Its main advantage is its widespread nature: Nearly all Linux distros bundle VNC, and clients are available for a wide selection of platforms.

By default, Fedora installs the VNC server component but not the client component. Go to the Add or Remove Packages dialog box and select System Tools. Then select vnc to install the client, go to Network Servers, and select vnc-server to install the server.

With that done, all that remains is to tell Fedora who should be allowed to connect to your session. This is done from the Remote Desktop option on the Preferences menu. By default, your desktop is not shared, so check Allow Other Users to View Your Desktop to share it. You should also check Allow Other Users to Control Your Desktop; otherwise, people will be able to see what you are doing but not interact with the desktop—which is not very helpful.

The second set of options on that screen is important. If you are using this as a remote way to connect to your own desktop, deselect Ask You for Confirmation. If this is not done, when you try to connect from your remote location, Fedora will pop up a message box on the local machine asking Should this person be allowed to connect? Because you are not there to click Yes, the connection will fail. If you want to let someone else remotely connect to your system, keep this box enabled so you know when people are connecting. You should always enter a password, no matter who it is that will connect. VNC, like XDMCP, should not be considered secure over the Internet, or even on untrusted networks.

Reference

- http://www.openssh.com—The home page of the OpenSSH implementation of SSH that Fedora Core Linux uses. It is run by the same team as OpenBSD, a secure BSD-based operating system.

- http://www.realvnc.com—The home page of the team that made VNC at AT&T's Cambridge Research Laboratory. It has since started RealVNC Ltd., a company dedicated to developing and supporting VNC.

- http://www.tightvnc.com—Here you can find an alternative to VNC called TightVNC that has several key advances over the stock VNC release. The most important feature is that TightVNC can use SSH for encryption, guaranteeing security.

- http://www.nomachine.com/—Another alternative to VNC is in the pipeline, called NX. The free implementation, FreeNX, is under heavy development at the time of writing but promises to work much faster than VNC.

One book on SSH that stands out from the crowd is known as "The Snail Book" because of the picture on the cover. It covers all the SSH suite and is called *SSH: The Secure Shell* (O'Reilly), ISBN: 0-596-00011-1.

25

CHAPTER **26**

Managing DNS

Computers on a network need to be found to be useful, which means we need to be able to identify each computer so we can connect to them and communicate with them. Most of today's networks use the Internet Protocol (IP), so each computer on these networks has a unique IP address to identify it.

An IP address is a very large 32-bit number, but we have a shortcut method of displaying that number called the "dotted quad" address. The dotted quad form of the address is made of four 8-bit numbers separated by dots. For example, a computer with the address 3232250992 has the dotted quad form 192.168.60.112. It's easier to use and remember the dotted quad form of an IP address, but even then remembering a lot of numbers becomes quite difficult. The domain name system (DNS) enables you to allocate hostnames that are much easier to remember to these IP addresses. These names, such as fedora.redhat.com, are translated by DNS into the dotted quad IP address, saving time—and memory! This translation process is called name resolution and is performed by software known as a resolver. For the average user, local configuration involves the DNS client, which queries a remote DNS server to exchange information. The DNS servers are typically maintained by Internet service providers (ISPs) and large corporate networks, although anyone can configure and run their own DNS server. All computers on networks need to have a properly configured DNS client.

This chapter introduces DNS concepts and practice using Berkeley Internet Name Domain (BIND), the de facto standard DNS software for Unix. In this chapter, you learn some of the concepts that are basic to DNS and its functions, including how DNS structure information is stored, how DNS serves name information to users, and how name resolution actually works. You learn how to use BIND to configure nameservers and how to provide DNS for a domain. This chapter also teaches you some important techniques for keeping DNS functions secure, as well as some of the most important troubleshooting techniques for tracking down potential problems related to your DNS functions.

If you are not going to be a DNS administrator, much of the information in this chapter will be of no practical use to you. That said, the knowledge of DNS that you can gain in this chapter might help you understand DNS problems that occur—so you will realize that it is not your computer that is broken!

You will also see how, after you register a domain name, you can obtain third-party DNS service so that you do not have to maintain a DNS server. Also, the commonly used DNS-related tools are explained with a focus on how they can be used to troubleshoot domain name resolution problems that you're likely to encounter.

DNS is essential for many types of network operations, and especially so when providing connectivity to the outside world via the Internet. DNS was designed to make the assignment and translation of hostnames fast and reliable and to provide a consistent, portable namespace for network resources. Its database is maintained in a distributed fashion to accommodate its size and the need for frequent updates. Performance and bandwidth utilization is improved by the extensive use of local caches. Authority over portions of the database is delegated to people who are able and willing to maintain the database in a timely manner, so updates are no longer constrained by the schedules of a central authority.

DNS is a simple—but easily misconfigured—system. Hostname resolution errors might manifest themselves in ways that are far from obvious, long after the changes that caused the errors were made. Such naming errors can lead to unacceptable and embarrassing service disruptions.

An understanding of the concepts and processes involved in working with BIND will help to make sure that your experiences as a DNS manager are pleasant ones.

Configuring DNS for Clients

Later in the chapter, we will focus on setup and configuration in order to provide DNS. In this section, we will briefly examine the setup and configuration required for a computer to use DNS services. The important user setup and configuration processes for DNS will likely have been accomplished during the initial installation of Fedora Core. After the initial installation, further DNS configuration can be accomplished by one or more of these methods:

Using Dynamic Host Control Protocol (DHCP)—in which case, some system settings are updated by the `dhclient` command without intervention by a local or remote administrator or user

Using the `system-config-network` GUI configuration tool

Manually editing the system's `/etc/host.conf` configuration file to specify the methods and order of name resolution

Manually editing the system's /etc/nsswitch.conf configuration file to specify the methods and order of name resolution

Manually editing the system's /etc/hosts file which lists specific hostnames and IP addresses

Manually editing the system's /etc/resolv.conf configuration file to add nameserver, domain, or search definition entries

Successful DNS lookups depend on the system's networking being enabled and correctly configured. You can learn more about how to accomplish that in Chapter 17, "Network Connectivity."

When an application needs to resolve a hostname, it calls system library functions to do the name resolution. If the GNU C library installed is version 2 or greater, then the /etc/nsswitch.conf configuration file is used. Older versions of the library use /etc/host.conf. Fedora uses the newer GNU C library, but /etc/host.conf is still provided for applications that have been statically linked with other libraries. The two files should be kept in sync.

Understanding the /etc/host.conf **File**

The file /etc/host.conf, known as the resolver configuration file, specifies which services to use for name resolution and what order they are to be used. This file has been superceded by /etc/nsswitch.conf, but is still provided for applications that use other libraries.

By default with Fedora, this file contains

```
order hosts,bind
```

The order shown here is to first consult /etc/hosts for a hostname. If the hostname is found in /etc/hosts, use the IP address specified there. If it is not found in /etc/hosts, then try and resolve the name using DNS (BIND).

One other option is available, although not set by default. This is nis, which is Sun's Network Information Service.

Understanding the /etc/nsswitch.conf **File**

The file /etc/nsswitch.conf is the System Databases and Name Service Switch configuration file. It contains methods for many types of lookups, but here we are concerned with DNS resolution, so the line we are interested in is the hosts line. This line defines the methods to be used for resolving hostnames and the order in which to apply them. The methods used are

db—Local database files (*.db)

files—Use the local file /etc/hosts

dns—Use BIND

nis—Use Sun's NIS (Network Information Service)

nisplus—Use Sun's NIS+

The default line with Fedora Core is

```
hosts: files dns
```

With this default, the same methods and order are specified as in the default
`/etc/host.conf`. First, `/etc/hosts` is searched, and then DNS is used.

Another example would be

```
hosts: files dns nisplus nis
```

In this example, name searches that fail in `/etc/hosts` and with DNS will continue to the
NIS services (`nisplus` and `nis`). NIS included with Fedora Core is the `ypserv` daemon.

When you are testing your configuration, you may want to halt name searching at a
specific point. You can use the entry `[NOTFOUND=return]`. For example, to stop searching
after looking in /etc/hosts, you would use the line

```
hosts: files [NOTFOUND=return] dns nisplus nis
```

Understanding the `/etc/hosts` **File**

The file `/etc/hosts` contains a table of local hosts (hostnames and IP addresses) used for
local DNS-type lookups. The file is used if the keyword hosts is included in the order line
of `/etc/host.conf`.

Using `/etc/hosts` to provide hostnames and hostname aliases can be effective when used
on small networks. For example, a short `/etc/hosts` might look like this:

```
...
192.168.1.3    wind.maximumhoyt.com      wind webserver #always breaks
192.168.1.4    marvin.maximumhoyt.com     marvin mailserver
192.168.1.5    titan.maximumhoyt.com      titan cvshost
192.168.1.6    hp.maximumhoyt.com      hp
...
```

This example shows a short list of hosts. The format of the file is an IP address, a
`hostname/domain name`, and aliases (such as `marvin` and `mailserver`). Using this
approach, a system administrator would maintain and update a master hosts list, and
then replicate the complete `/etc/hosts` file to every computer on the LAN. Users are then
able to access other systems by simply using the hostname alias (such as `marvin`). The
format of `/etc/hosts` is easy to understand and easy to maintain, and can be used in
conjunction with DNS, and in conjunction with a Dynamic Host Configuration Protocol
(DHCP) server on the same network.

Two disadvantages of using `/etc/hosts` become readily apparent on a large network:
maintenance and replication. Maintaining huge lists of IP addresses, hostnames, and
aliases—along with ensuring that changes are regularly updated to every host on the
network—can be a challenge.

The /etc/hosts file can be edited with a text editor, or by using the system-config-network GUI configuration tool which can be launched from the Network menu item in the System Settings menu. The Hosts tab allows editing the file.

Understanding the /etc/resolv.conf File

The file /etc/resolv.conf specifies how DNS searches are made. The file contains a list of nameservers (DNS servers to connect to) and some options.

For example, a simple, but usable /etc/resolv.conf generally contains at least two nameserver entries, specifying a primary and secondary nameserver. This example uses fictitious internal IP addresses:

```
nameserver 192.168.1.1
nameserver 192.168.1.2
search mydomain.com
```

The IP addresses listed in the /etc/resolv.conf file are usually assigned by an ISP and represent the remote nameservers. Other optional keywords, such as domain and search, are used to specify a local domain and search list for queries; the two terms are mutually exclusive, however (and we will explain these terms shortly). If you have both, the last one listed will be used.

The information in /etc/resolv.conf can be configured from the system-config-network tool by launching the tool from the Network menu item in the System settings menu. The DNS tab allows you to enter or edit the DNS information, as shown in Figure 26.1.

FIGURE 26.1   The GUI Network Configuration tool is one of Fedora Core's best-designed GUI tools, permitting extensive network configuration.

Understanding the Changes Made by DHCP

If your system is set to use DHCP, when the DHCP connection is made any existing /etc/resolv.conf is saved as resolv.conf.predhclient and a new /etc/resolv.conf is created with the DNS information supplied by DHCP. When DHCP is released, the saved file is moved back as /etc/resolv.conf.

Essential DNS Concepts

We begin with a look at the ideas behind DNS, prior to discussing the details of the software used to implement it. An understanding at this level is invaluable in avoiding the majority of problems administrators commonly experience with DNS, as well as in diagnosing and quickly solving the ones that do occur. The following overview omits several small details in the protocol because they are not relevant to the everyday tasks of a DNS administrator. If you need more information about DNS, consult the DNS standards, especially RFC 1034. (The RFCs related to DNS are distributed with BIND. Fedora Core installs them in /usr/share/doc/bind-*/rfc/.)

The domain namespace is structured as a tree. Each domain is a node in the tree and has a name. For every node, there are *resource records (RRs)*—each of which stores a single fact about the domain. (Who owns it? What is its IP address?) Domains can have any number of children, or subdomains. The root of the tree is a domain named . (similar to the / root directory in a file system.)

Each of the resource records belonging to a domain store a different type of information. For example,

- **A (Address)**—Records store the IP address associated with a name.

- **NS (Nameserver)**—Records name an authoritative nameserver for a domain.

- **SOA (Start of Authority)**—Records contain basic properties of the domain and the domain's zone.

- **PTR (Pointer)**—Records contain the real name of the host to which the IP belongs.

- **MX (Mail Exchanger)**—Records specify a mail server for the zone.

Each record type is discussed in detail later in this chapter.

Every node has a unique name that specifies its position in the tree, just as every file has a unique path that leads from the root directory to that file. That is, in the domain name, one starts with the root domain "." and prepends to it each name in the path, using a dot to separate the names. The root domain has children named com., org., net., de., and so on. They, in turn, have children named ibm.com., wiw.org., and gmx.de..

In general, a fully qualified domain name (FQDN) is one that contains the machine name, and the domain name, such as

foo.example.com.

is similar to the following path:

```
/com/example/foo
```

Contrary to the example, the trailing dot in an FQDN is often omitted. This reverse order is the source of confusion to many people who first examine DNS.

How Nameservers Store DNS Structure Information

Information about the structure of the tree, and its associated resource records, is stored by programs called nameservers. Every domain has an authoritative nameserver that holds a complete local copy of the data for the domain; the domain's administrators are responsible for maintaining the data. A nameserver can also cache information about parts of the tree for which the server has no authority. For administrative convenience, nameservers can delegate authority over certain subdomains to other, independently maintained, nameservers.

The authoritative nameserver for a zone knows about the nameservers to which authority over subdomains has been delegated. The authoritative nameserver might refer queries about the delegated zones to those nameservers. So, we can always find authoritative data for a domain by following the chain of delegations of authority from . (the root domain) until we reach an authoritative nameserver for the domain. This is what gives DNS its distributed tree structure.

How DNS Provides Name Service Information to Users

Users of DNS need not be aware of these details. To them, the namespace is just a single tree—any part of which they can request information about. The task of finding the requested RRs from the resource set for a domain is left to programs called *resolvers*. Resolvers are aware of the distributed structure of the database. They know how to contact the root nameservers (which are authoritative for the root domain) and how to follow the chain of delegations until they find an authoritative nameserver that can give them the information they are looking for.

At the risk of stretching the analogy too far, you can think of domains as directories in a file system and resource records as files in these directories. The delegation of authority over subdomains is similar to having an NFS file system mounted under a subdirectory: Requests for files under that directory would go to the NFS server, rather than this file system. The resolver's job is to start from the root directory and walk down the directory tree (following mount points) until it reaches the directory that contains the files they are interested in. For efficiency, they can then cache the information they find for some time. This is why things appear to be listed in "reverse" order. This process is examined in detail next.

In practice, there are several authoritative nameservers for a domain. One of them is the master (or primary) nameserver, where the domain's data is held. The others are known as slave (or secondary) nameservers, and they hold automatically updated copies of the master data. Both the master and the slaves serve the same information, so it doesn't matter which one a resolver asks. The distinction between master and slave is made purely for reasons of reliability—to ensure that the failure of a single nameserver does not result in the loss of authoritative data for the domain. As a bonus, this redundancy also distributes the network load between several hosts so that no one nameserver is over-whelmed with requests for authoritative information.

> **NOTE**
>
> As a DNS administrator, it is your responsibility to ensure that your nameservers provide suffi-cient redundancy for your zones. Your slaves should be far away from the master so that power failures, network outages, and other catastrophes do not affect your name service.

Despite these precautions, the load on DNS servers would be crushing without the exten-sive use of local caches. As mentioned before, nameservers are allowed to cache the results of queries and intermediate referrals for some time so that they can serve repeated requests for data without referring to the source each time. If they did not do this, root nameservers (and the nameservers for other popular zones) would be contacted by clients all over the world for every name lookup, wasting a huge amount of resources.

Name Resolution in Practice

When a web browser issues a request for an IP address, the request is sent to a local name-server, which resolves the name, stores the result in its cache, and returns the IP address. To better understand this process, take a moment to see what happens behind the scenes when a web browser issues a request for the IP address of www.ibm.com. This example mimics the actions of the resolver by using the incredibly useful dig utility to follow the chain of delegations between zones until you find the A record you are looking for. Because most nameservers would follow the delegations for you, this example uses the +norec dig parameter to turn off recursion. That is, if the nameserver does not know how to answer your query, it will not issue further queries on its own.

> **NOTE**
>
> There are 13 root nameservers around the world. Several are located in the United States—Virginia, California, and Maryland. Others are located in London, Stockholm, and Tokyo. These root servers do not hold "master lists" of IP addresses and domain names, but simply hand off requests to other nameservers.
>
> After a recent DOS (Denial of Service) attack on the root servers, at least one of them now runs an alternative application to BIND.

Begin by randomly selecting one of the 13 root nameservers (ranging from a.root-servers.net to m.root-servers.net; we picked e), and ask what it knows about an A record for www.ibm.com:

```
$ dig @e.root-servers.net www.ibm.com A +norec
```

```
; <<>> DiG 9.1.3 <<>> @e.root-servers.net www.ibm.com A +norec
;; global options:  printcmd
;; Got answer:
;; ->>HEADER<<- opcode: QUERY, status: NOERROR, id: 52356
;; flags: qr; QUERY: 1, ANSWER: 0, AUTHORITY: 13, ADDITIONAL: 13

;; QUESTION SECTION:
;www.ibm.com.                    IN      A

;; AUTHORITY SECTION:
com.                    172800  IN      NS      A.GTLD-SERVERS.NET.
com.                    172800  IN      NS      G.GTLD-SERVERS.NET.
com.                    172800  IN      NS      H.GTLD-SERVERS.NET.
com.                    172800  IN      NS      C.GTLD-SERVERS.NET.
com.                    172800  IN      NS      I.GTLD-SERVERS.NET.
com.                    172800  IN      NS      B.GTLD-SERVERS.NET.
com.                    172800  IN      NS      D.GTLD-SERVERS.NET.
com.                    172800  IN      NS      L.GTLD-SERVERS.NET.
com.                    172800  IN      NS      F.GTLD-SERVERS.NET.
com.                    172800  IN      NS      J.GTLD-SERVERS.NET.
com.                    172800  IN      NS      K.GTLD-SERVERS.NET.
com.                    172800  IN      NS      E.GTLD-SERVERS.NET.
com.                    172800  IN      NS      M.GTLD-SERVERS.NET.

;; ADDITIONAL SECTION:
A.GTLD-SERVERS.NET.     172800  IN      A       192.5.6.30
G.GTLD-SERVERS.NET.     172800  IN      A       192.42.93.30
H.GTLD-SERVERS.NET.     172800  IN      A       192.54.112.30
C.GTLD-SERVERS.NET.     172800  IN      A       192.26.92.30
I.GTLD-SERVERS.NET.     172800  IN      A       192.36.144.133
B.GTLD-SERVERS.NET.     172800  IN      A       192.33.14.30
D.GTLD-SERVERS.NET.     172800  IN      A       192.31.80.30
L.GTLD-SERVERS.NET.     172800  IN      A       192.41.162.30
F.GTLD-SERVERS.NET.     172800  IN      A       192.35.51.30
J.GTLD-SERVERS.NET.     172800  IN      A       210.132.100.101
K.GTLD-SERVERS.NET.     172800  IN      A       213.177.194.5
E.GTLD-SERVERS.NET.     172800  IN      A       192.12.94.30
M.GTLD-SERVERS.NET.     172800  IN      A       202.153.114.101

;; Query time: 819 msec
;; SERVER: 192.203.230.10#53(e.root-servers.net)
;; WHEN: Wed Sep 26 10:05:08 2001
;; MSG SIZE  rcvd: 461
```

26

The QUERY: 1, ANSWER: 0 in the response means that e.root-servers.net didn't know the answer to your question. It does know the authoritative nameservers for the com TLD, and it refers your query to them in the AUTHORITY section. Not too long ago, all the root-servers.net nameservers were themselves authoritative for the com TLD, but additional delegations were recently introduced.

The resolver's next step would be to select one of these listed servers at random, to use the IP addresses mentioned in the ADDITIONAL section of the response to connect to the server, and to repeat the question. This is what we do now, having chosen i.gtld-servers.net:

```
$ dig @i.gtld-servers.net www.ibm.com A +norec
; <<>> DiG 9.1.3 <<>> @i.gtld-servers.net www.ibm.com A +norec
;; global options:  printcmd
;; Got answer:
;; ->>HEADER<<- opcode: QUERY, status: NOERROR, id: 61562
;; flags: qr; QUERY: 1, ANSWER: 0, AUTHORITY: 5, ADDITIONAL: 5

;; QUESTION SECTION:
;www.ibm.com.                 IN      A

;; AUTHORITY SECTION:
ibm.com.               172800  IN      NS      INTERNET-SERVER.ZURICH.ibm.com.
  ibm.com.                     172800  IN      NS      NS.WATSON.ibm.com.
  ibm.com.                     172800  IN      NS      NS.ERS.ibm.com.
  ibm.com.                     172800  IN      NS      NS.ALMADEN.ibm.com.
  ibm.com.                     172800  IN      NS      NS.AUSTIN.ibm.com.

;; ADDITIONAL SECTION:
INTERNET-SERVER.ZURICH.ibm.com. 172800 IN A      195.212.119.252
NS.WATSON.ibm.com.             172800  IN      A      198.81.209.2
NS.ERS.ibm.com.                172800  IN      A      204.146.173.35
NS.ALMADEN.ibm.com.            172800  IN      A      198.4.83.35
NS.AUSTIN.ibm.com.             172800  IN      A      192.35.232.34

;; Query time: 8337 msec
;; SERVER: 192.36.144.133#53(i.gtld-servers.net)
;; WHEN: Wed Sep 26 10:06:46 2001
;; MSG SIZE  rcvd: 240
```

We still have 0 ANSWERs, but we are clearly getting closer. The response lists the names and IP addresses of five authoritative nameservers for the ibm.com domain. Notice the abnormally large query time—this tells us that our choice of i.gtld-servers.net was, for some reason, a poor one. Intelligent resolvers remember this fact, and would pick a different server in future. BIND only does this for the root servers, though.

We choose NS.WATSON.ibm.com, and repeat our question:

```
$ dig @NS.WATSON.ibm.com www.ibm.com A +norec

; <<>> DiG 9.1.3 <<>> @NS.WATSON.ibm.com www.ibm.com A +norec
;; global options:  printcmd
;; Got answer:
;; ->>HEADER<<- opcode: QUERY, status: NOERROR, id: 32287
;; flags: qr aa ra; QUERY: 1, ANSWER: 4, AUTHORITY: 5, ADDITIONAL: 5

;; QUESTION SECTION:
;www.ibm.com.                   IN      A

;; ANSWER SECTION:
www.ibm.com.           1800     IN      A       129.42.18.99
www.ibm.com.           1800     IN      A       129.42.19.99
www.ibm.com.           1800     IN      A       129.42.16.99
www.ibm.com.           1800     IN      A       129.42.17.99

;; AUTHORITY SECTION:
ibm.com.               600      IN      NS      ns.watson.ibm.com.
ibm.com.               600      IN      NS      ns.austin.ibm.com.
ibm.com.               600      IN      NS      ns.almaden.ibm.com.
ibm.com.               600      IN      NS      ns.ers.ibm.com.
ibm.com.               600      IN      NS
Âinternet-server.zurich.ibm.com.

;; ADDITIONAL SECTION:
ns.watson.ibm.com.     600      IN      A       198.81.209.2
ns.austin.ibm.com.     86400    IN      A       192.35.232.34
ns.almaden.ibm.com.    86400    IN      A       198.4.83.35
ns.ers.ibm.com.        259200   IN      A       204.146.173.35
internet-server.zurich.ibm.com. 1800 IN A       195.212.119.252

;; Query time: 441 msec
;; SERVER: 198.81.209.2#53(NS.WATSON.ibm.com)
;; WHEN: Wed Sep 26 10:08:21 2001
;; MSG SIZE  rcvd: 304
```

NS.WATSON.ibm.com knew the answer to our question, and for the first time, the response contains an ANSWER section that lists four A records for www.ibm.com. Most resolvers pick one at random and return it to the program that initiated the name resolution. This concludes our search.

Reverse Resolution

Given an IP address, it is often necessary to find the name associated with it (while writing web server logs, for example). This process is known as reverse resolution or reverse lookup, and is accomplished with the help of an elegant subterfuge. IP addresses (similar to filenames) are "backward" from the DNS point of view. Because we can only associate RRs with DNS names, we must find a way to write an IP address, with its left-to-right hierarchy (129.42.18.99 belongs to 129.*), as a DNS name with a right-to-left hierarchy (ibm.com belongs to com).

We do this by reversing the order of the octets in the address, and then appending .in-addr.arpa (a domain used exclusively to support reverse lookups) to the result. For example, 129.42.18.99 would be written as 99.18.42.129.in-addr.arpa. PTR (Pointer) records associated with this special name would then tell us the real name of the host to which the IP belongs.

We can look for PTR records in the usual fashion—by following a chain of delegations from a root server. We examine this process briefly by resolving 203.200.109.66 (which is one of the dial-up IP addresses that an ISP assigns to its customers). We ask a root name-server 66.109.200.203.in-addr.arpa:

```
- - - - - - - - - -
$ dig @a.root-servers.net 66.109.200.203.in-addr.arpa PTR +norec
; <<>> DiG 9.2.1 <<>> @a.root-servers.net 66.109.200.203.in-addr.arpa PTR +norec
;; global options:  printcmd
;; Got answer:
;; ->>HEADER<<- opcode: QUERY, status: NOERROR, id: 64298
;; flags: qr; QUERY: 1, ANSWER: 0, AUTHORITY: 5, ADDITIONAL: 1

;; QUESTION SECTION:
;66.109.200.203.in-addr.arpa.    IN      PTR

;; AUTHORITY SECTION:
203.in-addr.arpa.       86400   IN      NS      ns1.apnic.net.
203.in-addr.arpa.       86400   IN      NS      ns3.apnic.net.
203.in-addr.arpa.       86400   IN      NS      ns.ripe.net.
203.in-addr.arpa.       86400   IN      NS      rs2.arin.net.
203.in-addr.arpa.       86400   IN      NS      dns1.telstra.net.

;; ADDITIONAL SECTION:
ns.ripe.net.            172800  IN      A       193.0.0.193

;; Query time: 57 msec
;; SERVER: 198.41.0.4#53(a.root-servers.net)
;; WHEN: Wed Sep  4 21:15:24 2002
;; MSG SIZE  rcvd: 178
- - - - - - - - - -
```

Continuing with NS.TELSTRA.NET, we have

```
- - - - - - - - - -
$ dig @NS.TELSTRA.NET 66.109.200.203.in-addr.arpa PTR +norec

; <<>> DiG 9.2.1 <<>> @NS.TELSTRA.NET 66.109.200.203.in-addr.arpa PTR +norec
;; global options:  printcmd
;; Got answer:
;; ->>HEADER<<- opcode: QUERY, status: NOERROR, id: 12099
;; flags: qr ra; QUERY: 1, ANSWER: 0, AUTHORITY: 2, ADDITIONAL: 2

;; QUESTION SECTION:
;66.109.200.203.in-addr.arpa.     IN      PTR

;; AUTHORITY SECTION:
200.203.in-addr.arpa.    142315  IN      NS      dns.vsnl.net.in.
200.203.in-addr.arpa.    142315  IN      NS      ns3.vsnl.com.

;; ADDITIONAL SECTION:
dns.vsnl.net.in.         33557   IN      A       202.54.1.30
ns3.vsnl.com.            5370    IN      A       203.197.12.42

;; Query time: 293 msec
;; SERVER: 203.50.0.137#53(NS.TELSTRA.NET)
;; WHEN: Wed Sep  4 21:18:09 2002
;; MSG SIZE  rcvd: 132

- - - - - - - - - -
```

And then,

```
- - - - - - - - - -

$ dig @ns3.vsnl.com. 66.109.200.203.in-addr.arpa PTR +norec

; <<>> DiG 9.2.1 <<>> @ns3.vsnl.com. 66.109.200.203.in-addr.arpa PTR +norec
;; global options:  printcmd
;; Got answer:
;; ->>HEADER<<- opcode: QUERY, status: NXDOMAIN, id: 37848
;; flags: qr aa ra; QUERY: 1, ANSWER: 0, AUTHORITY: 1, ADDITIONAL: 0

;; QUESTION SECTION:
;66.109.200.203.in-addr.arpa.    IN      PTR
```

26

```
;; AUTHORITY SECTION:
200.203.in-addr.arpa.    86400    IN    SOA    dns.vsnl.net.in.
helpdesk.giasbm01.vsnl.net.in. 200001059 86400 7200 2592000 345600

;; Query time: 259 msec
;; SERVER: 203.197.12.42#53(ns3.vsnl.com.)
;; WHEN: Wed Sep  4 21:19:16 2002
;; MSG SIZE  rcvd: 114
----------
```

What happened here? In previous responses, the status has always been NOERROR, but this one has a status of NXDOMAIN (Nonexistent Domain), and the flags section has the aa (Authoritative Answer) flag. This means that the name we are looking for is known not to exist. In contrast, the response from the root nameservers did not have the aa flag set, and said "We do not know about this name: Ask somebody else." The authoritative answer from ns3.vsnl.com says "I know that this name doesn't exist, and you might as well stop looking."

The administrators at vsnl.net.in clearly have not bothered to set up PTR records for their dial-up IP address pool. If they had, the response would have looked like the ones we have seen before and would have included a PTR record. As it is, the response lists the SOA record for zone including the email address of the domain contact, helpdesk@giasbm01.vsnl.net.in, should we choose to complain about broken reverse resolution.

What Did the Resolver Learn?

Based on the work we have done up to this point, we have a list of names and addresses of the authoritative nameservers for the com TLD. In the future, if we are asked to resolve, say www.samspublishing.com, we can direct our query to gtld-servers.net from the start instead of wasting one query on a root server. However, the NS records have an expiry time (also known as Time To Live, or TTL, which you learn about in "The Zone File," later in this chapter) of 2D, meaning that the information is only guaranteed as accurate for two days. This lag time for updates is why you will see announcements made that it might take a few days for DNS changes to propagate throughout the Internet.

Similarly, we know the authoritative nameservers for ibm.com, which are for use in queries involving ibm.com during the next two days. For instance, a web browser might ask for the IP address of commerce.ibm.com when a user clicks on a link on the IBM web page. We can save two queries by asking NS.WATSON.ibm.com again. Of course, we also have the four A records for www.ibm.com in our cache, and we can return one of them if the browser asks us to resolve the name again.

All this information (including that gleaned from the reverse resolution process) can be cached by your computer until expiry and used to speed up further queries.

You have also learned some things that a resolver cannot remember or use. You can guess from the names, for instance, that the DNS administrators at IBM have, as recommended, delegated their DNS service to servers that are distant both geographically and on the network. You can see that IBM runs four web servers on the same network—perhaps to gracefully handle the load. We know that the DNS administrators at VSNL (a large ISP) are not as conscientious as they could be because they have only two nameservers for their entire domain and don't have correct reverse mappings.

DNS is endlessly fascinating, and a few hours of playing with dig is well rewarded. By doing so, you can learn some interesting things about DNS and you gain familiarity with dig queries and responses that will prove very useful in debugging problems with your own DNS setup.

Using DNS Tools

Fedora includes a number of standard tools that allow you to work with DNS. These tools, found in the bind-utils and whois packages, have everyday uses that do not require DNS administrator skills. If you want to know what domain name belongs to an IP address, or vice versa, these are the tools to use to track down that information. Forward lookups are where you map a name to an IP address; reverse lookups are where you map an address to a name.

Here are the tools you will use:

- dig (Domain Information Groper)
- host
- nslookup
- whois

The following sections briefly describe these tools and provide examples of their use.

dig

A command-line utility, the Domain Information Groper will query DNS nameservers. By default, dig uses the nameservers listed in /etc/resolv.conf and will perform an NS (Nameserver) query. Reverse lookups are accomplished with the -x argument with a default A (Address) query.

Here is an example of a forward lookup with dig:

```
$ dig www.pearson.com

; <<>> DiG 9.2.2 <<>> www.pearson.com
;; global options:  printcmd
;; Got answer:
;; ->>HEADER<<- opcode: QUERY, status: NOERROR, id: 59962
;; flags: qr rd ra; QUERY: 1, ANSWER: 1, AUTHORITY: 3, ADDITIONAL: 2
```

```
;; QUESTION SECTION:
;www.pearson.com.              IN      A

;; ANSWER SECTION:
www.pearson.com.        86400  IN      A       165.193.130.83

;; AUTHORITY SECTION:
pearson.com.            86400  IN      NS      ns1-p.dns.pipex.net.
pearson.com.            86400  IN      NS      ns.pearson.com.
pearson.com.            86400  IN      NS      ns0-p.dns.pipex.net.

;; ADDITIONAL SECTION:
ns0-p.dns.pipex.net.    66542  IN      A       158.43.129.80
ns1-p.dns.pipex.net.    66542  IN      A       158.43.193.80

;; Query time: 294 msec
;; SERVER: 64.83.0.10#53(64.83.0.10)
;; WHEN: Mon Sep  1 16:42:00 2003
;; MSG SIZE  rcvd: 151
```

A reverse lookup with dig:

```
$ dig -x 165.193.130.83

; <<>> DiG 9.2.2 <<>> -x 165.193.130.83
;; global options:  printcmd
;; Got answer:
;; ->>HEADER<<- opcode: QUERY, status: NOERROR, id: 63402
;; flags: qr rd ra; QUERY: 1, ANSWER: 1, AUTHORITY: 2, ADDITIONAL: 0

;; QUESTION SECTION:
;83.130.193.165.in-addr.arpa.   IN      PTR

;; ANSWER SECTION:
83.130.193.165.in-addr.arpa. 43200 IN   PTR
prs-sun-106-nyeh-peshr-hme0-4.digisle.net.

;; AUTHORITY SECTION:
130.193.165.in-addr.arpa. 43200 IN      NS      ns.digisle.net.
130.193.165.in-addr.arpa. 43200 IN      NS      ns1.digisle.net.

;; Query time: 41 msec
;; SERVER: 64.83.0.10#53(64.83.0.10)
;; WHEN: Mon Sep  1 16:42:21 2003
;; MSG SIZE  rcvd: 135
```

host

A command-line utility, host performs forward and reverse lookups by querying DNS nameservers, much as does dig.

Here's an example of a forward lookup with host:

```
$ host www.pearson.com
www.pearson.com has address 165.193.130.83
```

Here's a reverse lookup with host:

```
$ host 165.193.130.83
83.130.193.165.in-addr.arpa domain name pointer
prs-sun-106-nyeh-peshr-hme0-4.digisle.net.
```

nslookup

A command-line utility, nslookup can be used in an interactive and non-interactive manner to query DNS nameservers. Note that nslookup is outdated; try using dig instead.

Here's an example of a forward lookup using nslookup:

```
$ nslookup www.pearson.com
Note:  nslookup is deprecated and may be removed from future releases.
Consider using the `dig' or `host' programs instead.  Run nslookup with
the `-sil[ent]' option to prevent this message from appearing.
Server:        64.83.0.10
Address:       64.83.0.10#53

Non-authoritative answer:
Name:   www.pearson.com
Address: 165.193.130.83
```

Here's a reverse lookup using nslookup:

```
$ nslookup 165.193.130.83
Note:  nslookup is deprecated and may be removed from future releases.
Consider using the `dig' or `host' programs instead.  Run nslookup with
the `-sil[ent]' option to prevent this message from appearing.
Server:        64.83.0.10
Address:       64.83.0.10#53

Non-authoritative answer:
83.130.193.165.in-addr.arpa      name = prs-sun-106-nyeh-peshr-hme0-4.digisle.net.

Authoritative answers can be found from:
130.193.165.in-addr.arpa      nameserver = ns.digisle.net.
130.193.165.in-addr.arpa      nameserver = ns1.digisle.net.
```

26

Note that using a reverse lookup does not tell you the Fully Qualified Domain name of the server using that IP address. To determine that, we need to use the whois client.

whois

A command-line utility from the whois package, whois queries the database at whois.networksolutions.com.

For an IP lookup

```
$ whois 165.193.130.83
```

```
OrgName:    Cable & Wireless
OrgID:      CWUS
Address:    3300 Regency Pkwy
City:       Cary
StateProv:  NC
PostalCode: 27511
Country:    US

NetRange:   165.193.0.0 - 165.193.255.255
CIDR:       165.193.0.0/16
NetName:    CWDI-BLK6
NetHandle:  NET-165-193-0-0-1
Parent:     NET-165-0-0-0-0
NetType:    Direct Allocation
NameServer: NS.DIGISLE.NET
NameServer: NS1.DIGISLE.NET
Comment:
RegDate:
Updated:    2002-08-23

TechHandle: ZC221-ARIN
TechName:   Cable & Wireless
TechPhone:  +1-919-465-4023
TechEmail:  ip@gnoc.cw.net

OrgAbuseHandle: SPAMC-ARIN
OrgAbuseName:   SPAM COMPLAINTS
OrgAbusePhone:  +1-800-977-4662
OrgAbuseEmail:  abuse@cw.com

OrgNOCHandle: NOC99-ARIN
OrgNOCName:   Network Operations Center
OrgNOCPhone:  +1-800-977-4662
OrgNOCEmail:  trouble@cw.net
```

```
OrgTechHandle: UIAA-ARIN
OrgTechName:   US IP Address Administration
OrgTechPhone:  +1-800-977-4662
OrgTechEmail:  ipadmin@clp.cw.net

OrgTechHandle: GIAA-ARIN
OrgTechName:   Global IP Address Administration
OrgTechPhone:  +1-919-465-4096
OrgTechEmail:  ip@gnoc.cw.net

# ARIN WHOIS database, last updated 2003-08-31 19:15
# Enter ? for additional hints on searching ARIN's WHOIS database.
```

And for a domain name lookup (which is not what whois is used for)

```
$ whois www.pearson.com

Whois Server Version 1.3

Domain names in the .com and .net domains can now be registered
with many different competing registrars. Go to http://www.internic.net
for detailed information.

No match for "WWW.PEARSON.COM".
```

Configuring a Local Caching Nameserver

A caching nameserver builds a local cache of resolved domain names and provides them to other hosts on your LAN. This speeds up DNS searches and saves bandwidth by reusing lookups for frequently accessed domains and is especially useful on a slow dial-up connection or when your ISPs own nameservers malfunction.

If you have BIND and BIND-utils installed on your computer, you can configure a caching-nameserver by installing the caching-nameserver package. This sets up the configuration file /etc/named.conf, the /var/named directory, and the configuration files in /var/named (localhost.zone, named.ca, and named.local).

To start the caching nameserver, you can start the named service manually (see Chapter 14, "Automating Tasks") or use the system-config-services GUI configuration tool. This can be started by choosing the Services menu option in the Server Settings menu, which is in the System Settings menu, and then selecting named and using the Start button.

To get your local computer to use the caching nameserver, reconfigure the file /etc/resolv.conf to comment out any references to your ISP's nameservers, and set the only nameserver to be the localhost (127.0.0.1). The /etc/resolv.conf for the caching-nameserver host is

```
#/etc/resolv.conf
#nameserver 83.64.1.10
#nameserver 83.64.0.10
nameserver 127.0.0.1
```

Other machines on your network should have the IP of the local caching-nameserver in their /etc/resolv.conf files. Assuming that the IP address for the computer running the caching nameserver is 192.168.1.5, then the /etc/resolv.conf files on the other machines on your network should be

```
#/etc/resolv.conf
#nameserver 83.64.1.10
#nameserver 83.64.0.10
nameserver 192.168.1.5
```

Ad Blocking with a Caching Nameserver

Another advantage of setting up a caching nameserver, is that you can use it to block ads and objectionable sites by using bogus DNS zones to block specific domains. You do this by overriding the DNS lookup of the sites you want to block. Configuration is simple. First, determine the sites that you want to block. For example, you may want to block all access to doubleclick.net. Create an entry in /etc/named.conf like this

```
zone "doublelick.net" { type master; file "fakes"; };
```

Then create a new file /var/named/fakes. This should contain

```
$TTL 1D
@          IN        SOA       wind.maximumhoyt.com. hostmaster.maximumhoyt.com. (
                               2004081701 8H 2H 4W 1D)

@          IN        NS        wind.maximumhoyt.example.com.
@          IN        A         127.0.0.1
*          IN        A         127.0.0.1
```

where wind.maximumhoyt.com should be replaced by the hostname of the caching nameserver. This will point all DNS lookups of doubleclick.net to 127.0.0.1, where they will not be found. To make the change effective, you will need to restart named so that the new configuration information is read. Chapter 14 describes several different ways of restarting the named service, here is one of them:

```
# kill -HUP 'pidof named'
```

Once named has been restarted, attempts to resolve all doubleclick.net addresses will fail, the ads will not be loaded and will not be displayed, and your browsing experience will be faster.

Your Own Domain Name and Third-Party DNS

It is possible to have your own domain name and provide third-party DNS service for it, meaning that you do not have to configure and administer a DNS nameserver for yourself. You can even have a mail address for your domain without having a mail server.

Here is a summary of the major tasks involved in providing a third-party DNS service to your own domain name:

- **Register and pay for a unique domain name**—Several companies now offer to register these names, so shop around for the most reasonable price and perform some Google background checks on the company before using them.

- **Use a third-party DNS provider to provide DNS services**—One popular provider is ZoneEdit (www.maximumhoyt.com uses ZoneEdit as well, although there are a number of other free-of-cost providers) and provides detailed steps to use the service. ZoneEdit also provides mail forwarding services, so mail addressed to you@your.own.domain is forwarded to your regular ISP mail account. ZoneEdit also allows you to use DynamicDNS, which enables you to run a server on a dynamically assigned IP (from a cable or dial-up provider), yet still have DNS servers locate you. ZoneEdit can also provide a startup web page space for you or forward requests to an already established page with a long, complicated address.

- **Return to your domain name registrar and tell it what nameservers will be authoritative for your domain.**

Once you have completed the preceding tasks, it will take about three days for the information to propagate around the Internet.

Providing DNS for a Real Domain with BIND

BIND is the de facto standard DNS software suite for Unix. It contains a nameserver daemon (named) that answers DNS queries, a resolver library that enables programs to make such queries, and some utility programs. BIND is maintained by the ISC (Internet Software Consortium) at the website http://www.isc.org/bind/.

Three major versions of BIND are in common use today: 4, 8, and 9. The use of BIND 4 is now *strongly* discouraged (because of numerous security vulnerabilities and other bugs), and will not be discussed here. BIND 8, with many new features and bug fixes, is now quite widely deployed. It is actively maintained, but still vulnerable to a variety of attacks; its use is *strongly* discouraged as well. Fedora Core now provides BIND 9.

> **NOTE**
>
> If you are upgrading from BIND 8 to BIND 9, make sure to read the file /usr/share/doc/bind-9.2.3/misc/migration for any issues regarding configuration files (which will cause BIND not to run) and use of existing shell scripts. An HTML version of the BIND 9 manual is the file Bv9ARM.html under the /usr/share/doc/bind-9.2.3/arm directory.

In this chapter, we discuss the use of BIND 9, which ships with Fedora. BIND 9 was rewritten from scratch in an attempt to make the code more robust and leave behind the problems inherent in the old code. It is compliant with new DNS standards and represents a substantial improvement in features, performance, and security.

The `bind` RPM package contains the `named` daemon and a wealth of BIND documentation. The `bind-utils` RPM package contains, among other things, the invaluable `dig(1)` utility. If you choose to compile BIND yourself, you can download the source distribution from the ISC's website and follow the build instructions therein.

> **NOTE**
>
> You will also find build instructions in the file README under the `/usr/share/doc/bind-9.2.3` directory.

Once you install the RPMs, the following directories are of special interest because they contain the file used by BIND and contain the information shown in the listing:

```
- - - - - - - - - -

/etc/                        The rndc.conf, named.conf configuration files.
/usr/bin/                    dig, host, nslookup, nsupdate.
/usr/sbin/                   named, rndc, and various support programs.
/usr/share/doc/bind-9.2.3/   BIND documentation.
/usr/share/man/              Manual pages.
/var/named/*                 Zone files.

- - - - - - - - - -
```

If you install from source, the files will be in the locations you specified at configure time, with the default directories under `/usr/local/`.

The following example uses BIND to configure a nameserver, and then expand it as necessary to provide useful DNS service. To accomplish this, you must configure `named` (the nameserver daemon) and `rndc` components (a control utility that permits various interactions with a running instance of `named`). You also might need to configure the resolver software, as discussed later.

Three configuration files are used:

- `rndc.key` to specify the key used to authenticate between `rndc` and `named`

- `rndc.conf` to configure `rndc`

- `named.conf` to configure `named`

When `rndc` communicates with `named`, it uses cryptographic keys to digitally sign commands before sending them over the network to `named`. The configuration file, `/etc/rndc.key`, specifies the key used for the authentication.

The only authentication mechanism currently supported by named is the use of a secret key, encrypted with the HMAC-MD5 algorithm, and shared between rndc and named. The easiest way to generate a key is to use the dnssec-keygen utility. In the following example, you are asking the utility to generate a 128-bit HMAC-MD5 user key named rndc:

```
$ dnssec-keygen -a hmac-md5 -b 128 -n user rndc
Krndc.+157+14529
$ cat Krndc.+157+14529.private
Private-key-format: v1.2
Algorithm: 157 (HMAC_MD5)
Key: mKKd2FiHMFe1JqXl/z4cfw==
```

The utility creates two files with .key and .private extensions, respectively. The Key: line in the .private file tells us the secret that rndc and named need to share (mKKd2FiHMFe1JqXl/z4cfw==). When we have this, we can set up the rndc.key configuration file which is shared by both rndc.conf and named.conf.

```
key "rndc" {  algorithm    hmac-md5;  secret    "mKKd2FiHMFe1JqXl/z4cfw=="; };
----------
```

rndc.conf

rndc uses a TCP connection (on port 953) to communicate with named. The configuration file, /etc/rndc.conf by default, must specify a server to talk to, as well as include the corresponding key (which must be recognized by named) to use while talking to it:

```
----------
# Use the key named "rndc" when talking to the nameserver "localhost."
server localhost {
    key                "rndc";
};

# Defaults.
options {
    default-server     localhost;
    default-key        "rndc";
};

# Include the key to use
include "/etc/rndc.key;
----------
```

The file needs to have three sections:

- **Server section**—Defines a nameserver (localhost) and specifies a key (rndc) to be used while communicating with it.

26

- **Options section**—Sets up reasonable defaults (because the file might list multiple servers and keys).

- **Key section**—Includes the file we have already created, /etc/rndc.key.

Should you need it, the rndc(8) and rndc.conf(5) manual pages contain more information.

named.conf

You next must configure named itself. Its single configuration file (/etc/named.conf) has syntax very similar to rndc.conf; this section describes only the small subset of configuration directives essential to the configuration of a functional nameserver. For a more exhaustive reference, consult the BIND 9 ARM (Administrator Reference Manual); it is distributed with BIND, and Fedora Core installs it under /usr/share/doc/bind-*/arm/).

Only the options and named sections in the named.conf file are absolutely necessary. The options section must tell named where the zone files are kept, and named must know where to find the root zone ("."). We also set up a controls section to enable suitably authenticated commands from rndc to be accepted. Because clients (notably nslookup) often depend on resolving the nameserver's IP, we set up the 0.0.127.in-addr.arpa reverse zone as well.

We start with a configuration file similar to this:

```
----------options {     # This is where zone files are kept.     directory
        "/var/named"; };

# Allow rndc running on localhost to send us commands. controls {     inet
 127.0.0.1          allow { localhost; }        keys { rndc; }; };""include
 "/etc/rndc.key";

# Information about the root zone. zone "." {     type              hint;
file                "root.hints"; }; # Lots of software depends on being
able to resolve 127.0.0.1 zone "0.0.127.in-addr.arpa" {     type
master;    file               "rev/127.0.0"; };
----------
```

The options section is where we specify the directory in which named should look for zone files (as named in other sections of the file). You learn about using other options in later examples in this chapter.

Next, we instruct named to accept commands from an authenticated rndc. We include the key file, /etc/rndc.key, and the controls section saying that rndc will be connecting from localhost and using the specified key. (You can specify more than one IP address in the allow list or use an access control list as described in the section "Security.")

The . zone tells named about the root nameservers with names and addresses in the root.hints file. This information determines which root nameserver is initially consulted, although this decision is frequently revised based on the server's response time. Although the hints file can be obtained via FTP, the recommended, network-friendly way to keep it synchronized is to use dig. We ask a root nameserver (it doesn't matter which one) for the NS records of . and use the dig output directly:

```
# dig @j.root-servers.net. ns > /var/named/root.hints
# cat /var/named/root.hints
; <<>> DiG 8.2 <<>> @j.root-servers.net . ns
; (1 server found)
;; res options: init recurs defnam dnsrch
;; got answer:
;; ->>HEADER<<- opcode: QUERY, status: NOERROR, id: 6
;; flags: qr aa rd; QUERY: 1, ANSWER: 13, AUTHORITY: 0, ADDITIONAL: 13
;; QUERY SECTION:      ;; ., type = NS, class = IN

;; ANSWER SECTION:
.                   6D IN NS       H.ROOT-SERVERS.NET.
.                   6D IN NS       C.ROOT-SERVERS.NET.
.                   6D IN NS       G.ROOT-SERVERS.NET.
.                   6D IN NS       F.ROOT-SERVERS.NET.
.                   6D IN NS       B.ROOT-SERVERS.NET.
.                   6D IN NS       J.ROOT-SERVERS.NET.
.                   6D IN NS       K.ROOT-SERVERS.NET.
.                   6D IN NS       L.ROOT-SERVERS.NET.
.                   6D IN NS       M.ROOT-SERVERS.NET.
.                   6D IN NS       I.ROOT-SERVERS.NET.
.                   6D IN NS       E.ROOT-SERVERS.NET.
.                   6D IN NS       D.ROOT-SERVERS.NET.
.                   6D IN NS       A.ROOT-SERVERS.NET.

;; ADDITIONAL SECTION:
H.ROOT-SERVERS.NET.      5w6d16h IN A    128.63.2.53
C.ROOT-SERVERS.NET.      5w6d16h IN A    192.33.4.12
G.ROOT-SERVERS.NET.      5w6d16h IN A    192.112.36.4
F.ROOT-SERVERS.NET.      5w6d16h IN A    192.5.5.241
B.ROOT-SERVERS.NET.      5w6d16h IN A    128.9.0.107
J.ROOT-SERVERS.NET.      5w6d16h IN A    198.41.0.10
K.ROOT-SERVERS.NET.      5w6d16h IN A    193.0.14.129
L.ROOT-SERVERS.NET.      5w6d16h IN A    198.32.64.12
M.ROOT-SERVERS.NET.      5w6d16h IN A    202.12.27.33
I.ROOT-SERVERS.NET.      5w6d16h IN A    192.36.148.17
E.ROOT-SERVERS.NET.      5w6d16h IN A    192.203.230.10
D.ROOT-SERVERS.NET.      5w6d16h IN A    128.8.10.90
A.ROOT-SERVERS.NET.      5w6d16h IN A    198.41.0.4
```

26

```
;; Total query time: 4489 msec
;; FROM: lustre to SERVER: j.root-servers.net  198.41.0.10
;; WHEN: Mon Sep 10 04:18:26 2001
;; MSG SIZE  sent: 17  rcvd: 436
```

The Zone File

The zone `0.0.127.in-addr.arpa` section in `named.conf` says that we are a master name-server for that zone and that the zone data is in the file `127.0.0`. Before examining the first real zone file in detail, look at the general format of a resource record specification:

```
name        TTL     class   type    data
```

Here, `name` is the DNS name with which this record is associated. In a zone file, names ending with a "`.`" are fully qualified, whereas others are relative to the name of the zone. In the zone `example.com`, `foo` refers to the fully qualified name `foo.example.com`. The special name `@` is a short form for the name of the zone itself. If the name is omitted, the last specified name is used again.

The `TTL` (Time To Live) field is a number that specifies the time for which the record can be cached. This is explained in greater detail in the discussion of the `SOA` record in the next section. If it is omitted, the default `TTL` for the zone is assumed. `TTL` values are usually in seconds, but you can append an `m` for minutes, `h` for hours, or `d` for days.

BIND supports different record classes, but for all practical purposes, the only important class is `IN`, for Internet. If no class is explicitly specified, a default value of `IN` is assumed; to save a little typing, we do not mention the class in any of the zone files we write here.

The type field is mandatory and names the `RR` in use, such as `A`, `NS`, `MX`, or `SOA`. (We will only use a few of the existing `RR`s here. Consult the DNS standards for a complete list.) The data field (or fields) contains data specific to this type of record. The appropriate syntax will be introduced as we examine the use of each `RR` in turn.

Here is the zone file for the `0.0.127.in-addr.arpa` zone:

```
$TTL 2D
@       SOA     localhost. hostmaster.example.com. (
                        2001090101  ; Serial
                        24h         ; Refresh
                        2h          ; Retry
                        3600000     ; Expire (1000h)
                        1h)         ; Minimum TTL
        NS      localhost.

1       PTR     localhost.
```

The $TTL directive that should begin every zone file sets the default minimum time to live for the zone to two days. This is discussed further in the next section.

The Zone File's SOA Record

The second line in the zone file uses the special @ name that you saw earlier. Here, it stands for 0.0.127.in-addr.arpa, to which the SOA (Start of Authority) record belongs. The rest of the fields (continued until the closing parenthesis) contain SOA-specific data.

The first data field in the SOA record is the fully qualified name of the master nameserver for the domain. The second field is the email address of the contact person for the zone. It is written as a DNS name by replacing the @ sign with a ".."; foo@example.com would be written as foo.example.com.. (note the trailing ..).

Do not use an address such as a.b@example.com because it is written as a.b.example.com and will later be misinterpreted as a@b.example.com.

> **TIP**
>
> It is important to ensure that mail to the contact email address specified in the SOA field is frequently read because it is used to report DNS setup problems and other potentially useful information.

The next several numeric fields specify various characteristics of this zone. These values must be correctly configured, and to do so, you must understand each field. As shown in the comments (note that zone file comments are not the same syntax as named.conf comments), the fields are serial number, refresh interval, retry time, expire period, and minimum TTL.

Serial numbers are 32-bit quantities that can hold values between 0 and 4,294,967,295 (2^{32}-1). Every time the zone data is changed, the serial number must be incremented. This change serves as a signal to slaves that they need to transfer the contents of the zone again. It is conventional to assign serial numbers in the format YYYYMMDDnn; that is, the date of the change and a two-digit revision number (for example, 2001090101). For changes made on the same day, you increment only the revision. This reasonably assumes that you make no more than 99 changes to a zone in one day. For changes on the next day, the date is changed and the revision number starts from 01 again.

The refresh interval specifies how often a slave server should check whether the master data has been updated. It has been set to 24 hours here, but if the zone changes often, the value should be lower. (Slaves can reload the zone much sooner if they and the master both support the DNS NOTIFY mechanism. Most DNS software does.) The retry time is relevant only when a slave fails to contact the master after the refresh time has elapsed. It specifies how long it should wait before trying again. (It is set to two hours here.)

If the slave is consistently unable to contact the master for the length of the expire period (usually because of some catastrophic failure), it discards the zone data it already has and stops answering queries for the zone. Thus, the expire period should be long enough to allow for the recovery of the master nameserver. It has repeatedly been shown that a value of one or two weeks is too short. One thousand hours (about six weeks) is accepted as a good default.

As you read earlier, every RR has a TTL, which specifies how long it can be cached before the origin of the data must be consulted again. If the RR definition does not specify a TTL explicitly, the default TTL (set by the $TTL directive) is used instead. This enables individual RRs to override the default TTL as required.

The SOA TTL, the last numeric field in the SOA record, is used to determine how long negative responses (NXDOMAIN) should be cached. (That is, if a query results in an NXDOMAIN response, that fact is cached for as long as indicated by the SOA TTL.) Older versions of BIND used the SOA minimum TTL to set the default TTL, but BIND 9 no longer does so. The default TTL of 2 days and SOA TTL of 1 hour is recommended for cache friendliness.

The values used previously are good defaults for zones that do not change often. You might have to adjust them a bit for zones with very different requirements; in which case, the website http://www.ripe.net/docs/ripe-203.html is recommended reading.

The Zone File's Other Records

The next two lines in the zone file create NS and PTR records. The NS record has no explicit name specified, so it uses the last one, which is the @ of the SOA record. Thus, the nameserver for 0.0.127.in-addr.arpa is defined to be localhost.

The PTR record has the name 1, which becomes 1.0.0.127.in-addr.arpa (which is how you write the address 127.0.0.1 as a DNS name). When qualified, the PTR record name 1 becomes localhost. (You will see some of the numerous other RR types when we later configure our nameserver to be authoritative for a real domain.)

TXT Records and SPF (Sender Policy Framework)

One record not already mentioned is the TXT record. This record is usually used for documentation purposes in DNS, but a recent proposal is using the TXT record to help in the fight against email address forgery, spam, and phishing attacks.

One problem with email and SMTP is that when email is being delivered, the sender can claim that the email is coming from trusted.bank.com, when it really is coming from smalltime.crook.com. When the recipient of the email gets the email, it looks like valid instructions from trusted.bank.com, but if they do trust the email and follow the instructions, their bank accounts can become vulnerable.

These situations can be controlled by using SPF.

Domains can publish the valid IP address of their email servers in specially formatted TXT records. A TXT record could look like this:

```
trusted.bank.com. IN TXT "v=spf1 ip4:37.21.50.80 -all"
```

This record specifies that only one IP address is allowed to send mail for trusted.bank.com.

Receiving email servers can then do one extra check with incoming email. When an email arrives, they know the IP address that the email is coming from. They also know that the sender claims to be coming from trusted.bank.com, for example. The receiving email server can look up the DNS TXT record for trusted.bank.com, extract the allowed IP addresses, and compare them to the IP address that the email really is coming from. If they match, that is an extremely good indication that the email really is coming from trusted.bank.com. If they do not match, then that is a very good indication that the email is bogus and should be deleted or investigated further.

The SPF system does rely on cooperation between senders and receivers. Senders must publish their TXT records in DNS, and receivers must check the records with incoming email.

If you want more details on SPF, visit the home page at http://spf.pobox.com/.

Logging

We now have all the elements of a minimal functioning DNS server, but before we experiment further, some extra logging will allow us to see exactly what named is doing. Log options are configured in a logging section in named.conf, and the various options are described in detail in the BIND 9 ARM.

All log messages go to one or more channels—each of which can write messages to the syslog, to an ordinary file, to stderr, or to null. (Log messages written to null are discarded.) Categories of messages exist, such as those generated while parsing configuration files, those caused by OS errors, and so on. Your logging statement must define some channels and associate them with the categories of messages that you want to see.

BIND logging is very flexible, but complicated, so we will only examine a simple log configuration here.

The following addition to named.conf will set up a channel called custom, which writes time-stamped messages to a file and send messages in the listed categories to it:

```
logging {
    channel custom {
        file "/tmp/named.log";   # Where to send messages.
        print-time yes;          # Print timestamps?
        print-category yes;      # Print message category?
    };

    category config       { custom; };   # Configuration files
    category notify       { custom; };   # NOTIFY messages
    category dnssec       { custom; };   # TSIG messages
    category general      { custom; };   # Miscellaneous
    category security     { custom; };   # Security messages
    category xfer-out     { custom; };   # Zone transfers
    category lame-servers { custom; };
};
```

Resolver Configuration

The last step before running BIND is to set up the local resolver software. This involves configuring the /etc/hosts, /etc/resolv.conf, and /etc/nsswitch.conf files.

To avoid gratuitous network traffic, most Unix resolvers still use a hosts-like text file named /etc/hosts to store the names and addresses of commonly used hosts. Each line in this file contains an IP address and a list of names for the host. Add entries to this file for any hosts you want to be able to resolve independently from DNS. If the entry is found in /etc/hosts, the resolver does not have to contact a DNS server to resolve the name, which reduces network traffic.

/etc/resolv.conf specifies the addresses of preferred nameservers and a list of domains relative to which unqualified names will be resolved. You specify a nameserver with a line of the form nameserver 1.2.3.4 (where 1.2.3.4 is the address of the nameserver). You can use multiple nameserver lines (usually up to three). You can use a search line to specify a list of domains to search for unqualified names.

A search line such as search example.com example.net would cause the resolver to attempt to resolve the unqualified name xyz, first as xyz.example.com, and, if that fails, as xyz.example.net. Do not use too many domains in the search list because it slows down resolution.

A hosts: files dns line in /etc/nsswitch.conf will cause the resolver to consult /etc/hosts before using the DNS during the course of a name lookup. This allows you to override the DNS by making temporary changes to /etc/hosts, which is especially useful during network testing. (Older resolvers might require an order hosts, bind line in the /etc/host.conf file instead.)

Running the named Nameserver Daemon

Finally! You can now start named with /etc/rc.d/init.d/named start. You should see messages similar to the ones that follow in the syslog (or according to the logging configuration you have set up). One way to do this is to monitor the log file with the tail command; that will scroll the changes in the file down the screen:

```
#  tail -f /var/log/messages
- - - - - - - - - -
July 9 23:48:33 titan named[2605]: starting BIND 9.2.3 -u named
July 9 23:48:33 titan named[2605]: using 1 CPU
July 9 23:48:33 titan named[2608]: loading configuration from '/etc/named.conf'
July 9 23:48:33 titan named[2608]: no IPv6 interfaces found
```

```
July 9 23:48:33 titan named[2608]: listening on IPv4 interface lo, 127.0.0.1#53
July 9 23:48:33 titan named: named startup succeeded
July 9 23:48:33 titan named[2608]: listening on IPv4 interface\
 eth0, 192.168.2.68#53
July  9 23:48:33 titan named[2608]: command channel listening on 127.0.0.1#953
October  9 23:48:33 titan named[2608]: zone 0.0.127.in-addr.arpa/IN: \
loaded serial 1997022700
October  9 23:48:33 titan named[2608]: zone localhost/IN: loaded serial 42
October  9 23:48:33 titan named[2608]: running
- - - - - - - - - -
```

You can use rndc to interact with this instance of named. Running rndc without arguments displays a list of available commands, including the ability to reload or refresh zones, dump statistics and the database to disk, toggle query logging, and stop the server. Unfortunately, rndc does not yet implement all the commands that were supported by ndc—the control program shipped with earlier versions of BIND.

You should now be able to resolve 1.0.0.127.in-addr.arpa locally (try dig @localhost 1.0.0.127.in-addr.arpa PTR +norec) and other names via recursive resolution. If you cannot accomplish this resolution, something is wrong, and you should read the "Troubleshooting DNS" section later to diagnose and correct your problem before proceeding further. Remember to read the logs!

Providing DNS for a Real Domain

You can expand the minimal nameserver configuration you just created into one that performs useful name service for a real domain. Suppose that your ISP has assigned to you the IP addresses in the 192.0.2.0/29 range (which has six usable addresses: 192.0.2.1-6) and that you want to serve authoritative data for the domain example.com. A friend has agreed to configure her nameserver (192.0.2.96) to be a slave for the domain, as well as a backup mail server. In return, she wants the foo.example.com subdomain delegated to her own nameservers.

Forward Zone
First, we must introduce the zone to named.conf:

```
- - - - - - - - - -

    zone "example.com" {
        type master;
        file "example.com";
    };

- - - - - - - - - -
```

and create the zone file:

```
- - - - - - - - - -
    $TTL 2D
    @       SOA     ns1.example.com. hostmaster.example.com. (
                            2001090101  ; Serial
                            24h         ; Refresh
                            2h          ; Retry
                            3600000     ; Expire (1000h)
                            1h)         ; Minimum TTL
            NS      ns1.example.com.
            NS      ns2.example.com.
            MX 5    mx1.example.com.
            MX 10   mx2.example.com.
            A       192.0.2.1

    ; Addresses
    ns1     A       192.0.2.1           ; Nameservers
    ns2     A       192.0.2.96
    mx1     A       192.0.2.2           ; Mail servers
    mx2     A       192.0.2.96
    www     A       192.0.2.3           ; Web servers
     dev      A       192.0.2.4
    work    A       192.0.2.5           ; Workstations
    play    A       192.0.2.6

    ; Delegations
    foo     NS      dns1.foo.example.com.
    foo     NS      dns2.foo.example.com.
    dns1.foo A      192.0.2.96
    dns2.foo A      192.0.2.1
- - - - - - - - - -
```

The SOA record is similar to the one you saw before. Note that the next five records all use the implicit name @, which is short for example.com.

The two NS records define ns1.example.com (our own server, 192.0.2.1) and ns2.example.com (our friend's server, 192.0.2.96) as authoritative nameservers for example.com.

The MX (Mail Exchanger) records each specify a mail server for the zone. An MX RR takes two arguments: a priority number and the name of a host. In delivering mail addressed to example.com, the listed MXes are tried in increasing order of priority. In this case, mx1.example.com (our own machine, 192.0.2.2) has the lowest priority and is always tried first. If the attempt to deliver mail to mx1 fails (for whatever reason), the next listed MX, mx2.example.com (our friend's server), is tried.

The A record says that the address of example.com is 192.0.2.1, and the next few lines specify addresses for other hosts in the zone: our nameservers ns1 and ns2, mail servers mx1 and mx2, two web servers, and two workstations.

Next, we add NS records to delegate authority over the foo.example.com domain to dns1 and dns2.foo.example.com. The A records for dns1 and dns2 are known as *glue* records, and they enable resolvers to find the address of the authoritative nameservers so that they can continue the query. (If we were using dig, the NS records for dns1 and dns2 would be listed in the AUTHORITY section of the response, whereas the ADDITIONAL section would contain their addresses.)

Notice that dns2.foo.example.com is 192.0.2.1, our own nameserver. We are acting as a slave for the foo.example.com zone and must configure named accordingly. We introduce the zone as a slave in named.conf and specify the address of the master nameserver:

```
zone "foo.example.com" {
    type slave;
    file "foo.example.com";
    masters {
        192.0.2.96;
    };
};
```

Similarly, our friend must configure 192.0.2.96, which is a master for foo.example.com and a slave for example.com. (She must also configure her server to accept mail addressed to example.com. Usually, mx2 would just queue the mail until it could be delivered to mx1.)

Reverse Zone

Let us pretend that we live in a perfect world: Our highly competent ISP has successfully delegated authority of our reverse zone to us, and we must set up named to handle reverse resolution as well. This process is very similar to what you used to set up the reverse zone for 0.0.127.in-addr.arpa. Now, however, you must determine your zone's name.

DNS can only delegate authority at the "." in domain names; as a result, you can set up reverse zones for the whole of a class A, B, or C network because they are divided at octet boundaries in the IP address. This approach is clearly unsuitable for classless subnets such as ours because the divisions aren't at octet boundaries, but in the middle of an octet. In other words, our network cannot be described as x.* (class A), x.y.* (class B), or x.y.z.* (class C). The latter comes closest, but includes several addresses (such as 192.0.2.22) that don't belong to our tiny 192.0.2.0/29 network. To set up a reverse zone for our network, we must resort to the use of classless delegation (described in RFC 2317).

The ISP, which is authoritative for the 2.0.192.in-addr.arpa zone, must either maintain your reverse zone for you or add the following records into its zone file:

```
- - - - - - - - - -

¦    1          CNAME    1.1-6
¦    2          CNAME    2.1-6
¦    3          CNAME    3.1-6
¦    4          CNAME    4.1-6
¦    5          CNAME    5.1-6
¦    6          CNAME    6.1-6
¦
¦    1-6        NS       192.0.2.1
¦    1-6        NS       192.0.2.96
- - - - - - - - - -
```

The first CNAME record says that 1.2.0.192.in-addr.arpa is an alias for 1.1-6.2.0.
192._in-addr.arpa. (The others are similar. We don't have CNAME records for network and
broadcast addresses 0 and 7 because they do not need to resolve.) Resolvers already know
how to follow CNAME aliases while resolving names. When they ask about the 1-6 domain,
they find the NS records defined previously and continue with their query by asking our
nameserver about 1.1-6.2.0.192.in-addr.arpa.

So, we must set up a zone file for 1-6.2.0.192.in-addr.arpa. Apart from the peculiar
name, this zone file is similar in every respect to the reverse zone we set up earlier, and
should contain six PTR records (apart from the SOA and NS records). Note that we make
192.0.2.96 (ns2) a slave for the reverse zone as well, so the administrator must add a suitable zone statement to named.conf for it.

> **CAUTION**
>
> Be aware that in the real world you might have to wait for months for your ISP to get the
> reverse delegation right, and your reverse zone will remain broken until then.

Registering the Domain

You now have a working DNS setup, but external resolvers cannot see it because there is
no chain of delegations from the root nameservers to yours. You need to create this chain
by registering the domain; that is, by paying the appropriate registration fees to an
authority known as a registrar, who then delegates authority over the chosen zone to
your nameservers.

Nothing is magical about what a registrar does. It has authority over a certain portion of
the DNS database (say, the com. TLD), and, for a fee, it delegates authority over a subdomain (example.com) to you. This delegation is accomplished by the same mechanisms
that were explained earlier in our delegation of foo.example.com.

The site http://www.iana.org/domain-names.htm contains a list of all the TLDs and the
corresponding registrars (of which there are now several). The procedure and fees for

registering a domain vary wildly between them. Visit the website of the registrar in question and follow the procedures outlined there. After wading through the required amounts of red tape, your domain should be visible to the rest of the world.

Congratulations! Your job as a DNS administrator has just begun.

Troubleshooting DNS

Several sources offer good information about finding and fixing DNS errors. The DNSRD Tricks and Tips page at http://www.dns.net/dnsrd/trick.html and the comp.protocols. tcp-ip.domains FAQ (an HTML version is located at http://www.intac.com/~cdp/cptd-faq/) are good places to start. This section discusses some of the more common errors and their cures.

> **NOTE**
>
> RFC 1912, entitled "Common DNS Operational and Configuration Errors," discusses several of the most common DNS problems at length. It is available at http://www.intac.com/~cdp/cptd-faq/.

Delegation Problems

Your zone must be delegated to the nameservers authoritative for them, either by the root nameservers or the parents of the zone in question. Improper delegation can cause the name service for your domain to become dysfunctional, prevent some networks from using the name service, and numerous other problems. These problems typically occur only in the initial stages of setting up a domain when the delegations have not propagated widely yet.

If you experience such problems, you can use `dig` to follow delegation chains and find the point at which problems occur. Tools such as `dnswalk` might also be useful (see "Tools for Troubleshooting," later in this chapter).

Lame delegation is another common DNS delegation problem. *Lame delegation* occurs when a nameserver is listed as being authoritative for a zone, but in fact is not authoritative (it has not been configured to be a master for the zone); the nameserver in a lame delegation is called a lame server. Unfortunately, lame delegations are very common on the Internet. They can be the temporary result of domains being moved or (especially in the case of reverse zones) more permanent configuration errors that are never detected because of a lack of attention to detail.

If your registrar's bills for your domain are not promptly paid, the registrar might discontinue the delegation of authority for your zone. If this happens (and the `whois` record for your domain will usually mention this), the best thing to do is quickly pay the registrar and ask him to renew the delegation. It is better not to let it happen, though, because such changes can take a relatively long time to make and propagate.

26

Reverse Lookup Problems

Reverse lookup problems are often very hard to diagnose because they manifest themselves as failures in systems other than DNS. Many security sensitive services perform reverse lookups on the originating host for all incoming connections and deny the connection if the query fails.

Even if reverse resolution succeeds, many servers might reject connections from your host if your A and PTR records do not match. That is, the PTR record for a particular IP address refers to a name, and the A record for that name refers to a different IP address. They perform a double lookup to verify that the PTR and A records match to eliminate spoofing attacks. Maintain your reverse zones carefully at all times.

Delegation problems are a frequent source of woe. Unfortunately, many ISPs appear unable to understand, configure, or delegate reverse zones. In such cases, you often have little choice but to try and tell them what to do to fix the problem, and if they refuse to listen, find a new ISP (or live with broken DNS).

Another typical symptom of failing reverse lookups is an abnormally long delay on connection attempts. This happens when the server's query for a PTR record is not answered and times out (often because of network problems or the nameserver being down). This can be baffling to diagnose, but you should suspect DNS problems whenever you hear questions such as "Hey! Why is my web browser taking so long to connect?"

Maintaining Accurate Serial Numbers

Accurate serial numbers are very important to the correct operation of slave servers. An increase in the serial number of a zone causes slaves to reload the zone and update their local cache.

A very common mistake that system administrators make is forgetting to increment the serial number after a change to the zone data. If you make this mistake, secondary nameservers won't reload the zone, and will continue to serve old data. If you suspect that the data on the master and slave servers are out of sync, you can use dig to view the SOA record for the zone on each server (dig @master domain SOA and dig @slave domain SOA) and compare the serial numbers in the responses.

Another common problem is setting the serial number to an incorrect value—either too small or too large. A too small serial number causes slaves to think that they possess a more up-to-date copy of the zone data, but this is easily corrected by increasing the serial number as necessary. A too large serial number is more problematic and requires more elaborate measures to repair.

Serial number comparisons are defined in such a way that if a serial number—when subtracted from another with no overflow correction—results in a positive number, the second number is newer than the first, and a zone transfer is required. (See RFC 1982 "Serial Number Arithmetic" for details.) You can exploit this property by temporarily setting the serial number to 2^{32} (4,294,967,296), waiting for all the slaves to reload the zone, and then setting it to the correct number.

Troubleshooting Problems in Zone Files

The most common error in zone data is to forget that names in a zone file are relative to the origin of the zone, not to the root. Writing www.example.com in the zone file for example.com, and expecting it to be fully qualified, causes names such as www.example.com.example.com to show up in the DNS. You should either write www, which is qualified to the correct www.example.com, or write www.example.com. (with the trailing period) to indicate that the name is fully qualified.

The SOA record should contain (as the first field) the domain name of the master server (not a CNAME) and a contact address (with the @ replaced by a ".") to report problems to. Mail sent to this address should be read frequently. The other fields should contain sensible values for your zone, and the serial number should be correctly incremented after each change.

As discussed earlier, A and PTR records should always match; that is, the A record pointed to by a PTR should point back to the address of the PTR record. Remember to quote the two arguments of HINFO records if they contain any whitespace. Avoid the use of CNAME records for MX, NS, and SOA records.

In general, after making changes to zone data, it is a good idea to reload named and examine the logs for any errors that cause named to complain or reject the zone. Even better, you could use one of the verification tools such as dnswalk, discussed briefly next.

Tools for Troubleshooting

BIND includes the always useful dig program, as well as named-checkconf (to check /etc/named.conf for syntax errors) and named-checkzone (to do the same for zone files). We also especially recommend dnswalk and nslint. dnswalk is a Perl script that scans the DNS setup of a given domain for problems. It should be used in conjunction with RFC 1912, which explains most of the problems it detects. nslint, like the analogous lint utility for C programs, searches for common BIND and zone file configuration errors.

By occasionally using these programs to troubleshoot DNS problems (especially after non-trivial zone changes) you go far toward keeping your DNS configuration healthy and trouble free.

Using Fedora Core's BIND Configuration Tool

Fedora provides a dozen or more different graphical configuration tools system administrators can use to configure network (and system) services. One of these tools is system-config-bind, a deceptively simple BIND configuration tool that requires an active X session and must be run with root privileges.

You can launch this client by using the command system-config-bind from a terminal window or by selecting the domain name service menu item from the Server Settings menu. It is automatically installed if you select the Fedora configuration tools.

NOTE

Using `system-config-bind` and then saving any changes will overwrite existing settings! If you prefer to manually edit your `named` configuration files, do not use `system-config-bind`. Always make a backup of the configuration files in any event—you'll be glad you did.

After you type the root password and press Enter, the client launches. You will then see its main window, as shown in Figure 26.2.

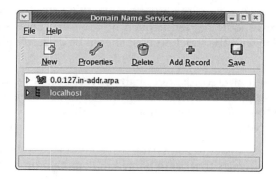

FIGURE 26.2   Fedora's `system-config-bind` utility can be used to create, modify, and save basic domain nameserver settings.

`system-config-bind` can be used to add a forward master zone, a reverse master zone, MX records or a slave zone. Click the Add Record button to select an entry for configuration, as shown in Figure 26.3.

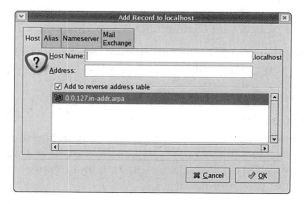

FIGURE 26.3   Use `system-config-bind` to add a new DNS record to your server or edit the existing settings.

Existing settings can be edited or deleted by first selecting and then clicking the Edit or Delete buttons in the `system-config-bind` dialog. When you have finished entering or editing your custom settings, select the Apply menu item from the File menu. Configuration files will be saved in /etc/named.conf and under the /var/named directory.

Managing DNS Security

Security considerations are of vital importance to DNS administrators because DNS was not originally designed to be a very secure protocol and a number of successful attacks against BIND have been found over the years. The most important defense is to keep abreast of developments in security circles and act on them promptly.

DNS is especially vulnerable to attacks known as poisoning and spoofing. *Poisoning* refers to placing incorrect data into the DNS database, which then spreads to clients and caches across the world, potentially causing hundreds of thousands of people to unwittingly use the bad data. Although DNS poisoning can occur because of carelessness, it has serious implications when performed deliberately. What if someone set up a clone of a common website, redirected users to it by DNS poisoning, and then asked them for their credit card numbers? *Spoofing* is the practice of forging network packets, and making nameservers believe that they are receiving a valid answer to a query is one of the ways malicious poisoning can be performed.

BIND has often been criticized as being very insecure, and although recent versions are greatly improved in this regard, DNS administrators today must take several precautions to ensure that its use is adequately protected from attacks. Of course, it is important to always run the latest recommended version of BIND.

> **TIP**
>
> One of your strongest defenses against DNS security risks is to keep abreast of developments in security circles and act on them promptly. The BugTraq mailing list, hosted at http://www.securityfocus.com/, and the SANS Institute at http://www.sans.org/ are good places to start.

Unix Security Considerations

The most important step in securing any Unix system is to configure the environment BIND runs in to use all the security mechanisms available to it through the operating system to its advantage. In short, this means that you should apply general security measures to your computer.

Run named with as few privileges as it needs to function. Don't run named as root. Even if an attacker manages to exploit a security hole in BIND, the effects of the break-in can be minimized if named is running as user nobody rather than as root. Of course, named needs to be started as root (because it needs to bind to port 53), but it can be instructed to switch to a given user and group with the -u and -g command-line options.

Starting named with a command such as named -u nobody -g nogroup is highly recommended. Remember, however, that if you run multiple services as nobody, you increase the risks of a compromise. In such a situation, it is best to create separate accounts for each service and use them for nothing else. Fedora Core runs named as the user named.

You can also use the `chroot` feature of Unix to isolate `named` into its own part of the file system. If correctly configured, such a file system "jail" will restrict attackers—if they manage to break in—to a part of the file system that contains little of value. It is important to remember that a *chroot jail* is not a panacea, and it does not eliminate the need for other defensive measures.

> **CAUTION**
>
> Programs that use `chroot` but do not take other precautions as well have been shown to be insecure. BIND does take such precautions. See the chroot-BIND HOWTO at http://www.ibiblio.org/pub/Linux/docs/HOWTO/other-formats/html_single/ Chroot-BIND-HOWTO.html.

For a `chroot` environment to work properly, you need to set up a directory that contains everything BIND needs to run. It is recommended that you start with a working configuration of BIND, create a directory, say `/usr/local/bind`, and copy over the files it needs into subdirectories under that one. For instance, you will need to copy the binaries, some system libraries, the configuration files, and so on. Consult the BIND documentation for details about exactly which files you need.

When your `chroot` environment is set up, you can start `named` with the `-t /usr/ local/bind` option (combined with the `-u` and `-g` options) to instruct it to chroot to the directory you have set up.

You might also want to check your logs and keep track of resource usage. `named` manages a cache of DNS data that can potentially grow very large; it will also happily hog CPU and bandwidth, making your server unusable. This is something that can be exploited by clever attackers, but you can configure BIND to set resource limits. Several such options in the `named.conf` file are available, including `datasize`, which limits the maximum size of the data segment (and thus the cache). One downside of this approach is that `named` might be killed by the kernel if it exceeds these limits, meaning that you have to run it in a loop that restarts it if it dies (or run it from `/etc/inittab`).

DNS Security Considerations

Several configuration options exist for `named` that can make it more resistant to various potential attacks. The most common ones are briefly described next.

For more detailed discussions of the syntax and use of these options, refer to the BIND 9 documentation.

> **TIP**
>
> The Security Level Configuration Tool (`system-config-securitylevel`) has been updated to make implementation of the firewall simpler. The new "on/off" choice (rather than "levels" as before) allows you to employ a firewall without requiring any special configuration for your DNS server.

Defining Access Control Lists

Specifying network and IP addresses multiple times in a configuration file is tedious and error prone. BIND allows you to define access control lists (ACLs), which are named collections of network and IP addresses. You use these collections to ease the task of assigning permissions.

Four predefined ACLs exist:

- any—Matches anything

- none—Matches nothing

- localhost—Matches all the network interfaces local to your nameserver

- localnets—Matches any network directly attached to a local interface

In addition, you can define your own lists in named.conf, containing as many network and IP addresses as you prefer, using the acl command as shown:

```
- - - - - - - - - -

acl trusted {
    192.0.2.0/29;          // Our own network is OK.
    localhost;             // And so is localhost.
    !192.0.2.33/29;        // But not this range.
};
- - - - - - - - - -
```

Here, you see that you can use a ! to negate members in an ACL. Once defined, you can use these ACLs in allow-query, allow-transfer, allow-recursion, and similar options, as discussed next.

Controlling Queries

As mentioned before, most nameservers will perform recursive resolution for any queries they receive unless specifically configured not to do so. (We suppressed this behavior by using dig +norec.) By repeatedly fetching data from a number of unknown and untrusted nameservers, recursion makes your installation vulnerable to DNS poisoning. (In other words, you get deliberately or inadvertently incorrect lists.) You can avoid this problem by explicitly denying recursion.

Recursive queries can be disabled by adding a recursion no statement to the options section of named.conf. It might still be desirable to allow recursive queries from some trusted hosts, however, and this can be accomplished by the use of an allow-recursion statement. This excerpt would configure named to disallow recursion for all but the listed hosts:

```
. . . . . . . . . .

options {
    ...

    recursion no;
    allow-recursion {
        192.0.2.0/29;
        localnets;           // Trust our local networks.
        localhost;           // And ourselves.
    };
};
. . . . . . . . . .
```

You can choose to be still more restrictive and allow only selected hosts to query your nameserver by using the `allow-query` statement (with syntax similar to `allow-recursion`, as described previously). Of course, this solution will not work if your server is authoritative for a zone. In that case, you will have to explicitly `allow-query { all; }` in the configuration section of each zone for which you want to serve authoritative data.

Controlling Zone Transfers

You also can use queries to enable only known slave servers to perform zone transfers from your server. Not only do zone transfers consume a lot of resources (they require a `named-xfer` process to be forked each time) and provide an avenue for denial of service attacks, but also there have been remote exploits via buffer overflows in `named-xfer` that allow attackers to gain root privileges on the compromised system. To prevent this, add sections such as the following to all your zone definitions:

```
. . . . . . . . . .

zone "example.com" {
    ...
    allow-transfer {
        192.0.2.96;          // Known slave.
        localhost;           // Often required for testing.
    };
};
. . . . . . . . . .
```

Alert named to Potential Problem Hosts

Despite all this, it might be necessary to single out a few troublesome hosts for special treatment. The server and black hole statements in `named.conf` can be used to tell `named` about known sources of poisoned information or attack attempts. For instance, if the host `203.122.154.1` is repeatedly trying to attack the server, the following addition to the options section of `named.conf` will cause our server to ignore traffic from that address. Of course, you can specify multiple addresses and networks in the black hole list.

```
- - - - - - - - - -

options {     ...
blackhole {          203.122.154.1;     };};
- - - - - - - - - -
```

For a known source of bad data, you can do something such as the following to cause your nameserver to stop asking the listed server any questions. This is different from adding a host to the black hole list. A server marked as bogus will never be sent queries, but it can still ask us questions. A black holed host is simply ignored altogether:

```
- - - - - - - - - -

server bogus.info.example.com {     bogus yes;};
- - - - - - - - - -
```

The AUS-CERT advisory AL-1999.004, which discusses denial of service attacks against DNS servers, also discusses various ways of restricting access to nameservers and is a highly recommended read. A copy is located at ftp://ftp.auscert.org.au/pub/auscert/ _advisory/AL-1999.004.dns_dos. Among other things, it recommends the most restrictive configuration possible and the permanent black-holing of some addresses known to be popular sources of spoofed requests and answers. It is a good idea to add the following ACL to the black hole list of all your servers:

```
- - - - - - - - - -

/* These are known fake source addresses. */acl "bogon" {
    0.0.0.0/8;      # Null address
    1.0.0.0/8;      # IANA reserved, popular fakes
    2.0.0.0/8;    192.0.2.0/24;  # Test address
    224.0.0.0/3;   # Multicast addresses

    /* RFC 1918 addresses may be fake too. Don't list these if you
       use them internally. */
    10.0.0.0/8;
    172.16.0.0/12;
    192.168.0.0/16;
};
- - - - - - - - - -
```

Using DNS Security Extensions

DNS Security Extensions (DNSSEC), a set of security extensions to the DNS protocol, provides data integrity and authentication by using cryptographic digital signatures. It provides for the storage of public keys in the DNS and their use for verifying transactions. DNSSEC still isn't widely deployed, but BIND 9 does support it for inter-server transactions (zone transfers, NOTIFY, recursive queries, dynamic updates). It is worth configuring the transaction signature (TSIG) if your slaves also run BIND 9. We briefly discuss using TSIG for authenticated zone transfers here.

To begin, use `dnssec-keygen`, as we did with `rndc`, to generate a shared secret key. This key is stored on both the master and slave servers. As before, we extract the Key: data from the `.private` file. The following command creates a 512-bit host key named `transfer`:

- - - - - - - - - -

```
$ dnssec-keygen -a hmac-md5 -b 512 -n host transfer
```
- - - - - - - - - -

Next, we set up matching key statements in `named.conf` for both the master and slave servers (similar to the contents of the `/etc/rndc.key` file which we created earlier). Remember not to transfer the secret key from one machine to the other over an insecure channel. Use `ssh`, `sftp` (secure FTP), or something similar. Remember also that the shared secrets shouldn't be stored in world readable files. The statements, identical on both machines, would look something similar to this:

- - - - - - - - - -
```
key transfer {
    algorithm "hmac-md5";
    secret "...";          # Key from .private file
};
```

- - - - - - - - - -

Finally, we set up a server statement on the master, to instruct it to use the key we just created when communicating with the slave, and enable authenticated zone transfers with the appropriate `allow-transfer` directives:

- - - - - - - - - -
```
server 192.0.2.96 {
    key { transfer; };
};
```

- - - - - - - - - -

The BIND 9 ARM contains more information on TSIG configuration and DNSSEC support in BIND.

Using Split DNS

BIND is often run on firewalls—both to act as a proxy for resolvers inside the network and to serve authoritative data for some zones. In such situations, many people prefer to avoid exposing more details of their private network configuration via DNS than is unavoidable (although there is some debate about whether this is actually useful). Those accessing your system from outside the firewall should only see information they are explicitly allowed access to, whereas internal hosts are allowed access to other data. This kind of setup is called split DNS.

Suppose you have a set of zones that you want to expose to the outside world and another set that you want to allow hosts on your network to see. You can accomplish this with a configuration such as the following:

```
- - - - - - - - - -
acl private {    localhost;    192.168.0.0/24;
    # Define your internal network suitably.
};
view private_zones {    match { private; };    recursion yes;
      # Recursive resolution for internal hosts.
zone internal.zone {        # Zone statements;    };
  # More internal zones.
};
view public_zones {    match { any; }    recursion no;
      zone external.zone {        # Zone statements;    };
      # More external zones.
};
- - - - - - - - - -
```

Further, you might want to configure internal hosts running named to forward all queries to the firewall and never try to resolve queries themselves. The forward only and forwarders options in named.conf do this. (forwarders specifies a list of IP addresses of the nameservers to forward queries to.)

The BIND 9 ARM discusses several details of running BIND in a secure split-DNS configuration.

26

Related Core and Linux Commands

You will use the following commands to manage DNS in Fedora:

dig—The domain information groper command, used to query remote DNS servers

host—A domain nameserver query utility

named—A domain nameserver included with Fedora

system-config-bind—A GUI tool to configure DNS information

nsupdate—A Dynamic DNS update utility

rndc—The nameserver control utility included with BIND

Reference

http://www.dns.net/dnsrd/—The DNS Resources Database.

http://www.isc.org/products/BIND/—The ISC's BIND web page.

http://archive.quadratic.net/docs/Bv9ARM.pdf—The BIND 9 Administrator Reference Manual.

The Concise Guide to DNS and BIND, by Nicolai Langfeldt (Que Publishing, 2000)—An in-depth discussion of both theoretical and operational aspects of DNS administration.

http://www.ibiblio.org/pub/Linux/docs/HOWTO/other-formats/html_single/ Chroot-BIND-HOWTO.html—A guide to how chroot works with BIND 9.

http://langfeldt.net/DNS-HOWTO/—The home page of the DNS HOWTO for BIND versions 4,8, and 9.

http://www.ibiblio.org/pub/Linux/docs/HOWTO/other-formats/html_single/ DNS-HOWTO.html#s3—Setting up a resolving, caching nameserver. Note that the file referenced as /var/named/root.hints is called /var/named/named.ca in Fedora Core.

http://spf.pobox.com/—The home page of Sender Policy Framework (SPF), a method of preventing email address forgery.

CHAPTER **27**

LDAP

IN THIS CHAPTER

- Configuring the Server
- Configuring Clients
- Administration
- Reference

The Lightweight Directory Access Protocol (LDAP, pronounced *ell-dap*) is one of those technologies that, while hidden, forms part of the core infrastructure in enterprise computing. Its job is simple: It stores information about users. However, its power comes from the fact that it can be linked into dozens of other services. LDAP can power login authentication, public key distribution, email routing, and address verification and, more recently, has formed the core of the push toward single sign-on technology.

> **TIP**
>
> Most people find the concept of LDAP easier to grasp when they think of it as a highly specialized form of database server. Behind the scenes, Fedora uses a database for storing all its LDAP information; however, LDAP does not offer anything as straightforward as SQL for data manipulation!
>
> OpenLDAP uses Sleepycat Software's Berkeley DB (BDB), and sticking with that default is highly recommended. That said, there are alternatives if you have specific needs.

This chapter looks at a relatively basic installation of an LDAP server, including how to host a company-wide directory service that contains the names and email addresses of employees. LDAP is a client/server system, meaning that an LDAP server hosts the data and an LDAP client queries it. Fedora Core Linux comes with OpenLDAP as its LDAP server, along with several LDAP-enabled email clients, including Evolution and Mozilla Thunderbird. We cover all three of these applications in this chapter.

Because LDAP data is usually available over the Internet— or at least your local network—it is imperative that you make every effort to secure your server. This chapter gives specific instruction on password configuration for OpenLDAP, and we recommend you follow our instructions closely.

Configuring the Server

If you have been using LDAP for years, you will be aware of its immense power and flexibility. On the other hand, if you are just trying LDAP for the first time, it will seem like the most broken component you could imagine. LDAP has very specific configuration requirements, is vastly lacking in graphical tools, and has a large number of acronyms to remember. On the bright side, all the hard work you put in will be worth it because, when it works, LDAP will hugely improve your networking experience.

The first step in configuring your LDAP server is to install the client and server applications. Select Add/Remove Applications, click the Details button next to Network Servers, and check openldap-servers. Then click the Details button next to System Tools and select openldap-clients. After you have installed them, close the dialog box and bring up a terminal.

Now, switch to the root user and edit /etc/openldap/slapd.conf in the text editor of your choice. This is the primary configuration file for slapd, the OpenLDAP server daemon. Scroll down until you see the lines database, suffix, and rootdn.

This is the most basic configuration for your LDAP system. What is the name of your server? The dc stands for *domain component*, which is the name of your domain as stored in DNS—for example, example.com. For our examples, we used hudzilla.org. LDAP considers each part of a domain name (separated by a period) to be a domain component, so the domain hudzilla.org is made up of a domain component hudzilla and a domain component org.

Change the suffix line to match your domain components, separated by commas. For example:

```
suffix    "dc=hudzilla,dc=org"
```

The next line defines the root DN, which is another LDAP acronym meaning *distinguished name*. A DN is a complete descriptor of a person in your directory: her name and the domain in which she resides. For example

```
rootdn    "cn=root,dc=hudzilla,dc=org"
```

CN is yet another LDAP acronym, this time meaning common name. A *common name* is just that—the name a person is usually called. Some people have several common names. Andrew Hudson is a common name, but that same user might also have the common name Andy Hudson. In our rootdn line, we define a complete user: common name root at domain hudzilla.org. These lines are essentially read backward. LDAP goes to org first, searches org for hudzilla, and then searches hudzilla for root.

The rootdn is important because it is more than just another person in your directory. The root LDAP user is like the root user in Linux. It is the person who has complete control over the system and can make whatever changes he wants to.

Now comes a slightly more complex part: We need to give the LDAP root user a password. The easiest way to do this is to open a new terminal window alongside your existing one. Switch to root in the new terminal also, and type **slappasswd**. This tool generates password hashes for OpenLDAP using the SHA1 hash algorithm. Enter a password when it prompts you. When you have entered and confirmed your password, you should see output like this:

```
{SSHA}qMVxFT2K1UUmrA89Gd7z6EK3gRLDIo2W
```

That is the password hash generated from your password. Yours will be different from the one shown here, but what is important is that it has {SSHA} at the beginning to denote it uses SHA1. You now need to switch back to the other terminal (the one editing slapd.conf) and add this line below the rootdn line:

```
rootpw <your password hash>
```

You should replace <your password hash> with the full output from slappasswd, like this:

```
rootpw {SSHA}qMVxFT2K1UUmrA89Gd7z6EK3gRLDIo2W
```

That sets the LDAP root password to the one you just generated with slappasswd. That is the last change you need to make in the slapd.conf file, so save your changes and close your editor.

Back in the terminal, run the slaptest command. This checks your slapd.conf file for errors and ensures you edited it correctly. Presuming there are no errors, run these two commands:

```
chkconfig ldap on
service ldap start
```

These tell Fedora to start OpenLDAP each time you boot up, and to start it right now.

The final configuration step is to tell Fedora which DN it should use if none is specified. This is done by going to System Settings and selecting Authentication. In the dialog box that appears, check Enable LDAP Support in both the User Information tab and Authentication tab. Next, click the Configure LDAP button, enter your DCs (for example, dc=hudzilla,dc=org) for the LDAP Search Base DN, and enter 127.0.0.1 for the LDAP Server. Click OK and then click OK again.

27

> **TIP**
>
> Checking Enable LDAP Support does not actually change the way in which your users log in. Behind the scenes, this forces Fedora to set up the ldap.conf file in /etc/openldap so that LDAP searches that do not specify a base search start point are directed to your DC.

Populating Your Directory

With LDAP installed, configured, and running, you can now fill the directory with people. This involves yet more LDAP acronyms and is by no means an easy task, so do not worry if you have to reread this several times before it sinks in.

First, create the file base.ldif. You will use this to define the base components of your system: the domain and the address book. LDIF is an acronym standing for LDAP Data Interchange Format, and it is the standard way of recording user data for insertion into an LDAP directory. Here are the contents we used for our example:

```
dn: dc=hudzilla,dc=org
objectClass: top
objectClass: dcObject
objectClass: organization
dc: hudzilla
o: Hudzilla Dot Org

dn: ou=People,dc=hudzilla,dc=org
ou: People
objectClass: top
objectClass: organizationalUnit
```

This file contains two individual entities, separated by an empty line. The first is our organization, hudzilla.org. The dn lines you know already, as they define each object uniquely in the scope of the directory. The objectClass directive specifies which attributes should be allowed for this entity and which attributes should be required. In this case, we use it to set the DC to hudzilla and to set o (the name of the organization) to Hudzilla Dot Org.

The next entity defines the address book, People, in which all our people will be stored. It is defined as an organizational unit, which is what the ou stands for. An *organizational unit* really is just an arbitrary partition of your company. You might have OUs for marketing, accounting, and management, for example.

You need to customize the file to your own requirements. Specifically, change the DCs to those you specified in your slapd.conf.

Next, create and edit a new file called people.ldif. This is where you will define entries for your address book, also using LDIF. Here are the people we used in our example:

```
dn: cn=Paul Hudson,ou=People,dc=hudzilla,dc=org
objectClass: inetOrgPerson
cn: Paul Hudson
cn: Hudzilla
mail: paul@hudzilla.org
jpegPhoto:< file:///home/paul/paulhudson.jpg
sn: Hudson
```

```
dn: cn=Andrew Hudson,ou=People,dc=hudzilla,dc=org
objectClass: inetOrgPerson
cn: Andrew Hudson
cn: IzAndy
mail: andrew@hudzilla.org
sn: Hudson

dn: cn=Nick Veitch,ou=People,dc=hudzilla,dc=org
objectClass: inetOrgPerson
cn: Nick Veitch
cn: CrackAttackKing
mail: nick@hudzilla.org
sn: Veitch
```

There are three entries there, again separated by empty lines. Each person has a DN that is made up of his common name (CN), organizational unit (OU), and domain components (DCs). He also has an `objectClass` definition, `inetOrgPerson`, which gives him standard attributes like an email address, a photograph, and a telephone number. Entities of type `inetOrgPerson` must have a CN and an SN (surname) so you will see them in this code.

Note also that each person has two common names: his actual name and a nickname. Not all LDAP clients support more than one CN, but there is no harm in having several as long as the main one comes first and is listed in the DN.

> **TIP**
>
> Having multiple key/value pairs, like multiple CNs, is one of the defining features of LDAP. In today's interconnected world, few people can be defined using a single set of attributes because they have home phone numbers, work phone numbers, cell phone numbers, pager numbers, plus several email addresses, and potentially even a selection of offices where they hot desk. Using multiple CNs and other attributes allows you to properly record these complex scenarios.

The `jpegPhoto` attribute for the first entity has very particular syntax. Immediately after the colon you use an opening angle bracket (<) followed by a space and then the location of the person's picture. Because the picture is local, it is prefixed with `file://`. It is in `/home/paul/paulhudson.jpg`, so the whole URL is `file:///home/paul/paulhudson.jpg`.

After you have edited the file to include the people in your organization, save it and close the editor. As root, issue these two commands:

```
ldapadd -x -W -D "cn=root,dc=hudzilla,dc=org" -f base.ldif
ldapadd -x -W -D "cn=root,dc=hudzilla,dc=org" -f people.ldif
```

The `ldapadd` command is used to convert LDIF into live directory content and, most importantly, can be executed while your LDAP server is running. The `-x` parameter means to use only basic authentication, which means you need to supply the root username and password. `-W` means to prompt you for the password. `-D` lets you specify a DN for your

27

username, and immediately after the -D, we specify the root DN as set earlier in `slapd.conf`. Finally, -f means to use the LDIF from the following file.

When you run them, you are prompted for the root password you set earlier. Upon entering it, you should see confirmation messages as your entries are added, like this:

```
adding new entry "cn=Paul Hudson,ou=People,dc=hudzilla,dc=org"
```

If you see an error such as `ldap_bind: Can't contact LDAP server (-1)`, you need to start the LDAP server by typing **service ldap start**. The most likely sources of other errors are typing errors. LDIF is a precise format, even down to its use of whitespace.

To test that the directory has been populated and that your configuration settings are correct, run this command:

```
ldapsearch -x 'objectclass=*'
```

The `ldapsearch` command does what you might expect: It queries the LDAP directory from the command line. Again, -x means to use simple authentication, although in this situation you do not need to provide any credentials because you are only reading from the directory. The `objectclass=*` search specifies to return any entry of any `objectclass`, so the search will return all the entries in your directory.

You can amend the search to be more specific, for example

```
ldapsearch -x 'cn=Ni*'
```

This returns all people with a common name that begins with *Ni*. If you get results for your searches, you are ready to configure your clients.

> **TIP**
>
> OpenLDAP needs specific permissions for its files. The `/var/lib/ldap` directory should be owned by user `ldap` and group `ldap`, with permissions `600`. If you experience problems, try running `chmod 600 /var/lib/ldap`.

Configuring Clients

Although Fedora comes with a selection of email clients, there is not enough room here to cover them all. So, we will discuss the two most frequently used clients: Evolution, the default, and Thunderbird. Both are powerful messaging solutions and so both work well with LDAP. Of the two, Thunderbird seems to be the easier to configure. We have had various problems with Evolution in the past in situations where Thunderbird has worked the first time.

Evolution

To configure Evolution for LDAP, click the arrow next to the New button and select Address Book. A new screen appears, the first option of which prompts you for the type of address book to create. Select On LDAP Servers.

For Name, just enter `Address book`, and for Server, enter the IP address of your LDAP server (or `127.0.0.1` if you are working on the server), as shown in Figure 27.1. Leave the port as 389, which is the default for `slapd`. Switch to the Details tab, and set Search Base to be the DN for your address book—for example, `ou=People,dc=hudzilla,dc=org`. Set Search Scope to be Sub so that Evolution will perform a comprehensive search. To finish, click Add Address Book.

Although Evolution is now configured to use your directory, it will not use it for email address autocompletion just yet. To enable that, go to the Tools menu and click Settings. From the options that appear on the left, click Autocompletion and select your LDAP server from the list. Click Close and then create a new email message. If everything has worked, typing part of someone's name should pop up a box with LDAP matches.

FIGURE 27.1   Configuring Evolution to use LDAP for addresses is easy for anonymous connections.

Thunderbird

Thunderbird is a little easier to configure than Evolution and tends to work better, particularly with entries that have multiple CNs. To enable autocompletion, go to the Tools menu, click Options, and then select Composition from the tab on the left.

Check the Directory Server box and click the Edit Directories button to its right. From the dialog box that appears, click Add to add a new directory. You can give it any name you want because this is merely for display purposes. As shown in Figure 27.2, set the Hostname field to be the IP address of your LDAP server (or 127.0.0.1 if you are working on the server). Set the Base DN to be the DN for your address book (for instance, ou=People,dc=hudzilla,dc=org), and leave the port number as 389. Click OK three times to get back to the main interface.

Now, click Write to create a new email message, and type the first few letters of a user in the To box. If everything has worked, Thunderbird should pop up a box with LDAP matches.

FIGURE 27.2   Thunderbird's options are buried deeper than Evolution's, but it does allow you to download the LDAP directory for offline use.

Administration

After you have your LDAP server and clients set up, they require little maintenance until something changes externally. Specifically, if someone in your directory changes jobs, changes her phone number, gets married (changing her surname), quits, or so forth, you need to be able to update your directory to reflect the change.

OpenLDAP comes with a selection of tools for manipulating directories, of which you have already met ldapadd. To add to that, you can use ldapdelete for deleting entries in your directory and ldapmodify for modifying entries. Both are hard to use but come with moderate amounts of documentation in their man pages.

A much smarter option is to use phpLDAPadmin, which is a GPLed LDAP administration tool that allows you to add and modify entries entirely through your web browser. You can learn more and download the product to try at http://www.phpldapadmin.com.

Reference

- http://www.openldap.org—The home page of the OpenLDAP project where you can download the latest version of the software and meet other users.

- http://www.kingsmountain.com/ldapRoadmap.shtml—A great set of links and resources across the Internet that explain various aspects of LDAP and its parent protocol, X500.

- http://ldap.perl.org/—The home of the Perl library for interacting with LDAP provides comprehensive documentation to get you started.

- http://www.ldapguru.com/—A gigantic portal for LDAP administrators around the world. From forums dedicated to LDAP to jobs specifically for LDAP admins, this site could very well be all you need.

The definitive book on LDAP is *LDAP System Administration* (O'Reilly), ISBN: 1-56592-491-6. It is an absolute must for the bookshelf of any Linux LDAP administrator. For more general reading, try *LDAP Directories Explained* (Addison-Wesley), ISBN: 0-201-78792-X. It has a much stronger focus on Microsoft's Active Directory LDAP implementation, though.

27

News Servers and Mailing Lists

There are many advantages to hosting your own local news server. If you have a number of clients on your network who need frequent access to a central site of information or you need to provide employees with a central collaboration site or forum, news servers can provide a simple way of getting information to them in a public and easy-to-use way.

News servers are notoriously difficult to configure and deploy, but follow the information in this chapter and you will be able to avoid many of the problems that are frequently encountered.

Types of News Servers

The InterNetNews (INN) package is the most popular news server software on Unix servers. The Internet Software Consortium (ISC) currently maintains it, along with the INN website (http://www.isc.org/products/INN/). The Fedora Core Linux distribution includes the INN package as a standard RPM file.

The following sections describe how the INN package works, how to install it, and how to configure it as a local news server. Because some users consider news servers to offer the greatest server-configuration challenges, these sections are quite detailed. The information you learn here will help you avoid some of the common pitfalls while configuring your local news server.

Unless you are an Internet service provider (ISP) or are planning to provide news services to a large group of people, you will likely not be setting up or administering a news server for your own use.

You can use a number of methods to implement a news server on a network, and the way you intend to use the news server determines how you must configure it. The following sections describe three of the most popular types of news servers on local networks: full newsfeed servers, leaf node servers, and local news servers.

Full Newsfeed Servers

A *full newsfeed news server* receives all the available Usenet newsgroup postings from an upstream news server (a large, commercial server). Because it receives all the newsgroups, it can serve as an upstream news server for other sites and provide newsfeeds to other servers. The other servers themselves might or might not subscribe to all the newsgroups. Besides providing newsfeeds for other sites, the full newsfeed news server can also support newsreader clients that connect to the news server to read and post articles to newsgroups.

Each news server receives newsfeeds and forwards postings to one or more remote news servers. The full newsfeed server must have enough storage capacity to maintain the newsfeeds for all the newsgroups it services. If the remote news servers don't connect to download their newsfeeds on a daily basis, the newsfeed server must be capable of maintaining all the newsfeeds for the intervening days. This can require a very large amount of data storage capacity beyond the capabilities of systems that are common among home users and many businesses.

Leaf Node Servers

A *leaf node news server* receives newsfeeds only from upstream news servers: It doesn't feed other news servers. This is the most common configuration for corporate news servers. Because the leaf node server doesn't have to feed other news servers, it doesn't have to retrieve all the newsgroups from its upstream newsfeed. You can pick and choose which newsgroups the news server retrieves from the newsfeed. The main role of the leaf node news server is to provide news services to newsreader clients.

The leaf node does, however, have to maintain a system for users to connect to the news server to read and post messages. This is often done using Unix, Microsoft Windows, or Apple Macintosh workstation software. Each client must connect to the leaf node to download articles from specific newsgroups, and it must upload postings made to the newsgroups. The leaf node must be capable of forwarding new postings to the newsfeed server.

Local News Servers

An organization that doesn't want to participate in the worldwide Usenet newsgroups still might want to use Usenet software to create its own news server to handle internal communications within the organization. Usually these communications need to remain private to the organization and don't need to be sent to all the Usenet newsfeed hosts around the world. This is likely the most common use of a news server you might be asked to configure.

Two methods are used to implement a local news server. An organization might create a standalone news server that doesn't receive any newsfeeds from Usenet servers. The server contains only local newsgroups that are used for internal corporate communications. Alternatively, on a Usenet news server you can create local newsgroups that aren't forwarded through any newsfeeds in the Usenet system. This enables organizations to create their own local newsgroups that their employees can participate in without sharing their information with the rest of the world.

Thus, local newsgroups can be created on news servers that either aren't connected to the Usenet network or that are connected to the Usenet network but do not forward the local groups to their upstream newsfeeds. Any postings to the local newsgroups appear only on the local news server. The Usenet news servers enable clients to post articles to both the local and Usenet newsgroups. However, only the articles posted to Usenet newsgroups are forwarded to the upstream news server. The local articles remain on only the local news server.

The INN Package and Configuration Files

The INN package (which is formed around the `innd` daemon) contains many executable programs and configuration files that enable the Fedora Core Linux server to work as a network news server. The standard INN RPM package contains all the files necessary for the installation. Table 28.1 describes some of the INN programs included in the distribution, in the order in which you'll find them in the file.

TABLE 28.1 INN Package Program Files

Program File	Description
ctlinnd	Allows the user to manually send control messages to the `innd` program
getlist	Obtains a list of newsgroups from a news server
grephistory	Queries the history database files for a specific message ID value and returns the record information
inncheck	Examines INN configuration files and databases
innconfval	Prints the values of parameters that are specified in the `innd` command line
innd	Handles all incoming newsfeeds and spawns INN programs as necessary
inndstart	Starts the `innd` daemon from the news user ID
innreport	Summarizes INN log files into readable reports
innstat	Prints a snapshot of the current status of the INN system
innwatch	Monitors the running INN system and, if necessary, throttles the newsfeeds to help reduce the load on the news server
mailpost	Manually sends a mail message into a specified newsgroup
makedbz	Creates binary indexed database files from the history file
makehistory	Creates a text history file of message IDs seen by the news server
news.daily	Runs as a cron job to perform daily maintenance on the news server
nnrpd	Communicates with newsreaders via the `innd` daemon
nntpget	Connects to a remote news server and retrieves articles that are specified on the standard input
nntpsend	Connects to a remote news server and posts articles to newsgroups

28

TABLE 28.1   Continued

Program File	Description
ovdb_recover	Attempts to repair a damaged INN database file
ovdb_upgrade	Attempts to upgrade an existing INN database file
prunehistory	Removes specific filenames from the history file
pullnews	Retrieves newsgroup articles from one news server and forwards them to another news server
rnews	Receives newsgroup articles from a news server by using a UUCP connection
scanlogs	Summarizes information in the INN log files and performs general cleaning and rotating of the log files
sm	Provides a command-line interface to the article storage manager

As you can see in Table 28.1, a number of the INN programs are used to help facilitate the news process on the server. The INN package also contains a number of configuration files that define how articles are handled. Table 28.2 lists and describes these files.

TABLE 28.2   INN Package Configuration Files

Configuration File	Description
control.ctl	Specifies how control messages are handled
expire.ctl	Specifies how articles are expired
incoming.conf	Specifies addresses and authentication information for servers that send newsfeeds to your news server
inn.conf	Acts as the primary general configuration file for the innd program
innfeed.conf	Specifies parameters for the incoming newsfeed handler
innwatch.ctl	Determines how the innwatch program monitors the INN system
moderators	Specifies email addresses for moderators of moderated newsgroups
motd.news	Specifies which information is posted to newsreaders when a list motd command is sent
newsfeeds	Specifies which newsgroups are fed to other news servers from this news server
nnrpd.track	Specifies newsreaders or servers that should have their activity recorded during an NNTP session
nntpsend.ctl	Specifies remote news servers that your news server will feed articles to in batch mode
passwd.nntp	Specifies passwords used to connect to remote news servers
readers.conf	Specifies authorized remote newsreader addresses and newsgroup permissions
sasl.conf	Specifies file locations for the encryption keys used for the SASL configuration
storage.conf	Specifies the storage method used for specific newsgroup articles
subscriptions	Specifies a list of newsgroups to which newsreaders can subscribe

Don't let the long list of configuration files in Table 28.2 worry you; most of the parameters defined in the configuration files work fine with their default settings. Typically, you need to make only a few changes to configure the INN news server to work in your particular network news environment.

Installing the INN Package

To work in your particular network news environment, Fedora uses two separate RPM files to install the INN package. The first package, simply called `inn`, installs the configuration and application files needed for the INN package to work on the system. The second package, called `inn-devel`, is used to install INN header files some external newsreader programs use to work with `innd`. You do not have to install the `inn-devel` package for INN, but if you are using other newsreader packages on the server, you should install it. The default INN installation also installs the `inews` and `cleanfeed` packages, which are used to forward articles to the server and filter out spam.

Configuring innd

After all the INN files are installed, you must begin the task of setting the proper parameters in the configuration files (installed in `/etc/news`) before you attempt to start the `innd` program. When you modify the INN configuration files, you must ensure that you are logged in as the news user or use the `su` command to become the news user (note that there is no password for the news user). If the ownership or permissions of any of the INN configuration files change, the `innd` package won't start.

Although there are many configuration files, only a handful of files need to be modified for a simple news server. The following sections describe common changes that must be made to the configuration files to make the news server operational.

The `inn.conf` File

The `/etc/news/inn.conf` file is the heart of the `innd` configuration. It defines the core features of the news server operation. Each parameter is listed on a separate line, using the following format:

```
parameter: value
```

Many parameters are defined in the `inn.conf` file, but fortunately most of them work just fine with their default values. Table 28.3 shows the parameters that should be changed in the `innd.conf` file to represent your news server environment.

TABLE 28.3   `innd.conf` Configuration Parameters

Parameter	Description
`mta`	The command used to invoke the system MTA mailer. The `%s` variable is included to replace the recipient address in the command line. If you have installed the default Fedora Core Sendmail package, `mta` should be set correctly.
`organization`	A text description of your organization. This value is used in the article header lines for all articles posted from your site, so be careful to enter accurate information.
`ovmethod`	The storage method used for the article indexes. The default, `tradindexed`, is usually fine for small sites but might not be fast enough for large sites.

28

TABLE 28.3   Continued

Parameter	Description
pathhost	The name of the host to place in the Path: article header line. This should represent your news server hostname. In the default file, it is shown as localhost and is commented out.
pathnews	The path to the news binaries, which is already set for your Fedora Core system.
domain	The complete domain name of your Internet domain. This parameter is blank until you fill it.
mailcmd	The command innd uses to send mail messages. Usually this should be the innmail program.
server	The name of a default NNTP server.
maxconnections	The maximum number of incoming NNTP connections your news server will support, based on your network's available bandwidth.
fromhost	The domain the INN system uses to construct email addresses. It should be set to your local system address.
moderatormailer	The email address to which messages posted to moderated newsgroups are sent if there is no corresponding entry in the moderator's file.
status	How frequently (in seconds) innd should create a status report. A value of 0 disables this feature. (A value of 0 is not recommended if you want to receive status reports, but it's the default Fedora Core setting. Set whatever you feel comfortable with.)
timer	How frequently (in seconds) innd should report performance statistics to the log files. A value of 0 disables this feature. (A value of 0 is not recommended, but it's the default Fedora Core setting. Set whatever you feel comfortable with.)

The inn.conf file is a text file you can modify by using any standard text editor. At a minimum, you should ensure that the organization, domain, mailcmd, mta, server, and fromhost parameters are specified. Listing 28.1 shows sample inn.conf file entries for a test server.

LISTING 28.1   Sample inn.conf Configuration File Entries

```
mta:              /usr/sbin/sendmail -oi -oem %s
organization:     Hoyt's MaximumNews
ovmethod:         tradindexed
domain:           maximumhoyt.com
mailcmd:          /usr/bin/innmail
status:           3600
timer:             3600
```

The sample configuration shown uses the standard Sendmail MTA for the mailer and the traditional indexed method for overview databases, and it creates new status reports every hour.

The `incoming.conf` File

The `/etc/news/incoming.conf` file is used to define the source from which the news server receives its newsfeeds. If you are building a standalone news server that doesn't receive newsfeeds, this file is still important because it also specifies the local address of the news server.

The `incoming.conf` file contains three types of data:

- Peer news server definitions
- Groups of news server definitions
- Parameter value definitions

Parameters can be defined globally, within peer definitions, and within group definitions. As you would expect, parameters defined globally apply to all peers and groups defined in the configuration file. Parameters defined within group definitions apply to all peers within the group definition and override any global definitions of the same parameter. Finally, parameters defined within peer definitions apply only to the peer, and they override any group or global definitions of the same parameter.

Ten parameters can be used to define the connection with a remote news server. In the case of a local news server only, you would not be accessing any incoming feeds, so the `incoming.conf` file can remain unmodified.

In addition, the `innfeed.conf` file that defines communication with peer news servers can remain unmodified, as can the `incoming.conf` file because no newsfeeds will be received.

The `storage.conf` File

Another important configuration file used by innd is the `/etc/news/storage.conf` file. This file tells the innd program how to store newsgroup articles on the news server. Fedora Core suggests two methods for storing articles on the news server:

- **Time hashed spool**—The time hashed spool method (`timehash`) stores articles on the news server by creating directories based on the arrival time of the articles. This creates more directories with fewer articles in each directory. Using `timehash` requires additional overhead for reading articles, however, because it is more difficult for the news server to find an individual article stored in this method.

- **Cyclic buffer spool**—The cyclic spool (`cnfs`) method speeds up the process of storing articles by using a preconfigured file buffer. As articles are received, they are placed in a preconfigured file of a set size. This greatly speeds up processing because no new files are created as articles are received.

Using `cnfs` does have a drawback, however. The buffer files are created at a set size, so when the articles fill up a buffer file, the file is overwritten, starting from the beginning. This method, therefore, forces an automatic expiration of articles on the news server. Although using a set buffer file size prevents the server from running out of disk space, it can cause premature article expiration, depending on the size of the buffer file. Most news administrators who use this method learn by trial and error the buffer file size necessary to handle the standard news traffic load at their sites.

> **CAUTION**
>
> If a newsgroup is not covered by a specific storage method, INN doesn't store the articles received for that newsgroup, and it produces an error message for each article. This can have a devastating effect on the news server. For a simple news server, it is best to select a single method of storage and configure the `storage.conf` file to use that method for all the newsgroups.

By default, the Fedora Core `/etc/news/storage.conf` file doesn't define any default storage method, but it is fully configured and commented out. You must define at least one method to use for INN to work properly; to do so, you can simply uncomment the desired section.

The `readers.conf` File

You use the `/etc/news/readers.conf` configuration file to define permissions for newsreaders that use your news server. If you are allowing your local users to connect to your news server to read articles, you must configure the `readers.conf` file to support them.

The `readers.conf` file consists of the following three types of data:

- An authentication definition
- An access definition
- Parameters and values

The authentication definition defines categories of users who will be accessing your news server. You can create several categories of users, based on various factors, such as remote address, newsgroups accessed, and type of authentication method used. The syntax of the authentication section is as follows:

```
auth name {
        hosts: hostlist
        auth: auth-program
        res: res-program
        default: defuser
        default-domain: defdomain
    }
```

The `name` value is used as a label to uniquely identify the authentication definition. The authentication definition uses parameters and values to identify its actions. The `hosts` parameter uses the `hostlist` value to identify individual remote hosts covered by the authentication definition. These can be listed by using either hostnames or numeric IP addresses, along with matching wildcard characters.

You can use the res parameter to specify an authentication program used to authenticate the connection based on its network information. Alternatively, you can use the auth parameter to specify an authentication program that can authenticate the connection by using a user ID/password pair. If you are interested in authenticating remote news servers, you should consult the INN documentation because it is a somewhat complicated process.

The access definition defines categories of access restrictions and permissions for groups of newsreaders. The syntax of the access definition is as follows:

```
access name {
            users: identity-wildcat
            newsgroups: group-wildcat
            access: permissions
}
```

The name value must match a corresponding authentication definition. The parameters defined in the access definition apply only to the hosts defined in the corresponding authentication definition. The users parameter limits the access rules to the specific set of users listed in the value. If the users parameter isn't present, the access rules apply to all users. The newsgroups parameter defines to which newsgroups the group has access, and the access parameter defines which access privileges the group has. The privileges are defined as follows:

- R—Read-only access is allowed.

- P—Posting articles is allowed.

- A—Posting approved articles is allowed (using a moderator).

- N—The NEWNEWS command is allowed.

- L—The group is allowed to post to newsgroups that are set to disallow local posting.

Here is a sample readers.conf file that allows all local newsreaders to read and post articles to all newsgroups:

```
# readers.conf
auth "localhost"
    hosts: "localhost, 127.0.0.1, 192.168.1.100, stdin"
    default: "<localhost>"
}

access "localhost" {
    users: "<localhost>"
    newsgroups: "*"
    access: RPA
}
```

28

```
auth "localnet" {
      hosts: "192.168.*"
      default: "<user>"
      default-domain: "isp.net"
      }

access "localnet" {
       users: "*@isp.net"
       newsgroups:  "*"
       access: "RP
}
```

The sample `readers.conf` file shown here defines two separate groups of users. The first group, called `localhost`, enables the local host, address `127.0.0.1`, address `192.168.1.100` (the local host's network address), and any connection using the standard input to connect to the news server. The unmodified `readers.conf` file provided by Fedora Core allows access only from users on the local host.

The second group defines any client located on the `192.168.` network; it allows both reading and posting of all newsgroups to any client on the network. You can adjust these addresses as necessary for your network.

The `active` and `newsgroups` Files

The `active` and `newsgroups` files, although not specifically identified as configuration files, are crucial to the operation of the news server. These files control which newsgroups your news server can handle. Each newsgroup handled by the news server must have an entry in both the `active` and `newsgroups` files. Both of these files are located in the `/var/lib/news` directory when they are installed by using the Fedora Core RPM package.

The syntax of the active file is as follows:

```
newsgroup      first     last     post
```

Each newsgroup handled by the news server is defined on a separate line in the active file. The default Fedora Core Linux INN configuration supplies a skeleton active file that defines several special newsgroups:

```
control 0000000000 0000000001 n
control.cancel 0000000000 0000000001 n
control.checkgroups 0000000000 0000000001 n
control.newgroup 0000000000 0000000001 n
control.rmgroup 0000000000 0000000001 n
junk 0000000000 0000000001 n
```

This default file is fine if you are running a standalone news server. The first field of this file defines the newsgroup name. The second and third fields define the first and last article sequence numbers. The final field defines whether posting is allowed for the news-group on the news server. The default newsgroups are set to n to prevent posting.

The control and control.cancel newsgroups are used to receive NNTP control articles for performing maintenance on the news server. As remote sites create new newsgroups and delete old ones, control articles are sent to the news servers to perform these tasks. The control series of newsgroups handles these articles. Also, the junk newsgroup is created to handle articles that have not been posted correctly and have no place to go.

The newsgroups file is parallel with the active file; it must contain the same newsgroup definitions as the active file.

The history Files

Also in the /var/lib/news directory are the INN history files. These files are used to keep a running index of each article posted to each newsgroup. It is crucial that these files not be tampered with because, if they get out of sync with the actual newsgroup articles, the news server has problems retrieving articles.

The history files have two separate parts: a text history file and a set of binary index files that are created by using a database program such as the common Berkeley db package. You must create both sets of files before you can start the innd daemon.

You use the /var/lib/news/bin/makehistory command to create the text history file based on the current newsgroup articles on the server (which should be none). Fedora Core provides a blank history file.

After you create the text history file, you create the binary index files. You use the /usr/lin/news/bin/makedbz program to convert the text history file into the binary index files. The makedbz -i command creates the following three separate binary files:

- history.n.dir
- history.n.index
- history.n.hash

You should rename these files to the standard history filenames (history.dir, history.index, and history.pag) so the innd program can recognize them. After the history files have been created, you are finally ready to start the news server.

Running innd

Using the /var/lib/news/bin/inndstart program is the best way to start the innd daemon, which in turn starts other INN package programs. The inndstart program must be run from the news user ID. It starts the innd program as well as the controlchan program in background mode.

The innd program listens for newsfeeds and newsreader requests on the NNTP TCP port. If a remote newsreader establishes a connection, the innd program spawns the active program to authenticate the remote connection and handle the newsreader requests. If the incoming articles are control articles, they are passed to the `controlchan` program for processing.

Fedora Core has thoughtfully configured the SystemV files that are necessary for starting the news server; you can use (in an appropriate way) `chkconfig`, `nytsysv`, `service`, or `system-config-services` to start the server. (See Chapter 14, "Automating Tasks," for details.) Here is an example:

```
# /sbin/service inn start
```

When the `innd` program is running, you can control it by using the `ctlinnd` program, with the following syntax:

```
ctlinnd [ -h ] [ -s ] [ -t timeout ] command [ argument...]
```

The `-s` option suppresses any output from the `ctlinnd` command. This option is often used in batch programs. The `-t` option specifies how long to wait for a response from the server (in seconds). If you are connecting to a server across a slow link or are connecting to a slow server, you can increase the value of `timeout`.

The command parameters define which actions the `ctlinnd` program should take with the `innd` news server. The `-h` option prints a summary of all the available command parameters that can be used with `ctlinnd`. For now, you can use the `newgroup` command to create a new local newsgroup that newsreaders can use to read and send messages:

```
$ ctlinnd newgroup local.linux.group y hoyt@maximumhoyt.com
```

The newgroup command uses three parameters:

- The name of the new newsgroup
- A flag to define which type of newsgroup to create (y stands for a regular open group and m stands for a moderated group)
- An email address for the maintainer of the new newsgroup

The `ctlinnd` program should be run from the news user ID. If the command is successful, it returns a simple OK message. You can use the `ctlinnd` command to check whether the new newsgroup has been added to the news server.

Filtering Spam with the `cleanfeed` Package

One problem that has plagued the Usenet newsgroup system is the proliferation of spam Usenet messages. Spam providers often attempt to post their messages to newsgroups to force messages to a large, captive audience. One of the most effective methods for blocking spam messages from being posted to a newsgroup is to use the `cleanfeed` package. The `cleanfeed` package is a Perl script that filters out spam before it hits your news server. You can configure this software by editing its configuration file, `cleanfeed.conf`, under the `/etc/news` directory.

The newsgroup example offered in this chapter is designed for a closed system and doesn't need to filter spam. But you can learn more about `cleanfeed` in the FAQ found at http://www.exit109.com/~jeremy/news/cleanfeed/.

Relevant Fedora Core Linux Commands

You can use the following commands to manage newsgroups and other collaborative communication processes in Fedora Core Linux:

`emacs`—The premier editing environment that can also be used to read Usenet news

`innd`—The INN daemon and its plethora of associated commands

`knode`—KDE's graphical Usenet newsreading client

`mozilla`—The mail and newsgroups component of the Open Source Mozilla browser

`pan`—An easy-to-use Usenet newsreader for GNOME

`pine`—A text-based mail client that can also read Usenet news

`slrn`—A text-based graphical Usenet newsreader

Reference

- http://www.faqs.org/rfcs/rfc977.html—RFC 977, which is the NNTP protocol

- http://www.faqs.org/rfcs/rfc1036.html—RFC 1036, which is the format of news messages

- http://www.list.org/—The home page for the Mailman mailing list manager

28

PART V

Programming Linux

IN THIS PART

Using Perl

Perl (Practical Extraction and Report Language) is a powerful scripting tool you can use to manage files, create reports, edit text, and perform many other tasks when using Linux. Perl is included with Fedora and could be considered an integral part of the distribution, as Fedora depends on Perl for many types of software services, logging activities, and software tools. If you do a full install from this book's CD-ROMs, you will find nearly 150 software tools written in Perl installed under the /usr/bin and /usr/sbin directories.

Following the birth of the World Wide Web in the early 1990s, Perl took off as the language of choice for Common Gateway Interface (CGI) programming, which is used to extend features of websites and make the Web more than just a resource for document publishing. With the recent interest in the Open Source movement, Perl has gotten almost as much press as Linux, although many experienced Linux users have been using Perl for quite some time.

Perl is perhaps not the easiest of programming languages to learn because it is designed for flexibility. This chapter shows how to create and use a Perl script on your system. You'll see what a Perl program looks like, how the language is structured, where you can find modules of prewritten code to help you write your own Perl scripts, and several examples of Perl used to perform a few common functions on a computer system.

This chapter also includes additional sources of information about Perl; consult the listing of websites, books, and online periodicals at the end of this chapter. The quest toward becoming a Perl hacker need not be long and arduous, but you will benefit from the generous help offered by other members of the Perl developer community. Perl works quickly and efficiently on a Linux system, but learning how to create good Perl programs will take some effort.

Using Perl with Linux

If you are familiar with some other programming languages, chances are you can write functional Perl code. Perl contains the best features of C, BASIC, and a variety of other programming languages—with a hearty dollop of awk, sed, and shell scripting thrown in. Perl was created in the mid-1980s by Larry Wall to overcome file-handling limitations of the awk command. Wall, a developer already responsible for a number of important Unix utilities, such as the patch command (used to easily update and insert changes into a program's source code), claims that Perl really stands for "Pathologically Eclectic Rubbish Lister."

Although originally designed as a data extraction and report generation language, Perl appeals to many Unix and Linux system administrators because it can be used to create new software tools that fill a gap between the capabilities of shell scripts and compiled C programs. Another advantage of Perl over other Unix tools is that it can process and extract data from binary files (those without line terminators or that contain binary data, such as some databases or compiled programs), whereas sed and awk cannot.

> **NOTE**
>
> In Perl, "there is more than one way to do it." This is the unofficial motto of Perl, and it comes up so often that it is usually abbreviated as TIMTOWTDI.

Perl interprets its language in text files known as Perl *scripts*. Although some consider Perl an interpreter, the programs are actually compiled in memory and then run by Perl's internal interpreter. You can use Perl at your shell's command line to execute one-line Perl programs, but most often the programs (usually ending in .pl) are run as a command. These programs will generally work on any computer platform, as Perl has been ported to just about every operating system. Perl is available by default when you install Fedora, and you will find its RPM files on the CD-ROMs included with this book.

Perl programs are used to support a number of Fedora services, such as system logging. For example, the logwatch.pl program is run every morning at 4:20 a.m. by the crond (scheduling) daemon on your system. The 690-line Perl program physically resides under the /etc/log.d/scripts/ directory, but is launched as the symbolic link named 00-logwatch under the /etc/cron.daily directory. This program (which can be configured by editing the configuration file logwatch.conf) generates and emails a short report after analyzing selected system logs.

Other Fedora services supported by Perl include

- Amanda for local and network backups
- Fax spooling with the faxrunqd program
- Printing supported by Perl document filtering programs
- Hardware sensor monitoring setup using the sensors-detect Perl program

Perl Versions

As of this writing, the current production version of Perl is 5.8.6 (which is Perl version 5 point 8, patch level 6).

You can download the code from http://www.perl.com/ and build Perl yourself from source. You will occasionally find updated versions in RPM format for Fedora, which can be installed by updating your system. See Chapter 7, "Managing Software and System Resources," to see how to quickly get a list of available updates for Fedora.

You can determine what version of Perl you installed by typing **perl -v** at a shell prompt. If you are installing the latest Fedora distribution, you should have the latest version of Perl.

A Simple Perl Program

This section introduces a very simple sample Perl program to get you started using Perl. Although trivial for experienced Perl hackers, a short example is necessary for new users who want to learn more about Perl.

> **NOTE**
>
> You will also find a Perl program named perlcc installed with Perl. This program can be used as a compiler to build executable commands out of Perl! The program can also be used to generate experimental C source code for use by the gcc compiler system (see Chapter 32, "C/C++ Programming Tools for Fedora").

To introduce you to the absolute basics of Perl programming, Listing 29.1 illustrates a simple Perl program that prints a short message.

LISTING 29.1   A Simple Perl Program

```
#!/usr/bin/perl
print "Look at all the camels!\n";
```

That's the entire program. Type that in and save it to a file called trivial.pl. Then make the file executable using the chmod command (see the following sidebar) and run it at the command prompt.

> **Command-Line Error**
>
> If you get the message bash: trivial.pl: command not found or bash: ./trivial.pl: Permission denied, it means that you either typed the command line incorrectly or forgot to make trivial.pl executable (with the chmod command):
>
> ```
> $ chmod +x trivial.pl
> ```

You can force the command to execute in the current directory as follows:

```
$ ./trivial.pl
```

Or you can use Perl to run the program like this:

```
$ perl trivial.pl
```

The sample program in the listing is a two-line Perl program. Typing in the program and running it (using Perl or making the program executable) shows how to create your first Perl program, a process duplicated by Linux users around the world every day!

> **NOTE**
>
> #! is often pronounced *she-bang,* which is short for *sharp* (the musicians name for the # character), and *bang,* which is another name for the exclamation point. The technical name of the # character is the *octothorpe,* a word coined by Bell Labs engineer Don Macpherson in the early 1960s. Another pronunciation of #! is *pound-bang* because most people refer to the # character on a telephone keypad as pound. This notation is also used in shell scripts. See Chapter 14, "Automating Tasks," for more information about writing shell scripts.

The #! line is technically not part of the Perl code at all. The # character indicates that the rest of the screen line is a comment. The comment is a message to the shell, telling it where it should go to find the executable to run this program. The interpreter ignores the comment line. Using a comment character is standard practice in shell programming.

Exceptions to this practice include when the # character is in a quoted string and when it is being used as the delimiter in a regular expression. Comments are useful to document your scripts, like this:

```
#!/usr/bin/perl
# a simple example to print a greeting
print "hello there\n";
```

A block of code, such as what might appear inside a loop or a branch of a conditional statement, is indicated with curly braces ({}). For example, here's an infinite loop:

```
#!/usr/bin/perl
# a block of code to print a greeting forever
while (1) {
        print "hello there\n";
};
```

Perl statements are terminated with a semicolon. A Perl statement can extend over several actual screen lines because Perl is not concerned about whitespace.

The second line of the simple program prints the text enclosed in quotation marks. \n is the escape sequence for a newline character.

Using the `perldoc` and `man` commands is an easy way to get more information about the version of Perl installed on your system. To learn how to use the `perldoc` command, enter the following:

```
$ perldoc perldoc
```

To get introductory information on Perl, you can use either of these commands:

```
$ perldoc perl
$ man perl
```

For an overview or table of contents of Perl's documentation, use the `perldoc` command like this:

```
$ perldoc perltoc
```

The documentation is extensive and well-organized. Perl includes a number of standard Linux manual pages as brief guides to its capabilities, but perhaps the best way to learn more about Perl is to read its *perlfunc* document, which lists all the available Perl functions and their usage. You can view this document by using the `perldoc` script and typing `perldoc perlfunc` at the command line. You can also find this document online at http://www.cpan.org/doc/manual/html/pod/perlfunc.html.

The next several sections provide an overview of Perl's language syntax and data handling.

Perl Variables and Data Structures

Perl is a *weakly typed* language, meaning that it does not require that you declare a data type, such as a type of value (data) to be stored in a particular variable. C, for example, makes you declare that a particular variable is an integer, a character, a structure, or whatever the case may be. Perl variables are whatever type they need to be, and can change type when you need them to.

Perl Variable Types

There are three variable types in Perl: *scalars*, *arrays*, and *hashes*. In an attempt to make each data type visually distinct, a different character is used to signify each variable type.

Scalar variables are indicated with the $ character, as in $penguin. Scalars can be numerical or strings, and they can change type from one to the other as needed. If you treat a number like a string, it becomes a string. If you treat a string like a number, it is translated into a number if it makes sense to do so; otherwise, it probably evaluates as 0.

For example, the string "76trombones" will evaluate as the number 76 if used in a numerical calculation, but the string "polar bear" will evaluate to 0.

Perl arrays are indicated with the @ character, as in @fish. An *array* is a list of values that are referenced by index number, starting with the first element numbered 0, just as in C and awk. Each element in the array is a scalar value. Because scalar values are indicated with the $ character, a single element in an array is also indicated with a $ character.

For example, $fish[2] refers to the third element in the @fish array. This tends to throw some people off, but is similar to arrays in C in which a first array element is 0.

Hashes are indicated with the % character, as in %employee. A *hash*, which used to go by the cumbersome name *associative array*, is a list of name and value pairs. Individual elements in the hash are referenced by name rather than by index (unlike an array). Again, because the values are scalars, the $ character is used for individual elements.

For example, $employee{name} gives you one value from the hash. Two rather useful functions for dealing with hashes are *keys* and *values*. The keys function returns an array containing all the keys of the hash, and values returns an array of the values of the hash. Using this approach, the Perl program in Listing 29.2 displays all the values in your environment, much like typing the bash shell's env command.

LISTING 29.2   Displaying the Contents of the env Hash

```
#!/usr/bin/perl
foreach $key (keys %ENV)  {
    print "$key = $ENV{$key}\n";
}
```

Special Variables

Perl has a wide variety of special variables. These usually look like punctuation—such as $_, $!, and $]—and are extremely useful for shorthand code. ($_ is the default variable, $! is the error message returned by the operating system, and $] is the Perl version number.)

$_ is perhaps the most useful of these, and you will see that variable used often in this chapter. $_ is the Perl default variable, which is used when no argument is specified. For example, the following two statements are equivalent:

```
chomp;
chomp($_);
```

The following loops are equivalent:

```
for $cow (@cattle) {
        print "$cow says moo.\n";
}
for (@cattle)         {
        print "$_ says moo.\n";
}
```

For a complete listing of the special variables, you should see the perlvar document that comes with your Perl distribution (such as in the perlvar manual page), or you can go online to http://theoryx5.uwinnipeg.ca/CPAN/perl/pod/perlvar.html.

Operators

Perl supports a number of operators to perform various operations. There are *comparison* operators (used to compare values, as the name implies), *compound* operators (used to combine operations or multiple comparisons), *arithmetic* operators (to perform math), and special string constants.

Comparison Operators

The comparison operators used by Perl are similar to those used by C, awk, and the csh shells, and are used to specify and compare values (including strings). Most frequently, a comparison operator is used within an if statement or loop. Perl has comparison operators for numbers and strings. Table 29.1 shows the numeric comparison operators and their behavior.

TABLE 29.1   Numeric Comparison Operators in Perl

Operator	Meaning
==	Is equal to
<	Less than
>	Greater than
<=	Less than or equal to
>=	Greater than or equal to
!=	Not equal to
..	Range of >= first operand to <= second operand
<=>	Returns –1 if less than, 0 if equal, and 1 if greater than

Table 29.2 shows the string comparison operators and their behaviors.

TABLE 29.2   String Comparison Operators in Perl

Operator	Meaning
eq	Is equal to
lt	Less than
gt	Greater than
le	Less than or equal to
ge	Greater than or equal to
ne	Not equal to
cmp	Returns -1 if less than, 0 if equal, and 1 if greater than
=~	Matched by regular expression
!~	Not matched by regular expression

Compound Operators

Perl uses compound operators, similar to those used by C or awk, which can be used to combine other operations (such as comparisons or arithmetic) into more complex forms of logic. Table 29.3 shows the compound pattern operators and their behavior.

29

TABLE 29.3   Compound Pattern Operators in Perl

Operator	Meaning
&&	Logical AND
¦ ¦	Logical OR
!	Logical NOT
( )	Parentheses; used to group compound statements

Arithmetic Operators

Perl supports a wide variety of math operations. Table 29.4 summarizes these operators.

TABLE 29.4   Perl Arithmetic Operators

Operator	Purpose
x**y	Raises x to the y power (same as x^y)
x%y	Calculates the remainder of x/y
x+y	Adds x to y
x-y	Subtracts y from x
x*y	Multiplies x times y
x/y	Divides x by y
-y	Negates y (switches the sign of y); also known as the *unary minus*
++y	Increments y by 1 and uses value (prefix increment)
y++	Uses value of y and then increments by 1 (postfix increment)
--y	Decrements y by 1 and uses value (prefix decrement)
y--	Uses value of y and then decrements by 1 (postfix decrement)
x=y	-Assigns value of y to x. Perl also supports operator-assignment operators (+=, -=, *=, /=, %=, **=, and others)

You can also use comparison operators (such as == or <) and compound pattern operators (&&, ¦¦, and !) in arithmetic statements. They evaluate to the value 0 for false and 1 for true.

Other Operators

Perl supports a number of operators that don't fit any of the prior categories. Table 29.5 summarizes these operators.

TABLE 29.5   Other Perl Operators

Operator	Purpose
~x	Bitwise not (changes 0 bits to 1 and 1 bits to 0)
x & y	Bitwise and
x ¦ y	Bitwise or
x ^ y	Bitwise exclusive or (XOR)
x << y	Bitwise shift left (shifts x by y bits)
x >> y	Bitwise shift right (shifts x by y bits)

TABLE 29.5   Continued

Operator	Purpose
x . y	Concatenate y onto x
a x b	Repeats string a for b number of times
x , y	Comma operator—evaluates x and then y
x ? y : z	Conditional expression—if x is true, y is evaluated; otherwise, z is evaluated. Provides the capability of an `if` statement anywhere you want (in the middle of a `print`, for instance)

Except for the comma operator and conditional expression, these operators can also be used with the assignment operator, similar to the way addition (+) can be combined with assignment (=), giving +=.

Special String Constants

Perl supports string constants that have special meaning or cannot be entered from the keyboard.

Table 29.6 shows most of the constants supported by Perl.

TABLE 29.6   Perl Special String Constants

Expression	Meaning
\ \	The means of including a backslash
\a	The alert or bell character
\b	Backspace
\cC	Control character (like holding the Ctrl key down and pressing the C character)
\e	Escape
\f	Formfeed
\n	Newline
\r	Carriage return
\t	Tab
\xNN	Indicates that NN is a hexadecimal number
\0NNN	Indicates that NNN is an octal (base 8) number

29

Conditional Statements: `if/else` and `unless`

Perl offers two conditional statements, `if` and `unless`, which function opposite one another. `if` enables you to execute a block of code only if certain conditions are met so that you can control the flow of logic through your program. Conversely, `unless` performs the statements when certain conditions are not met.

The following sections explain and demonstrate how to use these conditional statements when writing scripts for Linux.

if

The syntax of the Perl `if/else` structure is as follows:

```
if (condition) {
    statement or block of code
    }
elsif (condition) {
    statement or block of code
    }
else {
    statement or block of code
    }
```

condition can be a statement that returns a true or false value.

> **NOTE**
>
> Truth might be relative, but in 1844, the English mathematician George Boole introduced a new branch of mathematics known as *linguistic algebra*. The discipline continues to be used today in computing science as Boolean logic. His concepts of AND, NOT, and OR enable you to compare values that are in one of two mutually exclusive states and then make a decision based on the result of the comparison. Programmers refer to the states as off/on, zero/one, true/false, and so on. This logic is used to interpret 0s and 1s and is at the very foundation of computers. Perl implements Boolean logic in its conditional statements.

Truth is defined in Perl in a way that might be unfamiliar to you, so be careful. Everything in Perl is true except `0` (the digit zero), `"0"` (the string containing the number `0`), `""` (the empty string), and an undefined value. Note that even the string `"00"` is a true value because it isn't one of the four false cases.

The statement or block of code is executed if the test condition returns a true value.

For example, Listing 29.3 uses the `if/else` structure and shows conditional statements using the eq string comparison operator.

LISTING 29.3   `if/elsif/else`

```
if  ($favorite eq "chocolate") {
     print "I like chocolate too.\n";
} elsif ($favorite eq "spinach") {
     print "Oh, I don't like spinach.\n";
} else {
     print "Your favorite food is $favorite.\n";
}
```

> **NOTE**
>
> Perl was designed as a natural language, and it acknowledges idiomatic expressions that correspond with spoken English. The if statement is one good example. For example, you can say the following:
>
> ```
> }
> ```
>
> Alternatively, you could write it as you would more likely say it:
>
> ```
> print "Hello Rich!\n" if $name eq "Rich";
> ```

unless

unless works just like if, only backward. unless performs a statement or block if a condition is false:

```
unless ($name eq "Rich")          {
        print "Go away, you're not allowed in here!\n";
}
```

> **NOTE**
>
> You can restate the preceding example in more natural language, as you did in the if example.
>
> ```
> print "Go away!\n" unless $name eq "Rich";
> ```
>
> Although it isn't a rule, you should try to put the more important part of the statement (think of it as a sentence) on the left so that it is easier to read.

Looping

A *loop* is a way to repeat a program action multiple times. A very simple example is a countdown timer that performs a task (waiting for one second) 300 times before telling you that your egg is done boiling.

Looping constructs (also known as *control structures*) can be used to iterate a block of code as long as certain conditions apply, or while the code steps through (evaluates) a list of values, perhaps using that list as arguments.

Perl has four looping constructs: for, foreach, while, and until.

for

The for construct performs a *statement* (block of code) for a set of conditions defined as follows:

```
for (start condition; end condition; increment function) {
    statement(s)
}
```

29

The start condition is set at the beginning of the loop. Each time the loop is executed, the increment function is performed until the end condition is achieved. This looks much like the traditional for/next loop. The following code is an example of a for loop:

```
for ($i=1; $i<=10; $i++) {
     print "$i\n"
}
```

foreach

The foreach construct performs a statement block for each element in a list or array:

```
@names = ("alpha","bravo","charlie");
foreach $name (@names) {
   print "$name sounding off!\n";
}
```

The loop variable ($name in the example) isn't merely set to the value of the array elements; it is aliased to that element. That means if you modify the loop variable, you're actually modifying the array. If no loop array is specified, the Perl default variable $_ may be used:

```
@names = ("alpha","bravo","charlie");
foreach (@names) {
   print "$_ sounding off!\n";

}
```

This syntax can be very convenient, but it can also lead to unreadable code. Give a thought to the poor person who'll be maintaining your code. (It will probably be you.)

> **NOTE**
>
> foreach is frequently abbreviated as for.

while

while performs a block of statements as long as a particular condition is true:

```
while ($x<10) {
     print "$x\n";
     $x++;
}
```

Remember that the condition can be anything that returns a true or false value. For example, it could be a function call:

```
while ( InvalidPassword($user, $password) )          {
        print "You've entered an invalid password. Please try again.\n";
        $password = GetPassword;
}
```

until

until is the exact opposite of the while statement. It performs a block of statements as long as a particular condition is false—or, rather, until it becomes true:

```
until (ValidPassword($user, $password))   {
        print "You've entered an invalid password. Please try again.\n";
        $password = GetPassword;
}
```

last and next

You can force Perl to end a loop early by using a last statement. last is similar to the C break command—the loop is exited. If you decide you need to skip the remaining contents of a loop without ending the loop itself, you can use next, which is similar to the C continue command. Unfortunately, these statements don't work with do ... while.

On the other hand, you can use redo to jump to a loop (marked by a label) or inside the loop where called:

```
$a = 100;
while (1) {
   print "start\n";
   TEST: {
      if (($a = $a / 2) > 2) {
         print "$a\n";
         if (--$a < 2) {
            exit;
         }
         redo TEST;
      }
   }
}
```

In this simple example, the variable $a is repeatedly manipulated and tested in an endless loop. The word "start" will only be printed once.

do ... while and do ... until

The while and until loops evaluate the conditional first. The behavior is changed by applying a do block before the conditional. With the do block, the condition is evaluated last, which results in the contents of the block always executing at least once (even if the condition is false). This is similar to the C language do ... while (*conditional*) statement.

Regular Expressions

Perl's greatest strength is in text and file manipulation, which is accomplished by using the regular expression (regex) library. Regexes, which are quite different from the wildcard handling and filename expansion capabilities of the shell (see Chapter 14), allow complicated pattern matching and replacement to be done efficiently and easily.

For example, the following line of code replaces every occurrence of the string bob or the string mary with fred in a line of text:

```
$string =~ s/bob¦mary/fred/gi;
```

Without going into too many of the details, Table 29.7 explains what the preceding line says.

TABLE 29.7   Explanation of $string =~ s/bob¦mary/fred/gi;

Element	Explanation
$string =~	Performs this pattern match on the text found in the variable called $string.
s	Substitute.
/	Begins the text to be matched.
bob¦mary	Matches the text bob or mary. You should remember that it is looking for the text mary, not the word mary; that is, it will also match the text mary in the word maryland.
/	Ends text to be matched; begins text to replace it.
fred	Replaces anything that was matched with the text fred.
/	Ends replace text.
g	Does this substitution globally; that is, replaces the match text wherever in the string you match it (and any number of times).
i	The search text is not case sensitive. It matches bob, Bob, or bOB.
;	Indicates the end of the line of code.

If you're interested in the details, you can get more information using the regex (7) section of the manual.

Although replacing one string with another might seem a rather trivial task, the code required to do the same thing in another language (for example, C) is rather daunting unless supported by additional subroutines from external libraries.

Access to the Shell

Perl is useful for administrative functions because it has access to the shell. That means Perl can perform for you any process you might ordinarily perform by typing commands to the shell. To run Linux commands in your Perl programs, use the `` syntax. For example, the code in Listing 29.4 prints a directory listing.

LISTING 29.4   Using Backticks to Access the Shell

```
$curr_dir = `pwd`;
@listing = `ls -al`;
print "Listing for $curr_dir\n";
foreach $file (@listing) {
    print "$file";
}
```

> **NOTE**
>
> The `` notation uses the backtick found above the Tab key (on most keyboards), not the single quotation mark.

You can also use the Shell module to access the shell. Shell is one of the standard modules that comes with Perl; it allows creation and use of a shell-like command line. Look at the following code for an example:

```
use Shell qw(cp);
cp ("/home/httpd/logs/access.log", "/tmp/httpd.log");
```

This code almost looks like it is importing the command-line functions directly into Perl. Although that isn't really happening, you can pretend that the code is similar to a command line and use this approach in your Perl programs.

A third method of accessing the shell is via the system function call:

```
$rc = 0xffff & system('cp /home/httpd/logs/access.log /tmp/httpd.log');
if ($rc == 0) {
        print "system cp succeeded \n";
}
else {
        print "system cp failed $rc\n";
}
```

The call can also be used with the or die clause:

```
system('cp /home/httpd/logs/access.log /tmp/httpd.log') == 0
        or die "system cp failed: $?"
```

However, you can't capture the output of a command executed through the system function.

29

> **NOTE**
>
> Access to the command line is fairly common in shell scripting languages, but is less common in higher-level programming languages.

Switches

Perl has a variety of command-line options (*switches*) that can be used to change one or more aspects of Perl's behavior. Some switches will change how input data is handled (such as end-of-line characters), whereas others toggle Perl's internal behavior (such as to turn on debugging). These switches can appear on the command line or can be placed on the #! line at the beginning of the Perl program.

> **NOTE**
>
> Several command-line switches can be stacked together, so -pie is the same as -p -i -e.

The following list describes all available command-line switches:

-0[*digits*]—Specifies the input record separator ($/) as an octal number. $/ is usually a newline, so you get one line per record. For example, if you read a file into an array, this gives you one line per array element. The value 00 is a special case and causes Perl to read in your file one paragraph per record.

-a—Turns on Autosplit mode when used with an -n or -p. That means each line of input is automatically split into the @F array.

-C—Enables native support and system interfaces for wide characters (multibyte character sets).

-c—Tells Perl to perform syntax checking on the specified Perl program without executing it. This is invaluable, and the error messages given are informative, readable, and tell you where to begin looking for the problem, which is a rarity in error messages.

-D*flags*—Sets debugging flags. See perlrun for more details.

-d—Runs the script under the Perl debugger. See perldebug for more information.

-d:*foo*—Runs the script under the control of a debugging or tracing module installed as Devel::foo. For example, -d:Dprof executes the script using the Devel::DProf profiler. See perldebug for additional information on the Perl debugger.

-e *commandline*—Indicates that what follows is Perl code. This enables you to enter Perl code directly on the command line, rather than running code contained in a file:

```
$ perl -e 'print join " ", keys %ENV;'
```

-F*pattern*—Specifies the pattern to split on if -a is also in effect. This is " " by default, and -F enables you to set it to whatever works for you, such as ',' or ';'. The pattern can be surrounded by //, "", or ''.

-h—Typing perl -h lists all available command-line switches.

-Idirectory—Directories specified by -I are prepended to the search path for modules (@INC).

-i[extension]—This indicates that files are to be edited in place. If the extension is provided, the original is backed up with that extension. Otherwise, the original file is overwritten.

-l[octnum]—Enables automatic line-ending processing, which means that end-of-line characters are automatically removed from input and put back on to output. If the optional octal number is unspecified, this is just the newline character.

-m[-]module or *-M[-]module*—Loads the specified module before running your script. There's a subtle difference between m and M. See perlrun for more details.

-n—Causes Perl to loop around your script for each file provided to the command line. Does not print the output. The following example, from perlrun, deletes all files older than a week:

```
$ find . -mtime +7 -print ¦ perl -nle 'unlink;'
```

-P—This causes your script to be run through the C preprocessor before compilation by Perl.

-p—This is just like -n except that that each line is printed.

-S—This searches for the script using the PATH environment variable.

-s—This performs some command-line switch parsing and puts the switch into the corresponding variable in the Perl script. For example, the following script prints '1' if run with the -foobar switch. Your Perl code might look like this:

```
#!/usr/bin/perl -s
print $foobar;
```

When you execute it, you would enter

```
$ ./myperl -foobar
```

-T—This enables taint checking. In this mode, Perl assumes that all user input is tainted, or insecure, until the programmer tells it otherwise. This helps protect you from people trying to exploit security holes in your code and is especially important when writing CGI programs.

-U—This enables you to do unsafe things in your Perl program, such as unlinking directories while running as superuser.

-u—An available, but obsolete switch to tell Perl to dump core after compiling a program.

-V—This prints a summary of the major Perl configuration values and the current value of @INC.

-V:names

This parameter displays the value of the names configuration variable.

-v—This prints the version and patch level of your Perl executable. For example,

```
$ perl -v
This is perl, v5.8.4 built for i386-linux-thread-multi
(with 1 registered patch, see perl -V for more detail)
```

29

Copyright 1987-2003, Larry Wall

Perl may be copied only under the terms of either the Artistic License or the
GNU General Public License, which may be found in the Perl 5 source kit.

Complete documentation for Perl, including FAQ lists, should be found on
this system using `man perl' or `perldoc perl'. If you have access to the
Internet, point your browser at http://www.perl.com/, the Perl Home Page.

-W—This tells Perl to display all warning messages.

-w—This tells Perl to display warning messages about potential problems in the program, such as
variables used only once (might be a typo), using = instead of == in a comparison, and the like. This
is often used in conjunction with the -c flag to do a thorough program check.

```
$ perl -cw finalassignment.pl
```

-X—This tells Perl to disable all warning messages.

-x directory—This tells Perl that the script is embedded in something larger, such as an email
message. Perl throws away everything before a line starting with #!, containing the string 'perl',
and everything after _END__. If a directory is specified, Perl changes to the directory before executing the script.

> **NOTE**
>
> The Perl documentation is referred to a few times in this section. perldebug, perlrun, perlmod,
> and perlmodlib, for example, are documents from the Perl documentation. To see these docu-
> ments, just type **perldoc perlmodlib** at the shell prompt. You can also see all the Perl docu-
> ments online at http://www.cpan.org/doc/index.html or on any CPAN site. CPAN is the
> Comprehensive Perl Archive Network. See the "Modules and CPAN" section later in this chapter
> for more information.
>
> Perl documentation is written in POD (plain old documentation) format and can be converted
> into any other format, such as TeX, ASCII, or HTML, with the pod2* tools that ship with Perl. For
> example, to produce HTML documentation on the Fubar module, you would type pod2html
> Fubar.pm > Fubar.html.

Modules and CPAN

A great strength of the Perl community (and the Linux community) is the fact that it is
an open-source community. This community support is expressed for Perl via CPAN,
which is a network of mirrors of a repository of Perl code.

Most of CPAN is made up of *modules*, whichare reusable chunks of code that do useful
things, similar to software libraries containing functions for C programmers. These
modules help speed development when building Perl programs and free Perl hackers from
repeatedly reinventing the wheel when building a bicycle.

There are thousands of Perl modules that do everything from sending email to maintaining your Cisco router access lists to telling you whether a name is masculine or feminine to printing the time in some fancy format. If you can think of doing something with a Perl script, chances are pretty good that a module exists to help you. If there's no module that helps, you're encouraged to write one and share it with the rest of the community.

Perl comes with a set of standard modules installed. Those modules should contain much of the functionality that you will initially need with Perl. If you need to use a module not installed with Fedora, use the CPAN module (which is one of the standard modules) to download and install other modules onto your system. At http://www.perl.com/CPAN/, you will find the CPAN Multiplex Dispatcher, which will attempt to direct you to the CPAN site closest to you.

Typing the following command will put you into an interactive shell that gives you access to CPAN. You can type **help** at the prompt to get more information on how to use the CPAN program.

```
$ perl -MCPAN -e shell
```

After you have installed a module from CPAN (or written one of your own), you can load that module into memory where you can use it with the use function:

```
use Time::CTime;
```

use looks in the directories listed in the variable @INC for the module. In this example, use looks for a directory called Time, which contains a file called CTime.pm, which in turn is assumed to contain a package called Time::CTime. The distribution of each module should contain documentation on using that module.

For a list of all the standard Perl modules (those that come with Perl when you install it), see perlmodlib in the Perl documentation. You can read this document by typing **perldoc perlmodlib** at the command prompt.

Code Examples

Over the last few years, many people have picked up the notion that Perl is a CGI language, as though it weren't good for anything else. Nothing could be further from the truth. You can use Perl in every aspect of your system administration and as a building block in whatever applications you're planning to run on your shiny new Linux system.

The following sections contain a few examples of things you might want to do with Perl.

Sending Mail

There are several ways to get Perl to send email. One method that you see frequently is opening a pipe to the sendmail command and sending data to it (shown in Listing 29.5). Another method is using the Mail::Sendmail module (available through CPAN or directly at http://www.cpan.org/authors/id/M/MI/MIVKOVIC/), which uses socket connections directly to send mail (as shown in Listing 29.6). The latter method is faster because it does not have to launch an external process. Note that sendmail must be running on your system in order for the Perl program in Listing 29.5 to work.

LISTING 29.5   Sending Mail Using Sendmail

```perl
#!/usr/bin/perl
open (MAIL, "¦ /usr/sbin/sendmail -t"); # Use -t to protect from users
print MAIL <<EndMail;
To: dpitts\@mk.net
From: rbowen\@mk.net
Subject: Email notification

David,
 Sending email from Perl is easy!
Rich
.

EndMail
close MAIL;
```

> **NOTE**
>
> Note that the @ sign in the email addresses must be escaped so that Perl does not try to evaluate an array of that name. That is, dpitts@mk.net will cause a problem, so you need to use dpitts\@mk.net.
>
> The syntax used to print the mail message is called a *here document*. The syntax is as follows:
>
> ```perl
> print <<EndText;
> .....
> EndText
> ```
>
> The EndText value must be identical at the beginning and at the end of the block, including any whitespace.

LISTING 29.6   Sending Mail Using the Mail::Sendmail Module

```perl
#!/usr/bin/perl
use Mail::Sendmail;
%mail = ('To' => 'dpitts@mk.net',
        'From' => 'rbowen@mk.net'
        'Subject' => 'Email notification',
        'Message' => 'Sending email from Perl is easy!',
        );
sendmail(%mail);
```

Perl ignores the comma after the last element in the hash. It's convenient to leave it there; if you want to add items to the hash, you don't need to add the comma. This is purely a style decision.

Using Perl to Install a CPAN Module

You can use Perl to interactively download and install a Perl module from the CPAN archives by using the -M and -e commands. Start the process by using a Perl like this:

```
# perl -MCPAN -e shell
```

After you press Enter, you will see some introductory information and be asked to choose an initial automatic or manual configuration, which is required before any download or install takes place. Type **no** and press Enter to have Perl automatically configure for the download and install process; or, if desired, simply press Enter to manually configure for downloading and installation. If you use manual configuration, you will be asked a series of questions regarding paths, caching, terminal settings, program locations, and so on. Settings will be saved in a directory named .cpan in current directory.

When finished, you will see the CPAN prompt:

```
cpan>
```

To have Perl examine your system and then download and install a large number of modules, use the install keyword, specify Bundle at the prompt, and then press Enter like this:

```
cpan> install Bundle::CPAN
```

To download a desired module (using the example in Listing 29.6), use the get keyword like so:

```
cpan> get Mail::Sendmail
```

The source for the module will be downloaded into the .cpan directory. You can then build and install the module using the install keyword, like this:

```
cpan> install Mail::Sendmail
```

The entire process of retrieving, building, and installing a module can also be accomplished at the command line by using Perl's -e option like this:

```
# perl -MCPAN   -e "install Mail::Sendmail"
```

29

Note also that the @ sign did not need to be escaped within single quotation marks (' '). Perl does not *interpolate* (evaluate variables) within single quotation marks, but does within double quotation marks and here strings (similar to << shell operations).

Purging Logs

Many programs maintain some variety of logs. Often, much of the information in the logs is redundant or just useless. The program shown in Listing 29.7 removes all lines from a file that contain a particular word or phrase, so lines that you know are not important can be purged. For example, you might want to remove all the lines in the Apache error log that originate with your test client machine because you know those error messages were produced during testing.

LISTING 29.7   Purging Log Files

```
#!/usr/bin/perl
#       Be careful using this program!!
#       This will remove all lines that contain a given word
#       Usage:  remove <word> <file>
$word=@ARGV[0];
$file=@ARGV[1];
if ($file)  {
    # Open file for reading
    open (FILE, "$file") or die "Could not open file: $!";      @lines=<FILE>;
    close FILE;
    # Open file for writing
    open (FILE, ">$file") or die "Could not open file for writing: $!";
    for (@lines)  {
         print FILE unless /$word/;
    } # End for
    close FILE;
} else  {
    print "Usage:  remove <word> <file>\n";
}  #  End if...else
```

The code uses a few idiomatic Perl expressions to keep it brief. It reads the file into an array using the <FILE> notation; it then writes the lines back out to the file unless they match the pattern given on the command line.

The die function kills program operation and displays an error message if the open statements fail. $! in the error message, as mentioned in the section on special variables, is the error message returned by the operating system. It will likely be something like 'file not found' or 'permission denied'.

Posting to Usenet

If some portion of your job requires periodic postings to Usenet—a FAQ listing, for example—the following Perl program can automate the process for you. In the sample code, the posted text is read in from a text file, but your input can come from anywhere.

The program shown in Listing 29.8 uses the Net::NNTP module, which is a standard part of the Perl distribution. You can find more documentation on the Net::NNTP module by typing '**perldoc Net::NNTP**' at the command line.

LISTING 29.8   Posting an Article to Usenet

```perl
#!/usr/bin/perl
# load the post data into @post
open (POST, "post.file");
@post = <POST>;
close POST;
# import the NNTP module
use Net::NNTP;
$NNTPhost = 'news';
# attempt to connect to the remote host;
# print an error message on failure
$nntp = Net::NNTP->new($NNTPhost)
        or die "Cannot contact $NNTPhost: $!";
# $nntp->debug(1);
$nntp->post()
   or die "Could not post article: $!";
# send the header of the post
$nntp->datasend("Newsgroups: news.announce\n");
$nntp->datasend("Subject: FAQ - Frequently Asked Questions\n");
$nntp->datasend("From: ADMIN <root\@rcbowen.com>\n");
$nntp->datasend("\n\n");
# for each line in the @post array, send it
for (@post)     {
    $nntp->datasend($_);
} #  End for
$nntp->quit;
```

One-Liners

One medium in which Perl excels is the one-liner. Folks go to great lengths to reduce tasks to one line of Perl code. Perl has the rather undeserved reputation of being unreadable. The fact is that you can write unreadable code in any language. Perl allows for more than one way to do something, and this leads rather naturally to people trying to find the most arcane way to do things.

29

> **TIP**
>
> Just because you can do something is not a particularly good reason for doing it. For example, it can be more convenient to write somewhat lengthier pieces of Perl code for something that could be done in just one line, just for the sake of readability, and could save time later on. It can be irritating to go back to a piece of code reduced to one line for efficiency, but then later on have to spend 30 minutes trying to figure out what it does.
>
> Document your Perl scripts for readability. Use comments liberally because they will help you (or your co-workers who get to maintain your code) in the future.

Named for Randal Schwartz, a *Schwartzian Transform* is a way of sorting an array by something that is not obvious. The `sort` function sorts arrays alphabetically; that is pretty obvious. What if you want to sort an array of strings alphabetically by the third word? Perhaps you want something more useful, such as sorting a list of files by file size? A Schwartzian Transform creates a new list that contains the information that you want to sort by, referencing the first list. You then sort the new list and use it to figure out the order that the first list should be in. Here's a simple example that sorts a list of strings by length:

```
@sorted_by_length =
  map { $_ => [0] }            # Extract original list
  sort { $a=>[1] <=> $b=>[1] } # Sort by the transformed value
  map { [$_, length($_)] }     # Map to a list of element lengths
  @list;
```

Because each operator acts on the thing immediately to the right of it, it helps to read this from right to left (or bottom to top, the way it is written here).

The first thing that acts on the list is the `map` operator. It transforms the list into a hash in which the keys are the list elements and the values are the lengths of each element. This is where you put in your code that does the transformation by which you want to sort.

The next operator is the `sort` function, which sorts the list by the values.

Finally, the hash is transformed back into an array by extracting its keys. The array is now in the desired order.

Command-Line Processing

Perl is great at parsing the output of various programs. This is a task for which many people use tools such as `awk` and `sed`. Perl gives you a larger vocabulary for performing these tasks. The following example is very simple, but illustrates how you might use Perl to chop up some output and do something with it. In the example, Perl is used to list only those files that are larger than 10KB:

```
$ ls -la | perl -nae 'print "$F[8] is $F[4]\n" if $F[4] > 10000;'
```

The `-n` switch indicates that I want the Perl code run for each line of the output. The `-a` switch automatically splits the output into the `@F` array. The `-e` switch indicates that the Perl code is going to follow on the command line; refer to the "Switches" section earlier in this chapter for more information.

Related Fedora and Linux Commands

You will use these commands and tools when using Perl with Linux:

a2p—A filter used to translate awk scripts into Perl

find2perl—A utility used to create Perl code from command lines using the `find` command

pcregrep—A utility used to search data using Perl-compatible regular expressions

perlcc—A compiler for Perl programs

`perldoc`—A Perl utility used to read Perl documentation

`s2p`—A filter used to translate `sed` scripts into Perl

`vi`—The `vi` (actually `vim`) text editor

Reference

The first place to look is in the Perl documentation and Linux man pages.

Perl, all of its documentation, and millions of lines of Perl programs are all available free on the Internet. A number of Usenet newsgroups are also devoted to Perl, as well as shelves of books and a quarterly journal.

Books

Although your local bookstore might have dozens of titles on Perl, the following are some of the more highly recommended of these. You might also look at the *Camel Critiques* (Tom Christiansen; http://language.perl.com/critiques/index.html) for reviews of other available Perl books.

- *Advanced Perl Programming*, by Sriram Srinivasan, O'Reilly & Associates

- *Sams Teach Yourself Perl in 21 Days, Second Edition*, by Laura Lemay, Sams Publishing

- *Sams Teach Yourself Perl in 24 Hours, Second Edition,* by Clinton Pierce, Sams Publishing

- *Learning Perl, Third Edition*, by Randal L. Schwartz, Tom Phoenix, O'Reilly & Associates

- *Programming Perl, Third Edition*, by Larry Wall, Tom Christiansen, and Jon Orwant, O'Reilly & Associates

- *Effective Perl Programming: Writing Better Programs with Perl*, by Joseph Hall, Addison-Wesley Publishing Company

- *CGI Programming with Perl, Second Edition*, by Gunther Birznieks, Scott Guelich, Shishir Gundavaram, O'Reilly & Associates

- *Mastering Regular Expressions*, by Jeffrey Friedl, O'Reilly & Associates

Usenet

Check out the following on Usenet:

- `comp.lang.perl.misc`—Discusses various aspects of the Perl programming language. Make sure that your questions are Perl specific, not generic CGI programming questions. The regulars tend to flame folks who don't know the difference.

- `comp.infosystems.www.authoring.cgi`—Discusses authoring of CGI programs, so much of the discussion is Perl specific. Make sure that your questions are related to

CGI programming, not just Perl. The regulars are very particular about staying on topic.

WWW

Check these sites on the World Wide Web:

- http://www.perl.com/—Tom Christiansen maintains the Perl language home page. This is the place to find all sorts of information about Perl, from its history and culture to helpful tips. This is also the place to download the Perl interpreter for your system.

- http://www.perl.com/CPAN/—This is part of the site just mentioned, but it merits its own mention. CPAN (Comprehensive Perl Archive Network) is the place for you to find modules and programs in Perl. If you write something in Perl that you think is particularly useful, you can make it available to the Perl community here.

- http://www.perl.com/pub/q/FAQs—Frequently Asked Questions index of common Perl queries; this site offers a handy way to quickly search for answers about Perl.

- http://learn.perl.org/—One of the best places to start learning Perl online. If you master Perl, go to http://jobs.perl.org.

- http://www.hwg.org/—The HTML Writers Guild is a not-for-profit organization dedicated to assisting web developers. One of its services is a plethora of mailing lists. The hwg-servers mailing list and the hwg-languages mailing list are great places for asking Perl-related questions.

- http://www.pm.org/—The Perl Mongers are local Perl users groups. There might be one in your area. The Perl advocacy site is http://www.perl.org.

- http://www.tpj.com/—*The Perl Journal* is "a reader-supported monthly e-zine" devoted to the Perl programming language. *TPJ* is always full of excellent, amusing, and informative articles, and is an invaluable resource to both new and experienced Perl programmers.

- http://www-106.ibm.com/developerworks/linux/library/l-p101/—A short tutorial about one-line Perl scripts and code.

Other

Other valuable resources not falling into any of the preceding categories are Perl-related Internet Relay Chat channels. You can usually find several channels available on an IRC server. However, the questions, discussions, and focus of similarly named channels will vary from server to server.

For example, a #perlhelp channel is usually for general questions about installing, using, and learning about Perl. A #perl channel is generally for more advanced questions, but on some servers beginner questions might be welcomed. You might also find some helpful answers on #cgi and #html channels. Browse to http://perl-begin.berlios.de/irc/ for a list of servers.

# CHAPTER 30

Working with Python

As PHP has come to dominate the world of web scripting, Python is increasingly dominating the domain of command-line scripting. Python's precise and clean syntax makes it one of the easiest languages to learn, and it allows programmers to code more quickly and spend less time maintaining their code. Although PHP is fundamentally similar to Java and Perl, Python is closer to C and Modula-3, and so it might look unfamiliar at first.

Most of the other languages have a group of developers at their cores, but Python has Guido van Rossum—creator, father, and Benevolent Dictator For Life (BDFL). Although Guido spends less time working on Python now, he still essentially has the right of veto changes to the language, which has enabled it to remain consistent over the many years of its development. The end result is that, in Guido's own words, "even if you are in fact clueless about language design, you can tell that Python is a very simple language."

The following pages constitute a "quick start" tutorial to Python designed to give you all the information you need to put together basic scripts and to point you toward resources that can take you further.

Python on Linux

Fedora comes with Python installed by default, as do many other versions of Linux and Unix—even Mac OS X comes with Python preinstalled. Part of this is due to convenience because it is such a popular scripting language and it saves having to install it later if the user wants to run a script. However, in Fedora's case, part of the reason is that several of the core system programs are written in Python, including Yum itself.

If, for some reason, you manage to have a Fedora install without Python, you can install it using Yum using the command yum install python as root.

The Python binary is installed into /usr/bin/python; if you run that, you will enter the Python interactive interpreter where you can type commands and have them executed immediately. Although PHP also has an interactive mode (use php -a to activate it), it is neither as powerful or as flexible as Python's.

As with Perl, PHP, and other scripting languages, you can also execute Python scripts by adding a shebang line to the start of your scripts that point to /usr/bin/python and then setting the file to be executable.

The third and final way to run Python scripts is through mod_python, which is installed by default when you select the Web Server application group from the Add/Remove Packages dialog.

For the purposes of this introduction, we will be using the interactive Python interpreter because it provides immediate feedback on commands as you type them. Furthermore, knowledge of the interactive interpreter is essential for debugging when you start writing more advanced scripts.

Getting Interactive

We will be using the interactive interpreter for this chapter, so it is essential that you are comfortable using it. To get started, open a terminal and run the command python. You should see this:

```
[paul@caitlin ~]$ python
Python 2.3.4 (#1, Oct 26 2004, 16:42:40)
[GCC 3.4.2 20041017 (Red Hat 3.4.2-6.fc3)] on linux2
Type "help", "copyright", "credits" or "license" for more information.
>>>
```

The >>> is where you type your input, and you can set and get a variable like this:

```
>>> python = 'great'
>>> python
'great'
>>>
```

On line one, the variable python is set to the text great, and on line two that value is read back from the variable simply by typing the name of the variable you want to read. Line three shows Python printing the variable; on line four you are back at the prompt to type more commands.

Python remembers all the variables you use while in the interactive interpreter, which means you can set a variable to be the value of another variable.

When you are done, press Ctrl+D to exit. At this point, all your variables and commands are forgotten by the interpreter, which is why complex Python programs are always saved in scripts!

The Basics of Python

Python is a language wholly unlike most others, and yet it is so logical that most people can pick it up very quickly. You have already seen how easily you can assign strings, but in Python nearly everything is that easy—as long as you remember the syntax!

Numbers

The way Python handles numbers is fairly standard, although it is more precise than some other languages. It has all the normal operators—such as + for addition, - for subtraction, / for division, and * for multiplication—but it adds % for modulus (division remainder), ** for raise to the power, and // for floor division. It is also very specific about which type of number is being used, as this example shows:

```
>>> a = 5
>>> b = 10
>>> a * b
50
>>> a / b
0
>>> b = 10.0
>>> a / b
0.5
>>> a // b
0.0
```

The first division returns 0 because both a and b are integers (whole numbers), so Python calculates the division as an integer, giving 0. By converting b to 10.0, Python considers it to be a floating-point number and so the division is now calculated as a floating-point value, giving 0.5. Even with b being floating-point, using //—floor division—rounds it down.

Using **, you can easily see how Python works with integers:

```
>>> 2 ** 30
1073741824
>>> 2 ** 31
2147483648L
```

The first statement raises 2 to the power of 30 (that is, $2 \times 2 \times 2 \times 2 \times 2 \times ...$), and the second raises 2 to the power of 31. Notice how the second number has a capital L on the end of it—this is Python telling you that it is a long integer. The difference between long integers and normal integers is slight but important: Normal integers can be calculated using simple instructions on the CPU, whereas long integers—because they can be as big as you need them to be—need to be calculated in software and therefore are slower.

When specifying big numbers, you need not put the L at the end—Python will figure it out for you. Furthermore, if a number starts off as a normal number and then exceeds its boundaries, Python automatically converts it to a long integer. The same is not true the other way around: If you have a long integer and then divide it by another number so that it could be stored as a normal integer, it remains a long integer:

```
>>> num = 99999999999999999999999999999999L
>>> num = num / 100000000000000000000000000000000
>>> num
999L
```

You can convert between number types using typecasting, like this:

```
>>> num = 10
>>> int(num)
10
>>> float(num)
10.0
>>> long(num)
10L
>>> floatnum = 10.0
>>> int(floatnum)
10
>>> float(floatnum)
10.0
>>> long(floatnum)
10L
```

You need not worry whether you are using integers or long integers; Python handles it all for you, so you can concentrate on getting the code right.

More on Strings

Python stores strings as an immutable sequence of characters—a jargon-filled way of saying "it is a collection of characters that, once set, cannot be changed without creating a new string." Sequences are important in Python. There are three primary types, of which strings are one, and they share some properties. Mutability makes much sense when you learn about lists in the next section.

As you saw in the previous example, you can assign a value to strings in Python with just an equal sign, like this:

```
>>> mystring = 'hello';
>>> myotherstring = "goodbye";
>>> mystring
```

```
'hello'
>>> myotherstring;
'goodbye'
>>> test = "Are you really Bill O'Reilly?"
>>> test
"Are you really Bill O'Reilly?"
```

The first example encapsulates the string in single quotation marks and the second and third in double quotation marks. However, printing the first and second strings show them both in single quotation marks because Python does not distinguish between the two. The third example is the exception—it uses double quotation marks because the string itself contains a single quotation mark. Here, Python prints the string with double quotation marks because it knows it contains the single quotation mark.

Because the characters in a string are stored in sequence, you can index into them by specifying the character you are interested in. Like most other languages, these indexes are zero-based, which means you need to ask for character 0 to get the first letter in a string. For example:

```
>>> string = "This is a test string"
>>> string
'This is a test string'
>>> string[0]
'T'
>>> string [0], string[3], string [20]
('T', 's', 'g')
```

The last line shows how, with commas, you can ask for several indexes at the same time. You could print the entire first word using this:

```
>>> string[0], string[1], string[2], string[3]
('T', 'h', 'i', 's')
```

However, for that purpose you can use a different concept: slicing. A *slice* of a sequence draws a selection of indexes. For example, you can pull out the first word like this:

```
>>> string[0:4]
'This'
```

The syntax there means "take everything from position 0 (including 0) and end at position 4 (excluding it)." So, [0:4] copies the items at indexes 0, 1, 2, and 3. You can omit either side of the indexes, and it will copy either from the start or to the end:

```
>>> string [:4]
'This'
>>> string [5:]
```

30

```
'is a test string'
>>> string [11:]
'est string'
```

You can also omit both numbers, and it will give you the entire sequence:

```
>>> string [:]
'This is a test string'
```

Later you will learn precisely why you would want to do that, but for now there are a number of other string intrinsics that will make your life easier. For example, you can use the + and * operators to concatenate (join) and repeat strings, like this:

```
>>> mystring = "Python"
>>> mystring * 4
'PythonPythonPythonPython'
>>> mystring = mystring + " rocks! "
>>> mystring * 2
'Python rocks! Python rocks! '
```

In addition to working with operators, Python strings come with a selection of built-in methods. You can change the case of the letters with `capitalize()` (uppercases the first letter and lowercases the rest), `lower()` (lowercases them all), `title()` (uppercases the first letter in each word), and `upper()` (uppercases them all). You can also check whether strings match certain cases with `islower()`, `istitle()`, and `isupper()`; that also extends to `isalnum()` (returns `true` if the string is letters and numbers only) and `isdigit()` (returns `true` if the string is all numbers).

This example demonstrates some of these in action:

```
>>> string
'This is a test string'
>>> string.upper()
'THIS IS A TEST STRING'
>>> string.lower()
'this is a test string'
>>> string.isalnum()
False
>>> string = string.title()
>>> string
'This Is A Test String'
```

Why did `isalnum()` return `false`—our string contains only alphanumeric characters, doesn't it? Well, no. There are spaces in there, which is what is causing the problem. More importantly, we were calling `upper()` and `lower()` and they were not changing the contents of the string—they just returned the new value. So, to change our string from

`This is a test string` to `This Is A Test String`, we actually have to assign it back to the string variable.

Lists

Python's built-in list data type is a sequence, like strings. However, they are mutable, which means they can be changed. Lists are like arrays in that they hold a selection of elements in a given order. You can cycle through them, index into them, and slice them:

```
>>> mylist = ["python", "perl", "php"]
>>> mylist
['python', 'perl', 'php']
>>> mylist + ["java"]
['python', 'perl', 'php', 'java']
>>> mylist * 2
['python', 'perl', 'php', 'python', 'perl', 'php']
>>> mylist[1]
'perl'
>>> mylist[1] = "c++"
>>> mylist[1]
'c++'
>>> mylist[1:3]
['c++', 'php']
```

The brackets notation is important: You cannot use parentheses, ((and)) or braces ({ and }) for lists. Using + for lists is different from using + for numbers. Python detects you are working with a list and appends one list to another. This is known as *operator overloading*, and it is one of the reasons Python is so flexible.

Lists can be *nested*, which means you can put a list inside a list. However, this is where mutability starts to matter, and so this might sound complicated! If you recall, the definition of an immutable string sequence is that it is a collection of characters that, once set, cannot be changed without creating a new string. Lists are mutable as opposed to immutable, which means you can change your list without creating a new list.

This becomes important because Python, by default, copies only a reference to a variable rather than the full variable. For example:

```
>>> list1 = [1, 2, 3]
>>> list2 = [4, list1, 6]
>>> list1
[1, 2, 3]
>>> list2
[4, [1, 2, 3], 6]
```

Here we have a nested list. list2 contains 4, then list1, then 6. When you print the value of list2, you can see it also contains list1. Now, proceeding on from that:

```
>>> list1[1] = "Flake"
>>> list2
[4, [1, 'Flake', 3], 6]
```

In line one, we set the second element in list1 (remember, sequences are zero-based!) to be Flake rather than 2; then we print the contents of list2. As you can see, when list1 changed, list2 was updated also. The reason for this is that list2 stores a reference to list1 as opposed to a copy of list1; they share the same value.

We can show that this works both ways by indexing twice into list2, like this:

```
>>> list2[1][1] = "Caramello"
>>> list1
[1, 'Caramello', 3]
```

The first line says, "get the second element in list2 (list1) and the second element of that list, and set it to be 'Caramello'." Then list1's value is printed, and you can see it has changed. This is the essence of mutability: We are changing our list without creating a new list. On the other hand, editing a string creates a new string, leaving the old one unaltered. For example:

```
>>> mystring = "hello"
>>> list3 = [1, mystring, 3]
>>> list3
[1, 'hello', 3]
>>> mystring = "world"
>>> list3
[1, 'hello', 3]
```

Of course, this raises the question of how you copy without references when references are the default. The answer, for lists, is that you use the [:] slice, which we looked at earlier. This slices from the first element to the last, inclusive, essentially copying it without references. Here is how that looks:

```
>>> list4 = ["a", "b", "c"]
>>> list5 = list4[:]
>>> list4 = list4 + ["d"]
>>> list5
['a', 'b', 'c']
>>> list4
['a', 'b', 'c', 'd']
```

Lists have their own collections of built-in methods, such as sort(), append(), and pop(). The latter two add and remove single elements from the end of the list, with pop() also returning the removed element. For example:

```
>>> list5 = ["nick", "paul", "julian", "graham"]
>>> list5.sort()
```

```
>>> list5
['graham', 'julian', 'nick', 'paul']
>>> list5.pop()
'paul'
>>> list5
['graham', 'julian', 'nick']
>>> list5.append("Rebecca")
```

In addition, one interesting method of strings returns a list: split(). This takes a character to split by and then gives you a list in which each element is a chunk from the string. For example:

```
>>> string = "This is a test string";
>>> string.split(" ")
['This', 'is', 'a', 'test', 'string']
```

Lists are used extensively in Python, although this is slowly changing as the language matures.

Dictionaries

Unlike lists, *dictionaries* are collections with no fixed order. Instead, they have a *key* (the name of the element) and a *value* (the content of the element), and Python places them wherever it needs to for maximum performance. When defining dictionaries, you need to use braces ({ }) and colons (:). You start with an opening brace and then give each element a key and a value, separated by a colon, like this:

```
>>> mydict = { "perl" : "a language", "php" : "another language" }
>>> mydict
{'php': 'another language', 'perl': 'a language'}
```

This example has two elements, with keys perl and php. However, when the dictionary is printed, we find that php comes before perl—Python hasn't respected the order in which we entered them. We can index into a dictionary using the normal code:

```
>>> mydict["perl"]
'a language'
```

However, because a dictionary has no fixed sequence, we cannot take a slice, or index by position.

Like lists, dictionaries are mutable and can also be nested; however, unlike lists, you cannot merge two dictionaries by using +. This is because dictionary elements are located using the key. Therefore, having two elements with the same key would cause a clash. Instead, you should use the update() method, which merges two arrays by overwriting clashing keys.

You can also use the keys() method to return a list of all the keys in a dictionary.

30

Conditionals and Looping

So far, we have just been looking at data types, which should show you how powerful Python's data types are. However, you simply cannot write complex programs without conditional statements and loops.

Python has most of the standard conditional checks, such as > (greater than), <= (less than or equal to), and == (equal), but it also adds some new ones, such as in. For example, we can use in to check whether a string or a list contains a given character/element:

```
>>> mystring = "J Random Hacker"
>>> "r" in mystring
True
>>> "Hacker" in mystring
True
>>> "hacker" in mystring
False
```

The last example demonstrates how in is case sensitive. We can use the operator for lists, too:

```
>>> mylist = ["soldier", "sailor", "tinker", "spy"]
>>> "tailor" in mylist
False
```

Other comparisons on these complex data types are done item by item:

```
>>> list1 = ["alpha", "beta", "gamma"]
>>> list2 = ["alpha", "beta", "delta"]
>>> list1 > list2
True
```

list1's first element (alpha) is compared against list2's first element (alpha) and, because they are equal, the next element is checked. That is equal also, so the third element is checked, which is different. The *g* in gamma comes after the *d* in delta in the alphabet, so gamma is considered greater than delta and list1 is considered greater than list2.

Loops come in two types, and both are equally flexible. For example, the for loop can iterate through letters in a string or elements in a list:

```
>>> string = "Hello, Python!"
>>> for s in string: print s,
...
H e l l o ,   P y t h o n !
```

The for loop takes each letter in string and assigns it to s. This then is printed to the screen using the print command, but note the comma at the end; this tells Python not to insert a line break after each letter. The "..." is there because Python allows you to enter more code in the loop; you need to press Enter again here to have the loop execute.

The exact same construct can be used for lists:

```
>>> mylist = ["andi", "rasmus", "zeev"]
>>> for p in mylist: print p
...
andi
rasmus
zeev
```

Without the comma after the print statement, each item is printed on its own line.

The other loop type is the while loop, and it looks similar:

```
>> while 1: print "This will loop forever!"
...
This will loop forever!
This will loop forever!
This will loop forever!
This will loop forever!
This will loop forever!
(etc)
Traceback (most recent call last):
  File "<stdin>", line 1, in ?
KeyboardInterrupt
>>>
```

That is an infinite loop (it will carry on printing that text forever), so you need to press Ctrl+C to interrupt it and regain control.

If you want to use multiline loops, you need to get ready to use your Tab key: Python handles loop blocks by recording the level of indent used. Some people find this odious; others admire it for forcing clean coding on users. Most of us, though, just get on with programming!

For example:

```
>>> i = 0
>>> while i < 3:
...     j = 0
...     while j < 3:
...             print "Pos: " + str(i) + "," + str(j) + ")"
...             j += 1
...     i += 1
...
Pos: (0,0)
Pos: (0,1)
```

30

```
Pos: (0,2)
Pos: (1,0)
Pos: (1,1)
Pos: (1,2)
Pos: (2,0)
Pos: (2,1)
Pos: (2,2)
```

You can control loops using the `break` and `continue` keywords. `break` exits the loop and continues processing immediately afterward, and `continue` jumps to the next loop iteration.

Functions

The way Python handles functions is unique, fun, and quite unlike most other mainstream languages. The two basic tenets of Python functions are that they are defined at runtime and they are typeless.

Other languages—such as PHP—read and process an entire file before executing it, which means you can call a function before it is defined because the compiler will read the definition of the function before it tries to call it. Python is different: If the function definition has not been reached by the time you try to call it, you get an error. The reason behind this behavior is that Python actually creates an object for your function, and that in turns means two things. First, you can define the same function several times in a script and have the script pick the right one at runtime. Second, you can assign the function to another name just by using =.

Function definition starts with `def`, then the function name, then parentheses and a list of parameters, and then a colon. The contents of a function need to be indented at least one level beyond the definition. So, using function assignment and dynamic declaration, you can write a script that prints the right greeting in a roundabout manner:

```
>>> def hello_english(Name):
...     print "Hello, " + Name + "!"
...
>>> def hello_hungarian(Name):
...     print "Szia, " + Name + "!"
...
>>> hello = hello_hungarian
>>> hello("Paul")
Szia, Paul!
>>> hello = hello_english
>>> hello("Paul")
```

Notice that function definitions include no type information. Functions are typeless, like we said. The upside of this is that you can write one function to do several things:

```
>>> def concat(First, Second):
...     return First + Second
...
>>> concat(["python"], ["perl"])
['python', 'perl']
>>> concat("Hello, ", "world!")
'Hello, world!'
```

That demonstrates how the return statement sends a value back to the caller, but also how a function can do one thing with lists and another thing with strings. The magic here is being accomplished by the objects. We write a function that tells two objects to add themselves together, and the objects intrinsically know how to do that. If they don't—if, perhaps, the user passes in a string and an integer—Python catches the error for us. However, it is this hands-off, "let the objects sort themselves out" attitude that makes functions so flexible. Our concat() function could conceivably concatenate strings, lists, or *zonks*—a data type someone created herself that allows adding. The point is that we do not limit what our function can do—tacky as it might sound, the only limit is your imagination!

Object Orientation

After having read this far, you should not be surprised to hear that Python's object orientation is flexible and likely to surprise you if you have been using C-like languages for several years.

The best way to learn Python OOP is to just do it. So, here is a basic script that defines a class, creates an object of that class, and calls a function:

```
class dog(object):
    def bark(self):
        print "Woof!"

fluffy = dog()
fluffy.bark()
```

Defining a class starts, predictably, with the class keyword followed by the name of the class you are defining and a colon. The contents of that class need to be indented one level so Python knows where it stops. Note that the object inside parentheses is there for object inheritance, which is discussed later. For now, the least you need to know is that, if your new class is not based on an existing class, you should put object inside parentheses as shown in the previous code.

Functions inside classes work in much the same way as normal functions do (although they are usually called *methods*), with the main difference being that they should all take at least one parameter, usually called self. This parameter is filled with the name of the object the function was called on, and you need to use it explicitly.

30

Creating an instance of a class is done by assignment. You do not need any new keyword, as in some other languages—you just provide empty parentheses. Calling a function of that object is done using a period, the name of the class to call, with any parameters being passed inside parentheses.

The previous example is very basic and just prints Woof! The sole function requires no parameters, and there is no class inheritance. Let's make it a bit more complicated.

Class and Object Variables

Each object has its own set of functions and variables, and you can manipulate those variables independently of objects of the same type. Additionally, some class variables are set to a default value for all classes and can also be manipulated globally.

This script demonstrates two objects of the dog class being created, each with its own name:

```
class dog(object):
    name = "Lassie"
    def bark(self):
        print self.name + " says 'Woof!'"
    def setName(self, name):
        self.name = name
fluffy = dog()
fluffy.bark()
poppy = dog()
poppy.setName("Poppy")
poppy.bark()
```

That outputs the following:

```
Lassie says 'Woof!'
Poppy says 'Woof!'
```

There, each dog starts with the name Lassie, but it gets customized. Keep in mind that Python assigns by reference by default, meaning each object has a reference to the class's name variable, and as we assign that with the setName() method, that reference is lost. What this means is that any references we do not change can be manipulated globally. Thus, if we change a class's variable, it also changes in all instances of that class that have not set their own value for that variable. For example:

```
class dog(object):
    name = "Lassie"
    color = "brown"
fluffy = dog()
poppy = dog()
print fluffy.color
dog.color = "black"
```

```
print poppy.color
fluffy.color = "yellow"
print fluffy.color
print poppy.color
```

So, the default color of dogs is brown—both the `fluffy` and `poppy` dog objects start off as brown. Then, using `dog.color`, we set the default color to be black, and because neither of the two objects has set its own color value, they are updated to be black. The third to last line uses `poppy.color` to set a custom color value for the `poppy` object—`poppy` becomes yellow, while `fluffy` and the dog class in general remain black.

Constructors and Destructors

To help you automate the creation and deletion of objects, you can easily override two default methods: __init__ and __del__. These are the methods called by Python when a class is being instantiated and freed, known as the *constructor* and *destructor*, respectively.

Having a custom constructor is great for when you need to accept a set of parameters for each object being created. For example, you might want each dog to have its own name on creation, and you could implement that with this code:

```
class dog(object):
    def __init__(self, name):
        self.name = name
fluffy = dog("Fluffy")
print fluffy.name
```

If you do not provide a name parameter when creating the dog object, Python reports an error and stops. You can, of course, ask for as many constructor parameters as you want, although it is usually better to ask only for the ones you need and have other functions to fill in the rest.

On the other side of things is the destructor method, which allows you to have more control over what happens when an object is destroyed. Using the two, we can show the life cycle of an object by printing messages when it is created and deleted:

```
class dog(object):
    def __init__(self, name):
        self.name = name
        print self.name + " is alive!"
    def __del__(self):
        print self.name + " is no more!"
fluffy = dog("Fluffy")
```

The destructor is there to give you the chance to free up resources allocated to the object or perhaps log something to a file.

Class Inheritance

Python allows you to reuse your code by inheriting one class from one or more others. For example, lions, tigers, and bears are all mammals and so share a number of similar properties. In that scenario, you would not want to have to copy and paste functions between them; it would be smarter (and easier!) to have a mammal class that defines all the shared functionality and then inherit each animal from that.

Consider the following code:

```python
class car(object):
    color = "black"
    speed = 0
    def accelerateTo(self, speed):
        self.speed = speed
    def setColor(self, color):
        self.color = color
mycar = car()
print mycar.color
```

That creates a car class with a default color and also provides a setColor() function so people can change their own colors. Now, what do you drive to work? Is it a car? Sure it is, but chances are it is a Ford, or a Dodge, or a Jeep, or some other make—you don't get cars without a make. On the other hand, you do not want to have to define a class Ford, give it the methods accelerateTo(), setColor(), and however many other methods a basic car has and then do exactly the same thing for Ferrari, Nissan, and so on.

The solution is to use inheritance: Define a car class that contains all the shared functions and variables of all the makes and then inherit from that. In Python, you do this by putting the name of the class from which to inherit inside parentheses in the class declaration, like this:

```python
class car(object):
    color = "black"
    speed = 0
    def accelerateTo(self, speed):
        self.speed = speed
    def setColor(self, color):
        self.color = color

class ford(car): pass
class nissan(car): pass
mycar = ford()
print mycar.color
```

The pass directive is an empty statement—it means our class contains nothing new. However, because the ford and nissan classes inherit from the car class, they get color, speed, accelerateTo(), and setColor() provided by their parent class. Note that we do not need `object` after the classnames for `ford` and `nissan` because they are inherited from an existing class: `car`. This is not a strict requirement. Python 2.2 introduced these "new-style" classes, and they are recommended for use, but you can just use `class car:`. That said, those old-style ("classic") classes will be removed from the language in the future, so you might as well use the `(object)`.

By default, Python gives you all the methods the parent class has, but you can override that by providing new implementations for the classes that need them. For example:

```
class modelt(car):
    def setColor(self, color):
        print "Sorry, Model Ts only come in black!"

myford = ford()
ford.setColor("green")
mycar = modelt()
mycar.setColor("green")
```

The first car is created as a Ford, so `setColor()` will work fine because it uses the method from the car class. However, the second car is created as a Model T, which has its own `setColor()` method, so the call will fail.

This provides an interesting scenario: What do you do if you have overridden a method and yet want to call the parent's method also? If, for example, changing the color of a Model T was allowed but just cost extra, we would want to print a message saying, "You owe $50 more," but then change the color. To do this, we need to use the class object from which our current class is inherited—car in this example. Here's an example:

```
class modelt(car):
    def setColor(self, color):
        print "You owe $50 more"
        car.setColor(self, color)

mycar = modelt()
mycar.setColor("green")
print mycar.color
```

That prints the message and then changes the color of the car.

Multiple Inheritance

You can inherit as many classes as you need, building up functionality as you go. For example, you could have a class `animalia`, a subclass `chordata`, a sub-subclass `mammalia`, and a sub-sub-subclass `homosapiens`. Each one is more specific than its parent. However, an interesting addition in Python is the ability to have multiple inheritance—to take functionality from two classes simultaneously.

Again, this is best shown in code:

```
class car(object):
    def drive(self):
        print "We're driving..."

class timemachine(object):
    def timeTravel(self):
        print "Traveling through time..."

class delorian(car,timemachine): pass
mydelorian = delorian()
mydelorian.drive()
mydelorian.timeTravel()
```

In that example, we have a class car and a class timemachine. Both work by themselves, so you can have a car and drive around in it or a time machine and travel through time with it. However, we also have a delorian class that inherits from car and timemachine. As you can see, it is able to call both drive() (inherited from car) and timeTravel() (inherited from timemachine).

This introduces another interesting problem: What happens if both car and timemachine have a refuel() function? The answer is that Python picks the correct function to use based on the order in which you listed the parent classes. In the previous code, we use class delorian(car,timemachine), which means "inherit from car and then from timemachine." As a result, if both classes had a refuel() function, Python would pick car.refuel().

This situation becomes more complex when further inheritance is involved. That is, if car inherits its refuel() method from vehicle, Python still chooses it. What happens behind the scenes is that Python picks the first class you inherited from and searches it and all its parent classes for a matching method call. If it finds none, it goes to the next class and checks it and its parents. This process repeats until it finds a class that has the required method.

The Standard Library and the Vaults of Parnassus

A default Python install includes many modules (blocks of code) that allow you to interact with the operating system, open and manipulate files, parse command-line options, perform data hashing and encryption, and much more. This is one of the reasons most commonly cited when people are asked why they like Python so much—it comes stocked to the gills with functionality you can take advantage of immediately. In fact, the number of modules included in the Standard Library is so high that entire books have been written about them—try *Python Standard Library* (O'Reilly, ISBN: 0-596-00096-0) for a comprehensive, if slightly dated, list of them.

For unofficial scripts and add-ons for Python, the recommended starting place is called the Vaults of Parnassus: http://py.vaults.ca. There you can find about 20,000 public scripts and code examples for everything from mathematics to games.

Reference

The Python website (http://www.python.org) is packed with information and updated regularly. This should be your first stop, if only to read the latest Python news. Check out these other helpful sites:

- http://www.zope.org—The home page of the Zope Content Management System (CMS), it's one of the most popular CMSes around and, more importantly, written entirely in Python.

- http://www.jython.org/—Python also has an excellent Java-based interpreter to allow it to run on other platforms. If you prefer Microsoft's .NET, try http://www.ironpython.com.

- http://www.pythonline.com—Guido van Rossum borrowed the name for his language from *Monty Python's Flying Circus*, and a result many Python code examples use oblique *Monty Python* references. A visit to the official *Monty Python* site to hone your Python knowledge is highly recommended!

There are few truly great books about Python; however, you can find a list of what's on offer at http://www.python.org/moin/PythonBooks. If you are desperate to pick up a book immediately, you could do much worse than choose *Learning Python* (O'Reilly, ISBN: 0-596-00281-5).

30

CHAPTER **31**

Writing PHP Scripts

This chapter introduces you to the world of PHP programming, from the point of view of using it as a web scripting language and as a command-line tool. PHP originally stood for *personal home page* because it was a collection of Perl scripts designed to ease the creation of guest books, message boards, and other interactive scripts commonly found on home pages. However, since those early days, it has received two major updates (PHP 3 and PHP 4), plus a substantial revision in PHP 5, which is the version bundled with Fedora.

Part of the success of PHP has been its powerful integration with databases—its earliest uses nearly always took advantage of a database backend. In PHP 5, however, two big new data storage mechanisms were introduced: SQLite, which is a powerful and local database system, and SimpleXML, which is an API designed to make XML parsing and querying easy. As you will see over time, the PHP developers did a great job because both SQLite and SimpleXML are easy to learn and use.

If you used PHP prior to PHP 5, you should know that there has been a major evolution in the object-orientated system, and we strongly recommend you read the "Object Orientation" section.

> **NOTE**
>
> PHP's installation packages are under the Web Server category in Add/Remove Applications. The basic package is just called php, but you might also want to add extensions such as php_ldap, php_mysql, or php_pgsql. Choose only the extensions you plan to use; otherwise, it will waste system resources.

Introduction to PHP

In terms of the way it looks, PHP is a cross between Java and Perl, having taken the best aspects of both and merged them successfully into one language. The Java parts include a powerful object-orientation system, the capability to throw program exceptions, and the general style of writing that both languages borrowed from C. Borrowed from Perl is the "it should just work" mentality where ease of use is favored over strictness. As a result, you will find a lot of "there is more than one way to do it" in PHP.

If you have no previous experience using PHP, these next five sections are just for you: how to start and stop PHP processing, use variables, run operations, control program flow, and work with multiple files. If you have more experience, you can skip to the section "Basic Functions."

Entering and Exiting PHP Mode

Unlike PHP's predecessors, you embed your PHP code inside your HTML as opposed to the other way around. Before PHP, many websites had standard HTML pages for most of their content, linking to Perl CGI pages to do back-end processing when needed. With PHP, all your pages are capable of processing and containing HTML.

Each .php file is processed by PHP that looks for code to execute. PHP considers all the text it finds to be HTML until it finds one of four things:

- `<?php`

- `<?`

- `<%`

- `<script language="php">`

The first option is the preferred method of entering PHP mode because it is guaranteed to work. The second method, known as *short tags*, is disabled by default and is also likely to cause problems if you are serving XML documents along with your PHP. The third option is known as *ASP tags* because it mimics the manner in which Microsoft's ASP enters code blocks—this is rarely used. The last option is a last resort if you are using oddball code generators that don't like `<?php`—it looks like the same script blocks that are used to encapsulate JavaScript, and most editors leave it alone.

You can enter and exit PHP mode whenever you like, as often as you like, and—contrary to popular belief—there is little speed difference between printing your HTML in HTML mode or printing it in PHP mode.

Once in PHP mode, you can exit it by using `?>` (for `<?php` and `<?`); `%>` for `<%`) or `</script>` (for `<script language="php">`). This code example demonstrates entering and exiting PHP mode:

```
In HTML mode
<?php
    echo "In PHP mode";
```

```
?>
In HTML mode
In <?php echo "PHP"; ?> mode
```

Variables

All variables in PHP start with a dollar sign ($). Unlike many other languages, PHP does not have different types of variable for integers, floating-point numbers, arrays, or Booleans. They all start with a $, and all are interchangeable. As a result, PHP is a weakly typed language, which means you do not declare a variable as containing a specific type of data; you just use it however you want to.

This is best explained with some PHP code, so let's take a look at the most basic way of running PHP scripts: through your console. Save the code in Listing 31.1 into the script fedora1.php.

LISTING 31.1   Testing Types in PHP

```php
<?php
  $i = 10;
  $j = "10";
  $k = "Hello, world";
  echo $i + $j;
  echo $i + $k;
?>
```

To run that script, bring up a console and browse to where you saved it. Then type this command:

```
$ php fedora1.php
```

If PHP is installed correctly, you should see the output 2010, which is really two things. The 20 is the result of 10 + 10 ($i plus $j), and the 10 is the result of adding 10 to the text string Hello, world. Neither of those operations are really straightforward. Whereas $i is set to the number 10, $j is actually set to be the text value "10", which is not the same thing. Adding 10 to 10 gives 20, as you would imagine, but adding 10 to "10" (the string) forces PHP to convert $j to an integer on-the-fly before adding it.

Running $i + $k adds another string to a number, but this time the string is Hello, world and not just a number inside a string. PHP still tries to convert it, though, and converting any non-numeric string into a number converts it to 0. So, the second echo statement ends up saying $i + 0.

As you should have guessed by now, calling echo outputs values to the screen. Right now, that prints directly to your console, but internally PHP has a complex output mechanism that allows you to print to a console, send text through Apache to a web browser, send data over a network, and more.

Now that you have seen how PHP handles variables of different types, it is important that you understand the selection of types available to you:

Type	Stores
integer	Whole numbers; for example, 1, 9, or 324809873
float	Fractional numbers; for example, 1.1, 9.09, or 3.141592654
string	Characters; for example, "a", "sfdgh", or "Fedora Core Unleashed"
boolean	True or false
array	Several variables of any type
object	An instance of a class
resource	Any external data

The first four can be thought of as simple variables, and the last three as complex variables. Arrays are simply collections of variables. You might have an array of numbers (the ages of all the children in a class); an array of strings (the names of all Wimbledon tennis champions); or even an array of arrays, known as a *multidimensional array*. Arrays are covered in more depth in the next section because they are unique in the way in which they are defined.

Objects also have a section to themselves later in this chapter, but, briefly, they are used to define and manipulate a set of variables that belong to a unique entity. Each object has its own personal set of variables, as well as functions that operate on those variables. Objects are commonly used to model real-world things. You might define an object that represents a TV, with variables like $CurrentChannel (probably an integer), $SupportsHiDef (a Boolean), and so on. Don't worry if this does not make sense right now; objects are complex beasts, which is why they were grouped as *complex* variables!

Of all the complex variables, the easiest to grasp are resources. PHP has many extensions available to it that allow you to connect to databases, manipulate graphics, or even make calls to Java programs. Because they are all external systems, they need to have types of data unique to them that PHP cannot represent using any of the six other data types. So, PHP stores their custom data types in resources—data types that are meaningless to PHP but can be used by the external libraries that created them.

Arrays

Arrays are one of our favorite parts of PHP because the syntax is smart and easy to read and yet manages to be as powerful as you could want. There are four pieces of jargon you need to know to understand arrays:

- An array is made up of many *elements*.

- Each element has a *key* that defines its place in the array. An array can have only one element with a given key.

- Each element also has a *value*, which is the data associated with the key.

- Each array has a *cursor*, which points to the current key.

The first three are used regularly; the last one less so. The array cursor is covered later in this chapter in the section "Basic Functions," but we will look at the other three now. With PHP, your keys can be virtually anything: integers, strings, objects, or other arrays. You can even mix and match the keys so that one key is an array, another is a string, and so on. The one exception to all this is floating-point numbers: You cannot use floating-point numbers as keys in your arrays.

There are two ways of adding values to an array: with the [] operator, which is unique to arrays, and with the array() pseudo-function. You should use [] when you want to add items to an existing array and use array() to create a new array.

To sum all this up in code, Listing 31.2 shows a script that creates an array without specifying keys, adds various items to it both without keys and with keys of varying types, does a bit of printing, and then clears the array.

LISTING 31.2   Manipulating Arrays

```php
<?php
  $myarr = array(1, 2, 3, 4);

  $myarr[4] = "Hello";
  $myarr[] = "World!";
  $myarr["elephant"] = "Wombat";
  $myarr["foo"] = array(5, 6, 7, 8);

  echo $myarr[2];
  echo $myarr["elephant"];
  echo $myarr["foo"][1];

  $myarr = array();
?>
```

The initial array is created with four elements, to which we assign the values 1, 2, 3, and 4. Because no keys are specified, PHP automatically assigns keys for us starting at 0 and counting upward—giving keys 0, 1, 2, and 3. Then we add a new element with the [] operator, specifying 4 as the key and "Hello" as the value. Next, [] is used again to add an element with the value "World!" and no key and then again to add an element with the key "elephant" and the value "wombat". The line after that demonstrates using a string key with an array value—an array inside an array (a multidimensional array).

The next three lines demonstrate reading back from an array, first using a numeric key, then using a string key, and then using a string key and a numeric key. Remember, the "foo" element is an array in itself, so that third reading line retrieves the array and then prints the second element (arrays start at 0, remember). The last line blanks the array by simply using array() with no parameters, which creates an array with elements and assigns it to $myarr.

The following is an alternative way of using array() that allows you to specify keys along with their values:

```
$myarr = array("key1" => "value1", "key2" => "value2",
7 => "foo", 15 => "bar");
```

Which method you choose really depends on whether you want specific keys or want PHP to pick them for you.

Variable Variables

Although variable variables are not used frequently, it is at least important that you understand how they work so you will recognize them when you see them. A variable variable allows you to access the value of another variable indirectly by using its name as a string. That is, if you have a variable called $foo with a value "Hello, world!" and another variable called $bar set to "foo", you can use $$bar (yes, two dollar signs) to refer to "Hello, world!". When it sees two dollar signs, PHP looks at the value of the variable and treats that as the name of another variable; then it uses that value.

You can have as many layers of indirection as you like—for example, you could have $$$bar, $$$$$person, and so on. That said, anything past two dollar signs is probably not smart.

Listing 31.3 demonstrates variable variables in action.

LISTING 31.3 Variable Variables in Action

```
<?php
  $name = "Paul";
  $indirect1 = "name";
  $indirect2 = "indirect1";

  echo $name . "\n";
  echo $$indirect1 . "\n";
  echo $$$indirect2 . "\n";
?>
```

This code prints "Paul" three times.

Constants

As you have seen, variables hold values that can be changed during program flow and can vary. It should come as no surprise, then, that constants hold values that are fixed (constant) throughout the entire program. Constants are useful in compiled languages like C because they allow the compiler to allocate precisely enough memory to store them and there is no waste whatsoever. However, in PHP constants are no more efficient than variables and so are less useful.

However, they are used a great deal in functions that require specific values to be passed in. For example, a popular function is extract(), which takes all the values in an array and places them into variables in their own right. You can choose to change the name of the variables as they are extracted using the second parameter—send it a 0 and it over-writes variables with the same names as those being extracted, send it a 1 and it skips variables with the same names, send it 5 and it prefixes variables only if they exist already, and so on. Of course, no one wants to have to remember a lot of numbers for each function, so you can instead use EXTR_OVERWRITE for 0, EXTR_SKIP for 1, EXTR_PREFIX_IF_EXISTS for 5, and so on, which is much easier.

You can create constants of your own by using the define() function. Unlike variables, constants do not start with a dollar sign, which makes the code to define a constant look like this:

```php
<?php
  define("NUM_SQUIRRELS", 10);
  define("PLAYER_NAME", "Jim");
  define("NUM_SQUIRRELS_2", NUM_SQUIRRELS);
  echo NUM_SQUIRRELS_2;
?>
```

That script demonstrates how you can set constants to numbers, strings, or even the value of other constants, although that doesn't really get used much!

References

Using the equal sign (=) copies the value from one variable to another so they both have their own copy of the value. Another option here is to use references, which is where a variable does not have a value of its own; instead, it points to another variable. This enables you to share values and have variables mutually update themselves.

To copy by reference, use the & symbol, like this:

```php
<?php
  $a = 10;
  $b = &$a;
  echo $a . "\n";
  echo $b . "\n";

  $a = 20;
  echo $a . "\n";
  echo $b . "\n";
```

```
  $b = 30;
  echo $a . "\n";
  echo $b . "\n";
?>
```

If you run that script, you will see that updating $a also updates $b, but also that updating $b updates $a, too.

Comments

Although most people believe their code is so beautiful and easy to read that they do not need to write documentation, adding short comments to your code is recommended and usually a requirement in larger software houses. In PHP you have three options for commenting style: //, /* */, and #. The first option (two slashes) instructs PHP to ignore everything until the end of the line. The second (a slash and an asterisk) instructs PHP to ignore everything until it reaches */. The last (a hash symbol) works like // and is included because it is common amongst shell scripting languages.

This code example demonstrates the difference between // and /* */:

```
<?php
  echo "This is printed!";
  // echo "This is not printed";
  echo "This is printed!";
  /* echo "This is not printed";
  echo "This is not printed either"; */
?>
```

It is generally preferred to use // because it is a known quantity. On the other hand, it is easy to introduce coding errors with /* */ by losing track of where a comment starts and ends.

NOTE

Contrary to popular belief, having comments in your PHP script has almost no effect on the speed at which the script executes. What little speed difference exists is wholly removed if you use a code cache.

Escape Sequences

Some characters cannot be typed, and yet you will almost certainly want to use some of them from time to time. For example, you might want to use an ASCII character for new line, but you can't type it. Instead, you need to use an escape sequence: \n. Similarly, you can print a carriage return character with \r. It's important to know both of these because, on the Windows platform, you need to use \r\n to get a new line. If you do not plan to run your scripts anywhere else, you need not worry about this!

Going back to the first script we wrote, you will recall it printed 2010 because we added 10 + 10 and then 10 + 0. We can rewrite that using escape sequences, like this:

```php
<?php
  $i = 10;
  $j = "10";
  $k = "Hello, world";
  echo $i + $j;
  echo "\n";
  echo $i + $k;
  echo "\n";
?>
```

This time PHP prints a new line after each of the numbers, making it obvious that the output is 20 and 10 rather than 2010. Note that the escape sequences must be used in double quotation marks because they will not work in single quotation marks.

Three common escape sequences are \\, which means "ignore the backslash"; \", which means "ignore the double quote"; and \', which means "ignore the single quote." This is important when strings include quotation marks inside them. If we had a string such as "are you really Bill O'Reilly?", which has a single quotation mark in, this code would not work:

```php
<?php
  echo 'Are you really Bill O'Reilly?';
?>
```

PHP would see the opening quotation mark, read all the way up to the *O* in O'Reilly, and then see the quotation mark following the *O* as being the end of the string. The `Reilly?` part would appear to be a fragment of text and would cause an error. You have two options here: You can either surround the string in double quotation marks or escape the single quotation mark with \'.

If you choose the escaping route, it will look like this:

```php
echo 'Are you really Bill O\'Reilly?';
```

Although they are a clean solution for small text strings, you should be careful with overusing escape sequences. HTML is particularly full of quotation marks, and escaping them can get messy:

```php
$mystring = "<img src=\"foo.png\" alt=\"My picture\"
width=\"100\" height=\"200\" />";
```

In that situation, you are better off using single quotation marks to surround the text simply because it is a great deal easier on the eye!

Variable Substitution

PHP allows you to define strings using three methods: single quotation marks, double quotation marks, or heredoc notation. Heredoc is discussed in the next section because it really does need to be covered by itself, but single quotation marks and double quotation marks work identically, with one minor exception—variable substitution.

Consider the following code:

```php
<?php
  $age = 25
  echo "You are ";
  echo $age;
?>
```

That is a particularly clumsy way to print a variable as part of a string. Fortunately, if you put a variable inside a string, PHP performs *variable substitution*, replacing the variable with its value. That means we can rewrite the code like so:

```php
<?php
  $age = 25
  echo "You are $age";
?>
```

The output is the same. The difference between single quotation marks and double quotation marks is that single-quoted strings do not have their variables substituted. Here's an example:

```php
<?php
  $age = 25
  echo "You are $age";
  echo 'You are $age';
?>
```

The first echo prints "You are 25", but the second one prints "You are $age".

Heredoc Syntax

The third method for setting string variables is called *heredoc*, and it enables you to use anything you want to signify the start and end of your string. Heredoc uses <<< (three left angle brackets) followed by your string terminator. You can then enclose all the text you want in your string, including variables you want PHP to substitute. When you are done, simply print your terminator at column 0 on a line, followed by a semicolon.

That last part is important: You need to have your heredoc terminator as the first thing on a line by itself. You cannot even have any spaces before the terminator, so be extra careful.

Like many things, this becomes most apparent when you see it in code (see Listing 31.4).

LISTING 31.4   Using Heredoc Syntax to Define Strings

```php
<?php
  $variable = "heredoc";
  $mystring = <<<EOT
  This is some text
  This is some more text
  This is a $variable substitution
EOT;
  echo $mystring;
?>
```

There are two things to note here. First, the <<<EOT sets up the string "EOT" as the termi-nator for the heredoc; then that is printed as the first thing on the line to terminate it. We just picked EOT as standing for "end of text," but you can use whatever you like in your own scripts. Second, note there is no \n escape sequence to separate lines because we have physically hard-coded the new line breaks as needed.

Heredoc is generally reserved for situations in which you want to include a large amount of text in your script without having to worry about escaping quotation marks. As long as you ensure you use a heredoc terminator that does not appear in the string itself, you will be fine.

Operators

Now that we have data values to work with, we need some operators to use, too. We have already used + to add variables together, but many others in PHP handle arithmetic, comparison, assignment, and other operators. *Operator* is just a fancy word for something that performs an operation, like addition or subtraction. However, *operand* might be new to you. Consider this operation:

```php
$a = $b + c;
```

In this operation, = and + are operators and $a, $b, and $c are operands. Along with +, you will also already know – (subtract), * (multiply), and / (divide), but here are some more:

Operator	What It Does
=	Assigns the right operand to the left operand.
==	Returns true if the left operand is equal to the right operand.
!=	Returns true if the left operand is not equal to the right operand.
===	Returns true if the left operand is identical to the right operand. This is not the same as ==.
!==	Returns true if the left operand is not identical to the right operand. This is not the same as !=.
<	Returns true if the left operand is smaller than the right operand.

Operator	What It Does
>	Returns true if the left operand is greater than the right operand.
<=	Returns true if the left operand is equal to or smaller than the right operand.
&&	Returns true if both the left operand and the right operand are true.
¦¦	Returns true if either the left operand or the right operand is true.
++	Increments the operand by one.
--	Decrements the operand by one.
+=	Increments the left operand by the right operand.
-=	Decrements the left operand by the right operand.
.	Concatenates the left operand and the right operand (joins them together).
%	Divides the left operand by the right operand and returns the remainder.
¦	Performs a bitwise OR operation. It returns a number with bits that are set in either the left operand or the right operand.
&	Performs a bitwise AND operation. It returns a number with bits that are set both in the left operand and the right operand.

There are at least 10 other operators not listed, but to be fair you're unlikely to use them. Even some of the ones in this list are used infrequently—bitwise AND, for example. Having said that, the bitwise OR operator is used regularly because it allows you to combine values.

Here is a code example demonstrating some of the operators:

```php
<?php
  $i = 100;
  $i++; // $i is now 101
  $i--; // $i is now 100 again
  $i += 10; // $i is 110
  $i = $i / 2; // $i is 55
  $j = $i; // both $j and $i are 55
  $i = $j % 11; // $i is 0
?>
```

The last line uses modulus, which takes some people a little bit of effort to understand. The result of $i % 11 is 0 because $i is set to 55 and modulus works by dividing the left operand (55) by the right operand (11) and returning the remainder. 55 divides by 11 exactly five times, and so has the remainder 0.

The concatenation operator, a period, sounds scarier than it is: It just joins strings together. For example:

```php
<?php
  echo "Hello, " . "world!";
  echo "Hello, world!" . "\n";
?>
```

There are two "special" operators in PHP that are not covered here and yet are used frequently. Before we look at them, though, it's important that you see how the comparison operators (such as <, <=, and !=) are used inside conditional statements.

Conditional Statements

In a *conditional statement* you instruct PHP to take different actions depending on the outcome of a test. For example, you might want PHP to check whether a variable is greater than 10 and, if so, print a message. This is all done with the if statement, which looks like this:

```
if (your condition) {
   // action to take if condition is true
} else {
   // optional action to take otherwise
}
```

The *your condition* part can be filled with any number of conditions you want PHP to evaluate, and this is where the comparison operators come into their own. For example:

```
if ($i > 10) {
  echo "11 or higher";
} else {
  echo "10 or lower";
}
```

PHP looks at the condition and compares $i to 10. If it is greater than 10, it replaces the whole operation with 1; otherwise, it replaces it with 0. So, if $i is 20, the result looks like this:

```
if (1) {
  echo "11 or higher";
} else {
  echo "10 or lower";
}
```

In conditional statements, any number other than 0 is considered to be equivalent to the Boolean value true, so if (1) always evaluates to true. There is a similar case for strings—if your string has any characters in, it evaluates to true, with empty strings evaluating to false. This is important because you can then use that 1 in another condition through && or ¦¦ operators. For example, if you want to check whether $i is greater than 10 but less than 40, you could write this:

```
if ($i > 10 && $i < 40) {
  echo "11 or higher";
} else {
  echo "10 or lower";
}
```

If we presume that $i is set to 50, the first condition ($i > 10) is replaced with 1 and the second condition ($i < 40) is replaced with 0. Those two numbers are then used by the && operator, which requires both the left and right operands to be *true*. While 1 is equivalent to true, 0 is not, so the && operand is replaced with 0 and the condition fails.

=, ==, ===, and similar operators are easily confused and often the source of programming errors. The first, a single equal sign, assigns the value of the right operand to the left operand. However, all too often you see code like this:

```
if ($i = 10) {
  echo "The variable is equal to 10!";
} else {
  echo "The variable is not equal to 10";
}
```

That is incorrect. Rather than checking whether $i is equal to 10, it assigns 10 to $i and returns true. What is needed is ==, which compares two values for equality. In PHP, this is extended so that there is also === (three equal signs), which checks whether two values are identical—more than just equal.

The difference is slight but important: If you have a variable with the string value "10" and compare it against the number value of 10, they are equal. Thus, PHP converts the type and checks the numbers. However, they are not identical. To be considered identical, the two variables must be equal (that is, have the same value) and be of the same data type (that is, both are strings, both are integers, and so on).

> **NOTE**
>
> It is common practice to put function calls in conditional statements rather than direct comparisons. For example:
>
> ```
> if (do_something()) {
> ```
>
> If the do_something() function returns true (or something equivalent to true, such as a nonzero number), the conditional statement evaluates to true.

Special Operators

The ternary operator and the execution operator work differently from those we have seen so far. The ternary operator is rarely used in PHP, thankfully, because it is really just a condensed conditional statement. Presumably it arose through someone needing to make his code occupy as little space as possible because it certainly does not make PHP code any easier to read!

The ternary operator works like this:

```php
$age_description = ($age < 18) ? "child" : "adult";
```

Without explanation, that code is essentially meaningless; however, it expands into the following five lines of code:

```php
if ($age < 18) {
  $age_description = "child";
} else {
  $age_description = "adult";
}
```

The ternary operator is so named because it has three operands: a condition to check ($age < 18 in the previous code), a result if the condition is true ("child"), and a result if the condition is false ("adult"). Although we hope you never have to use the ternary operator, it is at least important to know how it works in case you stumble across it.

The other special operator is the execution operator, which is the back tick symbol, `. The position of the back tick key varies depending on your keyboard, but it is likely to be just to the left of the 1 key (above Tab). The execution operator executes the program inside the back ticks, returning any text the program outputs. For example:

```php
<?php
  $i = `ls -l`;
  echo $i;
?>
```

That executes the ls program, passing in -l (a lowercase *L*) to get the long format, and stores all its output in $i. You can make the command as long or as complex as you like, including piping to other programs. You can also use PHP variables inside the command.

Switching

Having multiple if statements in one place is ugly, slow, and prone to errors. Consider the code in Listing 31.5.

LISTING 31.5 How Multiple Conditional Statements Lead to Ugly Code

```php
<?php
  $cat_age = 3;

  if ($cat_age == 1) {
    echo "Cat age is 1";
  } else {
    if ($cat_age == 2) {
```

LISTING 31.5   Continued

```php
      echo "Cat age is 2";
    } else {
      if ($cat_age == 3) {
        echo "Cat age is 3";
      } else {
        if ($cat_age == 4) {
          echo "Cat age is 4";
        } else {
          echo "Cat age is unknown";
        }
      }
    }
  }
}
?>
```

Even though it certainly works, it is a poor solution to the problem. Much better is a switch/case block, which transforms the previous code into what's shown in Listing 31.6.

LISTING 31.6   Using a switch/case Block

```php
<?php
  $cat_age = 3;

  switch ($cat_age) {
    case 1:
      echo "Cat age is 1";
      break;
    case 2:
      echo "Cat age is 2";
      break;
    case 3:
      echo "Cat age is 3";
      break;
    case 4:
      echo "Cat age is 4";
      break;
    default:
      echo "Cat age is unknown";
  }
?>
```

Although it is only slightly shorter, it is a great deal more readable and much easier to maintain. A switch/case group is made up of a switch() statement in which you provide the variable you want to check, followed by numerous case statements. Notice the break statement at the end of each `case`. Without that, PHP would execute each `case` statement beneath the one it matches. Calling `break` causes PHP to exit the `switch/case`. Notice also that there is a `default case` at the end that catches everything that has no matching case.

It is important that you do not use `case default:` but merely `default:`. Also, it is the last `case` label, so it has no need for a `break` statement because PHP exits the `switch/case` block there anyway.

Loops

PHP has four ways you can execute a block of code multiple times: `while`, `for`, `foreach`, and `do...while`. Of the four, only `do...while` sees little use; the others are popular and you will certainly encounter them in other people's scripts.

The most basic loop is the `while` loop, which executes a block of code for as long as a given condition is true. So, we can write an infinite loop—a block of code that continues forever—with this PHP:

```php
<?php
  $i = 10;
  while ($i >= 10) {
    $i += 1;
    echo $i;
  }
?>
```

The loop block checks whether `$i` is greater or equal to 10 and, if that condition is true, adds 1 to `$i` and prints it. Then it goes back to the loop condition again. Because `$i` starts at 10 and we only ever add numbers to it, that loop continues forever. With two small changes, we can make the loop count down from 10 to 0:

```php
<?php
  $i = 10;
  while ($i >= 0) {
    $i -= 1;
    echo $i;
  }
?>
```

So, this time we check whether `$i` is greater than or equal to 0 and subtract 1 from it with each loop iteration. `while` loops are typically used when you are unsure of how many times the code needs to loop because `while` keeps looping until an external factor stops it.

With a `for` loop, you specify precise limits on its operation by giving it a declaration, a condition, and an action. That is, you specify one or more variables that should be set when the loop first runs (the *declaration*), you set the circumstances that will cause the loop to terminate (the *condition*), and you tell PHP what it should change with each loop iteration (the *action*). That last part is what really sets a `for` loop apart from a `while` loop: You usually tell PHP to change the condition variable with each iteration.

We can rewrite the script that counts down from 10 to 0 using a `for` loop:

```php
<?php
  for($i = 10; $i >= 0; $i -= 1) {
    echo $i;
  }
?>
```

This time we do not need to specify the initial value for `$i` outside the loop, and neither do we need to change `$i` inside the loop—it is all part of the `for` statement. The actual amount of code is really the same, but for this purpose the `for` loop is arguably tidier and therefore easier to read. With the `while` loop, the `$i` variable was declared outside the loop and so was not explicitly attached to the loop.

The third loop type is `foreach`, which is specifically for arrays and objects, although it is rarely used for anything other than arrays. A `foreach` loop iterates through each element in an array (or each variable in an object), optionally providing both the key name and the value.

In its simplest form, a `foreach` loop looks like this:

```php
<?php
  foreach($myarr as $value) {
    echo $value;
  }
?>
```

This loops through the `$myarr` array we created earlier, placing each value in the `$value` variable. We can modify that so we get the keys as well as the values from the array, like this:

```php
<?php
  foreach($myarr as $key => $value) {
    echo "$key is set to $value\n";
  }
?>
```

As you can guess, this time the array keys go in `$key` and the array values go in `$value`. One important characteristic of the `foreach` loop is that it goes from the start of the array to the end and then stops—and by *start* we mean the first item to be added rather than the lowest index number. This script shows this behavior:

```php
<?php
  $array = array(6 => "Hello", 4 => "World",
                 2 => "Wom", 0 => "Bat");
  foreach($array as $key => $value) {
    echo "$key is set to $value\n";
  }
?>
```

If you try this script, you will see that `foreach` prints the array in the original order of 6, 4, 2, 0 rather than the numerical order of 0, 2, 4, 6.

The `do...while loop` loop works like the `while` loop, with the exception that the condition appears at the end of the code block. This small syntactical difference means a lot, though,. because a `do...while` loop is always executed at least once. Consider this script:

```php
<?php
  $i = 10;
  do {
    $i -= 1;
    echo $i;
  } while ($i < 10);
?>
```

Without running the script, what do you think it will do? One possibility is that it will do nothing; `$i` is set to 10, and the condition states that the code must loop only while `$i` is less than 10. However, a `do...while` loop always executes once, so what happens is that `$i` is set to 10 and PHP enters the loop, decrements `$i`, prints it, and then checks the condition for the first time. At this point, `$i` is indeed less than 10, so the code loops, `$i` is decremented again, the condition is rechecked, `$i` is decremented again, and so on. This is in fact an infinite loop, and so should be avoided!

If you ever want to exit a loop before it has finished, you can use the same `break` statement, which we used earlier to exit a `switch/case` block. This becomes more interesting if you find yourself with *nested* loops—loops inside of loops. This is a common situation to be in. For example, you might want to loop through all the rows in a chessboard and, for each row, loop through each column. Calling `break` exits only one loop or `switch/case`, but you can use `break 2` to exit two loops or `switch/cases`, or `break 3` to exit three, and so on.

Including Other Files

Unless you are restricting yourself to the simplest programming ventures, you will want to share code amongst your scripts at some point. The most basic need for this is to have a standard header and footer for your website, with only the body content changing. However, you might also find yourself with a small set of custom functions you use frequently, and it would be an incredibly bad move to simply copy and paste the functions into each of the scripts that use them.

PHP gives you two ways to include other files into your current script. Both of them take the full content of the other script and merge it with the current script, allowing you to import functions, variables, or any other settings you have put in place. The basic way to include other files is with the `include` keyword. Save this script as `include1.php`:

```php
<?php
  for($i = 10; $i >= 0; $i -= 1) {
    include "echo_i.php";
  }
?>
```

Then save this script as echo_i.php:

```php
<?php
  echo $i;
?>
```

If you run include1.php, PHP loops from 10 to 0 and includes echo_i.php each time. For its part, echo_i.php just prints the value of $i, which is a crazy way of performing an otherwise simple operation, but it does demonstrate how included files share data. Note that the include keyword in include1.php is inside a PHP block, but we reopen PHP inside echo_i.php. This is important because PHP exits PHP mode for each new file, so you always have a consistent entry point.

The second way to include files is with the require keyword, which works in the same way as include except that, if PHP cannot find the file you ask for, it terminates execution immediately.

Basic Functions

PHP has a vast number of built-in functions that enable you to manipulate strings, perform mathematics, connect to databases, and more. There is not room here to cover even 10% of the functions; for more detailed coverage of functions, check the "References" section at the end of this chapter.

Strings

Several important functions are used for working with strings, and there are many more less frequently used ones for which there is not enough space here. We are going to look at the most important here, ordered by difficulty—easiest first!

The easiest function is strlen(), which takes a string as its parameter and returns the number of characters in there, like this:

```php
<?php
  $ourstring = "  The Quick Brown Box Jumped Over The Lazy Dog  ";
  echo strlen($ourstring);
?>
```

We will be using that same string in subsequent examples to save space. If you execute that script, it outputs 48 because 48 characters are in the string. Note the two spaces on either side of the text, which pad the 44-character phrase up to 48 characters.

We can fix that padding with the trim() function, which takes a string to trim and returns it with all the whitespace removed from either side. This is a commonly used function because all too often you encounter strings that have an extra new line at the end or a space at the beginning. This cleans it up perfectly.

Using `trim()`, we can turn our 48-character string into a 44-character string (the same thing, without the extra spaces), like this:

```
echo trim($ourstring);
```

Keep in mind that `trim()` returns the trimmed string, so that outputs `"The Quick Brown Box Jumped Over The Lazy Dog"`. We can modify that so `trim()` passes its return value to `strlen()` so the code trims it and then outputs its trimmed length:

```
echo strlen(trim($ourstring));
```

PHP always executes the innermost functions first, so the previous code takes $ourstring, passes it through `trim()`, uses the return value of `trim()` as the parameter for `strlen()`, and prints it.

Of course, everyone knows that boxes do not jump over dogs—the usual phrase is "the quick brown fox." Fortunately, there is a function to fix that problem: `str_replace()`. Note that it has an underscore in it; PHP is inconsistent on this matter, so you really need to memorize the function name.

The `str_replace()` function takes three parameters: the text to search for, the text to replace it with, and the string you want to work with. When working with search functions, people often talk about *needles* and *haystacks*—in this situation, the first parameter is the needle (the thing to find), and the third parameter is the haystack (what you are searching through).

So, we can fix our error and correct *box* to *fox* with this code:

```
echo str_replace("Box", "Fox", $ourstring);
```

There are two little addendums to make here. First, note that we have specified `"Box"` as opposed to `"box"` because that is how it appears in the text. The `str_replace()` function is a *case-sensitive* function, which means it does not consider `"Box"` to be the same as `"box"`. If you want to do a case-insensitive search and replace, you can use the `stri_replace()` function, which works in the same way.

The second addendum is that, because we are actually changing only one character (*B* to *F*), we need not use a function at all. PHP enables you to read (and change) individual characters of a string by specifying the character position inside braces ({ and }). As with arrays, strings are zero-based, which means in the $ourstring variable $ourstring{0} is *T*, $ourstring{1} is *h*, $ourstring{2} is *e*, and so on. We could use this instead of `str_replace()`, like this:

```
<?php
    $ourstring = "  The Quick Brown Box Jumped Over The Lazy Dog  ";
    $ourstring{18} = "F";
    echo $ourstring;
?>
```

Case sensitivity is something you will have to deal with many times throughout your programming career, particularly when dealing with passwords. Many sites do away with this problem by throwing away the letter case in passwords, either by uppercasing them all or lowercasing them all. PHP has two functions you can use for this purpose, `strtoupper()` and `strtolower()`. Both take a string as their parameter and return the string in all uppercase or all lowercase, respectively, as you would expect.

```
$ourstring = strtoupper($ourstring);
```

You can extract part of a string using the `substr()` function, which takes a string as its first parameter, a start position as its second parameter, and an optional length as its third parameter. Optional parameters are common in PHP. If you do not provide them, PHP assumes a default value. In this case, if you specify only the first two parameters, PHP copies from the start position to the end of the string. If you specify the third parameter, PHP copies that many characters from the start.

We can write a simple script to print `"Lazy Dog   "` by setting the start position to 38, which, remembering that PHP starts counting string positions from 0, copies from the 39th character to the end of the string:

```
echo substr($ourstring, 38);
```

If we just want to print the word `"Lazy,"` we need to use the optional third parameter to specify the length as 4, like this:

```
echo substr($ourstring, 38, 4);
```

The `substr()` function can also be used with negative second and third parameters. If you specify just parameter one and two and provide a negative number for parameter two, `substr()` counts backward from the end of the string. So, rather than specifying 38 for the second parameter, we can use –10, so it takes the last 10 characters from the string. Using a negative second parameter and positive third parameter counts backward from the end string and then uses a forward length. We can print `"Lazy"` by counting 10 characters back from the end and then taking the next four characters forward:

```
echo substr($ourstring, -10, 4);
```

Finally, we can use a negative third parameter, too, which also counts back from the end of the string. For example, using `"-4"` as the third parameter means to take everything except the last four characters. Confused yet? This code example should make it clear:

```
echo substr($ourstring, -19, -11);
```

That counts 19 characters backward from the end of the string (which places it at the O in Over) and then copies everything from there until 11 characters before the end of the string. That prints `"Over The"`. The same thing could be written using –19 and 8, or even 29 and 8—there is more than one way to do it!

Moving on, the strpos() function returns the position of a particular substring inside a string; however, it is most commonly used to answer the question, "Does this string contain a specific substring?" You need to pass it two parameters: a haystack and a needle (yes, that's a different order from str_replace()!).

In its most basic use, strpos() can find the first instance of "Box" in our phrase, like this:

```php
echo strpos($ourstring, "Box");
```

This outputs 18 because that is where the *B* in Box starts. If strpos() cannot find the substring in the parent string, it returns false rather than the position. Much more helpful, though, is the ability to check whether a string contains a substring; a first attempt to check whether our string contains the word *The* might look like this:

```php
<?php
  $ourstring = "The Quick Brown Box Jumped Over The Lazy Dog";
  if (strpos($ourstring, "The")) {
    echo "Found 'The'!\n";
  } else {
    echo "'The' not found!\n";
  }
?>
```

Note that we have temporarily taken out the leading and trailing whitespace from $ourstring and we are using the return value of strpos() for our conditional statement. This reads, "If the string is found, then print a message; if not, print another message." Or does it?

Run the script, and you will see it print the "not found" message. The reason for this is that strpos() returns false if the substring is not found and otherwise returns the position where it starts. If you recall, any nonzero number equates to true in PHP, which means that 0 equates to false. With that in mind, what is the string index of the first *The* in our phrase? Because PHP's strings are zero-based and we no longer have the spaces on either side of the string, the *The* is at position 0, which our conditional statement evaluates to false—hence, the problem.

The solution here is to check for identicality. We know that 0 and false are equal, but they are not identical because 0 is an integer, whereas false is a Boolean. So, we need to rewrite the conditional statement to see whether the return value from strpos() is identical to false. If it is, the substring was not found:

```php
<?php
  $ourstring = "The Quick Brown Box Jumped Over The Lazy Dog";
  if (strpos($ourstring, "The") !== false) {
    echo "Found 'The'!\n";
  } else {
    echo "'The' not found!\n";
  }
?>
```

Math

Like any modern programming language, PHP gives you a number of functions that handle a variety of mathematical functions, from calculating sine and cosine values to generating random numbers.

As with strings, we cover the most important subset, ordered from easiest to hardest.

First up are round(), floor(), and ceil(), which are functions that handle the rounding of floating-point numbers in different ways. The floor() function rounds a number down to its nearest whole integer, so 14.1, 14.5, and 14.9 all are rounded down to 14. The ceil() function does the opposite: It rounds numbers up to the nearest whole integer, meaning that 14.1, 14.5, and 14.9 are all rounded to 15. The round() function sits in the middle. If the fraction is 0.5 or greater, it rounds up; otherwise, it rounds down. Here's an example:

```php
<?php
  echo floor(14.5) . "\n";
  echo ceil(14.5) . "\n";
  echo round(14.5) . "\n";
  echo round(14.4) . "\n";
?>
```

That outputs 14, 15, 15, and 14 because floor() rounds 14.5 down, ceil() rounds 14.5 up, round() also rounds 14.5 up, but round() rounds 14.4 down.

Performing any sort of trigonometry makes sine, cosine, and tangent calculation a must, and PHP provides the sin(), cos(), and tan() functions for this purpose. Each of these accepts a parameter in radians and returns the sine value for that input. If you are used to working with degrees rather than radians, you can convert them with the deg2rad() function, like this:

```php
echo sin(deg2rad(90));
```

That returns the sine of 90°. Calculating cosine and tangent is as easy as replacing sin() with cos() or tan(). Keep in mind that the actual values of these mathematical functions are rounded internally by PHP and so cannot be relied on for very precise mathematics.

Another common mathematical function is calculating the square root of a number, which can be accomplished in PHP with the sqrt() function. This works precisely as you would imagine: You pass in the number you want to square root, and it returns the result:

```php
echo sqrt(2);
```

You can also calculate the square root of a number by using the pow() function, which is designed to raise a number to a certain power. Used normally, pow() takes two numerical parameters (we will call them X and Y) and returns the value of X multiplied by itself Y times. So, rather than writing $6 \times 6 \times 6 \times 6 \times 6 \times 6 \times 6 \times 6 \times 6 \times 6$, you can use pow(6, 10). If you use 0.5 as the second parameter, pow() calculates the square root of the first parameter.

There is a constant need to generate random numbers in programming. Not only is it crucial for computer games that need some variation between play periods, but it is also vital in cryptography and secure communications.

PHP has two ways of generating random numbers: fast and more predictable, and slow and less predictable. It is important to remember that true randomness is very difficult to achieve with computers, so many people refer to random number generators as *pseudo-random*, meaning they appear to be random but are not truly random.

The basic random generator is the rand() function, which takes two numbers as its two parameters: the lowest random number you want and the highest. So, using rand(1,10) could return 1, 10, or any whole number in between. The "more random" random number generator uses the Mersenne Twister algorithm and so is called mt_rand(). If all you are doing is printing a different greeting to your website visitors each time they come to your front page, rand() is more than enough!

Listing 31.7 demonstrates a script demonstrating the rand() function, but you can switch to the Mersenne Twister algorithm by swapping rand() for mt_rand().

LISTING 31.7   Varying Greeting Messages to Your Visitors

```php
<?php
  switch (rand(1,4)) {
    case 1:
      echo "Hello!";
      break;
    case 2:
      echo "Welcome!";
      break;
    case 3:
      echo "Greetings!";
      break;
    case 4:
      echo "Salutations!";
      break;
  }
?>
```

Arrays

Working with arrays is no easy task, but PHP makes it easier by providing a selection of functions that can sort, shuffle, intersect, and filter them. As with other functions, there is only space here to choose a selection; this is by no means a definitive reference to PHP's array functions.

The easiest function to use is array_unique(), which takes an array as its only parameter and returns the same array with all duplicate values removed. Also in the realm of "so easy you do not need a code example" is the shuffle() function, which takes an array as its parameter and randomizes the order of its elements. Note that `shuffle()` does not return the randomized array; it uses your parameter as a reference and scrambles it directly. The last too-easy-to-demonstrate function is `in_array()`, which takes a value as its first parameter and an array as its second and returns `true` if the value is in the array.

With those out of the way, we can focus on the more interesting functions, two of which are `array_keys()` and `array_values()`. They both take an array as their only parameter and return a new array made up of the keys in the array or the values of the array, respectively. The `array_values()` function is an easy way to create a new array of the same data, just without the keys. This is often used if you have numbered your array keys, deleted several elements, and want to reorder it.

The `array_keys()` function creates a new array where the values are the keys from the old array, like this:

```php
<?php
  $myarr = array("foo" => "red", "bar" => "blue", "baz" => "green");
  $mykeys = array_keys($myarr);
  foreach($mykeys as $key => $value) {
    echo "$key = $value\n";
  }
?>
```

That prints `"0 = foo"`, `"1 = bar"`, and `"2 = baz"`.

Several functions are used specifically for array sorting, but only two get much use: `asort()` and `ksort()`, the first of which sorts the array by its values and the second of which sorts the array by its keys. Given the array `$myarr` from the previous example, sorting by the values would produce an array with elements in the order bar/blue, baz/green, and foo/red. Sorting by key would give the elements in the order bar/blue, baz/green, and foo/red. As with the `shuffle()` function, both `asort()` and `ksort()` do their work *in place*, meaning they return no value, directly altering the parameter you pass in. For interest's sake, you can also use `arsort()` and `krsort()` for reverse value sorting and reverse key sorting, respectively.

This code example reverse sorts the array by value and then prints it as before:

```php
<?php
  $myarr = array("foo" => "red", "bar" => "blue", "baz" => "green");
  arsort($myarr);
  foreach($myarr as $key => $value) {
    echo "$key = $value\n";
  }
?>
```

Previously when discussing constants, we mentioned the `extract()` function that converts an array into individual variables; now it is time to start using it for real. You need to provide three variables: the array you want to extract, how you want the variables prefixed, and the prefix you want used. Technically, the last two parameters are optional, but practically you should always use them to properly namespace your variables and keep them organized.

The second parameter must be one of the following:

- EXTR_OVERWRITE—If the variable exists already, overwrites it.

- EXTR_SKIP—If the variable exists already, skips it and moves onto the next variable.

- EXTR_PREFIX_SAME—If the variable exists already, uses the prefix specified in the third parameter.

- EXTR_PREFIX_ALL—Prefixes all variables with the prefix in the third parameter, regardless of whether it exists already.

- EXTR_PREFIX_INVALID—Uses a prefix only if the variable name would be invalid (for example, starting with a number).

- EXTR_IF_EXISTS—Extracts only variables that already exist. We have never seen this used.

You can also, optionally, use the bitwise OR operator, ¦, to add in EXTR_REFS to have extract() use references for the extracted variables. In general use, EXTR_PREFIX_ALL is preferred because it guarantees namespacing. EXTR_REFS is required only if you need to be able to change the variables and have those changes reflected in the array.

This next script uses extract() to convert $myarr into individual variables, $arr_foo, $arr_bar, and $arr_baz:

```php
<?php
  $myarr = array("foo" => "red", "bar" => "blue", "baz" => "green");
  extract($myarr, EXTR_PREFIX_ALL, 'arr');
?>
```

Note that the array keys are "foo", "bar", and "baz" and that the prefix is "arr", but that the final variables will be $arr_foo, $arr_bar, and $arr_baz. PHP inserts an underscore between the prefix and array key.

The last group of functions we are going to look at are for the array cursor, mentioned earlier. If you recall, the array cursor is an invisible pointer to the current array element, but what defines the *current* element?

By default, this is the first element in the array, but you can move the array cursor around with prev(), next(), end(), and reset(). The first two move the cursor backward one place and forward one place, respectively, each time returning the value at the cursor. The last two move the cursor to the last element and the first element of the array, respectively, returning the value at that position. In addition, the current() function returns the value currently pointed to by the array cursor.

Listing 31.8 demonstrates these four in action.

LISTING 31.8   Browsing Arrays with the Array Cursor

```php
<?php
  $array = array("first\n", "second\n", "third\n", "fourth\n", "fifth\n");
  echo current($array);
  echo next($array);
  echo next($array);
  echo end($array);
  echo prev($array);
  echo reset($array);
?>
```

That outputs the following:

```
first
second
third
fifth
fourth
first
```

The array cursor is frequently used when the `foreach` loop is impractical, which is quite rare.

Files

As you will have learned from elsewhere in the book, the UNIX philosophy is that everything is a file. In PHP, this is also the case: A selection of basic file functions is suitable for opening and manipulating files, but those same functions can also be used for opening and manipulating network sockets. We cover both here.

Two basic read and write functions for files make performing these basic operations easy. They are `file_get_contents()`, which takes a filename as its only parameter and returns the file's contents as a string, and `file_put_contents()`, which takes a filename as its first parameter and the data to write as its second parameter.

Using these two, we can write a script that reads all the text from one file, `filea.txt`, and writes it to another, `fileb.txt`:

```php
<?php
  $text = file_get_contents("filea.txt");
  file_put_contents("fileb.txt", $text);
?>
```

Because PHP enables us to treat network sockets like files, we can also use `file_get_contents()` to read text from a website, like this:

```php
<?php
  $text = file_get_contents("http://www.slashdot.org");
  file_put_contents("fileb.txt", $text);
?>
```

The problem with using `file_get_contents()` is that it loads the whole file into memory at once; that's not practical if you have large files or even smaller files being accessed by many users. An alternative is to load the file piece by piece, which can be accomplished through the following five functions: `fopen()`, `fclose()`, `fread()`, `fwrite()`, and `feof()`. The *f* in those function names stands for *file*, so they open, close, read from, and write to files and sockets. The last function, `feof()`, returns `true` if the end of the file has been reached.

The `fopen()` function takes a bit of learning to use properly, but on the surface it looks straightforward. Its first parameter is the filename you want to open, which is easy enough. However, the second parameter is where you specify how you want to work with the file, and you should specify one of the following:

- r—Read only; it overwrites the file

- r+—Reading and writing; it overwrites the file

- w—Write only; it erases the existing contents and overwrites the file.

- w+—Reading and writing; it erases the existing content and overwrites the file

- a—Write only; it appends to the file

- a+—Reading and writing; it appends to the file

- x—Write only, but only if the file does not exist

- a+—Reading and writing, but only if the file does not exist

Optionally, you can also add b (for example, a+b or rb) to switch to binary mode. This is recommended if you want your scripts and the files they write to work smoothly on other platforms.

When you call `fopen()`, you should store the return value. It is a resource known as a *file handle*, which the other file functions all need to do their jobs. The `fread()` function, for example, takes the file handle as its first parameter and the number of bytes to read as its second, returning the content in its return value. The `fclose()` function takes the file handle as its only parameter and frees up the file.

So, we can write a simple loop to open a file, read it piece by piece, print the pieces, and then close the handle:

```php
<?php
  $file = fopen("filea.txt", "rb");
  while (!feof($file)) {
    $content = fread($file, 1024);
```

```
    echo $content;
  }
  fclose($file);
?>
```

That only leaves the `fwrite()` function, which takes the file handle as its first parameter and the string to write as its second. You can also provide an integer as the third parameter, specifying the number of bytes you want to write of the string, but if you exclude this, `fwrite()` writes the entire string.

If you recall, you can use a as the second parameter to `fopen()` to append data to a file. So, we can combine that with `fwrite()` to have a script that adds a line of text to a file each time it is executed:

```
<?php
  $file = fopen("filea.txt", "ab");
  fwrite($file, "Testing\n");
  fclose($file);
?>
```

To make that script a little more exciting, we can stir in a new function, `filesize()`, that takes a filename (not a file handle, but an actual filename string) as its only parameter and returns the file's size in bytes. Using that new function brings the script to this:

```
<?php
  $file = fopen("filea.txt", "ab");
  fwrite($file, "The filesize was" . filesize("filea.txt") . "\n");
  fclose($file);
?>
```

Although PHP automatically cleans up file handles for you, it is still best to use `fclose()` yourself so you are always in control.

Miscellaneous

Several functions do not fall under the other categories and so are covered here. The first one is `isset()`, which takes one or more variables as its parameters and returns `true` if they have been set. It is important to note that a variable with a value set to something that would be evaluated to `false`—such as 0 or an empty string—still returns `true` from `isset()` because it does not check the value of the variable. It merely checks that it is set; hence, the name.

The `unset()` function also takes one or more variables as its parameters, simply deleting the variable and freeing up the memory. With these two, we can write a script that checks for the existence of a variable and, if it exists, deletes it (see Listing 31.9).

LISTING 31.9   Setting and Unsetting Variables

```php
<?php
  $name = "Ildiko";
  if (isset($name)) {
    echo "Name was set to $name\n";
    unset($name);
  } else {
    echo "Name was not set";
  }

  if (isset($name)) {
    echo "Name was set to $name\n";
    unset($name);
  } else {
    echo "Name was not set";
  }
?>
```

That script runs the same isset() check twice, but it unset()s the variable after the first check. As such, it prints "Name was set to Ildiko" and then "Name was not set".

Perhaps the most frequently used function in PHP is exit, although purists will tell you that it is in fact a language construct rather than a function. exit terminates the processing of the script as soon as it is executed, meaning subsequent lines of code are not executed. That is really all there is to it; it barely deserves an example, but here is one just to make sure:

```php
<?php
  exit;
  echo "Exit is a language construct!\n";
?>
```

That script prints nothing because the exit comes before the echo.

One function we can guarantee you will use a lot is var_dump(), which dumps out information about a variable, including its value, to the screen. This is invaluable for arrays because it prints every value and, if one or more of the elements is an array, it prints all the elements from those, and so on. To use this function, just pass it a variable as its only parameter:

```php
<?php
  $drones = array("Graham", "Julian", "Nick", "Paul");
  var_dump($drones);
?>
```

The output from that script looks like this:

```
array(4) {
  [0]=>
  string(6) "Graham"
  [1]=>
  string(6) "Julian"
  [2]=>
  string(4) "Nick"
  [3]=>
  string(4) "Paul"
}
```

The var_dump() function sees a lot of use as a basic debugging technique because it is the easiest way to print variable data to the screen to verify it.

Finally, we briefly discuss regular expressions, with the emphasis on *briefly* because regular expression syntax is covered elsewhere in this book and the only unique thing relevant to PHP are the functions you will use to run the expressions. You have the choice of either Perl-Compatible Regular Expressions (PCRE) or POSIX Extended regular expressions, but there really is little to choose between them in terms of functionality offered. For this chapter, we will be using the PCRE expressions because, to the best of our knowledge, they see more use by other PHP programmers.

The main PCRE functions are preg_match(), preg_match_all(), preg_replace(), and preg_split(). We will start with preg_match() because it provides the most basic functionality by returning true if one string matches a regular expression. The first parameter to preg_match() is the regular expression you want to search for, and the second is the string to match. So, if we wanted to check whether a string had the word *Best, Test, rest, zest,* or any other word containing *est* preceded by any letter of either case, we could use this PHP code:

```
$result = preg_match("/[A-Za-z]est/", "This is a test");
```

Because the test string matches the expression, $result is set to 1 (true). If you change the string to a nonmatching result, you get 0 as the return value.

The next function is preg_match_all(), which gives you an array of all the matches it found. However, to be most useful, it takes the array to fill with matches as a by-reference parameter and saves its return value for the number of matches that were found.

We suggest you use preg_match_all() and var_dump() to get a feel for how the function works. This example is a good place to start:

```php
<?php
  $string = "This is the best test in the west";
  $result = preg_match_all("/[A-Za-z]est/", $string, $matches);
  var_dump($matches);
?>
```

That outputs the following:

```
array(1) {
  [0]=>
  array(3) {
    [0]=>
    string(4) "best"
    [1]=>
    string(4) "test"
    [2]=>
    string(4) "west"
  }
}
```

If you notice, the $matches array is actually multidimensional in that it contains one element, which itself is an array containing all the matches to our regular expression. The reason for this is because our expression has no *subexpressions*, meaning no independent matches using parentheses. If we had subexpressions, each would have its own element in the $matches array containing its own array of matches.

Moving on, preg_replace() is used to change all substrings that match a regular expression into something else. The basic manner of using this is quite easy: You search for something with a regular expression and provide a replacement for it. However, a more useful variant is *backreferencing*, using the match as part of the replacement. For our example, we will imagine you have written a tutorial on PHP but want to process the text so each reference to a function is followed by a link to the PHP manual.

PHP manual page URLs take the form http://www.php.net/<somefunc>—for example, http://www.php.net/preg_replace. The string we need to match is a function name, which is a string of alphabetic characters, potentially also mixed with numbers and underscores and terminated with two parentheses, (). As a replacement, we will use the match we found, surrounded in HTML emphasis tags (<em></em>), and then with a link to the relevant PHP manual page. Here is how that looks in code:

```php
<?php
  $regex = "/([A-Za-z0-9_]*)\(\)/";
  $replace = "<em>$1</em> (<a href=\"http://www.php.net/$1\">manual</A>)";
  $haystack = "File_get_contents()is easier than using fopen().";
  $result = preg_replace($regex, $replace, $haystack);
  echo $result;
?>
```

The $1 is our backreference; it will be substituted with the results from the first subexpression. The way we have written the regular expression is very exact. The [A-Za-z0-9_]* part, which matches the function name, is marked as a subexpression. After that is \(\), which means the exact symbols (and), not the regular expression meanings of them, which means that $1 in the replacement will contain fopen rather than , which is how it should be. Of course, anything that is not backreferenced in the replacement is removed, so we have to put the () after the first $1 (not in the hyperlink) to repair the function name.

After all that work, the output is perfect:

```
<em>File_get_contents()</em> (<a href="http://www.php.net/
file_get_contents">manual</A>) is easier than using <em>fopen()
</em> (<a href="http://www.php.net/fopen">manual</A>).
```

Object Orientation

Before PHP 5, the object orientation in PHP was little more than syntactic sugar—it looked nice but was little more than a fancy way of working, without offering any advantages. However, from v5 onward OOP is a powerful tool in the right hands. So, if you take the time to learn it fully, your code will benefit.

If you have used Java before, you will be at home with PHP because nearly everything from Java is in PHP, and with a very similar implementation. This chapter is aimed at people with no knowledge of object-oriented programming (OOP), so if you are already experienced, much of this will be review.

Introduction to OOP

Object-oriented programming is a system of expressing entities in your code as classes and objects. A *class* is a definition of an entity. For instance, you might define a car class or a pencil class. An *object* is an instance of a class. For instance, with your car class, you could create 10 car objects. As you define your car class, you can give it variables for storing car-related variables (color, model, and so on) and also car-specific functions (brake(), changeGear(), and so on). When you create an instance of a car, that object gets its own individual set of variables and functions that are not shared with other cars.

Defining a class is done with the class keyword and a list of functions and variables. You can then create instances of the class with the new operator, which returns a new object in the class. Here is how that looks in PHP:

```php
<?php
  class car {
    public function brake() {
      echo "Car is braking...\n";
    }

    public function changeGear($gear) {
      echo "Car is changing gear to $gear\n";
    }
  }
?>
```

Here we have our car class with two functions, brake() and changeGear(). Note the way the functions are written: The first letter is lowercase, with the first letter of subsequent words uppercased. This is known as *camel caps* or *studly caps*, and it is simply a coding convention that helps increase readability.

Second, note the word public before the function keyword. PHP implements a full PPP system, which means you have private functions and variables, public functions and variables, and protected functions and variables. Each do different things, and you need a firm grasp of the differences between them to understand OOP (we discuss them in the section "Access Modifiers").

Moving on, we need to create an instance of that car to use its functions:

```
$viper = new car;
$viper->changeGear(1);
$viper->changeGear(2);
$viper->brake();
```

That outputs the following:

```
Car is changing gear to 1
Car is changing gear to 2
Car is braking...
```

Object Variables and $this

Consider this code:

```
$viper = new car;
$concorde = new car;
$viper->changeGear(1);
$viper->changeGear(2);
$concorde->brake();
```

Although the code is very different, the output is identical because we have no way to distinguish between cars right now. We need to create a function, setName(), that gives each car a name. That means we need to store the name inside the car and print it when calling the other functions.

Adding the variable to the class is easy—add this line beneath the class car line:

```
public $name;
```

Again, notice that public is there; otherwise, you can ignore it. Put this setName() function immediately below the $name line:

```
public function setName($newname) {
  $this->name = $newname;
  echo "Car name changed to $newname\n";
}
```

The first line is standard, but the second line introduces the $this variable. Each instance of a class has its own set of variables, so PHP uses the $this variable to refer to whichever object had this function called upon it. If you call $concorde->brake(), $this is $concorde; if you call $viper->brake(), $this is $viper.

The way to set object variables is very specific. You do not use $name = ... or $this->$name = ...—that first one sets a new local variable called $name, and the second one looks up the value of the local variable name and uses it as a variable-variable. That is, if $name was wombat, it would set $this->wombat. Remember, unless you want to use variable-variables, PHP variables only ever have one dollar sign!

With the variable set, we can modify the other two functions to print the name so we can distinguish between the cars. The final script is shown in Listing 31.10.

LISTING 31.10   Multiple Cars, Distinguished by Name

```php
<?php
  class car {
    public $name;

    public function setName($newname) {
      $this->name = $newname;
      echo "Car name changed to $newname\n";
    }

    public function brake() {
      echo "Car $this->name is braking...\n";
    }

    public function changeGear($gear) {
      echo "Car $this->name is changing gear to $gear\n";
    }
  }

  $viper = new car;
  $concorde = new car;
  $viper->setName("Viper");
  $concorde->setName("Concorde");
  $viper->changeGear(1);
  $viper->changeGear(2);
  $concorde->brake();
?>
```

This time the output distinguishes between the cars.

Constructors and Destructors

Although having a function to set the name of cars is helpful, it should be obvious that every car needs a name. Rather than using setName() to set the initial value for the name, it makes more sense to use it only if, for some reason, we need to rename a car. Instead, because all cars need a name, we can force people to pass in the name when they are creating the car.

This is done through the *constructor* function, which is a magic function PHP calls whenever it creates an object of any class. If you have no constructor, like our current script, PHP skips this step. Constructors are used to set up initial values for objects. If you were creating a Human object, for example, it might set its age to 0 (just born), their birthday to today, and so on.

Because the constructor is a magic function (note: *magic function* is the actual term used to describe the constructor and others of its type), you must use a fixed name for it: __construct(). Note the two underscores at the beginning, which are a sure sign of a magic function.

If we want to set our car name during object creation, here is how the constructor should look (put this after the public $name line):

```
public function __construct($name) {
  $this->name = $name;
}
```

If we add that into the car class, save the script, and try running it, we will see that PHP now outputs warnings that we did not provide an initial name for our two cars. The constructor effectively replaces the setName() function for what we are doing; thus, we can rewrite the whole block of code at the bottom like this:

```
$viper = new car("Viper");
$concorde = new car("Concorde");
$viper->changeGear(1);
$viper->changeGear(2);
$concorde->brake();
```

Along with constructors come *destructors*, which work at the opposite end of objects and are called when your object is being destroyed. Object destruction takes place either explicitly (you use the unset() function) or implicitly (the script ends). Either way, PHP calls the __destruct() function for you, and you can do whatever you want with it, such as closing any file handles you opened in the constructor.

We can amend our car class to include a destructor by adding this code beneath the __construct() function:

```
public function __destruct() {
  echo "Car $this->name going to the scrap heap...\n";
}
```

Save your script and run it again; you should see the destructor being called for each car at the end of the script when PHP cleans up the objects.

Class Inheritance

PHP allows you to use one class as the base for another in what is known as *class inheritance*. Right now we have a car class, but what if we were to add a truck class and a bus class? We could just copy the changeGear() and brake() classes into each of them, but it makes maintenance much harder. If we find a bug in the brake() class later, for example, we'll need to remember to change it in various other places. Instead, we should create a class called vehicle that has all these shared functions and then have the car, truck, and bus classes that all inherit from vehicle.

When you inherit one class from another, it brings with it all the variables and functions that are declared as public, which is all of them so far. We can inherit a car class from a vehicle class by using the extends keyword in the class definition, like this:

```php
class car extends vehicle {
```

Then, by changing the car class over to a vehicle class, we can extend all three classes with the complete script shown in Listing 31.11.

LISTING 31.11   Multiple Vehicles, All Subclassed

```php
<?php
  class vehicle {
    public $name;

    public function __construct($name) {
      $this->name = $name;
    }

    public function __destruct() {
      echo "$this->name going to the scrap heap...\n";
    }

    public function setName($newname) {
      $this->name = $newname;
      echo "Name changed to $newname\n";
    }

    public function brake() {
      echo "$this->name is braking...\n";
    }

    public function changeGear($gear) {
      echo "$this->name is changing gear to $gear\n";
```

LISTING 31.11   Continued

```
    }
  }

  class car extends vehicle { }
  class truck extends vehicle { }
  class bus extends vehicle { }

  $viper = new car("Viper");
  $caterpillar = new truck("Caterpillar");
  $viper->changeGear(1);
  $caterpillar->brake();
?>
```

Because the class definitions for car, truck, and bus are all empty, they are identical to vehicle classes in all but name. However, having them separate means we can add individual functionality, such as a setFare() function for buses.

Although you can only inherit from one class at a time, you can inherit from an inherited class. That is, our car class inherits from vehicle, but we could create new classes that in turn inherit from car. Various terms are used to describe inheritance, with the most common being a parent/child relationship. In our example, car is the child class of vehicle, or, to put it another way, vehicle is the parent class of car. If we were to extend car further with classes like coupe or sedan, vehicle would be the grandparent of coupe.

Another common word for this is *subclassing*. So, car is a subclass of vehicle, coupe is a subclass of car, and so on. The opposite of a subclass is a superclass. In this case, then, vehicle is the superclass of car.

Access Modifiers

There is a lot more to PHP OOP than we have room to cover here, but access modifiers are so critical to a full understanding that they simply cannot be excluded.

We have already seen that public functions and variables are inherited by subclasses. Another property of public functions and variables is that they can be accessed by code outside the class. We call the brake() and changeGear() functions from the main body of the code.

Instead of public functions, we could use private functions, which do the opposite of everything public ones do. If the brake() function were to be declared private, it could not be called as it is in the example because private functions can be called only from within another class function. Similarly, private variables can be set only from within a class function. When inheriting, private variables are not accessible to any new functions introduced by the subclass. In our example, we have $name as public; changing that to private would still allow the car function to change the name through setName() because setName() is a vehicle function, not a car function.

The third alternative is protected, which is a slightly less strict version of private. Protected works like private in every way except inheriting. Protected variables are accessible to functions introduced by subclasses.

One of the basic tenets of OOP is *encapsulation* Classes should be encapsulated so programmers outside don't need to know how its internals work. If you have a class that implements a setName() function, programmers working with it should need to know only which parameters it takes and what its return value is. Although we could just do away with the setName() function and tell programmers to change the $name variable directly, it forces them to have explicit knowledge about how the object works.

Here is a list of functions that could be added to the vehicle class, along with the access method and explanation where needed:

- accelerate()—Public.

- setspeed()—Private/protected because programmers should not be able to arbitrarily define the speed of the car. Instead, they should use accelerate() or decelerate().

- soundHorn()—Public.

- crash()—Public because this is an external event happening to the car that triggers other events.

- inflateAirbag()—Private/protected because this should happen only as a result of something else—for example, someone calling crash().

If worse comes to worst and you simply cannot grasp private, protected, and public (even after having purchased a comprehensive PHP book), you can simply declare all your functions and variables as public. It is not preferable, but it works.

Handling HTML Forms

Given that PHP's primary role is handling web pages, you might wonder why this section has been left so late in the chapter. It's because handling HTML forms is so central to PHP that it is essentially automatic.

Consider this form:

```
<form method="POST" action="thispage.php">
User ID: <input type="text" name="UserID" /><br />
Password: <input type="password" name="Password" /><br />
<input type="submit" />
</form>
```

When a visitor clicks Submit, thispage.php is called again and this time PHP has the variables available to it inside the $_REQUEST array. Given that script, if the user enters 12345 and frosties as her user ID and password, PHP provides you with $_REQUEST['UserID'] set to 12345 and $_REQUEST['Password'] set to frosties. Note that it is important that you use HTTP post unless you specifically want GET. POST enables you to send a great deal more data and stops people from tampering with your URL to try to find holes in your script.

Is that it? Well, almost. That tells you how to retrieve user data, but you should be sure to sanitize it so users do not try to sneak HTML or JavaScript into your database as something you think is innocuous. PHP gives you the strip_tags() function for this purpose. It takes a string and returns the same string with all HTML tags removed.

Databases

The ease with which PHP can be used to create dynamic, database-driven websites is for many the key reason to use it. The stock build of PHP comes with support for MySQL, PostgreSQL, SQLite, Oracle, MS SQL Server, ODBC, plus several other popular databases, so you are sure to find something to work with your data.

If you want to, you can learn all the individual functions for connecting to and manipulating each database PHP supports, but a much smarter idea is to use PEAR::DB. PEAR::DB is an abstraction layer over the databases that PHP supports, which means you write your code once, and—with the smallest of changes—it will work on every database server.

PEAR is the script repository for PHP and contains numerous tools and prewritten solutions for common problems. PEAR::DB is perhaps the most popular part of the PEAR project, but it is worth checking out the PEAR site to see whether anything else catches your eye.

Introduction to PEAR::DB

To get basic use out of PEAR::DB, you need to learn how to connect to a database, run a SQL query, and work with the results. This is not a SQL tutorial, so we have assumed you are already familiar with the language. For the sake of this tutorial, we have also assumed you are working with a database called dentists and a table called patients that contains the following fields:

- **ID**—The primary key, autoincrementing integer for storing a number unique to each patient
- **Name**—A varchar(255) field for storing a patient name
- **Age**—Integer
- **Sex**—1 for male, 2 for female
- **Occupation**—A varchar(255) field for storing a patient occupation

Also for the sake of this tutorial, we will use a database server on IP address 10.0.0.1, running MySQL, with username fedora and password alm65z. You will need to replace these details with your own—use localhost for connecting to the local server.

The first step to using PEAR::DB is to include the standard PEAR::DB file, DB.php. Your PHP will be configured to look inside the PEAR directory for include() files, so you do not need to provide any directory information.

PEAR::DB is object-oriented, and you specify your connection details at the same time as you create the initial DB object. This is done using a URL-like system that specifies the database server type, username, password, server, and database name all in one. After you have specified the database server here, everything else is abstracted, meaning you only need to change the connection line to port your code to another database server.

This first script connects to our server and prints a status message (see Listing 31.12).

LISTING 31.12   Connecting to a Database Through PEAR::DB

```php
<?php
  include("DB.php");
  $dsn = "mysql://fedora:alm65z@10.0.0.1/dentists";
  $conn = DB::connect($dsn);

  if (DB::isError($conn)) {
    echo $conn->getMessage() . "\n";
  } else {
    echo "Connected successfully!\n";
  }
?>
```

You should be able to see how the connection string breaks down. It is server name first, then a username and password separated by a colon, then an @ symbol followed by the IP address to which to connect, and then a slash and the database name. Notice how the call to connect is DB::connect(), which calls PEAR::DB directly and returns a database connection object for storage in $conn. The variable name $dsn was used for the connection details because it is a common acronym standing for data source name.

If DB::connect() successfully connects to a server, it returns a database object we can use to run SQL queries. If not, we get an error returned that we can query using functions such as getMessage(). In the previous script we print the error message if we fail to connect, but we also just print a message if we succeed. Next, we will change that so we run an SQL query if we have a connection.

Running SQL queries is done through the query() function of our database connection, passing in the SQL we want to execute. This then returns a query result that can be used to get the data. This query result can be thought of as a multidimensional array because it has many rows of data, each with many columns of attributes. This is extracted using the fetchInto() function, which loops through the query result converting one row of data into an array that it sends back as its return value. You need to pass in two parameters to fetchInto() specifying where the data should be stored and how you want it stored.

Unless you have unusual needs, specifying DB_FETCHMODE_ASSOC for the second parameter is a smart move.

Listing 31.13 shows the new script.

LISTING 31.13   Running a Query Through PEAR::DB

```php
<?php
  include("DB.php");
  $dsn = "mysql://fedora:alm65z@10.0.0.1/dentists";
  $conn = DB::connect($dsn);

  if (DB::isError($conn)) {
    echo $conn->getMessage() . "\n";
  } else {
    echo "Connected successfully!\n";

    $result = $conn->query("SELECT ID, Name FROM patients;");

    while ($result->fetchInto($row, DB_FETCHMODE_ASSOC)) {
      extract($row, EXTR_PREFIX_ALL, 'pat');
      echo "$pat_ID is $pat_Name\n";
    }
  }
?>
```

The first half is identical to the previous script, with all the new action happening if we get a successful connection.

Going along with the saying "never leave to PHP what you can clean up yourself," the current script has problems. We do not clean up the query result, and we do not close the database connection. If this code were being used in a longer script that ran for several minutes, this would be a huge waste of resources. Fortunately, we can free up the memory associated with these two by calling $result->free() and $conn->disconnect(). If we add those two function calls to the end of the script, it will be complete.

Quick PEAR::DB Functions

Three special querying functions in PEAR::DB allow you to extract just one value, just one row, or just one column. In order, they are getOne(), getCol(), and getRow(). All three take a SQL query as their only parameter and immediately return either a single value (for getOne()) or an array of values (for the other two) that you can use immediately. This avoids the fetchInto() step entirely, which makes it faster and easier to read.

Listing 31.14 demonstrates all three functions in action.

LISTING 31.14   Extracting Data Without `fetchInto()`

```php
<?php
  include("DB.php");
  $dsn = "mysql://fedora:alm65z@10.0.0.1/dentists";
  $conn = DB::connect($dsn);

  echo $conn->getOne("SELECT AVG(Age) FROM patients;");
  echo "\n";

  $occupations = $conn->getCol("SELECT Occupation FROM patients;");
  var_dump($occupations);

  $patient = $conn->getRow("SELECT * FROM patients WHERE ID = 1;");
  var_dump($patient);
?>
```

Reference

Being as popular as it is, PHP gets a lot of coverage on the Internet. The best place to look for information, though, is the PHP online manual, at http://www.php.net. It is comprehensive, well-written, and updated regularly:

- http://www.phpbuilder.net—A large PHP scripts and tutorials site where you can learn new techniques and also chat with other PHP developers.

- http://www.zend.com—The home page of a company founded by two of the key developers of PHP. Zend develops and sells proprietary software, including a powerful IDE and a code cache, to aid PHP developers.

- http://pear.php.net/—The home of the PEAR project contains a large collection of software you can download and try, and it has thorough documentation for it all.

- http://www.phparch.com/—There are quite a few good PHP magazines around, but *PHP Architect* probably leads the way. It posts some of its articles online for free, and its forums are good, too.

Quality books on PHP abound, and you are certainly spoiled for choice. For beginning developers, the best available is *PHP and MySQL Web Development* (Sams Publishing), ISBN 0-672-32672-8. For a concise, to-the-point book covering all aspects of PHP, check out *PHP in a Nutshell* (O'Reilly). Finally, for advanced developers, you can consult *Advanced PHP Programming* (Sams Publishing), ISBN 0-672-32561-6.

# CHAPTER 32

C/C++ Programming Tools for Fedora

For many Linux users, coding means scripting. And why not? Most Linux distributions include Perl, Python, Tcl, and the bash, ksh, tcsh, and zsh shells—all of which support a wide range of commands that can be combined, in the form of scripts, into reusable programs. Command scripts for shell programs (and utilities such as GNU's gawk) can be all the programming that many users need in order to customize their computing environments. (You can learn more about scripting in Chapter 14, "Automating Tasks," and Chapter 29, "Using Perl.")

However, many programs that process scripts (such as the various Linux shells, the gawk command, and the Perl interpreter) are written in the C and C++ languages.

Learning how to use a computer language such as C or C++ can be more complex and difficult than learning shell scripting. You must learn to think in terms of machine resources and the way actions are accomplished within the computer, taking into account the operating system, language syntax, and assorted development tools, rather than think in terms of user-oriented commands.

Of course, the main benefit of learning C or C++ is that Linux and nearly all its related software is open source—if a program doesn't work the way you want it to, you can change it! You can also find a lot of "hidden" documentation in programmer comments inside the source to nearly all Linux programs.

Fedora comes with a diverse toolbox of program development software. There are C and C++ compilers, debuggers (used during the development process to find and diagnose errors), project organizing clients, graphical prototyping environments, and code management software. If you perform a full installation of Fedora from this book's CD-ROMs, you'll also be able to write Fortran 77, Java, and assembler (CPU-level) language programs.

This chapter focuses on C- and C++-related tools for Linux, such as the GNU C Compiler Collection (gcc) system, and prototyping environments for GNOME and the K Desktop Environment (KDE). The information presented here introduces some of the commands used to compile C and C++ programs, along with information about related programming tools.

Programming in C with Linux

C is the programming language most frequently associated with Unix-like operating systems such as Linux or BSD. Since the 1970s, the bulk of the Unix operating system and its applications have been written in C. Because the C language doesn't directly rely on any specific hardware architecture, Unix was one of the first portable operating systems. In other words, the majority of the code that makes up Unix does not know and doesn't care which computer it is actually running on. Machine-specific features are isolated in a few modules within the Unix kernel, which makes it easy for you to modify them when you are porting to different hardware architectures.

> **NOTE**
>
> In 1983, the American National Standards Institute (ANSI) established a committee to standardize the definition of C. The resulting standard is known as ANSI C, and it is the recognized standard for the language, the grammar, and a core set of libraries. The syntax is slightly different from that of the original C language, which is frequently called K&R, for Kernighan and Ritchie. There is also an International Standards Organization (ISO) C standard that is very similar to the ANSI C standard.

C is a *compiled* language, which means that your C source code is first analyzed by the *preprocessor* and then translated into assembly language first and then into machine instructions that are appropriate to the target CPU. An assembler then creates a binary, or *object*, file from the machine instructions. Finally, the object file is linked to any required external software support by the *linker*. A C program is stored in a text file that ends with a .c extension and always contains at least one routine, or function, such as main( ), unless the file is an *include* file (with a .h extension, also known as a *header* file) containing shared variable definitions or other data or declarations. *Functions* are the commands that perform each step of the task that the C program was written to accomplish.

> **NOTE**
>
> The Linux kernel is mostly written in C, which is why Linux works with so many different CPUs. To learn more about building the Linux kernel from source, see Chapter 38, "Kernel and Module Management."

Programming in C++

C++ is an object-oriented extension to C. Because C++ is a superset of C, C++ compilers compile C programs correctly, and it is possible to write non–object-oriented code in C++. The reverse is not true: C compilers cannot compile C++ code.

Object-oriented languages such as C++ allow programmers to define new abstract data types (including associated functions) and then derive subsequent data types from them. The notion of a new class of data objects, in addition to the built-in classes such as integer, floating-point number, and character, goes beyond the familiar capability to define complex data objects in C.

C++ extends the capabilities of C by providing the necessary features for object-oriented design and code. C++ also provides some features, such as the capability to associate functions with data structures, that do not require the use of class-based object-oriented techniques. For these reasons, the C++ language enables existing Unix programs to migrate toward the adoption of object orientation over time.

Support for C++ programming using Fedora is provided by gcc, which you run with the name g++ when you are compiling C++ code. KDE includes some intermediate C++ tools, such as moc (the Meta Object Compiler) for use when building KDE applications.

NOTE

You can read the C++ Programming HOWTO, available at http://www.tldp.org, for more information on programming using C++ and Linux.

Getting Started with Linux C/C++ Programming

Linux is popular with C and C++ programmers because of gcc and its suite of related software-development tools, such as gdb, autoconf, and make. Complex C programs might have dozens or hundreds of separate object files that are created during the build process. One, more, or all these (compiled) steps can be carried out automatically by the gcc compiler system, which is run by the make utility according to project rules contained in a makefile. After a program is compiled, it can be executed over and over without recompilation.

Writing C programs for Linux requires that you understand C syntax, have some understanding of how to interface with the Linux kernel (by using one or more of 1,100 different C functions, known as *system calls*), and know how to use Linux programming tools such as gcc and make. You'll learn about each of these concepts and processes in this chapter.

To get started, you need to make sure that you have installed all the necessary software development packages (perhaps by using the system-config-packages client; see Chapter 7, "Managing Software and System Resources") to support your project. Installation of basic development software requires more than 50 different software packages and 110MB of hard drive space. If you plan to build programs for the Linux kernel, you need the

Kernel development packages and an additional 180MB of storage space (not counting temporary disk space required when building a new kernel).

Developing programs for the X Window System requires installation of 20 software packages and about 40MB of software libraries, programming support files, and documentation. If you want to build GNOME clients, you need more than 60MB of additional space for nearly 50 software packages. And if you intend to develop programs for KDE, you should plan on reserving 220MB or so of your hard drive to store KDE's development software, contained in 20 different packages. Don't forget that you will also need lots of space for temporary files when you're building programs, as many intermediate files will be created during your programming sessions.

You should also become familiar with a good text editor. Although GNU purists use the emacs editing environment to write, edit, and compile programs, many other developers do just fine with an editor such as vi or nano for editing source and then use the command line to run development tools.

When programming for GNOME or KDE, you might find it most convenient to use a graphical development project manager, such as GNOME's Glade (the GTK+ User Interface Builder, glade-2), Trolltech's Qt Designer (designer), or KDE's KDevelop (the KDE development environment, kdevelop). These clients allow you to prototype an application with graphical drawing tools, which frees you to concentrate on your client's interface. You can use either to automatically generate all necessary project and source code files for skeletal applications. See the section "Graphical Development Tools," later in this chapter, for more information.

C Documentation

You will learn some of the basics of working in C in this chapter, and you also have a wealth of other information about C available to you on your Fedora Core system. You can use the man command to read online manual pages for the gcc C compiler and installed programming tools. You can use the info command to read the online GNU info files. You can get a general overview of how to use gcc by using the man command like this:

```
$ man gcc
```

For detailed information about using gcc, you can use the info command like this:

```
$ info gcc
```

Linux kernel and system calls are documented in manual pages in section 2, and manual pages for general Linux programming and helpful C routines (known as *library routines*) are found in section 3, known as the *Linux Programmer's Manual*. Linux programs use a number of support libraries, but the main routines are documented in the manual pages. For example, to see how to use the printf() function, you could use the man command like this:

```
$ man 3 printf
```

You can also gain additional insight into Linux programming by reading *Linux Programmer's Guide,* which is somewhat dated, but still useful, and is available at http://www.tldp.org/LDP/lpg/index.html. Or you can examine the source code for Linux programs. Later in this chapter you'll be introduced to the basics of using command-line development software and graphical program development tools for Linux.

The Process of Programming

Writing and building C programs when using Fedora Core Linux can be as easy as following a few simple steps, using several software tools. The basic steps are

1. Run a text editor, such as `vi` or a graphical programmer's editor, such as KDE's `kate`.

2. Type in C source code.

3. Save the changes.

4. Compile the program using the `gcc` compiler.

5. Run and test (debug) the program.

6. Edit the source code to implement new features or fix problems.

On the other hand, building a large and complex application can involve the efforts of many programmers, and require installing, configuring, and maintaining a source code control system (such as CVS, discussed later in this chapter), tracking program changes, developing software manuals, and using more complex software tools in the development process (such as `autoconf` or the `gdb` debugger).

Many Linux C programmers start by writing a program that solves an immediate need, such as a simple command-line program to download or upload phone numbers or other data to a cellular phone or handheld computer. Many beginners get started by becoming proficient in using a Linux text editor, researching any required software routines and reading documentation, browsing available Linux source code, learning how to run a compiler (such as `gcc`, discussed later in this chapter), and then launching into the iterative process of editing, compiling, executing, and testing.

The following sections in this chapter discuss some of the required or helpful software tools included with Fedora Core. You also see how to create, compile, and run a simple C program. You'll also see how to use several graphical prototyping tools (such as Glade, Designer, or KDevelop) to shorten the process of developing a user interface for graphical programs; these tools can free up time and effort on those tasks, allowing you to concentrate on the core functions of your new program.

Elements of the C/C++ Language

The C programming language has its own *syntax*—a specific form in which all commands and code must be written in order to be understood and processed by the computer system. The syntax you should understand when beginning to program in C includes the following:

- **Comments**—Comments are statements that document code and describe the program. A comment begins and ends with special characters, such as /* and */, that tell the compiler to ignore all content between those characters.

- **Identifiers**—You need to know how to properly name values, variables, and subroutines, such as &a, *p, and my_func().

- **Keywords**—Keywords are words that have special meaning to C and are therefore reserved for commands or parameters. The keywords int, char, and struct, for example, are used to declare variables, arrays, structures, and so on.

- **Constants**—You need to know how to use constants such as integers, floating-point numbers, characters, and character strings, such as 10, a, and "hello", and you need to know how to define symbolic constants, such as #define NULL 0.

- **Syntax notation**—You need to know how to use operators in expressions, which are used for calculations, retrieval, or assignment of values, such as for (;;) and line[n++] = a;.

You should also learn more about the software tools you will use for programming and the idiosyncrasies and features of the tools, such as GNU's gcc compiler system. (See the section "Using the GNU C Compiler," later in this chapter, for an overview of gcc.)

Using the C Programming Project Management Tools Provided with Fedora Core Linux

Fedora Core is replete with tools that make your life as a C/C++ programmer easier. There are tools to create programs (editors), compile programs (gcc), create libraries (ar), control the source (Revision Control System [RCS] and the Concurrent Versions System [CVS]), automate builds (make), debug programs (gdb and ddd), and determine where inefficiencies lie (gprof).

The following sections introduce some of the programming and project management tools included with Fedora. The discs included with this book contain many of these tools, which you can use to help automate software development projects. If you have some previous Unix experience, you will be familiar with most of these programs because they are traditional complements to a programmer's suite of software.

Building Programs with make

You use the make command to automatically build and install a C program, and for that use it is an easy tool. If you want to create your own automated builds, however, you need to learn the special syntax that make uses; the following sections walk you through a basic make setup.

Using Makefiles

The make command automatically builds and updates applications by using a *makefile*. A makefile is a text file that contains instructions about which options to pass on to the compiler preprocessor, the compiler, the assembler, and the linker. The makefile also specifies, among other things, which source code files need to be compiled (and the compiler command line) for a particular code module and which code modules are needed to build the program—a mechanism called *dependency checking*.

The beauty of the make command is its flexibility. You can use make with a simple makefile, or you can write complex makefiles that contain numerous macros, rules, or commands that work in a single directory or traverse your file system recursively to build programs, update your system, and even function as document management systems. The make command works with nearly any program, including text processing systems such as TeX.

You could use make to compile, build, and install a software package using a simple command like this:

```
# make install
```

You can use the default makefile (usually called Makefile, with a capital *M*), or you can use make's -f option to specify any makefile, such as MyMakeFile, like this:

```
# make -f MyMakeFile
```

Other options might be available, depending on the contents of your makefile.

Using Macros and Makefile Targets

Using make with macros can make a program portable. Macros allow users of other operating systems to easily configure a program build by specifying local values, such as the names and locations, or *pathnames*, of any required software tools. In the following example, macros define the name of the compiler (CC), the installer program (INS), where the program should be installed (INSDIR), where the linker should look for required libraries (LIBDIR), the names of required libraries (LIBS), a source code file (SRC), the intermediate object code file (OBS), and the name of the final program (PROG):

```
# a sample makefile for a skeleton program
CC= gcc
INS= install
INSDIR = /usr/local/bin
LIBDIR= -L/usr/X11R6/lib
LIBS= -lXm -lSM -lICE -lXt -lX11
SRC= skel.c
OBJS= skel.o
PROG= skel

skel:   ${OBJS}
        ${CC} -o ${PROG} ${SRC} ${LIBDIR} ${LIBS}

install: ${PROG}
        ${INS} -g root -o root ${PROG} ${INSDIR}
```

> **NOTE**
>
> The indented lines in the previous example are indented with tabs, not spaces. This is very important to remember! It is difficult for a person to see the difference, but make can tell. If make reports confusing errors when you first start building programs under Linux, you should check your project's makefile for the use of tabs and other proper formatting.

Using the makefile from the preceding example, you can build a program like this:

```
# make
```

To build a specified component of a makefile, you can use a target definition on the command line. To build just the program, you use make with the skel target, like this:

```
# make skel
```

If you make any changes to any element of a target object, such as a source code file, make rebuilds the target automatically. This feature is part of the convenience of using make to manage a development project. To build and install a program in one step, you can specify the target of install like this:

```
# make install
```

Larger software projects might have a number of traditional targets in the makefile, such as the following:

- test—To run specific tests on the final software
- man—To process an include a troff document with the man macros
- clean—To delete any remaining object files
- archive—To clean up, archive, and compress the entire source code tree
- bugreport—To automatically collect and then mail a copy of the build or error logs

Large applications can require hundreds of source code files. Compiling and linking these applications can be a complex and error-prone task. The make utility helps you organize the process of building the executable form of a complex application from many source files.

Using the autoconf Utility to Configure Code

The make command is only one of several programming automation utilities included with Fedora. There are others, such as pmake (which causes a parallel make), imake (which is a dependency-driven makefile generator that is used for building X11 clients), automake, and one of the newer tools, autoconf, which builds shell scripts that can be used to configure program source code packages.

Building many software packages for Linux that are distributed in source form requires the use of GNU's autoconf utility. This program builds an executable shell script named configure that, when executed, automatically examines and tailors a client's build from source according to software resources, or *dependencies* (such as programming tools, libraries, and associated utilities), that are installed on the target host (your Linux system). The idea is to increase software project portability and ease the task of the programmer who is faced with a software project expected to run on many compatible, yet potentially disparate, software platforms.

Many Linux commands and graphical clients for X downloaded in source code form include configure scripts. To configure the source package, build the software, and then install the new program, the root user might use the script like this (after uncompressing the source and navigating into the resulting build directory):

```
# ./configure ; make ; make install
```

The autoconf program uses a file named configure.in that contains a basic *ruleset*, or set of macros. The configure.in file is created with the autoscan command. Building a properly executing configure script also requires a template for the makefile, named Makefile.in. Although creating the dependency-checking configure script can be done manually, you can easily overcome any complex dependencies by using a graphical project development tool such as KDE's KDevelop or GNOME's Glade. (See the section "Graphical Development Tools," later in this chapter, for more information.)

Managing Software Projects with RCS and CVS

Although make can be used to manage a software project, larger software projects require document management, source code controls, security, and revision tracking as the source code goes through a series of changes during its development. RCS and CVS provide source code version control utilities for this kind of large software project management. You can find both of these utilities in RPM packages on your Fedora Core Linux CD-ROMs.

The RCS and CVS systems are used to track changes to multiple versions of files, and they can be used to backtrack or branch off versions of documents inside the scope of a project. They can also be used to prevent or resolve conflicting entries or changes made to source code files by multiple developers.

Although RCS and CVS provide similar features, RCS uses a locking and unlocking scheme to control access for making revisions; CVS, on the other hand, provides a modification and merging approach to working on older, current, or new versions of software. RCS uses different programs to check in or out of a revision under a directory; CVS uses a number of administrative files in a software repository of source code modules to merge and resolve change conflicts.

> **NOTE**
>
> Numerous changes to a source tree (directory of source code files) can also be accomplished using the patch command. Although patch does not offer the source control features of RCS

and CVS, it is very handy if there is a need to rapidly apply a "fix" to one or more files. You can use the diff command to create a patch, which is a text file that contains line-by-line differences between two files or directories of files. See "Patching the Kernel" in Chapter 38 for information on how to use patch to apply updates to the Linux kernel source tree.

RCS uses at least the following eight separate programs to track source code revisions:

- ci—Checks in revisions
- co—Checks out revisions
- ident—Starts the keyword utility for source files
- rcs—Changes file attributes
- rcsclean—Cleans up working files
- rcsdiff—Starts the revision comparison utility
- rcsmerge—Merges revisions
- rlog—Activates the logging and information utility

Source code control with CVS requires the use of at least the following six command options on the cvs command line:

- checkout—Checks out revisions
- update—Updates your sources with changes made by other developers
- add—Adds new files in cvs records
- import—Adds new sources to the repository
- remove—Eliminates files from the repository
- commit—Publishes changes to other repository developers

Note that some of these commands require you to use additional fields, such as the names of files.

RCS and CVS can be used for more than software development projects. These tools can be used for document preparation and workgroup editing of documents, and they can work with any text files. Both systems use registration and control files to accomplish revision management. Both systems also offer the opportunity to revisit any step or branch in a revision history and to restore previous versions of a project. This mechanism is extremely important in cross-platform development and for software maintenance.

Tracking information is usually contained in separate control files; each document within a project might contain information that is automatically updated with each change to a project. A process called *keyword substitution* is used to perform these automatic updates.

CVS and RCS use similar keywords, which are usually included inside C comment strings (/* */) near the top of a document. The following are some of the available keywords:

- $Author$—The username of the person who performed the last check-in

- $Date$—The date and time of the last check-in

- $Header$—The pathname of the document's RCS file, with the revision number, date and time, author, and state inserted

- Id—Same as $Header$, but without a full pathname

- $Name$—A symbolic name (see the co man page)

- $Revision$—The assigned revision number (such as 1.1)

- $Source$—The RCS file's full pathname

- $State$—The state of the document, such as Exp for experimental, Rel for released, or Stab for stable

You can also use these keywords to insert version information into compiled programs by using character strings in program source code. For example, given an extremely short C program named foo.c, you could use the following to assign version info to a variable (rsrcid in the example), which will then be embedded in the binary program:

```
/* $Header$ */
#include <stdio.h>
static char rsrcid[] = "$Header$";
main() {
    printf("Hello, Linus!\n");
}
```

The resulting $Header$ keyword might expand to this in an RCS document:

```
$Header: /home/bball/sw/RCS/foo.c,v 1.1 1999/04/20 15:01:07 root Exp Root $
```

Getting started with RCS is as simple as creating a project directory and an RCS directory under the project directory and then creating or copying initial source files in the project directory. You can then use the ci command to check in documents. Getting started with CVS requires that you initialize a repository by first setting the $CVSROOT environment variable with the full pathname of the repository and then using the init command option with the cvs command, like this:

```
# cvs init
```

You can find documentation for RCS and CVS in various man pages, under the /usr/share/doc directories for each of them, and in GNU information documents.

TIP

Even though they are free, CVS and RCS are powerful software project management tools. Many organizations use CVS and RCS to manage the source for their projects. Commercial code-management tools (also called *version-control programs*) also exist that include fancy interfaces, homogenous platform support, and greater flexibility than RCS and CVS. But those tools require dedicated administrators and might have significant licensing costs—both of which are major disadvantages.

Making Libraries with ar

C and C++ project management tools can help ease the process of building large applications; the ar command is an example of such a tool. If several different programs use the same functions, they can be combined into a single library archive. You use the ar command to build such a library. When you include the library on the compile line, the archive is searched to resolve any external symbols. Listing 32.1 shows an example of building and using a library.

LISTING 32.1   Building and Using a Library

```
$ gcc -c sine.c
$ gcc -c cosine.c
$ gcc -c tangent.c
$ ar c libtrig.a sine.o cosine.o tangent.o

$ gcc -c mainprog.c
$ gcc -o mainprog mainprog.o libtrig.a
```

Remember that gcc is the command that you use to invoke the GNU C compiler. (The section "Using the GNU C Compiler," later in this chapter, explains what -c and -o mean.)

Debugging Tools

Debugging is both a science and an art. Sometimes, the simplest tool—the code listing—is the best debugging tool. At other times, however, you need to use other debugging tools. Three of these tools are splint, gprof, and gdb.

Using splint to Check Source Code

The splint command is similar to the traditional Unix lint command: It statically examines source code for possible problems, and it also has many additional features. Even if your C code meets the standards for C and compiles cleanly, it might still contain errors. splint performs many types of checks and can provide extensive error information. For example, this simple program might compile cleanly and even run:

```
$ gcc -o tux tux.c
$ ./tux
```

But the splint command might point out some serious problems with the source:

```
$ splint tux.c
Splint 3.1.1 --- 17 Feb 2004

tux.c: (in function main)
tux.c:2:19: Return value (type int) ignored: putchar(t[++j] -...
   Result returned by function call is not used. If this is intended, can cast
   result to (void) to eliminate message. (Use -retvalint to inhibit warning)
Finished checking --- 1 code warning
```

You can use the splint command's -strict option, like this, to get a more verbose report:

```
$ splint -strict tux.c
```

The GNU C compiler also supports diagnostics through the use of extensive warnings (through the -Wall and -pedantic options):

```
$ gcc -Wall tux.c
tux.c:1: warning: return type defaults to `int'
tux.c: In function `main':
tux.c:2: warning: implicit declaration of function `putchar'
```

> **NOTE**
>
> If you would like to explore various C syntax-checking programs, navigate to
> http://www.ibiblio.org/pub/Linux/devel/lang/c/. The splint program is derived from lclint,
> which you can find in the lclint-2.2a-src.tar.gz file at the website.

Using gprof to Track Function Time

You use the gprof (profile) command to study how a program is spending its time. If a program is compiled and linked with -p as a flag, a mon.out file is created when it executes, with data on how often each function is called and how much time is spent in each function. gprof parses and displays this data. An analysis of the output generated by gprof helps you determine where performance bottlenecks occur. Using an optimizing compiler can speed up a program, but taking the time to use gprof's analysis and revising bottleneck functions significantly improves program performance.

Doing Symbolic Debugging with gdb

The gdb tool is a symbolic debugger. When a program is compiled with the -g flag, the symbol tables are retained, and a symbolic debugger can be used to track program bugs. The basic technique is to invoke gdb after a core dump (a file containing a snapshot of the memory used by a program that has crashed) and get a stack trace. The stack trace indicates the source line where the core dump occurred and the functions that were called to reach that line. Often, this is enough to identify a problem. It isn't the limit of gdb, though.

gdb also provides an environment for debugging programs interactively. Invoking gdb with a program enables you to set breakpoints, examine the values of variables, and monitor variables. If you suspect a problem near a line of code, you can set a breakpoint at that line and run gdb. When the line is reached, execution is interrupted. You can check variable values, examine the stack trace, and observe the program's environment. You can single-step through the program to check values. You can resume execution at any point. By using breakpoints, you can discover many bugs in code.

A graphical X Window interface to gdb is called the Data Display Debugger, or ddd.

NOTE

If you browse to http://www.ibiblio.org/pub/Linux/devel/debuggers/, you can find at least a dozen different debuggers.

Using the GNU C Compiler

If you elected to install the development tools package when you installed Fedora Core (or perhaps later on, using RPM, or other package tools), you should have the GNU C compiler (gcc). Many different options are available for the GNU C compiler, and many of them are similar to those of the C and C++ compilers that are available on other Unix systems. Table 32.1 shows the important switches for gcc. You can look at the man page or information file for gcc for a full list of options and descriptions

TABLE 32.1   GNU C Compiler Switches

Switch	Description
-x *language*	Specifies the language; C, C++, Java, and assembler are valid values.
-c	Compiles and assembles only; does not link.
-S	Compiles; does not assemble or link. Generates an assembly code (.s) file.
-E	Preprocesses only; does not compile, assemble, or link.
-o *file*	Specifies the output filename. a.out is the default.
-l *library*	Specifies the libraries to use.
-I *directory*	Searches the specified directory for include files.
-w	Inhibits warning messages.
-pedantic	Requires strict ANSI compliance.
-Wall	Prints additional warning messages.
-g	Produces debugging information for use with gdb.
-ggdb	Generates native-format debugging info and gdb extensions.
-p	Produces information required by gprof.
-pg	Produces information for use by gprof.
-O	Optimizes the compilation.

> **NOTE**
>
> Fedora Core always includes a recent release of gcc, but newer versions of gcc appear from time to time. You should be aware that if you use gcc to develop programs for earlier versions of Linux, your programs might not load or run because of software library incompatibilities. You can always install an older version of gcc and compatible development libraries to support building programs that work with older versions of Linux. These problems can occur because older and newer versions of software libraries might have different ideas about how standard routines are used.

When you build a C program using gcc, the compilation process takes place in several steps:

1. First, the C preprocessor parses the file. To do so, it sequentially reads the lines, includes header files, and performs macro replacement.

2. The compiler parses the modified code to determine whether the correct syntax is used. In the process, it builds a symbol table and creates an intermediate object format. Most symbols have specific memory addresses assigned, although symbols defined in other modules, such as external variables, do not.

3. The last compilation stage, linking, ties together different files and libraries and then links the files by resolving the symbols that had not previously been resolved.

> **NOTE**
>
> Most C programs compile with a C++ compiler if you follow strict ANSI rules. For example, you can compile the standard hello.c program (everyone's first program) with the GNU C++ compiler. Typically, you name the file something like hello.cc, hello.C, hello.c++, or hello.cxx. The GNU C++ compiler accepts any of these names.

A Simple C Program

This section provides a simple example of how to create an executable program for Linux by using gcc. One of the shortest programs you can write in C for Linux is the quintessential "hello, world" program (popularized by Brian W. Kernighan and Dennis M. Ritchie in their 1978 book *The C Programming Language*).

To get started, type in the following text, using your favorite Linux text editor:

```
main(){
    printf("hello, world.\n");
}
```

When you are finished, save the file as hello.c, and then compile the program by using the gcc compiler system, like this:

```
$ gcc -o hello hello.c
```

This command line creates an executable program named hello, using the file hello.c as input. You can then run the program like this:

```
$ ./hello
hello, world.
```

The C program contains only one function, named main(). The gcc command line specifies the name of the output program (using the -o option) and the input source file, hello.c. Note that in order to run the new hello command, you must specify it explicitly, using the period and forward-slash characters, as the program is not installed in a normal command directory (such as /usr/bin or /usr/local/bin).

> **NOTE**
>
> You can build large programs in C. C programs can be broken into any number of files, as long as no single function spans more than one file. To compile a program, you compile each source file into an intermediate object before you link all the objects into a single executable. The -c flag tells the compiler to stop at that stage. During the link stage, all the object files should be listed on the command line. Object files are identified by the .o suffix.

Graphical Development Tools

Fedora Core includes a number of graphical prototyping and development environments for use during X sessions. If you want to build client software for KDE or GNOME, you might find the KDevelop, Qt Designer, and Glade programs extremely helpful. You can use each of these programs to build graphical frameworks for interactive windowing clients, and you can use each of them to automatically generate the necessary skeleton of code needed to support a custom interface for your program.

Using the KDevelop Client

You can launch the KDevelop client (shown in Figure 32.1) from the desktop panel's start menu's Extras, Programming menu item or from the command line of a terminal window, like this:

```
$ kdevelop &
```

After you press Enter, the KDevelop Setup Wizard runs, and you are taken through several short wizard dialogs that set up and ensure a stable build environment. You must then run kdevelop again (either from the command line or by clicking its menu item under the desktop panel's Programming menu). You will then see the main KDevelop window and can start your project by selecting KDevelop's Project menu and clicking the New menu item.

You can begin building your project by stepping through the wizard dialogs. When you click the Create button, KDevelop automatically generates all the files that are normally found in a KDE client source directory (including the configure script, which checks dependencies and builds the client's makefile). To test your client, you can either first click the Build menu's Make menu item (or press F8) or just click the Execute menu item (or press F9), and the client is built automatically. You can use KDevelop to create KDE clients, plug-ins for the konqueror browser, KDE kicker panel applets, KDE desktop themes, Qt library–based clients, and even programs for GNOME.

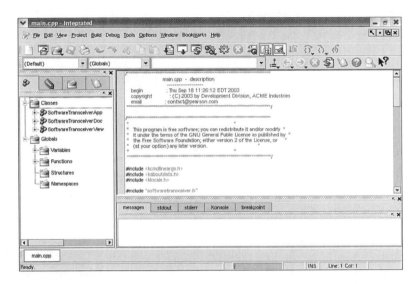

FIGURE 32.1   KDE's KDevelop is a rapid prototyping and client-building tool for use with Linux.

Trolltech's Qt Designer

A development environment that is related to KDevelop and is included with Fedora Core is Trolltech's Qt Designer. You can use this program to build user interface "forms" for cross-platform applications. Qt Designer has a complex interface that supports drawing of windows, buttons, and other client controls. You can start Qt Designer from the command line of a terminal window like this:

```
$ designer &
```

You can also start the prototyping environment by clicking its menu item under the Programming menu's More Programming tools menu. The Qt Designer main window (as shown in Figure 32.2) provides tools to quickly build and preview a graphical client. After first creating a directory to hold the project files, start by choosing File, New Menu to create a new project. Then, you can select a C++ project and save it with a name that ends with .pro.

FIGURE 32.2   Trolltech's Qt Designer is, like KDevelop, a capable prototyping and client-building tool for use with Linux and X.

Next, you can again use the File menu to add a file, but this time, you select a window, widget, or dialog, depending on the graphical interface you'd like to add to your project. After you design the program's GUI, you can preview your design by using the Preview menu. You can also test a build of the new client if you have added enough requisite code. You begin by navigating to your project's folder (using the cd command), and then you use the qmake and make commands, like this:

```
$ qmake –o Makefile myproject.pro
$ make
$ ./myproject
```

The Glade Client for Developing in GNOME

If you prefer to use GNOME and its development tools, the Glade GTK++ GUI builder (the glade-2 client) can help you save time and effort when building a basic skeleton for a program. You launch glade-2 from the desktop panel's Programming menu or from the command line of a terminal window, like this:

```
$ glade-2 &
```

> **TIP**
>
> Click the Contents menu item from the Glade Help menu to read a step-by-step guide on building a simple client interface. You'll also find an introductory tutorial on programming with Glade by Ishan Chattopadhyaya at http://wingtk.sourceforge.net/ishan/glade.html.

When you launch Glade, a directory named `Projects` is created in your home directory, and you see a main window, along with two floating palette and properties windows (see Figure 32.3, which shows a basic GNOME client with a calendar widget added to its main window). You can use Glade's File menu to save the blank project and then start building your client by clicking and adding user interface elements from the Palette window. For example, you can first click the Palette window's Gnome button and then click to create your new client's main window. A window with a menu and a toolbar appears—the basic framework for a new GNOME client!

FIGURE 32.3   The GNOME Glade client can be used to build and preview a graphical interface for a custom GNOME program.

When you have finished building the client, you can select Build Source Code from the Project window's File menu, and Glade builds the necessary source code and scripts for the project. You can then build the project's `configure` script by executing the `autogen.sh` script in the project directory, like so:

```
$ ./autogen.sh
```

After you set up the project, as with KDevelop projects, you are ready to configure, build, and install your project. To begin that process, execute the following:

```
# make install
```

You will need to add code to fill in the actions for your new KDE or GNOME client when using these rapid prototyping tools. But kdevelop, designer, and glade can help save development time and effort. Use these environments to create a working skeleton application, and then fine-tune your new client's user interface.

Related Fedora Core and Linux Commands

You will use many of these commands when programming in C and C++ for Linux:

ar—The GNU archive development tool

as—The GNU assembler

autoconf—The GNU configuration script generator

cervisia—A KDE client that provides a graphical interface to a CVS project

cvs—A project revision control system

designer—Trolltech's graphical prototyping tool for use with Qt libraries and X

gcc—The GNU C/C++ compiler system

gdb—The GNU interactive debugger

glade-2—The GNOME graphical development environment for building GTK+ clients

gprof—The GNU program profiler

kdevelop—The KDE C/C++ graphical development environment for building KDE, GNOME, or terminal clients

make—A GNU project management command

patch—Larry Wall's source patching utility

pmake—A BSD project management command

rcs—A suite of programs used to manage project documents

splint—The C source file checker

xmkmf—A shell script for X that is used to create a localized makefile for building an X client

---

Additional Resources

Unix and Linux were built on the C language. C is a platform-independent, compiled, procedural language based on functions and on the capability to derive new, programmer-defined data structures.

NOTE

Many people consider *The C Programming Language*, by Brian W. Kernighan and Dennis M. Ritchie, to be the definitive book for those who want to learn how to program in C.

If you are interested in learning more about C and C++, you should look for the following books:

- *Sams Teach Yourself C in 21 Days*, by Peter Aitken and Bradley Jones, Sams Publishing
- *Sams Teach Yourself C++ for Linux in 21 Days*, by Jesse Liberty and David B. Horvath, Sams Publishing

- *C How to Program* and *C++ How to Program*, both by Harvey M. Deitel and Paul J. Deitel, Deitel Associates

- *The C Programming Language*, by Brian W. Kernighan and Dennis M. Ritchie, Prentice Hall

- *The Annotated C++ Reference Manual*, by Margaret A. Ellis and Bjarne Stroustrup, ANSI Base Document

- *Programming in ANSI C*, by Stephen G. Kochan, Sams Publishing

Reference

http://gcc.gnu.org/java/compile.html—More information about GCC's Java support

http://www.gnu.org/software/autoconf/autoconf.html—More information about the GNU Project's autoconf utility and how to build portable software projects

http://sourcenav.sourceforge.net/—Home page for Red Hat's snavigator client, a source code analysis utility

http://www.trolltech.com/products/qt/tools.html—Trolltech's page for Qt Designer and a number of programming automation tools (including translators) that you can use with Fedora

http://glade.gnome.org/—Home page for the Glade GNOME developer's tool

http://www.kdevelop.org/—Site that hosts the KDevelop Project's latest versions of the KDE graphical development environment, KDevelop

PART VI

Fedora Housekeeping

IN THIS PART

CHAPTER **33**

Securing Your Machines

In today's world of interconnected computers and "always-on" access to the Internet, the importance of maintaining a secure computer has never been greater. Although there are a limited number of truly dangerous hackers in the world, only the FBI, CIA, and other world agencies need worry about them. The rest of us have to face script kiddies (unskilled hacker-wannabes who use prewritten hack programs), disgruntled employees, and fast-spreading worms—more than enough to keep our hands full.

As long as anyone has access to your system, whether physical or over a network, there is the threat that information stored on the network can be compromised. The more access given, the higher the threat. If your network is connected to the Internet, the threat of someone breaking into your computer is very real.

No home computer with a connection to the Internet is 100% safe. If this information causes you concern, it should. Although there is no way to stop a serious cracker who is intent on getting into your computer or network, there are ways to make it harder for him and to warn you when he does.

In this chapter, we discuss all aspects of securing your Linux machines. You might have wondered why we did not spread this information around the book wherever it was appropriate, but the reason is simple: If you ever have a security problem with Linux, you know you can turn to this page and start reading without having to search or try to remember where you saw a tip. Everything you need is here in this one chapter, and we strongly advise you read it from start to finish.

> **Built-in Protection in the Kernel**
>
> A number of networking and low-level protective services are built in to the Linux kernel. These services can be enabled, disabled, or displayed using the `sysctl` command, or by echoing a value (usually a 1 or a 0 to turn a service on or off) to a kernel process file under the `/proc` directory. One of the newest features is the ExecShield kernel enhancement. This feature protects your system by randomizing the location of processes in virtual memory and disallowing execution of parts of memory after a program loads. See the Fedora Release Notes for more information.

Understanding Computer Attacks

There are many ways in which computer attacks can be divided, but perhaps the easiest is *internal*, which are computer attacks done by someone with access to a computer on the local network, and *external*, which are attacks by someone with access to a computer through the Internet. This might sound like a trivial separation to make, but it is actually important: Unless you routinely hire talented computer hackers or allow visitors to plug computers into your network, the worst internal attack you are likely encounter is from a disgruntled employee.

> **Hacker Versus Cracker**
>
> In earlier days, there was a distinction made between the words *hacker* and *cracker*. A hacker was someone who used technology to innovate in new or unusual ways, whereas a cracker was someone who used technology to attack another's computers and cause harm.
>
> This distinction was lost on the general public, so the term *hacker* has now come to mean the same as *cracker*. This book follows general usage, so a *hacker* is a malicious person using his computer to cause problems for others.

Although you should never ignore the internal threat, you should arguably be more concerned with the outside world. The big bad Internet is a security vortex. Machines connected directly to the outside world can be attacked by people across the world, and invariably are, even only a few minutes after having been connected.

This situation is not a result of malicious users lying in wait for your IP address to do something interesting. Instead, canny virus writers have created worms that exploit a vulnerability, take control of a machine, and then spread it to other machines around them. As a result, most attacks today are the result of these autohacking tools; there are only a handful of true hackers around, and, to be frank, if one of these ever actually targets you seriously, it will take a mammoth effort to repel him regardless of which operating system you run.

Autohacking scripts also come in another flavor: prewritten code that exploits a vulnerability and gives its users special privileges on the hacked machine. These scripts are rarely used by their creators; instead, they are posted online and downloaded by wannabe hackers, who then use them to attack vulnerable machines.

So, the external category is itself made up of worms, serious day job hackers, and wannabe hackers (usually called *script kiddies*). Combined they will assault your Internet-facing servers, and it is your job to make sure your boxes stay up, happily ignoring the firefight around them.

On the internal front, things are somewhat more difficult. Users who sit inside your fire-wall are already past your primary source of defense and, worse, they might even have physical access to your machines.

Regardless of the source of the attack, there is a five-step checklist you can follow to secure your Fedora box:

1. Assess your vulnerability. Decide which machines can be attacked, which services they are running, and who has access to them.

2. Configure the server for maximum security. Only install what you need, only run what you must, and configure a local firewall.

3. Secure physical access to the server.

4. Create worst-case-scenario policies.

5. Keep up-to-date with security news.

Each of these is covered in the following sections, and each is as important as the others.

Assessing Your Vulnerability

It is a common mistake for people to assume that switching on a firewall makes them safe. This is not the case and, in fact, has never been the case. Each system has distinct security needs, and taking the time to customize its security layout will give you maximum security and the best performance.

The following list summarizes the most common mistakes:

- **Installing every package**—Do you plan to use the machine as a DNS server? If not, why have BIND installed? Go through the Add/Remove Applications dialog and ensure that you have only the software you need.

- **Enabling unused services**—Do you want to administer the machine remotely? Do you want people to upload files? If not, turn off SSH and FTP because they just add needless attack vectors. This goes for many other services.

- **Disabling the local firewall on the grounds that you already have a firewall at the perimeter**—In security, depth is crucial: The more layers someone has to hack through, the higher the likelihood she will give up or get caught.

- **Letting your machine give out more information than it needs to**—Many machines are configured to give out software names and version numbers by default, which is just giving hackers a helping hand.

- **Placing your server in an unlocked room**—If so, you might as well just turn it off now and save the worry. The exception to this is if all the employees at your company are happy and trustworthy. But why take the risk?

- **Plugging your machine into a wireless network**—Unless you need wireless, avoid it, particularly if your machine is a server. Never plug a server into a wireless network because it is just too fraught with security problems.

After you have ruled out these, you are onto the real problem: Which attack vectors are open on your server? In Internet terms, this comes down to which services are Internet-facing and which ports they are running on.

Two tools are often used to determine your vulnerabilities: Nmap and Nessus. Nessus scans your machine, queries the services running, checks their version numbers against its list of vulnerabilities, and reports problems.

Although Nessus sounds clever, it does not work well in many modern distributions (Fedora included) because of the way patches are made available to software. For example, if you're running Apache 2.0.52 and a bug is found that's fixed in 2.0.53, Fedora back-ports that patch to 2.0.52. This is done because the new release probably also includes new features that might break your code, so the Red Hat team takes only what is necessary and copies it into your version. As a result, Nessus will see the version 2.0.52 and think it is vulnerable to a bug that has in fact been backported.

The better solution is to use Nmap, which scans your machine and reports on any open TCP/IP ports it finds. Any service you have installed that responds to Nmap's query is pointed out, which enables you to ensure that you have locked everything down as much as possible.

To install Nmap, select System Settings, Add/Remove Applications. Near the bottom of the list of applications is System Tools, where you can select Nmap-frontend and Nmap. Although you can use Nmap from a command line, it is easier to use with the front end—at least until you become proficient. To run the front end, select Actions, Run Application and run `nmapfe`. If you want to enable all Nmap's options, you need to switch to root and run `nmapfe` from the console.

The best way to run Nmap is to use the SYN Stealth scan, with OS Detection and Version Probe turned on. You need to be root to enable the first two options (they are on by default when you are root), but it is well worth it. When you run Nmap (click the Scan button), it tests every port on your machine and checks whether it responds. If it does respond, Nmap queries it for version information and then prints its results onscreen.

The output lists the port numbers, service name (what usually occupies that port), and version number for every open port on your system. Hopefully, the information Nmap shows you will not be a surprise. If there is something open that you do not recognize, a hacker might have placed a backdoor on your system to allow herself easy access.

You should use the output from Nmap to help you find and eliminate unwanted services. The fewer services that are open to the outside world, the more secure you are.

Protecting Your Machine

After you have disabled all the unneeded services on your system, what remains is a core set of connections and programs that you want to keep. However, you are not finished yet: You need to clamp down your wireless network, lock your server physically, and put scanning procedures in place (such as Tripwire and promiscuous mode network monitors).

Securing a Wireless Network

Because wireless networking has some unique security issues, those issues deserve a separate discussion here. (General network security issues are discussed in "Securing Your Network," later in this chapter.)

Wireless networking, although convenient, can be very insecure by its very nature because transmitted data (even encrypted data) can be received by remote devices. Those devices could be in the same room; in the house, apartment, or building next door; or even several blocks away. Extra care must be used to protect the actual frequency used by your network. Great progress has been made in the past couple of years, but the possibility of a security breach is increased when the attacker is in the area and knows the frequency on which to listen. It should also be noted that the encryption method used by more wireless NICs is weaker than other forms of encryption (such as SSH) and should not be considered as part of your security plan.

> **TIP**
>
> Always use OpenSSH-related tools, such as `ssh` or `sftp`, to conduct business on your wireless LAN. Passwords are not transmitted as plain text, and your sessions are encrypted. See Chapter 25, "Remote Access with SSH and Telnet," to see how to connect to remote systems using `ssh`.

The better the physical security is around your network, the more secure it will be (this applies to wired networks as well). Keep wireless transmitters (routers, switches, and so on) as close to the center of your building as possible. Note or monitor the range of transmitted signals to determine whether your network is open to mobile network sniffing—now a geek sport known as *war driving*. (Linux software is available at http://sourceforge.net/project/showfiles.php?group_id=57253.) An occasional walk around your building not only gives you a break from work, but can also give you a chance to notice any people or equipment that should not be in the area.

Keep in mind that it takes only a single rogue wireless access point hooked up to a legitimate network hub to open access to your entire system. These access points can be smaller than a pack of cigarettes, so the only way to spot them is to scan for them with another wireless device.

Passwords and Physical Security

The next step toward better security is to use secure passwords on your network and ensure that users use them as well, especially the root password. If the root password on just one machine is cracked, the whole network is in trouble. For somewhat more physical security, you can force the use of a password with the LILO or GRUB bootloaders, remove bootable devices such as floppy and CD-ROM drives, or configure a network-booting server for Fedora. This approach is not well supported or documented at the time of this writing, but you can read about one way to do this in Brieuc Jeunhomme's Network Boot and Exotic Root HOWTO, available at http://www.tldp.org/HOWTO/Network-boot-HOWTO/. You can also read more about GRUB and LILO in Chapter 38, "Kernel and Module Management."

Also, keep in mind that some studies show that as much as 90% of network break-ins are by current or former employees. If a person no longer requires access to your network, lock out access or, even better, remove the account immediately. A good security policy also dictates that any data associated with the account first be backed up and retained for a set period of time to ensure against loss of important data. If you are able, remove the terminated employee from the system before he leaves the building.

Finally, be aware of physical security. If a potential attacker can get physical access to your system, getting full access becomes trivial. Keep all servers in a locked room, and ensure that only authorized personnel are given access to clients.

Configuring and Using Tripwire

Tripwire is a security tool that checks the integrity of normal system binaries and reports any changes to syslog or by email. Tripwire is a good tool for ensuring that your binaries have not been replaced by Trojan horse programs. *Trojan horses* are malicious programs inadvertently installed because of identical filenames to distributed (expected) programs, and they can wreak havoc on a breached system.

Fedora does not include the free version of Tripwire, but it can be used to monitor your system. To set up Tripwire for the first time, go to http://www.tripwire.org, and then download and install an open-source version of the software. After installation, run the `twinstall.sh` script (found under `/etc/tripwire`) as root like so:

```
# /etc/tripwire/twinstall.sh
----------------------------------------------
The Tripwire site and local passphrases are used to
sign a variety of files, such as the configuration,
policy, and database files.

Passphrases should be at least 8 characters in length
and contain both letters and numbers.

See the Tripwire manual for more information.

----------------------------------------------
Creating key files...
```

```
(When selecting a passphrase, keep in mind that good passphrases typically
have upper and lower case letters, digits and punctuation marks, and are
at least 8 characters in length.)

Enter the site keyfile passphrase:
```

You then need to enter a password of at least eight characters (perhaps best is a string of random madness, such as 5fwkc4ln) at least twice. The script generates keys for your site (host) and then asks you to enter a password (twice) for local use. You are then asked to enter the new site password. After following the prompts, the (rather extensive) default configuration and policy files (tw.cfg and tw.pol) are encrypted. You should then back up and delete the original plain-text files installed by Fedora's RPM package.

To then initialize Tripwire, use its --init option like so:

```
# tripwire --init
Please enter your local passphrase:
Parsing policy file: /etc/tripwire/tw.pol
Generating the database...
*** Processing Unix File System ***
....
Wrote database file: /var/lib/tripwire/shuttle2.twd
The database was successfully generated.
```

Note that not all the output is shown here. After Tripwire has created its database (which is a snapshot of your file system), it uses this baseline along with the encrypted configuration and policy settings under the /etc/tripwire directory to monitor the status of your system. You should then start Tripwire in its integrity checking mode, using a desired option. (See the tripwire manual page for details.) For example, you can have Tripwire check your system and then generate a report at the command line, like so:

```
# tripwire -m c
```

No output is shown here, but a report is displayed in this example. The output could be redirected to a file, but a report is saved as /var/lib/tripwire/report/hostname-YYYYMMDD-HHMMSS.twr (in other words, using your host's name, the year, the month, the day, the hour, the minute, and the seconds). This report can be read using the twprint utility, like so:

```
# twprint --print-report -r \
/var/lib/tripwire/report/shuttle2-20020919-181049.twr ¦ less
```

Other options, such as emailing the report, are supported by Tripwire, which should be run as a scheduled task by your system's scheduling table, /etc/crontab, on off-hours. (It can be resource intensive on less powerful computers.) The Tripwire software package also includes a twadmin utility you can use to fine-tune or change settings or policies or to perform other administrative duties.

33

Devices

Do not ever advertise that you have set a NIC to promiscuous mode. Promiscuous mode (which can be set on an interface by using `ifconfig`'s `promisc` option) is good for monitoring traffic across the network and can often allow you to monitor the actions of someone who might have broken into your network. The `tcpdump` command also sets a designated interface to promiscuous mode while the program runs; unfortunately, the `ifconfig` command does not report this fact while `tcpdump` is running! Keep in mind that this is one way a cracker will use to monitor your network to gain the ever-so-important root password.

NOTE

Browse to http://www.redhat.com/docs/manuals/ to read about how to detect unauthorized network intrusions or packet browsing (known as network *sniffing*). You can use the information to help protect your system. Scroll down the page and click the Security guide link.

Do not forget to use the right tool for the right job. Although a network bridge can be used to connect your network to the Internet, it would not be a good option. Bridges have almost become obsolete because they forward any packet that comes their way, which is not good when a bridge is connected to the Internet. A router enables you to filter which packets are relayed.

Viruses

In the right hands, Linux is every bit as vulnerable to viruses as Windows is. That might come as a surprise to you, particularly if you made the switch to Linux on the basis of its security record. However, the difference between Windows and Linux is that it is much easier to secure against viruses on Linux. Indeed, as long as you are smart, you need never worry about them. Here is why:

- Linux never puts the current directory in your executable path, so typing `ls` runs `/bin/ls` rather than any `ls` in the current directory.

- A nonroot user is only ever able to infect files he has write access to, which is usually only the files in his home directory. This is one of the most important reasons for never using the root account longer than you need to!

- Linux forces you to mark files as executable, so you can't accidentally run a file called `myfile.txt.exe`, thinking it was just a text file.

- By having more than one common web browser and email client, Linux has strength through diversity: Virus writers cannot target one platform and hit 90% of the users.

Despite saying all that, Linux is susceptible to being a carrier for viruses. If you run a mail server, your Linux box can send virus-infected mails on to Windows boxes. The Linux machine would be fine, but the Windows client would be taken down by the virus.

In this situation, you should consider a virus scanner for your machine. You have several to choose from, both free and commercial. The most popular free suite is Clam AV (www.clamav.net), but Central Command, BitDefender, F-Secure, Kaspersky, McAfee, and others all compete to provide commercial solutions—look around for the best deal before you commit.

Configuring Your Firewall

Always use a hardware-based or software-based firewall on computers connected to the Internet. Fedora includes a graphical firewall configuration client named `system-config-securitylevel`, along with a console-based firewall client named `lokkit`. Use these tools to implement selective or restrictive policies regarding access to your computer or LAN.

Start the `lokkit` command from a console or terminal window. You must run this command as root; otherwise, you will see an error message like this:

```
$ /usr/sbin/lokkit
ERROR - You must be root to run lokkit.
```

Use the su command to run `lokkit` like this:

```
$ su -c "/usr/sbin/lokkit"
```

After you press Enter, you see a dialog as shown in Figure 33.1. Press the Tab key to navigate to enable or disable firewalling. You can also customize your firewall settings to allow specific protocols access through a port and to designate an Ethernet interface for firewalling if multiple NICs are installed. Note that you can also use a graphical interface version of `lokkit` by running the `gnome-lokkit` client during an X session.

FIGURE 33.1   Fedora's `lokkit` command quickly generates firewall rules in memory for Linux.

Using `system-config-securitylevel` is a fast and easy way to implement a simple packet-filtering ruleset with filtering rules used to accept or reject TCP and UDP packets flowing through your host's Ethernet or designated device, such as `eth0` or `ppp0`. The rules are created on-the-fly and implemented immediately in memory using `iptables`.

Start `system-config-securitylevel` from the System Settings menu's Security level menu item. You are prompted for the root password and the client's window then appears. Figure 33.2 shows firewalling enabled for the `eth0` Ethernet device, allowing incoming secure shell and HTTP requests.

FIGURE 33.2   Fedora's `system-config-securitylevel` client can also be used to quickly generate and implement standard or simple custom firewall rules for Linux.

Fedora and Firewalling

Fedora also supports the older—but still popular—`ipchains` packet-filtering software, which can be used to construct effective firewalling rules on Linux firewalls, gateways, servers, and workstations. Linux also supports the more capable `iptables`, or NetFilter system, which offers additional controls and logging facilities used to build filtering *rulesets*, or filtering instructions.

Unfortunately, Fedora does not include any command-line or graphical interface utilities you can use to build, save, and test complex `iptables` rulesets, usually implemented as shell scripts. You need to do this if you want to control outgoing as well as incoming packets. However, you can write your own using a text editor such as vi. Many experienced Linux users hand-tune rulesets for specific application in advanced network situations, such as development of routing rules.

For a good overview and all the details about using `iptables` for a variety of gateway and firewall systems, read Robert L. Ziegler's excellent book, *Linux Firewalls, Second Edition*, available from New Riders. You can also browse to his site at http://www.linux-firewall-tools.com/linux/firewall/index.html, which offers a graphical, web-based firewall design and construction tool you can use to quickly build a custom `ipchains`-based ruleset file.

You can use Fedora to create a custom firewall, perhaps supporting IP masquerading (also known as *NAT*) by using either `ipchains` or `iptables`. You'll find two sample scripts under the `/usr/share/doc/rp-pppoe/configs` directory; these are used when connecting to the Internet using a digital subscriber line (DSL).

Forming a Disaster Recovery Plan

No one likes planning for the worst, which is why two thirds of people do not have wills. It is a scary thing to have your systems hacked: One or more criminals has broken through your carefully laid blocks and caused untold damage to the machine. Your boss, if you have one, will want a full report of what happened and why, and your users will want their email when they sit down at their desks in the morning. What to do?

If you ever do get hacked, nothing will take the stress away entirely. However, if you take the time to prepare a proper response in advance, you should at least avoid premature aging. Here are some tips to get you started:

- **Do not just pull the network cable out**—This alerts the hacker that he has been detected, which rules out any opportunities for security experts to monitor for that hacker returning and actually catch him.

- **Only inform the people who need to know**—Your boss and other IT people are at the top of the list; other employees are not. Keep in mind that it could be one of the employees behind the attack, and this tips them off.

- **If the machine is not required and you do not want to trace the attack, you can safely remove it from the network**—However, do not switch it off because some backdoors are only enabled when the system is rebooted.

- **Take a copy of all the log files on the system and store them somewhere else**—These might have been tampered with, but they might contain nuggets of information.

- **Check the `/etc/passwd` file and look for users you do not recognize**—Change all the passwords on the system, and remove bad users.

- **Check the output of `ps aux` for unusual programs running**—Also check to see whether any cron jobs are set to run.

- **Look in `/var/www` and see whether any web pages are there that should not be.**

- **Check the contents of the `.bash_history` files in the home directories of your users**—Are there any recent commands for the root user?

- **If you have worked with external security companies previously, call them in for a fresh audit**—Hand over all the logs you have, and explain the situation. They will be able to extract all the information from the logs that is possible.

- **Start collating backup tapes from previous weeks and months**—Your system might have been hacked long before you noticed, so you might need to roll back the system more than once to find out when the attack actually succeeded.

- **Download and install Rootkit Hunter from http://www.rootkit.nl/projects/ rootkit_hunter.html**—This searches for (and removes) the types of files that bad guys leave behind for their return.

Keep your disaster recovery plan somewhere safe; saving it as a file on the machine in question is a very bad move!

Keeping Up-to-Date on Linux Security Issues

A multitude of websites relate to security. One in particular hosts an excellent mailing list. The site is called Security Focus, and the mailing list is called BugTraq. BugTraq is well-known for its unbiased discussion of security flaws. Be warned: It receives a relatively large amount of traffic (20–100+ messages daily).

Often security holes are discussed on BugTraq before the software makers have even released the fix. The Security Focus site has other mailing lists and sections dedicated to Linux in general and is an excellent resource.

Related Fedora and Linux Commands
You will use these commands when managing security in your Fedora system:
Ethereal—GNOME graphical network scanner
gnome-lokkit—Fedora's basic graphical firewalling tool for X
lokkit—Fedora's basic graphical firewalling tool
ssh—The OpenSSH remote login client and preferred replacement for telnet
system-config-securitylevel—Fedora's graphical firewall configuration utility

Reference

http://www.redhat.com/docs/manuals/linux/RHL-9-Manual/custom-guide/ s1-basic-firewall-gnomelokkit.html—Red Hat's guide to basic firewall configuration. Newer documentation will appear at http://fedora.redhat.com.

http://www.insecure.org/nmap/—This site contains information on Nmap.

http://www.securityfocus.com/—The Security Focus website.

http://www.tripwire.org—Information and download links for the open-source version of Tripwire.

# CHAPTER 34

Performance Tuning

Squeezing extra performance out of your hardware might sound like a pointless task given how cheap commodity upgrades are today. To a certain degree that is true—for most of us, it is cheaper to buy a new computer than to spend hours fighting to get a 5% speed boost. But what if the speed boost were 20%? How about if it were 50%?

The amount of benefit you can get by optimizing your system varies depending on what kinds of tasks you are running, but there is something for everyone. Over the next few pages we will be looking at quick ways to optimize the Apache web server, both the KDE and Gnome desktop systems, both MySQL and PostgreSQL database servers, and more.

Before we start, you need to understand that *optimization* is not an absolute term: If we optimize a system, we have improved its performance, but it is still possible it could further be increased. We are not interested in getting 99.999% performance out of a system because optimization suffers from the law of diminishing returns—the basic changes make the biggest differences, but after that it takes increasing amounts of work to obtain decreasing speed improvements.

Hard Disk

Many Linux users love to tinker under the hood to increase the performance of their computers, and Linux gives you some great tools to do just that. Whereas Moms tell us, "Don't fix what's not broken," Dads often say, "Fix it until it breaks." In this section, you learn about many of the commands used to tune, or "tweak," your file system.

Before you undertake any "under the hood" work with Linux, however, keep a few points in mind. First, perform a benchmark on your system before you begin. Linux does not offer a well-developed benchmarking application, but availability changes rapidly. You can search online for the most up-to-date information for benchmarking applications for Linux. If you are a system administrator, you might choose to create your own benchmarking tests. Second, tweak only one thing at a time so you can tell what works, what does not work, and what breaks. Some of these tweaks might not work or might lock up your machine.

Always have a working boot floppy handy and remember that you are personally assuming all risks for attempting any of these tweaks.

Using the BIOS and Kernel to Tune the Disk Drives

One method of tuning involves adjusting the settings in your BIOS. Because the BIOS is not Linux and every BIOS seems different, always read your motherboard manual for better possible settings and make certain that all the drives are detected correctly by the BIOS. Change only one setting at a time.

Linux does provide a limited means to interact with BIOS settings during the boot process (mostly overriding them). In this section, you will learn about those commands.

Other options are in the following list, and are more fully outlined in the BOOTPROMPT HOWTO and the kernel documentation. These commands can be used to force the IDE controllers and drives to be optimally configured. Of course, YMMV (Your Mileage May Vary) because these do not work for everyone.

> `idex=dma`—This will force DMA support to be turned on for the primary IDE bus, where x=0, or the secondary bus, where x=1.
>
> `idex=autotune`—This command will attempt to tune the interface for optimal performance.
>
> `idex=ata66`—If you have ATA66 drives and controllers, this command will enable support for it.
>
> `hdx=ide-scsi`—This command will enable SCSI emulation of an IDE drive. This is required for some CD-RW drives to work properly in write mode and it might provide some performance improvements for regular CD-R drives as well.
>
> `idebus=xx`—This can be any number from 20 to 66; autodetection is attempted, but this can set it manually if dmesg says that it isn't autodetected correctly or if you have it set in the BIOS to a different value (overclocked). Most PCI controllers will be happy with 33.
>
> `pci=biosirq`—Some motherboards might cause Linux to generate an error message saying that you should use this. Look in dmesg for it; if you do not see it, you don't need to use it.

These options can be entered into `/etc/lilo.conf` or `/boot/grub/grub.conf` in the same way as other options are appended.

The hdparm Command

The hdparm utility can be used by root to set and tune the settings for IDE hard drives. You would do this to tune the drives for optimal performance.

Once a kernel patch and associated support programs, the `hdparm` program is now included with Fedora Core. You should only experiment with the drives mounted read-only because some settings can damage some file systems when used improperly. The `hdparm` command also works with CD-ROM drives and some SCSI drives.

The general format of the command is this:

```
# hdparm command device
```

This command runs a hard disk test:

```
hdparm -tT /dev/hda
```

You will need to replace /dev/hda with the location of your hard disk. `hdparm` will then run two tests—cached reads, and buffered disk reads. A good IDE hard disk should be getting 400–500MB/sec for the first test, and 20-30MB/sec for the second. Note down your scores, then try this command:

```
hdparm -m16 -d1 -u1 -c1 /dev/hda
```

That enables various performance-enhancing settings. Now try executing the original command again—if you see an increase, then you should run this command:

```
hdparm -m16 -d1 -u1 -c1 -k1 /dev/hda
```

The extra parameter tells `hdparm` to write the settings to disk so they will be used each time you boot up—ensuring optimal disk performance in the future.

The man entry for `hdparm` is extensive and contains useful detailed information, but since the kernel configuration selected by Fedora Core already attempts to optimize the drives, it might be that little can be gained through tweaking. Because not all hardware combinations can be anticipated by Fedora Core or by Linux and performance gains are always useful, you're encouraged to try.

TIP

You can use the `hdparm` command to produce a disk transfer speed result with

```
# hdparm -tT device
```

Be aware, however, that although the resulting numbers appear quantitative, they are subject to several technical qualifications beyond the scope of what is discussed and explained in this chapter. Simply put, do not accept values generated by `hdparm` as absolute numbers, but only as a relative measure of performance.

System-wide tweaks to `hdparm` are formally handled through the /etc/sysconfig/ harddisks files, but this file's use is poorly documented and, therefore, of little use.

> **TIP**
>
> You may find that your system turns off DMA for any CD-RW drives detected via a shell script command in `rc.sysinit`. This might not be appropriate for your hardware, so you can turn it back on simply by adding the line `options ide-cd dma=1` to `/etc/modules.conf`.

File System Tuning

Never content to leave things alone, Linux provides several tools to adjust and customize the file system settings. The belief is that hardware manufacturers and distribution creators tend to select conservation settings that will work well all the time, leaving some of the potential of your system leashed—that's why you have chosen Fedora Core Linux Unleashed to help you.

The Linux file system designers have done an excellent job of selecting default values used for file system creation and the 2.6 version of the Linux kernel now contains new code for the IDE subsystem that significantly improves I/O (input/output) transfer speeds over older versions, obviating much of the need for special tweaking of the file system and drive parameters if you use IDE disks. Although these values work well for most users, some server applications of Linux benefit from file system tuning. As always, observe and benchmark your changes.

> **Synchronizing the File System with `sync`**
>
> Because Linux uses buffers when writing to devices, the write will not occur until the buffer is full, until the kernel tells it to, or if you tell it to by using the `sync` command. Traditionally, the command is given twice, as in the following:
>
> `# sync ; sync`
>
> It is really overkill to do it twice. Still, it can be helpful prior to the unmounting of certain types of media with slow write speeds (such as some USB hard drives or PCMCIA storage media), but only because it delays the user from attempting to remove the media too soon, not because two syncs are better than one.

The `mke2fs` Command

`mke2fs -O sparse_super` will create a file system with sparse superblocks, reducing the space allocated to root for file system repair. This is not a performance enhancement per se, but it will free up additional space on a drive. This command only works on pre-2.2 kernels and is included here because a number of existing references don't make that distinction. With kernel version 2.2, the sparse superblock option has been moved to `tune2fs`, and this feature is turned "on" by default, so you will always create any new file systems with sparse superblocks.

`mke2fs -b blocksize` will set the block size. The block size chosen can also have an effect on the performance of the file system. A larger block size works better with large files and vice versa. There doesn't seem to be any hard and fast rule about this, and most advice is to accept the default block size of 1024KB unless you want to spend some time running benchmarks.

The tune2fs Command

With tune2fs, you can adjust the tunable file system parameters on an ext2 or ext3 file system. A few performance-related items of Note are as follows:

To disable file system checking, the -c 0 option sets the maximal mount count to zero.

The interval between forced checks can be adjusted with the -I option.

The -m option will set the reserved blocks percentage with a lower value, freeing more space at the expense of fsck having less space to write any recovered files.

Decrease the number of superblocks to save space with the -O sparse_super option. (Modern file systems use this by default.) Always run e2fsck after you change this value.

More space can be freed with the -r option that sets the number of reserved (for root) blocks.

Note that most of these uses of tune2fs free up space on the drive at the expense of the capability of fsck to recover data. Unless you really need the space and can deal with the consequences, just accept the defaults; large drives are now relatively inexpensive.

The e2fsck Command

This utility checks an ext2/ext3 file system . Some useful arguments taken from man e2fsck are as follows:

-c—Checks for bad blocks and then marks them as bad.

-f—Forces checking on a clean file system.

-v—Verbose mode.

The badblocks Command

Although not a performance tuning program per se, the utility badblocks checks a (preferably) unmounted partition for bad blocks. It is not recommended that you run this command by itself, but rather allow it to be called by fsck. It should only be used directly if you specify the block size accurately—don't guess or assume anything.

The options available for badblocks are detailed in the man page. They allow for very low-level manipulation of the file system that is useful for data recovery by file system experts or for file system hacking, but are beyond the scope of this chapter and the average user.

Disabling File Access Time

Whenever Linux reads a file, it changes the last access time—known as the *atime*. This is also true for your web server: If you are getting hit by 50 requests a second, your hard disk will be updating the atime 50 times a second. Do you really need to know the last time a file was accessed? If not, you can disable atime setting for a directory by typing this:

```
chattr -R +A /path/to/directory
```

The chattr command changes file system attributes, of which "don't update atime" is one. To set that attribute, use +A and specify -R so that it is recursively set. /path/to/directory gets changed, and so do all the files and subdirectories it contains.

Kernel

As the Linux kernel developed over time, developers sought a way to fine-tune some of the kernel parameters. Before sysctl, those parameters had to be changed in the kernel configuration and then the kernel had to be recompiled.

The sysctl command can change some parameters of a running kernel. It does this through the /proc file system, which is a "virtual window" into the running kernel. Although it might appear that a group of directories and files exist under /proc, that is only a representation of parts of the kernel. We can read values from and write values to those "files," referred to as *variables*. We can display a list of the variables as shown in the following. (An annotated list is presented because roughly 250 items [or more] exist in the full list.)

```
# sysctl -A
net.ipv4.tcp_max_syn_backlog = 1024
net.ipv4.tcp_rfc1337 = 0
net.ipv4.tcp_stdurg = 0
net.ipv4.tcp_abort_on_overflow = 0
net.ipv4.tcp_tw_recycle = 0
net.ipv4.tcp_syncookies = 0
net.ipv4.tcp_fin_timeout = 60
net.ipv4.tcp_retries2 = 15
net.ipv4.tcp_retries1 = 3
net.ipv4.tcp_keepalive_intvl = 75
net.ipv4.tcp_keepalive_probes = 9
net.ipv4.tcp_keepalive_time = 7200
net.ipv4.ipfrag_time = 30
```

The items shown are networking parameters, and actually tweaking these values is beyond the scope of this book. If we wanted to change a value, however, the -w command is used:

```
# sysctl -w net.ipv4.tcp_retries 2=20
```

This increases the value of that particular kernel parameter.

> **NOTE**
>
> Fedora Core provides a graphical interface to the `sysctl` command in `system-config-proc`. It's still a beta-quality application, and it must be launched from the command line. The interface itself is unremarkable, and it does not provide a means to manipulate all the possible values, but it does offer useful help for the kernel variables it addresses.

If you find that a particular setting is useful, you can enter it into the `/etc/sysctl.conf` file. The format is as follows, using the earlier example:

```
net.ipv4.tcp_retries 2=20
```

Of more interest to kernel hackers than regular users, `sysctl` is a potentially powerful tool that continues to be developed and documented.

> **TIP**
>
> The kernel does a good job of balancing performance for graphical systems, so there's not a great deal you can do tweak your desktop to run faster.
>
> Both GNOME and KDE are "heavyweight" desktop systems: They are all-inclusive, all-singing, and all-dancing environments that do far more than browse your file system. The drawback to this is that their size makes them run slow on older systems. On the flip side, Fedora also comes with the Xfce desktop, which is a great deal slimmer and faster than the other two. If you find GNOME and KDE are struggling just to open a file browser, Xfce is for you.
>
> Alternatively, if you simply cannot live without GNOME or KDE, take a look in the `/usr/share/autostart` directory, where you will see a list of files that are started when your graphical system boots. If you do not need any of them, simply move them out of there and into somewhere safe in case you ever need them again.

Apache

Despite being the most popular web server on the Internet, Apache is by no means the fastest. Part of the "problem" is that Apache has been written to follow every applicable standard to the letter, so much of its development work has been geared toward standards-compliancy rather than just serving web pages quickly. That said, with a little tweaking we can convert a $1,000 Dell server into something capable of surviving the Slashdot Effect.

> **NOTE**
>
> Slashdot.org is a popular geek news website that spawned the Slashdot Effect—the result of thousands of geeks descending on an unsuspecting website simultaneously. Our $1,000 Dell server had dual-2.8GHz Xeons with 1GB of RAM and SCSI hard disks—if you have more RAM, faster chips, and a high-end network card you can kick sand in Slashdot's face.

The first target for your tuning should be the `httpd.conf` file in `/etc/httpd/conf`, as well as the other files in `/etc/httpd/conf.d`. The more modules you have loaded, the more load Apache is placing on your server—take a look through the LoadModule list and comment out (start the line with a #) the ones you do not want. Some of these modules can be uninstalled entirely through the Add or Remove Packages dialog.

As a rough guide, you will almost certainly need `mod_mime` and `mod_dir`, and probably also `mod_log_config`. The default Apache configuration in Fedora is quite generic, so unless you are willing to sacrifice some functionality you may also need `mod_negotiation` (a speed killer if there ever was one), and `mod_access` (a notorious problem). Both of those last two modules can and should work with little or no performance decrease, but all too often they get abused and just slow things down.

Whatever you do, when you are disabling modules you should ensure you leave either `mod_deflate` or `mod_gzip` enabled, depending on your Apache version. Your bottleneck is almost certainly going to be your bandwidth rather than your processing power, and having one of these two compressing your content will usually turn 10Kb of HTML into 3Kb for supported browsers (most of them).

Next, ensure keepalives are turned off. Yes, you read that right: turn keepalives off. This adds some latency to people viewing your site, because they cannot download multiple files through the same connection. However, in turn it reduces the number of simultaneous open connections and so allows more people to connect.

If you are serving content that does not change, you can take the extreme step of enabling MMAP support. This allows Apache to serve pages directly from RAM without bothering to check whether they have changed, which works wonders for your performance. However, the downside is that when you do change your pages you need to restart Apache. Look for the `EnableMMAP` directive—it is probably commented out and set to off, so you will need to remove the comment and set it to on.

Finally, you should do all you can to ensure that your content is static: avoid PHP if you can, avoid databases if you can, and so on. If you know you are going to get hit by a rush of visitors, use plain HTML so that Apache is limited only by your bandwidth for how fast it can serve pages.

TIP

Some people, when questioned about optimizing Apache, will recommend you tweak the `HARD_SERVER_LIMIT` in the Apache source code and recompile. While we agree that compiling your own Apache source code is a great way to get a measurable speed boost if you know what you are doing, you should only ever need to change this directive if you are hosting a huge site.

The default value, 256, is enough to handle the Slashdot effect, and if you can handle that then you can handle most things.

MySQL

Tuning your MySQL server for increased performance is exceptionally easy to do, largely because you can see huge speed increases simply by getting your queries right. That said, there are various things you can tune in the server itself that help it cope with higher loads as long as your system has enough RAM.

The key is understanding its buffers—there are buffers and caches for all sorts of things, and finding out how full they are is crucial to maximizing performance. MySQL performs best when it has is making full use of its buffers, which in turn places a heavy demand on system RAM. Unless you have 4GB RAM or more in your machine, you do not have enough capacity to set very high values for all your buffers—you need to pick and choose.

Measuring Key Buffer Usage

When you add indexes to your data, it enables MySQL to find data faster. However, ideally you want to have these indexes stored in RAM for maximum speed, and the variable `key_buffer_size` defines how much RAM MySQL can allocate for index key caching. If MySQL cannot store its indexes in RAM, you will experience serious performance problems. Fortunately, most databases have relatively small key buffer requirements, but you should measure your usage to see what work needs to be done.

To do this, log in to MySQL and type **SHOW STATUS LIKE '%key_read%';**. That returns all the status fields that describe the hit rate of your key buffer—you should get two rows back: `Key_reads` and `Key_read_requests`, which are the number of keys being read from disk and the number of keys being read from the key buffer. From these two numbers you can calculate the percentage of requests being filled from RAM and from disk, using this simple equation:

$$100 - ((Key\_reads / Key\_read\_requests) \times 100)$$

That is, you divide `Key_reads` by `Key_read_requests`, multiply the result by 100 and then subtract the result from 100. For example, if you have `Key_reads` of 1000 and `Key_read_requests` of 100000, you divide 1000 by 100000 to get 0.01; then you multiply that by 100 to get 1.0, and subtract that from 100 to get 99. That number is the percentage of key reads being served from RAM, which means 99% of your keys are served from RAM.

Most people should be looking to get more than 95% served from RAM, although the primary exception is if you update or delete rows very often—MySQL can't cache what keeps changing. If your site is largely read only, this should be around 98%. Lower figures mean you might need to bump up the size of your key buffer.

If you are seeing problems, the next step is to check how much of your current key buffer is being used. Use the SHOW VARIABLES command and look up the value of the `key_buffer_size` variable. It is probably something like 8388600, which is eight million bytes, or 8MB. Now, use the SHOW STATUS command and look up the value of `Key_blocks_used`.

You can now determine how much of your key buffer is being used by multiplying Key_blocks_used by 1024, dividing by key_buffer_size, and multiplying by 100. For example, if Key_blocks_used is 8000, you multiply that by 1024 to get 8192000; then you divide that by your key_buffer_size (8388600) to get 0.97656, and finally multiplying that by 100 to get 97.656. Thus, almost 98% of your key buffer is being used.

Now, onto the important part: You have ascertained that you are reading lots of keys from disk, and you also now know that the reason for reading from disk is almost certainly because you do not have enough RAM allocated to the key buffer. A general rule of thumb is to allocate as much RAM to the key buffer as you can, up to a maximum of 25% of system RAM—128MB on a 512MB system is about the ideal for systems that read heavily from keys. Beyond that, you will actually see drastic performance decreases because the system has to use virtual memory for the key buffer.

Open /etc/my.cnf in your text editor, and look for the line that contains key_buffer_size. If you do not have one, you need to create a new one—it should be under the line [mysqld]. When you set the new value, do not just pick some arbitrarily high number. Try doubling what is there right now (or try 16MB if there's no line already); then see how it goes. To set 16MB as the key buffer size, you would need line like this:

```
[mysqld]
set-variable = key_buffer_size=16M
datadir=/var/lib/mysql
```

Restart your MySQL server with service mysqld restart, and then go back into MySQL and run SHOW VARIABLES again to see the key_buffer_size. It should be 16773120 if you have set it to 16M. Now, because MySQL just got reset, all its values for key hits and the like will also have been reset. You need to let it run for a while so you can assess how much has changed. If you have a test system you can run, this is the time to run it.

After your database has been accessed with normal usage for a short while (if you get frequent accesses, this might be only a few minutes), recalculate how much of the key buffer is being used. If you get another high score, double the size again, restart, and retest. You should keep repeating this until you see your key buffer usage is below 50% or you find you don't have enough RAM to increase the buffer further—remember that you should never allocate more than 25% of system RAM to the key buffer.

Using the Query Cache

Newer versions of MySQL allow you to cache the results of queries so that, if new queries come in that use exactly the same SQL, the result can be served from RAM. In some ways the query cache is quite intelligent: If, for example, part of the result changes due to another query, the cached results are thrown away and recalculated next time. However, in other ways it is very simple. For example, it uses cached results only if the new query is exactly the same as a cached query, even down to the capitalization of the SQL.

The query cache works well in most scenarios. If your site has an equal mix of reading and writing, the query cache will do its best but will not be optimal. If your site is mostly reading with few writes, more queries will be cached (and for longer), thus improving overall performance.

First, you need to find out whether you have the query cache enabled. To do this, use SHOW VARIABLES and look up the value of have_query_cache. All being well, you should get YES back, meaning that the query cache is enabled. Next, look for the value of query_cache_size and query_cache_limit—the first is how much RAM in bytes is allocated to the query cache, and the second is the maximum result size that should be cached. A good starting set of values for these two is 8388608 (8MB) and 1048576 (1MB).

Next, type **SHOW STATUS LIKE 'Qcache%';** to see all the status information about the query cache. You should get output like this:

```
mysql> SHOW STATUS LIKE 'qcache%';
+-------------------------+--------+
| Variable_name           | Value  |
+-------------------------+--------+
| Qcache_free_blocks      | 1      |
| Qcache_free_memory      | 169544 |
| Qcache_hits             | 698    |
| Qcache_inserts          | 38     |
| Qcache_lowmem_prunes    | 20     |
| Qcache_not_cached       | 0      |
| Qcache_queries_in_cache | 18     |
| Qcache_total_blocks     | 57     |
+-------------------------+--------+
8 rows in set (0.00 sec)
```

From that, we can see that only 18 queries are in the cache (Qcache_queries_in_cache), we have 169544 bytes of memory free in the cache (Qcache_free_memory), 698 queries have been read from the cache (Qcache_hits), 38 queries have been inserted into the cache (Qcache_inserts), but 20 of them were removed due to lack of memory (Qcache_lowmem_prunes), giving the 18 from before. Qcache_not_cached is 0, which means 0 queries were not cached—MySQL is caching them all.

From that, we can calculate how many total queries came in—it is the sum of Qcache_hits, Qcache_inserts, and Qcache_not_cached, which is 736. We can also calculate how well the query cache is being used by dividing Qcache_hits by that number and multiplying by 100. In this case, 94.84% of all queries are being served from the query cache, which is a great number.

In our example, we can see that many queries have been trimmed because there is not enough memory in the query cache. This can be changed by editing your /etc/my.cnf file and adding a line like this one, somewhere in the [mysqld] section:

```
set-variable = query_cache_size=32M
```

An 8MB query cache should be enough for most people, but larger sites might want 16MB or even 32MB if you are storing a particularly large amount of data. Very few sites will have need to go beyond a 32MB query cache, but keep an eye on the `Qcache_lowmem_prunes` value to ensure you have enough RAM allocated.

Using the query cache does not incur much of a performance hit. When MySQL calculates the result of a query normally, it simply throws it away when the connection closes. With the query cache, it skips the throwing away, and so there is no extra work being done. If your site does have many updates and deletes, be sure to check whether you get any speed boost at all from the query cache.

Miscellaneous Tweaks

If you have tuned your key buffer and optimized your query cache and yet still find your site struggling, there are a handful more smaller changes you make that will add some more speed.

When reading from tables, MySQL has to open the file that stores the table data. How many files it keeps open at a time is defined by the `table_cache` setting, which is set to 64 by default. You can increase this setting if you have more than 64 tables, but you should be aware that Fedora does impose limits on MySQL about how many files it can have open at a time. Going beyond 256 is not recommended unless you have a particularly DB-heavy site and know exactly what you are doing.

The other thing you can tweak is the size of the read buffer, which is controlled by `read_buffer_size` and `read_buffer_rnd_size`. Both of these are allocated per connection, which means you should be very careful to have large numbers. Whatever you choose, `read_buffer_rnd_size` should be three to four times the size of `read_buffer_size`, so if `read_buffer_size` is 1MB (suitable for very large databases), `read_buffer_rnd_size` should be 4MB.

Query Optimization

The biggest speed-ups can be seen by reprogramming your SQL statements so they are more efficient. If you follow these tips, your server will thank you:

- Select as little data as possible. Rather than SELECT *, select only the fields you need.

- If you only need a few fields, use LIMIT to select the number you need.

- Declare fields as NOT NULL when creating tables to save space and increase speed.

- Provide default values for fields, and use them where you can.

- Be very careful with table joins because they are the easiest way to write inefficient queries.

- If you must use joins, be sure you join on fields that are indexed.

- Find and fix slow queries. Add `log-long-format` and `log-slow-queries =
/var/log/slow-queries.log` to your `/etc/my.cnf` file, under `[mysqld]`, and MySQL
will tell you the queries that took a long time to complete.

- Use `OPTIMIZE TABLE tablename` to defragment tables and refresh the indexes.

Reference

http://www.coker.com.au/bonnie++/—The home page of bonnie, a disk benchmarking
tool. It also contains a link to RAID benchmarking utilities and Postal, a benchmarking
utility for SMTP servers.

http://httpd.apache.org/docs-2.0/misc/perf-tuning.html—The official Apache guide to
tuning your web server.

http://dev.mysql.com/doc/mysql/en/mysql-optimization.html—Learn how to optimize
your MySQL server direct from the source, the MySQL manual.

There is one particular MySQL optimization book that will really help you get more from
your system if you run a large site, and that is *High Performance MySQL* by Jeremy
Zawodny and Derek Balling (O'Reilly), ISBN: 0-596-00306-4.

34

CHAPTER **35**

Command-line Masterclass

In the earlier years of Linux, people made a big fuss of the graphical environments that were available—they rushed to tell new users that you really did not need to keep going back to the command line to type things. Now Linux is more mature, people accept that the command line is still a reality, and a welcome one. While the GUI does indeed make life easier for day-to-day tasks, your options are limited by what the developers wanted you to have—you cannot bring commands together in new ways, and neither can you use any of the GUI features if, for example, your GUI is broken. It does happen!

In his book *The Art of Unix Programming**, Eric Raymond wrote a short story that perfectly illustrates the power of the command line versus the GUI. It's reprinted here with permission, for your reading pleasure:

> One evening, Master Foo and Nubi attended a gathering of programmers who had met to learn from each other. One of the programmers asked Nubi to what school he and his master belonged. Upon being told they were followers of the Great Way of Unix, the programmer grew scornful.
>
> "The command-line tools of Unix are crude and backward," he scoffed. "Modern, properly designed operating systems do everything through a graphical user interface."
>
> Master Foo said nothing, but pointed at the moon. A nearby dog began to bark at the master's hand.
>
> "I don't understand you!" said the programmer.

Raymond, Eric. The Art of Unix Programming. Addison-Wesley, 2004.

Master Foo remained silent, and pointed at an image of the Buddha. Then he pointed at a window.

"What are you trying to tell me?" asked the programmer.

Master Foo pointed at the programmer's head. Then he pointed at a rock.

"Why can't you make yourself clear?" demanded the programmer.

Master Foo frowned thoughtfully, tapped the programmer twice on the nose, and dropped him in a nearby trash can.

As the programmer was attempting to extricate himself from the garbage, the dog wandered over and piddled on him.

At that moment, the programmer achieved enlightenment.

Whimsical as the story is, it does illustrate that there are some things that the GUI just does not do well. Enter the command line: It is a powerful and flexible operating environment on Linux, and—if you practice—can actually be quite fun, too!

In this chapter, you will learn how to master the command line so that you are able to perform common tasks through it, and also link commands together to create new command groups. We will also be looking at the two most popular Linux text editors: Vim and Emacs. The command line is also known as the shell, the console, the command prompt, and the CLI (command-line interpreter). For the purposes of this chapter these are interchangeable, although there are fine-grained differences between them!

Why Use the Shell?

Moving from the GUI to the command line is a conscious choice for most people, although it increasingly rare that it is an either/or choice. While in X, you can press Ctrl+Alt+F1 at any time to switch to a terminal, but most people tend to run an X terminal application that allows them to have the point-and-click applications and the command-line applications side by side.

Reasons for running the shell include:

- You want to chain two or more commands together.
- You want to use a command or parameter available only on the shell.
- You are working on a text-only system.
- You have used it for a long time and feel comfortable there.

Chaining two or more commands together is what gives the shell its real power. Hundreds of commands are available and, by combining them in different ways, you get hundreds of new commands. Some of the shell commands are available through the GUI, but these commands usually have only a small subset of their parameters available, which limits what you are able to do with them.

Working from a text-only system encapsulates both working locally with a broken GUI and also connecting to a remote, text-only system. If your Linux server is experiencing problems, the last thing you want to do is load it down with a GUI connection—working in text mode is faster and more efficient.

The last use is the most common: People use the shell just because it is familiar to them, with many people even using the shell to start GUI applications just because it saves them taking their hands off the keyboard for a moment! This is not a bad thing; it provides fluency and ease with the system and is a perfectly valid way of working.

Basic Commands

It is impossible to know how many commands the average shell citizen uses, but if we had to guess, we would place it at about 25:

- `cat`—Prints the contents of a file
- `cd`—Changes directories
- `chmod`—Changes file access permissions
- `cp`—Copies files
- `du`—Prints disk usage
- `emacs`—Text editor
- `find`—Finds files by searching
- `gcc`—The C/C++/Fortran compiler
- `grep`—Searches for a string in input
- `less`—Filter for paging through output
- `ln`—Creates links between files
- `locate`—Finds files from an index
- `ls`—Lists files in the current directory
- `make`—Compiles and installs programs
- `man`—The manual page reader
- `mkdir`—Makes directories
- `mv`—Moves files
- `ps`—Lists processes
- `rm`—Deletes files and directories
- `ssh`—Connects to other machines
- `tail`—Prints the last lines of a file
- `top`—Prints resource usage
- `vim`—A text editor

35

- which—Prints the location of a command

- xargs—Executes commands from its input

Of course, many other commands are available to you that get used fairly often—diff, nmap, ping, su, uptime, who, and so on—but if you are able to understand the 25 listed here, you will have sufficient skill to concoct your own command combinations.

Note that we say *understand* the commands—not know all their possible parameters and usages. This is because several of the commands, though commonly used, are used only in any complex manner by people with specific needs. gcc and make are good examples of this: Unless you plan to become a programmer, you need not worry about these beyond just typing make and make install now and then. If you want to learn more about these two, see Chapter 32, "C/C++ Programming Tools for Fedora."

Similarly, both Emacs and Vim are text editors that have a text-based interface all of their own, and SSH has already been covered in detail in Chapter 25, "Remote Access with SSH and Telnet."

What remains is 20 commands, each of which has many parameters to customize what it actually does. Again, we can eliminate much of this because many of the parameters are esoteric and rarely used, and, the few times in your Linux life that you need them, you can just read the manual page!

We will be going over these commands one by one, explaining the most common ways to use them. There is one exception to this: The xargs command requires you to understand how to join commands together, so it is bundled it in the section "Pipes and Output Redirection."

Most of these commands have been touched on elsewhere in the book, primarily in the "Using the Shell" section of Chapter 5, "First Steps with Fedora." The goal of that section was to give you "the least you need to know" to get by, whereas in this chapter each command is treated individually with an aim to giving you the confidence needed to be able to mix them together to create your own commands.

Printing the Contents of a File with cat

Many of Fedora's shell commands manipulate text strings, so if you want to be able to feed them the contents of files, you need to be able to output those files as text. Enter the cat command, which prints the contents of any files you pass to it.

Its most basic use is like this:

```
cat myfile.txt
```

That prints the contents of myfile.txt. For this usage there are two extra parameters that are often used: -n numbers the lines in the output, and -s ("squeeze") prints a maximum of one blank line at a time. That is, if your file has 1 line of text, 10 blank lines, 1 line of text, 10 blank lines, and so on, -s shows the first line of text, a single blank line, the next line of text, a single blank line, and so forth. When you combine -s and -n, cat numbers only the lines that are printed—the 10 blank lines shown as one will count as 1 line for numbering.

This command prints information about your CPU, stripping out multiple blank lines and numbering the output:

```
cat -sn /proc/cpuinfo
```

You can also use `cat` to print the contents of several files at once, like this:

```
cat -s myfile.txt myotherfile.txt
```

In that command, `cat` merges `myfile.txt` and `myotherfile.txt` on the output, stripping out multiple blank lines. The important thing is that `cat` does not distinguish between the files in the output—there are no filenames printed, and no extra breaks between the 2. This allows you to treat the 2 as 1 or, by adding more files to the command line, to treat 20 files as 1.

Changing Directories with `cd`

Changing directories is surely something that has no options, right? Not so. `cd` is actually more flexible than most people realize. Unlike most of the other commands here, `cd` is not a command in itself—it is built in to `bash` (or whichever shell interpreter you are using), but it is still used like a command.

The most basic usage of `cd` is this:

```
cd somedir
```

That looks in the current directory for the `somedir` subdirectory, then moves you into it. You can also specify an exact location for a directory, like this:

```
cd /home/paul/stuff/somedir
```

The first part of cd's magic lies in the characters (- and ~, a dash and a tilde). The first means "switch to my previous directory," and the second means "switch to my home directory." This conversation with `cd` shows this in action:

```
[paul@caitlin ~]$ cd /usr/local
[paul@caitlin local]$ cd bin
[paul@caitlin bin]$ cd -
/usr/local
[paul@caitlin local]$ cd ~
[paul@caitlin ~]$
```

In the first line, we change to /usr/local and get no output from the command. In the second line, we change to `bin`, which is a subdirectory of /usr/local. Next, `cd -` is used to change back to the previous directory. This time Bash prints the name of the previous directory so we know where we are. Finally, `cd ~` is used to change back to our home directory, although if you want to save an extra few keystrokes, just typing cd by itself is equivalent to cd ~.

The second part of cd's magic is its capability to look for directories in predefined locations. When you specify an absolute path to a directory (that is, one starting with a /), cd always switches to that exact location. However, if you specify a relative subdirectory—for example, cd subdir—you can tell cd where you would like that to be relative to. This is accomplished with the CDPATH environment variable. If this variable is not set, cd always uses the current directory as the base; however, you can set it to any number of other directories.

This next example shows a test of this. It starts in /home/paul/empty, an empty directory, and the lines are numbered for later reference:

```
1 [paul@caitlin empty]$ pwd
2 /home/paul/empty
3 [paul@caitlin empty]$ ls
4 [paul@caitlin empty]$ mkdir local
5 [paul@caitlin empty]$ ls
6 local
7 [paul@caitlin empty]$ cd local
8 [paul@caitlin local]$ cd ..
9 [paul@caitlin empty]$ export CDPATH=/usr
10 [paul@caitlin empty]$ cd local
11 /usr/local
12 [paul@caitlin empty]$ cd -
13 /home/paul/empty
14 [paul@caitlin empty]$ export CDPATH=.:/usr
15 [paul@caitlin empty]$ cd local
16 /home/paul/empty/local
17 [paul@caitlin local]$
```

Lines 1–3 show that we are in /home/paul/empty and that it is indeed empty—ls had no output. Lines 4–6 show the local subdirectory being made, so that /home/paul/empty/local exists. Lines 7 and 8 show you can cd into /home/paul/empty/local and back out again.

In line 9, CDPATH is set to /usr. This was chosen because Fedora has the directory /usr/local, which means our current directory (/home/paul/empty) and our CDPATH directory (/usr) both have a local subdirectory. In line 10, while in the /home/paul/empty directory, we use cd local. This time, Bash switches us to /usr/local and even prints the new directory to ensure we know what it has done.

Lines 12 and 13 move us back to the previous directory, /home/paul/empty. In line 14, CDPATH is set to be .:/usr. The : is the directory separator, so this means Bash should look first in the current directory, ., and then in the /usr directory. In line 15 cd local is issued again, this time moving to /home/paul/empty/local. Note that Bash has still printed the new directory—it does that whenever it looks up a directory in CDPATH.

Changing File Access Permissions with chmod

What you learned about chmod in Chapter 5 can be greatly extended through one simple parameter: -c. This instructs chmod to print a list of all the changes it made as part of its operation, which means we can capture the output and use it for other purposes. For example:

```
[paul@caitlin tmp]$ chmod -c 600 *
mode of `1.txt' changed to 0600 (rw-------)
mode of `2.txt' changed to 0600 (rw-------)
mode of `3.txt' changed to 0600 (rw-------)
[paul@caitlin tmp]$ chmod -c 600 *
[paul@caitlin tmp]$
```

There the chmod command is issued with -c, and you can see it has output the result of the operation: Three files were changed to rw------- (read and write by user only). However, when the command is issued again, no output is returned. This is because -c prints only the changes that it made. Files that already match the permissions you are setting are left unchanged and therefore are not printed.

There are two other parameters of interest: --reference and -R. The first allows you to specify a file to use as a template for permissions rather than specifying permissions yourself. For example, if you want all files in the current directory to have the same permissions as the file /home/paul/myfile.txt, you would use this:

```
chmod --reference /home/paul/myfile.txt *
```

You can use -R to enable recursive operation, which means you can use it to chmod a directory and it will change the permissions of that directory as well as all files and subdirectories under that directory. You could use chmod -R 600 /home to change every file and directory under /home become read/write to their owner.

Copying Files with cp

Like mv, which is covered later, cp is a command that is easily used and mastered. However, two marvelous parameters rarely see much use (which is a shame!) despite their power. These are --parents and -u, the first of which copies the full path of the file into the new directory. The second copies only if the source file is newer than the destination.

Using --parents requires a little explanation, so here is an example. You have a file, /home/paul/desktop/documents/work/notes.txt, and want to copy it to your /home/paul/backup folder. You could just do a normal cp, but that would give you /home/paul/backup/notes.txt, so how would you know where that came from later? If you use --parents, the file is copied to /home/paul/backup/desktop/documents/work/notes.txt.

The -u parameter is perfect for synchronizing two directories because it allows you to run a command like cp -Ru myfiles myotherfiles and have cp recopy only files that have changed. The -R parameter means *recursive* and allows you to copy directory contents.

Printing Disk Usage with du

The du command prints the size of each file and directory that is inside the current directory. Its most basic usage is as easy as it gets:

```
du
```

That outputs a long list of directories and how much space their files take up. You can modify that with the -a parameter, which instructs du to print the size of individual files as well as directories. Another useful parameter is -h, which makes du use human-readable sizes like 18M (18MB) rather than 17532 (the same number in bytes, unrounded). The final useful basic option is -c, which prints the total size of files.

So, using du we can get a printout of the size of each file in our home directory, in human-readable format, and with a summary at the end, like this:

```
du -ahc /home/paul
```

Two advanced parameters deal with filenames you want excluded from your count. The first is --exclude, which allows you to specify a pattern that should be used to exclude files. This pattern is a standard shell file matching pattern as opposed to a regular expression, which means you can use ? to match a single character or * to match 0 or many characters. You can specify multiple --exclude parameters to exclude several patterns. For example:

```
du --exclude="*.xml" --exclude="*.xsl"
```

Of course, typing numerous --exclude parameters repeatedly is a waste of time, so you can use -X to specify a file that has the list of patterns you want excluded. The file should look like this:

```
*.xml
*.xsl
```

That is, each pattern you want excluded should be on a line by itself. If that file were called xml_exclude.txt, we could use it in place of the previous example like this:

```
du -X xml_exclude.txt
```

You can make your exclusion file as long as you need, or you can just specify multiple -X parameters.

TIP

Running du in a directory where several files are hard-linked to the same inode counts the size of the file only once. If you want to count each hard link separately for some reason, use the -l parameter (lowercase *L*) .

Finding Files by Searching with `find`

The `find` command is one of the darkest and least understood areas of Linux, but it is also one of the most powerful. Admittedly, the `find` command does not help itself by using X-style parameters. The Unix standard is `-c`, `-s`, and so on, whereas the GNU standard is `--dosomething`, `--mooby`, and so forth. X-style parameters merge the two by having words preceded by only one dash.

However, the biggest problem with `find` is that it has more options than most people can remember—it truly is capable of doing most things you could want. The most basic usage is this:

```
find -name "*.txt"
```

That searches the current directory and all subdirectories for files that end in `.txt`. The previous search finds files ending in `.txt` but not `.TXT`, `.Txt`, or other case variations. To search without case sensitivity, use `-iname` instead of `-name`. You can optionally specify where the search should start before the `-name` parameter, like this:

```
find /home -name "*.txt"
```

Another useful test is `-size`, which lets you specify how big the files should be to match. You can specify your size in kilobytes and optionally also use + or - to specify greater than or less than. For example:

```
find /home -name "*.txt" -size 100k
find /home -name "*.txt" -size +100k
find /home -name "*.txt" -size -100k
```

The first brings up files of exactly 100KB, the second only files larger than 100KB, and the last only files under 100KB.

Moving on, the `-user` option enables you to specify the user who owns the files you are looking for. So, to search for all files in `/home` that end with `.txt`, are under 100KB, and are owned by user `paul`, you would use this:

```
find /home -name "*.txt" -size -100k -user paul
```

You can flip any of the conditions by specifying `-not` before them. For example, you can add a `-not` before `-user paul` to find matching files owned by everyone *but* `paul`:

```
find /home -name "*.txt" -size -100k -not -user paul
```

You can add as many `-not` parameters as you need, even using `-not` `-not` to cancel each other out! (Yes, that is pointless.) Keep in mind, though, that `-not` `-size` `-100k` is essentially equivalent to -size +100k, with the exception that the former will match files of exactly 100KB whereas the latter will not.

You can use `-perm` to specify which permissions a file should have for it to be matched. This is tricky, so read carefully. The permissions are specified in the same way as with the chmod command: u for user, g for group, o for others, r for read, w for write, and x for execute. However, before you give the permissions, you need to specify either a plus, a minus, or a blank space. If you specify neither a plus nor a minus, the files must exactly match the mode you give. If you specify -, the files must match all the modes you specify. If you specify +, the files must match any the modes you specify. Confused yet?

The confusion can be cleared up with some examples. This next command finds all files that have permission o=r (readable for other users). Notice that if you remove the -name parameter, it is equivalent to * because all filenames are matched.

```
find /home -perm -o=r
```

Any files that have o=r set are returned from that query. Those files also might have u=rw and other permissions, but as long as they have o=r, they will match. This next query matches all files that have o=rw set:

```
find /home -perm -o=rw
```

However, that query does not match files that are o=r or o=w. To be matched, a file must be readable *and* writeable by other users. If you want to match readable *or* writeable (or both), you need to use +, like this:

```
find /home -perm +o=rw
```

Similarly, this next query matches files only that are readable by user, group, and others:

```
find /home -perm -ugo=r
```

Whereas this query matches files as long as they are readable by the user, or by the group, or by others, or by any combination of the three:

```
find /home -perm +ugo=r
```

If you use neither + or -, you are specifying the exact permissions to search for. For example, the next query searches for files that are readable by user, group, and others but not writeable or executable by anyone:

```
find /home -perm ugo=r
```

You can be as specific as you need to be with the permissions. For example, this query finds all files that are readable for the user, group, and others and writeable by the user:

```
find /home -perm ugo=r,u=w
```

To find files that are not readable by others, use the -not condition, like this:

```
find /home -not -perm +o=r
```

Now, on to the most advanced aspect of the find command: the -exec parameter. This enables you to execute an external program each time a match is made, passing in the name of the matched file wherever you want it. This has very specific syntax: Your command and its parameters should follow immediately after -exec, terminated by \;. You can insert the filename match at any point using {} (an opening and a closing brace side by side).

So, you can match all text files on the entire system (that is, searching recursively from / rather than from /home as in our previous examples) over 10KB, owned by paul, that are not readable by other users, and then use chmod to enable reading, like this:

```
find / -name "*.txt" -size +10k -user paul -not -perm +o=r -exec chmod o+r {} \;
```

When you type your own -exec parameters, be sure to include a space before \;. Otherwise, you might see an error such as missing argument to `-exec'.

Do you see now why some people think the find command is scary? Many people learn just enough about find to be able to use it in a very basic way, but hopefully you will see how much it can do if you give it chance.

Searches for a String in Input with grep

The grep command, like find, is an incredibly powerful search tool in the right hands. Unlike find, though, grep processes any text, whether in files, or just in standard input.

The basic usage of grep is this:

```
grep "some text" *
```

That searches all files in the current directory (but not subdirectories) for the string some text and prints matching lines along with the name of the file. To enable recursive searching in subdirectories, use the -r parameter, like this:

```
grep -r "some text" *
```

Each time a string is matched within a file, the filename and the match are printed. If a file contains multiple matches, each of the matches is printed. You can alter this behavior with the -l parameter (lowercase L), which forces grep to print the name of each file that contains at least one match, without printing the matching text. If a file contains more than one match, it is still printed only once. Alternatively, the -c parameter prints each filename that was searched and includes the number of matches at the end, even if there were no matches.

You have a lot of control when specifying the pattern to search for. You can, as previously, specify a simple string like some text, or you can invert that search by specifying the -v parameter. For example, this returns all the lines of the file myfile.txt that do not contain the word hello:

```
grep -v "hello" myfile.txt
```

You can also use regular expressions for your search term. For example, you can search myfile.txt for all references to cat, sat, or mat with this command:

```
grep "[cms]at" myfile.txt
```

Adding the -i parameter to that removes case sensitivity, matching Cat, CAT, MaT, and so on:

```
grep -i [cms]at myfile.txt
```

The output can also be controlled to some extent with the -n and --color parameters. The first tells grep to print the line number for each match, which is where it appears in the source file. The --color parameter tells grep to color the search terms in the output, which helps them stand out when amongst all the other text on the line. You choose which color you want using the GREP_COLOR environment variable: export GREP_COLOR=36 gives you cyan, and export GREP_COLOR=32 gives you lime green.

This next example uses these two parameters to number and color all matches to the previous command:

```
grep -in --color [cms]at myfile.txt
```

Later you will see how important grep is for piping with other commands.

Paging Through Output with less

The less command enables you to view large amounts of text in a more convenient way than the cat command. For example, your /etc/passwd file is probably more than a screen long, so if you run cat /etc/passwd, you are not able to see what the lines at the top were. Using less /etc/passwd enables you to use the cursor keys to scroll up and down the output freely. Type q to quit and return to the shell.

On the surface, less sounds like a very easy command; however, it has the infamy of being one of the few Linux commands that have a parameter for every letter of the alphabet. That is, -a does something, -b does something else, -c, -d, -e ... -x, -y, -z—they all do things, with some letters even differentiating between upper- and lowercase. Furthermore, it is only the parameter used to invoke less. After you are viewing your text, even more commands are available to you. Make no mistake—less is a complex beast to master.

Input to less can be divided into two categories: what you type before running less and what you type while running it. The former category is easy, so we shall start there.

We have already discussed how many parameters less is capable of taking, but they can be distilled down to three that are very useful: -M, -N, and +. Adding -M (this is different from -m!) enables verbose prompting in less. Rather than just printing a colon and a flashing cursor, less prints the filename, the line numbers being shown, the total number of lines, and the percentage of how far you are through the file. Adding -N (again, this is different from -n) enables line numbering.

The last option, +, allows you to pass a command to less for it to execute as it starts. To use this, you first need to know the commands available to you in less, which means we need to move onto the second category of less input: what you type while less is running.

The basic navigation keys are the up, down, left, and right cursors; Home and End (for navigating to the start and end of a file); and Page Up and Page Down. Beyond that, the most common command is /, which initiates a text search. You type what you want to search for and press Enter to have less find the first match and highlight all subsequent matches. Type / again and press Enter to have less jump to the next match. The inverse of that is ?, which searches backward for text. Type ?, enter a search string, and press Enter to go to the first previous match of that string, or just use ? and press Enter to go to the next match preceding the current position. You can use / and ? interchangeably by searching for something with / and then using ? to go backward in the same search.

Searching with / and ? is commonly used with the + command-line parameter from earlier, which passes less a command for execution after the file has loaded. For example, you can tell less to load a file and place the cursor at the first match for the search hello, like this:

```
less +/hello myfile.txt
```

Or, to place the cursor at the last match for the search hello:

```
less +?hello myfile.txt
```

Beyond the cursor keys, the controls primarily involve typing a number and then pressing a key. For example, to go to line 50 and type 50g, or to go to the 75% point of the file and type 75p. You can also place invisible mark points through the file by pressing m and then typing a single letter. Later, while in the same less session, you can press ' (a single quote) and then type the letter, and it will move you back to the same position. You can set up to 52 marks, named a–z and A–Z.

One clever feature of less is that you can, at any time, press v to have your file opened inside your text editor. This defaults to Vim, but you can change that by setting the EDITOR environment variable to something else.

If you have made it this far, you can already use less better than most users. You can, at this point, justifiably skip to the next section and consider yourself proficient with less. However, if you want to be a less guru, there are two more things to learn: how to view multiple files simultaneously and how to run shell commands.

Like most other file-based commands in Linux, less can take several files as its parameters. For example:

```
less -MN 1.txt 2.txt 3.txt
```

That loads all three files into less, starting at 1.txt. When viewing several files, less usually tells you which file you are in, as well as numbering them: 1.txt (file 1 of 3)

35

should be at the bottom of the screen. That said, certain things will make that go away, so you should use -M anyway.

You can navigate between files by typing a colon and then pressing n to go to the next file or p to go to the previous file; these are referred to from now on as :n and :p. You can open another file for viewing by typing :e and providing a filename. This can be any file you have permission to read, including files outside the local directory. Use Tab to complete filenames. Files you open in this way are inserted one place after your current position, so if you are viewing file 1 of 4 and open a new file, the new file is numbered 2 of 5 and is opened for viewing straight away. To close a file and remove it from the list, use :d.

Viewing multiple files simultaneously has implications for searching. By default, less searches within only one file, but it is easy to search within all files. When you type / or ? to search, follow it with a *—you should see EOF-ignore followed by a search prompt. You can now type a search and it will search in the current file; if nothing is found, it looks in subsequent files until it finds a match. Repeating searches is done by press Esc and then either n or N. The lowercase option repeats the search forwards across files, and the uppercase repeats it backward.

The last thing you need to know is that you can get to a shell from less and execute commands. The simplest way to do this is just to type ! and press Enter. This launches a shell and leaves you free to type all the commands you want, as per normal. Type exit to return to less. You can also type specific commands by entering them after the exclamation mark, using the special character % for the current filename. For example, du -h % prints the size of the current file. Finally, you can use !! to repeat the previous command.

Creating Links Between Files with ln

Linux allows you to create links between files that look and work like normal files for the most part. Moreover, it allows you to make two types of links, known as *hard* links and *symbolic* links (*symlinks*). The difference between the two is crucial, although it might not be obvious at first!

Each filename on your system points to what is known as an *inode*, which is the absolute location of a file. Linux allows you to point more than one filename to a given inode, and the result is a hard link—two filenames pointing to exactly the same file. Each of these files shares the same contents and attributes. So, if you edit one, the other changes because they are both the same file.

On the other hand, a symlink—sometimes called a *soft* link—is a redirect to the real file. When a program tries to read from a symlink, it automatically is redirected to what the symlink is pointing at. The fact that symlinks are really just dumb pointers has two advantages: You can link to something that does not exist (and create it later if you want), and you can link to directories.

Both types of links have their uses. Creating a hard link is a great way to back up a file on the same disk. For example, if you delete the file in one location, it still exists untouched in the other location. Symlinks are popular because they allow a file to appear to be in a different location; you could store your website in /var/www/live and an under-construction holding page in /var/www/construction. Then you could have Apache point to a symlink /var/www/html that is redirected to either the live or construction directory depending on what you need.

> **TIP**
>
> The shred command overwrites a file's contents with random data, allowing for safe deletion. Because this directly affects a file's contents, rather than just a filename, this means that all file-names hard linked to an inode are affected.

Both types of link are created using the ln command. By default, it creates hard links, but you can create symlinks by passing it the -s parameter. The syntax is ln [-s] <something> <somewhere>, for example:

```
ln -s myfile.txt mylink
```

That creates the symlink mylink that points to myfile.txt. Remove the -s to create a hard link. You can verify that your link has been created by running ls -l. Your symlink should look something like this:

```
lrwxrwxrwx  1 paul paul    5 Feb 19 12:39 mylink -> myfile.txt
```

Note how the file properties start with l (lowercase *L*) for link and how ls -l also prints where the link is going. Symlinks are always very small in size; the previous link is 5 bytes in size. If you created a hard link, it should look like this:

```
-rw-rw-r  2 paul paul   341 Feb 19 12:39 mylink
```

This time the file has normal attributes, but the second number is 2 rather than 1. That number is how many hard links point to this file, which is why it is 2 now. The file size is also the same as that of the previous filename because it *is* the file as opposed to just being a pointer.

Symlinks are used extensively in Linux. Programs that have been superseded, such as sh, now point to their replacements (in this case bash), and library versioning is accomplished through symlinks. For example, applications that link against zlib load /usr/lib/libz.so. Internally, however, that is just a symlink that points to the actual zlib library: /usr/lib/libz.so.1.2.1.2. This enables multiple versions of libraries to be installed without applications needing to worry.

Finding Files from an Index with locate

When you use the find command, it searches recursively through each directory each time you request a file. This is slow, as you can imagine. Fortunately, Fedora ships with a cron job that creates an index of all the files on your system every night. Searching this index is extremely fast, which means that, if the file you are looking for has been around since the last index, this is the preferable way of searching.

To look for a file in your index, use the command `locate` followed by the names of the files you want to find, like this:

```
locate myfile.txt
```

On a relatively modern computer (1.5GHz or higher), `locate` should be able to return all the matching files in under a second. The trade-off for this speed is lack of flexibility. You can search for matching filenames, but, unlike `find`, you cannot search for sizes, owners, access permissions, or other attributes. The one thing you can change is case sensitivity; use the `-i` parameter to do a case-insensitive search.

Although Fedora rebuilds the filename index nightly, you can force a rebuild whenever you want by running the command `updatedb` as root. This usually takes a few minutes, but when it's done the new database is immediately available.

Listing Files in the Current Directory with `ls`

The `ls` command, like `ln`, is one of those you expect to be very straightforward. It lists files, but how many options can it possibly have? In true Linux style, the answer is many, although again you need only know a few to wield great power!

The basic usage is simply `ls`, which out the files and directories in the current location. You can filter that using normal wildcards, so all these are valid:

```
ls *
ls *.txt
ls my*ls *.txt *.xml
```

Any directories that match these filters are recursed into one level. That is, if you run `ls my*` and you have the files `myfile1.txt` and `myfile2.txt` and a directory `mystuff`, the matching files are printed first. Then `ls` prints the contents of the `mystuff` directory.

The most popular parameters for customizing the output of `ls` are

- `-a`—Includes hidden files.

- `-h`—Uses human-readable sizes.

- `-1`—A lowercase *L*, it enables long listing.

- `-r`—Reverse order.

- `-R`—Recursively lists directories.

- `-s`—Shows sizes.

- `--sort`—Sorts the listing.

All files that start with a period are hidden in Linux, so that includes the `.gnome` directory in your home directory, as well as `.bash_history` and the `.` and `..` implicit directories that signify the current directory and the parent. By default, `ls` does not show these files, but if you run ls -a, they are shown. You can also use ls -A to show all the hidden files except . and ...

The -h parameter needs to be combined with the -s parameter, like this:

```
ls -sh *.txt
```

That outputs the size of each matching file in a human-readable format, such as 108KB or 4.5MB.

Using the -l parameter enables much more information about your files. Instead of just providing the names of the files, you get output like this:

```
drwxrwxr-x 24 paul paul  4096 Dec 24 21:33 arch
-rw-r--r--  1 paul paul 18691 Dec 24 21:34 COPYING
-rw-r--r--  1 paul paul 88167 Dec 24 21:35 CREDITS
drwxrwxr-x  2 paul paul  4096 Dec 24 21:35 crypto
```

That shows four matches and prints a lot of information about each of them. The first row shows the arch directory; you can tell it is a directory because its file attributes starts with a d. The rwxrwxr-x following that shows the access permissions, and this has special meanings because it is a directory. Read access for a directory allows users to see the directory contents, write access allows you to create files and subdirectories, and execute access allows you to cd into the directory. If a user has execute access but not read access, he will be able to cd into the directory but not list files.

Moving on, the next number on the line is 24, which also has a special meaning for directories: It is the number of subdirectories, including . and ... After that is paul paul, which is the name of the user owner and the group owner for the directory. Next is the size and modification time, and finally the directory name itself.

The next line shows the file COPYING, and most of the numbers have the same meaning, with the exception of the 1 immediately after the access permissions. For directories, this is the number of subdirectories, but for files this is the number of hard links to this file. A 1 in this column means this is the only filename pointing to this inode, so if you delete it, it is gone.

Fedora comes configured with a shortcut command for ls -l: ll.

The --sort parameter allows you to reorder the output from the default alphabetical sorting. You can sort by various things, although the most popular are extension (alphabetically), size (largest first), and time (newest first). To flip the sorting (making size sort by smallest first), use the -r parameter also. So, this command lists all .ogg files, sorted smallest to largest:

```
ls --sort size -r *.ogg
```

Finally, the -R parameter recurses through subdirectories. For example, typing ls /etc lists all the files and subdirectories in /etc, but ls -R /etc lists all the files in and subdirectories in /etc, all the files and subdirectories in /etc/acpi, all the files and subdirectories in /etc/acpi/actions, and so on until every subdirectory has been listed.

Reading Manual Pages with man

Time for a much-needed mental break: The man command is easy to use. Most people use only the topic argument, like this: man gcc. However, two other commands work closely with man that are very useful—whatis and apropos.

The whatis command returns a one-line description of another command, which is the same text you get at the top of that command's man page. For example:

```
[paul@caitlin ~]$ whatis ls
ls    (1) - list directory contents
```

The output there explains what ls does but also provides the man page section number for the command so you can query it further.

On the other hand, the apropos command takes a search string as its parameter and returns all man pages that match the search. For example, apropos mixer gives this list:

```
alsamixer (1) - soundcard mixer for ALSA soundcard driver
mixer (1) - command-line mixer for ALSA soundcard driver
aumix (1) - adjust audio mixer
```

So, use apropos to help you find commands and use whatis to tell you what a command does.

Making Directories with mkdir

Making directories is as easy as it sounds, although there is one parameter you should be aware of: -p. If you are in /home/paul and you want to create the directory /home/paul/audio/sound, you will get an error like this:

```
mkdir: cannot create directory `audio/sound`: No such file or directory
```

At first glance this seems wrong because mkdir cannot create the directory because it does not exist. What it actually means is that it cannot create the directory sound because the directory audio does not exist. This is where the -p parameter comes in: If you try to make a directory within another directory that does not exist, like the previous, -p creates the parent directories, too. So:

```
mkdir -p audio/sound
```

That first creates the audio directory and then creates the sound directory inside it.

Moving Files with mv

This command is one of the easiest around. There are two helpful parameters to mv: -f, which overwrites files without asking, and -u, which moves the source file only if it is newer than the destination file. That is it!

Listing Processes with ps

This is the third and last "command that should be simple, but isn't" that is discussed here. The ps command lists processes and gives you an extraordinary amount of control over its operation.

The first thing to know is that ps is typically used with what are known as BSD-style parameters. Back in the section "Finding Files with find," we discussed Unix-style, GNU-style, and X-style parameters (-c, --dosomething, and -dosomething, respectively), but BSD-style parameters are different because they use single letters without a dash.

So, the default use of ps lists all processes that you are running that are attached to the terminal. However, you can ask it to list all your processes attached to any terminal (or indeed no terminal) by adding the x parameter: ps x. You can ask it to list all processes for all users with the a parameter or combine that with x to list all processes for all users, attached to a terminal or otherwise: ps ax.

However, both of these are timid compared with the almighty u option, which enables user-oriented output. In practice, that makes a huge difference because you get important fields like the username of the owner, how much CPU time and RAM are being used, when the process was started, and more. This outputs a lot of information, so you might want to try adding the f parameter, which creates a process forest by using ASCII art to connect parent commands with their children. You can combine all the options so far with this command: ps faux (yes, with a little imagination you spell words with the parameters!)

You can control the order in which the data is returned by using the --sort parameter. This takes either a + or a - (although the + is default) followed by the field you want to sort by: command, %cpu, pid, and user are all popular options. If you use the minus sign, the results are reversed. This next command lists all processes, ordered by CPU usage descending:

```
ps aux --sort=-%cpu
```

There are many other parameters for ps, including a huge amount of options for compatibility with other Unixes. If you have the time to read the man page, you should give it a try!

Deleting Files and Directories with rm

The rm command has only one parameter of interest: --preserve-root. By now, you should know that issuing rm -rf / as root will destroy your Linux installation because -r means *recursive* and -f means *force* (do not prompt for confirmation before deleting). It is possible for a clumsy person to issue this command by accident—not by typing the command on purpose, but by putting a space in the wrong place. For example:

```
rm -rf /home/paul
```

That command deletes the home directory of the user paul. This is not an uncommon command; after you have removed a user and backed up her data, you will probably want to issue something similar. However, if you add an accidental space between the / and the h in "home", you get this:

```
rm -rf / home/paul
```

This time the command means "delete everything recursively from / and then delete home/paul"—quite a different result! You can stop this from happening by using the --preserve-root parameter, which stops you from catastrophe with this message:

```
rm: it is dangerous to operate recursively on `/'
rm: use --no-preserve-root to override this failsafe.
```

Of course, no one wants to keep typing --preserve-root each time they run rm, so you should add this line to the .bashrc file in your home directory:

```
alias rm='rm --preserve-root'
```

That alias automatically adds --preserve-root to all calls to rm in future Bash sessions.

Printing the Last Lines of a File with tail

If you want to watch a log file as it is written to, or want to monitor a user's actions as they are occurring, you need to be able to track log files as they change. In these situations you need the tail command, which prints the last few lines of a file and updates as new lines are added. This command tells tail to print the last few lines of /var/log/httpd/access_log, the Apache hit log:

```
tail /var/log/httpd/access_log
```

To get tail to remain running and update as the file changes, add the -f parameter (follow):

```
tail -f /var/log/httpd/access_log
```

You can tie the lifespan of a tail follow to the existence of a process by specifying the --pid parameter. When you do this, tail continues to follow the file you asked for until it sees that the process identified by PID is no longer running, at which point it stops tailing.

If you specify multiple files on the command line, tail follows both, printing file headers whenever the input source changes. Press Ctrl+C to terminate tail when in follow mode.

Printing Resource Usage with top

The top command is unusual in this list because the few parameters it takes are rarely, if ever, used. Instead, it has a number of commands you can use while it is running to customize the information it shows you. To get the most from these instructions, open two terminal windows. In the first, run the program yes and leave it running; in the second, switch to root, and run top.

The default sort order in top shows the most CPU-intensive tasks first. The first command there should be the yes process you just launched from the other terminal, but there should be many others also. First, we want to filter out all the other uses and focus on the user running yes. To do this, press u and enter the username you used when you ran yes. When you press Enter, top filters out processes not being run by that user.

The next step is to kill the process ID of the yes command, so you need to understand what each of the important fields means:

- PID—The process ID
- User—The owner of the process
- PR—Priority
- NI—Niceness
- Virt—Virtual image size in kilobytes
- Res—Resident size in kilobytes
- Shr—Shared memory size in kilobytes
- S—Status
- %CPU—CPU usage
- %Mem—Memory usage
- Time+—CPU time
- Command—The command being run

Several of them are unimportant unless you have a specific problem. The ones we are interested in are PID, User, Niceness, %CPU, %MEM, Time+, and Command. The Niceness of a process is how much time the CPU allocates to it compared to everything else on the system: 19 is the lowest, and –19 is the highest.

With the columns explained, you should be able to find the process ID of the errant yes command launched earlier; it is usually the first number below PID. Now type k, enter that process ID, and press Enter. You are prompted for a signal number (the manner in which you want the process killed), with 15 provided as the default. Signal 15 (also known as SIGTERM, for "terminate") is a polite way of asking a process to shut down, and all processes that are not wildly out of control should respond to it. Give top a few seconds to update itself, and hopefully the yes command should be gone. If not, you need to be more forceful: type k again, enter the PID, and press Enter. When prompted for a signal to send, enter 9 and press Enter to send SIGKILL, or "terminate whether you like it or not."

You can choose the fields to display by pressing f. A new screen appears that lists all possible fields, along with the letter you need to press to toggle their visibility. Selected fields are marked with an asterisk and have their letter, for example:

```
* A: PID       = Process Id
```

If you press the a key, the screen changes to this:

```
a: PID         = Process Id
```

When you have made your selections, press Enter to return to the normal top view with your normal column selection.

You can also press F to select the field you want to use for sorting. This works in the same way as the field selection screen, except that you can select only one field at a time. Again, press Enter to get back to top after you have made your selection, and it will be updated with the new sorting.

If you press B, text bolding is enabled. By default, this bolds some of the header bar as well as any programs that are currently running (as opposed to sleeping), but if you press x you can also enable bolding of the sorted column. You can use y to toggle bolding of running processes.

The last command to try is r, which allows you to renice—or adjust the nice value—of a process. You need to enter the PID of the process, press Enter, and enter a new nice value. Keep in mind that 19 is the lowest and –20 is the highest; anything less than 0 is considered "high" and should be used sparingly.

Printing the Location of a Command with which

The purpose of which is to tell you the exact command that would be executed if you typed it. For example, which mkdir returns /bin/mkdir, telling you that running the command mkdir runs /bin/mkdir.

Combining Commands Together

So far, we have only been using commands individually, and for the large part that is what you will be doing in practice. However, some of the real power of these commands lies in the ability to join them together to get exactly what you want. There are some extra little commands that we have not looked at that are often used as glue because they do one very simple thing that enables a more complex process to work.

All the commands we have looked at have printed their information to the screen, but this is often flexible. There are two ways to control where output should go: piping and output redirection. A *pipe* is a connector between one command's output and another's input. Instead of sending its output to your terminal, a command sends that output directly to another command for input. Output redirection works in a similar way to pipes but is usually used for files. We will look at pipes first and then output redirection.

Two of the commands we have looked at so far are ps and grep: the process lister and the string matcher. We can combine the two to find out which users are playing Nethack right now:

```
ps aux ¦ grep nethack
```

That creates a list of all the processes running right now and sends that list to the grep command, which filters out all lines that do not contain the word nethack. Fedora Core Linux allows you to pipe as many commands as you can sanely string together. For example, we could add in the wc command, which counts the numbers of lines, words, and characters in its input, to count precisely how many times Nethack is being run:

```
ps aux ¦ grep nethack ¦ wc -l
```

The -l parameter to wc (lowercase *L*) prints only the line count.

Using pipes in this way is often preferable to using the -exec parameter to find, simply because many people consider find to be a black art and so anything that uses it less frequently is better! This is where the xargs command comes in: It converts output from one command into arguments for another.

For a good example, consider this mammoth find command from earlier:

```
find / -name "*.txt" -size +10k -user paul -not -perm +o=r -exec chmod o+r {} \;
```

That searches every directory from / onward for files matching *.txt that are greater than 10KB, are owned by user paul, and do not have read permission for others. Then it executes chmod on each of the files. It is a complex command, and people who are not familiar with the workings of find might have problems understanding it. So, what we can do is break it up into two—a call to find and a call to xargs. The most conversion would look like this:

```
find / -name "*.txt" -size +10k -user paul -not -perm +o=r ¦ xargs chmod o+r
```

That has eliminated the confusing {} \; from the end of the command, but it does the same thing, and faster, too. The speed difference between the two is because using -exec with find causes it to execute chmod once for each file. However, chmod accepts many files at a time and, because we are using the same parameter each time, we should take advantage of that. The second command, using xargs, is called once with all the output from find, and so saves many command calls. The xargs command automatically places the input at the end of the line, so the previous command might look something like this:

```
xargs chmod o+r file1.txt file2.txt file3.txt
```

Not every command accepts multiple files, though, and if you specify the -1 parameter, xargs executes its command once for each line in its input. If you want to check what it is doing, use the -p parameter to have xargs prompt you before executing each command.

For even more control, the -i parameter allows you to specify exactly where the matching lines should be placed in your command. This is important if you need the lines to appear before the end of the command or need it to appear more than once. Either way, using the -i parameter also enables the -l parameter so each line is sent to the command individually. This next command finds all files in /home/paul that are larger than 10,000KB in size (10MB) and copies them to /home/paul/archive:

```
find /home/paul -size +10000k | xargs -i cp {} ./home/paul/archive
```

Using find with xargs is a unique case. All too often, people use pipes when parameters would do the job just as well. For example, these two commands are identical:

```
ps aux --sort=-%cpu | grep -v `whoami`
ps -N ux --sort=-%cpu
```

The former prints all users and processes and then pipes that to grep, which in turn filters out all lines that contain the output from the program whoami (our username). So, line one prints all processes being run by other uses, sorted by CPU use. Line two does not specify the a parameter to ps, which makes it list only our parameters. It then uses the -N parameter to flip that, which means it is everyone but us, without the need for grep.

The reason people use the former is often just simplicity: Many people know only a handful of parameters to each command, so they can string together two commands simply rather than write one command properly. Unless the command is to be run regularly, this is not a problem. Indeed, the first line would be better because it does not drive people to the manual to find out what ps -N does!

Multiple Terminals

It is both curious and sad that many Linux veterans have not heard of the screen command. Curious because they needlessly go to extra effort to replicate what screen takes in its stride and sad because they are missing a powerful tool that would benefit them greatly.

Picture this scene: You connect to a server via SSH and are working at the remote shell. You need to open another shell window so you can have the two running side by side; perhaps you want the output from top in one window while typing in another. What do you do? Most people would open another SSH connection, but that is both wasteful and unnecessary. screen is a *terminal multiplexer*, which is a fancy term for a program that lets you run multiple terminals inside one terminal.

The best way to learn screen is to try it yourself, so open a console, type **screen**, and then press Enter. Your display will blank momentarily and then be replaced with a console; it will look like nothing has changed. Now, let's do something with that terminal. Run top and leave it running for the time being. Hold down the Ctrl key and press a (referred to as Ctrl+a from now on); then let go of them both and press c. Your prompt will clear again, leaving you able to type. Run the uptime command.

Pop quiz: What happened to the old terminal running top? It is still running, of course. You can type Ctrl+a and then press 0 to return to it. Type Ctrl+a and then press 1 to go back to your uptime terminal. While you are viewing other terminals, the commands in the other terminals carry on running as normal so you can multitask.

Many of screen's commands are case sensitive, so the lettering used here is very specific: Ctrl+a means press Ctrl and the a key", but Ctrl+A means press Ctrl and Shift and the a key" so you get a capital A. Ctrl+a+A means "press Ctrl and the a key, let them go, and then press Shift and the a key."

You have seen how to create new displays and how to switch between them by number. However, you can also bring up a window list and select windows using your cursor with Ctrl+a+" (that is, press Ctrl and a together, let go, and press the double quotes key [usually Shift and the single quote key]). You will find that the screens you create have the name bash by default, which is not very descriptive. Select a window and press Ctrl+a+A. You are prompted to enter a name for the current window, and your name is used in the window list.

Once you get past window 9, it becomes impossible to switch to windows using Ctrl+a and 0–9; as soon as you type the 1 of 10, screen switches to display 1. The solution is to use either the window list or the quick change option, in which you press Ctrl+a+' (single quote), enter either the screen number or the name you gave it, then press Enter. You can also change back to the previous window by pressing Ctrl+a+Ctrl+a. If you only work within a small set of windows, you can use Ctrl+a+n and Ctrl+a+p to move to the next and previous windows, respectively. Of course, if you are changing to and from windows only to see whether something has changed, you are wasting time because screen can monitor windows for you and report if anything changes. To enable (or disable) monitoring for a window, use Ctrl+a+M; when something happens, screen flashes a message. If you miss it (the messages disappear when you type something), use Ctrl+a+m to bring up the last message.

Windows close when you kill the main program inside. Using Ctrl+a+c, this window is Bash; type **exit** to quit. Alternatively, you can use Ctrl+a+K to kill a window. When all your windows are closed, screen terminates and prints a screen is terminating message so you know you are out.

However, there are two alternatives to quitting: locking and disconnecting. The first, activated with Ctrl+a+x, locks access to your screen data until you enter your system password. The second is the most powerful feature of screen: You can exit it and do other things for a while and then reconnect later and screen will pick up where you left off. For example, you could be typing at your desk, disconnect from screen, then go home, reconnect, and carry on as if nothing had changed. What's more, all the programs you ran from screen carry on running even while screen is disconnected. It even automatically disconnects for you if someone closes your terminal window while it is in a locked state (with Ctrl+a+x).

35

To disconnect from screen, press Ctrl+a+d. You are returned to the prompt from which you launched screen and can carry on working, close the terminal you had opened, or even log out completely. When you want to reconnect, run the command screen -r. You can, in the meantime, just run screen and start a new session without resuming the previous one, but that is not wise if you value your sanity! You can disconnect and reconnect the same screen session as many times you want, which potentially means you need never lose your session again.

Although this has been a mere taster of screen, hopefully you can see how useful it can be.

Reference

http://www.gnu.org/—The website of the GNU project, it contains manuals and downloads for lots of command-line software.

http://www.linuxdevcenter.com/linux/cmd/—A wide selection of Linux commands and explanations of what they do.

http://www.tuxfiles.org/linuxhelp/cli.html—Several short command-line tutorials, courtesy of tuXfiles.

http://www.linuxcommand.org/—Describes itself as "your one-stop command line shop!" It contains a wealth of useful information about the console.

http://www.tripwire.org—Information and download links for the open-source version of Tripwire.

Books

Understanding the way Unix works at the nuts and bolts level can be both challenging and rewarding, and there are several good books that will help guide you on your way. Perhaps the best is *The Art of Unix Programming* by Eric Raymond (Addison-Wesley, ISBN: 0-13-142901-9), which focuses on the philosophy behind Unix and manages to mix in much about the command line.

O'Reilly's *Unix CD Bookshelf* (ISBN: 0-596-00392-7) contains seven highly respected books in one, although it retails for more than $120 as a result! That said, it is incomparable in its depth and breadth of coverage.

36

Advanced Yum

One of the main things you will want to do with Fedora is to install your own choice of software, as if you had not got enough choice with the packages available with Fedora! Although Fedora provides a useful graphical configuration tool for adding and removing software, it is limited to the software that is supplied with Fedora. This means that you can't add anything else except what Fedora wants you to have, neither can you upgrade if a new release of software becomes available. The Yum tool (Yellowdog Updater, Modified) has been included with Fedora since version 1 and has become the tool of choice for installing and updating applications. In this chapter, we will take a look at how Yum works, its basic usage, and more advanced package and repository management.

Yum is controlled entirely from the command line, so you will have to memorize some useful switches to get the most from it.

Before I go into Yum itself, it is worthwhile understanding what goes on behind the scenes. How does Yum actually work?

It is easiest to think of Yum as a software layer that utilizes the rpm command. When you issue commands to Yum, it automatically accesses various repositories and downloads the rpm headers that are then queried using the rpm command. The advantage to this is that all the processing takes place locally, without the need to download the entire RPM itself. Typically, the RPM header makes up a very small portion of the file, which makes it easy to handle and quick to download. Yum builds and maintains a local cache of header files, attributed to the supplying repository, and queries this when you use Yum. Each time Yum is invoked, it checks the repositories for any updates. If any are found, it adds new headers to its cache, thereby making it as up-to-date as possible when you need to use it. Because Yum uses rpm, there should be no dependency problems, making it a fast and easy way to install and update software.

Yum is primarily controlled by its configuration file, yum.conf, and by the contents of the yum.repos.d directory, both of which can be found in /etc. By default, Yum uses the Red Hat and Fedora repositories for updates, but you can easily add more of your own if you want to install other software that is not available from Red Hat themselves.

Like apt, Yum is incredibly easy to use, requiring a single command with a switch to update all the software in Fedora.

Getting Started

First, open a terminal. Check that Yum is installed and working by simply typing

```
$ yum
```

This brings up the usage options for Yum and lets you know that you have it installed.

After you have verified that Yum is available, you should switch to super-user and enter the following command:

```
# yum check-update
```

This command initializes Yum and asks it to scan the installed RPMs on your machine, scan the repositories for header files, and then start building a cache of header file. After several minutes of frantic activity, Yum will have completed its local cache of header files and will be ready for you to start downloading and installing updates and new software.

To perform a quick and easy update of all the software on your system, enter the following command

```
# yum update
```

This asks Yum to download header information from the registered repositories, check that against your current installed packages, and update any that are marked as having new versions. This can take some time, depending on how often you run the command and how many packages you have installed on your system. Of course, if you have a cable or DSL connection, it will be quicker, but dial-up users should be warned that they might need to go away and make a few cups of coffee while Yum does its work.

When Yum has finished downloading the headers and working out dependencies, you are prompted with a list of the packages to be updated or installed and asked to give the go-ahead. Enter **y** at the command prompt and Yum commences downloading the RPM files.

After the download has finished, Yum runs the installation and a test to ensure that everything completed correctly. After Yum is satisfied that everything is present and correct, you are returned to the command prompt with a freshly updated system.

This is great when you want to update your entire system, but what if you want to update only certain packages? Again, Yum can easily take care of this for you. You can identify the package you want and then use Yum to check for its availability by using the command shown here:

```
# yum list <packagename>
```

This command asks Yum to cross-reference the package name with packages registered at the repositories and let you know what is available. You can use wildcards as part of the command to find out which associated packages are available. For instance, the command

```
# yum list kde*
```

searches for any packages containing kde, which is useful if you want to selectively update packages. Use the command shown here to update the single package:

```
# yum update <packagename>
```

Or use this command to update more than one package at a time:

```
# yum update <packagename1> <packagename2>
```

Of course, when Yum is processing the required packages, it also solves any dependency issues. You will get the opportunity to not only see the packages that will be updated, but also see which packages were required to satisfy dependency issues.

About Yum

Yum is not developed by Red Hat itself. Instead, Duke University has the honor of being the creators and maintainers of Yum and its related technology. In particular, Seth Vidal has spent a lot of time and effort ensuring that Yum improves in both speed and functionality. Subscribe to the Yum mailing list at https://lists.dulug.duke.edu/mailman/listinfo/yum for the latest information and updates on Yum.

Using Yum to Remove Packages

So far we have only looked at using Yum for installing software, but that is only a small part of its abilities.

It can also be used to remove packages that are no longer required, as well as give detailed information on installed and available packages.

The syntax is similar to the installation and update functions of Yum. In this section, we look at removing packages from the system using Yum.

As mentioned earlier, Yum interfaces with the rpm command to use it for querying the local package database. If you need to remove a package, you can use yum remove <packagename>. Yum then scans the local file system, finds the package named, and checks for potential dependency problems. This way, you will never remove a package that could crash your system. You will be prompted to give confirmation that you want to remove the required package; then Yum processes the packages and their dependencies to remove them safely.

Using Yum to Manage Package Inventory

Another useful feature of Yum is the capability to list several sets of packages. There are a few options that you can list, including packages that are currently installed, packages that are available to be installed, and packages that have updates available.

The command is as follows:

```
$ yum list <available> <updates> <installed> <extras>
```

- available—This lists the available packages in the configured repositories.
- updates—This lists the available updates for currently installed packages.
- installed—This lists the packages currently installed on the system.
- extras—This lists the installed packages that are not present in any of the configured repositories.

So, if I wanted to find out which packages I have installed on my system, I would use the command yum list installed to return a detailed summary of packages installed and their version numbers. You can take this one step further and query for individual packages. You might want to find out which version of OpenOffice.org you have installed and which version is available for installation. For this, you would use yum list openoffice.org—the results of which would show you which version was installed and which version was available for updating.

Yum can also search the headers and summaries for each RPM file so you can find specific information about packages that would not usually be available in just the package name itself.

For example, using yum search kdebindings would bring up entries matching kdebindings. The results of this command are shown here:

```
$ yum search kdebindings
Searching Packages:
Setting up Repo:  dries
Setting up Repo:  dag
Setting up Repo:  updates-released
Setting up Repo:  newrpms
Setting up Repo:  freshrpms
Setting up Repo:  base
Reading repository metadata in from local files
```

```
dries     : #################################################### 717/717
dag       : #################################################### 1808/1808
updates-re: #################################################### 722/722
newrpms   : #################################################### 385/385
freshrpms : #################################################### 477/477
base      : #################################################### 2622/2622


kdebindings.i386                    3.3.0-3              base
Matched from:
kdebindings


kdebindings-devel.i386              3.3.0-3              base
Matched from:
kdebindings-devel
Development files for kdebindings
Development files for the KDE bindings.

Install kdebindings-devel if you want to develop non-KDE
applications that talk to KDE.


kdebindings.i386                    3.3.1-1              updates-released
Matched from:
kdebindings


kdebindings-devel.i386              3.3.1-1              updates-released
Matched from:
kdebindings-devel
Development files for kdebindings
Development files for the KDE bindings.

Install kdebindings-devel if you want to develop non-KDE
applications that talk to KDE.


kdebindings-debuginfo.i386          3.3.1-1              updates-released
Matched from:
kdebindings-debuginfo
Debug information for package kdebindings
This package provides debug information for package kdebindings.
Debug information is useful when developing applications that use this
package or when debugging this package.
```

36

Configuring Yum

As mentioned earlier, Yum is primarily controlled by the contents of the yum.conf file and the /etc/yum.repos.d directory. Let's take a closer look at the contents of both of these so you can get a better understanding of how best to configure Yum.

When you initially install Fedora, there is a default yum.conf that provides several switches for the Yum command. It basically saves you having to type in a number of switches and keeps Yum simple. By default, Yum is configured to do the following:

- Keep a cache of headers in /var/cache/yum.
- Give minimal onscreen information during processing.
- Keep a log-file in /var/log/yum.log.
- Download only the most up-to-date packages.
- Be tolerant of errors in the process.
- Match packages to your processor architecture.
- Have a maximum retry limit of 20 times.
- Check for obsolete packages.
- Use GPG keys to ensure the identities of packages.

All these options are contained within the yum.conf file, letting you easily modify or even remove certain lines. For instance, you might need Yum to try only a maximum of five times, or you might need Yum to give you more visual information.

You can add repository information into the yum.conf file, but as of Fedora Core 3, there has been a change in the way Yum handles repositories. New to Fedora 3 was the yum.repos.d folder that allows you to create individual configuration files for each repository. By default, Fedora comes with repositories for their base packages, updated packages, updated packages that are in testing, and the more unstable development packages. Only the base and updated packages are enabled by default.

> **CAUTION**
>
> Unless you really know what you are doing, you should avoid the more unstable repositories of fedora-updates-testing and fedora-development. These repositories contain bleeding-edge packages that can break your system. You have been warned!

Opening a repository file shows you some details about the repository itself, including the path to it (either via HTTP, FTP, or local access), any lists of mirrors for that repository, whether that repository is enabled, and whether GPG checking is enabled.

If you want to add a new repository, you need to find out a few things before you can successfully add it to either its own repo file under /etc/yum.repos.d or in the yum.conf file.

Creating a Local Yum **Repository**

When Yum is active, it can download a lot of information in the form of RPM headers and files, which can easily eat up bandwidth.

If you have three or more Fedora-based machines on a local network, creating a local Yum repository can be a good way to conserve bandwidth.

Before we start setting up the repository, you need to have the `rsync` and `createrepo` packages installed because you will need them both. Use the command `yum install rsync createrepo` to make sure they are installed.

To begin, create a directory that will house your repository. In our example, we will use `/home/andrew/repo/` as our target directory.

Next, find the site you want to mirror (a selection of sites for the Fedora can be found at http://fedora.redhat.com/download/mirrors.html). For this example, we will use the UK Mirror service in Canterbury, Kent, which is rsync.mirror.ac.uk/fedora.redhat.com/ updates/3/i386/.

`rsync` itself is easy to use as follows:

```
# rsync rsync://rsync.mirror.ac.uk/fedora.redhat.com/updates
/3/i386/*.rpm /home/andrew/repo
```

`rsync` then starts to download the files it finds within that directory to `/home/andrew/repo`. This can take some time (at the time of writing, there is about 5GB of updates available at the previous address). To ensure that `rsync` really is working, navigate using Nautilus to `/home/andrew/repo`; here you should see a number of packages appearing one after the other.

After you have completed downloading the updates you want, you need to create your repository. This is where the `createrepo` command comes in.

Using Createrepo

Createrepo is a program designed to quickly and efficiently draw the relevant information from a collection of `rpm` files to make the metadata Yum requires to successfully install or update your currently installed package base.

The command is simply

```
createrepo /yourtargetdirectoryhere
```

So, if we were to use the example in the previous section, the syntax would look something like this:

```
$ createrepo /home/andrew/repo
```

36

This would give you the following output:

```
88/88 - alsa-lib-1.0.6-5.i386.rpm
Saving Primary metadata
Saving file lists metadata
Saving other metadata
```

This shows that 88 RPMs were cataloged and that the relevant metadata was saved. The program automatically uses the given directory, so you do not have to worry about making several copies of directories.

After this is done, you are ready to include your new repository into the /etc/yum.conf file or into its own file under /etc/yum.repo.d. Let's take a look at a typical configuration file for use with Yum:

```
$ cat /etc/yum.repos.d/local.repo
[local]
name=Fedora Core $releasever - $basearch - Updates
baseurl=http://192.168.2.5/repo
enabled=1
gpgcheck=0
```

This file is fairly easy to read. Line one is the name of the repository that is passed to Yum. The name must be enclosed in square brackets for it to be picked up; in this case, it is simply local. Line two gives us the display name for Yum to show while it is busy working; for this repository, it uses Fedora Core $releasever - $basearch – Updates, which prints the release version (in this case 4) and the base architecture (i386). Next comes the base URL, or the primary download point. This is used for Yum to scan and download the metadata it needs. The fourth line shows whether this repository is enabled: enabled=0 means it is disabled, and enabled=1 means it is enabled and able to be used. The final line determines whether the RPMs are checked using a GnuPG key. You are advised to obtain the relevant GnuPG key from the original repository to ensure that the packages you install have not been tampered with. This can then be imported into the RPM database by using the following command:

```
# rpm --import thiskey.txt
```

After the key has been imported into the database, Yum can use it to verify that the packages are intact and safe to use.

> **CAUTION**
>
> Notice that we say the use of GPG keys can make packages safer to use. This is certainly true, but be aware that sometimes packages can conflict with each other. You should be careful about which repositories you use because some are incompatible with others. When selecting a repository, always read any FAQs for warnings of incompatibilities. Check out http://fedoraproject.org/wiki/Extras_2fRepositoryMixingProblems for the official Fedora stance on this.

Reference

http://www.linux.duke.edu/projects/yum/—The home page of the Yum project, hosted at Linux@Duke (Duke University).

http://rpm.livna.org/—The Livna Yum repository.

http://freshrpms.net/—The FreshMeat Yum repository. It's part of the OSTG, which also includes slashdot and linux.com.

http://dag.wieers.com—The Yum repository of Dag Wieers.

http://atrpms.net—ATrpms Yum repository. It includes some highly unstable packages, so use it at your own risk!

http://apt.sw.be/dries/—Dries's Yum/apt repository.

http://www.fedorafaq.org/—A useful, but unofficial source of information. It gives locations of GPG keys for all the previously mentioned repositories.

# CHAPTER 37

Managing the File System

A Linux file system is more than just a format for your hard drive or floppy disk and more than just the disk itself or the formatting process. The file system is the structure and organization of data on a data storage device. In other words, it is how your data is organized and stored in files, disk drives, and removable media.

In this chapter, you learn about the structure of the disks themselves, the file systems that can be placed on them, and how to work with those file systems. You also learn some background and history about the file systems that Linux can use. This chapter also provides some basic information about the file system's default settings, as well as how you can adapt those settings to better match your system and its needs. At the end of the chapter, you learn how to build a test file system and use the loopback file system so that you can safely explore all the file system commands without risking any damage to your system.

Also covered are the use of the file system table, `fstab`, and instructions for formatting `ext3`, `reiserfs`, and DOS drives. This chapter also discusses the special files for character and block devices, as well as the device file system, `devfs`. The "Reference" section is full of sources with extensive information on file system-related topics.

The Fedora Core Linux File System Basics

The Fedora Core Linux file system, like all Unix file systems, is used for storing not only data, but also metadata—information about the files, such as who the file owner is, what permissions are associated with the file, and other file attributes.

The Fedora Core Linux file system is much more complex than most people care to know about. Its features are patterned after features found on commercial Unix systems, as well as those included in research or experimental file systems. In this section of the chapter, you learn what the Fedora Core Linux file system is, how it is structured, and how you work with it in the management of the Fedora Core Linux system—both as a user and a system administrator.

Fortunately, the native Linux file system is robust and works well with the default settings. Fedora Core has conveniently provided an easy-to-use setup tool for use during the installation, but here, you also learn how to manage file system settings manually.

Providing a great deal of flexibility, the file system support allows Linux users to access files on file systems used by other operating systems, many of which are obscure. A sampling of the Fedora Core kernel modules for supported file systems is as follows:

bfs—SCO Unixware Boot file system

coda—Carnegie Mellon University network file system

cramfs—Compressed ROM file system

ext3—Linux Extended File System 3 (adds journaling to ext2)

fat—Microsoft File Allocation Table file system: FAT 12 and FAT 16

freevxfs—Free version of the Veritas VxFS file system used by SCO: Unixware, Sun Solaris, HP-UX

hfs—Macintosh: Hierarchical file system

jfs—IBM's journaled file system

minix—Minix file system

msdos—Microsoft File Allocation Table -16

ncfps—Novell Corporation protocol file system

nfs—Network file system

ntfs—Windows NT, Windows 2000, Windows XP

reiserfs—Reiser file system

romfs—ROM file system

smbfs—File system based on the use of the Shared Message Block protocol used by Microsoft and Samba

sysv—System V Coherent file system: Xenix, System V, Coherent

udf—Universal Disk Format (DVD-ROM file system)

ufs—Unix file system used on BSD, Sun, and Mac OS X

umsdos—MS-DOS file system with Linux permissions

vfat—Microsoft File Allocation Table file system known as FAT32

Support for ext3, ext2, NFS, and iso9660 file systems is compiled into the Linux kernel; all others are available as modules.

There is not an exact correlation between the file system source code and the modules compiled for the default kernel. The kernel documentation for the file systems can be found at `/usr/src/linux-2.6/Documentation/file systems/`. The usage of some of these file system modules is mentioned in the man page for mount.

Physical Structure of the File System on the Disk

If you were to visualize the file system on the physical disk, it would resemble a series of boxes known as blocks. The first block on the disk is a special block that contains the boot sector; subsequent blocks contain the operating system, applications, and your data.

Each individual block is made up of smaller groups of data:

- A superblock (called by that name because it contains redundant information about the overall file system).

- Redundant file system descriptors—All the redundant information is useful for reliability and recovery from disasters and errors.

- A bitmap of the block.

- A bitmap of the inode table.

- Information from the inode table.

- The data blocks.

Inodes and File Attributes

The informationthat constitutes a file in the ext2/etx3 file system begins with the inode.

The inode contains the following description of the file: the file type, its access rights, its owners, several different time stamps, the file size, and pointers to data blocks that hold the file information. When you want to access a file, the kernel uses those pointers to calculate where the data resides physically on the disk.

File attributes are also stored in the inode. The chattr command enables the root operator to manipulate some special attributes of files on an ext2/3 file system. One of the most interesting uses of the chattr command is to make a file *immutable*, meaning that it cannot be deleted, renamed, written to, or modified by anyone, even root (at least until the immutable attribute is un-set). To make a file immutable (the word means unalterable; not capable of change)

```
# chattr +i filename
```

and to change it back

```
# chattr -i filename
```

Another interesting flag is the s flag, which tells the system to zero out all the blocks used for that file when the file is deleted.

37

To observe the existing attributes of a file, use

lsattr filename

The chattr utility is part of the e2fsprogs package.

A file's attributes include its access *permissions*. The traditional Unix systems of permissions is controlled with chmod. Posix Access Control Lists extend this functionality.

ACL supports permissions for users and groups beyond the traditional owner/group/world scheme. They enable finer-grained control of permissions for files.

To learn more about Access Control Lists, visit the Posix ACLs for Linux website: http://acl.bestbits.at/.

How big are these blocks? The default size is 1,024 bytes, but the size can be made smaller or larger when the file system is first created. The optimum size is determined by the application of the particular machine. If you typically use very large files, a larger block size can speed up disk I/O operations at the expense of slower I/O for smaller files; the reverse is also true. For an individual system, it might require monitoring over time and benchmarking before an optimal value is determined. For most users, the defaults have been found satisfactory.

File System Partitions

File system partitions are ways to organize blocks of data on the physical drive media and are parts of the overall file system on your computer. No single universal partition format exists. In addition to the commonly used DOS partition format (used by Linux as well), Fedora Core also provides support for the following partition types:

- Acorn

- Alpha OS (compiled into the kernel)

- Amiga

- Atari

- Macintosh (compiled into the kernel)

- BSD (compiled into the kernel)

- Minix (compiled into the kernel)

- SunOS/Solaris (compiled into the kernel)

- Unixware slices (compiled into the kernel)

- SGI (compiled into the kernel)

- Windows Logical Disk Manager

- DEC Ultrix (now owned by Hewlett Packard)

Network and Disk File Systems

We can separate file systems into two broad categories: those that can be used over a network and local disk file systems. You are provided with all the applications necessary to work with both categories of file systems when using Fedora Core Linux.

Network file systems are physically stored somewhere other than your local computer but appear as if they are mounted on your local computer.

Some common network file system types are

- NFS—The Network File System was developed by Sun and is in common use. It has no built-in security because it was originally designed to run over friendly networks. Although considered problematic by some, it is easy to implement. It is typically used between Unix peers. Fedora Core supports client and server installations of this file system.

- Coda—Similar to NFS, Coda offers support for disconnected operation and security caching (keeping a local copy of files in case the network connection is lost). Fedora Core only provides kernel compatibility with Coda; the actual client and server code is available from http://www.coda.cs.cmu.edu/.

- InterMezzo—Similar in features to Coda, InterMezzo is a GPL project. The server daemon can be obtained from http://www.inter-mezzo.org/.

- NCP—Used to mount Novelle Netware volumes, its use is more fully described in the Linux Network Administrators Guide at http://www.tldp.org/LDP/nag2/x-087-2-ipx.ncpfs.client.html.

- SMB—The network-focused Server Message Block protocol was developed by Microsoft. The Linux implementation is known as Samba and is one of the most advanced open-source projects available. It is typically used between Linux and Microsoft Windows peers. Netatalk is the Macintosh equivalent protocol.

37

Disk file systems are found on a physical device; they are the hard drive in your desktop or laptop computer. Some common disk file system types are

- FAT is a disk-oriented, table-based (a linked list) file system used by Microsoft. It has been regularly extended to add functionality. Microsoft's Enterprise-level file system is known as NTFS. (You learn more about this system in "DOS File Systems," later in this chapter.)

- ext2, ext3, and reiserfs are inode-based. (You learn about reiserfs in "The Reiser File System (reiserfs)," later in this chapter.)

The JFS (Journaled File System from IBM) and XFS (from Silicon Graphics) file systems are available for use with Fedora Core Linux, but primarily as migration aids for those migrating existing file systems to Linux.

A journaling file system adds a journal, or hidden file, to the data on the drive. Because of the way data is written to a disk, the kernel might be holding some of the data while it is deciding where to place it. If your computer were to suffer a failure, that cached data would be lost. A journaling file system keeps that data in a special place until the kernel decides to formally write it to the disk. If a system failure occurs, a special application (fsck) knows that the data was never formally written and will make certain that it is written in the correct place. This ensures that no data is lost. Journaling file systems are actually much more complex than this, but the mechanics of them are beyond the scope of this chapter. Journaling file systems such as ext3, reiserfs, JFS, and XFS are major improvements over older, non-journaling file systems.

Viewing Your System's File Systems

Your installation of Fedora Core Linux might have its own unique set of usable virtual file system modules. You can view the file systems that your system can access right now (and verify your kernel's support for these file systems) by using the following command:

```
# cat /proc/file systems
```

Your output will vary, depending on your system's hardware and kernel settings. The test system we used for this chapter presented this output:

```
nodev   rootfs
nodev   bdev
nodev   proc
nodev   sockfs
nodev   tmpfs
nodev   shm
nodev   pipefs
        ext2
nodev   ramfs
        iso9660
```

```
nodev   devpts
        ext3
nodev   usbdevfs
nodev   usbfs
        ReiserFS
        vfat
nodev   nfs
nodev   autofs
nodev   binfmt_misc
```

The entries not preceded by `nodev` are not of interest to us because they do not tell us any information about the file system. On this machine, the `ext2`, `ext3`, `vfat`, `reiserfs`, and `iso9660` file systems are supported. Modules for other file systems could be loaded if needed.

Working with the `ext3` File System

Red Hat had invested heavily in the development of the `ext3` file system and provides support for the `ext3` file system as the journaling file system for its distribution. Red Hat (and now Fedora Core) does not provide that level of support for other file systems. Other distributions such as SuSE and Mandrake support the Reiser file system, which is covered later.

The `ext3` file system is an update to the `ext2` file system, which has been one of the most popular Linux file systems for some time. You can choose to use the `ext3` file system during a fresh install or automatically convert to an `ext3` file system when you upgrade your present system to the current version of Fedora Core Linux. All the `ext2` tools provided by Fedora Core have been upgraded to work with both `ext2` and `ext3`. We mention the `ext2` tools only because you will see the `ext2` file system mentioned frequently; `ext3`, as supplied with Fedora Core Linux, is completely compatible with `ext2`.

Understanding the `ext3` File System Structure

Fedora Core's rationale for choosing `ext3` may be compelling. Although it provides availability, data integrity, and speed similar to other file system choices, `ext3` has one unique advantage: It is an easy transition from `ext2` to `ext3`, and the transition is forgiving of mistakes along the way. It is also potentially possible to recover a deleted file from an `ext3` file system; such a recovery is not possible at all for a `reiserfs` file system.

> **NOTE**
>
> The downside to using `ext3` seems to be performance related. A recent benchmarking evaluation (see http://fsbench.netnation.com/) of all Linux file systems placed `ext3` at the bottom for general performance. What the study really demonstrates is that you must match the file system to the application for best all-around performance.

37

The ext3 file system can accommodate files as large as 2TB, directories as large as 2TB, and a maximum filename length of 255 characters. (With special kernel patches, this limit can be increased to 1,024 characters if the standard length is insufficient for your use.) The ext3 file system can allocate and use empty space in a very efficient manner.

The usage of space is so efficient that ext3 file systems typically do not need defragmenting (rearranging the files to make them contiguous). The dynamic allocation of resources is also the source of one Achilles heel for the file system. When a file is deleted, its inode is erased and the data blocks associated with it are freed; they might very well be reallocated immediately, and the old data lost forever.

> **NOTE**
>
> A defragmentation program for the ext2 file system does exist, but it is infrequently used, is not typically included with standard Linux distributions such as Fedora Core Linux, and is not recommended for general use. The ext2/3 file system assigns blocks of space for files based on their parent directories; this spaces files out all over the physical disk, leaving room to keep files contiguous and reduce fragmentation. However, a file system full of files at 90% of its capacity can become badly fragmented.

Every file system varies in structure, depending on its efficiency, security, and even proprietary designs to limit cross-compatibility deliberately. The ext3 file systems were designed to follow Unix design concepts, particularly "everything is a file."

For example, a directory in the ext3 file system is simply a file; that file contains the names of the files to be found in that directory, and the locations of those files. The list of names is linked so that space is not wasted because of varying filename lengths.

Journaling Options in ext3

The ext3 file system has several options that, depending on your needs, allow you to select how much information is journaled. According to Red Hat, the typical journal requires a second or so to be read and recovered. The time needed to recover from an improper shutdown of a journaled file system is not dependent on the file system size, but the amount of data in the journal.

The default setting provided by Fedora Core is adequate for most needs. The optimal choice depends on so many factors (computer usage, hardware used, and testing and evaluation methods) that a meaningful discussion is beyond the scope of this chapter. You learn in this chapter what the choices are and how they differ, but whether a choice is right for you can only be determined on an individual basis.

Like all journaling file systems, the traditional file system check (fsck) is not necessary on an ext3 file system. Although only mildly annoying on a 20GB drive on your machine at home, imagine the seemingly endless hours that an fsck would take to run on a terabyte of data. This feature is shared in common with the other journaling file systems.

When choosing journaling options, you can trade off data integrity (keeping your data current and valid) for data transfer speed in your file system's operation; you cannot have both because of the nature of the file system design. You can choose to expose some of your data to potential damage in the case of an improper shutdown in exchange for faster data handling; or, you can sacrifice some speed to keep the state of the file system consistent with the state of the operating system.

Three modes available as options to ext3 are as follows:

writeback—Enables old data to stay in the file system, attaining the fastest speed possible. It does not schedule any data writes; it just enables the kernel's 30-second writeback code to flush the buffer.

ordered—Keeps the data consistent, but with some sacrifice in speed (the default mode for Fedora Core).

journal—Requires more disk space to journal more data. You might see slower performance because data is written twice, but there are some speed benefits if you are doing synchronous data writes as in database operations.

For most of us, the default selection represents a good trade-off. Fedora Core supports booting from an ext3 formatted root file system with the proper drivers loaded in the initrd image.

The mode is selected by using the appropriate mount option in /etc/fstab. For example, to set the file system mode to the fastest of the three modes, use data=writeback as the option. For more details, see man mount.

Verifying File Integrity in ext3 File Systems with the fsck Utility

The file system integrity is assured using fsck, or file system check, program—one of five commands in the library that are used to maintain and modify the ext3 file system.

When fsck is run, it performs a sequential analysis of the file system information available in the file system if it detects a directory that cannot be traced back to the root or an undeleted file with a zero link count. It places these directories and files in the /lost+found directory that is created on each physical partition by the file system formatting process. Some blocks are reserved for this and other uses of the superuser. It is possible to reduce this allocation to free additional space for regular users by special arguments to the formatting program mke2fs.

To run the fsck command, use the name of the file system as the argument. You will need to ensure that the file system you want to check is unmounted by using the umount command. If you want to fsck the file system at /dev/hdc, for example, do this:

```
# fsck /dev/hdc
```

> **TIP**
>
> If you are logged on as a regular user and su to root using su, you will not inherit root's environment and path, meaning that the preceding command will not work without using the full path: /usr/sbin/fsck.

> Either type the full path each time, or become root with su -, which causes you to inherit root's environment and path; you have less to type.

The file system state is tracked in the ext3 file systems. A special field in the superblock tells the kernel that, after the file system is mounted read/write, it is marked as not clean; when it is properly unmounted, it is marked as clean. If a file system is not unmounted properly, it could contain corrupt data because all the file data might not have been written to it. (This is what the journaling file systems such as ext3 strive to eliminate.) When the system is booted, this flag is checked and if it is not clean, the program fsck is run. Internally, fsck is actually a wrapper program that runs the appropriate version of fsck for the file system in use: fsck.minix, fsck.ext2, fsck.ext3, fsck.reiserfs, fsck.msdos, and fsck.vfat. If the kernel detects an inconsistency in the superblock field, the file system is marked erroneous, and the file system check is forced even if other indicators suggest that fsck does not need to be run.

By default, the system will run fsck on a file system after a periodic number of reboots, regardless of the status of the clean flag. This behavior is triggered by a mount counter kept in the superblock or after a predetermined amount of time has elapsed since the last reboot (information also kept in the superblock). These parameters can be adjusted through the tune2fs command; this command can also be used to modify how the kernel handles the erroneous flag and, interestingly, the number of blocks reserved for the superuser, also known as root. This latter option is useful on very large or very small disks to make more disk space available to the user.

Other File Systems Available to Fedora Core Linux

Although ext3 is certainly an acceptable root file system, there are other alternatives. No operating systems can support as many root file systems as Linux, but you should be aware that every file system has its strengths and weaknesses. Some are better with small files, some are better with large files, some are better at writing data, and some better at reading data. Unfortunately, there is no one perfect file system. The following sections discuss some of the other common file systems available for use with Fedora Core Linux.

The Reiser File System (reiserfs)

The other popular journaling file system for Linux is the written-from-scratch Reiser file system, reiserfs. It is used primarily in the SUSE and Mandrake distributions, which support booting from a reiserfs root file system. reiserfs offers similar features to ext3, but there is no easy migration path from an already existing ext2 partition, as you learn to do in "Converting an Existing ext2 File System to ext3," later in this chapter. In the past, reiserfs didn't work well over NFS mounts, but recent versions of the nfsd daemon have fixed those problems. Fedora Core does offer reiserfs, but does not offer support for booting from it as the root partition file system, nor does it offer the choice to format non-root partitions as reiserfs during the installation process.

reiserfs is offered primarily for compatibility with existing reiserfs partitions you might want to access. Although the Reiser file system can be used as a root file system (meaning that Linux can be booted from a Reiser file system), Fedora Core has chosen not to support that option. The main problem is that reiserfs does not, at the time of writing, play nicely with SELinux and is therefore not recommended either by Red Hat or the NSA (SELinux's developers).

> **NOTE**
>
> The reiserfs file system has undergone a major update and release with Reiser4. The project, sponsored by The Defense Advanced Research Projects Agency (DARPA), aims to introduce improvements in a number of areas, such as maximum number of directories, files, links, sizes of individual files and size of the file system (nearly 18 terabytes). Other improvements include performance improvements and encryption.

JFS and XFS File Systems

Two commercial Unix file systems have been ported (rewritten) to allow them to be used in Linux. IBM has provided its Journaled File System (JFS) that is used with its commercial Unix named AIX. Silicon Graphics, Inc. (SGI) has provided its XFS file system used by its commercial Unix named IRIX. Because these file systems are generally suited for enterprise systems rather than home or small office systems, it seems likely that they are offered in Fedora Core Linux to ease the transition of IRIX and AIX users to Linux by eliminating the need for these users to reformat their very large file systems.

Beginning with kernel 2.6, XFS is fully supported in the kernel.

DOS File Systems

The extent of DOS file system support in Linux is often surprising to newcomers, but the DOS file system proved to be a viable option in the early years of Linux. Because Microsoft has been the dominant operating system on Intel computers, Linux has always worked toward coexistence with DOS.

Microsoft DOS and the consumer-oriented Windows operating systems use a file system known as FAT (File Allocation Table). FAT32 is the typical system used today. The number following the FAT name indicates the size of the space for naming address pointers; the more space, the larger a section of contiguous space can be identified and accessed. FAT32 is the most recent version of FAT, and it is backward-compatible with other versions of FAT. Older versions are not forward compatible.

The Fedora Core Linux kernel can access all versions of FAT formatted partitions (including floppy disks) using the vfat kernel module.

CD-ROM File Systems

If you use CD-ROM or DVD-ROM media, you need to understand a little bit about the file system and how it works with Linux. To the average user, the file system of a CD-ROM

37

looks just like a native Linux file system. It is not the native file system, but the features of the Virtual File System make it possible for it to appear that way. The CD-ROM file system standards continue to evolve to accommodate new technology.

iso9660

The file system typically used on a CD-ROM is known as iso9660, the name of the standard that defines the format. Each operating system translates the iso9660 file system into the native file system of the operating system (with some restrictions). Several extensions have been created to address certain special needs. The Rock Ridge extension allows long filenames and Unix-like symbolic links. The Joliet extension allows Unicode characters and long filenames, useful when dealing with non-English languages. El Torito CDs contain a bootable image and, with a suitable BIOS, can boot an operating system from the CD.

Universal Disk Format

The Universal Disk Format (UDF) is the file system used on DVD discs. UDF has a number of built-in features such as allowing larger files, having improved file descriptors, and packet writing that the iso9660 file system cannot easily accommodate. The UDF format is the next step in compact disc technology.

Creating a File System

To create a file system on a disk that has never had a partition table on it or to change the partition table (called repartitioning the disk), you must first create the new partition table. In this section, you begin by learning about the basic structure and workings of the disk as a storage device. This information is fundamental to your understanding of the file system creation process. You then learn to create a partition table using the fdisk and GNUparted commands. As with all similar Linux commands, each has its own strengths and weaknesses and none is a perfect choice for all situations. In the end, the partition table you create will be the same no matter which command you use. You then learn to create the file system, using commands appropriate for the type of file system you want to create.

> **NOTE**
>
> The Microsoft version of fdisk creates both a partition table and the bootloader. In Linux, fdisk only creates the partition table. The bootloader is created later by LILO, GRUB, or another bootloader; no bootloader is necessary to create a file system and store data on a disk, just a partition table.
>
> In fact, IDE disks physically installed as something other than /dev/hda (such as /dev/hdc, the secondary master drive) will not have a bootloader written to them; the space where the bootloader code normally resides will likely be blank. For SCSI disks, the drive designated in the BIOS as the bootable drive will have the bootloader written to it.

The Disk As a Storage Device

Because data storage devices are central to the file system, it is important to understand the workings of the most common data storage device—the hard disk drive. Although they work with a different medium, the basic storage functions of floppy disks and removable disk drives are similar to those of the hard disk.

Mechanically, the hard drive is a metal box that encloses disks, also known as platters, which have a magnetic coating on each side. Multiple disks are typically connected to the same spindle and rotated by a motor. The read and write heads for each side of the disk are moved by a second motor to position them over the area of the disk where the data you are looking for is stored. Each platter is organized into cylinders (the default size is 512 bytes) and sectors, and each platter has a head. Each drive has some electronics on a controller card that, along with the disk controller card on the motherboard of the computer, are capable of placing the heads at the correct space to retrieve the data.

The three components, cylinders, heads, and sectors (CHS), are referred to as the drive geometry and are used to identify specific locations on the drive. The CHS information for the drive is detected by the system BIOS and passed on to the operating system.

The first sector of the disk is called the MBR, or Master Boot Record. It is the most important sector on the disk because it contains the bootloader code and the partition table (the table containing pointers to beginning and end of the logical partitions on the disk). The BIOS gets the system's hardware ready, and then executes the bootloader code. The bootloader code and the bootloader program load the kernel and turn over control of the system to the kernel. Then, Linux is on its way to providing us with one of the best operating system experiences in the world.

The MBR sector is 512 bytes long; the first 446 bytes contain the bootloader code. The next 64 bytes contain the partition table, and the final 2 bytes contain a special code (the hexadecimal values of 55 and AA, respectively) that identifies that sector as the MBR. More details about the MBR can be found Chapter 16, "Backing Up, Restoring, and Recovery."

Creating the Partition Table

Fedora Core provides several tools to create, examine, and modify the partition table.

Because not all the tools we review are likely to be installed on your system (or other system you might be working on for now), this chapter describes making a partition table using some command-line and graphical tools that Fedora Core Linux provides.

The partition table only has enough room for four partitions. When the format was first created, it must have been assumed that four would be plenty. Complex, modern systems with very large hard drives make multiple partitions desirable for any number of unique reasons. To get around this problem, one of the four partitions—typically, partition number four—can be used as an *extended* partition. In other words, in the partition table, it looks like a big partition taking up the rest of the disk. Actually, it is a link to a table that contains the offsets to as many as 63 partitions for IDE disks and 15 for SCSI disks. One extended partition is chained to the next one in this manner.

> **CAUTION**
>
> Fedora and Red Hat have modified their supplied version of fdisk to limit the number of IDE partitions to 15 to match the limit for SCSI disks. That's a problem if you already have more than 15 IDE partitions as fdisk will simply delete those partitions without warning if you use it! If you have less than 15 partitions, there will be no problem. If this causes a problem for you, compile your own fdisk from pristine sources and file a bug report with Fedora/Red Hat.

> **NOTE**
>
> Zip disks are typically delivered with a single partition numbered 4. This has some arcane relevance to Apple computer users, but is of no importance to Linux users who are free to use any valid number they choose.

The fdisk Command

The Linux fdisk command edits the partition table.

You must be the superuser (root) before you can run fdisk (also said in Linux shorthand as "run fdisk as root"). Only hard drives (IDE and SCSI) can be accessed with fdisk, and you must use the device name as an argument. USB hard drives are accessed under SCSI emulation and are treated just as if they were SCSI devices. For example, to open fdisk and use it on the first IDE hard drive on the system, you would type this

```
# fdisk /dev/hda
```

and you would see something like this:

```
# fdisk /dev/hda
The number of cylinders for this disk is set to 4982. There is nothing wrong
➥with that, but this is larger than 1024, and in certain setups could
➥cause problems with software that runs at boot time:
1) software that runs at boot time (e.g., old versions of LILO)
2) booting and partitioning software from other OSes (e.g., DOS FDISK or the
   ➥OS/2 FDISK)
```

Pressing the m key displays the help screen as follows:

```
Command (m for help): m
Command action
   a   toggle a bootable flag
   b   edit bsd disklabel
   c   toggle the dos compatibility flag
   d   delete a partition
   l   list known partition types
   m   print this menu
   n   add a new partition
   o   create a new empty DOS partition table
```

```
p   print the partition table
q   quit without saving changes
s   create a new empty Sun disklabel
t   change a partition's system id
u   change display/entry units
v   verify the partition table
w   write table to disk and exit
x   extra functionality (experts only)
```

Pressing the p key will display the volume's partition information as follows (note that your drive information will be different):

```
Command (m for help): p

Disk /dev/hda: 255 heads, 63 sectors, 4982 cylinders
Units = cylinders of 16065 * 512 bytes

   Device Boot    Start      End    Blocks   Id  System
/dev/hda1    *        1      383   3076416    b  Win95 FAT32
/dev/hda2            384      387     32130   83  Linux
/dev/hda3            388     1025   5124735   83  Linux
/dev/hda4           1026     4982 31784602+   5  Extended
/dev/hda5           1026     1042    136521   82  Linux swap
/dev/hda6           1043     1552  4096543+   83  Linux
/dev/hda7           1553     4102 20482843+   83  Linux
/dev/hda8           4103     4500  3196903+   83  Linux
/dev/hda9           4501     4982  3871633+   83  Linux
```

Older versions of fdisk would default to /dev/hda. The author of fdisk decided that wasn't a good thing, so now you must always type the device name.

> **TIP**
>
> The fdisk command is only dangerous to explore if you write the changes to the partition table. Because you are specifically asked whether you want to do this, poke around to satisfy your curiosity and avoid pressing the w key when you're done; just use q to quit. Armed with this knowledge, do not feel too shy if you're curious about the partition table. But if you really do not want to take a chance on breaking anything, play it safe and use the -l (that's the letter L, not the numeral 1) as in
>
> ```
> # fdisk -l /dev/had
> ```
>
> fdisk happily prints the contents of the partition table to the screen (often referred to as stdout, or standard output) and exits without placing you in the edit mode.
>
> It is always a good idea to keep a hard copy of your edited partition table. You can redirect the output of fdisk -l to a file
>
> ```
> # fdisk -l device > mypartitiontable.txt
> ```

37

or send it to the printer with

```
# fdisk -l device | kprinter
```

In the first example, a redirector symbol (>) is used to redirect the listing from stdout to a file. In the second example, we used a pipe (|) to send the output directly to the printer (assuming that you have one connected).

Now that you are running fdisk as root, you can create a partition table. We will assume that you have installed a brand-new drive as /dev/hdb (the Primary Slave IDE device) and want to partition the entire drive as a single partition. Launch fdisk with

```
# fdisk /dev/hdb
```

Use the n key to create a new partition, and fdisk will prompt you for the beginning cylinder:

```
First Cylinder (1-9729, default 1) :
```

Press the Enter key to accept the default of 1. Now, fdisk prompts

```
Using the default value of 1
Last Cylinder or +size or +sixeM or +sizeK (2-9729, default 9729) :
```

Here, you can give the size in cylinders, the size in kilobytes, the size in megabytes, or accept the default value (which is the last cylinder on the disk). Press the Enter key to accept the default.

```
Using default value of 9729
```

And we are back at the fdisk prompt:

```
Command (m for help) :
```

Enter the w command to write the new partition table to the disk, and fdisk will exit, returning you to the command prompt.

The parted Command

In the past, Red Hat used a partition editor during its installation process named Disk Druid; the underlying code for Disk Druid has been replaced by GNUparted (also known simply as parted, the name of the command itself). GNUparted is the GNU partition editor and a very powerful utility. You use parted to create, delete, move, resize, and copy ext2, ext3, and FAT32 partitions. Although GNUparted displays a GUI interface during the installation process, it really is a console utility. GNUparted can be used from the command line.

Creating the File System on the Partitioned Disk

After you have partitioned the disk for a specific file system, you can create the file system on it. In the DOS world, this two-part process is described by DOS as low-level formatting (creating the partitions and partition table) and formatting (creating the file system). In the Unix world, the latter is known as creating a file system. In this section, you learn how to create a file system in Linux.

An unformatted disk storage device (a floppy disk, hard disk drive, or removable media) typically arrives to you with a low-level format, which has been done with a tool such as fdisk or superformat. Although the disk might have a boot block and partition information, it typically lacks the file structure needed for a file system.

> **NOTE**
>
> If you are preparing to create a file system on any device other than a floppy disk, examine it with fdisk or another utility of your choice and modify the partition table accordingly (following the instructions you saw in the preceding sections of this chapter).

To create the file system structure, you need to do what is sometimes referred to as a high-level format. For FAT file systems, this is accomplished by the format command. In Linux, you use the mke2fs -j command to create an ext3 file system.

> **NOTE**
>
> If you are creating a Reiser file system, use the mkreiserfs command. To create a DOS file system, use the mkdosfs command. Other commands for other file systems include
>
> mkfs.bfs—The SCO file system
>
> mkfs.ext2—The ext2 file system
>
> mkfs.minix—The minix file system
>
> mkfs.msdos—The MS-DOS file system
>
> mkfs.vfat—The FAT32 file system

Using mke2fs to Create the File System

The mke2fs command is used to create both the ext2 and the ext3 file systems. At its simplest, the command is used as

```
# mke2fs psrtition
```

such as

```
# mke2fs /dev/hdc4
```

Here are some of the most useful options for `mke2fs`:

-c—This option checks for bad blocks during file system creation.

-N—This option overrides the default number of inodes created. (The default number is usually a good choice, but you might need to use this option to allow additional usable disk space.)

-m—This option frees up some space on the disk, but you do so at your peril. By default, the system allocates 5% of the blocks to the superuser—to be used in file recovery during `fsck`. You can lower that allocation, but you might not leave enough blocks for `fsck` to recover enough files.

-L—This option gives the volume a label, which is useful if you need to be reminded what the file system is used for; it also provides some flexibility in identifying volumes in `/etc/fstab`.

-S—This option is a last-ditch effort for recovering a broken file system; it writes only the superblock and descriptors, leaving the information in the inodes unchanged. Always run `fsck` after using this option.

As you can see, `mke2fs` offers a few options to make more space available for the regular users. But that extra space always comes from the superuser's space for recovering damaged files. The default settings accommodate most users, so think carefully before using one of these options. Hard disks are getting less expensive all the time, so adding another might be a better solution.

Using `mkfs.ext3`

To make a new `ext3` file system, you use the `mke2fs` command with the `-j` or `-J` option, or call the command as `mkfs.ext3`. Use the `tune2fs` command on an existing `ext2` file system to add journaling. You learn how to convert an existing `ext2` file system into an `ext3` file system later in this chapter. Here, *x* represents a partition:

```
# tune2fs /dev/hdx -j
```

Some arguments you can use with this command include

-j—This option adds an `ext3` journal to the new file system using the default values. Note that you must be using a kernel that has `ext3` support to actually make use of the journal.

-J `journal-options`—This option overrides the default `ext3` journal parameters so that you can choose the options you desire. The following journal options are comma separated and can take an argument using the = sign.

`size=journal-size`—This option creates a journal of journal-size megabytes. With a minimum size of 1,024 blocks, it cannot be more than 102,400 blocks. There must be enough free space in the file system to create a journal of that size.

`device=external-journal`—This option associates the file system with a journal not contained within the file system (one that must have already been created with the command `mke2fs -O journal_device journal_name`); in other words, the journal and the data files do not have to be on the same device.

37

> **NOTE**
>
> The latter two options in the arguments list are mutually exclusive.

To select the `ext3` journaling mode, you must add the appropriate entry in `/etc/fstab`.

Because the `ext3` file system is a new version of the `ext2` file system with journaling added, it supports the same options as `ext2`, as well as the following additions:

`noload`—This option disables the `ext3` file system's journal when mounting; it becomes an `ext2` file system.

`data=journal` / `data=ordered` / `data=writeback`—This option specifies the journaling mode; "ordered" is the default. Metadata is always journaled.

`journal`—The slowest, but most secure mode because all the data is written to the journal before it is written to the regular file system.

`ordered`—This is the default mode in which all data is written to the main file system prior to its metadata being committed to the journal.

`writeback`—With this option, data can be written into the main file system after its metadata has been committed to the journal. This option enables old data to appear in files after a crash and journal recovery, but it is the fastest option.

Using `mkreiserfs`

The Reiser file system journals file data and handles smaller files more efficiently than the `ext3` file system. Although it is suitable for use as the root file system, Fedora Core does not officially support its use in that way. You use the `mkreiserfs` command to create a Reiser file system. The default values for `mkreiserfs` work well. To create a Reiser file system, use

```
# mkreiserfs device
```

Creating a DOS File System with `mkdosfs`

It is possible to create DOS file systems without owning any Microsoft software using the `mkdosfs` command. To create a DOS file system in an image file, use the `-C` option. The `-n` option allows you to specify a volume label. To create a 1.4M DOS file system as an image file with the label `dosfloppy`, the sector size (`-S`) should be `512` and the block count should be `1440`. Use the `-v` option to provide verbose output so that we can observe what happens.

```
# mkdosfs -n dosfloppy -v -C floppy.img -S 512 1440
```

> **TIP**
>
> To create a DOS file system on a floppy disk drive, use `# fdformat device`.

A complete review of all the argument options and syntax for creating a DOS file system can be found in man mkdosfs. The new file system must be mounted (as described in the following section) and then formatted with the mformat command.

Mounting File Systems

File Systems in Unix are very flexible in that they need not be physically present on your computer; you can have network access to other file systems on other machines. The Linux file system structure (the Virtual File System we spoke of at the beginning of the chapter) makes it appear as if all the file systems, regardless of type and location, are local and mounted somewhere on the root file system. As the system administrator, you decide what file systems are to be made available and where they will be attached, or mounted, to the root file system. The standard arrangement of the file system tree is that installed by default by Fedora Core Linux. The source of that standard arrangement is found in the File System Hierarchy Standards. Although a detailed discussion of those standards is beyond the scope of this section, they can be examined at http://www.pathname.com/fhs/. In this section, you learn how to mount file systems to the root file system and add file systems to the system, and you learn the traditional mount points of commonly used file systems as well.

In Linux (and its Unix cousins), all file systems—whether local, remote, images on a disk, or in memory—are mounted on a single point known as root (which is not the same as the root operator, also known as the superuser). This mount point is written as a forward slash, /, which is read and pronounced "root." The resulting file directory hierarchy all starts from /. Once mounted, the physical location of the files is unimportant because they all appear to be local.

Even if the file systems are different (FAT, ext2, HPFS, ntfs, and so on), the Linux kernel modules and the VFS make them all appear as part of the directory tree as native files. Listing the file systems as native files obviates the need for any applications to be aware of the physical location of the file or the true nature of the native file system. As a result, programming these applications is simplified because the applications only have to work with what they think are local, native files.

Any file system can be mounted anywhere, but some places are more traditional than others. Removable media devices are traditionally mounted under the /mnt directory (for example, floppy drives on /mnt/floppy and CD-ROM drives on /mnt/cdrom). The /mnt directory is the traditional place to mount removable or remote file systems that are unrelated to the local system directories that branch from the root mount point.

The mount Command

File systems are mounted with the mount command and unmounted, curiously enough, with the umount command.

During the installation, you have the opportunity to decide where and how your partitions will be mounted. You indicate your choices, and Fedora Core automatically stores them in /etc/fstab, the File System Table, for you. The mount command looks at

/etc/fstab and mounts the file system according to those set preferences. You learn more about the File System Table later in this section.

The syntax for mount is

```
mount -t type file system_to_be mounted mount_point
```

Here are the components of the mount command, and a brief explanation of each:

> type—Always preceded by the -t argument and followed by a space, and then the type of file system you are mounting. Typical file systems types are: ext2, ext3, vfat, iso9660, hpfs, hfs, ntfs, and others. For many file systems, mount can detect what type they are automatically, and the -t argument is superfluous (and is replaced with auto).

> file system_to_be mounted (as represented by the partition on which it resides)—This is the device name of the file system you want to mount, typically in the form of /dev/hdx, /dev/scx, or /dev/fdx.

> mount_point—The place in the directory tree where you want to mount the file system. Curiously, you can mount a file system over part of an existing file system. For example, if you have an existing directory at /foo with a single file named bar, and you mount a file system at /foo that includes a file named snafu, a listing of the directory /foo will not show the file bar, but only the file snafu. To show both files is a feature called *transparency*, which unfortunately is not in the current Linux repertoire.

The only real restriction to "mount anything anywhere" is that the critical system files in /bin, /etc, /lib, /dev, /proc, and /tmp need to be accessed at bootup, which typically means that they need to be on the same physical disk. If they cannot be accessed at bootup, Linux will not load and run.

Here are a few examples of using the mount command:

Mounting a floppy:

```
# mount -t vfat /dev/fd0 /mnt/floppy
```

Mounting a CD-ROM:

```
# mount -t iso9660 /dev/scd0 /mnt/cdrom
```

Mounting a Network File System (NFS) volume:

```
# mount -t nfs remote_host:/dir [options] mount_point
```

Numerous mount options exist. These options are used primarily in the /etc/fstab file. You can invoke a mount option by preceding it (or a comma-delimited string of options) with the -o switch. The mount options are listed in the fstab section of this chapter.

The umount **Command**

To unmount a file system, use the umount command with the following syntax:

umount mount_point

You can also unmount by device name:

umount device_name

> **CAUTION**
>
> Do not use umount -a to unmount everything that the system does not require to run (or is not currently using). Unmounting *everything* is a particularly bad idea on a multiuser, networked system because your users will undoubtedly lose access to some or all their files. So, as any good sysadmin will tell you, do not do that.

Mounting Automatically with /etc/fstab

A special file, /etc/fstab, exists to provide the system with predetermined options and mount points so that the file systems can be automatically or manually mounted with minimal typing and without having to recall arcane Linux syntax.

The /etc/fstab file can only be written to by the superuser. The commands fsck, mount, and umount all read information from /etc/fstab. Each file system gets its own line with the information separated by tabs.

On each line of fstab, the first field indicates the block device or remote file system that will be mounted. The second field identifies the mount point on the local system where the file system will be mounted. The third field is the file system type, and the fourth field is a comma-delimited list of mount options. Options include

exec—If this option is specified, binaries can be executed from this file system.

noauto—This means that the -a option will not cause the file system to be mounted and it will not be mounted at bootup.

noexec—If this option is specified, binaries cannot be executed from this file system.

nosuid—This option does not permit set-user-identifier or set-group-identifier bits to take effect.

ro—This option mounts the file system as read-only.

rw—This option mounts the file system as read/write.

sync—Reading from and writing to the files are done synchronously.

user—This option allows a regular (not just root) user to mount the file system, but it includes the options noexec, nosuid, and nodev by default unless they are overridden by exec, dev, and suid.

For `iso9660` file systems, the interesting option is `unhide`, which shows hidden and associated files.

The `fstab` man pages contain an in-depth description of `fstab` and its options.

The fifth field of `/etc/fstab` is used by `dump` (a traditional Unix backup program) to determine whether the file system should be dumped (backed up); 1 is yes, and 0 is no. Default values are set for you during the initial installation. They are of concern only if you actually use `dump`; then you would set the value to 1 for the file systems you wanted to back up.

The sixth field is used by `fsck` to determine how `fsck` needs to interact the file system—0 means that `fsck` is never run on the file system (a FAT32 file system, for example); 1 means that `fsck` will be run on the drive at a predetermined time. 2 is recommended for non-root file systems so that `fsck` is not run on them as frequently.

Here is a simple `/etc/fstab` file from a system with a RAID0 ext3 root partition and dual-booted with MS Windows.

```
LABEL=/12      /              ext3    defaults                1 1
none           /dev/pts       devpts  gid=5,mode=620          0 0
none           /proc          proc    defaults                0 0
none           /dev/shm       tmpfs   defaults                0 0
/dev/hda11     swap           swap    defaults                0 0
/dev/cdrom     /mnt/cdrom     iso9660 noauto,owner,kudzu,ro   0 0
/dev/fd0       /mnt/floppy    auto    noauto,owner,kudzu      0 0
/dev/hda1      /mnt/win_c     vfat    auto,quiet,exec         0 0
```

Notice the two entries marked with the `kudzu` option. This is the result of the actions of `updfstab`, which keeps `fstab` synchronized with the state of any removable devices on the system such as CD-ROMs, floppy drives, Zip and Jaz drives, LS-120 drives, and some digital cameras. The `quiet` option shown for the Windows partition will suppress error messages and is recommended if you use the Wine application.

> **NOTE**
>
> Device labels can be very useful. You can use the label in `/etc/fstab`, and if you have many devices, their labels might be easier for you to remember and track than would their device names. You can also shuffle around partitions without editing `fstab`, just by changing their labels. The `e2label` command is easier to remember than the analogous `tune2fs` command.
>
> The command `e2label` can display or change the label of a device. (You also can change a device label with `tune2fs -L`.) For example, to change the label of `/dev/hda4` to archives, use
>
> `# e2label /dev/hda4 archives`

As mentioned earlier, you record mounting preferences in `/etc/fstab` during installation. You only need to modify `/etc/fstab` if you make changes to your mounts or desire to change the default settings to address the specific needs of your system.

As long as the superuser understands the syntax and options of the fstab file, she can edit the file with any text editor.

GUI Tools to Mount File Systems

The usermount graphical file system management client is available for use with Fedora Core Linux. Although Fedora Core provides usermount as the default file system mounting tool, it is not as feature-rich as KDiskFree, which is installed when you select the KDE desktop during installation.

The K Desktop Environment (KDE) provides several disk- and file system-related utilities. You might find one or more available on your Fedora Core system if you select KDE for installation. Found in the Extras menu under System Tools, the KDiskFree menu item (it is kdf from a command line) displays all the file systems noted in the /etc/fstab file, presents information about them, and allows you to easily mount and unmount them (see Figure 37.1). KWikDisk enables mounts and unmounts from a panel applet.

TIP

KWikDisk is the KDE panel applet for KDiskFree. You would normally right-click on the KDE panel and add the applet to the panel. Fedora Core has omitted KWikDisk from the KDE applet menu, but still includes it with Fedora Core. Launch it from a command line, and it will appear on the KDE panel or on the GNOME desktop. Clicking on the KwikDisk panel icon launches an abbreviated version of KDiskFree:

```
$ kwikdisk &
```

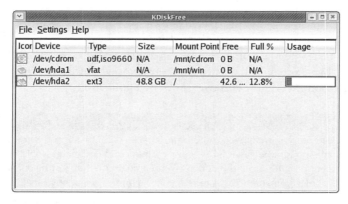

FIGURE 37.1   KDiskFree provides a graphical interface to tools used to configure custom mount options, as well as mount, or unmount disks.

The User Mount Tool, accessed from the System Tools menu as the Disk Management menu item, is a convenient way to mount and unmount file systems (see Figure 37.2). It also allows you to format floppy disks.

Floppy Formatter is a KDE tool to easily format a floppy in `ext2` or `FAT` format. You can start it by choosing System Tools, Floppy Formatter. Floppy Formatter can format floppy disks in 3.5" and 5.25" high- and low-density formats (see Figure 37.3).

FIGURE 37.2   The User Mount Tool is the default Fedora Core disk management GUI tool. It can mount and unmount file systems, as well as the cdrom device.

FIGURE 37.3   Point and click for floppy formatting makes it easy. A larger choice of formatting options (like a 1.7MB 3.5" floppy) would be nicer. The Floppy Formatter is found under the System Tools menu.

> ### Automounting with the Automount Daemon (amd) and `autofs`
>
> The `automount` daemon will watch specified devices and will mount the devices when they are accessed and unmount them when there has been no activity. The configuration files are `/etc/auto.master` and `/etc/auto.misc`. The former file contains only comments; the latter contains examples and the sole entry used by Fedora Core to automount the CD-ROM drive. If you insert a CD, after a long pause, a file browser will appear on your desktop. Many people find this behavior annoying and prefer to disable `automount`.

Because `autofs` is started at boot time and controls the `automount` daemon, simply do not run `autofs`. Use the `checkconfig`, `ntsysv`, or GUI clients to edit the startup scripts for your runlevel (see Chapter 14, "Automating Tasks," for details).

Relocating a File System

Many home users start with a single disk partition that mounts not only the root file system files, but also all the other files. Although this might work quite well for most home users, there might come a time when the physical disk becomes full. Adding another drive and moving part of the file system there is not difficult, but it is the source of many questions from new Linux users. This section of the chapter explains how to do this kind of file system relocation.

In this example, we will install a new IDE hard drive to `/dev/hdb` (the primary slave drive), create a single partition on it, format it as an `ext3` file system, and move all of the user files located in `/home` to it. Once done, we will make it mount, by default, at the `/home` mount point by editing the `/etc/fstab` file.

Installing the New Drive

First, physically install the drive, making certain that the master/slave jumpers are set correctly to set the drive as a slave drive. Also be certain that the jumpers are set correctly on the existing master drive. (Some drives require a different jumper setting, depending on whether they are a single master drive or a master drive with a slave drive; others offer a "cable-select" option to automatically set the drive status.) Failing to ensure that the jumpers are set correctly is a common error made even by people who are familiar with computer hardware.

After you have installed the drive, it must be correctly detected by the BIOS. Many modern BIOSes have an autodetect feature, or you can manually enter the drive CHS information in the BIOS (found on the drive label or documentation).

> **NOTE**
>
> Linux can ignore the BIOS-provided CHS information and use information that you provide when loading the kernel, passing it as a kernel argument. Although this is a very powerful Linux option, it is now only used when working with obsolete BIOSes from more than three or four years ago and when you are attempting to use a hard drive that is larger than the BIOS was designed to address. In these cases, the CHS information helps the bootloader program know where the kernel is on the disk and helps the kernel understand how the data on the drive is organized, enabling Linux to make older hardware remain useful long after it has become obsolete. For more detailed information, you can look at the Large Disk HOWTO and the BootPrompt HOWTO if you have problems with drive geometry and the BIOS.

Most modern large drives use the LBA setting (Logical Block Addressing) to deal with the BIOS size limitations. If the drive is not detected, check the power connection, the IDE cable connection (the red stripe usually goes next to the power connector, but always double-check), and the master/slave jumpers. If all these are fine, you might have a bad drive, or the two hard drives if made by different manufactures) might not be playing nice with each other (especially if they were made by different manufacturers).

To check further, reset the jumper of the new drive to make it the master drive, disconnect the old drive, and plug in the new one in its place. If the new drive is now correctly detected, suspect some incompatibility between the drives. Always make cable changes to the drives with the power off, or you will damage the drive.

TIP

If you were to examine the partition table with a hexadecimal editor, you would find that with only 10 bits in which to store the partition's cylinder offset (an index to data on the disk); no disk can have any more than 1,024 cylinders.

One creative way to get around that limitation is to increase the number of heads so that the number of cylinders can remain small enough to fit the partition table. This scheme is known as Logical Block Addressing, or LBA. Modern BIOSes (post-1998 or so) support it, but older ones do not. But because Linux is capable of being told about the drive geometry at boot time, it is not as big a problem to Linux users as it is to users of other operating systems. For more detailed information, you can look at the Large Disk HOWTO and the BootPrompt HOWTO if you have problems with large hard disks.

Creating the Partition Table and Formatting the Disk

Once installed and recognized by the BIOS, a partition table needs to be created. Use `fdisk` (or the program of your choice) to create a single partition on the drive, remembering to write the changes to the MBR before you exit the program (see "Creating the Partition Table," earlier in this chapter).

Formatting the drive is next. Because we are creating a new `ext3` file system, we use the j option, as

```
# mke2fs -cj /dev/hdb1
```

Notice that we are checking the drive (using the `-c` option) for bad blocks as we format. Even though it adds considerable time to formatting the drive, an initial bad block check is always a good idea. The program will identify bad blocks and not use them; bad blocks would only corrupt our data if we didn't mark the file system to ignore them.

Mount the New Partition and Populating It with the Relocated Files

For the example that follows, it is assumed that /home was a directory that was part of the partition mounted at /, not a separate partition to begin with.

Here, we create a temporary mount point and mount the new partition:

```
# mkdir /mnt/newpartition
```

```
# mount -t ext3 /dev/hdb1 /mnt/newpartition
```

It is now time to copy all the files from /home to /mnt/newpartition. It is important that we preserve the time and date stamps for the files and the permissions. We're copying entire directories and subdirectories, so we use one of our three basic copying methods (tar, cpio, or cp) that best accommodates this:

```
# cp -a /home/* /mnt/newpartition
```

We need to modify /etc/fstab so that our new ext3 partition will be mounted correctly:

```
/dev/hdb1    /home ext3  defaults     1 2
```

Here, we have chosen to use the default mount options for the ext3 partition. The defaults are identical to those for the ext2 file system, as well as additionally selecting the default data=ordered journaling mode.

Anytime we reboot, the new partition containing the copied files will automatically be mounted at /home. But before we do that, cd to /home and enter this:

```
# touch thisistheoldhomepartition
```

Now we can mount the new partition:

```
# umount /mnt/newpartition
```

```
# mount /dev/hdb1 /home
```

Note that if you do an

```
# ls -al /home
```

you will not see the thisistheoldhomepartition file we created with the touch command. So what happened to the old files? They are still there, but just hidden because we mounted a directory "over" them. When we are satisfied that all is well, we can unmount our newly created home partition and delete the files in the partition that contains the thisistheoldhomepartition file.

> **TIP**
>
> You can use the previously explained technique as a placeholder or warning for any temporarily mounted file system so that you do not mistakenly think that the file system is mounted when it is not.

Logical Volume Management

The previous example showed you how to add a new drive to overcome a lack of disk space. What if this could be done without all the mounting and file copying? That's where Logical Volume Management (LVM) is useful. Using LVM, disk space from multiple drives can be pooled into a single logical volume.

As with any new technology, there is a steep learning curve involved in using LVM, not the least of which is its vocabulary. Within this vocabulary, partitions are known as physical volumes, or pv. We add pvs to a volume group that defines a logical volume on which we can create our file system.

On a heavily used system, the files being backed up can change during the backup, and the restored files might be in an unstable condition. LVM can also make snapshots of the logical volume that can then be mounted and backed up.

For more information on LVM under Linux, read the LVM HOWTO at http://tldp.org/HOWTO/LVM-HOWTO/, which explains the terminology and provides a guide to setting up and using LVM on a Linux system.

File System Manipulation

Different people have various learning styles. For those of you who prefer examples rather than lectures, here are a few practical examples in which you learn how to create a file system within a file and mount it using the *loopback file system*—a special file system that allows us to accomplish this useful feat. You can use the file system you create to experiment with and practice almost all the commands found in this chapter with no fear of damaging your system.

Creating a File System for Testing

Because most of us do not have a spare computer or hard drive on which to experiment and practice, we can make one of our own by creating an image file containing the file system of our choice and using the loopback file system to mount it. That way, we do not run the risk of accidentally wreaking havoc on the system itself. Although you could also use a floppy drive for these same exercises, their small size limits your flexibility.

Step 1—Make a Blank Image File

Use the dd command to create a file with a block size of 1,024 bytes (a megabyte) and create a file that is 10MB in size. (You need to have enough free space on your hard drive to hold a file this big, so adjust the size accordingly.) We want 10,000 1KB (1,024-byte) blocks, so we select a count of 10000.

If we wanted a floppy-sized image, we would have selected a block size (bs) of 512 and a count of 2880 for a 1.4MB floppy or 5760 for a 2.88MB floppy. Here's how to do that:

```
# dd if=/dev/zero of=/tmp/fedoratest.img bs=1024 count=10000
```

We see the computer respond with the following:

```
10000+0 records in
10000+0 records out
```

37

If we check our new `file` command, we see this:

```
# file /tmp/fedoratest.img
/tmp/fedoratest.img: data
```

Step 2—Make a File System

Now we need to make the system think that the file is a block device instead of an ASCII file, so we use `losetup`, a utility that associates loop devices with regular files or block devices; we will be using the loopback device, `/dev/loop0`.

```
# losetup /dev/loop0 /tmp/fedoratest.img
```

Now we can format the file as an `ext2` file system:

```
# mke2fs /dev/loop0
```

We see the computer respond as follows:

```
mke2fs 1.27 (8-Mar-2003)
File System label=
OS type: Linux
Block size=1024 (log=0)
Fragment size=1024 (log=0)
2512 inodes, 10000 blocks
500 blocks (5.00%) reserved for the super user
First data block=1
2 block groups
8192 blocks per group, 8192 fragments per group
1256 inodes per group
Superblock backups stored on blocks:
    8193

Writing inode tables: done
Writing superblocks and file system accounting information: done

This file system will be automatically checked every 21 mounts or 180 days, \
whichever comes first. Use tune2fs -c or -i to override.
```

Step 3—Mount Our Test File System

After your test file system has been created, you can experiment with the different options for the formatting commands you will be using. It will be useful to make a mount point for our image file

```
# mkdir /mnt/image
```

and then mount it

```
# mount /dev/loop0 /mnt/image
```

We can do this now because we already have the loopback file system associated with the image file. Later on if we remount it, we must use the following format to use the loopback option:

```
# mount -o loop /tmp/fedoratest.img /mnt/image
```

After mounting the new file system, we can look at it and see that the /lost+found directory has been created on it and that the df command returns

```
# df -h /mnt/image
File System      Size Used Avail Use% Mounted on /dev/loop0      \
9.5M  13k 8.9M   1% /mnt/image
```

To unmount it, use this:

```
# umount /mnt/image
```

Make a backup of the image just in case we break the original:

```
# cp /tmp/fedoratest.img fedoratest.bak
```

After the test file system is created, you can create directories, copy files to it, delete files, attempt to recover them, and, in general, create controlled chaos on your computer while you are learning and practicing valuable skills. If you damage the file system on the image beyond repair, unmount it, delete it, and create a new one (or copy a new one from that backup).

Using dumpe2fs

You can use the program dumpe2fs to examine the structure of your ext3 file system.

The syntax for the command is

```
dumpe2fs [ -bfhixV ] [ -ob superblock ] [ -oB blocksize ] device
```

To examine our image file system using dumpe2fs, first unmount it, and then use this:

```
# dumpe2fs /tmp/fedoratest.img
```

```
dumpe2fs 1.27 (8-Mar-2003)
File System volume name:  <none>
Last mounted on:          <not available>
File System UUID:         03644acf-581c-410f-b4b6-10958992016e
File System magic number: 0xEF53
File System revision #:   1 (dynamic)
File System features:     filetype sparse_super
File System state:        not clean
Errors behavior:          Continue
File System OS type:      Linux
```

```
Inode count:             2512
Block count:             10000
Reserved block count:    500
Free blocks:             9664
Free inodes:             2501
First block:             1
Block size:              1024
Fragment size:           1024
Blocks per group:        8192
Fragments per group:     8192
Inodes per group:        1256
Inode blocks per group:  157
Last mount time:         Fri May 16 14:36:33 2003
Last write time:         Fri May 16 14:37:09 2003
Mount count:             2
Maximum mount count:     21
Last checked:            Fri May 16 14:35:39 2003
Check interval:          15552000 (6 months)
Next check after:        Wed Nov 12 13:35:39 2003
Reserved blocks uid:     0 (user root)
Reserved blocks gid:     0 (group root)
First inode:             11
Inode size:              128

Group 0: (Blocks 1-8192)
 Primary Superblock at 1, Group Descriptors at 2-2
 Block bitmap at 3 (+2), Inode bitmap at 4 (+3)
 Inode table at 5-161 (+4)
 8018 free blocks, 1245 free inodes, 2 directories
 Free blocks: 175-8192
 Free inodes: 12-1256
Group 1: (Blocks 8193-9999)
 Backup Superblock at 8193, Group Descriptors at 8194-8194
 Block bitmap at 8195 (+2), Inode bitmap at 8196 (+3)
 Inode table at 8197-8353 (+4)
 1646 free blocks, 1256 free inodes, 0 directories
 Free blocks: 8354-9999
 Free inodes: 1257-2512
```

A *lot* of information is in the metadata for the file: Every conceivable bit of information about the file system is displayed. Most of it is of use only to file system developers, not system administrators. Match up the information shown with the file system characteristics presented previously in this chapter to get a better picture of how it all fits together and what can be useful to you.

You can use the -b option to display a list of the blocks that are marked as "bad" and use the -f option to force dumpe2fs to ignore any problems it might have with file system flags it cannot read.

You can use the next two options in recovering lost data. The stressed out and desperate system administrator (that's you) would be the "file system wizard" referred to.

> -ob *superblock*—Use a specific alternate superblock when examining the file system. This option is not usually needed except by a file system wizard who is examining the remains of a very badly corrupted file system.
>
> -oB *blocksize*—Use blocks of "blocksize" bytes when examining the file system. This option is not usually needed except by a file system wizard who is examining the remains of a very badly corrupted file system.

Another program, debugfs, can be used to manipulate a file system as well as repair and recover a damaged file system. Because it is such a powerful command, it does not run by default with the capability to write any changes to the file system; that functionality must be explicitly enabled when the command is run. By entering the help command at the debugfs prompt, a menu of command options is displayed; the q command exits the program.

Mounting a Partition As Read-Only on a Running System

Remember that to do almost any kind of file system manipulation (formatting, checking, and so on), you should unmount the file system; by doing so, you avoid having any writes made to the file system, which would corrupt it.

How do you remount partitions on a running system? For example, to remount the /home partition (assuming that it is on a separate physical partition from root) as read-only to run fsck on it and then remount it as read-write, use the remount option for mount:

```
# mount -o ro,remount /home
```

> **NOTE**
>
> Remounting will not work if a normal user is logged in because /home will be busy (in use). You might need to switch to runlevel 1 (init 1), which is single-user mode, to remount /home.

Now we can run fsck on the partition. When done,

```
# mount -o rw,remount /home
```

puts it back in service.

If you reboot your system to mount the root file system read-only for maintenance (enter the maintenance mode, s, as described in Chapter 14.

```
# mount -o rw,remount /
```

will remount it read-write and you can continue on. That's easier than unmounting and remounting the device.

Converting an Existing ext2 File System to ext3

An existing `ext2` file system is easily converted to `ext3` to take advantage of the benefits of journaling. After you convert an existing file system, any other operating system—including BeOS, Windows (with the appropriate drivers), and other Unix systems that have drivers to access `ext2` partitions can access `ext3` partitions. To those operating systems (and their drivers), your converted file system still looks just like an `ext2` file system.

To begin the conversion to `ext3`, you use the `tune2fs` utility to add the journal to an existing `ext2` file system. In this example, you are changing `/dev/hda2`, an already formatted `ext2` partition.

```
# tune2fs -j /dev/hda2
```

It does not matter if `hda2` is mounted or unmounted at the time of the migration; if it is mounted, you will see a new file, `.journal`, in the directory.

Next, edit the line for `/dev/hda2` in `/etc/fstab` and change the value from `ext2` to `ext3`. It will be mounted as an `ext3` file system the next time you reboot.

> **NOTE**
>
> If you have decided to convert your root file system to take advantage of the benefits of the `ext3` file system, bear in mind that you cannot run `tune2fs -j` on it while it is unmounted because you cannot unmount the root file system. Because the file system is mounted when you run `tune2fs -j`, the `.journal` file on it will be visible when you finish the migration.
>
> When compiling a new kernel, make certain to include `ext3` file system support in your new kernel by selecting that choice in your kernel configuration (see Chapter 38, "Kernel and Module Management"). Also, note that you do not need to perform the actions described in the next section if you have just freshly installed Fedora Core Linux.

Making an Initial Ramdisk

You need to create an `initrd` image file to load the `ext3` driver and mount the root partition as an `ext3` partition. The `initrd` file is an initial ramdisk that contains a small kernel and enough of the Linux OS to load drivers so that the real kernel and the rest of the operating system can load.

> **NOTE**
>
> If you forget to create the `initrd` file, your system will still boot, but it will mount the root partition as `ext2`. That's very clever—none of the other journaling file systems are as forgiving.

To create the file, run the `mkinitrd` utility before you reboot.

```
# mkinitrd /boot/initrd-2.6.7-1.478.img 2.6-7-1.478
```

The first argument is the name of the `initrd` file that will be placed in the `/boot` directory. The name can be anything; the name shown here follows the usual naming convention; you can find a number of other naming options in the `mkinitrd` man page. The second argument after the `mkinitrd` command is the version of the kernel you want to use. The value you enter here does not have to be the version you are currently using, but it must match the version you use when you boot (and the kernel must support `ext3`).

After you run the utility, edit `/boot/grub.conf` or `/etc/lilo.conf` to change the `initrd` loaded at boot time. For GRUB, add this same line beneath the kernel line in the section that references your kernel:

```
initrd (hd0,0)/boot/initrd-2.6.7-1.478.img
```

If you use LILO, add the following line to the appropriate LILO stanza:

```
initrd=/boot/initrd-2.6.7-1.478.img
```

> **NOTE**
>
> LILO is no longer used in Fedora, but you may have it on an older system upgraded to Fedora.

Examine an `initrd` Image File

The `initrd.img` file is automatically created during the installation process (if necessary) or with the `mkinitrd` command. You never need to examine it, but if you are curious about what's in the `initrd.img` file, just take a look: It is really just a gzipped `ext2` file system. To examine it, first copy it to the `/tmp` directory and add the `.gz` suffix to it:

```
# cp /boot/initrd-2.6.7-1.478.img /tmp/initrd-2.6.7-1.478.img.gz
```

If your system does not have an `initrd.img` file in `/boot`, mount your boot floppy and see if it has one. Next, uncompress it as follows:

```
# gunzip /tmp/initrd-2.6.7-1.478.img.gz
```

Mount it as follows:

```
# mount -o loop /tmp/initrd-2.6.7-1.478.img /mnt/image
```

and browse the directory to your heart's content.

Not every system will have an `initrd.img` file. It is typically used to load device drivers for file systems (such as Reiser) or hardware (such as the Promise RAID IDE controller) that must be in place before the system can continue booting. Some floppy-based Linux distributions use initrd.img to load a minimal operating system that can then uncompress and load the working file system from the floppy.

You can also mount .iso images in the same way, but remember that they are always read-only because of the nature of the underlying iso9660 file system; you can write to the other images unless you explicitly mount them as read-only. If you want to read and write to the files in an ISO file system, you must first copy the files to a device that is mounted read-write, make your changes, and then use mkisofs to create a new .iso image. This is a common "gotcha" for many users.

Examine a Floppy Image File

The floppy boot images on the installation CD have different configurations to address special situations, as explained in their accompanying documentation. If you find the need to modify one for your unique situation or if you are curious to know what's in any of the boot floppy images that are on the install CD, mount the image using the mount command as follows:

```
# mount -o loop /image /mnt/image
```

Managing Files for Character Devices, Block Devices, and Special Devices

For Unix and Linux, *everything* is a file. In this section, you learn about special types of files found in Linux that represent all the devices found on your system and handle all the input and output on your system. You also learn how to identify and create them.

If you have installed the kernel documentation, it will contain a text file named /usr/src/linux-2.6/Documentation/devices.txt, an excerpt of which reads

```
3 char   Pseudo-TTY slaves
     0 = /dev/ttyp0      First PTY slave
     1 = /dev/ttyp1      Second PTY slave
    ...
   255 = /dev/ttyef  256th PTY slave

  These are the old-style (BSD) PTY devices; Unix98
  devices are on major 136 and above.

  block  First MFM, RLL and IDE hard disk/CD-ROM interface
      0 = /dev/hda       Master: whole disk (or CD-ROM)
     64 = /dev/hdb       Slave: whole disk (or CD-ROM)

   For partitions, add to the whole disk device number:
      0 = /dev/hd?       Whole disk
      1 = /dev/hd?1      First partition
```

```
 2 = /dev/hd?2      Second partition
 ...
63 = /dev/hd?63  63rd partition
```

```
For Linux/i386, partitions 1-4 are the primary
partitions, and 5 and above are logical partitions.
Other versions of Linux use partitioning schemes
appropriate to their respective architectures.
```

The number 3 at the upper left of the preceding listing represents the *major number* that identifies a class of device. In this case, major 3 identifies both character devices (Pseudo-TTY slaves) and block devices (IDE drives). The columns of numbers that follow under the device types are called the *minor numbers*; any device can be identified uniquely by its major and minor number. Linux uses these numbers internally; you usually see the name of the device as it is listed in the /dev directory. The major/minor numbers do show up in kernel error messages from time to time, and understanding the numbers helps you debug the problem. As you'll see in the next section, the mknod command needs to be told those numbers in order to create a device. Take some time to browse the entire file because it contains some interesting information that provides answers to many frequently asked questions.

The /dev directory contains all the special files known as device files. The files are placed in /dev during the original installation, and you can also create device files to go there if you need them.

During the normal operation of Linux, you never need to bother with the files in /dev, but if you want to look at all the files in /dev, use this command:

```
# ls -l --sort=none /dev ¦ less
```

The --sort=none argument keeps the devices mostly grouped by major numbers for your viewing convenience; redirecting the output of the command (known as piping) through the less command allows you to use the PageUp and PageDown keys to navigate the long list rather than have it scroll off the screen. There are too many devices to list here, but they will all be either *block* or *character* devices.

A character device is a file that handles data one character at a time and processes data sequentially. Examples include TTY (display console) devices, SCSI tape drives, the keyboard, audio devices, the Coda network file system, among others.

Block devices are files that have a beginning, an end, and a fixed size; data can be written and read from anywhere inside them in any order. Because a block device can be much larger than the data it contains, utilities such as tar and cpio work with the files' data rather than the size, so they can store and retrieve the data directly off the block device rather than require a formatted file on a block device. (You can see how those commands are used in Chapter 16.) This works especially well with tape devices because they are character devices rather than block devices and are not formatted in the way that block devices are formatted.

37

Special devices are block or character devices established for a special purpose. Two special devices of interest are

- /dev/null—This is the null device, also called the "bit bucket." Any output written to it is discarded. It is useful to redirect messages to it when you do not want them displayed on the standard output or written to a file. For example,

```
$ ls 2> /dev/null
```

will display the file listing to the screen, but will not display any error messages even though the ls command might generate one; we redirected the standard error messages (2>) to /dev/null. Almost all commands generate messages to the standard output and standard error when run, and sometimes, as when running a script, it is useful to not see the messages.

- /dev/zero—This device has an inexhaustible supply of zeros; use all you want—it makes more. It is very useful for writing strings of zeros to a device or file, such as when preparing an image of a file system (perhaps to be copied onto compact flash or other media).

Naming Conventions Used for Block and Character Devices

The traditional naming system for block and character devices has been in use for a while. In /usr/src/linux-2.6/Documentation/devices.txt, the device name for the first partition of the first IDE disk would be /dev/hda1. If it were a SCSI disk, it would be /dev/sda1 (shown elsewhere in devices.txt file).

All device names are included in devices.txt, and all the devices that have been created on your system are listed in the /dev directory. That directory also can hold links; for example, /dev/cdrom can actually be a link back to the actual device that is your CD-ROM (perhaps /dev/hdc? or /dev/scd0?). /dev/mouse and /dev/modem are commonly used symbolic links in the /dev directory.

Using mknod to Create Devices

If you need a device file in /dev that's not already there for some reason, you can create the special file with the mknod command. You might have noticed that /dev lists devices that you do not have. That's because the device's listing must appear in /dev before the system can use the actual device; if you install the hardware at some point in the future, the system will not create the device files on-the-fly. So, if you're preparing to install a device, and you check /dev but find that it does not contain the device's file, you can create the file with mknod.

Creating files with mknod is a straightforward process as long as you know what type of device you are creating the file for and what the device's major and minor numbers are.

The syntax of mknod is

```
# mknod [OPTION].. NAME TYPE [MAJOR MINOR]
```

The useful option -m allows you to set the mode at file creation instead of doing it separately with the chmod command.

You can obtain the values for NAME, TYPE, MAJOR, and MINOR from devices.txt, which even has a block of experimental numbers if you are inclined to experiment.

The Device File System—devfs

An alternative device file system known as the Device File System (devfs) will soon come into common use in Linux. It only has entries for devices that you have attached to your system, and the naming convention is different from the traditional system. It can be used in tandem with the traditional system. Although Fedora Core supports devfs in the kernel sources, it is not enabled by default because Red Hat does not yet believe it is stable for Enterprise use.

Naming conventions are different with devfs. For example, /dev/hda1 is named /dev/ide/hd/c0b0t0u0p1 and is a symbolic link to /dev/ide/host0/bus0/target0/lun0/part1.

The Device File System is similar to the /proc file system in that it is a virtual file system; the devices exist in memory and not as actual files on the drive.

Why use devfs? There are some limitations to the use of major and minor numbers (128 maximum are available), which is why H. Peter Anvin maintains devices.txt, and access to new device numbers is limited. The address space could be enlarged, but this creates some performance issues. It also gets around the requirement that the /dev directory be on the root file system, making read-only root file systems difficult to use. You cannot share a root file system using NFS, and you cannot embed it in a ROM file system. The workaround requires creating a ramdisk and copying the contents of /dev there.

Non-Unix file systems cannot be mounted as the root file system because they do not support the special characteristics of Unix file systems. devfs can solve these types of problems and provide even more flexibility to Linux. FreeBSD, BeOS, Plan9, and QNX use devfs; so it is not a new concept, just new to Linux.

For additional details, read the Linux DEVFS FAQ at http://www.atnf.csiro.au/~rgooch/linux/docs/devfs.html.

37

Relevant Fedora Core and Linux Commands

You use these commands when managing file systems in Fedora Core Linux:

df—Shows free disk space

du—Displays disk usage

dump—An ext2 file system backup utility

dumpe2fs—Shows information about an ext2 file system

e2fsadm—Administers an LVM/ext2 file system

e2image—Creates an image file of ext2 file system data

fdisk—The standard Linux partition table editor

fsck—Checks or repairs a file system

lsraid—Displays information about Linux RAID devices

mformat—Formats a DOS floppy disk; part of the Mtools suite of tools

mkfs—Creates various file systems and acts as a wrapper for the actual programs that do the work

mkisofs—Creates a CD-ROM file system in iso960 format

mkreiserfs—Creates a Linux reiserfs file system

mkswap—Prepares a Linux swap device

mount—Mounts a supported file system

parted—The GNU partition editor and resizing utility

reiserfsck—Checks a Linux reiserfs file system

resize_reiserfs—Resizes a Linux reiserfs file system

smbmount—Mounts an smbfs file system

stat—Shows file or file system status

swapon—Displays swap usage or start using system swap device

swapoff—Turns off swap usage

sync—Flushes file system buffers

tune2fs—Changes file system parameters on ext2 file systems

umount—Unmounts a file systems

usermount—The Fedora Core graphical file system mounting and formatting tool

Reference

http://www.ibiblio.org/pub/Linux/docs/HOWTO/other-formats/html_single/
File Systems-HOWTO.html—In the File Systems HOWTO, you'll find extensive information on native Linux file systems, as well as more exotic file systems.

http://www.ibiblio.org/pub/Linux/docs/HOWTO/other-formats/html_single/
Partition.html—A great deal of detailed information is contained in the Linux Partition HOWTO on partitions and their requirements.

http://batleth.sapienti-sat.org/projects/FAQs/ext3-faq.html—The Linux ext3 FAQ is an unofficial FAQ with some useful info, especially for converting an ext3 partition back to ext2.

http://www.ibiblio.org/pub/Linux/docs/HOWTO/other-formats/html_single/
Ext2fs-Undeletion.html—You deleted a file on your ext2/3 partition? The Linux Ext2fs Undeletion mini HOWTO is there to help you out.

http://www.ibiblio.org/pub/Linux/docs/HOWTO/other-formats/html_single/
Ext2fs-Undeletion-Dir-Struct.html—You deleted a directory on your ext2/3 partition? Read the Ext2fs Undeletion of Directory Structures HOWTO to see how to rescue your data.

http://www.ibiblio.org/pub/Linux/docs/HOWTO/other-formats/html_single/
Loopback-Root-FS.html—Here's the concept: Not only can we have a traditional file

system, but also we can have a file system inside a large file located on some other file system. The Loopback Root File System HOWTO examines how this is done.

http://www.ibiblio.org/pub/Linux/docs/HOWTO/other-formats/html_single/ Loopback-Encrypted-File System-HOWTO.html—You can use the loopback device to mount an encrypted file system, for example /home, for security reasons.

http://www.ibiblio.org/pub/Linux/docs/HOWTO/other-formats/html_single/ LVM-HOWTO.html—Throw away those concepts that marry physical disks to finite-sized file systems; the Logical Volume Manager HOWTO explains how to overcome that kind of restrictive thinking.

http://linux.org.mt/article/lvm—A good overview and discussion of Logical Volume Managers.

http://www.coda.cs.cmu.edu/—The Coda network file system home page.

http://www.inter-mezzo.org/—The InterMezzo network file system home page.

http://www.math.ualberta.ca/imaging/snfs/—Secure NFS via an SSH Tunnel is a very interesting attempt to address a security shortcoming of NFS over a public network.

http://www.ibiblio.org/pub/Linux/docs/HOWTO/other-formats/html_single/ UMSDOS-HOWTO.html—If you are interested in using the umsdos file system, the UMSDOS HOWTO provides ample information to you.

http://www.ibiblio.org/pub/Linux/docs/HOWTO/other-formats/html_single/ NFS-Root.html—The NFS-Root mini HOWTO.

http://www.ibiblio.org/pub/Linux/docs/HOWTO/other-formats/html_single/ NFS-Root-Client-mini-HOWTO.html—Explains in detail how to set up and use NFS for exporting root file systems.

http://www.ibiblio.org/pub/Linux/docs/HOWTO/other-formats/html_single/ Multi-Disk-HOWTO.html—The Multi Disk System Tuning HOWTO contains explanations of the drive and controller hardware that are useful, as well as discussion of file systems. It offers an interesting section on optimizing multidisk setups.

http://www.ibiblio.org/pub/Linux/docs/HOWTO/other-formats/html_single/ Software-RAID-HOWTO.html—The Software-RAID HOWTO is an excellent tour de force of software RAID.

http://www.ibiblio.org/pub/Linux/docs/HOWTO/other-formats/html_single/ Tips-HOWTO.html—The Linux Tips HOWTO provides some useful tips that make it worth the time to read because it addresses some file system problems such as "Is there enough free space?" and "How do I move directories between file systems?"

http://www.ibiblio.org/pub/Linux/docs/HOWTO/other-formats/html_single/ Large-Disk-HOWTO.html—Still unsure about drive geometry, the limits to LILO and GRUB, and those very large disks? The Large Disk HOWTO goes into useful detail about that. It also tells you how to handle disks that use disk managers such as OnTrack and EZ_Drive.

http://www.ibiblio.org/pub/Linux/docs/HOWTO/other-formats/html_single/
BootPrompt-HOWTO.html—The BootPrompt HOWTO informs you of boot time
arguments that can be passed to the kernel to deal with misbehaving hardware, configure
non-PNP devices, and so on. For this chapter, section 7, "Hard Disks," is most useful.

http://www.atnf.csiro.au/~rgooch/linux/docs/devfs.html—It is coming. It is a new technology to Linux, and you should start to learn about it from the Linux Devfs (Device File
System) FAQ.

http://www.namesys.com/—Details about the improvements in `reiserfs` and the release
of Reiser4 (see http://www.namesys.com/v4/v4.html).

http://www.linux-usb.org/USB-guide/x498.html—The USB Guide for mass storage and
other USB devices. If you have a USB device and need to know if it is supported and how
to access it, check here. (Tip: USB storage devices are emulated as SCSI devices.)

# CHAPTER 38

Kernel and Module Management

A kernel is a complex piece of software that manages the processes and process interactions that take place within an operating system. As a user, you rarely, if ever, interact directly with it. Instead, you work with the applications that the kernel manages.

The Linux kernel is Linux. It is the result of years of cooperative (and sometimes contentious) work by numerous people around the world. There is only one common kernel source tree, but each major Linux distribution massages and patches its version slightly to add features, performance, or options. Each Linux distribution, including Fedora Core Linux, comes with its own precompiled kernel as well as the kernel source code, providing you with absolute authority over the Linux operating system. In this chapter, we will examine the kernel and learn what it does for us and for the operating system.

In this chapter, you also learn how to obtain the kernel sources, as well as how and when to patch the kernel. The chapter leads you through an expert's tour of the kernel architecture and teaches you essential steps in kernel configuration, how to build and install modules, and how to compile drivers in Fedora Core Linux. This chapter also teaches you important aspects of working with GRUB, the default Fedora Core Linux boot loader. Finally, the chapter's troubleshooting information will help you understand what to do when something goes wrong with your Linux kernel installation or compilation process. As disconcerting as these problems can seem, this chapter shows you some easy fixes for many kernel problems.

Most users find that the precompiled Fedora Core Linux kernel suits their needs. At some point, you might need to recompile the kernel to support a specific piece of hardware or add a new feature to the operating system. If you have heard horror stories about the difficulties of recompiling the Linux kernel, you can relax; this chapter gives you all the information you need to understand when recompiling is necessary and how to painlessly work through the process.

The Linux Kernel

The Linux kernel is the management part of the operating system that many people call "Linux." Although many think of the entire distribution as Linux, the only piece that can correctly be called Linux is the kernel. Fedora Core Linux, like many Linux distributions, includes a kernel packaged with add-on software that interacts with the kernel so that the user can interface with the system in a meaningful manner.

The system utilities and user programs enable computers to become valuable tools to a user.

> **The First Linux Kernel**
>
> In 1991, Linus Torvalds released version .99 of the Linux kernel as the result of his desire for a powerful, Unix-like operating system for his Intel 80386 personal computer. Linus wrote the initial code necessary to create what is now known as the Linux kernel and combined it with Richard Stallman's GNU tools. Indeed, because many of the Linux basic system tools come from the GNU Project, many people refer to the operating system as GNU/Linux. Since then, Linux has benefited as thousands of contributors add their talents and time to the Linux project. Linus still maintains the kernel, deciding on what will and will not make it into the kernel as official releases, known to many as the "vanilla" or "Linus" Linux kernel.

The Linux Source Tree

The source code for the Linux kernel is kept in a group of directories called the kernel source tree. The structure of the kernel source tree is important because the process of compiling (building) the kernel is automated; it is controlled by scripts interpreted by the make application. These scripts, known as makefiles, expect to find the pieces of the kernel code in specific places or they will not work. You will learn how to use make to compile a kernel later in this chapter.

It is not necessary for the Linux kernel source code to be installed on your system for the system to run or for you to accomplish typical tasks such as email, web browsing, or word processing. It is necessary that the kernel sources be installed, however, if you want to compile a new kernel. In the next section, we will show you how to install the kernel source files and how to set up the special symbolic link required. That link is /usr/src/linux-2.6, and it is how we will refer to the directory of the kernel source tree as we examine the contents of the kernel source tree.

The /usr/src/linux-2.6 directory contains the .config and the Makefile files among others. The .config file is the configuration of your Linux kernel as it was compiled. There is no .config file by default; you must select one from the /configs subdirectory.

There, you will find configuration files for each flavor of the kernel Fedora provides; simply copy the one appropriate for your system to the default directory and rename it .config.

We have already discussed the contents of the /configs subdirectory, so let us examine the other directories found under /usr/src/linux-2.6. The most useful for us is the Documentation directory. In it and its subdirectories, you will find almost all the documentation concerning every part of the kernel. The file 00-INDEX (each Documentation subdirectory also contains a 00-INDEX file as well) contains a list of the files in the main directory and a brief explanation of what they are. Many files are written solely for kernel programmers and application writers, but a few are useful to the intermediate or advanced Linux user when attempting to learn about kernel and device driver issues. Some of the more interesting and useful documents are

> devices.txt—A list of all possible Linux devices that are represented in the /dev directory, giving major and minor numbers and a short description. If you have ever gotten an error message that mentions char-major-*xxx*, this file is where that list is kept. Devices are mentioned in Chapter 37, "Managing the File System."

> ide.txt—If your system uses IDE hard drives, this file discusses how the kernel interacts with them and lists the various kernel commands that can be used to solve IDE-related hardware problems, manually set data transfer modes, and otherwise manually manage your IDE drives. Most of this management is automatic, but if you want to understand how the kernel interacts with IDE devices, this file explains it.

> initrd.txt—Chapter 37 also discusses the initial ramdisk. This file provides much more in-depth knowledge of initial ramdisks, giving details on the loopback file system used to create and mount them and explaining how the kernel interacts with them.

> kernel-parameters.txt—This file is a list of most of the arguments that you can pass at boot time to configure kernel or hardware settings, but it does not appear too useful at first glance because it is just a list. However, knowing that a parameter exists and might relate to something you are looking for can assist you in tracking down more information because now you have terms to enter into an Internet search engine such as http://www.google.com/linux.

> sysrq.txt—If you have ever wondered what that key on you keyboard marked "SysRq" was used for, this file has the answer. Briefly, it is a key combination hardwired into the kernel that can help you recover from a system lockup. Fedora Core disables this function by default for security reasons. You can re-enable it by entering the command # echo "1" > /proc/sys/kernel/sysrq and disable it by echoing a value of 0 instead of 1.

In the other directories found in Documentation, you will find similar text files that deal with the kernel modules for CD-ROM drivers, file system drivers, gameport and joystick drivers, video drivers (not graphics card drivers—those belong to X11R6 and not to the kernel), network drivers, and all the other drivers and systems found in the Linux operating system. Again, these documents are usually written for programmers, but they can provide useful information to the intermediate and advanced Linux user as well.

38

The directory named `scripts` contains many of the scripts that `make` uses. It really does not contain anything of interest to anyone who is not a programmer or a kernel developer (also known as a kernel hacker).

After a kernel is built, all the compiled files will wind up in the `arch` directory and its subdirectories. Although you can manually move them to their final location, we will show you later in this chapter how the `make` scripts will do it for you. In the early days of Linux, this post-compilation file relocation was all done by hand; you should be grateful for `make`.

> **Note**
>
> The `make` utility is a very complex program. Complete documentation on the structure of `make` files, as well as the arguments that it can accept, can be found at http://www.gnu.org/software/make/manual/make.html.

The remainder of the directories in `/usr/src/linux-2.6` contain the source code for the kernel and the kernel drivers. When you install the kernel sources, these files are placed there automatically. When you patch kernel sources, these files are altered automatically. When you compile the kernel, these files are accessed automatically. Although you never need to touch the source code files, they can be useful. The kernel source files are nothing more than text files with special formatting, which means that we can look at them and read the programmers' comments. Sometimes, a programmer will write an application, but cannot (or often will not) write the documentation. The comments he puts in the source code are often the only documentation that exists for the code.

Small testing programs are even "hidden" in the comments of some of the code, along with comments and references to other information. Because the source code is written in a language that can be read as easily—almost—as English, a non-programmer might be able to get an idea of what the application or driver is actually doing (see Chapter 32, "C/C++ Programming Tools for Fedora"). This information might be of use to an intermediate to advanced Linux user when he is confronted by kernel- and driver-related problems.

> **Note**
>
> The interaction and control of hardware is handled by a small piece of the kernel called a *device driver*. The driver tells the computer how to interact with a modem, a SCSI card, a keyboard, a mouse, and so on in response to a user prompt. Without the device driver, the kernel does not know how to interact with the associated device.

Types of Kernels

In the early days of Linux, kernels were a single block of code containing all the instructions for the processor, the motherboard, and the other hardware. If you changed hardware, you were required to recompile the kernel code to include what you needed and discard what you did not. Including extra, unneeded code carried a penalty since the kernel became larger and occupied more memory. On older systems that had only 4MB–8MB of memory, wasting precious memory for unnecessary code was considered unacceptable. Kernel compiling was something of a "black art" as early Linux users attempted to wring the most performance from their computers. These kernels compiled as a single block of code are called *monolithic kernels*.

As the kernel code grew larger and the number of devices that could be added to a computer increased, the requirement to recompile became onerous. A new method of building the kernel was developed to make the task of compiling easier. The part of the kernel's source code that composed the code for the device drivers could be optionally compiled as a module that could be loaded and unloaded into the kernel as required. This is known as the *modular* approach to building the kernel. Now, all the kernel code could be compiled at once—with most of the code compiled into these modules. Only the required modules would be loaded; the kernel could be kept smaller, and adding hardware was much simpler.

The typical Fedora Core kernel has some drivers compiled as part of the kernel itself (called *in-line* drivers) and others compiled as modules. Only device drivers compiled in-line are available to the kernel during the boot process; modular drivers are only available after the system has been booted.

> **Note**
>
> As a common example, drivers for SCSI disk drives must be available to the kernel if you intend to boot from SCSI disks. If the kernel is not compiled with those drivers in-line, the system will not boot because it will not be able to access the disks.
>
> A way around this problem for modular kernels is to use an initial Ram disk (`initrd`) discussed later in "Creating an Initial RAM Disk Image." The `initrd` loads a small kernel and the appropriate device driver, which then can access the device to load the actual kernel you want to run.

Some code can only be one or the other (for technical reasons unimportant to the average user), but most code can be compiled either as modular or in-line. Depending on the application, some system administrators prefer one way over the other, but with fast modern processors and abundant system memory, the performance differences are of little concern to all but the most ardent Linux hackers.

When compiling a kernel, the step in which you make the selection of modular or in-line is part of the `make config` step that we will detail later in this chapter. Unless you have a specific reason to do otherwise, we suggest that you select the modular option when given a choice. The process of managing modules is addressed in the next section because you will be managing them more frequently than you will be compiling a kernel.

Managing Modules

When using a modular kernel, special tools are required to manage the modules. Modules must be loaded and unloaded, and it would be nice if that were done as automatically as possible. We also need to be able to pass necessary parameters to modules when we load them—things such as memory addresses and interrupts. (That information varies from module to module, so you will need to look at the documentation for your modules to determine what, if any, information needs to be passed to it.) In this section, we will cover the tools provided to manage modules and then look at a few examples of using them.

Linux provides the following module management tools for our use. All these commands (and `modprobe.conf`) have man pages:

> `lsmod`—This command lists the loaded modules. It is useful to pipe this through the `less` command because the listing is usually more than one page long.
>
> `insmod`—This command loads the specified module into the running kernel. If a module name is given without a full path, the default location for the running kernel, `/lib/modules/*/`, will be searched. Several options are offered for this command—the most useful is `-f`, which forces the module to be loaded.
>
> `rmmod`—This command unloads (removes) the specified module from the running kernel. More than one module at a time can be specified.
>
> `modprobe`—A more sophisticated version of `insmod` and `rmmod`, it uses the dependency file created by `depmod` and automatically handles loading, or with the `-r` option, removing modules. There is no force option, however. A useful option to modprobe is `–t`, which causes `modprobe` to cycle through a set of drivers until it finds one that matches your system. If you were unsure of what module would work for your network card, you would use this command:
>
> `# modprobe -t net`
>
> The term `net` is used because that is the name of the directory (`/lib/modules/*/kernel/net`) where all the network drivers are kept. It will try each one in turn until it loads one successfully.
>
> `modinfo`—This will query a module's object file and provide a list of the module name, author, license, and any other information that is there. It often is not very useful.
>
> `depmod`—This program creates a dependency file for kernel modules. Some modules need to have other modules loaded first; that is, they "depend" on the other modules. (A lot of the kernel code is like this because it eliminates redundancy in the code base.) During the boot process, one of the startup files contains the command `depmod -a` and it is run every time you boot to re-create the file `/lib/modules/*/modules.dep`. If you make changes to the file `/etc/modprobe.conf`, run depmod `-a` manually. The `depmod` command, its list of dependencies, and the `/etc/modprobe.conf` file enable kernel modules to be automatically loaded as needed.
>
> `/etc/modprobe.conf`—This is not a command, but a file that controls how `modprobe` and `depmod` behave; it contains kernel module variables. Although the command syntax can be quite complex, most actual needs are very simple. The most common use is to alias a module and then pass it some parameters. For example, in the following code, we alias a device name (from `devices.txt`) to a more descriptive word and then pass some information to an associated module. The `i2c-dev`

device is used to read the CPU temperature and fan speed on our system. These lines for
`/etc/modprobe.conf` were suggested for our use by the program's documentation. We added them
with a text editor.

```
alias char-major-89 i2c-dev
options eeprom ignore=2,0x50,2,0x51,2,0x52
```

A partial listing of `lsmod` is shown here, piped through the `less` command, allowing us to
view it a page at a time:

```
# lsmod ¦ less
Module            Size  Used by
parport_pc       19392  1
Module            Size  Used by
parport_pc       19392  1
lp                8236  0
parport          29640  2 parport_pc,lp
autofs4          10624  0
sunrpc          101064  1
```

The list is actually much longer, but here we see that the input module is being used by
the `joydev` (joystick device) module, but the joystick module is not being used. This
computer has a joystick port that was autodetected, but no joystick is connected. A
scanner module is also loaded, but because the USB scanner is unplugged, the module is
not being used. You would use the `lsmod` command to determine whether a module was
loaded and what other modules were using it. If you examine the full list, you would see
modules for all the devices attached to your computer.

To remove a module, `joydev` in this example, use

```
# rmmod joydev
```

or

```
# modprobe -r joydev
```

A look at the output of `lsmod` would now show that it is no longer loaded. If we removed
`input` as well, we could then use `modprobe` to load both `input` and `joydev` (one depends
on the other, remember) with a simple

```
# modprobe joydev
```

If Fedora Core Linux were to balk at loading a module (because it had been compiled
using a different kernel version from what we are currently running; for example, the
NVIDIA graphics card module), we could force it to load like this:

```
# insmod -f nvidia
```

We would ignore the complaints (error messages) in this case if the kernel generated any.

In Chapter 10, "Multimedia Applications," we talked about loading a scanner module; in the example there, we manually loaded the scanner module and passed it the vendor ID. The scanner was not included in the lookup list because it is not supported by the GPL scanner programs; as a result, the scanner module was not automatically detected and loaded. However, the scanner will work with a closed-source application after the module is loaded. Automatic module management is nice when it works, but sometimes it is necessary to work with modules directly.

When to Recompile

Fedora Core systems use a modified version of the plain vanilla Linux kernel (a modified version is referred to as a *patched* kernel) with additional drivers and other special features compiled into it.

Fedora Core has quite an intensive testing period for all distribution kernels and regularly distributes updated versions. The supplied Fedora Core kernel is compiled with as many modules as possible to provide as much flexibility as possible. A running kernel can be further tuned with the `sysctl` program, which enables direct access to a running kernel and permits some kernel parameters to be changed (see "Kernel Tuning with `sysctl`" at the end of the chapter). As a result of this extensive testing, configurability, and modularity, the precompiled Fedora Core Linux kernel does everything most users need it to do. Most users only need to recompile the kernel to

- Accommodate an esoteric piece of new hardware.

- Conduct a system update when Fedora Core has not yet provided precompiled kernels.

- Experiment with the system capabilities.

Fedora Core supplies several precompiled versions of the kernel for Athlon and Pentium processors, for single- and multi-processor motherboards, and for Enterprise-class systems (higher security; uses 4GB of memory). These kernel versions are provided in RPM format. Installing them is as easy as

```
# rpm -Uvh new_kernel.rpm
```

The kernel (but not the source) RPM files include installation scripts that will automatically alter your bootloader configuration, making the new kernel the default. If you do not want that to happen, just manually edit the `/etc/lilo.conf` or `/boot/grub/grub.conf` files and change them back.

CAUTION
You always `rpm -U` (upgrade), rather than `rpm -i` (install), a new kernel rpm to avoid overwriting the old, but still working, kernel. This is done as a safety measure. What if the new one does not work?

Kernel Versions

The Linux kernel is in a constant state of development. As new features are added, bugs are fixed, and new technology is incorporated into the code base, it becomes necessary to provide stable releases of the kernel for use in a production environment. It is also important to have separate releases that contain the newest code for developers to test. To keep track of the kernels, version numbers are assigned to them. Programmers enjoy using sequential version numbers that have abstract meaning. Is version 8 twice as advanced as version 4 of the same application? Is version 1 of one application less developed than version 3 of another? The version numbers cannot be used for this kind of qualitative or quantitative comparison. It is entirely possible that higher version numbers can have fewer features and more bugs than older versions. The numbers exist solely to differentiate and organize sequential revisions of software.

For the latest development version of the kernel at the time of writing, for example, the kernel version number is 2.6.10-1.

The kernel version can be broken down into four sections:

- major version—This is the major version number, now at 2.
- minor version—This is the minor version number, now at 6.
- sublevel number—This number indicates the current iteration of the kernel; here it is number 10.
- extraversion level—This is the number representing a collection of patches and additions made to the kernel by the Red Hat engineers to make the kernel work for them (and you). Each collection is numbered, and the number is indicated here in the kernel name. From our preceding example, it is 1.

Typing uname -r at the command prompt displays your current kernel version.

```
# uname -r
2.6.10-1
```

Even-numbered minor versions are stable kernels, whereas odd-numbered minor versions are development releases. Version 2.6.x is the stable production kernel, whereas version 2.5.x is the development Linux kernel. When a new version of the development kernel is started, it will be labeled 2.7.x.

For production machines, you should always use the kernels with even minor numbers. The odd minor numbers introduce new features, so you might want to use those on a test machine if you need features they provide.

Obtaining the Kernel Sources

The Linux kernel has always been freely available to anyone who wants it. If you just want to recompile the existing kernel, install the kernel-sources RPM from the CD. To get the very latest "vanilla" version, open an FTP connection to ftp.kernel.org using your favorite FTP client and log in as anonymous. Because you are interested in the 2.6 kernel, change directories to /pub/linux/kernel/v2.6. The latest stable kernel as of this writing is 2.6.11.

> **Note**
>
> ftp.kernel.org receives more than its share of requests for download. It is considered a courtesy to use a mirror site to reduce the traffic that ftp.kernel.org bears. http://www.kernel.org/mirrors/ has a list of all mirrors around the world. Find one close to your geographic location and substitute that address for ftp.kernel.org.

A number of different entries are on the FTP archive site for each kernel version, but because you are only interested in the full kernel it is only necessary to get the full package of source code. There are two of these packages:

```
linux-2.6.11.tar.gz
linux-2.6.11.bz2
```

Although these are the same kernel packages, they are built using different compression utilities: The .gz extension is the gzip package, found on almost every Linux system available. The .bz2 extension is the newer bzip2 utility, which has better compression than gzip. Both packages have the same content, so download the one compressed with the program you use.

Once downloaded, move the package to a directory other than /usr/src and unpack it. If you downloaded the .gz package, the unpacking command is tar -xzvf linux-2.6.11. tar.gz. Otherwise, the bzip2 unpack command is tar -xjvf linux-2.6.11.tar.bz2. Once unpacked, the package will create a new directory, linux-2.6.11. Copy it to /usr/src or move it there. Then, create a symbolic link of linux-2.6 to linux-2.6.11 (otherwise, some scripts will not work). Here is how to create the symbolic link:

```
# rm /usr/src/linux-2.6
# ln -s /usr/src/linux-2.6.11 /usr/src/linux-2.6
```

By creating a symbolic link to /usr/src/linux-2.6, it is possible to allow multiple kernel versions to be compiled and tailored for different functions: You will just change the symbolic link to the kernel directory you want to work on.

> **CAUTION**
>
> The correct symbolic link is critical to the operation of make. Always have the symbolic link point to the version of the kernel sources you are working with.

Patching the Kernel

It is possible to patch a kernel to the newest Linux kernel version as opposed to downloading the entire source code. This choice can be beneficial for those who are not using a high-speed broadband connection. (A typical compressed kernel source file is nearly 30MB for a download time of about 10 minutes on a 512Kb DSL connection; adjust accordingly for your connection.) Whether you are patching existing sources or downloading the full source, the end results will be identical.

Patching the kernel is not a mindless task. It requires the user to retrieve all patches from her current version to the version she wants to upgrade to. For example, if you are currently running 2.6.1 (and have those sources) and want to upgrade to 2.6.8, you must retrieve the 2.6.2, and 2.6.3 patch sets, and so on. Once downloaded, these patches must be applied in succession to upgrade to 2.6.8. This is more tedious than downloading the entire source, but useful for those who keep up with kernel hacking and want to perform incremental upgrades to keep their Linux kernel as up-to-date as possible.

To patch up to several versions in a single operation, you can use the patch-kernel script located in the kernel source directory for the kernel version you currently use. This script applies all necessary version patches to bring your kernel up to the latest version.

The format for using the patch-kernel script looks like this:

```
patch-kernel source_dir patch_dir stopversion
```

The source directory defaults to /usr/src/linux if none is given, and the patch_dir defaults to the current working directory if one is not supplied.

For example, assume that you have a 2.6.6 kernel code tree that needs to be patched to the 2.6.8 version. The 2.6.7 and 2.6.8 patch files have been downloaded from ftp.kernel.org and are placed in the /patch directory in the source tree. You issue the following command in the /usr/src/linux-2.6 directory:

```
# scripts/patch-kernel /usr/src/linux-2.6.6 /usr/src/linux-2.6.6/patch
```

Each successive patch file is applied, eventually creating a 2.6.8 code tree. If any errors occur during this operation, files named xxx# or xxx.rej are created, where xxx is the version of patch that failed. You will have to resolve these failed patches manually by examining the errors and looking at the source code and the patch. An inexperienced person will not have any success with this because you need to understand C programming and kernel programming to know what is broken and how to fix it. Because this was a stock 2.6.6 code tree, the patches were all successfully applied without errors. If you are attempting to apply a nonstandard third-party patch, the patch might likely fail.

When you have successfully patched the kernel, you are ready to begin compiling this code tree as if we started with a fresh, stock 2.6.8 kernel tree.

Using the patch Command

If you have a special, nonstandard patch to apply—such as a third-party patch for a commercial product, for example—you can use the patch command rather than the special patch-kernel script that is normally used for kernel source updates. Here are some quick steps and an alternative method of creating patched code and leaving the original code alone.

1. Create a directory in your home directory and name it something meaningful, like `mylinux`.

2. Copy the pristine Linux source code there with

   ```
   cp -ravd /usr/src/linux-2.6/* ~/mylinux
   ```

3. Copy the patch file to that same directory with

   ```
   cp patch_filename ~/mylinux
   ```

4. Change to the `~/mylinux` directory with

   ```
   cd ~/mylinux
   ```

5. Apply the patch with

   ```
   patch -p1 < patch_filename  > mypatch.log 2>&1
   ```

   (This last bit of code saves the message output to a file so that you can look at it later.)

6. If the patch applies successfully, you are done and have not endangered any of the pristine source code. In case the newly patched code does not work, you will not have to reinstall the original, pristine source code.

7. Copy your new code to `/usr/src` and make that special symbolic link described elsewhere in the chapter.

Compiling the Kernel

If you want to update the kernel from new source code you have downloaded, or you have applied a patch to add new functionality or hardware support, you will need to compile and install a new kernel to actually use that new functionality. Compiling the kernel involves translating the kernel's contents from human-readable code to binary form. Installing the kernel involves putting all the compiled files where they belong in `/boot` and `/lib` and making changes to the bootloader.

The process of compiling the kernel is almost completely automated by the `make` utility as is the process of installing. By providing the necessary arguments and following the steps covered next, you can recompile and install a custom kernel for your use.

Here is a checklist of steps to compile and configure the kernel:

1. Verify a working bootdisk for the old kernel to be able to reboot your system in case something goes wrong with the new kernel.

CAUTION

Before making any changes to your current, working kernel, make sure that you have a backup copy on a floppy disk. This will allow you to boot into your system with a known working kernel in case something goes wrong during configuration. The command to do this is as follows:

```
# mkbootdisk --device /dev/fd0 `uname -r`
```

This assumes that your floppy drive is /dev/fd0. (Here is a good shell script tip: the ` character tells the shell to execute what is within ` first and then returns that output as part of the input of the mkbootdisk command.) On this machine, the result is

```
# mkbootdisk --device /dev/fd0 2.6.7-1
```

This command will not be echoed to your screen, but it is what the system will execute.

2. Apply all patches, if any, so that you have the features you desire. See the previous section for details.

3. Back up the .config file, if it exists, so that you can recover from the inevitable mistake. Use the following cp command:

```
# cp .config .config.bak
```

> **NOTE**
>
> If you are recompiling the Fedora Core default kernel, the /usr/src/linux-2.6/configs direc-tory contains several versions of configuration files for different purposes.
>
> Fedora Core provides a full set of .config files in the subdirectory configs, all named for the type of system they were compiled for. For example, kernel-2.6.7-i686-smp.config is a configuration file for a multiprocessor Pentium-class computer. If you want to use one of these default configurations as the basis for a custom kernel, simple copy the appropriate file to /usr/src/linux-2.6 and rename it .config.

4. Run the make mrproper directive to prepare the kernel source tree, cleaning out any old files or binaries.

5. Restore the .config file that the command make mrproper deleted, and edit the Makefile to change the EXTRAVERSION number.

> **NOTE**
>
> If you want to keep any current version of the kernel that was compiled with the same code tree, manually edit the Makefile with your favorite text editor and add some unique string to the EXTRAVERSION variable.
>
> You can use any description you prefer, however.

6. Modify the kernel configuration file using make config, make menuconfig, or make xconfig—we recommend the latter, but read the "Choosing a Configuration Interface" section for details.

7. Run make dep to create the code dependencies used later in the compilation process.

38

If you have a multiprocessor machine, you can use both processors to speed the make process by inserting `-jx` after the `make` command, where as a rule of thumb, x is one more than the number of processors you have. You might try a larger number and even try this on a single processor machine (we have used `-j8` successfully on an SMP machine); it will only load up your CPU. For example,

```
# make -j3 bzImage
```

All the make processes except `make dep` will work well with this method of parallel compiling.

8. Run `make clean` to prepare the sources for the actual compilation of the kernel.

9. Run `make bzImage` to create a binary image of the kernel.

Several choices of directives exist, although the most common ones are as follows:

`zImage`—This directive compiles the kernel, creating an uncompressed file called `zImage`.

`bzImage`—This directive creates a compressed kernel image necessary for some systems that require the kernel image to be under a certain size for the BIOS to be able to parse them; otherwise, the new kernel will not boot. It is the most commonly used choice. However, the Fedora kernel compiled with `bzImage` is still too large to fit on a floppy, so a smaller version with some modules and features removed is used for the boot floppies. Fedora recommends that you boot from the rescue CD-ROM.

`bzDisk`—This directive does the same thing as `bzImage`, but it copies the new kernel image to a floppy disk for testing purposes. This is helpful for testing new kernels without writing kernel files to your hard drive. Make sure that you have a floppy disk in the drive because you will not be prompted for one.

10. Run `make modules` to compile any modules your new kernel needs.

11. Run `make modules_install` to install the modules in `/lib/modules` and create dependency files.

12. Run `make install` to automatically copy the kernel to `/boot`, create any other files it needs, and modify the bootloader to boot the new kernel by default.

13. Using your favorite text editor, verify the changes made to `/etc/lilo.conf` or `/boot/grub/grub.conf`; fix if necessary and rerun `/sbin/lilo` if needed.

14. Reboot and test the new kernel.

15. Repeat the process if necessary, choosing a Configuration Interface.

Over time, the process for configuring the Linux kernel has changed. Originally, you configured the kernel by responding to a series of prompts for each configuration parameter (this is the `make config` utility described shortly). Although you can still configure

Linux this way, most users find this type of configuration confusing and inconvenient; moving back through the prompts to correct errors, for instance, is impossible.

The make config utility is a command-line tool. The utility presents a question regarding kernel configuration options. The user responds with a Y, N, M, or ?. (It is not case sensitive.) Choosing M configures the option to be compiled as a module. A response of ? displays context help for that specific options, if available. (If you choose ? and no help is available, you can turn to the vast Internet resources to find information.) We recommend that you avoid the make config utility, shown in Figure 38.1.

FIGURE 38.1 The make config utility in all its Spartan glory.

If you prefer to use a command-line interface, you can use make menuconfig to configure the Linux kernel. menuconfig provides a graphical wrapper around a text interface. Although it is not as raw as make config, menuconfig is not a fancy graphical interface either; you cannot use a mouse, but must navigate through it using keyboard commands. The same information presented in make config is presented by make menuconfig, but as you can see in Figure 38.2, it looks a little nicer. Now, at least, you can move back and forth in the selection process in case you change your mind or have made a mistake.

In make menuconfig, you use the arrow keys to move the selector up and down and the spacebar to toggle a selection. The Tab key moves the focus at the bottom of the screen to either Select, Exit, or Help.

If a graphical desktop is not available, menuconfig is the best you can do. However, both menuconfig and xconfig (see below) offer an improvement over editing the .config file directly. If you want to configure the kernel through a true graphical interface—with

mouse support and clickable buttons—make xconfig is the best configuration utility
option. To use this utility, you must have the X Window System running. The application
xconfig is really nothing but a Tcl/Tk graphics *widget set* providing borders, menus, dialog
boxes, and the like. Its interface is used to wrap around data files that are parsed at execution time. Figure 38.3 shows the main menu of xconfig for the 2.6.7 kernel.

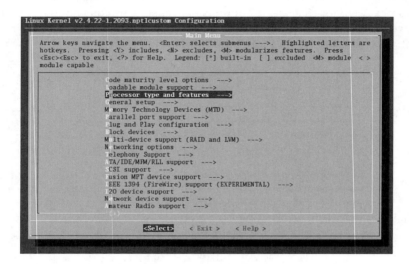

FIGURE 38.2   The make menuconfig utility, a small improvement over make config.

After loading this utility, you use it by clicking on each of the buttons that list the configuration options. Each button you click opens another window that has the detail configuration options for that subsection. Three buttons are at the bottom of each window: Main
Menu, Next, and Prev(ious). Clicking the Main Menu button closes the current window
and displays the main window. Clicking Next takes you to the next configuration section.
When configuring a kernel from scratch, click the button labeled Code Maturity Level
Options, and then continue to click the Next button in each subsection window to
proceed through all the kernel configuration choices. When you have selected all options,
the main menu is again displayed. The buttons on the lower right of the main menu are
for saving and loading configurations. Their functions are self-explanatory. If you just
want to have a look, go exploring! Nothing will be changed if you elect not to save it.

If you are upgrading kernels from a previous release, it is not necessary to go though the
entire configuration from scratch. Instead, you can use the directive make oldconfig; it
uses the same text interface that make config uses, and it is noninteractive. It will just
prompt for changes for any new code.

Using xconfig to Configure the Kernel

For simplicity's sake, during this brisk walk-through, we will assume that you are using
make xconfig. Prior to this point, we also assume that you will have completed the first
five steps in our kernel compilation checklist shown previously.

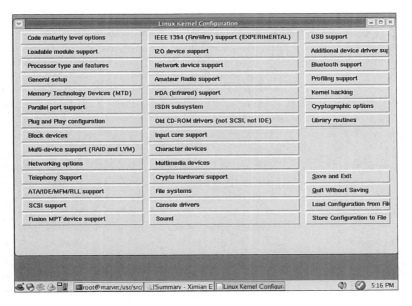

FIGURE 38.3   The much nicer `make xconfig` GUI interface. We recommend that you use this interface if you are able.

As you learned in the preceding section, you configure the kernel using `make xconfig` by making choices in several configuration subsection windows. Each subsection window contains specific kernel options. With hundreds of choices, the kernel is daunting to configure. We cannot really offer you detailed descriptions of which options to choose because your configuration will not match your own system and setup.

Table 38.1 provides a brief description of each subsection's options so that you can get an idea of what you might encounter. We recommend that you copy your kernel's `.config` file to `/usr/src/linux-2.6` and run `make xconfig` from there. Explore all the options. As long as you do not save the file, absolutely nothing will be changed on your system.

TABLE 38.1   Kernel Subsections for Configuration

Name	Description
Code maturity level options	Enables development code to be compiled into the kernel even if it has been marked as obsolete or as testing code only. This option should only be used by kernel developers or testers because of the possible unusable state of the code during development.
General setup	This section contains several different options covering how the kernel talks to the BIOS, whether it should support PCI or PCMCIA, whether it should use APM or ACPI, and what kind of Linux binary formats will be supported. Contains several options for supporting kernel structures necessary to run binaries compiled for other systems directly without recompiling the program.

TABLE 38.1   Continued

Name	Description
Loadable module support	Determines whether the kernel enables drivers and other nonessential code to be compiled as loadable modules that can be loaded and unloaded at runtime. This option keeps the basic kernel small so that it can run and respond more quickly; in that regard, choosing this option is generally a good idea.
Processor type and features	Several options dealing with the architecture that will be running the kernel.
Power management options	Options dealing with ACPI and APM power management features
Bus options	Configuration options for the PCMCIA bus found in laptops and PCI hotplug devices
Memory Technology Devices (MTD)	Options for supporting flash memory devices, such as EEPROMS. Generally, these devices are used in embedded systems.
Parallel port support	Several options for configuring how the kernel will support parallel port communications.
Plug-and-play configuration	Options for supporting Plug and Play PCI, ISA, and plug-and-play BIOS support. Generally, it is a good idea to support plug-and-play for PCI and ISA devices.
Block devices	Section dealing with devices that communicate with the kernel in blocks of characters instead of streams. This includes IDE and ATAPI devices connected via parallel ports, as well as enabling network devices to communicate as block devices.
ATA/IDE/MFM/RLL support	Large collection of options to configure the kernel to communicate using different types of data communication protocols to talk to mass storage devices, such as hard drives. Note that this section does not cover SCSI.
SCSI device support	Options for configuring the kernel to support Small Computer Systems Interface. This subsection covers drivers for specific cards, chipsets, and tunable parameters for the SCSI protocol.
Old CD-ROM drivers	Configuration options to support obscure, older CD-ROM devices that do not conform to the SCSI or IDE standards. These are typically older CD-ROM drivers that are usually a proprietary type of SCSI (not SCSI, not IDE).
Multi-device support	Options for enabling the kernel to support RAID devices in (RAID and LVM) software emulation and the different levels of RAID. Also contains options for support of a logical volume manager.
Fusion MPT device support	Configures support for LSI's Logic Fusion Message Passing Technology. This technology is for high performance SCSI and local area network interfaces.
IEEE1394 (firewire) support	Experimental support for Firewire devices.
I2O device support	Options for supporting the Intelligent Input/Output architecture. This architecture enables the hardware driver to be split from the operating system driver, thus enabling a multitude of hardware devices to be compatible with an operating system in one implementation.

TABLE 38.1   Continued

Name	Description
Networking support	Several options for the configuration of networking in the kernel. The options are for the types of supported protocols and configurable options of those protocols.
Amateur radio support	Options for configuring support of devices that support the AX25 protocol.
IrDA (infrared) support	Options for configuring support of the infrared Data Association suite of protocols and devices that use these protocols.
Bluetooth support	Support for the Bluetooth wireless protocol. Includes options to support the Bluetooth protocols and hardware devices.
ISDN subsystem	Options to support Integrated Services Digital Networks protocols and devices. ISDN is a method of connection to a large area network digitally over conditioned telephone lines, largely found to connect users to ISPs.
Telephony support	Support for devices that enable the use of regular telephone lines to support VOIP applications. This section does not handle the configuration of modems.
Input device support	Options for configuring Universal Serial Bus (USB) Human Interface Devices (HID). These include keyboards, mice, and joysticks.
Character devices	Configuration options for devices that communicate to the server in sequential characters. This is a large subsection containing the drivers for several motherboard chipsets.
Multimedia devices	Drivers for hardware implementations of video and sound devices such as video capture boards, TV cards, and AM/FM radio adapter cards.
Graphics support	Configures VGA text console, video mode selection, and support for frame buffer cards.
Sound	Large subsection to configure supported sound card drivers and chipset support for the kernel.
USB support	Universal Serial Bus configuration options. Includes configuration for USB devices, as well as vendor-specific versions of USB.
File system	Configuration options for supported file system types. See Chapter 37 for a description of the file systems supported by the kernel.
Additional device driver support	A section for third-party patches.
Profiling support	Profiling kernel behavior to aid in debugging and development.
Kernel hacking	This section determines whether the kernel will contain advanced debugging options. Most users will not want to include this option in their production kernels because it increases the kernel size and slows performance by adding extra routines.
Security options	Determines whether NSA Security Enhanced Linux (SELinux) is enabled.
Cryptographic options	Support for cryptography hardware (Fedora patches not found in the "vanilla" kernel sources).
Library routines	Contains zlib compression support.

38

After you select all the options you want, you can save the configuration file and continue with step 7 in the kernel compiling checklist shown earlier.

Creating an Initial RAM Disk Image

If you require special device drivers to be loaded in order to mount the root file system (for SCSI drives, network cards or exotic file systems, for example), you must create an initial RAM disk image named /boot/initrd.img. For most users, it is not necessary to create this file, but if you are not certain, it really does not hurt. We covered the initrd.img in Chapter 37. To create an initrd.img file, use the shell script /sbin/ mkinitrd.

The format for the command is the following:

```
/sbin/mkinitrd file_name kernel_version
```

Where *file_name* is the name of the image file you want created.

mkinitrd looks at /etc/fstab, /etc/modprobe.conf, and /etc/ raidtab to obtain the information it needs to determine which modules should be loaded during boot. For our system, we use

```
# mkinitrd initrd-2.6.7-1.img 2.6.7-1
```

When Something Goes Wrong

Several things might go wrong during a kernel compile and installation, and several clues will point to the true problem. You will see error messages printed to the screen, and some error messages will be printed to the file /var/log/messages, which can be examined with a text editor. If you have followed our directions for patching the kernel, you will need to examine a special error log as well. Do not worry about errors because many problems are easily fixed with some research on your part. Some errors may be unfixable, however, depending on your skill level and the availability of technical information.

Errors During Compile

Although it is rare that the kernel will not compile, there is always a chance that something has slipped though the regression testing. Let's take a look at an example of a problem that might crop up during the compile.

It is possible that the kernel compile will crash and not complete successfully, especially if you attempt to use experimental patches, add untested features, or build newer and perhaps unstable modules on an older system. For example, the kernel compile will fail on an older stock Red Hat 7.2 installation using the 2.4.9 kernel when selecting the NTFS file system, either as a loadable module or inline, as shown here:

```
gcc -D__KERNEL__  -I/usr/src/linux-2.4.9/include -Wall -Wstrict-prototypes
-Wno-trigraphs -O2 -fomit-frame-pointer -fno-strict-aliasing -fno-common
-pipe -mpreferred-stack-boundary=2 -march=athlon  -DMODULE -DMODVERSIONS
```

```
-include /usr/src/linux-2.4.9/include/linux/modversions.h
➥-DNTFS_VERSION=\"1.1.16\" Â\
  -c -o unistr.o unistr.c
unistr.c: In function `ntfs_collate_names':
unistr.c:99: warning: implicit declaration of function `min'
unistr.c:99: parse error before `unsigned'
unistr.c:99: parse error before `)'
unistr.c:97: warning: `c1' might be used uninitialized in this function
unistr.c: At top level:
unistr.c:118: parse error before `if'
unistr.c:123: warning: type defaults to `int' in declaration of `c1'
unistr.c:123: `name1' undeclared here (not in a function)
unistr.c:123: warning: data definition has no type or storage class
unistr.c:124: parse error before `if'
make[2]: *** [unistr.o] Error 1
make[2]: Leaving directory `/usr/src/linux-2.4.9/fs/ntfs'
make[1]: *** [_modsubdir_ntfs] Error 2
make[1]: Leaving directory `/usr/src/linux-2.4.9/fs'
make: *** [_mod_fs] Error 2
```

At this juncture, you have two options:

- Fix the errors and recompile.

- Remove the offending module or option and wait for the errors to be fixed by the
  kernel team.

Most users will be unable to fix some errors because of the complexity of the kernel code,
although you should not rule out this option. It is possible that someone else discovered
the same error during testing of the kernel and developed a patch for the problem: check
the Linux kernel mailing list archive. If the problem is not mentioned there, a search on
Google might turn up something.

The second option, removing the code, is the easiest and is what most people do in cases
in which the offending code is not required. In the case of the NTFS module failing, it is
almost expected because NTFS support is still considered experimental and subject to
errors. This is primarily because the code for the file system is reverse-engineered instead
of implemented via documented standards. Read-only support has gotten better in recent
kernels; write support is still experimental.

Finally, should you want to take on the task of trying to fix the problem yourself, this is a
great opportunity to get involved with the Linux kernel and make a contribution that
could help many others.

If you are knowledgeable about coding and kernel matters, you might want to look in the
MAINTAINERS file in the /usr/src/linux-2.6/ directory of the kernel source and find the
maintainer of the code. The recommended course of action is to contact the maintainer
and see if he is aware of the problems you are having. If nothing has been documented

for the specific error, submitting the error to the kernel mailing list is an option. The guidelines for doing this are in the README file in the base directory of the kernel source under the section "If Something Goes Wrong."

Runtime Errors, Boot Loader Problems, and Kernel Oops

Runtime errors occur as the kernel is loading. Error messages are displayed on the screen or written to the /var/log/messages file. Bootloader problems display messages to the screen; no log file is produced. *Kernel oops* are errors in a running kernel, and error messages are written to the /var/log/messages file.

Excellent documentation on the Internet exists for troubleshooting just about every type of error that LILO, GRUB, or the kernel could give during boot. The best way to find this documentation is to go to your favorite search engine and type in the keywords of the error you received. You will need to adjust the keywords you use as you focus your search.

In this category, the most common problems deal with LILO configuration issues. Diagnosis and solutions to these problems can be found in the LILO mini-HOWTO found on the Linux Documentation project's website at http://www.ibiblio.org/pub/Linux/docs/HOWTO/other-formats/html_single/LILO.html.

If you have GRUB problems, the GRUB manual is online at http://www.gnu.org/software/grub/manual/.

> **TIP**
>
> For best results, go to http://www.google.com/linux to find all things Linux on the Internet. Google has specifically created a Linux area of its database, which should allow faster access to information on Linux than any other search engine.
>
> The Usenet newsgroup postings are searchable at http://www.google.com/grphp.
>
> Mail list discussions can be searched in the Mailing listARChives (MARC) at http://marc.theaimsgroup.com/.

> **Relevant Fedora Core and Linux Commands**
>
> You will use the following commands when managing the kernel and its modules in Fedora Core Linux:
>
> gcc—The GNU compiler system
>
> make—GNU project and file management command
>
> mkbootdisk—Fedora Core's boot disk creation tool
>
> sysctl—The interface to manipulating kernel variables at runtime
>
> mkinitrd—Create a RAM-disk file system for bootloading support

Reference

http://www.kernel.org/—Linux Kernel Archives. The source of all development discussion for the Linux kernel.

http://www.kerneltraffic.org/kernel-traffic/index.html—Linux Kernel Traffic. Summarized version and commentary of the Linux Kernel mailing list produced weekly.

http://www.gnu.org/—Free Software Foundation. Source of manuals and software for programs used throughout the kernel compilation process. Tools such as `make` and `gcc` have their official documentation here.

http://slashdot.org/article.pl?sid=01/08/22/1453228&mode=thread—The famous AC Patches from Alan Cox, for whom they are named.

http://www.digitalhermit.com/linux/Kernel-Build-HOWTO.html—The Linux Kernel Rebuild Guide; configuration, compilation, and troubleshooting.

http://www.ibiblio.org/pub/Linux/docs/HOWTO/other-formats/html_single/KernelAnalysis-HOWTO.html—KernelAnalysis HOWTO. Describes the mysterious inner workings of the kernel.

http://www.tldp.org/HOWTO/Module-HOWTO/—Kernel Module HOWTO. Includes a good discussion about unresolved symbols.

http://www.ibiblio.org/pub/Linux/docs/HOWTO/other-formats/html_single/Modules.html—The Linux Kernel Modules Installation HOWTO; an older document discussing recompiling kernel modules.

http://www.tldp.org/—The Linux Documentation Project. The Mecca of all Linux documentation. Excellent source of HOWTO documentation, as well as FAQs and online books, all about Linux.

http://www.minix.org/—The unofficial minix website. It contains a selection of links to information about minix and a link to the actual homepage. Although minix is still copyrighted, the owner has granted unlimited rights to everyone. See for yourself the OS used to develop Linux.

http://jungla.dit.upm.es/~jmseyas/linux/kernel/hackers-docs.html—Web page with links to Linux kernel documentation, books, hacker tomes, and other helpful information for budding and experienced Linux kernel and kernel module developers. This list will also be found in the file `/usr/src/linux-2.6/Documentation/kernel-docs.txt` if you install the Fedora Core Linux kernel sources.

PART VII

Appendix

IN THIS PART

Fedora and Linux Internet Resources

Linux enjoys a wealth of Internet support in the form of websites with technical information, specific program documentation, targeted whitepapers, bug fixes, user experiences, third-party commercial technical support, and even free versions of specialized, fine-tuned clone distributions.

This appendix lists many of the supporting websites, FTP repositories, Usenet newsgroups, and electronic mailing lists that you can use to get more information and help with your copy of Fedora.

If You Need Help 24/7

If you are a small business, corporate, or enterprise-level Red Hat Linux user, don't forget that you can always turn to the source, Red Hat, or third-party companies, such as Levanta (http://www.levanta.com/) for commercial technical support on a 24/7 onsite basis, by phone, by electronic mail, or even on a per-incident basis. Red Hat offers a spectrum of support options for its software products. You can read more about support options when you purchase Red Hat software at http://www.redhat.com/software/rhel/purchase/. Remember that Fedora is not an officially supported product from Red Hat. If you want help, try http://fedoraproject.org.

The appendix is divided into the following sections:

- Websites with Linux information arranged by category

- Usenet newsgroups pertaining to Linux

- Mailing lists providing Linux user and developer discussions

- Internet Relay Chat groups for Linux information

This appendix also lists websites that might be of general interest when using Fedora or specific components such as Xorg. Every effort has been made to ensure the accuracy of the URLs, but keep in mind that the Internet is always in flux!

Keep Up-to-Date with *up2date* **or** *yum*

Keeping informed about bug fixes, security updates, and other errata is critical to the success and health of a Fedora system. To keep abreast of the most important developments when using Fedora, be sure to register with the Fedora Announcements mailing list. This will tell you which updates have been issued and what has been fixed as a result. Go to http://www.redhat.com/mailman/listinfo/fedora-announce-list to register for this mailing list. You should also use the yum command (as root) to keep up with bug fixes, new software packages, or security updates.

Websites and Search Engines

Literally thousands of websites exist with information about Linux and Fedora. The key to getting the answers you need right away involves using the best search engines and techniques. Knowing how to search can mean the difference between frustration and success when troubleshooting problems. This section provides some Internet search tips and lists Red Hat, Fedora, and Linux-related sites sorted by various topics. The lists are not comprehensive, but have been checked and were available at the time of this writing.

Web Search Tips

Troubleshooting problems with Linux by searching the Web can be an efficient and productive way to get answers to vexing problems. One of the most basic rules for conducting productive searches is to use specific search terms to find specific answers. For example, if you simply search for "Fedora Linux," you will end up with too many links and too much information. But if you search for "Fedora Core sound," you are more likely to find the information you need. If you've received an error message, use it; otherwise, use the Linux kernel diagnostic message as your search criterion.

Other effective techniques include

- Using symbols in the search string, such as the plus sign (+) to force matches of web pages containing both strings (if such features are supported by the search engine used by web search site)

- Searching within returned results

- Sorting results (usually by date to get the latest information)

- Searching for related information

- Stemming searches; for example, specifying returns for not only "link" but also "linking" and "linked"

Invest some time and experiment with your favorite search engine's features—the result will be more productive searches. In addition to sharpening your search skills, also take the time to choose the best search engine for your needs.

Google Is Your Friend

Some of the fastest and most comprehensive search engines on the Web are powered by Linux, so it makes sense to use the best available resources. Out of the myriad number of websites with search engines, http://google.com stands out from the crowd, with 10 million or more users per month. The site uses advanced hardware and software to bring speed and efficiency to your searches. If you are looking for specific Linux answers, take advantage of Google's Linux page at http://google.com/linux.

Why is Google (named after a math number) so powerful? You can find get a quick idea from the Google folks at http://www.google.com/technology/index.html. Part of its success is because of great algorithms, good programming, and simple interface design, but most users really seem to appreciate Google's uncanny capability to provide links to what you are looking for in the first page of a search return. Google's early success was also assured because the site ran its search engine on clusters of thousands of PCs running a version of Red Hat Linux!

Google has the largest database size of any search engine on the Web, with more than eight billion web pages searched and indexed. The database size is important because empty search results are useless to online users, and the capability to return hits on esoteric subjects can make the difference between success and failure or satisfaction and frustration. Some of Google's features include a GoogleScout link to return similar pages on the results page, the capability to see the exact version of a web page as returned to a search engine (known as a "cached" feature), advanced searches, and more recently, a link to an active Usenet news feed!

To get a better idea of what Google can offer you, browse to http://www.google.com/options/. You will find links to more than two dozen different services and tools covering specialized searches, databases, information links, translators, and other helpful browsing tools.

Fedora Package Listings

You can quickly and easily view a list of the installed RPM packages installed on your Fedora system, along with a short description of each package, by using the rpm command:

```
$ rpm -qai ¦ less
```

Fedora users can also use the yum command to view package names and information about not only installed packages, but any available updated packages, like this:

```
$ yum info ¦ less
```

A

If you use Fedora and only want to see info about your installed packages, use the yum command's installed list option like so:

```
$ yum info installed ¦ less
```

However, the Fedora Project conveniently provides a list and description of each package in each Fedora release at http://fedora.redhat.com/projects/package-list/. A list of packages included with the last free Linux distribution from Red Hat, Red Hat Linux 9, can be found at http://www.fedora.us/pkglists/fedora-9-stable.html l.

Certification

Linux certification courses are part of the rapidly growing information technology train-ing industry. Hundreds of different vendors now offer courses about and testing of Linux skill sets. However, because Linux is open-source software, there are no formal rules or mandates concerning what knowledge or level of expertise is required for certification. If you are interested in certification using Red Hat Linux and would like to pursue a career or obtain employment with a company using Red Hat Linux, you really should seek train-ing from the one best and most qualified company: Red Hat.

That said, the following websites might be of interest if you'd like to pursue a certification track for Red Hat or other Linux distributions:

- http://www.lpi.org—The Linux Professional Institute, with Linux vendor- and distri-bution-neutral programs

- http://www.redhat.com/training/—Entry page to Red Hats Global Learning Services and information about the Red Hat Certified Engineer program

Commercial Support

Commercial support for Linux and Red Hat Linux is an essential ingredient to the success of Linux in the corporate and business community. Although hundreds, if not thousands, of consultants well versed in Linux and Unix are available on call for a fee, here is a short list of the best-known Linux support providers:

- http://www.redhat.com/apps/support/—Red Hat's main support page with links to its various support programs.

- http://www.levanta.com—Home page for Levanta—formerly known as Linuxcare—providing local and remote technical support for many types of installations and customers.

- http://www.ibm.com/linux/—Linux services offered by IBM include e-business solu-tions, Open Source consulting, database migration, clustering, servers, and support. In addition to service-oriented support companies, nearly every commercial distrib-utor of Linux has some form of easily purchased commercial support. There are various ways in which to take advantage of support services (such as remote management, onsite consulting, device driver development, and so on), but needs will vary according to customer circumstances and installations.

> **The Benefits of Joining a Linux User Group**
>
> Join a local Linux Users Group (LUG)! Joining and participating in a local LUG has many benefits. You will be able to get help, trade information, and learn many new and wonderful things about Linux. Most LUGs do not have membership dues, and many often sponsor regular lectures and discussions from leading Linux, GNU, and open-source experts. For one great place to start, browse to http://www.tux.org/luglist.html.

Documentation

Nearly all Linux distributions include thousands of pages of documentation in the form of manual pages, HOWTO documents (in various formats, such as text and HTML), mini-HOWTO documents, or software package documentation (usually found under the /usr/share/doc/ directory). However, the definitive site for reading the latest versions of these documents is the Linux Documentation Project, found at http://www.tldp.org.

Linux Guides

If you are looking for more extensive and detailed information concerning a Linux subject, try reading one of the many Linux guides. These guides, available for a number of subjects, dwell on technical topics in more detail and at a more leisurely pace than a HOWTO. You find copies of

- "Advanced Bash-Scripting Guide," by Mendel Cooper; a guide to shell scripting using bash

- "LDP Author Guide," by Mark F. Komarinski; how to write LDP documentation

- "Linux Administration Made Easy," by Steve Frampton

- "Linux Administrator's Security Guide," by Kurt Seifried

- "Linux Consultants Guide," by Joshua Drake; a worldwide listing of commercial Linux consultants

- "Linux from Scratch," by Gerard Beekmans; creating a Linux distribution from software

- "Linux Kernel 2.4 Internals," by Tigran Aivazian; a guide to the 2.4 kernel

- "Linux Kernel Module Programming Guide," by Ori Pomerantz; a somewhat dated guide to building 2.0 and 2.2 series modules

- "Securing and Optimizing Linux," by Gerhard Mourani; specific to Red Hat Linux

A

- Linux certification

- "The Linux Network Administrator's Guide, Second Edition," by Olaf Kirch and Terry Dawson; a comprehensive Net admin guide

The Fedora Project

- http://fedora.redhat.com—Home page for the Fedora Project, Red Hat community-based free Linux distribution. Fedora Core is the main release of this Linux distribution, and includes thousands of software packages that form the core of an up-to-date, cutting-edge Linux-based desktop.

- http://www.fedoraproject.org/—Home page for the community side of Fedora. You will find a lot of support and HOWTOs here.

Red Hat Linux

- http://www.redhat.com—Home page for Red Hat's distribution of Red Hat Enterprise Linux for multiple processors and architectures. Support is also provided for older, but now discontinued, versions of the SPARC.

- http://www.redhat.com/apps/support/documentation.html—Specific web page with links to current official Red Hat manuals and guides, FAQs, HOWTOs, whitepapers, free books, mailing list archives, hardware compatibility lists, and other documentation.

Mini-CD Linux Distributions

Mini-CD Linux distributions are used for many different purposes. Some distributions are used to boot to a read-only firewall configuration; others are used to provide as complete a rescue environment as possible; whereas others are used to either install or help jump-start an install of a full distribution. Mini-CDs are available in a wide variety of sizes, such as 3" CD-Rs (or CD-RW) with sizes ranging from 185 to 210MB. You can also download an .iso image and create a Linux bootable business card, typically fitting on a 40 or 50MB credit card–sized CD-R (consider using a mini–CD-RW, especially if you want to upgrade your distribution often). Here are some links to these distributions:

- http://www.lnx-bbc.org—Home page for the Linux BBC, a 40MB image hosting a rather complete live Linux session with X, a web browser, and a host of networking tools.

- http://crux.nu/—Home page of the CRUX i686–optimized Linux distribution.

- http://www.trustix.net/—Home page for the free version of the Trustix Secure Linux distribution, which currently uses the latest 2.4 kernel. Trustix is RPM based.

- http://www.smoothwall.org/community/home/—The 22MB SmoothWall distribution, which easily fits on a bootable business card and is used to install a web-administered firewall, router, or gateway with SSH, HTTP, and other services.

- http://www.phy.olemiss.edu/debian-cd/—A 185MB Debian 3.0 (Woody) distribution with enough software to bring up a working Debian system. X is not included, so you must download and install other packages to expand the system.

Floppy-Based Linux Distributions

- http://www.linuxrouter.org—Home page for the Linux Router Project

- http://floppix.ccai.com/index.html—A Debian-based floppy

- http://www.toms.net/rb/—Tom's root and boot disk distribution

- http://www.coyotelinux.com/—Secure routing and embedded Linux disk distributions

- http://trinux.sourceforge.net—An ultra-secure Linux distribution on floppy

- http://PenguinBackup.sourceforge.net/—A unique, floppy-based distribution that allows quick backup of your Palm-type PDA

Various Intel-Based Linux Distributions

Choosing a Linux distribution (distro) for an Intel-based PC is generally a matter of personal preference or need. Many Linux users prefer Red Hat's distro because of its excellent support, commercial support options, and widespread use around the world. However, many different Linux distributions are available for download. One of the best places to start looking for a new distro or new version of your favorite distro is http://www.distrowatch.com:

- http://www.xandros.net—New home of the original and improved version of Corel's Debian-based Linux

- http://www.debian.org—The Debian Linux distribution, consisting only of software distributed under the GNU GPL license

- http://www.independence.seul.org—A newer Red Hat–based Linux distribution

- http://www.libranet.com—A Linux distribution based on Debian

- http://www.slackware.com—Home page for download of the newest version of one of the oldest Linux distributions, Slackware

- http://www.suse.com—Home page for SuSE Linux, also available for the PowerPC

- http://www.mandrakelinux.com—A Pentium-optimized, RPM-based distribution, originally based on Red Hat's Linux distribution

A

PowerPC-Based Linux Distributions

- http://penguinppc.org/—Home page for the PowerPC GNU/Linux distribution

- http://www.suse.com—SuSE PPC Linux; moving to UnitedLinux

- http://www.yellowdoglinux.com—Home page for Terra Soft Solutions' Yellow Dog Linux for the PowerPC, which is based on Red Hat

Linux on Laptops and PDAs

One of the definitive sites for getting information about running Linux on your laptop is Kenneth Harker's Linux Laptop site. Although not as actively updated as in the past, this site (http://www.linux-laptop.net) still contains the world's largest collection of Linux and laptop information, with links to user experiences and details concerning specific laptop models.

Another site to check is Werner Heuser's Tuxmobil-Mobile Unix website at http://www.tuxmobil.org. You'll find links to information such as IrDA, Linux PDAs, and cell phones. Linux Zaurus PDA users can browse to http://www.openzaurus.org to download a complete open-source replacement operating system for the Zaurus 5000 and 5500 models.

The X Window System

Although much technical information is available on the Internet regarding the X Window System, finding answers to specific questions when troubleshooting can be problematic. If you are having a problem using X, first try to determine whether the problem is software or hardware related. When searching or asking for help (such as on Usenet's comp.os.linux.x newsgroup, which you can access through Google's Groups link; see the next section for other helpful Linux newsgroups), try to be as specific as possible. Some critical factors or information needed to adequately assess a problem include the Linux distribution in use; the kernel version used; the version of X used; the brand, name, and model of your video card; the names, brands, and models of your monitor and other related hardware.

This section lists just some of the basic resources for Linux XFree86 users. Definitive technical information regarding X is available from http://www.X.org:

- http://www.lesstif.org/—Home page for the GPL'd OSF/Motif clone, LessTif

- http://www.motifzone.net—Site for download of the open-source version of Motif for Linux, Open Motif

- http://www.rahul.net/kenton/index.shtml—Ken Lee's X and Motif website with numerous links to tutorial, development, and other information about X

- http://www.xfree86.org—Home page for The XFree86 Project, developers of XFree86, used with Red Hat Linux

- http://www.xig.com/—Home page for a commercial version of X for Linux (along with other software products)

Usenet Newsgroups

Linux-related Usenet newsgroups are another good source of information if you're having trouble using Linux. (Refer to Chapter 28, "News Servers and Mailing Lists," for more information about using newsgroups.) If your ISP does not offer a comprehensive selection of Linux newsgroups, you can browse to http://groups.google.com/.

The primary Linux and Linux-related newsgroups are

- `alt.os.linux.dial-up`—Using PPP for dial-up
- `alt.os.linux.mandrake`—All about Mandrake Linux
- `alt.os.linux.redhat`—Alternative discussions about Red Hat Linux
- `alt.os.linux.slackware`—Using Slackware Linux
- `alt.os.linux.suse`—Using SuSE Linux
- `comp.os.linux.admin`—Administering Linux
- `comp.os.linux.advocacy`—Heated discussions about Linux and other related issues
- `comp.os.linux.alpha`—Using Linux on the Alpha CPU
- `comp.os.linux.announce`—General Linux announcements
- `comp.os.linux.answers`—Releases of new Linux FAQs and other information
- `comp.os.linux.development.apps`—Using Linux development tools
- `comp.os.linux.development.system`—Building the Linux kernel
- `comp.os.linux.embedded`—Linux embedded device development
- `comp.os.linux.hardware`—Configuring Linux for various hardware devices
- `comp.os.linux.help`—Help with Linux
- `comp.os.linux.m68k`—Linux on Motorola's 68K-family CPUs
- `comp.os.linux.misc`—Miscellaneous Linux topics
- `comp.os.linux.networking`—Networking and Linux
- `comp.os.linux.portable`—Using Linux on laptops
- `comp.os.linux.powerpc`—Using PPC Linux
- `comp.os.linux.questions`—Questions about Linux
- `comp.os.linux.redhat`—All about Red Hat Linux
- `comp.os.linux.security`—Linux security issues
- `comp.os.linux.setup`—Linux installation topics
- `comp.os.linux.x`—Linux and the X Window System

A

- `comp.windows.x.apps`—Using X-based clients

- `comp.windows.x.i386unix`—X for Unix PCs

- `comp.windows.x.intrinsics`—X Toolkit library topics

- `comp.windows.x.kde`—Using KDE and X discussions

- `comp.windows.x.motif`—All about Motif programming

- `comp.windows.x`—Discussions about X

- `linux.admin.*`—Two newsgroups for Linux administrators

- `linux.debian.*`—30 newsgroups about Debian

- `linux.dev.*`—25 or more Linux development newsgroups

- `linux.help`—Get help with Linux

- `linux.kernel`—The Linux kernel

- `linux.redhat.*`—Red Hat-based discussions: `linux.redhat.announce`, `linux.redhat.list`, `linux.redhat.applixware`, `linux.redhat.misc`, `linux.redhat.devel`, `linux.redhat.pam`, `linux.redhat.development`, `linux.redhat.ppp`, `linux.redhat.digest`, `linux.redhat.rpm`, `linux.redhat.install`, `linux.redhat.sparc`, `linux.redhat.axp`

> **Fedora Usenet Newsgroups**
>
> By the time you read this, you might find that Fedora-related newsgroups have been voted on and formed, perhaps with names beginning with `linux.fedora.*`.

Mailing Lists

Mailing lists are interactive or digest-form electronic discussions about nearly any topic. To use a mailing list, you must generally send an email request to be subscribed to the list, and then verify the subscription with a return message from the master list mailer. After subscribing to an interactive form of list, each message sent to the list will appear in your email inbox. However, many lists provide a digest form of subscription in which a single- or half-day's traffic is condensed in a single message. The digest form is generally preferred unless you have set up electronic mail filtering (Chapter 28 also discusses the use of mailing lists in Fedora Core).

The main Fedora Project mailing lists are detailed here, but there are quite a few Linux-related lists. Red Hat's offerings are also provided here. You can search for nearly all online mailing lists by using a typical mailing list search web page, such as the one at http://www.lsoft.com/lists/list_q.html.

GNOME and KDE Mailing Lists

GNOME users and developers should know that more than two dozen mailing lists are available through http://mail.gnome.org/. KDE users will also benefit by perusing the KDE-related mailing lists at http://www.kde.org/mailinglists.html.

Fedora Project Mailing Lists

The Fedora Project is still in its infancy at the time of this writing. You will find many other knowledgeable users with answers to your questions by participating in one of Fedora's mailing lists. The lists are focused on using, testing, and developing and participating in Fedora Core's development:

- `fedora-devel-list@redhat.com`—Developer information exchanges
- `fedora-docs-list@redhat.com`—For Fedora users working on project documentation
- `fedora-list@redhat.com`—Discussions among users of Fedora Core releases
- `fedora-test-list@redhat.com`—Queries and reports from testers of Fedora Core test releases

Red Hat Mailing Lists

Red Hat provides a comprehensive archive and mailing list management web page at http://www.redhat.com/mailman/listinfo/. You can use this page to subscribe to one of more than 40 mailing lists related to Red Hat Linux. Some of the more pertinent lists are

- `redhat-announce-list`—General announcements about Red Hat Linux
- `redhat-devel-list`—Information for developers using Red Hat Linux
- `redhat-install-list`—Installation issues about Red Hat Linux
- `redhat-list`—A general Red Hat Linux discussion list
- `redhat-ppp-list`—Issues regarding PPP and dial-up under Red Hat Linux
- `redhat-secure-server`—Using Red Hat, Inc.'s secure server
- `redhat-watch-list`—Announcements of bug fixes, updates for Red Hat Linux
- `rpm-list`—Using the Red Hat Package Manager
- `under-the-brim`—Red Hat's helpful electronic newsletter

Internet Relay Chat

Internet Relay Chat (IRC) is a popular form and forum of communication for many Red Hat Linux developers and users because it allows an interactive, real-time exchange of information and ideas. To use IRC, you must have an IRC client and the address of a network and server hosting the desired chat channel for your discussions.

You can use the `irc.freenode.net` IRC server, or one listed at http://www.freenode.net/ to chat with other Fedora Project users. Two current channels are

- `#fedora channel`—General chat about Fedora

- `#fedora-devel`—Hangout for a number of Fedora Project developers

One comprehensive list of active Linux-related IRC channels can be found at http://www.helsinki.fi/~rvaranka/Computer/Linux/IRC.shtml. To get help with getting started with IRC, browse to http://www.irchelp.org/. Some of the channels of interest might be

- `#linux`—General discussions about Linux

- `#linuxhelp`—A help chat discussion for new users

Most IRC networks provide one or more Linux channels, although some providers require sign up and registration before you can access any chat channel.

Index

NUMBERS

A

B

C

How can we make this index more useful? Email us at indexes@samspublishing.com

H

How can we make this index more useful? Email us at indexes@samspublishing.com

mounting

   file systems

      /etc/fstab files, 972-974

      amd, 975

      defining, 955

      Floppy Formatter (KDE), 975

      KDiskFree (KDE), 974

      KwikDisk (KDE), 974

      loopback file systems, 980-981

      mount command, 970-971

      umount command, 972

      User Mount Tool (KDE), 974-975

      usermount graphical file system management client, 974

   initrd files, 985

   partitions

      read-only partitions, 983

      relocating file systems, 977-978

   Samba shares, 593

mouse devices

   button assignment, 130

   changing, X Window System updates, 167

   configuring, 63, 125

   .gpm drivers, 92

   gpm servers, button assignment, 130-131

   scrolling, enabling, 92

   system reboots/shutdowns, 130-131

   text, copying/pasting in consoles, 130

   three-button

      emulation, 130

      Linux configuration, 90

   two-button, Linux configuration, 90

   X Window System configurations, 166-167

mouseconfig command, 88, 184

   three-button mouse emulation, 130

   two-button mouses, Linux support, 90

mouseconfig tool, 84

mov video file format, 275

moving files via mkdir shell command, 933

mozilla command, 771

Mozilla Firefox web browser, 208-209, 552, 684

Mozilla Mail email client, 217

Mozilla news client, 227

Mozilla Suite web browser, 209

Mozilla Thunderbird

   email client, 216

   news client, 228-229

Mozilla web browser

   Flash plug-in (Macromedia), 276

   Java plug-ins, 288

MP3 files, 270

MPEG files

   Fedora support, 270

   streaming audio, 272

   video files, 275

MPlayer video viewer, 277

MPM (multiprocessing modules), Apache web server configuration, 524-525

mpm_common MPM (multiprocessing module), 525

mput command, FTP text-based client interface, 614

MS Exchange Server, 677-678

msdos modules, 952

MTAs (mail transport agents), 660

   choosing, 662

   defining, 211

   Exim, 661

Q

How can we make this index more useful? Email us at indexes@samspublishing.com

V

Y

How can we make this index more useful? Email us at indexes@samspublishing.com

Z

Your Guide to Computer Technology

www.informit.com

What's On the DVD

The book's DVD includes the binary version of Fedora Core 4—the equivalent of four CDs.

DESKTOPS

- X.Org 6.8.2
- GNOME 2.10
- K Desktop Environment 3.4

APPLICATIONS

Editors

- Joe's Own Editor (JOE)
- Emacs
- Vi IMproved (VIM)
- Vi IMproved for X11
- XEmacs

Engineering and Scientific

- Parallel Virtual Machine (PVM)
- Gnuplot Version
- Local Area Multicomputer (LAM)
- units

Graphical Internet

- X-Chat
- Firefox
- Thunderbird
- gFTP
- Epiphany
- Evolution
- Evolution Connector
- Gaim
- GnomeMeeting

Text-based Internet

- Slang Read News (slrn)
- Mutt
- ELinks
- fetchmail
- Lynx
- EPIC
- cadaver

Office/Productivity

- KDE-PIM
- Gnumeric 1.2.13-6
- MagicPoint 1.11b-1
- GnuCash
- Xpdf
- OpenOffice.org
- TeTeX-xdvi

Office/Productivity (continued)

- Evince
- Planner

Sound and Video

- Totem
- K3b
- Rhythmbox
- tvtime
- SoX
- Advanced Linux Sound Architecture (ALSA) utilities
- zisofs tools
- mkisofs
- HelixPlayer
- MikMod
- Kdemultimedia
- Sound Juicer
- Cdparanoia
- Cdrecord
- dvgrab
- cdda2wav
- X-CD-Roast
- Vorbis Tools

Authoring and Publishing

- DocBook slides, styles, and utilities
- Simplified DocBook
- Linux Documentation Tools
- xmlto
- XHTML DTDs
- TeTeX and utilities

Graphics

- ImageMagick
- GIMP Print plugin
- GIMP Animation Package
- netpbm-progs
- libsane-hpoj
- Xfig
- XSane GIMP plugin
- GIMP
- SANE Frontends
- GIMP Data Extras
- XSane
- Kdegraphics
- Dia

Games and Entertainment

- GNOME games
- KDE games
- KDE edutainment
- joystick

SERVERS AND NETWORKING

Server Configuration Tools

- Server configuration tools

Web Server

- Apache HTTPD Server
- Apache Tomcat
- distcache
- mod_authz_ldap
- mod_ssl
- mod_auth_kerb
- tomcat5-admin-webapps
- tomcat5-webapps
- php-odbc
- mod_auth_mysql
- php-pgsql
- mod_auth_pgsql
- Squid
- php-ldap
- mod_perl
- Tux
- cryptoutils
- PHP
- PHP-MySQL
- httpd-manual
- Webalizer
- mod_python

Mail

- Sendmail
- SquirrelMail
- SpamAssassin
- Mailman
- Dovecot
- Postfix

Windows Files Server

- SAMBA

DNS/Name

- BIND
- CachingNameServer
- bind-chroot

FTP

- Very Secure FTP Daemon (vsftpd)

PostgreSQL Database

- postgresql-jdbc
- postgresql-contrib
- postgresql-docs
- postgresql-test
- rhdb-utiils
- postgresql-pl
- postgresql-odbc
- postgresql-python
- postgresql-tcl
- qt-ODBC
- PostgreSQL server
- perl-DBD-Pg
- unixODBC

MySQL Database

- MySQL server
- libdbi-dbd-mysql
- perl-DBD-MySQL
- mysql-bench
- qt-MySQL
- mysql-devel
- MyODBC
- php-mysql
- qt-ODBC
- MySQL-python
- mod_auth_mysql

News Server

- INN

Network Servers

- Netdump
- OpenLDAP
- Finger 0.17-26
- FreeRADIUS
- Virtual Network Computing (VNC)
- Quagga
- Router Advertisement Daemon (RADVD)